STUDY GUIDE
to accompany
McConnell and Brue
ECONOMICS

STUDY GUIDE
to accompany
McConnell and Brue
ECONOMICS

Fourteenth Edition

WILLIAM B. WALSTAD
PROFESSOR OF ECONOMICS
UNIVERSITY OF NEBRASKA–LINCOLN

ROBERT C. BINGHAM
LATE PROFESSOR OF ECONOMICS
KENT STATE UNIVERSITY

Boston Burr Ridge, IL Dubuque, IA Madison, WI New York San Francisco St. Louis
Bangkok Bogotá Caracas Lisbon London Madrid
Mexico City Milan New Delhi Seoul Singapore Sydney Taipei Toronto

McGraw-Hill

A Division of The McGraw-Hill Companies

Study Guide to Accompany Economics
Principles, Problems, and Policies

3 4 5 6 7 8 9 0 QPD QPD 9 4 3 2 1 0 9 8

ISBN 0-07-289837-2

Editorial director: Michael Junior
Publisher: Gary Burke
Sponsoring editor: Lucille Sutton
Developmental editor: Marilea Fried
Marketing manager: Nelson Black
Project manager: Eva Marie Strock
Production supervisor: Louis Swaim
Cover designer: Francis Owens
Editorial assistant: Lee Hertel
Compositor: York Graphic Services, Inc.
Typeface: Helvetica
Printer: Quebecor Printing

Back cover illustration by Jacques Cournoyer

http://www.mhhe.com

About the Authors

William B. Walstad is a professor of economics at the University of Nebraska–Lincoln, where he directs the National Center for Research in Economic Education. He received his Ph.D. degree from the University of Minnesota. Professor Walstad has been honored with a Distinguished Teaching Award at Nebraska. He also received the Henry H. Villard Research Award for his published research in economic education. He coedited *Teaching Undergraduate Economics: A Handbook for Instructors* (McGraw-Hill) and serves as an associate editor of the *Journal of Economic Education.*

Robert C. Bingham was an undergraduate student at DePauw University and obtained M.A. and Ph.D. degrees from Northwestern University. He taught at the University of Nebraska–Lincoln, where he was a colleague of Professor McConnell before moving to Kent State University, from which he retired in 1985. He was the author of several other study guides and supplements for the principles of economics courses.

To

Tammie, Laura, and Kristin, and Eileen

Contents

How to Use the Study Guide to Learn Economics

This *Study Guide* is designed to help you read and understand Campbell R. McConnell and Stanley L. Brue's textbook, *Economics,* fourteenth edition. If used properly, a study guide can be a great aid to you for what is probably your first course in economics.

No one pretends that the study of economics is easy, but it can be made easier. Of course, a study guide will not do your work for you, and its use is no substitute for reading the text. You must be willing to read the text, spend time on the subject, and work at learning if you wish to understand economics.

Many students do read their text and work hard on their economics course and still fail to learn the subject. This occurs because principles of economics is a new subject for these students, and they have had no previous experience in learning economics. They want to learn but do not know just how to go about it. Here is where the *Study Guide* can help. Let's first see what the *Study Guide* contains and then how to use it.

■ WHAT THE STUDY GUIDE IS

The *Study Guide* contains 40 chapters—one for each chapter in *Economics*—and a **glossary.** Each *Study Guide* chapter has 11 sections. The first 5 sections identify and explain the basic content and concepts in each chapter.

1. An **introduction** explains what is in the chapter of the text and how it is related to material in earlier and later chapters. It points out topics to which you should give special attention and reemphasizes difficult or important principles and facts.

2. A **checklist** tells you the things you should be able to do when you have finished the chapter.

3. A **chapter outline** shows how the chapter is organized and summarizes briefly the essential points made in the chapter.

4. Selected **hints and tips** for each chapter help you master the material and make connections with any previous discussion of a topic.

5. A list of the **important terms** in the chapter points out what you must be able to define in order to understand the material in the chapter. A definition of each term is in the glossary at the end of the *Study Guide.*

The next 6 sections of the *Study Guide* allow you to **self-test** your understanding of the chapter material.

6. Fill-in questions (short-answer and list questions) help you learn and remember the important generalizations and facts in the chapter.

7. True-false questions test your understanding of the material in the chapter.

8. Multiple-choice questions also give you a chance to check your knowledge of the chapter content and prepare for this type of course examination.

9. Problems help you learn and understand economic concepts by requiring different skills—drawing a graph, completing a table, or finding relationships—to solve the problems.

10. Short answer and **essay questions** can be used as a self-test, to identify important questions in the chapter, and to prepare for examinations.

11. Answers to fill-in questions, problems and projects, true-false questions, and multiple-choice questions are found at the end of each chapter. References to the specific pages in the textbook for each true-false, multiple-choice, and short answer or essay question are also provided.

■ HOW TO STUDY AND LEARN WITH THE HELP OF THE *STUDY GUIDE*

1. *Read and outline.* For best results, quickly read the introduction, outline, list of terms, and checklist in the *Study Guide* before you read the chapter in *Economics.* Then read the chapter in the text slowly, keeping one eye on the *Study Guide* outline and the list of terms. Highlight the chapter as you read it by identifying the *major and minor* points and by placing *Study Guide* outline numbers or letters (such as I or A or 1 or a) in the margins. When you have completed the chapter, you will have the chapter highlighted, and the *Study Guide* outline will serve as a handy set of notes on the chapter.

2. *Review and reread.* After you have read the chapter in the text once, return to the introduction, outline, and list of terms in the *Study Guide.* Reread the introduction and outline. Does everything there make sense? If not, go back to the text and reread the topics that you do not remember well or that still confuse you. Look at the outline. Try to recall each of the minor topics or points that were contained in the text under each of the major points in the outline. When you come to the list of terms, go over them one by one. *Define or explain each to yourself and then look for the definition of the term either in the text chapter or in the glossary*. Compare your own definition or explanation with that in the *text or glossary.* The quick way to find the definition of a term in the text is to look in the text index for the page(s) in which that term or concept is mentioned. Make any necessary correction or change in your own definition or explanation.

3. *Test and check answers.* When you have done all this, you will have a general idea of what is in the text chapter. *Now look at the fill-in questions, true-false questions, multiple-choice questions, and problems.* Tackle each of these four sections one at a time, using the following procedure. (**1**) Answer as many questions as you can without looking in the text or in the answers section. (**2**) Check the text for whatever help you need. It is a good idea to do more than merely look for answers in the text. Reread any section for which you were not able to answer questions. (**3**) Consult the answers section at the end of the chapter for the correct answers and reread any section of the text for which you missed questions. (See the text page references given with the answer to each true-false or multiple-choice question.)

The questions in these four sections are not all equally difficult. Do not expect to get them all right the first time. Some are designed to pinpoint things of importance that you will probably miss the first time you read the text and to get you to read about them again. None of the questions are unimportant. Even those that have no definite answers will bring you to grips with many important economic questions and increase your understanding of economic principles and problems.

The *short answer and essay questions* cover the major points in the chapter. For some of the easier questions, all you may do is mentally outline your answer. For the more difficult questions, you may want to write out a brief outline of the answer or a full answer. Do not avoid the difficult questions just because they are more work. Answering these questions is often the most valuable work you can do toward acquiring an understanding of economic relationships and principles.

Although no answers are given in the *Study Guide* to the short answer and essay questions, the answer section does list text page references for each question. You are *strongly* encouraged to read those text pages for an explanation of the question or for better insight into the question content.

4. *Double check.* Before you turn to the next chapter in the text and *Study Guide,* return to the checklist. If you cannot honestly check off each item in the list, you have not learned what the authors of the text and of this *Study Guide* hoped you would learn.

■ ANSWERS TO KEY QUESTIONS IN *ECONOMICS*

In addition to the self-test in the *Study Guide,* there are end-of-chapter questions in *Economics* that you can answer to double check your understanding. Some of these questions are similar to the questions in the *Study Guide,* but none are identical. It is highly recommended that you try to answer the ***key questions*** at the end of each chapter in *Economics.* You can then check your work against the Answers sections in the *Study Guide.*

■ SOME FINAL WORDS

Perhaps the method of using the *Study Guide* outlined above seems like a lot of work. It is! Study and learning necessarily entail work on your part. This is a fact you must accept if you are to learn economics.

After you have used the *Study Guide* to study three or four chapters, you will find that some sections are more valuable to you than others. Let your own experience determine how you will use it. But do not discontinue use of the *Study Guide* after three or four chapters merely because you are not sure whether it is helping you. ***Stick with it.***

■ ACKNOWLEDGMENTS

The late Professor Robert Bingham prepared the first 10 editions of the *Study Guide.* He worked with great care and wanted the *Study Guide* to be a valuable aid for students. Many past users of the *Study Guide* will attest to his success. Although Professor Bingham did not participate directly in this revision, his work remains a major contribution to this edition.

I also want to acknowledge the help I received from many others. Campbell McConnell and Stanley Brue offered many insightful comments on the *Study Guide* over the years and encouraged my work. I received valuable suggestions and corrections for this edition from Loretta Fairchild, Joyce Gleason, Richard Harmstone, Ralph Lewis, Peter Kerr, Dave Rosenbaum, Mary Stevenson, and Joshua Stull. Ken Rebeck helped me proof and check the self-test questions and identify text page numbers for answers. Students in my principles of economics classes at the University of Nebraska–Lincoln continue to give me feedback that has helped improve the *Study Guide* with each edition. Sharon Nemeth was of invaluable assistance in helping proof portions of the manuscript. Finally, the team at McGraw-Hill, especially Lucille Sutton, provided good editorial and production support. Despite the many contributions from others, all responsibility for any errors or omissions are mine. I encourage *Study Guide* users to send me comments or suggestions at any time.

William B. Walstad

STUDY GUIDE
to accompany
McConnell and Brue
ECONOMICS

CHAPTER 1

The Nature and Method of Economics

Chapter 1 introduces you to economics—the study of how people decide how to use scarce productive resources to satisfy material wants. The purpose of this chapter is to explain the nature of the subject and to describe the methods that economists use to study economic questions.

The first section of the chapter describes the three key features of the ***economic perspective.*** This perspective first recognizes that all choices involve costs and that these costs must be involved in an economic decision. The economic perspective also incorporates the view that to achieve a goal, people make decisions which reflect their rational self-interest. The third feature considers that people compare marginal benefits against marginal costs when making decisions and will choose the situation where the marginal benefit is greater than the marginal cost. You will develop a better understanding of these features and the meaning of the economic perspective as you read about the economic issues in this book.

As you begin your study of economics, you might be wondering if the work you will do to learn the chapter material is worthwhile. It most certainly is. Knowledge of economics is important because it is essential for well-informed citizenship and has many practical applications to professional and personal decisions.

Economists use two different approaches to examine economic topics. Theoretical economics, or ***economic analysis,*** is the systematic gathering of relevant facts and the derivation of principles with these facts using inductive or deductive methods. ***Policy economics*** entails the formulation of policies or recommended solutions to economic problems.

The heart of the chapter is the discussion of ***economic principles*** in the economic methodology section. These principles are generalizations, imprecise and subject to exceptions because economists cannot conduct laboratory experiments to test the generalizations. Economics is a science, but not an exact science. Economic principles are also simplifications—approximations of a complex world—for analyzing problems in ***microeconomics*** and ***macroeconomics*** and for finding solutions to these problems.

The choice of an economic policy depends on economic principles *and* on the value judgments and weights given to economic goals. Here we move from ***economic theory*** and ***positive economics,*** which investigates what is, to ***normative economics,*** which incorporates subjective or value-laden views of what ought to be. Many of the apparent disagreements among economists are over normative policy issues and involve deciding which economic goals for our economy are most important in making the case for a policy solution.

Clear thinking about economic questions requires that beginning students avoid many pitfalls. Errors of commission and omission can occur from bias, loaded terminology, imprecise definitions, fallacies of composition, and causation fallacies. Awareness of these pitfalls will help you think more objectively about the economic issues you will read about throughout this book.

■ CHECKLIST

When you have studied this chapter you should be able to

☐ Write a formal definition of economics.
☐ Describe the three key features of an economic perspective.
☐ Give examples of the application of an economic perspective.
☐ Give two good reasons for studying economics.
☐ Describe theoretical economics or economic analysis.
☐ Distinguish between induction and deduction in economic reasoning.
☐ Explain what an economic principle is and how economic principles are obtained.
☐ Discuss how economic principles are generalizations and abstractions.
☐ Explain what the "other things equal" (***ceteris paribus***) assumption is and why this assumption is employed in economics.
☐ Define policy economics.
☐ List three steps in economic policymaking.
☐ Identify eight economic goals widely accepted in the United States and many other nations.
☐ Discuss the conflicting or complementary nature of economic goals.
☐ Distinguish between macroeconomics and microeconomics.
☐ Give examples of positive and normative economics.
☐ Identify the five pitfalls to objective thinking when given examples.

■ CHAPTER OUTLINE

1. Economics is concerned with the efficient use of limited productive resources to achieve the maximum satisfaction of human material wants.

2. The *economic perspective* has three interrelated features.

a. It recognizes scarcity requires choice and that all choices entail a cost.

b. It views people as rational decision makers who make choices based on their self-interest.

c. It uses marginal analysis to assess how the marginal costs of a decision compare with the marginal benefits.

3. Citizens in a democracy must understand elementary economics to comprehend the present-day problems of their society and to make intelligent decisions when they vote. Economics is an academic rather than a vocational subject, but a knowledge of it is valuable to business executives, consumers, and workers.

4. Economic methodology includes both theoretical economics and policy economics.

a. *Theoretical economics* is the gathering and analysis of relevant facts to derive economic principles. Economists use both inductive and deductive reasoning to develop economic principles. Induction creates principles from factual observations, or goes from the particular to the general. Deduction formulates a hypothesis and then tests it for validity, or goes from the general to the particular. Economic principles and theories are meaningful statements about economic behavior in the economy.

(1) They are also called laws and models.

(2) Each principle and theory is a generalization that shows a tendency or average effect.

(3) The "other things equal" (ceteris paribus) assumption is used to limit the influence of other factors when making a generalization.

(4) Economic principles and theories are abstractions from reality.

(5) Many economic principles or models can be illustrated graphically.

b. *Policy economics* is the use of economic principles to develop a course of action to solve economic problems.

(1) The three steps in creating economic policy are stating the goal, considering the options, and evaluating the results.

(2) Eight major economic goals are considered important in the United States and many other nations: economic growth, full employment, economic efficiency, price-level stability, economic freedom, economic security, an equitable distribution of income, and a balance of trade. Economic goals can be complementary, or they can conflict and require tradeoffs. The interpretation of economic goals and the setting of priorities can be difficult and cause problems in economic policymaking.

5. Economic analysis is conducted at two levels, and might be positive or normative.

a. *Macroeconomics* looks at the entire economy or its major aggregates or sectors, such as households, businesses, or government.

b. *Microeconomics* studies the economic behavior of individuals, particular markets, firms, or industries.

c. *Positive economics* focuses on facts and is concerned with what is, or the scientific analysis of economic behavior.

d. *Normative economics* suggests what ought to be and answers policy questions based on value judgments. Most disagreements among economists involve normative economics.

6. Objective thinking in the study and use of economic principles requires strict application of the rules of logic, in which personal emotions are irrelevant, if not detrimental. The pitfalls beginning students encounter when studying and applying economic principles include the following:

a. Bias of preconceived beliefs not warranted by facts

b. Loaded terminology or the use of terms in a way which appeals to emotion and leads to a nonobjective analysis of the issues

c. The definition of terms by economists in ways which may not be the same as the ways in which these terms are more commonly used

d. The fallacy of composition or the assumption that what is true of the part is necessarily true of the whole

e. Two causation fallacies confuse cause and effect.

(1) The after this, therefore because of this fallacy ***(post hoc, ergo propter hoc)*** is the mistaken belief that when one event precedes another, the first event is the cause of the second.

(2) The other fallacy is to confuse correlation with causation. Two factors may be related, but that does not mean that one factor caused the other.

■ HINTS AND TIPS

1. The economic perspective presented in the first section of the chapter has three features related to decision making: scarcity and the necessity of choice, rational self-interest in decision making, and marginal analysis of the costs and benefits of decisions. Although these features may seem strange to you at first, they are central to the economic thinking used to examine decisions and problems throughout the book.

2. The chapter introduces important pairs of terms: inductive and deductive reasoning; microeconomics and macroeconomics; and positive economics and normative economics. Make sure you understand what each pair means.

3. Objective thinking about economic problems is difficult and requires that you be able to recognize the major pitfalls—loaded terminology, inaccurate definitions, fallacy of composition, *post hoc* fallacy, and confusing correlation with causation. One way to remember these pitfalls is to associate each one with a practical example.

■ IMPORTANT TERMS

Note: See Glossary in the back of the book for definitions of terms.

economics	**economic analysis**
economic perspective	**marginal analysis**

economic theory
economic principles
induction
deduction
generalizations
ceteris paribus
policy economics
tradeoffs
macroeconomics
aggregate
microeconomics
positive economics
normative economics
fallacy of composition
post hoc, ergo propter hoc

SELF-TEST

■ FILL-IN QUESTIONS

1. Economics is the study of the efficient use of (unlimited, limited) _____ resources to achieve (minimum, maximum) _____ satisfaction of human wants.

2. The economic perspective recognizes that (resources, scarcity) _____ requires choice and that choice has an opportunity (benefit, cost) _____. "There is no such thing as a free lunch" in economics because scarce resources have (unlimited, alternative) _____ uses.

3. The economic perspective also assumes that people make choices based on their self-interest and that they are (irrational, rational) _____. It also is based on comparisons of the (partial, marginal) _____ costs and benefits of an economic decision.

4. An understanding of economics is essential if we are to be well-informed (citizens, technicians) _____, and such an understanding has many personal and professional applications even though it is a(n) (vocational, academic) _____ and not a(n) _____ subject.

5. The systematic arranging of facts, the interpretation of them, and the drawing of generalizations based on them is called (policy, theoretical) _____ economics.

6. When economists develop economic principles from studying facts, they are using the (deductive, inductive) _____ method, whereas the _____ method uses facts to test the validity of hypotheses or economic theories.

7. Economic principles are also called (facts, laws) _____, or (theories, policies) _____, or (models, tradeoffs) _____.

8. Economic principles are often imprecise quantitative statements or (fallacies, generalizations) _____ about people's economic behavior, and they necessarily involve (abstractions, distractions) _____ from reality to simplify complex situations.

9. When economists assume that other factors are held constant and do not change when studying an economic relationship, they are using the (*post hoc,* other things equal) _____ assumption.

10. The formulation of recommended solutions or remedies for economic problems is referred to as (theoretical, policy) _____ economics.

11. The three steps in the formulation of economic policy are (1) stating the economic (theory, goal) _____, (2) determining the policy (results, options) _____, and (3) implementing and evaluating policy (assumptions, effectiveness) _____.

12. Eight widely accepted economic goals in the United States and many nations are

a. _____
b. _____
c. _____
d. _____
e. _____
f. _____
g. _____
h. _____

13. Increases in economic growth that promote full employment would be an example of a set of (conflicting, complementary) _____ economic goals. Efforts to achieve an equitable distribution of income that at the same time reduce economic efficiency would be an example of a set of (conflicting, complementary) _____ economic goals, indicating that there are (tradeoffs, causal effects) _____ among economic goals.

14. The study of the total output of the economy or the general level of prices is the subject of (microeconomics, macroeconomics) _____, whereas the study of output in a particular industry or of a particular product is the subject of _____.

15. The collection of specific units which are being added and treated as if they were one unit is an (assumption, aggregate) _____.

16. Two different types of statements can be made about economic topics. A (positive, normative) _____ statement explains what is by offering a scientific proposition about economic behavior that is based on economic theory and facts, but a _____ statement includes a value judgment about an economic policy or the economy that suggests what ought to be. Many of the reported disagreements among economists usually involve (positive, normative) ______________ statements.

17. Holding a preconceived notion, such as thinking that corporate profits are always excessive, is an example of a(n) (aggregate, bias) ______________ pitfall in economic thinking.

18. Pitfalls to economic thinking can also occur because terminology is (theoretical, loaded) ______________ and definitions are based on (common, economic) ______________ usage.

19. The statement that "what is good for the individual is also good for the group" may not be correct because of the fallacy of (complexity, composition) ______________.

20. The person who believes that "washing a car will cause it to rain tomorrow" is expressing a(n) (other things equal, *post hoc*) ______________ fallacy.

■ TRUE-FALSE QUESTIONS

Circle the T if the statement is true, the F if it is false.

1. Economics deals with the activities by which humans can earn a living and improve their standard of living. **T F**

2. From an economic perspective, "there is no such thing as a free lunch." **T F**

3. Rational self-interest is the same thing as being selfish. **T F**

4. The economic perspective views individuals or institutions as making rational choices based on the marginal analysis of the costs and benefits of decisions. **T F**

5. Economics is academic and of little value because it does not teach the student how to earn a living. **T F**

6. Systematically arranging facts, interpreting them, and using them to derive economic principles is called economic analysis. **T F**

7. The deductive method is the scientific method and the method used to derive economic principles from economic facts. **T F**

8. Deduction and induction are complementary rather than opposing techniques of investigation. **T F**

9. Economic principles enable us to predict the economic consequences of many human actions. **T F**

10. In economics, the terms "law," "principle," "theory," and "model" essentially mean the same thing. **T F**

11. The "other things equal" or *ceteris paribus* assumption is made to simplify the reasoning process. **T F**

12. Economic principles, or theories, are abstractions. **T F**

13. The first step in the formulation of an economic policy, the statement of goals, may be occasion for disagreement because different people may have different and conflicting goals to be achieved. **T F**

14. Once a single goal or end has been determined as the sole objective of economic policy, there is seldom any question of which policy to adopt to achieve that goal. **T F**

15. One of the widely (although not universally) accepted economic goals of people in the United States is an equal distribution of income. **T F**

16. A tradeoff is a situation in which some of one economic goal is sacrificed to obtain some of another economic goal. **T F**

17. Macroeconomic analysis is concerned with the economic activity of specific firms or industries. **T F**

18. Microeconomic analysis is concerned with the performance of the economy as a whole or its major aggregates. **T F**

19. The statement that "the legal minimum wage should be raised to give working people a decent income" is an example of a normative statement. **T F**

20. When value judgments are made about the economy or economic policy, this is called positive economics. **T F**

21. The belief that lending money is always superior to borrowing money is an example of a bias in objective thinking about economic issues. **T F**

22. The fallacy of composition would be calling profits "excessive" or an unemployed worker "lazy." **T F**

23. If you speak of "capital" to most people, they understand that you are referring to money. The economist, therefore, is obligated to use the term "capital" to mean money. **T F**

24. The *post hoc, ergo propter hoc* fallacy is the belief that "what is true for the individual or part of a group is necessarily true for the group or whole." **T F**

25. A person who concludes that more education increases income may be confusing correlation with causation. **T F**

■ MULTIPLE-CHOICE QUESTIONS

Circle the letter that corresponds to the best answer.

1. What statement would best complete a short definition of economics? "Economics is the study of
- **(a)** how businesses produce goods and services"
- **(b)** the efficient use of scarce productive resources"
- **(c)** the equitable distribution of society's income and wealth"
- **(d)** the printing and circulation of money throughout the economy"

2. The idea in economics that "there is no such thing as a free lunch" means that

(a) the marginal benefit of such a lunch is greater than its marginal cost
(b) businesses cannot increase their market share by offering free lunches
(c) scarce resources have alternative uses or opportunity costs
(d) consumers are irrational when they ask for a free lunch

3. A major feature of the economic perspective is
(a) equating rational self-interest with selfishness
(b) comparing marginal benefits with marginal costs
(c) the validity of normative economics for decision making
(d) the recognition of the abundance of economic resources

4. From an economic perspective, when a business decides to employ more workers, the business decision maker has most likely concluded that the marginal
(a) costs of employing more workers have decreased
(b) benefits of employing more workers has increased
(c) benefits of employing more workers are greater than the marginal costs
(d) costs of employing more workers is not an opportunity cost for the business because more workers are needed to increase production

5. Economic analysis that derives economic principles about how individuals behave or institutions act is called
(a) policy economics
(b) macroeconomics
(c) normative economics
(d) theoretical economics

6. When economic principles or theories are derived from factual evidence, this method of economic reasoning is called
(a) *post hoc*
(b) deduction
(c) induction
(d) hypothesis testing

7. The development of an economic hypothesis through intuition, insight, or logic is associated with
(a) induction
(b) deduction
(c) policy economics
(d) normative economics

8. When economists state that "consumer spending rises when personal income increases," this is an example of
(a) a generalization
(b) loaded terminology
(c) a normative statement
(d) a fallacy of composition

9. Another term for the assumption that "other things are equal" is
(a) *ceteris paribus*
(b) the correlation fallacy
(c) the fallacy of composition
(d) *post hoc, ergo propter hoc*

10. An economic principle states that the lower the price of a product, the greater the quantity consumers will wish to purchase. This principle is based on the critical assumption that
(a) the whole is not greater than the sum of the parts
(b) economic goals are complementary and not conflicting
(c) economic analysis is normative
(d) there are no other important changes affecting the demand for the product

11. The three basic steps in economic policymaking are
(a) gather facts, make abstractions, show findings
(b) state the goal, determine the options, evaluate results
(c) create the theory, analyze assumptions, derive conclusions
(d) form hypotheses, simplify the model, assume other things are equal

12. The production of more goods and services and the development of higher standard of living would be associated with what economic goal?
(a) economic security
(b) economic freedom
(c) economic growth
(d) full employment

13. Which economic goal is associated with the idea that we want to get the maximum benefit at the minimum cost from the limited productive resources available?
(a) economic security
(b) economic freedom
(c) economic growth
(d) economic efficiency

14. Which economic goal would be most abstract and difficult to measure?
(a) full employment
(b) economic efficiency
(c) economic freedom
(d) price-level stability

15. To say that two economic goals are conflicting means
(a) it is impossible to quantify both goals
(b) there is a tradeoff in the achievement of the two goals
(c) the two goals are not fully accepted as important economic goals
(d) the attainment of one goal also results in the attainment of the other goal

16. If economic growth tends to produce a more equitable distribution of income among people in a nation, this relationship between the two economic goals appears to be
(a) deductive
(b) conflicting
(c) complementary
(d) mutually exclusive

17. When we look at the whole economy or its major aggregates, our analysis would be at the level of
(a) microeconomics
(b) macroeconomics
(c) positive economics
(d) normative economics

18. Which would be studied in microeconomics?
- **(a)** the output of the entire economy
- **(b)** the total number of workers employed in the United States
- **(c)** the general level of prices in the U.S. economy
- **(d)** the output and price of wheat in the United States

19. Which is a normative economic statement?
- **(a)** the consumer price index rose 5.6% last month
- **(b)** the unemployment rate of 6.8% is too high
- **(c)** the average rate of interest on loans is 8.6%
- **(d)** the economy grew at an annual rate of 2.6%

20. Sandra states that "there is a high correlation between consumption and income." Arthur replies that the correlation occurs because "people consume too much of their income and don't save enough."
- **(a)** Both Sandra's and Arthur's statements are positive.
- **(b)** Both Sandra's and Arthur's statements are normative.
- **(c)** Sandra's statement is positive and Arthur's statement is normative.
- **(d)** Sandra's statement is normative and Arthur's statement is positive.

21. What pitfall to objective thinking is reflected in a person's view that corporate profits are always excessive?
- **(a)** bias
- **(b)** definition
- **(c)** the fallacy of composition
- **(d)** confusing correlation and causation

22. During World War II, the United States used price control to prevent inflation; some people said this was "a fascist and arbitrary restriction of economic freedom," while others said it was "a necessary and democratic means of preventing ruinous inflation." Both labels are examples of
- **(a)** economic bias
- **(b)** the fallacy of composition
- **(c)** the misuse of commonsense definitions
- **(d)** loaded terminology

23. If a farmer grows a larger crop one year, he or she will likely receive more income. Therefore, to reason that if all farmers grew larger crops one year they will likely receive more income is an example of
- **(a)** the after this, therefore because of this fallacy
- **(b)** the fallacy of composition
- **(c)** economic bias
- **(d)** using loaded terminology

24. The government increases its expenditures for road construction equipment, and later the average price of this equipment falls. The belief that the lowered price was the result of the increase in government expenditures is an example of:
- **(a)** the after this, therefore because of this fallacy
- **(b)** the fallacy of composition
- **(c)** imprecise definition
- **(d)** using loaded terminology

25. You observe that more education is associated with more income and conclude that more income leads to more education. This would be an example of
- **(a)** the fallacy of composition
- **(b)** confusing correlation and causation
- **(c)** using the other things equal assumption
- **(d)** the after this, therefore because of this fallacy

■ PROBLEMS

1. Use the appropriate number to match the terms with the phrase.

1. economics	**5. microeconomics**
2. theoretical economics	**6. positive economics**
3. policy economics	**7. normative economics**
4. macroeconomics	**8. empirical economics**

a. The formulation of courses of action to bring about desired economic outcomes or to prevent undesired occurrences. ________

b. The attempt to establish scientific statements about economic behavior; a concern with "what is" rather than what ought to be." ________

c. Part of economics that involves value judgments about what the economy should be like or the way the economic world should be. ________

d. Social science concerned with the efficient use of scarce resources to achieve maximum satisfaction of human material wants. ________

e. Part of economics concerned with the whole economy or its major sectors. ________

f. The testing of economic hypotheses and theories. ________

g. Deriving economic principles from relevant economic facts. ________

h. Part of economics concerned with the economic behavior of individual units such as households, firms, and industries (particular markets). ________

2. ***News report:*** "The worldwide demand for wheat from the United States increased and caused the price of wheat in the United States to rise." This is a *specific* instance of a more *general* economic principle. Of which economic *generalization* is this a particular example? ________

____

____

3. Following are four statements. Each is an example of one of the pitfalls frequently encountered in the study of economics. Indicate in the space following each statement the type of pitfall involved.

a. "Investment in stocks and bonds is the only way to build real capital assets." ________

b. "An unemployed worker can find a job if the worker looks diligently and conscientiously for employment; therefore, all unemployed workers can find employment if they are diligent and conscientious in looking for a job."

____

c. ***McConnell:*** "Regulation of public utilities in the United States is an immoral and unconscionable interference with the divine right of private property and, as you know, there is no private property in the socialist nations." ***Brue:*** "It is far from that. You know perfectly well that it is an attempt to limit the unmitigated avarice of mammoth corporations in order, as the Constitution commands, to promote the general welfare of a democratic America." ______________________

____

d. "The stock market crash of 1929 was followed by and resulted in 10 years of depression." ____________

____

4. Following is a list of economic statements. Indicate in the space to the right of each statement whether it is positive (P) or normative (N). Then, in the last four lines below, write two of your own examples of positive economic statements and two examples of normative economic statements.

a. New York City should control the rental price of apartments. ____

b. Consumer prices rose at an annual rate of 5% last year. ____

c. Most people who are unemployed are just too lazy to work. ____

d. Generally, if you lower the price of a product, people will buy more of that product. ____

e. The profits of drug companies are too large and ought to be used to conduct research on new medicines. ____

f. Government should do more to help the poor. ____

g. ______________________ P

h. ______________________ P

i. ______________________ N

j. ______________________ N

■ SHORT ANSWER AND ESSAY QUESTIONS

1. Define economics in both a less and a more sophisticated way. In your latter definition, explain the meaning of "resources" and "wants."

2. What are the three interrelated features of the economic perspective?

3. What is the economic meaning of the statement "there is no such thing as a free lunch"?

4. What is the difference between rational self-interest and selfishness?

5. How do economists use marginal analysis?

6. What are the principal reasons for studying economics?

7. Define the terms "induction" and "deduction" and give an example of each.

8. Define and explain the relationships between economic theory and policy economics.

9. What is the relationship between fact and theory?

10. What is a "laboratory experiment under controlled conditions"? Does the science of economics have any kind of laboratory? Why do economists use the "other things equal" assumption?

11. Why are economic principles and models necessarily generalized and abstract?

12. What does it mean to say that economic principles can be used for prediction?

13. What procedure should be followed in formulating sound economic policies?

14. Of the eight economic goals listed in the text, which one would you *rank* first, second, third, etc.? Would you add any other goals to this list? If economic goals 2 and 4 were conflicting, which goal would you prefer? Why? If goals 1 and 5 were conflicting, which would you prefer? Why?

15. How can the concept "tradeoffs" be applied to the discussion of economic goals? Give an example.

16. Explain the difference between macroeconomics and microeconomics.

17. Why do economists disagree?

18. What are some current examples of positive economic statements and normative economic statements?

19. Explain each of the following terms:

(a) fallacy of composition

(b) loaded terminology

(c) the *post hoc, ergo propter hoc* fallacy

20. Use an example to describe how correlation differs from causation.

ANSWERS

Chapter 1 The Nature and Method of Economics

FILL-IN QUESTIONS

1. limited, maximum
2. scarcity, cost, alternative
3. rational, marginal
4. citizen, academic, vocational
5. theoretical
6. inductive, deductive
7. laws, theories, models
8. generalizations, abstractions
9. other things equal (or *ceteris paribus*)
10. policy
11. goal, options, effectiveness
12. *a.* economic growth; *b.* full employment; *c.* economic efficiency; *d.* price stability; *e.* economic freedom; *f.* equitable distribution of income; *g.* economic security; *h.* balance of trade (*any order for a–h*)
13. complementary, conflicting, tradeoffs
14. macroeconomics, microeconomics

15. aggregate
16. positive, normative, normative
17. bias
18. loaded, common
19. composition
20. *post hoc*

TRUE-FALSE QUESTIONS

1. T, p. 3	**8.** T, p. 7	**15.** T, p. 9	**22.** F, p. 11
2. T, p. 4	**9.** T, p. 7	**16.** T, p. 9	**23.** F, p. 11
3. F, p. 4	**10.** T, p. 7	**17.** F, pp. 9-10	**24.** F, p. 11
4. T, pp. 4-5	**11.** T, p. 8	**18.** F, pp. 9-10	**25.** T, pp. 11-13
5. F, pp. 5-6	**12.** T, p. 8	**19.** T, p. 10	
6. T, pp. 6-7	**13.** T, pp. 8-9	**20.** F, p. 10	
7. F, p. 7	**14.** F, p. 8	**21.** T, pp. 10-11	

MULTIPLE-CHOICE QUESTIONS

1. b, p. 3	**8.** a, pp. 7–8	**15.** b, p. 9	**22.** d, p. 11
2. c, p. 4	**9.** a, p. 8	**16.** c, p. 9	**23.** b, p. 11
3. b, pp. 4-5	**10.** d, p. 8	**17.** b, pp. 9-10	**24.** a, p. 11
4. c, pp. 4-5	**11.** b, pp. 8-9	**18.** d, p. 10	**25.** b, pp. 11-13
5. d, pp. 6-7	**12.** c, p. 9	**19.** b, p. 10	
6. c, p. 7	**13.** d, p. 9	**20.** c, p. 10	
7. b, p. 7	**14.** c, p. 9	**21.** a, pp. 10-11	

PROBLEMS

1. *a.* 3; *b.* 6; *c.* 7; *d.* 1; *e.* 4; *f.* 8; *g.* 2; *h.* 5
2. An increase in the demand for an economic good will cause the price of that good to rise.
3. *a.* definitions; *b.* the fallacy of composition; *c.* loaded terminology; *d.* the after this, therefore because of this fallacy.
4. *a.* N; *b.* P; *c.* N; *d.* P; *e.* N; *f.* N

SHORT ANSWER AND ESSAY QUESTIONS

1. p. 3	**6.** pp. 5-6	**11.** pp. 7-8	**16.** pp. 9-10
2. pp. 4-5	**7.** p. 7	**12.** pp. 7-8	**17.** p. 10
3. p. 4	**8.** pp. 6-9	**13.** pp. 8-9	**18.** p. 10
4. p. 4	**9.** pp. 6-8	**14.** p. 9	**19.** p. 11
5. pp. 4-5	**10.** p. 8	**15.** p. 9	**20.** pp. 11-13

APPENDIX TO CHAPTER 1

Graphs and Their Meaning

This appendix introduces graphing in economics. Graphs help illustrate and simplify the economic theories and models presented throughout this book. The old saying that "a picture is worth 1000 words" applies to economics; graphs are the way that economists "picture" relationships between economic variables.

You must master the basics of graphing if these "pictures" are to be of any help to you. The appendix explains how to achieve that mastery. It shows you how to construct a graph from a table of data of two variables, such as income and consumption. Economists usually, but not always, place the ***independent variable*** (income) on the horizontal axis and the ***dependent variable*** (consumption) on the vertical axis of the graph. Once the data points are plotted and a line drawn to connect the plotted points, you can determine whether there is a ***direct*** or an ***inverse relationship*** between the variables. Identifying a direct and an inverse relationship between variables is an essential skill used repeatedly in this book.

Information from data in graphs and tables can be written in an equation. This work involves determining the ***slope*** and ***intercept*** from a straight line in a graph or data in a table. Using values for the slope and intercept, you can write a ***linear equation*** that will enable you to calculate what the dependent variable would be for a given level of the independent variable.

Some graphs used in the book are *nonlinear.* With ***nonlinear curves,*** the slope of the line is no longer constant throughout but varies as one moves along the curve. This slope can be estimated at a point by determining the slope of a straight line that is drawn tangent to the curve at that point. Similar calculations can be made for other points to see how the slope changes along the curve.

■ APPENDIX CHECKLIST

After you have studied this appendix you should be able to

☐ Explain why economists use graphs.
☐ Construct a graph of two variables using the numerical data from a table.
☐ Make a table with two variables from data on a graph.
☐ Distinguish between a direct and an inverse relationship when given data on two variables.
☐ Identify dependent and independent variables in economic examples and graphs.
☐ Describe how economists use the other things equal (*ceteris paribus*) assumption in graphing two variables.
☐ Calculate the slope of a straight line between two points when given the tabular data, and indicate whether the slope is positive or negative.
☐ Describe how slopes are affected by the choice of the units of measurement for either variable.
☐ Explain how slopes are related to marginal analysis.
☐ Graph infinite or zero slopes and explain their meaning.
☐ Determine the vertical intercept for a straight line in a graph with two variables.
☐ Write a linear equation using the slope of a line and the vertical intercept; when given values for the dependent variable, determine values for the independent variable.
☐ Estimate the slope of a nonlinear curve at a point using a line that is tangent to the curve at that point.

■ APPENDIX OUTLINE

1. Graphs illustrate the relationship between variables and give economists and students another way, in addition to verbal explanation, of understanding economic phenomena. Graphs are aids in describing economic theories and models.

2. The construction of a simple graph involves plotting the numerical data of two variables from a table.

a. Each graph has a horizontal and a vertical axis that can be labeled for each variable and then scaled for the range of the data point that will be measured on the axis.
b. Data points are plotted on the graph by drawing perpendiculars from the scaled points on the two axes to the place on the graph where the perpendiculars intersect.
c. A line or curve can then be drawn to connect the points plotted on the graph.

3. A graph provides information about relationships between variables.

a. An upward-sloping line to the right on a graph indicates that there is a positive or *direct relationship* between two variables: an increase in one is associated with an increase in the other; a decrease in one is associated with a decrease in the other.
b. A downward-sloping line to the right means that there is a negative or *inverse relationship* between the two variables: An increase in one is associated with a

decrease in the other; a decrease in one is associated with an increase in the other.

4. Economists are often concerned with determining cause and effect in economic events.

a. A dependent variable changes (increases or decreases) because of a change in another variable.

b. An independent variable produces or "causes" the change in the dependent variable.

c. In a graph, mathematicians place an independent variable on the horizontal axis and a dependent variable on the vertical axis; economists are more arbitrary about which variable is placed on an axis.

5. Economic graphs are simplifications of economic relationships. When graphs are plotted, usually an implicit assumption is made that all other factors are being held constant. This "other things equal" or *ceteris paribus* assumption is used to simplify the analysis so the study can focus on the two variables of interest.

6. The *slope* of a straight line in a two-variable graph is the ratio of the vertical change to the horizontal change between two points.

a. A *positive* slope indicates that the relationship between the two variables is *direct.*

b. A *negative* slope indicates that there is an *inverse* relationship between the two variables.

c. Slopes are affected by the *measurement units* for either variable.

d. Slopes measure *marginal* changes.

e. Slopes can be *infinite* (line parallel to vertical axis) or *zero* (line parallel to horizontal axis).

7. The vertical *intercept* of a straight line in a two-variable graph is the point where the line intersects the vertical axis of the graph.

8. The slope and intercept of a straight line can be expressed in the form of a *linear equation,* which is written as $y = a + bx$. Once the values for the intercept (a) and the slope (b) are calculated, then given any value of the independent variable (x), the value of the dependent variable (y) can be determined.

9. The slope of a straight line is constant, but the slope of a nonlinear curve changes throughout. To estimate the slope of a nonlinear curve at a point, the slope of a line tangent to the curve at that point is calculated.

■ HINTS AND TIPS

1. This appendix will help you understand the graphs and problems presented throughout the book. Do not skip reading the appendix or working on the self-test questions and problems in this *Study Guide.* The time you invest now will pay off in improved understanding in later chapters. Graphing is a basic skill for economic analysis.

2. Positive and negative relationships in graphs often confuse students. To overcome this confusion, draw a two-variable graph with a positive slope and another two-variable graph with a negative slope. In each graph, show what happens to the value of one variable when there is a change in the value of the other variable.

3. A straight line in a two-variable graph can be expressed in an equation. Make sure you know how to interpret each part of the linear equation.

■ IMPORTANT TERMS

vertical and horizontal axes
direct (positive) and inverse (negative) relationships
dependent and independent variables
slope of a straight line
vertical intercept
linear equation
nonlinear curve
tangent

SELF-TEST

■ FILL-IN QUESTIONS

1. The relationship between two economic variables can be visualized with the aid of a two-dimensional ______________, which has a ______________ axis and a ______________ axis.

2. Customarily, the (dependent, independent) ______________ variable is placed on the horizontal axis and the ______________ is placed on the vertical axis. The ______________ variable is said to change because of a change in the ______________ variables.

3. The vertical and horizontal (scales, ranges) ______________ of the graph are calibrated to reflect the ______________ of values in the table of data points on which the graph is based.

4. The graph of a straight line that slopes downward to the right indicates that there is a(n) (direct, inverse) ______________ relationship between the two variables. A graph of a straight line that slopes upward to the right tells us that the relationship is (direct, inverse) ______________. When the value of one variable increases and the value of the other variable increases, then the relationship is ______________; when the value of one increases, while the other decreases, the relationship is ______________.

5. In interpreting an economic graph, the "cause" or the "source" is the (dependent, independent) ______________ variable and the "effect" or "outcome" is the ______________ variable.

6. Other variables, beyond the two in a two-dimensional graph, that might affect the economic relationship are assumed to be (changing, held constant) ______________. This assumption is also referred to as the "other things equal" assumption or as (*post hoc, ceteris paribus*) ______________.

7. The slope of a straight line between two points is defined as the ratio of the (vertical, horizontal) ______________ change to the ______________ change.

8. When two variables move in the same direction, the slope will be (negative, positive) ______________; when the variables move in opposite directions, the slope will be ______________.

9. The slope of a line will be affected by the (units of measurement, vertical intercept) ______________.

10. The concept of a slope is important to economists because it reflects the (marginal, total) ______________ change in one variable on another variable.

11. A graph of a line with an infinite slope is (horizontal, vertical) ______________, while a graph of a line with a zero slope is ______________.

12. The point at which the slope of the line meets the vertical axis is called the vertical (tangent, intercept) ______________.

13. We can express the graph of a straight line with a linear equation that can be written as $y = a + bx$.

a. a is the (slope, intercept) ______________ and b is the ______________

b. y is the (dependent, independent) ______________ variable and x is the ______________ variable.

c. If a were 2, b were 4, and x were 5, then y would be ______________. If the value of x changed to 7, then y would be ______________. If the value of x changed to 3, then y would be ______________.

14. The slope of a (straight line, nonlinear curve) ______________ is constant throughout; the slope of a ______________ varies from point to point.

15. An estimate of the slope of a nonlinear curve at a certain point can be made by calculating the slope of a straight line that is (tangent, perpendicular) ______________ to the point on the curve.

■ TRUE-FALSE QUESTIONS

Circle the T if the statement is true, the F if it is false.

1. Economists design graphs to confuse people. T F

2. If the straight line on a two-variable graph slopes downward to the right, then there is a positive relationship between the two variables. T F

3. A variable that changes as a consequence of a change in another variable is considered a dependent variable. T F

4. Economists always put the independent variable on the horizontal axis and the dependent variable on the vertical axis of a two-variable graph. T F

5. *Ceteris paribus* means that other variables are changing at the same time. T F

6. In the ratio for the calculation of the slope of a straight line, the vertical change is in the numerator and the horizontal change is in the denominator. T F

7. If the slope of the linear relationship between consumption and income was .90, then it tells us that for every $1 increase in income there will be a $.90 increase in consumption. T F

8. The slope of a straight line in a two-variable graph will *not* be affected by the choice of the units for either variable. T F

9. The slopes of lines measure marginal changes. T F

10. The absence of a relationship between a change in the price of variable *A* and the quantity of variable *B* would be described by a line parallel to the horizontal axis. T F

11. A line with an infinite slope in a two-variable graph is parallel to the horizontal axis. T F

12. In a two-variable graph, income is graphed on the vertical axis and the quantity of snow is graphed on the horizontal axis. If income was independent of the quantity of snow, then this independence would be represented by a line parallel to the horizontal axis. T F

13. If a linear equation is $y = 10 + 5x$, the vertical intercept is 5. T F

14. When a line is tangent to a nonlinear curve, then it intersects the curve at a particular point. T F

15. If the slope of a straight line on a two-variable (x, y) graph were .5 and the vertical intercept were 5, then a value of 10 for x would mean that y is also 10. T F

16. A slope of −4 for a straight line in a two-variable graph indicates that there is an inverse relationship between the two variables. T F

17. If x is an independent variable and y is a dependent variable, then a change in y results in a change in x. T F

18. An upward slope for a straight line that is tangent to a nonlinear curve indicates that the slope of the nonlinear curve at that point is positive. T F

19. If one pair of x, y points was (13, 10) and the other pair was (8, 20), then the slope of the straight line between the two sets of points in the two-variable graph, with x on the horizontal axis and y on the vertical axis, would be 2. T F

20. When the value of x is 2, a value of 10 for y would be calculated from a linear equation of $y = -2 + 6x$. T F

■ MULTIPLE-CHOICE QUESTIONS

Circle the letter that corresponds to the best answer.

1. If an increase in one variable is associated with a decrease in another variable, then we can conclude that the variables are
(a) nonlinear
(b) directly related
(c) inversely related
(d) positively related

2. The ratio of the absolute vertical change to the absolute horizontal change between two points of a straight line is the
(a) slope
(b) vertical intercept
(c) horizontal intercept
(d) point of tangency

3. There are two sets of x, y points on a straight line in a two-variable graph, with y on the vertical axis and x on the horizontal axis. If one set of points was (0, 5) and the other set (5, 20), the linear equation for the line would be
(a) $y = 5x$
(b) $y = 5 + 3x$
(c) $y = 5 + 15x$
(d) $y = 5 + .33x$

4. In a two-variable graph of data on the price and quantity of a product, economists place
(a) price on the horizontal axis because it is the independent variable and quantity on the vertical axis because it is the dependent variable
(b) price on the vertical axis because it is the dependent variable and quantity on the horizontal because it is the independent variable
(c) price on the vertical axis even though it is the independent variable and quantity on the horizontal axis even though it is the dependent variable
(d) price on the horizontal axis even though it is the dependent variable and quantity on the vertical axis even though it is the independent variable

5. In a two-dimensional graph of the relationship between two economic variables, an assumption is usually made that
(a) both variables are linear
(b) both variables are nonlinear
(c) other variables are held constant
(d) other variables are permitted to change

6. When the slope of a straight line to a point tangent to a nonlinear curve is zero, then the straight line is
(a) vertical
(b) horizontal
(c) upward sloping
(d) downward sloping

Questions 7, 8, 9, and 10 are based on the following four data sets. In each set, the independent variable is in the left column and the dependent variable is in the right column.

(1)		(2)		(3)		(4)	
A	*B*	*C*	*D*	*E*	*F*	*G*	*H*
0	1	0	12	4	5	0	4
3	2	5	8	6	10	1	3
6	3	10	4	8	15	2	2
9	4	15	0	10	20	3	1

7. There is an inverse relationship between the independent and dependent variable in data sets
(a) 1 and 4
(b) 2 and 3
(c) 1 and 3
(d) 2 and 4

8. The vertical intercept is 4 in data set
(a) 1
(b) 2
(c) 3
(d) 4

9. The linear equation for data set 1 is
(a) $B = 3A$
(b) $B = 1 + 3A$
(c) $B = 1 + .33A$
(d) $A = 1 + .33B$

10. The linear equation for data set 2 is
(a) $C = 12 - 1.25D$
(b) $D = 12 + 1.25C$
(c) $D = 12 - .80C$
(d) $C = 12 - .80D$

Answer Questions 11, 12, 13, and 14 on the basis of the following diagram.

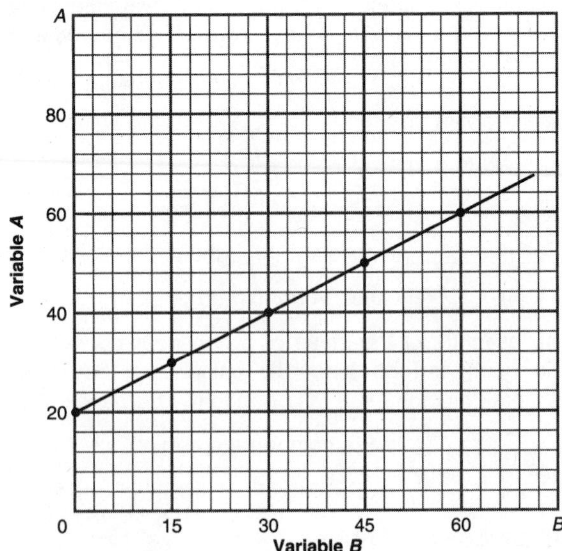

11. The variables A and B are:
(a) positively related
(b) negatively related
(c) indirectly related
(d) nonlinear

12. The slope of the line is
(a) .33
(b) .67
(c) 1.50
(d) 3.00

13. The vertical intercept is
(a) 80
(b) 60
(c) 40
(d) 20

14. The linear equation for the slope of the line is
(a) $A = 20 + .33B$
(b) $B = 20 + .33A$
(c) $A = 20 + .67B$
(d) $B = 20 + .67A$

Answer Questions 15, 16, and 17 on the basis of the following diagram.

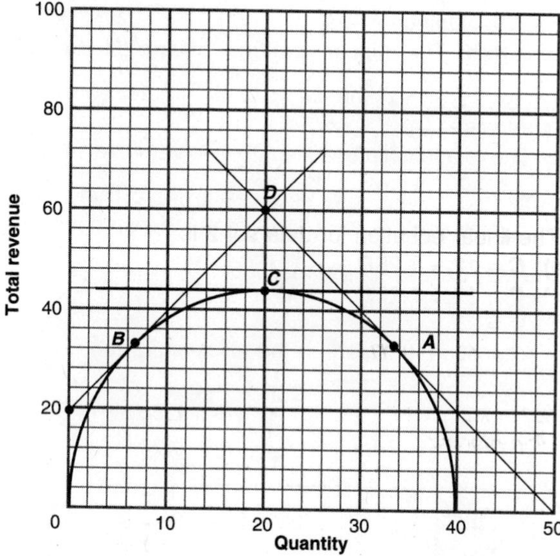

15. The slope of the line tangent to the curve at point ***A*** is
(a) 2
(b) −2
(c) −1.5
(d) −0.5

16. The slope of the line tangent to the curve at point ***B*** is
(a) −2
(b) 2
(c) 3
(d) 0.5

17. The slope of the line tangent to the curve at point ***C*** is
(a) −1
(b) 1
(c) 0
(d) undefined

18. Assume that the relationship between concert ticket prices and attendance is expressed in the equation $P = 25 - 1.25Q$, where ***P*** equals ticket price and ***Q*** equals concert attendance in thousands of people. On the basis of this equation, it can be said that
(a) more people will attend the concert when the price is high compared to when the price is low
(b) if 12,000 people attended the concert, then the ticket price was \$10
(c) if 18,000 people attend the concert, then entry into the concert was free
(d) an increase in ticket price by \$5 reduces concert attendance by 1000 people

19. If you know that the equation relating consumption (***C***) to income (***Y***) is $C = \$7{,}500 + .2Y$, then
(a) consumption is inversely related to income
(b) consumption is the independent variable and income is the dependent variable
(c) if income is \$15,000, then consumption is \$10,500
(d) if consumption is \$30,000, then income is \$10,000

20. If the dependent variable changes by 22 units when the independent variable changes by 12 units, then the slope of the line is
(a) 0.56
(b) 1.83
(c) 2.00
(d) 3.27

■ PROBLEMS

1. Following are three tables for making graphs. On the graphs, plot the economic relationships contained in each table. Be sure to label each axis of the graph and indicate the unit measurement and scale used on each axis.

a. Use the table at the top of the next page to graph national income on the horizontal axis and consumption expenditures on the vertical axis below; connect the seven points and label the curve "Consumption." The relationship between income and consumption is a(n) (direct, inverse) _______________ one and the consumption curve a(n) (up-, down-) _______________ sloping curve.

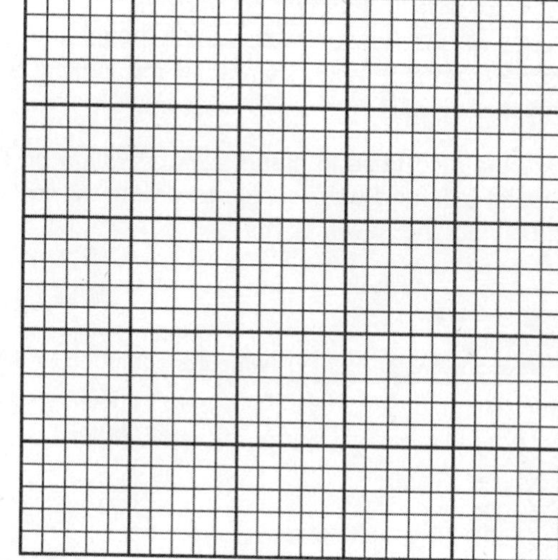

National income, billions of dollars	Consumption expenditures, billions of dollars
$ 600	$ 600
700	640
800	780
900	870
1000	960
1100	1050
1200	1140

b. Use the next table to graph investment expenditures on the horizontal axis and the rate of interest on the vertical axis; connect the seven points and label the curve "Investment." The relationship between the rate of interest and investment expenditures is a(n) (direct, inverse) ______________ one and the investment curve is a(n) (up-, down-) ___________ sloping curve.

Rate of interest, %	Investment expenditures, billions of dollars
8	$220
7	280
6	330
5	370
4	400
3	420
2	430

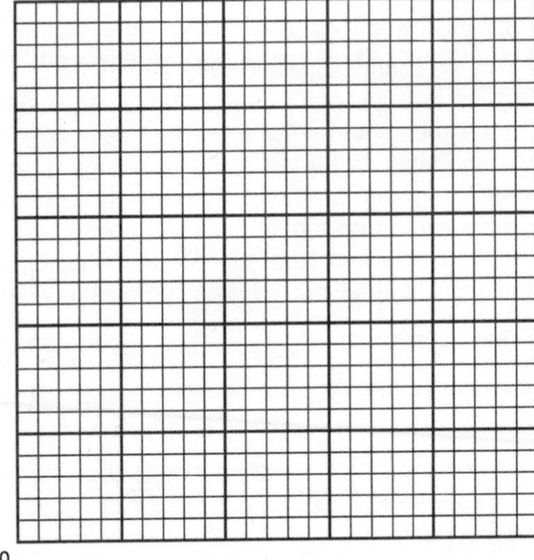

0

c. Use the next table to graph average salary on the horizontal axis and wine consumption on the vertical axis; connect the seven points.

Average salary, U.S. college professors	Annual per capita wine consumption in liters
$52,000	11.5
53,000	11.6
54,000	11.7
55,000	11.8
56,000	11.9
57,000	22.0
58,000	22.1

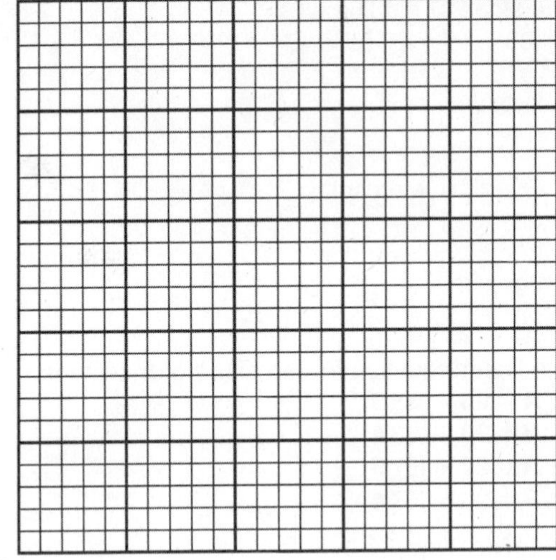

0

(1) The average salary of a college professor and wine consumption (are, are not) are not *correlated.* The higher average salary (is, is not) ______________ the *cause* of the greater consumption of wine.

(2) The relationship between the two variables may be purely ______________; or, as is more likely, both the higher salaries and the greater consumption of wine may be the result of the higher ______________ in the U.S. economy.

2. This question is based on the following graph.

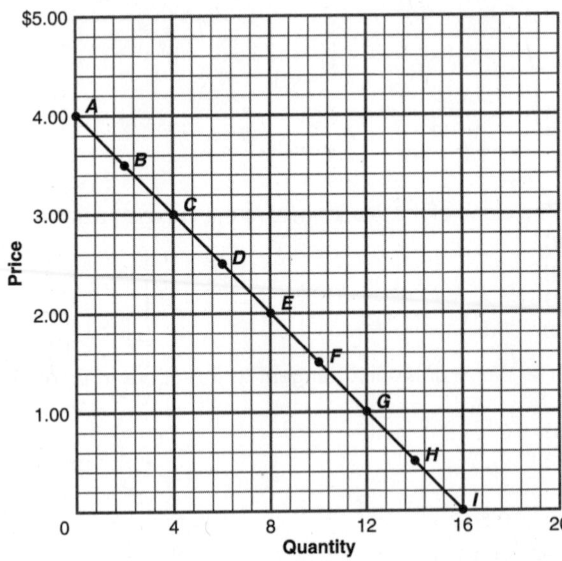

a. Construct a table for points ***A–I*** from the data shown in the graph.

b. According to economists, price is the (independent, dependent) ______________ variable and quantity is the ______________ variable.

c. Write a linear equation that summarizes the data.

3. The following three sets of data each show the relationship between an independent variable and a dependent variable. For each set, the independent variable is in the left column and the dependent variable is in the right column.

(1)		*(2)*		*(3)*	
A	***B***	***C***	***D***	***E***	***F***
00	10	0	100	0	20
10	30	10	75	50	40
20	50	20	50	100	60
30	70	30	25	150	80
40	90	40	0	200	100

a. Write an equation that summarizes the data for sets (1), (2), and (3).

b. State whether each data set shows a positive or an inverse relationship between the two variables.

c. Plot data sets 1 and 2 on the following graph. Use the same horizontal scale for both sets of independent variables and the same vertical scale for both sets of dependent variables.

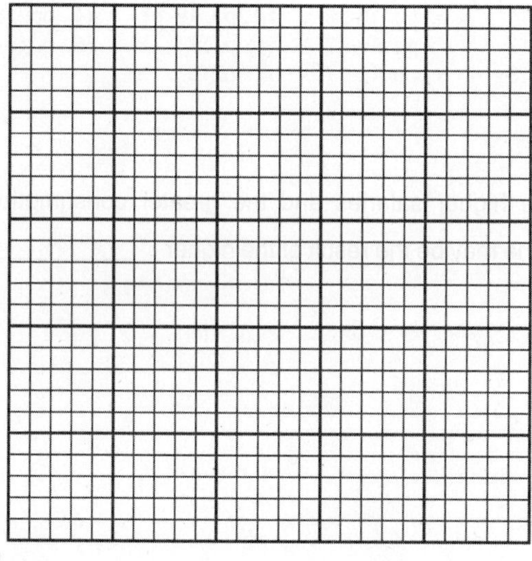

4. This problem is based on the following graph.

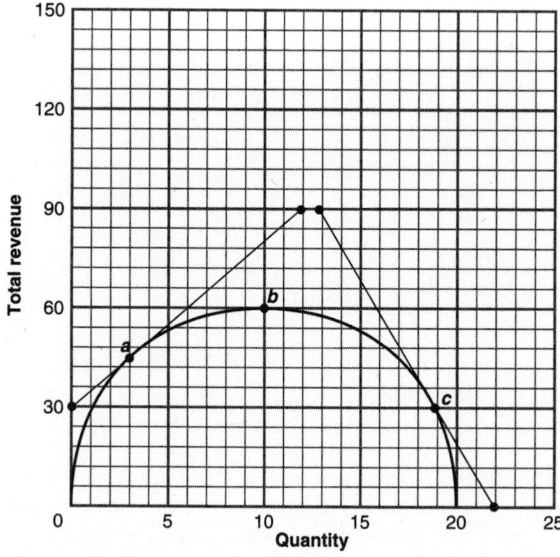

a. The slope of the straight line through point ***a*** is?

b. The slope of the straight line through point ***b*** is?

c. The slope of the straight line through point ***c*** is?

■ SHORT ANSWER AND ESSAY QUESTIONS

1. Why do economists use graphs in their work?

2. Give two examples of a graph that illustrates the relationship between two economic variables.

3. What does the slope tell you about a straight line? How would you interpret a slope of 4? A slope of −2? A slope of .5? A slope of −.25?

4. If the vertical intercept increases in value but the slope of a straight line stays the same, what happens to the graph of the line? If the vertical intercept decreases in value, what will happen to the line?

5. How do you interpret a vertical line on a two-variable graph? How do you interpret a horizontal line?

6. When you know that the price and quantity of a product are inversely related, what does this tell you about the slope of a line? What do you know about the slope when the two variables are positively related?

7. Which variable is the dependent and which is the independent in the following economic statement: "A decrease in business taxes had a positive effect on investment spending."

8. How do you tell the difference between a dependent and independent variable when examining economic relationships?

9. Why is an assumption made that all other variables are held constant when we construct a two-variable graph of the price and quantity of a product?

10. How do mathematicians and economists differ at times in how they construct two-dimensional graphs? Give an example.

11. How is the slope of a straight line in a two-variable graph affected by the choice of the units for either variable? Explain and give an example.

12. What is the relationship between the slopes of lines and marginal analysis?

13. Describe a case in which a straight line in a two-variable graph would have an infinite slope and a case in which the slope of a line would be zero.

14. If you know that the equation relating consumption (***C***) to income (***Y***) is $C = 10{,}000 + 5Y$, then what would consumption be when income is $5000? Construct an income-consumption table for five different levels of income.

15. How do the slopes of a straight line and a nonlinear curve differ? How do you estimate the slope of a nonlinear curve?

ANSWERS

Appendix to Chapter 1 Graphs and Their Meaning

FILL-IN QUESTIONS

1. graph, horizontal, vertical (either order for last two)
2. independent, dependent, dependent, independent
3. scales, ranges
4. inverse, direct, direct, inverse
5. independent, dependent
6. held constant, *ceteris paribus*
7. vertical, horizontal
8. positive, negative
9. units of measurement
10. marginal
11. vertical, horizontal
12. intercept
13. *a.* intercept, slope; *b.* dependent, independent; *c.* 22, 30, 14
14. straight line, nonlinear curve
15. tangent

TRUE-FALSE QUESTIONS

1. F, p. 15	**6.** T, p. 17	**11.** F, p. 18	**16.** T, pp. 17
2. F, pp. 15-16	**7.** T, pp. 17-18	**12.** T, p. 18	**17.** F, pp. 16-17
3. T, p. 16	**8.** F, p. 17	**13.** F, p. 18	**18.** T, p. 19
4. F, p. 17	**9.** T, p. 18	**14.** F, p. 19	**19.** F, pp. 16-17
5. F, p. 17	**10.** T, p. 18	**15.** T, pp. 18-19	**20.** T, pp. 18-19

MULTIPLE-CHOICE QUESTIONS

1. c, pp. 15-16	**6.** b, pp. 18-19	**11.** a, pp. 15-16	**16.** b, p. 17
2. a, p. 17	**7.** d, pp. 15-16	**12.** b, p. 17	**17.** c, pp. 17-19
3. b, pp. 17-19	**8.** d, p. 18	**13.** d, p. 18	**18.** b, pp. 18 -19
4. c, p. 17	**9.** c, p. 18	**14.** c, pp. 18-19	**19.** c, pp. 18-19
5. c, p. 17	**10.** c, p. 18	**15.** b, p. 17	**20.** b, p. 17

PROBLEMS

1. *a.* direct, up-; *b.* inverse, down-; *c.* (1) are, is not; (2) coincidental, incomes (standard of living, or similar answer)
2. *a.*; *b.* independent, dependent; *c.* $P = 4.00 - .25Q$

Point	Price	Quantity
A	$4.00	0
B	3.50	2
C	3.00	4
D	2.50	6
E	2.00	8
F	1.50	10
G	1.00	12
H	.50	14
I	.00	16

3. *a.* (1) $B = 10 + 2A$; (2) $D = 100 - 2.5C$; (3) $F = 20 + .4E$; *b.* (1) positive; (2) inverse; (3) positive
4. *a.* 5; *b.* 0; *c.* −10

■ SHORT ANSWER AND ESSAY QUESTIONS

1. p. 15	**5.** p. 18	**9.** p. 17	**13.** p. 18
2. p. 16	**6.** pp. 15-16	**10.** pp. 18-19	**14.** pp. 18-19
3. p. 17	**7.** pp. 16-17	**11.** p. 17	**15.** p. 19
4. p. 18	**8.** pp. 16-17	**12.** p. 18	

CHAPTER 2

The Economizing Problem

Chapter 2 explains the central problem of economics: Resources—the ultimate means of satisfying material wants—are scarce *relative* to the insatiable wants of society. Economics as a science is the study of the various aspects of the behavior of society in its effort to allocate the scarce resources—land, labor, capital, and entrepreneurial ability—in order to satisfy as best it can its unlimited desire for consumption.

Economics is called the science of efficiency. To understand what efficiency means, however, you must first define its two characteristics: ***full employment*** and ***full production.*** Full employment means that all productive resources available to the economy are being used. Full production requires that two types of efficiency—allocative and productive—are being achieved. ***Allocative efficiency*** means that resources are being devoted to the production of the goods and services society most highly values. ***Productive efficiency*** entails producing this optimal product mix in the least costly way.

The ***production possibilities curve*** is used in this chapter's tables and graphs to discuss the major concerns of economics. The production possibilities model is a valuable device for illustrating the meaning of many concepts defined in the chapter—scarcity, choice, the law of increasing opportunity cost, allocative and productive efficiency, unemployment, and economic growth. It can also be applied to many real economic situations involving budgeting, wartime production, discrimination, productivity, economic growth comparisons, environmental protection, international trade, famine, and central planning. This basic economic model is the first and one of the most important ones presented in the text that you will be using to understand the economic world.

Every economy is faced with the problem of scarce resources and has to find ways to respond to the economic problem. No economy answers the problem in the same way that another economy does. Between the extremes of pure (or laissez-faire) capitalism and the command economy (socialism) are various economic systems; all these systems are different devices—different methods of organization—for finding an answer to the economic problem of relative scarcity. Chapters 3 through 6 explain in greater detail how the U.S. economy is organized and operates to address the economizing problem.

The ***circular flow model*** (or diagram) is a device which illustrates for a capitalistic economy the relation between households and businesses, the flow of money and economic goods and services between households and businesses, their dual role as buyers and sellers, and the two basic types of markets essential to the capitalist process.

■ CHECKLIST

When you have studied this chapter you should be able to

- ☐ Explain the economizing problem in terms of wants and resources.
- ☐ Identify four types of economic resources.
- ☐ Describe the resource payments made in return for each economic resource.
- ☐ Write a definition of economics that incorporates the relationship between resources and wants.
- ☐ Explain why full employment and full production are necessary for the efficient use of resources.
- ☐ Distinguish between allocative efficiency and productive efficiency.
- ☐ State the four assumptions made when a production possibilities table or curve is constructed.
- ☐ Construct a production possibilities curve when you are given the appropriate data.
- ☐ Define opportunity cost and utilize a production possibilities curve to explain the concept.
- ☐ State the law of increasing opportunity costs.
- ☐ Show how the law of increasing opportunity cost is reflected in the shape of the production possibilities curve.
- ☐ Explain the economic rationale for the law of increasing opportunity cost.
- ☐ Use marginal analysis to define allocative efficiency.
- ☐ Explain how allocative efficiency determines the optimal point on a production possibilities curve.
- ☐ Use a production possibilities curve to illustrate unemployment and productive inefficiency.
- ☐ Use the production possibilities curve to illustrate economic growth.
- ☐ Explain how international trade affects a nation's production possibilities curve.
- ☐ Give examples of the application of the production possibilities model.
- ☐ Define pure capitalism, command economy, and traditional economy.
- ☐ Use two characteristics to compare and contrast pure capitalism with a command economy.
- ☐ Explain why many economies can be described as mixed economic systems.

☐ Draw the circular flow diagram; correctly label the real and money flows and the two major types of markets.
☐ Draw the circular flow model, correctly labeling the two markets and the real and money flows between the two sectors in this simplified economy.

■ CHAPTER OUTLINE

1. The study of economics rests on the bases of two facts:
   a. Society's material wants are unlimited.
   b. The economic resources which are the ultimate means of satisfying these wants are scarce in relation to the wants.
   (1) Economic resources are classified as land, capital, labor, and entrepreneurial ability.
   (2) The payments received by those who provide the economy with these four resources are rental income, interest income, wages, and profits, respectively.
   (3) Because these resources are scarce (or limited), the output that the economy is able to produce is also limited.

2. Economics, then, is the study of how society's scarce resources are used (administered) to obtain the greatest satisfaction of its material wants. To be efficient in the use of its resources, an economy must achieve both full employment and full production.
   a. *Full employment* means that the economy is using all available resources.
   b. *Full production* means that all resources used for production should contribute to the maximum satisfaction of society's material wants. Full production implies that there is
   (1) *productive efficiency,* in which the goods and services society desires are being produced in the least costly way.
   (2) *allocative efficiency,* in which resources are devoted to the production of goods and services society most highly values.
   c. The production possibilities table indicates the alternative combinations of goods and services an economy is capable of producing when it has achieved full employment and full production.
   (1) The four assumptions usually made when a production possibilities table is constructed is that economic efficiency, fixed resources, fixed technology, and two products are being considered.
   (2) The table illustrates the fundamental choice every society must make: what quantity of each product it wants produced.
   d. The data in the production possibilities table can be plotted on a graph to obtain a production possibilities curve.
   e. The opportunity cost of producing an additional unit of one product is the total amount of other products that are sacrificed. The law of increasing opportunity costs reflects that the opportunity cost of producing additional units of a product increases as more of that product is produced.
   (1) The law of increasing opportunity costs results in a production possibilities curve that is concave (from the origin).
   (2) The opportunity cost of producing additional units of a product increases as more of the product is produced because resources are not completely adaptable to alternative uses.
   f. Allocative efficiency means that resources are devoted to the optimal product mix for society. This optimal mix is determined by assessing marginal costs and benefits.
   (1) The marginal-cost curve for a product rises because of the law of increasing opportunity costs; the marginal-benefit curve falls because the consumption of a product yields less and less satisfaction.
   (2) There will be *underallocation* of resources to production of a product when the marginal benefit is greater than the marginal cost, and *overallocation* when the marginal cost is greater than the marginal benefit.
   (3) Allocative efficiency is achieved when the marginal cost of a product equals the marginal benefit of a product.

3. Different outcomes will occur when assumptions underlying the production possibilities model are relaxed.
   a. ***Unemployment.*** The economy may be operating at a point inside the production possibilities curve if the assumption of full production and productive efficiency no longer holds. In this case, there will be an unemployment of resources and production will not occur in the least costly way.
   b. ***Economic Growth.*** The production possibilities curve can move outward if the assumption of fixed resources or the assumption of no technological change is dropped.
   (1) Economic growth can occur when there is an expansion in the quantity and quality of resources, or when there is technological advancement.
   (2) The combination of goods and services an economy chooses to produce today helps determine its production possibilities in the future.
   c. International trade and specialization allow a nation to obtain more goods and services than what is indicated by its production possibilities curve, and thus the effect is similar to an increase in economic growth.

4. There are many applications of the production possibilities model. Seven are discussed in the chapter: society's production of military or consumer goods, discrimination, land-use controversies, women in the labor force, economic growth in Japan and the United States, famine in Africa, and emerging technologies.

5. Different economic systems differ as to how they respond to the economizing problem.
   a. At one extreme is pure capitalism, which relies on the private ownership of its economic resources and the market system.
   b. At the other extreme, the command economy uses the public ownership of its resources and central planning.
   c. Economies in the real world lie between these two extremes and are hybrid systems.

d. Some less-developed nations have traditional (or customary) economies which are shaped by the society's customs and traditions.

6. The circular flow model is a device used to clarify the relationships between households and business firms in a purely capitalistic economy.

a. In resource markets, households supply and firms demand resources, and in product markets, the firms supply and households demand products. Households use the incomes they obtain from supplying resources to purchase the goods and services produced by the firms, and in the economy there is a real flow of resources and products and a money flow of incomes and expenditures.

b. The circular flow model has several limitations.

■ HINTS AND TIPS

1. Chapter 2 presents many economic definitions and classifications. Spend time learning these definitions *now* because they are used in later chapters, and you must know them if you are to understand what follows.

2. The production possibilities graph is a simple and extremely useful economic model. Practice your understanding of it by using it to explain the following economic concepts: scarcity, choice, opportunity cost, the law of increasing opportunity costs, full employment, full production, productive efficiency, allocative efficiency, unemployment, and economic growth.

3. Opportunity cost is always measured in terms of a foregone alternative. From a production possibilities table, you can easily calculate how many units of one product you forgo when you get another unit of a product. The ratio of what you forgo to what you get measures the opportunity cost of a choice in a production possibilities table.

■ IMPORTANT TERMS

economizing problem	**production possibilities curve**
utility	**opportunity cost**
economic resources	**law of increasing opportunity costs**
land, capital, labor, and entrepreneurial ability	**economic growth**
investment	**unemployment**
factors of production	**economic systems**
economics	**pure capitalism**
full employment	**market systems**
full production	**command economies**
allocative efficiency	**traditional economies**
productive efficiency	**resource market**
consumer goods	**product market**
capital goods	**circular flow model**
production possibilities table	

SELF-TEST

■ FILL-IN QUESTIONS

1. The economizing problem arises because society's material wants are (limited, unlimited) __unlimited__ and economic resources are __limited__.

2. Consumers want to obtain goods and services that provide (resources, utility) __utility__. Some products that meet this objective are (capital goods, necessities) __necessities__, while others are (investment goods, luxuries) __luxuries__.

3. The four types of resources are

a. __labor__

b. __land__

c. __capital__

d. __entrepreneurial ability__

4. Both consumer goods and capital goods satisfy human wants. The consumer goods satisfy these wants (directly, indirectly) ______________, and the capital goods satisfy them ______________.

5. The income individuals receive from supplying land or natural resources is (interest, rental) ______________ income, whereas the income received from supplying capital goods is ______________ income. The income received by individuals who supply labor is (wage, profit) ______________ income; the income received from entrepreneurial ability is ______________ income.

6. Economics is the social science concerned with the problem of using (unlimited, scarce) ______________ resources to attain the maximum fulfillment of society's ______________ wants.

7. Economic efficiency requires full (employment, allocation) ______________ so that all available resources can be used and that there be full (production, distribution) ______________ so that the employed resources contribute to the maximum satisfaction of material wants.

8. Full production implies that two types of efficiency are achieved: Resources are devoted to the production of the mix of goods and services society most wants, or there is (allocative, productive) ______________ efficiency and the goods and services will be produced in the least costly way, or there will be ______________ efficiency.

9. When a production possibilities table or curve is constructed, four assumptions are made:

a. ______________________________

b. ______________________

c. ______________________

d. ______________________

10. In a two-product world, the quantity of other goods and services an economy must give up to produce more housing is the opportunity (benefit, cost) ______________ of producing the additional housing.

11. The law of increasing opportunity costs explains why the production possibilities curve is (convex, concave) ______________ from the origin. The economic rationale for the law is that economic resources (are, are not) ______________ completely adaptable to alternative uses.

12. Allocative efficiency is determined by assessing the marginal costs and benefits of the output from the allocation of resources to production.

a. The marginal cost curve for a product rises because of increasing (satisfaction, opportunity costs) ______________, and the marginal benefit curve falls because of less ______________ from the additional consumption of a product.

b. When the marginal benefit is greater than the marginal cost, there will be (over, under) ______________-allocation of resources to the production of a product, but when the marginal cost is greater than the marginal benefit, there will be an ______________-allocation.

c. Optimal allocation of resources occurs when the marginal costs of the product output are (greater than, less than, equal to) ______________ the marginal benefits.

13. Following is a production possibilities curve for capital goods and consumer goods.

Capital goods

A

•Y

B

•X

0

Consumer goods

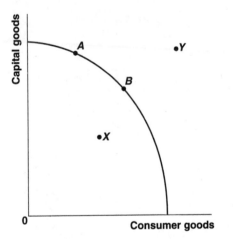

a. If the economy moves from point ***A*** to point ***B***, it will produce (more, fewer) ______________ capital goods and (more, fewer) ______________ consumer goods.

b. If the economy is producing at point ***X***, some resources in the economy are either (not available, unemployed) ______________ or (underemployed, overemployed) ______________.

c. If the economy moves from point ***X*** to point ***B*** (more, fewer) ______________ capital goods and (more, fewer) ______________ consumer goods will be produced.

d. If the economy is to produce at point ***Y***, there must be (unemployment, economic growth) ______________. This can occur because of a resource supply (decrease, increase) ______________ or a technological (decline, improvement) ______________.

14. The more an economy consumes its current production, the (more, less) ______________ it will be capable of producing in future years if other things are equal.

15. The United States' experience with World War II or the Vietnam War can be used to illustrate the production possibilities curve by placing (labor resources, military goods) ______________ on one axis and (capital resources, civilian goods) ______________ on the other axis and then drawing a curve (bowed out from, bowed into) ______________ the origin.

16. Technological advance can shift a nation's production possibilities curve (inward, outward) __outward__ because the effects are similar to an increase in (economic growth, unemployment) __ec growth__.

17. The institutional arrangements and coordinating mechanisms used to respond to the economic problem is called (a traditional economy, an economic system) ______________.

18. In pure capitalism, property resources are (publicly, privately) __privately__ owned. The means used to direct and coordinate economic acitivity is the (command, market) __market__ system.

19. In a command economy, property resources are (publicly, privately) __publicly__ owned. The coordinating device in this economic system is (planning, markets) __planning__.

20. In the circular flow model,

a. Households are demanders and businesses are suppliers in (product, resource) __product__ markets, and businesses are demanders and households are suppliers in __resource__ markets.

b. The flow of economic resources and finished goods and services is the (money, real) ______________ flow, and the flow of income and expenditures is the ______________ flow.

■ TRUE-FALSE QUESTIONS

Circle the T if the statement is true, the F if it is false.

1. The conflict between the scarce material wants of society and its unlimited economic resources gives rise to the economizing problem. **T F**

2. The wants with which economics is concerned include only those wants which can be satisfied by goods and services. **T F**

3. Money is a resource and is classified as "capital." **T F**

4. From the economist's perspective, investment refers to the production and purchase of capital goods. **T F**

5. The payment to entrepreneurial ability is interest income. **T F**

6. Resources are scarce because society's material wants are unlimited and productive resources are limited. **T F**

7. Economic efficiency requires that there be both full employment of resources and full production. **T F**

8. Allocative efficiency means that goods and services are being produced by society in the least costly way. **T F**

9. Only allocative efficiency is necessary for there to be full production. **T F**

10. The opportunity cost of producing antipollution devices is the other goods and services the economy is unable to produce because it has decided to produce these devices. **T F**

11. The opportunity cost of producing a good tends to increase as more of it is produced because resources less suitable to its production must be employed. **T F**

12. Drawing a production possibilities curve concave to the origin is the geometric way of stating the law of increasing opportunity costs. **T F**

13. Economic rationale for the law of increasing opportunity cost is that economic resources are fully adaptable to alternative uses. **T F**

14. Allocative efficiency is determined by assessing the marginal costs and benefits of the output from the allocation of resources to production. **T F**

15. The marginal-cost curve for a product rises because of increasing satisfaction from the consumption of the product. **T F**

16. Given full employment and full production, it is not possible for an economy capable of producing just two goods to increase its production of both. **T F**

17. Economic growth means an increase in the production of goods and services, and it is shown by a movement of the production possibilities to the right. **T F**

18. The more capital goods an economy produces today, the greater will be the total output of all goods it can produce in the future, other things being equal. **T F**

19. International trade and specialization can shift the production possibilities of a nation outward, similar to what would occur if there were increased economic growth. **T F**

20. If a country has unemployed resources at the outset of a war, it can increase its production of military goods without having to decrease its production of civilian goods. **T F**

21. Pure capitalism is also called laissez-faire capitalism. **T F**

22. A command economy is characterized by the private ownership of resources and the use of markets and prices to coordinate and direct economic activity. **T F**

23. Most real-world economies contain features exhibiting both pure capitalism and a command economy. **T F**

24. In the circular flow model, the household functions on the demand side of the resource and product markets. **T F**

25. One limitation of the simple model of the circular flow is that flows of output and income are constant. **T F**

■ MULTIPLE-CHOICE QUESTIONS

Circle the letter that corresponds to the best answer.

1. Which is the correct match of an economic resource and payment for that resource?
(a) land and wages
(b) labor and interest income
(c) capital and rental income
(d) entrepreneurial ability and profit

2. An "innovator" is defined as an entrepreneur who
(a) makes basic policy decisions in a business firm
(b) combines factors of production to produce a good or service
(c) invents a new product or process for producing a product
(d) introduces new products on the market or employs a new method to produce a product

3. An economy is efficient when it has achieved
(a) full employment
(b) full production
(c) either full employment or full production
(d) both full employment and full production

4. Allocative and productive efficiency are conditions that best characterize
(a) full employment
(b) full production
(c) traditional economies
(d) command economies

5. When a production possibilities schedule is written (or a production possibilities curve is drawn) in this chapter, four assumptions are made. Which of the following is one of those assumptions?
(a) more than two products are produced

(b) the state of technology changes
(c) the economy has both full employment and full production
(d) the quantities of all resources available to the economy are variable, not fixed

Answer Questions 6, 7, 8, and 9 based on the following graph.

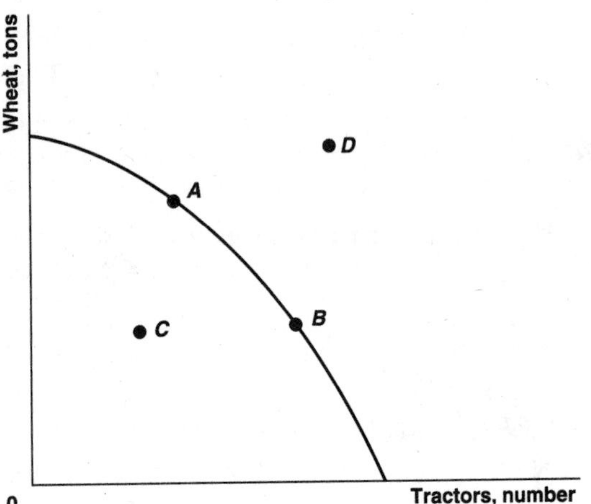

6. At point ***A*** on the production possibilities curve in the above illustration,
(a) wheat production is inefficient
(b) tractor production is inefficient
(c) the economy is employing all its resources
(d) the economy is not employing all its resources

7. Unemployment and production inefficiency would best be represented in the graph by point:
(a) ***A***
(b) ***B***
(c) ***C***
(d) ***D***

8. The choice of point ***B*** over point ***A*** as the optimal product mix for society would be based on
(a) productive efficiency
(b) full employment of resources
(c) the law of increasing opportunity costs
(d) a comparison of marginal costs and benefits

9. Economic growth could be represented by
(a) a movement from point ***A*** to point ***B***
(b) a movement from point ***B*** to point ***A***
(c) a shift in the production possibilities curve out to point ***C***
(d) a shift in the production possibilities curve out to point ***D***

10. The production possibilities curve is
(a) concave
(b) convex
(c) linear
(d) positive

11. What is the economic rationale for the law of increasing opportunity cost?
(a) full production and full employment of resources have not been achieved
(b) economic resources are not completely adaptable to alternative uses
(c) economic growth is being limited by the pace of technological advancement
(d) an economy's present choice of output is determined by fixed technology and fixed resources

12. If there is an increase in the resources available within the economy,
(a) more goods and services will be produced in the economy
(b) the economy will be capable of producing more goods and services
(c) the standard of living in the economy will rise
(d) the technological efficiency of the economy will improve

13. If the production possibilities curve below moves from position ***A*** to position ***B***, then
(a) the economy has increased the efficiency with which it produces wheat
(b) the economy has increased the efficiency with which it produces tractors
(c) the economy has put previously idle resources to work
(d) the economy has gone from full employment to less than full employment

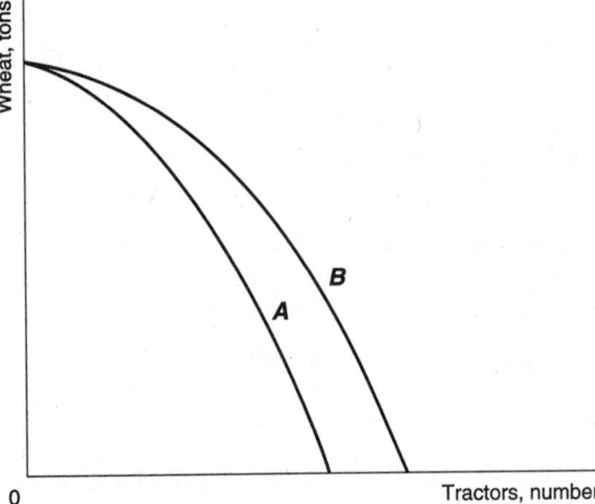

14. Which would be the best example of allocative efficiency? When society devoted resources to the production of
(a) slide rules instead of hand-held calculators
(b) horse-drawn carriages instead of automobiles
(c) word processors instead of manual typewriters
(d) long-playing records instead of compact discs or cassette tapes

15. Which situation would most likely shift the production possibilities curve for a nation in an outward direction?
(a) deterioration in product quality
(b) reductions in the supply of resources
(c) increases in technological advances
(d) rising levels of discrimination

16. The opportunity cost of a new public stadium is the
(a) money cost of hiring guards and staff for the new stadium

(b) cost of constructing the new stadium in a future year
(c) change in the real estate tax rate to pay off the new stadium
(d) other goods and services that must be sacrificed to construct the new stadium

17. Which situation would most likely cause a nation's production possibilities curve to shift inward?
(a) investing more resources in new plants and equipment
(b) eliminating discrimination based on race and ethnic background
(c) increasing international trade or incurring a trade deficit
(d) going to war with another nation and suffering a major defeat

18. The combination of products in society's production possibilities table which is the most valued or optimal is determined
(a) at the midpoint of the production possibilities table
(b) at the endpoint of the production possibilities table
(c) where the marginal benefits equal marginal costs
(d) where the opportunity costs are maximized

19. The underallocation of resources by society to the production of a product means that the
(a) marginal benefit is greater than the marginal cost
(b) marginal benefit is less than the marginal cost
(c) opportunity cost of production is rising
(d) consumption of the product is falling

Answer Questions 20, 21, and 22 on the basis of the data given in the following production possibilities table.

	Production possibilities (alternatives)					
	A	B	C	D	E	F
Capital goods	100	95	85	70	50	0
Consumer goods	0	100	180	240	280	300

20. The choice of alternative **B** compared with alternative **D** would tend to promote
(a) a slower rate of economic growth
(b) a faster rate of economic growth
(c) increased consumption in the present
(d) central economic planning

21. If the economy is producing at production alternative **D**, the opportunity cost of 40 more units of consumer goods is about
(a) 5 units of capital goods
(b) 10 units of capital goods
(c) 15 units of capital goods
(d) 20 units of capital goods

22. In the table, the law of increasing opportunity costs is suggested by the fact that
(a) greater and greater quantities of consumer goods must be given up to get more capital goods
(b) smaller and smaller quantities of consumer goods must be given up to get more capital goods
(c) capital goods are relatively more scarce than consumer goods
(d) the production possibilities curve will eventually shift outward as the economy expands

23. The private ownership of property resources and use of the market system to direct and coordinate economic activity is characteristic of
(a) pure capitalism
(b) the command economy
(c) market socialism
(d) the traditional economy

24. The two kinds of markets found in the circular flow model are
(a) real and money markets
(b) real and traditional markets
(c) money and authoritarian markets
(d) product and resource markets

25. In the circular flow model, businesses
(a) demand both products and resources
(b) supply both products and resources
(c) demand products and supply resources
(d) supply products and demand resources

PROBLEMS

1. Following is a list of resources. Indicate in the space to the right of each whether the resource is land (LD), capital (C), labor (LR), entrepreneurial ability (EA), or some combinations of these resources.

a. Fishing grounds in the North Atlantic ______
b. A cash register in a retail store ______
c. Uranium deposits in Canada ______
d. An irrigation ditch in Nebraska ______
e. The work performed by Bill Gates ______
f. The oxygen breathed by human beings ______
g. An IBM plant in Rochester, Minnesota ______
h. The food on the shelf of a grocery store ______
i. The work done by a robot in an auto plant ______
j. The tasks accomplished in perfecting a new computer for commercial sales ______
k. A carpenter building a house ______

2. Following is a production possibilities table for two commodities: wheat and automobiles. The table is constructed using the usual assumptions. Wheat is measured in units of 100,000 bushels and automobiles in units of 100,000.

Combination	Wheat	Automobiles
A	0	7
B	7	6
C	13	5
D	18	4
E	22	3
F	25	2
G	27	1
H	28	0

a. Follow the general rules for making graphs (see the appendix to Chapter 1); plot the data from the table on the graph below to obtain a production possibilities curve. Place wheat on the vertical axis and automobiles on the horizontal axis.
b. Fill in the following table showing the opportunity cost per unit of producing the 1st through the 7th automobile.

Automobiles	Cost of production
1st	_____
2d	_____
3d	_____
4th	_____
5th	_____
6th	_____
7th	_____

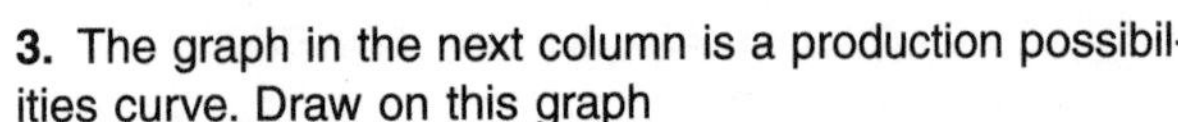

3. The graph in the next column is a production possibilities curve. Draw on this graph
a. a production possibilities curve which indicates greater efficiency in the production of good **A**
b. a production possibilities curve which indicates greater efficiency in the production of good **B**
c. a production possibilities curve which indicates an increase in the resources available to the economy

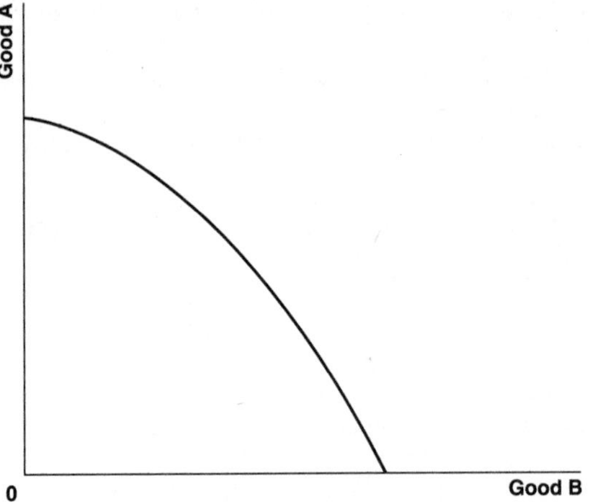

4. Following is a list of 12 economic goods. Indicate in the space to the right of each good whether it is a consumer good (CON), a capital good (CAP), or that it depends (DEP) on who is using it and for what purpose.

a. An automobile _____
b. A tractor _____
c. A taxicab _____
d. A house _____
e. A factory building _____

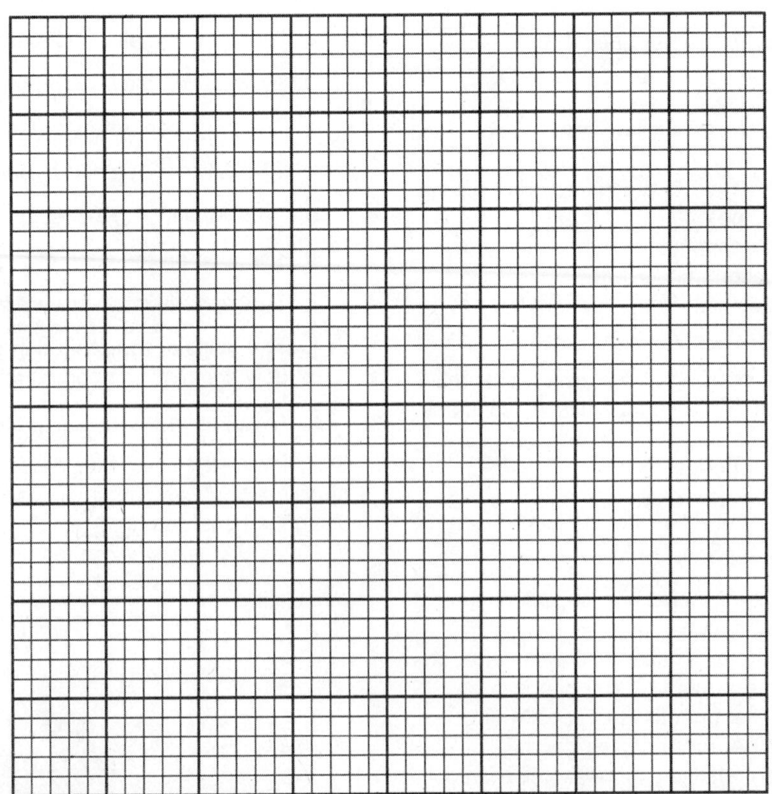

f. An office building ______

g. An ironing board ______

h. A refrigerator ______

i. A telephone ______

j. A quart of a soft drink ______

k. A cash register ______

l. A screwdriver ______

5. In the circular flow diagram below, the upper pair of flows (***a*** and ***b***) represent the resource market and the lower pair (***c*** and ***d***) the product market.

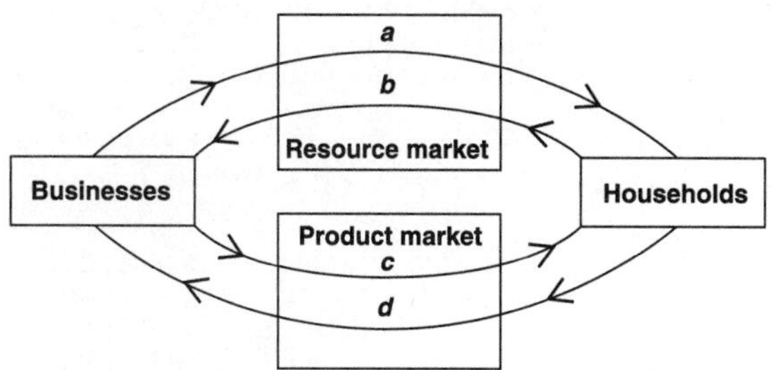

Supply labels or explanations for each of the four flows:

a. ______________________________

b. ______________________________

c. ______________________________

d. ______________________________

■ SHORT ANSWER AND ESSAY QUESTIONS

1. Explain what the term "economizing problem" means. Why are resources scarce?

2. In what sense are wants satiable or insatiable?

3. What are the four economic resources? How is each resource defined?

4. What is the income each economic resource earns?

5. When is a society economically efficient? What does "full production" mean, and how does it differ from "full employment"?

6. Explain why full production implies both allocative and productive efficiency.

7. What four assumptions are made in drawing a production possibilities curve or schedule?

8. What is opportunity cost? Give an example.

9. What is the law of increasing opportunity cost? Why do costs increase?

10. What determines the optimal product mix for society's production possibilities?

11. How can unemployment be illustrated with the production possibilities curve?

12. What will be the effect of increasing resource supplies on production possibilities?

13. Describe how technological advances will affect the production possibilities curve.

14. Explain the tradeoff between goods for the present and goods for the future and the effect on economic growth.

15. What qualification does international trade make for the interpretation of production possibilities?

16. Describe how going to war can be illustrated by the production possibilities curve.

17. Give examples of other real-world applications of the production possibilties curve.

18. Pure capitalism and the command economy differ in two important ways. Compare the two economic systems with each other and with authoritarian capitalism and market socialism.

19. In the circular flow model, what are the two markets? What roles do households play and what role do businesses play in each market?

20. In the circular flow model, what two income flows are pictured in money terms and in real terms? What two expenditure flows are pictured in money terms and in real terms?

ANSWERS

Chapter 2 The Economizing Problem

FILL-IN QUESTIONS

1. unlimited, limited
2. utility, necessities, luxuries
3 *a.* land or natural resources, *b.* capital, *c.* labor, *d.* entrepreneurial ability
4. directly, indirectly
5. rental, interest, wage, profit
6. scarce, unlimited
7. employment, production
8. allocative, productive
9. *a.* the economy is operating at full employment and full production; *b.* the available supplies of the factors of production are fixed; *c.* technology does not change during the course of the analysis; *d.* the economy produces only two products
10. cost
11. concave, are not
12. *a.* opportunity costs, satisfaction; *b.* under, over; *c.* equal to
13. *a.* fewer, more; *b.* unemployed, underemployed; *c.* more, more; *d.* economic growth, increase, improvement
14. less
15. military goods, civilian goods, bowed out from
16. outward, economic growth
17. economic system
18. privately, market
19. publicly, planning
20. *a.* product, resource; *b.* real, money

TRUE-FALSE QUESTIONS

1. F, pp. 22 **3.** F, pp. 23-24 **5.** F, p. 24 **7.** T, p. 24
2. T, pp. 22-23 **4.** T. p. 23 **6.** T, p. 24 **8.** F, p. 25

9. F, p. 25
10. T, pp. 27-28
11. T, pp. 27-28
12. T, p. 28
13. F, p. 28
14. T, pp. 28-29
15. F, pp. 27-28
16. T, pp. 26-27
17. T, pp. 30-31
18. T, pp. 31-32
19. T, pp. 32-33
20. T, p. 33
21. T, p. 34
22. F, p. 35
23. T, p. 35
24. F, pp. 36-37
25. T, p. 36

MULTIPLE-CHOICE QUESTIONS

1. d, p. 24
2. d, p. 24
3. d, p. 24
4. b, p. 25
5. c, pp. 25-26
6. c, p. 26
7. c, pp. 29-30
8. d, p. 28-29
9. d, p. 31
10. a, p. 28
11. b, p. 28
12. b, p. 30
13. b, pp. 30-32
14. c, pp. 28-29
15. c, pp. 30-31
16. d, p. 27
17. d, p. 34
18. c, pp. 28-29
19. a, pp. 28-29
20. b, p. 31-32
21. d, p. 27-28
22. a, pp. 27-28
23. a, p. 34
24. d, p. 36
25. d, p. 36

PROBLEMS

1. *a.* LD; *b.* C; *c.* LD; *d.* C; *e.* EA; *f.* LD; *g.* C; *h.* C; *i.* C; *j.* EA; *k.* LR

2. *b.* 1, 2, 3, 4, 5, 6, 7 units of wheat

3. *a.* curve will shift outward along good A axis but stay at the same point on good B axis; *b.* curve will shift outward along good B axis but stay at the same point on good A axis; *c.* entire curve will shift outward

4. *a.* DEP; *b.* CAP; *c.* CAP; *d.* DEP; *e.* CAP; *f.* CAP; *g.* DEP; *h.* DEP; *i.* DEP; *j.* DEP; *k.* CAP; *l.* DEP

5. *a.* money income payments (wages, rent, interest, and profit); *b.* services or resources (land, labor, capital, and entrepreneurial ability); *c.* goods and services; *d.* expenditures for goods and services

SHORT ANSWER AND ESSAY QUESTIONS

1. pp. 22-24
2. p. 23
3. pp. 23-24
4. p. 24
5. pp. 24-25
6. p. 25
7. pp. 25-26
8. pp. 4; 27
9. pp. 27-28
10. pp. 28-29
11. p. 30
12. p. 30
13. pp. 30-31
14. pp. 31-32
15. p. 32
16. pp. 33-34
17. pp. 33-34
18. pp. 34-35
19. pp. 35-37
20. pp. 36-37

CHAPTER 3

Understanding Individual Markets: Demand and Supply

Chapter 3 introduces you to the most fundamental tools of economic analysis: demand and supply. To progress successfully into the later chapters, it is essential that you understand what is meant by demand and supply and how to use these powerful tools.

Demand and supply are simply "boxes" or categories into which all the forces and factors that affect the price and the quantity of a good bought and sold in a competitive market are placed. Demand and supply determine price and quantity exchange, and it is necessary to see *why* and *how* they do this.

Many students never do understand demand and supply because they never learn to *define* demand and supply *exactly.* They never learn (1) what an increase or decrease in demand or supply means, (2) the important distinctions between "demand" and "quantity demanded" and between "supply" and "quantity supplied," and (3) the equally important distinctions between an increase (or decrease) in demand and an increase (or decrease) in quantity demanded and between an increase (or decrease) in supply and an increase (or decrease) in quantity supplied.

Having learned these, however, it is no great trick to comprehend the so-called law of supply and demand. The equilibrium price—that is, the price which will tend to prevail in the market as long as demand and supply do not change—is simply the price at which ***quantity demanded*** and ***quantity supplied*** are equal. The quantity bought and sold in the market (the equilibrium quantity) is the quantity demanded and supplied at the equilibrium price. If you can determine the equilibrium price and quantity under one set of demand and supply conditions, you can determine them under any other set and so will be able to analyze for yourself the effects of changes in demand and supply upon equilibrium price and quantity.

This chapter includes a brief examination of the factors that determine demand and supply and the ways in which changes in these determinants will affect and cause changes in demand and supply. A graphic method is used in this analysis in order to facilitate an understanding of demand and supply, equilibrium price and quantity, changes in demand and supply, and the resulting changes in equilibrium price and quantity. In addition to understanding the *specific* definitions of demand and supply, it is necessary to understand the two counterparts of demand and supply: the ***demand curve*** and the ***supply curve.*** These are graphic (or geometric) representations of the same data contained in the schedules of demand and supply.

You will use supply and demand over and over. It will turn out to be as important to you in economics as jet propulsion is to the pilot of a Boeing 767: You can't get off the ground without it.

■ CHECKLIST

When you have studied this chapter you should be able to

- ☐ Define a market.
- ☐ Define demand and state the law of demand.
- ☐ Graph the demand curve when you are given a demand schedule.
- ☐ Explain the difference between individual and market demand.
- ☐ List the major determinants of demand and explain how each one shifts the demand curve.
- ☐ Distinguish between change in demand and change in the quantity demanded.
- ☐ Define supply and state the law of supply.
- ☐ Graph the supply curve when you are given a supply schedule.
- ☐ List the major determinants of supply and explain how each shifts the supply curve.
- ☐ Distinguish between change in supply and change in the quantity supplied.
- ☐ Define surplus and shortage.
- ☐ Describe how the equilibrium price and quantity are determined in a competitive market.
- ☐ Determine, when you are given the demand for and the supply of a good, the equilibrium price and the equilibrium quantity.
- ☐ Predict the effects of changes in demand and supply on equilibrium price and equilibrium quantity; and on the prices of substitute and complementary goods.
- ☐ Explain the meaning of the rationing function of prices.
- ☐ Explain why violations of the "other things equal" assumption may cause confusion about the validity of the laws of demand and supply.
- ☐ Give a real-world application of supply and demand.

■ CHAPTER OUTLINE

1. A market is any institution or mechanism that brings together buyers and sellers of a particular good or service. This chapter assumes that markets are highly competitive.

2. *Demand* is a schedule of prices and the quantities which buyers would purchase at each of these prices during a selected period of time.

a. As price rises, other things being equal, buyers will purchase smaller quantities, and as price falls they will purchase larger quantities; this is the law of demand.
b. The demand curve is a graphic representation of demand and the law of demand.
c. Market (or total) demand for a good is a summation of the demands of all individuals in the market for that good.
d. The demand for a good depends on the tastes, income, and expectations of buyers; the number of buyers in the market; and the prices of related goods.
e. A change (either an increase or a decrease) in demand is caused by a change in any of the factors (in **d**) which determine demand and means that the demand schedule and demand curve have changed.
f. A change in demand and a change in the quantity demanded are *not* the same thing.

3. *Supply* is a schedule of prices and the quantities which sellers will sell at each of these prices during some period of time.

a. The supply schedule shows, other things equal, that as the price of the good rises larger quantities will be offered for sale, and that as the price of the good falls, smaller quantities will be offered for sale.
b. The supply curve is a graphic representation of supply and the law of supply; the market supply of a good is the sum of the supplies of all sellers of the good.
c. The supply of a good depends on the techniques used to produce it, the prices of the resources employed in its production, the extent to which it is taxed or subsidized, the prices of other goods which might be produced, the price expectations of sellers, and the number of sellers of the product.
d. Supply will change when any of these determinants of supply changes; a change in supply is a change in the entire supply schedule or curve.
e. A change in supply must be distinguished from a change in quantity supplied.

4. The market or ***equilibrium price*** of a product is that price at which quantity demanded and quantity supplied are equal; the quantity exchanged in the market (the equilibrium quantity) is equal to the quantity demanded and supplied at the equilibrium price.

a. The rationing function of price is the elimination of shortages and surpluses of the commodity.
b. A change in demand, supply, or both changes both the equilibrium price and the equilibrium quantity in specific ways.
c. When demand and supply schedules (or curves) are drawn up, it is assumed that all the nonprice determinants of demand and supply remain unchanged. This assumption is often stated as "other things equal."
d. There are many real-world examples of the application of supply and demand.

■ HINTS AND TIPS

1. This chapter is the most important one in the book. Make sure you spend extra time on it and master the material. If you do, your long-term payoff will be a much easier understanding of the applications in later chapters.

2. One mistake students often make is to confuse ***change in demand*** with ***change in quantity demanded.*** A change in demand causes the entire demand curve to *shift,* whereas a change in quantity demanded is simply a *movement* along an existing demand curve.

3. It is strongly recommended that you draw supply and demand graphs as you work on supply and demand problems so you can see a picture of what happens when demand shifts, supply shifts, or both demand and supply shift.

4. Make a chart and related graphs that show the eight possible outcomes from changes in demand and supply. Figure 3-6 in the text illustrates the *four single shift* outcomes:

(1) **D**↑: **P**↑, **Q**↑ (3) **S**↑: **P**↓, **Q**↑
(2) **D**↓: **P**↓, **Q**↓ (4) **S**↓: **P**↑, **Q**↓

Four shift combinations are described in Table 3-9 of the text. Make a figure to illustrate each combination.

(1) **S**↑, **D**↓: **P**↓, **Q**? (3) **S**↑, **D**↑: **P**?, **Q**↑
(2) **S**↓, **D**↑: **P**↑, **Q**? (4) **S**↓, **D**↓: **P**?, **Q**↓

5. Make sure you understand the other things equal assumption described at the end of the chapter. It will help you understand why the law of demand is not violated even if the price and quantity of a product increase over time.

■ IMPORTANT TERMS

market
demand
demand schedule (curve)
law of demand
diminishing marginal utility
quantity demanded
income effect
substitution effect
demand curve
individual demand
total or market demand
determinant of demand
increase (or decrease) in demand
normal good
inferior good
substitute goods
complementary goods
supply
supply schedule (curve)
quantity supplied
supply curve
determinant of supply
increase (or decrease) in supply
equilibrium price
equilibrium quantity
rationing function of prices
other things equal assumption

SELF-TEST

■ FILL-IN QUESTIONS

1. A market is the institution or mechanism that brings together buyers or (demanders, suppliers) demanders and sellers or suppliers of a particular good or service.

2. In resource markets prices are determined by the demand decisions of (businesses, households) businesses and the supply decisions of households.

3. In product markets prices are determined by demand decisions of (businesses, households) households and the supply decisions of businesses.

4. The relationship between price and quantity in the demand schedule is a(n) (direct, inverse) inverse relationship; in the supply schedule the relationship is a(n) direct one.

5. The added satisfaction or pleasure a consumer obtains from additional units of a product decreases as the consumer's consumption of the product increases. This phenomenon is called deminishing marginal (equilibrium, utility) utility.

6. A consumer tends to buy more of a product as its price falls because

a. The purchasing power of the consumer is increased and the consumer tends to buy more of this product (and of other products), this is called the (income, substitution) income effect;

b. The product becomes less expensive relative to similar products and the consumer tends to buy more of the original product and less of a similar product, which is called the Substitution effect.

7. When demand or supply is graphed, price is placed on the (horizontal, vertical) vertical axis and quantity on the horizontal axis.

8. The change from an individual to a market demand schedule involves (adding, multiplying) adding the quantities demanded by each consumer at the various possible (incomes, prices) prices.

9. When the price of one product and the demand for another product are directly related, the two products are called (substitutes, complements) Substitutes; however, when the price of one product and the demand for another product are inversely related, the two products are called Complements.

10. When a consumer demand schedule or curve is drawn up, it is assumed that five factors that determine demand are fixed and constant. These five determinants of consumer demand are

a. ________________

b. ________________

c. ________________

d. ________________

e. ________________

11. A decrease in demand means that consumers will buy (larger, smaller) Smaller quantities at every price, or will pay (more, less) less for the same quantities.

12. A change in income or in the price of another product will result in a change in the (demand for, quantity demanded of) ________________ the given product, while a change in the price of the given product will result in a change in the ________________ the given product.

13. An increase in supply means that producers will make and be willing to sell (larger, smaller) larger quantities at every price, or will accept (more, less) less for the same quantities.

14. A change in resource prices or the prices of other goods that could be produced will result in a change in the (supply, quantity supplied) ________________ of the given product, but a change in the price of the given product will result in a change in the ________________.

15. The fundamental factors which determine the supply of any commodity in the product market are

a. ________________

b. ________________

c. ________________

d. ________________

e. ________________

f. ________________

16. If quantity demanded is greater than quantity supplied, price is (above, below) below the equilibrium price; and the (shortage, surplus) Shortage will cause the price to (rise, fall) rise. If quantity demanded is less than the quantity supplied, price is (above, below) above the equilibrium price, and the (shortage, surplus) surplus will cause the price to (rise, fall) fall.

17. The equilibrium price of a product is the price at which quantity demanded is (greater than, equal to) ________________ quantity supplied, and there (is, is not) ________________ a surplus or a shortage at that price.

18. In the space next to **a–h,** indicate the effect [*increase* (+), *decrease* (−), or *indeterminate* (?)] on equilibrium price (***P***) and equilibrium quantity (***Q***) of each of these changes in demand and/or supply.

	P	*Q*
a. Increase in demand, supply constant	___	___
b. Increase in supply, demand constant	___	___
c. Decrease in demand, supply constant	___	___
d. Decrease in supply, demand constant	___	___
e. Increase in demand, increase in supply	___	___
f. Increase in demand, decrease in supply	___	___
g. Decrease in demand, decrease in supply	___	___
h. Decrease in demand, increase in supply	___	___

19. If supply and demand establish a price for a good so that there is no shortage or surplus of a product, then price is successfully performing its (utility, rationing) ______________ function. The price that is set is a market-(changing, clearing) ______________ price.

20. To assume that all the determinants of demand and supply do not change is to employ the (marginal utility, other things equal) ______________ assumption.

■ TRUE-FALSE QUESTIONS

Circle the T if the statement is true, the F if it is false.

1. A market is any arrangement that brings together the buyers and sellers of a particular good or service. **T F**

2. Demand is the amount of a good or service which a buyer will purchase at a particular price. **T F**

3. The law of demand states that as price increases, other things being equal, the quantity of the product demanded increases. **T F**

4. The law of diminishing marginal utility is one explanation of why there is an inverse relationship between price and quantity demanded. **T F**

5. The substitution effect suggests that, at a lower price, you have the incentive to substitute the more expensive product for similar products which are relatively less expensive. **T F**

6. There is no difference between individual demand schedules and the market demand schedule for a product. **T F**

7. In graphing supply and demand schedules, supply is put on the horizontal axis and demand on the vertical axis. **T F**

8. If price falls, there will be an increase in demand. **T F**

9. If consumer tastes or preferences for a product decreases, the demand for the product will tend to decrease. **T F**

10. An increase in income will tend to increase the demand for a product. **T F**

11. When two products are substitute goods, the price of one and the demand for the other will tend to move in the same direction. **T F**

12. If two goods are complementary, an increase in the price of one will tend to increase the demand for the other. **T F**

13. A change in the quantity demanded means that there has been a change in demand. **T F**

14. Supply is a schedule which shows the amounts of a product a producer can make in a limited time period. **T F**

15. An increase in resource prices will tend to decrease supply. **T F**

16. A government subsidy for the production of a product will tend to decrease supply. **T F**

17. An increase in the prices of other goods that could be made by producers will tend to decrease the supply of the current good that the producer is making. **T F**

18. A change in supply means that there is a movement along an existing supply curve. **T F**

19. A surplus indicates that the quantity demanded is less than the quantity supplied at that price. **T F**

20. If the market price of a product is below its equilibrium price, the market price will tend to rise because demand will decrease and supply will increase. **T F**

21. The equilibrium price of a good is the price at which the demand and the supply of the good are equal. **T F**

22. The rationing function of prices is the elimination of shortages and surpluses. **T F**

23. If the supply of a product increases and demand decreases, the equilibrium price and quantity will increase. **T F**

24. If the demand for a product increases and the supply of the product decreases, the equilibrium price will increase and equilibrium quantity will be indeterminant. **T F**

25. Economists often make the assumption of other things equal to hold constant the effects of other factors when examining the relationship between prices and quantities demanded and supplied. **T F**

■ MULTIPLE-CHOICE QUESTIONS

Circle the letter that corresponds to the best answer.

1. The markets examined in this chapter
(a) sell nonstandard or differentiated products
(b) have buyers cooperating to determine prices
(c) are controlled by a single producer
(d) are highly competitive

2. A schedule which shows the various amounts of a product consumers are willing and able to purchase at each price in a series of possible prices during a specified period of time is called
(a) supply
(b) demand
(c) quantity supplied
(d) quantity demanded

3. The reason for the law of demand can best be explained in terms of
(a) supply
(b) complementary goods
(c) the rationing function of prices
(d) diminishing marginal utility

4. Assume that in a competitive market video tape players (VCRs) double in price. What will most likely happen in that market to the equilibrium price and quantity of video tapes?
(a) price will increase; quantity will decrease
(b) price will decrease; quantity will increase
(c) price will decrease; quantity will decrease
(d) price will increase; quantity will increase

5. Given the following individuals' demand schedules for product X, and assuming these are the only three consumers of X, which set of prices and output levels below will be on the market demand curve for this product?

Price X	Consumer 1 Q_{dx}	Consumer 2 Q_{dx}	Consumer 3 Q_{dx}
$5	1	2	0
4	2	4	0
3	3	6	1
2	4	8	2
1	5	10	3

(a) ($5, 2); ($1, 10)
(b) ($5, 3); ($1, 18)
(c) ($4, 6); ($2, 12)
(d) ($4, 0); ($1, 3)

6. Which factor will decrease the demand for a product?
(a) a favorable change in consumer tastes
(b) an increase in the price of a substitute good
(c) a decrease in the price of a complementary good
(d) a decrease in the number of buyers

7. The income of a consumer decreases and the consumer's demand for a particular good increases. It can be concluded that the good is
(a) normal
(b) inferior
(c) a substitute
(d) a complement

8. Which of the following could cause a decrease in consumer demand for product X?
(a) a decrease in consumer income
(b) an increase in the prices of goods which are good substitutes for product X
(c) an increase in the price which consumers expect will prevail for product X in the future
(d) a decrease in the supply of product X

9. If two goods are substitutes for each other, an increase in the price of one will necessarily
(a) decrease the demand for the other
(b) increase the demand for the other
(c) decrease the quantity demanded of the other
(d) increase the quantity demanded of the other

10. If two products, A and B, are complements, then
(a) an increase in the price of A will decrease the demand for B
(b) an increase in the price of A will increase the demand for B
(c) an increase in the price of A will have no significant effect on the price of B
(d) a decrease in the price of A will decrease the demand for B

11. If two products, X and Y, are independent goods, then
(a) an increase in the price of X will significantly increase the demand for Y
(b) an increase in the price of Y will significantly increase the demand for X
(c) an increase in the price of Y will have no significant effect on the demand for X
(d) a decrease in the price of X will significantly increase the demand for Y

12. The law of supply states that, other things being constant, as price increases
(a) supply increases
(b) supply decreases
(c) quantity supplied increases
(d) quantity supplied decreases

13. If the supply curve moves from S_1 to S_2 on the graph below, there has been
(a) an increase in supply
(b) a decrease in supply
(c) an increase in quantity supplied
(d) a decrease in quantity supplied

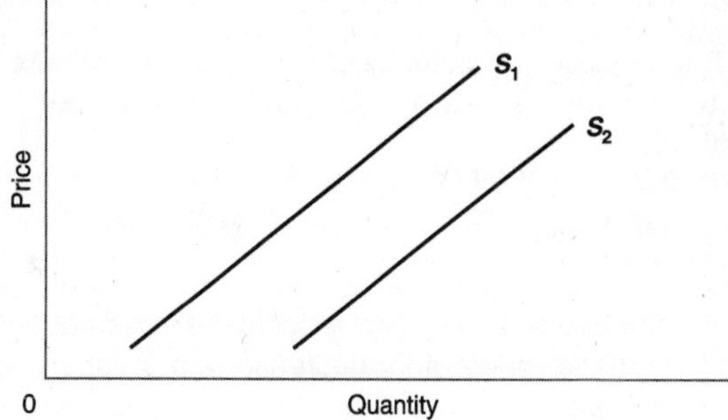

14. A decrease in the supply of a product would most likely be caused by
(a) an increase in business taxes
(b) an increase in consumer incomes
(c) a decrease in resource costs for production
(d) a decrease in the price of a complementary good

15. Which of the following could *not* cause an increase in the supply of cotton?
(a) an increase in the price of cotton
(b) improvements in the art of producing cotton
(c) a decrease in the price of the machinery and tools employed in cotton production
(d) a decrease in the price of corn

16. If the quantity supplied of a product is greater than the quantity demanded for a product, then
(a) there is a shortage of the product
(b) there is a surplus of the product
(c) the product is a normal good
(d) the product is an inferior good

17. When government sets the price of a good and that price is below the equilibrium price, the result will be
(a) a surplus of the good
(b) a shortage of the good
(c) an increase in the demand for the good
(d) a decrease in the supply of the good

Answer Questions 18, 19, and 20 on the basis of the data in the the following table. Consider the following supply and demand schedules for corn.

Price	Quantity demanded	Quantity supplied
$20	395	200
22	375	250
24	350	290
26	320	320
28	280	345
30	235	365

18. The equilibrium price in this market is
(a) $22
(b) $24
(c) $26
(d) $28

19. An increase in the cost of labor lowers the quantity supplied by 65 units at each price. The new equilibrium price would be
(a) $22
(b) $24
(c) $26
(d) $28

20. If the quantity demanded at each price increases by 130 units, then the new equilibrium quantity will be
(a) 290
(b) 320
(c) 345
(d) 365

21. A decrease in supply and a decrease in demand will
(a) increase price and decrease the quantity exchanged
(b) decrease price and increase the quantity exchanged
(c) increase price and affect the quantity exchanged in an indeterminate way
(d) affect price in an indeterminate way and decrease the quantity exchanged

22. An increase in demand and a decrease in supply will
(a) increase price and increase the quantity exchanged
(b) decrease price and decrease the quantity exchanged
(c) increase price and the effect upon quantity exchanged will be indeterminate
(d) decrease price and the effect upon quantity exchanged will be indeterminate

23. An increase in supply and an increase in demand will:
(a) increase price and increase the quantity exchanged
(b) decrease price and increase the quantity exchanged
(c) affect price in an indeterminate way and decrease the quantity exchanged
(d) affect price in an indeterminate way and increase the quantity exchanged

24. A cold spell in Florida devastates the orange crop. As a result, California oranges command a higher price. Which of the following statements best explains the situation?
(a) the supply of Florida oranges decreases, causing the supply of California oranges to increase and their price to increase
(b) the supply of Florida oranges decreases, causing their price to increase and the demand for California oranges to increase
(c) the supply of Florida oranges decreases, causing the supply of California oranges to decrease and their price to increase
(d) the demand for Florida oranges decreases, causing a greater demand for California oranges and an increase in their price

Answer Questions 25, 26, 27, 28, and 29 based on the following graph showing the market supply and demand for a product.

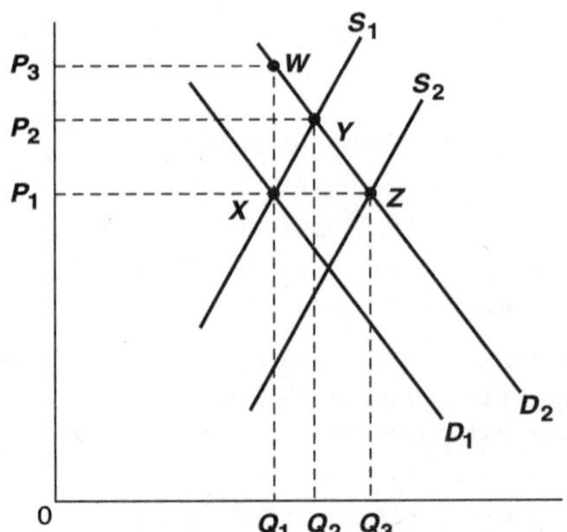

25. Assume that the market is initially in equilibrium where D_1 and S_1 intersect. If there is an increase in the number of buyers, then the new equilibrium would most likely be at point
(a) *W*
(b) *X*
(c) *Y*
(d) *Z*

26. Assume that the equilibrium price and quantity in the market are P_2 and Q_2. Which factor would cause the equilibrium price and quantity to shift to P_1 and Q_3?
(a) an increase in product price
(b) an increase in demand
(c) an increase in supply
(d) a decrease in quantity

27. If the market equilibrium was at point *Y* but the price of the product was set at P_1, then there would be a
(a) surplus of $Q_3 - Q_1$
(b) shortage of $Q_3 - Q_1$
(c) surplus of $Q_1 - Q_2$
(d) shortage of $Q_2 - Q_1$

28. What would cause a shift in the equilibrium price and quantity from point *Z* to point *X*?
(a) a decrease in prodution costs and more favorable consumer tastes for the product
(b) an increase in the number of suppliers and an increase in consumer incomes
(c) an increase in production costs and decrease in consumer incomes
(d) an improvement in production technology and decrease in the price of a substitute good

29. Assume that the market is initially in equilibrium where D_1 and S_1 intersect. If consumer incomes increased and the technology for making the product improved, then new equilibrium would most likely be at
(a) P_1 and Q_1
(b) P_2 and Q_2
(c) P_1 and Q_3
(d) P_3 and Q_1

30. The demand curve and its inverse relationship between price and quantity demanded is based on the assumption of
(a) other things equal
(b) changing expectations
(c) complementary goods
(d) increasing marginal utility

■ PROBLEMS

1. Using the demand schedule at the top of the next column, plot the demand curve on the graph below the schedule. Label the axes and indicate for each axis the units being used to measure price and quantity.

Price	Quantity demanded, 1000 bushels of soybeans
$7.20	10
7.00	15
6.80	20
6.60	25
6.40	30
6.20	35

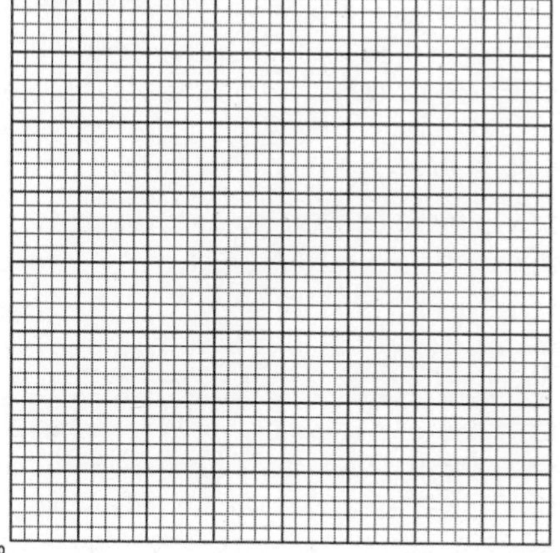

a. Plot the following supply schedule on the same graph.

Price	Quantity supplied, 1000 bushels of soybeans
$7.20	40
7.00	35
6.80	30
6.60	25
6.40	20
6.20	15

b. The equilibrium price of soybeans will be $______.
c. How many thousand bushels of soybeans will be exchanged at this price? __________
d. Indicate clearly on the graph the equilibrium price and quantity by drawing lines from the intersection of the supply and demand curves to the price and quantity axes.
e. If the Federal government supported a price of $7.00 per bushel there would be a (shortage, surplus) __________ of __________ bushels of soybeans.

2. The demand schedules of three individuals (Robert, Charles, and Lynn) for loaves of bread are shown in the following table. Assuming there are only three buyers of bread, determine and graph the total or market demand schedule for bread.

	Quantity demanded, loaves of bread			
Price	Robert	Charles	Lynn	Total
$.40	1	4	0	____
.36	3	5	1	____
.32	6	6	5	____
.28	10	7	10	____
.24	15	8	16	____

3. Following is a demand schedule for bushels of apples. In columns 3 and 4 insert *any* new figures for quantity which represent in column 3 an increase in demand and in column 4 a decrease in demand.

(1) Price	(2) Quantity demanded	(3) Demand increases	(4) Demand decreases
$6.00	400	____	____
5.90	500	____	____
5.80	600	____	____
5.70	700	____	____
5.60	800	____	____
5.50	900	____	____

4. Assume that O'Rourke has, when his income is $100 per week, the demand schedule for good A shown in columns 1 and 2 of the following table and the demand schedule for good B shown in columns 4 and 5. Assume that the prices of A and B are $.80 and $5, respectively.

Demand for A (per week)			*Demand for B (per week)*		
(1) Price	(2) Quantity demanded	(3) Quantity demanded	(4) Price	(5) Quantity demanded	(6) Quantity demanded
$.90	10	0	$5.00	4	7
.85	20	10	4.50	5	8
.80	30	20	4.00	6	9
.75	40	30	3.50	7	10
.70	50	40	3.00	8	11
.65	60	50	2.50	9	12
.60	70	60	2.00	10	13

a. How much A will O'Rourke buy? ____________

How much B? ____________

b. Suppose that as a consequence of a $10 increase in O'Rourke's weekly income, the quantities demanded of A become those shown in column 3 and the quantities demanded of B become those shown in column 6.

(1) How much A will he now buy? ____________

How much B? ____________

(2) Good A is (normal, inferior) ____________.

(3) Good B is ____________.

5. The market demand for good X is shown in columns 1 and 2 of the following table. Assume the price of X to be $2 and constant.

(1) Price	(2) Quantity demanded	(3) Quantity demanded	(4) Quantity demanded
$2.40	1,600	1,500	1,700
2.30	1,650	1,550	1,750
2.20	1,750	1,650	1,850
2.10	1,900	1,800	2,000
2.00	2,100	2,000	2,200
1.90	2,350	2,250	2,450
1.80	2,650	2,550	2,750

a. If as the price of good Y rises from $1.25 to $1.35 the quantities demanded of good X become those shown in column 3, it can be concluded that X and Y are (substitute, complementary) ____________ goods.

b. If as the price of good Y rises from $1.25 to $1.35 the quantities of good X become those shown in column 4, it can be concluded that X and Y are ____________ ____________ goods.

6. In a local market for hamburger on a given date, each of 300 identical sellers of hamburger has the following supply schedule.

(1) Price	(2) Quantity supplied—one seller, lb	(3) Quantity supplied—all sellers, lb
$2.05	150	____________
2.00	110	____________
1.95	75	____________
1.90	45	____________
1.85	20	____________
1.80	0	____________

a. In column 3 construct the market supply schedule for hamburger.

b. Following is the market demand schedule for hamburger on the same date and in the same local market as that given above.

Price	Quantity demanded, lb
$2.05	28,000
2.00	31,000
1.95	36,000
1.90	42,000
1.85	49,000
1.80	57,000

If the Federal government sets a price on hamburger at $1.90 a pound, the result would be a (shortage, surplus) ____________ of ____________ pounds of hamburger in this market.

7. Each of the following events would tend to increase or decrease either the demand for or the supply of computer games and, as a result, will increase or decrease the price of these games. In the first blank indicate the effect on demand or supply (increase, decrease); in the second blank, indicate the effect on price (increase, decrease).

a. It becomes known that a local department store is going to have a sale on these games 3 months from now. ____________;

____

b. The workers who produce the games go on strike for over 2 months. ____________; ____________

c. The workers in the industry receive a $1 an hour wage increase. _______________; _______________

d. The average price of movie tickets increases. _______________; _______________

e. The price of business software, a product also supplied by the computer software producers, rises. _______________; _______________

f. It is announced by a private research institute that children who play computer games also improve their grades in school. _______________; _______________

g. Because of the use of mass production techniques, the amount of labor necessary to produce a game decreases. _______________; _______________

h. The price of computers increases. _______________; _______________

i. The average consumer believes that a shortage of games is developing in the economy. _______________; _______________

j. The Federal government imposes a $5 per game tax on the manufacturers of computer games. _______________; _______________

■ SHORT ANSWER AND ESSAY QUESTIONS

1. What is a market? Define it and give examples.

2. Define demand and the law of demand.

3. What are three possible explanations for the inverse relationship between price and quantity demanded?

4. Two decades ago, the price of coffee in the United States rose significantly as a result of bad weather in coffee-producing regions. Use the income effect and the substitution effect concepts to explain why the quantity of coffee demanded in the United States significantly decreased.

5. Use the diminishing marginal utility concept to explain why the quantity demanded of a product will tend to rise when the price of the product falls.

6. What is the difference between individual and market demand? What is the relationship between these two types of demand?

7. Explain the difference between an increase in demand and an increase in the quantity demanded.

8. What are the factors that cause a change in demand? Use supply and demand graphs to illustrate what happens to price and quantity when demand increases.

9. How are inferior, normal, and superior goods defined? What is the relationship between these goods and changes in income?

10. Why does the effect of a change in the price of related goods depend on whether a good is a substitute or complement? What are substitutes and complements?

11. A newspaper reports that "blue jeans have become even more popular and are now the standard clothing that people wear for both play and work." How will this change affect the demand and supply of blue jeans? What will happen to the price and quantity of blue jeans sold in the market? Explain and use a supply and demand graph to illustrate your answer.

12. Compare and contrast the supply schedule with the demand schedule.

13. Supply does not remain constant for long because the factors which determine supply change. What are these factors? How do changes in them affect supply?

14. Explain the difference between an increase in supply and an increase in the quantity supplied.

15. Describe and illustrate with a supply and demand graph the effect of an increase in supply on price and quantity. Do the same for a decrease in supply.

16. The U.S. Congress passes a law that raises the excise tax on gasoline by $1 per gallon. What effect will this change have on the demand and supply of gasoline? What will happen to gasoline price and quantity? Explain and use a supply and demand graph to illustrate your answer.

17. What is the relationship between the price of a product and a shortage of the product? What is the relationship between the price of a product and surplus of the product?

18. Given the demand for and the supply of a commodity, what price will be the equilibrium price of this commodity? Explain why this price will tend to prevail in the market and why higher (lower) prices, if they do exist temporarily, will tend to fall (rise).

19. Analyze the following quotation and explain the fallacies contained in it: "An increase in demand will cause price to rise; with a rise in price, supply will increase and the increase in supply will push price down. Therefore, an increase in demand results in little change in price because supply will increase also."

20. Suppose an industry sells 2000 units of a product at $10 per unit one year, 3000 units at $12 the next year, and 4000 units at $14 the third year. Is this evidence that the law of demand is violated? Explain.

ANSWERS

Chapter 3 Understanding Individual Markets: Demand and Supply

FILL-IN QUESTIONS

1. demanders, suppliers
2. businesses, households
3. households, businesses
4. inverse, direct
5. utility
6. *a.* income; *b.* substitution
7. vertical, horizontal

8. adding, prices
9. substitutes, complements
10. *a.* the tastes or preferences of consumers; *b.* the number of consumers in the market; *c.* the money income of consumers; *d.* the prices of related goods; *e.* consumer expectations with respect to future prices and income (any order for *a–e*)
11. smaller, less
12. demand for, quantity demanded of
13. larger, less
14. supply, quantity supplied
15. *a.* the technology of production; *b.* resource prices; *c.* taxes and subsidies; *d.* prices of other goods; *e.* price expectations; *f.* the number of sellers in the market (any order for *a–f*)
16. below, shortage, rise, above, surplus, fall
17. equal to, is not
18. *a.* +, +; *b.* −, +; *c.* −, −; *d.* +, −; *e.* ?, +; *f.* +, ?; *g.* ?, −; *h.* −, ?
19. rationing, clearing
20. other things equal

TRUE-FALSE QUESTIONS

1. T, p. 42
2. F, pp. 43; 47-48
3. F, P. 43
4. T, p. 43
5. F, p. 44
6. F, pp. 44-45
7. F, p. 53
8. F, pp. 47-48
9. T, pp. 45-46
10. T, pp. 46-47
11. T, p. 47
12. F, p. 47
13. F, pp. 47-48
14. F, p. 48
15. T, pp. 49-50
16. F, p. 50
17. T, p. 50
18. F, p. 51
19. T, p. 52
20. F, pp. 52-53
21. F, pp. 52-53
22. T, p. 53
23. F, pp. 53-54
24. T, pp. 54-55
25. T, p. 57

MULTIPLE-CHOICE QUESTIONS

1. d, p. 42
2. b, p. 43
3. d, p. 43
4. c, pp. 47; 53
5. b, pp. 44-45
6. d, pp. 45-47
7. b, p. 47
8. a, pp. 45-47
9. b, p. 47
10. a, p. 47
11. c, p. 47
12. c, p. 49
13. a, p. 50
14. a, pp. 49-50; 53
15. a, p. 51
16. b, p. 52
17. b, p. 52
18. c, pp. 52-53
19. d, pp. 52-53
20. d, pp. 52-53
21. d, p. 56
22. c, pp. 54-55
23. d, p. 55
24. b, pp. 47; 53
25. c, pp. 46; 53
26. c, p. 53
27. b, pp. 52; 54
28. c, pp. 45-47; 49-51; 56
29. c, pp. 46-47; 50; 55
30. a, pp. 43; 57

PROBLEMS

1. *b.* 6.60; *c.* 25,000; *e.* surplus, 20,000
2. Total: 5, 9, 17, 27, 39
3. Each quantity in column 3 is greater than in column 2, and each quantity in column 4 is less than in column 2.
4. *a.* 30, 4; *b.* (1) 20, 7; (2) inferior; (3) normal (superior)
5. *a.* complementary; *b.* substitute
6. *a.* 45,000; 33,000; 22,500; 13,500; 6,000; 0 *b.* shortage, 28,500
7. *a.* decrease demand, decrease price; *b.* decrease supply, increase price; *c.* decrease supply, increase price; *d.* increase demand, increase price; *e.* decrease supply, increase price; *f.* increase demand, increase price; *g.* increase supply, decrease price; *h.* decrease demand, decrease price; *i.* increase demand, increase price; *j.* decrease supply, increase price

SHORT ANSWER AND ESSAY QUESTIONS

1. p. 42
2. p. 43
3. pp. 43-44
4. p. 44
5. p. 43
6. pp. 44-45
7. pp. 47-48
8. pp. 45; 53
9. p. 46-47
10. p. 47
11. pp. 45-46; 53
12. pp. 43; 48-49
13. pp. 49-51
14. p. 51
15. p. 53
16. pp. 50; 53
17. p. 52
18. pp. 52-53
19. p. 51
20. p. 53

CHAPTER 4

Pure Capitalism and the Market System

Chapter 4 describes the characteristics of pure capitalism, identifies three practices found in all modern economies, and offers a detailed explanation of the operation of the market system.

The first part of Chapter 4 describes the *ideological* and *institutional* characteristics of pure capitalism. In a pure capitalist system, most of the resources are owned by its citizens, who are free to use them as they wish in their own self-interest. Prices and markets express the self-interests of resource owners, consumers, and business firms. Competition regulates self-interest—to prevent the self-interest of any person or any group from working to the disadvantage of the economy and to make self-interest work for the benefit of the entire economy. The role of government is also limited under pure capitalism.

The three practices of all modern economies are the employment of large amounts of ***capital,*** the development of ***specialization,*** and the *use of money.* Economies use capital and engage in specialization because it is a more efficient use of their resources; it results in larger total output and the greater satisfaction of wants. When workers, business firms, and regions within an economy specialize, they become dependent on each other for the goods and services they do not produce for themselves. To obtain these goods and services they must engage in trade. Trade is made more convenient by using money as a medium of exchange.

The latter part of Chapter 4 describes the operation of the competitive market system. There are ***Five Fundamental Economic Questions*** that any economic system must answer in its attempt to use its scarce resources to satisfy its material wants. The five questions or problems are: (1) How much output is to be produced? (2) What is to be produced? (3) How is the output to be produced? (4) Who is to receive the output? (5) Can the economic system adapt to change? Only the last four questions will be discussed in this chapter; the first question will be discussed in the chapter on macroeconomics.

The explanation of how the market system finds answers to the last four of the Five Fundamental Economic Questions is only an approximation—a simplified version or a model—of the methods actually employed by the U.S. economy. Yet this simple model, like all good models, contains enough realism to be truthful and is general enough to be understandable. If the aims of this chapter are accomplished, you can begin to understand the market system and methods our economy uses to solve the economizing problem presented in Chapter 2.

■ CHECKLIST

When you have studied this chapter you should be able to

☐ Identify the six important institutional or ideological characteristics of capitalism.
☐ Describe the significance of property rights in capitalism.
☐ Distinguish between freedom of enterprise and freedom of choice.
☐ Explain why self-interest is a driving force of capitalism.
☐ Identify two features of competition.
☐ Explain the role of a market system in capitalism.
☐ Describe the size of government in capitalism.
☐ List three characteristics of all modern economies.
☐ Explain why the production of capital goods entails roundabout production.
☐ Discuss how specialization improves efficiency.
☐ Describe the advantages of money over barter for the exchange of goods and services.
☐ List the Five Fundamental Economic Questions about the operation of an economy.
☐ Explain how a competitive market system determines what will be produced.
☐ Distinguish between normal profit and economic profit.
☐ Predict what will happen to the price charged by and the output of an expanding and a declining industry, and explain why these events will occur.
☐ Explain how consumer sovereignty and dollar votes work in a market economy.
☐ Describe market restraints on economic freedom.
☐ Explain how production is organized in a competitive market system.
☐ Find the least costly combination of resources when given the technological data and the prices of the resources.
☐ Explain how a competitive market system determines the distribution of total output.
☐ Describe the guiding function of prices to accommodate change in the competitive market system.
☐ Explain how the competitive market system initiates change by fostering technological advances and capital accumulation.
☐ State how the "invisible hand" in the competitive market system tends to promote public or social interests.
☐ List three virtues of the competitive market system.

■ CHAPTER OUTLINE

1. The U.S. economy is not pure capitalism, but it is a

close approximation of pure capitalism. Pure capitalism has the following six features that distinguish it from other economic systems.

a. Private individuals and organizations own and control their property resources by means of the institution of private property.

b. These individuals and organizations possess both the freedom of enterprise and the freedom of choice.

c. Each of them is motivated largely by self-interest.

d. Competition prevents them, as buyers and sellers, from exploiting others.

e. Markets and prices (the market system) are used to communicate and coordinate the decisions of buyers and sellers.

f. The role of government is limited in a competitive and capitalist economy.

2. In common with other advanced economies of the world, the U.S. economy has three major characteristics.

a. It employs complicated and advanced methods of production and large amounts of capital equipment to produce goods and services efficiently.

b. It is a highly specialized economy, and this specialization increases the productive efficiency of the economy.

c. It uses money extensively to facilitate trade and specialization.

3. Five Fundamental Economic Questions must be answered by the competitive market system.

a. How much output is to be produced?

b. What is to be produced?

c. How is output to be produced?

d. Who is to receive the output?

e. Can the economic system adapt to change?

4. The system of prices and markets and households' and business firms' choices furnish the economy with answers to the last four Fundamental Economic Questions.

a. The demands of consumers for products and the desires of business firms to maximize their profits determine what and how much of each product is produced and what price it will be set at.

b. The desires of business firms to maximize profits by keeping their costs of production as low as possible guide them to use the most efficient techniques of production and determine their demands for and prices of the various resources; competition forces them to use the most efficient techniques and ensures that only the most efficient will be able to stay in business.

c. With resource prices determined, the money income of each household is determined; and with product prices determined, the quantity of goods and services these money incomes will buy is determined.

d. The market system is able to accommodate itself to changes in consumer tastes, technology, and resource supplies.

(1) The desires of business firms for maximum profits and competition lead the economy to make the appropriate adjustments in the way it uses its resources.

(2) Competition and the desire to increase profits promotes better techniques of production and capital accumulation.

5. Competition in the economy compels firms seeking to promote their own interests to promote (as though led by an "invisible hand") the best interest of society as a whole: an allocation of resources appropriate to consumer wants, production by the most efficient means, and the lowest possible prices.

a. Three noteworthy merits of the market system are

(1) The *efficient* use of resources

(2) The *incentive* the system provides for productive activity

(3) The personal *freedom* allowed participants as consumers, producers, workers, or investors.

■ HINTS AND TIPS

1. The first section of the chapter describes pure capitalism, which is an idealized framework based on *six* characteristics and institutions. After reading the section, check your understanding by listing the six points and writing a short explanation of each one.

2. There are *three* other characteristics of all modern economies that you should know. Can you list and explain them to yourself or to a fellow student? If not, make sure you reread that section of the chapter.

3. The section on the "Market System At Work" is both the most important and the most difficult part of the chapter. A market economy, or any economic system, must answer *Five Fundamental Economic Questions.* Detailed answers to four of the five questions are given in this section of the chapter. If you examine each one individually and in the order in which each is presented, you will more easily understand how the market system works. (Actually, the market system finds the answers simultaneously, but make your learning easier for now by considering them one by one.)

4. Be sure to understand the *importance* and *role* of each of the following in the operation of the market system: (1) the rationing and directing functions of prices, (2) the profit motive of business firms, (3) the entry into and exodus of firms from industries, (4) competition, and (5) consumer sovereignty.

■ IMPORTANT TERMS

private property
freedom of choice
freedom of enterprise
self-interest
competition
roundabout production
specialization
division of labor
medium of exchange
barter
coincidence of wants
Five Fundamental Questions
economic cost
normal profit
economic profit
expanding industry
declining industry
consumer sovereignty
dollar votes
derived demand
guiding function of prices
invisible hand

SELF-TEST

FILL-IN QUESTIONS

1. The ownership of property resources by private individuals and organizations is the institution of private (resources, property) ______________. The freedom of private businesses to obain resources and use them to produce goods and services is the freedom of (choice, enterprise) ______________, while the freedom to dispose of property or money as a person sees fit is the freedom of ______________.

2. Self-interest means that each economic unit attempts to do what is best for itself, but this might lead to an abuse of power in a capitalist economy if it were not directed and constrained by (government, competition) ______________. Self-interest and selfishness (are, are not) ______________ the same thing in a market economy.

3. According to the economist, competition is present if two conditions prevail; these two conditions are

 a. ______________________________
 ____

 b. ______________________________
 ____

4. In a capitalist economy, individual buyers communicate their demands and individual sellers communicate their supplies in the system of (markets, prices) ______________, and the outcomes from economic decisions are a set of product and resource ______________ that are determined by demand and supply.

5. In the ideology of pure capitalism, government is assigned a(n) (limited, extensive) ______________ role.

6. Modern economies make extensive use of capital goods and engage in roundabout production because it is more (efficient, inefficient) ______________ than direct production; they practice specialization and the division of labor because the self-sufficient producer or worker tends to be an ______________ one.

7. In modern economies money functions chiefly as a medium of (commerce, exchange) ______________. Barter between two individuals will take place only if there is a coincidence of (resources, wants) ______________.

8. List the Five Fundamental Economic Questions every economy must answer.

 a. ______________________________

 b. ______________________________

 c. ______________________________

 d. ______________________________

 e. ______________________________

9. A ***normal profit*** (is, is not) ______________ an economic cost because it is a payment that (must, need not) ______________ be paid to (workers, entrepreneurs) ______________, but an ***economic profit*** (is, is not) ______________ an economic cost because it (must, need not) ______________ be paid to them to obtain and retain the services they provide to the firm.

10. Pure or economic profit is equal to the total (revenue, cost) ______________ of a firm less its total ______________.

11. Business firms tend to produce those products from which they can obtain at least a(n) (economic, normal) ______________ profit and a maximum ______________ profit.

12. If firms in an industry are obtaining economic profits, firms will (enter, leave) ______________ the industry, the price of the industry's product will (rise, fall) ______________, the industry will employ (more, fewer) ______________ resources, produce a (larger, smaller) ______________ output, and the industry's economic profits will (increase, decrease) ______________ until they are equal to (zero, infinity) ______________.

13. Consumers vote with their dollars for the production of a good or service when they (sell, buy) __________ it, and because of this, consumers are said to be (dependent, sovereign) ______________ in a market economy. The buying decisions of consumers (restrain, expand) ______________ the freedom of firms and resource suppliers.

14. Firms are interested in obtaining the largest economic profits possible, so they try to produce a product in the (most, least) ______________ costly way. The most efficient production techniques depend on the available (income, technology) ______________ and the (prices, quotas) ______________ of needed resources.

15. The market system determines how the total output of the economy will be distributed among its households by determining the (incomes, expenditures) ______________ of each household and by determining the (prices, quality) ______________ for each good and service produced.

16. In industrial economies, change is almost continuous in consumer (preferences, resources) ______________, in the supplies of ______________,

and in technology. To make the appropriate adjustments to these changes, a marekt economy allows price to perform its (monopoly, guiding) _______________ function.

17. The competitive market system tends to foster technological change. The incentive for a firm to be the first to use a new and improved technique of production or to produce a new and better product is a greater economic (profit, loss) _______________, and the incentive for other firms to follow its lead is the avoidance of _______________.

18. Technological advance will require additional (capital, consumer) _______________ goods, so the entrepreneur uses profit obtained from the sale of _______________ goods to accquire (capital, consumer) _______________ goods.

19. A purely competitive market system promotes (unity, disunity) _______________ between private and public interests. Firms and resource suppliers seem to be guided by a(n) (visible, invisible) _______________ hand to allocate the economy's resources efficiently.

20. The two *economic* arguments for a market system are that it promotes (public, efficient) _______________ use of resources and that it uses (incentives, government) _______________ for directing economic activity. The major *noneconomic* argument for the market system is that it allows for personal (wealth, freedom) _______________.

■ TRUE-FALSE QUESTIONS

Circle the T if the statement is true, the F if it is false.

1. The U.S. economy can correctly be called "pure capitalism." **T F**

2. In the United States, there are legal limits to the right of private property. **T F**

3. The freedom of business firms to produce a particular consumer good is always limited by the desires of consumers for that good. **T F**

4. The pursuit of economic self-interest is the same thing as selfishness. **T F**

5. When a market is competitive, the individual sellers of the commodity are unable to reduce the supply of the commodity enough to drive its price upward. **T F**

6. The market system is also a communication system. **T F**

7. The employment of capital to produce goods and services requires that there be "roundabout production" and it is more efficient than "direct" production. **T F**

8. Increasing the amount of specialization in an economy generally leads to the more efficient use of its resources. **T F**

9. One way human specialization can be achieved is through a division of labor in productive activity. **T F**

10. Money is a device for facilitating the exchange of goods and services. **T F**

11. "Coincidence of wants" means that two persons want to acquire the same good or service. **T F**

12. Cigarettes may serve as money if sellers are generally willing to accept them as money. **T F**

13. One of the Five Fundamental Questions is who will control the output. **T F**

14. Business firms try to maximize their normal profits. **T F**

15. Industries in which economic profits are earned by the firms in the industry will attract the entry of new firms. **T F**

16. If firms have sufficient time to enter industries, the economic profits of an industry will tend to disappear. **T F**

17. Business firms are only free to produce whatever they want in any way they wish if they do not want to maximize profits or to minimize losses. **T F**

18. The derived demand of a resource depends on the demands for the products the resource produces. **T F**

19. Resources will tend to be used in those industries capable of earning normal or economic profits. **T F**

20. Economic efficiency requires that a given output of a good or service be produced in the least costly way. **T F**

21. If the market price of resource A decreases, firms will tend to employ smaller quantities of resource A. **T F**

22. Changes in the tastes of consumers are reflected in changes in consumer demand for products. **T F**

23. The incentive which the market system provides to induce technological improvement is the opportunity for economic profits. **T F**

24. The tendency for individuals pursuing their own self-interests to bring about results which are in the best interest of society as a whole is often called the "invisible hand." **T F**

25. A basic economic argument for the market system is that it promotes an efficient use of resources. **T F**

■ MULTIPLE-CHOICE QUESTIONS

Circle the letter that corresponds to the best answer.

1. Which is one of the main features of pure capitalism?
(a) central economic planning
(b) limits on freedom of choice

(c) the right to own private property
(d) an expanded role for government in the economy

2. In pure capitalism, freedom of enterprise means that
(a) businesses are free to produce products that consumers want
(b) consumers are free to buy goods and services that they want
(c) resources are distributed freely to businesses that want them
(d) government is free to direct the actions of businesses

3. The maximization of profit tends to be the driving force in the economic decision making of
(a) entrepreneurs
(b) workers
(c) consumers
(d) legislators

4. How do consumers typically express self-interest?
(a) by minimizing their economic losses
(b) by maximizing their economic profits
(c) by seeking the lowest price for a product
(d) by seeking jobs with the highest wages and benefits

5. Which of the following is a characteristic of competition as the economist sees it?
(a) the widespread diffusion of economic power
(b) a small number of buyers in product markets
(c) several sellers of all products
(d) the relatively difficult entry into and exit from industries by producers

6. To decide how to use its scarce resources to satisfy human wants pure capitalism relies on
(a) central planning
(b) roundabout production
(c) markets and prices
(d) barter

7. In pure capitalism, the role of government is best described as
(a) nonexistent
(b) limited
(c) significant
(d) extensive

8. What is roundabout production?
(a) the division of labor that results from specialization in the production of a good or service
(b) the production and use of capital goods to help make consumer goods
(c) the production of a good and service and the payment for it with money
(d) the production of a consumer good and its sale to consumers

9. In an economy that possesses full employment and full production, constant amounts of resources, and unchanging technology,
(a) increasing the production of capital goods requires an increase in the production of consumer goods
(b) decreasing the production of capital goods necessitates a decrease in the production of consumer goods
(c) increasing the production of capital goods is impossible
(d) increasing the production of capital goods requires a decrease in the production of consumer goods

10. When workers specialize in various tasks to produce a commodity, the situation is referred to as
(a) double coincidence of wants
(b) roundabout production
(c) freedom of choice
(d) division of labor

11. Which is a prerequisite of specialization?
(a) having a convenient means of exchanging goods
(b) letting government create a plan for the economy
(c) business firms making an economic profit
(d) business firms making a normal profit

12. The competitive market system is a method of
(a) communicating and synchronizing the decisions of consumers, producers, and resource suppliers
(b) centrally planning economic decisions
(c) promoting productive efficiency, but not allocative efficiency
(d) promoting allocative efficiency, but not productive efficiency

13. Which of the following best defines economic costs?
(a) total payments made to workers, landowners, suppliers of capital, and entrepreneurs
(b) only total payments made to workers, landowners, suppliers of capital, and entrepreneurs which must be paid to obtain the services of their resources
(c) total payments made to workers, landowners, suppliers of capital, and entrepreneurs less normal profits
(d) total payments made to workers, landowners, suppliers of capital, and entrepreneurs plus normal profits

14. If a business' total economic cost of producing 10,000 units of a product is $750,000 and this output is sold to consumers for $1,000,000, then the firm would earn
(a) a normal profit of $750,000
(b) an economic profit of $750,000
(c) an economic profit of $250,000
(d) a normal profit of $1,750,000

15. If less-than-normal profits are being earned by the firms in an industry, the consequences will be that
(a) lower-priced resources will be drawn into the industry
(b) firms will leave the industry, causing the price of the industry's product to fall
(c) firms will leave the industry, causing the price of the industry's product to rise
(d) the price of the industry's product will fall and thereby cause the demand for the product to increase

16. Which of the following would necessarily result, sooner or later, from a decrease in consumer demand for a product?

(a) a decrease in the profits of firms in the industry
(b) an increase in the output of the industry
(c) an increase in the supply of the product
(d) an increase in the prices of resources employed by the firms in the industry

17. The demand for resources is
(a) increased when the price of resources falls
(b) most influenced by the size of government in a capitalist economy
(c) derived from the demand for the products made with the resources
(d) decreased when the product that the resources produce becomes popular

Answer Questions 18, 19, and 20 on the basis of the following information.

Suppose 50 units of product X can be produced by employing just labor and capital in the four ways shown below. Assume the prices of labor and capital are $5 and $4, respectively.

	A	B	C	D
Labor	1	2	3	4
Capital	5	3	2	1

18. Which technique is economically most efficient in producing product X?
(a) A
(b) B
(c) C
(d) D

19. If the price of product X is $1, the firm will realize
(a) an economic profit of $28
(b) an economic profit of $27
(c) an economic profit of $26
(d) an economic profit of $25

20. Now assume that the price of labor falls to $3 and the price of capital rises to $5. Which technique is economically most efficient in producing product X?
(a) A
(b) B
(c) C
(d) D

21. Which is the primary factor determining the share of the total output of the economy received by a household?
(a) the tastes of the household
(b) the medium of exchange used by the household
(c) the prices at which the household sells its resources
(d) ethical considerations in the operation of a market economy.

22. If an increase in the demand for a product and the resulting rise in the price of the product cause the quantity of the product supplied, the size of the industry producing the product, and the amounts of resources devoted to the production of the product to expand, price is successfully performing its
(a) guiding function
(b) rationing function
(c) medium-of-exchange function
(d) standard-of-value function

23. In a capitalist economy characterized by competition, if one firm introduces a new and better method of production, other firms will be forced to adopt the improved technique
(a) to avoid less-than-normal profits
(b) to obtain economic profits
(c) to prevent the price of the product from falling
(d) to prevent the price of the product from rising

24. Which of the following would be an indication that competition does not exist in an industry?
(a) less-than-normal profits in the industry
(b) inability of the firms in the industry to expand
(c) inability of firms to enter the industry
(d) wages are lower than the average wage in the economy

25. The chief economic virtue of the competitive market system is that it
(a) allows extensive personal freedom
(b) efficiently allocates resources
(c) provides an equitable distribution of income
(d) eliminates the need for decision making

■ PROBLEMS

1. Use the appropriate number to match the term with the phrase.

1. invisible hand	**5. consumer sovereignty**
2. coincidence of wants	**6. derived demand**
3. division of labor	**7. specialization**
4. guiding function of prices	**8. roundabout production**

a. The construction and use of capital goods to aid in the production of consumer goods. _____
b. The ability of price changes to bring about changes in the quantities of products and resources demanded and supplied. _____
c. Using the resources of an individual, a firm, a region, or a nation to produce one (or a few) goods and services. _____
d. The tendency of firms and resource suppliers seeking to further their own self-interest while also promoting the interests of society in a market economy. _____
e. The demand for a resource that depends on the demand for the product it can be used to produce. _____
f. Splitting the work required to produce a product into a number of different tasks that are performed by different workers. _____
g. A situation in which the product that one trader desires to obtain is the same as that which another trader desires to give. _____
h. Determination by consumers of the types and quanti-

ties of goods and services that will be produced in a market economy. _____

2. Assume that a firm can produce *either* product A, product B, or product C with the resources it currently employs. These resources cost the firm a total of $50 per week. Assume, for the purposes of the problem, that the firm's employment of resources cannot be changed. The market prices of and the quantities of A, B, and C these resources will produce per week are given below. Compute the firm's profit when it produces A, B, or C, and enter these profits in the table below.

Product	Market price	Output	Economic profit
A	$7.00	8	$_____
B	4.50	10	_____
C	.25	240	_____

a. Which product will the firm produce? _____

b. If the price of A rose to $8, the firm would _____

_____

(Hint: You will have to recompute the firm's profit from the production of A.)

c. If the firm were producing A and selling it at a price of $8, what would tend to happen to the number of firms producing A? _____

_____

3. Suppose that a firm can produce 100 units of product X by combining labor, land, capital, and entrepreneurial ability in three different ways. If it can hire labor at $2 per unit, land at $3 per unit, capital at $5 per unit, and entrepreneurship at $10 per unit, and if the amounts of the resources required by the three methods of producing 100 units of product X are indicated in the table, answer the following questions.

	Method		
Resource	**1**	**2**	**3**
Labor	8	13	10
Land	4	3	3
Capital	4	2	4
Entrepreneurship	1	1	1

a. Which method is the least expensive way of producing 100 units of X? _____

b. If X sells for 70 cents per unit, what is the economic profit of the firm? $_____

c. If the price of labor should rise from $2 to $3 per unit and if the price of X is 70 cents,

(1) the firm's use of

labor would change from _____ to _____

land would change from _____ to _____

capital would change from _____ to _____

entrepreneurship would not change

(2) The firm's economic profit would change from $_____ to $_____

■ SHORT ANSWER AND ESSAY QUESTIONS

1. Explain the several elements—institutions and assumptions—embodied in pure capitalism.

2. What do each of the following seek if they pursue their own self-interest: consumers, resource owners, and business firms?

3. Explain what economists mean by competition. For a market to be competitive, why is it important that there be buyers and sellers and easy entry and exit?

4. What are the advantages of indirect or roundabout production?

5. How does an economy benefit from specialization and the division of labor?

6. Give an example of how specialization can benefit two separate and diversely endowed geographic regions.

7. What is money? What important function does it perform? Explain how money performs this function and how it overcomes the disadvantages associated with barter.

8. For an item to be useful as money, what is its necessary major characteristic? Can you think of other characteristics that might be favorable?

9. What are the Five Fundamental Economic Questions?

10. In what way do the desires of entrepreneurs to obtain economic profits and avoid losses make consumer sovereignty effective?

11. Why is the ability of firms to enter industries which are prosperous important to the effective functioning of competition?

12. Explain *in detail* how an increase in the consumer demand for a product will result in more of the product being produced and more resources being allocated to its production.

13. To what extent are firms "free" to produce what they wish by methods which they choose? Do resource owners have freedom to use their resources as they wish?

14. What are the two important functions of prices? Explain the difference between these two functions.

15. Households use the dollars obtained by selling resource services to "vote" for the production of consumer goods and services. Who "votes" for the production of capital goods, why do they "vote" for capital-goods production, and where do they obtain the dollars needed to cast these "votes"?

16. What is meant when it is said that competition is the mechanism which "controls" the market system? How does competition do this?

17. "An invisible hand operates to identify private and public interests." What are private interests and what is the public interest?

18. What is it that leads the economy to operate as if it were directed by an invisible hand?

19. If the basic economic decisions are not made in a capitalist economy by a central authority, how are they made?

20. Describe three virtues of the market system.

ANSWERS

Chapter 4 Pure Capitalism and the Market System

FILL-IN QUESTIONS

1. property, enterprise, choice
2. competition, are not
3. *a.* large numbers of independently acting buyers and sellers operating in the markets; *b.* freedom of buyers and sellers to enter or leave these markets
4. markets, price
5. limited
6. efficient, inefficient
7. exchange, wants
8. *a.* How much of a society's resources should be used?; *b.* What goods and services are to be produced?; *c.* How is that output to be produced?; *d.* How is the output to be distributed among economic units of the economy?; *e.* Can the economic system adapt to change?
9. is, must, entrepreneurs, is not, need not
10. revenue, cost
11. normal, economic
12. enter, fall, more, larger, decrease, zero
13. buy, sovereign, restrain
14. least, technology, prices
15. incomes, prices
16. preferences, resources, guiding
17. profit, losses
18. capital, consumer, capital
19. unity, invisible
20. efficient, incentives, freedom

TRUE-FALSE QUESTIONS

1. F, p. 61	**8.** T, p. 65	**15.** T, p. 68	**22.** T, pp. 71-72
2. T, p. 62	**9.** T, p. 65	**16.** T, p. 68	**23.** T, pp. 72-73
3. T, P. 62	**10.** T, pp. 65-66	**17.** T, p. 69	**24.** T, p. 73
4. F, p. 63	**11.** F, p. 66	**18.** T, p. 69	**25.** T, p. 73
5. T, p. 63	**12.** T, p. 66	**19.** T, pp. 69-70	
6. T, p. 64	**13.** F, p. 67	**20.** T, p. 70	
7. T, pp. 64-65	**14.** F, p. 68	**21.** F, p. 70	

MULTIPLE-CHOICE QUESTIONS

1. c, p. 61	**8.** b, ppw. 64-65	**15.** c, pp. 68-69	**22.** c, pp. 70-71
2. a, p. 62	**9.** d, p. 65	**16.** a, p. 69	**23.** a, p. 62
3. a, p. 63	**10.** d, p. 65	**17.** c, pp. 69-70	**24.** c, pp. 69-70
4. c, p. 63	**11.** a, pp. 65-66	**18.** b, p. 70	**25.** b, p. 70
5. a, p. 63	**12.** a, p. 67	**19.** a, pp. 68; 70	
6. c, p. 64	**13.** b, p. 68	**20.** d, p. 70	
7. b, p. 64	**14.** c, p. 68	**21.** c, pp. 70-71	

PROBLEMS

1. *a.* 8; *b.* 4; *c.* 7; *d.* 1; *e.* 6; *f.* 3; *g.* 2; *h.* 5
2. \$6, −\$5, \$10; *a.* C; *b.* produce A and have an economic profit of \$14; *c.* it would increase
3. *a.* method 2; *b.* 15; *c.* (1) 13, 8; 3, 4; 2, 4; (2) 15, 4

SHORT ANSWER AND ESSAY QUESTIONS

1. pp. 61-67	**6.** p. 65	**11.** pp. 68-69	**16.** p. 73
2. p. 63	**7.** pp. 65-66	**12.** p. 69	**17.** p. 73
3. p. 63	**8.** pp. 66-67	**13.** p. 69	**18.** p. 73
4. pp. 64-65	**9.** p. 67	**14.** pp. 68-69	**19.** p. 73
5. p. 65	**10.** p. 68	**15.** p. 73	**20.** pp. 73-74

CHAPTER 5

The Mixed Economy: Private and Public Sectors

The U.S. economy is divided into a private sector and public sector. The first half of Chapter 5 discusses the private sector—the characteristics of the millions of households and business firms. The second half of Chapter 5 describes the public sector—the functions and financing of the Federal, state, and local governments. Learning about these two sectors will give you the basic facts and framework you need for understanding the U.S. economy.

Chapter 5 begins with an examination of the ***households*** of the economy, the distribution of income in the United States, and the uses to which the households put their incomes. Two different distributions of income are examined. Households in the United States earn five kinds of income and receive transfer payments. The way in which the total personal income received by all U.S. households is divided among the five types of earned income and transfer payments is called the ***functional distribution of income.*** The way in which the total personal income received by all households is distributed among the various income classes is called the ***personal distribution of income.***

Business firms in the United States are also a focus of the chapter. It is apparent that what most characterizes U.S. business is the differences among firms in size and legal form, as well as in the products they produce. You should note the distinctions between a proprietorship, a partnership, and a corporation and the advantages and disadvantages of each form. Also, big business is an important characteristic of the U.S. economy because corporations account for the major source of production in the economy.

Chapter 5 also introduces you to the five basic functions performed by the Federal, state, and local governments in the mixed capitalist economy of the United States. The discussion points out the degree and the ways in which government causes the U.S. economy to differ from pure capitalism. The chapter does not attempt to list all the *specific* ways in which government affects the behavior of the economy; instead, it provides a *general* classification of the tasks government performs.

This chapter also discusses the two major functions of government: (1) the legal and social framework for the operation of the market system as provided by government; (2) government actions that can be taken to maintain competition in the economy. In addition, the chapter explains how government influences the market system in three other ways: by redistributing wealth and income, altering domestic output, and stabilizing the economy.

The chapter also returns to the ***circular flow model*** first presented in Chapter 2. The model has now been modified to include government along with businesses and households. The addition of government changes the real and monetary flows in the model. The 12 links among the household, business, and government sectors in the model are described in detail.

The facts of *government finance* in the United States are presented in the final sections of Chapter 5. The organization of the discussion is relatively simple. First, the trends for taxes collected and expenditures made by all levels of government—Federal, state, and local—are examined briefly. Second, a closer look is taken at the major items upon which the Federal government spends its income, the principal taxes it levies to obtain its income, and the relative importance of these taxes. Third, the chapter looks at the major expenditures and taxes of the state and local governments and will take a brief look at fiscal federalism and lotteries.

■ CHECKLIST

When you have studied this chapter you should be able to

□ Define and distinguish between a functional and a personal distribution of income.
□ State the relative size of the five sources of personal income in the functional distribution.
□ List the three uses to which households put their personal incomes and state the relative size of each.
□ Distinguish among durable goods, nondurable goods, and services in personal consumption expenditures.
□ Explain the differences among a plant, a firm, a conglomerate, and an industry.
□ State the difference between limited and unlimited liability.
□ State the advantages and disadvantages of the three legal forms of business enterprise.
□ Report the relative importance of each of the legal forms of business enterprise in the U.S. economy.
□ Cite evidence to indicate that large corporations dominate the economy.
□ Explain in one or two sentences why the U.S. economy is ***mixed capitalism*** rather than ***pure capitalism.***
□ Enumerate the five economic functions of government

in the United States and explain the difference between the purpose of the first two and the purpose of the last three functions.
☐ Define monopoly and explain why government wishes to prevent monopoly and to preserve competition in the economy.
☐ Explain why government feels it should redistribute income and list the three principal policies it employs for this purpose.
☐ Define spillover cost and spillover benefit.
☐ Explain why a competitive market fails to allocate resources efficiently when there are spillover costs and benefits.
☐ List two actions government can take to reduce spillover costs.
☐ List three actions goverment can take to encourage spillover benefits.
☐ Give definitions of a public good and a quasipublic good.
☐ Explain how the government reallocates resources from the production of private goods to the production of public or quasipublic goods.
☐ Describe the stabilization role of government and the two main economic problems it is designed to address.
☐ Draw the circular flow diagram that includes businesses, households, and government, labeling all the flows and illustrating the role of government.
☐ Explain the difference between government purchases and transfer payments and the affect of each on the composition of national output.
☐ Identify the four largest categories of Federal expenditures.
☐ List the three main sources of Federal tax revenues.
☐ Define and explain the differences between marginal and average tax rates.
☐ Identify the four largest sources of expenditures for state and local government.
☐ Describe how state and local governments raise tax revenue.
☐ Discuss the affect of fiscal federalism and lotteries on state and local government finance.

■ CHAPTER OUTLINE

1. *Households* play a dual role in the economy. They supply the economy with resources, and they purchase the greatest share of the goods and services produced by the economy. They obtain their personal incomes in exchange for the resources they furnish the economy and from the transfer payments they receive from government.

  a. The functional distribution of income indicates the way in which total personal income is divided among the five sources of earned income (wages and salaries, proprietors' income, corporate profits, interest, and rents) and transfer payments.
  b. The personal distribution of income indicates the way in which total personal income is divided among households in different income classes.

2. Households use their incomes to purchase consumer goods, to pay taxes, and to accumulate savings.

  a. Personal taxes constitute a deduction from a household's personal income; what remains after taxes can be either saved or spent.
  b. Saving is what a household does not spend of its after-tax income.
  c. Households spend for durable goods, nondurable goods, and services.

3. The *business population* of the U.S. economy consists of three major types of entities. A ***plant*** is a physical structure that produces a product. A *business firm* is an organization which owns and operates plants. (Multiplant firms may own horizontal, vertical, or conglomerate combinations of plants.) An ***industry*** is a group of firms producing the same or similar goods or services.

4. The three principal *legal forms* of business firms are the *proprietorship, partnership,* and *corporation.* Each has special characteristics and advantages and disadvantages.

  a. The proprietorship is easy to form, lets the owner be boss, and allows great freedom. Disadvantages are lack of access to large amounts of financial capital, difficulty of managerial specialization, and the owner's unlimited liability.
  b. The partnership is also easy to form and allows for more access to financial capital and permits more managerial specialization. Potential disadvantages are that partners may disagree, there are still limits to financial capital or managerial specialization, continuity of the firm over time is a problem, and partners face unlimited liability.
  c. The corporation can raise financial capital through the sale of stocks and bonds, has limited liability for owners, can become large in size, and has an independent life. Chief disadvantages are the double taxation of some corporate income, potential for abuse of this legal entity, and legal or regulatory expenses. There can also be a principal-agent problem with the separation of ownership and control of the firm.
  d. Large corporations are a major characteristic of the U.S. economy; they dominate most industries and produce most of the nation's output.

5. The U.S. economy is "mixed," with government and markets directing economic activity. *Government* performs five economic functions. The first two (**6** and **7** following) are designed to make the market systems operate more effectively; the other three (**8**, **9**, and **10**) are used to eliminate the shortcomings of a purely market-type economy.

6. The first of these functions is to provide the legal and social framework that makes the effective operation of the market system possible.

7. The second function is the maintenance of competition and the regulation of monopoly.

8. Government performs its third function when it redistributes income to reduce income inequality.

9. When government reallocates resources it performs its fourth function:

a. It reallocates resources to take account of spillover costs and benefits.

b. It also reallocates resources to provide society with public (social) goods and services.

c. It levies taxes and uses the tax revenues to purchase or produce the public goods.

10. Its fifth function is stabilization of the price level and maintenance of full employment.

11. *A circular flow* diagram that includes the public sector as well as business firms and households in the private sector of the economy reveals that government purchases public goods from private businesses, collects taxes from and makes transfer payments to these firms, purchases labor services from households, collects taxes from and makes transfer payments to these households, and can alter the distribution of income, reallocate resources, and change the level of economic activity by affecting the real and monetary flows in the diagram.

12. Government spending consists of *purchases* of goods and services and *transfer* payments, but they have different effects on the economy. Purchases are exhaustive because they directly use the economy's resources, while transfers are nonexhaustive. Government spending is equal to about one-third of domestic output.

13. At the Federal level of government,

a. most spending goes for pensions and income security, national defense, health care, or interest on the public debt.

b. the major sources of revenue are personal income taxes, payroll taxes, and corporate income taxes.

14. At the other government levels,

a. state governments depend largely on sales, excise, and personal income taxes, and they spend their revenues on public welfare, education, health care, and highways.

b. local governments rely heavily on property taxes; they spend much of the revenue on education.

c. state and local governments often receive transfers and grants from the Federal government in a process called fiscal *federalism*; they sometimes use *lotteries* to supplement tax revenues.

■ HINTS AND TIPS

1. This chapter is a long one, so do not try to learn everything at once. Break the chapter into its three natural parts and work on each one separately. The first part describes features of the private sector. The second part explains the functions of government. The third part looks at government finance.

2. There are many descriptive statistics about the private and public sectors. Avoid memorizing these statistics. Instead, look for the trends and generalizations which these statistics illustrate about the private or public sector. For example, the discussion of government finance describes recent trends in government expenditures and taxes, and indicates the relative importance of taxes and expenditures at each level of government.

■ IMPORTANT TERMS

functional distribution of income
personal distribution of income
personal taxes
personal saving
personal consumption expenditures
durable good
nondurable good
services
plant
firm
horizontal combination
vertical combination
conglomerate combination
industry
sole proprietorship
partnership
corporation
stocks
bonds
limited liability
double taxation
principal-agent problem
monopoly
spillover (externality)
spillover cost
spillover benefit
exclusion principle
public goods
free-rider problem
quasipublic goods
government purchase
government transfer payment
personal income tax
marginal tax rate
average tax rate
payroll tax
corporate income tax
sales tax
excise tax
property tax
fiscal federalism
lotteries

SELF-TEST

■ FILL-IN QUESTIONS

1. The approximately 101 million (businesses, households) ________________ in the United States play a dual role in the economy because they (sell, buy) ________________ resources and ________________ most of total output of the economy.

2. The largest single source of income in the United States is (profits, interest, wages and salaries) ________________ and is equal to about (26, 51, 71) _____% of total income.

3. In the United States the poorest (1, 20) _____% of all families receive about 4% of total personal income, and the richest (1, 20) _____% of these families receive about 47% of total personal income.

4. The total income of households is disposed of in three ways: personal ________________, personal ________________, and personal ________________.

5. Households use about 14% of their total income to pay for personal (taxes, consumption expenditures) ______________ and about 80% for personal ______________.

6. If a product has an expected life of 3 years or more it is a (durable, nondurable) ______________ good, whereas if it has an expected life of less than 3 years it is a ______________ good.

7. Today there are about 22 million business (firms, industries) ______________ in the United States. The legal form of the great majority of them is the (sole proprietorship, partnership, corporation) ______________, but the legal form that produces 90 percent of the sales of the U.S. economy is the ______________.

8. The liabilities of a sole proprietor and of partners are (limited, unlimited) ______________, but the liabilities of stockholders in a corporation are ______________.

9. The separation of ownership and control in a corporation may create a (free-rider, principal-agent) ______________ problem. In this case, stockholders would be the (riders, principals, agents) ______________ and managers would be the ______________.

10. List the five economic functions of government.

a. ______________

b. ______________

c. ______________

d. ______________

e. ______________

11. To control monopoly, the U.S. government has created commissions to (tax, regulate) ______________ natural monopolies, and in cases at the local level, government has become an (agent, owner) ______________. Government has also enacted (trust, antitrust) ______________ laws to maintain competition.

12. The market system, because it is an impersonal mechanism, results in an (equal, unequal) ______________ distribution of income. To redistribute income from the upper- to the lower-income groups, the government has provided (transfer, tax) ______________ payments, engaged in (military, market) ______________ intervention, and used the (income, sales) ______________ tax to raise much of its revenues.

13. Government frequently reallocates resources when it finds instances of (market, public) ______________ failure. The two major cases of such failure occur when the competitive market system either

a. ______________;

b. ______________

14. Competitive markets bring about an efficient allocation of resources only if there are no (private, spillover) ______________ costs or benefits in the consumption and production of the good or service.

15. There is an externality whenever some of the costs of producing a product accrue to people other than the (seller, buyer) ______________ or some of the benefits from consuming a product accrue to people other than the ______________.

16. What two things can government do to

a. make the market reflect spillover costs?

(1) ______________

(2) ______________

b. make the market reflect spillover benefits?

(1) ______________

(2) ______________

17. Public goods tend to be goods which are not subject to the (inclusion, exclusion) ______________ principle and which are (divisible, indivisible) ______________. Quasipublic goods are goods which could be subjected to the (inclusion, exclusion) ______________ principle but are provided by government because they have large spillover (costs, benefits) ______________.

18. To reallocate resources from the production of private to the production of public and quasipublic goods, government reduces the demand for private goods by (taxing, subsidizing) ______________ consumers and then uses the (profits, tax revenue) ______________ to buy public or quasipublic goods.

19. To stabilize the economy with less than full employment, government will (increase, decrease) ______________ total spending by (increasing, decreasing) ______________ its expenditures for public goods and services and by (increasing, decreasing) ______________ taxes. When there are inflationary pressures, the government will (decrease, increase) ______________ total spending by (decreasing, increasing) ______________ its expenditures for public goods and services and by ______________ taxes.

20. An examination of the public sector of the U.S. economy reveals that

a. since 1960 government *purchases* of goods and services as a percentage of total output (increased, remained relatively constant) ______________ and since the early 1950s have been about (10, 20, 30) _____% of the domestic output;

b. but government *transfer payments* as a percentage of domestic output during the past 35 years (increased, decreased, remained constant) ______________;

c. and the tax revenues required to finance both government expenditures and transfer payments are today about (one-third, two-thirds) ______________ of domestic output.

21. Government transfer payments are (exhaustive, nonexhaustive) ______________, whereas government purchases of goods and services are ______________ because they absorb resources.

22. The most important source of revenue for the Federal government is the (personal income, payroll) ______________ tax; next in importance is the ______________ tax. The three largest categories of Federal expenditures ranked by budget size are (health, national defense, pensions, and income security) ______________, ______________, and ______________.

23. Federal income tax rates are progressive, which means that people with (lower, higher) ______________ incomes pay a larger percentage of that income as taxes than do persons with ______________ incomes. The tax paid on an additional unit of income is the (average, marginal) ______________, while the total tax paid divided by the total taxable income is the ______________ tax rate.

24. Many state governments rely primarily on (property, sales, and excise) ______________ taxes and (personal, corporate) ______________ income taxes for their revenue, which they spend mostly on (national defense, public welfare) ______________ and (interest, education) ______________.

25. At local levels of government the single most important source of revenue is the (income, property) ______________ tax and the single most important expenditure is for (public safety, education) ______________.

■ TRUE-FALSE QUESTIONS

Circle the T if the statement is true, the F if it is false.

1. The personal distribution of income describes the manner in which society's total personal income is divided among wages and salaries, corporate profits, proprietors' income, interest, and rents. **T F**

2. In both relative and absolute terms, personal taxes have risen since World War II. **T F**

3. Most of the personal saving in the U.S. economy is done by those households in the top 10% of its income receivers. **T F**

4. ***Dissaving*** means that personal consumption expenditures exceed after-tax income. **T F**

5. A durable good is defined as a good which has an expected life of 3 years or more. **T F**

6. A plant is defined as a group of firms under a single management. **T F**

7. An industry is a group of firms that produce the same or nearly the same products. **T F**

8. Limited liability refers to the fact that all members of a partnership are liable for the debts incurred by one another. **T F**

9. The corporate form of organization is the least used by firms in the United States. **T F**

10. The corporation in the United States today always has a tax advantage over other legal forms of business organization. **T F**

11. Whether a business firm should incorporate or not depends chiefly on the amount of money capital it must have to finance the enterprise. **T F**

12. Corporations produce about 90% of the total sales (output) produced by privately owned business firms in the United States. **T F**

13. The U.S. economy is a mixed economy because there are both households and businesses. **T F**

14. The Pure Foods and Drug Act is an example of the reallocation function of government. **T F**

15. When the Federal government provides for a monetary system, it is doing so primarily to maintain competition. **T F**

16. Transfer payments are one means government uses to redistribute income. **T F**

17. If demand and supply reflected all the benefits and costs of producing a product, there would be efficient resource use. **T F**

18. When there are spillover costs, more resources are allocated to the production of the product and more is produced than is efficient. **T F**

19. One way for government to correct for spillover costs from a product is to increase its demand. **T F**

20. When there are spillover benefits from a product, there will be an overallocation of resources for its production. **T F**

21. One way for government to correct spillover benefits from a product is to subsidize consumers of the product. **T F**

22. Using the exclusion principle, government provides public goods so as to exclude private businesses from providing them. **T F**

23. Obtaining the benefits of private goods requires that they be purchased; obtaining benefits from public goods requires only that they be produced. **T F**

24. Governments have provided lighthouse services because these services have public benefits and because private producers of such services experience the free-rider problem. **T F**

25. When the Federal government takes actions to control unemployment or inflation it is performing the allocative function of government. **T F**

26. Government purchases of goods and services are called *nonexhaustive expenditures* and government transfer payments are called *exhaustive expenditures.* **T F**

27. When a government levies taxes and uses the tax revenue to make transfer payments, it shifts resources from the production of private goods to the production of public goods. **T F**

28. The chief source of revenue for the Federal government is the corporate income tax. **T F**

29. If the marginal tax rate is higher than the average tax rate, the average tax rate will fall as income rises. **T F**

30. Property taxes are the largest percentage of the total budget of local governments. **T F**

■ MULTIPLE-CHOICE QUESTIONS

Circle the letter that corresponds to the best answer.

1. The functional distribution for the United States shows that the largest part of the personal income is
(a) wages and salaries
(b) proprietors' income
(c) corporate profits
(d) interest and rents

2. The part of after-tax income which is not consumed is defined as
(a) saving
(b) capital investment
(c) wages and salaries
(d) nondurable goods expenditure

3. If personal consumption expenditures were 80% of income and personal taxes were 8% of income, then personal savings would be
(a) 8% of income
(b) 10% of income
(c) 12% of income
(d) 88% of income

4. Which is a true statement?
(a) The durable goods and services parts of personal consumption expenditures vary more over time than do the expenditures for nondurables.
(b) Expenditures for nondurables vary more than do the expenditures for durable goods and services.
(c) Expenditures for nondurables vary more than the expenditures for services and less than the expenditures for durables.
(d) Expenditures for nondurables vary more than the expenditures for durables and less than the expenditures for services.

5. A group of three plants which is owned and operated by a single firm and which consists of a farm growing wheat, a flour-milling plant, and a plant which bakes and sells bakery products is an example of
(a) a horizontal combination
(b) a vertical combination
(c) a conglomerate combination
(d) a corporation

6. Limited liability is associated with
(a) only proprietorships
(b) only partnerships
(c) both proprietorships and partnerships
(d) only corporations

7. Which form of business organization can most effectively raise money capital?
(a) corporation
(b) partnership
(c) proprietorship
(d) vertical combination

8. The separation of ownership and control in a corporation may create
(a) a free-rider problem
(b) a principal-agent problem
(c) a horizontal combination
(d) limited liability

9. One major means that government uses to deal with monopoly is to
(a) increase the demand for its product
(b) decrease the supply of its product
(c) stabilize incomes
(d) regulate the firm

10. Government uses all the following ways to redistribute income, *except*
(a) transfer payments
(b) market intervention
(c) limited liability
(d) taxation

11. To redistribute income from high-income to low-income households, government might
(a) increase transfer payments to high-income and decrease transfer payments to low-income households

(b) increase the taxes paid by high-income and increase the transfer payments to low-income households
(c) increase the taxes paid by low-income and decrease the taxes paid by high-income households
(d) decrease the taxes paid by high-income and decrease the transfer payments to low-income households

12. Which is the best example of a good or service providing the economy with a spillover cost?
(a) a textbook
(b) an automobile
(c) a business suit
(d) an audit of a business firm's books

13. Which economic situation would result in overallocation of resources to the production of a good?
(a) spillover benefits
(b) spillover costs
(c) a free-rider program
(d) inflation

14. How does government correct for spillover benefits?
(a) by taxing consumers
(b) by taxing producers
(c) by subsidizing producers
(d) by separating ownership from control

15. Which is characteristic of public goods?
(a) they are indivisible
(b) they are sold in competitive markets
(c) they are subject to the exclusion principle
(d) they can be produced only if large spillover costs are incurred

16. There is a free-rider problem when people
(a) are willing to pay for what they want
(b) are not willing to pay for what they want
(c) benefit from a good without paying for its cost
(d) want to buy more than is available for purchase in the market

17. Quasipublic goods are goods and services
(a) to which the exclusion principle could not be applied
(b) which have large spillover benefits
(c) which would not be produced by private producers through the market system
(d) which are indivisible

18. In the circular flow model, government provides goods and services and receives net taxes from
(a) colleges and universities
(b) businesses and households
(c) resource and product markets
(d) foreign nations and corporations

19. Which accounts for the largest percentage of all Federal expenditures?
(a) income security
(b) national defense
(c) interest on the public debt
(d) veterans' services

20. Which is the largest source of the tax revenues of the Federal government?
(a) sales and excise taxes
(b) property taxes
(c) payroll taxes
(d) personal income taxes

21. A tax that would most likely alter consumer expenditures on a product would be
(a) an excise tax
(b) a general sales tax
(c) a personal income tax
(d) a corporate income tax

22. Which pair represents the chief source of income and the most important type of expenditure of state governments?
(a) personal income tax and expenditures for education
(b) personal income tax and expenditures for highways
(c) sales and excise taxes and expenditures for highways
(d) sales and excise taxes and expenditures for public welfare

23. Which pair represents the chief source of income and the most important type of expenditure of *local* governments?
(a) property tax and expenditures for highways
(b) property tax and expenditures for education
(c) sales and excise taxes and expenditures for public welfare
(d) sales and excise taxes and expenditures for police, fire, and general government

Questions 24 and 25 are based on the tax table given below.

Taxable income	Total tax
$ 0	$ 0
30,000	5,000
70,000	15,000
150,000	42,000

24. The marginal tax rate at the $70,000 level of taxable income is
(a) 16.6
(b) 21.4
(c) 25.0
(d) 28.0

25. The average tax rate at the $150,000 level of taxable income is
(a) 21.4
(b) 28.0
(c) 31.5
(d) 33.8

■ PROBLEMS

1. The following table shows the functional distribution of total income in the United States in 1997.

	Billions of dollars
Wages and salaries	$4,703
Proprietors' income	545
Corporate profits	804
Interest	450
Rents	148
Total earnings	6,650

Of the total earnings about ______% were wages and salaries, and about ______% were corporate profits.

2. Indicate in the space to the right of **a–i** whether these business characteristics are associated with the proprietorship (PRO), partnership (PART), corporation (CORP), two of these, or all three of these legal forms.

a. Much red tape and legal expense in beginning the firm ______

b. Unlimited liability ______

c. No specialized management ______

d. Has a life independent of its owner(s) ______

e. Double taxation of income ______

f. Greatest ability to acquire funds for the expansion of the firm ______

g. Permits some but not a great degree of specialized management ______

h. Possibility of an unresolved disagreement among owners over courses of action ______

i. The potential for the separation of ownership and control of the business ______

3. Following is a list of various government activities. Indicate in the space to the right of each into which of the five classes of government functions the activity falls. If it falls under more than one of the functions, indicate this.

a. Maintaining an army ______

b. Providing for a system of unemployment compensation ______

c. Establishment of the Federal Reserve Banks ______

d. Insuring employees of business firms against industrial accidents ______

e. Establishment of an Antitrust Division in the Department of Justice ______

f. Making it a crime to sell stocks and bonds under false pretenses ______

g. Providing low-cost lunches to school children ______

h. Taxation of whisky and other spirits ______

i. Regulation of organized stock, bond, and commodity markets ______

j. Setting tax *rates* higher for larger incomes than for smaller ones ______

4. The following circular flow diagram includes business firms, households, and the government (the public sector). Also shown are the product and resource markets.

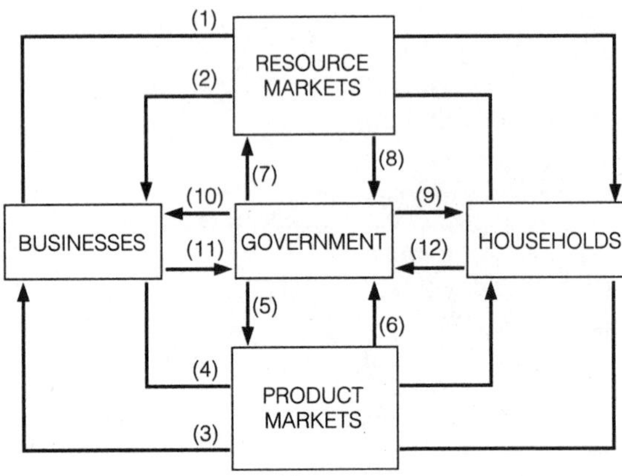

a. Supply a label or an explanation for each of the 12 flows in the model:

(1) ______

(2) ______

(3) ______

(4) ______

(5) ______

(6) ______

(7) ______

(8) ______

(9) ______

(10) ______

(11) ______

(12) ______

b. If government wished to

(1) expand output and employment in the economy, it would increase expenditure flows ______ or ______, decrease net tax flows ______ or ______, or do both;

(2) increase the production of public (social) goods and decrease the production of private goods in the economy, it would increase flows ______ and ______ or ______;

(3) redistribute income from high-income to low-income households, it would (increase, decrease) ______ the net taxes (taxes minus transfers) paid by the former and ______ the net taxes paid by the latter in flow ______.

5. In the following table are several levels of taxable income and hypothetical marginal tax rates for each $1000 increase in income.

Taxable income	Marginal tax rate, %	Tax	Average tax rate, %
$1500		$300	20
2500	22	520	20.8
3500	25	_____	_____
4500	29	_____	_____
5500	34	_____	_____
6500	40	_____	_____

a. At the four income levels compute the tax and the average tax rate
b. As the marginal tax rate
(1) increases the average tax rate (increases, decreases, remains constant) _____________________
_____________________.
(2) decreases the average tax rate _______________.
c. This tax is _______________ because the average tax rate increases as income _____________.

■ SHORT ANSWER AND ESSAY QUESTIONS

1. Explain the difference between a functional and a personal distribution of income. Rank the five types of earned income in the order of their size.

2. Which would result in greater total saving and less consumption spending out of a national income of a given size: a more or less nearly equal distribution of income?

3. The purchase of what type of consumer goods is largely postponable? Why is this? How is it possible for a family's personal consumption expenditures to exceed its after-tax income?

4. What is the difference between a plant and a firm? Between a firm and an industry? Which of these three concepts is the most difficult to apply in practice? Why? Distinguish between a horizontal, a vertical, and a conglomerate combination.

5. What are the principal advantages and disadvantages of each type of the three legal forms of business organization? Which of the disadvantages of the proprietorship and partnership accounts for the employment of the corporate form among the big businesses of the U.S. economy?

6. Explain what "separation of ownership and control" of the modern corporation means. What problem does this separation create for stockholders and managers?

7. Is the U.S. economy and manufacturing in the United States dominated by big business? What evidence do you use to reach this conclusion?

8. Why is it proper to refer to the U.S. economy as "mixed"?

9. What are the five economic functions of government in the U.S. mixed capital economy? Explain what the performance of each function requires government to do.

10. Would you like to live in an economy in which government undertook only the first two functions listed in the text? What would be the advantages and disadvantages of living in such an economy?

11. Why does the market system provide some people with lower income than it provides others?

12. What is meant by a spillover in general and by spillover cost and spillover benefit in particular?

13. How does the existence of spillover costs and benefits affect the allocation of resources and the prices of products?

14. What methods does government use to
(a) redistribute income
(b) reallocate resources to take account of spillover costs
(c) reallocate resources to take account of spillover benefits?

15. Distinguish between a private and a public good. Include in your answer an explanation of the "exclusion principle," the distinction between divisible and indivisible goods, and the free-rider problem.

16. What basic method does government in the United States use to reallocate resources away from the production of private goods and toward the production of public and quasipublic goods?

17. What is the stabilization function of government? What are the two economic problems that this function addresses?

18. In a circular flow diagram that includes not only business firms and households but also government (or the public sector), what are the four flows of money into or out of the government sector of the economy? Using this diagram, explain how government redistributes income, reallocates resources from the private to the public sector, and stabilizes the economy.

19. What is the present size of government spending and taxation in the U.S. economy?

20. Government expenditures fall into two broad classes: expenditures for goods and services and transfer payments. Explain the difference between these, and give examples of expenditures which fall into each of the two classes.

21. Explain precisely the difference between the marginal tax rate and the average tax rate.

22. Explain how the Federal personal income tax enables the Federal government to perform three (of the five) economic functions.

23. Explain in detail the differences that exist among Federal, state, and local governments in the taxes upon which they primarily rely for their revenues and the major purposes for which they use these revenues.

24. Why does the Federal government share its tax revenues with state and local governments? How has this fiscal federalism changed in recent years?

25. What points do critics and defenders make about the lotteries state or local governments use?

ANSWERS

Chapter 5 The Mixed Economy: Private and Public Sectors

FILL-IN QUESTIONS

1. households, sell, buy
2. wages and salaries, 71
3. 20, 20
4. consumption, saving, taxes (any order)
5. taxes, consumption expenditures
6. durable, nondurable
7. firms, sole proprietorship, corporation
8. unlimited, limited
9. principal-agent, principals, agents
10. *a.* provide legal foundation and social environment; *b.* maintain competition; *c.* redistribute income and wealth; *d.* reallocate resources; *e.* stabilize the economy (any order for *a–e*)
11. regulate, owner, antitrust
12. unequal, transfer, market, income
13. market; *a.* produces the "wrong" amounts of certain goods and services; *b.* fails to allocate any resources to the production of certain goods and services whose production is economically justified
14. spillover
15. seller, buyer
16. *a.* (1) enact legislation, (2) pass special taxes; *b.* (1) subsidize consumers, (2) subsidize suppliers, (3) government financing or production of the product
17. exclusion, indivisible, exclusion, benefits
18. taxing, tax revenue
19. increase, increasing, decreasing, decrease, decreasing, increasing
20. *a.* 20; *b.* increased; *c.* one-third
21. nonexhaustive, exhaustive
22. personal income, payroll, pensions and income security, national defense, health
23. higher, lower, marginal, average
24. sales and excise, personal, public welfare, education
25. property, education

TRUE-FALSE QUESTIONS

1. F, p. 78
2. T, pp. 78-79
3. T, P. 79
4. T, p. 79
5. T, p. 79
6. F, p. 80
7. T, p. 80
8. F, p. 83
9. F, p. 81
10. F, pp. 82-83
11. T, p. 82
12. T, p. 82
13. F, p. 84
14. F, p. 84
15. F, pp. 84-85
16. T, p. 85
17. T, p. 86
18. T, p. 86
19. F, p. 86
20. F, p. 86-87
21. T, p. 87
22. F, p. 87
23. T, p. 87
24. T, p. 87-88
25. F, p. 88-89
26. F, p. 91
27. F, p. 91
28. F, p. 92
29. F, p. 93
30. T, p. 94-95

MULTIPLE-CHOICE QUESTIONS

1. a, p. 77
2. a, p. 78
3. c, pp. 78-79
4. a, p. 79
5. b, p. 80
6. d, p. 81-83
7. a, p. 82-83
8. b, p. 83
9. d, p. 85
10. c, pp. 85-86
11. b, pp. 85-86
12. b, p. 86
13. b, p. 86
14. c, p. 87
15. a, p. 87
16. c, p. 88
17. b, p. 88
18. b, p. 90
19. a, p. 93
20. d, p. 93
21. a, p. 94
22. d, p. 94
23. b, p. 95
24. c, p. 93
25. b, p. 93

PROBLEMS

1. 71, 12
2. *a.* CORP; *b.* PRO and PART; *c.* PRO; *d.* CORP; *e.* CORP; *f.* CORP; *g.* PART; *h.* PART; *i.* CORP
3. *a.* reallocates resources; *b.* redistributes income; *c.* provides a legal foundation and social environment *and* stabilizes the economy; *d.* reallocates resources; *e.* maintains competition; *f.* provides a legal foundation and social environment *and* maintains competition; *g.* redistributes income; *h.* reallocates resources; *i.* provides a legal foundation and social environment; *j.* redistributes income
4. *a.* (1) businesses pay costs for resources that become money income for households; (2) households provide resources to businesses; (3) household expenditures become receipts for businesses; (4) businesses provide goods and services to households; (5) government spends money in product market; (6) government receives goods and services from product market; (7) government spends money in resource market; (8) government receives resources from resource market; (9) government provides goods and services to households; (10) government provides goods and services to businesses; (11) businesses pay net taxes to government; (12) households pay net taxes to government; *b.* (1) 5, 7 (either order), 11, 12 (either order); (2) 9, 10, 11 (either order); (3) increase, decrease, 12
5. *a.* tax: $770, 1,060, 1,400, 1,800; average tax rate: 22%, 23.6%, 25.5%, 27.7%; *b.* (1) increases, (2) decreases; *c.* progressive, increases

SHORT ANSWER AND ESSAY QUESTIONS

1. pp. 77-78
2. p. 79
3. p. 79
4. p. 80
5. pp. 81-83
6. p. 83
7. p. 84
8. p. 84
9. p. 84
10. pp. 84-85
11. p. 85
12. pp. 86-87
13. pp. 86-87
14. pp. 85-87
15. pp. 87-88
16. p. 88
17. pp. 88-89
18. pp. 89-91
19. pp. 91-95
20. pp. 91-92
21. pp. 93-94
22. pp. 84, 92
23. pp. 92-95
24. pp. 95-96
25. p. 96

CHAPTER 6

The United States in the Global Economy

Chapter 6 introduces you to the global economy and its influence on the United States. International trade is important to the United States for many reasons, as you learn in the first section of the chapter. In *relative* terms, other nations have exports and imports which are a larger percentage of their GDPs—about 25 to 35%—because they often have a small domestic market and a limited resource base. By contrast, the United States exports and imports only about 12 to 14% of its GDP because it has a larger domestic market and a more abundant resource base. In *absolute* terms, however, the United States is the world's largest trading nation. Exports were $857 billion and imports were $972 billion in 1996, exceeding all other nations. Most of the trade is with other industrially advanced nations such as Canada, Japan, and Germany. This volume of trade has grown over the years with expansion of the global economy, the rise of multinational corporations, and with the emergence of new trading nations such as the "Asian tigers" [Hong Kong (now part of China), Singapore, South Korea, and Taiwan] and China.

The second section of the chapter briefly returns to the circular flow. Now the global economy ("rest of the world") can be added to the model by connecting it to the product market of that model to make it more complete. Four links are made to the model: *Export flows* are paid for by *foreign expenditure flows*; *import flows* are paid for by *U.S. expenditure flows.*

In the third section, you learn about the principle of ***comparative advantage,*** which is the basis for all trade between individuals, regions, and nations. A nation, for example, will specialize in the production of a product at which it has a lower domestic opportunity cost and trade to obtain those products for which its domestic opportunity cost is higher. Thus, specialization and trade increase productivity within a nation and increase a nation's output and standard of living.

Trading in a global economy requires a ***foreign exchange market*** in which national currencies are exchanged, as you discover in the fourth section of the chapter. This market is competitive, so the principles of supply and demand that you read about in Chapter 3 apply to it. Changes in supply and demand for currency will affect the price of a national currency. When the U.S. dollar price of another currency has increased, the value of the U.S. dollar has ***depreciated*** relative to the other currency. Conversely, when the U.S. dollar price of another currency has increased, the value of the U.S. dollar has ***appreciated*** in value relative to the other currency.

Government actions and policies can affect international trade in many ways. Governments can impose protective tariffs, import quotas,and nontariff barriers, or they can foster exports through subsidies. The reasons for the interventions are difficult to explain given the strong economic rationale for free trade based on the principle of comparative advantage. Nevertheless, as you learn in the fifth section of the chapter, public misunderstanding of the gains from trade, or political considerations designed to protect domestic industries, often lead to government policies that create trade barriers and distort the free flow of products between the nations, thus increasing costs for society.

The sixth section discusses *multilateral* agreements among nations and the creation of free-trade zones that have been designed to reduce trade barriers and increase world trade. In the United States, the process of gradual tariff reduction began with the Reciprocal Trade Agreement Act of 1934. Since 1947, worldwide multilateral negotiations to reduce trade barriers have been conducted through the General Agreements on Tariffs and Trade (GATT). The Uruguay round of GATT negotiations were completed in 1993, and this new agreement included many provisions to improve trade among nations. The other major development has been the formation of free-trade zones. The European Union (originally the Common Market) is a trading bloc of 15 European nations. In 1993, the North American Free Trade Agreement (NAFTA) created a free-trade zone covering the United States, Canada, and Mexico. These trade blocs have the potential to create more trade frictions or lead to freer worldwide trade.

The final section of the chapter explores the issue of whether U.S. businesses can *compete* in a global economy. Foreign competition has certainly changed production practices and employment in U.S. industry since the 1960s. Some industries face a comparative *dis*advantage in world markets. Many U.S. firms, however, have adapted to the changes in the global economy by increasing productivity to reduce costs, improve product quality, and expand export markets.

■ CHECKLIST

When you have studied this chapter you should be able to

□ Explain the importance of international trade to the U.S. economy in terms of volume, dependence, trade patterns, and financial linkages.

□ Describe several factors that have facilitated the rapid growth of international trade since World War II.
□ Identify the key participating nations in international trade.
□ Add the international trade dimension to the circular flow model.
□ Explain the basic principle of comparative advantage based on an individual example.
□ Compute the comparative costs of production from production possibilities data when you are given an example with cost data for 2 countries.
□ Determine which of 2 economic countries have a comparative advantage in the example.
□ Indicate the range in which the terms of trade will be found in the example.
□ Show the gains from specialization and trade in the example.
□ Define the main characteristics of the foreign exchange market.
□ Demonstrate how supply and demand analysis applies to the foreign exchange market.
□ Distinguish between the appreciation and depreciation of a currency.
□ Identify four types of trade impediments and subsidies.
□ Discuss two reasons why governments intervene in international trade.
□ Estimate the cost to society from trade restrictions.
□ List the major features of the Reciprocal Trade and Agreements Act of 1934 and the General Agreements on Tariffs and Trade (GATT) of 1947.
□ Identify the major provisions of the Uruguay round of GATT negotiations.
□ Describe the history, goals, and results from the European Union.
□ Explain the features and significance of the North American Free Trade Agreement (NAFTA).
□ Discuss the prospects for frictions among trading blocs or further trade integration among nations.
□ Discuss the capability of U.S. business to compete in the global economy.

■ CHAPTER OUTLINE

1. *Trade* among nations is large and unique, and thus warrants special attention.

a. Although the relative importance of international trade to the United States is less than it is for other nations, it is still of considerable importance.
(1) Exports and imports are about 12–14% of GDP, and the United States is the largest trading nation in the world.
(2) The U.S. economy depends on international trade for vital raw materials and a variety of finished products.
(3) There are some patterns in U.S. trade: most are with industrially advanced nations, with Canada being the largest trade partner; overall imports exceed exports, but the deficits are greatest with Japan and OPEC countries.
(4) International trade must be financed, and, in the case of the United States, large trade deficits have required the selling of business ownership (securities) to companies in other nations.

b. Factors that have facilitated trade since World War II include improvements in transportation and communications technology, along with a general decline in tariffs and worldwide peace.

c. The major participants in international trade are the United States, Japan, and the nations of western Europe. Newer participants include the Asian tigers (Hong Kong, Singapore, South Korea, and Taiwan) and China. The collapse of communism in the former Soviet Union and the nations of Eastern Europe significantly changed trade patterns in that region.

2. The ***circular flow model*** of Chapter 5 can be expanded to include the international trade dimension by adding the "rest of the world" box to the model. This box would be connected to the U.S. product market, through flows of imports and exports, and U.S. and foreign expenditures.

3. Specialization and trade among economic units (individuals, firms, states, regions, or nations) are based on the principle of *comparative advantage.* Specialization and trade increase productivity and the output of goods and services.

a. The basic principle can be illustrated with an example using two individuals.
(1) Suppose that an accountant wants to have her house painted. The accountant can either do it herself or hire a professional painter to do the job. The law of comparative advantage suggests that the accountant will specialize in that work where the opportunity cost is lower relative to the work where the opportunity cost is higher.
(2) The same principle applies to the professional painter in deciding whether to prepare his own tax return or hire an accountant to prepare the tax return.
(3) Given the hypothetical labor time and wage data in the textbook example, both the accountant and the painter reduce their opportunity costs when they specialize in their respective jobs and exchange money for other services they desire.

b. The concept can also be illustrated with a hypothetical example of trade between two nations that produce two different products.
(1) Suppose that the production possibilities for each nation are a straight line (there is a constant cost ratio).
(2) Each nation will find it profitable to trade because there is a comparative (cost) advantage in the production of one of the two products; each nation can produce one of the products at a lower opportunity cost than the other.

c. The terms of trade between nations—the ratio at which one product is traded for another—lies between the cost ratios for the two nations.

d. Each nation gains from this trade because specialization allows for more total production from the same resources and permits a better allocation of resources; specialization and trade have the effect of easing the fixed constraints of the production possibilities curve for each nation.

4. National currencies are traded in a *foreign exchange market.* This market is competitive and establishes the exchange rate of a domestic currency for foreign currency. The price of a domestic currency, or its exchange rate, is the price paid in the domestic currency to buy 1 unit of another currency ($0.01 U.S. = 1 Japanese yen). Exchange rates are unusual prices because they link the prices of the currencies of nations.

a. The exchange rate for a nation's currency is determined by the supply of and demand for that currency. When the supply or demand changes, then the exchange rate of the currency changes (for example, a change from $0.01 U.S. = 1 yen to $0.02 U.S. = 1 yen).

b. The exchange value of a currency can depreciate or appreciate.

(1) Increases in the exchange rate or price of a unit of foreign currency (the dollar price of a yen increases) means that there has been a *depreciation* in the value of one currency (the dollar) relative to the foreign currency.

(2) Decreases in the exchange rate for a foreign currency (a decrease in the dollar price of yen) means that there has been an *appreciation* in the value of one currency (the dollar) relative to the foreign currency (the yen).

5. Governments develop *trade policies* that can reduce trade between nations.

a. Government policies that restrict trade between nations include protective tariffs, import quotas, nontariff barriers, and export subsidies.

b. The reason for trade restrictions is that governments may not understand the gains from trade, or there are political concerns, such as the protection of businesses or groups in a nation against international competition.

c. But the costs of these restrictive trade policies outweigh the benefits, and as a consequence consumers pay higher prices and the nation makes less efficient use of its resources.

6. International trade policies have changed over the years with the development of *multilateral agreements* and ***free-trade*** zones.

a. United States trade policy has been significantly affected by the Reciprocal Trade Agreements Act of 1934 and by the General Agreements on Tariffs and Trade (GATT) begun in 1947.

(1) Until 1934, the United States steadily increased tariff rates to protect private-interest groups, but since the passage of the 1934 act, tariff rates have been substantially reduced. This act gave the president the authority to negotiate with foreign nations and included ***most-favored-nation (MFN) status*** clauses.

(2) GATT provided equal treatment of all member nations and sought to reduce tariffs and eliminate import subsidies by multilateral negotiations.

(3) The Uruguay round of GATT negotiations started in 1986 and was completed in 1993. The major provisions, which will be phased in through 2005, reduce tariffs on products, cut restrictive rules applying to services, phase out quotas on textiles and apparel, and decrease subsidies for agriculture. A World Trade Organization was established to settle disputes among nations.

b. The European Union (EU) is an example of a regional free-trade zone or trade bloc among 15 nations. It abolished tariffs among member nations and developed common policies on various economic issues, such as the tariffs on goods to and from nonmember nations. The EU has produced freer trade and increased economies of scale for production in its member nations, but such a trading bloc creates trade frictions with nonmember nations like the United States.

c. In 1993, the North American Free Trade Agreement (NAFTA) created a free-trade zone covering the United States, Mexico, and Canada. Critics of this agreement fear job losses and the potential for abuse by other nations using Mexico as a base for production. Defenders cite the mutual advantages from freer trade and the fact that increased worldwide investment in Mexico will stimulate growth in that nation and trade with the United States.

d. Free-trade agreements may create hostile trading blocs or serve as leverage for reducing trade restrictions. The United States is working toward freer trade though the Asian-Pacific Economic Cooperation (APEC) forum and by expanding NAFTA coverage to Chile and Mercosur nations (Brazil, Argentina, Uruguay, and Paraguay).

7. Increased international trade has resulted in more competitive pressure on U.S. businesses, which raises the question of whether the United States can compete in global markets. Most firms have been able to meet the competitive change by lowering production costs, improving products, or using new technology. Some firms and industries have had difficulty remaining competitive and continue to lose market share and employment. Overall, increased trade has produced substantial benefits for U.S. consumers (lower prices and more products) and enabled the nation to make more efficient use of its scarce resources.

■ HINTS AND TIPS

1. Comparative advantage is directly related to the opportunity cost concept and production possibilities you learned about in Chapter 2.

a. A nation has a comparative advantage in the production of a product when it can produce the product at a lower domestic opportunity cost than can a trading partner. A nation will specialize in the production of a product for which it is the low (opportunity) cost producer.

b. When a production possibilities schedule for two nations and two products has a constant cost ratio, you can reduce the complicated production possibilities schedule to a 2 × 2 table. Put the two products in the two columns and the two nations in the two rows of the matrix. In each cell of the matrix put the *maximum* of each product that can be produced by a nation. Then for each nation, divide the maximum of one product into the maximum amount of the other product to get the domestic opportunity cost of one product in terms of the other.

c. This last point can be illustrated with an example from problem 2 in this study guide chapter. Lilliput can produce a *maximum* of 40 pounds of apples or 20 pounds of bananas. Brobdingnag can produce a *maximum* of 75 pounds of apples or 25 pounds of bananas. The 2 × 2 matrix would look like this:

	Apples	Bananas
Lilliput	40	20
Brobdingnag	75	25

For Lilliput, the domestic opportunity cost of producing 1 pound of apples is $\frac{1}{2}$ pound of bananas. In Brobdingnag, the domestic opportunity cost of producing 1 pound of apples is $\frac{1}{3}$ pound of bananas. Brobdingnag is the lower (opportunity) cost producer of apples and will specialize in the production of that product. Lilliput is the lower (opportunity) cost producer of bananas because producing 1 pound of bananas requires giving up 2 pounds of apples, whereas in Brobdingnag producing 1 pound of bananas requires giving up 3 pounds of apples.

2. Foreign exchange rates often confuse students because they can be expressed in two ways: the U.S. dollar price of a unit of foreign currency ($1.56 for 1 British pound), or the amount of foreign currency that can be purchased by one U.S. dollar ($1 can purchase .64 British pounds). If you know the exchange rate in one way, you can easily calculate it the other way. Using the information from the first way, dividing $1.56 into 1 British pound gives you the British pound price for 1 U.S. dollar (1/1.56 = .64 of a British pound). Using information from the second way, dividing .64 of a British pound into 1 U.S. dollar gives you the dollar price of a British pound (1/.64 = 1.56). Both ways may be used, although one way may be used more often than the other. Rates for British pounds or Canadian dollars are usually expressed the first way, in terms of U.S. dollars. Rates for the Swiss franc, Japanese yen, or German mark are expressed in the second way, per U.S. dollar.

■ IMPORTANT TERMS

multinational corporations
"Asian tigers"
comparative advantage
terms of trade
foreign exchange market
exchange rates
depreciation
appreciation
protective tariffs
import quotas
nontariff barriers
export subsidies
Smoot-Hawley Tariff Act
Reciprocal Trade Agreements Act
free-trade zones
most-favored-nation clauses
General Agreements on Tariffs and Trade (GATT)
World Trade Organization
European Union (EU)
trade bloc
North American Free Trade Agreement (NAFTA)

SELF-TEST

■ FILL-IN QUESTIONS

1. The importance of international trade varies by nation. Nations in which exports account for a relatively high percentage of GDP tend to have a (limited, diversified) ______________ resource base and domestic market, whereas nations in which exports account for a lower percentage of GDP tend to have a ______________ resource base and domestic market. An example of a higher exporting nation would be the (United States, Netherlands) ______________, and a lower exporting nation would be the ______________.

2. In relative terms, the imports and exports of the United States amount to about (12–14, 25–27) ______% of the economy's GDP. In absolute terms, the United States is the world's (smallest, largest) ______________ trading nation.

3. The bulk of the trade of the United States is with (less developed, industrially advanced) ______________ nations. The largest trading partner for the United States is (Canada, Japan) ______________. The United States has a large trade deficit with (Canada, Japan) ______________.

4. Factors that have helped increase the growth of world trade since World War II include improvement in ______________ and ______________ technology, a general decline in ______________, and ______________ relations between the major trading partners in the world.

5. The top participants in international trade include the ______________, ______________ and the nations of western Europe. These participants serve as the headquarters for most (national, multinational) ______________ corporations and dominate world trade. The new industrializing economies of Hong Kong, Singapore, South Korea, and Taiwan, known as the "______________," have expanded their share of the world trade to over 10%.

6. In the circular flow model that adds the "rest of the world," foreign expenditures pay for U.S. (imports, exports) ______________ and U.S. expenditures pay for ______________.

7. Specialization and trade (increase, decrease) ______________ the productivity of a nation's resources and ______________ total output more than would be the case without it.

8. When one nation has a lower opportunity cost of producing a product relative to another state or nation it has a (nontariff barrier, comparative advantage) _______ _______________. The amount of one product that must be given up to obtain 1 unit of another product is the (foreign exchange, terms of trade) _______________.

9. When the dollar price of foreign currency increases, there has been a(n) (appreciation, depreciation) _______________ in value of the dollar. When the dollar price of foreign currency decreases, there has been a(n) _______________ in value of the dollar. For example, if the dollar price of a German mark (DM) decreases from $0.60 = 1 DM to $0.50 = 1 DM, then it means that there has been a(n) (appreciation, depreciation) _______________ in the value of the dollar; but if the dollar price of a German mark increases from $0.40 = 1 DM to $0.55 = 1 DM, then it means that there has been a(n) _______________ in the value of the dollar.

10. In the market for Japanese yen, an increase in the (demand for, supply of) _______________ yen will decrease the dollar price of yen, while an increase in the _______________ yen will increase the dollar price of yen. If the dollar price of the yen increases, then Japanese goods imported into the United States will be (more, less) _______________ expensive.

11. The major government policies that restrict trade include
a. excise taxes or duties on imported goods that are called _______________,
b. limits on the quantities or total value of specific items that may be imported, referred to as _______________,
c. licensing requirements, unreasonable standards, and red tape for a product, which are _______________,
d. government payments to domestic producers of export goods, known as _______________.

12. Governments may intervene in trade between nations because they mistakenly think of (exports, imports) _______________ as helpful and _______________ as harmful for a national economy. In fact, there are important gains from trade in the form of the extra output obtained from abroad. Trade makes it possible to obtain (exports, imports) _______________ at a lower cost than would be the case if they were produced using domestic resources, and the earnings from _______________ help a nation pay for these lower cost (exports, imports) _______________.

13. Another reason why governments interfere with free trade is based on (private, political) _______________ considerations. Groups and industries seek protection from foreign competition through (GATT, tariffs) _______________ and import (quotas, subsidies) _______________, or other kinds of trade restrictions. The costs of trade protectionism are (clear to, hidden from) _______________ consumers in the protected product so there is little opposition to demands for protectionism.

14. Tariffs and quotas (benefit, cost) _______________ domestic firms in the protected industries, but _______________ domestic consumers in the form of (lower, higher) _______________ prices than would be the case if there were free trade. They also (benefit, cost) _______________ domestic firms that use the protected goods as inputs in their production processes.

15. Until 1934, the trend of tariff rates in the United States was (upward, downward) _______________. The trend has been (upward, downward) _______________ since the 1934 passage of the (Smoot-Hawley Tariff, Reciprocal Trade Agreements) _______________ Act. This act empowered the President to lower (tariffs, quotas) _______________ by up to 50% in return for a reduction in foreign restrictions on U.S. goods and incorporated (quotas, most-favored-nation) _______________ clauses in U.S. trade agreements.

16. The three cardinal principles established in the General Agreements on Tariffs and Trade are
a. _______________
b. _______________
c. _______________

17. The major provisions of the Uruguay round of (NAFTA, GATT) _______________ negotiations include (exchange rate, tariff) _______________ reductions, coverage of legal, financial, and other (goods, services) _______________ by GATT, cuts in agricultural (import quotas, subsidies) _______________, and protection of (collective, intellectual) _______________ property against piracy. It also created the successor to GATT, called the (Reciprocal, World) _______________ Trade Organization.

18. An example of a free-trade zone or trade bloc is the (Mercosur, European) _______________ Union that was originally started in 1958 as the Common Market.
a. The specific aims of the Common Market were the abolition of (exchange rates, tariffs and quotas) _______________, the establishment of (uniform, different) _______________ tariffs on goods imported from outside the Common Market, the (restricted, free) _______________ movement of capital and labor within the Common Market, and common policies on other matters.
b. The Union created (small, large) _______________ markets and stimulated production that has allowed in-

dustries to achieve (higher, lower) ______________ costs. The economic effects of the Union on nonmember nations such as the United States are mixed because economic growth in the Union will cause U.S. exports to the Union to (decrease, increase) ______________ while the tariffs barrier will cause U.S. exports to ______________.

19. The North American Free Trade Agreement (NAFTA) formed a trade (barrier, bloc) ______________ among the United States, Canada, and Mexico. This agreement eliminated (terms of trade, tariffs) ______________ among the nations. Critics in the United States say that it will (increase, decrease) ______________ jobs, but defenders say that it will ______________ total output.

20. The evidence shows that many U.S. firms (can, cannot) ______________ compete and be successful in the global economy; however, some firms that have benefitted from past trade protection may find it difficult to adjust to foreign (control, competition) ______________ and may go out of business.

■ TRUE-FALSE QUESTIONS

Circle the T if the statement is true, the F if it is false.

1. For the United States, the volume of international trade has been increasing relatively but not absolutely. **T F**

2. The U.S. economy's share of world trade has decreased since 1947. **T F**

3. The United States exports and imports goods and services with a dollar value greater than any other nation in the world. **T F**

4. The United States is completely dependent on trade for certain commodities which cannot be obtained in domestic markets. **T F**

5. Canada is the most important trading partner for the United States in terms of the volume of exports and imports. **T F**

6. If a person, firm, or region has a comparative advantage in the production of a particular commodity, it should specialize in the production of that commodity. **T F**

7. If one nation has a comparative advantage in the production of a commodity than another nation, then it has a higher opportunity cost of production relative to the other nation. **T F**

8. The economic effects of specialization and trade between nations are similar to increasing the quantity of resources or to achieving technological progress. **T F**

9. The interaction of the demand for, and supply of, Japanese yen will establish the dollar price of Japanese yen. **T F**

10. An increase in incomes in the United States would tend to cause the dollar price of the Japanese yen to fall. **T F**

11. When the dollar price of another nation's currency increases, there has been an appreciation in the value of the dollar. **T F**

12. When the dollar depreciates relative to the value of the currencies of the trading partners of the United States, then goods imported into the United States will tend to become more expensive. **T F**

13. Export subsidies are government payments to reduce the price of a product to buyers from other nations. **T F**

14. Nontariff barriers include excise taxes or duties placed on imported goods. **T F**

15. Through world trade, an economy can reach a point beyond its domestic production possibilities curve. **T F**

16. One reason that trade restrictions get public support is that the alleged benefits of the restrictions are often immediate and clear-cut, but the adverse affects are often obscure and dispersed over the economy. **T F**

17. Tariffs and quotas benefit domestic firms in the protected industries and also help domestic consumers by lowering the prices for those products. **T F**

18. The Smoot-Hawley Tariff Act of 1930 reduced tariffs in the United States to the lowest level ever in an attempt to pull the nation out of the Great Depression. **T F**

19. If the United States concludes a tariff agreement which lowers the tariff rates on goods imported from another nation and that trade agreement contains a most-favored-nation (MFN) clause, the lower tariff rates are then applied to those goods when they are imported from other MFNs. **T F**

20. The members of the European Union (EU) have experienced freer trade since it was formed. **T F**

21. The economic integration of nations creates larger markets for firms within the nations that integrate and makes it possible for these firms and their customers to benefit from the economies of large-scale (mass) production. **T F**

22. The formation of the European Union (EU) may make it more difficult for U.S. firms to compete for European customers with firms located within the Union. **T F**

23. The 1993 North American Free Trade Agreement (NAFTA) includes all Central American nations. **T F**

24. NAFTA is an example of the gains to be obtained from voluntary export restrictions. **T F**

25. The evidence is clear that major U.S. firms are unable to compete in world markets without significant protection from foreign competition. **T F**

■ MULTIPLE-CHOICE QUESTIONS

Circle the letter that corresponds to the best answer.

1. Which nation is the world's leading trading nation in terms of absolute volumes of imports and exports?

(a) Japan
(b) China
(c) Germany
(d) United States

2. Which nation is our most important trading partner in terms of the quantity of trade volume?
(a) Japan
(b) Canada
(c) Germany
(d) United Kingdom

3. Which of the following is true?
(a) Exports as a percentage of GDP is greatest in the United States.
(b) The United States is almost totally dependent on other nations for aircraft, machine tools, and coal.
(c) Most of the exports and imports trade of the United States is with industrially advanced nations.
(d) The United States has a trade surplus with Japan.

4. How is most of the trade deficit financed by a nation such as the United States?
(a) by buying securities or assets from other nations
(b) by selling securities or assets to other nations
(c) by borrowing from the Federal government
(d) by lending to the Federal government

5. Which factor has greatly facilitated international trade since World War II?
(a) expanded export subsidies
(b) greater import quotas
(c) increased nontariff barriers
(d) improved communications

6. "Asian tigers" refers to the
(a) nations of Japan and China
(b) nations of Hong Kong, Singapore, South Korea, and Taiwan
(c) aggressive export strategies of the Philippines and Thailand
(d) multinational corporations located in Asian countries

7. In the circular flow model of the economy, U.S.
(a) imports are paid for by foreign expenditures
(b) exports are paid for by U.S. expenditures
(c) imports are paid for by U.S. expenditures
(d) exports are paid for by U.S. multinational corporations

8. Why do nations specialize and engage in trade?
(a) to protect multinational corporations
(b) to increase output and income
(c) to improve communications
(d) to control other nations

Answer Questions 9, 10, 11, and 12 on the basis of the data given for two regions, Slobovia and Utopia, which have the following production possibilities tables.

SLOBOVIA PRODUCTION POSSIBILITIES TABLE

	Production alternatives					
Product	**A**	**B**	**C**	**D**	**E**	**F**
Cams	1,500	1,200	900	600	300	0
Widgets	0	100	200	300	400	500

UTOPIA PRODUCTION POSSIBILITIES TABLE

	Production alternatives				
Product	**A**	**B**	**C**	**D**	**E**
Cams	4,000	3,000	2,000	1,000	0
Widgets	0	200	400	600	800

9. In Slobovia, the comparative cost of
(a) 1 cam is 3 widgets
(b) 1 widget is $\frac{1}{3}$ cam
(c) 1 cam is $\frac{1}{3}$ widget
(d) 3 widgets is 1 cam

10. Which of the following statements is *not* true?
(a) Slobovia should specialize in the production of widgets.
(b) Slobovia has a comparative advantage in the production of widgets.
(c) Utopia should specialize in the production of widgets.
(d) Utopia has a comparative advantage in the production of cams.

11. The terms of trade will be
(a) greater than 7 cams for 1 widget
(b) between 7 cams for 1 widget and 5 cams for 1 widget
(c) between 5 cams for 1 widget and 3 cams for 1 widget
(d) less than 3 cams for 1 widget

12. Assume that if Slobovia did not specialize it would produce alternative C and that if Utopia did not specialize it would select alternative B. The gains from specialization are
(a) 100 cams and 100 widgets
(b) 200 cams and 200 widgets
(c) 400 cams and 500 widgets
(d) 500 cams and 400 widgets

13. If the dollar-yen exchange rate is $1 for 110 yen, then a Sony VCR priced at 27,500 yen would cost a U.S. consumer
(a) $200
(b) $250
(c) $275
(d) $300

14. If the equilibrium exchange rate changes so that the dollar price of Japanese yen increases
(a) the dollar has appreciated in value
(b) the dollar has depreciated in value
(c) U.S. citizens will be able to buy more Japanese goods
(d) Japanese will be able to buy fewer U.S. goods

15. A decrease in the United States demand for Japanese goods will
(a) increase the demand for Japanese yen and increase the dollar price of yen
(b) increase the demand for Japanese yen but decrease the dollar price of yen
(c) decrease the demand for Japanese yen and decrease the dollar price of yen
(d) decrease the demand for Japanese yen but increase the dollar price of yen

16. If the exchange rate for one United States dollar changes from 1.4 German marks to 1.7 German marks, then there has been

(a) an appreciation in the value of the mark
(b) a depreciation in the value of the dollar
(c) a depreciation in the value of the mark
(d) an increase in the price of the mark

17. Which of the following is designed to restrict trade?

(a) GATT
(b) NAFTA
(c) import quotas
(d) multinational corporations

18. Why do governments often intervene in international trade?

(a) to expand a nation's production possibilities
(b) to improve the position of multinational corporations
(c) to protect domestic industries from foreign competition
(d) to increase revenue from tariff duties and excise taxes

19. Tariffs and quotas in a nation benefit domestic

(a) consumers and foreign producers of the protected product
(b) consumers and producers of the protected product
(c) producers of the protected product, but harm domestic consumers of the product
(d) foreign producers of the protected product, but harm domestic producers of the product

20. Which one of the following specifically empowered the president of the United States to reduce its tariff rates up to 50% if other nations would reduce their tariffs on American goods?

(a) the Smoot-Hawley Tariff Act of 1930
(b) the Reciprocal Trade Agreements Act of 1934
(c) the General Agreement on Tariffs and Trade of 1947
(d) North American Free Trade Agreement of 1993

21. Which of the following is characteristic of the General Agreement on Tariffs and Trade? Nations signing the agreement were committed to

(a) the expansion of import quotas
(b) the reciprocal increase in tariffs by negotiation
(c) the nondiscriminatory treatment of all member nations
(d) the establishment of a world customs union

22. One important outcome from the Uruguay round of GATT was

(a) removal of voluntary export restraints in manufacturing
(b) reduction of trade barriers and subsidies in agriculture
(c) abolishment of patent, copyright, and trademark protection
(d) an increase in tariff barriers on services

23. One of the potential problems with the European Union is that

(a) an unregulated free flow of labor and capital may reduce productivity
(b) economies of large-scale production may increase consumer prices
(c) tariffs may reduce trade with nonmember nations
(d) governments may have difficulty covering the shortfall from the elimination of duties and taxes

24. An example of the formation of a trade bloc would be the

(a) Smoot-Hawley Tariff Act
(b) North American Free Trade Agreement
(c) Reciprocal Trade Agreements Act
(d) General Agreements on Tariffs and Trade

25. The Mercosur is

(a) the controlling body of the European Union
(b) one of the provisions of the North American Free Trade Agreement
(c) the name of the organization resulting from the latest GATT negotiations
(d) a free-trade zone covering Brazil, Argentina, Uruguay, and Paraguay

■ PROBLEMS

1. The following problem will help you understand the principle of comparative advantage and the benefits of specialization. A tailor named Hart has the production possibilities table for trousers and jackets as given. He chooses production alternative D.

HART'S PRODUCTION POSSIBILITIES TABLE

	Production alternatives					
Product	**A**	**B**	**C**	**D**	**E**	**F**
Trousers	75	60	45	30	15	0
Jackets	0	10	20	30	40	50

Another tailor, Schaffner, has the following production possibilities table and produces production alternative E.

SCHAFFNER'S PRODUCTION POSSIBILITIES TABLE

	Production alternatives						
Product	**A**	**B**	**C**	**D**	**E**	**F**	**G**
Trousers	60	50	40	30	20	10	0
Jackets	0	5	10	15	20	25	30

a. To Hart,

(1) the cost of one pair of trousers is _____ jackets

(2) the cost of one jacket is _____ pairs of trousers

b. To Schaffner,

(1) the cost of one pair of trousers is _____ jackets

(2) the cost of one jacket is _____ pairs of trousers

c. If Hart and Schaffner were to form a partnership to make suits,

(1) _______________ should specialize in the making of trousers because he can make a pair of trousers at the cost of _____ of a jacket while it costs his partner ___________ of a jacket to make a pair of trousers.

(2) ________ should specialize in the making of jackets because he can make a jacket at the cost of _____ pairs of trousers while it costs his partner _____ pairs of trousers to make a jacket.

d. Without specialization, Hart and Schaffner were able to make 50 pairs of trousers and 50 jackets. If each specializes completely in the item in the production of which he has a comparative advantage, their combined production will be _____ pairs of trousers and _____ jackets. Thus the gain from specialization is ____.

e. When Hart and Schaffner come to divide the income of the partnership between them, the manufacture of a pair of trousers should be treated as the equivalent of from _____ to _____ jackets (or a jacket should be treated as the equivalent of from _____ to _____ pairs of trousers).

2. The countries of Lilliput and Brobdingnag have the production possibilities tables for apples and bananas shown below.

Note that the costs of producing apples and bananas are constant in both countries.

LILLIPUT PRODUCTION POSSIBILITIES TABLE

	Production alternatives					
Product (lb)	**A**	**B**	**C**	**D**	**E**	**F**
Apples	40	32	24	16	8	0
Bananas	0	4	8	12	16	20

BROBDINGNAG PRODUCTION POSSIBILITIES TABLE

	Production alternatives					
Product (lb)	**A**	**B**	**C**	**D**	**E**	**F**
Apples	75	60	45	30	15	0
Bananas	0	5	10	15	20	25

a. In Lilliput the cost of producing

(1) 8 apples is _____ bananas

(2) 1 apple is _____ bananas

b. In Brobdingnag the cost of producing

(1) 15 apples is _____ bananas

(2) 1 apple is _____ bananas

c. In Lilliput the cost of producing

(1) 4 bananas is _____ apples

(2) 1 banana is _____ apples

d. In Brobdingnag the cost of producing

(1) 5 bananas is _____ apples

(2) 1 banana is _____ apples

e. The cost of producing 1 apple is lower in the country of ____________ and the cost of producing 1 banana is lower in the country of ____________.

f. Lilliput has a comparative advantage in the production of ____________ and Brobdingnag has a comparative advantage in the production of ____________.

g. The information in this problem is not sufficient to determine the exact terms of trade, but the terms of trade will be *greater* than _____ apples for 1 banana and *less* than _____ apples for 1 banana. Put another way, the terms of trade will be between _____ bananas for 1 apple and _____ bananas for 1 apple.

h. If neither nation could specialize, each would produce production alternative C. The combined production of apples in the two countries would be _____ apples and the combined production of bananas would be _____ bananas.

(1) If each nation specializes in producing the fruit for which it has a comparative advantage, their combined production will be _____ apples and _____ bananas.

(2) Their gain from specialization will be _____ apples and _____ bananas.

3. Use the following table that shows 10 different currencies and how much of each currency can be purchased with a U.S. dollar.

		Currency per U.S. $		
Country	**Currency**	**Year 1**	**Year 2**	**A or D**
Brazil	Real	0.85	0.91	_____
Britain	Pound	0.65	0.59	_____
Canada	Dollar	1.41	1.51	_____
France	Franc	5.44	5.22	_____
Germany	Mark	1.58	1.69	_____
India	Rupee	31.39	34.55	_____
Japan	Yen	100.15	110.23	_____
Mexico	Peso	4.65	5.09	_____
Norway	Krone	6.88	6.49	_____
Thailand	Bhat	25.12	23.22	_____

a. In the far right column of the table, indicate whether the U.S. dollar has appreciated (A) or depreciated (D) from year 1 to year 2.

b. In year 1, a U.S. dollar would purchase _____ French francs, but in year 2, it would purchase _____ French francs. The U.S. dollar has (appreciated, depreciated) ____________ against the French franc from year 1 to year 2.

c. In year 1, a U.S. dollar would purchase ______ Japanese yen, but in year 2, it would purchase ______ Japanese yen. The U.S. dollar has (appreciated, depreciated) ______________ against the Japanese yen from year 1 to year 2.

4. This problem asks you to calculate prices based on exchange rates. Use the data in the table for Problem 3 to answer the following items.

a. Using the exchange rates shown for year 1, what would be the U.S. dollar cost for the following products?
(1) Japanese television costing 30,000 yen. $______
(2) French scarf costing 600 francs. $______
(3) Thai artwork costing 3,768 bhats. $______
(4) German auto costing 79,000 marks. $______
(5) Mexican silver bracelet costing 1,376 pesos. $______

b. Using the exchange rates shown for year 2, what would be the U.S. dollar cost of the following products?
(1) Japanese television costing 30,000 yen. $______
(2) French scarf costing 600 francs. $______
(3) Thai artwork costing 3,768 bhats. $______
(4) German auto costing 79,000 marks. $______
(5) Mexican silver bracelet costing 1,376 pesos. $______

c. Indicate whether the U.S. dollar cost of each product in **4b** has increased (+) or decreased (−) from year 1 to year 2. ______ ______ ______ ______

d. What is the relationship between your answers in **4c** to the ones you gave for the corresponding nations in **3a**?
(1) When the U.S. dollar *appreciates* in value against a foreign currency, the U.S. dollar cost of a product from that nation will (increase, decrease) ______________.
(2) When the U.S. dollar *depreciates* in value against a foreign currency, the U.S. dollar cost of a product from that nation will (increase, decrease) ______________.

■ SHORT ANSWER AND ESSAY QUESTIONS

1. In relative and absolute terms, how large is the volume of the international trade of the United States? What has happened to these figures over the past 30 or so years?

2. What are the principal exports and imports of the U.S. economy? What commodities used in the economy come almost entirely from abroad, and what American industries sell large percentages of their outputs abroad?

3. Which nations are the principal trading partners of the United States? How much of this trade is with the developed and how much of it is with the developing nations of the world?

4. Give several factors that have facilitated trade since World War II.

5. Who are the major participants in international trade? Describe the relative influence of the key players.

6. Describe how the international trade component can be added to the circular flow model of the economy.

7. Use an example of two individuals to describe the basic principle of comparative advantage.

8. What is meant by comparative cost and comparative advantage?

9. Explain how comparative advantage determines the terms of trade between nations.

10. What is the gain for a nation that results from specialization in the production of products for which there is a comparative advantage?

11. Describe the characteristics of a foreign exchange market and of exchange rates. Why is an exchange rate an unusual price?

12. Illustrate with a supply and demand graph how equilibrium is determined in a dollar-yen market. Be sure to label axes and curves.

13. Why might an appreciation of the value of the U.S. dollar relative to the Japanese yen depress the U.S. economy and stimulate the Japanese economy? Why might a government intervene in the foreign exchange market and try to increase or decrease the value of its currency?

14. What are the major trade impediments and subsidies? How do they restrict international trade?

15. Why do governments intervene in international trade and develop restrictive trade policies?

16. What is the cost to society from trade protectionism? Who benefits and who is hurt by trade protectionism?

17. What was the Smoot-Hawley Tariff Act of 1930? What international trade problems are illustrated by this act?

18. Explain the basic provisions of the Reciprocal Trade Agreements Act of 1934.

19. What were the cardinal principles contained in the General Agreements on Tariffs and Trade (GATT)?

20. What were the basic provisions and important results of the Uruguay round of GATT negotiations?

21. What is the European Union? What were its original goals under the Common Market?

22. Discuss the potential trade effects of the European Union on the United States.

23. What is the North American Free Trade Agreement (NAFTA)? What do its critics and defenders say about the agreement?

24. What are the prospects for friction among trading blocs or further integration of worldwide trade among nations?

25. Can U.S. firms compete in a global economy? Evaluate the competitive abilities of U.S. firms in a global economy.

ANSWERS

Chapter 6 The United States in the Global Economy

FILL-IN QUESTIONS

1. limited, diversified, Netherlands, United States
2. 12–14, largest
3. industrially advanced, Canada, Japan
4. transportation, communications (any order), tariffs, peaceful
5. United States, Japan (any order), multinational, Asian tigers
6. exports, imports
7. increase, increase
8. comparative advantage, terms of trade
9. depreciation, appreciation, appreciation, depreciation
10. supply of, demand for, more
11. *a.* protective tariffs; *b.* import quotas; *c.* nontariff barriers; *d.* export subsidies
12. exports, imports, imports, exports, imports
13. political, tariffs, quotas, hidden from
14. benefit, cost, higher cost
15. upward, downward, Reciprocal Trade Agreements, tariffs, most-favored-nation
16. *a.* equal, nondiscriminatory treatment of all member nations; *b.* reduction of tariffs by multilateral negotiations; *c.* elimination of import quotas
17. GATT, tariff, services, subsidies, intellectual, World
18. European; *a.* tariffs and quotas, uniform, free; *b.* large, large, lower, increase, decrease
19. bloc, tariffs, decrease, increase
20. can, competition

TRUE-FALSE QUESTIONS

1. F, p. 102
2. T, p. 102
3. T, p. 102
4. T, p. 102
5. T, p. 103
6. T, p. 109
7. F, p. 109
8. T, p. 110
9. T, p. 111
10. F, pp. 111-112
11. F, pp. 111-112
12. T, pp. 111-112
13. T, p. 113
14. F, p. 113
15. T, p. 113
16. T, pp. 113-114
17. F, pp. 113-114
18. F, p. 114
19. T, p. 114
20. T, p. 116
21. T, p. 116
22. T, p. 116
23. F, p. 116
24. F, pp. 116-117
25. F, pp. 117-118

MULTIPLE-CHOICE QUESTIONS

1. d, p. 102
2. b, p. 103
3. c, p. 103
4. b, p. 104
5. d, p. 104
6. b, p. 105
7. c, pp. 105-106
8. b, pp. 107-108
9. c, pp. 108-109
10. c, pp. 108-109
11. c, pp. 108-109
12. a, pp. 108-109
13. b, p. 111
14. b, p. 111
15. c, p. 111
16. c, pp. 111-112
17. c, p. 113
18. c, p. 113
19. c, p. 113
20. b, p. 114
21. c, pp. 115-116
22. b, pp. 115-116
23. c, p. 116
24. b, p. 116
25. d, p. 117

PROBLEMS

1. *a.* (1) 2/3, (2) 1 1/2; *b.* (1) 1/2, (2) 2; *c.* (1) Schaffner, 1/2, 2/3; (2) Hart, 1 1/2, 2; *d.* 60, 50, 10 pairs of trousers; *e.* 1/2, 2/3, 1 1/2, 2

2. *a.* (1) 4, (2) 1/2; *b.* (1) 5, (2) 1/3; *c.* (1) 8, (2) 2; *d.* (1) 15, (2) 3; *e.* Brobdingnag, Lilliput; *f.* bananas, apples; *g.* 2, 3, 1/3, 1/2; *h.* 69, 18, (1) 75, 20, (2) 6, 2

3. *a.* A, D, A, D, A, A, A, A, D, D; *b.* 5.44, 5.22, depreciated; *c.* 100.15, 110.23, appreciated

4. *a.* (1) 299.55 (2) 110.29 (3) 150 (4) 50,000 (5) 295.91; *b.* (1) 272.16 (2) 114.94 (3) 162.27 (4) 46,745.56 (5) 270.33; *c.* 1 – (2) + (3) + (4) – (5)–; *d.* (1) decrease (2) increase

SHORT ANSWER AND ESSAY QUESTIONS

1. p. 102
2. p. 103
3. p. 103
4. p. 104
5. pp. 104-105
6. pp. 105-107
7. p. 108
8. pp. 108-109
9. p. 109
10. pp. 109-110
11. pp. 110-111
12. p. 111
13. pp. 111-112
14. pp. 112-113
15. pp. 113-114
16. pp. 113-114
17. p. 114
18. pp. 114-115
19. p. 115
20. pp. 115-116
21. p. 116
22. p. 116
23. pp. 116-117
24. p. 117
25. pp. 117-118

CHAPTER 7

Measuring Domestic Output, National Income, and the Price Level

The subject of Chapter 7 is national income accounting. The first measure that you will learn about in the chapter is the ***gross domestic product (GDP).*** The GDP is an important economic statistic because it provides the best estimate of the total market value of all final goods and services produced by our economy in 1 year. You will also discover why GDP is a monetary measure that counts only the value of final goods and services and excludes nonproductive transactions such as secondhand sales.

National income accounting involves estimating output, or income, for the nation's society as a whole, rather than for an individual business firm or family. Note that the terms "output" and "income" are interchangeable because the nation's domestic output and its income are identical. The value of the nation's output equals the total expenditures for this output, and these expenditures become the income of those who have produced this output. Consequently, there are two equally acceptable methods—expenditures or income—for determining GDP.

From an expenditure perspective, GDP is composed of four expenditure categories: personal consumption expenditures ($\boldsymbol{C}$), gross private domestic investment (I_g), government purchases ($\boldsymbol{G}$), and net exports (X_n). These expenditures become income for people when they are paid out in the form of employee compensation, rents, interest, proprietor's income, and corporate profits, with adjustments made for indirect business taxes, depreciation, and net foreign factor income earned in the United States. In national income accounting, the amount spent to purchase this year's total output is equal to money income derived from production of this year's output.

This chapter also explains the relationship of GDP to other national accounts. These accounts include ***net domestic product*** (NDP), ***national income*** (NI) as derived from NDP, ***personal income*** (PI), and ***disposable income*** (DI). The relationship between GDP, NDP, NI, PI, and DI is shown in Table 7-4 of the text. The circular flow using the expenditures and income approaches to GDP are illustrated in Figure 7-3 of the text.

By measuring the ***price level,*** economists are able to determine how much inflation (an increase in the price level) or deflation (a decrease in the price level) has occurred in the economy. This information is important because income-output measures are expressed in monetary units, so if accurate comparisons are to be made between years, these monetary measures must be adjusted to take account of changes in the price level. A simple example is presented to show how a GDP price index, or deflator, is constructed, and then the index is used to adjust nominal GDP to determine real GDP for comparison purposes. The GDP price index and the consumer price index as measures of the rate of inflation will also be explained.

The last section of the chapter looks at the relationship between GDP and economic well-being. You will learn about economic factors that are excluded from GDP measurement—nonmarket or illegal transactions, changes in leisure and product quality, differences in the composition and distribution of output, and the environmental effects of GDP production—and how their exclusion can lead to an under- or overstatement of economic well-being. Although national income accounts are not perfect measures of all economic conditions, they are still reasonably accurate and useful indicators of the performance of the national economy.

Chapter 7 is the essential background for Parts 2 and 3 of the text, which explain the history of and the factors that determine the level of domestic output and income in the economy. Chapter 7 is important because it explains the several methods used to measure the performance of the economy in a given year and make the adjustments necessary to ensure accurate measurements of performance over time.

■ CHECKLIST

When you have studied this chapter you should be able to

☐ Identify three ways national income accounting can be used for economic decision making.

☐ Give a definition of the gross domestic product (GDP).

☐ Explain why GDP is a monetary measure.

☐ Describe how GDP measures value added and avoids multiple counting.

☐ Give examples of two types of nonproduction transactions that are excluded from GDP.

☐ Describe the relationship between the expenditures and income approaches to GDP accounting.

☐ List the two types of goods included in personal consumption expenditures (C).

☐ Identify three items included in gross private domestic investment (I_g).

☐ Explain why changes in inventories are an investment.

☐ Distinguish between gross and net investment.

☐ Discuss how differences in the amount of net investment affect economic growth in an economy.
☐ List the items included in government purchases (G).
☐ Describe the meaning and calculation of net exports (X_n).
☐ Compute GDP using the expenditures approach when given national income accounting data.
☐ Identify the five income items that make up U.S. national income.
☐ List three things that can happen to corporate profits.
☐ Explain the indirect business taxes adjustment to national income accounts.
☐ Define depreciation and discuss how it affects national income accounts.
☐ Describe the effect of net foreign factor income on national income accounts.
☐ Compute GDP using the income approach when given national income accounting data.
☐ Define net domestic product (NDP).
☐ Show how to derive U.S. national income (NI) from net domestic product (NDP).
☐ Define personal income (PI) in national income accounts.
☐ Explain how to obtain disposable income (DI) from personal income (PI).
☐ Use Figure 7-3 in the text to describe the circular flow model for GDP.
☐ Distinguish between nominal and real GDP.
☐ Construct a price index when given the necessary price and quantity data.
☐ Obtain a price index when given data on nominal and real GDP.
☐ Discuss some real-world factors that affect the GDP price index.
☐ Distinguish between the GDP and the consumer price index (CPI).
☐ List seven reasons why GDP may understate or overstate economic well-being.

■ CHAPTER OUTLINE

1. National income accounting consists of concepts which enable those who use them to measure the economy's output, to compare it with past outputs, to explain its size and the reasons for changes in its size, and to formulate policies designed to increase it.

2. The market value of all final goods and services produced in the economy during the year is measured by the gross domestic product (GDP).

a. GDP is measured in dollar terms rather than in terms of physical units of output.

b. To avoid multiple counting, GDP includes only *final* goods and services (goods and services that will not be processed further during the *current* year).

c. Nonproduction transactions are not included in GDP; purely financial transactions and second-hand sales are therefore excluded.

d. Measurement of GDP can be accomplished by either the expenditures or the income method, but the same result is obtained by the two methods.

3. Computation of the GDP by the ***expenditures approach*** requires the addition of the total amounts of the four types of spending for final goods and services.

a. Personal consumption expenditures (C) are the expenditures of households for durable and nondurable goods and for services.

b. Gross private domestic investment (I_g) is the sum of the spending by business firms for machinery, equipment, and tools; spending by firms and households for new buildings; and the changes in the inventories of business firms.

(1) A change in inventories is included in investment because it is the part of output of the economy which was not sold during the year.

(2) Investment does not include expenditures for stocks or bonds or for second-hand capital goods.

(3) Gross investment exceeds net investment by the value of the capital goods worn out during the year.

(4) An economy in which net investment is positive (zero, negative) is an expanding (a static, a declining) economy.

c. Government purchases (G) are the expenditures made by all governments in the economy for products produced by business firms and for resource services from households.

d. Net exports (X_n) in an economy equal the expenditures made by foreigners for goods and services produced in the economy less the expenditures made by the consumers, governments, and investors of the economy for goods and services produced in foreign nations.

e. In equation form, $\boldsymbol{C + I_g + G + X_n}$ = GDP

4. Computation of GDP by the ***income approach*** requires adding the income derived from the production and sales of final goods and services. The five income items are

a. Compensation of employees (the sum of wages and salaries *and* wage and salary supplements).

b. Rents.

c. Interest (only the interest payments made by business firms are included, and the interest payments made by government are excluded).

d. Proprietors' income (the profits or net income of unincorporated firms).

e. Corporate profits which are subdivided into

(1) Corporate income taxes

(2) Dividends

(3) Undistributed corporate profits

f. Three additions are made to the income side to balance it with expenditures.

(1) Indirect business taxes are added because they are initially income that later gets paid to government.

(2) Depreciation, or the consumption of fixed capital, is added because it is initially income to businesses that later gets deducted in calculating profits.

(3) Net foreign factor income is added because it reflects income from all domestic output regardless of the foreign or domestic ownership of domestic resources.

5. In addition to GDP, four other national income measures are important in evaluating the performance of the economy. Each has a distinct definition and can be computed by making additions to or deductions from another measure.

a. NDP is the annual output of final goods and services over and above the capital goods worn out during the year. It is equal to the GDP minus depreciation (consumption of fixed capital).

b. NI is the total income **earned** by U.S. owners of land and capital and by the U.S. suppliers of labor and entrepreneurial ability during the year. It equals NDP *minus* net foreign factor income earned in the United States and *minus* indirect business taxes.

c. PI is the total income **received**—whether it is earned or unearned—by the households of the economy before the payment of personal taxes. It is found by **adding** transfer payments to and **subtracting** social security contributions, corporate income taxes, and undistributed corporate profits from the NI.

d. DI is the total income available to households after the payment of personal taxes. It is equal to PI less personal taxes and also equal to personal consumption expenditures plus personal saving.

e. The relations among the five income-output measures are summarized in Table 7-4.

f. Figure 7-3 is a more realistic and complex circular flow diagram that shows the flows of expenditures and incomes among the households, business firms, and governments in the economy.

6. Because price levels change from year to year, it is necessary to adjust the nominal GDP (or money GDP) computed for any year to obtain the real GDP before year-to-year comparison between the outputs of final goods and services can be made.

a. There are two methods for deriving ***real GDP*** from ***nominal GDP.*** The first method involves computing a ***price index.***

(1) This index is a ratio of the price of a market basket in a given year to the price of the same market basket in a base year, with the ratio multiplied by 100.

(2) To obtain real GDP, divide nominal GDP by the price index expressed in hundredths.

b. In the second method, nominal GDP is broken down into prices and quantities for each year. Real GDP is found by using base-year prices and multiplying them times each year's physical quantities. The GDP price index for a particular year is the ratio of nominal to real GDP for that year.

c. In the real world, complex methods are used to calculate the GDP price index. The price index is useful for calculating real GDP. The price index number for a reference period is arbitrarily set at 100.

(1) For years when the price index is below 100, dividing nominal GDP by the price index (in hundredths) inflates nominal GDP to obtain real GDP.

(2) For years when the price index is greater than 100, dividing nominal GDP by the price index (in hundredths) deflates nominal GDP to obtain real GDP.

d. The consumer price index (CPI) is a fixed-weight price index that measures the ratio of the current price of a fixed, base-period market basket to the base period price of the same market basket, multiplied by 100. It is designed to measure the cost of a constant standard of living.

7. The GDP is not, for the following reasons, a measure of economic well-being.

a. It excludes the value of final goods and services not bought and sold in the markets of the economy.

b. It excludes the amount of leisure the citizens of the economy are able to have.

c. It does not record the improvements in the quality of products which occur over the years.

d. It does not measure changes in the composition and the distribution of the domestic output.

e. It is not a measure of per capita output because it does not take into account changes in the size of the economy's population.

f. It does not record the pollution costs to the environment of producing final goods and services.

g. It does not measure the market value of the final goods and services produced in the underground sector of the economy.

■ HINTS AND TIPS

1. This chapter is fairly difficult, and the only way to learn the material is to sit down and read through the chapter several times. A careful reading will enable you to avoid the necessity of memorizing. Begin by making sure you know precisely what GDP means and what is included in and excluded from measurement of this most important statistic.

2. Accounting is essentially an adding-up process. This chapter explains in detail and lists the items which must be added to obtain GDP by the *expenditures approach* or *income approach.* It is up to you to learn what to add on the expenditure side, and what to add on the income side. Figure 7-1 is an important accounting reference for this task.

3. Changes in the price level have a significant effect on the measurement of GDP, and thus it is critical that you practice converting nominal GDP to real GDP using a price index. Problems 4 and 5 in this *Study Guide* should help you understand nominal and real GDP and the conversion process.

4. GDP is a good measure of the market value of the output of final goods and services that are produced in an economy in 1 year; however, the measure is not perfect, so you should be aware of its limitations, which are noted at the end of the chapter.

■ IMPORTANT TERMS

national income accounting
price level
gross domestic product (GDP)
final goods
intermediate goods
multiple counting
value added
expenditures approach
income approach
personal consumption expenditures

gross private domestic investment
net private domestic investment
government purchases
net exports
national income (NI)
indirect business taxes
consumption of fixed capital (depreciation)
net domestic product (NDP)
personal income (PI)
disposable income (DI)
nominal GDP
real GDP
price index
consumer price index

SELF-TEST

■ **FILL-IN QUESTIONS**

1. National income accounting is valuable because it provides a means of keeping track of the level of (unemployment, production) ______________ in the economy and the course it has followed over the long run and the information needed to make public (policies, payments) ______________ that will improve the performance of the economy.

2. Gross domestic product (GDP) measures the total (market, nonmarket) ______________ value of all (intermediate, final) ______________ goods and services produced in a country (in 1 year, over 2 years) ______________.

3. GDP for a country includes goods and services produced (within, outside) ______________ its geographic boundaries and (does, does not) ______________ treat resources supplied by U.S. citizens differently from resources supplied by citizens of other countries.

4. GDP is a (monetary, nonmonetary) ______________ measure that permits comparison of the (relative, absolute) ______________ worth of goods and services.

5. In measuring GDP only (intermediate, final) ______________ goods and services are included; if ______________ goods and services were included, the accountant would be (over, under) ______________stating GDP, or (single, multiple) ______________ counting.

6. A firm buys materials for $2000 from other firms in the economy and produces from them a product which sells for $3015. The value added by the firm is ($1015, $2000, $3015) ______________.

7. GDP accounting excludes (production, nonproduction) ______________ transactions. These include (financial, nonfinancial) ______________ transactions such as public or private transfer payments or the sale of securities, and (first, second) ______________hand sales.

8. Personal consumption expenditures are the expenditures of households for goods such as automobiles, which are (durable, nondurable) ______________, and goods such as food, which are ______________, plus expenditures for (housing, services) ______________.

9. Gross private domestic investment basically includes the final purchases of (capital, consumer) ______________ goods by businesses, all (construction of new, sales of existing) ______________ buildings and houses, and changes in (services, inventories) ______________.

10. The difference between gross and net private domestic investment is equal to (depreciation, net exports) ______________, or the (production, consumption) ______________ of fixed capital.

11. If gross private domestic investment is less than depreciation, net private domestic investment is (positive, zero, negative) ______________ and the production capacity of the economy is (static, declining, expanding) ______________.

12. An economy's *net* exports equal its exports (minus, plus) ______________ its imports. If exports are less than imports, net exports are (positive, negative) ______________, but if exports are greater than imports, net exports are ______________.

13. Using the expenditure approach, the GDP equation equals ($NDP + NI + PI$, $C + I_g + G + X_n$) ______________.

14. The compensation of employees in the system of social accounting consists of actual wages and salaries (plus, minus) ______________ wage and salary supplements. Salary supplements are the payments employers make to social security or (public, private) ______________ insurance programs and to ______________ pension, health, and welfare funds.

15. Corporate profits are disposed of in three ways: corporate income (taxes, interest) ______________, (depreciation, dividends) ______________, and undistributed corporate (taxes, profits) ______________.

16. Three adjustments are added to national income to obtain (GDP, DI) ______________. They are (direct, indirect) ______________ business taxes, the consumption of (variable, fixed) ______________ capital, and (gross, net) ______________ foreign factor income earned in the United States.

17. Gross domestic product overstates the economy's production because it fails to make allowance for (multiple counting, depreciation) ________________ or the need to replace (consumer, capital) ______________ goods. When this adjustment is made, the calculations produce (net domestic product, national income) ________________.

18. National income is equal to net domestic product (plus, minus) ______________ indirect business taxes plus (gross, net) ______________ foreign factor income earned in the United States.

19. Personal income equals national income (plus, minus) ______________ transfer payments ______________ the sum of social security contributions, corporate income taxes, and undistributed corporate profits.

20. Disposable income equals (national, personal) ______________ income (plus, minus) ______________ personal taxes.

21. A GDP which reflects the prices prevailing when the output is produced is called unadjusted, or (nominal, real) ______________ GDP, but a GDP figure which is deflated or inflated for price level changes is called adjusted or ______________ GDP.

22. To calculate a price index in a given year, the combined price of a market basket of goods and services in that year is (divided, multiplied) ______________ by the combined price of the market basket in the base year. The result is then ______________ by 100.

23. Real GDP is calculated by dividing (the price index, nominal GDP) ______________ by ______________. The price index expressed in hundredths is calculated by dividing (real, nominal) ________________ GDP by ______________ GDP.

24. The consumer price index (CPI) is a (variable, fixed) ________________-weight price index that measures the change in the cost of a (constant, variable) ______________ standard of living.

25. For several reasons, GDP is not a measure of social welfare in an economy.

a. It does not include the (market, nonmarket) ______________ transactions that result in the production of goods and services or the amount of (work, leisure) ______________ of participants in the economy.

b. It fails to record improvements in the (quantity, quality) ______________ of the products produced, or the changes in the (level, composition) ______________, and distribution of the economy's total output.

c. It does not take into account the undesirable effects of GDP production on the (government, environment) ______________ or the goods and services produced in the (market, underground) ______________ economy.

d. Because it is a measure of the *total* output of the economy, it does not measure the (marginal, per capita) ______________ output of the economy.

■ TRUE-FALSE QUESTIONS

Circle the T if the statement is true, the F if it is false.

1. National income accounting allows us to assess the performance of the economy and make policies to improve that performance. **T F**

2. Gross domestic product measures at their market values the total output of all goods and services produced in the economy during a year. **T F**

3. GDP is simply a count of the quantity of output and is not a monetary measure. **T F**

4. The total market value of the wine produced in the United States during a year is equal to the number of bottles of wine produced in that year multiplied by the (average) price at which a bottle sold during that year. **T F**

5. GDP includes the sale of intermediate goods and excludes the sale of final goods. **T F**

6. The total value added to a product and the value of the final product are equal. **T F**

7. Social security payments and other public transfer payments are counted as part of GDP. **T F**

8. The sale of stocks and bonds are excluded from GDP. **T F**

9. In computing gross domestic product, private transfer payments are excluded because they do not represent payments for currently produced goods and services. **T F**

10. The two approaches to the measurement of the gross domestic product yield identical results because one approach measures the total amount spent on the products produced by business firms during a year while the second approach measures the total income of business firms during the year. **T F**

11. Personal consumption expenditures only include expenditures for durable and nondurable goods. **T F**

12. The expenditure made by a household to have a new home built is a personal consumption expenditure. **T F**

13. In national income accounting, any increase in the inventories of business firms is included in gross private domestic investment. **T F**

14. If gross private domestic investment is greater than depreciation during a given year, the economy's production capacity has declined during that year. **T F**

15. Government purchases include spending by all units of government on the finished products of business, but excludes all direct purchases of resources such as labor. **T F**

16. The net exports of an economy equal its exports of goods and services less its imports of goods and services. **T F**

17. The income approach to GDP include compensation of employees, rents, interest income, proprietor's income, and corporate profits. **T F**

18. Indirect business taxes are the difference between gross private domestic investment and net private domestic investment. **T F**

19. Net foreign factor income is the difference between the earnings of foreign-owned resources in the United States and the earnings from U.S.-supplied resources abroad. **T F**

20. Comparison of a gross domestic product with the gross domestic product of an earlier year when the price level has risen between the two years necessitates "inflating" of the GDP figure in the later year. **T F**

21. To adjust nominal gross domestic product for a given year, it is necessary to divide nominal GDP by the price index—expressed in hundredths—for that year. **T F**

22. The consumer price index (CPI) is the price index used to adjust nominal GDP to measure real GDP. **T F**

23. The GDP is a good measure of the economic well-being of society. **T F**

24. The productive services of a homemaker are included in GDP. **T F**

25. The spillover costs from pollution and other activities associated with the production of the GDP are deducted from total output. **T F**

■ MULTIPLE-CHOICE QUESTIONS

Circle the letter that corresponds to the best answer.

1. Which is a primary use for national income accounting?
(a) it provides a basis for assessing the performance of the economy.
(b) it measures economic efficiency in specific industries.
(c) it estimates expenditures on nonproduction transactions.
(d) it analyzes the cost of pollution to the economy.

2. Gross domestic product (GDP) is defined as
(a) personal consumption expenditures and gross private domestic investment
(b) the sum of wage and salary compensation of employees, corporate profits, and interest income
(c) the market value of final goods and services produced within a country in 1 year
(d) the market value of all final and intermediate goods and services produced by the economy in 1 year

3. GDP provides an indication of society's evaluation of the relative worth of goods and services because it
(a) provides an estimate of the value of secondhand sales
(b) gives increased weight to security transactions
(c) is an estimate of income received
(d) is a monetary measure

4. To include the value of the parts used in producing the automobiles turned out during a year in gross domestic product for that year would be an example of
(a) including a nonmarket transaction
(b) including a nonproduction transaction
(c) including a noninvestment transaction
(d) multiple counting

5. Which of the following is a security transaction?
(a) the sale of a used (secondhand) ironing board at a garage sale
(b) the sale of shares of stock in the United States Steel Corporation
(c) the payment of social security benefits to a retired worker
(d) the birthday gift of a check for $5 sent by a grandmother to her grandchild

6. The sale in 1999 of an automobile produced in 1998 would not be included in the gross domestic product for 1999; doing so would involve
(a) including a nonmarket transaction
(b) including a nonproduction transaction
(c) including a noninvestment transaction
(d) multiple counting

7. The service a babysitter performs when she stays at home with her baby brother while her parents are out and for which she receives no payment is not included in the gross domestic product because
(a) this is a nonmarket transaction
(b) this is a nonproduction transaction
(c) this is a noninvestment transaction
(d) multiple counting would be involved

8. According to national income accounting, money income derived from the production of this year's output is equal to
(a) corporate profits and indirect business taxes
(b) the amount spent to purchase this year's total output
(c) the sum of interest income and the compensation of employees
(d) gross private domestic investment less the consumption of fixed capital

9. Which would be considered an investment according to economists?

(a) the purchase of newly issued shares of stock in Microsoft
(b) the construction of a new computer chip factory by Intel
(c) the resale of stock originally issued by the General Motors Corporation
(d) the sale of a retail department store building by Sears to JC Penney

10. A refrigerator was produced by its manufacturer in 1998, sold to a retailer in 1998, and sold by the retailer to a final consumer in 1999. The refrigerator was

(a) counted as consumption in 1998
(b) counted as investment in 1999
(c) counted as investment in 1998
(d) not included in the gross domestic product of 1998

11. If gross private domestic investment is greater than depreciation, the economy will most likely be

(a) static
(b) expanding
(c) declining
(d) experiencing inflation

12. GDP in an economy is $3452 billion. Consumer expenditures are $2343 billion, government purchases are $865 billion, and gross investment is $379 billion. Net exports are

(a) +$93 billion
(b) +$123 billion
(c) −$45 billion
(d) −$135 billion

13. The annual charge which estimates the amount of capital equipment used up in each year's production is called

(a) indirect business taxes
(b) inventory reduction
(c) depreciation
(d) investment

14. The income approach to GDP sums the total income earned by U.S. resource suppliers, adds net foreign factor income earned in the United States, and also adds two adjustments:

(a) net investment and the consumption of fixed capital
(b) the consumption of fixed capital and indirect business taxes
(c) indirect business taxes and undistributed corporate profits
(d) undistributed corporate profits and financial transactions

15. What can happen to the allocation of corporate profits?

(a) It is paid to proprietors as income.
(b) It is paid to to stockholders as dividends.
(c) It is paid to the government as interest income.
(d) It is retained by the corporation as rents.

Questions 16 through 22 use the national income accounting data given in the following table.

	Billions of dollars
Net private domestic investment	$ 32
Personal taxes	39
Transfer payments	19
Indirect business taxes	8
Corporate income taxes	11
Personal consumption expenditures	217
Consumption of fixed capital	7
U.S. exports	15
Dividends	15
Government purchases	51
Net foreign factor income earned in the U.S.	0
Undistributed corporate profits	10
Social security contributions	4
U.S. imports	17

16. Gross private domestic investment is equal to

(a) $32 billion
(b) $39 billion
(c) $45 billion
(d) $56 billion

17. Net exports are equal to

(a) −$2 billion
(b) $2 billion
(c) −$32 billion
(d) $32 billion

18. The gross domestic product is equal to

(a) $298 billion
(b) $302 billion
(c) $317 billion
(d) $305 billion

19. Corporate profits are equal to

(a) $15 billion
(b) $25 billion
(c) $26 billion
(d) $36 billion

20. The net domestic product is equal to

(a) $298 billion
(b) $302 billion
(c) $317 billion
(d) $321 billion

21. National income is equal to

(a) $245 billion
(b) $278 billion
(c) $290 billion
(d) $310 billion

22. Personal income is equal to

(a) $266 billion
(b) $284 billion
(c) $290 billion
(d) $315 billion

23. If both nominal gross domestic product and the level of prices are rising, it is evident that

(a) real GDP is constant
(b) real GDP is rising but not so rapidly as prices

(c) real GDP is declining
(d) no conclusion can be drawn concerning the real GDP of the economy on the basis of this information

24. Suppose nominal GDP rose from $500 billion to $600 billion while the GDP deflator increased from 125 to 150. The real GDP
(a) remained constant
(b) increased
(c) decreased
(d) cannot be calculated from these figures

25. In an economy, the total expenditures for a market basket of goods in year 1 (the base year) was $4000 billion. In year 2, the total expenditure for the same market basket of goods was $4500 billion. What was the GDP price index for the economy in year 2?
(a) .88
(b) 1.13
(c) 188
(d) 113

26. Nominal GDP is less than real GDP in an economy in year 1. In year 2, nominal GDP is equal to real GDP. In year 3, nominal GDP is slightly greater than real GDP. In year 4, nominal GDP is significantly greater than real GDP. Which year is most likely to be the base year that is being used to calculate the price index for this economy?
(a) 1
(b) 2
(c) 3
(d) 4

27. Nominal GDP was $3774 billion in year 1 and the GDP deflator was 108 and nominal GNP was $3989 in year 2 and the GDP deflator that year was 112. What was real GDP in years 1 and 2, respectively?
(a) $3494 billion and $3562 billion
(b) $3339 billion and $3695 billion
(c) $3595 billion and $3725 billion
(d) $3643 billion and $3854 billion

28. A price index one year was 145, and the next year it was 167. What is the approximate percentage change in the price level from one year to the next as measured by that index?
(a) 12%
(b) 13%
(c) 14%
(d) 15%

29. GDP accounting includes
(a) the goods and services produced in the underground economy
(b) expenditures for equipment to reduce the pollution of the environment
(c) the value of the leisure enjoyed by citizens
(d) the goods and services produced but not bought and sold in the markets of the economy

30. Which is a major reason why GDP is *not* an accurate index of society's economic well-being?
(a) It includes population changes.
(b) It excludes many improvements in product quality.
(c) It includes transactions from the underground economy.
(d) It excludes transactions from the buying and selling of stocks.

■ PROBLEMS

1. Following are national income accounting figures for the United States.

	Billions of dollars
Exports	$ 367
Dividends	60
Consumption of fixed capital	307
Compensation of employees	1722
Government purchases	577
Rents	33
Indirect business taxes	255
Gross private domestic investment	437
Corporate income taxes	88
Transfer payments	320
Interest	201
Proprietors' income	132
Personal consumption expenditures	1810
Imports	338
Social security contributions	148
Undistributed corporate profits	55
Personal taxes	372
Net foreign factor income earned in the U.S.	0

a. In the following table, use any of these figures to prepare an Income Statement for the economy similar to the one found in Table 7-3 of the text.

Receipts: Expenditures approach		*Allocations: Income approach*	
Item	**Amount**	**Item**	**Amount**
______	$______	______	$______
______	$______	______	$______
______	$______	______	$______
______	$______	______	$______
		______	$______
		______	$______
		______	$______
		National income	$______
		______	$______
		______	$______
		______	$______
Gross domestic product	$______	Gross domestic product	$______

b. Use the other national accounts to find

(1) Net domestic product is $______________

(2) National income is $______________

(3) Personal income is $______________

(4) Disposable income is $______________

2. A farmer owns a plot of ground and sells the right to pump crude oil from his land to a crude oil producer. The crude oil producer agrees to pay the farmer $20 a barrel for every barrel pumped from the farmer's land.

a. During one year 10,000 barrels are pumped.

(1) The farmer receives a payment of $__________ from the crude oil producer.

(2) The value added by the farmer is $__________.

b. The crude oil producer sells the 10,000 barrels pumped to a petroleum refiner at a price of $25 a barrel.

(1) The crude oil producer receives a payment of $__________ from the refiner.

(2) The value added by the crude oil producer is $__________.

c. The refiner employs a pipeline company to transport the crude oil from the farmer's land to the refinery and pays the pipeline company a fee of $1 a barrel for the oil transported.

(1) The pipeline company receives a payment of $________ from the refiner.

(2) The value added by the company is $__________.

d. From the 10,000 barrels of crude oil, the refiner produces 315,000 gallons of gasoline and various by-products which are sold to distributors and gasoline service stations at an average price of $1 per gallon.

(1) The total payment received by the refiner from its customers is $__________.

(2) The value added by the refiner is $__________.

e. The distributors and service stations sell the 315,000 gallons of gasoline and by-products to consumers at an average price of $1.30 a gallon.

(1) The total payment received by distributors and service stations is $__________.

(2) The value added by them is $__________.

f. The total value added by the farmer, crude oil producer, pipeline company, refiner, and distributors and service stations is $__________, and the market value of the gasoline and by-products (the final good) is $__________.

3. Following is a list of items which may or may not be included in the five income-output measures of the national income accounts (GDP, NDP, NI, PI, DI). Indicate in the space to the right of each which of the income-output measures includes this item; it is possible for the item to be included in none, one, two, three, four, or all of the measures. If the item is included in none of the measures, indicate why it is not included.

a. Interest on the national debt ____________________

____

b. The sale of a used computer ____________________

c. The production of shoes which are not sold by the manufacturer ____________________

d. The income of a bootlegger in a dry state ________

e. The purchase of a share of common stock on the New York Stock Exchange ____________________

f. The interest paid on the bonds of the General Motors Corporation ____________________

g. The labor performed by a homemaker ____________

h. The labor performed by a paid babysitter ________

i. The monthly check received by an idler from his rich aunt ____________________

j. The purchase of a new tractor by a farmer ________

k. The labor performed by an assembly line worker in repapering his own kitchen ____________________

l. The services of a lawyer ____________________

m. The purchase of shoes from the manufacturer by a shoe retailer ____________________

n. The monthly check received from the Social Security Administration by a college student whose parents have died ____________________

o. The rent a homeowner would receive if she did not live in her own home ____________________

4. Following is hypothetical data for a market basket of goods in year 1 and year 2 for an economy.

a. Compute the expenditures for year 1.

MARKET BASKET FOR YEAR 1 (BASE YEAR)

Products	Quantity	Price	Expenditures
Toys	3	$10	$____
Pencils	5	2	$____
Books	7	5	$____
Total			$____

b. Compute the expenditures for year 2.

MARKET BASKET FOR YEAR 2

Products	Quantity	Price	Expenditures
Toys	3	$11	$____
Pencils	5	3	$____
Books	7	6	$____
Total			$____

c. In the space below, show how you computed the GDP price index for year 2.

____

5. The following table shows nominal GDP figures for 3 years and the price indices for each of the 3 years. (The GDP figures are in billions.)

Year	Nominal GDP	Price index	Real GDP
1929	$104	121	$____
1933	56	91	$____
1939	91	100	$____

a. Use the price indices to compute the real GDP in each year. (You may round your answers to the nearest billion dollars.) Write answers in the table.
b. Which of the 3 years appears to be the base year?

____

c. Between
(1) 1929 and 1933 the economy experienced (inflation, deflation) ______________.
(2) 1933 and 1939 it experienced ______________.
d. The nominal GDP figure
(1) for 1929 was (deflated, inflated, neither) ______________.
(2) for 1933 was ______________.
(3) for 1939 was ______________.
e. The price level
(1) fell by ______________ % from 1929 to 1933.
(2) rose by ______________ % from 1933 to 1939.

■ SHORT ANSWER AND ESSAY QUESTIONS

1. Of what use is national income accounting to economists and policymakers?

2. What is the definition of GDP? How are the values of output produced at a U.S.-owned factory in the United States and a foreign-owned factory in the United States treated in GDP accounting?

3. Why is GDP a monetary measure?

4. How does GDP accounting avoid multiple counting and exaggeration of the value of GDP?

5. Why does GDP accounting exclude nonproduction transactions?

6. What are the two principal types of nonproduction transactions? List examples of each type.

7. What are the two sides to GDP accounting? What is the meaning and relationship between the two sides?

8. What would be included in personal consumption expenditures by households?

9. How is gross private domestic investment defined?

10. Is residential construction counted as investment or consumption? Explain.

11. Why is a change in inventories an investment?

12. How do you define a static, an expanding, and a declining production capacity using the concepts of gross private domestic investment and depreciation?

13. What do government purchases include and what do they exclude?

14. How are imports and exports handled in GDP accounting?

15. What are five income components of GDP that add up to national income? Define and explain the characteristics of each component.

16. What are three adjustments made to the income approach to GDP accounting to get it to balance with expenditures? Define and explain the characteristics of each one.

17. Explain how to calculate net domestic product (NDP), national income (NI), personal income (PI), and disposable income (DI).

18. What is the difference between real and nominal GDP? Describe two methods economists use to determine real GDP. Illustrate each method with an example.

19. Explain the difference between the GDP price index and the consumer price index (CPI).

20. Why might GDP not be considered an accurate measure of the economic well-being of society? Identify seven reasons why GDP might understate or overstate economic well-being.

ANSWERS

Chapter 7 Measuring Domestic Output, National Income, and the Price Level

FILL-IN QUESTIONS

1. production, policies
2. market, final, in 1 year
3. within, does not
4. monetary, relative
5. final, intermediate, over, multiple
6. $1015
7. nonproduction, financial, second
8. durable, nondurable, services
9. capital, construction of new, inventories
10. depreciation, consumption
11. negative, declining
12. minus, negative, positive
13. $C + I_g + G + X_n$
14. plus, public, private
15. taxes, dividends, profits
16. GDP, indirect, fixed, net
17. depreciation, capital, net domestic product
18. minus, net
19. plus, minus
20. personal, minus
21. nominal, real
22. divided, multiplied
23. nominal GDP, the price index, nominal, real
24. fixed, constant
25. *a.* nonmarket, leisure; *b.* quality, composition; *c.* environment, underground; *d.* per capita

TRUE-FALSE QUESTIONS

1. T, p. 125	**4.** T, p. 125	**7.** F, p. 126	**10.** F, p. 127
2. F, p. 125	**5.** F, pp. 125-126	**8.** T, p. 127	**11.** F, p. 128
3. F, P. 125	**6.** T, p. 126	**9.** T, pp. 126-127	**12.** F, p. 128

13. T, pp. 128-129
14. F, pp. 129-131
15. F, p. 131
16. T, p. 131
17. T, pp. 132-133
18. F, p. 133
19. T, p. 134
20. F, pp. 135-137
21. T, p. 138
22. F, pp. 137-138, 140
23. F, p. 140
24. F, p. 140
25. F, p. 142

MULTIPLE-CHOICE QUESTIONS

1. a, pp. 124-125
2. c, p. 125
3. d, p. 125
4. d, pp. 125-126
5. b, p. 127
6. b, p. 127
7. a, p. 140
8. b, p. 127
9. b, p. 128
10. c, pp. 128-129
11. b, p. 129
12. d, p. 132
13. c, p. 133
14. b, pp. 132-134
15. b, p. 133
16. b, p. 129
17. a, p. 131
18. d, p. 132
19. d, p. 133
20. a, p. 134
21. c, p. 135
22. b, p. 135
23. d, pp. 136-138
24. b, pp. 138-139
25. d, p. 139
26. b, pp. 138-139
27. a, p. 139
28. d, p. 141
29. b, pp. 140-144
30. b, p. 143

PROBLEMS

1. *a.* See the following table; *b.* (1) 2546, (2) 2291, (3) 2320, (4) 1948

Receipts: Expenditures approach		Allocations: Income approach	
Personal consumption expenditures	$1810	Compensation of employees	$1722
Gross private domestic investment	437	Rents	33
Government purchases	577	Interest	201
Net exports	29	Proprietors' income	132
		Corporate income taxes	88
		Dividends	60
		Undistributed corporate profit	55
		National income	$2291
		Indirect business taxes	255
		Consumption of fixed capital	307
		Net foreign factor income earned in the U.S.	0
Gross domestic product	$2853	Gross domestic product	$2853

2. *a.* (1) 200,000, (2) 200,000; *b.* (1) 250,000, (2) 50,000; *c.* (1) 10,000, (2) 10,000; *d.* (1) 315,000, (2) 55,000; *e.* (1) 409,500, (2) 94,500; *f.* 409,500, 409,500

3. *a.* personal income and disposable income, a public transfer payment; *b.* none, a secondhand sale; *c.* all, represents investment (additions to inventories); *d.* all, illegal production and incomes are included when known; *e.* none, a purely financial transaction; *f.* all; *g.* none, a nonmarket transaction; *h.* all; *i.* none, a private transfer payment; *j.* all; *k.* none, a nonmarket transaction; *l.* all; *m.* all, represents additions to the inventory of the retailer; *n.* personal income and disposable income, a public transfer payment; *o.* all, estimate of rental value of owner-occupied homes is included in rents as if it were income and in personal consumption expenditures as if it were payment for a service

4. *a.* 30, 10, 35, 75; *b.* 33, 15, 42, 90; *c.* ($90/$75) 100 = 120

5. *a.* 86, 62, 91; *b.* 1939; *c.* (1) deflation, (2) inflation; *d.* (1) deflated, (2) inflated, (3) neither; *e.* (1) 24.8 (2) 9.9

SHORT ANSWER AND ESSAY QUESTIONS

1. pp. 124-125
2. p. 125
3. p. 125
4. pp. 125-126
5. p. 126
6. pp. 126-127
7. p. 127
8. p. 128
9. p. 128
10. p. 128
11. pp. 128-129
12. pp. 129-131
13. p. 131
14. p. 131
15. pp. 132-133
16. pp. 133-134
17. pp. 134-135
18. pp. 136-140
19. p. 141
20. pp. 141-144

CHAPTER 8

Macroeconomic Instability: Unemployment and Inflation

In the last chapter you learned how to define and how to compute the gross and net domestic product and domestic, personal, and disposable income in any year. This chapter begins the explanation of what determines how large each of these five income-output measures will be. In the chapters that follow, you will learn what influences the income and output levels of the economy, what causes them to change, and how they might be controlled for the welfare of society.

Chapter 8 is concerned with the instability of the American economy. The first major section of the chapter discusses the ***business cycle:*** the ups and downs in the employment of labor and the real output of the economy that occur over the years. That there have been expansions and contractions in economic (or business) activity since the end of the American Civil War is evident from even a casual look at U.S. economic history. What is not immediately evident, however, is that these alternating and relatively short periods of prosperity and hard times have taken place over a longer period in which the trends in output, employment, and the standard of living have been upward. During this long history booms and busts have occurred quite irregularly; their duration and intensity have been so varied that it is better to think of economic instability than of business cycles.

Two principal problems result from the instability of the economy. The first problem is described in the second major section of the chapter. Here you will find an examination of the ***unemployment*** that accompanies a downturn in the level of economic activity in the economy. You will discover that there are three different kinds of unemployment, that ***full employment*** means about 5.5% of the labor force is unemployed, and that there are at least three problems encountered in measuring the percentage of the labor force actually unemployed at any time. You will also learn that unemployment has an ***economic cost,*** and that this cost is unequally distributed among different sectors of our society. You probably will not be too surprised to discover that widespread unemployment can be the cause of other social problems.

The second problem that results from economic instability is ***inflation;*** it is examined in the remainder of the chapter. Inflation is an increase in the general (or average) level of prices in an economy. It does not have a unique cause: It may result from increases in demand, from increases in costs, or from both. Regardless of its cause, it works a real hardship on certain sectors within the economy. If it occurs at too rapid a rate, it may bring about a severe breakdown in the economy.

Understanding the meaning of unemployment and inflation is important. They are the twin problems of the macroeconomy.

■ CHECKLIST

When you have finished this chapter you should be able to

☐ Explain what the business cycle means.
☐ Describe the four phases of an idealized business cycle.
☐ Identify the immediate determinant or cause of the cyclical changes in the levels of real output and employment.
☐ Identify the two types of noncyclical fluctuations.
☐ Distinguish the differences among the impact of cyclical fluctuations on industries producing capital and consumer durable goods, the impact on those producing consumer nondurable goods, and the impact on high- and low-concentration industries.
☐ Distinguish among frictional, structural, and cyclical unemployment, and explain the causes of these three kinds of unemployment.
☐ Define full employment and the full-employment unemployment rate (the natural rate of unemployment).
☐ Describe the process used by the Bureau of Labor Statistics (BLS) to measure the rate of unemployment, and list the two criticisms of the BLS data.
☐ Identify the economic cost of unemployment.
☐ Define the GDP gap and state Okun's law.
☐ Discuss the unequal burdens of unemployment.
☐ Define inflation and the rate of inflation.
☐ Make international comparisons of inflation rate and unemployment rate data.
☐ Define demand-pull inflation and explain its effects in ranges 1, 2, and 3 of a price level and real domestic output graph.
☐ Define cost-push inflation and its relation to per unit production costs.
☐ Identify two variants of cost-push or supply-side inflation.
☐ Describe the complexities involved in distinguishing between demand-pull and cost-push inflation.
☐ Distinguish between real and nominal income and calculate real income when given data on nominal income and the price level.

□ List groups that are hurt by and groups that benefit from unanticipated inflation.
□ Describe how the redistributive effects of inflation are changed when it is anticipated.
□ Present three scenarios that describe the possible effects of inflation on real output and employment.

■ CHAPTER OUTLINE

1. The history of the U.S. economy is a record of exceptional economic growth.
a. But this growth has been accompanied by periods of inflation, recession, or both.
b. The ***business cycle*** means alternating periods of prosperity and recession. These recurrent periods of ups and downs in employment, output, and prices are irregular in their duration and intensity, but the typical pattern is **peak, recession, trough,** and **recovery** to another peak.
c. Changes in the levels of output and employment are largely the result of changes in the level of total spending in the economy.
d. Not all changes in employment and output which occur in the economy are cyclical; some are due to seasonal and secular influences.
e. The business cycle affects almost the entire economy, but it does not affect all parts in the same way and to the same degree: The production of capital and durable consumer goods fluctuates more than the production of consumer nondurable goods during the cycle because
(1) the purchase of capital and durable consumer goods can be postponed.
(2) the industries producing these goods are largely dominated by a few large firms that hold prices constant and let production and employment decline when demand falls.

2. Full employment does not mean that all workers in the labor force are employed and that there is no unemployment; some unemployment is normal.
a. There are at least three types of unemployment.
(1) ***Frictional unemployment*** is due to workers searching for new jobs or waiting to take new jobs; this type of unemployment is generally desirable.
(2) ***Structural unemployment*** is due to the changes in technology and in the types of goods and services consumers wish to buy; these changes affect the total demand for labor in particular industries or regions.
(3) ***Cyclical unemployment*** is due to insufficient total spending in the economy; this type of unemployment arises during the recession phase of the businesss cycle.
b. Because some frictional and structural unemployment is unavoidable, the full-employment unemployment rate (the ***natural rate of unemployment***) is the sum of frictional and structural unemployment, is achieved when cyclical unemployment is zero (the real output of the economy is equal to its potential output), and is about 5.5% of the labor force. This natural rate is not automatically achieved and changes over time.
c. Surveying some 60,000 households each month, the Bureau of Labor Statistics (BLS) finds the unemployment rate by dividing the number of persons in the labor force who are unemployed by the number of persons in the labor force. The figures collected in the survey have been criticized for at least two reasons:
(1) They include part-time workers.
(2) They exclude "discouraged" workers who have left the labor force.
d. Unemployment has an economic cost.
(1) The economic cost is the unproduced output (or the ***GDP gap***). ***Okun's law*** is that for every 1% the actual unemployment rate exceeds the natural rate of unemployment, there is a GDP gap of about 2%.
(2) This cost is unequally distributed among different groups of workers in the labor force.
e. Unemployment also leads to serious social problems.

3. Over its history, the U.S. economy has experienced not only periods of unemployment but periods of inflation.
a. *Inflation* is an increase in the general level of prices in the economy; a decline in the level of prices is deflation.
b. The rate of inflation in any year is equal to the percentage change in the price index between that year and the preceding year. The rule of 70 can be used to calculate the number of years it will take for the price level to double at any given rate of inflation.
c. The United States has experienced both inflation and deflation, but the past half century has been a period of inflation. Inflation is also experienced by other industrial nations.
d. There are at least two causes of inflation, and these two causes may operate separately or simultaneously to raise the price level.
(1) ***Demand-pull inflation*** is the result of excess total spending in the economy. While increases in total spending do not increase the price level, when the unemployment rate is high (in a depression) they do bring about inflation as the economy nears and reaches full employment.
(2) ***Cost-push*** or ***supply-side inflation*** is the result of factors that raise per unit production costs. This average cost is found by dividing the total cost of the resource inputs by the amount produced. Two variants explain this rise in costs: (*a*) excessive wage increases that push up unit costs, and (*b*) supply shock from an increase in the prices of resource inputs. With cost-push inflation, output and employment decline as the price level rises.
It is difficult to distinguish between demand-pull and cost-push inflation in the real world.

4. Even if the total output of the economy did not change, inflation would arbitrarily redistribute real income and wealth, and it would benefit some groups and hurt other groups in the economy.
a. Whether someone benefits or is hurt by inflation is measured by what happens to real income. Inflation injures those whose real income falls and benefits those whose real income rises.
(1) ***Real income*** is determined by dividing nominal income by the price level expressed in hundredths.

(2) The percentage change in real income can be approximated by subtracting the percentage change in the price level from the percentage change in nominal income.

b. Inflation injures savers because it decreases the real value of any savings.

c. It benefits debtors and hurts creditors because it lowers the real value of debts.

d. When the inflation is anticipated and people can adjust their nominal incomes to reflect the expected rise in the price level, the redistribution of income and wealth is lessened.

e. Since World War II inflation in the United States has redistributed wealth from the household to the public sector of the economy.

f. If short in duration, inflation acts to tax some groups and to subsidize other groups.

5. Inflation may also affect the total output of the economy, but economists disagree over whether it is likely to expand or contract total output.

a. Mild demand-pull inflation seems likely to expand output and employment in the economy.

b. Cost-push inflation is apt to contract output and employment.

c. Hyperinflation may well lead to the breakdown of the economy.

■ HINTS AND TIPS

1. Some students get confused by the seemingly contradictory term "full-employment unemployment rate" and related unemployment concepts. Full employment does not mean that everyone who wants to work has a job; it means that the economy is achieving its potential output and has a *natural rate of unemployment.* Remember that there are three types of unemployment: frictional, structural, and cyclical. There will always be some unemployment arising from frictional reasons (e.g., people searching for jobs) or structural reasons (e.g., changes in industry demand), and these two types of unemployment are "natural" for an economy. Cyclical reasons (e.g., a downturn in the business cycle) for unemployment, however, are not natural for an economy. Thus, full-employment unemployment rate means that there are no cyclical reasons causing unemployment, only frictional or structural reasons.

2. To verify your understanding of how to calculate the unemployment rate, GDP gap, or inflation rate after reading the chapter, do Problems 1, 2, and 3 in this *Study Guide* chapter.

3. Inflation is a rise in the general level of prices, not just a rise in the prices of a few products. An increase in product price is caused by supply or demand factors. You now know why the prices for many products rise in an economy. The macroeconomic reasons given in Chapter 8 for the increase in the general level of prices are different from the microeconomic reasons for a price increase that you learned about in Chapter 3.

■ IMPORTANT TERMS

business cycle
peak
recession
trough
recovery
seasonal variation
secular trend
unemployment
frictional unemployment
structural unemployment
cyclical unemployment
full-employment unemployment rate
natural rate of unemployment
potential output
unemployment rate
labor force
discouraged workers
GDP gap
Okun's law
inflation
deflation
rule of 70
demand-pull inflation
cost-push inflation
supply-side inflation
per unit production cost
nominal income
real income
anticipated inflation
unanticipated inflation
cost-of-living adjustment (COLA)
inflation premium
nominal interest rate
real interest rate
hyperinflation

SELF-TEST

■ FILL-IN QUESTIONS

1. The history of the U.S. economy is one of (steady, unsteady) ______________ economic growth. At times its growth has been accompanied by price (stability, inflation) ______________, and at other times its expansion has been interrupted by (increasing, decreasing) ______________ levels of output of goods and services and ______________ unemployment of workers.

2. The business cycle is a term which encompasses the recurrent ups, or (decreases, increases) ______________, and downs, or ______________, in the level of business activity in the economy.

3. The order of the four phases of a typical business cycle are peak, (recovery, trough, recession) ______________, ______________, and ______________.

4. The basic determinant of the levels of employment and output in an economy is the level of (monopoly power, total spending) ______________.

5. In addition to the changes brought about by the operation of the business cycle, noncyclical fluctuations in output and employment may be due to (secular, seasonal) ______________ variations and a ______________ trend.

6. Expansion and contraction of the economy affect to a greater extent the production and employment in the consumer (durables, nondurables) _______________ and (capital, consumer) _______________ goods industries than they do (durable, nondurable) _______________ goods industries, and prices vary to a greater extent in the (low-, high-) _______________ concentration industries.

7. When workers are searching for a new job or waiting to start a new job, this type of unemployment is called (structural, frictional, cyclical) _______________, but when workers are laid off because of changes in the consumer demand and technology in industries or regions, this unemployment is called _______________; when workers are unemployed because of insufficient total spending in the economy, this type of unemployment is called _______________.

8. The full-employment unemployment rate is called the (Okun, natural) _______________ rate of unemployment. It is equal to the total of (frictional and structural, cyclical and frictional) _______________ unemployment in the economy. It is realized when the (frictional, cyclical) _______________ unemployment in the economy is equal to zero and when the actual output of the economy is (less than, equal to) _______________ its potential output. It is assumed in this chapter to be about (2.5, 5.5, 7.5) _____%.

9. When the economy achieves its natural rate of unemployment, the number of job seekers is (greater than, less than, equal to) _______________ the number of job vacancies and the price level is (rising, falling, constant) _______________.

10. The *unemployment rate* is found by dividing the number of (employed, unemployed) _______________ persons by the (population, labor force) _______________ and (multiplying, dividing) _______________ by 100.

11. The GDP gap is equal to the potential GDP (minus, plus) _______________ the actual GDP. For every percentage point the unemployment rate rises above the natural rate, the GDP gap will, according to Okun's law, (increase, decrease) _______________ by (1, 2, 5) _____%.

12. The burdens of unemployment are borne more heavily by (black, white) _______________, (adult, teenage) _______________, and (white-collar, blue-collar) _______________ workers, and the percentage of the labor force unemployed for 15 or more weeks is much (greater, less) _______________ than the unemployment rate.

13. Inflation means (an increase, a decrease) _______________ in the general level of (unemployment, prices) _______________ in the economy. To calculate the rate of inflation from year 1 to year 2, subtract the price index for year 1 from year 2, then (multiply, divide) _______________ the result by the price index for year 1, and _______________ by 100.

14. To find the approximate number of years it takes the price level to double, (multiply, divide) _______________ 70 by the percentage annual increase in the rate of inflation. This approximation is called (Okun's law, rule of 70) _______________.

15. Since the 1920s, the experience of the United States with inflation has varied. The price level decreased during the early years of the Great Depression, which means (inflation, deflation) _______________ was occurring in the economy. In the United States, the post–World War II period (1945–1948) was characterized by (high, low) _______________ rates of inflation, the 1961–1965 period was a period of _______________ inflation, and the mid-to-late 1970s was a period of (high, low) _______________ inflation.

16. The basic cause of

a. demand-pull inflation is (a(n) (increase, decrease) _______________ in total spending beyond the full employment output rate in the economy.

b. cost-push inflation is explained in terms of factors that raise per unit (inflation, production) _______________ costs. This type of inflation is also called (demand, supply) _______________-side inflation and is caused by (decreases, increases) _______________ in wages and prices of nonwage inputs.

c. In practice, it is (easy, difficult) _______________ to distinguish the two types of inflation.

17. The amount of goods and services one's nominal income can buy is called (variable, real) _______________ income.

a. If one's nominal income rises by 10% and the price level rose by 7%, the percentage of increase in (variable, real) _______________ income would be (1, 2, 3) _______.

b. If nominal income was $30,000 and the price index, expressed in hundredths, was 1.06, then (variable, real) _______________ income would be ($28,302, $29,855) _______________.

18. Inflation hurts those whose nominal incomes are relatively (fixed, flexible) _______________, penalizes savers when the inflation is (expected, unexpected) _______________, hurts (creditors, debtors) _______________ and benefits _______________, and has, since World War II, shifted wealth from (the public sector, households) _______________ to _______________.

19. The redistributive effects of inflation are less severe when it is (anticipated, unanticipated) _______________.

a. Clauses in labor contracts that call for automatic adjustments of workers' income from the effects of inflation are called (unemployment benefits, cost-of-living) _______________ adjustments.

b. The percentage increase in purchasing power that the lender receives from the borrower is the (real rate of interest, nominal rate of interest) _______________; the percentage increase in money that the lender receives is the _______________.

20. Despite considerable disagreement and uncertainty among economists, it seems that demand-pull inflation, unless there is full employment in the economy, will (increase, decrease) _______________ total output and employment, cost-push inflation will _______________ output and employment in the economy, and an economic collapse or breakdown can result from (cost-push, hyperinflation) _______________.

■ TRUE-FALSE QUESTIONS

Circle the T if the statement is true, the F if it is false.

1. The U.S. economy has always experienced steady economic growth, price stability, and full employment. **T F**

2. The business cycle is best defined as alternating periods of increases and decreases in the rate of inflation in the economy. **T F**

3. Individual business cycles tend to be of roughly equal duration and intensity. **T F**

4. Not all changes which occur in output and employment in the economy are due to the business cycle. **T F**

5. Industries which are highly concentrated show small relative decreases in output and large relative decreases in prices during a downswing of the business cycle. **T F**

6. Frictional unemployment is not only inevitable but largely desirable. **T F**

7. The essential difference between frictionally and structurally unemployed workers is that the former *do not have* and the latter *do have* salable skills. **T F**

8. When the number of people seeking employment is less than the number of job vacancies in the economy, the actual rate of unemployment is less than the natural rate of unemployment, and the price level will tend to rise. **T F**

9. If unemployment in the economy is at its natural rate, the actual and potential outputs of the economy are equal. **T F**

10. The natural rate of unemployment in the U.S. economy is a constant 7% of the labor force. **T F**

11. An economy cannot produce an actual real GDP that exceeds its potential real GDP. **T F**

12. The unemployment rate is equal to the number of people in the labor force divided by the number of people who are unemployed. **T F**

13. The percentage of the labor force unemployed for 15 or more weeks is always less than the unemployment rate and tends to rise during a recession. **T F**

14. The economy's GDP gap is measured by deducting its actual GDP from its potential GDP. **T F**

15. The economic cost of cyclical unemployment is the goods and services that are not produced. **T F**

16. Inflation is defined as an increase in the total output of an economy. **T F**

17. From one year to the next, the consumer price index rose from 311.1 to 322.2. The rate of inflation was therefore 5.6%. **T F**

18. If the price level increases by 10% each year, the price level will double every 10 years. **T F**

19. With a moderate amount of unemployment in the economy, an increase in aggregate spending will generally increase both the price level and the output of the economy. **T F**

20. The theory of cost-push inflation explains rising prices in terms of factors which increase per unit production cost. **T F**

21. A person's real income is the amount of goods and services which the person's nominal (or money) income will enable him or her to purchase. **T F**

22. Whether inflation is anticipated or unanticipated, the effects of inflation on the distribution of income are much the same. **T F**

23. Suppose a household has $10,000 on deposit in a savings and loan association and earns 7% interest during a year, and the rate of inflation is 9% in that year. By the end of the year the purchasing power of the $10,000 and the interest it has earned will have decreased to about $9,817. **T F**

24. Unemployment and inflation rates vary among major industrialized nations. **T F**

25. Inflation in the United States has transferred wealth from the public sector to the households of the economy. **T F**

■ MULTIPLE-CHOICE QUESTIONS

Circle the letter that corresponds to the best answer.

1. Which is one of the four phases of an idealized business cycle?

(a) inflation

(b) recession
(c) unemployment
(d) seasonal variation

2. Most economists believe that the immediate determinant of the levels of domestic output and employment is
(a) the price level
(b) the size of the civilian labor force
(c) the nation's stock of capital goods
(d) the level of total spending

3. Total output in December of this year was greater than total output in December of 1928. This is no doubt due to the effect of
(a) seasonal variations
(b) secular trend
(c) the business cycle
(d) business fluctuations

4. If employment in the agricultural sector of the U.S. economy during August and September is typically 112% of what it normally is in the other months of the year, this is probably a consequence of
(a) seasonal variations
(b) secular trend
(c) the business cycle
(d) both seasonal variations and the business cycle

5. Production and employment in which of the following industries would be least affected by a depression?
(a) nondurable consumer goods
(b) durable consumer goods
(c) capital goods
(d) iron and steel

6. A worker who loses a job at a petroleum refinery because consumers and business firms switch from the use of oil to the burning of coal is an example of
(a) frictional unemployment
(b) structural unemployment
(c) cyclical unemployment
(d) disguised unemployment

7. A worker who has quit one job and is taking 2 weeks off before reporting to a new job is an example of
(a) frictional unemployment
(b) structural unemployment
(c) cyclical unemployment
(d) disguised unemployment

8. Insufficient total spending in the economy results in
(a) frictional unemployment
(b) structural unemployment
(c) cyclical unemployment
(d) disguised unemployment

9. The full-employment unemployment rate in the economy has been achieved when
(a) frictional unemployment is zero
(b) structural unemployment is zero
(c) cyclical unemployment is zero
(d) the natural rate of unemployment is zero

10. Which has decreased the natural rate of unemployment in the United States in recent years?
(a) the increased size of unemployment benefits
(b) more workers covered by unemployment programs
(c) fewer young workers in the labor force
(d) less competition in product and labor markets

11. The labor force includes those who are
(a) less than 16 years of age
(b) in mental institutions
(c) not seeking work
(d) employed

12. The unemployment rate in an economy is 8%. The total population of the economy is 250 million, and the size of the civilian labor force is 150 million. The number of employed workers in this economy is
(a) 12 million
(b) 20 million
(c) 138 million
(d) 140 million

13. The price has doubled in about 14 years. The approximate annual percentage rate of increase in the price level over this period has been
(a) 2%
(b) 3%
(c) 4%
(d) 5%

14. The unemployment data collected by the Bureau of Labor Statistics have been criticized because
(a) part-time workers are not counted in the number of workers employed
(b) discouraged workers are not considered a part of the labor force
(c) it covers frictional unemployment, but not cyclical unemployment, which inflates unemployment figures.
(d) the underground economy may understate unemployment

15. Okun's law predicts that when the actual unemployment rate exceeds the natural rate of unemployment by two percentage points, the GDP gap will equal
(a) 2% of the potential GDP
(b) 3% of the potential GDP
(c) 4% of the potential GDP
(d) 5% of the potential GDP

16. If the GDP gap were equal to 6% of the potential GDP, the actual unemployment rate would exceed the natural rate of unemployment by
(a) two percentage points
(b) three percentage points
(c) four percentage points
(d) five percentage points

17. The burden of unemployment is *least* felt by
(a) white-collar workers
(b) teenagers
(c) blacks
(d) males

18. If the consumer price index was 110 in one year and 117 in the next year, then the rate of inflation from one year to the next was
(a) 3.5%
(b) 4.7%

(c) 6.4%
(d) 7.1%

Use the following graph to answer Question 19.

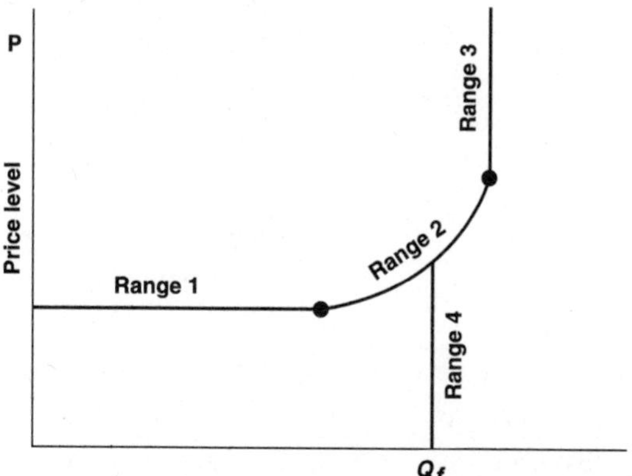

19. In which range does the price level begin to rise as the economy either approaches or surpasses the full employment level of output?
- **(a)** range 1
- **(b)** range 2
- **(c)** range 3
- **(d)** range 4

20. Only two resources, capital and labor, are used in an economy to produce an output of 300 million units. If the total cost of capital resources is $150 million and the total cost of labor resources is $50 million, then the per unit production costs in this economy are
- **(a)** $0.67 million
- **(b)** $1.50 million
- **(c)** $2.00 million
- **(d)** $3.00 million

21. If the economy can supply no more resources to production, an increase in aggregate spending will cause
- **(a)** output and employment to increase
- **(b)** output and prices to increase
- **(c)** nominal income and prices to increase
- **(d)** employment and nominal income to increase

22. If the economy is experiencing a depression with substantial unemployment, an increase in total spending will cause
- **(a)** a decrease in the *real* income of the economy
- **(b)** little or no increase in the level of prices
- **(c)** an increase in the *real* income and a decrease in the *nominal* income of the economy
- **(d)** proportionate increases in the price level, output, and income in the economy

23. If a person's nominal income increases by 8% while the price level increases by 10%, the person's real income
- **(a)** increases by 2%
- **(b)** increases by 18%
- **(c)** decreases by 18%
- **(d)** decreases by 2%

24. If the average level of nominal income is $21,000 and the price level index is 154, the average real income would be about
- **(a)** $12,546
- **(b)** $13,636
- **(c)** $15,299
- **(d)** $17,823

25. With no inflation, a bank would be willing to lend a business firm $10 million at an annual interest rate of 8%. But, if the rate of inflation was anticipated to be 6%, the bank would charge the firm an annual interest rate of
- **(a)** 2%
- **(b)** 6%
- **(c)** 8%
- **(d)** 14%

26. Who would be hurt by unanticipated inflation?
- **(a)** those living on incomes with cost-of-living adjustments
- **(b)** those who find prices rising less rapidly than their nominal incomes
- **(c)** those who lent money at a fixed interest rate
- **(d)** those who became debtors when prices were lower

27. Some economists argue that mild demand-pull inflation at less than full employment results in
- **(a)** rising real output and employment
- **(b)** falling real output and employment
- **(c)** a rising price level and falling employment
- **(d)** a falling price level and rising employment

28. Which contributes to cost-push inflation?
- **(a)** an increase in employment and output
- **(b)** an increase in per unit production costs
- **(c)** a decrease in resource prices
- **(d)** an increase in unemployment

29. Which is *not* associated with hyperinflation?
- **(a)** war or its aftermath
- **(b)** rising output in the economy
- **(c)** the hoarding of goods and speculation
- **(d)** a halt to the use of money as both a medium of exchange and a standard of value

30. If an economy has experienced an inflation rate of over 3000% per year, this economic condition would best be described as
- **(a)** a wage-price inflationary spiral
- **(b)** a cost-of-living adjustment
- **(c)** cost-push inflation
- **(d)** hyperinflation

■ PROBLEMS

1. The following table gives statistics on the labor force and total employment during year 1 and year 5. Make the computations necessary to complete the table. (Numbers of persons are in thousands.)

	Year 1	Year 5
Labor force	84,889	95,453
Employed	80,796	87,524
Unemployed	____	____
Unemployment rate	____	____

a. How is it possible that *both* employment and unemployment increased? ______________________

____

b. In relative terms, if unemployment increases, employment will decrease. Why? ______________________

____

____

c. Would you say that year 5 was a year of full employment? ______________________

____

d. Why is the task of maintaining full employment over the years more than just a problem of finding jobs for those who happen to be employed at any given time?

____

2. Suppose that in year 1 an economy is at full employment, has a potential and actual real GDP of $3000 billion, and has an unemployment rate of 5.5%.

a. Compute the GDP gap in year 1 and enter it in the table below.

Year	Potential GDP	Actual GDP	GDP gap
1	$3000	$3000.0	$____
2	3800	3724.0	____
3	4125	3712.5	____

b. The potential and actual real GDPs in years 2 and 3 are also shown in the table. Compute and enter into the table the GDP gaps in these 2 years.

c. In year 2, the actual real GDP is ______% of the potential real GDP. (*Hint:* divide the actual real GDP by the potential real GDP and multiply by 100.)

(1) The actual real GDP is ______% *less* than the potential real GDP.

(2) Using Okun's law, the unemployment rate will rise from 5.5% in year 1 and be ______% in year 2.

d. In year 3 the actual real GDP is ______% of the potential real GDP.

(1) The actual real GDP is ______% *less* than the potential real GDP.

(2) The unemployment rate, according to Okun's law, will be _____%.

3. The following table shows the price index in the economy at the end of four different years.

Year	Price index	Rate of inflation
1	100.00	
2	112.00	_____%
3	123.20	_____
4	129.36	_____

a. Compute and enter in the table the rates of inflation in years 2, 3, and 4.

b. Employing the rule of 70, how many years would it take for the price level to double at each of these three inflation rates? ______________________

____

c. If nominal income increased by 15% from year 1 to year 2, what was the approximate percentage change in real income? ____________

d. If nominal income increased by 7% from year 2 to year 3, what was the approximate percentage change in real income? ____________

e. If nominal income was $25,000 in year 2, what was real income that year? ____________

f. If nominal income was $25,000 in year 3, what was real income that year? ____________

g. If the nominal interest rate was 14% to borrow money from year 1 to year 2, what was the approximate real rate of interest over that period? ____________

h. If the nominal interest rate was 8% to borrow money from year 3 to year 4, what was the approximate real rate of interest over that period? ____________

4. Indicate in the space below each of the following the most likely effect—beneficial (B), detrimental (D), or indeterminate (I)—of unanticipated inflation on these persons:

a. A retired business executive who now lives each month by spending a part of the amount that was saved and deposited in a fixed-rate savings account for a long term. ____________

b. A retired private-school teacher who lives on the dividends received from the shares of stock owned.

____

c. A farmer borrowed $500,000 from a bank at a fixed rate; the loan must be repaid in the next 10 years.

____

d. A retired couple whose sole source of income is the pension they receive from a former employer.

____

e. A widow whose income consists entirely of interest received from the corporate bonds she owns.

____

f. A public school teacher. ____________

g. A member of a union who works for a firm that produces computers. ____________

5. Indicate for each of the following situations the effects of an increase in total spending on *real GDP, nominal GDP*, the *unemployment rate,* and the *price level,* respectively, using the following symbols: A, little, or no effect; B, increase; C, decrease; and D, sharp increase.

a. Depression and widespread unemployment

________ ________ ________ ________

b. Prosperity, but moderate unemployment

________ ________ ________ ________

c. Prosperity and full employment

________ ________ ________ ________

6. On the following two graphs, the price *level* is measured along the vertical axis and real *domestic* output is measured along the horizontal axis. The demand for and the supply of domestic output are shown by the curves labeled ***D*** and ***S***.

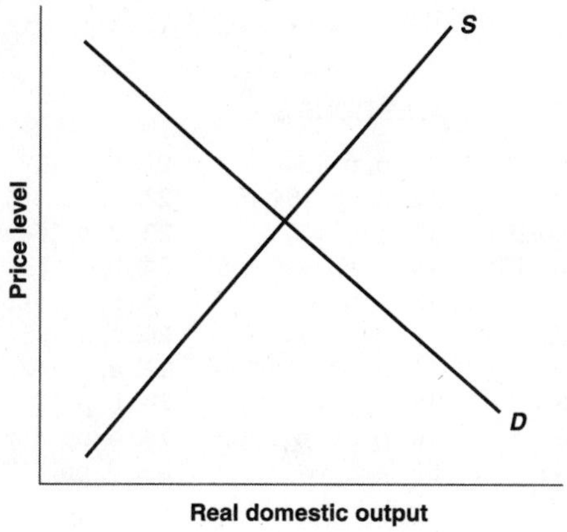

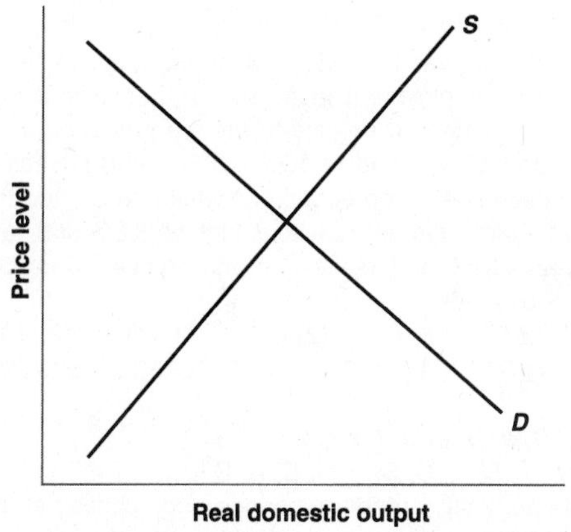

Price level

S

D

Real domestic output

Price level

S

D

Real domestic output

a. Applying the principles of demand and supply which you learned in Chapter 3, the equilibrium price level is the price level at which the domestic output demanded and the domestic output supplied are ________ and the equilibrium domestic output is ________ ________.

b. On the first graph, draw a new demand curve which represents an *increase* in the demand for domestic output.

(1) The effect of this increase in demand is a rise in the equilibrium price level and a(n) ________ in the equilibrium domestic output.

(2) This rise in the price level is an example of ________ ________ inflation.

c. On the second graph, draw a new supply curve which represents a *decrease* in the supply of domestic output.

(1) The effect of this decrease in supply is a ________ in the equilibrium price level and a ________ in the equilibrium domestic output.

(2) These effects are an example of ________ ________.

■ SHORT ANSWER AND ESSAY QUESTIONS

1. What is the historical record of the U.S. economy with respect to economic growth, full employment, and price-level stability?

2. Define the business cycle. Why do some economists prefer the term "business fluctuations" to "business cycle"?

3. Describe the four phases of an idealized business cycle.

4. In the opinion of most economists, what is the immediate determinant or cause of the levels of output and employment in the economy?

5. The business cycle is only one of three general causes of changes in output and employment in the economy. What are the other influences which affect these variables?

6. Compare the manner in which the business cycle affects output and employment in the industries producing capital and durable goods with industries producing nondurable goods and services. What causes these differences?

7. Distinguish among frictional, structural, and cyclical unemployment.

8. When is there full employment in the U.S. economy? (Answer in terms of the unemployment rate, the actual and potential output of the economy, and the markets for labor.)

9. What is the natural rate of unemployment? Will the economy always operate at the natural rate? Why is the natural rate subject to revision?

10. How is the unemployment rate measured in the United States? What criticisms have been made of the method the Bureau of Labor Statistics uses to determine the unemployment rate?

11. What is the economic cost of unemployment, and how is this cost measured? What is the quantitative relationship (called Okun's law) between the unemployment rate and the cost of unemployment?

12. What groups in the economy tend to bear the burdens of unemployment? How are women affected by unemployment, and how is the percentage of the labor force unemployed 15 or more weeks related to the unemployment rate in the economy?

13. How does the unemployment rate in the United States compare with those for other industrialized nations in recent years?

14. What is inflation, and how is the rate of inflation measured?

15. What has been the experience of the United States with inflation since the 1920s? How does the inflation rate in the United States compare with those for other industrialized nations in recent years?

16. Compare and contrast demand-pull and cost-push inflation.

17. What groups benefit from and what groups are hurt by inflation, and how has the public sector of the economy been affected by it?

18. What is the difference between the effects of unanticipated and the effects of anticipated inflation on the redistribution of real incomes in the economy?

19. Explain what will tend to happen to employment, output, nominal and real income, and the price level if total spending increases and the resources of the economy are (*a*) widely unemployed, (*b*) moderately unemployed, and (*c*) fully employed. If total spending *decreased* would the effects on employment, output, income, and the price level be just the opposite?

20. Write three scenarios that describe the effects of inflation on the domestic output.

ANSWERS

Chapter 8 Macroeconomic Instability: Unemployment and Inflation

FILL-IN QUESTIONS

1. unsteady, inflation, decreasing, increasing
2. increases, decreases
3. recession, trough, recovery
4. total spending
5. seasonal, secular
6. durable, capital, nondurable, low-
7. frictional, structural, cyclical
8. natural, frictional and structural, cyclical, equal to, 5.5
9. equal to, constant
10. unemployed, labor force, multiplying
11. minus, increase, 2
12. black, teenage, blue-collar, less
13. an increase, prices, divide, multiply
14. divide, rule of 70
15. deflation, high, low, high
16. *a.* an increase; *b.* production, supply, increases; *c.* difficult
17. real; *a.* real, 3; *b.* real, $28,302
18. fixed, unexpected, creditors, debtors, households, the public sector
19. anticipated; *a.* cost-of-living; *b.* real rate of interest, nominal rate of interest
20. increase, decrease, hyperinflation

TRUE-FALSE QUESTIONS

1. F, p. 148 **8.** T, pp. 153-154 **15.** T, p. 156 **22.** F, p. 164
2. F, p. 149 **9.** T, p. 153 **16.** F, p. 159 **23.** T, p. 164
3. F, P. 149 **10.** F, p. 154 **17.** F, p. 160 **24.** T, pp. 159, 161
4. T, p. 150 **11.** F, p. 156 **18.** F, p. 160 **25.** F, p. 165
5. F, p. 151 **12.** F, p. 154 **19.** T, p. 162
6. T, p. 152 **13.** T, p. 158 **20.** T, p. 163
7. F, p. 153 **14.** T, p. 156 **21.** T, p. 164

MULTIPLE-CHOICE QUESTIONS

1. b, p. 149 **11.** d, p. 154 **21.** c, p. 162
2. d, p. 150 **12.** c, pp. 154-155 **22.** b, pp. 161-162
3. b, pp. 150-151 **13.** d, p. 160 **23.** d, p. 164
4. a, pp. 150-151 **14.** b, pp. 155-156 **24.** b, p. 164
5. a, p. 151 **15.** c, p. 156 **25.** d, pp. 165-166
6. b, pp. 152-153 **16.** b, p. 156 **26.** c, p. 165
7. a, p. 152 **17.** a, pp. 156-158 **27.** a, p. 167
8. c, p. 153 **18.** c, p. 160 **28.** b, p. 163
9. c, p. 153 **19.** b, pp. 161-162 **29.** b, pp. 167-169
10. c, p. 154 **20.** a, p. 163 **30.** d, pp. 167-169

PROBLEMS

1. year 1: 4,093, 4.8; year 5: 7,929, 8.3; *a.* the labor force increased more than employment increased; *b.* because unemployment and employment in relative terms are percentages of the labor force and *always* add to 100%, and if one increases the other must decrease; *c.* no economist would argue that the full-employment unemployment rate is as high as 8.3% and year 5 was not a year of full employment; *d.* the number of people looking for work expands
2. *a.* 0; *b.* 76, 412.5; *c.* 98, (1) 2, (2) 6.5; *d.* 90, (1) 10, (2) 10.5
3. *a.* 12, 10, 5; *b.* 5.8, 7, 14; *c.* 3; *d.* −3; *e.* $22,321; *f.* $20,292; *g.* 2; *h.* 3
4. *a.* D; *b.* I; *c.* B; *d.* D; *e.* D; *f.* I; *g.* I
5. *a.* B, B, C, A; *b.* B, B, C, B; *c.* A, D, A, D
6. *a.* equal, the domestic output demanded and supplied at the equilibrium price level; *b.* (1) increase, (2) demand-pull; *c.* (1) rise, fall, (2) cost-push inflation

SHORT ANSWER AND ESSAY QUESTIONS

1. p. 149 **8.** pp. 153-154 **15.** p. 161
2. pp. 149-150 **9.** pp. 153-154 **16.** pp. 161-163
3. p. 149 **10.** pp. 154-156 **17.** pp. 164-165
4. p. 150 **11.** p. 156 **18.** pp. 165-166
5. pp. 150-151 **12.** pp. 156-158 **19.** p. 167
6. p. 151 **13.** p. 159 **20.** pp. 167-169
7. pp. 152-153 **14.** pp. 159-160

CHAPTER 9

Building the Aggregate Expenditures Model

This chapter is the first of two chapters that develops the first macroeconomic model of the economy presented in the textbook—the ***aggregate expenditures model.*** In the chapter you will find out what determines the demand for real domestic output (real GDP) and how an economy achieves an equilibrium level of output (and employment).

The first section of Chapter 9 offers a brief historical perspective on the aggregate expenditures model. Here you will learn about classical economics and its conclusion that the economy will automatically function to produce the maximum output it is capable of producing and provide employment for all those who are willing and able to work. This conclusion is based on ***Say's law,*** which holds that production automatically provides the income necessary to purchase all output, or **supply creates its own demand.**

The Great Depression and the work of John Maynard Keynes showed that there is no guarantee of maximum output and full employment. Depression or inflation can prevail with no automatic tendency for it to be corrected by the economy. **Keynesian** analysis of the expenditure components of the economy became the basis for the aggregate expenditures model.

A major section of the chapter describes the largest component of aggregate expenditures—consumption. An examination of consumption, however, also entails a study of saving because saving is simply the part of disposable income that is not consumed. This section develops the consumption and saving schedules and describes their main characteristics. Other key concepts are also presented: ***average propensities to consume*** (APC), and ***save*** (APS), ***marginal propensities to consume*** (MPC), and ***save*** (MPS), and the nonincome determinants of consumption and saving.

Investment expenditures is the subject of the next section of the chapter. The purchase of capital goods depends on the rate of return which business firms *expect* to earn from an investment and on the real rate of interest they have to pay for the use of money. Because firms are anxious to make profitable investments and to avoid unprofitable ones, they undertake all investments which have an expected rate of return greater than (or equal to) the real rate of interest and do not undertake an investment when the expected rate of return is less than the real interest rate. This relationship between the real interest rate and the level of investment spending is an inverse one: The lower the interest rate, the greater the investment spending. It is illustrated by an ***investment demand curve*** which is downsloping. This curve can also be shifted by five factors which can change the expected rate of return on investment.

The investment decisions of individual firms can be aggregated to construct an investment schedule, which shows the amount firms collectively intend to invest at each possible level of GDP. A simplifying assumption is made that investment is independent of GDP. Unlike the consumption schedule, which is relatively stable over time, the investment schedule is unstable for several reasons and often shifts upward or downward.

The next two sections of the chapter explain the equilibrium level of real GDP with tables and graphs, first by using the ***expenditures-output approach*** and then by employing the ***leakages-injections approach.*** These two approaches are complementary and are two different ways of analyzing the same process and reaching the same conclusions. For each approach it is important for you to know, given the consumption (or saving) schedule and the level of investment expenditures, what real GDP will tend to be produced and why this will be the real GDP which will be produced.

The final section discusses the distinction between ***planned investment*** and ***actual investment.*** Saving and actual investment are always equal because they are defined in exactly the same way: the output of the economy minus its consumption. But saving and planned investment are not equal by definition. Saving and planned investment are equal only when real GDP is at its equilibrium level. When real GDP is *not* at its equilibrium level, saving and planned investment are *not* equal even though saving and actual investment are, as always, equal because the actual investment includes *un*planned investment or disinvestment. Remember: Equilibrium real GDP is achieved when saving and *planned* investment—*not* saving and *actual* investment—are equal.

The tools and ideas explained in Chapter 9 are important because they are used to form a complete picture of how aggregate expenditures determine the level of GDP in the next chapter.

■ CHECKLIST

When you have studied this chapter you should be able to

□ Describe Say's law and the main ideas of classical economics.

☐ Explain the major ideas of Keynesian economics and how it differs from classical economics.
☐ List four simplifying assumptions in this chapter for building the aggregate expenditures model and two implications of those assumptions.
☐ State what determines the amount of goods and services produced and the level of employment in the Keynesian theory.
☐ Explain how consumption and saving are related to disposable income.
☐ Draw a graph to illustrate the relationship among consumption, saving, and disposable income.
☐ Construct a hypothetical consumption schedule.
☐ Construct a hypothetical saving schedule, and identify the level of break-even income.
☐ Compute the four propensities (APC, APS, MPC, and MPS) when given the necessary data.
☐ State the relationship between APC and APS as income increases.
☐ Demonstrate that MPC is the slope of the consumption schedule and MPS is the slope of the saving schedule.
☐ Explain how each of the four nonincome determinants of consumption and saving affect the consumption and saving schedules.
☐ Explain the difference between a change in the amount consumed (or saved) and a change in the consumption (or saving) schedule.
☐ Describe the marginal benefit and marginal cost in an investment decision.
☐ Draw a graph of an investment demand curve for the business sector.
☐ Explain how each of the five noninterest determinants of investment will shift the investment demand curve.
☐ Construct an investment schedule showing the relationship between intended investment and GDP.
☐ Give two reasons why a higher level of business activity may induce additional investment spending.
☐ Give four explanations of why investment spending tends to be unstable.
☐ When given the necessary data, use a table or graph to find equilibrium GDP using the aggregate expenditures—domestic output approach.
☐ When given the necessary data, use a table or graph to find equilibrium GDP using the leakages-injection approach.
☐ Explain why the economy will tend to produce its equilibrium GDP rather than at some small or larger level real GDP.
☐ State the difference between planned and actual investment.
☐ Explain how it is possible for saving and actual investment to be equal when saving and planned investment are not equal.
☐ State the conditions for inventories and investment at equilibrium GDP.

■ CHAPTER OUTLINE

1. The context for the development of the aggregate expenditures model developed in this chapter is historical debate between classical and Keynesian economics.

a. ***Classical economics*** concluded that the economy would automatically tend to full employment of resources and maximum output and that laissez faire is the best policy for the government to pursue. These employment and output conclusions are based on Say's law, which states that supply creates its own demand. If there were an excess supply of goods or an excess supply of labor, price and wages would fall until the excesses were eliminated and full employment and maximum output were again achieved.

b. The Great Depression and the ideas of J. M. Keynes, in *The General Theory of Employment, Interest and Money,* laid the foundation for a rejection of classical economics and the development of the aggregate expenditures model. Keynes challenged Say's law and showed that an economy can be inherently unstable and experience a long period of recession. Wages and prices are inflexible downward, and saving and investment decisions may not be coordinated, so there is no guarantee of full employment and maximum output. The economy is not self-regulating, so government policies are necessary to counteract economic instability.

2. To simplify the explanation of the aggregate expenditures model, four *assumptions* are made: The economy is "closed," government neither spends nor collects taxes, all saving is personal saving, and depreciation and net foreign factor income earned in the United States are zero. These assumptions have two important implications: Only consumption and investment are considered in the model, and output or income measures (GDP, NI, PI, DI) are treated as equal to each other.

3. Aggregate output and employment in the aggregate expenditures theory are directly related to the level of total or aggregate expenditures in the economy. To understand what determines the level of total expenditures at any time, it is necessary to explain the factors which determine the levels of consumption and investment expenditures.

4. Consumption is the largest component of aggregate expenditures, and saving is disposable income not spent for consumer goods.

a. Disposable income is the most important determinant of both consumption and saving; the relationships between income and consumption and between income and saving are both direct (positive) ones.

b. The consumption schedule shows the amounts that households plan to spend for consumer goods at various levels of income, given a price level.

c. The saving schedule indicates the amounts households plan to save at different income levels, given a price level.

d. The average propensity to consume (APC) and the average propensity to save (APS) and the marginal propensity to consume (MPC) and the marginal propensity to save (MPS) can be computed from the consumption and saving schedules.

(1) The APC and the APS are, respectively, the percentages of income spent for consumption and saved, and their sum is equal to 1.

(2) The MPC and the MPS are, respectively, the percentages of *additional* income spent for consumption and saved; and their sum is equal to 1.
(3) The MPC is the slope of the consumption schedule, and the MPS is the slope of the saving schedule when the two schedules are graphed.

e. In addition to income, there are several other important determinants of consumption and saving, and changes in these nonincome determinants will cause the ***consumption*** and ***saving schedules*** to change. The four nonincome determinants include wealth, expectations, household debt, and taxation.

f. Three other considerations need to be noted:
(1) A change in the amount consumed (or saved) is not the same thing as a change in the consumption (or saving) schedule.
(2) Changes in wealth, expectations, and household debt shift consumption and saving schedules in opposite directions; taxation shifts them in the same direction.
(3) Both consumption and saving schedules tend to be stable over time.

5. The two important determinants of the level of **investment spending** in the economy are the expected rate of return (*r*) from the purchase of additional capital goods and the real rate of interest (*i*).

a. The expected rate of return is directly related to the net profits (revenues less operating costs) that are expected to result from an investment. It is the marginal benefit of investment for a business.

b. The rate of interest is the price paid for the use of money. It is the marginal cost of investment for a business. When the expected real rate of return is greater (less) than the real rate of interest, a business will (will not) invest because the investment will be profitable (unprofitable).

c. For this reason, the lower (higher) the real rate of interest, the greater (smaller) will be the level of investment spending in the economy; the investment demand curve (schedule) indicates this inverse relationship between the real rate of interest and the level of spending for capital goods. The amount of investment by the business sector is determined at the point where the marginal benefit of investment (*r*) equals the marginal cost (*i*).

d. There are at least five noninterest determinants of investment demand, and a change in any of these determinants will shift the investment demand curve (schedule). These determinants include acquisition, maintenance, and operating costs; business taxes; technological change; the stock of capital on hand; and expectations.

e. The investment decisions of businesses in an economy can be aggregated to form an investment schedule which shows the amounts business firms collectively plan to invest at each possible level of GDP. A simplifying assumption is made that investment is independent of disposable income or real GDP.

f. Investment is inherently unstable, and the investment schedule will shift up or down. Factors that contribute to this variability are the durability of capital goods, innovations, changes in profits, and altered expectations.

6. Employing the ***aggregate expenditures—domestic output approach,*** the equilibrium real GDP is the real GDP at which

a. aggregate expenditures (consumption plus planned investment) equal the real GDP, or

b. in graphical terms, the aggregate expenditures curve crosses the 45 degree line and its slope is equal to the marginal propensity to consume.

7. Using the ***leakages-injections approach,*** the equilibrium real GDP is the real GDP at which

a. saving and planned investment are equal, or

b. in graphical terms, the saving schedule crosses the planned investment schedule.

8. The ***investment schedule*** indicates what investors plan to do. Actual investment consists of both planned and unplanned investment (unintended changes in inventory investment).

a. At above equilibrium levels of GDP, saving is greater than planned investment, and there will be unintended or unplanned investment through increases in inventories. At below equilibrium levels of GDP, planned investment is greater than saving, and there will be unintended or unplanned disinvestment through a decrease in inventories.

b. Equilibrium is achieved when planned investment equals saving and there is no unplanned investment.

■ HINTS AND TIPS

1. The most important graph in the chapter is the consumption schedule (see Key Graph 9-2). Know how to interpret it. There are two lines on the graph. The 45 degree reference line shows all points where disposable income equals consumption (there is no saving). The consumption schedule line shows the total amount of disposal income spent on consumption at each and every income level. Where the two lines *intersect,* all disposable income is spent (consumed). At all income levels to the right of the intersection, the consumption line lies below the 45 degree line, and not all disposable income is spent (there is saving). To the left of the intersection, the consumption line lies above the 45 degree line and consumption exceeds disposable income (there is dissaving).

2. Always remember that *marginal propensities* sum to 1 (MPC + MPS = 1). The same is true for average propensities (APC + APS = 1). Thus, if you know the value of one marginal propensity (e.g., MPC), you can always figure out the value of the other one (e.g., 1 − MPC = MPS).

3. Do not confuse the *investment demand curve* for the business sector with the *investment schedule* for an economy. The former shows the inverse relationship between the expected rate of return and the amount of total investment by the business sector, whereas the latter shows the collective investment intentions of business firms at each possible level of disposable income or real GDP.

4. The distinction between *actual* and *planned* investment is important for determining the equilibrium level of real GDP. *Actual* investment includes both *planned* and *unplanned* investment. At any level of real GDP, *saving* and *actual* investment will always be equal by definition, but *saving* and *planned* investment may not equal real GDP because there may be *unplanned* investment (unplanned changes in inventories). Only at the equilibrium level of real GDP will *saving* and *planned* investment be equal (this is no *unplanned* investment).

■ IMPORTANT TERMS

Say's law
Keynesian economics
consumption schedule
saving schedule
break-even income
average propensity to consume (APC)
average propensity to save (APS)
marginal propensity to consume (MPC)
marginal propensity to save (MPS)
expected rate of return
real rate of interest
investment demand curve
investment schedule
aggregate expenditures—domestic output approach
aggregate expenditures schedule
equilibrium (real) GDP
45 degree line
expenditures-output approach
leakages-injections approach
leakage
injection
planned investment
actual investment

SELF-TEST

■ FILL-IN QUESTIONS

1. Classical economists believe a market (or capitalistic) economy will tend to produce an output at which its labor force is (fully, less than fully) _______________ employed; Keynesian economists argue it will often tend to produce an output at which its labor force is _______________ employed.

2. According to the classical way of thinking, if total output exceeded the level of spending, prices, wages, and interest rates would (rise, fall) _______________. These changes would (increase, decrease) _______________ consumer spending, _______________ employment, _______________ investment spending. After these adjustments, the supply of goods and workers would be (greater than, less than, equal to) _______________ the demand for them.

3. According to Say's law, the production of goods and services creates an equal (supply of, demand for) _______________ these goods and services.

4. J. M. Keynes (accepted, rejected) _______________ Say's law and showed that an economy can be inherently (stable, unstable) _______________ and experience long periods of (recession, economic growth) _______________. According to Keynes, wages and prices are (flexible, inflexible) _______________ downward, and thus costly unemployment can occur for (short, long) _______________ periods.

5. Four simplifying assumptions used throughout most of the chapter are that the economy is a(n) (open, closed) _______________ economy, the economy is (private, public) _______________, all saving is (personal, business) _______________ saving, and depreciation and net foreign factor income earned in the United States is (positive, negative, zero) _______________. Two implications of these assumptions are

a. Aggregate spending = ____________ + ____________

b. GDP = ____________ = ____________ = ____________

6. In modern capitalism, domestic output and employment depend on the level of (marginal, aggregate) _______________ expenditures in the economy. The most important determinant of consumption and saving is the economy's disposable (production, income) _______________. The consumption schedule shows the various amounts that households plan to (save, consume) _______________ at various levels of disposable income, while the saving schedule shows the various amounts that households plan to _______________.

7. Both consumption and saving are (directly, indirectly) _______________ related to the level of disposable income. At lower levels of disposable income, households tend to spend a (smaller, larger) _______________ proportion of this income and save a _______________ proportion, but at higher levels of disposable income, they tend to spend a (smaller, larger) _______________ proportion of this income and save a _______________ proportion. At the break-even income, consumption is (greater than, less than, equal to) _______________ disposable income.

8. As disposable income falls, the average propensity to consume (APC) will (rise, fall) _______________ and the average propensity to save (APS) will _______________. The sum of APC and APS is equal to (0, 1) _____.

9. The marginal propensity to consume (MPC) is the change in (consumption, saving, income) ______________ divided by the change in ______________; it is the numerical value of the slope of the ______________ schedule. The marginal propensity to save (MPS) is the change in (consumption, saving, income) ______________ divided by the change in ______________; it is the numerical value of the slope of the ______________ schedule. The sum of MPC and MPS is equal to (0, 1) ____.

10. The most important determinants of consumption spending, other than the level of income, are

a. ______________

b. ______________

c. ______________

d. ______________

11. A change in the consumption (or saving) schedule means that the amount consumers plan to consume (save) will (be the same, change) ______________ at every level of income, but a change in the amount consumed (or saved) means that the level of income has (stayed the same, changed) ______________ and that consumers will (not change, change) ______________ their planned consumption (saving) as a result.

12. Investment is defined as spending for additional (consumer, capital) ______________ goods, and the total amount of investment spending in the economy depends on the expected rate of (interest, return) ______________ and the real rate of ______________. A business firm will increase the amount of investment if the expected rate of (interest, return) ______________ on this investment is (greater, less) ______________ than the real rate of (interest, return) ______________ it must pay for the use of money.

13. The relationship between the rate of interest and the total amount of investment in the economy is (direct, inverse) ______________ and is shown in the investment-(supply, demand) ______________ curve. This curve shows that if the real rate of interest rises, the quantity of investment will (increase, decrease) ______________, but if the real rate of interest falls, the quantity of investment will ______________.

14. Five noninterest determinants of investment demand are

a. ______________

b. ______________

c. ______________

d. ______________

e. ______________

15. The consumption schedule and the saving schedule tend to be (stable, unstable) ______________, while investment demand tends to be ______________.

16. The demand for new capital goods tends to be unstable because of the (durability, nondurability) ______________ of capital goods, the (regularity, irregularity) ______________ of innovation, and the (stability, variability) ______________ of actual and expected profits.

17. Two complementary approaches used to explain the equilibrium level of real domestic output are

a. ______________

b. ______________

18. Assuming a private and closed economy, the equilibrium level of real GDP is determined where aggregate expenditures are (greater than, less than, equal to) ______________ real domestic output, consumption plus investment is ______________ real domestic output, and the aggregate expenditures schedule or curve intersects the (90 degree, 45 degree) ______________ line.

19. A leakage is (an addition to, a withdrawal from) ______________ the income expenditure stream, whereas an injection is ______________ to the income expenditure stream. In this chapter, the only leakage considered is (investment, saving) ______________, and the only injection considered is ______________.

20. At every level of GDP, saving is equal to (planned, actual) ______________ gross investment.

a. If aggregate expenditures are greater than the real domestic output, saving is (greater than, less than, equal to) ______________ planned investment, there is unplanned (investment, disinvestment) ______________ in inventories, and the real GDP will (rise, fall) ______________.

b. If aggregate expenditures are less than the real domestic output, saving is (greater than, less than, equal to) ______________ planned investment, there is unplanned (investment, disinvestment) ______________ in inventories, and the real GDP will (rise, fall) ______________.

c. If aggregate expenditures are equal to the real domestic output, saving is (greater than, less than, equal to) ______________ planned investment, unplanned investment in inventories is (negative, positive, zero) ______________, and the real GDP will neither rise nor fall.

■ TRUE-FALSE QUESTIONS

Circle the T if the statement is true, the F if it is false.

1. In the aggregate expenditures model of the economy, the price level is constant. **T F**

2. According to the classical economists, full employment is normal in market economies. **T F**

3. The classical economists believed that when the economy deviated from full employment, there would be automatic adjustments in prices, wages, and interest rates within the market to restore the full-employment equilibrium. **T F**

4. Say's law states that demand for goods and services creates an equal supply of goods and services. **T F**

5. Classical economists contend that prices and wages would be sufficiently flexible to ensure full employment. **T F**

6. The level of saving in the economy, according to the Keynesians, depends primarily on the level of its disposable income. **T F**

7. The consumption schedule used as an analytical tool is also a historical record of the relationship of consumption to disposable income. **T F**

8. Empirical data suggest that households tend to spend a similar proportion of a small disposable income than of a larger disposable income. **T F**

9. The average propensity to save is equal to the level of saving divided by the level of consumption. **T F**

10. The marginal propensity to consume is the change in consumption divided by the change in income. **T F**

11. The slope of the saving schedule is equal to the average propensity to save. **T F**

12. An increase in wealth will increase the consumption schedule (shift the consumption curve upward). **T F**

13. An increase in the taxes paid by consumers will decrease both the amount they spend for consumption and the amount they save. **T F**

14. Both the consumption schedule and the saving schedule tend to be relatively stable over time. **T F**

15. The *real* interest rate is the nominal interest rate minus the rate of inflation. **T F**

16. A business firm will purchase additional capital goods if the real rate of interest it must pay exceeds the expected rate of return from the investment. **T F**

17. An increase in the stock of capital goods on hand will decrease the investment-demand curve. **T F**

18. The relationship between the rate of interest and the level of investment spending is called the investment schedule. **T F**

19. The investment schedule tends to be relatively stable over time. **T F**

20. The irregularity of innovations and the variability of business profits contribute to the instability of investment expenditures. **T F**

21. The equilibrium level of GDP is that GDP level corresponding to the intersection of the aggregate expenditures schedule with the 45 degree line. **T F**

22. Saving is an injection into and investment is a leakage from the income expenditures stream. **T F**

23. The investment schedule is a schedule of planned investment rather than a schedule of actual investment. **T F**

24. Saving and actual investment are always equal. **T F**

25. Saving at any level of real GDP equals planned investment plus unplanned investment (or minus unplanned disinvestment). **T F**

■ MULTIPLE-CHOICE QUESTIONS

Circle the letter that corresponds to the best answer.

1. Classical economics suggests that in capitalist economies

(a) unemployment may persist for extended periods
(b) the market system will ensure full employment
(c) a slump in output will increase prices, wages, and interest rates
(d) demand creates its own supply

2. From the perspective of classical economics, if total output were greater than total spending, competition would tend to force

(a) prices and wages up
(b) prices and wages down
(c) prices down and wages up
(d) prices up and wages down

3. Which would be considered part of Keynes' criticism of classical economics?

(a) Investment spending will increase when the interest rate increases.
(b) Prices and wages are flexible downward in modern capitalist economies.
(c) The act of producing goods generates an amount of income equal to the value of the goods produced.
(d) Saving and investment decisions are not always completely synchronized.

4. If the economy is closed, government neither taxes nor spends, all saving done in the economy is personal saving, and depreciation and net foreign factor income earned in the United States are zero, then

(a) gross domestic product equals personal consumption expenditures
(b) gross domestic product equals personal saving
(c) gross domestic product equals disposable income
(d) disposable income equals personal consumption expenditures

5. The level of output and employment in the economy depends

(a) directly on the level of total expenditures
(b) inversely on the quantity of resources available
(c) inversely on the level of disposable income
(d) directly on the rate of interest

6. As disposable income decreases, *ceteris paribus*

(a) both consumption and saving increase
(b) consumption increases and saving decreases
(c) consumption decreases and saving increases
(d) both consumption and saving decrease

7. If consumption spending increases from $358 to $367 billion when disposable income increases from $412 to $427 billion, it can be concluded that the marginal propensity to consume is

(a) 0.4
(b) 0.6
(c) 0.8
(d) 0.9

8. If disposable income is $375 billion when the average propensity to consume is 0.8, it can be concluded that

(a) the marginal propensity to consume is also 0.8
(b) consumption is $325 billion
(c) saving is $75 billion
(d) the marginal propensity to save is 0.2

9. As the disposable income of the economy increases

(a) both the APC and the APS rise
(b) the APC rises and the APS falls
(c) the APC falls and the APS rises
(d) both the APC and the APS fall

10. The slope of the consumption schedule or line for a given economy is the

(a) marginal propensity to consume
(b) average propensity to consume
(c) marginal propensity to save
(d) average propensity to save

Answer Questions 11 and 12 on the basis of the following diagram.

11. This diagram indicates that

(a) consumption decreases after the $60 billion level of GDP
(b) the marginal propensity to consume decreases after the $60 billion level of GDP
(c) consumption decreases as a percentage of GDP as GDP increases
(d) consumption increases as GDP decreases

12. If the relevant saving schedule were constructed, one would find that

(a) the marginal propensity to save is negative up to the $60 billion level of GDP
(b) the marginal propensity to save increases after the $60 billion level of GDP
(c) saving is zero at the $60 billion level of GDP
(d) saving is $20 billion at the $0 level of GDP

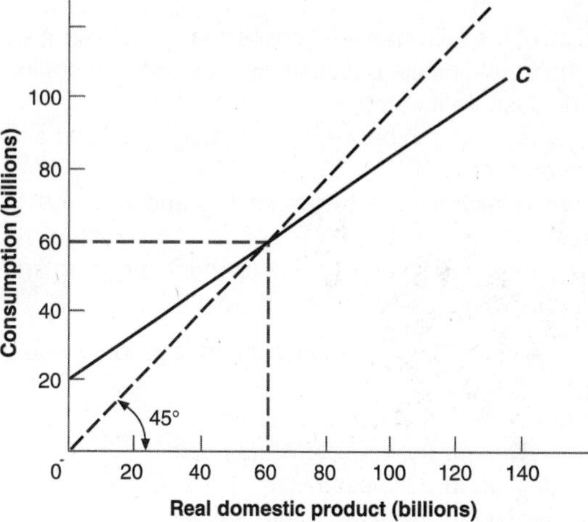

*Answer Questions 13, 14, and 15 on the basis of the following disposable income (**DI**) and consumption (**C**) schedules for a private, closed economy. All figures are in billions of dollars.*

DI	*C*
$ 0	$ 4
40	40
80	76
120	112
160	148
200	184

13. If plotted on a graph, the slope of the consumption schedule would be

(a) 0.6
(b) 0.7
(c) 0.8
(d) 0.9

14. At the $160 billion level of disposable income, the average propensity to save is

(a) 0.015
(b) 0.075
(c) 0.335
(d) 0.925

15. If consumption increases by $5 billion at each level of disposable income, then the marginal propensity to consume will

(a) change, but the average propensity to consume will *not* change
(b) change, and the average propensity to consume will change
(c) *not* change, but the average propensity to consume will change
(d) *not* change, and the average propensity to consume will *not* change

16. If the slope of a linear saving schedule decreases in a private, closed economy, then it can be concluded that the
(a) MPS has decreased
(b) MPC has decreased
(c) income has decreased
(d) income has increased

17. Which of the following relationships is an inverse one?
(a) the relationship between consumption spending and disposable income
(b) the relationship between investment spending and the rate of interest
(c) the relationship between saving and the rate of interest
(d) the relationship between investment spending and gross domestic product

18. A decrease in the level of investment spending would be a consequence of
(a) a decline in the rate of interest
(b) a decline in the level of wages paid
(c) a decline in business taxes
(d) a decline in expected future sales

19. Which would increase investment demand?
(a) an increase in business taxes
(b) an increase in the cost of acquiring capital goods
(c) a decrease in the rate of technological change
(d) a decrease in the stock of capital goods on hand

20. Which one of the following best explains the variability of investment?
(a) the predictable useful life of capital goods
(b) constancy or regularities in business innovations
(c) instabilities in the level of profits
(d) business pessimism about the future

21. On a graph, the equilibrium real GDP is found at the intersection of the 45 degree line and
(a) the consumption curve
(b) the investment demand curve
(c) the saving curve
(d) the aggregate expenditures curve

22. Which of the following is an injection?
(a) investment
(b) saving
(c) taxes
(d) imports

23. When the economy's real GDP exceeds its equilibrium real GDP,
(a) there is unplanned investment in the economy
(b) planned investment exceeds saving
(c) aggregate expenditures exceed the real domestic output
(d) leakages equal injections

24. If real GDP is $275 billion, consumption is $250 billion, and investment is $30 billion, real GDP
(a) will tend to remain constant
(b) will tend to increase
(c) will tend to decrease
(d) equals aggregate expenditures

25. If saving is greater than planned investment
(a) businesses will be motivated to increase their investments
(b) aggregate expenditures will be greater than the real domestic output
(c) real GDP will be greater than planned investment plus consumption
(d) saving will tend to increase

■ PROBLEMS

1. The following table is a consumption schedule. Assume taxes and transfer payments are zero and that all saving is personal saving.

GDP	*C*	*S*	APC,%	APS,%
$1500	$1540	$_____	1.027	−.027
1600	1620	_____	1.013	−.013
1700	1700	_____	_____	_____
1800	1780	_____	.989	.011
1900	1860	_____	.979	.021
2000	1940	_____	_____	_____
2100	2020	_____	.962	.038
2200	2100	_____	_____	_____

a. Compute saving at each of the eight levels of GDP and the missing average propensities to consume and to save.

b. The break-even level of income (GDP) is $_____.
c. As GDP rises, the marginal propensity to consume remains constant. Between each two GDPs the MPC can be found by dividing $________ by $________, and is equal to ________.
d. The marginal propensity to save also remains constant when the GDP rises. Between each two GDPs the MPS is equal to $________ divided by $________, or to ________.
e. Plot the consumption schedule, the saving schedule, and the 45 degree line on the graph on the next page.
(1) The numerical value of the slope of the consumption schedule is ________, and the term that is used to describe it is the ________.
(2) If the relevant saving schedule were constructed, the numerical value of the slope of the saving schedule would be ________, and the term that is used to describe it is the ________.

2. Indicate in the space to the right of each of the following events whether the event will tend to increase (+) or decrease (−) the *saving* schedule.
a. Development of consumer expectations that prices will be higher in the future _____

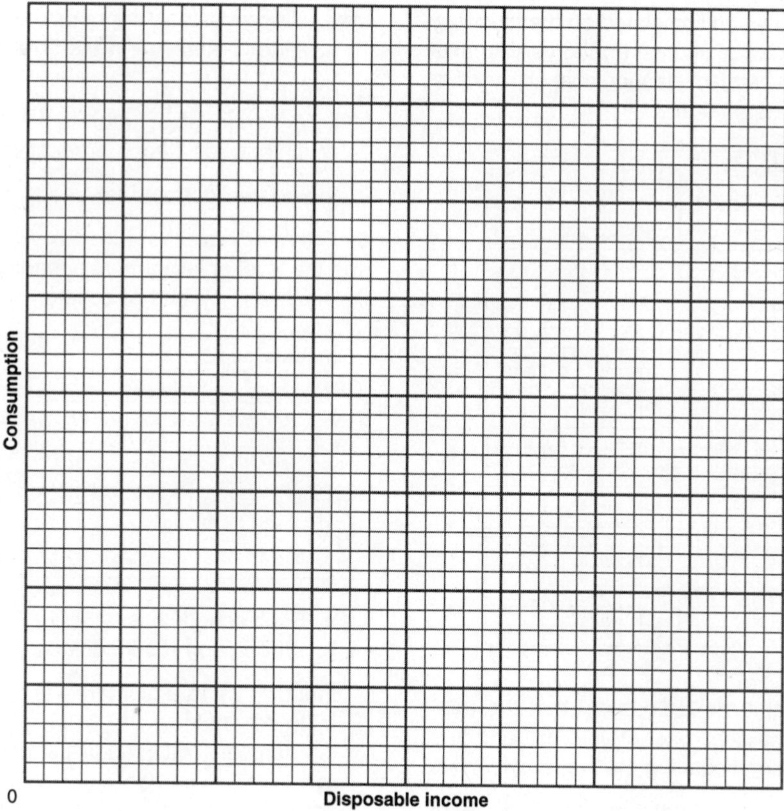

b. Gradual shrinkage in the quantity of real assets owned by consumers _____

c. Increase in the volume of consumer indebtedness _____

d. Growing belief that disposable income will be lower in the future _____

e. Rumors that a current shortage of consumer goods will soon disappear _____

f. Rise in the actual level of disposable income _____

g. A build-up in the dollar size of the financial assets owned by consumers _____

h. Development of a belief by consumers that the Federal government can and will prevent recessions in the future _____

3. The following schedule has eight different expected rates of return, and the dollar amounts of the investment projects expected to have each of these return rates.

Expected rate of return profit	Investment projects (billions)
18%	$ 0
16	10
14	20
12	30
10	40
8	50
6	60
4	70

a. If the real rate of interest in the economy were 18%, business firms would plan to spend $_______ billion for investment, but if the real interest rate were 16%, they would plan to spend $_______ for investment.

b. Should the real interest rate be 14%, they would still wish to make the investments they were willing to make at real interest rates of 18% and 16%, they would plan to spend an additional $_______ billion for investment, and their total investment would be $_______ billion.

c. Were the real rate of interest 12% they would make all the investments they had planned to make at higher real interest rates plus an additional $_______ billion, and their total investment spending would be $_______ billion.

d. Complete the following table by computing the amount of planned investment at the four remaining real interest rates.

Real rate of interest	Amount of investment (billions)
18%	$ 0
16	10
14	30
12	60
10	_____
8	_____
6	_____
4	_____

e. Graph the schedule you completed on the following graph. Plot the real rate of interest on the vertical axis and the amount of investment planned at each real rate of interest on the horizontal axis.

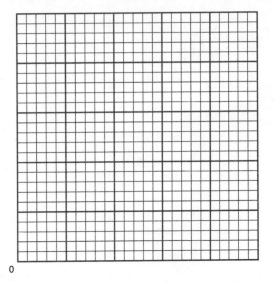

0

f. Both the graph and the table show that the relationship between the real rate of interest and the amount of investment spending in the economy is ______________. This means that when the real rate of interest

(1) increases, investment will (increase, decrease) ______________.

(2) decreases, investment will ______________.

g. It also means that should we wish to

(1) increase investment, we would need to ________ the real rate of interest.

(2) decrease investment, we would have to ________ the real rate of interest.

h. This graph (or table) is the ______________ ______________ curve.

4. Indicate in the space to the right of the following events whether the event would tend to increase (+) or decrease (−) investment expenditures.

a. Rising stock market prices ____

b. Development of expectations by business executives that business taxes will be higher in the future ____

c. Step up in the rates at which new products and new production processes are being introduced ____

d. Business belief that wage rates may be lower in the future and labor and capital are complementary resources ____

e. An expectation of a recession ____

f. A belief that business is "too good" and the economy is due for a period of "slow" consumer demand ____

g. Rising costs in the construction industry ____

h. A rapid increase in the size of the economy's population ____

i. A period of a high level of investment spending which has resulted in productive capacity in excess of the current demand for goods and services ____

5. Following are two schedules showing several GDPs and the level of investment spending (*I*) at each GDP. (All figures are in billions of dollars.)

Schedule number 1		*Schedule number 2*	
GDP	***I***	**GDP**	***I***
$1850	$90	$1850	$ 75
1900	90	1900	80
1950	90	1950	85
2000	90	2000	90
2050	90	2050	95
2100	90	2100	100
2150	95	2150	105

a. Each schedule is an ______________ schedule.

b. When such a schedule is drawn up, it is assumed that the real rate of interest is ______________.

c. In schedule

(1) number 1, GDP and *I* are (unrelated, directly related) ______________.

(2) number 2, GDP and *I* are ______________.

d. Should the real rate of interest rise, investment spending at each GDP would (increase, decrease) ______________ and the curve relating GDP and investment spending would shift (upward, downward) ______________.

■ SHORT ANSWER AND ESSAY QUESTIONS

1. According to the classical economists, what level of employment would tend to prevail in the economy? Why?

2. In classical analysis, Say's law made it certain that whatever was produced would be sold. How did flexible prices, flexible wages, and competition drive the economy to full employment and maximum output?

3. On what grounds did J. M. Keynes argue that flexible interest rates would not ensure the operation of Say's law?

4. What are the four simplifying assumptions used in this chapter, and what are the two implications of these assumptions?

5. Describe the relationship between consumption and disposable income, called the consumption schedule, and the one between saving the disposable income, known as the saving schedule.

6. Define the two average propensities and the two marginal propensities.

7. Explain briefly how the average propensity to consume and the average propensity to save vary as dis-

posable income varies. Why do APC and APS behave this way? What happens to consumption and saving as disposable income varies?

8. Why do the sum of the APC and the APS and the sum of the MPC and the MPS always equal exactly 1?

9. What is the relationship between MPC and MPS and the consumption and saving schedule?

10. Explain briefly and explicitly *how* changes in the four nonincome determinants will affect the consumption schedule and the saving schedule and *why* such changes will affect consumption and saving in the way you have indicated.

11. Explain the marginal cost and marginal benefit of an investment decision. How is the marginal cost and the marginal benefit of investment measured?

12. Draw an investment demand curve. Use it to explain why investment spending tends to rise when the real rate of interest falls, and vice versa.

13. Identify and explain how five noninterest determinants of investment spending can increase or decrease the amount of investment. Illustrate the changes with a graph.

14. What is the difference between an investment demand curve and an investment schedule?

15. What assumption is made about the relationship between investment and disposable income? Is this assumption a reasonable one?

16. Why does the level of investment spending tend to be highly unstable?

17. Explain why the amount consumers spend and the amount investors spend matter to the performance of the economy.

18. Why is the equilibrium level of real GDP that level of real GDP at which domestic output equals aggregate expenditures? What will cause real GDP to rise if it is below this level, and what will cause it to fall if it is above this level?

19. Explain what is meant by a leakage and by an injection. Which leakage and which injection are considered in this chapter? Why is the equilibrium real GDP the real GDP at which the leakages equal the injections?

20. Why is it important to distinguish between planned and actual investment in explaining how a private, closed economy achieves its equilibrium level of real GDP?

ANSWERS

Chapter 9 Building the Aggregate Expenditures Model

FILL-IN QUESTIONS

1. fully, less than fully
2. fall, increase, increase, increase, equal to
3. demand for
4. rejected, unstable, recession, inflexible, long
5. closed, private, personal, zero; *a.* consumption, investment; *b.* national income, personal income, disposable income
6. aggregate, income, consume, save
7. directly, larger, smaller, smaller, larger, equal to
8. rise, fall, one
9. consumption, income, consumption, saving, income, saving, one
10. *a.* wealth (real and financial assets); *b.* household expectations; *c.* household debt; *d.* taxation of consumer income
11. change, changed, change
12. capital, return, interest, return, greater, interest
13. inverse, demand, decrease, increase
14. *a.* the cost of acquiring, maintaining, and operating the capital goods; *b.* business taxes; *c.* technological change; *d.* the stock of capital goods on hand; *e.* expectations
15. stable, unstable
16. durability, irregularity, variability
17. *a.* aggregate expenditures—domestic output; *b.* leakages-injections
18. equal to, equal to, 45 degree
19. a withdrawal from, an addition to, saving, investment
20. actual; *a.* less than, disinvestment, rise; *b.* greater than, investment, fall; *c.* equal to, zero

TRUE-FALSE QUESTIONS

1. T, p. 172	**10.** T, p. 178	**19.** F, pp. 186-187
2. T, pp. 172-173	**11.** F, p. 179	**20.** T, p. 187
3. T, pp. 172-173	**12.** T, p. 179	**21.** T, p. 190
4. F, p. 173	**13.** T, p. 180	**22.** F, pp. 190-191
5. T, pp. 172-173	**14.** T, p. 181	**23.** T, pp. 185, 188, 193
6. T, p. 175	**15.** T, pp. 181-182	**24.** T, p. 193
7. F, pp. 175-176	**16.** F, p. 182	**25.** T, p. 193
8. F, p. 176	**17.** T, p. 184	
9. F, p. 178	**18.** F, p. 185	

MULTIPLE-CHOICE QUESTIONS

1. b, p. 174	**8.** c, p. 178	**15.** c, p. 178	**22.** a, pp. 190-192
2. b, p. 173	**9.** c, p. 178	**16.** a, p. 179	**23.** a, pp. 193-195
3. d, p. 173	**10.** a, p. 179	**17.** b, pp. 182-184	**24.** b, pp. 189-190
4. c, p. 174	**11.** c, p. 178	**18.** d, pp. 184-185	**25.** c, pp. 192-193
5. a, p. 174	**12.** c, p. 176	**19.** d, pp. 184-185	
6. d, p. 175	**13.** d, p. 178	**20.** c, pp. 186-187	
7. b, p. 178	**14.** b, p. 178	**21.** d, p. 190	

PROBLEMS

1. *a.* S: −40, −20, 0, 20, 40, 60, 80, 100; APC: 1.000, 0.970, 0.955; APS: 0.000, 0.030, 0.045; *b.* 1700; *c.* 80, 100, .8; *d.* 20, 100, .20; *e.* (1) .8, MPC, (2) .2, MPS
2. *a.* −; *b.* +; *c.* −; *d.* +; *e.* +; *f.* none; *g.* −; *h.* −
3. *a.* 0, 10; *b.* 20, 30; *c.* 30, 60; *d.* 100, 150, 210, 280; *f.* inverse, (1) decrease, (2) increase; *g.* (1) lower, (2) raise; *h.* investment-demand
4. *a.* +; *b.* −; *c.* +; *d.* +; *e.* −; *f.* −; *g.* −; *h.* +; *i.* −
5. *a.* investment; *b.* constant (given); *c.* (1) unrelated, (2) directly related; *d.* decrease, downward

SHORT ANSWER AND ESSAY QUESTIONS

1. pp. 172-173	**6.** p. 178	**11.** pp. 181-182	**16.** pp. 186-187
2. pp. 172-173	**7.** p. 178	**12.** pp. 182-184	**17.** pp. 188-190
3. pp. 173-174	**8.** p. 178	**13.** pp. 184-185	**18.** pp. 188-190
4. p. 174	**9.** p. 179	**14.** p. 185	**19.** pp. 190-192
5. pp. 175-176	**10.** pp. 179-180	**15.** pp. 185-186	**20.** pp. 193-195

CHAPTER **10**

Aggregate Expenditures: The Multiplier, Net Exports, and Government

Chapter 10 extends the aggregate expenditures model of a private closed economy developed in Chapter 9. You now learn what causes real GDP to rise and fall. Changes in investment spending have an added effect on real GDP because of the multiplier. Including net exports in the aggregate expenditures model transforms the analysis from a closed economy to an open economy, and changes in net exports will change the equilibrium level of real GDP. Government spending and taxation make the economy mixed instead of private, and changes in public spending or taxes also shift the equilibrium real GDP.

The consumption (and the saving) schedule and the investment schedule—especially the latter—are subject to change, and when they change, equilibrium real GDP will also change. The relationship between an initial change in the investment or consumption schedules and a change in equilibrium real GDP is called the ***multiplier.*** Three things to note here are: how the multiplier is defined, why there is a multiplier effect, and upon what the size of the multiplier depends.

The aggregate expenditures model of the economy can be extended by adding the ***net exports*** of an economy to the aggregate expenditures schedule. Net exports are nothing more than the economy's exports less its imports of goods and services. Like investment, the exports of a nation are an injection into its circular flow of income and an increase in the flow. But imports are, like saving, a leakage from the circular flow and a decrease in the flow.

The generalization used to find the **equilibrium** real GDP in an open economy (one that exports and imports) is the same one as for a closed economy: The economy will tend to produce a real GDP which is equal to aggregate expenditures. The only difference is that the aggregate expenditures include not only consumption and investment expenditures but the expenditures for net exports. So the equilibrium real GDP will equal $C + I_g + X_n$ (when X_n is the symbol used for net exports). An increase in X_n, like an increase in I_g, will increase the equilibrium real GDP; a decrease in X_n will decrease the equilibrium real GDP. And like a change in I_g, a change in X_n has a multiplier effect on real GDP.

The section titled "Adding the Public Sector" introduces **government** taxing and spending into the analysis of equilibrium real GDP. Government purchases of goods and services add to aggregate expenditures and taxation reduces the disposable income of consumers, thereby reducing both the amount of consumption and the amount of saving that will take place at any level of real GDP. Both approaches are again employed, and you are warned that you must know what real GDP will tend to be produced and why. Special attention should be directed to the exact effect taxes have on the consumption and saving schedules and to the multiplier effects of changes in government purchases and taxes.

It is important to be aware that the equilibrium real GDP is not necessarily the real GDP at which full employment with inflationary pressures is achieved. Aggregate expenditures may be greater or less than the full-employment noninflationary real GDP; if they are greater there is an ***inflationary gap,*** and if they are less there exists a ***recessionary gap.*** Be sure that you know how to measure the size of each gap: the amount by which the aggregate expenditures schedule (or curve) must change to bring the economy to its full-employment real GDP without there being inflation in the economy. Several historical examples—the Great Depression and the Vietnam war inflation—are described to help you see the application of the recessionary and inflationary gaps concepts.

The aggregate expenditures model that you have learned about is a valuable tool for explaining such economic events as recession, inflation, prosperity, and economic growth. The model, however, has limitations. The last section of the chapter describes the major shortcomings and how later chapters address some of these deficiencies.

■ CHECKLIST

When you have studied this chapter you should be able to

☐ Illustrate how equilibrium real GDP changes when the investment schedule shifts upward or downward.
☐ Define the multiplier effect in words, with a ratio, and using an equation.
☐ Make three clarifying points about the multiplier.
☐ Cite two facts on which the multiplier is based.
☐ Discuss the relationship between the multiplier and the marginal propensities.
☐ Find the value of the multiplier when you are given the necessary information.
☐ Explain the difference between the simple and the complex multiplier.
☐ Use the concept of net exports to define aggregate expenditures in an open economy.

- ☐ Explain what the equilibrium real GDP in an open economy will be when net exports are positive and when net exports are negative.
- ☐ Find the equilibrium real GDP in an open economy when you are given the appropriate data.
- ☐ Give examples of how circumstances or policies abroad can affect domestic GDP.
- ☐ List five simplifying assumptions used to add the public sector to the aggregate expenditures model.
- ☐ Find the equilibrium real GDP in an economy in which the government purchases goods and services and levies net taxes when you are given the necessary data.
- ☐ Determine the effect on the equilibrium real GDP of a change in government purchases of goods and services and in net taxes.
- ☐ Explain why the balanced-budget multiplier is equal to 1.
- ☐ Distinguish between the equilibrium real GDP and the full-employment noninflationary level of real GDP.
- ☐ Find the recessionary and the inflationary gaps when you are provided the relevant data.
- ☐ Apply the concepts of recessionary and inflationary gaps to historical economic events.
- ☐ Explain four shortcomings of aggregate expenditures theory.

■ CHAPTER OUTLINE

1. Changes in investment (or in the consumption and saving schedules) will cause the equilibrium real GDP to change in the same direction by an amount greater than the initial change in investment (or consumption).

a. This is called the ***multiplier effect;*** the multiplier is equal to the ratio of the change in the real GDP to the initial change in spending.

(1) The multiplier effect occurs because a change in the dollars spent by one person alters the income of another person in the same direction and because any change in the income of one person will change the person's consumption and saving in the same direction by a fraction of the change in income.

(2) The value of the simple multiplier is equal to the reciprocal of the marginal propensity to save (1/MPS).

(3) The significance of the multiplier is that relatively small changes in the spending plans of business firms or households bring about large changes in the equilibrium real GDP.

(4) The simple multiplier has this value only in an economy in which the only leakage is saving; the complex multiplier takes into account such other leakages as taxes and imports.

2. In an ***open economy*** the exports (***X***) of a nation increase and its imports (***M***) decrease aggregate expenditures in that economy; aggregate expenditures are equal to the sum of consumption spending, investment spending, and net exports (X_n) when X_n is defined as ***X*** minus ***M***.

a. The equilibrium real GDP in an open economy is the real GDP equal to consumption plus investment plus net exports, and

b. Any increase (decrease) in its X_n will increase (decrease) its equilibrium real GDP with a multiplier effect.

c. In an open economy model, circumstances and policies abroad, such as a change in the level of national incomes of trading partners, changes in tariffs or quotas, or changes in exchange rates can affect domestic GDP.

3. Changes in government spending and tax rates can offset cyclical fluctuations and increase economic growth.

a. Five assumptions are made in order to simplify the explanation of the effects of government spending and taxes on the equilibrium real GDP.

b. ***Government purchases*** of goods and services add to the aggregate expenditures schedule and increase equilibrium real GDP; an increase in these purchases has a multiplier effect on equilibrium real GDP.

c. *Taxes* decrease consumption and the aggregate expenditures schedule by the amount of the tax times the MPC (and decrease saving by the amount of the tax times the MPS); an increase in taxes has a negative multiplier effect on the equilibrium real GDP. When government both taxes and purchases goods and services, the equilibrium GDP is the GDP at which

(1) aggregate expenditures (consumption + investment + net exports + government purchases of goods and services) = the real domestic output (consumption + saving + taxes), or

(2) using the leakages-injections approach, at which investment + exports + government purchases of goods and services = saving + imports + taxes.

d. Equal increases (decreases) in taxes and in government purchases increase (decrease) equilibrium real GDP by the amount of the change in taxes (or in expenditures).

4. The equilibrium level of real GDP may turn out to be an equilibrium at less than full employment, at full employment, or at full employment with inflation.

a. If the equilibrium real GDP is *less* than the real GDP consistent with full employment, there exists a *recessionary gap*; the size of the recessionary gap equals the amount by which the aggregate expenditures schedule must increase (shift upward) to increase the real GDP to its full-employment noninflationary level.

b. If equilibrium real GDP is *greater* than the real GDP consistent with stable prices there is an *inflationary gap*. The size of the inflationary gap equals the amount by which the aggregate expenditures schedule must decrease (shift downward) if the economy is to achieve full employment without inflation.

5. The concepts of recessionary and inflationary gaps from the aggregate expenditures model can be applied to two events in U.S. history.

a. The Great Depression is an example of a severe recessionary (or depressionary) gap as investment spending declined by 82%, thus reducing aggregate expenditures. Four reasons explain this decline in investment spending:

(1) overcapacity in production and increased business indebtedness during the 1920s

(2) a decline in residential construction in the mid-to-late 1920s
(3) the stock market crash of 1929 and its secondary effects
(4) a sharp decline in the money supply
b. The economic expansion during the Vietnam war produced an inflationary gap in the U.S. economy, as inflation went from 1.6% in 1965 to 5.7% by 1970. This inflationary gap occurred because of various factors that significantly increased aggregate expenditures. These factors included the tax cuts in 1962 and 1964 that increased investment and consumption spending, increased government expenditures from 1965–1968 to pay for the escalating Vietnam war, and a tightened labor market because of the military draft.

6. There are four shortcomings of the aggregate expenditures model: an inability to measure price-level changes or the rate of inflation, no explanation for why demand-pull inflation can occur before the economy reaches its full-employment level of output, no insights into why the economy can expand beyond its full-employment level of real GDP, and no coverage of cost-push inflation. These shortcomings are overcome in the aggregate demand—aggregate supply model of the next chapter.

■ HINTS AND TIPS

1. The multiplier effect is a key concept in this chapter and in the ones that follow, so make sure you understand how it works.
a. The multiplier is simply the ratio of the change in real GDP to the *initial* changes in spending. Multiplying the *initial* change in spending by the multiplier gives you the amount of change in real GDP.
b. The multiplier effect works in both positive and negative directions. An *initial* decrease in spending will result in a larger decrease in real GDP, or an *initial* increase in spending will create a larger increase in real GDP.
c. The multiplier is directly related to the marginal propensities. The multiplier equals 1/MPS. The multiplier also equals 1/ (1 − MPC).
d. The main reason for the multiplier effect is that the *initial* change in income (spending) induces additional rounds of income (spending) that add progressively less each round as some of the income (spending) gets saved because of the marginal propensity to save (see Table 10-1 of the text).

2. There is an important difference between equilibrium and full-employment GDP in the aggregate expenditures model. Equilibrium means no tendency for the economy to change its output (or employment) level. Thus, an economy can experience a low level of output and high unemployment and still be at equilibrium. The recessionary gap shows how much aggregate expenditures need to increase, so that when this increase is multiplied by the multiplier, it will shift the economy to a higher equilibrium and to the full-employment level of real GDP. Remember that you multiply the needed increase in aggregate expenditures (the recessionary gap) by the multiplier to calculate the change in real GDP that moves the economy from below- to full-employment equilibrium.

■ IMPORTANT TERMS

multiplier	**balanced-budget multiplier**
net exports	**recessionary gap**
lump-sum tax	**inflationary gap**

SELF-TEST

■ FILL-IN QUESTIONS

1. An upshift in the aggregate expenditures schedule will (increase, decrease) ______________ the equilibrium GDP. The upshift in the aggregate expenditures schedule can result from a(n) (increase, decrease) ______________ in the consumption schedule or a(n) ______________ in the investment schedule.

2. The multiplier is the change in real GDP (multiplied, divided) ______________ by an initial change in spending; when the initial change in spending is ______________ by the multiplier, the result equals the change in real GDP.

3. The multiplier has a value equal to 1 divided by the marginal propensity to (consume, save) ______________, which is the same thing as 1 divided by the quantity of 1 minus the marginal propensity to ______________.

4. The multiplier is based on two facts:
a. an initial increase in spending by business firms or consumers will increase the (debts, income) ______________ of households in the economy
b. this increase in (debts, income) ______________ will increase and expand the (consumption, investment) ______________ spending of households by an amount equal to the incomes times the marginal propensity to (consume, save) ______________.

5. When investment spending increases, the equilibrium real GDP (increases, decreases) ______________, and when investment spending decreases, the equilibrium real GDP ______________.
a. The changes in the equilibrium real GDP are (greater, less) ______________ than the changes in investment spending.
b. The size of the multiplier varies (directly, inversely) ______________ with the size of the marginal propensity to consume.

6. The (simple, complex) _______________ multiplier is 1 divided by the marginal propensity to (consume, save) _______________ because it reflects only the leakage of saving. The (simple, complex) _______________ multiplier takes into account other leakages such as (exports, imports) _______________ or (taxes, government spending) _______________ along with saving.

7. In an open economy, a nation's net exports are equal to its exports (plus, minus) _______________ its imports. In the open economy, aggregate expenditures are equal to consumption (plus, minus) _______________ investment (plus, minus) _______________ net exports.

8. What would be the effect—increase (+) or decrease (−)—of each of the following upon an open economy's equilibrium real GDP?

a. an increase in imports _____

b. an increase in exports _____

c. a decrease in imports _____

d. a decrease in exports _____

e. an increasing level of national income among trading partners _____

f. an increase in trade barriers imposed by trading partners _____

g. a depreciation in the value of the economy's currency _____

9. Increases in public spending will (decrease, increase) _______________ the aggregate expenditures schedule and equilibrium real GDP, but decreases in public spending will _______________ the aggregate expenditures schedule and equilibrium real GDP.

10. Taxes tend to reduce consumption at each level of real GDP by an amount equal to the taxes multiplied by the marginal propensity to (consume, save) _______________; saving will decrease by an amount equal to the taxes multiplied by the marginal propensity to _______________.

11. In an economy in which government both taxes and purchases goods and services, the equilibrium level of real GDP is the real GDP at which

a. aggregate (output, expenditures) _______________ equals domestic _______________.

b. real GDP is equal to consumption (plus, minus) _______________ investment (plus, minus) _______________ net exports (plus, minus) _______________ purchases of goods and services by government.

12. When the public sector is added to the model, the equation for the leakages-injection approach shows (consumption, investment) _______________ plus (imports, exports) _______________, plus purchases of goods and services by government equals (consumption, saving) _______________ plus (exports, imports) _______________ plus taxes.

13. Equal increases in taxes and government purchases will (increase, decrease) _______________ real GDP by an amount equal to the _______________ in taxes and government purchases. In this case, the balanced-budget multiplier is (1, 0) _______________.

14. A recessionary gap exists when equilibrium real GDP is (greater, less) _______________ than the full-employment real GDP. To bring real GDP to the full-employment level, the aggregate expenditures schedule must (increase, decrease) _______________ by an amount equal to the difference between the equilibrium and the full-employment real GDP (multiplied, divided) _______________ by the multiplier.

15. The amount by which aggregate spending at the full-employment GDP exceeds the full-employment level of real GDP is a(n) (recessionary, inflationary) _______________ gap. To eliminate this gap, the aggregate expenditures schedule must (increase, decrease) _______________ by the amount by which current GDP exceeds the full-employment noninflationary GDP divided by the multiplier.

16. The Great Depression is a historical example of a(n) (inflationary, recessionary) _______________ gap, whereas the period of the escalation of the Vietnam war is a historical example of a(n) _______________ gap.

17. List the factors that caused the steep decline in investment spending during the Great Depression.

a. _______________________________

b. _______________________________

c. _______________________________

d. _______________________________

18. The inflation of the Vietnam war was caused by tax (increases, decreases) _______________ during the early-to-mid-1960s, _______________ in government spending from 1965–1968, and (increases, decreases) _______________ in the demand for labor because of the military draft.

19. One problem with the aggregate expenditures model is that it can explain (cost-push, demand-pull) _______________ but not _______________ inflation. Another problem is that the model also has no way of measuring the rate of (interest, inflation) _______________ because there is no price level.

20. Two other deficiencies of the aggregate expenditures model are its inability to explain premature (demand-pull, cost-push) _______________ inflation or how the economy can expand (to, beyond) _______________ the full-employment level of output.

■ TRUE-FALSE QUESTIONS

Circle the T if the statement is true, the F if it is false.

1. The equilibrium level of GDP will change in response to changes in the investment schedule or the saving-consumption schedules. **T F**

2. If there is a decrease in the investment schedule, there will be an upshift in the aggregate expenditures schedule. **T F**

3. If the expected rate of return from investment increases in an economy, there will most likely be an upshift in the investment schedule for that economy. **T F**

4. A decrease in the real rate of interest will, other things equal, result in a decrease in the equilibrium real GDP. **T F**

5. The multiplier is equal to the change in real GDP multiplied by the initial change in spending. **T F**

6. The initial change in spending for the multiplier refers to an upshift or downshift in the aggregate expenditures schedule due a change in one of its components. **T F**

7. The multiplier effect works only in a positive direction in changing GDP. **T F**

8. The multiplier is based on the idea that any change in income will cause both consumption and saving to vary in the same direction as a change in income and by a fraction of that change in income. **T F**

9. The larger the marginal propensity to consume, the larger the size of the multiplier. **T F**

10. If the slope of a linear consumption schedule is steeper in economy A than economy B, then the MPC is less in economy A than economy B. **T F**

11 The value of the complex multiplier will usually be greater than the value of the simple multiplier because there will be more injections into the economy. **T F**

12. The net exports of an economy equal the sum of its exports and imports of goods and services. **T F**

13. An increase in the volume of a nation's exports, other things being equal, will expand the nation's real GDP. **T F**

14. An increase in the imports of a nation will increase the exports of other nations. **T F**

15. An appreciation of the dollar will increase net exports. **T F**

16. If the MPS were 0.3 and taxes were levied by the government so that consumers paid $20 in taxes at each level of real GDP, consumption expenditures at each level of real GDP would be $14 less. **T F**

17. If taxes are reduced by only $10 at all levels of real GDP and the marginal propensity to save is 0.4, equilibrium real GDP will rise by $25. **T F**

18. Equal increases in government purchases and taxes expand GDP by an amount equal to the increase. **T F**

19. The equilibrium real GDP is the real GDP at which there is full employment in the economy. **T F**

20. The existence of a recessionary gap in the economy is characterized by the full employment of labor. **T F**

21. One major cause of the Great Depression was the decline in the level of government spending. **T F**

22. The main reasons for the inflationary gap that developed in the economy during the 1960s was the increases in investment spending resulting from tax cuts and added government purchases of goods and services for the Vietnam war. **T F**

23. The aggregate expenditures model is valuable because it indicates how much the price level will rise when aggregate expenditures are excessive relative to the economy's capacity. **T F**

24. The aggregate expenditures model bars real GDP beyond the full-employment level of output. **T F**

25. The aggregate expenditures model provides a good explanation for cost-push inflation. **T F**

■ MULTIPLE-CHOICE QUESTIONS

Circle the letter that corresponds to the best answer.

Questions 1 and 2 are based on the following consumption schedule.

Real GDP	*C*
$200	$200
240	228
280	256
320	284
360	312
400	340
440	368
480	396

1. If investment is $60, the equilibrium level of real GDP will be

(a) $320
(b) $360
(c) $400
(d) $440

2. If investment were to increase by $5, the equilibrium real GDP would increase by
(a) $5.00
(b) $7.14
(c) $15.00
(d) $16.67

3. If the value of the marginal propensity to consume is 0.6 and real GDP falls by $25, this was caused by a decrease in the aggregate expenditures schedule of
(a) $10.00
(b) $15.00
(c) $16.67
(d) $20.00

4. If the marginal propensity to consume is 0.67 and if both planned gross investment and the saving schedule increase by $25, real GDP will
(a) increase by $75
(b) not change
(c) decrease by $75
(d) increase by $25

5. If in an economy a $150 billion increase in investment spending creates $150 billion of new income in the first round of the multiplier process and $105 billion in the second round, the multiplier and the marginal propensity to consume will be, respectively
(a) 5.00 and 0.80
(b) 4.00 and 0.75
(c) 3.33 and 0.70
(d) 2.50 and 0.40

Answer Questions 6, 7, and 8 on the basis of the following table for a private, closed economy. All figures are in billions of dollars.

Expected rate of return	Investment	Consumption	GDP
10%	$ 0	$200	$200
8	50	250	300
6	100	300	400
4	150	350	500
2	200	400	600
0	250	450	700

6. If the real rate of interest is 4%, then the equilibrium level of GDP will be
(a) $300 billion
(b) $400 billion
(c) $500 billion
(d) $600 billion

7. An increase in the interest rate by 4% will
(a) increase the equilibrium level of GDP by $200 billion
(b) decrease the equilibrium level of GDP by $200 billion
(c) decrease the equilibrium level of GDP by $100 billion
(d) increase the equilibrium level of GDP by $100 billion

8. The multiplier for this economy is
(a) 2.00
(b) 2.50
(c) 3.00
(d) 3.33

Use the data in the following table to answer Questions 9, 10, and 11.

Real GDP	$C + I_g$	Net exports
900	$ 913	$3
920	929	3
940	945	3
960	961	3
980	977	3
1,000	993	3
1,020	1,009	3

9. The equilibrium real GDP is
(a) $960
(b) $980
(c) $1,000
(d) $1,020

10. If net exports are increased by $4 billion at each level of GDP, the equilibrium real GDP would be
(a) $960
(b) $980
(c) $1,000
(d) $1,020

11. If the marginal propensity to save in this economy is 0.2, a $10 increase in its net exports would increase its equilibrium real GDP by
(a) $40
(b) $50
(c) $100
(d) $200

12. Other things remaining constant, which of the following would increase an economy's real GDP and employment?
(a) the imposition of tariffs on goods imported from abroad
(b) a decrease in the level of national income among the trading partners for this economy
(c) a depreciation of the dollar relative to foreign currencies
(d) an increase in the exchange rate for foreign currencies

13. An increase in the real GDP of an economy will, other things remaining constant,
(a) increase its imports and the real GDPs in other economies
(b) increase its imports and decrease the real GDPs in other economies
(c) decrease its imports and increase the real GDPs in other economies
(d) decrease its imports and the real GDPs in other economies

14. The economy is operating at the full-employment level of output. A depreciation of the dollar will most likely result in
- **(a)** a decrease in exports
- **(b)** an increase in imports
- **(c)** a decrease in real GDP
- **(d)** an increase in the price level

Questions 15, 16, 17, and 18 are based on the following consumption schedule. Investment figures are for planned investment.

Real GDP	C
$300	$290
310	298
320	306
330	314
340	322
350	330
360	338

15. If taxes were zero, government purchases of goods and services $10, investment $6, and net exports zero, equilibrium real GDP would be
- **(a)** $310
- **(b)** $320
- **(c)** $330
- **(d)** $340

16. If taxes were $5, government purchases of goods and services $10, investment $6, and net exports zero, equilibrium real GDP would be
- **(a)** $300
- **(b)** $310
- **(c)** $320
- **(d)** $330

17. Assume investment is $42, taxes are $40, net exports are zero, and government purchases of goods and services zero. If the full-employment level of real GDP is $340, the gap can be eliminated by reducing taxes by
- **(a)** $8
- **(b)** $10
- **(c)** $13
- **(d)** $40

18. Assume that investment is zero, taxes are zero, net exports are zero, and the government purchases of goods and services are $20. If the full-employment level of real GDP is $330, the gap can be eliminated by decreasing government expenditures by
- **(a)** $4
- **(b)** $5
- **(c)** $10
- **(d)** $20

19. If the marginal propensity to consume is 0.67 and both taxes and government purchases of goods and services increase by $25, real GDP will
- **(a)** fall by $25
- **(b)** rise by $25
- **(c)** fall by $75
- **(d)** rise by $75

20. Which of the following policies would do the *most* to reduce inflation?
- **(a)** increase taxes by $5 billion
- **(b)** reduce government purchases of goods and services by $5 billion
- **(c)** increase taxes and government expenditures by $5 billion
- **(d)** reduce both taxes and government purchases by $5 billion

21. If MPS is 0.10, a simultaneous increase in both taxes and government spending of $30 billion will
- **(a)** reduce consumption by $27 billion, increase government spending by $27 billion, and increase GDP by $30 billion
- **(b)** reduce consumption by $27 billion, increase government spending by $30 billion, and increase GDP by $27 billion
- **(c)** reduce consumption by $24 billion, increase government spending by $30 billion, and increase GDP by $30 billion
- **(d)** reduce consumption by $24 billion, increase government spending by $24 billion, and increase GDP by $24 billion

Answer Questions 22, 23, and 24 on the basis of the following diagram.

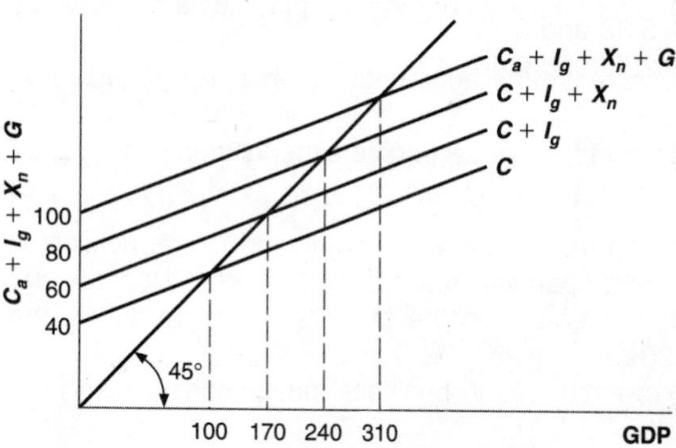

22. The size of the multiplier associated with changes in government spending in this economy is approximately
- **(a)** 0.29
- **(b)** 1.50
- **(c)** 2.50
- **(d)** 3.50

23. If this were an open economy without a government sector, the level of GDP would be
- **(a)** $100
- **(b)** $170
- **(c)** $240
- **(d)** $310

24. In this diagram it is assumed that investment, net exports, and government expenditures
- **(a)** vary inversely with GDP
- **(b)** vary directly with GDP
- **(c)** are independent of GDP
- **(d)** are all negative

25. If the MPC in an economy is 0.75, government could eliminate a recessionary gap of $50 billion by decreasing taxes by
- **(a)** $33.3 billion
- **(b)** $50 billion
- **(c)** $66.7 billion
- **(d)** $80 billion

26. In which of the following situations for an open mixed economy will the level of GDP contract?
- **(a)** when $C_a + S + M$ is less than $I_g + X + T$
- **(b)** when $I_g + M + T$ is less than $C + X + S$
- **(c)** when $S_a + M + T$ is less than $I_g + X + G$
- **(d)** when $I_g + X + G$ is less than $S_a + M + T$

27. If the economy's full-employment real GDP is $1200 and its equilibrium real GDP is $1100, there is a recessionary gap of
- **(a)** $100
- **(b)** $100 divided by the multiplier
- **(c)** $100 multiplied by the multiplier
- **(d)** $100 times the reciprocal of the marginal propensity to consume

28. To eliminate an inflationary gap of $50 in an economy in which the marginal propensity to save is 0.1, it will be necessary to
- **(a)** decrease the aggregate expenditures schedule by $50
- **(b)** decrease the aggregate expenditures schedule by $5
- **(c)** increase the aggregate expenditures schedule by $50
- **(d)** increase the aggregate expenditures schedule by $5

29. Which of the following contributed to the decline in investment spending that led to the Great Depression?
- **(a)** a decrease in the business capacity during the 1920s
- **(b)** an increase in business indebtedness during the 1920s
- **(c)** a decrease in net exports during the 1930s
- **(d)** an increase in the money supply during the 1930s

30. One of the deficiencies of the aggregate expenditures model is that it
- **(a)** fails to account for demand-pull inflation
- **(b)** gives more weight to cost-push then demand-pull inflation
- **(c)** explains recessionary gaps but not inflationary gaps
- **(d)** has no way of measuring the rate of inflation

■ PROBLEMS

1. Assume the marginal propensity to consume is 0.8 and the change in investment is $10. Complete the following table modeled after Table 10-1 in the textbook.

	Change in income	Change in consumption	Change in saving
Increase in gross investment of $10	$ + 10	$____	$____
Second round	____	____	____
Third round	____	____	____
Fourth round	____	____	____
Fifth round	____	____	____
All other rounds	16.38	13.10	3.28
Totals	____	____	____

2. The following table shows consumption and saving at various levels of real GDP. Assume the price level is constant, the economy is closed to international trade, and there is no government, no business savings, no depreciation, and no net foreign factor income earned in the United States.

Real GDP	C	S	I_g	$C + I_g$	UI
$1,300	$1,290	$10	$22	$1312	−12
1,310	1,298	12	22	1320	−10
1,320	1,306	14	____	____	____
1,330	1,314	16	____	____	____
1,340	1,322	18	____	____	____
1,350	1,330	20	____	____	____
1,360	1,338	22	____	____	____
1,370	1,346	24	____	____	____
1,380	1,354	26	____	____	____
1,390	1,362	28	22	1384	+6
1,400	1,370	30	22	1392	+8

a. The next table is an investment demand schedule which shows the amounts investors plan to invest at different rates of interest. Assume the rate of interest is 6%. In the previous table, complete the gross investment, the consumption-plus-investment, and the unplanned investment (***UI***) columns—showing unplanned investment with a + and unplanned disinvestment with a −.

Interest rate	I_g
10%	$ 0
9	7
8	13
7	18
6	22
5	25

b. The equilibrium real GDP will be $ ____________.

c. The value of the marginal propensity to consume in this problem is ____________, and the value of the marginal propensity to save is ____________.

d. The value of the simple multiplier is ____________.

e. If the rate of interest should fall from 6% to 5%, investment would (increase, decrease) ____________

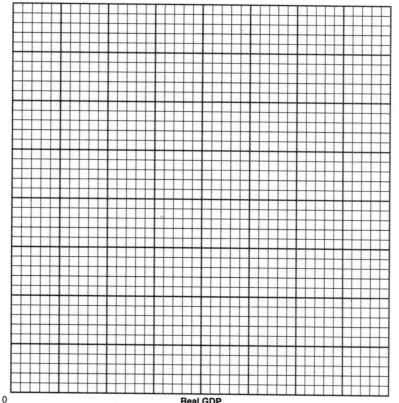

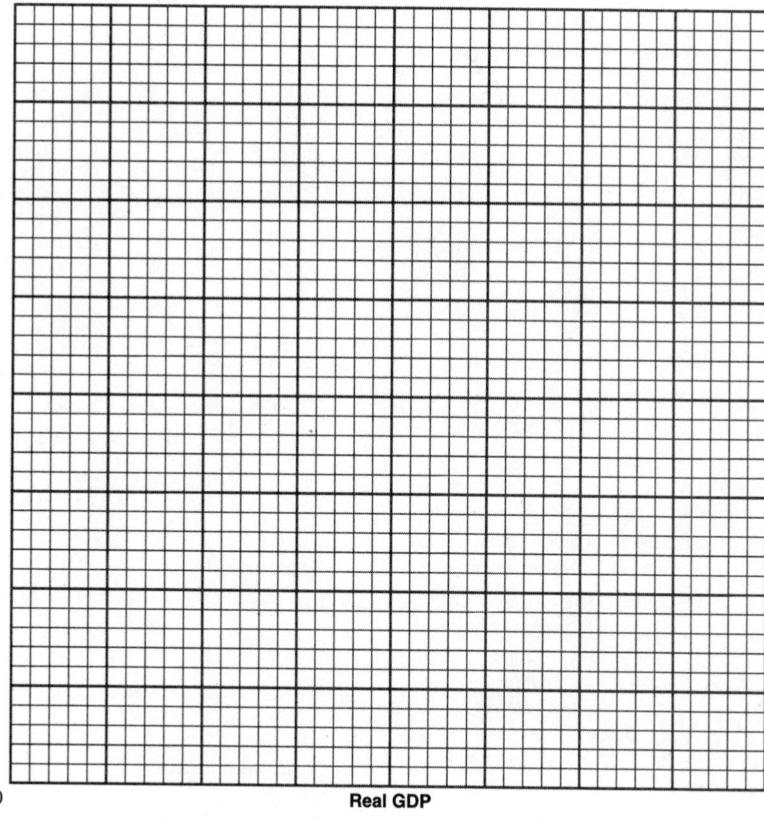

by $______________; and the equilibrium real GDP would, as a result, (increase, decrease) ____________ by $______________.

f. Suppose the rate of interest were to rise from 6% to 7%. Investment would ______________ by $____________, and the equilibrium real GDP would ____________ by $ ____________.

g. Assume the rate of interest is 6%,

(1) on the following graph, plot ***S*** and I_g and indicate the equilibrium real GDP, and

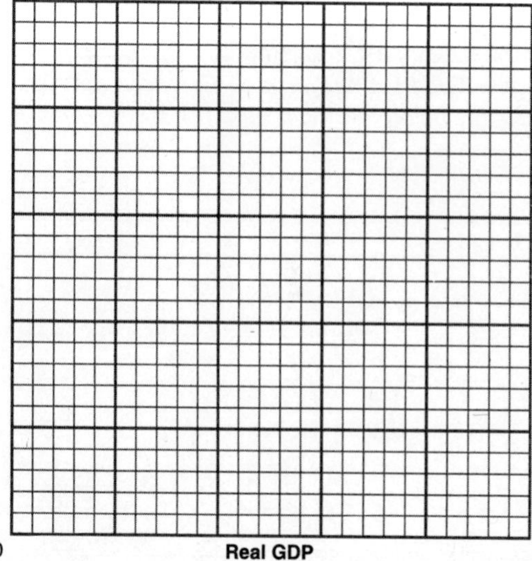

(2) on the above graph, plot ***C***, ***C*** + I_g, and the 45 degree line, and indicate the equilibrium real GDP.

3. Following is a saving and investment schedule (I_g) indicating that planned investment is constant.

Real GDP	*S*	I_g
320	9	15
330	11	15
340	13	15
350	15	15
360	17	15
370	19	15

a. The equilibrium real GDP is $ ____________ and saving and investment are both $ ______.

b. The marginal propensity to save is ____________, and the simple multiplier is ____________.

c. A $2 rise in the I_g schedule will cause real GDP to rise by $ ____________.

d. Use the investment schedule given in the table and assume a $2 increase in the saving schedule in the table—that is, saving at every real GDP increases by $2.

(1) Equilibrium real GDP will ______________ to $____________, and at this real GDP, saving will be $____________.

(2) The amount by which real GDP changes depends on the size of the change in the saving schedule and the size of ____________________.

Possible levels of real GDP (billions)	Aggregate expenditures, closed economy (billions)	Exports (billions)	Imports (billions)	Net exports (billions)	Aggregate expenditures, open economy (billions)
$ 750	$ 776	$90	$86	$_____	$_____
800	816	90	86	_____	_____
850	856	90	86	_____	_____
900	896	90	86	_____	_____
950	936	90	86	_____	_____
1,000	976	90	86	_____	_____
1,050	1,016	90	86	_____	_____

4. Above is a schedule showing what aggregate expenditures (consumption plus investment) would be at various levels of real domestic product in a closed economy.

a. Were this economy to become an open economy, the volume of exports would be a constant $90 billion, and the volume of imports would be a constant $86 billion. At each of the seven levels of real GDP, net exports would be $__________ billion.

b. Compute aggregate expenditures in this open economy at the seven real GDP levels and enter them in the table.

c. The equilibrium real GDP in this open economy, would be __________ billion.

d. The value of the multiplier in this open economy is equal to __________.

e. A $10 billion increase in

(1) exports would (increase, decrease) __________ the equilibrium real GDP by $__________ billion.

(2) imports would (increase, decrease) __________ the equilibrium real GDP by $__________ billion.

5. Following are consumption and saving schedules.

a. Assume government levies a lump sum tax of $100. Also assume that imports are $5.

(1) Because the marginal propensity to consume in this problem is __________, the imposition of this tax will reduce consumption at all levels of real GDP by $__________. Complete the C_a column to show consumption at each real GDP after this tax has been levied.

(2) Because the marginal propensity to save in this problem is __________, this tax will reduce saving at all levels of real GDP by $__________. Complete the S_a column to show saving at each real GDP after this tax has been levied.

b. Compute the (after-tax) saving-plus-imports-plus-taxes at each real GDP and put them in the $S_a + M + T$ column.

c. Suppose that investment is $150, exports are $5, and government purchases of goods and services equal $200. Complete the investment-plus-exports-plus-government-purchases column ($I_g + X + G$) and the (after-tax) consumption-plus-investment-plus-net-exports-plus-government-purchases column ($C_a + I_g + X_n + G$).

d. The equilibrium real GDP is $__________.

e. On the two graphs on p. 111, plot

(1) C_a, $I_g + X_n + G$, $C_a + I_g + X_n + G$, and the 45 degree line. Show the equilibrium real GDP.

(2) $S_a + M + T$ and $I_g + X + G$. Show the real equilibrium GDP. (To answer the questions that follow, it is *not* necessary to recompute C, S, $S + M + T$, $I_g + X + G$, or $C + I_g + X_n + G$. They can be answered by using the multipliers.)

Real GDP	C	S	C_a	S_a	$S_a + M + T$	$I_g + X + G$	$C_a + I_g + X_n + G$
$1,500	$1,250	$250	$_____	$_____	$_____	$_____	$_____
1,600	1,340	260	_____	_____	_____	_____	_____
1,700	1,430	270	_____	_____	_____	_____	_____
1,800	1,520	280	_____	_____	_____	_____	_____
1,900	1,610	290	_____	_____	_____	_____	_____
2,000	1,700	300	_____	_____	_____	_____	_____
2,100	1,790	310	_____	_____	_____	_____	_____

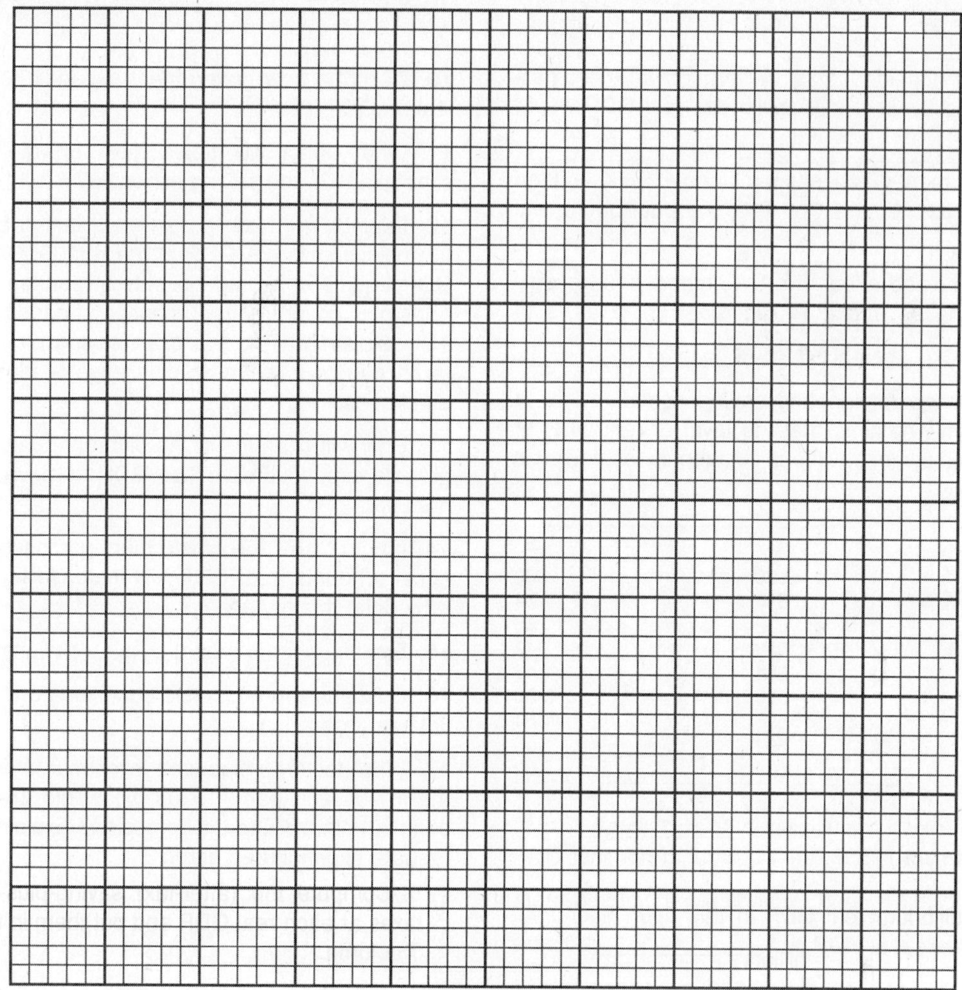
0
Real GDP

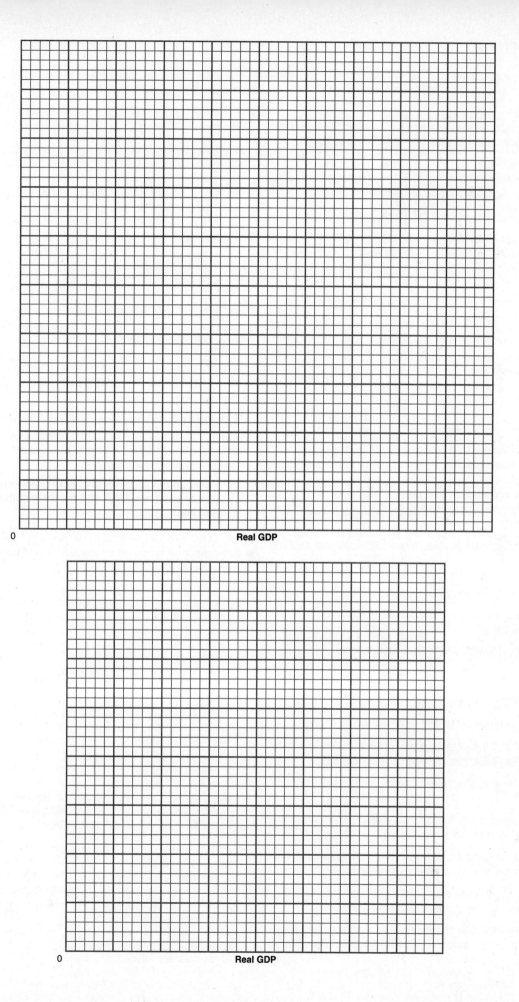

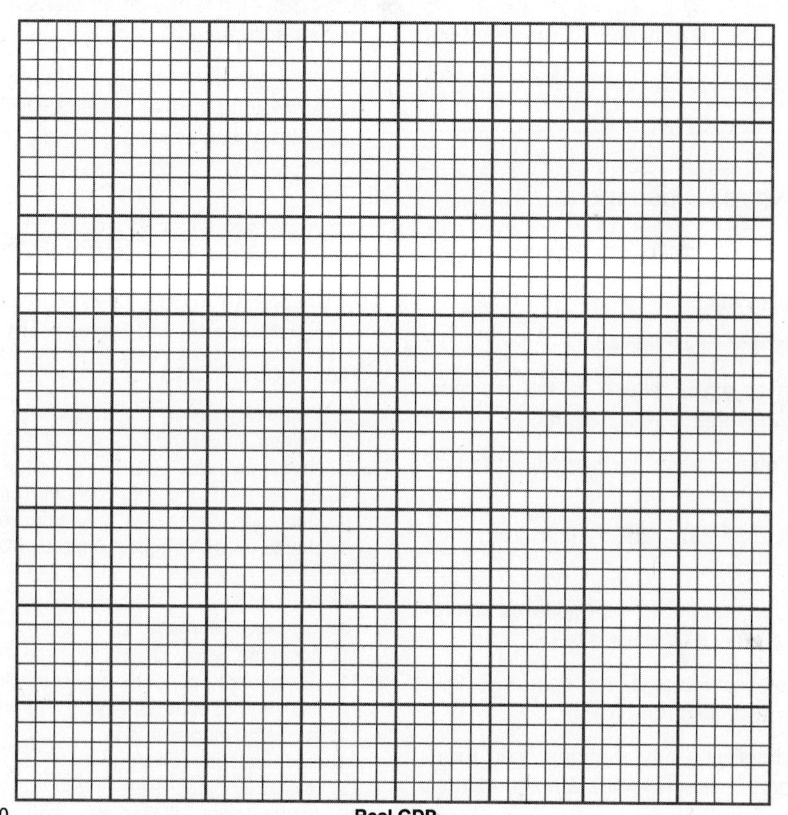
0
Real GDP

f. If taxes remained at $100 and government purchases rose by $10, the equilibrium real GDP would (rise, fall) ______________ by $ ______________.

g. If government purchases remained at $200 and the lump-sum tax increased by $10, the equilibrium real GDP would ______________ by $ ______________.

h. The combined effect of a $10 increase in government purchases *and* a $10 increase in taxes is to ______________ real GDP by $ ______________.

6. Here are consumption and saving schedules for a closed economy. Assume that the level of real GDP at which full employment without inflation is achieved is $590.

Real GDP	*C*	*S*
$550	$520	$30
560	526	34
570	532	38
580	538	42
590	544	46
600	550	50
610	556	54
620	562	58
630	568	62

a. The value of the multiplier is ______________.

b. If investment is $58, the equilibrium nominal GDP is $ ______________ and exceeds the full-employment noninflationary real GDP by $______________. There is a(n) ______________ gap of $ ______________.

c. If investment is $38, the equilibrium real GDP is $ ______________ and is less than full-employment real GDP by $ ______________. There is a(n) ______________ gap of $ ______________.

■ SHORT ANSWER AND ESSAY QUESTIONS

1. Why does the equilibrium level of real GDP change?

2. What is the multiplier effect?

3. Give a rationale for the multiplier effect.

4. How is the multiplier effect related to the marginal propensities? Explain in words and equations.

5. Explain the difference between the simple and complex multiplier.

6. How do exports and imports get included in the aggregate expenditures model?

7. What happens to the aggregate expenditures schedule when net exports increase or decrease?

8. Give some examples of international economic linkages affecting the domestic level of GDP.

9. Explain the five simplifying assumptions used to include the public sector in the aggregate expenditures model.

10. Describe how government expenditures affect equilibrium GDP.

11. What effect will taxes have on the consumption schedule? On the saving schedule?

12. Explain why, with government taxing and spending, the equilibrium real GDP is the real GDP at which real GDP equals consumption plus investment plus net exports plus government purchases of goods and services. Also explain why in this case saving plus imports plus taxes equals investment plus exports plus government purchases.

13. How will changes in the different components of aggregate expenditures cause GDP to move to its equilibrium level?

14. If both taxes and government purchases increase by equal amounts, real GDP will increase by that amount. Why does this happen?

15. Explain what is meant by a recessionary gap.

16. Describe the economic conditions that create an inflationary gap.

17. What factors influenced investment spending during the 1920s and early 1930s? How did these conditions contribute to the Great Depression? Explain using an aggregate expenditures graph.

18. What events led to the Vietnam war inflation of the 1960s? How can this event be characterized using the aggregate expenditures model?

19. What are the limitations of the aggregate expenditures model in terms of the measurement of the price level or demand-pull inflation?

20. Is it possible for the economy to expand beyond its full-employment level of real GDP? How does the aggregate expenditures model handle this situation?

ANSWERS

Chapter 10 Aggregate Expenditures: The Multiplier, Net Exports, and Government

FILL-IN QUESTIONS

1. increase, increase, increase
2. divided, multiplied
3. save, consume
4. *a.* income; *b.* income, consumption, consume
5. increases, decreases; *a.* greater; *b.* directly
6. simple, save, complex, imports, taxes
7. minus, plus, plus
8. *a.* −; *b.* +; *c.* +; *d.* −; *e.* +; *f.* −; *g.* +
9. increase, decrease
10. consume, save
11. *a.* expenditures, output; *b.* plus, plus, plus
12. investment, exports, saving, imports
13. increase, increase, one
14. less, increase, divided
15. inflationary, decrease
16. recessionary, inflationary

17. *a.* overcapacity and business indebtedness; *b.* decline in residential construction; *c.* the stock market crash; *d.* shrinking money supply (any order)
18. decreases, increases, increases
19. demand-pull, cost-push, inflation
20. demand-pull, beyond

TRUE-FALSE QUESTIONS

1. T, p. 199
2. F, pp. 200-201
3. T, p. 200
4. F, pp. 200-201
5. F, p. 201
6. T, p. 201
7. F, p. 201
8. T, p. 201
9. T, p. 203
10. F, p. 203
11. F, pp. 203-204
12. F, p. 204
13. T, pp. 205-206
14. T, pp. 206-207
15. F, p. 207
16. T, pp. 209-210
17. F, pp. 209-210
18. T, p. 212
19. F, p. 213
20. F, p. 213
21. F, pp. 214-217
22. T, p. 217
23. F, p. 217
24. T, p. 218
25. F, p. 218

MULTIPLE-CHOICE QUESTIONS

1. c, pp. 199-200
2. d, pp. 199-200
3. a, pp. 202-203
4. b, pp. 202-203
5. c, pp. 201-202
6. c, pp. 199-200
7. b, pp. 199-200
8. a, p. 201
9. b, p. 204
10. c, p. 204
11. b, pp. 205-206
12. c, p. 207
13. a, p. 206
14. d, p. 207
15. c, pp. 207-208
16. b, pp. 200-210
17. b, p. 213
18. a, p. 213
19. b, pp. 212-213
20. b, pp. 212-213
21. a, pp. 212-213
22. d, p. 201
23. c, p. 205
24. c, p. 207
25. c, pp. 209-210
26. d, pp. 211-212
27. b, p. 213
28. a, p. 213
29. b, p. 215
30. d, p. 217

PROBLEMS

1. Change in income: 8.00, 6.40, 5.12, 4.10, 50; Change in consumption: 8.00, 6.40, 5.12, 4.10, 3.28, 40.00; Change in saving: 2.00, 1.60, 1.28, 1.02, 0.82, 10.00
2. *a.* I_g: 22, 22, 22, 22, 22, 22, 22; $C + I_g$: 1,328, 1,336, 1,344, 1,352, 1,360, 1,368, 1,376; ***UI***: −8, −6, −4, −2, 0, +2, +4; *b.* 1,360; *c.* 0.8, 0.2; *d.* 5; *e.* increase, 3, increase, 15; *f.* decrease, 4, decrease, 20
3. *a.* 350, 15; *b.* 0.20, 5; *c.* 10; *d.* (1) decrease, 340, 15, (2) the multiplier
4. *a.* $4 (and put $4 in each of the seven net exports values in the table); *b.* $780, 820, 860, 900, 940, 980, 1,020; *c.* $900; *d.* 5; *e.* (1) increase, $50, (2) decrease, $50
5. *a.* (1) 0.9, 90; C_a: 1,160, 1,250, 1,340, 1,430, 1,520, 1,610, 1,700, (2) 0.1, 10, S_a: 240, 250, 260, 270, 280, 290, 300; *b.* $S_a + M + T$: 345, 355, 365, 375, 385, 395, 405; *c.* $I_g + X + G$: 355, 355, 355, 355, 355, 355, 355; $C_a + I_g + X_n + G$: 1510, 1600, 1690, 1780, 1870, 1960, 2050; *d.* 1600; *f.* rise, 100; *g.* fall, 90; *h.* raise, 10
6. *a.* 2 1/2; *b.* 620, 30, inflationary, 12; *c.* 570, 20, recessionary, 8

SHORT ANSWER AND ESSAY QUESTIONS

1. pp. 199-201
2. p. 201
3. pp. 201-202
4. pp. 202-203
5. pp. 203-204
6. pp. 204-205
7. pp. 205-206
8. pp. 206-207
9. p. 207
10. pp. 207-208
11. pp. 209-210
12. pp. 211-212
13. pp. 199-213
14. pp. 212-213
15. p. 213
16. p. 213
17. pp. 214-217
18. p. 217
19. p. 217
20. p. 218

CHAPTER 11

Aggregate Demand and Aggregate Supply

Chapter 11 introduces another macro model of the economy, one based on aggregate demand and aggregate supply. This model overcomes a limitation of the aggregate expenditures model because **the price level is allowed to vary rather than be fixed.** The aggregate demand–aggregate supply model allows you to both determine the size of real domestic output or the level of prices at any time and understand what causes output and the price level to change.

The ***aggregate demand (AD) curve*** is **downsloping** because of the wealth, interest rate, and foreign-purchases effects on changes in the price level. With a downsloping aggregate demand curve, changes in the price level have an inverse effect on the level of spending by domestic consumers, businesses, government, and foreign buyers, and thus on real domestic output, assuming *other things equal.* This change would be equivalent to a movement along an existing aggregate demand curve: A lower price level increases the quantity of real domestic output, and a higher price level decreases the quantity of real domestic output.

Although the aggregate expenditures model is a fixed-price level model and the aggregate demand–aggregate supply model is a variable-price level model, there is a close relationship between the two models. The important thing to understand is that prices can be fixed or constant at different levels. The AD curve can be derived from the aggregate expenditures model by letting price be **constant at different levels.** In this case, the lower (the higher) the level at which prices are constant in the aggregate expenditures model, the larger (the smaller) will be the equilibrium real GDP in that model of the economy. Various output-price level combinations can be traced to derive an AD curve that slopes downward.

The **aggregate demand curve can increase or decrease.** The curve shifts because of a change in the non-price level determinants of aggregate demand. The determinants include changes in factors affecting consumer, investment, government, or net export spending. These determinants are similar to the components of the aggregate expenditures model. It is easy to show the relationship between the shifts in the two models. A change in spending will cause a shift (upward or downward) in the aggregate expenditures schedule. The initial change in spending when multiplied times the multiplier would be equal to the size of the horizontal shift in AD, assuming a constant price level.

The ***aggregate supply (AS) curve*** differs from the shape of the aggregate demand curve because it reflects what happens to per unit production costs as real domestic output increases or decreases. For the purposes of this analysis, it has three ranges: (1) At a low level of real domestic output, the price level is relatively constant, so the aggregate supply curve in this range is horizontal; (2) at a high level of real domestic output, the aggregate supply curve is vertical; and (3) in the intermediate range, the level of real domestic output rises along with the price level, so the curve is upsloping.

You should remember that an assumption has also been made that other things are equal when one moves along an aggregate supply curve. When other things change, then the aggregate supply curve can shift. The determinants of aggregate supply include changes in input prices, changes in productivity, and changes in the legal and institutional environment for production.

The **intersection** of the aggregate demand and aggregate supply curves determines ***equilibrium output*** and the ***price level.*** Assuming that the determinants of aggregate demand and aggregate supply do not change, there are competitive pressures that will tend to keep the economy at equilibrium. If, however, a determinant changes, then aggregate demand, aggregate supply, or both, can shift.

When aggregate demand increases, this can lead to changes in real domestic output and the price level, depending on the range on the aggregate supply curve in which the economy is operating. In the intermediate and vertical ranges of AS, a change in AD demand will cause an increase in the price level. Thus, in these ranges the change in AD may not have its full multiplier effect on the real GDP of the economy, and it will result in demand-pull inflation.

There can also be a decrease in aggregate demand, but it is less certain what the effects will be. Some economists think that there is a ***ratchet effect*** that occurs because prices are inflexible downward. This effect may arise for several reasons, as you will learn from the chapter.

Aggregate supply may also increase or decrease. An increase in aggregate supply gives a double bonus for the economy because the price level falls and output (and employment) increase. Conversely, a decrease in aggregate supply doubly harms the economy because the price level increases and output (and employment) falls, and thus the economy experiences cost-push inflation.

The aggregate demand–aggregate supply model is an important framework for determining the equilibrium level of real domestic output and prices in an economy. The model will be used extensively throughout the next eight chapters to analyze how different parts of the economy function.

■ CHECKLIST

When you have studied this chapter you should be able to

☐ Contrast the aggregate expenditures and the aggregate demand–aggregate supply models by comparing the variability of the price level and real GDP.
☐ Define aggregate demand.
☐ Explain why the aggregate demand curve slopes downward.
☐ Derive the aggregate demand curve from the aggregate expenditures model.
☐ Identify the four major spending determinants of aggregate demand and their underlying components.
☐ Explain how the four major spending determinants of aggregate demand and their underlying components can increase or decrease aggregate demand.
☐ Explain the effect of a change in aggregate expenditures on the aggregate demand curve.
☐ Define aggregate supply.
☐ Describe the shape of the aggregate supply curve and name the three ranges on it.
☐ Identify the three major spending determinants of aggregate supply and their underlying components.
☐ Explain how the three major determinants of aggregate supply and their underlying components can increase or decrease aggregate supply.
☐ Explain what the real domestic output and price level will be in equilibrium and why the economy will tend to produce this output and price level (rather than another combination).
☐ State the effects on the real domestic output and on the price level of an increase in aggregate demand when the economy is in the horizontal, vertical, and intermediate ranges.
☐ Explain what determines how large the multiplier effect on the equilibrium real GDP will be in the aggregate demand–aggregate supply model.
☐ Use a graph to illustrate the operation of the ratchet effect.
☐ Give six reasons for downward price-level inflexibility.
☐ Predict the effects of a change in aggregate supply on the price level and the equilibrium real GDP.

■ CHAPTER OUTLINE

1. This chapter introduces the aggregate demand–aggregate supply model of the economy to explain why real domestic output *and* the price level fluctuate. This model has an advantage over the aggregate expenditures model because it allows the price level to vary (rise and fall) rather than be constant or fixed as in the aggregate expenditures model.

2. Aggregate demand is a curve which shows the total quantity of goods and services that will be purchased (demanded) at different price levels.

a. The aggregate demand curve slopes downward for three reasons:
(1) Wealth effect: An increase in the price level also decreases the purchasing power of financial assets with a fixed money value, and because those who own such assets are now poorer, they spend less for goods and services; a decrease in the price level has the opposite effects.
(2) Interest-rate effect: With the supply of money fixed, an increase in the price level increases the demand for money, increases interest rates, and as a result reduces those expenditures (by consumers and business firms) which are sensitive to increased interest rates; a decrease in the price level has the opposite effects.
(3) Foreign purchases effect: An increase in the price level (relative to foreign price levels) will reduce U.S. exports, expand U.S. imports, and decrease the quantity of goods and services demanded in the U.S. economy; a decrease in the price level (relative to foreign price levels) will have opposite effects.

b. The aggregate demand curve is derived from the intersections of the aggregate expenditures curves and the 45 degree curve. As the price level falls, the aggregate expenditures curve shifts upward and the equilibrium real GDP increases, but as the price level rises, the aggregate expenditures curve shifts downward and the equilibrium real GDP decreases. The inverse relationship between the price level and equilibrium real GDP is the aggregate demand curve. Note that for the aggregate expenditures model, changes in
(1) wealth increase or decrease the consumption schedule;
(2) the interest rate increase or decrease the investment schedule;
(3) imports or exports shift the net export schedule.

3. Spending by domestic consumers, businesses, government, and foreign buyers that is independent of changes in the price level shifts aggregate demand, as outlined in Figure 11-3.

a. For domestic consumers, increases in wealth, improved expectations, reductions in indebtedness, or lower taxes can increase consumer spending and aggregate demand; decreases in consumer wealth, less positive expectations, increases in indebtedness, and higher taxes decrease consumer spending and aggregate demand.

b. For businesses, lower interest rates, higher expected returns on investment, lower taxes, improved technology, and less excess capacity may increase investment spending and aggregate demand, whereas higher interest rates, lower expected returns on investment, higher taxes, and more excess capacity may retard investment spending and aggregate demand.

c. More government spending tends to increase aggregate demand and less government spending will decrease it, assuming that tax collections and interest rates do not change as a result.

d. Net export spending and aggregate demand are increased by increases in the national incomes of other nations and by a dollar depreciation; declines in the incomes of foreign buyers and a dollar appreciation tend to reduce net exports and aggregate demand.

e. If the price level is constant, any change in the nonprice-level determinants of consumption and planned investment that shifts the aggregate expenditures curve upward (downward) will increase (decrease) the equilibrium real GDP and shift the AD curve to the right (left) by an amount equal to the initial increase (decrease) in aggregate expenditures times the multiplier.

4. Aggregate supply is a curve that shows the total quantity of goods and services that will be produced (supplied) at different price levels. The curve has three ranges:

a. In the horizontal range (when the economy is in a severe recession or depression), the aggregate supply curve is horizontal; the price level need not rise to induce producers to supply larger quantities of goods and services.

b. In the vertical range (when the economy is at full employment), the aggregate supply curve is vertical; a rise in the price level cannot result in an increase in the quantity of goods and services supplied.

c. Between these two ranges is the intermediate range in which the supply curve slopes upward; the price level must rise to induce producers to supply larger quantities of goods and services.

5. Factors that shift the aggregate supply curve include changes in the prices of inputs for production, changes in productivity, and changes in the legal and institutional environment in the economy, as outlined in Figure 11-6.

a. Lower prices for productive domestic resources (land, labor, capital, and entrepreneurial ability) and imported resources tend to reduce unit costs of production and increase aggregate supply, whereas higher input prices, which may be brought about by more market power on the part of resource suppliers, will tend to decrease aggregate supply.

b. As productivity improves, per-unit production costs fall and aggregate supply increases; the converse occurs when productivity falls.

c. A decrease in the level of business taxation or reduced regulation of business may improve the business environment and increase aggregate supply; the opposite actions may reduce aggregate supply.

6. The equilibrium real domestic output and the equilibrium price level are at the intersection of the aggregate demand and the aggregate supply curves. Were the actual output greater (less) than the equilibrium output, producers would find that their inventories were increasing (decreasing), and they would contract (expand) their output to the equilibrium output.

7. The aggregate demand and aggregate supply curves shift to change equilibrium.

a. An increase in aggregate demand in

(1) the horizontal range would result in an increase in real output, but the price level would remain unchanged,

(2) the vertical range would result in an increase in the price level, but the real domestic output would remain unchanged,

(3) the intermediate range would result in an increase in both real domestic output and the price level.

b. If the economy is operating along the

(1) horizontal range of the AS curve, an increase in AD will have no effect on the price level and the increase in the equilibrium real GDP will equal the full multiplier effect of the increase in aggregate expenditures,

(2) intermediate range the increase in AD will increase the price level and the increase in the equilibrium real GDP will be less than the full multiplier effect of the increase in aggregate expenditures,

(3) vertical range the increase in AD will increase the price level and have no effect on the equilibrium real GDP.

c. But a decrease in aggregate demand may not have the opposite effect on the price level because prices tend to be inflexible (sticky) downward. This ratchet effect occurs for at least six interrelated reasons: long-term wage contracts, efficiency wages, investments in training, the minimum wage, menu costs, and fear of price wars.

d. A decrease in aggregate supply means there will be a decrease in real domestic output (economic growth) and employment along with a rise in the price level, or cost-push inflation.

e. An increase in aggregate supply, however, has the beneficial effects of improving real domestic output and employment while simultaneously reducing the price level.

■ HINTS AND TIPS

1. Demand and supply are the tools used to explain what determines the economy's real output and price level. These tools, however, are different from the demand and supply used in Chapter 3 to explain what determines the output and price of a *particular* product. Instead of thinking about the quantity of a *particular* good or service demanded or supplied, it is necessary to think about the total or *aggregate* quantity of all final goods and services demanded (purchased) and supplied (produced). You will have no difficulty with the way demand and supply are used in this chapter once you switch from thinking about a *particular* good or service and its price to the *aggregate* of all final goods and services and its average price.

2. The aggregate supply curve has a strange shape because there are three ranges—horizontal, upsloping (intermediate), and vertical. Make sure you understand the rationale for each range. Also, the shape of the aggregate supply curve means that graphically an *increase* in aggregate supply will move aggregate supply both *downward* (in the horizontal range) and *outward* (in the upsloping and vertical ranges). The opposite is the case for a decrease in aggregate supply. Check your understanding of this point by referring to Figure 11-6 in the text.

3. Make sure you know the difference between a movement along an aggregate demand or supply curve and a shift in an aggregate demand or supply curve. Figures 11-3 and 11-6 in the text are extremely valuable summaries of the determinants of aggregate demand and aggregate supply that shift each curve.

■ IMPORTANT TERMS

aggregate demand (AD) curve
wealth or real balances effect
interest-rate effect
foreign purchases effect
determinants of aggregate demand
aggregate supply (AS) curve
determinants of aggregate supply
productivity
horizontal range
vertical range
intermediate range
equilibrium price level
equilibrium real domestic output
demand-pull inflation
ratchet effect
efficiency wages
menu costs
cost-push inflation

SELF-TEST

■ FILL-IN QUESTIONS

1. In the aggregate demand–aggregate supply model, the price level is (fixed, variable) ______________, but in the aggregate expenditures model, the price level is ______________.

2. Aggregate demand and aggregate supply together determine the equilibrium real domestic (price, output) ______________ and the equilibrium ______________ level.

3. The aggregate demand curve shows the quantity of goods and services that will be (supplied, demanded) ______________ or purchased at various price levels. It slopes (upward, downward) ______________ because of the (wealth, consumption) ______________ effect, the (profit, interest) ______________-rate effect, and the (domestic, foreign) ______________ purchases effects.

4. For the aggregate demand curve, an increase in the price level leads to a(n) (increase, decrease) ______________ in the quantity of real domestic output, whereas a decrease in the price level leads to a(n) ______________ in the quantity of real domestic output, assuming other things equal.

5. In the aggregate expenditures model, a lower price level would (raise, lower) ______________ the consumption, investment, and aggregate expenditures curves, and the equilibrium level of real GDP would (rise, fall) ______________. A higher price level would (raise, lower) ______________ the consumption, investment, and aggregate expenditures curves, and the equilibrium level of real GDP would (rise, fall) ______________. This (direct, inverse) ______________ relationship between the price level and equilibrium real GDP in the aggregate expenditures model can be used to derive the aggregate (demand, supply) ______________ curve (or schedule).

6. In the aggregate demand curve, when the price level changes, there is a (movement along, change in) ______________ the curve. When the entire aggregate demand curve shifts, there is a change in (the quantity of real output demanded, aggregate demand) ______________.

7. List the determinants of aggregate demand from changes in consumer spending:

a. ______________
b. ______________
c. ______________
d. ______________

8. List the determinants of aggregate demand from changes in investment spending:

a. ______________
b. ______________
c. ______________
d. ______________
e. ______________

9. Aggregate demand can also shift because of changes in government (spending, regulation) ______________; it may also shift because of a change in national income abroad or exchange rates that affect net (import, export) ______________ spending.

10. If the price level were constant, an increase in the aggregate expenditures curve would shift the aggregate demand curve to the (right, left) ______________ by an amount equal to the upward shift in aggregate expenditures times the (interest rate, multiplier) ______________. A decrease in the aggregate expenditures curve would shift the aggregate demand curve to the (right, left) ______________ by an amount equal to the (upward, downward) ______________ shift in aggregate expenditures times the (interest rate, multiplier) ______________.

11. The aggregate supply curve shows the quantity of goods and services that will be (demanded, supplied) _____ or produced at various price levels. In the horizontal range of the aggregate supply curve, as domestic output increases, the price level (is constant, increases) _____; in the intermediate range, as domestic output increases, the price level _____; and in the vertical range, domestic output remains constant and the price level _____.

12. The basic cause of a decrease in aggregate supply is a(n) (increase, decrease) _____ in the per-unit costs of producing goods and services, and the basic cause of an increase in aggregate supply is a(n) _____ in the per-unit costs of production, all other things equal.

13. Aggregate supply shift may result from

a. a change in input prices caused by a change in

(1) _____

(2) _____

(3) _____

b. from a change in (consumption, productivity) _____

c. from a change in the legal and institutional environment caused by a change in

(1) _____

(2) _____

14. The equilibrium real domestic output and price level are found at the (zero values, intersection) _____ of the aggregate demand and the aggregate supply curves. At this price level, the aggregate quantity of goods and services purchased (demanded) is (greater than, less than, equal to) _____ the aggregate quantity of goods and services produced (supplied). And at this real domestic output, the prices producers are willing to (pay, accept) _____ are equal to the prices buyers are willing to _____.

15. Were the actual real domestic output greater than the equilibrium domestic output, producers would find that their inventories were (increasing, decreasing) _____ and they would (expand, reduce) _____ their production. At less than the equilibrium domestic output, producers would find that their inventories were (increasing, decreasing) _____ and they would (expand, reduce) _____ their production.

16. When the economy is producing in the horizontal range of aggregate supply, an increase in aggregate demand will (increase, decrease, have no effect on) _____ real domestic output and will _____ the price level; in the intermediate range, an increase in aggregate demand will _____ real domestic output and will _____ the price level; and in the vertical range, an increase in aggregate demand will _____ real domestic output and will _____ the price level.

17. Were aggregate demand to increase, the flatter the aggregate supply curve, the (greater, smaller) _____ would be the multiplier effect on the real equilibrium GDP and the _____ would be the effect on the equilibrium price level; the steeper the aggregate supply curve, the _____ would be the multiplier effect on the equilibrium real GDP and the _____ would be the effect on the equilibrium price level.

18. The tendency for prices to be inflexible downward when aggregate demand decreases is called the (interest-rate, ratchet) _____ effect. This effect occurs because wage contracts are (short, long) _____-term, workers are paid (efficiency, inefficiency) _____ wages, businesses have (invested in, reduced) _____ training for workers, there is a (maximum, minimum) _____ wage, businesses experience menu (benefits, costs) _____, and there is fear of (price, cold) _____ wars.

19. An increase in aggregate supply will (increase, decrease) _____ real domestic output and _____ the price level. A decrease in aggregate supply will (increase, decrease) _____ real output and _____ the price level.

20. Demand-pull inflation is the result of a(n) (increase, decrease) _____ in aggregate demand and is accompanied by a (rise, fall) _____ in real output, but cost-push inflation is the result of a(n) _____ in aggregate supply and is accompanied by a _____ in real output.

■ TRUE-FALSE QUESTIONS

Circle the T if the statement is true, the F if it is false.

1. Aggregation in macroeconomics is the process of combining all the prices of individual products and services into a price level and merging all the equilibrium quantities into real domestic output. **T F**

2. The aggregate demand curve slopes downward. **T F**

3. A fall in the price level increases the real value of financial assets with fixed money values and, as a result, increases spending by the holders of these assets. **T F**

4. A fall in the price level reduces the demand for money in the economy and drives interest rates upward. **T F**

5. A rise in the price level of an economy (relative to foreign price levels) tends to increase that economy's exports and to reduce its imports of goods and services. **T F**

6. The higher the price level, the smaller the wealth of consumers and the lower the consumption schedule (curve). **T F**

7. An increase in the price level will shift the aggregate expenditures schedule upward. **T F**

8. A change in aggregate demand is caused by a change in the price level, *other things equal.* **T F**

9. A fall in excess capacity, or unused existing capital goods, will retard the demand for new capital goods and therefore reduce aggregate demand. **T F**

10. The wealth effect is one of the determinants of aggregate demand. **T F**

11. A high level of household indebtedness will tend to increase consumption spending and aggregate demand. **T F**

12. Appreciation of the dollar relative to foreign currencies will tend to increase net exports and aggregate demand. **T F**

13. The aggregate supply curve has a downsloping range. **T F**

14. When the determinants of aggregate supply change, they alter the per-unit production cost and thereby aggregate supply. **T F**

15. Productivity is a measure of real output per unit of input. **T F**

16. A change in the degree of market power or monopoly power held by sellers of resources can affect input prices and aggregate supply. **T F**

17. Per-unit production cost is determined by dividing total input cost by units of output. **T F**

18. At the equilibrium price level, the real domestic output purchased is equal to the real domestic output produced. **T F**

19. In the intermediate range on the aggregate supply curve, an increase in aggregate demand will increase both the price level and the real domestic output. **T F**

20. In the horizontal range on the aggregate supply curve, an increase in aggregate demand will have no effect on the real equilibrium GDP of the economy and will raise its price level. **T F**

21. The greater the increase in the price level that results from an increase in aggregate demand, the greater will be the increase in the equilibrium real GDP. **T F**

22. Inflation has no effect on the strength of the multiplier. **T F**

23. A decrease in aggregate demand will lower the price level by the same amount as an equal increase in aggregate demand would have raised it because of the ratchet effect. **T F**

24. An increase in aggregate supply increases both the equilibrium real domestic output and the full-employment output of the economy. **T F**

25. A decrease in aggregate supply is "doubly good" because it increases the real domestic output and prevents inflation. **T F**

■ MULTIPLE-CHOICE QUESTIONS

Circle the letter that corresponds to the best answer.

1. The aggregate demand curve is the relationship between the
- **(a)** price level and the real domestic output purchased
- **(b)** price level and the real domestic output produced
- **(c)** price level and what producers will supply
- **(d)** real domestic output purchased and the real domestic output produced

2. When the price level rises,
- **(a)** holders of financial assets with fixed money values increase their spending
- **(b)** the demand for money and interest rates rise
- **(c)** spending which is sensitive to interest-rate changes increases
- **(d)** holders of financial assets with fixed money values have more purchasing power

3. The slope of the aggregate demand curve is the result of
- **(a)** the wealth effect
- **(b)** the interest-rate effect
- **(c)** the foreign purchases effect
- **(d)** all of the above effects

4. If the price level in the aggregate expenditures model were lower, the consumption and aggregate expenditures curves would be
- **(a)** lower, and the equilibrium real GDP would be smaller
- **(b)** lower, and the equilibrium real GDP would be larger
- **(c)** higher, and the equilibrium real GDP would be larger
- **(d)** higher, and the equilibrium real GDP would be smaller

5. A decrease in the price level will shift the
- **(a)** consumption, investment, and net exports curves downward
- **(b)** consumption, investment, and net exports curves upward
- **(c)** consumption and investment curves upward, but the net exports curve downward
- **(d)** consumption and net export curves upward, but the investment curve downward

6. The aggregate demand curve will tend to be increased by
(a) a decrease in the price level
(b) an increase in the price level
(c) an increase in the excess capacity of factories
(d) a depreciation in the value of the U.S. dollar

7. A sharp decline in the real value of stock prices, which is independent of a change in the price level, would best be an example of
(a) the wealth effect
(b) the real balance effect
(c) a change in real wealth
(d) a change in household indebtedness

8. An increase in aggregate expenditures shifts the aggregate demand curve to the
(a) right by the amount of the increase in aggregate expenditures
(b) right by the amount of the increase in aggregate expenditures times the multiplier
(c) left by the amount of the increase in aggregate expenditures
(d) left by the amount of the increase in aggregate expenditures times the multiplier

9. The aggregate supply curve is the relationship between the
(a) price level and the real domestic output purchased
(b) price level and the real domestic output produced
(c) price level which producers are willing to accept and the price level purchasers are willing to pay
(d) real domestic output purchased and the real domestic output produced

10. In the intermediate range, the aggregate supply curve is
(a) upsloping
(b) downsloping
(c) vertical
(d) horizontal

Suppose that real domestic output in an economy is 50 units, the quantity of inputs is 10, and the price of each input is $2. Answer Questions 11, 12, 13, and 14 on the basis of this information.

11. The level of productivity in this economy is
(a) 5
(b) 4
(c) 3
(d) 2

12. The per unit cost of production is
(a) $0.40
(b) $0.50
(c) $2.50
(d) $3.50

13. If real domestic output in the economy rose to 60 units, then per-unit production costs would
(a) remain unchanged and aggregate supply would remain unchanged
(b) increase and aggregate supply would decrease
(c) decrease and aggregate supply would increase
(d) decrease and aggregate supply would decrease

14. All else equal, if the price of each input increases from $2 to $4, productivity would
(a) decrease from $4 to $2 and aggregate supply would decrease
(b) decrease from $5 to $3 and aggregate supply would decrease
(c) decrease from $4 to $2 and aggregate supply would increase
(d) remain unchanged and aggregate supply would decrease

15. If the prices of imported resources increase, then this event would most likely
(a) decrease aggregate supply
(b) increase aggregate supply
(c) increase aggregate demand
(d) decrease aggregate demand

16. If Congress passed much stricter laws to control the air pollution from business, this action would tend to
(a) increase per-unit production costs and shift the aggregate supply curve to the right
(b) increase per-unit production costs and shift the aggregate supply curve to the left
(c) increase per-unit production costs and shift the aggregate demand curve to the left
(d) decrease per-unit production costs and shift the aggregate supply curve to the left

17. An increase in business taxes will tend to
(a) decrease aggregate demand but not change aggregate supply
(b) decrease aggregate supply but not change aggregate demand
(c) decrease aggregate demand and decrease aggregate supply
(d) decrease aggregate supply and increase aggregate demand

18. If the real domestic output is less than the equilibrium real domestic output, producers find
(a) their inventories decreasing and expand their production
(b) their inventories increasing and expand their production
(c) their inventories decreasing and contract their production
(d) their inventories increasing and contract their production

Answer Questions 19, 20, 21, and 22 on the basis of the following aggregate demand–aggregate supply schedule for a hypothetical economy.

Real domestic output demanded (in billions)	Price level	Real domestic output supplied (in billions)
$1,500	170	$4,000
$2,000	150	$4,000
$2,500	125	$3,500
$3,000	100	$3,000
$3,500	75	$2,500
$4,000	75	$2,000

19. The equilibrium price level and quantity of real domestic output will be
(a) 100 and $2,500
(b) 100 and $3,000
(c) 125 and $3,500
(d) 150 and $4,000

20. The horizontal range of the aggregate supply curve is associated with the quantity supplied of
(a) $4,000
(b) $4,000 and $3,500
(c) $3,500 and $3,000
(d) $2,500 and $2,000

21. If the quantity of real domestic output demanded increased by $2,000 at each price level, the new equilibrium price level and quantity of real domestic output would be
(a) 175 and $4,000
(b) 150 and $4,000
(c) 125 and $3,500
(d) 100 and $3,000

22. Using the original data from the table, if the quantity of real domestic output demanded *increased* by $500 and the quantity of real domestic output supplied *decreased* by $500 at each price level, the new equilibrium price level and quantity of real domestic output would be
(a) 175 and $4,000
(b) 150 and $4,000
(c) 125 and $3,000
(d) 100 and $3,500

23. When the economy is in the horizontal range, an increase in aggregate demand will
(a) increase the price level and have no effect on real domestic output
(b) increase the real domestic output and have no effect on the price level
(c) increase both real output and the price level
(d) increase the price level and decrease the real domestic output

24. An increase in aggregate demand will increase the equilibrium real GDP if the economy is operating in the
(a) horizontal range only
(b) intermediate range only
(c) horizontal or intermediate ranges
(d) vertical range only

25. An increase in aggregate demand will increase both the equilibrium real GDP and the price level if the economy is operating in the
(a) horizontal range
(b) intermediate range
(c) intermediate or vertical ranges
(d) vertical range

26. In the aggregate demand–aggregate supply model, an increase in the price level will
(a) increase the marginal propensity to consume
(b) increase the strength of the multiplier
(c) decrease the strength of the multiplier
(d) have no effect on the strength of the multiplier

27. If aggregate demand decreases but the price level does not fall as much as would be expected if price were flexible, then this situation could be the result of
(a) an increase in aggregate supply
(b) the foreign purchases effect
(c) lower interest rates
(d) a ratchet effect

28. The ratchet effect is the result of
(a) a price level that is inflexible upward
(b) a price level that is inflexible downward
(c) a domestic output that cannot be increased
(d) a domestic output that cannot be decreased

29. An increase in aggregate supply will
(a) reduce the price level and real domestic output
(b) reduce the price level and increase the real domestic output
(c) increase the price level and real domestic output
(d) reduce the price level and have no effect on real domestic output

30. If there were cost-push inflation in the economy that decreased aggregate supply,
(a) both the real domestic output and the price level would decrease
(b) the real domestic output would increase and rises in the price level would become smaller
(c) the real domestic output would decrease and the price level would rise
(d) both the real domestic output and rises in the price level would become greater

■ PROBLEMS

1. Following is an aggregate supply schedule.

Price level	Real domestic output supplied
250	2,000
225	2,000
200	1,900
175	1,700
150	1,400
125	1,000
125	500
125	0

a. The economy is in the
(1) horizontal range when the real domestic output is between ____________ and ____________.
(2) vertical range when the real domestic output is ____________ and the price level is ____________ or more.
(3) intermediate range when the real domestic output is between ____________ and ____________.
b. Plot this aggregate supply schedule on the accompanying graph.
c. The following table has three aggregate demand schedules.

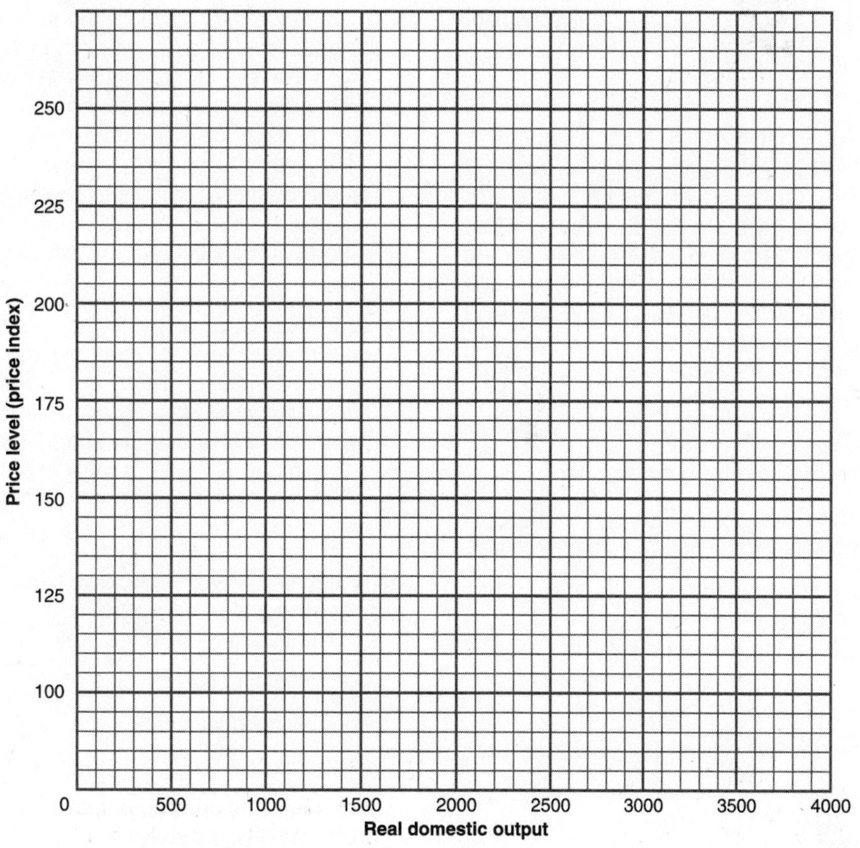

Price level	Real domestic output demanded		
(1)	(2)	(3)	(4)
250	1,400	1,900	400
225	1,500	2,000	500
200	1,600	2,100	600
175	1,700	2,200	700
150	1,800	2,300	800
125	1,900	2,400	900
100	2,000	2,500	1,000

(1) On the graph, plot the aggregate demand curve shown in columns 1 and 2; label this curve **AD**$_1$. At this level of aggregate demand, the equilibrium real domestic output is ______________

and the equilibrium price level is ______________.

(2) On the same graph, plot the aggregate demand curve shown in columns 1 and 3; label this curve **AD**$_2$. The equilibrium real domestic output is ________

and the equilibrium price level is ______________.

(3) On the same graph, plot the aggregate demand curve shown in columns 1 and 4; label it **AD**$_3$. The equilibrium real domestic output is ______________

and the equilibrium price level is ______________.

2. Column 1 of the following table shows the real GDP an economy might produce.

(1) Real GDP	(2) $AE_{1.20}$	(3) $AE_{1.00}$	(4) $AE_{0.80}$
$2,100	$2,110	$2,130	$2,150
2,200	2,200	2,220	2,240
2,300	2,290	2,310	2,330
2,400	2,380	2,400	2,420
2,500	2,470	2,490	2,510
2,600	2,560	2,580	2,600

a. If the price level in this economy were $1.20, the aggregate expenditures (AE) at each real GDP would be those shown in column 2 and the equilibrium real GDP would be $______________.

b. If the price level were $1.00, the aggregate expenditures at each real GDP would be those shown in column 3 and the equilibrium real GDP would be $________.

c. If the price level were $0.80, the aggregate expenditures at each real GDP would be those shown in column 4 and the equilibrium real GDP would be $________.

d. Show in the following schedule the equilibrium real GDP at each of the three price levels.

Price level	Equilibrium real GDP
$1.20	$_____
1.00	_____
0.80	_____

(1) This schedule is the ______________ schedule.

(2) The equilibrium real GDP is ______________ related to the price level.

3. In the following list, what will most likely happen as a result of each event to (1) aggregate demand (AD); (2) aggregate supply (AS); (3) the equilibrium price level (***P***); and (4) equilibrium real domestic output (***Q***)? Assume that all other things remain constant when the event occurs and that the economy is operating in the intermediate range of the aggregate supply curve. Use the following symbols to indicate the expected effects: ***I*** = increase, ***D*** = decrease, ***S*** = remains the same, and ***U*** = uncertain.

a. A decrease in labor productivity.

AD_____ AS_____ *P*_____ *Q*_____

b. A fall in the interest rate for business loans.

AD_____ AS_____ *P*_____ *Q*_____

c. Consumer incomes decline as the economy moves into a recession.

AD_____ AS_____ *P*_____ *Q*_____

d. The price of oil on the world market falls to a low level.

AD_____ AS_____ *P*_____ *Q*_____

e. There is an appreciation in the value of the U.S. dollar.

AD_____ AS_____ *P*_____ *Q*_____

4. Following are hypothetical data showing the relationships between the real domestic output and the quantity of input resources needed to produce each level of output.

Output	Input	*Productivity* (1)	(2)	*Per unit cost* (3)	(4)	(5)
2500	500	_____	_____	_____	_____	_____
2000	400	_____	_____	_____	_____	_____
1500	300	_____	_____	_____	_____	_____

a. In column 1, compute the level of productivity at each level of real domestic output.

b. In column 2, compute the level of productivity if there is a doubling in the quantity of inputs required to produce each level of output.

c. In column 3, compute the per-unit production cost at each level of output if each unit of input costs $15, given the level of productivity in column 1.

d. In column 4, compute the new per-unit production cost at each level of output if each unit of input costs $15, given that there has been a doubling in the required quantity of inputs to produce each level of output as shown in column 2. What will happen to the aggregate supply curve if this situation occurs? ______________

____

e. In column 5, compute the new per-unit production cost at each level of output, given that input price is now $10 instead of $15 but the level of productivity stays as it was originally shown in column 1. What will happen to the aggregate supply curve if this situation occurs? ______________________________

____

5. Columns 1 and 2 in the table below are the aggregate supply schedule of an economy.

a. The economy is in the

(1) vertical range when its real GDP is $__________ and the price level is $__________ or higher.

(2) horizontal range when its real GDP is $__________ or less and its price level is $__________.

b. If the aggregate demand in the economy were columns 1 and 3, the equilibrium real GDP would be $__________ and the equilibrium price level would be $__________, and if aggregate demand should increase by $100 to that shown in columns 1 and 4, the equilibrium real GDP would increase by $__________ and the price level would be __________.

c. Should aggregate demand be that shown in columns 1 and 5, the equilibrium real GDP would be $__________ and the equilibrium price would be $__________, and if aggregate demand should increase by $100 to that shown in columns 1 and 6, the equilibrium real GDP would increase by $__________ and the price level would rise to $__________.

(1) Price level	(2) Real GDP	(3) AD_1	(4) AD_2	(5) AD_3	(6) AD_4	(7) AD_5	(8) AD_6
$2.60	$2,390	$ 840	$ 940	$1,900	$2,000	$2,190	$2,290
2.40	2,390	940	1,040	2,000	2,100	2,290	2,390
2.20	2,390	1,040	1,140	2,100	2,200	2,390	2,490
2.00	2,390	1,140	1,240	2,200	2,300	2,490	2,590
1.90	2,350	1,190	1,290	2,250	2,350	2,540	2,640
1.80	2,300	1,240	1,340	2,300	2,400	2,590	2,690
1.60	2,200	1,340	1,440	2,400	2,500	2,690	2,790
1.40	2,090	1,440	1,540	2,500	2,600	2,790	2,890
1.20	1,970	1,540	1,640	2,600	2,700	2,890	2,990
1.00	1,840	1,640	1,740	2,700	2,800	2,990	3,090
1.00	1,740	1,640	1,740	2,700	2,800	2,990	3,090
1.00	1,640	1,640	1,740	2,700	2,800	2,990	3,090

d. And if aggregate demand were that shown in columns 1 and 7, the equilibrium real GDP would be

$__________ and the equilibrium price level would

be $__________, but if aggregate demand increased by $100 to that shown in columns 1 and 8,

the price level would rise to $__________ and the

equilibrium real GDP would __________.

6. The following diagram shows an aggregate supply curve and six aggregate demand curves.

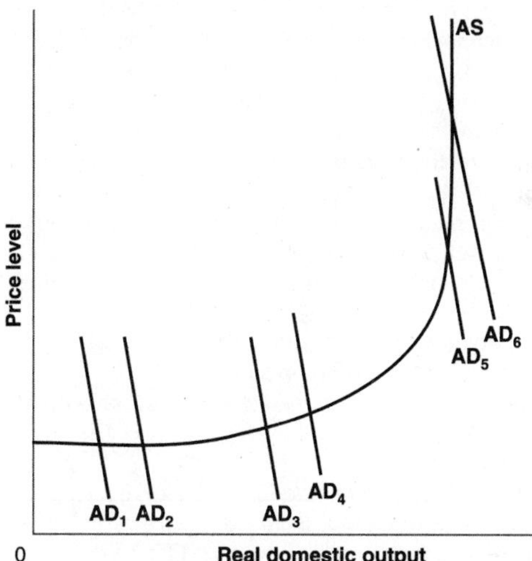

a. The movements of the aggregate demand curves from **AD_1** to **AD_2**, from **AD_3** to **AD_4**, and from **AD_5** to **AD_6** all portray (increases, decreases) __________ in aggregate demand.

(1) The movement from **AD_1** to **AD_2** increases the (real domestic output, price level) __________

but does not change the __________.

(2) The movement from **AD_3** to **AD_4** will (raise, lower)

__________ the price level and will (expand,

contract) __________ the real domestic output.

(3) The movement from **AD_5** to **AD_6** will __________

__________.

b. The movements of the aggregate demand curves to the left all portray (increases, decreases) __________ in aggregate demand.

(1) If prices are flexible in a downward direction, what effects will these changes in aggregate demand have upon the real domestic output and the price level?

____

____

(2) If prices are *not* flexible in a downward direction, what effects will these changes in aggregate demand

have? __________

____

7. The following diagram shows two aggregate supply curves and three aggregate demand curves.

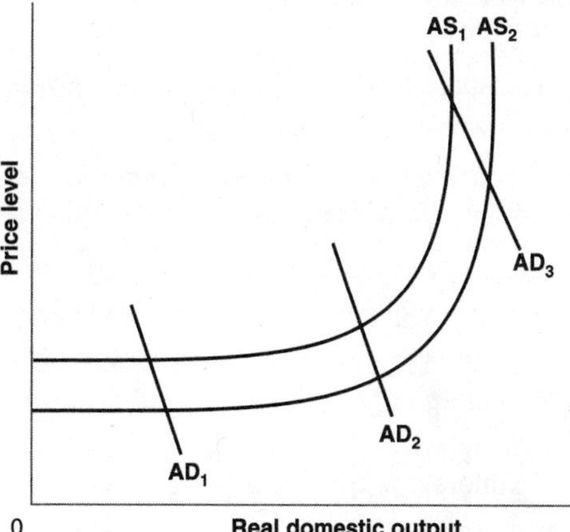

a. The movement of the aggregate supply curve from **AS_1** to **AS_2** represents a(n) (increase, decrease)

__________ in aggregate supply.

(1) If the price level is flexible downward and upward, this change in aggregate supply in each of the three ranges along the aggregate supply curve will (raise,

lower) __________ the price level and (expand,

contract) __________ the real domestic output.

(2) But if prices are inflexible in a downward direction, this change in aggregate supply will (increase, decrease)

__________ real domestic output but (will, will

not) __________ affect the price level.

b. The movement of aggregate supply from **AS_2** to **AS_1**

portrays a(n) __________ in aggregate supply

and in each of the three ranges will __________

the price level and __________ the real domestic output.

■ SHORT ANSWER AND ESSAY QUESTIONS

1. What is the aggregate demand curve? Draw a graph of one and explain its features.

2. Explain
(a) the interest-rate effect
(b) the wealth effect
(c) the foreign purchases effect of a change in the price level on the quantity of goods and services demanded in an economy

3. What roles do the expectations of consumers and businesses play in influencing aggregate demand?

4. Explain the difference between the wealth effect and "a change in the real value of consumer wealth" for the interpretation of aggregate demand.

5. What is the effect of an increase in aggregate expenditures on the aggregate demand curve? Explain in words and with a graph.

6. The aggregate supply curve is divided into three distinct ranges. Describe the slope of this curve in each of the three ranges. What conditions prevail in the economy in each of the ranges?

7. Why does the aggregate supply curve slope upward in the intermediate range?

8. How does an increase or decrease in per-unit production costs change aggregate supply? Give examples.

9. How does the legal and institutional environment affect the price level and real domestic output? Give examples.

10. Explain how a change in business taxes affects aggregate demand and aggregate supply.

11. Describe how changes in the international economy influence aggregate demand or aggregate supply.

12. What is the relationship between the production possibilities curve and aggregate supply?

13. What real domestic output is the equilibrium real domestic output? Why will business firms that produce the domestic output reduce or expand their production when they find themselves producing more or less than the equilibrium output?

14. What are the effects on the real domestic output and the price level when aggregate demand increases in each of the three ranges along the aggregate supply curve?

15. How are the three ranges of the aggregate supply curve, the price level, and the multiplier related? What is the relationship between the effect of an increase in aggregate demand on real GDP and the rise in the price level that accompanies it?

16. If prices were as flexible downward as they are upward, what would be the effects on real domestic output and the price level of a decrease in aggregate demand in each of the three ranges along the aggregate supply curve?

17. Prices in the economy tend to be "sticky" or inflexible in a downward direction. Why? Explain in terms of wages, prices, and costs.

18. What are the effects on the real domestic output and the price level of a decrease in aggregate supply? What are the effects of an increase in aggregate supply on the real domestic output, the price level, and the maximum real output the economy is able to produce?

19. Why is a decrease in aggregate supply "doubly bad" and an increase in aggregate supply "doubly good"?

20. Using the aggregate demand and aggregate supply concepts, explain the difference between demand-pull and cost-push inflation.

ANSWERS

Chapter 11 Aggregate Demand and Aggregate Supply

FILL-IN QUESTIONS

1. variable, fixed
2. output, price
3. demanded, downward, wealth, interest, foreign
4. decrease, increase
5. raise, rise, lower, fall, inverse, demand
6. movement along, aggregate demand
7. *a.* consumer wealth; *b.* consumer expectations; *c.* household indebtedness; *d.* personal taxes (any order)
8. *a.* interest rates; *b.* expected returns on investment; *c.* business taxes; *d.* technology; *e.* degree of excess capacity (any order)
9. spending, export
10. right, multiplier, left, downward, multiplier
11. supplied, is constant, increases, increases
12. increase, decrease
13. *a.* (1) domestic resource availability, (2) prices of imported resources, (3) market power (any order); *b.* productivity; *c.* (1) business taxes and subsidies, (2) government regulation (either order)
14. intersection, equal to, accept, pay
15. increasing, reduce, decreasing, expand
16. increase, have no effect on, increase, increase, have no effect on, increase
17. greater, smaller, smaller, greater
18. ratchet, short, efficiency, invested in, minimum, costs, price
19. increase, decrease, decrease, increase
20. increase, rise, decrease, fall

TRUE-FALSE QUESTIONS

1. T, p. 221
2. T, pp. 221-222
3. T, p. 222
4. F, pp. 222-223
5. F, p. 223
6. T, p. 223
7. F, p. 223
8. F, pp. 223-224
9. F, p. 226
10. F, p. 225
11. F, p. 225
12. F, p. 227
13. F, pp. 228-229
14. T, p. 229-230
15. T, p. 232
16. T, pp. 231-232
17. T, pp. 232
18. T, pp. 233-234
19. T, p. 234
20. F, p. 234
21. F, pp. 234-236
22. F, pp. 234-236
23. F, p. 236
24. T, p. 239
25. F, pp. 237-239

MULTIPLE-CHOICE QUESTIONS

1. a, pp. 221-222
2. b, pp. 222-223
3. d, pp. 222-223
4. c, p. 223
5. b, p. 223
6. d, pp. 226-227
7. c, pp. 224-225
8. b, p. 227
9. b, p. 227
10. a, p. 229
11. a, p. 232
12. a, p. 232
13. c, p. 232
14. d, p. 232
15. a, p. 231
16. b, p. 232
17. c, p. 232
18. a, p. 234
19. b, pp. 233-234
20. d, pp. 228-229
21. b, p. 234
22. c, pp. 234, 237-239
23. b, p. 234
24. c, p. 234
25. b, p. 234
26. c, pp. 234-236
27. d, p. 236
28. b, p. 236
29. b, pp. 237-239
30. c, pp. 237-239

PROBLEMS

1. *a.* (1) 0, 1,000, (2) 2,000, 225, (3) 1,000, 2,000; *c.* (1) 1,700, 175, (2) 2,000, 225, (3) 900, 125

2. *a.* 2,200; *b.* 2,400; *c.* 2,600; *d.* 2,200, 2,400, 2,600, (1) aggregate demand, (2) inversely

3. *a. S, D, I, D; b. I, S, I, I; c. D, S, D, D; d. I, I, U, I; e. D, I, D, U*

4. *a.* 5, 5, 5; *b.* 2.5, 2.5, 2.5; *c.* \$3, \$3, \$3; *d.* \$6, \$6, \$6, it will decrease; *e.* \$2, \$2, \$2, it will increase

5. *a.* (1) 2,390, 2.00, (2) 1,840, 1.00; *b.* 1,640, 1.00, 100, remain constant; *c.* 2,300, 1.80, 50, 1.90; *d.* 2,390, 2.20, 2.40, remain constant

6. *a.* increases, (1) real domestic output, price level, (2) raise, expand, (3) increase the price level but will not affect domestic output; *b.* decreases, (1) decrease the price level in the vertical and intermediate ranges and decrease domestic output in the intermediate and horizontal ranges, (2) decrease only output in the intermediate, vertical, and horizontal ranges

7. *a.* increase, (1) lower, expand, (2) increase, will not; *b.* decrease, increase, decrease

SHORT ANSWER AND ESSAY QUESTIONS

1. pp. 221-222
2. pp. 222-223
3. pp. 225-226
4. pp. 224-225
5. pp. 227-228
6. pp. 228-229
7. p. 229
8. pp. 230-231
9. p. 232
10. pp. 226, 232
11. pp. 226-227, 231
12. p. 239
13. pp. 233-234
14. p. 234
15. pp. 234-236
16. p. 236
17. pp. 236-237
18. pp. 237-239
19. pp. 237-239
20. pp. 234, 237

CHAPTER 12

Fiscal Policy

Principles of economics are generalizations about how the economy works. These principles are studied to help devise policies to solve real problems. Over the past 100 years or so, the most serious macroeconomic problems have been those resulting from the swings of the business cycle. Learning what determines the equilibrium level of real output and prices in an economy and what causes them to fluctuate makes it possible to find ways to achieve maximum output, full employment, and stable prices. In short, macroeconomic principles suggest policies to lessen both recession and inflation in an economy.

As you will discover in Chapter 12, government can use ***fiscal policy*** to influence the economy's output, employment, and price level. These policies involve the use of the Federal government's spending and taxing powers to improve economic conditions. The brief first section of this chapter explains how Congress, in the Employment Act of 1946, committed the Federal government to achieving three goals: economic growth, full employment, and stable prices. This act also established the Council of Economic Advisors (CEA) to advise the president and the Joint Economic Committee (JEC) to advise Congress on national economic policies.

The second section of the chapter discusses ***discretionary fiscal policy,*** which can be either ***expansionary*** or ***contractionary.*** Here you will learn how these fiscal policies affect aggregate demand and the Federal budget. Expansionary fiscal policy is used to stimulate the economy and pull it out of a slump or recession. This type of policy can be achieved by increasing government spending, decreasing taxes, or some combination of the two. Contractionary fiscal policy is enacted to counter inflationary pressure in the economy. The policy actions taken to dampen inflation include cutting government spending, raising taxes, or a combination of the two. As you will learn, each policy can have a significant effect on aggregate demand and the Federal budget. If the government has a budget deficit or surplus, the way the government finances it can affect the economy's operation as much as the size of the deficit or surplus.

Discretionary fiscal policy requires that Congress take action to change tax rates, transfer payment programs, or purchases of goods and services. *Non*discretionary fiscal policy does not require Congress to take any action and is a ***built-in stabilizer*** of the economy. You should be sure that you understand *why* net taxes increase when the GDP rises and decrease when the GDP falls and *how* this tends to stabilize the economy.

Unfortunately, nondiscretionary fiscal policy by itself may not be able to eliminate any recessionary or inflationary gap that might develop, and discretionary fiscal policy may be necessary if the economy is to produce its full-employment GDP and avoid inflation. The built-in stabilizers make it more difficult to use discretionary fiscal policy to achieve this goal because they create the illusion that the Federal government's policy is expansionary or contractionary when in fact its policy is just the opposite.

The illusions created by the built-in stabilizers have led economists to develop a ***full-employment budget*** and to distinguish between a ***cyclical deficit*** and a ***structural deficit.*** This analysis enables economists to determine whether Federal fiscal policy is expansionary or contractionary and to determine what policy should be enacted to improve the economy's economic performance.

Fiscal policy is not without its *problems, criticisms,* or *complications.* There are timing problems in getting it implemented, and there are political problems in getting it accepted. In addition, there are three major criticisms of or complications with fiscal policy. Some economists are concerned that expansionary fiscal policy, which requires the Federal government to borrow money, will raise interest rates and crowd out investment spending, thus reducing the expansionary effect of the fiscal policy. A second complication arises from the connection of the domestic economy to the world economy. Aggregate demand shocks from abroad or a net export effect may increase or decrease the effectiveness of a given fiscal policy. The third concern is whether an expansionary fiscal policy might actually increase the price level and have little effect on real output, especially if the economy is operating near its full-employment level of output.

Most of the discussion of fiscal policy focuses on its effects on aggregate demand. Some economists, however, argue that a reduction in tax rates will not only increase aggregate demand but also expand *aggregate supply.* In this way, fiscal policy can be used to increase real GDP with little or no rise in the price level.

By mastering this chapter on fiscal policy, you will gain an understanding of one of the two major policies used to influence outcomes from the economy. Mastery of this chapter will also prepare you for learning about monetary policy, a topic for Part 3 of the text.

■ CHECKLIST

When you have studied this chapter you should be able to

☐ State the responsibility imposed on the Federal government by the Employment Act of 1946 and the roles of the CEA and JEC in fulfilling this responsibility.
☐ Distinguish between discretionary and nondiscretionary fiscal policy.
☐ Explain expansionary fiscal policy and the effect of different policy options on aggregate demand.
☐ Describe contractionary fiscal policy and the effect of different policy options on aggregate demand.
☐ Explain how the expansionary effect of a budget deficit depends on the method used to finance it.
☐ Describe how the deflationary effect of a budget surplus depends on the method used to finance it.
☐ Assess whether it is preferable to use government spending or taxes to eliminate recession and inflation.
☐ Indicate how the built-in stabilizers help to eliminate recession and inflationary pressures.
☐ Describe the relationship among progressive, proportional, and regressive tax systems and the built-in stability of the economy.
☐ Distinguish between the actual budget and the full-employment budget.
☐ Define structural deficit and cyclical deficit and relate them to the full-employment budget.
☐ Make historical comparisons between the full-employment budget and actual budget since 1962.
☐ Evaluate the economic effects of a balanced-budget amendment.
☐ Outline three timing problems that may arise with fiscal policy.
☐ Discuss four political problems with fiscal policy.
☐ Explain and use a graph to illustrate the crowding-out effect of an expansionary fiscal policy.
☐ State the major criticisms of the crowding-out effect.
☐ Show with a graph how the effects of an expansionary fiscal policy differ across different ranges of the aggregate supply curve.
☐ Describe two ways that the effectiveness of fiscal policy changes from interdependency with the world economy.
☐ Explain how supply-side fiscal policy affects real GDP and the price level.

■ CHAPTER OUTLINE

1. Fiscal policy is the manipulation by the Federal government of its expenditures and tax receipts in order to expand or contract the economy; and by doing this manipulation, the Federal government either increases its real output (and employment) or decreases its rate of inflation.

2. The Employment Act of 1946 set the goals of fiscal policy in the United States and provided for a Council of Economic Advisers to the president and the Joint Economic Committee.

3. *Discretionary fiscal policy* involves changes in government spending or taxation by Congress which is designed to change the level of real GDP, employment, incomes, or the price level. Specific action needs to be taken by Congress to initiate this policy, in contrast to nondiscretionary fiscal policy that occurs automatically (see item 4 below).

a. *Expansionary fiscal policy* is generally used to counteract the negative economic effects of a recession or cyclical downturn in the economy (a decline in real GDP and rising unemployment). The purpose of the policy is to stimulate the economy by increasing aggregate demand. Three policy options are used: an **increase in government spending;** a **reduction in taxes** (which increases consumer spending); or a **combination** of an increase in government spending and a tax reduction. These policy actions will create a ***budget deficit*** if the budget were in balance before the policy actions were taken. The stimulative effect on the economy from the initial increase in spending from the policy change will be increased by the multiplier effect.

b. *Contractionary fiscal policy* is a restrictive form of fiscal policy generally used to control demand-pull inflation. The purpose of this policy is to reduce aggregate demand pressures that increase the price level. Three policy options are used: a **decrease in government spending;** an **increase in taxes** (which reduces consumer spending); or a **combination** of a reduction in government spending and a tax increase. If the government budget is balanced before the policy actions are taken, it will create a ***budget surplus.*** The contractionary effect on the economy from the initial reduction in spending from the policy actions will be reinforced by the multiplier effect.

c. In addition to the size of the deficit or surplus, the manner in which government finances its deficit or disposes of its surplus affects the level of total spending in the economy.

(1) To finance a deficit, the government can either borrow money from the public or issue new money to creditors, with the latter action being more expansionary.

(2) Budget surpluses may be used for debt reduction, or the funds may be impounded, with the latter action being more contractionary.

d. Whether government purchases or taxes should be altered to reduce recession and inflation depends to a large extent on whether an expansion or a contraction of the public sector is desired.

4. In the U.S. economy, net tax revenues (tax revenues minus government transfer payments) are not a fixed amount or lump sum; they increase as the GDP rises and decrease as the GDP falls.

a. This net tax system serves as a *built-in stabilizer* of the economy because it reduces purchasing power during periods of inflation and expands purchasing during periods of recession.

(1) As GDP increases, the average tax rates will increase in progressive systems, remain constant in proportional systems, and decrease in regressive systems;

there is more built-in stability for the economy in progressive tax systems.
(2) Built-in stabilizers can only reduce and cannot eliminate economic fluctuations.
b. The *full-employment budget* is a better index than the actual budget of the direction of government fiscal policy because it indicates what the Federal budget deficit or surplus would be if the economy were to operate at full employment. In the case of a budget deficit, the full employment budget
(1) removes the cyclical portion that is produced by swings in the business cycle, and
(2) reveals the size of the structural deficit, indicating how expansionary fiscal policy was that year.
(3) Historical comparisons between the actual budget and full-employment budget show which years the discretionary fiscal policy has been expansionary in recent decades.
c. The large annual deficit the United States has experienced since the 1980s has led to calls for a balanced-budget amendment. In its strict form, this amendment would eliminate the use of discretionary fiscal policy to counter recessions and would be contractionary at a time when expansionary fiscal policy is needed.

5. Certain *problems, criticisms,* and *complications* arise in enacting and applying fiscal policy.
a. There will be problems of timing because it requires time to recognize the need for fiscal policy, to take the appropriate steps in the Congress, and for the action taken there to affect output, employment, and the rate of inflation in the economy.
b. There will also be political problems because
(1) the economy has goals other than full employment and stable prices,
(2) the fiscal policies of state and local government run counter to Federal fiscal policy,
(3) there is an expansionary bias (for budget deficits and against surpluses),
(4) there may be a political business cycle (if politicians lower taxes and increase expenditures before and then do the opposite after elections).
c. An expansionary fiscal policy may, by raising the level of interest rates in the economy, reduce (or crowd out) investment spending and weaken the effect of the policy on real GDP; but this crowding-out effect may be small and can be offset by an expansion in the nation's money supply.
d. The effect of an expansionary fiscal policy on the real GDP will also be weakened to the extent that it results in a rise in the price level (inflation). Aggregate demand and aggregate supply curves can be used to show how crowding out and inflation weaken the effects of an expansionary fiscal policy on real GDP.
e. The connection of the domestic economy to a world economy means that fiscal policy may be inappropriate or less effective because of aggregate demand shocks from the world economy or a net export effect that counteracts or reinforces domestic fiscal policy.
f. But an expansionary fiscal policy that includes a reduction in taxes (tax rates) may, by increasing aggregate supply in the economy, expand real GDP (and employment), and reduce inflation. Many economists, however, are skeptical about these supply-side effects.

■ HINTS AND TIPS

1. Fiscal policy is a broad concept that covers various taxation and spending policies of the Federal government; it is not limited to one policy. You will need to know the distinctions between the several kinds of fiscal policies. The main difference is between discretionary and nondiscretionary fiscal policy. *Discretionary* fiscal policy is *active* and means that Congress took specific actions to change taxes or government spending to influence the economy. It can also be *expansionary* or *contractionary. Nondiscretionary* fiscal policy is *passive,* or automatic, because changes in taxes or government spending will occur without specific action by Congress.

2. An increase in government spending that is equal to a cut in taxes will not have an equal effect on real GDP. To understand this point, assume that the MPC is .75, the increase in government spending is $8 billion, and the decrease in taxes is $8 billion. The multiplier would be 4 because it equals 1/(1 − .75). The increase in government spending will increase real GDP by $32 billion ($8 billion × 4). Of the $8 billion decrease in taxes, however, one-quarter of it will be saved ($6 billion × .25 = $2 billion) and just three-quarters will be spent ($8 billion × .75 = $6 billion). Thus, the tax cut results in an increase in *initial* spending in the economy of $6 billion, not $8 billion as was the case with the increase in government spending. The tax cut effect on real GDP is $24 billion ($6 × 4), not $32 billion.

3. A large part of the chapter deals with six problems (or criticisms and complications) of fiscal policy. Do not miss the big picture and get lost in the details of each one. The six include (a) timing, (b) politics, (c) crowding out, (d) inflation reducing the multiplier effect, (e) net export effect offsetting fiscal policy, and (f) supply-side effect offsetting or reinforcing demand-side effects.

■ IMPORTANT TERMS

fiscal policy
Employment Act of 1946
Council of Economic Advisers
discretionary fiscal policy
expansionary fiscal policy
budget deficit
contractionary fiscal policy
budget surplus
built-in stabilizers
progressive tax
proportional tax
regressive tax
actual budget
full-employment budget
cyclical deficit
structural deficit
political business cycle
crowding-out effect
net export effect
supply-side fiscal policy

SELF-TEST

■ FILL-IN QUESTIONS

1. The use of monetary and fiscal policy to reduce inflation and recession became national economic policy in the (Employment, Unemployment) ______________ Act of 1946. To assist and advise the president, the act established the (Joint Economic Committee, Council of Economic Advisers) ______________, and to aid Congress in investigating economic matters, the act established the ______________.

2. Policy actions taken by Congress designed to change government spending or taxation are (discretionary, nondiscretionary) ______________ fiscal policy, but when the policy takes effect automatically or independent of Congress, then it is ______________ fiscal policy.

3. Expansionary fiscal policy is generally designed to (increase, decrease) ______________ aggregate demand and thus ______________ real GDP and employment in the economy. Contractionary fiscal policy is generally used to (increase, decrease) ______________ aggregate demand and ______________ the level of prices.

4. Expansionary fiscal policy can be achieved with an increase in (government spending, taxes) ______________, a decrease in ______________, or a combination of the two; contractionary fiscal policy can be achieved by a decrease in (government spending, taxes) ______________, an increase in ______________, or a combination of the two.

5. An increase of government spending of $5 billion from an expansionary fiscal policy for an economy ultimately produces an increase in real GDP of $20 billion. This magnified effect occurs because of the (multiplier, crowding-out) ______________ effect, which has a size of (4, 5) _____ for this economy.

6. If the Federal budget is balanced and Congress passes legislation supporting an expansionary fiscal policy, then this action is likely to produce a budget (deficit, surplus) ______________, but if Congress passes legislation supporting a contractionary fiscal policy, then the action will result in a budget ______________.

7. If fiscal policy is to have a countercyclical effect, it probably will be necessary for the Federal government to incur a budget (surplus, deficit) ______________ during a recession and a budget ______________ during inflation.

8. Of the two principal means available to the Federal government for financing budget deficits, the one that is more expansionary is (borrowing money from the public, creating new money) ______________.
Of the two principal means available to the Federal government for using funds from a budget surplus, the one that is more contractionary is (impounding funds, debt reduction) ______________.

9. Net taxes equal taxes (plus, minus) ______________ transfer payments and are called "taxes" in this chapter. In the United States, as GDP increases, tax revenue will (increase, decrease) ______________, and as the GDP decreases, tax revenues will ______________.

10. Because tax revenues are (directly, indirectly) ______________ related to the GDP, the economy has some (artificial, built-in) ______________ stability. If the GDP increases, then tax revenue will increase, and the budget surplus will (increase, decrease) ______________, thus (stimulating, restraining) ______________ the economy when it is needed. When GDP decreases, tax revenues decrease, and the budget deficit (increases, decreases) ______________, thus (stimulating, restraining) ______________ the economy when it is needed.

11. As GDP increases, the average tax rates will increase with a (progressive, proportional, regressive) ______________ tax, remain constant with a ______________ tax, and decrease with a ______________ tax. With a progressive tax, there is (more, less) ______________ built-in stability for the economy.

12. If there is a deficit in the full-employment budget, then fiscal policy is (contractionary, expansionary) ______________. A deficit produced by swings in the business cycle is (structural, cyclical) ______________, whereas a deficit produced through government taxation and spending decisions is ______________. The full-employment budget deficit is also called the (cyclical, structural) ______________ deficit.

13. If government has a balanced-budget requirement and the economy moves into recession, then the government must either (increase, decrease) ______________ taxes, ______________ government spending, or some combination of the two. These actions would (improve, worsen) ______________ economic conditions in the economy.

14. There is a problem of timing in the use of discretionary fiscal policy because of the time between the beginning of a recession or inflation and awareness of it, or a(n) (administrative, operational, recognition) ______________ lag; the time needed for Congress to adjust fiscal policy, or a _______________ lag; and the time needed for fiscal policy to take effect, or an _______________ lag.

15. Political problems arise in the application of discretionary fiscal policy to stabilize the economy because government has (one, several) _______________ economic goals, state and local fiscal policies may (reinforce, counter) _______________ Federal fiscal policy, voters have a bias in favor of budget (surpluses, deficits) _______________, and politicians may use fiscal policies in a way that creates a(n) (international, political) _______________ business cycle.

16. When the Federal government employs an expansionary fiscal policy to increase real GDP and employment in the economy, it usually has a budget (surplus, deficit) _______________ and (lends, borrows) _______________ in the money market. These actions will (raise, lower) _______________ interest rates in the economy and (contract, expand) _______________ investment spending. This change in investment spending is the (net export, crowding-out) _______________ effect of the expansionary fiscal policy, and it tends to (weaken, strengthen) _______________ the influence of the expansionary fiscal policy on real GDP and employment.

17. An expansionary fiscal policy when the economy is operating in the intermediate range of the aggregate supply curve will increase the real GDP and employment in the economy and (raise, lower) _______________ the price level. This change in the price level will (weaken, strengthen) _______________ the impact of the expansionary fiscal policy on output and employment in the economy.

18. Fiscal policy is subject to further complications from (independence from, interdependency with) _______________ the world economy. For example, the domestic economy can be influenced by aggregate demand (inflation, shocks) _______________ from abroad that alter GDP and might reinforce or offset fiscal policy.

19. International trade can also produce a (crowding-out, net export) _______________ effect that influences aggregate demand and partially offsets fiscal policy.

a. When fiscal policy is expansionary, it tends to (increase, decrease) _______________ interest rates, which in turn tends to _______________ the value of the dollar, (increase, decrease) _______________ net exports, and _______________ aggregate demand.

b. When fiscal policy is contractionary, it tends to (increase, decrease) _______________ interest rates, which in turn tends to _______________ the value of the dollar, (increase, decrease) _______________ net exports, and _______________ aggregate demand.

20. If an expansionary fiscal policy is the result of reduction in taxes, the supply-side effects of the policy may be to (increase, decrease) _______________ aggregate supply, to _______________ productivity capacity of the economy, to (increase, decrease) _______________ real GDP and employment, to _______________ the rate of inflation, and to (weaken, strengthen) _______________ the impact of the fiscal policy on output and employment.

■ TRUE-FALSE QUESTIONS

Circle the T if the statement is true, the F if it is false.

1. The Council of Economic Advisers was established to give economic advice to Congress. **T F**

2. Discretionary fiscal policy is independent of Congress and left to the discretion of state and local governments. **T F**

3. Expansionary fiscal policy during a recession or depression will create a budget deficit or add to an existing budget deficit. **T F**

4. A decrease in taxes is one of the options that can be used to pursue a contractionary fiscal policy. **T F**

5. To increase initial consumption by a specific amount, government must reduce taxes by more than that amount because some of the tax cut will be saved by households. **T F**

6. A full-employment budget deficit is contractionary. **T F**

7. A reduction in taxes and an increase in government spending during a recession would tend to contract the public sector of the economy. **T F**

8. Built-in stabilizers are not sufficiently strong to prevent recession or inflation, but they can reduce the severity of a recession or inflation. **T F**

9. The less progressive the tax system, the greater the economy's built-in stability. **T F**

10. The full-employment budget indicates how much government must spend and tax if there is to be full employment in the economy. **T F**

11. A cyclical deficit is the result of countercyclical actions by government to stimulate the economy. **T F**

12. If an economy achieved a full-employment level of output but tax revenues were less than government expenditures, then a structural deficit is created. **T F**

13. The key to assessing discretionary fiscal policy is to disregard the actual budget deficit and instead observe the change in the full-employment budget. **T F**

14. A balanced-budget requirement will use fiscal policy to lessen the effects of recession and stabilize the economy. **T F**

15. Recognition, administrative, and operational lags in the timing of Federal fiscal policy make fiscal policies more effective in reducing the rate of inflation and decreasing unemployment in the economy. **T F**

16. State and local governments' fiscal policies have tended to assist and reinforce the efforts of the Federal government to counter recession and inflation. **T F**

17. The Federal government spending and taxing policies are designed solely to reduce unemployment and limit inflation in the economy. **T F**

18. It is generally easier to induce U.S. senators and representatives to vote for decreases in tax rates and for increases in government purchases than for increased taxes and decreased purchases. **T F**

19. Economists who see evidence of a political business cycle argue that members of Congress tend to increase taxes and reduce expenditures before and to reduce taxes and increase expenditures after elections. **T F**

20. The crowding-out effect occurs when an expansionary fiscal policy decreases the interest rate, increases investment spending, and strengthens fiscal policy. **T F**

21. Critics contend that the crowding-out effect will be greatest when the economy is in a recession. **T F**

22. With an upsloping aggregate supply curve, some portion of the potential effect of an expansionary fiscal policy on real GDP may be lost because of an increase in the price level. **T F**

23. For a domestic economy, there are gains for specialization and trade but also complications from the interdependency with the world economy. **T F**

24. A net export effect may partially offset an expansionary fiscal policy. **T F**

25. Supply-side economists maintain that reduction in tax rates decrease aggregate supply and are, therefore, inflationary. **T F**

■ MULTIPLE-CHOICE QUESTIONS

Circle the letter that corresponds to the best answer.

1. Which of the following was instrumental in assigning to the Federal government the basic responsibility for promoting economic stability in the U.S. economy?
- **(a)** the Employment Act of 1946
- **(b)** the Tax Reform Act of 1986
- **(c)** the Ricardian equivalence theorem
- **(d)** the balanced-budget multiplier

2. If the government wishes to increase the level of real GDP, it might reduce
- **(a)** taxes
- **(b)** its purchases of goods and services
- **(c)** transfer payments
- **(d)** the size of the budget deficit

3. If Congress passes legislation to make a substantial increase in government spending to counter the effects of severe recession, this would be an example of a
- **(a)** supply-side fiscal policy
- **(b)** contractionary fiscal policy
- **(c)** discretionary fiscal policy
- **(d)** nondiscretionary fiscal policy

4. Which combination of policies would be the most expansionary?
- **(a)** an increase in government spending and taxes
- **(b)** a decrease in government spending and taxes
- **(c)** an increase in government spending and a decrease in taxes
- **(d)** a decrease in government spending and an increase in taxes

5. An economy is in a recession and the government decides to increase spending by $4 billion. The MPC is .8. What would be the full increase in real GDP from the change in government spending assuming the increase would be in the horizontal range of the aggregate supply curve?
- **(a)** $3.2 billion
- **(b)** $4 billion
- **(c)** $16 billion
- **(d)** $20 billion

6. Which combination of fiscal policies would be the most contractionary?
- **(a)** an increase in government spending and taxes
- **(b)** a decrease in government spending and taxes
- **(c)** an increase in government spending and a decrease in taxes
- **(d)** a decrease in government spending and an increase in taxes

7. Which is a more expansionary way for government to finance a budget deficit?
- **(a)** borrowing money in the money market
- **(b)** decreasing government spending
- **(c)** creating new money
- **(d)** increasing taxes

8. Which would be the most contractionary use of funds from a budget surplus?
- **(a)** cutting tax rates
- **(b)** impounding the funds
- **(c)** using the funds to retire outstanding government debt
- **(d)** increasing government spending on social programs

9. When government tax revenues change automatically and in a countercyclical direction over the course of the business cycle, this is an example of
- **(a)** the political business cycle
- **(b)** nondiscretionary fiscal policy
- **(c)** the full-employment budget
- **(d)** crowding out

10 If the economy is to have built-in stability, when real GDP falls,

(a) tax revenues and government transfer payments both should fall
(b) tax revenues and government transfer payments both should rise
(c) tax revenues should fall and government transfer payments should rise
(d) tax revenues should rise and government transfer payments should fall

Answer Questions 11, 12, and 13 on the basis of the following diagram.

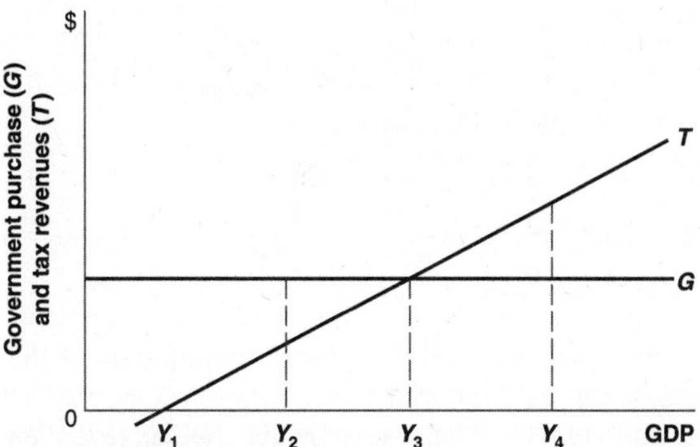

11. If the slope of the line *T* were steeper, there would be
(a) more built-in stability for the economy
(b) less built-in stability for the economy
(c) no change in the built-in stability for the economy
(d) the need for more emphasis on discretionary fiscal policy

12. If the slope of the line *T* were flatter, there would be
(a) larger cyclical deficits produced as GDP moved from Y_3 to Y_2
(b) smaller cyclical deficits produced as GDP moved from Y_3 to Y_2
(c) larger structural deficits produced as GDP moved from Y_3 to Y_2
(d) smaller structural deficits produced as GDP moved from Y_3 to Y_2

13. Actions by the Federal government to raise marginal tax rates would tend to
(a) flatten the slope of line *T* and increase built-in stability
(b) flatten the slope of line *T* and decrease built-in stability
(c) steepen the slope of line *T* and increase built-in stability
(d) steepen the slope of line *T* and decrease built-in stability

14. With a proportional tax system, as the level of income increases in an economy, the average tax rate will
(a) increase
(b) decrease
(c) remain the same
(d) either increase or decrease

15. In any given year, the full-employment deficit is equal to the
(a) structural deficit
(b) cyclical deficit
(c) actual deficit
(d) zero-employment budget

16. If the full-employment budget shows a deficit of about $200 billion and the actual budget shows a deficit of about $250 billion over a several-year period, it can be conducted that there is
(a) a structural deficit but not a cyclical deficit
(b) a cyclical deficit but not a structural deficit
(c) neither a cyclical nor structural deficit
(d) both a cyclical and structural defict

17. When the actual budget deficit is greater than the full-employment deficit, it can be concluded that
(a) discretionary fiscal policy is contractionary
(b) the economy is at less than full employment
(c) the tax system for the economy is regressive
(d) the structural deficit has increased

18. A balanced-budget amendment that required the Federal government to balance its budget each year would be
(a) expansionary at a time when fiscal policy should be contractionary
(b) contractionary at a time when fiscal policy should be expansionary
(c) expansionary at a time when fiscal policy should be expansionary
(d) contractionary at a time when fiscal policy should be contractionary

19. The length of time involved for the fiscal action taken by Congress to affect output, employment, or the price level is referred to as the
(a) administrative lag
(b) operational lag
(c) recognition lag
(d) fiscal lag

20. The crowding-out effect of an expansionary (deficit) fiscal policy is the result of government borrowing in the money market which
(a) increases interest rates and net investment spending in the economy
(b) increases interest rates and decreases net investment spending
(c) decreases interest rates and increases net investment spending
(d) decreases interest rates and net investment spending

21. The effect of an expansionary fiscal policy on the real GDP of an economy operating in the horizontal range of the aggregate supply curve is partially or fully
(a) reinforced by the crowding-out effect
(b) offset by the crowding-out effect
(c) reinforced by raising rax rates
(d) offset by lowering tax rates

22. The effect of an expansionary fiscal policy on the real GDP of an economy operating in the upsloping portion of the aggregate supply curve is
(a) increased by the net export effect
(b) decreased by the creation of new money

(c) increased by the crowding-out effect
(d) decreased by a rise in the price level

23. Suppose the United States pursued an expansionary fiscal policy to stimulate its economy and eliminate a recession. The net export effect suggests that net exports would
(a) decrease, thus decreasing aggregate demand and partially offsetting the fiscal policy
(b) decrease, thus increasing aggregate demand and partially offsetting the fiscal policy
(c) increase, thus decreasing aggregate demand and partially offsetting fiscal policy
(d) increase, thus increasing aggregate demand and partially reinforcing the fiscal policy

24. Suppose the United States pursued a contractionary fiscal policy to reduce the level of inflation. The net export effect suggests that net exports would
(a) decrease, thus decreasing aggregate demand and partially reinforcing the fiscal policy
(b) decrease, thus increasing aggregate demand and partially offsetting the fiscal policy
(c) increase, thus decreasing aggregate demand and partially reinforcing the fiscal policy
(d) increase, thus increasing aggregate demand and partially offsetting the fiscal policy

25. Supply-side fiscal policy is generally enacted through
(a) a decrease in tax rates
(b) a decrease in investment spending
(c) an increase in government spending
(d) an increase in automatic stabilizers

■ PROBLEMS

1. Columns 1 and 2 in the following table are the aggregate supply schedule, and columns 1 and 3 are the aggregate demand schedule.

(1) Price level	(2) Real GDP_1	(3) AD_1	(4) AD_2	(5) Real GDP_2
220	2,390	2,100	2,200	2,490
200	2,390	2,200	2,340	2,490
190	2,350	2,250	2,350	2,450
180	2,300	2,300	2,400	2,400
160	2,200	2,400	2,500	2,300

a. The equilibrium real GDP is $____________ and the price level is ____________.
b. Suppose that an expansionary fiscal policy increases aggregate demand from that shown in columns 1 and 3 to that shown in columns 1 and 4.
(1) If the price level remained constant, the equilibrium real GDP would increase to $____________.
(2) But the increase in aggregate demand does raise the price level to ____________, and this rise in the price level results in real GDP increasing to only $____________.
c. If the expansionary fiscal policy that increased aggregate demand also has supply-side effects and increased aggregate supply from that shown in columns 1 and 2 to that shown in columns 1 and 5,
(1) the equilibrium real GDP would increase to $____________.
(2) the price level would ____________.

2. The following table shows seven real GDPs and the net tax revenues of government at each real GDP.

Real GDP	Net tax revenues	Government purchases	Government deficit/surplus
$ 850	$170	$____	$____
900	180	____	____
950	190	____	____
1,000	200	____	____
1,050	210	____	____
1,100	220	____	____
1,150	230	____	____

a. Looking at the two columns on the left side of the table, it can be seen that
(1) when real GDP increases by $50, net tax revenues (increase, decrease) ____________ by $____________.
(2) when real GDP decreases by $100, net tax revenues (increase, decrease) ____________ by $____________.
(3) the relationship between real GDP and net tax revenues is (direct, inverse) ____________.
b. Assume the simple multiplier has a value of 10 and that investment spending in the economy decreases by $10.
(1) *If* net tax revenues remained constant, the equilibrium real GDP would decrease by $____________.
(2) But when real GDP decreases, net tax revenues also decrease; and this decrease in net tax revenues will tend to (increase, decrease) ____________ the equilibrium real GDP.
(3) And, therefore, the decrease in real GDP brought about by the $10 decrease in investment spending will be (more, less) ____________ than $100.
(4) The direct relationship between net tax revenues and real GDP has (lessened, expanded) ____________ the impact of the $10 decrease in investment spending on real GDP.
c. Suppose the simple multiplier is also 10 and government wishes to increase the equilibrium real GDP by $50.
(1) *If* net tax revenues remained constant, government would have to increase its purchases of goods and services by $____________.
(2) But when real GDP rises, net tax revenues also rise, and this rise in net tax revenues will tend to (increase, decrease) ____________ the equilibrium real GDP.

(3) The effect, therefore, of the $5 increase in government purchases will also be to increase the equilibrium real GDP by (more, less) ______ than $50.
(4) The direct relationship between net tax revenues and real GDP has (lessened, expanded) ______ the effect of the $5 increase in government purchases, and to raise the equilibrium real GDP by $50, the government will have to increase its purchases by (more, less) ______ than $5.

d. Imagine that the full-employment real GDP of the economy is $1150 and that government purchases of goods and services are $200.
(1) Complete the table on the previous page by entering the government purchases and computing the budget deficit or surplus at each of the real GDPs. (Show a government deficit by placing a minus sign in front of the amount by which expenditures exceed net tax revenues.)
(2) The full-employment surplus equals $______.
(3) Were the economy in a recession and producing a real GDP of $900, the budget would show a (surplus, deficit) ______ of $______.
(4) This budget deficit or surplus makes it appear that government is pursuing a(n) (expansionary, contractionary) ______ fiscal policy, but this deficit or surplus is not the result of countercyclical fiscal policy but the result of the ______.
(5) If government did not change its net tax *rates,* it could increase the equilibrium real GDP from $900 to the full-employment real GDP of $1150 by increasing its purchases by (approximately) $70. At the full-employment real GDP the budget would show a (surplus, deficit) ______ of $______.
(6) If government did not change its purchases, it would increase the equilibrium real GDP from $900 to the full-employment real GDP of $1150 by decreasing net tax revenues at all real GDPs by a lump sum of (approximately) $80. The full-employment budget would have a (surplus, deficit) ______ of $______.

3. a. Complete the table below by computing the average tax rates, given the net tax revenue data in columns 2, 4, and 6. Calculate the average tax rate in percentage to one decimal place (for example, 5.4%).

b. As real GDP increases in column 1, the average tax rate (increases, decreases, remains the same) ______ in column 3, ______ in column 5, and ______ in column 7. The tax system is (progressive, proportional, regressive) ______ in column 2, ______ in column 4, and ______ in column (6).

c. On the graph below, plot the real GDP, net tax revenue, and government spending data given in columns 1, 2, 4, 6, and 8.

(1) Real GDP	(2) Net tax revenue	(3) Average tax rate	(4) Net tax revenue	(5) Average tax rate	(6) Net tax revenue	(7) Average tax rate	(8) Government spending
$1,000	$100	____%	$100	____%	$100	____%	$120
$1,100	$120	____	$110	____	$108	____	$120
$1,200	$145	____	$120	____	$115	____	$120
$1,300	$175	____	$130	____	$120	____	$120
$1,400	$210	____	$140	____	$123	____	$120

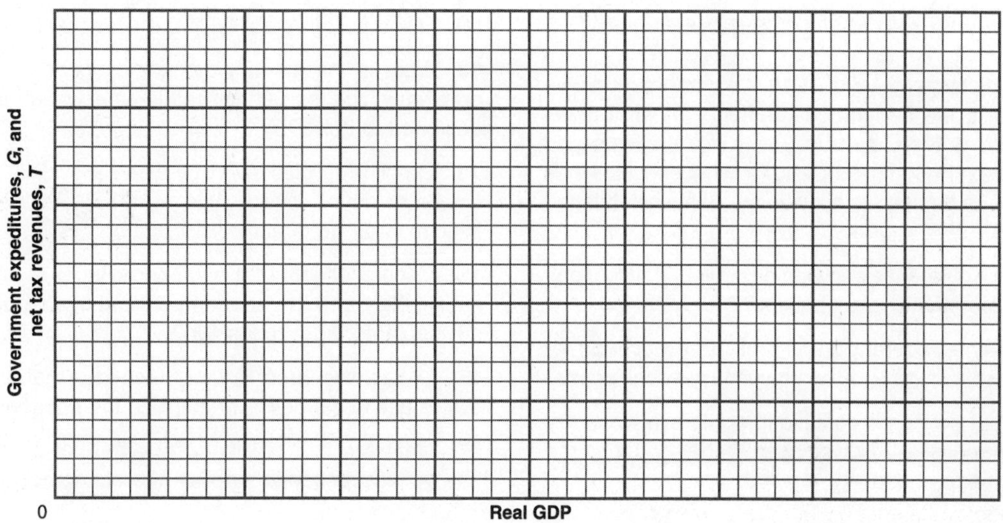

(1) Year	(2) Actual budget surplus (+) or deficit (−)	(3) Full-employment budget surplus (+) or deficit (−)	(4) Direction of fiscal policy
1	−$10 billion	+$10 billion	________
2	+$10 billion	−$20 billion	________
3	−$20 billion	+$0 billion	________
4	−$120 billion	−$120 billion	________
5	−$150 billion	−$130 billion	________

Tax revenue system with the steepest slope is found in column ________, and it is (progressive, proportional, regressive) ________ while the one with the flat test slope is found in column ________, and it is ________.

4. a. Complete the table above by stating whether the direction of discretionary fiscal policy was contractionary, expansionary, or had no effect, given the hypothetical budget data for an economy.

b. The best gauge of the direction of fiscal policy is the (actual, full-employment) ________ budget deficit or surplus because it removes the (cyclical, structural) ________ component from the discussion of the budget situation.

c. (1) In what years were there cyclical deficits, and what was the amount of the cyclical deficit in each of those years? ________________

____

(2) In what years were there cyclical deficits, and what was the size of the cyclical deficits in each of those years? ________________

____

■ SHORT ANSWER AND ESSAY QUESTIONS

1. In the Employment Act of 1946, (*a*) what responsibility was given to the Federal government, (*b*) what tasks were assigned to the Council of Economic Advisers and the Joint Economic Committee, and (*c*) what specific kinds of policy were to be used to achieve the goals established by the act?

2. What is the difference between discretionary fiscal policy and nondiscretionary fiscal policy?

3. What are the Federal government's three options for conducting expansionary or contractionary fiscal policy?

4. Under what economic conditions would expansionary or contractionary fiscal policy be used? What would be the effect on the Federal budget?

5. Compare and contrast the effect of expansionary and contractionary fiscal policy on aggregate demand. Draw a graph to illustrate the likely effects.

6. What is the effect of the simple multiplier on the initial change in spending from fiscal policy? When the government wants to increase initial consumption by a specific amount, why must the government reduce taxes by more than that amount?

7. In the real world, is the purpose of fiscal policy to restore a previously lower price level? How do "sticky" prices affect events?

8. What are the alternative means of financing deficits and disposing of surpluses available to the Federal government? What is the difference between these methods insofar as their expansionary and contractionary effect is concerned?

9. Explain the fiscal policy that would be advocated during a recession and during a period of inflation by those who (*a*) wish to expand the public sector and (*b*) wish to contract the public sector.

10. What is a built-in stabilizer? How do the built-in stabilizers work to reduce rises and falls in the level of nominal GDP?

11. What is the economic importance of the direct relationship between tax receipts and GDP?

12. Supply a definition of a progressive, proportional, and regressive tax. What are the implications of each type of tax for the built-in stability of the economy?

13. What is the full-employment budget? What was the problem which the use of the full-employment budget was designed to solve?

14. Explain the distinction between a cyclical deficit and structural deficit. Which type of deficit provides the best indication of the direction of fiscal policy? Why?

15. Discuss effects of a balanced-budget requirement on fiscal policy and the economy. Would this requirement be advisable during a recession?

16. Explain the three kinds of time lags that make it difficult to use fiscal policy to stabilize the economy.

17. What are four political problems that complicate the use of fiscal policy to stabilize the economy?

18. How do (*a*) crowding out and (*b*) inflation reduce the effect of an expansionary (deficit) fiscal policy on real GDP and employment?

19. What complications for fiscal policy arise from interdependency with the world economy? Explain how aggregate demand shocks from abroad and the net export effect influence fiscal policy.

20. What might be the supply-side effects of a reduction in tax rates on the capacity output of the economy, the equilibrium levels of real GDP and employment, and the price level?

ANSWERS

Chapter 12 Fiscal Policy

FILL-IN QUESTIONS

1. Employment, Council of Economic Advisers, Joint Economic Committee
2. discretionary, nondiscretionary
3. increase, increase, decrease, decrease
4. government spending, taxes, government spending, taxes
5. multiplier, 4
6. deficit, surplus
7. deficit, surplus
8. creating new money, impounding funds
9. minus, increase, decrease
10. directly, built-in, increase, restraining, increases, stimulating
11. progressive, proportional, regressive, more
12. expansionary, cyclical, structural, structural
13. increase, decrease, worsen
14. recognition, administrative, operational
15. several, counter, deficits, political
16. deficit, borrows, raise, contract, crowding-out, weaken
17. raise, weaken
18. interdependency with, shocks
19. net export *a.* increase, increase, decrease, decrease; *b.* decrease, decrease, increase, increase
20. increase, increase, increase, decrease, strengthen

TRUE-FALSE QUESTIONS

1. F, p. 244
2. F, p. 244
3. T, p. 244
4. F, p. 245
5. T, p. 245
6. F, pp. 250-251
7. F, pp. 245-246
8. T, p. 249
9. F, p. 249
10. F, p. 250
11. F, p. 250
12. T, p. 250
13. T, p. 250
14. F, p. 251-252
15. F, p. 253
16. F, p. 253
17. F, pp. 253
18. T, pp. 253-254
19. F, p. 254
20. F, p. 254
21. F, p. 255
22. T, pp. 255-256
23. T, p. 256
24. T, p. 256
25. F, pp. 257-258

MULTIPLE-CHOICE QUESTIONS

1. a, pp. 243-244
2. a, p. 245
3. c, p. 244
4. c, pp. 244-246
5. d, pp. 244-245
6. d, pp. 246-247
7. c, p. 247
8. b, p. 247
9. b, p. 248
10. c, pp. 248-249
11. a, p. 249
12. b, pp. 249-250
13. c, p. 249
14. c, p. 249
15. a, p. 250
16. d, pp. 249-250
17. b, pp. 249-250
18. b, p. 252
19. b, p. 253
20. b, p. 254
21. b, pp. 254-255
22. d, pp. 255-256
23. a, pp. 256-257
24. d, pp. 256-257
25. a, pp. 257-258

PROBLEMS

1. *a.* 2,300, 180; *b.* (1) 2,400, (2) 190, 2,350; *c.* (1) 2,400, (2) remain constant
2. *a.* (1) increase, $10, (2) decrease, $20, (3) direct; *b.* (1) $100, (2) increase, (3) less, (4) lessened; *c.* (1) $5, (2) decrease, (3) less, (4) lessened, more; *d.* (1) government expenditures are $200 at all GDPs, government surplus or deficit: −30, −20, −10, 0, 10, 20, 30, (2) $30, (3) deficit, $20, (4) expansionary, recession, (5) deficit, $40, (6) deficit, $50
3. *a.* column 3: 10.0, 10.9, 12.1, 13.5, 15.0; column 5: 10.0 at each GDP level; column 7: 10.0, 9.8, 9.6, 9.2, 8.8; *b.* increases, remains the same, decrease; progressive, proportional, regressive; *c.* 2, progressive, 6, regressive
4. *a.* contractionary, expansionary, no effect, expansionary, expansionary; *b.* full-employment, cyclical; *c.* (1) year 1 ($20 billion), year 3 ($20 billion), year 5 ($20 billion), (2) year 2 ($20 billion), year 4 ($120 billion), year 5 ($130 billion)

SHORT ANSWER AND ESSAY QUESTIONS

1. pp. 243-244
2. pp. 244, 248
3. pp. 244-247
4. pp. 244-247
5. pp. 244-247
6. pp. 244-245
7. p. 246
8. p. 247
9. pp. 247-248
10. pp. 248-249
11. p. 248
12. p. 249
13. pp. 249-250
14. pp. 249-250
15. pp. 251-252
16. p. 253
17. pp. 253-254
18. pp. 254-256
19. p. 256
20. pp. 257-258

CHAPTER 13

Money and Banking

Chapter 13 explains how the financial system affects the operation of the economy. The chapter is largely descriptive and factual. Pay particular attention to the following: (1) what money is and the functions it performs, what types of money exist in the U.S. economy and their relative importance, and how the three measures of the money supply (***M***1, ***M***2, and ***M***3) are defined; (2) what gives value to or backs U.S. money; (3) why people want to have money in their possession and what determines how much money they want to have on hand at any time; (4) how the total demand for money and the money supply together determine the equilibrium rate of interest; and (5) the principal institutions of the U.S. financial system and their functions.

Several points are worth repeating here because so much depends on your full understanding of them. First, money is whatever performs the three functions of money, and in the United States money consists largely of the debts (promises to pay) of the Federal Reserve Banks and depository institutions. In the United States, this money is backed by the goods and services for which its owners can exchange it and not by gold.

Second, the total **demand for money** is made up of a ***transactions demand for money*** and an ***asset demand for money.*** Because money is used as a medium of exchange, consumers and business firms wish to have money on hand to use for transaction purposes. The quantity of money they demand for this purpose is directly related to the size of the economy's nominal (or money) gross domestic product. This means that when either the price level or the real gross domestic product increases, they will want to have more money on hand to use for transactions.

Money is also used as a store of value. Consumers and firms who own assets may choose to have some of their assets in the form of money (rather than in stocks, bonds, goods, or property). There is, therefore, also an asset demand for money. Holding money, however, imposes a cost on those who hold it. This cost is the interest they lose when they own money rather than, as an example, bonds. This means that people will demand less money for asset purposes when the rate of interest (the cost of holding money) is high and more when the rate of interest is low: the quantity of money demanded for this purpose is inversely related to the interest rate.

The total demand for money is the sum of the transactions demand and the asset demand, and therefore, it is affected by both nominal GDP and the rate of interest. It is this total demand and the supply of money that determines interest rates in the money market. The inverse relationship between bond prices and interest rates help this market adjust to shortages or surpluses.

Third, the ***central bank*** in the United States consists of the 12 Federal Reserve Banks and the Board of Governors of the Federal Reserve System which oversees their operation. These banks, while privately owned by the commercial banks, are operated more or less as an agency of the Federal government. They are not for profit but are primarily to regulate the nation's money supply in the best interests of the economy as a whole and secondarily to perform other services for the banks, the government, and the economy. They are able to perform their primary function because they are bankers' banks in which depository institutions (commercial banks and the thrifts) can deposit and borrow money. They do not deal directly with the public.

Fourth, these depository institutions accept deposits and make loans, but they also are able to create money by lending checkable deposits. Because they are able to do this, they have a strong influence on the size of the money supply and the value of money. The Federal Reserve Banks exist primarily to regulate the money supply and its value by influencing and controlling the amount of money depository institutions create.

The final section of Chapter 13 discusses recent developments in money and banking, of which three are particularly noteworthy. Since the early 1980s, the relative decline of banks and thrifts has significantly altered the financial services industry. Also, financial markets are now global and more highly integrated than in previous decades. In addition, technological advances have changed the character of money. As you will learn, each development has and will continue to shape money and banking in the United States and other nations.

■ CHECKLIST

When you have studied this chapter you should be able to

☐ List and explain the three functions of money.
☐ Give an ***M***1 definition of money that explains its two major components.
☐ Describe the two major types of institutions offering checkable deposits.

☐ Give an ***M*2** definition of money that explains its relationship to ***M*1** and four near-money components.
☐ Give an ***M*3** definition of money and its major components.
☐ State three reasons why near-monies are important.
☐ Distinguish between credit cards and money.
☐ Explain why money is debt in the U.S. economy and who holds that debt.
☐ State three reasons why currency and checkable deposits are money and have value.
☐ Use an equation to explain the relationship between the value of money and the price level.
☐ Explain what role government plays in maintaining or stabilizing the value of money.
☐ Give a definition of the transactions demand for money that describes how it varies with nominal GDP.
☐ Give a definition of the asset demand for money that describes how it varies with the rate of interest.
☐ Illustrate graphically how the transactions and asset demands for money combine to form the total money demand.
☐ Describe the money market and what determines the equilibrium rate of interest.
☐ Explain how changes in nominal GDP and in the money supply affect the interest rate.
☐ Illustrate with an example how disequilibrium in the money market is corrected through changes in bond prices.
☐ Describe the relationship between the major units of the Federal Reserve System.
☐ Explain why the Federal Reserve Banks are central, quasipublic, and bankers' banks.
☐ List and explain the seven major functions of the Federal Reserve System and indicate which one is most important.
☐ Discuss both sides of the controversy over the independence of the Federal Reserve.
☐ Explain the relative decline of banks and thrifts and the three types of actions that have been taken to respond to it.
☐ Describe the globalization of financial markets.
☐ Explain how technological progress has changed the characteristics of money.

■ CHAPTER OUTLINE

1. Money is whatever performs the three basic functions of money: a medium of exchange, a unit of account, and a store of value.

2. In the U.S. economy, ***money*** is whatever is generally used as a medium of exchange and consists of the debts of the Federal government and of commercial banks and other financial institutions.

a. The narrowly defined money supply is called ***M*1** and has two principal components.

(1) The smaller component is currency: coins which are token money and paper money largely in the form of Federal Reserve Notes.

(2) The larger and more important component is checkable deposits in commercial banks and thrift institutions.

(3) These checkable deposits include demand deposits (checking accounts), negotiable order of withdrawal (NOW) accounts, automatic transfer service (ATS) accounts, and share draft accounts, all of which give the depositor the ability to write checks.

(4) Currency and checkable deposits owned by the Federal government, commercial banks and savings institutions, and the Federal Reserve Banks are not, however, included in ***M*1** or any of the more broadly defined money supplies.

b. ***M*2** and ***M*3** are the more broadly defined money supplies and include not only the currency and checkable deposits in ***M*1** but such near-monies as noncheckable savings deposits and time deposits in commercial banks and savings institutions.

(1) ***M*2** includes ***M*1** plus noncheckable savings deposits plus small time deposits (less than $100,000) plus money market deposit accounts (MMDA) plus money market mutual funds (MMMF).

(2) ***M*3** includes ***M*2** plus large time deposits ($100,000 or more).

(3) There are advantages to each of the different measures of money, but since ***M*1** is included in all the definitions and the principles that apply to it are applicable to the other measures, that narrow definition is used for the textbook discussion unless noted otherwise.

c. Near-monies held by the public are important because they affect spending habits, serve as a stabilizing force in economic activity, and provide different definitions of money for the conduct of monetary policy.

d. Credit cards are not money but are a device by which the cardholders obtain a loan (credit) from the issuer of the card.

3. In the United States,

a. Money is the promise of a commercial bank, a savings (thrift) institution, or a Federal Reserve Bank to pay, but these debts cannot be redeemed for anything tangible.

b. Money has value only because people can exchange it for desirable goods and services.

c. The value of money is inversely related to the price level.

d. Money is backed by the confidence which the public has that the value of money will remain stable; the Federal government can use monetary and fiscal policy to keep the value of money relatively stable.

4. Business firms and households wish to hold and, therefore, demand money for two reasons.

a. Because they use money as a medium of exchange, they have a transactions demand which is directly related to the nominal gross domestic product of the economy.

b. Because they also use money as a store of value, they have an asset demand which is inversely related to the rate of interest.

c. Their *total demand for money* is the sum of the transactions and asset demands.

5. In the ***money market,*** the demand for money and the supply of money determine the interest rate. Graphically, the demand for money is a downsloping line and the supply of money is a vertical line, and their intersection determines the interest rate. Disequilibrium in this market is corrected by changes in bond prices and their inverse relationship with interest rates.

a. If there is a shortage of money, bonds will be sold. The increase in supply of bonds will drive down bond prices, causing interest rates to rise until the shortage is eliminated.

b. If there is a surplus of money, bonds will be bought. The increased demand for bonds will drive up bond prices, causing interest rates to fall until the surplus is eliminated.

6. The financial sector of the economy is significantly influenced by the ***Federal Reserve System (Fed)*** and the nation's banks and thrift institutions.

a. The banking system remains centralized and regulated by government because historical problems led to different kinds of money and the mismanagement of the money supply.

b. The Board of Governors of the Fed exercises control over the supply of money and the banking system. The U.S. president appoints the seven members of the Board of Governors.

c. Four important bodies help the Board of Governors establish and conduct policy: the *Federal Open Market Committee* (*FOMC*), which establishes policy over the buying and selling of government securities; and three *Advisory Councils* that provide input from commercial banks, thrift institutions, and consumer-related organizations.

d. The 12 Federal Reserve Banks of the Fed serve as central banks, quasipublic banks, and bankers' banks.

e. The U.S. banking system contains thousands of commercial banks and thrift institutions that are directly affected by the Fed's decisions.

f. The Fed performs seven functions: issuing currency, setting reserve requirements and holding reserves, lending money to banks and thrifts, collecting and processing checks, serving as the fiscal agent for the Federal government, supervising banks, and controlling the money supply. The last function is the most important.

g. There is a continuing controversy about the independence of the Fed because it limits congressional and presidential control, but most economists think this is necessary to protect the Fed from strong political pressure and from making poor economic decisions.

7. Three *recent developments* have affected money and banking in the United States.

a. There has been a relative decline in the number of banks and thrift institutions since the early 1980s. Three responses to this change have been the expansion of services by banks and thrifts, an increase in the number of bank and thrift mergers, and a push for regulatory reform to deregulate banks and thrifts and permit more competition in the financial services industry.

b. Financial markets are now more globalized and integrated because of advances in computer and communications technology.

c. The character of money has changed with the shift to use of electronic money and other forms of payment.

■ HINTS AND TIPS

1. Most students think of currency as the major component of the money supply, but it is a very small component relative to checkable deposits. Actually, there are several definitions of the ***money supply*** that you must know about, from the narrow ***M*1** to the broader ***M*2** and ***M*3**.

2. Spend extra time learning how the total demand for money is determined (see Figure 13-2 in the text). The total demand for money is composed of a transactions and an asset demand for money. The transactions demand is influenced by the level of nominal GDP and not affected by the interest rate, so it *is graphed as a vertical line.* The asset demand for money is affected by the interest rate, so it *is graphed as a downsloping curve.* The total demand for money is also graphed as a *downsloping curve* because of the influence of asset demand, but the curve is shifted farther to the right than the asset demand curve because of the influence of transactions demand.

3. One of the most difficult concepts to understand is the inverse relationship between bond prices and interest rates. The simple explanation is that interest yield from a bond is the ratio of the *fixed* annual interest payment to the bond price. The numerator is fixed, but the denominator (bond price) is variable. If the bond price falls, the interest yield on the bond rises because the fixed annual interest payment is being divided by a smaller denominator.

■ IMPORTANT TERMS

medium of exchange
unit of account
store of value
money supply
***M*1, *M*2, and *M*3**
token money
intrinsic value
Federal Reserve Note
checkable deposit
thrift (savings) institutions
savings and loan associations
mutual savings banks
credit unions
near-monies
noncheckable savings account
money market deposit accounts
national banks
E-cash (electronic money)
time deposits
money market mutual funds
legal tender
fiat money
transactions demand for money
asset demand for money
total demand for money
money market
bonds
Federal Reserve System
Board of Governors
Federal Open Market Committee (*FOMC*)
Advisory Councils
Federal Reserve Banks
commercial banks
state banks
smart cards

SELF-TEST

■ FILL-IN QUESTIONS

1. When money is usable for buying and selling goods and services, it functions as (a unit of account, a store of value, a medium of exchange) ______________ ______________, but when money serves as a measure of relative worth, it functions as ______________, and when money serves a liquid asset it functions as a ______________.

2. All coins in circulation in the United States are (paper, token) ______________ money, which means that their intrinsic value is (less, greater) ______________ than the face value of the coin.

3. Paper money and coins are considered (currency, checkable deposits) ______________. The major component of ***M*1** is (currency, checkable deposits) ______________, and the minor component is ______________.

4. ***M*2** is equal to (***M*1**, ***M*3**) ______________ plus (checkable, noncheckable) ______________ savings deposits, (small, large) ______________ time deposits, and money market (deposit accounts, mutual funds) ______________ and ______________.

5. ***M*3** is equal to ***M*2** plus (small, large) ______________ time deposits. These deposits have a face value of (less than $100,000; $100,000 or greater) ______________.

6. List three reasons why the existence of near-monies is important.

a. ______________________________

____

b. ______________________________

____

c. ______________________________

____

7. Credit cards (are, are not) ______________ considered money but rather a form of (paper money, loan) ______________ from the institution that issued the card.

8. Paper money is the circulating debt of (banks and thrifts, the Federal Reserve Banks) ______________ ______________, while checkable deposits are the debts of ______________. In the United States, currency and checkable deposits (are, are not) ______________ backed by gold and silver.

9. Money has value because it is (unacceptable, acceptable) ______________ in exchange for products and resources, because it is (legal, illegal) ______________ tender, and because it is relatively (abundant, scarce) ______________.

10. The value of money varies (directly, inversely) ______________ with the price level. To find the value of $1 (multiply, divide) ______________ 1 by the price level.

11. The transactions demand varies (directly, inversely) ______________ with (the rate of interest, nominal GDP) ______________, and asset demand varies (directly, inversely) ______________ with (the rate of interest, nominal GDP) ______________.

12. The sum of the transactions and asset demands for money is the total (demand, supply) ______________ of money, and the intersection of it with the ______________ of money determines the equilibrium (interest rate, price level) ______________.

13. When the quantity of money demanded exceeds the quantity of money supplied, bond prices (increase, decrease) ______________ and interest rates ______________. When the quantity of money demanded is less than the quantity of money supplied, bond prices (increase, decrease) ______________ and interest rates ______________.

14. The Federal Reserve System is composed of the Board of (Control, Governors) ______________ that is assisted by the powerful (U.S. Mint, Federal Open Market Committee) ______________ and (3, 12) ______ Advisory Councils. There are also (10, 12) ______ Federal Reserve Banks.

15. The Federal Reserve Banks are (private, quasipublic) ______________ banks, serve as (consumers', bankers') ______________ banks, and are (local, central) ______________ banks whose policies are coordinated by the Board of Governors.

16. The workhorses of the U.S. banking system are the more than 9,000 (thrifts, commercial banks) ______________, two-thirds of which are (national, state) ______________, banks and one-third of which are ______________ banks.

17. The seven major functions of the Fed are

a. ______________________________
____

b. ______________________________
____

c. ______________________________
____

d. ______________________________
____

e. ______________________________
____

f. ______________________________
____

g. ______________________________
____

Of these, the most important function is ______________
______________________________.

18. The independence of the Fed is a matter of continuing controversy. Opponents say that it is (democratic, undemocratic) ______________, while supporters contend that the Fed must be protected from political pressure if it is to control (recession, inflation) ______________.

19. Banks and thrifts have responded to their relative decline in recent years by (contracting, expanding) ______________ financial services, (starting up, merging with) ______________ other banks and thrifts, and pushing for (bankruptcy, regulatory) ______________ reform.

20. Two other recent developments in money and banking are the (localization, globalization) ______________ of financial markets, and the use of (paper, electronic) ______________ money.

■ TRUE-FALSE QUESTIONS

Circle the T if the statement is true, the F if it is false.

1. When the price of a product is stated in terms of dollars and cents, then money is functioning as a unit of account. **T F**

2. The money supply designated ***M*1** is the sum of currency and noncheckable deposits. **T F**

3. The currency component of ***M*1** includes both coins and paper money. **T F**

4. If a coin is token money, its face value is less than its intrinsic value. **T F**

5. Both commercial banks and thrift institutions accept checkable deposits. **T F**

6. The checkable deposits of the Federal government at the Federal Reserve Banks are a component of ***M*1**. **T F**

7. ***M*2** exceeds ***M*1** by the amount of noncheckable savings, small time deposits, and money market deposit accounts and money market mutual funds. **T F**

8. A *small* time deposit is one that is less than $100,000. **T F**

9. ***M*2** is less than ***M*3** by the amount of small time deposits in depository institutions. **T F**

10. Economists and public officials are in general agreement on how to define the money supply in the United States. **T F**

11. A near-money is a medium of exchange. **T F**

12. Currency and checkable deposits are money because they are acceptable to sellers in exchange for goods and services. **T F**

13. If money is to have a fairly stable value, its supply must be limited relative to the demand for it. **T F**

14. There is a transactions demand for money because households and business firms use money as a store of value. **T F**

15. An increase in the price level would, *ceteris paribus,* increase the transactions demand for money. **T F**

16. An increase in the nominal GDP, other things remaining the same, will increase both the total demand for money and the equilibrium rate of interest in the economy. **T F**

17. Bond prices and interest rates are inversely related. **T F**

18. Members of the Board of Governors of the Federal Reserve System are appointed by the president of the United States and confirmed by the Senate. **T F**

19. The Federal Open Market Committee (FOMC) is responsible for keeping the stock market open and regulated. **T F**

20. The Federal Reserve Banks are owned and operated by the U.S. government. **T F**

21. Federal Reserve Banks are bankers' banks because they make loans to and accept deposits from depository institutions. **T F**

22. At times, the Fed lends money to banks and thrifts, charging them an interest rate called the *bank and thrift rate.* **T F**

23. Defenders of Fed independence contend that the Fed must be protected from political pressure so that it can effectively control the money supply and maintain price stability. **T F**

24. In recent years, banks and thrifts have increased their share of the financial services industry and control of financial assets. **T F**

25. It is expected that electronic cash and smart cards will reduce problems for the Federal Reserve in controlling the money supply. **T F**

■ MULTIPLE-CHOICE QUESTIONS

Circle the letter that corresponds to the best answer.

1. Which one is an economic function of money?
(a) a medium of communications
(b) a factor of production
(c) a store of bonds
(d) a unit of account

2. The largest element of the currency component of *M*1 is
(a) coins
(b) United States Notes
(c) silver certificates
(d) Federal Reserve Notes

3. Which of the following constitutes the largest element in the *M*1 money supply?
(a) currency
(b) Federal Reserve Notes
(c) time deposits
(d) checkable deposits

4. Checkable deposits are money because they are
(a) legal tender
(b) fiat money
(c) token money
(d) a medium of exchange

5. The supply of money *M*1 consists almost entirely of the debts of
(a) the Federal government
(b) the Federal Reserve Banks
(c) depository institutions
(d) the Federal Reserve Banks and depository institutions

Use the following table to answer Questions 6, 7, and 8 about the money supply, given the following hypothetical data for the economy.

Item	Billions of dollars
Checkable deposits	1,775
Small time deposits	345
Currency	56
Large time deposits	1,230
Noncheckable savings deposits	945
Money market deposit accounts	256
Money market mutual funds	587

6. The size of the ***M*1** money supply is
(a) $1,775
(b) $1,831
(c) $2,176
(d) $3,019

7. The size of the ***M*2** money supply is
(a) $2,176
(b) $3,146
(c) $3,964
(d) $4,532

8. The size of the ***M*3** money supply is
(a) $4,532
(b) $5,194
(c) $5,339
(d) $6,007

9. Which of the following *best* describes the backing of money in the United States?
(a) the gold bullion stored in Fort Knox, Kentucky
(b) the belief of holders of money that it can be exchanged for desirable goods and services
(c) the willingness of banks and the government to surrender something of value in exchange for money
(d) the faith and confidence of the public in the ability of government to pay its debts

10. If the price level increases 20%, the value of money decreases
(a) 14.14%
(b) 16.67%
(c) 20%
(d) 25%

11. To keep the value of money fairly constant, the Federal Reserve
(a) uses price and wage controls
(b) employs fiscal policy
(c) controls the money supply
(d) buys stock

12. The total quantity of money demanded is
(a) directly related to nominal GDP and the rate of interest
(b) directly related to nominal GDP and inversely related to the rate of interest
(c) inversely related to nominal GDP and directly related to the rate of interest
(d) inversely related to nominal GDP and the rate of interest

13. There is an asset demand for money because money is
(a) a medium of exchange
(b) a measure of value
(c) a store of value
(d) a standard of deferred payment

14. If the dollars held for transactions purposes are, on the average, spent five times a year for final goods and services, then the quantity of money people will wish to hold for transactions is equal to
(a) five times the nominal GDP
(b) 20% of the nominal GDP

(c) five divided by the nominal GDP
(d) 20% divided by the nominal GDP

15. An increase in the rate of interest would increase
(a) the opportunity cost of holding money
(b) the transactions demand for money
(c) the asset demand for money
(d) the prices of bonds

Use the table below to answer Questions 16 and 17.

Interest rate	Asset demand (billions)
14%	$100
13	150
12	200
11	250

16. Suppose the transactions demand for money is equal to 10% of the nominal GDP, the supply of money is $450 billion, and the asset demand for money is that shown in the table. If the nominal GDP is $3,000 billion, the equilibrium interest rate is
(a) 14%
(b) 13%
(c) 12%
(d) 11%

17. If the nominal GDP remains constant, an increase in the money supply from $450 billion to $500 billion would cause the equilibrium interest rate to
(a) rise to 14%
(b) fall to 11%
(c) fall to 12%
(d) remain unchanged

18. The stock of money is determined by the Federal Reserve System and does not change when the interest rate changes; therefore the
(a) supply of money curve is downward sloping
(b) demand for money curve is downward sloping
(c) supply of money curve is upward sloping
(d) supply of money curve is vertical

19. If the legal ceiling on the interest rate was set below equilibrium, the
(a) quantity of money demanded would be greater than the quantity of money supplied
(b) quantity of money demanded would be less than the quantity of money supplied
(c) supply of money would increase and the demand for money would decrease
(d) demand for money would increase and the supply of money would decrease

20. Which one of the following points would be true?
(a) Bond prices and the interest rate are directly related.
(b) A lower interest rate raises the opportunity cost of holding money.
(c) The supply of money is directly related to the interest rate.
(d) The total demand for money is inversely related to the interest rate.

Answer Questions 21 and 22 on the basis of the following information: Bond price = $10,000; bond fixed annual interest payment = $1,000; bond annual rate of interest = 10%.

21. If the price of this bond decreases by $2,500, the interest rate in effect will
(a) decrease by 1.1 percentage points
(b) decrease by 1.9 percentage points
(c) increase by 2.6 percentage points
(d) increase by 3.3 percentage points

22. If the price of this bond increases by $2,000, the interest rate in effect will
(a) decrease by 1.7 percentage points
(b) decrease by 2.4 percentage points
(c) increase by 1.1 percentage points
(d) increase by 2.9 percentage points

23. The Federal Open Market Committee (FOMC) of the Federal Reserve System is primarily responsible for
(a) supervising the operation of banks to make sure they follow regulation and monitoring banks so they do not engage in fraud
(b) handling the Fed's collection of checks and adjusting legal reserves among banks
(c) setting the Fed's monetary policy and directing the buying and selling of government securities
(d) acting as the fiscal agent for the Federal government and issuing currency

24. The most important function of the Federal Reserve System is
(a) issuing currency
(b) controlling the money supply
(c) supervising commercial banks
(d) lending money to banks and thrifts

25. According to the text, which would be a recent development in the banking industry?
(a) an increase in the number of banks and thrifts
(b) increased integration of world financial markets
(c) increased use of coins and currency as a medium of exchange
(d) a decrease in the financial services and activities of banks and thrifts

■ PROBLEMS

1. From the figures in the following table it can be concluded that

Item	Billions of dollars
Small time deposits	630
Large time deposits	645
Money market deposit accounts	575
Money market mutual funds	425
Checkable deposits	448
Noncheckable savings deposits	300
Currency	170

a. *M*1 is equal to the sum of $________ and $________, so it totals $________ billion.

b. $M2$ is equal to $M1$ plus $________ and $________ and $________ and $________, so it totals $________ billion.

c. $M3$ is equal to $M2$ plus $________, so it totals $________ billion.

2. Complete the following table showing the relationship between a percentage change in the price level and the percentage change in the value of money. Calculate the percentage change in the value of money to one decimal place.

Change in price level	Change in value of money
a. *rise* by:	
5%	–____.__%
10%	–____.__
15%	–____.__
20%	–____.__
25%	–____.__
b. *fall* by:	
5%	+____.__%
10%	+____.__
15%	+____.__

3. The total demand for money is equal to the transaction plus the asset demand for money.

a. Assume each dollar held for transaction purposes is spent (on the average) four times per year to buy final goods and services.

(1) This means that transaction demand for money will be equal to (what fraction or percent) ________ of the nominal GDP, and,

(2) if the nominal GDP is $2000 billion, the transaction demand will be $________ billion.

b. The following table shows the number of dollars demanded for asset purposes at each rate of interest.

(1) Given the transactions demand for money in (*a*), complete the table.

(2) On the graph below, plot the *total* demand for money (D_m) at each rate of interest.

Interest rate	Amount of money demanded (billions): For asset purposes	Total
16%	$ 20	$____
14	40	____
12	60	____
10	80	____
8	100	____
6	120	____
4	140	____

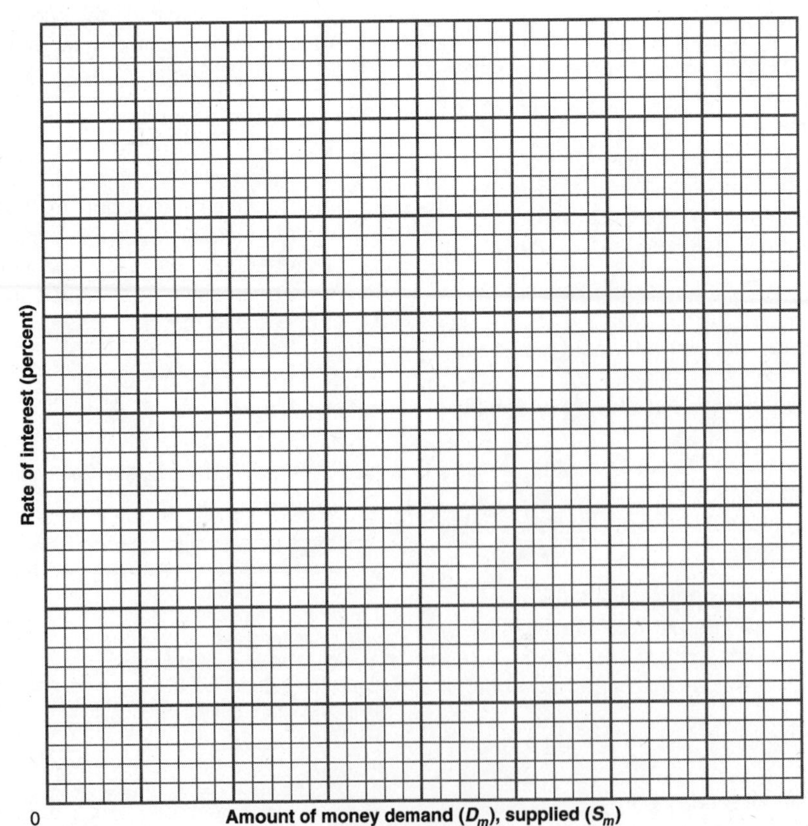

c. Assume the money supply (S_m) is $580 billion.
(1) Plot this money supply on the graph.
(2) Using either the graph or the table, the equilibrium rate of interest is ______________ %.

d. Should the money supply
(1) increase to $600 billion, the equilibrium interest rate would (rise, fall) ____________ to __________ %.
(2) decrease to $540 billion, the equilibrium interest rate would ______________ to __________ %.

e. If the nominal GDP
(1) increased by $80 billion, the total demand for money would (increase, decrease) ______________ by $______________ billion at each rate of interest and the equilibrium rate of interest would (rise, fall) ______________ by ______________ %.
(2) decreased by $120 billion, the total demand for money would ______________ by $__________ billion at each rate of interest and the equilibrium interest rate would ______________ by __________ %.

4. Suppose a bond with no expiration date pays a fixed $500 annually and sells for its face value of $5,000.

a. Complete the following table and calculate the interest rate (to one decimal place) that would be obtained from the bond when the bond price is given or calculate the bond price when the interest rate is given.

Bond price	Interest rate
$4,000	_____._____%
$_____	11.0
$5,000	_____._____
$5,500	_____._____
$_____	8.0

b. Based on the results of the table, as the price increases on a bond with a fixed annual payment, the interest yield on the bond (decreases, increases) ______________, but when the price of a bond decreases, the interest yield ______________. Given this situation in an economy, you can conclude that a higher price for bonds ______________ interest rates and that a lower price for bonds ______________ interest rates.

■ SHORT ANSWER AND ESSAY QUESTIONS

1. How would you define money based on its three functions?

2. What are the components of the $M1$ supply of money in the United States? Which of these components is larger?

3. What are checkable deposits, and what are the different types of institutions offering checkable deposits?

4. What is a near-money? What are the more important near-monies in the U.S. economy?

5. Define $M2$ and $M3$, and explain why the existence of near-monies is important.

6. For what reasons are checkable deposits included in the money supply?

7. What backs the money used in the United States? What determines the value of money?

8. Explain the relationship between the value of money and the price level.

9. What must government do if it is to stabilize the value of money?

10. What are the two reasons people wish to hold money? How are these two reasons related to the functions of money?

11. Explain the determinant of each of the two demands for money and how a change in the size of these determinants will affect the amount of money people wish to hold.

12. The rate of interest is a price. Of what good or service is it the price? Explain how demand and supply determine this price.

13. Describe how changes in bond prices correct disequilibrium in the money market. What is the relationship between bond prices and interest rates?

14. Outline the structure of the Federal Reserve System and explain the chief functions of each of the four parts of the system.

15. As briefly as possible, outline the three characteristics of the Federal Reserve Banks and explain the meaning of these characteristics.

16. What are the chief functions the Federal Reserve Banks perform? Explain briefly the meaning of each function. Which of the chief functions is the most important?

17. What are the basic arguments for and against the independence of the Federal Reserve System?

18. Describe three different responses by banks and thrifts to the relative decline of these institutions in recent years.

19. Discuss the meaning and effects of increased integration of world financial market.

20. Explain how electronic money changes the way money is stored and transferred and how these changes will affect banks, thrifts, and the Federal Reserve.

ANSWERS

Chapter 13 Money and Banking

FILL-IN QUESTIONS

1. a medium of exchange, unit of account, store of value
2. token, less

3. currency, checkable deposits, currency

4. *M*1, noncheckable, small, deposit accounts, mutual funds (either order for the last two)

5. large, $100,000 or greater

6. *a.* they influence consuming-saving habits; *b.* conversion from near-money to money or from money to near-money may affect the stability of the economy; *c.* they are important when monetary policy is to be used

7. are not, loan

8. the Federal Reserve Banks, banks and thrifts, are not

9. acceptable, legal, scarce

10. inversely, divide

11. directly, nominal GDP, inversely, the rate of interest

12. demand, supply, interest rate

13. decrease, increase, increase, decrease

14. Governors, Federal Open Market Committee, 3, 12

15. quasipublic, bankers', central

16. commercial banks, state, national

17. *a.* issuing currency; *b.* setting reserve requirements and holding reserves; *c.* lending money to banks and thrifts; *d.* collecting and processing checks; *e.* serving as fiscal agent for the Federal government; *f.* bank supervision; *g.* controlling the money supply; controlling the money supply

18. undemocratic, inflation

19. expanding, merging with, regulatory

20. globalization, electronic

TRUE-FALSE QUESTIONS

1. T, p. 265
2. F, p. 265
3. T, p. 265
4. F, p. 265
5. T, pp. 266-267
6. F, pp. 266-267
7. T, p. 267
8. T, p. 267
9. F, p. 267-268
10. F, p. 265
11. F, p. 267
12. T, pp. 269-270
13. T, pp. 270-272
14. F, p. 272
15. T, p. 272
16. T, p. 274
17. T, pp. 274-275
18. T, pp. 276-277
19. F, p. 277
20. F, p. 278
21. T, p. 278
22. F, p. 279
23. T, pp. 279-280
24. F, p. 280
25. F, p. 284

MULTIPLE-CHOICE QUESTIONS

1. d, p. 265
2. d, p. 266
3. d, p. 266
4. d, p. 266
5. d, p. 269
6. b, p. 266
7. c, p. 266
8. b, p. 266
9. b, pp. 269-270
10. b, pp. 270-271
11. c, pp. 271-272
12. b, pp. 272-274
13. c, pp. 272-273
14. b, p. 272
15. a, p. 274
16. b, pp. 273-275
17. c, pp. 273-275
18. d, p. 274
19. a, pp. 274-275
20. d, p. 274
21. d, pp. 274-275
22. a, pp. 274-275
23. c, p. 277
24. b, p. 279
25. b, p. 282

PROBLEMS

1. *a.* 170, 448 (either order), 618; *b.* 300, 630, 575, 425 (either order), 2,548; *c.* 645, 3,193

2. *a.* 4.8, 9.1, 13, 16.7, 20; *b.* 5.3, 11.1, 17.6

3. *a.* (1) 1/4 (25%), (2) 500; *b.* (1) 520, 540, 560, 580, 600, 620, 640; *c.* (2) 10; *d.* (1) fall, 8, (2) rise, 14; *e.* (1) increase, 20, rise, 2, (2) decrease, 30, fall, 3

4. *a.* 12.5%, $4,545, 10.0%, 9.1%, $6,250; *b.* decreases, increases, decreases, increases

SHORT ANSWER AND ESSAY QUESTIONS

1. pp. 264-265
2. pp. 265-266
3. pp. 266-267
4. p. 267
5. pp. 267-268
6. p. 266
7. pp. 269-270
8. pp. 270-271
9. pp. 271-272
10. pp. 272-274
11. pp. 272-274
12. pp. 273-275
13. pp. 274-275
14. pp. 276-278
15. pp. 277-278
16. p. 279
17. pp. 279-280
18. pp. 280-282
19. pp. 282-283
20. pp. 282-284

CHAPTER 14

How Banks Create Money

Chapter 13 explained the institutional structure of banking in the United States today, the functions which banks and the other depository institutions and money perform, and the composition of the money supply. Chapter 14 explains how banks create money—***demand-deposit*** money—and the factors which determine and limit the money-creating ability of commercial banks. The other depository institutions also create checkable deposits, but this chapter focuses on the commercial banks because they have created and will continue to create a very large part of the total amount of money created by all depository institutions in the United States.

The convenient and simple device used to explain commercial banking operations and money creation is the ***balance sheet.*** All banking transactions affect this balance sheet, and the first step to understanding how money is created is to understand how various simple and typical transactions affect the commercial bank balance sheet.

In reading this chapter you must analyze for yourself the effect of each and every banking transaction discussed on the balance sheet. The important items in the balance sheet are demand deposits and reserves because **demand deposits are money,** and the ability of a bank to create new demand deposits is determined by the amount of reserves the bank has. Expansion of the money supply depends on the possession by commercial banks of excess reserves. Excess reserves do not appear explicitly in the balance sheet but do appear there implicitly because excess reserves are the difference between the actual reserves and the required reserves of commercial banks.

Two cases—the single commercial bank and the banking system—are presented to help you build an understanding of banking and money creation. It is important to understand that the money-creating potential of a single commercial bank differs from the money-creating potential of the entire banking system; it is equally important to understand how the money-creating ability of many single commercial banks is *multiplied* and influences the money-creating ability of the banking system as a whole.

Certain assumptions are used throughout most of this chapter to analyze money creation; in certain instances these assumptions may not be completely realistic and may need to be modified. The chapter concludes with a discussion of how the earlier analysis must be modified—but not changed in its essentials—to take account of slightly unrealistic assumptions.

You will also learn that the money-creating actions of banks have a procyclical effect on the economy which needs to be controlled by the Federal Reserve System—a topic discussed in more detail in the next chapter.

■ CHECKLIST

When you have studied this chapter you should be able to

☐ Define the basic items in a bank's balance sheet.

☐ Recount the story of how goldsmiths came to issue paper money and became bankers who created money and held fractional reserves.

☐ Cite two significant characteristics of the fractional reserve banking system today.

☐ Explain the effects of the deposit of currency in a checking account on the composition and size of the money supply.

☐ Compute a bank's required and excess reserves when you are given the needed balance-sheet figures.

☐ Explain why a commercial bank is required to maintain a reserve and why this reserve is not sufficient to protect the depositors from losses.

☐ Indicate how the deposit of a check drawn on one commercial bank and deposited into another will affect the reserves and excess reserves of the two banks.

☐ Show what happens to the money supply when a commercial bank makes a loan (or buys government securities).

☐ Show what happens to the money supply when a loan is repaid (or a bank sells government securities).

☐ Explain what happens to a commercial bank's reserves and demand deposits after it has made a loan, a check has been written on the newly created demand deposit and deposited in another commercial bank and cleared, and explain what happens to the reserves and demand deposits of the commercial bank in which the check was deposited.

☐ Describe what would happen to a commercial bank's reserves if it made loans (or bought government securities) in an amount that exceeded its excess reserves.

☐ State the money-creating potential of a commercial bank (the amount of money a commercial bank can safely create by lending or buying securities).

☐ Explain how the Federal funds market helps reconcile the goals of profits and liquidity for commercial banks.
☐ State the money-creating potential of the banking system.
☐ Explain how it is possible for the banking system to create an amount of money which is a multiple of its excess reserves when no individual commercial bank ever creates money in an amount greater than its excess reserve.
☐ Compute the size of the monetary multiplier and the money-creating potential of the banking system when you are provided with the necessary data.
☐ Illustrate with an example using the monetary multiplier how money can be destroyed in the banking system.
☐ List the two leakages which reduce the money-creating potential of the banking system.
☐ Explain why the size of the money supply needs to be controlled by the Federal Reserve System.

■ CHAPTER OUTLINE

1. The *balance sheet* of the commercial bank is a statement of the assets, liabilities, and net worth (capital stock) of the bank at a specific time; and in the balance sheet, the bank's assets equal its liabilities plus its net worth.

2. The history of the early goldsmiths illustrates how paper money came into use in the economy. This history also shows how goldsmiths became bankers when they began making loans and issuing money in excess of their gold holdings. The goldsmiths' fractional reserve system is similar to today's fractional banking system, which has two significant characteristics:

a. Banks can create money in such a system.
b. Banks are subject to "panics" or "runs" in a fractional banking system and thus need government regulation.

3. By examining the ways the balance sheet of the commercial bank is affected by various transactions, it is possible to understand how a *single commercial bank* in a multibank system can create money.

a. Once a commercial bank has been founded,
(1) by selling shares of stock and obtaining cash in return;
(2) and acquiring the property and equipment needed to carry on the banking business;
(3) the deposit of cash in the bank does not affect the total money supply; it only changes its composition by substituting demand deposits for currency in circulation;
(4) three reserve concepts are vital to an understanding of the money-creating potential of a commercial bank.
(a) The ***legal reserve deposit*** (required reserve), which a bank *must* maintain at its Federal Reserve Bank (or as vault cash—which can be ignored), equals the reserve ratio multiplied by the deposit liabilities of the commercial bank;
(b) the ***actual reserves*** of a commercial bank are its deposits at the Federal Reserve Bank (plus the vault cash which is ignored);
(c) the ***excess reserves*** equal to the actual reserves less the required reserve.
(5) The writing of a check on the bank and its deposit in a second bank results in a loss of reserves and deposits for the first and a gain in reserves and deposits for the second bank.

b. When a single commercial bank lends or buys government securities, it increases its own deposit liabilities and therefore the supply of money by the amount of the loan or security purchase. But the bank only lends or buys securities in an amount equal to its excess reserves because it fears the loss of reserves to other commercial banks in the economy.
c. When a single commercial bank receives loan repayments or sells government securities, its deposit liabilities and therefore the supply of money are described by the amount of the loan repayments or securities sale.
d An individual commercial bank balances its desire for profits (which result from the making of loans and the purchase of securities) with its desire for liquidity or safety (which it achieves by having excess reserves or vault cash).
e. The Federal funds market allows banks with excess reserves to lend funds overnight to banks which are short of reserves. The interest rate paid on the overnight loans is the Federal funds rate.

4. The ability of a *banking system* composed of many individual commercial banks to lend and to create money is a multiple (greater than 1) of its excess reserves and is equal to the excess reserves of the banking system multiplied by the demand-deposit (or monetary) multiplier.

a. The banking system as a whole can do this even though no single commercial bank ever lends an amount greater than its excess reserve because the banking system, unlike a single commercial bank, does not lose reserves.
b. The monetary (or demand-deposit) multiplier is equal to the reciprocal of the required reserve ratio for demand deposits, and the maximum expansion of demand deposits is equal to the excess reserves in the banking system times the monetary multiplier.
c. The potential lending ability of the banking system may not be fully achieved if there are leakages because borrowers choose to have additional currency or bankers choose to have excess reserves.
d If bankers lend as much as they are able during periods of prosperity and less than they are able during recessions, they add to the instability of the economy. To reduce this instability, the Federal Reserve Banks must control the size of the money supply.

■ HINTS AND TIPS

1. Note that several terms are used interchangeably in this chapter: (1) "Commercial bank" (or "bank") is sometimes called "thrift institution"; (2) "checkable deposit" is sometimes called "demand deposit" or "depository institution."

2. A bank's balance sheet must balance. The bank's assets are either claimed by owners (net worth) or by nonowners (liabilities). Assets = liabilities + net worth.

3. Make a running balance sheet in writing for yourself as you read about each of the eight transactions in the text for the Wahoo Bank. Then determine if you understand the material by telling yourself (or a friend) the story for each transaction without using the text.

4. The maximum amount of **demand-deposit expansion** is determined by multiplying two factors: the excess reserves by the monetary multiplier. Each factor, however, is affected by the required reserve ratio. The monetary multiplier is calculated by dividing one by the required reserve ratio. Excess reserves are determined by multiplying the required reserve ratio by the amount of new deposits. Thus, a change in the required reserve ratio will change the monetary multiplier *and* the amount of excess reserves. For example, a required reserve ratio of 25% gives a monetary multiplier of 4. For $100 in new money deposited, required reserves are $25 and excess reserves are $75. The maximum demand-deposit expansion is $300 (4 × $75). If the reserve ratio drops to 20%, the monetary multiplier is 5 and excess reserves are $80, so the maximum demand-deposit expansion is $400. Both factors have changed.

5. Be aware that the monetary multiplier can result in money destruction as well as money creation in the banking system. You should know how the monetary multiplier reinforces effects in one direction or the other.

■ IMPORTANT TERMS

balance sheet	**reserve ratio**
assets	**actual reserve**
liabilities	**excess reserve**
net worth	**Federal funds rate**
fractional reserve system of banking	**commercial banking system**
vault cash (till money)	**monetary (demand-deposit) multiplier**
required reserves	

SELF-TEST

■ FILL-IN QUESTIONS

1. In this chapter, a commercial bank may also be called a (checkable, thrift) ______________ institution and a demand deposit may also be called a ______________ deposit.

2. The balance sheet of a commercial bank is a statement of the bank's (gold account, assets) ______________, the claims of the owners of the bank, [called (net worth, liabilities) ______________], and claims of the nonowners (called ______________). This relationship would be written in equation form as:

____.

3. The banking system used today is a (total, fractional) ______________ reserve system, which means that (100%, less than 100%) ______________ of the money deposited in a bank is kept on reserve.

4. There are two significant characteristics to the banking system of today.

a. Banks can create (reserves, money) ______________ depending on the amount of ______________ they hold.

b. Banks are susceptible to (panics, regulation) ______________ or "runs," and to prevent this situation from happening, banks are subject to government ______________.

5. The coins and paper money which a bank has in its possession are (petty, vault) ______________ cash or (till, capital) ______________ money.

6. When a person deposits cash in a commercial bank and receives a demand deposit in return, the size of the money supply has (increased, decreased, not changed) ______________.

7. The legal reserve of a commercial bank (ignoring vault cash) must be kept on deposit at (a branch of the U.S. Treasury, its district Federal Reserve Bank) ______________ ______________.

8. The reserve ratio is equal to the commercial bank's (required, gold) ______________ reserves divided by its demand deposit (assets, liabilities) ______________.

9. The authority to establish and vary the reserve ratio within limits legislated by Congress is given to the (U.S. Treasury, Fed) ______________.

10. If commercial banks are allowed to accept (or create) deposits in excess of their reserves, the banking system is operating under a system of (fractional, currency) ______________ reserves.

11. The excess reserves of a commercial bank equal its (actual, required) ______________ reserves minus its ______________ reserves.

12. The basic purpose for having member banks deposit a legal reserve in the Federal Reserve Bank in their district is to provide (liquidity for, control of) ______________ the banking system by the Fed.

13. When a commercial bank deposits a legal reserve in its district Federal Reserve Bank, the reserve is (a liabil-

ity, an asset) ______________ to the commercial bank and ______________ to the Federal Reserve Bank.

14. When a check is drawn on Bank X, deposited in Bank Y, and cleared, the reserves of Bank X are (increased, decreased, not changed) ______________ and the reserves of Bank Y are ______________; deposits in Bank X are (increased, decreased, not changed) ______________ and deposits in Bank Y are ______________.

15. A single commercial bank in a multibank system can safely make loans or buy government securities equal in amount to the (required, excess) ______________ reserves of that commercial bank.

16. When a commercial bank makes a new loan of $10,000, the supply of money (increases, decreases) ______________ by $______________, but when a loan is repaid, the supply of money (increases, decreases) by $______________.

17. When a commercial bank sells a $10,000 government bond to a securities dealer, the supply of money (increases, decreases) ______________ $ ______________, but when a commercial bank buys a $10,000 government bond from a securities dealer, the supply of money (increases, decreases) ______________ by $______________.

18. A bank ordinarily pursues two conflicting goals; one goal is the desire to make money, or (profits, liquidity) ______________, and the other goal is the need for safety, or ______________.

19. When a bank lends temporary excess reserves held at its Federal Reserve Bank to other commercial banks that are temporarily short of legal reserves, it is participating in the (government securities, Federal funds) ______________ market. The interest rate paid on these overnight loans is called the (government securities, Federal funds) ______________ rate.

20. The monetary multiplier is equal to 1 divided by the (excess, required) ______________ reserve ratio.

21. The greater the reserve ratio, the (larger, smaller) ______________ the monetary multiplier.

22. The banking system can make loans (or buy government securities) and create money in an amount equal to its (required, excess) ______________ reserves multiplied by the (required reserve ratio, monetary multiplier) ______________.

23. Assume that the required reserve ratio is 16.67% and the banking system is $6 million short of required reserves. If the banking system is unable to increase its reserves, the banking system must (increase, decrease) ______________ the money supply by ($6, $36) ______________ million.

24. The money-creating potential of the commercial banking system is lessened by the (addition, withdrawal) ______________ of currency from banks and by banks not lending (required, excess) ______________ reserves.

25. Commercial banks in the past have kept excess reserves during periods of (prosperity, recession) ______________ and have kept few or no excess reserves during periods of ______________. By acting this way, they have made the economy (more, less) ______________ stable, which has given rise to the need for monetary control by the Federal Reserve System.

■ TRUE-FALSE QUESTIONS

Circle the T if the statement is true, the F if it is false.

1. The balance sheet of a commercial bank shows the transactions in which the bank has engaged during a given period of time. **T F**

2. A commercial bank's assets plus its net worth equal the bank's liabilities. **T F**

3. Goldsmiths increased the money supply when they accepted deposits of gold and issued paper receipts to the depositors. **T F**

4. Modern banking systems use gold as the basis for the fractional reserve system. **T F**

5. Cash held by a bank is sometimes called vault cash. **T F**

6. Mary Lynn, a music star, deposits a $30,000 check in a commercial bank and receives a demand deposit in return; 1 hour later the Manfred Iron and Coal Company borrows $30,000 from the same bank. The money supply has increased $30,000 as a result of the two transactions. **T F**

7. A commercial bank may maintain its legal reserve either as a deposit in its Federal Reserve Bank or as government bonds in its own vault. **T F**

8. The legal reserve which a commercial bank maintains must equal at least its own deposit liabilities multiplied by the required reserve ratio. **T F**

9. Legal reserves permit the Board of Governors of the Federal Reserve System to influence the lending ability of commercial banks. **T F**

10. The actual reserves of a commercial bank equal excess reserves plus required reserves. **T F**

11. The reserve of a commercial bank in the Federal Reserve Bank is an asset of the Federal Reserve Bank. **T F**

12. A check for $1,000 drawn on bank X by a depositor and deposited in bank Y will increase the excess reserves in bank Y by $1,000. **T F**

13. A single commercial bank can safely lend an amount equal to its excess reserves multiplied by the monetary multiplier ratio. T F

14. When a borrower repays a loan of $500, either in cash or by check, the supply of money is reduced by $500. T F

15. The granting of a $5,000 loan and the purchase of a $5,000 government bond from a securities dealer by a commercial bank have the same effect on the money supply. T F

16. The selling of a government bond by a commercial bank will increase the money supply. T F

17. A commercial bank seeks both profits and liquidity, but these are conflicting goals. T F

18. The Federal funds rate is the interest rate at which the Federal government lends funds to commercial banks. T F

19. The reason that the banking system can lend by a multiple of its excess reserves, but each individual bank can only lend "dollar for dollar" with its excess reserves, is that reserves lost by a single bank are not lost to the banking system as a whole. T F

20. The monetary multiplier is excess reserves divided by required reserves. T F

21. The maximum demand-deposit expansion is equal to excess reserves divided by the monetary multiplier. T F

22. If the banking system has $10 million in excess reserves and if the reserve ratio is 25%, it can increase its loans by $40 million. T F

23. When borrowers from a commercial bank wish to have cash rather than demand deposits, the money-creating potential of the banking system is increased. T F

24. A desire by banks to hold excess reserves may reduce the size of the monetary multiplier. T F

25. There is a need for the Federal Reserve System to control the money supply because profit-seeking banks tend to make changes in the money supply that are procyclical. T F

■ MULTIPLE-CHOICE QUESTIONS

Circle the letter that corresponds to the best answer.

1. The fractional reserve system of banking started when goldsmiths began
   - **(a)** accepting deposits of gold for safe storage
   - **(b)** issuing receipts for the gold stored with them
   - **(c)** using deposited gold to produce products for sale to others
   - **(d)** issuing paper money in excess of the amount of gold stored with them

2. When cash is deposited in a demand-deposit account in a commercial bank, there is
   - **(a)** a decrease in the money supply
   - **(b)** an increase in the money supply
   - **(c)** no change in the composition of the money supply
   - **(d)** a change in the composition of the money supply

3. A commercial bank has actual reserves of $9000 and liabilities of $30,000, and the required reserve ratio is 20%. The excess reserves of the bank are
   - **(a)** $3,000
   - **(b)** $6,000
   - **(c)** $7,500
   - **(d)** $9,000

4. The primary reason commercial banks must keep required reserves on deposit at the Federal Reserve Banks is to
   - **(a)** protect the deposits in the commercial bank against losses
   - **(b)** provide the means by which checks drawn on the commercial bank and deposited in other commercial banks can be collected
   - **(c)** add to the liquidity of the commercial bank and protect it against a "run" on the bank
   - **(d)** provide the Fed with a means of controlling the lending ability of the commercial bank

5. A depositor places $750 in cash in a commercial bank, and the reserve ratio is 33 1/3%; the bank sends the $750 to the Federal Reserve Bank. As a result, the *reserves* and the *excess reserves* of the bank have been increased, respectively, by
   - **(a)** $750 and $250
   - **(b)** $750 and $500
   - **(c)** $750 and $750
   - **(d)** $500 and $500

6. A commercial bank has no excess reserves until a depositor places $600 in cash in the bank. The bank then adds the $600 to its reserves by sending it to the Federal Reserve Bank. The commercial bank then lends $300 to a borrower. As a consequence of these transactions the size of the money supply has
   - **(a)** not been affected
   - **(b)** increased by $300
   - **(c)** increased by $600
   - **(d)** increased by $900

7. A commercial bank has excess reserves of $500 and a required reserve ratio of 20%; it grants a loan of $1,000 to a borrower. If the borrower writes a check for $1,000 which is deposited in another commercial bank, the first bank will be short of reserves, after the check has been cleared, in the amount of
   - **(a)** $200
   - **(b)** $500
   - **(c)** $700
   - **(d)** $1,000

8. A commercial bank sells a $1,000 government security to a securities dealer. The dealer pays for the bond in cash, which the bank adds to its vault cash. The money supply has
   - **(a)** not been affected
   - **(b)** decreased by $1,000

(c) increased by $1,000
(d) increased by $1,000 multiplied by the reciprocal of the required reserve ratio

9. A commercial bank has deposit liabilities of $100,000, reserves of $37,000, and a required reserve ratio of 25%. The amount by which a *single commercial bank* and the amount by which the *banking system* can increase loans are, respectively
(a) $12,000 and $48,000
(b) $17,000 and $68,000
(c) $12,000 and $60,000
(d) $17,000 and $85,000

10. If the required reserve ratio were 12 1/2%, the value of the monetary multiplier would be
(a) 5
(b) 6
(c) 7
(d) 8

11. The commercial banking system has excess reserves of $700, makes new loans of $2,100, and is just meeting its reserve requirements. The required reserve ratio is
(a) 20%
(b) 25%
(c) 30%
(d) 33 1/3%

12. The commercial banking system, because of a recent change in the required reserve ratio from 20% to 30%, finds that it is $60 million short of reserves. If it is unable to obtain any additional reserves it must decrease the money supply by
(a) $60 million
(b) $180 million
(c) $200 million
(d) $300 million

13. Only one commercial bank in the banking system has an excess reserve, and its excess reserve is $100,000. This bank makes a new loan of $80,000 and keeps an excess reserve of $20,000. If the required reserve ratio for all banks is 20%, the potential expansion of the money supply is
(a) $80,000
(b) $100,000
(c) $400,000
(d) $500,000

14. The money-creating potential of the banking system is reduced when
(a) bankers choose to hold excess reserves
(b) borrowers choose to hold none of the funds they have borrowed in currency
(c) the Federal Reserve lowers the required reserve ratio
(d) bankers borrow from the Federal Reserve

15. The excess reserves held by banks tend to
(a) rise during periods of prosperity
(b) fall during periods of recession
(c) rise during periods of recession
(d) fall when interest rates in the economy fall

16. Unless controlled, the money supply will
(a) fall during periods of prosperity
(b) rise during periods of recession
(c) change in a procyclical fashion
(d) change in an anticyclical fashion

Use the following balance sheet for the First National Bank to answer Questions 17, 18, 19, 20, and 21. Assume the required reserve ratio is 20%.

Assets		Liabilities and Net Worth	
Reserves	$ 50,000	Demand Deposits	$150,000
Loans	70,000	Capital Stock	100,000
Securities	30,000		
Property	100,000		

17. This commercial bank has excess reserves of
(a) $10,000
(b) $20,000
(c) $30,000
(d) $40,000

18. This bank can safely expand its loans by a maximum of
(a) $50,000
(b) $40,000
(c) $30,000
(d) $20,000

19. Using the original bank balance sheet, assume that the bank makes a loan of $10,000 and has a check cleared against it for the amount of the loan; then its reserves and demand deposits will now be
(a) $40,000 and $140,000
(b) $40,000 and $150,000
(c) $30,000 and $150,000
(d) $60,000 and $140,000

20. Using the original bank balance sheet, assume that the bank makes a loan of $15,000 and has a check cleared against it for the amount of the loan; then it will have excess reserves of
(a) $5,000
(b) $10,000
(c) $15,000
(d) $20,000

21. If the original bank balance sheet was for the commercial banking *system,* rather than a single bank, loans and deposits could have been expanded by a maximum of
(a) $50,000
(b) $100,000
(c) $150,000
(d) $200,000

22. The claims of the owners of the bank against the bank assets is the bank's
(a) net worth
(b) liabilities
(c) balance sheet
(d) fractional reserves

23. The selling of government bonds by commercial banks is most similar to the

(a) making of loans by banks because both actions increase the money supply
(b) making of loans by banks because both actions decrease the money supply
(c) repayment of loans to banks because both actions decrease the money supply
(d) repayment of loans to banks because both actions increase the money supply

Answer Questions 24 and 25 on the basis of the following consolidated balance sheet for the commercial banking system. All figures are in billions. Assume that the required reserve ratio is 12.5%.

Assets		Liabilities and Net Worth	
Reserves	$ 40	Demand Deposits	$200
Loans	80	Capital Stock	120
Securities	100		
Property	200		

24. The maximum amount by which this commercial banking system can expand the supply of money by lending is
(a) $120 billion
(b) $240 billion
(c) $350 billion
(d) $440 billion

25. If there is a deposit of $20 billion of new currency into checking accounts in the banking system, excess reserves will increase by
(a) $16.5 billion
(b) $17.0 billion
(c) $17.5 billion
(d) $18.5 billion

■ PROBLEMS

1. The following table shows the simplified balance sheet of a commercial bank. Assume that the figures given show the bank's assets and demand-deposit liabilities *prior to each of the following four transactions.* Draw up the balance sheet as it would appear after each of these transactions is completed and place the balance-sheet figures in the appropriate column. Do *not* use the figures you place in columns a, b, and c when you work the next part of the problem; start all parts of the problem with the printed figures.

		(a)	(b)	(c)	(d)
Assets:					
Cash	$100	$____	$____	$____	$____
Reserves	200	____	____	____	____
Loans	500	____	____	____	____
Securities	200	____	____	____	____
Liabilities and net worth:					
Demand deposits	900	____	____	____	____
Capital stock	100	100	100	100	100

a. A check for $50 is drawn by one of the depositors of the bank, given to a person who deposits it in another bank, and cleared (column a).
b. A depositor withdraws $50 in cash from the bank, and the bank restores its vault cash by obtaining $50 in additional cash from its Federal Reserve Bank (column b).
c. A check for $60 drawn on another bank is deposited in this bank and cleared (column c).
d. The bank sells $100 in government bonds to the Federal Reserve Bank in its district (column d).

2. Following are five balance sheets for a single commercial bank (columns 1a–5a). The required reserve ratio is 20%.

a. Compute the required reserves (A), ignoring vault cash, the excess reserves (B) of the bank (if the bank is short of reserves and must reduce its loans or obtain additional reserves, show this by placing a minus sign in front of the amounts by which it is short of reserves), and the amount of new loans it can extend (C).

	(1a)	(2a)	(3a)	(4a)	(5a)
Assets:					
Cash	$ 10	$ 20	$ 20	$ 20	$ 15
Reserves	40	40	25	40	45
Loans	100	100	100	100	150
Securities	50	60	30	70	60
Liabilities and net worth:					
Demand deposits	175	200	150	180	220
Capital stock	25	20	25	50	50
A. Required reserve	$____	$____	$____	$____	$____
B. Excess reserve	____	____	____	____	____
C. New loans	____	____	____	____	____

b. In the following table, draw up for the individual bank the five balance sheets as they appear after the bank has made the new *loans* that it is capable of making.

	(1b)	(2b)	(3b)	(4b)	(5b)
Assets:					
Cash	$____	$____	$____	$____	$____
Reserves	____	____	____	____	____
Loans	____	____	____	____	____
Securities	____	____	____	____	____
Liabilities and net worth:					
Demand deposits	____	____	____	____	____
Capital stock	____	____	____	____	____

3. The table on the top of the next page shows several reserve ratios. Compute the monetary multiplier for each reserve ratio and enter the figures in column 2. In column 3 show the maximum amount by which a single commercial bank can increase its loans for each dollars worth of excess reserves it possesses. In column 4 indicate the maximum amount by which the banking system can increase its loans for each dollar's worth of excess reserves in the system.

(1)	(2)	(3)	(4)
12 1/2%	$____	$____	$____
16 2/3%	____	____	____
20%	____	____	____
25%	____	____	____
30%	____	____	____
33 1/3%	____	____	____

4. At the bottom of the page is the simplified consolidated balance sheet for *all* commercial banks in the economy. Assume that the figures given show the banks' assets and liabilities *prior to each of the following three transactions* and that the reserve ratio is 20%. Do *not* use the figures you placed in columns 2 and 4 when you begin parts **b** and **c** of the problem; start parts **a, b,** and **c** of the problem with the printed figures.

a. The public deposits $5 in cash in the banks and the banks send the $5 to the Federal Reserve, where it is added to their reserves. Fill in column 1. If the banking system extends the maximum amount of new loans which it is capable of extending, show in column 2 the balance sheet as it would then appear.

b. The banking system sells $8 worth of securities to the Federal Reserve. Complete column 3. Assuming the system extends the maximum amount of credit of which it is capable, fill in column 4.

c. The Federal Reserve lends $10 to the commercial banks; complete column 5. Complete column 6 showing the condition of the banks after the maximum amount of new loans which the banks are capable of making is granted.

SHORT ANSWER AND ESSAY QUESTIONS

1. Why does a bank's balance sheet balance?

2. How did the early goldsmiths come to issue paper money and then become bankers?

3. Explain the difference between a 100% and fractional reserve system of banking.

4. What are two significant characteristics of a fractional reserve system of banking?

5. Explain what happens to the money supply when a bank accepts deposits of cash.

6. What are legal reserves? How are they determined? How are legal reserves related to the reserve ratio?

7. Define the meaning of excess reserves. How are they calculated?

8. Explain why bank reserves can be an asset to the depositing commercial bank but a liability to the Federal Reserve Bank receiving them.

9. Commercial banks seek both profits and safety. Explain how the balance sheet of the commercial banks reflects the desires of bankers for profits and for liquidity.

10. What is the Federal funds rate?

11. Discuss how the Federal funds market helps banks reconcile the two goals of profits and liquidity.

12. Do the reserves held by commercial banks satisfactorily protect the bank's depositors? Are the reserves of commercial banks needed? Explain your answers.

13. Explain why the granting of a loan by a commercial bank increases the supply of money. Why does the repayment of a loan decrease the supply of money?

14. How does the buying or selling of government securities by commercial banks influence the money supply?

15. The owner of a sporting goods store writes a check on his account in a Kent, Ohio, bank and sends it to one of his suppliers who deposits it in his bank in Cleveland, Ohio. How does the Cleveland bank obtain payment from the Kent bank? If the two banks were in Kent and New York City, how would one bank pay the other? How are the excess reserves of the two banks affected?

16. Why is a single commercial bank able to lend safely only an amount equal to its excess reserves?

		(1)	(2)	(3)	(4)	(5)	(6)
Assets:							
Cash	$ 50	$____	$____	$____	$____	$____	$____
Reserves	100	____	____	____	____	____	____
Loans	200	____	____	____	____	____	____
Securities	200	____	____	____	____	____	____
Liabilities and net worth:							
Demand deposits	500	____	____	____	____	____	____
Capital stock	50	50	50	50	50	50	50
Loans for Federal Reserve	0	____	____	____	____	____	____
Excess reserves		____	____	____	____	____	____
Maximum possible expansion of the money supply		____	____	____	____	____	____

17. No one commercial bank ever lends an amount greater than its excess reserve, but the banking system as a whole is able to extend loans and expand the money supply by an amount equal to the system's excess reserves multiplied by the reciprocal of the reserve ratio. Explain why this is possible and how the multiple expansion of deposits and money takes place.

18. What is the monetary multiplier? How does it work?

19. On the basis of a given amount of excess reserves and a given reserve ratio, a certain expansion of the money supply may be possible. What are two reasons why the potential expansion of the money supply may not be fully achieved?

20. Why is there a need for monetary control in the U.S. economy?

ANSWERS

Chapter 14 How Banks Create Money

FILL-IN QUESTIONS

1. thrift, checkable
2. assets, net worth, liabilities, assets = liabilities + net worth
3. fractional, less than 100%
4. *a.* money, reserves; *b.* panics, regulation
5. vault, till
6. not changed
7. its district Federal Reserve Bank
8. required, liabilities
9. Fed
10. fractional
11. actual, required
12. control of
13. an asset, a liability
14. decreased, increased, decreased, increased
15. excess
16. increases, 10,000, decreases, 10,000
17. decreases, 10,000, increases, 10,000
18. profits, liquidity
19. Federal funds, Federal funds
20. required
21. smaller
22. excess, monetary multiplier
23. decrease, $36
24. withdrawal, excess
25. recession, prosperity, less

TRUE-FALSE QUESTIONS

1. F, p. 287
2. F, pp. 287-288
3. F, p. 288
4. F, p. 288
5. T, p. 289
6. T, pp. 289, 293-294
7. F, p. 290
8. T, p. 290
9. T, p. 291
10. T, p. 291
11. F, p. 291
12. F, pp. 291-293
13. F, p. 295
14. T, p. 295
15. T, p. 295
16. F, p. 296
17. T, p. 296
18. F, p. 296
19. T, pp. 296-299
20. F, p. 299
21. F, p. 299
22. T, p. 299
23. F, p. 300
24. T, p. 300
25. T, pp. 300-302

MULTIPLE-CHOICE QUESTIONS

1. b, p. 288
2. d, pp. 289
3. a, pp. 290-291
4. d, pp. 291
5. b, pp. 291-293
6. b, p. 293-294
7. b, pp. 293-295
8. b, pp. 295-296
9. a, pp. 296-299
10. d, p. 299
11. d, p. 299
12. c, p. 299
13. c, pp. 299-300
14. a, p. 300
15. c, p. 302
16. c, p. 302
17. b, pp. 290-291
18. d, pp. 293-295
19. b, pp. 293-294
20. a, pp. 293-294
21. b, p. 299
22. a, pp. 287-288
23. c, p. 295
24. a, pp. 291, 299
25. c, p. 291

PROBLEMS

1.

	(a)	(b)	(c)	(d)
Assets:				
Cash	$100	$100	$100	$100
Reserves	150	150	260	300
Loans	500	500	500	500
Securities	200	200	200	100
Liabilities and net worth:				
Demand deposits	850	850	960	900
Capital stock	100	100	100	100

2. a.

	(1a)	(2a)	(3a)	(4a)	(5a)
A. Required reserve	$35	$40	$30	$36	$44
B. Excess reserve	5	0	−5	4	1
C. New loans	5	0	*	4	1

b.

	(1b)	(2b)	(3b)	(4b)	(5b)
Assets:					
Cash	$ 10	$ 20	$ 20	$ 20	$ 15
Reserves	40	40	25	40	45
Loans	105	100	*	104	151
Securities	50	60	30	70	60
Liabilities and net worth:					
Demand deposit	180	200	*	184	221
Capital stock	25	20	25	50	50

*If an individual bank is $5 short of reserves it must either obtain additional reserves of $5 by selling loans, securities, or its own IOUs to the reserve bank or contract its loans by $25.

3.

(1)	(2)	(3)	(4)
12 1/2%	$8	$1	$8
16 2/3%	6	1	6
20%	5	1	5
25%	4	1	4
30%	3 1/3	1	3 1/3
33 1/3%	3	1	3

4. see top of following page

SHORT ANSWER AND ESSAY QUESTIONS

1. pp. 287-288
2. p. 288
3. p. 288
4. p. 288
5. p. 289-290
6. p. 290
7. p. 291
8. pp. 291-292
9. p. 296
10. p. 296
11. p. 296
12. p. 291
13. pp. 293-295
14. pp. 295-296
15. pp. 292-293
16. pp. 293-295
17. pp. 296-299
18. pp. 299-300
19. p. 300
20. pp. 300-302

	(1)	(2)	(3)	(4)	(5)	(6)
Assets:						
Cash	$ 50	$ 50	$ 50	$ 50	$ 50	$ 50
Reserves	105	105	108	108	110	110
Loans	200	220	200	240	200	250
Securities	200	200	192	192	200	200
Liabilities and net worth:						
Demand deposit	505	525	500	540	500	550
Capital stock	50	50	50	50	50	50
Loans from Federal Reserve	0	0	0	0	10	10
Excess reserves	4	0	8	0	10	0
Maximum possible expansion of the money supply	20	0	40	0	50	0

CHAPTER 15

Monetary Policy

Chapter 15 is the third chapter dealing with money and banking. It explains how the Board of Governors of the Federal Reserve System and the Federal Reserve Banks affect output, income, employment, and the price level of the economy. Central-bank policy designed to affect these variables is called monetary policy, the goal of which is full employment without inflation.

The first half of the chapter explains how the *Federal Reserve* achieves its basic goal. In this discussion, attention should be paid to the following: (1) the important items on the balance sheet of the Federal Reserve Banks; (2) the three major controls available to the Federal Reserve, and how the employment of these controls can affect the reserves, excess reserves, actual money supply, and money-creating potential of the banking system; (3) the actions the Federal Reserve would take if it were pursuing a ***tight money policy*** to curb inflation, and the actions it would take if it were pursuing an ***easy money policy*** to reduce unemployment, and (4) the relative importance of the three major controls which the Federal Reserve uses or has used to influence the economy.

Following the examination of "The Tools of Monetary Policy," Professors McConnell and Brue explain how the demand for and the supply of money determine the interest rate (in the "money market"), and how the interest rate and the investment-demand schedule determine the level of equilibrium GDP. How an easy money policy and a tight money policy work through this cause-effect chain is illustrated with examples and summarized in Table 15-3.

This explanation of monetary policy makes it clear that the effect of a change in the money supply depends on just how steep or flat the money-demand and investment-demand curves are. There may also be feedback effects from an easy money policy because the increased economic activity may cause interest rates to rise and partially offset interest-rate decreases started by the easy money policy. Changes in monetary policy and aggregate demand also have different output and price-level outcomes depending on the range of the aggregate supply curve where the changes in aggregate demand occur.

A major section of the chapter discusses the strengths and shortcomings of or problems with monetary policy as a stabilization tool. Its strengths are related to its speed, flexibility, and its isolation from political pressures. Its weaknesses are its potential ineffectiveness during recessions, while changes in the velocity of money can offset the policy effects.

Monetary policy can be used in different ways in the real world, and it can be subject to complications. In recent years, the Federal Reserve has made changes in monetary policy by adjusting its targets for the Federal fund rates. These rates in turn have an effect on other interest rates in the economy, such as the prime interest rate. The effectiveness of monetary policy is also complicated by linkages with the international economy. Monetary policy can affect exchange rates and net exports, which in turn can strengthen or weaken its intended effects.

The final section of the chapter is short but extremely important. Figure 15-3 in that section gives you an overview of the economic factors and government policies that affect aggregate demand and supply. It summarizes much of the economic theory and policy that have been discussed in this chapter and the eight others that preceded it.

■ CHECKLIST

When you have studied this chapter you should be able to

□ State the fundamental objective of monetary policy.
□ List the important assets and liabilities of the Federal Reserve Banks.
□ Identify the three tools of monetary policy.
□ Explain how the Federal Reserve expands or contracts the money supply by buying or selling government bonds.
□ Describe how an increase or decrease in reserve requirement can increase or decrease the money supply.
□ Illustrate how an increase or decrease in the discount rate increases or decreases the money supply.
□ Describe three actions the Fed can take to pursue an easy money policy.
□ Describe three actions the Fed can take to pursue a tight money policy.
□ Discuss the relative importance of monetary policy tools.
□ Draw the demand-for-money and the supply-of-money curves and use them to show how a change in the supply of money will affect the interest rate.
□ Draw an investment-demand curve to explain the effects of changes in the interest rate on investment spending.
□ Construct an aggregate supply and demand graph to show how aggregate demand and the equilibrium level of

GDP are affected by changes in interest rates and investment spending.

☐ Use a cause-effect chain to explain the links between a change in the money supply and a change in the equilibrium level of GDP when there is an easy money policy and a tight money policy.

☐ State precisely how the steepness of the demand-for-money and of the investment-demand curves affects the impact of a change in the money supply on the equilibrium GDP.

☐ Explain the feedback effects from different monetary policies.

☐ Use the ranges of the aggregate supply curve to explain how a change in aggregate demand is divided between changes in real output and the price level.

☐ List three strengths of monetary policy.

☐ Discuss five shortcomings of or problems with monetary policy.

☐ Describe the relationship among the Federal funds rate, the prime interest rate, and monetary policy in recent years.

☐ Describe how the effectiveness of an easy money policy or a tight money policy is influenced by net exports and how these policies affect international trade deficits.

☐ Use Figure 15-4 to summarize the key factors and policies affecting aggregate supply and demand, and the level of output, employment, income, and prices in an economy.

■ CHAPTER OUTLINE

1. The fundamental *objective* of monetary policy is full employment without inflation. The Federal Reserve can accomplish this objective by exercising control over the amount of excess reserves held by commercial banks and thereby influencing the size of the money supply and the level of aggregate expenditures.

2. By examining the consolidated *balance sheet* and the principal assets and liabilities of the Federal Reserve Banks, an understanding of the ways the Federal Reserve can control and influence the reserves of commercial banks and the money supply can be obtained.

a. The principal assets of the Federal Reserve Banks (in order of size) are U.S. government securities and loans to commercial banks.

b. Their principal liabilities are Federal Reserve Notes, the reserve deposits of commercial banks, and U.S. Treasury deposits.

3. The Federal Reserve Banks use *three principal tools* (techniques or instruments) to control the reserves of banks and the size of the money supply.

a. The Federal Reserve can buy and sell government securities in the open market.

(1) Buying securities in the open market from either banks or the public increases the reserves of banks.

(2) Selling securities in the open market to either banks or the public decreases the reserves of banks.

b. It can raise or lower the reserve ratio.

(1) Raising the reserve ratio decreases the excess reserves of banks and the size of the monetary (demand-deposit) multiplier.

(2) Lowering the reserve ratio increases the excess reserves of banks and the size of the monetary multiplier.

c. It can also lower the discount rate to encourage banks to borrow reserves from the Fed and raise it to discourage them from borrowing reserves from the Fed.

d. Monetary policy can be easy or tight.

(1) An easy money policy can be implemented by actions of the Federal Reserve to buy government bonds in the open market, decrease the discount rate, or decrease the reserve ratio.

(2) A tight money policy can be implemented by actions of the Federal Reserve to sell government bonds in the open market, increase the discount rate, or increase the reserve ratio.

e. Open-market operations are the most important of the three monetary tools.

4. Monetary policy affects the equilibrium GDP in many ways.

a. In the money market the demand-for- and the supply-of-money curves determine the real interest rate, the investment-demand curve and this rate of interest determine investment spending, and investment spending affects aggregate demand and the equilibrium levels of real output and prices.

b. If unemployment and deflation are the problems, the Federal Reserve takes policy actions to increase the money supply, causing the interest rate to fall and investment spending to increase, thereby increasing aggregate demand and increasing real GDP by a multiple of the increase in investment.

c. But if inflation is the problem, the Federal Reserve uses its tools to decrease the money supply, causing the interest rate to rise and investment spending to decrease, thereby reducing aggregate demand and inflation.

d. There are refinements and feedback effects to monetary policy that must be considered.

(1) The steeper the demand-for-money curve and the flatter the investment-demand curve, the greater will be the effect on the equilibrium GDP of a change in the money supply.

(2) Changes in the equilibrium GDP that result from a change in the money supply will alter the demand for money and dampen the effect of the change in the money supply on the GDP.

e. The aggregate supply curve will influence how the change in investment spending and aggregate demand is divided between change in real output and changes in the price level.

5. Whether monetary policy is effective in promoting full employment without inflation is a debatable question because monetary policy has both *strengths* and *shortcomings* or problems in fighting recession and inflation.

a. Its strengths are that it can be more quickly changed than fiscal policy, it is more isolated from political pressure than fiscal policy, and it has been successful when it was used in recent situations.

b. Its five shortcomings or problems are that it

(1) may be subject to less control by the Federal Reserve because of recent changes in banking practices,

(2) is more effective in fighting inflation than it is in curbing recession,
(3) can be offset by changes in the velocity of money,
(4) may not have a significant effect on investment spending, and
(5) may produce changes in interest income and expenses that have offsetting effects.

c. The recent focus of the monetary policy of the Federal Reserve has been interest rates.
(1) The Federal Reserve can influence the ***Federal funds rate*** by buying or selling bonds. When the Federal Reserve buys bonds, it becomes cheaper for banks to borrow excess reserves overnight because the Federal funds rate falls; conversely, when the Federal Reserve sells bonds, the Federal funds rates rise and it becomes more expensive for banks to borrow funds.
(2) The ***prime interest rate*** is the rate that banks charge their most creditworthy customers; it tends to rise and fall with the Federal funds rate.

d. There are **international linkages** to monetary policy.
(1) An easy money policy to bring the economy out of recession or slow growth will tend to lower domestic interest rates and cause the dollar to depreciate. In this situation, net exports will increase, thus increasing aggregate demand and reinforcing the effect of the easy money policy.
(2) A tight money policy to reduce inflation will tend to raise domestic interest rates and cause the dollar to appreciate. These events will decrease net exports and reduce aggregate demand, thereby strengthening the tight money policy.
(3) An easy policy is compatible with the goal of correcting a balance of trade deficit, but a tight money policy conflicts with this economic goal.

6. The equilibrium levels of output, employment, income, and prices are determined by the interaction of aggregate supply and demand.

a. There are four expenditure components of aggregate demand: consumption, investment, net export spending, and government spending.

b. There are three major components of aggregate supply: the prices of inputs or resources, factors affecting the productivity with which resources are used, and the legal and institutional environment.

c. Fiscal, monetary, or other government policies may have an effect on the components of aggregate demand or supply, which in turn affect the level of output, employment, income, and prices.

■ HINTS AND TIPS

1. To acquire a thorough knowledge of how the Federal Reserve transactions affect reserves, excess reserves, the actual money supply, and the potential money supply, carefully study each of the sets of balance sheets which are used to explain these transactions. The items to watch are the reserves and demand deposits. Be sure that you know why a change is made in each balance sheet, and be able to make the appropriate balance-sheet entries as you trace through the effects of each transaction. Problem 2 in this chapter provides additional practice.

2. You must understand and remember the cause-effect chain of monetary policy. The best way to learn it is to draw your own chain (diagram or table) that shows the links for an easy money policy and a tight money policy. Then check your work against Table 15-3 in the text. Draw another chain for describing monetary policy and the net export effect. Check your cause-effect chain against Table 15-4 in the text.

3. The single most important figure for the macroeconomics part of the textbook is probably Figure 15-4. It gives an excellent overview and summary of the determinants of aggregate supply and demand and identifies the key policy variables that have been discussed in this chapter and Chapters 7–14.

■ IMPORTANT TERMS

monetary policy
open-market operations
reserve ratio
discount rate
easy money policy
tight money policy
velocity of money
Federal funds rate
prime interest rate

SELF-TEST

■ FILL-IN QUESTIONS

1. The objective of monetary policy in the United States is a full-employment (inflationary, noninflationary) ______________ level of total output. Responsibility for monetary policy rests with the (Secretary of the Treasury, Federal Board of Governors) ____________________, and they are put into effect by the 12 (largest commercial banks, Federal Reserve Banks) ____________________.

2. The two important assets of the Federal Reserve Banks are (Treasury deposits, government securities) ____________________ and (reserves of, loans to) ______________ commercial banks. The three major liabilities are (Treasury deposits, government securities) ____________________, (reserves of, loans to) ______________ commercial banks, and (government securities, Federal Reserve Notes) ________________.

3. The three tools the monetary authority uses to control the money supply are (open, closed) ______________-market operations, changing the (loan, reserve) ______________ ratio, and changing the (prime interest, discount) ______________ rate.

4. When the Federal Reserve Banks buy government securities in the open market, the reserves of commercial banks will (increase, decrease) ______________ and when they sell government securities in the open market, the reserves of commercial banks will ______________.

5. If the Federal Reserve Banks were to sell $10 million in government bonds to the *public* and the reserve ratio were 25%, the supply of money would immediately be reduced by $______________, the reserves of commercial banks would be reduced by $______________, and the excess reserves of the banks would be reduced by $______________. But if these bonds were sold to the commercial banks, the supply of money would immediately be reduced by $______________, the reserves of the banks would be reduced by $______________, and the excess reserves of the banks would be reduced by $______________.

6. An increase in the reserve ratio will (increase, decrease) ______________ the size of the monetary multiplier and ______________ the excess reserves held by commercial banks, thus causing the money supply to (increase, decrease) ______________. A decrease in the reserve ratio will (increase, decrease) ______________ the size of the monetary multiplier and ______________ the excess reserves held by commercial banks, thus causing the money supply to (increase, decrease) ______________.

7. If the Federal Reserve Banks were to lower the discount rate, commercial banks would tend to borrow (more, less) ______________ from them, and this would (increase, decrease) ______________ their excess reserves.

8. To increase the supply of money, the Federal Reserve Banks should (raise, lower) ______________ the reserve ratio, (buy, sell) ______________ securities in the open market, and/or (increase, decrease) ______________ the discount rate.

9. An easy money policy would be characterized by actions of the Federal Reserve to (increase, decrease) ______________ the discount rate, ______________ reserve ratios, and (buy, sell) ______________ government bonds, whereas a tight money policy would include actions taken to (increase, decrease) ______________ the discount rate, ______________ reserve ratios, and (buy, sell) ______________ government bonds.

10. The most effective and most often used tool of monetary policy is a change in (the discount rate, the reserve ratio, open-market operations) ______________, and a rarely used tool is a change in ______________; an announcement effect is created by a change in ______________, but it is relatively weak because banks may not be inclined to borrow even at a lower rate.

11. There is cause-effect chain of monetary policy.

a. In the money market, the demand for and the supply of money determine the equilibrium rate of (discount, interest) ______________.

b. This rate in turn determines the level of (government, investment) ______________ spending based on the ______________-demand curve.

c. This spending in turn affects aggregate (demand, supply) ______________, and the intersection of aggregate supply and demand determine the equilibrium level of real (interest, GDP) ______________ and the (discount, price) ______________ level.

d. When there is an increase in the supply-of-the money curve, the real interest rate will (increase, decrease) ______________, investment spending will ______________, aggregate demand will (increase, decrease) ______________, and real GDP will ______________.

12. To eliminate inflationary pressures in the economy, the traditional view holds that the monetary authority should seek to (increase, decrease) ______________ the reserves of commercial banks; this would tend to______________ the money supply and to (increase, decrease) ______________ the rate of interest, and this in turn would cause investment spending, aggregate demand, and GDP to ______________. This action by monetary authorities would be considered a(n) (easy, tight) ______________ money policy.

13. If there were a serious problem with unemployment in the economy, the traditional view would be that the Federal Reserve should pursue a(n) (easy, tight) __________ money policy, in which case the Federal Reserve would (buy, sell)______________ government bonds as a way of (increasing, decreasing) ______________ the money supply, and thereby ______________ interest rates; these events would have the effect of (increasing, decreasing) ______________ investment spending and thus ______________ real GDP.

14. The effect of a $1 billion increase or decrease in the money supply upon the equilibrium GDP is greater the (flatter, steeper) ________________ the demand-for-money curve and the ______________ the investment-demand curve.

15. An increase in the money supply will shift the aggregate (supply, demand) ______________ curve to the (right, left) ______________.

a. In the horizontal (or recession) range along the aggregate supply curve, this increase in the money supply will have a (small, large) ______________ effect on real domestic output and a ______________ effect on the price level.

b. In the vertical range along the aggregate supply curve, this increase in the money supply will have a (small, large) ______________ effect on real domestic output and a ______________ effect on the price level.

16. Monetary policy has strengths. Compared to fiscal policy, monetary policy is speedier and (more, less) ______________ flexible, ______________ isolated from political pressure, and (more, less) ______________ successfully used to counter inflation and recession in recent years.

17. Monetary policy has shortcomings or problems, too.

a. It may be subject to (more, less) ______________ control by the Federal Reserve because of recent changes in banking practices that give the Fed ______________ control of the money supply.

b. It may be more effective in counteracting (recession, inflation) ______________ than ______________.

c. It may be offset when the velocity of money changes in the (same, opposite) ______________ direction as the money supply.

d. It will not be effective if changes in the interest rate have (little, significant) ______________ effect on investment spending.

e. It will cause changes in interest income that (offset, reinforce) ______________ the intended effects on consumer or investment spending.

18. The interest rate that banks charge one another for overnight loans is the (prime interest, Federal funds) ‘ ______________ rate, but the rate banks charge their most creditworthy customers is the ______________ rate. The (prime interest, Federal funds) ______________ rate has been the recent focus of the monetary policy of the Federal Reserve.

19. An easy money policy (increases, decreases) ______________ net exports; a tight money policy ______________ net exports. The net export effect from an easy money policy thus (strengthens, weakens) ______________ domestic monetary policy, and the net export effect from a tight money policy ______________ it.

20. An easy money policy is (compatible, incompatible) ______________ with the economic goal of reducing a balance of trade deficit, but a tight money policy is ______________ with this economic goal.

■ TRUE-FALSE QUESTIONS

Circle the T if the statement is true, the F if it is false.

1. The fundamental goal of monetary policy is to stabilize interest rates. **T F**

2. The securities owned by the Federal Reserve Banks are almost entirely U.S. government bonds. **T F**

3. If the Federal Reserve Banks buy $15 in government securities from the public in the open market, the effect will be to increase the excess reserves of commercial banks by $15. **T F**

4. When the Federal Reserve sells bonds in the open market, the price of these bonds falls. **T F**

5. A change in the reserve ratio will affect the multiple by which the banking system can create money, but it will not affect the actual or excess reserves of member banks. **T F**

6. If the reserve ratio is lowered, some required reserves are turned into excess reserves. **T F**

7. When commercial banks borrow from the Federal Reserve Banks, they increase their excess reserves and their money-creating potential. **T F**

8. If the monetary authority wished to follow a tight money policy, it would sell government bonds in the open market. **T F**

9. An increase in the required reserve ratio tends to reduce the profits of banks. **T F**

10. The least effective and used tool of monetary policy is the open-market operation, in which government securities are bought and sold. **T F**

11. The equilibrium rate of interest is found at the intersection of the demand-for-money and the supply-of-money curves. **T F**

12. An increase in the equilibrium GDP will shift the demand-for-money curve to the left and increase the equilibrium interest rate. **T F**

13. Consumer spending is more sensitive to changes in the rate of interest than is investment demand. **T F**

14. There can be a feedback effect from an easy money policy because an increase in GDP resulting from the policy will also cause an increase in the demand for money, partially offsetting the interest-reducing effect of the policy. **T F**

15. When the economy is at or near full employment, an increase in the money supply tends to be inflationary. **T F**

16. It is generally agreed that fiscal policy is more effective than monetary policy in controlling the business cycle because fiscal policy is more flexible. **T F**

17. Monetary policy is subject to more political pressure than fiscal policy. **T F**

18. A tight money policy suffers from a "You can lead a horse to water, but you can't make him drink" problem. **T F**

19. A combination of a relatively flat money-demand curve and a relatively steep investment-demand curve will mean that a particular change in the money supply will cause a large change in investment and, thus, a large change in equilibrium GDP. **T F**

20. When interest rates increase, the reduction in spending for purchases of capital goods, homes, and autos is partially offset by the increase in spending by those who receive increased interest income. **T F**

21. In recent years, the Federal Reserve has announced its changes in monetary policy by changing its targets for the Federal funds rate. **T F**

22. The prime interest rate is the rate that banks charge other banks for overnight loans of excess reserves at Federal Reserve banks. **T F**

23. An easy money policy decreases net exports. **T F**

24. A tight money policy will tend to cause the dollar to appreciate. **T F**

25. A tight money policy is compatible with the goal of correcting a trade deficit. **T F**

■ MULTIPLE-CHOICE QUESTIONS

Circle the letter that corresponds to the best answer.

1. The agency directly responsible for monetary policy in the United States is
(a) the 12 Federal Reserve Banks
(b) the Board of Governors of the Federal Reserve System
(c) the Congress of the United States
(d) the U.S. Treasury

2. The largest single asset in the Federal Reserve Banks' consolidated balance sheet is
(a) securities
(b) the reserves of commercial banks
(c) Federal Reserve Notes
(d) loans to commercial banks

3. The largest single liability of the Federal Reserve Banks is
(a) securities
(b) the reserves of commercial banks
(c) Federal Reserve Notes
(d) loans to commercial banks

4. Assuming that the Federal Reserve Banks sell $20 million in government securities to commercial banks and the reserve ratio is 20%, then the effect will be
(a) to reduce the actual supply of money by $20 million
(b) to reduce the actual supply of money by $4 million
(c) to reduce the potential money supply by $20 million
(d) to reduce the potential money supply by $100 million

5. Which of the following is the most important control used by the Federal Reserve Banks to regulate the money supply?
(a) changing the reserve ratio
(b) open-market operations
(c) changing the discount rate
(d) changing the Federal funds rate

6. Assume that there is a 20% reserve ratio and that the Federal Reserve buys $100 million worth of government securities. If the securities are purchased from the public, this action has the potential to increase bank lending by a maximum of
(a) $500 million, but only by $400 million if the securities are purchased directly from commercial banks
(b) $400 million, but by $500 million if the securities are purchased directly from commercial banks
(c) $500 million, and also by $500 million if the securities are purchased directly from commercial banks
(d) $400 million, and also by $400 million if the securities are purchased directly from commercial banks

7. In the traditional or Keynesian chain of cause and effect between changes in the excess reserves of commercial banks and the resulting changes in output and employment in the economy,
(a) an increase in excess reserves will decrease the money supply
(b) a decrease in the money supply will increase the rate of interest
(c) an increase in the rate of interest will increase aggregate demand
(d) an increase in aggregate demand will decrease output and employment

8. Which of the following is more likely to be affected by changes in the rate of interest?
(a) consumer spending
(b) investment spending

(c) the spending of the Federal government
(d) the exports of the economy

9. The economy is experiencing inflation and the Federal Reserve decides to pursue a tight money policy. Which set of actions by the Fed would be most consistent with this policy?
(a) buying government securities and lowering the discount rate
(b) buying government securities and lowering the reserve ratio
(c) selling government securities and raising the discount rate
(d) selling government securities and lowering the discount rate

10. A newspaper headline reads: "Fed Cuts Discount Rate for Third Time This Year." This headline indicates that the Federal Reserve is most likely trying to
(a) reduce inflationary pressures in the economy
(b) increase the Federal funds rate
(c) reduce the cost of credit and stimulate the economy
(d) increase the value of the dollar

11. A change in the money supply has the *least* effect on the equilibrium GDP when
(a) both the demand-for-money and the investment-demand curves are steep
(b) both the demand-for-money and the investment-demand curves are flat
(c) the demand-for-money curve is flat and the investment-demand curve is steep
(d) the demand-for-money curve is steep and the investment-demand curve is flat

12. Which explanation best describes the feedback effects of an easy money policy? The increase in GDP resulting from the policy will
(a) decrease the demand for money, and partially offset the interest-reducing effect of the policy
(b) increase the demand for money, and partially offset the interest-increasing effect of the policy
(c) increase the demand for money, and partially offset the interest-reducing effect of the policy
(d) decrease the demand for money, and partially offset the interest-increasing effect of the policy

13. An increase in the money supply will have little or no effect on the price level in
(a) the horizontal range of the aggregate supply curve
(b) the intermediate range of the aggregate supply curve
(c) the vertical range of the aggregate supply curve
(d) any of the three ranges of the aggregate supply curve

Use the following graph to answer Questions 14, 15, and 16.

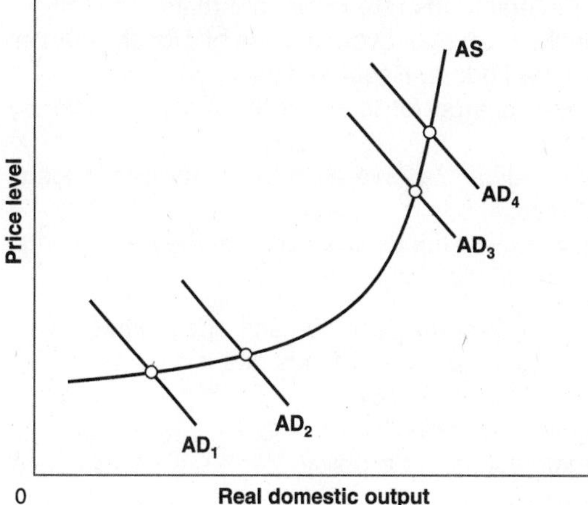

14. A shift from AD_1 to AD_2 would be most consistent with
(a) an increase in the prime interest rate
(b) an increase in the discount rate by the Federal Reserve
(c) the buying of securities by the Federal Reserve
(d) the selling of securities by the Federal Reserve

15. Which shift would be most consistent with the potential effects of tight money policy in an inflationary period in an economy where prices are flexible?
(a) AD_1 to AD_2
(b) AD_3 to AD_4
(c) AD_4 to AD_3
(d) AD_2 to AD_1

16. If the Federal Reserve adopted an easy money policy in a period of high unemployment, the situation can best be characterized by a shift from
(a) AD_1 to AD_2
(b) AD_3 to AD_4
(c) AD_4 to AD_3
(d) AD_2 to AD_1

17. Which one is considered a *strength* of monetary policy compared to fiscal policy?
(a) feedback effects
(b) cyclical asymmetry
(c) isolation from political pressure
(d) effect on changes in the velocity of money

18. An increase in the money supply is *least* effective in stimulating aggregate expenditures when the velocity of money
(a) falls as the money supply increases
(b) remains constant
(c) rises as the money supply increases
(d) is equal to 5

19. A shortcoming of monetary policy is that actions taken to increase the interest rate
(a) decrease investment spending and decrease interest income, thus doubling the effect
(b) increase investment spending and increase interest income, thus doubling the effect
(c) decrease investment spending but increase interest income, thus offsetting the effect
(d) increase investment spending but decrease interest income, thus offsetting the effect

20. The Federal funds rate is the rate that
(a) banks charge for overnight use of excess reserves held at the Federal Reserve banks
(b) banks charge for loans to the most creditworthy customers
(c) the Federal Reserve charges for short-term loans to commercial banks
(d) government bonds are sold at in the open-market operations of the Federal Reserve

21. When the Federal Reserve uses open-market operations to reduce the Federal funds rate it is pursuing a(n)
(a) easier money policy
(b) tighter money policy
(c) prime interest rate policy
(d) discretionary fiscal policy

22. When the Federal Reserve Banks decide to buy government bonds, the demand for government bonds will
(a) decrease, bond prices will decrease, and the interest rate will decrease
(b) increase, bond prices will increase, and the interest rate will decrease
(c) increase, bond prices will increase, and the interest rate will increase
(d) decrease, bond prices will increase, and the interest rate will decrease

23. A tight money policy in the United States is most likely to
(a) increase domestic interest rates and cause the value of the dollar to depreciate
(b) decrease domestic interest rates and cause the value of the dollar to appreciate
(c) increase domestic interest rates and cause the value of the dollar to appreciate
(d) decrease domestic interest rates and cause the value of the dollar to depreciate

24. Which policy combination would tend to reduce net exports?
(a) tight money policy and expansionary fiscal policy
(b) easy money policy and expansionary fiscal policy
(c) tight money policy and contractionary fiscal policy
(d) easy money policy and contractionary fiscal policy

25. A tight money policy that is used to reduce inflation in the domestic economy
(a) is best conducted by reducing the required reserve ratios at commercial banks
(b) increases net exports and the effectiveness of the policy
(c) conflicts with the economic goal of correcting a trade deficit
(d) causes the dollar to depreciate

■ PROBLEMS

1. Assume that the following consolidated balance sheet is for all commercial banks. Assume also that the required reserve ratio is 25% and that cash is *not* a part of the commercial banks' legal reserve.

Assets		Liabilities	
Cash	$ 50	Demand deposits	$400
Reserves	100	Loans from Federal Reserve	25
Loans	150	Net worth	75
Securities	200		
	$500		$500

a. To *increase* the supply of money by $100, the Fed could (buy, sell) ______________ securities worth $______________ in the open market.
b. To *decrease* the supply of money by $50, the Fed could (buy, sell) ______________ securities worth $______________ in the open market.

2. On the next page are the consolidated balance sheets of the Federal Reserve and of the commercial banks. Assume that the reserve ratio for commercial banks is 25%, that cash is *not* a part of a bank's legal reserve, and that the figures in column 1 show the balance sheets of the Federal Reserve and the commercial banks *prior to each of the following five transactions.* Place the new balance-sheet figures in the appropriate columns and complete A, B, C, D, and E in these columns. Do *not* use the figures you place in columns 2 through 5 when you work the next part of the problem; start all parts of the problem with the printed figures in column 1.
a. The Federal Reserve Banks sell $3 in securities to the public, which pays by check (column 2).
b. The Federal Reserve Banks buy $4 in securities from the commercial banks (column 3).
c. The Federal Reserve Banks lower the required reserve ratio for commercial banks to 20% (column 4).
d. The U.S. Treasury buys $5 worth of goods from U.S. manufacturers and pays the manufacturers by checks drawn on its accounts at the Federal Reserve Banks (column 5).
e. Because the Federal Reserve Banks have raised the discount rate, commercial banks repay $6 which they owe to the Federal Reserve (column 6).

3. On the following graph is the demand-for-money curve which shows the amounts of money consumers and firms

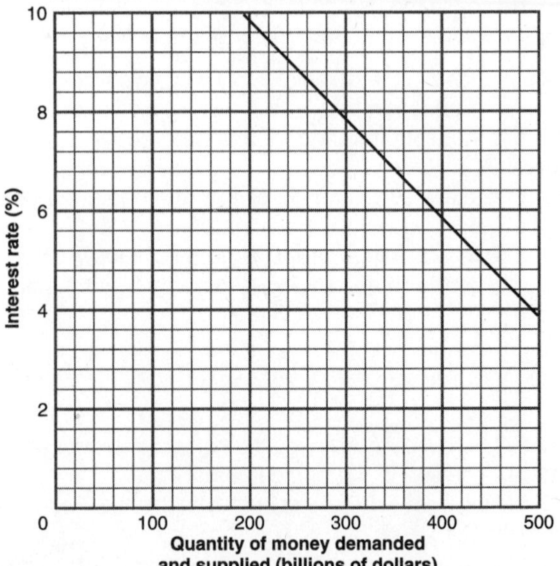

	(1)	(2)	(3)	(4)	(5)	(6)
	Federal Reserve Banks					
Assets:						
Gold certificates	$ 25	$____	$____	$____	$____	$____
Securities	30	____	____	____	____	____
Loans to commercial banks	10	____	____	____	____	____
Liabilities:						
Reserves of commercial banks	50	____	____	____	____	____
Treasury deposits	5	____	____	____	____	____
Federal Reserve Notes	10	____	____	____	____	____
	Commercial Banks					
Assets:						
Reserves	$ 50	$____	$____	$____	$____	$____
Securities	70	____	____	____	____	____
Loans	90	____	____	____	____	____
Liabilities:						
Demand deposits	200	____	____	____	____	____
Loans from Federal Reserve	10	____	____	____	____	____
A. Required reserves		____	____	____	____	____
B. Excess reserves		____	____	____	____	____
C. How much has the money supply changed?		____	____	____	____	____
D. How much ***more*** can the money supply change?		____	____	____	____	____
E. What is the total of C and D?		____	____	____	____	____

wish to hold at various rates of interest (when the nominal GDP in the economy is given).

a. Suppose the supply of money is equal to $300 billion. (1) Draw the supply-of-money curve on the graph on page 168. (2) The equilibrium rate of interest in the economy is____________ %.

b. Below is a graph of an investment-demand curve which shows the amounts of planned investment at various rates of interest. Given your answer to (2) above, how much will investors plan to spend for capital goods? $__________ billion.

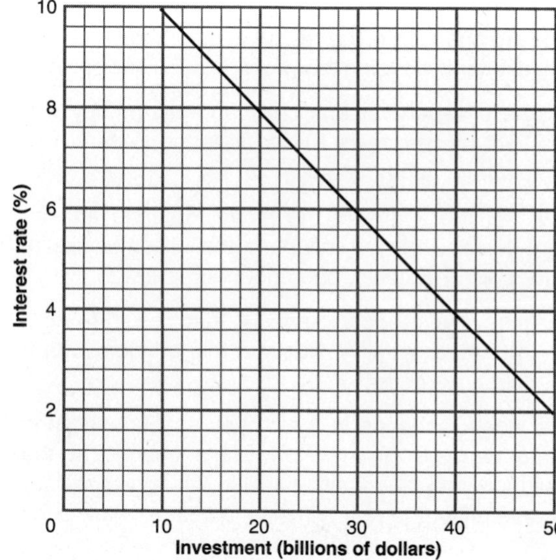

c. The following figure shows the aggregate supply (**AS**) curve in this economy. On the graph, draw an aggregate demand curve (**AD$_1$**) so that it crosses the **AS** curve in the horizontal range of aggregate supply. Label the price level (***P$_1$***) and output level (***Q$_1$***) associated with the intersection of **AD$_1$** and **AS**.

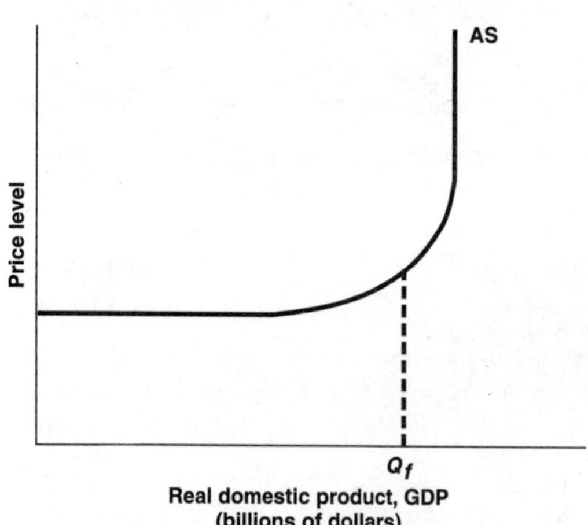

d. Now assume that monetary authorities increase the money supply to $400.

(1) On the graph on page 168, plot the new money supply curve. The new equilibrium interest rate is ______________ %.

(2) On the investment graph, determine the level of investment spending that is associated with this new interest rate: $______________ billion. By how much

has investment spending increased as a result of the change in the interest rate? $____________ billion.
(3) Assume that the marginal propensity to consume is .75. What is the multiplier? ____________ By how much will the new investment spending increase aggregate demand? $____________ billion.
(4) On the previous figure, indicate how the change in investment spending affects aggregate demand. Draw a new aggregate demand curve (**AD_2**) so that it crosses the **AS** curve in the intermediate range of aggregate supply at the output level (**Q_f**). Also label the new price level (**P_2**) associated with the intersection of **AD_2** and **AS**.

4. Columns 1 and 2 of the following table show the aggregate supply schedule. (The price level is a price index, and real domestic output is measured in billions of dollars.)

(1) Price level	(2) Real output	(3) AD_1	(4) AD_2	(5) AD_3	(6) AD_4	(7) AD_5	(8) AD_6
.30	$1500	$1600	$1700	$2070	$2400	$2920	$3020
.30	1600	1600	1700	2070	2400	2920	3020
.30	1700	1600	1700	2070	2400	2920	3020
.40	1790	1500	1600	1970	2300	2820	2920
.50	1870	1400	1500	1870	2200	2720	2820
.60	1940	1300	1400	1770	2100	2620	2720
.70	2000	1200	1300	1670	2000	2520	2620
.80	2050	1100	1200	1570	1900	2420	2520
.90	2090	1000	1100	1470	1800	2320	2420
1.00	2120	900	1000	1370	1700	2220	2320
1.10	2120	800	900	1270	1600	2120	2220
1.20	2120	700	800	1170	1500	2020	2120

a. The horizontal range on this aggregate supply schedule is from a real domestic output of zero to $____________ billion.
b. The vertical range on this aggregate supply curve is at the real domestic output of $____________ billion.
c. If the aggregate demand schedule were that shown in columns 1 and 3, the equilibrium real domestic output would be $____________ billion and the price level would be ____________.
d. If the aggregate demand schedule increased from that shown in columns 1 and 3 to the one shown in columns 1 and 4, the equilibrium real domestic output would ____________ and the price level would ____________.
e. If the aggregate demand schedule increased from that shown in columns 1 and 5 to the one shown in columns 1 and 6, the equilibrium real domestic output would ____________ and the price level would ____________.
f. If the aggregate demand schedule increased from that shown in columns 1 and 7 to the one shown in columns 1 and 8, the equilibrium real domestic output would ____________ and the price level would ____________.

■ SHORT ANSWER AND ESSAY QUESTIONS

1. What is the basic goal of monetary policy? What actions are taken to achieve this goal during recession or during a period of high inflation?

2. What are the important assets and liabilities of the Federal Reserve Banks?

3. Explain how the monetary policy tools of the Federal Reserve Banks would be used to contract the supply of money. How would they be used to expand the supply of money?

4. What is the difference between the effects of the Federal Reserve's buying (selling) government securities in the open market from (to) commercial banks and from (to) the public?

5. Which of the monetary policy tools available to the Federal Reserve is most effective? Why is it more important than other tools?

6. Using three graphs, explain what determines (*a*) the equilibrium interest rate, (*b*) investment spending, and (*c*) the equilibrium GDP. Now use these three graphs to show the effects of a decrease in the money supply upon the equilibrium GDP.

7. Using your answers to Question 6, (*a*) what determines how large the effect of the decrease in the money supply on the equilibrium GDP will be, and (*b*) how would the change in the equilibrium GDP affect the demand-for-money curve, the interest rate, investment spending, and the GDP itself?

8. Explain how the Board of Governors and the Federal Reserve Banks can influence income, output, employment, and the price level. In your explanation, employ the following concepts: reserves, excess reserves, the supply of money, the availability of bank credit, and the rate of interest.

9. Why are changes in the rate of interest more likely to affect investment spending than consumption and saving?

10. What are the characteristics of an easy money policy or a tight money policy? How does the Federal Reserve implement such policies?

11. How will the shape of the money-demand and investment-demand curves influence the effectiveness of monetary policy? Explain, and show with a graph.

12. Describe the feedback effects that result from a change in monetary policy. Illustrate this problem with a graph.

13. How does a change in the money supply affect the aggregate demand curve? How will a change in the money supply and the resulting shift in the aggregate demand curve affect the real domestic output and the price level in (*a*) the horizontal range and (*b*) the vertical range, along the aggregate supply curve?

14. What are the major strengths of monetary policy?

15. How might recent changes in banking practices affect control of monetary policy?

16. Why is monetary policy more effective in controlling inflation than in reducing unemployment?

17. Why might a change in velocity reduce the effectiveness of monetary policy?

18. What is the prime interest rate, and how is it related to the Federal funds rate? What happens to the Federal funds rate when the Federal Reserve expands or contracts the money supply through open-market operations?

19. Explain how the net export effect influences the effectiveness of a tight or an easy money policy.

20. What type of monetary policy would you recommend to correct a balance of trade deficit? Why?

ANSWERS

Chapter 15 Monetary Policy

FILL-IN QUESTIONS

1. noninflationary, Federal Board of Governors, Federal Reserve Banks
2. government securities, loans to, Treasury deposits, reserves of, Federal Reserve Notes
3. open, reserve, discount
4. increase, decrease
5. 10 million, 10 million, 7.5 million, 0, 10 million, 10 million
6. decrease, decrease, decrease, increase, increase, increase
7. more, increase
8. lower, buy, decrease
9. decrease, decrease, buy, increase, increase, sell
10. open-market operations, the reserve ratio, the discount rate
11. *a.* interest; *b.* investment, investment; *c.* demand, GDP, price; *d.* decrease, increase, increase, increase
12. decrease, decrease, increase, decrease, tight
13. easy, buy, increasing, decreasing, increasing, increasing
14. steeper, flatter
15. demand, right; *a.* large, small; *b.* small, large
16. more, more, more
17. *a.* less, less; *b.* inflation, recession; *c.* opposite; *d.* little; *e.* offset
18. Federal funds, prime interest, Federal funds
19. increases, decreases, strengthens, strengthens
20. compatible, incompatible

TRUE-FALSE QUESTIONS

1. F, p. 306
2. T, p. 306-307
3. F, p. 308-309
4. T, pp. 310-311
5. F, pp. 311-312
6. T, p. 311
7. T, p. 312
8. T, p. 313
9. T, p. 313
10. F, p. 313
11. T, pp. 314-316
12. F, pp. 314-316
13. F, p. 316
14. T, p. 318
15. T, p. 318
16. F, p. 318
17. F, p. 319
18. F, pp. 319-320
19. F, p. 320
20. T, p. 320
21. T, pp. 320-321
22. F, p. 321
23. F, pp. 322-323
24. T, pp. 322-323
25. F, pp. 323-324

MULTIPLE-CHOICE QUESTIONS

1. b, p. 305
2. a, pp. 306-307
3. c, pp. 306-307
4. d, pp. 309-310
5. b, p. 313
6. b, pp. 307-309
7. b, pp. 314-316
8. b, p. 316
9. c, p. 313
10. c, pp. 316-317
11. c, p. 318
12. c, p. 318
13. a, p. 318
14. c, pp. 315-317
15. c, pp. 315, 317
16. a, pp. 315-317
17. c, p. 319
18. a, p. 320
19. c, p. 320
20. a, pp. 320-321
21. a, pp. 320-321
22. b, pp. 310-311
23. c, pp. 322-323
24. a, pp. 322-323
25. c, pp. 323-324

PROBLEMS

1. *a.* buy, 25; *b.* sell, 12 1/2
2. see below

	(2)	(3)	(4)	(5)	(6)
			Federal Reserve Banks		
Assets:					
Gold certificates	$ 25	$ 25	$ 25	$ 25	$ 25
Securities	27	34	30	30	30
Loans to commercial banks	10	10	10	10	4
Liabilities:					
Reserves of commercial banks	47	54	50	55	44
Treasury deposits	5	5	5	0	5
Federal Reserve Notes	10	10	10	10	10
			Commercial Banks		
Assets:					
Reserves	$ 47	$ 54	$ 50	$ 55	$ 44
Securities	70	66	70	70	70
Loans	90	90	90	90	90
Liabilities:					
Demand deposits	197	200	200	205	200
Loans from Federal Reserve	10	10	10	10	4
A. Required reserves	49.25	50	40	51.25	50
B. Excess reserves	−2.25	4	10	3.75	−6
C. How much has the money supply changed?	−3	0	0	+5	0
D. How much ***more*** can the money supply change?	−9	+16	+50	+15	−24
E. What is the total of C and D?	−12	+16	+50	+20	−24

3. *a.* (2) 8; *b.* 20; *c.* see Figure 15-2 in text; *d.* (1) 6, (2) 30, 10, (3) 4, 40, (4) see Figure 15-2 in text

4. *a.* 1700; *b.* 2120; *c.* 1600, .30; *d.* rise to $1700 billion, remain constant; *e.* rise from $1870 billion to $2000 billion, rise from .50 to .70; *f.* remain constant at $2120 billion, rise from 1.10 to 1.20

SHORT ANSWER AND ESSAY QUESTIONS

1. p. 306
2. pp. 306-307
3. pp. 312-313
4. pp. 307-311
5. p. 313
6. pp. 314-317
7. pp. 317-318
8. pp. 314-317
9. p. 316
10. pp. 316-317
11. p. 318
12. p. 318
13. p. 318
14. pp. 318-319
15. p. 319
16. pp. 319-320
17. p. 320
18. pp. 320-321
19. pp. 322-323
20. pp. 323-324

CHAPTER 16

Extending the Analysis of Aggregate Supply

Chapter 16 extends the basic aggregate demand–aggregate supply (AD–AS) model first introduced in Chapter 11. This addition will give you the analytical tools to improve your understanding of the relationship between unemployment and inflation. The chapter also offers different economic perspectives on the appropriateness of government policy for controlling inflation and reducing unemployment.

The major extension to the AD–AS model is the distinction between the short-run aggregate supply curve and the long-run aggregate supply curve. In the ***short run,*** nominal wages are fixed, so an increase in the price level increases business profits and real output. In the ***long run,*** nominal wages are flexible, so business profits and employment return to their original level. Thus, the ***long-run aggregate supply curve*** is vertical at the full-employment level of output.

The distinction between the short-run and long-run aggregate supply curve requires a reinterpretation of ***demand-pull inflation*** and ***cost-push inflation.*** Although demand-pull inflation will increase the price level and real output in the short run, once nominal wages increase, the temporary increase in output is gone, but the price level will be higher at the full-employment level of output. Cost-push inflation will increase the price level and decrease real output in the short run, but again, once nominal wages fall, output and the price level will return to their original positions. If government policymakers try to counter cost-push inflation by increasing aggregate demand, they may make matters worse by increasing the price level and causing the short-run aggregate supply curve to decrease, thereby setting off an inflationary spiral.

The relationship between inflation and unemployment has been studied for many years. One influential observation, supported by data from the 1950s and 1960s, was embodied in the ***Phillips Curve,*** which suggested that there was a stable and predictable tradeoff between the rate of inflation and the unemployment rate. During the 1960s, it was thought that this tradeoff could be used for formulating sound monetary and fiscal policy to manage the economy.

The ***stagflation*** of the 1970s, however, called into question the shape and stability of the Phillips Curve because the economy was experiencing both higher rates of inflation and unemployment. One widely accepted explanation of events was that the aggregate supply shocks of this period shifted the Phillips Curve rightward. When these shocks dissipated in the 1980s, the Phillips Curve began to shift back to its original position.

An alternative explanation of the stagflation of the 1970s and early 1980s came from the ***natural rate hypothesis.*** Two variants of this hypothesis were ***adaptive expectations theory*** and ***rational expectations theory*** **(RET).** Both theories contend that the downsloping Phillips Curve is actually a vertical line in the long run at the natural rate of unemployment. In this view, government attempts to reduce the unemployment rate below the natural rate simply result in inflation. The major difference between adaptive and rational expectations is that the former believes there are time lags in wage and price adjustments in the economy which can bring about a decline in unemployment in the short run, whereas the latter sees no distinction between short-run and long-run adjustments.

Another perspective on aggregate supply comes from ***supply-side economics,*** which gained visibility during the Reagan administration (1981–1988). Supply-side economists pointed to the role of the Federal government in causing the slump in productivity and economic growth in the 1970s. The solutions, which became the program of Reaganomics, were to come from large cuts in personal and corporate income taxes and reduced government regulation. It was thought that the tax cuts would increase incentive to work, save, and invest, thus increasing productivity and aggregate supply. Despite its successes, this economic program has been criticized for the failure of the tax cuts to increase aggregate supply beyond its historical rate.

Chapter 16 is important because it provides the analytical foundation for understanding disputes over macroeconomic theory and policy. These disputes will be the focus of Chapter 17.

■ CHECKLIST

When you have studied this chapter you should be able to

☐ Give a definition of the short run and long run in macroeconomics.
☐ Distinguish between a change in real wages and a change in nominal wages.
☐ Draw the short-run aggregate supply curve and describe its characteristics.
☐ Explain how the long-run aggregate supply curve is determined.
☐ Draw a graph that illustrates equilibrium in the extended AD-AS model.

☐ Explain demand-pull inflation using the extended AD-AS model and identify its short-run and long-run outcomes.
☐ Describe cost-push inflation using the extended AD-AS model.
☐ Give two generalizations about the policy dilemma for government in dealing with cost-push inflation.
☐ Explain recession and the process of adjustment using the extended AD-AS model.
☐ Describe how to derive a Phillips Curve from an AD-AS model.
☐ Draw a Phillips Curve and identify the basic tradeoffs.
☐ Define stagflation and contrast it with the conclusion from the Phillips Curve.
☐ Explain how aggregate supply shocks contributed to the stagflation of the 1970s and how they might have shifted the Phillips Curve.
☐ List events that contributed to stagflation's demise and their effect on the price level and output.
☐ Contrast the traditional view of the Phillips Curve with the natural rate hypothesis.
☐ Use adaptive expectations theory and its view of the short and long-run Phillips Curve to explain inflation and disinflation.
☐ Describe how rational expectations theory differs from adaptive expectations theory.
☐ Discuss the changing interpretations of the Phillips Curve and the current perspective on the issue.
☐ List the three tax-transfer disincentives identified by supply-side economists.
☐ Use the Laffer Curve to explain the hypothesized relationship between marginal tax rates and tax revenues.
☐ State three criticisms of the Laffer Curve.
☐ Give examples of how overregulation adversely affects the economy.
☐ Describe how supply-side economics was embodied in Reaganomics.
☐ Evaluate the effectiveness of Reaganomics.

■ CHAPTER OUTLINE

1. The aggregate supply curve has short- and long-run characteristics. The short-run curve also shifts because of an increase in nominal wages. These factors make the analysis of aggregate supply and demand more complex.

a. The short run is a period in which nominal wages (and other input prices) remain fixed as the price level changes. The long run is a period in which nominal wages are fully responsive to changes in the price level.

b. The *short-run aggregate supply curve* is upward sloping: An increase in the price level increases business revenues and profits because nominal wages are fixed; in contrast, when the price level decreases, business revenue and profits decline, and so does real output.

c. The *long-run aggregate supply curve* is vertical at the potential level of output. Increases in the price level will increase nominal wages and cause a decrease (shift left) in the short-run aggregate supply curve, or declines in the price level reduce nominal wages and increase (shift right) the short-run aggregate supply curve. In either case, although the price level changes, output returns to its potential level, and the long-run aggregate supply curve is vertical at the full-employment level of output.

d. Equilibrium in the extended AD-AS model occurs at the price level and output where the aggregate demand crosses the long-run aggregate supply curve and also crosses the short-run aggregate supply curve.

2. The extended AD-AS model can be applied to explain conditions of inflation and recession in an economy.

a. *Demand-pull inflation* will increase (shift right) the aggregate demand curve, which increases the price level and causes a temporary increase in real output. In the long run, workers will realize that their real wages have fallen and will demand raises in their nominal wages. The short-run aggregate supply curve, which was based on fixed nominal wages, now decreases (shifts left), resulting in an even higher price level and with real output returning to its initial level.

b. *Cost-push inflation* will decrease (shift left) the short-run aggregate supply curve. This situation will increase the price level and temporarily decrease real output, causing a recession. It creates a policy dilemma for government.

(1) If government takes actions to counter the cost-push inflation and recession by increasing aggregate demand, the price level will move to an even higher level, and the actions may set off an inflationary spiral.

(2) If government takes no action, the recession will eventually reduce nominal wages, and eventually the short-run aggregate supply curve will shift back to its original position.

c. If aggregate demand decreases, it will result in a recession. If prices and wages are flexible downward, the price level will fall and increase real wages. Eventually, nominal wages will fall to restore the original real wages. This change will increase short-run aggregate supply and end the recession, but not without a long period of high unemployment and lost output.

3. The *Phillips Curve* is important for examining the short- and long-run relationship between inflation and unemployment.

a. If aggregate supply is constant and the economy is operating in the upsloping range of aggregate supply, then the greater the rate of increase in aggregate demand, the higher the rate of inflation (and output) and the lower the rate of unemployment. This inverse relationship between the rate of inflation and unemployment is known as the Phillips Curve.

b. In the 1960s, economists thought there was a predictable tradeoff between unemployment and inflation. All society had to do was to choose the combination of inflation and unemployment on the Phillips Curve.

c. Events of the 1970s and 1980s called into question the stability of the Phillips Curve. In that period, the economy experienced both higher rates of inflation and unemployment (*stagflation*). The data suggested that the Phillips Curve had either shifted right or that there was no dependable tradeoff between inflation and unemployment.

d. The stagflation of the 1970s and early 1980s was most likely caused by aggregate supply shocks from an increase in resource prices (oil), shortages in agricultural production, higher wage demands, and declining productivity. These shocks decreased the short-run aggregate supply curve, which increased the price level and decreased output (and unemployment).

e. The demise of stagflation came in the 1982–1989 period because of such factors as a severe recession in 1981–1982 that reduced wage demands, increased foreign competition that restrained price increases, and a decline in OPEC's monopoly power. The short-run aggregate supply curve increased, and the price level and unemployment rate fell. This meant that the Phillips Curve may have shifted back (left). Recent unemployment-inflation data are now similar to the Phillips Curve of the 1960s.

4. The *natural rate hypothesis* questions the existence of a downsloping Phillips Curve and views the economy as stable in the long run at the natural rate of unemployment. There are two variants to this hypothesis.

a. *Adaptive expectations theory* suggests that an increase in aggregate demand sponsored by government may temporarily reduce unemployment as the price level increases and profits expand, but the actions also set into motion other events.

(1) The increase in the price level reduces the real wages of workers who demand and obtain higher nominal wages; these actions return unemployment to its original level.

(2) Back at the original level, there is now a higher actual and expected rate of inflation for the economy, so the short-run Phillips Curve has shifted upward.

(3) The process is repeated when government tries again to reduce unemployment, and the rise in the price level accelerates as the short-run Phillips Curve shifts upward.

(4) In the long run, the Phillips Curve is stable only as a vertical line at the natural rate of unemployment; there is no tradeoff between unemployment and inflation.

b. *Rational expectations theory (RET)* assumes that workers fully anticipate that government policies to reduce unemployment will also be inflationary, and they increase their nominal wage demands to offset the expected inflation; thus there will not even be a temporary decline in unemployment or even a short-run Phillips Curve.

c. The interpretations of the Phillips Curve have changed over the past three decades based on the adaptive and rational expectations analysis. This consensus view of economists is that there is a short-run tradeoff between unemployment and inflation, but not a long-run tradeoff. Most economists also now acknowledge that both aggregate supply shocks and misguided government policies contributed to the stagflation of the 1970s.

5. *Supply-side economics* views aggregate supply as active rather than passive in explaining changes in the price level and unemployment.

a. It argues that higher marginal tax rates and a widespread system for public transfer payments reduce incentives to work and that high taxes also reduce incentives to save and invest. These policies lead to a misallocation of resources, less productivity, and a decrease in aggregate supply. To counter these effects, supply-side economists call for a cut in marginal tax rates.

b. The Laffer Curve suggests that it is possible to lower tax rates and increase tax revenues, thus avoiding a budget deficit because the policies will result in less tax evasion and reduced transfer payments.

c. Critics of *supply-side economics* and the Laffer Curve suggest that the policy of cutting tax rates will not work because

(1) It has only a small and uncertain effect on incentives to work (or on aggregate supply).

(2) It would increase aggregate demand relative to aggregate supply and thus reinforce inflation when there is full employment.

(3) The expected tax revenues from tax rate cuts depend on assumptions about the position on the Laffer Curve. If tax cuts reduce tax revenues, it only contributes to problems with existing budget deficits.

d. Another tenet of supply-side economics is that overregulation of the economy by government (both industrial and social regulation) has decreased productivity, led to higher costs, and reduced economic growth.

e. The economic program of the Reagan administration (1981–1988), or *Reaganomics,* was based on supply-side ideas. This program reduced government regulation and cut personal and corporate income taxes.

(1) The record shows that by the late 1980s, there was a reduction in inflation and interest rates, an economic expansion, and the achievement of full employment.

(2) The supply-side approach can also be criticized. There is little evidence to show that the tax cuts increased aggregate supply beyond its historic pace, or provided strong incentives to work, or increased saving or investment. The economic expansion may also be attributed to the expansionary effect of the tax cuts on aggregate demand. The tax cuts also increased U.S. budget deficits and were not financed by increasing tax revenues as predicted by the Laffer Curve.

■ HINTS AND TIPS

1. Chapter 16 is a more difficult chapter because the AD-AS model is made more complex. Spend extra time mastering this material, but do not try to read everything at once. Break the chapter into its logical sections, and practice drawing each graph.

2. Be sure you understand the distinction between the short-run and long-run aggregate supply curve. Then use these ideas to explain demand-pull inflation, cost-push inflation, and recession. Doing problem 2 will be especially helpful.

3. Be sure you understand the different perspectives on the shape and stability of the controversial Phillips Curve.

4. Use Figure 16-9 in the text to help you understand the distinction between adaptive and rational expectations. Problem 4 will help your understanding of this complicated graph.

IMPORTANT TERMS

short-run aggregate supply curve	**adaptive expectations theory**
long-run aggregate supply curve	**disinflation**
Phillips Curve	**rational expectations theory (RET)**
stagflation	**supply-side economics**
aggregate supply shocks	**Laffer Curve**
natural rate hypothesis	**Reaganomics**

SELF-TEST

FILL-IN QUESTIONS

1. In an AD-AS model with a stable aggregate supply curve, when the economy is producing in the upsloping portion of the aggregate supply curve, an increase in aggregate demand will (increase, decrease) ______________ real output and employment, but a decrease in aggregate supply will ______________ real output and employment.

2. In the short run, nominal wages are (fixed, variable) ______________, and in the long run, nominal wages are ______________. In the short run, the aggregate supply curve is (upsloping, vertical) ______________, and in the long run the curve is ______________.

3. Demand-pull inflation will shift the aggregate demand curve (right, left) ______________, which will (decrease, increase) ______________ the price level and temporarily ______________ real output. As a consequence, the (short-run, long-run) ______________ aggregate supply curve will shift left because of a rise in (real, nominal) ______________ wages, producing a (lower, higher) ______________ price level at the original level of real output.

4. Cost-push inflation will shift the short-run aggregate supply curve (right, left) ______________; thus the price level will (increase, decrease) ______________ and real output will temporarily ______________.

5. If government takes no actions to counter the cost-push inflation, the resulting recession will (increase, decrease) ______________ nominal wages and shift the short-run aggregate supply curve back to its original position, yet if the government tries to counter the cost-push inflation and recession with a(n) ______________ in aggregate demand, the price level will move even higher.

6. A recession will occur when there is a(n) (increase, decrease) ______________ in aggregate demand. If the controversial assumption is made that prices and wages are flexible downward, then the price level (rises, falls) ______________. Real wages will then (increase, decrease) ______________, but eventually nominal wages will ______________ and the aggregate supply curve will (increase, decrease) ______________ and end the recession.

7. Along the upsloping portion of the short-run aggregate supply curve, the greater the increase in aggregate demand, the (greater, smaller) ______________ the increase in the rate of inflation, the ______________ the increase in real output, and the (greater, smaller) ______________ the unemployment rate.

8. The Phillips Curve indicates that there will be a(n) (direct, inverse) ______________ relationship between the rate of inflation and the unemployment rate. This means that high rates of inflation will be associated with a (high, low) ______________ unemployment rate, or that low rates of inflation will be associated with a ______________ unemployment rate.

9. The policy tradeoff based on a stable Phillips Curve was that for the economy to reduce the unemployment rate, the rate of inflation must (increase, decrease) ______________, and to reduce the rate of inflation, the unemployment rate must ______________.

10. During the 1970s and early 1980s, the Phillips Curve was (stable, unstable) ______________ because of aggregate (demand, supply) ______________ shocks. These shocks produced (demand-pull, cost-push) ______________ inflation that resulted in a simultaneous increase in the inflation rate and the unemployment rate.

11. Factors that contributed to stagflation's demise during the 1982–1989 period include the 1981–1982 (inflation, recession) ______________ largely caused by a(n) (tight, easy) ______________ money policy. There was also (increased, decreased) ______________ foreign competition and the ______________ monopoly power of OPEC. These factors (increased, decreased) ______________ the short-run aggregate supply curve; thus the inflation ______________ and the unemployment rate (increased, decreased) ______________.

12. The standard explanation for the Phillips Curve is that during the stagflation of the 1970s, the Phillips Curve shifted (right, left) ______________, and during the demise of stagflation from 1982–1989, the Phillips Curve shifted ______________. In this view, there is a tradeoff between the unemployment rate and rate of inflation, but changes in (short-run, long-run) ______________ aggregate supply can shift the Phillips Curve.

13. Another explanation for stagflation is the (inflation, natural) ______________ rate hypothesis. It suggests that the inverse relationship between the rate of inflation and the rate of unemployment (does, does not) ________ exist in the long run, and the economy is stable at its natural rate of (unemployment, inflation) ______________.

14. The theory of adaptive expectations suggests that people form their expectations of inflation based on experience and (immediately, gradually) ______________ change expectations. With this theory, the (short-run, long-run) ______________ Phillips Curve may be downsloping, but the ______________ Phillips Curve is vertical at the natural rate of unemployment, and attempts by government to reduce the unemployment rate result in a(n) (increase, decrease) ______________ in the rate of inflation.

15. In the view of adaptive expectations, when the actual rate of inflation is higher than the expected rate, profits temporarily (fall, rise) ______________ and the unemployment rate temporarily falls, but when the actual rate of inflation is lower than the expected rate, profits temporarily ______________ and the unemployment rate temporarily rises. The latter case would occur during a period of (inflation, disinflation) ______________.

16. Rational expectations theory suggests that the inflation resulting from a government policy to reduce the unemployment rate will be (unanticipated, anticipated) ________________, and this will (reinforce, offset) ________________ the intent of the government policy. Workers will try to keep their (real, nominal) __________ wages constant by obtaining an increase in their ______________ wages. This action brings about (a rise, a fall, no change) ______________ in the price level and ______________ in the unemployment rate.

17. It is the view of supply-side economics that high marginal tax rates (increase, decrease) ______________ incentives to work, save, invest, and take risks. According to supply-side economists, the remedy for stagflation is a substantial (increase, decrease) ______________ in marginal tax rates that would ______________ economic growth through a(n) (increase, decrease) ______________ in aggregate supply.

18. The Laffer Curve depicts the relationship between tax rates and tax revenues. In theory, as the tax rates increase from 0%, tax revenues will (increase, decrease) ______________ to some maximum level, after which tax revenues will ______________ as the tax rates increase, or as tax rates are reduced from 100%, tax revenues will (increase, decrease) ______________ to some maximum level, after which tax revenues will ______________ as tax rates decrease.

19. Criticisms of the Laffer Curve are that the effects of a cut in tax rates on incentives to work, save, and invest are (large, small) ______________; the tax cuts generate an increase in aggregate (demand, supply) ______________ that outweigh any increase in aggregate ______________ and may lead to inflation in a full-employment situation; and tax cuts can produce a (gain, loss) ______________ in tax revenues that only adds to a budget deficit.

20. The two principal elements of Reaganomics were calls for (more, less) ______________ regulation by government and ______________ taxation of personal and corporate incomes. These changes were designed to increase productivity and economic growth by stimulating aggregate (demand, supply) ______________. The evidence suggests that supply-side economics ideas (did, did not) __________ work as proposed in Reaganomics. The cut in tax rates primarily (increased, decreased) ______________ aggregate demand, and the tax cuts ______________ tax revenues that added to budget deficits. The effect of tax cuts on saving, investment, and productivity was (minimal, substantial) ______________.

■ TRUE-FALSE QUESTIONS

Circle the T if the statement is true, the F if it is false.

1. The short run in macroeconomics is a period in which nominal wages are fully responsive to changes in the price level. **T F**

2. The short-run aggregate supply curve has a negative slope. **T F**

3. The long-run aggregate supply curve is vertical because nominal wages eventually change by the same amount as changes in the price level. **T F**

4. Demand-pull inflation will increase the price level and real output in the short run, but in the long run, only the price level will increase. **T F**

5. Cost-push inflation results in a simultaneous increase in the price level and real output. **T F**

6. When the economy is experiencing cost-push inflation, an inflationary spiral is likely to result when the government enacts policies to maintain full employment. **T F**

7. A recession is the result of an increase in the short-run aggregate supply curve. **T F**

8. If the economy is in a recession, prices and nominal wages will presumably fall, and the short-run aggregate supply curve will increase, so that real output returns to its full-employment level. **T F**

9. The Phillips Curve shows an inverse relationship between the rate of inflation and the unemployment rate. **T F**

10. Stagflation refers to a situation in which both the price level and the unemployment rate are rising. **T F**

11. The data from the 1970s suggest that the Phillips Curve shifted to the left. **T F**

12. One important explanation for the stagflation of the 1970s and early 1980s was a series of aggregate supply shocks. **T F**

13. The factors that contributed to the demise of stagflation during the 1980s tended to shift the Phillips Curve to the right. **T F**

14. The natural rate hypothesis suggests that there is a natural rate of inflation for the economy. **T F**

15. The adaptive expectations theory indicates that there may be a short-run tradeoff between inflation and unemployment, but no long-run tradeoff. **T F**

16. From the adaptive expectations perspective, when the actual rate of inflation is higher than the expected rate, the unemployment rate will rise. **T F**

17. Adaptive expectations theory can be used to explain disinflation. **T F**

18. An implication of rational expectations theory is that labor will anticipate the inflationary effects of government policies to reduce unemployment and increase its wage demands, so the policy will increase inflation. **T F**

19. According to rational expectations theory, the Phillips Curve is horizontal at the current rate of inflation. **T F**

20. Most economists reject the idea of a short-run tradeoff between the unemployment and inflation rates but accept the long-run tradeoff. **T F**

21. Supply-side economists contend that aggregate demand is the active factor in determining the price level and real output in an economy. **T F**

22. One proposition of supply-side economics is that the marginal tax rates on earned income should be reduced to increase the incentives to work. **T F**

23. The Laffer Curve suggests that lower tax rates will increase the rate of inflation. **T F**

24. The economic effects of overregulation on the economy is an increase in costs and prices and a decrease in economic growth. **T F**

25. There is considerable evidence that the tax cuts made as part of Reaganomics increased aggregate supply more rapidly than its historical pace. **T F**

■ MULTIPLE-CHOICE QUESTIONS

Circle the letter that corresponds to the best answer.

1. For macroeconomics, the short run is a period in which nominal wages
- **(a)** remain fixed as the price level stays constant
- **(b)** change as the price level stays constant
- **(c)** remain fixed as the price level changes
- **(d)** change as the price level changes

2. Once sufficient time has elapsed for wage contracts to expire and nominal wage adjustments to occur, the economy enters
- **(a)** the short run
- **(b)** the long run
- **(c)** a period of inflation
- **(d)** a period of unemployment

3. A graph of the short-run aggregate supply curve is
- **(a)** downsloping, and a graph of the long-run aggregate supply is upsloping
- **(b)** upsloping, and a graph of the long-run aggregate supply is vertical
- **(c)** upsloping, and a graph of the long-run aggregate supply is downsloping
- **(d)** vertical, and a graph of the long-run aggregate supply is upsloping

4. Assume that initally your nominal wage was $10 an hour and the price index was 100. If the price level increases to 110, then your
- **(a)** real wage has increased to $11.00
- **(b)** real wage has decreased to $9.09
- **(c)** nominal wage has increased to $11.00
- **(d)** nominal wage has decreased to $9.09

5. In the extended AD-AS model, demand-pull inflation occurs because of an increase in aggregate demand that will eventually produce
- **(a)** an increase in real wages, thus a decrease in the short-run aggregate supply curve
- **(b)** an increase in nominal wages, thus an increase in the short-run aggregate supply curve
- **(c)** a decrease in nominal wages, thus a decrease in the short-run aggregate supply curve
- **(d)** an increase in nominal wages, thus a decrease in the short-run aggregate supply curve

6. In the short run, demand-pull inflation increases real
- **(a)** output and decreases the price level
- **(b)** wages and nominal wages
- **(c)** output and the price level
- **(d)** wages and decreases nominal wages

7. In the long run, demand-pull inflation
- **(a)** decreases real wages
- **(b)** increases the price level
- **(c)** increases the unemployment rate
- **(d)** decreases real output

8. A likely result of the government trying to reduce the unemployment associated with cost-push inflation through stimulative fiscal policy or monetary policy is
(a) an inflationary spiral
(b) stagflation
(c) a recession
(d) disinflation

9. What will occur if the government adopts a hands-off approach to cost-push inflation?
(a) an increase in real output
(b) a fall in unemployment
(c) demand-pull inflation
(d) a recession

10. If prices and wages are flexible, a recession will increase real wages as the price level falls. Eventually, nominal wages will
(a) fall to the previous real wages, and the short-run aggregate supply will increase
(b) rise to the previous real wages, and the short-run aggregate supply will increase
(c) fall to the previous real wages, and the short-run aggregate supply will decrease
(d) rise to the previous real wages, and the short-run aggregate supply will decrease

11. The traditional Phillips Curve is based on the idea that with a constant short-run aggregate supply curve, the greater the increase in aggregate demand
(a) the greater the increase in the unemployment rate
(b) the greater the increase in the rate of inflation
(c) the greater the increase in real output
(d) the smaller the increase in nominal wages

12. The traditional Phillips Curve shows the
(a) inverse relationship between the rate of inflation and the unemployment rate
(b) inverse relationship between the nominal and the real wage
(c) direct relationship between unemployment and demand-pull inflation
(d) tradeoff between the short run and the long run

13. Supply shocks which cause a leftward shift in the aggregate supply curve, aggregate demand remaining constant, will
(a) decrease the price level
(b) decrease the unemployment rate
(c) increase real output
(d) increase both the price level and the unemployment rate

14. Which would be a factor contributing to the demise of stagflation during the 1982–1989 period?
(a) a lessening of foreign competition
(b) a strengthening of the monopoly power of OPEC
(c) a recession brought on largely by a tight monetary policy
(d) an increase in regulation of airline and trucking industries

15. The shift in the Phillips Curve during the 1982–1989 period was the consequence of a
(a) rightward shift in aggregate demand
(b) rightward shift in aggregate supply
(c) leftward shift in aggregate demand
(d) leftward shift in aggregate supply

16. The natural rate hypothesis suggests that the economy is stable only in the
(a) short run at the natural rate of unemployment
(b) short run at the natural rate of inflation
(c) long run at the natural rate of unemployment
(d) long run at the natural rate of inflation

17. The adaptive expectations theory suggests that if increases in nominal wage rates lag behind increases in the price level and government attempts to reduce unemployment by using fiscal and monetary policies, then employment
(a) and the price level increase in the long run
(b) remains constant and the price level increases in the short run
(c) increases and the price level remains constant in the short run
(d) remains constant and the price level increases in the long run

18. The rational expectations theorists contend that when government attempts to reduce unemployment by using monetary and fiscal policies, unemployment decreases
(a) temporarily and the price level rises
(b) permanently and the price level rises
(c) both temporarily and permanently and the price level rises
(d) neither temporarily nor permanently and the price level rises

19. In the view of natural rate theorists, the long-run Phillips Curve is
(a) horizontal
(b) vertical
(c) upsloping
(d) downsloping

20. Disinflation, or reductions in the rate of inflation, can be explained based on the natural rate conclusion that when the
(a) actual rate of inflation is lower than the expected rate, the unemployment rate will rise to bring the expected and actual rates into balance
(b) expected rate of inflation is lower than the actual rate, the unemployment rate will rise to bring the expected and actual rates into balance
(c) actual rate of inflation is higher than the expected rate, the unemployment rate will fall to bring the expected and actual rates into balance
(d) expected rate of inflation is higher than the actual rate, the unemployment rate will fall to bring the expected and actual rates into balance

21. The natural rate theory suggests that the aggregate supply curve
(a) is stable in the short run so long as nominal wages do not increase in the short run in response to the increase in the price level
(b) is stable in the long run because real wages are continually changing

(c) will shift to the right when the price of capital increases
(d) will shift to the right when nominal wages increase

22. Supply-side economists contend that the U.S. system of taxation reduces
(a) unemployment but causes inflation
(b) incentives to work, save, and invest
(c) transfer payments to the poor
(d) the effects of cost-push inflation

23. Based on the Laffer Curve, a cut in the tax rate from 100% to a point before the maximum level of tax revenue will
(a) increase the price level
(b) increase tax revenues
(c) decrease real output
(d) decrease the real wages

24. In the case of cuts in tax rates, most economists think that
(a) the demand-side effects exceed the supply-side effects
(b) the supply-side effects exceed the demand-side effects
(c) the demand-side and supply-side effects offset each other
(d) there are only supply-side effects

25. One general criticism of Reaganomics of the 1981–1988 period was that it failed to have a significant effect on
(a) cuts in personal and corporate income tax rates
(b) increases in saving and investment
(c) reductions in government regulation
(d) renewed interest in entrepreneurship

■ PROBLEMS

1. In columns 1 and 2 of the following table is a portion of a short-run aggregate supply schedule. Column 3 shows the number of full-time workers (in millions) that would have to be employed to produce each of the seven real domestic outputs (in billions) in the short-run aggregate supply schedule. The labor force is 80 million workers and the full-employment output of the economy is $______.

a. If the aggregate demand schedule were that shown in columns 1 and 4,

(1) the price level would be ______ and the real output would be $______.

(2) the number of workers employed would be ______, the number of workers unemployed would be ______, and the unemployment *rate* would be ______%.

b. If aggregate demand were to increase to that shown in columns 1 and 5 and short-run aggregate supply remained constant,

(1) the price level would rise to ______ and the real output would rise to $______.

(2) employment would increase by ______ workers and the unemployment rate would fall to ______%.

(3) the price level would increase by ______ and the rate of inflation would be ______%.

c. If aggregate demand were to decrease to that shown in columns 1 and 6 and short-run aggregate supply remained constant,

(1) the price level would fall to ______ and the real output would fall to $______.

(2) employment would decrease by ______ compared with situation a, and workers and the unemployment rate would rise to ______%.

(3) the price level would decrease and the rate of inflation would be (positive, negative) ______.

2. On the top of the next page is an aggregate demand and aggregate supply model. Assume that the economy is initially in equilibrium at **AD_1** and **AS_1**. The price level will be ______ and the real domestic output will be ______.

a. If there is demand-pull inflation, then

(1) in the short run, the new equilibrium is at point ______, with the price level at ______ and real output at ______;

(2) in the long run, nominal wages will rise so the aggregate supply curve will shift from ______ to ______. The equilibrium will be at point ______ with the price level at ______ and real output at ______, so the increase in

(1) Price level	(2) Real output supplied	(3) Employment (in millions)	(4) Real output demanded	(5) Real output demanded	(6) Real output demanded
130	$ 800	69	$2300	$2600	$1900
140	1300	70	2200	2500	1800
150	1700	72	2100	2400	1700
160	2000	75	2000	2300	1600
170	2200	78	1900	2200	1500
180	2300	80	1800	2100	1400
190	2300	80	1700	2000	1300

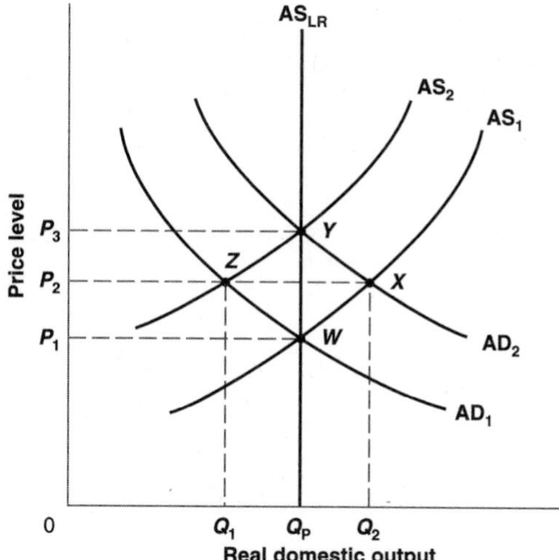

aggregate demand has only moved the economy along its __________ curve.

b. Now assume that the economy is initially in equilibrium at point ***W***, where AD_1 and AS_1 intersect. If there is cost-push inflation, then

(1) in the short run, the new equilibrium is at point __________, with the price level at __________ and real output at __________.

(2) if the government tries to counter the cost-push inflation with expansionary monetary and fiscal policy, then aggregate demand will shift from __________ to __________, with the price level becoming __________ and real output __________, but this policy has a trap because the price level has shifted from __________ to __________ and the new level of inflation might shift __________ leftward.

(3) if government does not counter the cost-push inflation, the price level will eventually move to __________ and real output to __________ as the recession reduces nominal wages and shifts the aggregate supply curve from __________ to __________.

c. Now assume that the economy is initially in equilibrium at point ***Y***, where AD_2 and AS_2 intersect. If there is a recession that reduces investment spending, then

(1) aggregate demand decreases and real output shifts from __________ to __________, and, assuming that prices and wages are flexible downward, the price level shifts from __________ to __________.

(2) these events cause real wages to (rise, fall) __________, and eventually nominal wages __________ to restore the previous real wages.

(3) when this happens, the short-run aggregate supply curve shifts from __________ to __________ to its new equilibrium at point __________. The equilibrium price level is __________ and the equilibrium level of output is __________ at the long-run aggregate supply curve __________.

3. Following is a traditional Phillips Curve.

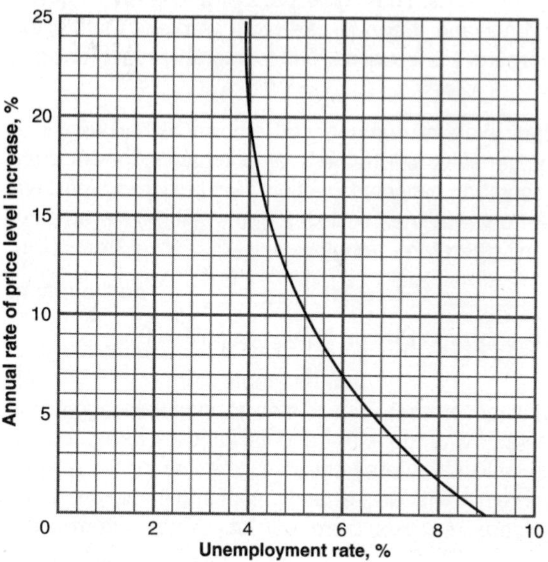

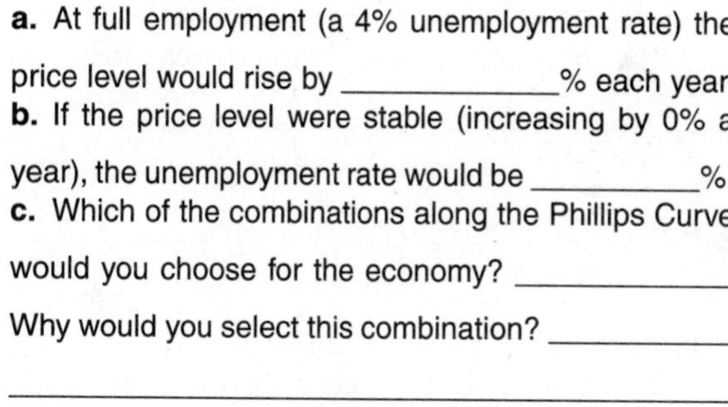

a. At full employment (a 4% unemployment rate) the price level would rise by __________% each year.

b. If the price level were stable (increasing by 0% a year), the unemployment rate would be __________%.

c. Which of the combinations along the Phillips Curve would you choose for the economy? __________

Why would you select this combination? __________

____

4. Following is an adaptive expectations model of the short- and long-run Phillips Curve.

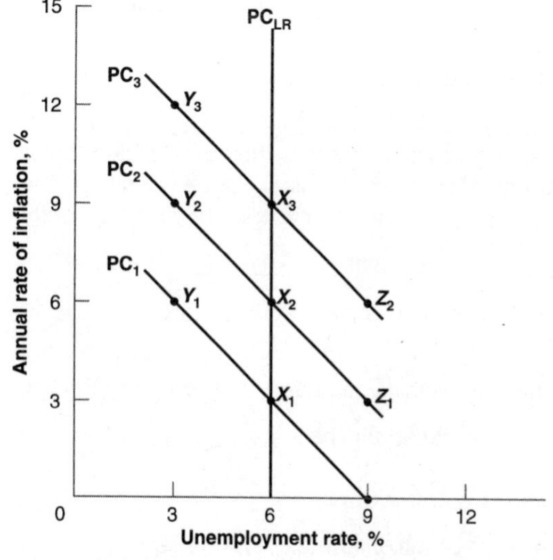

a. Suppose you begin at point X_1 and an assumption is made that nominal wages are set on the original expectation that a 3% rate of inflation will continue in the economy.

(1) If government invokes expansionary monetary and fiscal policy to reduce the unemployment rate from 6% to 3%, then the actual rate of inflation will move to _________%. The higher product prices will lift profits of firms and they will hire more workers; thus in the short run the economy will temporarily move to point ____________.

(2) If workers demand and receive higher wages to compensate for the loss of purchasing power from higher than expected inflation, then business profits will fall from previous levels and firms will reduce employment; therefore, employment will move from point ___________ to point ____________ on the graph. The short-run Phillips Curve has shifted from _______ to ____________ on the graph.

(3) If government again tries to stimulate aggregate demand with monetary and fiscal policy to reduce the unemployment rate from 6% to 3%, then prices will rise before nominal wages, and output and employment will increase, so that there will be a move from point ___________ to point ____________ on the graph.

(4) But when workers get nominal wage increases, profits fall, and employment moves from point ______________ at ______________% to point ____________ at _____________%. The short-run Phillips Curve has now shifted from ___________ to ____________ on the graph.

(5) The long-run Phillips Curve is the line ________.

b. Suppose you begin at point X_3, where the expected and actual rate of inflation is 9% and the unemployment rate is 6%.

(1) If there should be a decline in aggregate demand because of a recession and if the actual rate of inflation should fall to 6%, well below the expected rate of 9%, then business profits will fall and the unemployment rate will decrease to 9% as shown by the movement from point X_3 to point ____________.

(2) If firms and workers adjust their expectation to the 6% rate of inflation, the nominal wages will fall, profits will rise, and the economy will move from point ___________ to point ____________. The short-run Phillips Curve has shifted from ____________ to ____________.

(3) If this process is repeated, the long-run Phillips Curve will be traced as line ____________.

5. Following is a Laffer Curve.

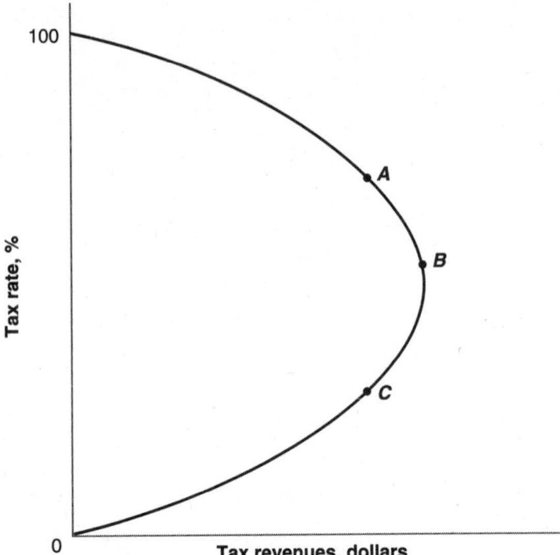

a. The point of maximum tax revenue is ________. As tax rates decrease from 100% to point ***B***, tax revenues will (increase, decrease) ______________. As tax rates increase from 0% to point ***B***, tax revenues will ______________.

b. Supply-side economists would contend that it would be beneficial for government to cut tax rates if they are (below, above) __________ point ***B***, whereas critics of supply-side economics contend that it would be harmful for government to cut tax rates if they are ____________ point ***B***.

■ SHORT ANSWER AND ESSAY QUESTIONS

1. What distinguishes the short run from the long run in macroeconomics?

2. Identify the basic difference between a short-run and a long-run aggregate supply curve. Explain what happens to aggregate supply when an increase in the price level results in an increase in nominal wages.

3. Explain how to find equilibrium in the extended AD-AS model.

4. Describe the process of demand-pull inflation in the short run and in the long run. How does demand-pull inflation influence the aggregate supply curve?

5. What two generalizations emerge from the analysis of cost-push inflation? Describe the two scenarios that provide the basis for the generalizations.

6. What is a Phillips Curve? Explain how a Phillips Curve with a negative slope may be derived by holding aggregate supply constant and mentally increasing aggregate demand.

7. What policy dilemma does the traditional Phillips Curve illustrate? Does the manipulation of aggregate demand through monetary and fiscal policy move the Phillips Curve or cause a movement along the Phillips Curve?

8. Were the rates of inflation and of unemployment consistent with the Phillips Curve in the 1960s? What do these two rates suggest about the curve in the 1970s and early 1980s?

9. What were the aggregate supply shocks to the U.S. economy during the 1970s and early 1980s? How did these shocks affect the Phillips Curve in the United States?

10. Describe the factors that contributed to stagflation's demise during the 1982–1989 period. What do many economists contend happened to the Phillips Curve during this period compared to the 1970s and early 1980s?

11. Explain the natural rate hypothesis, and briefly describe the two variants of the interpretation of the unemployment-inflation rate data of the 1970s and early 1980s.

12. What does "adaptive" refer to in the adaptive expectations theory? Illustrate how this theory is used to explain both inflation and disinflation in the economy.

13. What are the views of the adaptive expectations theory on the
(a) effects of expansionary monetary and fiscal policy on employment in the short run and on the short-run Phillips Curve, and
(b) long-run Phillips Curve? How does it reach these conclusions?

14. How does rational expectations theory explain expansionary monetary and fiscal policy effects on the price level and employment in the short run and the long run? What assumptions are made to reach this conclusion?

15. Compare and contrast the theories of rational expectations and adaptive expectations in terms of views on inflationary expectations, the interpretation of the Phillips Curve, and the effectiveness of monetary policy and fiscal policy.

16. Discuss three ways that supply-side economists contend there are tax and transfer payment disincentives in the economy.

17. Draw a Laffer Curve showing the relationship between tax rates and tax revenues. Outline the three criticisms of the ideas expressed in the Laffer Curve.

18. What are the two types of government regulation? How might this regulation affect economic growth?

19. Identify the major feature of Reaganomics. Make a case for its success.

20. Discuss the evidence on the effects of Reaganomics on saving, investment, productivity, economic growth, and aggregate supply. Did supply-side economics work during the 1980s?

ANSWERS

Chapter 16 Extending the Analysis of Aggregate Supply

FILL-IN QUESTIONS

1. increase, decrease
2. fixed, variable, upsloping, vertical
3. right, increase, increase, short-run, nominal, higher
4. left, increase, decrease
5. decrease, increase
6. decrease, falls, increase, decrease, increase
7. greater, greater, smaller
8. inverse, low, high
9. increase, increase
10. unstable, supply, cost-push
11. recession, tight, increased, decreased, increased, decreased, decreased
12. right, left, short-run
13. natural, does not, unemployment
14. gradually, short-run, long-run, increase
15. rise, fall, disinflation
16. anticipated, offset, real, nominal, a rise, no change
17. decrease, decrease, increase, increase
18. increase, decrease, increase, decrease
19. small, demand, supply, loss
20. less, less, supply, did not, increased, decreased, minimal

TRUE-FALSE QUESTIONS

1. F, p. 331
2. F, pp. 331-332
3. T, p. 332
4. T, p. 333
5. F, pp. 334-335
6. T, p. 335
7. F, pp. 335-336
8. T, pp. 335-336
9. T, pp. 336-337
10. T, pp. 337-338
11. F, p. 338
12. T, pp. 338-339
13. F, p. 339
14. F, pp. 339-340
15. T, pp. 340-341
16. F, p. 341
17. T, pp. 341-342
18. T, p. 342
19. F, p. 342
20. F, p. 342
21. F, p. 343
22. T, p. 343
23. F, pp. 343-344
24. T, p. 345
25. F, p. 345

MULTIPLE-CHOICE QUESTIONS

1. c, p. 331
2. b, p. 331
3. b, pp. 332-333
4. b, p. 331
5. d, p. 333
6. c, p. 333
7. b, pp. 333-334
8. a, p. 335
9. d, p. 335
10. a, pp. 335-336
11. b, pp. 336-337
12. a, pp. 336-337
13. d, pp. 338-339
14. c, p. 339
15. b, p. 339
16. c, pp. 339-340
17. d, pp. 340-341
18. d, p. 342
19. b, p. 341
20. a, pp. 341-342
21. a, p. 340
22. b, p. 343
23. b, pp. 343-344
24. a, p. 344
25. b, p. 345

PROBLEMS

1. 2300; *a.* (1) 160, 2,000, (2) 75, 5, 6.25; *b.* (1) 170, 2,200, (2) 3, 2.5, (3) 6.25; *c.* (1) 150, 1,700, (2) 3, 10, (3) negative
2. P_1, Q_p; *a.* (1) X, P_2, Q_2, (2) AS_1, AS_2, Y, P_3, Q_p, AS_{LR}; *b.* (1) Z, P_2, Q_1, (2) AD_1, AD_2, P_3, Q_p, P_2, P_3, AS_2, (3) P_1, Q_p, AS_2, AS_1; *c.* (1). Q_p, Q_1, P_3, P_2, (2) rise, fall, (3) AS_2, AS_1, W, P_1, Q_p, AS_{LR}
3. *a.* 20; *b.* 9
4. *a.* (1) 6, Y_1; (2) Y_1, X_2, PC_1, PC_2, (3) X_2, Y_2, (4) Y_2, 3, X_3, 6, PC_2, PC_3, (5) PC_{LR}; *b.* (1) Z_2, (2) Z_2, X_2, PC_3, PC_2, (3) PC_{LR}
5. *a.* B, increase, decrease; *b.* above, below

SHORT ANSWER AND ESSAY QUESTIONS

1. p. 331
2. pp. 331-333
3. p. 333
4. pp. 333-334
5. pp. 334-335
6. pp. 336-337
7. pp. 336-337
8. pp. 337-338
9. pp. 338-339
10. p. 339
11. pp. 340-342
12. pp. 340-342
13. pp. 340-342
14. p. 342
15. pp. 340-342
16. p. 343
17. pp. 343-344
18. p. 345
19. p. 345
20. p. 345

CHAPTER 17

Disputes in Macro Theory and Policy

Now that you understand the basic theory and models of the macro economy, you are ready to learn about different perspectives on how the economy functions and the major disputes in macro theory and policy.

Economics has always been an arena in which conflicting theories and policies oppose each other. This field of intellectual combat, in major engagements, has seen Adam Smith do battle with the defenders of a regulated economy. It witnessed the opposition of Karl Marx to the orthodox economics of his day. In the 1930s, it saw Keynes oppose the classical economists. Around the major engagements have been countless minor skirmishes between opposing viewpoints. Out of these major and minor confrontations have emerged not winners and losers but the advancement of economic theory and the improvement of economic policy.

Chapter 17 sets the foundation for understanding the modern debates by comparing **classical** and **Keynesian** views of macroeconomic theory. The now familiar aggregate demand–aggregate supply model is used to illustrate the classical view that aggregate supply is vertical and aggregate demand relatively stable. Keynesians, however, saw aggregate supply as being horizontal (to full-employment output), aggregate demand as being highly unstable, and a need for government intervention to stabilize the macro economy.

The chapter then turns to the first of three major questions: *What causes macro instability in the economy?* Four different perspectives on the issues are given. First, from the Keynesian-based *mainstream* view, this instability arises primarily from volatility in investment that shifts aggregate demand or from occasional shocks to aggregate supply. Second, *monetarists* focus on the money supply and assume that the competitive market economy has a high degree of stability, except when there is inappropriate monetary policy. The monetarist analysis is based on the equation of exchange and the assumption that the velocity of money is stable. Changes in the money supply, therefore, directly affect the level of nominal GDP. Third, ***real-business-cycle*** theorists see instability as coming from the aggregate supply side of the economy and from real factors that affect the long-term growth rather than monetary factors that affect aggregate demand. Fourth, some economists think that macroeconomic instability is the result of *coordination failures* that do not permit people to act jointly to determine the optimal level of output, and the equilibrium in the economy changes as expectations change.

The next question the chapter discusses is: *Does the economy self-correct its macro instability?* The view of new classical economics is that internal mechanisms in the economy allow it to self-correct. The two variants of this new classical perspective are based on ***monetarism*** and ***rational expectations theory (RET).*** Monetarists think the economy will self-correct to its long-run level of output, although there can be short-run changes in the price level and real output. Rational expectations theory suggests that the self-correction process is quick and does not change the price level or real output, except when there are price-level surprises.

By contrast, mainstream economists contend that the downward inflexibility of wages limits the self-correction mechanisms in the economy. Several explanations are offered for this inflexibility. There can be long-term wage contracts that support wages. Firms may also pay an efficiency wage to encourage work effect, reduce turnover, and prevent shirking. Firms may also be concerned about maintaining the support and teamwork of key workers (insiders), so they do not cut wages even when other workers (outsiders) might be willing to accept a lower wage.

The different perspectives on macro instability and self-correction set the stage for discussion of the third and final question: *Should the macro economy be guided by policy rules* or *discretion?* To restrict monetary policy, monetarists and rational expectations economists call for a monetary rule that would have monetary authorities allow the money supply to grow in proportion to the long-term growth in the productive capacity of the economy. Both monetarists and rational expectations economists also oppose the use of fiscal policy, and a few call for a balanced budget requirement to limit the use of discretionary fiscal policy.

Mainstream economists see value in discretionary monetary and fiscal policy. They suggest that a monetary rule would be ineffective in achieving growth and would destabilize the economy. A balanced-budget requirement would also have a procyclical effect that would reinforce recessionary or inflationary tendencies in the economy. And, since government has taken a more active role in the economy, the historical record shows that discretionary monetary and fiscal actions have reduced macro instability.

As was the case in the past, macroeconomic theory and policy have changed because of the debates among economists. The disputes among mainstream economists, monetarists, rational expectationists, and real business cycle theorists have produced new insights about how the macro economy operates. In particular, it is now recognized that "money matters" and that the money supply has a significant effect on the economy. More attention is also being given to the influence of people's expectations on policy and coordination failures in explaining macroeconomic events. The factors that influence aggregate supply and long-term growth in the economy are also being considered. The disputes in macroeconomics in the past 30 years forced economists to reconsider previous conclusions and led to the incorporation of new ideas into mainstream thinking about macro theory and policy.

■ CHECKLIST

When you have studied this chapter you should be able to

☐ Compare and contrast the classical and Keynesian views of the aggregate demand curve and the aggregate supply curve.
☐ Describe the mainstream view of stability in the macro economy and the two potential sources of instability.
☐ Explain the monetarist view of stability in the macro economy.
☐ Write the equation of exchange and define each of the four terms in the equation.
☐ Explain why monetarists think the velocity of money is stable.
☐ Write a brief scenario which explains what monetarists believe will happen to change the nominal GDP and to ***V*** (velocity of money) when ***M*** (money supply) is increased.
☐ Discuss the monetary causes of instability in the macro economy.
☐ Describe the real-business-cycle view of stability in the macro economy.
☐ Give a noneconomic and macroeconomic example of the coordination failures view of stability in the macro economy.
☐ Use a graph to explain the new classical view of self-correction in the macro economy.
☐ Discuss the differences between the monetarist and rational expectations views on the speed of adjustment for self-correction in the macro economy.
☐ State the two basic assumptions of the rational expectations theory (RET).
☐ Use a graph to explain how RET views unanticipated and fully anticipated changes in the price level.
☐ Describe the mainstream view of self-correction in the macro economy.
☐ Give two reasons why there may be downward wage inflexibility.
☐ State three reasons why a higher wage might result in greater efficiency.
☐ Use ideas from insider-outsider theory to explain the downward inflexibility of wages.
☐ State the rationale for why monetarists think there should be a monetary rule, and illustrate it using an aggregate demand and aggregate supply model.
☐ Describe how monetarists and new classical economists view the effectiveness of fiscal policy.
☐ Offer a mainstream defense of discretionary stabilization policy and a critique of a monetary rule and balanced-budget requirement.
☐ Describe the possible reasons for increased stability in the macro economy since 1946.
☐ Offer a summary of the four alternative views on issues affecting the macro economy.

■ CHAPTER OUTLINE

1. Classical and Keynesian economics can be compared by examining their aggregate demand–aggregate supply models of the economy.

a. In the *classical model,*
(1) the aggregate supply curve is vertical at the economy's full-employment output, and a decrease in aggregate demand will lower the equilibrium price level and have no effect on the real output (or employment) in the economy because of Say's law and flexible, responsive prices and wages.
(2) the aggregate demand curve slopes downward because (with a fixed money supply in the economy) a fall in the price level increases the purchasing power of money and enables consumers and business firms to purchase a larger real output. Aggregate demand will be reasonably stable if the nation's monetary authorities maintain a constant supply of money to accomodate long-term growth.

b. In the *Keynesian model,*
(1) the aggregate supply curve is horizontal at the current price level, and a decrease in aggregate demand will lower the real output (and employment) in the economy and have no effect on the equilibrium price level because of the downward inflexibility of prices and wages.
(2) aggregate demand is viewed as being unstable over time, even if the supply of money is held constant, partly because of fluctuations in investment spending. A decline in aggregate demand decreases real domestic output but has no effect on the price level, thereby causing output to stay permanently below the full-employment level.

2. There are four different views among economists on stability and instability in the macro economy.

a. The *mainstream view* is Keynesian-based and holds that instability in the economy arises from
(1) the volatility in investment spending that makes aggregate demand unstable, and
(2) occasional aggregate supply shocks which cause cost-push inflation and recession.

b. *Monetarists* focus on the money supply. They think markets are highly competitive and that government intervention destabilizes the economy.
(1) In monetarism, the equation of exchange is $MV = PQ$, where M is the money supply, V the velocity of money, P the price level, and Q the quantity of goods and services produced.
(2) Monetarists think that velocity is stable or that the quantity of money demanded is a stable percentage of

GDP (GDP/***M*** is constant). If velocity is stable, there is a predictable relationship between ***M*** and nominal GDP (= ***PQ***). An increase in ***M*** will leave firms and households with more money than they wish to have, so they will increase spending and boost aggregate demand. This causes nominal GDP and the amount of money they wish to hold to rise until the demand for money is equal to ***M*** and nominal GDP/***M*** = ***V***.

(3) Monetarists view macroeconomic instability as a result of inappropriate monetary policy. An increase in the money supply will increase aggregate demand, output, and the price level; it will also reduce unemployment. Eventually, nominal wages rise to restore real wages and real output, and the unemployment rate falls back to its natural level at long-run aggregate supply.

c. *Real-business-cycle theorists* see macroeconomic instability as being caused by real factors influencing aggregate supply instead of monetary factors causing shifts in aggregate demand. Changes in technology and resources will affect productivity and thus the long-run growth rate of aggregate supply.

d. A fourth view of instability in the macro economy attributes the reasons to *coordination failures.* These failures occur when people are not able to coordinate their actions to achieve an optimal equilibrium. A self-fulfilling prophecy can lead to recession because if households and firms expect it, they individually cut back on spending and employment. If, however, they were to act jointly, they could take actions to counter the recession expectations to achieve an optimal equilibrium.

3. Economists also debate the issue of *whether the macro economy self-corrects.*

a. The *new classical view* of economics, held by monetarists and rational expectations economists, is that the economy may deviate from the full-employment level of output, but it eventually returns to this output level because there are self-corrective mechanisms in the economy.

(1) Graphically, if aggregate demand increases, it temporarily raises real output and the price level. Nominal wages rise and productivity falls, so short-run aggregate supply decreases, thus bringing the economy back to its long-run output level.

(2) There is disagreement about the speed of adjustment. The monetarists adopt the adaptive expectations view that there will be a slower, temporary change in output but that in the long run it will return to its natural level. Other new classical economists adopt the *rational expectations theory (RET)* view that there will be a rapid adjustment with little or no change in output. RET is based on two assumptions: People understand how the economy works so that they quickly anticipate the effect on the economy of an economic event, and all markets in the economy are so competitive that equilibrium prices and quantities quickly adjust to changes in policy.

(3) In RET, unanticipated price-level changes, called price-level surprises, cause short-run changes in real output because they cause misperceptions about the economy among workers and firms.

(4) In RET, fully anticipated price-level changes do not change real output even in the short run because workers and firms anticipate and counteract the effects of the changes.

b. The *mainstream view of self-correction* suggests that price and wages may be inflexible downward in the economy.

(1) Graphically, a decrease in aggregate demand will decrease real output but not the price level because nominal wages will not decline and cause the short-run aggregate supply curve to shift right.

(2) Downward wage inflexibility primarily arises because of wage contracts and the legal minimum wage, but they may also occur from efficiency wages and insider-outsider relationships, according to new Keynesian economics.

(3) An efficiency wage minimizes the firm's labor cost per unit of output but may be higher than the market wage. This higher wage may result in greater efficiency because it stimulates greater work effort, requires less supervision costs, and reduces job turnover.

(4) Insider-outsider relationships may also produce downward wage inflexibility. During a recession, outsiders (who are less essential to the firm) may try to bid down wages to try to keep their jobs, but the firm may not lower wages because it does not want to alienate insiders (who are more essential to the firm) and disrupt the cooperative environment in the firm needed for production.

4. The debates over macro policy also focus on the need for *policy rules* or *discretion.*

a. Monetarists and new classical economists argue for policy rules to reduce government intervention in the economy. They believe this intervention causes macroeconomic instability.

(1) In regard to monetary policy, monetarists have proposed a monetary rule that the money supply be increased at the same annual rate as the potential annual rate of increase in the real GDP. A monetary rule would shift aggregate demand rightward to match a shift in the long-run aggregate supply curve that occurs because of economic growth, thus keeping the price level stable over time.

(2) Monetarists and new classical economists question the value of fiscal policy, and some would like to see a balanced Federal budget over time. An expansionist fiscal policy will tend to crowd out investment and cause only a temporary increase in output. RET economists also think that fiscal policy is ineffective and that people will anticipate it and their acts will counteract its intended effects.

b. Mainstream economists think that discretionary fiscal and monetary policy can be effective and are opposed to a monetary rule and a balanced-budget requirement.

(1) They see the velocity of money as relatively unstable and a loose link beween changes in the money supply and aggregate demand. This means that a monetary rule might produce too great a shift in aggregate demand (and demand-pull inflation) or too small a shift

(and deflation) to match the shift in aggregate supply. Such a rule would contribute to price instability, not price stability.

(2) They support the use of fiscal policy during a recession or to counter growing inflation. Fiscal policy, however, should be reserved for those situations where monetary policy is relatively ineffective. They also oppose a balanced-budget amendment because its effects would be procyclical rather than countercyclical and would reinforce recessionary or inflationary tendencies.

c. Mainstream ecconomists also note that there has been greater stability in the macro economy since 1946, when discretionary monetary and fiscal policy was more actively used to moderate the effects of the business cycle.

5. The *disputes* in macroeconomics in the past two decades have led to the incorporation of several ideas from monetarism, rational expectations theory, real-business-cycle theory, and supply-side economics into mainstream thinking about macroeconomics. First, monetarists have gotten mainstream economists to recognize that changes in the money supply are important in explaining long-lasting and rapid inflation. Second, mainstream economists now recognize that expectations matter because of rational expectations theory and that there are coordination failures in the economy. Third, real-business-cycle theory and supply-side economics have forced mainstream economists to give more attention to government policies that promote long-run economic growth. Table 17-1 summarizes the four alternative views of macroeconomics.

■ HINTS AND TIPS

1. The chapter may appear complex because many alternative viewpoints are presented. To simplify matters, first focus on the three questions that the chapter addresses: What causes macro instability in the economy? Does the economy self-correct? Should policymakers use rules or discretion? For each question, identify how different types of economists answer each question.

2. Review the discussions of aggregate demand and aggregate supply in Chapters 11 and 16 as preparation for the comparison of alternate views of the macro economy presented in this chapter.

3. Monetarist and mainstream views of the macro economy are two approaches of looking at the same thing. The similarities can best be seen in equations in nominal form. The monetarist equation of exchange is $MV = PQ$. The Keynesian-based mainstream equation is $C_a + I_g + X_n + G = GDP$. The MV term is the monetarist expression for the mainstream equilibrium $C_a + I_g + X_n + G$. The PQ term is the monetarist expression for GDP. Monetarists give more emphasis to the role of money and assume that velocity is relatively stable. Mainstream economists give more emphasis to the instability caused by investment spending and to influences on GDP from consumption, net export, and government spending.

■ IMPORTANT TERMS

classical economics
Keynesianism
monetarism
equation of exchange
velocity
real-business-cycle theory
coordination failures
new classical economics
price-level surprises
new Keynesian economics
efficiency wage
insider-outsider theory
monetary rule
rational expectations theory (RET)

SELF-TEST

■ FILL-IN QUESTIONS

1. The aggregate supply curve of the classical economists is (horizontal, vertical) ______________, and the aggregate supply curve of the Keynesian economists is ______________ up to the full-employment level of output. Therefore, a decrease in aggregate demand will have no effect on price level and will decrease output and employment in the (classical, Keynesian) ______________ model, but a decrease in aggregate demand will decrease the price level and have no effect on output and employment in the ______________ model.

2. In the classical way of thinking, changes in the money supply shift the aggregate (demand, supply) __________ curve. If the money supply increases, then the curve will (increase, decrease) ______________, and if the money supply decreases, then the curve will ______________. If the nation's monetary authorities maintain a constant supply of money, this curve will be (stable, unstable) ______________.

3. From the Keynesian perspective, aggregate demand is (stable, unstable) ______________, even if there are no changes in the supply of money, largely because of the volatility in (investment, government) ______________ spending.

4. The mainstream view is that macro instability is caused by changes in investment spending which shift the aggregate (demand, supply) ________________ curve. If it increases too rapidly, then (inflation, recession) ______________ can occur, but if it decreases, then the economy can experience ______________. Occasionally, adverse aggregate (demand, supply) ______________ shocks also cause instability.

5. Monetarists argue that capitalism is inherently (stable, unstable) ______________ because most of its markets are (competitive, noncompetitive) ______________.

They believe that government intervention in the economy has contributed to macroeconomic (stability, instability) ________________ and has promoted (flexibility, inflexibility) ________________ in wages.

6. The basic equation of the monetarists is ______ = ______. Indicate what each of the four letters in the following equation represents:

a. ***M:*** ________________
b. ***V:*** ________________
c. ***P:*** ________________
d. ***Q:*** ________________

7. Monetarists believe that ***V*** is (stable, unstable) ______________ because people have a ______________ desire to hold money relative to holding other financial and real assets or for making purchases. The amount of money people will want to hold will depend on the level of (real, nominal) ______________ GDP.

8. An increase in ***M***, to the monetarist's way of thinking, will leave the public with (more, less) ______________ money than it wishes to have, induce the public to (increase, decrease) ______________ its spending for consumer and capital goods, which will result in a(n) ______________ in aggregate demand and nominal GDP until nominal GDP equals ***MV.***

9. Monetarists believe that the most significant cause of macroeconomic instability has been inappropriate (fiscal, monetary) ______________ policy. Too rapid increases in ***M*** cause (recession, inflation) ______________; insufficient growth of ***M*** causes ______________.

10. The theory that changes in resource availability and technology (real factors), which alter productivity, are the main causes of instability in the macro economy is held by (real-business-cycle, rational expectations) ______________ economists. In this theory, shifts in the economy's long-run aggregate (demand, supply) ______________ curve change real output. As a consequence, money demand and money supply change, shifting the aggregate demand curve in the (opposite, same) ______________ direction as the initial change in long-run aggregate supply. Real output thus can change (with, without) ______________ a change in the price level.

11. A coordination failure is said to occur when people (do, do not) ______________ reach a mutually beneficial equilibrium because they lack some way to jointly coordinate their actions. In this view, there is (one, a number of) ______________ equilibrium position(s) in the economy. Macroeconomic instability is the result of changing (the money supply, expectations) ______________ that result in changing in the equilibrium position(s).

12. Monetarists and rational expectations economists view the economy as (capable, incapable) ______________ of self-correction when it deviates from the full-employment level of real output. Monetarists suggest that this adjustment occurs (gradually, rapidly) ______________, while rational expectations economists argue that it occurs ______________.

13. Rational expectations theory assumes that with sufficient information, peoples' beliefs about future economic outcomes (are, are not) ______________ accurate reflections of the likelihood of the outcomes occurring. It also assumes that markets are highly competitive, meaning that prices and wages are (flexible, inflexible) ______________.

14. In rational expectations theory, changes in aggregate demand that change the price level and real output are (anticipated, unanticipated) ______________, while changes in aggregate demand that only change in the price level and not real output are ______________.

15. The view of mainstream economists is that many prices and wages are (flexible, inflexible) ______________ downward for (short, long) ______________ periods of time. This situation (increases, decreases) ______________ the ability of the economy to automatically self-correct for deviations from full-employment output.

16. A higher wage can result in more efficiency because of results in (greater, less) ______________ work effort, supervision costs that are (lower, higher) ______________, and (more, less) ______________ turnover in jobs. Efficiency wages (increase, decrease) ______________ the downward inflexibility of wages because it makes firms more reluctant to cut wages when aggregate demand declines.

17. Monetarists and rational expectations economists support a monetary rule because they believe that discretionary monetary policy tends to (stabilize, destabilize) ______________ the economy. With this rule the money supply would be increased at a rate (greater than, less than, equal to) ______________ the long-run growth of potential GDP; graphically, this can be shown by a shift in aggregate demand that would be ______________ the shift in long-run aggregate supply resulting from economic growth.

18. Proponents of the rational expectations theory contend that discretionary monetary policy is (effective, ineffective) ______________ and like the monetarists favor (rules, discretion) ______________. When considering discretionary fiscal policy, most monetarists and RET economists (do, do not) ______________ advocate its use.

19. Mainstream economists (support, oppose) ______________ a monetary rule and a balanced-budget requirement. They view discretionary monetary policy as (effective, ineffective) ______________, and think discretionary fiscal policy is ______________ but should be held in reserve when monetary policy works too slowly. They say the use of discretionary monetary and fiscal policy since 1946 has produced (more, less) ______________ stability in the macro economy.

20. Many ideas from alternative views of the macro economy have been absorbed into mainstream thinking about macroeconomics. There is more recognition that excessive growth of the money supply is a major cause of (recession, inflation) ______________, that expectations and coordination failures are (important, unimportant) ______________, and that government needs to focus more attention on policy that shifts aggregate (demand, supply) ______________.

■ TRUE-FALSE QUESTIONS

Circle the T if the statement is true, the F if it is false.

1. The classical view is that the aggregate supply curve is vertical. **T F**

2. Classical economists consider the aggregate demand curve to be unstable. **T F**

3. Keynesians think that the aggregate supply curve is horizontal (to full-employment output). **T F**

4. Keynesians suggest that full employment is the norm in the economy. **T F**

5. The mainstream view is that macro instability is caused by the volatility of investment spending, which shifts the aggregate demand curve. **T F**

6. Monetarists argue that the market system would provide for macroeconomic stability were it not for government interference in the economy. **T F**

7. In the equation of exchange, the left side, ***MV***, represents the total amount received by sellers of output, while the right side, ***PQ***, represents the total amount spent by purchasers of that output. **T F**

8. Monetarists argue that ***V*** in the equation of exchange is stable and that a change in ***M*** will bring about a direct and proportional change in ***PQ***. **T F**

9. Most monetarists believe that an increase in the money supply has no effect on real output and employment in the short run. **T F**

10. In the monetarist view, a major cause of the Great Depression was the decline in investment spending. **T F**

11. Real-business-cycle theory views changes in resource availability and technology, which alter productivity, as the main cause of macroeconomic instability. **T F**

12. In real-business-cycle theory, real output changes only with a change in the price level. **T F**

13. A coordination failure is said to occur when people do not reach a mutually beneficial equilibrium because they lack some way to jointly coordinate their actions to achieve it. **T F**

14. Peoples' expectations have no effect on coordination failures. **T F**

15. Neoclassical economists see the economy as automatically correcting itself when disturbed from its full-employment level of real output. **T F**

16. Rational expectations theory assumes that both product and resource markets are uncompetitive and that wages and prices are inflexible. **T F**

17. In rational expectations theory, a fully anticipated price-level change results in a change in real output. **T F**

18. Mainstream economists contend that wages are inflexible downward. **T F**

19. An efficiency wage is a below-market wage that spurs greater work effort and gives the firm more profits because of lower wage costs. **T F**

20. Insider-outsider theory offers one explanation for the downward inflexibility of wages in the economy. **T F**

21. Monetarists believe that a monetary rule would reduce instability in the macro economy. **T F**

22. Rational expectations economists argue that monetary policy should be left to the discretion of government. **T F**

23. Monetarists support the use of fiscal policy, especially as a means of controlling inflation. **T F**

24. Mainstream economists believe that discretionary monetary policy is an effective tool for stabilizing the economy. **T F**

25. The mainstream view of the economy since 1946 believes that it has become inherently less stable because of the use of fiscal policy. **T F**

■ MULTIPLE-CHOICE QUESTIONS

Circle the letter that corresponds to the best answer.

1. Classical economists suggest that full employment is
- **(a)** best achieved through government interventions
- **(b)** not possible in an unstable market economy
- **(c)** inversely related to the price level
- **(d)** the norm in a market economy

2. The aggregate supply curve of classical economists
- **(a)** is vertical
- **(b)** is horizontal

(c) slopes upward
(d) slopes downward

3. Classical theory concludes that the production behavior of firms will *not* change when the price level decreases because input costs would
(a) rise along with product prices to leave real profits and output unchanged
(b) fall along with product prices to leave real profits and output unchanged
(c) fall, but product prices would rise, offsetting any change in real profits or output
(d) rise, but product prices would rise, offsetting any change in real profits or output

4. In classical economics, a decrease in aggregate demand results in
(a) a decrease in both the price level and domestic output
(b) a decrease in the price level and no change in domestic output
(c) no change in the price level and a decrease in domestic output
(d) no change in either the price level or domestic output

5. The aggregate supply curve in the Keynesian model is
(a) vertical at the full-employment output level
(b) horizontal to the full-employment output level
(c) positively sloped to the full-employment output level
(d) negatively sloped to the full-employment output level

6. In the Keynesian model, a decrease in aggregate demand results in
(a) a decrease in both the price level and domestic output
(b) a decrease in the price level and no change in domestic output
(c) no change in the price level and a decrease in domestic output
(d) no change in either the price level or domestic output

7. The mainstream view of the economy holds that
(a) government intervention in the economy is not desirable
(b) product and labor markets are highly competitive and flexible
(c) changes in investment spending lead to changes in aggregate demand
(d) economic growth is best achieved through implementation of a monetary rule

8. In the monetarist perspective
(a) discretionary monetary policy is the most effective way to moderate swings in the business cycle
(b) government policies have reduced macroeconomic stability
(c) macroeconomic stability results from adverse aggregate supply shocks
(d) markets in a capitalistic economy are largely noncompetitive

9. Which is the equation of exchange?
(a) $PQ/M + V = GDP$
(b) $V = M + PQ$
(c) $MV = PQ$
(d) $V + I_g + M = GDP$

10. In the equation of exchange, if V is stable, an increase in M will necessarily increase
(a) the demand for money
(b) government spending
(c) nominal GDP
(d) velocity

11. When nominal gross domestic product (GDP) is divided by the money supply (***M***), then you will obtain the
(a) velocity of money
(b) monetary multiplier
(c) equation of exchange
(d) monetary rule

12. Monetarists argue that the amount of money the public will want to hold depends primarily on the level of
(a) nominal GDP
(b) investment
(c) consumption
(d) prices

13. Real-business-cycle theory suggests that
(a) velocity changes gradually and predictably; thus it is able to accommodate the long-run changes in nominal GDP
(b) the volatility of investment is the main cause of the economy's instability
(c) inappropriate monetary policy is the single most important cause of macroeconomic instability
(d) changes in technology and resources affect productivity, and thus the long-run growth of aggregate supply

14. In real-business-cycle theory, if the long-run aggregate supply increased, then aggregate demand would increase by
(a) an equal amount, so real output and the price level would increase
(b) less than an equal amount, so real output would increase and the price level would decrease
(c) greater than an equal amount, so real output and the price level would increase
(d) an equal amount, so real output would increase and the price level would be unchanged

15. If aggregate demand declined and the economy experienced a recession due to a self-fulfilling prophecy, this would be an example of
(a) real-business-cycle theory
(b) insider-outsider theory
(c) a coordination failure
(d) a change in velocity

16. In the new classical view, when the economy diverges from its full-employment output,

(a) internal mechanisms within the economy would automatically return it to its full-employment output
(b) discretionary monetary policy is needed to return it to its full-employment output
(c) discretionary fiscal policy is needed to return it to its full-employment output
(d) the adoption of an efficiency wage in the economy would return it to its full-employment output

17. The views about the speed of adjustment for self-correction in the economy suggest that
(a) monetarists think it would be gradual and rational expectations economists think it would be quick
(b) monetarists think it would be quick and rational expectations economists think it would be gradual
(c) monetarists and mainstream economists think it would be quick
(d) real-business-cycle theorists and rational expectations economists think it would be gradual

18. Proponents of rational expectations theory argue that people
(a) are not as rational as monetarists assume them to be
(b) make forecasts that are based on poor information, causing economic policy to be driven by a self-fulfilling prophecy
(c) form beliefs about future economic outcomes that accurately reflect the likelihood that those outcomes will occur
(d) do not respond quickly to changes in wages and prices, causing a misallocation of economic resources in the economy

19. In the rational expectations theory, a temporary change in real output would occur from a
(a) fully anticipated price-level change
(b) downward wage inflexibility
(c) coordination failure
(d) price-level surprise

20. The conclusion mainstream economists draw about the downward price and wage inflexibility is that
(a) the effects can be reversed relatively quickly
(b) efficiency wages do not contribute to the problem
(c) the economy can be mired in recession for long periods
(d) wage and price controls are needed to counteract the situation

21. According to mainstream economists, which contributes to the downward inflexibility of wages?
(a) price-level surprises
(b) insider-outsider relationships
(c) adverse aggregate supply shocks
(d) inadequate investment spending

22. The rule suggested by the monetarists is that the money supply should be increased at the same rate as the
(a) price level
(b) interest rate
(c) velocity of money
(d) potential growth in real GDP

23. To stabilize the economy, monetarist and rational expectations economists advocate
(a) the use of price-level surprises and adoption of an efficiency wage
(b) a monetary rule and a balanced-budget requirement
(c) the use of discretionary fiscal policy instead of discretionary monetary policy
(d) the use of discretionary monetary policy instead of discretionary fiscal policy

24. Mainstream economists support
(a) increasing the money supply at a constant rate
(b) eliminating insider-outsider relationships in business
(c) the use of discretionary monetary and fiscal policy
(d) a balanced-budget requirement and a monetary rule

25. Which would be an idea from monetarism which has been absorbed into mainstream macroeconomics?
(a) how changes in investment spending change aggregate demand
(b) the importance of money and the money supply in the economy
(c) using discretion rather than rules for guiding economic policy
(d) building the macro foundations for microeconomics

■ PROBLEMS

1. Assume that you are a monetarist in this problem and that ***V*** is stable and equal to 4. In the following table is the aggregate supply schedule: the real output ***Q*** which producers will offer for sale at seven different price levels ***P***.

P	*Q*	*PQ*	*MV*
$1.00	100	$____	$____
2.00	110	____	____
3.00	120	____	____
4.00	130	____	____
5.00	140	____	____
6.00	150	____	____
7.00	160	____	____

a. Compute and enter in the table above the seven values of ***PQ***.
b. Assume ***M*** is $90. Enter the values of ***MV*** on each of the seven lines in the table. The equilibrium

(1) nominal domestic output (***PQ*** or ***MV***) is $________.

(2) price level is $________________.

(3) real domestic output (***Q***) is $________________.

c. When ***M*** increases to $175, ***MV*** at each price level is $____________ and the equilibrium

(1) nominal domestic output is $________________.

(2) price level is $________________.

(3) real domestic output is $________________.

2. Indicate what perspective(s) of economics would be most closely associated with each position. Use the following abbreviations: **MAI** (mainstream economics), **MON** (monetarism), **RET** (rational expectations theory), and **RBC** (real-business-cycle theory).

a. macro instability from investment spending ________

b. macro instability from inappropriate monetary policy ________

c. macro instability from changes in resource availability and technology ________

d. equation of exchange ________

e. fiscal policy can be effective ________

f. unanticipated price-level changes ________

g. downward inflexibility of wages and prices ________

h. monetary rule ________

i. neutral fiscal policy ________

j. economy automatically self-corrects ________

k. monetary policy is effective ________

3. Following are price-level (***PL***) and output (***Q***) combinations to describe aggregate demand and aggregate supply curves: (1) **PL** and $\mathbf{Q_1}$ is $\mathbf{AD_1}$. (2) ***PL*** and Q_2 is $\mathbf{AD_2}$. (3) ***PL*** and Q_3 is $\mathbf{AS_{LR1}}$. (4) ***PL*** and Q_4 is $\mathbf{AS_{LR2}}$.

PL	Q_1	Q_2	Q_3	Q_4
250	0	200	400	600
200	200	400	400	600
150	400	600	400	600
100	600	800	400	600
50	800	1,000	400	600

a. Use the following to graph $\mathbf{AD_1}$, $\mathbf{AD_2}$, $\mathbf{AS_{LR1}}$, and $\mathbf{AS_{LR2}}$. Label the vertical axis as the price level and the horizontal axis as real output (***Q***).

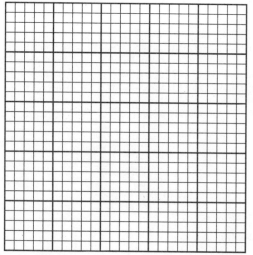

0

b. If the economy is initially in equilibrium where $\mathbf{AD_1}$ and $\mathbf{AS_{LR1}}$ intersect, the price level will be ________ and real output will be ________.

c. If, over time, the economy grows from $\mathbf{AS_{LR1}}$ to $\mathbf{AS_{LR2}}$, the equilibrium price level will be ________ and real output will be ________.

d. Assume a monetary rule is adopted that increases the money supply proportionate to the increase in aggregate supply. Aggregate demand will increase from $\mathbf{AD_1}$ to $\mathbf{AD_2}$, making the price level ________ and real output ________.

e. Mainstream economists would argue that velocity is unstable, so a constant increase in the money supply might not shift $\mathbf{AD_1}$ all the way to $\mathbf{AD_2}$. In this case, the price level would fall below the target of ________. It might also be the case that the constant increase in the money supply might shift $\mathbf{AD_1}$ beyond $\mathbf{AD_2}$, so the price level would rise above the target of ________.

■ SHORT ANSWER AND ESSAY QUESTIONS

1. What is the difference between the classical and Keynesian aggregate supply curve? Draw a graph showing the difference. What is the justification for each viewpoint?

2. What is the effect of a decrease in aggregate demand on the price level and real domestic output in the classical and Keynesian model? Show the change in a graph.

3. Why did classical economists consider the aggregate demand curve to be stable? What is the response of Keynesians to this position?

4. Why does the classical aggregate demand curve have a negative (downward) slope?

5. Explain the two causes of macroeconomic instability in the view of mainstream economists.

6. What do monetarists see as the cause of economic instability in the economy? Explain, using the equation of exchange, how a change in the money supply will affect nominal GDP.

7. Why do monetarists argue that the velocity of money is stable? If the money supply increases, how will people respond from a monetarist perspective?

8. Compare and contrast the monetarist and mainstream view on the causes of macroeconomic instability. How do monetarists explain the Great Depression?

9. Explain the real-business-cycle view of macroeconomic instability using an aggregate demand and supply graph.

10. Give a macroeconomic example of how coordination failures cause macroeconomic instability.

11. Explain the monetarist view of self-correction in the macro economy. Contrast that perspective with that of rational expectations in terms of the real output, the price level, and the speed of adjustment.

12. Describe the two assumptions on which rational expectations is based. How realistic is to expect that people will be able to accurately forecast economic outcomes?

13. Use a graph to illustrate and explain the mainstream view of self-correction in the macro economy.

14. Why would an efficiency wage lead to downward inflexibility in prices?

15. Give an example of insider-outsider relationships and explain how it affects wage flexibility.

16. What is the monetary rule? Why do monetarists suggest this rule to replace discretionary monetary policy?

17. What is the perspective of rational expectations economists on a monetary rule and the conduct of monetary policy?

18. What is the position of some monetarist and rational expectations economists on a requirement for a balanced budget? Why do they adopt such a position?

19. How do mainstream economists defend the use of discretionary monetary and fiscal policy? What interpretation do mainstream economists make of the historical evidence on the relationship between macroeconomic policy and instability?

20. What influence has monetarism, rational expectations theory, real-business-cycle theory, and supply-side economics had on mainstream macroeconomic theory and policy? Give three examples of ideas that have changed mainstream thinking.

ANSWERS

Chapter 17 Disputes in Macro Theory and Policy

FILL-IN QUESTIONS

1. vertical, horizontal, Keynesian, classical
2. demand, increase, decrease, stable
3. unstable, investment
4. demand, inflation, recession, supply
5. stable, competitive, instability, inflexibility
6. ***MV = PQ;*** *a.* the money supply; *b.* the velocity of money; *c.* the average price of each unit of physical output; *d.* the physical volume of goods and services produced
7. stable, stable, nominal
8. more, increase, increase
9. monetary, inflation, recession
10. real-business-cycle, supply, same, without
11. do not, a number of, expectations
12. capable, gradually, rapidly
13. are, flexible
14. unanticipated, anticipated
15. inflexible, long, decreases
16. greater, lower, less, increase
17. destabilize, equal to, equal to
18. ineffective, rules, do not
19. oppose, effective, effective, more
20. inflation, important, supply

TRUE-FALSE QUESTIONS

1. T, p. 351
2. F, p. 350
3. T, P. 352
4. F, p. 352
5. T, p. 353
6. T, p. 353
7. F, p. 353
8. T, p. 354
9. F, p. 354
10. F, p. 355
11. T, p. 355
12. F, p. 355
13. T, p. 356
14. F, p. 356
15. T, pp. 356-357
16. F, p. 358
17. F, p. 358
18. T, p. 359
19. F, p. 359
20. T, p. 360
21. T, pp. 360-361
22. F, p. 361
23. F, pp. 361-362
24. T, p. 363
25. F, p. 363

MULTIPLE-CHOICE QUESTIONS

1. d, p. 351
2. a, p. 351
3. b, p. 351
4. b, pp. 351-352
5. b, p. 352
6. c, pp. 351-352
7. c, p. 353
8. b, p. 353
9. c, p. 353
10. c, p. 354
11. a, p. 354
12. a, p. 354
13. d, p. 355
14. d, p. 355
15. c, p. 356
16. a, p. 356
17. a, pp. 357-358
18. c, pp. 357-358
19. d, p. 358
20. c, p. 359
21. b, pp. 359-360
22. d, p. 360
23. b, pp. 360-361
24. c, p. 363
25. b, p. 364

PROBLEMS

1. *a.* 100, 220, 360, 520, 700, 900, 1120; *b.* 360, 360, 360, 360, 360, 360, 360, (1) 360, (2) 3.00, (3) 120; *c.* 700, (1) 700, (2) 5.00, (3) 140
2. *a.* MAI; *b.* MON, RET; *c.* RBC; *d.* MON; *e.* MAI; *f.* RET; *g.* MAI; *h.* MON, RET; *i.* MON, RET; *j.* MON, RET; *k.* MAI
3. *a.* graph similar to Figure 17-4 in the text; *b.* 150, 400; *c.* 100, 600; *d.* 150, 600; *e.* 150, 150

SHORT ANSWER AND ESSAY QUESTIONS

1. pp. 350-352
2. pp. 351-352
3. p. 352
4. p. 352
5. p. 353
6. pp. 353-354
7. p. 354
8. pp. 353-355
9. p. 355
10. p. 356
11. pp. 356-358
12. pp. 357-358
13. pp. 358-359
14. p. 359
15. p. 360
16. pp. 360-361
17. p. 361
18. pp. 361-363
19. pp. 363-364
20. p. 364

CHAPTER 18

Economic Growth

The United States has experienced an impressive record of economic growth since 1900. In Chapter 18 you will learn about the major factors that have contributed to this long-term economic growth.

The chapter begins by defining economic growth and explaining its significance. The text then analyzes the six factors that make growth possible. The four ***supply factors*** increase the output potential of the economy. Whether the economy actually produces its full potential—that is, whether the economy has both full employment and full production—depends upon two other factors: the level of aggregate demand (the ***demand factor***) and the efficiency with which the economy allocates resources (the ***efficiency factor***).

The next section of the chapter places the factors contributing to economic growth in graphical perspective with the use of two familiar models. The ***production possibilities model*** was originally presented in Chapter 2 and is now used to discuss how the two major supply factors—labor input and labor productivity—shift the production possibilities curve outward. The second model is the ***aggregate demand–aggregate supply model*** that was first explained in Chapter 11 and was discussed in more detail in Chapter 16. Here you learn how both the short-run and the long-run shifts in aggregate supply combined with shifts in aggregate demand (and the factors underlying those shifts) affect the output and the price level.

The growth record of the United States has been impressive both in terms of increases in real GDP and in real GDP per capita. What accounts for this long-term economic growth of the United States? First, the U.S. population and the size of its labor force have grown. Second and more important, the productivity of the labor force in the United States has increased. The increase in the productivity of labor is the result of technological advances, the expansion of the stock of capital goods in the U.S. economy, the improved education and training of its labor force, economies of scale, the reallocation of resources, the generous quantities of natural resources with which the U.S. economy was endowed, and its social, cultural, and political environment. (Note, however, that the regulations of government tend to slow the rates at which the productivity of labor and the output of the economy grows.) In addition, macroeconomic instability has limited the economy from achieving its full potential output.

The rate of increase in labor productivity was less in the 1970s and 1980s compared with previous decades and also less when compared with some of our major trading partners. This slowdown in labor productivity is significant for several reasons related to our standard of living, inflation, and the competitiveness of the United States in world markets. As you will learn, the decline stems from at least five major problems experienced by the economy in the past two decades.

Although productivity growth has increased modestly in recent years, the resurgence may be transitory and low productivity may continue to limit the long-term potential for economic growth. It is still too early to tell if the recent upsurge in productivity and economic growth heralds a "new economy" or is a short-term change to be followed by macroeconomic instability.

The last section of the chapter describes two major types of growth policies. The demand-side policies include discretionary monetary and fiscal policies that you learned about in previous chapters. The supply-side policies are varied and include efforts to improve education and training, and changes in tax policies to increase incentives to work, save, and invest. These policies may also include deregulation of industries or international trade agreements both of which increase the long-term growth potential of the economy.

■ CHECKLIST

When you have studied this chapter you should be able to

☐ Define economic growth in two different ways.
☐ Explain why economic growth is important to any economy.
☐ Use the rule of 70 to demonstrate how different growth rates affect real domestic output over time.
☐ Identify four supply factors in economic growth.
☐ Explain demand and efficiency factors in economic growth.
☐ Show graphically how economic growth shifts the production possibilities curve.
☐ Explain the equation for total output.
☐ Illustrate graphically how economic growth shifts the short-run and long-run aggregate supply curve and the aggregate demand curve.
☐ Describe the growth record of the U.S. economy since 1940 and its rates of economic growth since 1948.

☐ Compare the relative importance of the two major means of increasing the real GDP in the United States since 1929.
☐ List the sources of growth in the productivity of labor in the United Sates since 1929, and state their relative importance.
☐ Identify the chief detriment to growth and indicate how much it has reduced real output in the United States since 1929.
☐ Describe the other contributing factors which affect an economy's growth rate.
☐ Explain why the actual rate of growth in the United States has been less than its potential rate of growth and why it has been unstable.
☐ Give three reasons why the slowdown in productivity is significant.
☐ Enumerate the five principal causes of the slowdown in the rate of labor productivity in the United States.
☐ Discuss whether there has been a resurgence of productivity growth and the development of a "new economy."
☐ Outline two growth policies and give examples of each.

■ CHAPTER OUTLINE

1. *Growth economics* deals with the long-run changes in production capacity over time.

  a. ***Economic growth*** means an increase in the per capita real output of an economy and is measured in terms of the annual percentage rate of growth of per capita real output.
  b. Economic growth is important because it lessens the burden of scarcity; it provides the means of satisfying existing wants more fully and fulfilling new wants.
  c. One or two percentage point differences in the rate of growth result in substantial differences in annual increases in the economy's output.

2. Whether economic growth *can* occur depends on supply, demand, and efficiency factors:

  a. ***supply factors*** include the quantity and quality of resources (natural, human, and capital), and technology;
  b. ***demand factors*** influence the level of aggregate demand in the economy that is important for sustaining full employment of resources; and
  c. ***efficiency factors*** affect the efficient use of resources to obtain maximum production of goods and services (productive efficiency) and allocates them to their highest and best use by society (allocative efficiency).

3. Two familiar economic models can be used for the analysis of economic growth.

  a. In the *production possibilities model,* economic growth shifts the production possibilities curve outward because of improvement in supply factors that
  (1) increase real output by increasing the labor inputs and by increasing the productivity of labor (in equation terms: total output = worker-hours × labor productivity);
  (2) however, whether the economy operates on the frontier of the curve depends on demand factors affecting the full employment of resources efficiency factors affecting full production.
  b. In the *aggregate demand–aggregate supply model,* economic growth is also affected by these supply, demand, and efficiency factors.
  (1) Supply factors that contribute to economic growth shift the vertical long-run aggregate supply to the right in the model.
  (2) But since the price level has increased over time, this suggests that the increase in potential output has been accompanied by an even greater shift in aggregate demand (and its underlying demand and allocative factors).

4. Over the past 50 years, the *growth record* of the U.S. economy has been impressive, but economic growth in America has been less impressive than the record of many advanced industrialized nations in recent decades.

  a. Economic well-being may be understated by economic growth figures because the figures do not take into account improvements in product quality or increase in leisure time.
  b. But growth may have adverse effects on the environment or the quality of life that are not reflected in growth figures, thus the figures may overstate the benefits of growth.

5. Many factors account for the economic growth of the United States since 1929.

  a. Two-thirds of this growth was the result of the increased productivity of labor, and one-third of it was the result of the increased quantity of labor employed in the economy.
  b. During this period the U.S. population and its labor force expanded, and despite decreases in the length of the workweek and birthrates, the increased participation of women in the labor force and the growth of its population continue to expand the size of the labor force by two million workers a year.
  c. Technological advance is combining given amounts of resources in new ways that result in a larger output, and since 1929, it accounted for 28% of the increase in real national income.
  d. Saving and investment have expanded the U.S. economy's stock of capital; increased the quantity of tools, equipment, and machinery with which each worker has to work; and accounted for 20% of the increase in real national income since 1929.
  e. Increased investment in human capital (in the training and education of workers) expands the productivity of workers, and accounted for 12% of the increase in real national income.
  f. Economies of scale *and* the improved allocation of resources also expand the productivity of workers; since 1929, each has contributed 8% to the U.S. real national income.
  g. But such detriments (or deterrents) to the growth of productivity as the government regulation of industry, pollution, and worker health and safety divert investment away from productivity-increasing additions to

capital. They accounted for a *negative* 9% of the increased real national income since 1929.

h. Other factors that are difficult to quantify, such as a general abundance of natural resources and social-cultural-political environment, have also contributed to economic growth in the United States.

i. While the actual economic growth in the United States averaged 2.9% per year since 1929, it would have been higher by .2 to .3 percentage points if the economy had achieved its potential level of output and not experienced depression or recession.

6. The annual rates of growth in labor productivity in the United States declined substantially during the 1970s and rose only modestly during the 1980s and early 1990s. Productivity rates achieved in the United States are also less than those found in other major industrial nations such as Japan or Germany.

a. The slowdown in the growth of labor productivity is significant because it affects the standard of living, inflation, and the prices of U.S. goods in world markets.

b. The suggested causes of the productivity slowdown have included

(1) *labor quality*—a decline in the quality (education, training, and experience) of the U.S. labor force;

(2) *less technological progress*—a decline in research and development expenditures as a percentage of GDP;

(3) *low investment*—reduced investment in capital goods as a percentage of GDP than in previous periods stemming from low saving rates, import competition, regulation, and less spending for infrastructure;

(4) *high energy prices*—higher prices in 1973–1975 and 1978–1980 increased production costs and had inflationary and adverse macro policy effects on the economy;

(5) *low growth of service productivity*—the lack of substitute resources, less competitive pressure, and the demand for higher quality services contributed to this condition.

7. Productivity and economic growth showed substantial improvement in the 1990s compared with the 1970s and 1980s. These developments caused some economists to wonder whether a "new economy" has developed based on improvements in computer technology, communications, and global capitalism. The question is whether these increases in the rates of productivity and economic growth represent a long-run trend or a short-run boom to be followed by macroeconomic instability.

8. Two economic policies have been discussed for achieving more economic growth in the United States.

a. ***Demand-side policies*** focus on the use of monetary and fiscal policies to influence aggregate demand and maintain full employment and full production of resources.

b. ***Supply-side policies*** call for expansion of the economy's output potential and often involve changes in education and training and new tax policies to increase investment, saving, and work effort.

■ HINTS AND TIPS

1. Chapter 18 contains very little economics that should be new to you. You learned about real GDP and how to measure its growth in Chapter 7. Chapter 2 introduced you to the production possibilities model that is now discussed in more detail. In Chapters 11 and 16 you learned about the aggregate demand–aggregate supply models that are now used to discuss economic growth. You might review these concepts and models from previous chapters before reading Chapter 18.

2. Table 18-2 is important if you want to understand the factors that influence economic growth in the United States. The figures in the table indicate the relative importance of each factor. About two-thirds of American economic growth comes from eight factors that affect labor productivity, and one-third comes from the increase in the quantity of labor.

■ IMPORTANT TERMS

economic growth
supply factor
demand factor
efficiency factor
labor productivity
labor force participation rate
infrastructure

SELF-TEST

■ FILL-IN QUESTIONS

1. Growth economics is concerned with an economy whose productive capacity (increases, decreases) ______________ over time.

2. Economic growth is best measured either by an increase in (nominal, real) ______________ GDP over a time period or by an increase in ______________ GDP per capita over a time period.

3. A rise in real output per capita (increases, decreases) ______________ the standard of living and ______________ the burden of scarcity in the economy.

4. Assume an economy has a GDP of $3600 billion. If the growth rate is 5%, real GDP will increase by ($360, $180) ______________ billion next year; but if the rate of growth is only 3%, the annual increase in GDP will be ($54, $108) ______________ billion. A two percentage point difference in the growth rate results in a ($72, $254) ________ billion difference in the annual increase in GDP.

5. The four supply factors in economic growth are

a. ______________________________

b. ____________

c. ____________

d. ____________

6. To realize its growing production potential, a nation must fully employ its expanding supplies of resources, which is the (efficiency, demand) ____________ factor in economic growth, and it must also achieve productive and allocative ____________, the other factor contributing to economic growth.

7. In the production possibilities model, economic growth increases primarily because of (demand, supply) ____________ factors that shift the production possibilities curve to the (left, right) ____________; but if there is less than full employment and production, the economy (may, may not) ____________ realize its potential.

8. Real GDP of any economy in any year is equal to the quantity of labor employed (divided, multiplied) ____________ by the productivity of labor. The quantity of labor is measured by the number of (workers, hours of labor) ____________ employed. Productivity is equal to real GDP per (capita, worker-hour) ____________.

9. The quantity of labor employed in the economy in any year depends on the size of the (unemployed, employed) ____________ labor force and the length of the average workweek. The size element depends on the size of the working-age population and the labor-force (unemployment, participation) ____________ rate.

10. In the aggregate demand–aggregate supply framework, economic growth is illustrated by an (increase, decrease) ____________ in the long-run aggregate supply curve; when the price level also increases, it indicates that the aggregate demand curve has increased (more, less) ____________ rapidly than the long-run aggregate supply.

11. Since 1940, real GDP has increased (threefold, sixfold) ____________ and real GDP per capita has increased ____________. These figures do not fully account for (better, worse) ____________ products and services, (more, less) ____________ leisure, (positive, negative) ____________ environmental effects, and the fact that the growth rate in the United States is (less, more) ____________ impressive than many other industrial nations.

12. Economist Edward Denison studied economic growth in the United States since 1929 and found that the increase in the quantity of labor accounted for (one-third, two-thirds) ____________ of economic growth and increases in labor productivity accounted for ____________ of economic growth.

13. Factors contributing to labor productivity include

a. technological ____________

b. increases in the quantity of ____________ employed and in the quantity employed per ____________

c. the improved ____________ and ____________ of workers

d. economies of ____________

e. the improved ____________ of resources.

14. An increase in the stock of capital of a nation is the result of saving and (consumption, investment) ____________. In the United States the stock of capital has historically grown (more, less) ____________ rapidly than the quantity of labor employed.

15. The principal detriment to growth of real output since 1929 seems to have been government regulations which diverted (consumption, investment) ____________ spending away from uses that would have increased the (cost, productivity) ____________ of labor.

16. Two other factors that have led to economic growth in the United States are its abundant (labor, natural) ____________ resources and its social-cultural-political (parties, environment) ____________.

17. Denison's analysis is designed to explain (actual, potential) ____________ real national income, but when there is macroeconomic instability such as a recession the ____________ rate of economic growth falls short of the (actual, potential) ____________ rate.

18. In the 1970s and to a lesser extent the 1980s, the annual rates of increase in the productivity of labor (rose, fell) ____________. The significance of this development is that it can cause a (rise, fall) ____________ in the standard of living and a ____________ in inflationary pressure. It can also result in a loss of international markets for (United States, foreign) ____________ producers of goods and services.

19. The slowdown in productivity growth is a result of problems with labor (quantity, quality) ____________, (more, less) ____________ technological progress, relatively (high, low) ____________ levels of investment spending as a percent of GDP, energy prices that are (high, low) ____________ in certain years, and (faster, slower) ____________ growth in service productivity. Some of these problems have lessened in the past two decades, and productivity has (increased, decreased) _______________ as a consequence, but it is not known whether the change is permanent and signals the development of a (new, old) ____________ economy.

20. Two basic types of growth policies have been suggested for stimulating economic growth in the United States. Policies that involve the use of discretionary monetary and fiscal policies to sustain and expand full employment in the economy are (supply, demand) _____________-side policies, whereas ______________-side policies focus primarily on tax changes to stimulate work, saving, investment, education, and training policies.

■ TRUE-FALSE QUESTIONS

Circle the T if the statement is true; the F if it is false.

1. Growth economics examines why an economy's production capacity increases over time. **T F**

2. The better of the two definitions of economic growth for comparing living standards is an increase in the per capita real output of the economy. **T F**

3. Suppose two economies both have GDPs of $500 billion. If the GDPs grow at annual rates of 3% in the first economy and 5% in the second economy, the difference in their amounts of growth in 1 year is $10 billion. **T F**

4. If the rate of growth in real GDP averages 2.5% a year, it will take about 28 years for real GDP to double. **T F**

5. The potential of an enhanced productive capacity in an economy will not be completely realized unless there is full employment of resources and full production in the economy. **T F**

6. An increase in economic growth will increase the long-run aggregate supply curve and the short-run aggregate supply curve, but will decrease the aggregate demand curve. **T F**

7. The demand factor in economic growth refers to the ability of the economy to expand its production as the demand for products grows. **T F**

8. To reach its production potential, a nation must achieve not only full employment but also economic efficiency. **T F**

9. The real GDP of an economy in any year is equal to its input of labor divided by the productivity of labor. **T F**

10. Real GDP has tended to increase more rapidly than real per capita GDP in the United States. **T F**

11. Growth and rates-of-growth estimates generally attempt to take account of changes in the quality of goods produced and in the amount of leisure members of the economy enjoy. **T F**

12. Increased labor productivity has been more important than increased labor inputs in the growth of the U.S. economy since 1929. **T F**

13. Since 1929 improved technology has accounted for about 28% of the increase in real output in the United States. **T F**

14. More often than not technological progress requires the economy to invest in new machinery and equipment. **T F**

15. The single most important source of the growth of labor productivity in the United States since 1929 has been the increase in the size of the U.S. labor force. **T F**

16. The expanded regulation of industry, the environment, and worker health and safety tends to reduce the rate at which labor productivity grows. **T F**

17. The availability of natural resources in the United States has been a significant factor in the growth of the U.S. economy. **T F**

18. Over the past 60 years, the U.S. social, cultural, and political environment has slowed the economic growth of the United States. **T F**

19. Increases in labor productivity can, at least in the U.S. economy, be taken pretty much for granted because the rate of increase has been nearly constant for well over half a century. **T F**

20. Productivity growth is the basic source of improvements in real wage rates and the standard of living. **T F**

21. Productivity increases offset increases in nominal wage rates, partly or fully lessening cost-push inflationary pressures. **T F**

22. There was a significant improvement in the education, employment training, and work experience of workers in the 1970s and 1980s that contributed to increased labor productivity in those decades. **T F**

23. During the 1970s and 1980s the United States invested a larger percentage of its GDP in capital goods. **T F**

24. The slowdown in U.S. productivity growth has been greater in the manufacturing sector than in the service sector. **T F**

25. An example of a supply-side policy for economic growth would be programs for education and training of the labor force. **T F**

■ MULTIPLE-CHOICE QUESTIONS

Circle the letter that corresponds to the best answer.

1. Which of the following is a benefit of real economic growth to a society?

(a) Everyone enjoys a greater nominal income.
(b) The standard of living increases.
(c) The burden of scarcity increases.
(d) The society is less able to satisfy new wants.

2. If the real output of an economy were to increase from \$2,000 billion to \$2,100 billion in 1 year, the rate of growth of real output during that year would be
(a) 0.5%
(b) 5%
(c) 10%
(d) 50%

3. Suppose an economy has a real GDP of \$700 billion and an annual growth rate of 5%. Over a 2-year period real GDP will increase by
(a) \$14 billion
(b) \$35 billion
(c) \$70 billion
(d) \$71 3/4 billion

4. If a nation's real GDP is growing by 2% per year, then approximately how many years will it take for real GDP to double?
(a) 25 years
(b) 30 years
(c) 35 years
(d) 40 years

5. Which of the following is *not* a supply factor in economic growth?
(a) an expansion in purchasing power
(b) an increase in the economy's stock of capital goods
(c) more natural resources
(d) technological progress

Use the following graph to answer Questions 6 and 7.

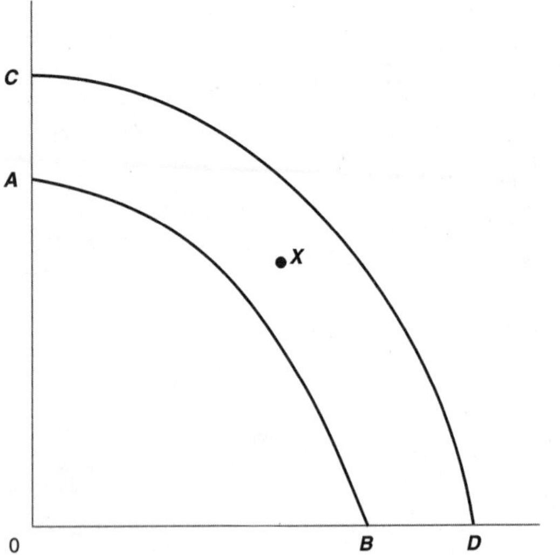

6. If the production possibilities curve of an economy shifts from ***AB*** to ***CD***, it is most likely caused by
(a) supply factors
(b) demand factors
(c) efficiency factors
(d) industrial policy

7. If the production possibilities curve for an economy is at ***CD*** but the economy is operating at point ***X***, the reasons are most likely to be because of
(a) supply and environmental factors
(b) demand and efficiency factors
(c) labor inputs and labor productivity
(d) technological progress

8. Total output or real GDP in any year is equal to
(a) labor inputs divided by resource outputs
(b) labor productivity multiplied by real output
(c) worker-hours multiplied by labor productivity
(d) worker-hours divided by labor productivity

9. Assume that an economy has 1,000 workers, each working 2,000 hours per year. If the average real output per worker-hour is \$9, then total output or real GDP will be
(a) \$2 million
(b) \$9 million
(c) \$18 million
(d) \$24 million

Use the graph below to answer Questions 10 and 11.

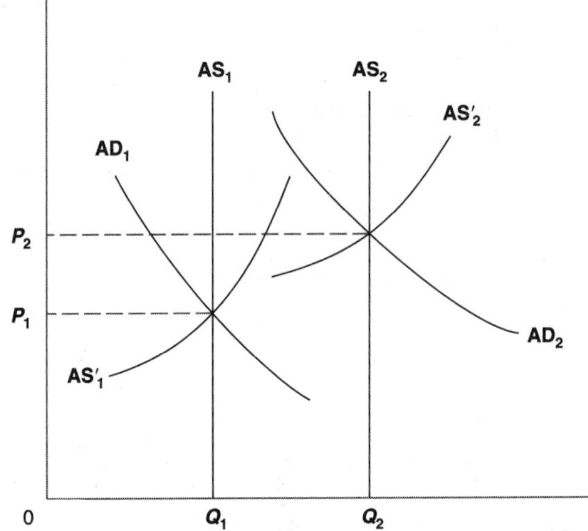

10. A shift from Q_1 to Q_2 is caused by a shift in the
(a) level of prices
(b) aggregate demand curve
(c) short-run aggregate supply curve
(d) long-run aggregate supply curve

11. Which combination would best explain a shift in the price level from P_1 to P_2 and an increase in real domestic output from Q_1 to Q_2?
(a) an increase in the long-run aggregate supply **(AS_1** to **AS_2**) and in short-run aggregate supply (**AD_1** to **AD_2**).
(b) an increase in aggregate demand (**AD_1** to **AD_2**) and a decrease in long-run aggregate supply (**AS_2** to **AS_1**).
(c) an increase in the long-run aggregate supply **(AS_1** to **AS_2**), an increase in aggregate demand (**AD_1** to **AD_2**), and an increase in short-run aggregate supply (**AS'_1** to **AS'_2**).
(d) a decrease in the long-run aggregate supply (**AS_2** to **AS_1**), a decrease in aggregate demand (**AD_2** to

AD_1), and a decrease in short-run aggregate supply (AS'_2 to AS'_1)

12. Since 1940 real GDP in the United States has increased about
(a) onefold
(b) twofold
(c) fourfold
(d) sixfold

13. The real GDP of the U.S. economy since 1948 increased at an average *annual* rate of about
(a) .5%
(b) 2.1%
(c) 3.1%
(d) 5.4%

14. Real GDP per capita in the United States since 1948 increased at an average annual rate of about
(a) 1%
(b) 2%
(c) 3%
(d) 4%

15. Data on real GDP, real GDP per capita, and the respective growth rates of those measured in the United States take into account
(a) improvement in product quality
(b) increases in available leisure time
(c) environmental problems
(d) changes in domestic output

16. About what fraction of the growth in the real national income of the United States since 1929 has been due to increases in the quantity of labor employed?
(a) one-fourth
(b) one-third
(c) one-half
(d) two-thirds

17. The factor accounting for the largest increase in the productivity of labor in the United States since 1929 has been
(a) economies of scale
(b) technological advance
(c) the quantity of capital
(d) the education and training of workers

18. A major factor that has negatively affected economic growth since 1929 has been
(a) the decreased quantity of labor
(b) education and training
(c) diseconomies of scale
(d) government regulation

19. The average annual growth rate in the United States has been
(a) increased by periods of recession
(b) increased by periods of inflation
(c) decreased by periods of recession
(d) not affected by periods of inflation

20. Which labor factor contributed to the slowdown in the growth rate of productivity in the 1970s and 1980s?
(a) a decline in the number of high school dropouts
(b) a decline in the level of work experience
(c) a decline in the size of the labor force
(d) a rise in the number of jobs

21. Which best explains why there was a lower level of capital investment in the United States in the 1970s and 1980s?
(a) less regulation of business practices
(b) less competition from imported goods
(c) greater spending for infrastructure
(d) lower rates of saving

22. A factor that helped slow the growth rate of productivity in the 1970s and 1980s was
(a) a rise in the growth rate of manufacturing productivity
(b) a fall in the growth rate of service productivity
(c) a rise in the quality of labor
(d) a fall in energy prices

23. Which factor has contributed to the resurgence of productivity growth in recent years?
(a) increased inflation
(b) higher energy prices
(c) more experienced workers
(d) greater government regulation

24. If the Federal Reserve acted to cut interest rates to stimulate investment, this would be an example of
(a) a supply-side policy
(b) a demand-side policy
(c) an industrial policy
(d) a fiscal policy

25. A program which provides tuition tax credits that are designed to increase college enrollment would be an example of
(a) monetary policy
(b) regulatory policy
(c) supply-side policy
(d) demand-side policy

■ PROBLEMS

1. The table below shows the quantity of labor (measured in hours) and the productivity of labor (measured in real GDP per hour) in a hypothetical economy in three different years.

Year	Quantity of labor	Productivity of labor	Real GDP
1	1000	$100	$ _____
2	1000	105	_____
3	1100	105	_____

a. Compute the economy's real GDP in each of the three years and enter them in the table.
b. Between years 1 and 2, the quantity of labor remained constant, but

(1) the productivity of labor increased by ________%, and

(2) as a consequence, real GDP increased by

________%.

c. Between years 2 and 3, the productivity of labor remained constant, but

(1) the quantity of labor increased by ________%, and
(2) as a consequence, real GDP increased by

________%.

d. Between years 1 and 3

(1) real GDP increased by ________%, and
(2) this rate of increase is approximately equal to the

sum of the rates of increase in the ____________

and the ____________ of labor.

2. Suppose the real GDP and the population of an economy in seven different years were those shown in the next table.

Year	Population, million	Real GDP, billions of dollars	Per capital real GDP
1	30	$ 9	$ 300
2	60	24	_____
3	90	45	_____
4	120	66	_____
5	150	90	_____
6	180	99	_____
7	210	105	_____

a. How large would the real per capita GDP of the economy be in each of the other six years? Put your figures in the table.

b. What would have been the size of the optimum population of this economy? ____________

c. What was the *amount* of growth in real GDP between year 1 and year 2? $ ____________

d. What was the *rate* of growth in real GDP between year 3 and year 4? ____________ %

3. Given the hypothetical data in the table below, calculate the average annual rates of growth in real GDP and real per capita GDP over the period given.

Year	Real GDP	Annual growth in %	Real GDP per capita	Annual growth in %
1	$2,416		$11,785	
2	2,695	_____	12,593	_____
3	3,187	_____	13,978	_____
4	3,618	_____	15,139	_____
5	3,995	_____	16,240	_____
6	4,545	_____	17,110	_____

■ SHORT ANSWERS AND ESSAY QUESTIONS

1. What is meant by economic growth? Why should the citizens of the United States be concerned with economic growth?

2. What are the six basic ingredients of economic growth? What is the essential difference between the supply factors and the other two factors? Is there any relationship between the strength of the supply factors and the strength of the demand factor?

3. What is the relationship between the real GDP produced in any year and the quantity of labor employed and labor productivity?

4. In what units are the quantity of labor and the productivity of labor measured?
(a) What are the two principal determinants of the quantity of the labor input?
(b) What determines the size of the labor force?

5. How does economic growth affect production possibilities? What demand and efficiency assumptions are necessary to achieve maximum productive potential?

6. Describe how economic growth can be illustrated in an aggregate demand–aggregate supply framework. What has happened to aggregate demand compared to long-run aggregate supply when the price level and real domestic output both increase?

7. What has been the growth record of the U.S. economy? Compare recent U.S. growth rates with those in other nations.

8. What have been the sources of the growth of the real national income in the United States since 1929? What has tended to slow the increase in labor productivity and in real national income?

9. What changes have occurred in the size of the U.S. population and labor force since 1929? What factor has slowed the rate of growth of the former, and what factor has speeded the growth of the latter?

10. What is the relationship between investment and the stock of capital? What is the connection between increases in the capital stock and the rate of economic growth?

11. What is technological advance, and why are technological advance and capital formation closely related processes?

12. What tends to increase the "quality" of labor? How is this quality usually measured?

13. What are the economic consequences if the economy fails to achieve its potential output year after year? What are the long-term consequences of this macroeconomic instability?

14. By how much did the annual increases in the productivity of labor decline in the United States between the mid-1960s and 1981? What are three significant features of this decline in this productivity growth?

15. What are five causes of the slowdown in the growth of labor productivity since the mid-1960s? Explain how each cause affects productivity.

16. How might changes in labor quality dampen productivity growth? What factors in the United States have contributed to this situation?

17. What is the relationship between the capital investment and productivity growth? What four conditions in the United States have affected the relative level of investment?

18. Explain the three possible reasons for slower productivity growth in services relative to manufacturing since the 1970s.

19. Has there been a resurgence in economic growth? What trends are suggested by the evidence? Do you think this is a long-term or short-term development in the economy?

20. What are the basic differences between demand-side and supply-side policies to stimulate economic growth? Give examples of each type.

ANSWERS

Chapter 18 Economic Growth

FILL-IN QUESTIONS

1. increases
2. real, real
3. increases, decreases
4. $180, $108, $72
5. *a.* quantity and quality of natural resources; *b.* quantity and quality of human resources; *c.* the supply or stock of capital goods; *d.* technology (any order for a–d)
6. demand, efficiency
7. supply, right, may not
8. multiplied, hours of labor, worker-hour
9. employed, participation
10. increase, more
11. sixfold, threefold, better, more, negative, less
12. one-third, two-thirds
13. *a.* progress (advance); *b.* capital, worker; *c.* education, training; *d.* scale; *e.* allocation
14. investment, more
15. investment, productivity
16. natural, environment
17. actual, actual, potential
18. fell, fall, rise, United States
19. quality, less, low, high, slower, increased, new
20. demand, supply

TRUE-FALSE QUESTIONS

1. T, p. 368
2. T, pp. 368-369
3. T, pp. 368-369
4. T, p. 369
5. T, pp. 369-370
6. F, pp. 371-372
7. F, p. 369
8. T, pp. 369-370
9. F, pp. 370-371
10. T, p. 372
11. F, p. 373
12. T, pp. 373-374
13. F, p. 374
14. T, p. 374
15. F, pp. 373-376
16. T, p. 376
17. T, p. 377
18. F, p. 377
19. F, p. 378
20. T, p. 378
21. T, p. 378
22. F, pp. 378-379
23. F, p. 380
24. T, pp. 381-382
25. T, p. 383

MULTIPLE-CHOICE QUESTIONS

1. b, p. 369
2. b, p. 369
3. d, p. 369
4. c, p. 369
5. a, p. 369
6. a, p. 370
7. b, p. 370
8. c, pp. 370-371
9. c, pp. 370-371
10. d, pp. 371-372
11. c, pp. 371-372
12. d, p. 372
13. c, p. 373
14. b, p. 373
15. d, p. 373
16. b, pp. 373-374
17. b, p. 374
18. d, p. 376
19. c, p. 377
20. b, p. 379
21. d, p. 380
22. b, pp. 381-382
23. c, p. 382
24. b, p. 383
25. c, p. 383

PROBLEMS

1. *a.* 100,000, 105,000, 115,500; *b.* (1) 5, (2), 5; *c.* (1) 10, (2) 10; *d.* (1) 15.5, (2) quantity, productivity
2. *a.* 400, 500, 550, 600, 550, 500; *b.* 150 million; *c.* $15 billion; *d.* 46.7%
3. *real GDP:* years 1–2 (2.3%); years 2–3 (3.7%); years 3–4 (2.7%); years 4–5 (3.5%); years 5–6 (4.6%); *real GDP per capita:* years 1–2 (1.4%); years 2–3 (2.2%); years 3–4 (1.7%); years 4–5 (2.4%); years 5–6 (1.8%)

SHORT ANSWER AND ESSAY QUESTIONS

1. pp. 368-369
2. pp. 369-370
3. pp. 370-371
4. pp. 370-371
5. p. 370
6. pp. 371-372
7. pp. 372-373
8. pp. 373-377
9. p. 374
10. pp. 374-375
11. p. 374
12. p. 375
13. p. 377
14. p. 378
15. pp. 378-382
16. p. 379
17. p. 380
18. pp. 381-382
19. pp. 382-383
20. pp. 383

CHAPTER 19

Budget Deficits and the Public Debt

Over the past 35 years, the Federal government has had budget deficits in all but one year. In the past decade these budget deficits have grown quite large and have caused problems for the U.S. economy. Chapter 19 looks at the data and issues surrounding ***budget deficits*** and the related ***public debt.***

The Federal government can operate with a budget deficit, a budget surplus, or a balanced budget during a year. Any budget surplus or deficit affects the size of the public (sometimes called national) debt; surpluses decrease it and deficits increase it. After a budget deficit and the public debt have been defined, three budget philosophies are discussed. Be aware that the philosophies the Federal government adopts have a significant impact on output and employment in the economy and on the public debt.

The chapter then discusses how four major *factors—wars, recessions, tax cuts,* and *lack of political will*—have contributed to increases in the public debt since 1929. The increased public debt resulting from these factors is placed into perspective with a quantitative description of the size of the public debt (and interest payments for it) relative to the size of the economy (GDP), how the public debt in the United States compares with that in other industrial nations, who owns the debt, and measurement problems caused by accounting and inflation.

The two middle sections of the chapter examine the economic implications or consequences of the public debt and deficits. These economic problems do not include bankrupting the Federal government because the government has three ways that it can meet its obligations. Nor does the public debt simply shift the economic burden to future generations because the public debt is a public credit for the many people who hold that debt in the form of government bonds. Rather, the public debt and payment of interest on the debt contribute to five important problems: increased inequality in income, reduced incentives for work and production, decreased standard of living when part of the debt is paid to foreigners, curbs on fiscal policy, and less capital investment.

The crowding out of investment in plant and equipment in the United States is probably the most serious of these five problems. You should understand how crowding out works and how it may impose a burden on future generations by reducing the growth of the nation's capital stock. Whether it does impose a burden on a future generation depends on how the increased government spending is financed. Raising taxes to pay for increased spending imposes a burden on the current taxpayers, whereas government borrowing to finance increased spending tends to reduce private investment and future capital stock.

The final sections of the chapter offer an extensive discussion of the macroeconomic problems with the Federal deficits of the past two decades. The recent deficits are of great concern because of their relatively large size, high interest cost, and the problems they pose for domestic macroeconomic and trade policy. Be sure that you study each link in the chain of events that lead to the contractions of output and employment in the U.S. economy as a result of large deficits. There is not any new economic theory in this discussion, just an application of theory you learned in previous chapters. The chapter then concludes with an explanation of three different policy responses to eliminate or reduce Federal budget deficits.

■ CHECKLIST

When you have studied this chapter you should be able to

☐ Define a budget deficit and the public debt, and explain how they are related.
☐ List three budget philosophies.
☐ Describe the characteristics of an annually balanced budget.
☐ State the rationale for a cyclically balanced budget.
☐ Explain how functional finance works as a budget philosophy.
☐ Identify the four principal causes of the public debt and discuss their relative importance.
☐ Describe the absolute and relative sizes of the public debt and interest payments since 1929.
☐ Compare the relative size of the public debt to those of other industrial nations.
☐ State who owns the public debt.
☐ Explain how inflation and accounting issues affect the public debt.
☐ Give three reasons why a large public debt will not bankrupt the government.
☐ Discuss whether the public debt imposes a burden on future generations.
☐ List five substantive issues related to the public debt.
☐ State the effect of the public debt on income distribution.
☐ Explain how the public debt affects incentives.
☐ Compare the effects of an internal debt with the effects of an external debt on the economy.
☐ Explain how large budget deficits curb the use of fiscal policy.

☐ Describe the crowding-out effect from a public debt.
☐ Compare taxation with borrowing as a way to finance a public debt and and qualify this comparison in two ways.
☐ Describe five concerns with the budget deficits and the public debt during the past two decades.
☐ Discuss the cause and effect linkage between the budget deficits and the balance of trade deficits and three related complications.
☐ Explain three major policy responses to large budget deficits and the expanding public debt.
☐ State how the public debt plays a positive role in the economy.

■ CHAPTER OUTLINE

1. The *budget deficit* of the Federal government is the amount by which its expenditures exceed its revenues in any year, and the *public debt* at any time is the sum of the Federal government's previous annual deficits (less any annual surpluses).

2. If the Federal government uses fiscal policy to combat recession and inflation, its budget is not likely to be balanced in any particular year. Three *budget philosophies* may be adopted by the government; the adoption of any of these philosophies will affect employment, real output, and the price level of the economy.

a. Proponents of an ***annually balanced budget*** would have government expenditures and tax revenues equal in every year. Such a budget is pro- rather than countercyclical; but conservative economists favor it to prevent the expansion of the public sector (and the contraction of the private sector) of the economy without the increased payment of taxes by the public.

b. Those who advocate a ***cyclically balanced budget*** propose matching surpluses (in years of prosperity) with deficits (in depression years) to stabilize the economy, but there is no assurance that the surpluses will equal the deficits over the years.

c. Advocates of ***functional finance*** contend that deficits, surpluses, and the size of the debt are of minor importance and that the goal of full employment without inflation should be achieved regardless of the effects of the necessary fiscal policies on the budget and the size of the public debt.

3. Any government deficit increases the size of the public debt. The public debt has grown substantially since 1929.

a. There are four basic *causes of the debt:*
(1) *wars* require increased Federal borrowing to finance the war effort;
(2) *recessions* result in budget deficits because of the built-in stability of the economy (tax revenues fall and domestic spending rises);
(3) *cuts in tax rates* without offsetting reductions in expenditures contribute to budget deficits, as occurred during the early 1980s; and
(4) *a lack of political will* to control expenditures for popular entitlement programs or raise taxes to pay for them adds to budget deficits.

b. The public debt in 1997 was $5.4 trillion.
(1) The size of the debt as a percentage of the economy's GDP did not grow as rapidly as the absolute size of the debt between 1940 and 1997, but relative to the GDP, it has increased significantly since the early 1980s.
(2) Other industrial nations have relative public debts similar to or greater than the United States.
(3) Since the 1970s the interest payments on the debt (because of increases in the size of the debt and higher interest rates in the economy) have also increased significantly, and interest payments as a percentage of the economy's GDP have grown dramatically.
(4) More than one-third (37%) of the public debt is owed to government agencies and the Federal Reserve Banks. Less than two-thirds (63%) is owed to others, including 23% owed to foreign citizens, firms, and governments.
(5) Because the accounting system the Federal government uses records its debts but not its assets, the public debt is not a true picture of its financial position. Adjusting for inflation further decreases the size of budget deficits and the public debt.

4. The contentions that a large debt will eventually *bankrupt* the government and that borrowing to finance expenditures passes the cost on to future generations are false.

a. The debt cannot bankrupt the government because the government
(1) need not retire (reduce) the debt and can refund (or refinance) it,
(2) has the constitutional authority to levy and collect taxes, and
(3) can always print (or create) money to pay both the principal and the interest on it.

b. The debt cannot shift the burden of the debt to future generations because the debt is largely internally held, and repayment of any portion of the principal and the payment of interest on it does not reduce the wealth or purchasing power of U.S. citizens.

5. The public debt does create real and potential problems in the economy.

a. The payment of interest on the debt probably increases the extent of income inequality.

b. The payment of taxes to finance these interest payments may reduce the incentives to bear risks, to innovate, to invest, and to save, and therefore they slow economic growth in the economy.

c. The portion of the debt that is externally held (by foreign citizens and institutions) requires the repayment of principal and the payment of interest to foreign citizens and institutions. This transfers a part of the real output of the U.S. economy to them.

d. It creates political problems for the use of fiscal policy as an antirecessionary measure because increasing government expenditures or cutting taxes during a recession adds to the public debt.

e. An increase in government spending may or may not impose a burden on future generations.
(1) If the increase in government spending is financed by increased personal taxes, the burden of the in-

creased spending is on the present generation whose consumption is reduced, but if it is financed by an increased public debt, the increased borrowing of the Federal government will raise interest rates and crowd out investment spending, and future generations will inherit a smaller stock of capital goods.

(2) The burden imposed on future generations is lessened if the increase in government expenditures is for real or human capital or if the economy were initially operating at less than full employment (and it stimulates an increase in investment demand).

6. Federal budget deficits during the past two decades have been the focus of national interest for many economic reasons.

a. The absolute size of the annual Federal budget deficit grew enormously during the 1980s and 1990s.

b. Recent budget deficits may be understated because surpluses from social security are being used to offset current government spending.

c. Interest costs of the debt have risen.

d. The deficits have taken place in an economy operating close to full employment, which means there is great potential for the crowding out of real private investment and for demand-pull inflation.

e. Large budget deficits make it difficult for a nation to achieve a balance in its international trade.

7. These large Federal budget deficits produced a cause-and-effect chain of events with the *balance of trade deficits.*

a. They increased interest rates, which crowded out real private investment and increased foreign financial investment in the United States. The greater foreign investment increased the international value of the dollar, which in turn reduced U.S. exports and increased U.S. imports, resulting in trade deficits.

b. There are three loose ends to the complex chain of events as described in **a**:

(1) The inflow of foreign funds helped keep interest rates lower than would otherwise be the case and diminished the size of the crowding-out effect.

(2) High interest rates in the United States resulting from large deficits placed an increased burden on developing countries, thereby contributing to the world debt problem and banking problems in the United States.

(3) The unfavorable trade balance meant that the United States had to borrow heavily from other nations and to sell assets to foreign investors, thereby affecting the course of economic growth in the future.

8. Several *policy responses* have lessened the effect of the large Federal budget deficits and the expanding public debt.

a. Deficit reduction legislation has been passed in recent years, including the Deficit Reduction Act of 1993 and a 1996 tax and spending package designed to reduce the deficit to zero by 2002.

b. In 1995 Congress gave the president authority to veto individual spending items.

c. Congress has considered an amendment to the U.S. Constitution that would require Congress to balance the Federal budget each year.

9. Private and public debt play a positive role in the economy. As an economy grows, saving increases. This saving is borrowed and spent by consumers and businesses, and private debt is created. If, however, consumers and businesses do not borrow sufficient amounts, the public debt will need to be increased to absorb some saving so that the economy can maintain full employment and achieve its growth potential.

■ HINTS AND TIPS

1. Make sure you know the difference between the public debt and the budget deficit. The two are often confused.

2. The best way to gauge public debt and budget deficit is to calculate each one as a percentage of real GDP. The absolute size of the public debt or the deficit is not a good indicator of whether it causes problems for the economy.

3. Try to understand the real rather than the imagined problems caused by the public debt. The debt will not cause the country to go bankrupt, nor will it be the burden on future generations that people often state that it will. Carefully read the section on the false issues and the real issues.

■ IMPORTANT TERMS

public debt	**external debt**
annually balanced budget	**public investments**
cyclically balanced budget	**balanced budget amendment**
functional finance	**line-item veto**
entitlement programs	

SELF-TEST

■ FILL-IN QUESTIONS

1. The Federal government's budget deficit in any year is equal to its (expenditures, revenues) ______________ less its ______________ in that year. The public debt is equal to the sum of the Federal government's past budget (deficts, surpluses) ______________ minus its budget ______________.

2. An annually balanced budget is (pro, counter) ______________-cyclical because governments would have (raised, lowered) ______________ taxes and ______________ their purchases of goods and services during a recession (and have done just the opposite during an inflation).

3. A cyclically balanced budget suggests that to ensure full employment without inflation, the government would incur deficits during periods of (inflation, recession)

_______________ and surpluses during periods of _______________, with the deficits and surpluses equaling each other over the business cycle.

4. The budget philosophy that has as its main goal the achievement of full employment without inflation is (external debt, functional finance) _______________. It regards budget deficits and increases in the public debt as of (primary, secondary) _______________ importance to this goal.

5. The principal causes of the public debt are the expense of paying for (wars, inflation) _______________, changes in the economy such as (a recession, an expansion) _______________, tax rate (cuts, increases) _______________ without offsetting reductions in government expenditures, and the lack of (monopoly power, political will) _______________ to control entitlement spending or increase taxes to balance the budget.

6. There are several quantitative aspects to the public debt.

a. The most meaningful way to measure the public debt is relative to (interest rates, GDP) _______________, and in 1997 it was _______________%.

b. In 1997 the public debt as a percentage of GDP was (higher, lower) _______________ in Japan and Canada and _______________ in Britain and Australia.

c. Federal government agencies and our central banks hold about (one-third, two-thirds) _______________ of the debt, and commercial banks, financial institutions, state and local governments, and foreign individuals and institutions hold about_______________ of the debt.

d. Most of the public debt is (internal, external) _______________ because foreigners hold only about _______________% of the public debt.

e. The public debt and budget deficits are subject to measurement problems because the accounting procedures the Federal government uses reflect (assets, debts) _______________ but do not reflect _______________.

f. If the Federal government used a capital budget which included depreciation costs, the Federal budget deficit would be (increased, decreased) _______________; if the Federal budget was adjusted for the effects of inflation, the budget deficit would be _______________.

7. The possibility that the Federal government will go bankrupt is a false issue. It does not need to reduce its debt; it can retire maturing securities by (taxing, refinancing) _______________ them or by (destroying, creating) _______________ money. The government can also pay its debts by increasing (interest, taxes) _______________.

8. As long as the government expenditures which lead to the increase in the public debt are not financed by borrowing from foreigners, the public debt of the United States is a(n) (liability, asset) _______________ of the U.S. citizens who own government securities; the cost of a government program financed by borrowing from the U.S. public is equal to the public's decreased consumption of goods and services and is a burden on the (present, future) _______________ generation.

9. The public debt is a burden on an economy if it is (internally, externally) _______________ held. Also, it and the payment of interest on it may (increase, decrease) _______________ income inequality in the economy, _______________ the incentives to work, take risks, save, and invest in the economy, and (increase, decrease) _______________ the crowding out of private investment.

10. A public debt which is internally held imposes a burden on future generations if the borrowing done to finance an increase in government expenditures (increases, decreases) _______________ interest rates, _______________ investment spending, and (increases, decreases) _______________ the stock of capital goods for future generations.

11. If the increased government expenditures are financed by an increase in the taxes on personal income, the present generation will have (more, less) _______________ consumer goods, and the burden of the increased government expenditures will be on the (future, present) _______________ generation.

12. The size of the burden of increased government expenditures financed by borrowing on future generations is weakened if the government expenditures finance (increases, decreases) _______________ in physical or human capital or if the economy had been operating at (full, less than full) _______________ employment.

13. The increased concern of the public about the Federal deficit and the expanding public debt in the past two decades is the result of the (small, large) _______________ size of these deficits, the use of funds from (external debt, social security) _______________ that offset and understate the deficit, the fact that interest costs have (fallen, risen) _______________, the use of macroeconomic policies that were (appropriate, inappropriate) _______________ for dealing with the economy, and the difficulty of achieving a (surplus, balance) _______________ in international trade.

14. Large deficits during times of full employment raise two problems. First, there is great potential for crowding out or (increasing, decreasing) _______________ real private investment. Second, the stimulus to the economy from the deficits may create the conditions for (cost-push, demand-pull) ______________ inflation.

15. Large budget deficits create an unfavorable balance of trade by (increasing, decreasing) ______________ imports and ______________ exports. This trade imbalance has contributed to making the United States a (creditor, debtor) ______________ nation and (increased, decreased) ______________ the selling of domestic assets to foreign investors.

16. The deficits of the Federal government tend to (increase, decrease) ______________ interest rates in the money markets.

a. This change in interest rates (expands, contracts) ______________ private investment spending and makes financial investments by foreigners in the United States (more, less) ______________ attractive.

b. This change in the financial investments of foreigners in the United States (increases, decreases) ______________ the external debts of the United States and (raises, lowers) ______________ the international value of the dollar.

c. This change in the international value of the dollar (expands, contracts) ______________ U.S. exports, ______________ U.S. imports, and (expands, contracts) ______________ *net* exports.

17. Other complications must be considered in the chain of events from the budget deficits of the 1980s. First, the inflow of funds from abroad (raised, lowered) ______________ domestic interest rates and therefore (strengthened, weakened) ______________ the crowding-out effect. Second, the high interest rates in the United States placed greater burden on (developed, developing) ______________ countries that trade with the United States. Third, the value of imports became greater than exports, so the United States had to (lend, borrow) ______________ from foreigners and (buy, sell) ______________ more assets.

18. In 1993, the Congress passed the Deficit Reduction Act, which was designed to (decrease, increase) ______________ tax revenues by $250 billion over a 5-year period and ______________ government spending by a similar amount.

19. In 1995 Congress passed a (balanced-budget amendment, line-item veto) ______________ to give the president more budget control. Congress has also considered the merit of a more extreme proposal, a ______________, as another policy response to budget deficits.

20. Public and private debts play a positive role if they absorb a sufficient amount of (investment, saving) ______________ to enable an economy that is (stationary, growing) ______________ to remain at full employment.

■ TRUE-FALSE QUESTIONS

Circle the T if the statement is true, the F if it is false.

1. The budget deficit of the Federal government in any year is equal to its revenues less its expenditures. **T F**

2. An annually balanced budget is economically neutral in its effects on the economy. **T F**

3. A cyclically balanced budget is procyclical, not countercyclical. **T F**

4. Proponents of functional finance argue that a balanced budget, whether it is balanced annually or over the business cycle, is of minor importance when compared with the objective of full employment without inflation. **T F**

5. A major reason for the increase in the public debt since 1929 is the government spending associated with recessions. **T F**

6. One reason for the growth in the public debt is the difficulty of getting political support for specific proposals to cut government spending or raise taxes to pay for government programs. **T F**

7. The defense spending for new weapons programs by the U.S. government is an example of an entitlement program. **T F**

8. The public debt as a percentage of GDP is higher in the United States than in most other industrial nations. **T F**

9. Interest payments as a percent of GDP reflect the level of taxation (average tax rate) required to service the public debt. **T F**

10. Most of the public debt is owned by foreign individuals and institutions. **T F**

11. Inflation increases the real value of the public debt. **T F**

12. A large public debt will bankrupt the Federal government. **T F**

13. The public debt is a public credit. **T F**

14. The payment of interest on the public debt probably increases income inequality. **T F**

15. The additional taxes required to pay the interest on the public debt increase incentives to work, save, invest, and bear risks. **T F**

16. Selling government securities to foreigners to finance increased expenditures by the Federal government imposes a burden on future generations. **T F**

17. A large and growing public debt makes it politically difficult to use fiscal policy during a recession. **T F**

18. The crowding-out effect is caused by a rise in interest rates resulting from an increase in government borrowing in the money market to finance government expenditures. **T F**

19. The crowding-out effect increases the investment-demand curve and investment in capital goods. **T F**

20. If government spending is for investment-type projects, then this spending can increase the economy's future production capacity. **T F**

21. The size of recent annual Federal budget deficits may be understated because they include items such as the social security surplus that offsets some current government spending. **T F**

22. Large budget deficits can increase interest rates and lead to an appreciation in the value of the dollar that contributes to trade deficits. **T F**

23. The 1993 Deficit Reduction Act is a constitutional amendment that requires a balanced Federal budget by the year 2010. **T F**

24. In 1995, Congress gave the president the authority to veto individual spending items in legislation passed by Congress. **T F**

25. The process by which saving is transferred to spenders in an economy is debt creation, and it plays a positive role in a growing economy. **T F**

■ MULTIPLE-CHOICE QUESTIONS

Circle the letter that corresponds to the correct answer.

1. The public debt is the sum of all previous
(a) expenditures of the Federal government
(b) budget deficits of the Federal government
(c) budget deficits less the budget surpluses of the Federal government
(d) budget surpluses less the current budget deficit of the Federal government

2. Which of the following would involve reducing government expenditures and increasing tax rates during a recession?
(a) an annually balanced budget policy
(b) functional finance
(c) a cyclically balanced budget policy
(d) a policy employing built-in stability

3. A cyclically balanced budget philosophy is
(a) procyclical
(b) countercyclical
(c) functional finance
(d) economically neutral

4. What three factors largely explain why the public debt has increased since 1929?
(a) interest payments on the public debt, spending for social security, and depreciation of the dollar
(b) deficit spending to finance a war, effects of automatic stabilizers on the budget during recessions, and tax cuts not offset by spending cuts
(c) deficit spending caused by depressions, borrowing funds from other nations, and increased government spending to cover economic problems such as the saving and loan bailout
(d) interest payments on the public debt, government spending for welfare programs, and the crowding out of investment spending

5. Since the 1980s, the public debt relative to GDP has
(a) increased and interest payments relative to GDP have increased
(b) decreased and interest payments relative to GDP have decreased
(c) decreased, but interest payments relative to GDP have decreased
(d) increased, but interest payments relative to GDP have decreased

6. To place the public debt in perspective based on the wealth and productive capacity of the economy, it is more meaningful to
(a) examine its absolute size
(b) calculate the interest payments on the debt
(c) measure it relative to the gross domestic product
(d) compare it to import, exports, and the trade deficit

7. The public debt of the United States as a percentage of its GDP is
(a) larger than all other industrial nations
(b) smaller than all other industrial nations
(c) less than all other industrial nations except Japan
(d) greater than some industrial nations but less than others

8. Foreign individuals and institutions hold about what percentage of the public debt?
(a) 5%
(b) 14%
(c) 23%
(d) 34%

9. The accounting procedures the Federal government uses record
(a) only its assets
(b) only its debts
(c) both its assets and debts
(d) its net worth

10. Inflation is a tax on the
(a) holders of the public debt, and it reduces the real size of the public debt
(b) holders of the public debt, and expands the real size of the public debt
(c) Federal government, and reduces the real size of the public debt
(d) Federal government, and expands the real size of the public debt

11. The public debt cannot bankrupt the Federal government because the Federal government
(a) has the power to levy taxes

(b) is able to refinance the debt
(c) can create money to repay the debt and pay the interest on it
(d) all of the above

12. Incurring an internal debt to finance a war does not pass the cost of the war on to future generations because
(a) the opportunity cost of the war is borne by the generation that fights it
(b) the government need not pay interest on internally held debts
(c) there is never a need for government to refinance the debt
(d) wartime inflation reduces the relative size of the debt

13. Which would be a consequence of the retirement of the internally held portion of the public debt?
(a) a reduction in the nation's productive capacity
(b) a reduction in the nation's standard of living
(c) a redistribution of the nation's wealth among its citizens
(d) an increase in aggregate expenditures in the economy

14. Which of the following is an important consequence of the public debt of the United States?
(a) It increases incentives to work and invest.
(b) It transfers a portion of the U.S. output of goods and services to foreign nations.
(c) It reduces income inequality in the United States.
(d) It leads to greater saving at every level of disposable income.

15. A large and growing public debt creates political problems for the Congress and the president to adopt
(a) an easy money policy
(b) a tight money policy
(c) an antirecessionary fiscal policy
(d) a trade policy calling for increased U.S. exports and decreased U.S. imports

16. The crowding-out effect of borrowing in the money market to finance an increase in government expenditures
(a) reduces current private investment expenditures
(b) decreases the rate at which the privately owned stock of real capital increases
(c) imposes a burden on future generations
(d) does all of the above

17. The crowding-out effect from government borrowing is reduced
(a) when the economy is operating at less than full employment
(b) when the expenditures expand human capital in the economy
(c) when the government's deficit financing improves the profit expectations of business firms
(d) when any one or more of the above are true

18. Which is *not* one of the sources of the concern with the deficits of the Federal government and the growth of the public debt during the past two decades?
(a) the large increases in the size of the deficits and in the public debt
(b) the operation of the economy substantially below full employment throughout the decade
(c) the rising interest costs of the debt
(d) problems with the balance of trade

19. Deficits in the early 1990s were primarily increased by
(a) an increase in spending for social security
(b) a recession and a bailout of the savings and loan industry
(c) an increased demand by foreigners for government securities
(d) an easy money policy of the Federal Reserve

20. The increased foreign demand for U.S. securities that results from higher interest rates in the United States
(a) increases the external debts of the United States and the international value of the dollar
(b) increases the external debts of the United States and decreases the international value of the dollar
(c) decreases the external debts of the United States and increases the international value of the dollar
(d) decreases the external debts of the United States and the international value of the dollar

21. When the international value of the dollar rises,
(a) U.S. exports tend to increase
(b) U.S. imports tend to decrease
(c) U.S. net exports tend to decrease
(d) U.S. net exports tend to increase

22. High interest rates in the United States which were related to Federal budget deficits
(a) contributed to the debt burden of developing nations that traded with the United States
(b) reduced the flow of funds from foreign nations to the United States
(c) increased the long-term economic growth and domestic investment of foreign nations that transferred funds to the United States
(d) enabled the United States to become a major creditor nation

23. The Deficit Reduction Act of 1993 was legislation passed by Congress and signed by the president; it was designed to
(a) decrease marginal tax rates on personal income, but increase corporate income taxes and the Federal tax on gasoline
(b) increase taxes on personal income and corporations and hold all discretionary government spending to 1993 nominal levels
(c) use fiscal policy to stimulate the sluggish U.S. economy during 1993
(d) coordinate fiscal policy with the monetary policy of the Federal Reserve to achieve a budget balance by the year 2010

24. A serious proposal to eliminate annual Federal budget deficits that Congress has recently considered is
(a) the changing of accounting procedures
(b) a balanced-budget amendment
(c) a moratorium on debt payments
(d) a reduction in interest rates

25. The process by which saving is transferred to spenders is
- **(a)** public investment
- **(b)** functional finance
- **(c)** debt creation
- **(d)** crowding out

■ PROBLEMS

1. The following table gives data on the public debt and the GDP for selected 5-year periods from 1961–1997. Data for the public debt and the GDP are in billions of dollars.

Year	Debt	GDP	Debt/GDP
1961	$ 292.6	$ 531.8	_____ %
1966	328.5	769.8	_____
1971	408.2	1097.2	_____
1976	629.0	1768.4	_____
1981	994.3	3030.6	_____
1986	2120.1	4268.6	_____
1991	3599.0	5671.8	_____
1996	4921.0	7265.4	_____
1997	5369.7	8083.4	_____

a. Calculate the ratio of the public debt to GDP expressed as a percentage of GDP. Enter the numbers into the last column of the table.
b. On the graph below, plot the year on the horizontal axis and plot the public debt as a percentage of GDP on the vertical axis.
c. Explain what happened to the public debt as a percentage of GDP from 1961–1997.

____

____

____

2. The following table gives data on interest rates and investment demand (in billions of dollars) in a hypothetical economy.

Interest rate	I_{d1}	I_{d2}
10%	$250	$300
8	300	350
6	350	400
4	400	450
2	450	500

a. Use the I_{d1} schedule. Assume that the government needs to finance a budget deficit and this public borrowing increases the interest rate from 4% to 6%. How much crowding out of private investment will occur?

____

b. Now assume that the deficit is used to improve the performance of the economy and that, as a consequence, the investment-demand schedule changes from I_{d1} to I_{d2}. At the same time, the interest rate rises from 4% to 6% as the government borrows money to finance the deficit. How much crowding out of private investment will occur in this case? _______________
c. Graph the two investment-demand schedules on the graph on page 213 and show the difference between the two events. Put the interest rate on the vertical axis and the quantity of investment demanded on the horizontal axis.

3. Columns 1 and 2 in the following table are the investment-demand schedules and show planned investment (I) at different rates of interest (i). Assume the marginal propensity to consume in the economy is 0.8.

(1) i	(2) I	(3) I'
.08	$115	$125
.07	140	150
.06	165	175
.05	190	200
.04	215	225

a. If the Federal government were to spend an additional $20 for goods and services, the equilibrium real

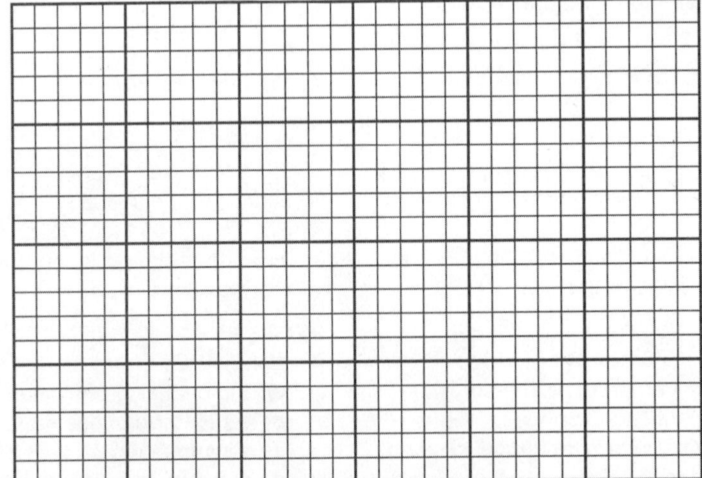

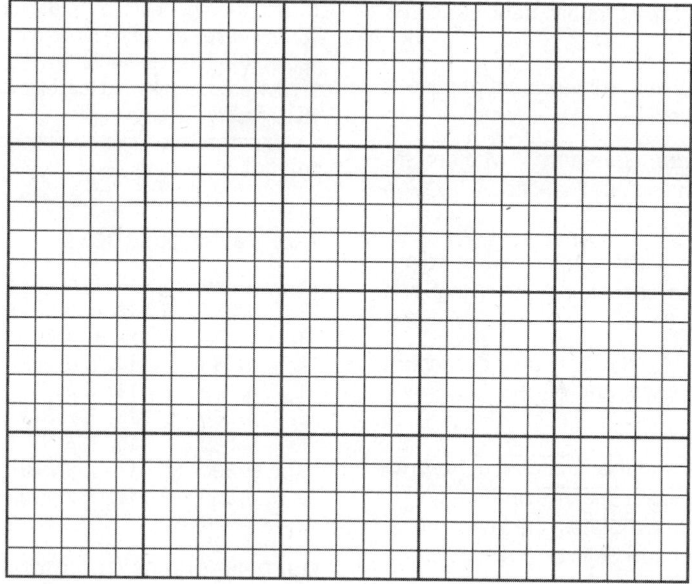

GDP would (increase, decrease) ______________

by $______________.

b. If the Federal government had obtained the additional $20 by

(1) increasing taxes by $20, the equilibrium real GDP would have (increased, decreased) ______________ by a total of $ ______________;

(2) borrowing $20 in the money market and this borrowing had increased the interest rate from 5% to 6%,

(a) planned investment spending would have (increased, decreased) ______________ by $__________,

(b) the equilibrium real GDP would have __________ by $ __________, and

(c) the net effect of the increased government spending of the $20 borrowed in the money market would have been to ______________ the equilibrium real GDP by $______________.

c. But if the government deficit spending had improved business profit expectations and shifted the investment-demand schedule to the one shown in columns 1 and 3 in the preceding table, the total effect of the increased government spending of the $20 borrowed in the money market would have been to ______________ the equilibrium real GDP by $______________.

■ SHORT ANSWER AND ESSAY QUESTIONS

1. What is the difference between the (Federal) budget deficit and the public debt?

2. Explain why an annually balanced budget is not neutral and how it can intensify, rather than reduce, the tendencies for GDP to rise and fall.

3. How does a cyclically balanced budget philosophy differ from the philosophy of functional finance? Why do advocates of functional finance argue that budget deficits and a mounting national debt are of secondary importance?

4. What are the four basic causes of the public debt over the past 55 years?

5. How does the lack of political will and entitlement programs affect the public debt and Federal budget deficits?

6. How big is the public debt of the United States absolutely and relative to the GDP? How large are the interest payments on this debt absolutely and relative to the GDP? What has happened to the size of the debt and the interest payments on it absolutely and relatively since 1930 and since 1980? Why have these changes occurred?

7. In what way do the accounting procedures of the Federal government misstate its actual financial position (its net worth)? How does inflation effect the *real* size of the public debt and the real size of the Federal government's budget deficits?

8. Why can't the public debt result in the bankruptcy of the Federal government?

9. Explain the difference between an internally held and an externally held public debt. If the debt is internally held, government borrowing to finance a war does not pass the cost of the war on to future generations. Why?

10. How does the public debt and the payment of interest on this debt affect

(a) the distribution of income and

(b) incentives?

11. Who owns the public debt? What percentage is held by the two major groups? What percentage of the public debt is held by foreigners? What are the economic implications of the portion of the public debt held by foreigners?

12. Why can a large and growing public debt put curbs on the use of fiscal policy?

13. How does the crowding out of investment impose a burden on future generations?

14. Does it matter to future generations whether increases in government spending are financed by taxation or increased public debt?

15. What two qualifications might lessen the crowding-out effect on the size of the economic burden that has shifted to future generations?

16. What are four reasons for the heightened concern about Federal budget deficits during the past two decades?

17. How do budget deficits and the increase in the public debt affect interest rates, domestic investment, foreign financial investment in the United States, the international value of the dollar, and the trade deficit?

18. Explain three complications arising from the relationship between budget and trade deficits.

19. Describe the major policy responses to concerns about large budget deficits and the expanding public debt.

20. How does debt play a positive role in a growing economy?

ANSWERS

Chapter 19 Budget Deficits and the Public Debt

FILL-IN QUESTIONS

1. expenditures, revenues, deficits, surpluses
2. pro, raised, lowered
3. recession, inflation
4. functional finance, secondary
5. wars, a recession, cuts, political will
6. *a.* GDP, 66; *b.* higher, lower; *c.* one-third, two-thirds; *d.* internal, 23; *e.* debts, assets; *f.* decreased, decreased
7. refinancing, creating, taxes
8. asset, present
9. externally, increase, decrease, increase
10. increases, decreases, decreases
11. less, present
12. increases, less than full
13. large, social security, risen, inappropriate, balance
14. decreasing, demand-pull
15. increasing, decreasing, debtor, increased
16. increase; *a.* contracts, more; *b.* increases, raises; *c.* contracts, expands, contracts
17. lowered, weakened, developing, borrow, sell
18. increase, decrease
19. line-item veto, balanced-budget amendment
20. saving, growing

TRUE-FALSE QUESTIONS

1. F, p. 386
2. F, p. 387
3. F, p. 387
4. T, p. 388
5. T, p. 389
6. T, p. 389
7. F, p. 389
8. F, p. 390
9. T, p. 390
10. F, pp. 390-391
11. F, p. 391
12. F, p. 391
13. T, p. 392
14. T, p. 393
15. F, p. 393
16. T, p. 393
17. T, p. 393
18. T, p. 393
19. F, pp. 394-395
20. T, p. 394
21. T, pp. 395-396
22. T, pp. 396-397
23. F, pp. 398-399
24. T, p. 399
25. T, p. 400

MULTIPLE-CHOICE QUESTIONS

1. c, p. 386
2. a, p. 387
3. b, p. 387
4. b, pp. 389-390
5. a, pp. 388, 390
6. c, p. 390
7. d, p. 390
8. c, p. 390
9. b, p. 391
10. a, p. 391
11. d, pp. 391-392
12. a, p. 392
13. c, pp. 392-393
14. b, p. 393
15. c, p. 393
16. d, p. 393
17. d, pp. 394-395
18. b, pp. 395-396
19. b, p. 395
20. a, pp. 396-397
21. c, pp. 396-397
22. a, p. 397
23. b, pp. 398-399
24. b, p. 400
25. c, p. 400

PROBLEMS

1. *a.* 55, 43, 37, 36, 33, 50, 63, 69, 68, 66; *c.* The debt as a percentage of GDP fell from 1961 to 1981 and then rose substantially from 1981 to 1995. It has fallen slightly since 1995.
2. *a.* $50 billion; *b.* none
3. *a.* increase, 100; *b.* (1) increased, 20 (2) (a) decreased, 25, (b) decreased, 125 (c) decrease, 25; *c.* increase, 25

SHORT ANSWER AND ESSAY QUESTIONS

1. p. 386
2. p. 387
3. pp. 387-388
4. pp. 389-390
5. pp. 389-390
6. pp. 388, 390
7. p. 391
8. pp. 391-392
9. pp. 392-393
10. pp. 392-393
11. pp. 390-391, 393
12. p. 393
13. p. 393
14. pp. 393-394
15. pp. 394-395
16. pp. 395-396
17. pp. 396-397
18. pp. 397-398
19. pp. 398-400
20. p. 400

CHAPTER 20

Demand and Supply: Elasticities and Applications

Chapter 20 is basically a continuation of Chapter 3, as you might have guessed from the chapter title. In the earlier part of the book, you needed only an elementary knowledge of supply and demand. Now the economic principles, problems, and policies to be studied require a more detailed discussion of supply and demand. Therefore, before you start reading Chapter 20, you are urged—you would be commanded if this were possible—to read and study Chapter 3 again. It is absolutely essential that you master Chapter 3 before reading Chapter 20.

The concept of ***price elasticity of demand,*** to which the major portion of Chapter 20 is devoted, is of great importance for studying material found in the remainder of the text. You must understand (1) what price elasticity measures; (2) how the price-elasticity formula is applied to measure the price elasticity of demand; (3) the difference between price elastic, price inelastic, and unit elasticity; (4) how total revenue varies by the type of price elasticity of demand; (5) the meaning of perfect price elasticity and perfect price inelasticity of demand; (6) the four major determinants of price elasticity of demand; and (7) the practical application of the concept to many economic issues.

When you have become thoroughly acquainted with the concept of price elasticity of demand, you will find that you have very little trouble understanding the ***price elasticity of supply.*** The transition requires no more than the substitution of the words "quantity supplied" for the words "quantity demanded." Attention should be concentrated on the meaning of price elasticity of supply and the effect of time on it.

The chapter also introduces you to two other elasticity concepts. The ***cross elasticity of demand*** measures the sensitivity of a change in the quantity demanded for one product due to a change in the price of another product. This concept is especially important to identifying substitute, complementary, or independent goods. The ***income elasticity of demand*** assesses the change in the quantity demanded of a product resulting from a change in consumer incomes. It is useful for categorizing products as superior, normal, or inferior.

The final section of the chapter discusses ***price ceilings*** and ***price floors*** that are created when government imposes legal prices on the competitive market. Note that these ceilings and floors prevent supply and demand from determining the equilibrium price and quantity of a product in the market. The economic consequence of this interference in the market will be shortages or surpluses of the product. Among the applications presented in this section to illustrate the economic effects of price ceilings or price floors are (1) price controls during World War II, (2) rent controls, (3) limits on interest rates for credit cards, and (4) price supports for agricultural products.

The concepts of demand and supply, which have been expanded in Chapter 20 to include discussion of elasticity and price ceilings and price floors, are the foundations of the next 10 chapters in the text. If you master the topics in Chapter 20, you will be prepared to understand the material in these chapters.

■ CHECKLIST

When you have studied this chapter you should be able to

☐ Define price elasticity of demand and compute the coefficient for it when you are given the demand data.
☐ State two reasons why the formula for price elasticity of demand uses percentages rather than absolute amounts in measuring consumer responsiveness.
☐ Explain the meaning of elastic, inelastic, and unit elasticity as they relate to demand.
☐ Define and illustrate graphically the concepts of perfectly price elastic and perfectly price inelastic demand.
☐ State the midpoint formula for price elasticity of demand and explain how it refines the original formula for price elasticity.
☐ Describe the relationship between price elasticity of demand and the price range for most demand curves.
☐ Explain why the slope of the demand curve is *not* a sound basis for judging price elasticity.
☐ Apply the total-revenue test to determine whether demand is elastic, inelastic, or unit elastic.
☐ Illustrate graphically the relationship between price elasticity of demand and total revenue.
☐ List the four major determinants of the price elasticity of demand, and explain how each determinant affects price elasticity.
☐ Describe six practical applications of the concept of price elasticity of demand.
☐ Define the price elasticity of supply and compute the coefficient for it when given the relevant data.
☐ Explain the effect of time on price elasticity of supply.
☐ Define cross elasticity of demand and compute the coefficient for it when given relevant data.

☐ Define income elasticity of demand and compute the coefficient for it when given relevant data.
☐ Explain the economic consequences of price ceilings and give four examples of the use of price ceilings.
☐ Describe how price floors affect the price and quantity of a product in a market.
☐ Identify the controversial tradeoffs arising from price ceilings or price floors.

■ CHAPTER OUTLINE

1. Price elasticity of demand is a measure of the responsiveness or sensitivity of quantity demanded to changes in the price of a product. When quantity demanded is relatively responsive to a price change, demand is said to be ***elastic.*** When quantity demanded is relatively unresponsive to a price change, demand is said to be ***inelastic.***

a. The exact degree of elasticity can be measured by using a formula to compute the elasticity coefficient.
(1) The changes in quantity demanded and in price are comparisons of consumer responsiveness to price changes of different products.
(2) Because price and quantity demanded are inversely related to each other, the price elasticity of demand coefficient is a negative number, but economists ignore the minus sign in front of the coefficient and focus their attention on its absolute value.

b. The coefficient of price elasticity has several interpretations.
(1) Demand is ***elastic*** when the percentage change in quantity is greater than the percentage change in price. The elasticity coefficient is greater than 1.
(2) Demand is ***inelastic*** when the percentage change in quantity is less than the percentage change in price. The elasticity coefficient is less than 1.
(3) Demand is ***unit elastic*** when the percentage change in quantity is equal to the percentage change in price. The elasticity coefficient is equal to 1.
(4) ***Perfectly inelastic*** demand means that a change in price results in no change in quantity demanded of a product, whereas ***perfectly elastic*** demand means that a small change in price causes buyers to purchase all they desire of a product.

c. A *midpoints* formula calculates price elasticity across a price and quantity range to overcome the problem of selecting the reference points for price and this. In this formula, the average of the two quantities and the average of the two prices are used as reference points.

d. Note several points about the graph of the demand curve and price elasticity of demand.
(1) It is not the same at all prices, and demand is typically elastic at higher and inelastic at lower prices.
(2) It cannot be judged from the slope of the demand curve.

e. The way in which total revenue changes (increases, decreases, or remains constant) when price changes is a test of the elasticity of demand for a product.
(1) When demand is *elastic,* a decrease in price will increase total revenue and an increase in price will decrease total revenue.
(2) When demand is *inelastic,* a decrease in price will decrease total revenue and an increase in price will increase total revenue.
(3) When demand is *unit elastic,* an increase or decrease in price will not affect total revenue.

f. The relationship between price elasticity of demand and total revenue can be shown by graphing demand and total revenue, one above the other. In this case, the horizontal axis for each graph uses the same quantity scale. The vertical axis for demand represents price. The vertical axis for the total revenue graph measures total revenue.
(1) When demand is price elastic, as price declines and quantity increases along the demand curve, total revenue increases in the total revenue graph.
(2) Conversely, when demand is price inelastic, as price declines and quantity increases along the demand curve, total revenue decreases.
(3) When demand is unit elastic, as price and quantity change along the demand curve, total revenue remains the same.

g. The price elasticity of demand for a product depends on the number of good substitutes for the product, its relative importance in the consumer's budget, whether it is a necessity or a luxury, and the period of time under consideration.

h. Price elasticity of demand is of practical importance in matters of public policy and in the setting of prices by the individual business firm. The concept is relevant to bumper crops in agriculture, automation, airline deregulation, excise taxes, drugs and street crime, and minimum wage laws.

2. Price elasticity of supply is a measure of the sensitivity of quantity supplied to changes in the price of a product.

a. There is both a general formula and a midpoints formula that is similar to those for the price elasticity of demand, but "quantity supplied" replaces "quantity demanded."

b. The price elasticity of supply depends primarily on the amount of time sellers have to adjust to a price change; supply will tend to be more price inelastic in the short run than in the long run.

c. There is no total-revenue test for price elasticity of supply because price and total revenue move in the same direction regardless of the degree of price elasticity of supply.

3. Two other elasticity concepts are important.

a. The cross elasticity of demand measures the degree to which the quantity demanded of one product is affected by a change in the price of another product; cross elasticities of demand are positive for substitute goods, negative for complementary goods, and essentially zero for independent goods.

b. The income elasticity of demand measures the effect of a change in income on the quantity demanded of a product; income elasticities of demand are positive for normal or superior goods, and negative for inferior goods.

4. Supply and demand analysis and the elasticity concepts have many important applications.

a. Price ceilings and price floors set by government prevent price from performing its rationing function.

(1) A price ceiling results in a shortage of the product, may bring about formal rationing by government and a black market, and causes a misallocation of resources.

(2) A price floor creates a surplus of the product, and may induce government to undertake measures either to increase the demand for or to decrease the supply of the product.

b. There are many examples of price ceilings and shortages created by government-controlled prices.

(1) Price controls were imposed on many products during World War II.

(2) Rent controls have been established by cities in an attempt to restrain rent increases in housing markets.

(3) Bills have been introduced in Congress to restrict the interest rate that can be charged to holders of credit cards.

c. Setting prices below the equilibrium price is not just practiced by government. Businesses may price a product below the market-clearing price to generate excess demand. For example, rock stars may price concert tickets below the market-clearing price to generate publicity and enthusiasm for the concert.

d. There are also illustrations of price floors resulting from prices set by government to support the price of some agricultural products.

■ TIPS AND HINTS

1. This chapter is an extension of the material in Chapter 3. Be sure you thoroughly review the contents and exercises in Chapter 3 before you do the self-test exercises for this chapter.

2. You should *not* judge the price elasticity of demand based on the slope of the demand curve unless it is horizontal (perfectly elastic) or vertical (perfectly inelastic). Remember that elasticity varies from elastic to inelastic along a downsloping, linear demand curve. The price elasticity equals 1 at the midpoint of a downsloping linear demand curve.

3. Master the total-revenue test for assessing the price elasticity of demand (review Table 20-2). For many problems, the total-revenue test is easier to use than the midpoints formula for identifying the type of elasticity (elastic, inelastic, unit), and the test has many practical applications.

4. Do not just memorize the elasticity formulas in this chapter. Instead, work on understanding what they mean and how they are used for economic decisions. The elasticity formulas simply measure the *responsiveness* of a percentage change in *quantity* to a percentage change in some other characteristic (price or income). The elasticity formulas all have a similar structure: A percentage change in some type of *quantity* (demanded, supplied) is divided by a percentage change in the other variable. The price elasticity of demand measures the responsiveness of a percentage change in *quantity demanded* for a product to a percentage change in its *price.* The cross elasticity of demand measures the percentage change in the *quantity demanded of product X* to a percentage change in the *price of product Y.* The income elasticity of demand is the percentage change in *quantity demanded* for a product to a percentage change in *income.* The price elasticity of supply is the percentage change in the *quantity supplied* of a product to a percentage change in its *price.*

5. Practice always helps in understanding graphs. Without looking at the textbook, draw a supply and demand graph with a price ceiling below the equilibrium price and show the resulting shortage in the market for a product. Then, draw a supply and demand graph with a price floor above the equilibrium price and show the resulting surplus. Explain to yourself what the graphs show. Check your graphs and your explanations by referring to textbook Figures 20-4 and 20-5 and the related explanations.

■ IMPORTANT TERMS

price elasticity of demand
elastic demand
inelastic demand
unit elasticity
perfectly inelastic demand
perfectly elastic demand
total revenue
total-revenue test
price elasticity of supply
elastic supply
inelastic supply
market period
short run
long run
cross elasticity of demand
income elasticity of demand
price ceiling
price floor

SELF-TEST

■ FILL-IN QUESTIONS

1. The present chapter begins the study of (macro, micro) ___macro___ economics. This requires an analysis of the (revenues, markets) ___markets___ and how (actions, prices) ___prices___ are determined in them.

2. If a relatively large change in price results in a relatively small change in quantity demanded, demand is (elastic, inelastic) ___inelastic___. If a relatively small change in price results in a relatively large change in quantity demanded, demand is (elastic, inelastic) ___elastic___.

3. The price elasticity formula is based on (absolute amounts, percentages) ___percentages___ because it avoids the problems caused by arbitrary choice of units and permits meaningful comparisons of consumer (responsiveness, incomes) ________ to changes in the prices of different products.

4. If a change in price causes no change in quantity demanded, demand is perfectly (elastic, inelastic) ________ and the demand curve is (horizontal, vertical) ________. If an extremely small change in price causes an extremely large change in quantity demanded, demand is perfectly (elastic, inelastic) ________ and the demand curve is (horizontal, vertical) ________.

5. The midpoints formula for the price elasticity of demand uses the (total, average) ________ of the two quantities as a reference point in calculating the percentage change in quantity and the (total, average) ________ of the two prices as a reference point in calculating the percentage change in price.

6. Two characteristics of the price elasticity of a linear demand curve are that elasticity (is constant, varies) ________ over the different price ranges, and the slope is a(n) (sound, unsound) ________ basis for judging its elasticity.

7. Assume the price of a product declines.

a. When demand is inelastic; the loss of revenue due to the lower price is (less, greater) ________ than the gain in revenue due to the greater quantity demanded.

b. When demand is elastic; the loss of revenue due to the lower price is (less, greater) ________ than the gain in revenue due to the greater quantity demanded.

c. When demand is unit elastic; the loss of revenue due to the lower price (exceeds, is equal to) ________ the gain in revenue due to the greater quantity demanded.

8. If demand is elastic, price and total revenue are (directly, inversely) ________ related, but if demand is inelastic, price and total revenue are (directly, inversely) ________ related.

9. Complete the following summary table.

If demand is	The elasticity coefficient is	If price rises, total revenue will	If price falls, total revenue will
Elastic	____	____	____
Inelastic	____	____	____
Unit elastic	____	____	____

10. What are the four most important determinants of the price elasticity of demand?

a. ________

b. ________

c. ________

d. ________

11. The price elasticity of supply measures the percentage change in (price, quantity supplied) ________ divided by the percentage change in ________.

12. The most important factor affecting the price elasticity of supply is (revenues, costs, time) ________. Typically, the price elasticity of supply is (more, less) ________ elastic in the short run than in the long run.

13. The measure of the sensitivity of the consumption of one product given a change in the price of another product is the (cross, income) ________ elasticity of demand, while the measure of the responsiveness of consumer purchases to changes in income is the ________ elasticity of demand.

14. When the cross elasticity of demand is positive, two products are (complements, substitutes, independent) ________, but when the cross elasticity of demand is negative, they are ________; a zero cross elasticity suggests that two products are ________.

15. If consumers increase purchases of a product as consumer incomes increase, then a good is classified as (inferior, normal or superior) ________, but if consumers decrease purchases of a product as consumer incomes increase, then a good is classified as ________.

16. The demand and supply schedules for a certain product are those given in the following table. Answer the related questions.

Quantity demanded	Price	Quantity supplied
12,000	$10	18,000
13,000	9	17,000
14,000	8	16,000
15,000	7	15,000
16,000	6	14,000
17,000	5	13,000
18,000	4	12,000

a. The equilibrium price of the product is $________ and the equilibrium quantity is ________.

b. If the government imposes a price ceiling of $5 on this product, there would be a (shortage, surplus) ________ of ________ units.

c. If the government supports a price of $8, there would be a ______________ of ______________ units.

17. A price ceiling is the (minimum, maximum) ______________ a seller may charge for a product or service, whereas price floors are ______________ prices fixed by government.

18. If the price ceiling is below the market equilibrium price, a (surplus, shortage) ______________ will arise in the market, and if a price floor is above the market equilibrium price, a (surplus, shortage) ______________ will arise in the market.

19. Price ceilings imposed by the U.S. government usually have occurred during (peace, war) ______________ time. They cause a rationing problem because the available (demand, supply) ______________ must be apportioned among interested buyers and they can create (legal, illegal) ______________ black markets.

20. An example of a price ceilings is (rent controls, minimum wage) ______________, while an example of a price floor is ______________.

■ TRUE-FALSE QUESTIONS

Circle the T if the statement is true, the F if it is false.

1. If the percentage change in price is greater than the percentage change in quantity demanded, the price elasticity coefficient is greater than 1. **T F**

2. If the quantity demanded for a product increases from 100 to 150 units when the price decreases from $14 to $10, the price elasticity of demand for this product in this price range is 1.2. **T F**

3. A product with a price elasticity of demand equal to 1.5 is described as price inelastic. **T F**

4. The flatness or steepness of a demand curve is based on absolute changes in price and quantity, while elasticity is based on relative or percentage changes in price and quantity. **T F**

5. Demand tends to be inelastic at higher prices and elastic at lower prices. **T F**

6. Price elasticity of demand and the slope of the demand curve are two different things. **T F**

7. If the price of a product increases from $5 to $6 and the quantity demanded decreases from 45 to 25, then according to the total-revenue test, the product is price inelastic in this price range. **T F**

8. Total revenue will not change when price changes if the price elasticity of demand is unitary. **T F**

9. When the absolute value of the price elasticity coefficient is greater than 1 and the price of the product decreases, then the total revenue will increase. **T F**

10. The demand for most agricultural products is inelastic. Consequently, an increase in supply will reduce the total income of producers of agricultural products. **T F**

11. A state government seeking to increase its excise-tax revenues is more likely to increase the tax rate on restaurant meals than on automobile tires. **T F**

12. In general, the larger the portion of a household budget required to buy a product, the greater the price elasticity of demand for the product will tend to be. **T F**

13. Studies indicate that the short-run demand for gasoline is price elastic, while the long-run response is price inelastic. **T F**

14. If the demand for soybeans is highly inelastic, a bumper crop may reduce farm incomes. **T F**

15. If an increase in product price results in no change in the quantity supplied, supply is perfectly elastic. **T F**

16. The immediate market period is a time so short that producers cannot respond to a change in demand and price. **T F**

17. The price elasticity of supply will tend to be more inelastic in the long run. **T F**

18. For a complementary good, the coefficient of the cross price elasticity of demand is positive. **T F**

19. Cross elasticity of demand is measured by the percentage change in quantity demanded over the percentage change in income. **T F**

20. A negative cross elasticity of demand for two goods indicates that they are complements. **T F**

21. Inferior goods have a positive income elasticity of demand. **T F**

22. If the government imposes a price ceiling below what would be the free-market price of a product, a shortage of the product will develop. **T F**

23. A price floor set by government will raise the equilibrium price and quantity in a market. **T F**

24. If the price floor set by government is above the equilibrium price, shortages will develop in the market. **T F**

25. A government-imposed ceiling on interest rates charged by issuers of bank credit cards would probably lead to actions by the issuers to reduce costs or to increase revenues. **T F**

■ MULTIPLE-CHOICE QUESTIONS

Circle the letter that corresponds to the best answer.

1. If, when the price of a product rises from $1.50 to $2, the quantity demanded of the product decreases from 1,000 to 900, the price elasticity of demand coefficient is

(a) 3.00
(b) 2.71
(c) 0.37
(d) 0.33

2. If a 1% fall in the price of a product causes the quantity demanded of the product to increase 2%, demand is
(a) inelastic
(b) elastic
(c) unit elastic
(d) perfectly elastic

3. In the following diagram, D_1 is a
(a) perfectly elastic demand curve
(b) perfectly inelastic demand curve
(c) unit elastic demand curve
(d) a long-run demand curve

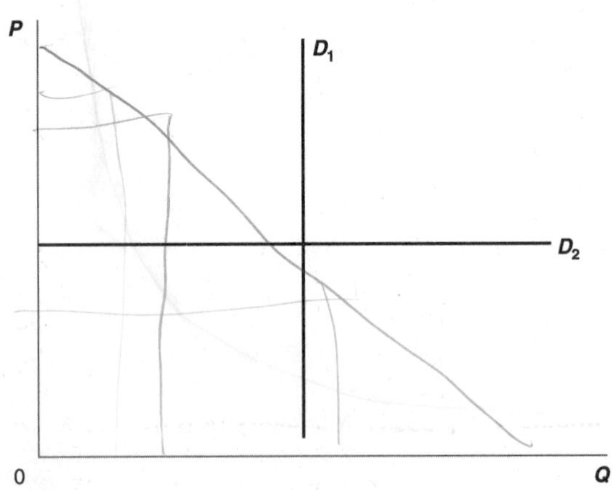

4. Compared to the lower-right portion, the upper-left portion of most demand curves tends to be
(a) more inelastic
(b) more elastic
(c) unit elastic
(d) perfectly inelastic

5. In which range of the demand schedule is demand price inelastic?

Price	Quantity demanded
$11	50
9	100
7	200
5	300
3	400

(a) $11–$9
(b) $9–$7
(c) $7–$5
(d) $5–$3

6. If a business increased the price of its product from $7 to $8 when the price elasticity of demand was inelastic, then
(a) total revenues decreased
(b) total revenues increased
(c) total revenues remain unchanged
(d) total revenues were perfectly inelastic

7. You are the sales manager for a pizza company and have been informed that the price elasticity demand for your most popular pizza is greater than 1. To increase total revenues, you should
(a) increase the price of the pizza
(b) decrease the price of the pizza
(c) hold pizza prices constant
(d) decrease demand for your pizza

8. Assume Amanda Herman finds that her total spending on compact discs remains the same after the price of compact discs falls, other things equal. Which of the following is true about Amanda's demand for compact discs with this price change?
(a) It is unit price elastic.
(b) It is perfectly price elastic.
(c) It is perfectly price inelastic.
(d) It increased in response to the price change.

Questions 9, 10, and 11 are based on the following graph.

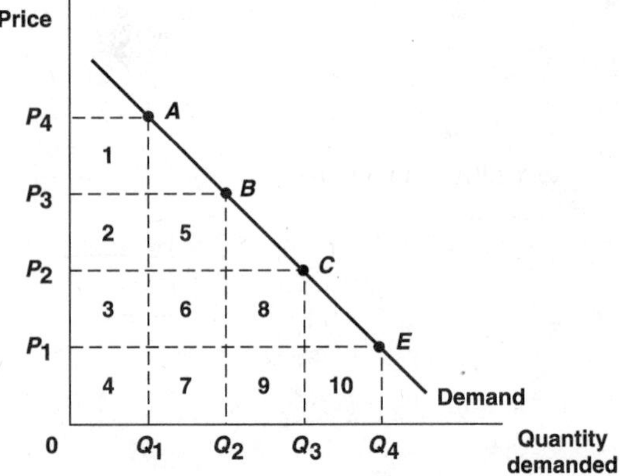

9. If price is P_3, then total revenue is measured by the area
(a) $0P_3\,CQ_3$
(b) $0P_3\,BQ_2$
(c) $0P_3\,BQ_3$
(d) $0P_3\,CQ_2$

10. If price falls from P_2 to P_1, then in this price range demand is
(a) relatively inelastic because the loss in total revenue (areas 3 + 6 + 8) is greater than the gain in total revenue (area 10)
(b) relatively elastic because the loss in total revenue (areas 3 + 6 + 8) is greater than the gain in total revenue (area 10)
(c) relatively inelastic because the loss in total revenue (area 10) is less than the gain in total revenue (areas 3 + 6 + 8)
(d) relatively inelastic because the loss in total revenue (areas 4 + 7 + 9 + 10) is greater than the gain in total revenue (areas 3 + 6 + 8)

11. As price falls from P_4 to P_3, you know that demand is
(a) elastic because total revenue decreased from $0P_4\,AQ_1$ to $0P_3\,BQ_2$

(b) inelastic because total revenue decreased from $0P_3\ BQ_2$ to $0P_4\ AQ_1$
(c) elastic because total revenue increased from $0P_4\ AQ_1$ to $0P_3\ BQ_2$
(d) inelastic because total revenue decreased from $0P_4\ AQ_1$ to $0P_3\ BQ_2$

12. Which product is most likely to be the most price elastic?
(a) bread
(b) clothing
(c) restaurant meals
(d) local telephone service

13. Which of the following is characteristic of a product whose demand is elastic?
(a) The price elasticity coefficient is less than 1.
(b) Total revenue decreases if price decreases.
(c) Buyers are relatively insensitive to price changes.
(d) The percentage change in quantity is greater than the percentage change in price.

14. The demand for Nike basketball shoes is more price elastic than the demand for basketball shoes as a whole. This is best explained by the fact that
(a) Nike basketball shoes are a luxury good, not a necessity
(b) Nike basketball shoes are the best made and widely advertised
(c) there are more complements for Nike basketball shoes than for basketball shoes as a whole
(d) there are more substitutes for Nike basketball shoes than for basketball shoes as a whole

15. Which of the following is characteristic of a good whose demand is inelastic?
(a) There are a large number of good substitutes for the good for consumers.
(b) The buyer spends a small percentage of total income on the good.
(c) The good is regarded by consumers as a luxury.
(d) The period of time for which demand is given is relatively long.

16. From a time perspective, the demand for most products is
(a) less elastic in the short run and unit elastic in the long run
(b) less elastic in the long run and unit elastic in the short run
(c) more elastic in the short run than in the long run
(d) more elastic in the long run than in the short run

17. If a 5% fall in the price of a commodity causes quantity supplied to decrease by 8%, supply is
(a) inelastic
(b) unit elastic
(c) elastic
(d) perfectly inelastic

18. In the following diagram, what is the price elasticity of supply between points ***A*** and ***C?***
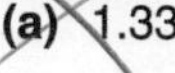
(a) 1.33

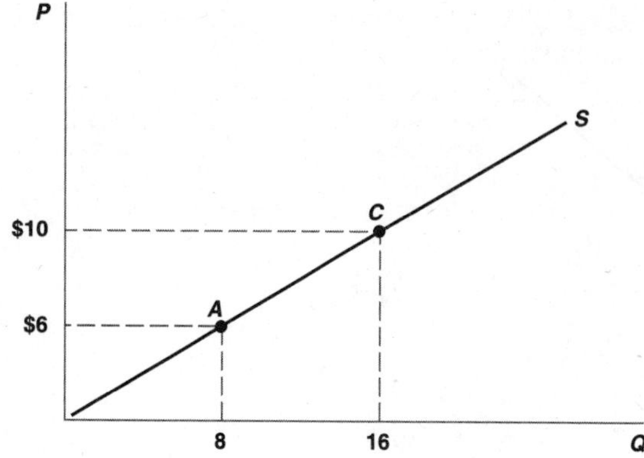

(b) 1.67
(c) 1.85
(d) 2.46

19. If supply is inelastic and demand decreases, the total revenue of sellers will
(a) increase
(b) decrease
(c) decrease only if demand is elastic
(d) increase only if demand is inelastic

20. The chief determinant of the price elasticity of supply of a product is
(a) the number of good substitutes the product has
(b) the length of time sellers have to adjust to a change in price
(c) whether the product is a luxury or a necessity
(d) whether the product is a durable or a nondurable good

21. A study shows that the coefficient of the cross price elasticity of Coke and Sprite is negative. This information indicates that Coke and Sprite are
(a) normal goods
(b) complementary goods
(c) substitute goods
(d) independent goods

22. If a 5% increase in the price of one good results in a decrease of 2% in the quantity demanded of another good, then it can be concluded that the two goods are
(a) complements
(b) substitutes
(c) independent
(d) normal

23. Most goods can be classified as *normal* goods rather than inferior goods. The definition of a normal good means that
(a) the percentage change in consumer income is greater than the percentage change in price of the normal good
(b) the percentage change in quantity demanded of the normal good is greater than the percentage change in consumer income
(c) as consumer income increases, consumer purchases of a normal good increase
(d) the income elasticity of demand is negative

24. Based on the information in the table, which product would be an inferior good?

Product	% change in income	% change in quantity demanded
A	−10	+10
B	+10	+10
C	+5	+5
D	−5	−5

(a) Product A
(b) Product B
(c) Product C
(d) Product D

25. For which product is the income elasticity of demand most likely to be negative?
(a) automobiles
(b) bus tickets
(c) computers
(d) tennis rackets

26. In the following diagram, a legal price floor of $9.00 will result in
(a) a surplus of 20 units
(b) a surplus of 10 units
(c) a shortage of 20 units
(d) no shortage or surplus

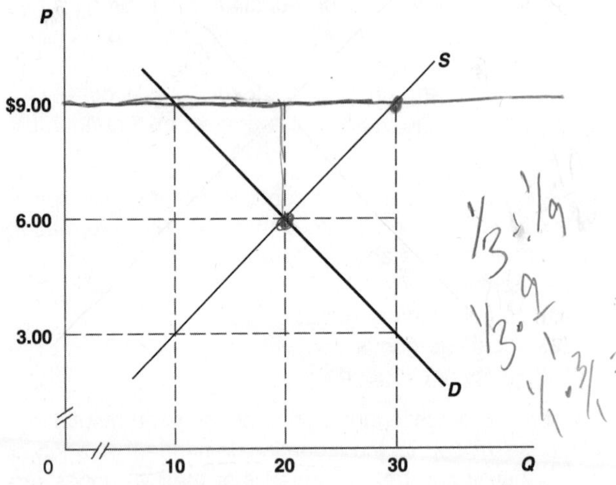

Questions 27, 28, and 29 relate to the following table that shows a hypothetical supply and demand schedule for a product.

Quantity demanded (pounds)	Price (per pound)	Quantity supplied (pounds)
200	$4.40	800
250	4.20	700
300	4.00	600
350	3.80	500
400	3.60	400
450	3.40	300
500	3.20	200

27. The equilibrium price and quantity is
(a) $4.00 and 600 pounds
(b) $3.80 and 350 pounds
(c) $3.60 and 400 pounds
(d) $3.40 and 300 pounds

28. If a legal price floor is established at $4.20, there will be a
(a) shortage of 450 pounds
(b) surplus of 450 pounds
(c) shortage of 300 pounds
(d) surplus of 300 pounds

29. A shortage of 150 pounds of the product will occur if a legal price is established at
(a) $3.20
(b) $3.40
(c) $3.80
(d) $4.00

30. Which of the following would be an example of a price floor?
(a) controls on apartment rent in major cities
(b) limiting interest charged by credit card companies
(c) price controls during World War II
(d) price supports for agricultural products

■ PROBLEMS

1. In the following table, using the demand data given, complete the table by computing total revenue at each of the seven prices and the six price elasticity coefficients between each of the seven prices, and indicate whether demand is elastic, inelastic, or unit elastic between each of the seven prices.

Price	Quantity demanded	Total revenue	Elasticity coefficient	Character of demand
$1.00	300	$ ____		
.90	400	____	____	____
.80	500	____	____	____
.70	600	____	____	____
.60	700	____	____	____
.50	800	____	____	____
.40	900	____	____	____

2. Use the data from the table for this problem. On the *first* of the two graphs on page 223, plot the demand curve (price and quantity demanded) and indicate the elastic, inelastic, and unit elastic portions of the demand curve. On the *second* graph, plot the total revenue on the vertical axis and the quantity demanded on the horizontal axis. (*Note:* The scale for quantity demanded that you plot on the horizontal axis of each graph should be the same on both graphs.)

a. As price decreases from $1.00 to $0.70, demand is (elastic, inelastic, unit elastic) ____________ and total revenue (increases, decreases, remains the same) ____________.

b. As price decreases from $0.70 to $0.60, demand is (elastic, inelastic, unit elastic) ____________ and total revenue (increases, decreases, remains the same) ____________.

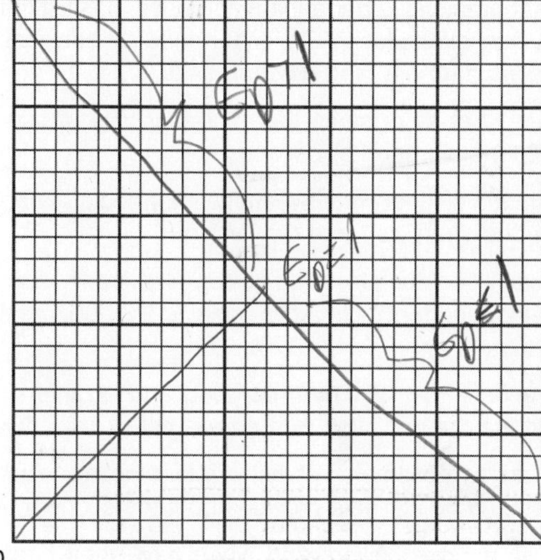

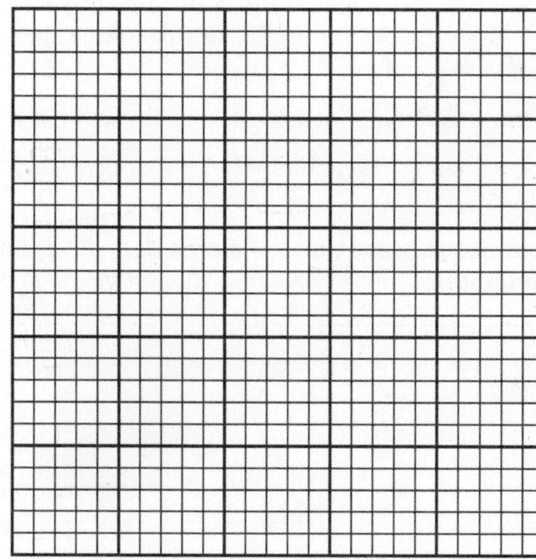

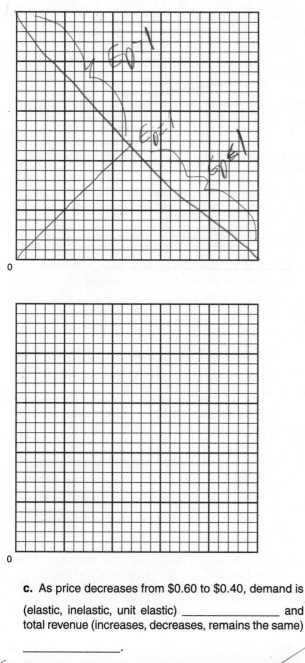

c. As price decreases from $0.60 to $0.40, demand is (elastic, inelastic, unit elastic) _______________ and total revenue (increases, decreases, remains the same) _______________.

3. Using the supply data in the following schedule, complete the table by computing the six price elasticity of supply coefficients between each of the seven prices, and indicate whether supply is elastic, inelastic, or unit elastic.

Price	Quantity supplied	Elasticity coefficient	Character of supply
$1.00	800		
.90	700	____	____
.80	600	____	____
.70	500	____	____
.60	400	____	____
.50	300	____	____
.40	200	____	____

4. The following graph shows three different supply curves (S_1, S_2, and S_3) for a product bought and sold in a competitive market.

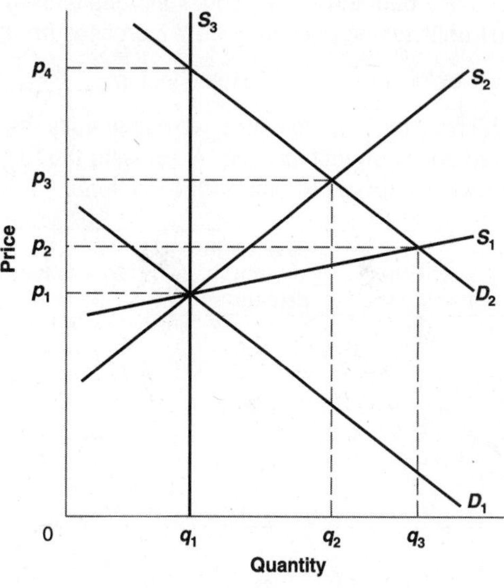

a. The supply curve for the

(1) market period is the one labeled _______________.

(2) short run is the one labeled _______________.

(3) long run is the one labeled _______________.

b. No matter what the period of time under consideration, if the demand for the product were D_1, the equilibrium price of the product would be _______________ and the equilibrium quantity would be _______________.

(1) If demand were to increase to D_2 in the market period the equilibrium price would increase to _______________ and the equilibrium quantity would _______________.

(2) In the short run the price of the product would increase to _______________ and the quantity would increase to _______________.

(3) In the long run the price of the product would be _______________ and the quantity would be _______________.

c. The longer the period of time allowed to sellers to adjust their outputs the (more, less) _______________ elastic is the supply of the product.

d. The more elastic the supply of a product, the (greater, less) _______________ the effect on equilibrium price and the _______________ the effect on equilibrium quantity of an increase in demand.

5. For the following three cases, use a midpoints formula to calculate the coefficient for the cross elasticity of demand and identify the relationship between the two goods (complement, substitute, or independent).

a. The quantity demanded for good A increases from 300 to 400 as the price of good B increases from $1 to $2. Coefficient: __________ Relationship: __________

b. The quantity demanded for good J decreases from 2000 to 1500 as the price of good K increases from $10 to $15. Coefficient: ________ Relationship: ________

c. The quantity demanded for good X increases from 100 to 101 units as the price of good Y increases from $8 to $15. Coefficient: ________ Relationship: ________

6. Use the information in the following table to identify the income characteristic of each product A–E using the following labels: N = normal (or superior), I = inferior.

Product	% change in income	% change in quantity demanded	Income type (N or I)
A	10	10	N
B	1	15	N
C	5	−12	I
D	5	−2	I
E	10	1	N

■ SHORT ANSWER AND ESSAY QUESTIONS

1. Define and explain the price elasticity of demand in terms of the relationship between the relative (percentage) change in quantity demanded and the relative (percentage) change in price. Use the elasticity coefficient in your explanation.

2. Define and explain the price elasticity of demand in terms of the change in total revenue when price changes.

3. What is meant by perfectly elastic demand? By perfectly inelastic demand? What does the demand curve look like when demand is perfectly elastic and when it is perfectly inelastic?

4. In computing the price elasticity coefficient, it usually makes a considerable difference whether the higher price and lower quantity or the lower price and higher quantity are used as a point of reference. What have economists done to eliminate the confusion which would arise if the price elasticity of demand coefficient varied and depended upon whether a price rise or fall were being considered?

5. Demand seldom has the same elasticity at all prices. What is the relationship between the price of most commodities and the price elasticity of demand for them?

6. What is the relationship—if there is one—between the price elasticity of demand and the slope of the demand curve?

7. When the price of a commodity declines, the quantity demanded of it increases. When demand is elastic, total revenue is greater at the lower price, but when demand is inelastic, total revenue is smaller. Explain why total revenue will sometimes increase and why it will sometimes decrease.

8. What are the factors which together determine the price elasticity of demand for a product?

9. Of what practical importance is the price elasticity of demand? Cite examples of its importance to business firms, workers, farmers, and governments.

10. Explain what determines the price elasticity of supply of an economic good or service.

11. Explain the distinction between the intermediate market period, the short run, and the long run.

12. How can goods be classified as complementary, substitute, or independent? On what basis is this judgment made?

13. Give a definition of a normal good and an inferior good. Illustrate the definition with an example.

14. What are two examples of insights that income elasticity of demand coefficients provide about the economy?

15. What is a price ceiling, and when have they been used in the United States? Give examples.

16. What are the consequences of a price ceiling for a product if it is set below the equilibrium price? Illustrate your answer with a graph.

17. What two problems arise from price ceilings?

18. What are price floors, and how have they been used by government?

19. What are the consequences of a price floor if it is set above the equilibrium price? Illustrate your answer with a graph.

20. Why do price floors and ceilings result in controversial tradeoffs?

ANSWERS

Chapter 20 Demand and Supply: Elasticities and Applications

FILL-IN QUESTIONS

1. micro, markets, prices
2. inelastic, elastic
3. percentages, responsiveness
4. inelastic, vertical, elastic, horizontal
5. average, average
6. varies, unsound
7. *a.* greater; *b.* less; *c.* is equal to
8. inversely, directly
9. Elastic: greater than 1, decrease, increase; Inelastic: less than 1, increase, decrease; Unit elastic: equal to 1, remain constant, remain constant
10. *a.* The number of good substitute products; *b.* The relative importance of the product in the total budget of the buyer; *c.* Whether the good is a necessity or a luxury; *d.* The period of time in which demand is being considered (any order a–d)
11. quantity supplied, price
12. time, less
13. cross, income
14. substitutes, complements, independent
15. normal or superior, inferior
16. *a.* 7.00, 15,000; *b.* shortage, 4,000; *c.* surplus, 2,000
17. maximum, minimum

18. shortage, surplus
19. war, supply, illegal
20. rent controls, minimum wage

TRUE-FALSE QUESTIONS

1. F, p. 405
2. T, p. 405
3. F, p. 405
4. T, p. 407
5. F, p. 407
6. T, p. 407
7. F, pp. 408-409
8. T, p. 409
9. T, pp. 405, 408
10. T, pp. 408-409
11. F, pp. 410, 412
12. T, p. 410
13. F, p. 411
14. T, p. 411
15. F, p. 414
16. T, p. 414
17. F, p. 415
18. F, p. 415
19. F, p. 415
20. T, p. 415
21. F, p. 416
22. T, p. 417
23. F, p. 419
24. F, p. 419
25. T, p. 418

MULTIPLE-CHOICE QUESTIONS

1. c, pp. 406-407
2. b, p. 405
3. b, p. 406
4. b, p. 406
5. d, pp. 406-407
6. b, pp. 408-409
7. b, p. 408
8. a, p. 409
9. b, p. 408
10. a, pp. 408-409
11. c, pp. 408-409
12. c, pp. 409-411
13. d, p. 405
14. d, pp. 409-410
15. b, p. 410
16. d, p. 411
17. c, p.413
18. a, p. 413
19. b, pp. 408, 413
20. b, p. 413
21. b, p. 415
22. a, p. 415
23. c, p. 416
24. a, p. 416
25. b, p. 416
26. a, p. 419
27. c, p. 417
28. b, p. 419
29. b, p. 417
30. d, p. 419

PROBLEMS

1. Total revenue: $300, 360, 400, 420, 420, 400, 360; Elasticity coefficient: 2.71, 1.89, 1.36, 1, 0.73, 0.53; Character of demand: elastic, elastic, elastic, unit elastic, inelastic, inelastic
2. *a.* elastic, increases; *b.* unit elastic, remains the same; *c.* inelastic, decreases
3. Elasticity coefficient: 1.27, 1.31, 1.36, 1.44, 1.57, 1.8; Character of supply: elastic, elastic, elastic, elastic, elastic, elastic
4. *a.* (1) S_3; (2) S_2; (3) S_1; *b.* p_1, q_1; *c.* (1) p_4, remain at q_1; (2) p_3, q_2; (3) p_2, q_3; *c.* more; *d.* less, greater
5. *a.* 43, substitute; *b.* −.71, complement; *c.* .02, independent
6. N, N, I, I, N

SHORT ANSWER AND ESSAY QUESTIONS

1. pp. 404-405
2. pp. 408-409
3. p. 406
4. pp. 406-407
5. p. 407
6. p. 407
7. pp. 408-409
8. pp. 409-411
9. pp. 411-413
10. pp. 413-415
11. pp. 414-415
12. p. 415
13. p. 416
14. p. 416
15. pp. 417-419
16. p. 417
17. pp. 417-418
18. pp. 419-420
19. p. 419
20. pp. 419-420

CHAPTER 21

Consumer Behavior and Utility Maximization

Previous chapters explained that consumers typically buy more of a product as its price decreases and less of a product as its price increases. Chapter 21 looks behind this law of demand to explain why consumers behave this way.

Two explanations for the law of demand are presented. The first explanation is a general and simple one based on ***income effects*** and ***substitution effects.*** From this perspective, a change in the price of a product changes the amount consumed because of a change in the real income and a change in the price of this good relative to other products that could be purchased. The other explanation is more detailed and abstract because it is based on the concept of ***marginal utility.*** In this view, the additional satisfaction (or marginal utility) that a consumer obtains from the consumption of each additional unit of a product will tend to decline; therefore a consumer will have an incentive to purchase additional units of a product only if its price falls. (A third explanation of consumer demand that is more complete than the first two is based on the use of indifference curves; this more complex topic is discussed in the appendix to the chapter.)

Most of this chapter presents the marginal-utility view of consumer behavior. This explanation requires that you first understand the concepts and assumptions on which this theory of consumer behavior rests, and second, do some rigorous reasoning using these concepts and assumptions. It is an exercise in logic, but be sure that you follow the reasoning. To help you, several problems are provided so that you can work things out for yourself.

No one believes that consumers actually perform these mental gymnastics before they spend their incomes or make a purchase. But we study the marginal-utility approach to consumer behavior because the consumers behave as if they made their purchases on the basis of very fine calculations. Thus, this approach explains what we do in fact observe and makes it possible for us to predict with a good deal of precision how consumers will react to changes in their incomes and the prices of products.

The final section of the chapter describes how the theory of consumer behavior can be used to explain many economic events in the real world. The five applications discussed are the takeover by compact discs of the market for recorded music, the water-diamond paradox, the value of time in consumption, the reasons for increased consumer expenditures on health care, and the economic effects of cash and noncash transfers. Be sure you understand how consumer theory is used to explain these five phenomena.

■ CHECKLIST

When you have studied this chapter you should be able to

□ Define and distinguish between the income and the substitution effects of a price change.
□ Use the income and the substitution effects to explain why a consumer will buy more of a product when its price falls and less of a product when its price rises.
□ Define marginal utility, total utility, and the law of diminishing marginal utility.
□ Explain the relationship of the law of diminishing marginal utility to demand and elasticity.
□ List four dimensions of the typical consumer's situation.
□ State the utility-maximizing rule.
□ Use the utility-maximizing rule to determine how consumers would spend their fixed income when you are given the utility and price data.
□ Derive a consumer's demand for a product from utility, income, and price data.
□ Give examples of how consumer theory can be used to explain such economic phenomena as the
(1) compact discs' takeover of music recordings,
(2) diamond-water paradox,
(3) value of time in consumption
(4) increased consumer expenditures on health care, and
(5) tradeoffs between cash and transfer payments.

■ CHAPTER OUTLINE

1. The law of consumer demand can be explained by using either the income-effect and substitution-effect concepts or the concept of marginal utility.

a. Consumers buy more of a product when its price falls because their money income will go further (the income effect) and the product is now less expensive relative to other products (the substitution effect).

b. The essential assumption made in the alternative explanation is that the more the consumer buys of any product, the smaller becomes the marginal (extra) utility obtained from it.

2. The assumption (or law) of **diminishing marginal utility** is the basis of the theory that explains how consumers will spend their income.

a. It is assumed that the typical consumer is rational, knows marginal-utility schedules for the various goods available, has a limited money income to spend, and must pay a price to acquire each of the goods which yield utility.

b. Given these assumptions, the consumer maximizes the total utility obtained when the marginal utility of the last dollar spent on each product is the same for all products.

c. Algebraically, total utility is a maximum when the marginal utility of the last unit of a product purchased divided by its price is the same for all products (that is, marginal utility per dollar is equal for all products).

3. To find a consumer's demand for a product, the ***utility-maximizing rule*** is applied to determine the amount of the product the consumer will purchase at different prices, with income, tastes, and the prices of other products remaining constant.

a. A numerical example is used to illustrate the rule using two products, A and B, and assuming that all money income is spent on one of the two products.

b. In making the decision, the rational consumer must compare the extra or marginal utility from each product with its added cost (as measured by its price). Thus, marginal utility is compared on a per-dollar basis.

c. The allocation rule states that consumers will maximize their satisfaction when they allocate their money income so that the last dollar spent on each product yields the same marginal utility. In the two-product case, this can be stated algebraically as

$$\frac{\text{Marginal utility of A}}{\text{Price of A}} = \frac{\text{marginal utility of B}}{\text{price of B}}$$

4. Five of the many *applications* and *extensions* of consumer theory for the real world are discussed in this chapter.

a. Compact discs now dominate the market for recorded music because of the change in consumer preferences and the fall in the price of CD players.

b. Diamonds are high in price, but of limited usefulness, while water is low in price, but essential for life. This diamond-water paradox is explained by distinguishing between marginal and total utility. Water is low in price because it is generally in plentiful supply and thus has low marginal utility. Diamonds are high in price because they are relatively scarce and thus have high marginal utility. Water, however, is considered more useful than diamonds because it has much greater total utility.

c. The facts that consumption takes time and time is a scarce resource can be included in marginal-utility theory. The full price of any consumer good or service is equal to its market price plus the value of time taken to consume it (i.e., the income the consumer could have earned had he or she used that time for work).

d. The consumption of health care services has increased in the past few decades because of the financing of health care through insurance. Under this system, the consumer does not pay the full price of health care services and thus has an incentive to consume more than would be the case if the consumer paid the full price.

e. Cash transfers or gifts tend to be more efficient for consumers because they are more likely to match consumer preferences and increase the total utility compared to noncash transfers or gifts that restrict consumer choice.

■ HINTS AND TIPS

1. Remember that a change in the price of a good has both an **income effect** and a **substitution effect**. For most products, a price decrease gives consumers more income to spend on that product and other products, so the quantity demanded for that product increases. The three steps in the logic for typical product A are (1)$P_A\downarrow$, (2) income$\uparrow$, and (3) $Q_{dA}\uparrow$. A price decrease also makes product A more attractive to buy relative to its substitutes, so the demand for these substitutes decrease and the quantity demanded for product A increases. Again, there are three steps in the logic: (1) $P_A\downarrow$, (2) demand for substitutes $\downarrow$, and (3) $Q_{dA}\uparrow$. In both cases, the end result is the same: $Q_{dA}\uparrow$. Practice your understanding by showing the logic for an increase in the price of product A.

2. ***Utility*** is simply an abstraction useful for explaining consumer behavior. Do not become overly concerned with the precise measurement of utility or satisfaction. What you should focus on is the relative comparison of the additional satisfaction (marginal utility) from a dollar spent on one good to the additional satisfaction obtained from a dollar spent on another good. The choice of producing more additional utility satisfaction than the other will maximize the consumer satisfaction. Thus, you just need to know which good won the contest, not the final score (how much additional utility was added).

3. Master the difference between marginal and total utility. Once you think you understand the difference, use those concepts to explain to someone the diamond-water paradox discussed at the end of the chapter.

■ IMPORTANT TERMS

income effect	**marginal utility**
substitution effect	**law of diminishing marginal utility**
utility	**utility-maximizing rule**
total utility	

SELF-TEST

■ FILL-IN QUESTIONS

1. The law of demand can be explained in terms of income and (complements, substitution) ______________ effects or by the law of (increasing, diminishing) ______________ marginal utility.

2. A fall in the price of a product tends to (increase, decrease) ______________ a consumer's real income, and a rise in its prices tends to ______________ real income. This is called the (substitution, income) ______________ effect.

3. When the price of a product increases, the product becomes relatively (more, less) ______________ expensive than it was and the prices of other products become relatively (higher, lower) ______________ than they were; the consumer will therefore buy (less, more) ______________ of the product in question and ______________ of the other products. This is called the (substitution, income) ______________ effect.

4. The overall satisfaction a consumer gets from consuming a good or service is (marginal, total) ______________ utility, but the extra or additional satisfaction that a consumer gets from a good or service is (marginal, total) ______________ utility. Utility is a(n) (objective, subjective) ______________ concept and (is, is not) ______________ the same thing as usefulness.

5. The law of diminishing marginal utility states that marginal utility will (increase, decrease) ______________ as a consumer increases the quantity consumed of a product.

6. A graph of total and marginal utility shows that when total utility is increasing, marginal utility is (increasing, decreasing) ______________, and when total utility is at a maximum, marginal utility is at (a maximum, zero, a minimum) ______________.

7. Assuming all other things equal, if the marginal utility of a product decreases rapidly as additional units are consumed, then demand is likely to be (elastic, inelastic) ______________, but if marginal utility decreases slowly as consumption increases, then it suggests that demand is ______________.

8. The marginal-utility theory of consumer behavior assumes that the consumer is (wealthy, rational) rational and has certain (preferences, discounts) preferences for various goods.

9. A consumer cannot buy every good and service desired because income is (subsidized, limited) ______________ and goods and services are (unlimited, scarce) ______________ in relation to the demand for them; thus they have (prices, quantities) ______________ attached to them.

10. When the consumer is maximizing the utility the consumer's income will obtain, the ratio of the marginal utility of the (first, last) ______________ unit purchased of a product to its price is (the same, greater than) ______________ for all the products brought.

11. If the marginal utility of the last dollar spent on one product is greater than the marginal utility of the last dollar spent on another product, the consumer should (increase, decrease) ______________ purchases of the first and ______________ purchases of the second product.

12. Assume there are only two products, X and Y, that a consumer can purchase with a fixed income. The consumer is maximizing utility algebraically when:

a. ______________ / **b.** ______________ = **c.** ______________ / **d.** ______________

13. In deriving a consumer's demand for a particular product, the two factors (other than the tastes of the consumer) which are held constant are

a. ______________________________

b. ______________________________

14. The utility-maximizing rule and the demand curve are logically (consistent, inconsistent) ______________. Because marginal utility declines, a lower price is needed to get the consumer to buy (less, more) ______________ of a particular product.

15. When consumer preferences changed from long-playing records and cassette tapes to CDs, and the prices of CDs (increased, decreased) ______________ significantly, this led to (increased, decreased) ______________ purchases of compact discs.

16. Water is low in price because its (total, marginal) ______________ utility is low, while diamonds are high in price because their ______________ utility is high. Water, however, is more useful than diamonds because the (total, marginal) ______________ utility of water is much greater than the ______________ utility of diamonds.

17. The theory of consumer behavior has been generalized to account for (supply, time) ______________. This is a valuable economic resource because it is (limited, unlimited) ______________. Its value is (greater than, equal to) ______________ the income that can be earned with it. The full price to the consumer of any product is, therefore, the market (time, price) ______________ plus the value of the consumption ______________.

18. With health insurance coverage, the price consumers pay is less than the "true" price or opportunity (benefit, cost) ______________. The lower price to consumers encourages them to consume (more, less) ______________ health care services.

19. A comparison of food consumption at an all-you-can-eat buffet with a pay-per-item cafeteria would show that people tend to eat (less, more) ______________ at the buffet because the marginal utility of an extra food item is (positive, zero) ______________ while its price is ______________.

20. Noncash transfer payments are (less, more) ______________ efficient than cash transfer payments because they yield (less, more) ______________ utility to consumers.

■ TRUE-FALSE QUESTIONS

Circle the T if the statement is true, the F if it is false.

1. An increase in the real income of a consumer will result from an increase in the price of a product the consumer is buying. **T F**

2. The income and substitution effects will induce the consumer to buy more of normal good Z when the price of Z increases. **T F**

3. Utility and usefulness are not synonymous. **T F**

4. Marginal utility is the change in total utility from consuming one more unit of a product. **T F**

5. Because utility cannot actually be measured, the marginal-utility theory cannot really explain how consumers will behave. **T F**

6. A consumer's demand curve for a product is downsloping because total utility decreases as more of the product is consumed. **T F**

7. If total utility is increasing, then marginal utility is positive and may be either increasing or decreasing. **T F**

8. There is a significant, positive relationship between the rate of decrease in marginal utility and the price elasticity of demand. **T F**

9. When marginal utility falls slowly as more of a good is consumed, demand will tend to be inelastic. **T F**

10. The theory of consumer behavior assumes that consumers act rationally to get the most from their money. **T F**

11. All consumers are subject to the budget restraint. **T F**

12. To find a consumer's demand for a product, the price of the product is varied while tastes, income, and the prices of other products remain unchanged. **T F**

13. The theory of consumer behavior assumes that consumers attempt to maximize marginal utility. **T F**

14. If the marginal utility per dollar spent on product A is greater than the marginal utility per dollar spent on product B, then to maximize utility, the consumer should purchase less of A and more of B. **T F**

15. When consumers are maximizing total utility, the marginal utilities of the last unit of every product they buy are identical. **T F**

16. The marginal utility of product X is 15 and its price is \$5, while the marginal utility of product Y is 10 and its price is \$2. The utility-maximizing rule suggests that there should be *less* consumption of product Y. **T F**

17. In most cases, a change in incomes will cause a change in the portfolio of goods and services purchased by consumers. **T F**

18. A fall in the price of CD players will decrease the demand for CDs. **T F**

19. The diamond-water paradox is explained by the fact that the total utility derived from water is low while the total utility derived from diamonds is high. **T F**

20. If a consumer can earn \$10 an hour and it takes 2 hours to consume a product, the value of the time required for the consumption of the product is \$5. **T F**

21. Paying \$300 to fly from one city to another may be cheaper than paying \$50 for a bus trip between the two cities when the economic value of time is taken into account. **T F**

22. A decrease in the productivity of labor will tend over time to increase the value of time. **T F**

23. One reason for the increased use of health care services is that consumers pay only part of the full price of the services. **T F**

24. Social security is an example of a cash transfer payment. **T F**

25. Noncash transfer payments are more efficient than cash transfer payments. **T F**

■ MULTIPLE-CHOICE QUESTIONS

Circle the letter that corresponds to the best answer.

1. The reason the substitution effect works to encourage a consumer to buy more of a product when its price decreases is

(a) the real income of the consumer has been increased
(b) the real income of the consumer has been decreased
(c) the product is now relatively less expensive than it was
(d) other products are now relatively less expensive than they were

2. Kristin Hansen buys only two goods, food and clothing. Both are normal goods for Kristin. Suppose the price of food decreases. Kristin's consumption of clothing will

(a) decrease due to the income effect
(b) increase due to the income effect
(c) increase due to the substitution effect
(d) decrease due to the substitution effect

3. Which of the following best expresses the law of diminishing marginal utility?

(a) The more a person consumes of a product, the smaller becomes the utility which he receives from its consumption.
(b) The more a person consumes of a product, the smaller becomes the additional utility which she re-

ceives as a result of consuming an additional unit of the product.
(c) The less a person consumes of a product, the smaller becomes the utility which she receives from its consumption.
(d) The less a person consumes of a product, the smaller becomes the additional utility which he receives as a result of consuming an additional unit of the product.

The following table shows a hypothetical total utility schedule for a consumer of chocolate candy bars. Use the table to answer Questions 4, 5, and 6.

Number consumed	Total utility
0	0
1	9
2	19
3	27
4	35
5	42
6	42
7	40

4. This consumer begins to experience diminishing marginal utility when he consumes the
(a) first candy bar
(b) second candy bar
(c) third candy bar
(d) fourth candy bar

5. Marginal utility becomes negative with the consumption of the
(a) fourth candy bar
(b) fifth candy bar
(c) sixth candy bar
(d) seventh candy bar

6. Based on the data, you can conclude that the
(a) marginal utility of the fourth unit is 6
(b) marginal utility of the second unit is 27
(c) total utility of 5 units is 42
(d) total utility of 3 units is 55

7. After eating eight chocolate chip cookies, you are offered a ninth cookie. You turn down the cookie. Your refusal indicates that the
(a) marginal utility for chocolate chip cookies is negative
(b) total utility for chocolate chip cookies is negative
(c) marginal utility is positive for the eighth and negative for the ninth cookie
(d) total utility was zero because you ate one cookie and refused the other

8. Other things being equal, demand is likely to be *elastic* if the marginal utility of a product
(a) decreases rapidly as additional units are consumed
(b) decreases slowly as additional units are consumed
(c) increases rapidly as additional units are consumed
(d) increases slowly as additional units are consumed

9. Which of the following is *not* an essential assumption of marginal-utility theory of consumer behavior?
(a) The consumer has a small income.
(b) The consumer is rational.
(c) Goods and services are not free.
(d) Goods and services yield decreasing amounts of marginal utility as the consumer buys more of them.

10. A consumer is making purchases of products A and B such that the marginal utility of product A is 20 and the marginal utility of product B is 30. The price of product A is $10 and the price of product B is $20. The utility-maximizing rule suggests that this consumer should increase consumption of product
(a) B and decrease consumption of product A
(b) B and increase consumption of product A
(c) A and decrease consumption of product B
(d) make no change in consumption of A or B

Answer Questions 11, 12, and 13 based on the following table showing the marginal-utility schedules for goods X and Y for a hypothetical consumer. The price of good X is $1 and the price of good Y is $2. The income of the consumer is $9.

Good X		*Good Y*	
Quantity	**MU**	**Quantity**	**MU**
1	8	1	10
2	7	2	8
3	6	3	6
4	5	4	4
5	4	5	3
6	3	6	2
7	2	7	1

11. To maximize utility, the consumer will buy
(a) 7*X* and 1*Y*
(b) 5*X* and 2*Y*
(c) 3*X* and 3*Y*
(d) 1*X* and 4*Y*

12. When the consumer purchases the utility-maximizing combination of goods *X* and *Y*, total utility will be
(a) 36
(b) 45
(c) 48
(d) 52

13. Suppose that the consumer's income increased from $9 to $12. What would be the utility-maximizing combination of goods *X* and *Y*?
(a) 5*X* and 2*Y*
(b) 6*X* and 3*Y*
(c) 2*X* and 5*Y*
(d) 4*X* and 4*Y*

14. Suppose that the prices of A and B are $3 and $2, respectively, that the consumer is spending her entire income and buying 4 units of A and 6 units of B, and that the marginal utility of both the fourth unit of A and the sixth unit of B is 6. It can be concluded that
(a) the consumer is in equilibrium
(b) the consumer should buy more of A and less of B
(c) the consumer should buy less of A and more of B
(d) the consumer should buy less of both A and B

15. A decrease in the price of product Z will
(a) increase the marginal utility per dollar spent on Z

(b) decrease the marginal utility per dollar spent on Z
(c) decrease the total utility per dollar spent on Z
(d) cause no change in the marginal utility per dollar spent on Z

16. Robert Woods is maximizing his satisfaction consuming two goods, X and Y. If the marginal utility of X is half that of Y, what is the price of X if the price of Y is $1.00?
(a) $0.50
(b) $1.00
(c) $1.50
(d) $2.00

17. Summing the marginal utilities of each unit consumed will determine total
(a) cost
(b) revenue
(c) utility
(d) consumption

Answer Questions 18, 19, 20, and 21 on the basis of the following total utility data for products A and B. Assume that the prices of A and B are $6 and $8, respectively, and that consumer income is $36.

Units of A	Total utility	Units of B	Total utility
1	18	1	32
2	30	2	56
3	38	3	72
4	42	4	80
5	44	5	84

18. What is the level of total utility for the consumer in equilibrium?
(a) 86
(b) 102
(c) 108
(d) 120

19. How many units of the two products will the consumer buy?
(a) 1 of A and 4 of B
(b) 2 of A and 2 of B
(c) 2 of A and 3 of B
(d) 3 of A and 4 of B

20. If the price of A decreases to $4, then the utility-maximizing combination of the two products is
(a) 2 of A and 2 of B
(b) 2 of A and 3 of B
(c) 3 of A and 3 of B
(d) 4 of A and 4 of B

21. Which of the following represents the demand curve for A?

(a)		*(b)*		*(c)*		*(d)*	
P	Q_d	*P*	Q_d	*P*	Q_d	*P*	Q_d
$6	1	$6	2	$6	2	$6	2
4	4	4	5	4	3	4	4

22. The price of water is substantially less than the price of diamonds because
(a) the marginal utility of a diamond is significantly less than the marginal utility of a gallon of water
(b) the marginal utility of a diamond is significantly greater than the marginal utility of a gallon of water
(c) the total utility of diamonds is greater than the total utility of water
(d) diamonds have a low marginal utility

23. The full price of a product to a consumer is
(a) its market price
(b) its market price plus the value of its consumption time
(c) its market price less the value of its consumption time
(d) the value of its consumption time less its market price

24. A consumer has two basic choices: rent a videotape movie for $4.00 and spend 2 hours of time watching it or spend $15 for dinner at a restaurant that takes 1 hour of time. If the marginal utilities of the movie and the dinner are the same, and the consumer values time at $15 an hour, the rational consumer will most likely
(a) rent more movies and buy fewer restaurant dinners
(b) buy more restaurant dinners and rent fewer movies
(c) buy fewer restaurant dinners and rent fewer movies
(d) make no change in the consumption of both

25. Most economists contend that noncash transfers are
(a) of greater total utility but of less marginal utility
(b) of less total utility but of greater marginal utility
(c) more efficient because they do not waste scarce resources
(d) less efficient because they may not match recipient's preferences

■ PROBLEMS

1. Suppose that when the price of bread is $2 per loaf, the Robertson family buys six loaves of bread in a week.
a. When the price of bread falls from $2 to $1.60, the Robertson family will increase its bread consumption to seven loaves.
(1) Measured in terms of bread, the fall in the price of bread will ______________ their real income by ______________ loaves. (*Hint:* How many loaves of bread *could* they now buy without changing the amount they spend on bread?)
(2) Is the Robertsons' demand for bread elastic or inelastic? ______________
b. When the price of bread rises from $2 to $2.40 per loaf, the Robertson family will decrease its bread consumption to four loaves.
(1) Measured in terms of bread, this rise in the price of bread will ______________ their real income by ______________ loaf.
(2) Is the Robertsons' demand for bread elastic or inelastic? ______________

Good A			Good B			Good C		
Quantity	Total utility	Marginal utility	Quantity	Total utility	Marginal utility	Quantity	Total utility	Marginal utility
1	21	21	1	7	7	1	23	23
2	41	20	2	13	6	2	40	17
3	59	18	3	18	5	3	52	12
4	74	15	4	22	4	4	60	8
5	85	11	5	25	3	5	65	5
6	91	6	6	27	2	6	68	3
7	91	0	7	28.2	1.2	7	70	2

2. Assume that Harriet Palmer finds only three goods, A, B, and C, for sale and that the amounts of utility which their consumption will yield her are as shown in the table above. Compute the marginal utilities for successive units of A, B, and C and enter them in the appropriate columns.

3. Using the marginal-utility data for goods A, B, and C which you obtained in problem 2, assume that the prices of A, B, and C are $5, $1, and $4, respectively and that Palmer has an income of $37 to spend.

a. Complete the following table by computing the *marginal utility per dollar* for successive units of A, B, and C.

b. Palmer would *not* buy 4 units of A, 1 unit of B, and 4 units of C because ______________.

c. Palmer would *not* buy 6 units of A, 7 units of B, and 4 units of C because ______________.

d. When Palmer is maximizing her utility, she will buy ______________ units of A, ______________ units of B, ______________ units of C; her total utility will be ______________, and the marginal utility of the last dollar spent on each good will be ______________.

e. If Palmer's income increased by $1, she would spend it on good ______________, assuming she can buy fractions of a unit of a good, because ______________ ______________.

4. Sam Thompson has an income of $36 to spend each week. The only two goods he is interested in purchasing are H and J. The marginal-utility schedules for these two goods are shown in the table at the bottom of the page.

The price of J does not change from week to week and is $4. The marginal utility per dollar from J is also shown in the table. But the price of H varies from one week to the next. The marginal utility per dollar from H when the price of H is $6, $4, $3, $2, and $1.50 is shown in the table.

Good A		Good B		Good C	
Quantity	Marginal utility per dollar	Quantity	Marginal utility per dollar	Quantity	Marginal utility per dollar
1	____	1	____	1	____
2	____	2	____	2	____
3	____	3	____	3	____
4	____	4	____	4	____
5	____	5	____	5	____
6	____	6	____	6	____
7	____	7	____	7	____

	Good H						Good J	
Quantity	MU	MU/$6	MU/$4	MU/$3	MU/$2	MU/$1.50	MU	MU/$4
1	45	7.5	11.25	15	22.5	30	40	10
2	30	5	7.5	10	15	20	36	9
3	20	3.33	5	6.67	10	13.33	32	8
4	15	2.5	3.75	5	7.5	10	28	7
5	12	2	3	4	6	8	24	6
6	10	1.67	2.5	3.33	5	6.67	20	5
7	9	1.5	2.25	3	4.5	6	16	4
8	7.5	1.25	1.88	2.5	3.75	5	12	3

a. Complete the table below to show how much of H Thompson will buy each week at each of the five possible prices of H.

Price of H	Quantity of H demanded
$6.00	_____
4.00	_____
3.00	_____
2.00	_____
1.50	_____

b. What is the table you completed in part **a** called?

____

5. Assume that a consumer can purchase only two goods: *R* (recreation) and *M* (material goods). The market price of *R* is $2 and the market price of *M* is $1. The consumer spends all her income in such a way that the marginal utility of the last unit of *R* she buys is 12 and the marginal utility of the last unit of *M* she buys is 6.

a. If we ignore the time it takes to consume *R* and *M*, is the consumer maximizing the total utility she obtains from the two goods?_______________

b. Suppose it takes 4 hours to consume each unit of *R*, 1 hour to consume each unit of *M*, and the consumer can earn $2 an hour when she works.

(1) The full price of a unit of *R* is $_______________.

(2) The full price of a unit of *M* is $_______________.

c. If we take into account the full price of each of the commodities, is the consumer maximizing her total utility? _______________ How do you know this?

____

d. If the consumer is not maximizing her utility, should she increase her consumption of *R* or of *M*? ________

Why should she do this?_______________

e. Will she use more or less of her time for consuming *R*? _______________

SHORT ANSWER AND ESSAY QUESTIONS

1. Explain, employing the income-effect and substitution-effect concepts, the reasons consumers buy more of a product at a lower price than at a higher price and vice versa.

2. Why is utility a "subjective concept"?

3. Define total and marginal utility. What is the relationship between total and marginal utility?

4. How can the law of diminishing marginal utility be used to explain the law of demand?

5. How does the subjective nature of utility limit the practical usefulness of the marginal-utility theory of consumer behavior?

6. What is the relationship of marginal utility to the price elasticity of demand?

7. What essential assumptions are made about consumers and the nature of goods and services in developing the marginal-utility theory of consumer behavior?

8. What is meant by "budget restraint"?

9. When is the consumer in equilibrium and maximizing total utility? Explain why any deviation from this equilibrium will decrease the consumer's total utility.

10. Why must the amounts of extra utility derived from differently priced goods mean that marginal utility must be put on a per-dollar-spent basis? Give an example.

11. How can saving be incorporated into the utility-maximizing analysis?

12. Give and explain an algebraic restatement of the utility-maximizing rule.

13. Using the marginal-utility theory of consumer behavior, explain how an individual's demand schedule for a particular consumer good can be obtained.

14. Why does the demand schedule that is developed based on the marginal-utility theory almost invariably result in an inverse or negative relationship between price and quantity demanded?

15. What aspects of the theory of consumer behavior explain why consumers started buying CDs in larger numbers instead of cassette tapes or long-playing records in the past decade?

16. Why does water have a lower price than diamonds despite the fact that water is more useful than diamonds?

17. Explain how a consumer might determine the value of his or her time. How does the value of time affect the full price the consumer pays for a good or service?

18. What does taking time into account explain that the traditional approach to consumer behavior does not explain?

19. How does the way that we pay for goods and services affect the quantity purchased? Explain by using health care as an example.

20. Why are noncash transfers less efficient for consumers than cash transfers?

ANSWERS

Chapter 21 Consumer Behavior and Utility Maximization

FILL-IN QUESTIONS

1. substitution, diminishing
2. increase, decrease, income
3. more, lower, less, more, substitution
4. total, marginal, subjective, is not
5. decrease
6. decreasing, zero

7. inelastic, elastic
8. rational, preferences
9. limited, scarce, prices
10. last, the same
11. increase, decrease
12. *a.* MU of product *X*; *b.* price of *X*; *c.* MU of product *Y*; *d.* price of *Y*
13. *a.* the income of the consumer; *b.* the prices of other products
14. consistent, more
15. decreased, increased
16. marginal, marginal, total, total
17. time, limited, equal to, price, time
18. cost, more
19. more, positive, zero
20. less, less

TRUE-FALSE QUESTIONS

1. F, pp. 424-425
2. F, pp. 424-425
3. T, p. 425
4. T, p. 425
5. F, p. 425
6. F, p. 427
7. T, pp. 425-427
8. F, p. 427
9. F, p. 427
10. T, p. 428
11. T, p. 428
12. T, p. 431
13. F, p. 428
14. F, pp. 429-430
15. F, p. 429
16. F, pp. 429-430
17. T, pp. 431-432
18. F, p. 432
19. F, pp. 433
20. F, pp. 433-434
21. T, pp. 433-434
22. F, pp. 433-434
23. T, pp. 434-435
24. T, p. 435
25. F, p. 435

MULTIPLE-CHOICE QUESTIONS

1. c, p. 425
2. b, pp. 424-425
3. b, pp. 425-427
4. c, pp. 425-427
5. d, pp. 425-427
6. c, pp. 425-427
7. c, pp. 425-427
8. b, p. 427
9. a, p. 428
10. c, pp. 429-431
11. b, pp. 429-431
12. c, pp. 425, 429-431
13. b, pp. 429-431
14. c, pp. 429-431
15. a, p. 429
16. a, pp. 430-431
17. c, pp. 425-427
18. b, pp. 430-431
19. c, pp. 430-431
20. c, pp. 430-431
21. c, p. 431
22. b, p. 433
23. b, pp. 433-434
24. b, pp. 433-434
25. d, pp. 435

PROBLEMS

1. *a.* (1) increase, 1 1/2; (2) inelastic; *b.* (1) decrease, 1; (2) elastic
2. marginal utility of good A: 21, 20, 18, 15, 11, 6, 0; marginal utility of good B: 7, 6, 5, 4, 3, 2, 1.2; marginal utility of good C: 23, 17, 12, 8, 5, 3, 2
3. *a.* marginal utility per dollar of good A: 4.2, 4, 3.6, 3, 2.2, 1.2, 0; marginal utility per dollar of good B: 7, 6, 5, 4, 3, 2, 1.2; marginal utility per dollar of good C, 5.75, 4.25, 3, 2, 1.25, .75, .5; *b.* the marginal utility per dollar spent on good B (7) is greater than the marginal utility per dollar spent on good A (3), and the latter is greater than the marginal utility per dollar spent on good C (2); *c.* she would be spending more than her $37 income; *d.* 4, 5, 3, 151, 3; *e.* A, she would obtain the greatest marginal utility for her dollar (2.2)
4. *a.* 2, 3, 4, 6, 8; *b.* the demand schedule (for good H)
5. *a.* yes; *b.* (1) 10, (2) 3; *c.* no, the marginal utility to price ratios are not the same for the two goods; *d.* of M, because its MU/P ratio is greater; *e.* less

SHORT ANSWER AND ESSAY QUESTIONS

1. pp. 424-425
2. p. 425
3. pp. 425-427
4. pp. 425-427
5. p. 425
6. p. 427
7. p. 428
8. p. 428
9. p. 429
10. pp. 429-430
11. p. 430
12. pp. 430-431
13. p. 431
14. p. 431
15. pp. 432
16. pp. 433
17. pp. 433-434
18. pp. 433-434
19. pp. 434-435
20. pp. 435

APPENDIX TO CHAPTER 21

Indifference Curve Analysis

This brief appendix contains the third explanation or approach to the theory of consumer behavior. In it you are introduced first to the ***budget line*** and then to the ***indifference curve***. These two geometrical concepts are then combined to explain when a consumer is purchasing the combination of two products that maximizes the total utility obtainable with his or her income. The last step is to vary the price of one of the products to find the consumer's demand (schedule or curve) for the product.

■ CHECKLIST

When you have studied this appendix you should be able to

☐ Define the concept of a budget line.
☐ Explain how to measure the slope of a budget line and determine the location of the budget line.
☐ Define the concept of an indifference curve.
☐ State two characteristics of indifference curves.
☐ Explain the meaning of an indifference map.
☐ Given an indifference map, determine which indifference curves bring more or less total utility to consumers.
☐ Use indifference curves to identify which combination of two products maximizes the total utility of consumers.
☐ Derive a consumer's demand for a product using indifference curve analysis.
☐ Compare and contrast the marginal-utility and the indifference curve analyses of consumer behavior.

■ APPENDIX OUTLINE

1. A *budget line* shows graphically the different combinations of two products a consumer can purchase with a particular money income; a budget line has a negative slope.

a. An increase (decrease) in the money income of the consumer will shift the budget line to the right (left) without affecting its slope.

b. An increase (decrease) in the prices of both products shifts it to the left (right), but an increase (decrease) in the price of the product the quantity of which is measured horizontally (the price of the other product remaining constant) pivots the budget line around a fixed point on the vertical axis in a clockwise (counterclockwise) direction.

2. An *indifference curve* shows graphically the different combinations of two products which bring a consumer the same total utility.

a. An indifference curve is downsloping; if utility is to remain the same when the quantity of one product increases, the quantity of the other product must decrease.

b. An indifference curve is also convex to the origin; the more a consumer has of one product, the smaller the quantity of a second product he is willing to give up to obtain an additional unit of the first product.

c. The consumer has an indifference curve for every level of total utility; the nearer (farther) a curve is to (from) the origin in this indifference map, the smaller (larger) is the utility of the combinations on that curve.

3. The consumer is in *equilibrium* and purchasing the combination of two products that brings the maximum utility to him where the budget line is tangent to an indifference curve.

4. In the marginal-utility approach to consumer behavior, it is assumed that utility is measurable, but in the indifference curve approach, it need only be assumed that a consumer can say whether a combination of products has more utility than, less utility than, or the same amount of utility as another combination.

5. The *demand* (schedule or curve) for one of the products is derived by varying the price of that product and shifting the budget line, holding the price of the other product and the consumer's income constant, and finding the quantity of the product the consumer will purchase at each price when in equilibrium.

■ HINTS AND TIPS

1. This appendix simplifies the analysis by limiting consumer choice to just two goods. The budget line shows the consumer what is possible to purchase in the two-good world, given an income. Make sure that you understand what a budget line is. To test your understanding, practice with different income levels and prices. For example, assume you had an income of \$100 to spend for two goods (A and B). Good A costs \$10 and Good B costs

$5. Draw a budget line to show the possible combinations of A and B that you could purchase.

2. Indifference curves and the marginal rate of substitution are perhaps the most difficult concepts to understand in this appendix. Remember that the points on the curve show the possible combinations of two goods for which the consumer is *indifferent,* and thus does not care what combination is chosen. The marginal rate of substitution is the rate at which the consumer gives up units of one good for units of another along the indifference curve. This rate will change (diminish) as the consumer moves down an indifference curve because the consumer is less willing to *substitute* one good for the other.

3. The material in this appendix is more advanced, but do not forget its basic purpose: to provide another explanation for the downsloping demand curve.

■ IMPORTANT TERMS

budget line
indifference curve
marginal rate of substitution
indifference map
equilibrium position

SELF-TEST

■ FILL-IN QUESTIONS

1. A schedule or curve that shows the various combinations of two products a consumer can buy with a specific ______________ is called a ______________ line.

2. Given two products X and Y, and a graph with the quantities of X measured horizontally and the quantities of Y measured vertically, the budget line has a slope equal to the ratio of the ______________ to the ______________.

3. When a consumer's income increases, the budget line shifts to the (left, right) ______________, while a decrease in income shifts the budget line to the ______________.

4. Given two products, A and B, and a budget line graph with the quantities of A measured horizontally and the quantities of B measured vertically, an increase in the price of A will fan the budget line (outward, inward) ______________, and a decrease in the price of A will fan the budget line ______________ around a fixed point on the ______________ axis.

5. A(n) (demand, indifference) ______________ curve shows the various combinations of two products that give a consumer the same total satisfaction or total (cost, utility) ______________.

6. An indifference curve slopes (upward, downward) ______________ and is (concave, convex) ______________ to the origin.

7. The slope of the indifference curve at each point measures the (marginal, total) ______________ rate of substitution of the combination represented by that point.

8. The more a consumer has of one product, the (greater, smaller) ______________ is the quantity of a second product the consumer will give up to obtain an additional unit of the first product. As a result, the marginal rate of substitution (MRS) of the first for the second product (increases, decreases) ______________ as a consumer moves from left to right (downward) along an indifference curve.

9. A set of indifference curves reflects different levels of (marginal, total) ______________ utility and is called an indifference (plan, map) ______________.

10. The farther from the origin an indifference curve lies, the (greater, smaller) ______________ the total utility obtained from the combinations of products on that curve.

11. A consumer obtains the greatest attainable total utility or satisfaction when he or she purchases that combination of two products at which his or her budget line is ______________ ______________. At this point the consumer's marginal rate of substitution is equal to ______________ ______________ ______________

12. Were a consumer to purchase a combination of two products which lie on her budget line and at which her budget line is steeper than the indifference curve intersecting that point, she could increase her satisfaction by trading (down, up) ______________ her budget line.

13. The marginal-utility approach to consumer behavior requires that we assume utility (is, is not) ______________ numerically measurable; the indifference curve approach (does, does not) ______________ require we make this assumption.

14. When quantities of product X are measured along the horizontal axis, a decrease in the price of X

a. fans the budget line (inward, outward) ______________ and to the (right, left) ______________;

b. puts the consumer, when in equilibrium, on a (higher, lower) ______________ indifference curve; and

c. normally induces the consumer to purchase (more, less) ______________ of product X.

15. Using indifference curves and different budget lines to determine how much of a particular product an individual consumer will purchase at different prices makes it possible to derive that consumer's (supply, demand) ______________ curve or schedule for that product.

■ TRUE-FALSE QUESTIONS

Circle the T if the statement is true, the F if it is false.

1. The slope of the budget line when quantities of F are measured horizontally and quantities of G vertically is equal to the price of G divided by the price of F. **T F**

2. An increase in the money income of a consumer shifts the budget line to the right. **T F**

3. The closer to the origin an indifference curve lies, the smaller the total utility a consumer obtains from the combinations of products on that indifference curve. **T F**

4. If a consumer moves from one combination (or point) on an indifference curve to another combination (or point) on the same curve, the total utility obtained by the consumer does not change. **T F**

5. A consumer maximizes total utility when she or he purchases the combination of the two products at which her or his budget line crosses an indifference curve. **T F**

6. A consumer is unable to purchase any of the combinations of two products which lie below (or to the left) of the consumer's budget line. **T F**

7. An indifference curve is concave to the origin. **T F**

8. A decrease in the price of a product normally enables a consumer to reach a higher indifference curve. **T F**

9. It is assumed in the marginal-utility approach to consumer behavior that utility is numerically measurable. **T F**

10. In both the marginal-utility and indifference curve approaches to consumer behavior, it is assumed that a consumer is able to say whether the total utility obtained from combination A is greater than, equal to, or less than the total utility obtained from combination B. **T F**

11. The budget line shows all combinations of two products which the consumer can purchase, given money income and the prices of the products. **T F**

12. On an indifference map, the further from the origin, the lower the level of utility associated with each indifference curve. **T F**

13. The marginal rate of substitution shows the rate, at the margin, at which the consumer is prepared to substitute one good for the other so as to remain equally satisfied. **T F**

14. On an indifference map, the consumer's equilibrium position will be where the slope of the highest attainable indifference curve equals the slope of the budget line. **T F**

15. There can be an intersection of consumer indifference curves. **T F**

■ MULTIPLE-CHOICE QUESTIONS

Circle the letter that corresponds to the best answer.

1. Suppose a consumer has an income of $8, the price of R is $1, and the price of S is $0.50. Which of the following combinations is on the consumer's budget line?
- **(a)** 8R and 1S
- **(b)** 7R and 1S
- **(c)** 6R and 6S
- **(d)** 5R and 6S

2. If a consumer has an income of $100, the price of U is $10, and the price of V is $20, the maximum quantity of U the consumer is able to purchase is
- **(a)** 5
- **(b)** 10
- **(c)** 20
- **(d)** 30

3. When the income of a consumer is $20, the price of T is $5, the price of Z is $2, and the quantity of T is measured horizontally, the slope of the budget line is
- **(a)** .4
- **(b)** 2.5
- **(c)** 4
- **(d)** 10

4. Assume that everything else remains the same, but there is a decrease in a consumer's money income. The most likely effect is
- **(a)** an inward shift in the indifference curves because the consumer can now satisfy fewer wants
- **(b)** an inward shift in the budget line because the consumer can now purchase less of both products
- **(c)** an increase in the marginal rate of substitution
- **(d)** no change in the equilibrium of the consumer

5. An indifference curve is a curve which shows the different combinations of two products that
- **(a)** give a consumer equal marginal utilities
- **(b)** give a consumer equal total utilities
- **(c)** cost a consumer equal amounts
- **(d)** have the same prices

6. In the following schedule for an indifference curve, how much of G is the consumer willing to give up to obtain the third unit of H?
- **(a)** 3
- **(b)** 4
- **(c)** 5
- **(d)** 6

Quantity of G	Quantity of H
18	1
12	2
7	3
3	4
0	5

7. The slope of the indifference curve measures the
(a) slope of the budget line
(b) total utility of a good
(c) space on an indifference map
(d) marginal rate of substitution

8. The marginal rate of substitution
(a) may rise or fall, depending on the slope of the budget line
(b) rises as you move downward along an indifference curve
(c) falls as you move downward along an indifference curve
(d) remains the same along a budget line

9. Which of the following is characteristic of indifference curves?
(a) They are concave to the origin.
(b) They are convex to the origin.
(c) Curves closer to the origin have the highest level of total utility.
(d) Curves closer to the origin have the highest level of marginal utility.

10. To derive the demand curve of a product, the price of the product is varied. For the indifference curve analysis, the
(a) budget line is held constant
(b) money income of the consumer changes
(c) tastes and preferences of the consumer are held constant
(d) prices of other products the consumer might purchase change

Questions 11, 12, 13, and 14 are based on the diagram below.

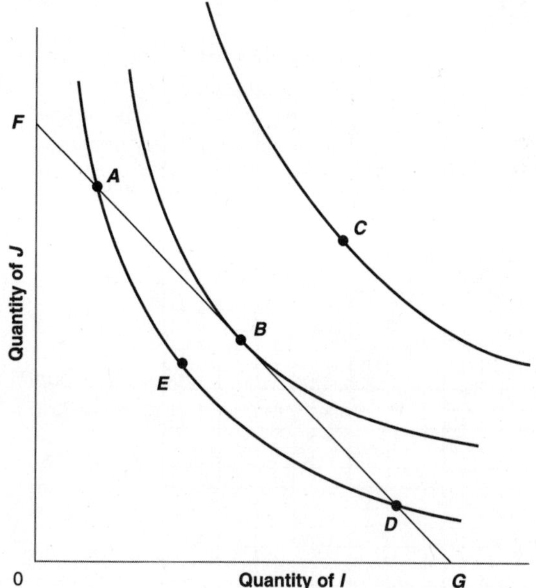

11. The budget line is best represented by line
(a) *AB*
(b) *AD*
(c) *FG*
(d) *DG*

12. Which combination of goods ***I*** and ***J*** will the consumer purchase?
(a) *A*
(b) *B*
(c) *C*
(d) *E*

13. Suppose the price of good ***I*** increases. The budget line will shift
(a) inward around a point on the ***J*** axis
(b) outward around a point on the ***J*** axis
(c) inward around a point on the ***I*** axis
(d) outward around a point on the ***I*** axis

14. If the consumer chooses the combination of goods ***I*** and ***J*** represented by point ***E***, then the consumer could
(a) obtain more goods with the available money income
(b) not obtain more goods with the available money income
(c) shift the budget line outward so that it is tangent with point ***C***
(d) shift the budget line inward so that it is tangent with point ***E***

15. In indifference curve analysis, the consumer will be in equilibrium at the point where the
(a) indifference curve is concave to the origin
(b) budget line crosses the vertical axis
(c) two indifference curves intersect and are tangent to the budget line
(d) budget line is tangent to the highest attainable indifference curve

16. If a consumer is initially in equilibrium, a decrease in money income will
(a) move the consumer to a new equilibrium on a lower indifference curve
(b) move the consumer to a new equilibrium upon a higher indifference curve
(c) make the slope of the consumer's indifference curves steeper
(d) have no effect on the equilibrium position

Questions 17, 18, 19, and 20 are based on the graph at the top of page 240.

17. If the budget line shifts from **BL #1** to **BL #2,** it is because the price of
(a) ***K*** increased
(b) ***K*** decreased
(c) ***L*** increased
(d) ***L*** decreased

18. If the budget line shifts from **BL #2** to **BL #1,** it is because the price of
(a) ***K*** increased
(b) ***K*** decreased
(c) ***L*** increased
(d) ***L*** decreased

19. When the budget line shifts from **BL #2** to **BL #1,** the consumer will buy
(a) more of ***K*** and ***L***
(b) less of ***K*** and ***L***

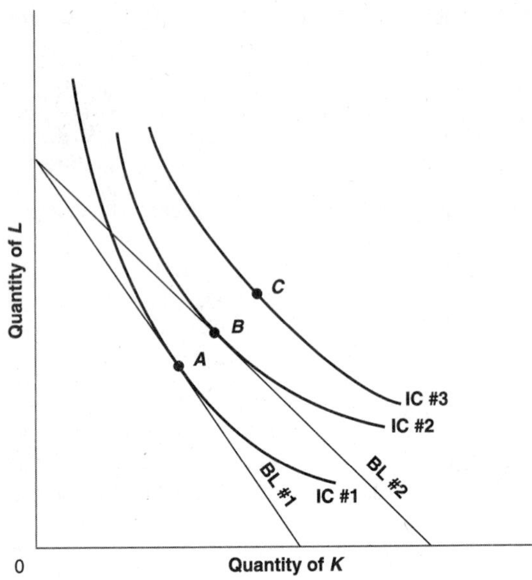

(c) more of K and less of L
(d) less of K and more of L

20. Point C on indifference curve **IC #3** can be an attainable combination of products K and L, if
(a) the price of K increases
(b) the price of L increases
(c) money income increases
(d) money income decreases

■ PROBLEMS

1. Following are the schedules for three indifference curves.

Indifference schedule 1		*Indifference schedule 2*		*Indifference schedule 3*	
A	**B**	**A**	**B**	**A**	**B**
0	28	0	36	0	45
1	21	1	28	1	36
2	15	2	21	2	28
3	10	3	15	3	21
4	6	4	11	4	15
5	3	5	7	5	10
6	1	6	4	6	6
7	0	7	1	7	3
		8	0	8	1
				9	0

a. On the graph below, measure quantities of A along the horizontal axis (from 0 to 9) and quantities of B along the vertical axis (from 0 to 45).
(1) Plot the 8 combinations of A and B from indifference schedule 1 and draw through the 8 points a curve which is in no place a straight line. Label this curve **IC #1.**

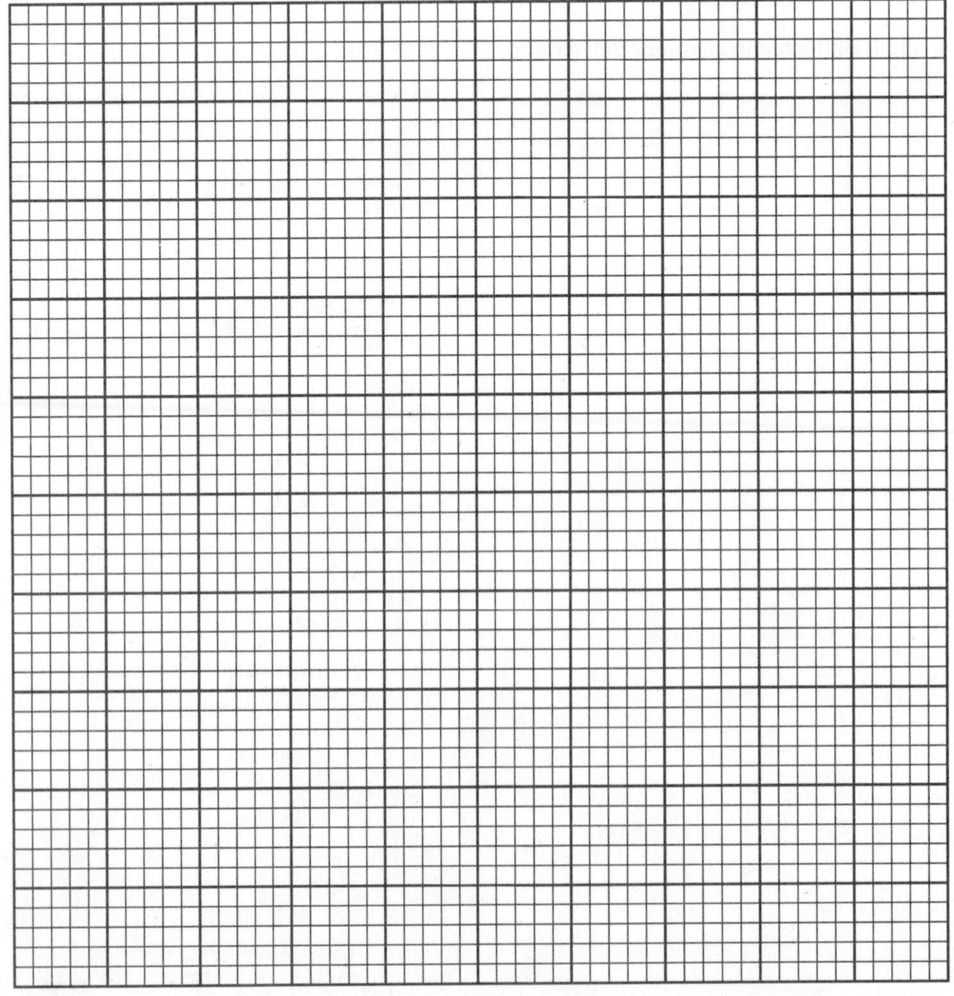

(2) Do the same for the 9 points in indifference schedule 2 and label it **IC #2.**

(3) Repeat the process for the 10 points in indifference schedule 3 and label the curve **IC #3.**

b. Assume the price of A is $12, the price of B is $2.40, and a consumer has an income of $72.

(1) Complete the following table to show the quantities of A and B this consumer is able to purchase.

A	B
0	_____
1	_____
2	_____
3	_____
4	_____
5	_____
6	_____

(2) Plot this budget line on the graph you completed in part **a.**

(3) This budget line has a slope equal to __________.

c. To obtain the greatest satisfaction or utility from his income of $72 this consumer will

(1) purchase ________ units of A and ________ of B;

(2) and spend $________ on A and $________ on B.

2. Following is a graph with three indifference curves and three budget lines. This consumer has an income of $100, and the price of **Y** remains constant at $5.

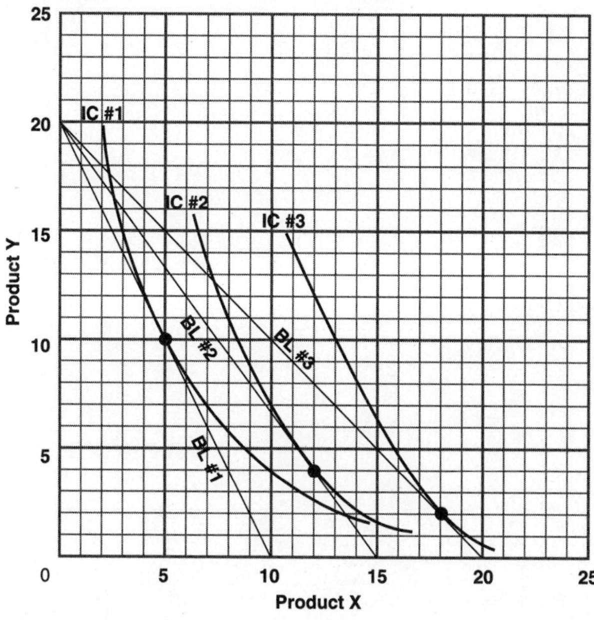

a. When the price of **X** is $10, the consumer's budget line is **BL #1** and the consumer

(1) purchases ____________ **X** and ____________ **Y**;

(2) and spends $________ on **X** and $________ on **Y**.

b. If the price of **X** is $6, 2/3 the budget line is **BL #2** and the consumer

(1) purchases ____________ **X** and ____________ **Y**;

(2) and spends $________ for **X** and $________ for **Y**.

c. And when the price of **X** is $5, the consumer has budget line **BL #3** and

(1) buys ____________ **X** and ____________ **Y**; and

(2) spends $________ on **X** and $________ on **Y**.

d. On the following graph, plot the quantities of X demanded at the three prices.

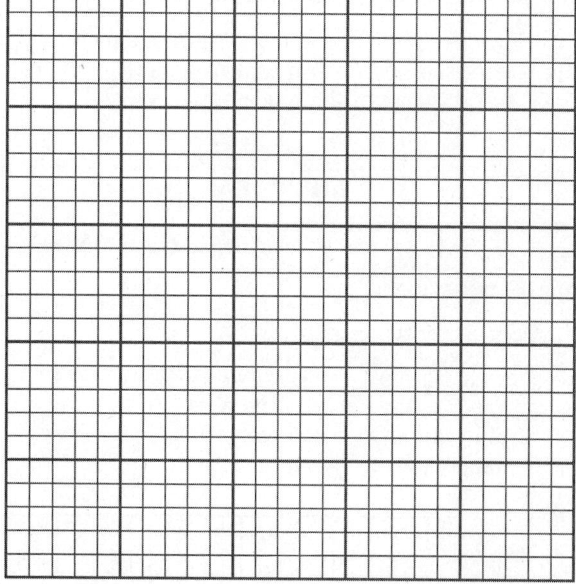

e. Between $10 and $5 this consumer's demand for X is (elastic, inelastic) ______________, and for him products X and Y are (substitutes, complements) ______________.

■ SHORT ANSWER AND ESSAY QUESTIONS

1. Why is the slope of the budget line negative?

2. How will each of the following events affect the budget line?

(a) a decrease in the money income of the consumer
(b) an increase in the prices of both products
(c) a decrease in the price of one of the products

3. Explain why the budget line can be called "objective" and an indifference curve "subjective."

4. What is the relationship between an indifference curve and total utility? Between an indifference map and total utility?

5. Why is the slope of an indifference curve negative and convex to the origin?

6. You are given two products, X and Y. Why will the utility-maximizing combination of the two products be the one lying on the highest attainable indifference curve?

7. Suppose a consumer purchases a combination of two products that is on her budget line but the budget line is not tangent to an indifference curve at that point. Of which product should the consumer buy more, and of which should she buy less? Why?

8. What is the important difference between the marginal-utility theory and the indifference-curve theory of consumer demand?

9. Explain how the indifference map of a consumer and the budget line are utilized to derive the consumer's demand for one of the products. In deriving demand, what is varied and what is held constant?

10. How does a change in the price of one product shift the budget line and determine a new equilibrium point? Explain and illustrate with a graph.

ANSWERS

Appendix to Chapter 21 Indifference Curve Analysis

FILL-IN QUESTIONS

1. income, budget
2. price of X, price of Y
3. right, left
4. inward, outward, B
5. indifference, utility
6. downward, convex
7. marginal
8. smaller, decreases
9. total, map
10. greater
11. tangent to an indifference curve, the ratio of the price of the product measured on the horizontal axis to the price of the product measured on the vertical axis (or the slope of her or his budget line)
12. up
13. is, does not
14. *a.* outward, right; *b.* higher; *c.* more
15. demand

TRUE-FALSE QUESTIONS

1. F, pp. 438-439
2. T, p. 439
3. T, p. 440
4. T, p. 439
5. F, p. 441
6. F, pp. 438-439
7. F, p. 440
8. T, p. 442
9. T, p. 441
10. T, pp. 441-442
11. T, p. 438
12. F, p. 440
13. T, p. 440
14. T, p. 441
15. F, pp. 439-440

MULTIPLE-CHOICE QUESTIONS

1. d, pp. 438-439
2. b, pp. 438-439
3. b, pp. 438-439
4. b, p. 439
5. b, p. 439
6. c, p. 440
7. d, p. 440
8. c, p. 440
9. b, p. 440
10. c, p. 442
11. c, p. 438
12. b, p. 441
13. a, p. 439
14. a, p. 438
15. d, p. 441
16. a, pp. 439, 441
17. b, p. 439
18. a, p. 439
19. b, p. 442
20. c, p. 439

PROBLEMS

1. *b.* (1) 30, 25, 20, 15, 10, 5, 0; (3) −5; *c.* (1) 3, 15; (2) 36, 36
2. *a.* (1) 5, 10; (2) 50, 50; *b.* (1) 12, 4; (2) 80, 20; *c.* (1) 18, 2; (2) 90, 10; *e.* elastic, substitutes

SHORT ANSWER AND ESSAY QUESTIONS

1. pp. 438-439
2. p. 439
3. pp. 438-440
4. pp. 439-440
5. pp. 439-440
6. p. 441
7. p. 441
8. pp. 441-442
9. p. 442
10. p. 442

CHAPTER 22

The Costs of Production

Previous chapters discussed consumer behavior and its effect on product demand. This chapter switches the focus to producer behavior and the business firms. It explains how a firm's costs of production change as the firm's output changes, both in the short run and the long run.

This chapter begins with a definition of cost and profit. You should be somewhat familiar with these terms because they were first introduced in Chapters 2 and 4. The explanation of the terms in Chapter 22, however, is more detailed. There are several definitions of cost and profit, and you must know the distinctions if you are to understand the true meaning of ***economic cost*** and ***economic profit.***

The second and third sections of the chapter focus on **short-run production costs.** You are first introduced to the important ***law of diminishing returns,*** which defines the relationship between the quantity of resources used by the firm and the output the firm produces in the short run. The chapter discussion then shifts to costs because resource prices are associated with the fixed and variable resources the typical firm uses to produce its output. The three basic types of short-run costs—total, average, and marginal—vary for the firm as the quantity of resources and output changes. The chapter describes the relationship among the various cost curves and how they are shaped by the law of diminishing returns.

The fourth section of the chapter looks at production costs in the long run. All resources, and also production costs, are variable in the long run. You will learn that the long-run cost curve for the typical firm is based on the short-run cost curves for firms of different sizes. In the long run, firms can experience ***economies of scale*** and ***diseconomies of scale*** that will shape the long-run cost curve for the firm. The chapter concludes with several practical applications of the concept of scale economies.

It is important that you master this material on the costs of production because it sets the foundation for understanding the price and output decisions of a firm operating under different market structures that you will be reading about in the next three chapters.

■ CHECKLIST

When you have studied this chapter you should be able to

☐ Define economic cost.
☐ Distinguish between an explicit and an implicit cost.
☐ Explain the difference between normal profit and economic profit and why the former is a cost and the latter is not a cost.
☐ Distinguish between the short run and the long run in production.
☐ Define marginal product, average product, and total product.
☐ State the law of diminishing returns and explain its rationale with examples.
☐ Compute marginal and average product when you are given the necessary data.
☐ Explain the relationship between marginal and average product.
☐ Explain the difference between a fixed cost and a variable cost.
☐ Define total cost and average cost.
☐ Compute and graph average fixed cost, average variable cost, average total cost, and marginal cost when you are given total-cost data.
☐ Explain the difference between average cost and marginal cost.
☐ State the relationship between average product and average variable cost and between marginal product and marginal cost.
☐ Explain why cost curves might shift.
☐ Explain the difference between short-run costs and long-run costs.
☐ State why the long-run average total cost curve is expected to be U-shaped.
☐ List the causes of the economies and the diseconomies of scale.
☐ Indicate the relationship between long-run average total costs and the structure and competitiveness of an industry.
☐ Give examples of economies and diseconomies of scale in the real world.
☐ Explain the concept of minimum efficient scale.

■ CHAPTER OUTLINE

1. Because resources are scarce and may be employed to produce many different products, the economic cost of using resources to produce any one of these products is an opportunity cost: The amount of other products that cannot be produced.

a. In money terms, the costs of employing resources to produce a product are also an opportunity cost: the payments a firm must make to the owners of resources to attract these resources away from their best alternative opportunities for earning incomes. These costs may be either explicit or implicit.

b. ***Normal profit*** is an implicit cost and is the minimum payment that entrepreneurs must receive for performing the entrepreneurial functions for the firm.

c. ***Economic,*** or pure, ***profit*** is the revenue a firm receives in excess of all its explicit and implicit economic (opportunity) costs. (The firm's accounting profit is its revenue less only its ***explicit costs***.)

d. The firm's economic costs vary as the firm's output varies, and the way in which costs vary with output depends on whether the firm is able to make short-run or long-run changes in the amounts of resources it employs. The firm's plant is a fixed resource in the short run and a variable resource in the long run.

2. In the *short run* the firm cannot change the size of its plant and can vary its output only by changing the quantities of the variable resources it employs.

a. The *law of diminishing returns* determines the manner in which the costs of the firm change as it changes its output in the short run.

b. The **total** short-run costs of a firm are the sum of its fixed and variable costs. As output increases,

(1) the fixed costs do not change;

(2) at first the variable costs increase at a decreasing rate, and then increase at an increasing rate;

(3) and at first total costs increase at a decreasing rate and then increase at an increasing rate.

c. **Average** fixed, variable, and total costs are equal, respectively, to the firm's fixed, variable, and total costs divided by the output of the firm. As output increases,

(1) average fixed cost decreases;

(2) at first average variable cost decreases and then increases;

(3) and at first average total cost also decreases and then increases.

d. **Marginal** cost is the extra cost incurred in producing one additional unit of output.

(1) Because the marginal product of the variable resource increases and then decreases (as more of the variable resource is employed to increase output), marginal cost decreases and then increases as output increases.

(2) At the output at which average variable cost is a minimum, average variable cost and marginal cost are equal, and at the output at which average total cost is a minimum, average total cost and marginal cost are equal.

(3) On a graph, marginal cost will always intersect average variable cost at its minimum point and marginal cost will always intersect average total cost at its minimum point. These intersections will always have marginal cost approaching average variable cost and average total cost from below.

(4) Changes in either resource prices or technology will cause the cost curves to shift.

3. In the *long run,* all the resources employed by the firm are variable resources, and therefore all its costs are variable costs.

a. As the firm expands its output by increasing the size of its plant, average total cost tends to fall at first because of the economies of large-scale production, but as this expansion continues, sooner or later, average total cost begins to rise because of the diseconomies of large-scale production.

b. The *economies and diseconomies of scales* encountered in the production of different goods are important factors influencing the structure and competitiveness of various industries.

(1) ***Minimum efficient scale (MES)*** is the smallest level of output at which a firm can minimize long-run average costs. This concept explains why relatively large and small firms could coexist in an industry and be viable when there is an extended range of constant returns to scale.

(2) In other industries the long-run average cost curve will decline over a range of output. Given consumer demand, efficient production will be achieved only with a small number of large firms.

(3) When economies of scale extend beyond the market size, the conditions for a ***natural monopoly*** are produced, wherein unit costs are minimized by having a single firm produce a product.

■ HINTS AND TIPS

1. Many different cost terms are described in this chapter. Make yourself a glossary so that you can distinguish among them. You need to know what each one means if you are to master the material in the chapter. If you try to learn them in the order in which you encounter them, you will have little difficulty because the later terms build on the earlier ones.

2. Make sure you know the difference between marginal and average relationships in this chapter. ***Marginal product (MP)*** shows the *change* in total output associated with each additional input. ***Average product (AP)*** is simply the output per unit of resource input. ***Marginal cost (MC)*** shows the *change* in total cost associated with producing another unit of output. ***Average cost*** shows the per unit cost of producing a level of output.

3. Practice drawing the different sets of cost curves used in this chapter: (1) short-run total cost curves, (2) short-run average and marginal cost curves, and (3) long-run cost curves. Also, explain to yourself the relationship between the curves in each set that you draw.

4. In addition to learning *how* the costs of the firm vary as its output varies, be sure to understand *why* the costs vary the way they do. In this connection note that the behavior of short-run costs is the result of the law of diminishing returns and that the behavior of long-run costs is the consequence of economies and diseconomies of scale.

■ IMPORTANT TERMS

economic cost	**explicit cost**
opportunity cost	**implicit cost**

economic (pure) profit
short run
long run
law of diminishing returns
normal profit
marginal product (MP)
average product (AP)
fixed resource
variable resource
fixed cost
variable cost
total cost (TC)
average fixed cost (AFC)
average variable cost (AVC)
total product (TP)
average total cost (ATC)
marginal cost (MC)
economies of scale
diseconomies of scale
constant returns to scale
minimum efficient scale (MES)
natural monopoly

SELF-TEST

■ FILL-IN QUESTIONS

1. The value or worth of any resource is what it can earn in its best alternative use and is called the (out-of-pocket, opportunity) _______________ cost of that resource.

2. The economic cost of producing a product is the amount of money or income the firm must pay or provide to (government, resource owners) to _______________ attract land, labor, and capital goods away from alternative uses in the economy. The monetary payments, or out-of-pocket payments, are (explicit, implicit) _______________ costs, and the costs of self-owned or self-employed resources are _______________ costs.

3. Normal profit is a cost because it is the payment which the firm must make to obtain the services of the (workers, entrepreneurs) _______________. Accounting profit is equal to the firm's total revenue less its (explicit, implicit) _______________ costs. Economic profit is not a cost and is equal to the firm's total (costs, revenues) _______________ less its total _______________.

4. In the short run the firm can change its output by changing the quantity of the (fixed, variable) _______________ resources it employs, but it cannot change the quantity of the _______________ resources. This means that the firm's plant capacity is fixed in the (short, long) _______________ run and variable in the _______________ run.

5. The law of diminishing returns is that as successive units of a (fixed, variable) _______________ resource are added to a _______________ resource beyond some point the (total, marginal) _______________ product of the former resource will decrease. The law assumes that all units of inputs are of (equal, unequal) _______________ quality.

6. If the total product increases at an increasing rate, the marginal product is (rising, falling) _______________. If it increases at a decreasing rate, the marginal product is (positive, negative, zero) _______________, but (rising, falling) _______________.

7. If total product is at a maximum, the marginal product is (positive, negative, zero) _______________, but if it decreases, the marginal product is _______________.

8. If the marginal product of any input exceeds its average product the average product is (rising, falling) _______________, but if it is less than its average product the average product is _______________. If marginal product is equal to its average product the average product is at a (minimum, maximum) _______________.

9. Those costs which in total do not vary with changes in output are (fixed, variable) _______________ costs, but those costs which in total change with the level of output are _______________ costs. The sum of fixed and variable costs at each level of output is (marginal, total) _______________ cost.

10. The law of diminishing returns explains why a firm's average variable, average total, and marginal cost may at first tend to (increase, decrease) _______________ but ultimately _______________ as the output of the firm increases.

11. Marginal cost is the increase in (average, total) _______________ variable cost or _______________ cost which occurs when the firm increases its output by one unit.

12. If marginal cost is less than average variable cost, average variable cost will be (rising, falling, constant) _______________ but if average variable cost is less than marginal cost, average variable cost will be _______________.

13. Assume that labor is the only variable input in the short run and that the wage rate paid to labor is constant.

a. When the marginal product of labor is rising, the marginal cost of producing a product is (rising, falling) _______________.

b. When the average variable cost of producing a product is falling, the average product of labor is (rising, falling) _______________.

c. At the output at which marginal cost is at a minimum, the marginal product of labor is at a (minimum, maximum) _______________.

d. At the output at which the average product of labor is at a maximum, the average variable cost of producing the product is at a (minimum, maximum) ______________.

e. At the output at which the average variable cost is at a minimum, average variable cost and (marginal, total) ______________ cost are equal and average product and ______________ product are equal.

14. Changes in either resource prices or technology will cause cost curves to (shift, remain unchanged) ______________. If average fixed costs increase, then the average fixed costs curve will (shift up, shift down, remain unchanged) ______________ and the average total cost curve will ______________, but the average variable cost curve will ______________ and the marginal cost curve will (shift up, shift down, remain unchanged) ______________.

15. If average variable costs increase, then the average variable cost curve will (shift up, shift down, remain unchanged) ______________ and the average total cost curve will ______________, and the marginal cost curve will (shift up, shift down, remain unchanged) ______________, but the average fixed cost curve would ______________.

16. The short-run costs of a firm are fixed and variable costs, but in the long run all costs are (fixed, variable) ______________. The long-run average total cost of producing a product is equal to the lowest of the short-run costs of producing that product after the firm has had all the time it requires to make the appropriate adjustments in the size of its (workforce, plant) ______________.

17. List the three important sources of economies of scale:

a. ______________________________

b. ______________________________

c. ______________________________

18. When the firm experiences diseconomies of scale, it has (higher, lower) ______________ average total costs as output increases. Where diseconomies of scale are operative, an increase in all inputs will cause a (greater, less) ______________-than-proportionate increase in output. The factor which gives rise to diseconomies of large scale is managerial (specialization, problems) ______________.

19. The smallest level of output at which a firm can minimize long-run average costs is (maximum, minimum) ______________ efficient scale. Relatively large and small firms could coexist in this type of industry and be equally viable when there is an extended range of (increasing, decreasing, constant) ______________ returns to scale.

20. In some industries, the long-run average cost curve will (increase, decrease) ______________ over a long range of output and efficient production will be achieved with only a few (small, large) ______________ firms. The conditions for a natural monopoly are created when unit costs are minimized by having a single firm produce a product, so that (economies, diseconomies) ______________ of scale extend beyond the market's size.

■ TRUE-FALSE QUESTIONS

Circle the T if the statement is true, the F if it is false.

1. The economic costs of a firm are the payments it must make to resource owners to attract their resources from alternative employments. **T F**

2. Economic or pure profit is an explicit cost, while normal profit is an implicit cost. **T F**

3. In the short run the size (or capacity) of a firm's plant is fixed. **T F**

4. The resources employed by a firm are all variable in the long run and all fixed in the short run. **T F**

5. The law of diminishing returns states that as successive amounts of a variable resource are added to a fixed resource, beyond some point total output will diminish. **T F**

6. An assumption of the law of diminishing returns is that all units of variable inputs are of equal quality. **T F**

7. When total product is increasing at a decreasing rate, marginal product is positive and increasing. **T F**

8. When average product is falling, marginal product is greater than average product. **T F**

9. When marginal product is negative, total production (or output) is decreasing. **T F**

10. The larger the output of a firm, the smaller the fixed cost of the firm. **T F**

11. The law of diminishing returns explains why increases in variable costs associated with each 1-unit increase in output become greater and greater after a certain point. **T F**

12. Fixed costs can be controlled or altered in the short run. **T F**

13. Total cost is the sum of fixed and variable costs at each level of output. **T F**

14. Marginal cost is the change in fixed cost divided by the change in output. **T F**

15. The marginal-cost curve intersects the average-total-cost (ATC) curve at the ATC curve's minimum point. T F

16. If the fixed cost of a firm increases from one year to the next (because the premium it must pay for the insurance on the buildings it owns has been increased) while its variable-cost schedule remains unchanged, its marginal-cost schedule will also remain unchanged. T F

17. Marginal cost is equal to average variable cost at the output at which average variable cost is a minimum. T F

18. When the marginal product of a variable resource increases, the marginal cost of producing the product will decrease, and when marginal product decreases, marginal cost will increase. T F

19. If the price of a variable input should increase, the average variable cost, average total cost, and marginal cost curves would all shift upward, but the position of the average fixed cost curve would remain unchanged. T F

20. One explanation why the long-run average-total-cost curve of a firm rises after some level of output has been reached is the law of diminishing returns. T F

21. The primary cause of diseconomies of scale is increased specialization of labor. T F

22. If a firm has constant returns to scale in the long run, the total costs of producing its product do not change when it expands or contracts its output. T F

23. Many firms appear to be larger than is necessary for them to achieve the minimum efficient scale. T F

24. If a firm increases all its inputs by 30% and its output increases by 20%, the firm is encountering economies of scale. T F

25. Minimum efficient scale occurs at the largest level of output at which a firm can minimize long-run average costs. T F

■ MULTIPLE-CHOICE QUESTIONS

Circle the letter that corresponds to the best answer.

1. Suppose that a firm produces 100,000 units a year and sells them all for $5 each. The explicit costs of production are $350,000 and the implicit costs of production are $100,000. The firm has an accounting profit of

(a) $200,000 and economic profit of $25,000
(b) $150,000 and economic profit of $50,000
(c) $125,000 and economic profit of $75,000
(d) $100,000 and economic profit of $50,000

2. Economic profit for a firm is defined as the total revenues of the firm minus its

(a) accounting profit
(b) explicit costs of production
(c) implicit costs of production
(d) opportunity cost of all inputs

3. Which would best describe the short run for a firm as defined by economists?

(a) The plant capacity for a firm is variable.
(b) The plant capacity for a firm is fixed.
(c) There are diseconomies of scale.
(d) There are economies of scale.

4. The change in total product divided by the change in resource input defines

(a) total cost
(b) average cost
(c) average product
(d) marginal product

5. The law of diminishing returns is most useful for explaining the

(a) shape of the short-run marginal cost curve
(b) shape of the long-run average cost curve
(c) decline in average fixed costs as output increases
(d) decline in total fixed costs as output increases

Use the following table to answer Questions 6 and 7. Assume that the only variable resource used to produce output is labor.

Amount of labor	Amount of output
1	3
2	8
3	12
4	15
5	17
6	18

6. The marginal product of the fourth unit of labor is

(a) 2 units of output
(b) 3 units of output
(c) 4 units of output
(d) 15 units of output

7. When the firm hires four units of labor the average product of labor is

(a) 3 units of output
(b) 3.75 units of output
(c) 4.25 units of output
(d) 15 units of output

8. Because the marginal product of a variable resource initially increases and later decreases as a firm increases its output,

(a) average variable cost decreases at first and then increases
(b) average fixed cost declines as the output of the firm expands
(c) variable cost at first increases by increasing amounts and then increases by decreasing amounts
(d) marginal cost at first increases and then decreases

9. Because the marginal product of a resource at first increases and then decreases as the output of the firm increases,

(a) average fixed cost declines as the output of the firm increases
(b) average variable cost at first increases and then decreases

(c) variable cost at first increases by increasing amounts and then increases by decreasing amounts
(d) total cost at first increases by decreasing amounts and then increases by increasing amounts

For Questions 10, 11, and 12, use the data given in the following table. The fixed cost of the firm is $500, and the firm's total variable cost is indicated in the table.

Output	Total variable cost
1	$ 200
2	360
3	500
4	700
5	1,000
6	1,800

10. The average variable cost of the firm when 4 units of output are produced is
(a) $175
(b) $200
(c) $300
(d) $700

11. The average total cost of the firm when 4 units of output are being produced is
(a) $175
(b) $200
(c) $300
(d) $700

12. The marginal cost of the sixth unit of output is
(a) $200
(b) $300
(c) $700
(d) $800

13. Marginal cost and average variable cost are equal at the output at which
(a) marginal cost is a minimum
(b) marginal product is a maximum
(c) average product is a maximum
(d) average variable cost is a maximum

14. Average variable cost may be either increasing or decreasing when
(a) marginal cost is decreasing
(b) marginal product is increasing
(c) average fixed cost is decreasing
(d) average total cost is increasing

15. Why does the short-run marginal-cost curve eventually increase for the typical firm?
(a) diseconomies of scale
(b) minimum efficient scale
(c) the law of diminishing returns
(d) economic profit eventually decreases

16. If the price of labor or some other variable resource increased, the
(a) AVC curve would shift downward
(b) AFC curve would shift upward
(c) AFC curve would shift downward
(d) MC curve would shift upward

Questions 17, 18, 19, and 20 are based on the following figure.

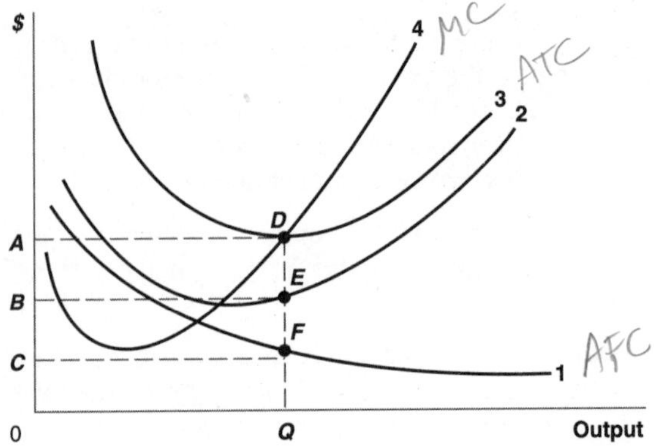

17. In the figure, curves **1, 3,** and **4,** respectively, represent
(a) average variable cost, marginal cost, and average total cost
(b) average total cost, average variable cost, and marginal cost
(c) average fixed cost, average total cost, and marginal cost
(d) marginal cost, average total cost, and average variable cost

18. At output level ***Q,*** the average fixed cost is measured by vertical distance represented by
(a) ***DE***
(b) ***DF***
(c) ***DQ***
(d) ***EF***

19. As output increases beyond the level represented by ***Q,***
(a) marginal product is rising
(b) marginal product is falling
(c) total fixed costs are rising
(d) total costs are falling

20. If the firm is producing at output level ***Q,*** then the total variable costs of production are represented by area
(a) 0 ***QFC***
(b) 0 ***QEB***
(c) 0 ***QDC***
(d) ***CFEB***

21. At an output of 10,000 units per year, a firm's total variable costs are $50,000 and its average fixed costs are $2. The total costs per year for the firm are
(a) $50,000
(b) $60,000
(c) $70,000
(d) $80,000

22. A firm has total fixed costs of $4,000 a year. The average variable cost is $3.00 for 2000 units of output. At this level of output, its average total costs are
(a) $2.50
(b) $3.00
(c) $4.50
(d) $5.00

23. If you know that total fixed cost is $100, total variable cost is $300, and total product is 4 units, then

(a) marginal cost is $50
(b) average fixed cost is $45
(c) average total cost is $125
(d) average variable cost is $75

24. If the short-run average variable costs of production for a firm are falling, then this indicates that

(a) average variable costs are above average fixed costs
(b) marginal costs are below average variable costs
(c) average fixed costs are constant
(d) total costs are falling

25. Which of the following is most likely to be a long-run adjustment for a firm which manufactures jet fighter planes on an assembly line basis?

(a) an increase in the amount of steel the firm buys
(b) a reduction in the number of shifts of workers from three to two
(c) a changeover from the production of one type of jet fighter to the production of a later-model jet fighter
(d) a changeover from the production of jet fighters to the production of sports cars.

Answer Questions 26 and 27 using the following table. Three short-run cost schedules are given for three plants of different sizes which a firm might build in the long run.

Plant 1		*Plant 2*		*Plant 3*	
Output	**ATC**	**Output**	**ATC**	**Output**	**ATC**
10	$10	10	$15	10	$20
20	9	20	10	20	15
30	8	30	7	30	10
40	9	40	10	40	8
50	10	50	14	50	9

26. What is the *long-run* average cost of producing 40 units of output?

(a) $7
(b) $8
(c) $9
(d) $10

27. At what output is long-run average cost a minimum?

(a) 20
(b) 30
(c) 40
(d) 50

28. Which of the following is *not* a factor which results in economies of scale?

(a) more efficient utilization of the firm's plant
(b) increased specialization in the use of labor
(c) greater specialization in the management of the firm
(d) utilization of more efficient equipment

29. The long-run average costs of producing a particular product are one of the factors that determine

(a) the competition among the firms producing the product
(b) the number of firms in the industry producing the product
(c) the size of each of the firms in the industry producing the product
(d) all of the above

30. A firm is encountering constant returns to scale when it increases all of its inputs by 20% and its output increases by

(a) 10%
(b) 15%
(c) 20%
(d) 25%

■ PROBLEMS

1. On the following graph, sketch the way in which the average product and the marginal product of a resource change as the firm increases its employment of that resource.

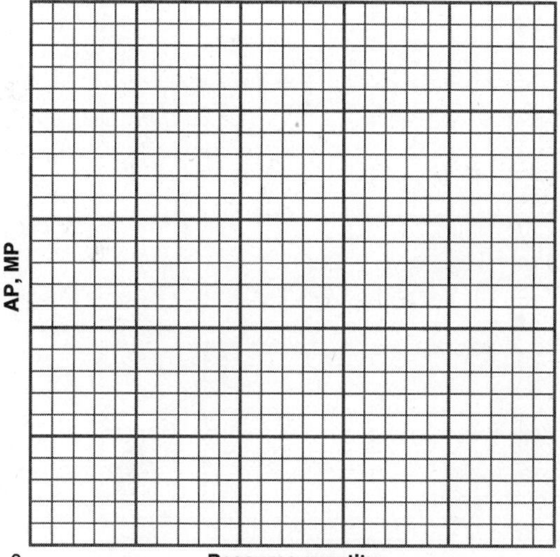

2. The following table shows the total production of a firm as the quantity of labor employed increases. The quantities of all other resources employed are constant.

a. Compute the marginal products of the first through the eighth unit of labor and enter them in the table.

Units of labor	Total production	Marginal product of labor	Average product of labor
0	0		0
1	80	80	80
2	200	120	100
3	330	130	110
4	400	70	100
5	450	50	90
6	480	30	80
7	490	10	70
8	480	-10	60

b. Now compute the average products of the various quantities of labor and enter them in the table.

c. There are increasing returns to labor from the first through the ______________ unit of labor and decreasing returns from the ______________ through the eighth unit.

d. When total production is increasing, marginal product is (positive, negative) ______________ and when total production is decreasing, marginal product is ______________.

e. When marginal product is greater than average product, then average product will (rise, fall) ____________, and when marginal product is less than average product, the average product will ______________.

3. On the following graph, sketch the manner in which fixed cost, variable cost, and total cost change as the output the firm produces in the short run changes.

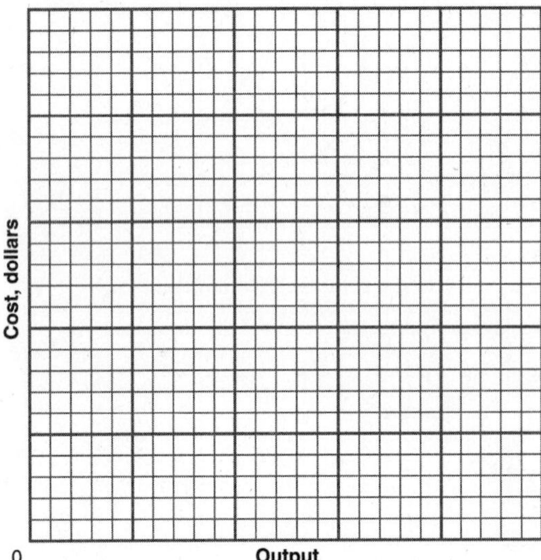

4. Assume that a firm has a plant of fixed size and that it can vary its output only by varying the amount of labor it employs. The table at the bottom of the page shows the relationships between the amount of labor employed, the output of the firm, the marginal product of labor, and the average product of labor.

a. Assume each unit of labor costs the firm $10. Compute the total cost of labor for each quantity of labor the firm might employ, and enter these figures in the table.

b. Now determine the marginal cost of the firm's product as the firm increases its output. Divide the *increase* in total labor cost by the *increase in total output* to find the marginal cost. Enter these figures in the table.

c. When the marginal product of labor

(1) increases, the marginal cost of the firm's product (increases, decreases) ______________.

(2) decreases, the marginal cost of the firm's product ______________.

d. If labor is the only variable input, the total labor cost and total variable cost are equal. Find the average variable cost of the firm's product (by dividing the total labor cost by total output) and enter these figures in the table.

e. When the average product of labor

(1) increases, the average variable cost (increases, decreases) ______________.

(2) decreases, the average variable cost ____________.

5. The law of diminishing returns causes a firm's average variable, average total, and marginal cost to decrease at first and then to increase as the output of the firm increases.

Sketch these three cost curves on the graph on page 251 in such a way that their proper relationship to each other is shown.

Quantity of labor employed	Total output	Marginal product of labor	Average product of labor	Total cost	Marginal cost	Average variable cost
0	0	—	—	$_____	—	—
1	5	5	5	_____	$_____	$_____
2	11	6	5.50	_____	_____	_____
3	18	7	6	_____	_____	_____
4	24	6	6	_____	_____	_____
5	29	5	5.80	_____	_____	_____
6	33	4	5.50	_____	_____	_____
7	36	3	5.14	_____	_____	_____
8	38	2	4.75	_____	_____	_____
9	39	1	4.33	_____	_____	_____
10	39	0	3.90	_____	_____	_____

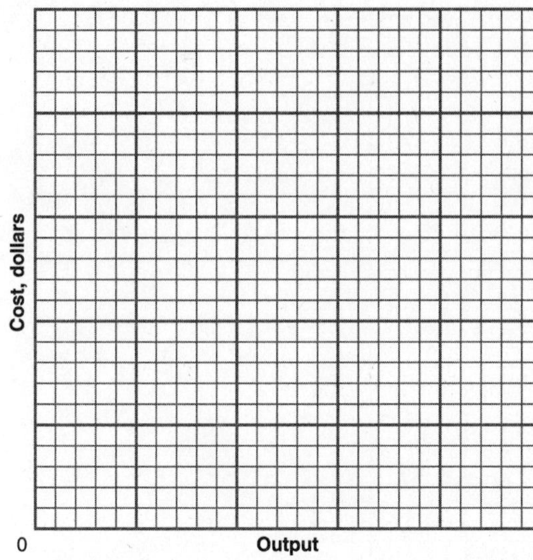

6. The table at the bottom of the page is a schedule of a firm's fixed cost and variable cost.

a. Complete the table by computing total cost, average fixed cost, average total cost, and marginal cost.

b. On the first graph on page 252, plot and label fixed cost, variable cost, and total cost.

c. On the second graph on page 252, plot average fixed cost, average variable cost, average total cost, and marginal cost. Label the four curves.

7. Following are the short-run average-cost curves of producing a product with three different sizes of plants, **Plant 1, Plant 2,** and **Plant 3.** Draw the firm's long-run average cost on this graph.

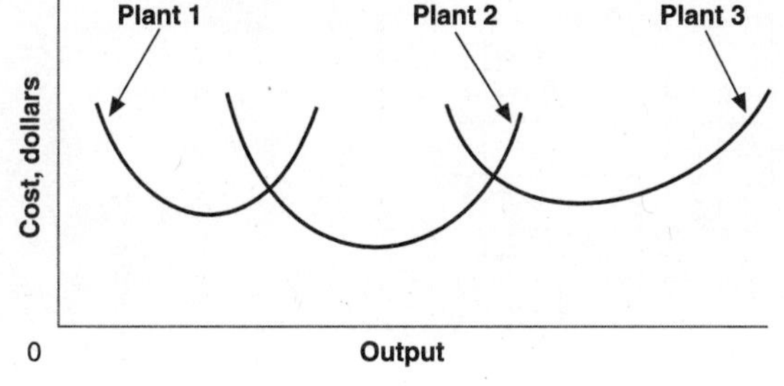

8. Following are the short-run average-total-cost schedules for three plants of different sizes which a firm might build to produce its product. Assume that these are the only possible sizes of plants which the firm might build.

Plant size A		*Plant size B*		*Plant size C*	
Output	ATC	Output	ATC	Output	ATC
10	$ 7	10	$17	10	$53
20	6	20	13	20	44
30	5	30	9	30	35
40	4	40	6	40	27
50	5	50	4	50	20
60	7	60	3	60	14
70	10	70	4	70	11
80	14	80	5	80	8
90	19	90	7	90	6
100	25	100	10	100	5
110	32	110	16	110	7
120	40	120	25	120	10

a. Complete the *long-run* average-cost schedule for the firm in the following table.

Output	Average cost	Output	Average cost
10	$____	70	$____
20	____	80	____
30	____	90	____
40	____	100	____
50	____	110	____
60	____	120	____

b. For outputs between

(1) ________________ and ________________, the firm should build Plant A.

(2) ________________ and ________________, the firm should build Plant B.

(3) ________________ and ________________, the firm should build Plant C.

Output	Total fixed cost	Total variable cost	Total cost	Average fixed cost	Average variable cost	Average total cost	Marginal cost
$ 0	$200	$ 0	$____				
1	200	50	____	$____	$50.00	$____	$____
2	200	90	____	____	45.00	____	____
3	200	120	____	____	40.00	____	____
4	200	160	____	____	40.00	____	____
5	200	220	____	____	44.00	____	____
6	200	300	____	____	50.00	____	____
7	200	400	____	____	57.14	____	____
8	200	520	____	____	65.00	____	____
9	200	670	____	____	74.44	____	____
10	200	900	____	____	90.00	____	____

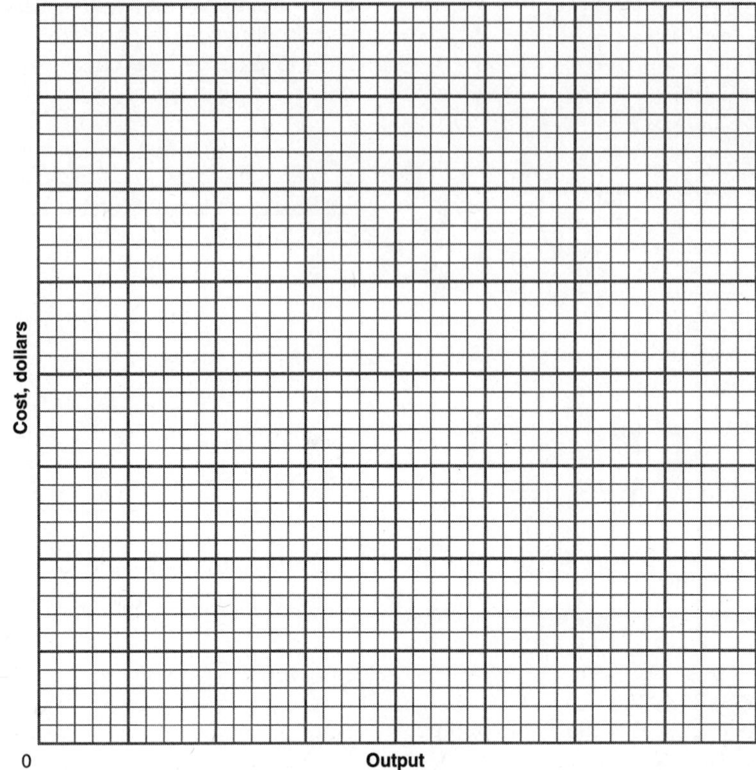
Cost, dollars
0
Output

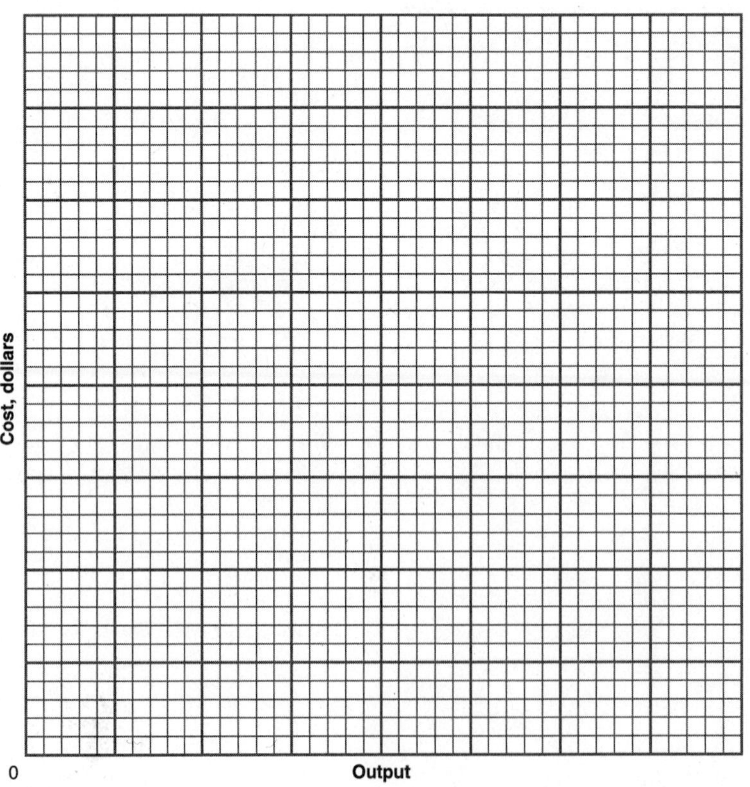
Cost, dollars
0
Output

■ SHORT ANSWER AND ESSAY QUESTIONS

1. Explain the meaning of the opportunity cost of producing a product and the difference between an explicit and an implicit cost. How would you determine the implicit money cost of a resource?

2. What is the difference between normal and economic profit? Why is the former an economic cost? How do you define accounting profit?

3. What type of adjustments can a firm make in the long run that it cannot make in the short run? What adjustments can it make in the short run? How long is the short run?

4. Why is the distinction between the short run and the long run important?

5. State precisely the law of diminishing returns. Exactly what is it that diminishes, and why does it diminish?

6. Distinguish between a fixed cost and a variable cost.

7. Why are short-run total costs partly fixed and partly variable costs, and why are long-run costs entirely variable?

8. Why do short-run variable costs increase at first by decreasing amounts and later increase by increasing amounts?

9. How does the behavior of short-run variable cost influence the behavior of short-run total costs?

10. Describe the way in which short-run average fixed cost, average variable cost, average total cost, and marginal cost vary as the output of the firm increases.

11. What is the connection between marginal product and marginal cost, and between average product and average variable cost? How will marginal cost behave as marginal product decreases and increases? How will average variable cost change as average product rises and falls?

12. What is the precise relationship between marginal cost and minimum average variable cost, and between marginal cost and minimum average total cost? Why are these relationships necessarily true?

13. What happens to the average total costs, average variable cost, average fixed cost, and marginal cost curves when the price of a variable input increases or decreases? Describe what other factor can cause short-run cost curves to shift.

14. What does the long-run average-cost curve of a firm show? What relationship is there between long-run average cost and the short-run average-total-cost schedules of the different-sized plants which a firm might build?

15. Why is the long-run average-cost curve of a firm U-shaped?

16. What is meant by economies of scale? What are some of the more important factors that explain its existence?

17. What are four factors that explain why there are economies of scale?

18. What is meant by and what causes diseconomies of large scale?

19. Describe at least three real-world examples of economies and diseconomies of scale.

20. Why are the economies and diseconomies of scale of great significance, and how do they influence the size of firms in an industry and the number of firms in an industry?

ANSWERS

Chapter 22 The Costs of Production

FILL-IN QUESTIONS

1. opportunity
2. resource owners, explicit, implicit
3. entrepreneurs, explicit, revenues, costs
4. variable, fixed, short, long
5. variable, fixed, marginal, equal
6. rising, positive, falling
7. zero, negative
8. rising, falling, maximum
9. fixed, variable, total
10. decrease, increase
11. total, total
12. falling, rising
13. *a.* falling; *b.* rising; *c.* maximum; *d.* minimum; *e.* marginal, marginal
14. shift, shift up, shift up, remain unchanged, remain unchanged
15. shift up, shift up, shift up, remain unchanged
16. variable, plant
17. *a.* labor specialization; *b.* managerial specialization; *c.* more efficient use
18. higher, less, problems
19. minimum, constant
20. decrease, large, economies

TRUE-FALSE QUESTIONS

1. T, p. 445	**10.** F, p. 449	**19.** T, pp. 454-455
2. F, pp. 445-446	**11.** T, p. 449	**20.** F, pp. 456, 460
3. T, p. 446	**12.** F, p. 449	**21.** F, p. 460
4. F, p. 446	**13.** T, p. 449	**22.** F, p. 461
5. F, p. 447	**14.** F, pp. 449, 452	**23.** T, p. 460
6. T, pp. 447-448	**15.** T, pp. 453-454	**24.** F, p. 459
7. F, pp. 448-450	**16.** T, p. 454	**25.** F, p. 462
8. F, pp. 448-450	**17.** T, pp. 453-454	
9. T, pp. 448, 450	**18.** T, p. 453	

MULTIPLE-CHOICE QUESTIONS

1. b, p. 445	**11.** c, pp. 451-452	**21.** c, pp. 449, 451
2. d, pp. 445-446	**12.** d, pp. 452-453	**22.** d, pp. 449, 451
3. b, p. 446	**13.** c, pp. 447-454	**23.** d, pp. 449, 451
4. d, p. 447	**14.** c, p. 451	**24.** b, pp. 453-454
5. a, p. 453	**15.** c, p. 453	**25.** d, p. 446
6. b, pp. 447-448	**16.** d, pp. 454-455	**26.** b, p. 456
7. b, pp. 447-448	**17.** c, pp. 453-454	**27.** b, p. 446
8. a, p. 451	**18.** a, p. 452	**28.** a, pp. 457-459
9. d, p. 449	**19.** b, p. 453	**29.** d, pp. 462-463
10. a, p. 451	**20.** b, pp. 451-452	**30.** c, p. 461

PROBLEMS

1. see Figure 22-2(b) of the text
2. *a.* 80, 120, 130, 70, 50, 30, 10, −10; *b.* 80, 100, 110, 100, 90, 80, 70, 60; *c.* third, fourth; *d.* positive, negative; *e.* rise, fall
3. see Figure 22-3 of the text
4. *a.* $0, 10, 20, 30, 40, 50, 60, 70, 80, 90, 100; *b.* $2.00, 1.67, 1.43, 1.67, 2.00, 2.50, 3.33, 5.00, 10.00, NA; *c.* (1) decreases, (2) increases; *d.* 2.00, 1.82, 1.67, 1.67, 1.72, 1.82, 1.94, 2.11, 2.31, 2.56; *e.* (1) decreases, (2) increases
5. see Figure 22-5 of the text
6. *a.*

Total cost	Average fixed cost	Average total cost	Marginal cost
$ 200	—	—	—
250	$200.00	$250.00	$ 50
290	100.00	145.00	40
320	66.67	106.67	30
360	50.00	90.00	40
420	40.00	84.00	60
500	33.33	83.33	80
600	28.57	85.71	100
720	25.00	90.00	120
870	22.22	96.67	150
1,100	20.00	110.00	230

7. see Figures 22-7 and 22-8 of the text
8. *a.* $7.00, 6.00, 5.00, 4.00, 4.00, 3.00, 4.00, 5.00, 6.00, 5.00, 7.00, 10.00; *b.* (1) 10, 40; (2) 50, 80; (3) 90, 120

SHORT ANSWER AND ESSAY QUESTIONS

1. pp. 444-445
2. pp. 445-446
3. p. 446
4. p. 446
5. pp. 447-448
6. p. 449
7. pp. 449, 455
8. p. 449
9. p. 449
10. pp. 449-454
11. pp. 453, 455
12. pp. 453-454
13. pp. 454-455
14. pp. 456-457
15. pp. 456-457
16. pp. 457-459
17. pp. 457-459
18. p. 460
19. pp. 461-462
20. pp. 462-463

CHAPTER 23

Pure Competition

Chapter 23 is the first of three chapters that bring together the previous discusion of demand and production costs. These chapters examine demand and production costs under four different market structures: pure competition, monopoly, oligopoly, and monopolistic competition. This chapter focuses exclusively on the pure competition market structure, which is characterized by (1) a large number of firms, (2) the selling of a standardized product, (3) firms which are price takers rather than price makers, and (4) ease of entry into and exit from the industry.

The main section of the chapter describes profit maximization for the firm in the short run. Although two approaches to profit maximization are presented, the one given the greatest emphasis is the marginal revenue–marginal cost approach. You will learn the rule that a firm maximizes profit or minimizes losses by producing the output level at which marginal revenue equals marginal cost. Finding this equality provides the answers to the three central questions each firm has to answer: (1) Should we produce? (2) If so, how much output? (3) What profit (or loss) will be realized?

Answers to the these questions also give insights about the short-run supply curve for the individual firm. The firm will find it profitable to produce at any output level where marginal revenue is greater than marginal costs. The firm will also produce in the short run, but it will experience losses if marginal revenue is les than marginal costs and greater than the minimum of average total cost. You will be shown how to construct the ***short-run supply curve*** for the purely competitive firm given price and output data. The market supply curve for the industry is the sum of all supply curves for individual firms.

This chapter also discusses what happens to competitive firms in the long run as equilibrium conditions change. Over time, new firms will enter an industry that is making economic profits and existing firms will exit an industry that is experiencing economic losses, changing price and output in the industry. Here you will learn that the shape of the ***long-run supply curve*** is directly affected by whether the industry is one characterized by constant costs, increasing costs, or decreasing costs as output increases.

In the long run, pure competition produces almost ideal conditions for ***economic efficiency.*** These ideal conditions and their qualifications are discussed in detail near the end of the chapter. Pure competition produces products in the least costly way, and thus it is ***productively efficient.*** Pure competition also allocates resources to firms so that they produce the products most wanted by society, and therefore it is ***allocatively efficient.*** You will find out that these two efficiency conditions can be expressed in the triple equality: Price (and marginal revenue) = marginal cost = minimum of average total cost.

You must understand the purely competitive model because it is the efficiency standard or norm for evaluating different market structures. You will be using it often for comparison with the monopoly model presented in Chapter 24 and with the oligopoly and monopolistically competitive models described in Chapter 25.

■ CHECKLIST

When you have studied this chapter you should be able to

☐ List the five characteristics of each of the four basic market models.
☐ Give examples of industries that reflect the characteristics of the four basic market models.
☐ Describe the major features of pure competition.
☐ Explain why a purely competitive firm is a price taker.
☐ Describe the firm's view of the demand for its product and the marginal revenue from the sale of additional units.
☐ Compute average, total, and marginal revenue when you are given the demand schedule faced by a purely competitive firm.
☐ Use the total-revenue and total-cost approach to determine the output that a purely competitive firm will produce in the short run in the profit maximizing case, and explain why the firm will produce this output.
☐ Use the marginal-revenue and marginal-cost approach to determine the output that a purely competitive firm will produce in the short run under three different conditions, and explain why the firm will produce this output.
☐ Find the firm's short-run supply curve when you are given the firm's short-run cost schedules.
☐ Explain the links among the law of diminishing returns, production costs, and product supply in the short run.
☐ Graph a shift in the firm's short-run supply curve and cite factors that cause the curve to increase or decrease.
☐ Find the industry's short-run supply curve (or schedule) when you are given the typical firm's short-run cost schedules.
☐ Determine, under short-run conditions, the price at which the product will sell, the output of the industry, and the output of the individual firm.

☐ Describe the basic goal for long-run adjustments in pure competition.
☐ Determine, under long-run conditions, the price at which the product will sell, the output of the firm, and the output of the industry.
☐ Explain the role played by the entry and exit of firms in a purely competitive industry in achieving equilibrium in the long run.
☐ Describe the characteristics and rationale for the long-run supply curve in a constant-cost industry, in an increasing-cost industry, and in a decreasing-cost industry.
☐ Distinguish between productive and allocative efficiency.
☐ Explain the significance of MR (= *P*) = MC = minimum ATC.
☐ Discuss how pure competition makes dynamic adjustments.
☐ Identify four potential barriers to achieving allocative and productive efficiency in a competitive market.

■ CHAPTER OUTLINE

1. The ***price*** a firm charges for the good or service it produces and its ***output*** of that product depend not only on the demand for and the cost of producing it but on the character (or structure) of the market (industry) in which it sells the product.

2. The models of the markets in which firms sell their products are pure competition, pure monopoly, monopolistic competition, and oligopoly. These four models are defined in terms of the number of firms in the industry, whether the product they sell is standardized or differentiated, and how easy it is for new firms to enter the industry.

3. This chapter examines pure competition, in which a large number of independent firms, no one of which is able by itself to influence market price, sell a standardized product in a market where firms are free to enter and to leave in the long run. Although pure competition is rare in practice, it is the standard against which the *efficiency* of the economy and other market models can be compared.

4. A firm selling its product in a purely competitive industry cannot influence the price at which the product sells and is a price taker.

a. The demand for its product is *perfectly price elastic.*
b. Average revenue (or price) and marginal revenue are equal and constant at the fixed (equilibrium) market price, and total revenue increases at a constant rate as the firm increases its output.
c. The demand (average revenue) and marginal revenue curves faced by the firm are horizontal and identical at the market price.
d. The total revenue curve has a constant positive slope.

5. The purely competitive firm operating in the short run is a price taker that can maximize profits (or minimize losses) only by changing its level of output. Two ways are used to determine the optimal output for the firm.

a. The ***total revenue–total cost approach*** to profit maximization sets the level of output at that quantity where the difference between total revenue minus total cost is greatest.
b. The ***marginal revenue–marginal cost approach*** to profit maximization basically sets the level of output at the quantity where marginal revenue (or price) equals marginal cost. There are three possible cases to consider when using this approach.
(1) The firm will **maximize profits** when MR = MC at an output level where price is greater than average total cost.
(2) The firm will **minimize losses** when MR = MC at an output level where price is greater than the minimum of average variable cost (but less than average total cost).
(3) The firm will **shut down** when MR = MC at an output level where price is less than average variable cost.

6. There are a number of relationships between marginal cost and the supply curve for the purely competitive firm and industry.

a. The *short-run supply curve* for the purely competitive firm is the portion of the marginal-cost curve that lies above average variable cost.
b. There are links among the law of diminishing returns, production costs, and product supply. The law of diminishing returns suggests that marginal costs will increase as output expands. The firm must receive more revenue (get higher prices for its product) if it is to expand output.
c. Changes in variable inputs will change the marginal-cost or supply curve for the purely competitive firm. For example, an improvement in technology that increases productivity will decrease the marginal cost curve (shift it downward).
d. The short-run supply curve of the industry (which is the sum of the supply curves of the individual firms) and the total demand for the product determine the short-run equilibrium price and equilibrium output of the industry. Firms in the industry may be either prosperous or unprosperous in the short run.

7. In the *long run,* the price of a product produced under conditions of pure competition will equal the minimum average total cost, and firms in the industry will neither earn economic profits nor suffer economic losses.

a. If economic profits are being received in the industry in the short run, firms will enter the industry in the long run (attracted by the profits), increase total supply, and thereby force price down to the minimum average total cost, leaving only a normal profit.
b. If losses are being suffered in the industry in the short run, firms will leave the industry in the long run (seeking to avoid losses), reduce total supply, and thereby force price up to the minimum average total cost, leaving only a normal profit.

c. If an industry is a ***constant-cost industry,*** the entry of new firms will not affect the average-total-cost schedules or curves of firms in the industry.
(1) An increase in demand will result in no increase in the long-run equilibrium price, and the industry will be able to supply larger outputs at a constant price.
(2) Graphically, the long-run supply curve in a constant-cost industry is horizontal at the minimum of the average-total-cost curve, indicating that firms make only normal profits, but not economic profits.

d. If an industry is an ***increasing-cost industry,*** the entry of new firms will raise the average-total-cost schedules or curves of firms in the industry.
(1) An increase in demand will result in an increase in the long-run equilibrium price, and the industry will be able to supply larger outputs only at higher prices.
(2) Graphically, the long-run supply curve in an increasing-cost industry is upsloping at the minimum of the average-total-cost curve, indicating that firms make only normal profits but not economic profits.

e. If an industry is a ***decreasing-cost industry,*** the entry of new firms will lower the average-total-cost schedules or curves of firms in the industry.
(1) An increase in demand will result in a decrease in the long-run equilibrium price, and the industry will be able to supply larger outputs only at lower prices.
(2) Graphically, the long-run supply curve in a decreasing-cost industry is downsloping at the minimum of the average-total-cost curve, indicating that firms make only normal profits, but not economic profits.

8. In the long run, each purely competitive firm is compelled by competition to produce that output at a price at which marginal revenue, average cost, and marginal cost are equal and average cost is a minimum.

a. An economy in which all industries were purely competitive would use its resources efficiently.
(1) Goods are **efficiently produced** when the average total cost of producing them is at a minimum; buyers benefit most from this efficiency when they are charged a price just equal to minimum average total cost.
(2) Resources are **efficiently allocated** when goods are produced in such quantities that the total satisfaction obtained from the economy's resources is at a maximum or when the price of each good is equal to its marginal cost.

b. Even in a purely competitive economy, the allocation of resources may not, for at least four reasons, be the most efficient.
(1) Spillover costs and benefits and the production of public goods may not be taken into account in the allocation of resources in the competitive market model.
(2) There may be economies of scale that make production by a large number of small firms less productively efficient than production by a few large-scale firms.
(3) The rate of technological advance may be slower and use of the best-known productive techniques may be less widespread in purely competitive industries.
(4) The range of consumer choice and the development of new products may be restricted in a purely competitive economy.

■ HINTS AND TIPS

1. The purely competitive model is extremely important for you to master even if examples of it in the real world are rare. The model is the standard against which the other market models—pure monopoly, monopolistic competition, and oligopoly—will be compared for effects on economic efficiency. Spend extra time learning the material in this chapter so you can make model comparisons in later chapters.

2. Make sure that you understand why a purely competitive firm is a price "taker" and not a price "maker." The purely competitive firm has no influence over the price of its product and can only make decisions about the level of output.

3. Construct a table for explaining how the purely competitive firm maximizes profits or minimizes losses in the short run. Ask yourself the three questions in the table: (1) Should the firm produce? (2) What quantity should be produced to maximize profits? (3) Will production result in economic profit? Answer the questions using a marginal-revenue–marginal-cost approach. Check your answers against those presented in the text.

4. The average purely competitive firm in long-run equilibrium will not make economic profits. Find out why by following the graphical analysis in Figures 23-8 and 23-9.

5. The triple equality of MR (= ***P***) = MC = minimum ATC is the most important equation in the chapter because it allows you to judge the allocative and productive efficiency of a purely competitive economy. Check your understanding of this triple equality by explaining what happens to productive efficiency when ***P*** > minimum ATC, or to allocative efficiency when ***P*** < MC or ***P*** > MC.

■ IMPORTANT TERMS

pure competition
pure monopoly
monopolistic competition
oligopoly
imperfect competition
price taker
total revenue
average revenue
marginal revenue
break-even point
short-run supply curve
long-run supply curve
constant-cost industry
increasing-cost industry
decreasing-cost industry
productive efficiency
allocative efficiency

SELF-TEST

■ FILL-IN QUESTIONS

1. The four market models examined in this and the next three chapters are

a. ______________________

b. ______________________

c. ______

d. ______

2. The four market models differ in terms of the (size, number) ______ of firms in the industry, whether the product is (a consumer good, standardized) ______ or (a producer good, differentiated) ______, and how easy or difficult it is for new firms to (enter, leave) ______ the industry.

3. What are the four specific conditions which characterize pure competition?

a. ______

b. ______

c. ______

d. ______

4. The individual firm in a purely competitive industry is a price (maker, taker) ______ and finds that the demand for its product is perfectly (elastic, inelastic) ______.

5. The firm's demand schedule is also a (cost, revenue) ______ schedule. The price per unit to the seller is (marginal, total, average) ______ revenue, price multiplied by the quantity the firm can sell is ______ revenue, and the extra revenue that results from selling one more unit of output is ______ revenue.

6. In pure competition, product price (rises, falls, is constant) ______ as an individual firm's output increases. Marginal revenue is (less than, greater than, equal to) ______ product price.

7. Economic profit is total revenue (plus, minus) ______ total cost. If the firm is making only a normal profit, total revenue is (greater than, equal to) ______ total cost. In the latter case, this output level is called the (profit, break-even) ______ point by economists.

8. If a purely competitive firm produces any output at all, it will produce that output at which its profit is a (maximum, minimum) ______ or its loss is a ______. Or, said another way, the output at which marginal cost is (equal to, greater than) ______ marginal revenue.

9. A firm will be willing to produce at an economic loss in the short run if the price which it receives is greater than its average (fixed, variable, total) ______ cost.

10. In the short run, the individual firm's supply curve in pure competition is that portion of the firm's (total, marginal) ______ cost curve which lies (above, below) ______ the average variable cost curve.

11. The short-run market supply curve is the (average, sum) ______ of the (short-run, long-run) ______ supply curves of all firms in the industry.

12. In the short run in a purely competitive industry, the equilibrium price is the price at which quantity demanded is equal to (average cost, quantity supplied) ______, and the equilibrium quantity is the quantity demanded and ______ at the equilibrium price.

13. In a purely competitive industry, in the short run the number of firms in the industry and the sizes of their plants are (fixed, variable) ______, but in the long run they are ______.

14. When a purely competitive industry is in long-run equilibrium, the price which the firm is paid for its product is equal to (total, average, marginal) ______ revenue, and to long-run ______ cost. In this case, the long-run average cost is a (maximum, minimum) ______.

15. An industry will be in long-run equilibrium when firms are earning (normal, economic) ______ profits, but firms tend to enter an industry if the firms in the industry are earning ______ profits. Firms will tend to leave an industry when they are realizing economic (profits, losses) ______.

16. If the entry of new firms into an industry tends to raise the costs of all firms in the industry, the industry is said to be a(n) (constant-, increasing-, decreasing-) ______ cost industry. Its long-run supply curve is (horizontal, downsloping, upsloping) ______.

17. If the entry of new firms into an industry tends to lower costs of all firms in the industry, the industry is said to be a(n) (constant-, increasing-, decreasing-) ______ cost industry. Its long-run supply curve is (horizontal, downsloping, upsloping) ______.

18. The purely competitive economy achieves productive efficiency in the long run because price and (total, average) ______ cost are equal and the latter is a (maximum, minimum) ______.

19. In the long run the purely competitive economy is allocatively efficient because price and (total, marginal) _______________ cost are equal.

20. List four reasons why conclusions about the productive and allocative efficiency of a purely competitive market system need to be qualified.

a. ____

b. ____

c. ____

d. ____

■ TRUE-FALSE QUESTIONS

Circle the T if the statement is true, the F if it is false.

1. The structures of the markets in which business firms sell their products in the U.S. economy are very similar. **T F**

2. A large number of sellers does not necessarily mean that the industry is purely competitive. **T F**

3. Only in a purely competitive industry do individual firms have no control over the price of their product. **T F**

4. Imperfectly competitive markets are defined as all markets except those which are purely competitive. **T F**

5. One reason for studying the pure competition model is that many industries are almost purely competitive. **T F**

6. The purely competitive firm views an average revenue schedule as identical to its marginal revenue schedule. **T F**

7. The demand curves for firms in a purely competitive industry are perfectly inelastic. **T F**

8. Under purely competitive conditions, the product price charged by the firm increases as output increases. **T F**

9. The purely competitive firm can maximize its economic profit (or minimize its loss) only by adjusting its output. **T F**

10. Economic profit is the difference between total revenue and average revenue. **T F**

11. The break-even point means that the firm is realizing normal profits, but not economic profits. **T F**

12. A purely competitive firm that wishes to produce and not close down will maximize profits or minimize losses at that output at which marginal costs and marginal revenue are equal. **T F**

13. Assuming that the purely competitive firm chooses to produce and not close down, to maximize profits or minimize losses it should produce at that point where price equals average cost. **T F**

14. If a purely competitive firm is producing output less than its profit-maximizing output, marginal revenue is greater than marginal cost. **T F**

15. If at the profit-maximizing level of output for the purely competitive firm price exceeds the minimum average variable cost but is less than average total cost, the firm will make profit. **T F**

16. A purely competitive firm will produce in the short run the output at which marginal cost and marginal revenue are equal provided that the price of the product is greater than its average variable cost of production. **T F**

17. The short-run supply curve of a purely competitive firm tends to slope upward from left to right because of the law of diminishing returns. **T F**

18. The long-run supply curve for a competitive, increasing-cost industry is upwardsloping. **T F**

19. When firms in a purely competitive industry are earning profits which are less than normal, the supply of the product will tend to decrease in the long run. **T F**

20. If a purely competitive firm is in short-run equilibrium and its marginal cost is greater than its average total cost, firms will leave the industry in the long run. **T F**

21. Pure competition, if it could be achieved in all industries in the economy, would result in the most efficient allocation of resources. **T F**

22. Under conditions of pure competition, firms are forced to employ the most efficient production methods available to survive. **T F**

23. The marginal costs of producing a product are society's measure of the marginal worth of alternative products. **T F**

24. In a purely competitive market, product price measures the marginal benefit, or additional satisfaction, which society obtains from producing additional units of the product. **T F**

25. The production of goods that results in external benefits tends to be overproduced in a purely competitive economy. **T F**

■ MULTIPLE-CHOICE QUESTIONS

Circle the letter that corresponds to the best answer.

1. For which market model is there a very large number of firms?

(a) monopolistic competition
(b) oligopoly
(c) pure monopoly
(d) pure competition

2. In which of the following market models is the individual seller of a product a price taker?

(a) pure competition
(b) pure monopoly
(c) monopolistic competition
(d) oligopoly

3. Which of the following industries comes *closest* to being purely competitive?
(a) wheat
(b) shoes
(c) electricity
(d) automobile

4. In a purely competitive industry,
(a) each existing firm will engage in various forms of nonprice competition
(b) new firms are free to enter and existing firms are able to leave the industry very easily
(c) individual firms have a price policy
(d) each firm produces a differentiated (nonstandardized) product

5. The demand schedule or curve confronted by the individual purely competitive firm is
(a) perfectly inelastic
(b) inelastic but not perfectly inelastic
(c) perfectly elastic
(d) elastic but not perfectly elastic

6. Total revenue for producing 10 units of output is $6. Total revenue for producing 11 units of output is $8. Given this information, the
(a) average revenue for producing 11 units is $2.
(b) average revenue for producing 11 units is $8.
(c) marginal revenue for producing the 11th unit is $2.
(d) marginal revenue for producing the 11th unit is $8.

7. In pure competition, product price is
(a) greater than marginal revenue
(b) equal to marginal revenue
(c) equal to total revenue
(d) greater than total revenue

8. The individual firm's short-run supply curve is that part of its marginal-cost curve lying above its
(a) average total-cost curve
(b) average variable-cost curve
(c) average fixed-cost curve
(d) average revenue curve

9. Which statement is true of a purely competitive industry in short-run equilibrium?
(a) Price is equal to average total cost.
(b) Total quantity demanded is equal to total quantity supplied.
(c) Profits in the industry are equal to zero.
(d) Output is equal to the output at which average total cost is a minimum.

10. Suppose that when 2000 units of output are produced, the marginal cost of the 2001st unit is $5. This amount is equal to the minimum of average total cost, and marginal cost is rising. If the optimal level of output in the short run is 2500 units, then at that level,
(a) marginal cost is greater than $5 and marginal cost is less than average total cost
(b) marginal cost is greater than $5 and marginal cost is greater than average total cost
(c) marginal cost is less than $5 and marginal cost is greater than average total cost
(d) marginal cost is equal to $5 and marginal cost is equal to average total cost

11. The Zebra, Inc., is selling in a purely competitive market. Its output is 250 units, which sell for $2 each. At this level of output, marginal cost is $2 and average variable cost is $2.25. The firm should
(a) produce zero units of output
(b) decrease output to 200 units
(c) continue to produce 250 units
(d) increase output to maximize profits

Questions 12, 13, 14, and 15 are based on the following graph.

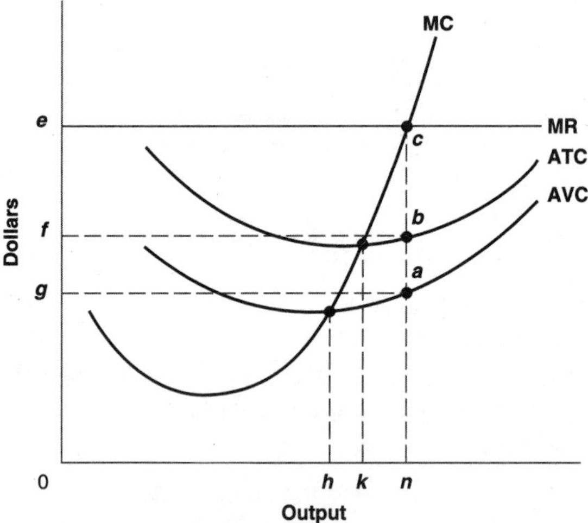

12. If the firm is producing at output level 0***n***, the rectangular area ***fecb*** is
(a) total variable cost
(b) total fixed costs
(c) total revenue
(d) total economic profit

13. At the profit-maximizing output, average fixed cost is
(a) ***ab***
(b) ***ac***
(c) ***na***
(d) ***nb***

14. At the profit-maximizing output, the total variable costs are equal to the area
(a) 0***fbn***
(b) 0***ecn***
(c) 0***gan***
(d) ***gfba***

15. The demand curve for this firm is equal to
(a) **MR**, and the supply curve is the portion of the **MC** curve where output is greater than level ***n***
(b) **MR**, and the supply curve is the portion of the **MC** curve where output is greater than level ***k***
(c) **MR**, and the supply curve is the portion of the **MC** curve where output is greater than level ***h***
(d) **MR**, and the supply curve is the portion of the **ATC** curve where output is greater than level ***k***

Answer Questions 16, 17, 18, 19, and 20 on the basis of the following cost data for a firm that is selling in a purely competitive market.

Output	AFC	AVC	ATC	MC
1	$300	$100	$400	$100
2	150	75	225	50
3	100	70	170	60
4	75	73	148	80
5	60	80	140	110
6	50	90	140	140
7	43	103	146	180
8	38	119	156	230
9	33	138	171	290
10	30	160	190	360

16. If the market price for the firm's product is $140, the competitive firm will produce
(a) 5 units at an economic loss of $150
(b) 6 units and break even
(c) 7 units and break even
(d) 8 units at an economic profit of $74

17. If the market price for the firm's product is $290, the competitive firm will produce
(a) 7 units at an economic profit of $238
(b) 8 units at an economic profit of $592
(c) 9 units at an economic profit of $1071
(d) 10 units at an economic profit of $1700

18. If the product price is $179, the *per unit* economic profit at the profit-maximizing output is
(a) $15
(b) $23
(c) $33
(d) $39

19. The total fixed costs are
(a) $100
(b) $200
(c) $300
(d) $400

Assume there are 100 identical firms in this industry and total or market demand is as shown.

Price	Quantity demanded
$360	600
290	700
230	800
180	900
140	1000
110	1100
80	1200

20. The equilibrium price will be
(a) $140
(b) $180
(c) $230
(d) $290

21. Assume that the market for wheat is purely competitive. Currently, firms growing wheat are experiencing economic losses. In the long run, we can expect this market's
(a) supply curve to increase
(b) demand curve to increase
(c) supply curve to decrease
(d) demand curve to decrease

22. The long-run supply curve under pure competition will be
(a) downsloping in an increasing-cost industry and upsloping in a decreasing-cost industry
(b) horizontal in a constant-cost industry and upsloping in a decreasing-cost industry
(c) horizontal in a constant-cost industry and upsloping in an increasing-cost industry
(d) upsloping in an increasing-cost industry and vertical in a constant-cost industry

23. The long-run supply curve in a constant-cost industry will be
(a) perfectly elastic
(b) perfectly inelastic
(c) unit elastic
(d) income elastic

24. In a decreasing-cost industry, the long-run
(a) demand curve would be perfectly inelastic
(b) demand curve would be perfectly elastic
(c) supply curve would be upsloping
(d) supply curve would be downsloping

25. Increasing-cost industries find that their costs rise as a consequence of an increased demand for the product because of
(a) the diseconomies of scale
(b) diminishing returns
(c) higher resource prices
(d) a decreased supply of the product

26. When a purely competitive industry is in long-run equilibrium, which statement is true?
(a) Firms in the industry are earning normal profits.
(b) Price and long-run average total cost are not equal to each other.
(c) Marginal cost is at its minimum level.
(d) Marginal cost is equal to total revenue.

27. It is contended that which of the following triple identities results in the most efficient use of resources?
(a) $P =$ MC = minimum ATC
(b) $P =$ AR = MR
(c) $P =$ MR = minimum MC
(d) TR = MC = MR

28. An economy is producing the goods most wanted by society when, for each and every good, its
(a) price and average cost are equal
(b) price and marginal cost are equal
(c) marginal revenue and marginal cost are equal
(d) price and marginal revenue are equal

29. The marginal costs and prices of a purely competitive market system accurately measure
(a) both spillover costs and spillover benefits
(b) spillover costs but not spillover benefits
(c) spillover benefits but not spillover costs
(d) neither spillover costs nor spillover benefits

30. In an economy where markets are purely competitive and there is no government sector,
(a) public goods will be underproduced
(b) scarce resources will be underallocated in all markets
(c) goods which entail spillover costs will be underproduced
(d) goods which entail spillover benefits will not be produced at all

■ PROBLEMS

1. Using the following set of terms, complete the following table by inserting the appropriate letter or letters in the blanks.

a. one
b. few
c. many
d. a very large number
e. standardized
f. differentiated
g. some
h. considerable
i. very easy
j. blocked
k. fairly easy
l. fairly difficult
m. none
n. unique

	Market model			
Market characteristics	**Pure competition**	**Pure monopoly**	**Monopolistic competition**	**Oligopoly**
Number of firms	____	____	____	____
Type of product	____	____	____	____
Control over price	____	____	____	____
Conditions of entry	____	____	____	____
Nonprice competition	____	____	____	____

2. Following is the demand schedule facing the individual firm.

Price	Quantity demanded	Average revenue	Total revenue	Marginal revenue
$10	0	$____	$____	—
10	1	____	____	$____
10	2	____	____	____
10	3	____	____	____
10	4	____	____	____
10	5	____	____	____
10	6	____	____	____

a. Complete the table by computing average revenue, total revenue, and marginal revenue.
b. Is this firm operating in a market which is purely competitive? ____________ How can you tell?

____

c. The coefficient of the price elasticity of demand is the same between every pair of quantities demanded. What is it? ____________

d. What relationship exists between average revenue and marginal revenue? ____________________

____

e. On the first graph on page 263, plot the demand schedule, average revenue, total revenue, and marginal revenue; label each curve.
f. The demand, average-revenue, and marginal-revenue curves are all ____________ lines at a price of $____________ across all quantities.
g. The total-revenue curve is an upsloping line with a ____________ slope because marginal revenue is ____________.

3. Assume that a purely competitive firm has the following schedule of costs.

Output	TFC	TVC	TC
0	$300	$ 0	$300
1	300	100	400
2	300	150	450
3	300	210	510
4	300	290	590
5	300	400	700
6	300	540	840
7	300	720	1020
8	300	950	1250
9	300	1240	1540
10	300	1600	1900

a. Complete the following table to show the total revenue and total profit of the firm at each level of output the firm might produce. Assume the market price is $200.

	Market price = $200	
Output	**Revenue**	**Profit**
0	$____	$____
1	____	____
2	____	____
3	____	____
4	____	____
5	____	____
6	____	____
7	____	____
8	____	____
9	____	____
10	____	____

b. Indicate what output the firm would produce and what its profits would be at a price of $200, output of ____________, and profit of ____________.
c. Plot the cost data for total variable cost and total cost on the second graph on page 263. Then plot the total revenue when the price is $200. For this price, indicate the level of output and the economic profit or loss on the graph.

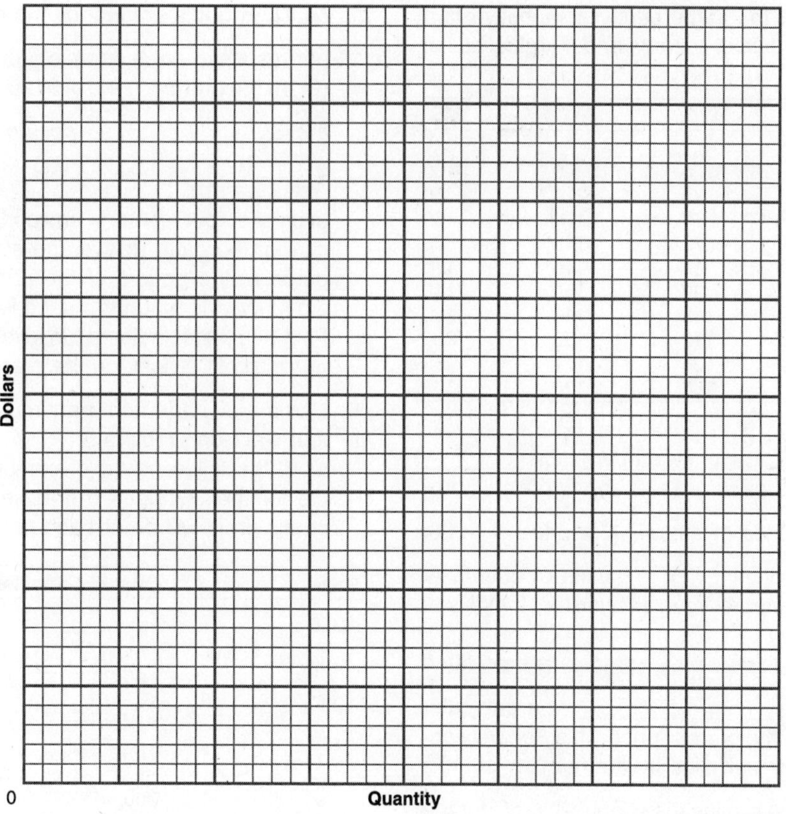
Dollars
0
Quantity

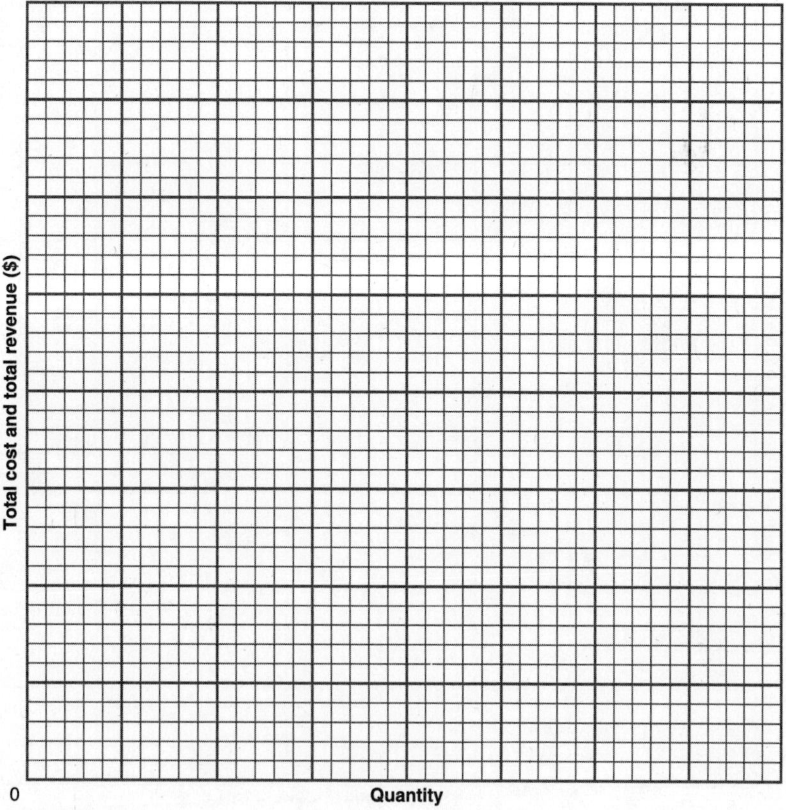
Total cost and total revenue ($)
0
Quantity

4. Now assume that the same purely competitive firm has the following schedule of average and marginal costs:

Output	AFC	AVC	ATC	MC
0				
1	$300	$100	$400	$100
2	150	75	225	50
3	100	70	170	60
4	75	73	148	80
5	60	80	140	110
6	50	90	140	140
7	43	103	146	180
8	38	119	156	230
9	33	138	171	290
10	30	160	190	360

a. At a price of $55, the firm would produce ________ units of output. At a price of $120, the firm would produce ________ units of output. At a price of $200, the firm would produce ________ units of output. At the $200 price compare your answers to those you gave in problem 3.

b. The *per unit* economic profit (or loss) is calculated by subtracting ________________ at a particular level of output from the product price. This *per unit* economic profit is then multiplied by the number of units of ________ to determine the economic profit for the competitive firm.

(1) At the product price of $200, the average total costs are $______, so *per unit* economic profit is $______. Multiplying this amount by the number of units of output results in an economic profit of $________.

(2) At the product price of $120, the average total costs are $__________, so *per unit* economic losses are $________. Multiplying this amount by the number of units of output results in an economic loss of $_______.

c. Plot the data for average and marginal cost in the graph at the bottom of the page. Then plot the marginal revenue when the price is $55, $120, and $200. For each price, indicate the level of output and the economic profit or loss on the graph.

5. Use the average and marginal cost data in problem 4 in your work on problem 5.

a. In the following table, complete the supply schedule for the competitive firm and state what the economic profit will be at each price.

Price	Quantity supplied	Profit
$360	____	$____
290	____	____
230	____	____
180	____	____
140	____	____
110	____	____
80	____	____
60	____	____

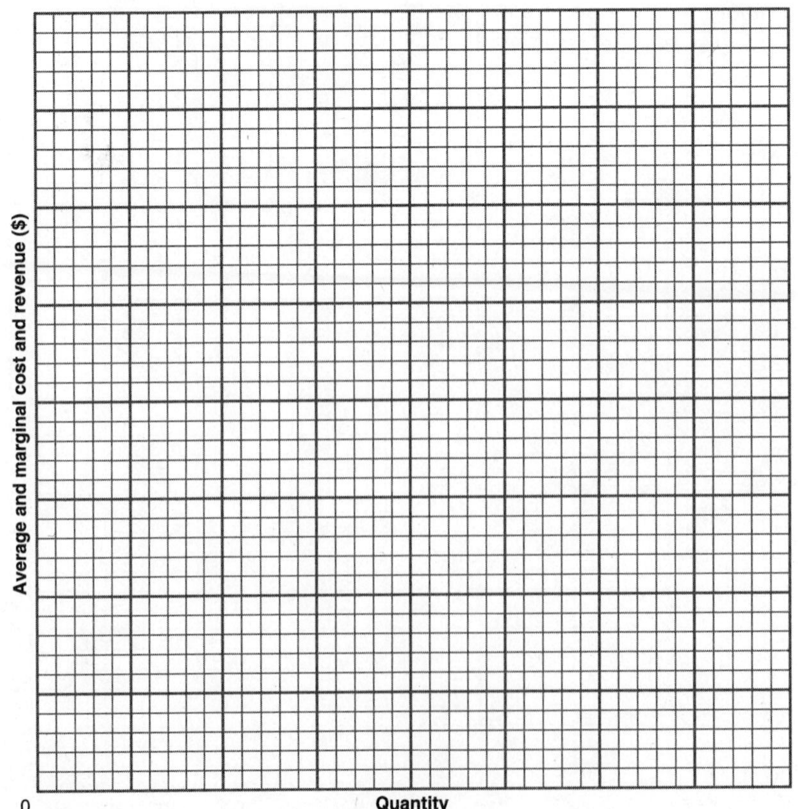

b. If there are 100 firms in the industry and all have the same cost schedule,

(1) complete the market supply schedule in the following table.

Quantity demanded	Price	Quantity supplied
400	$360	____
500	290	____
600	230	____
700	180	____
800	140	____
900	110	____
1,000	80	____

(2) Using the demand schedule given in (1):

(*a*) What will the market price of the product be? $________

(*b*) What quantity will the individual firm produce? ________

(*c*) How large will the firm's profit be? $________

(*d*) Will firms tend to enter or leave the industry in the long run? ________ Why? ________

____

____

6. If the average total costs assumed for the individual firm in problem 4 were long-run average total costs and if the industry were a constant-cost industry,

a. what would be the market price of the product in the long run? $________

b. what output would each firm produce when the industry was in long-run equilibrium? ________

c. approximately how many firms would there be in the industry in the long run, given the present demand for the product as shown in the table in **5b**? ________

____

d. if the following table were the market demand schedule for the product, how many firms would there be in the long run in the industry? ________

Price	Quantity demanded
$360	500
290	600
230	700
180	800
140	900
110	1,000
80	1,100

7. On the following graph, draw a long-run supply curve of

a. a constant-cost industry

b. an increasing-cost industry

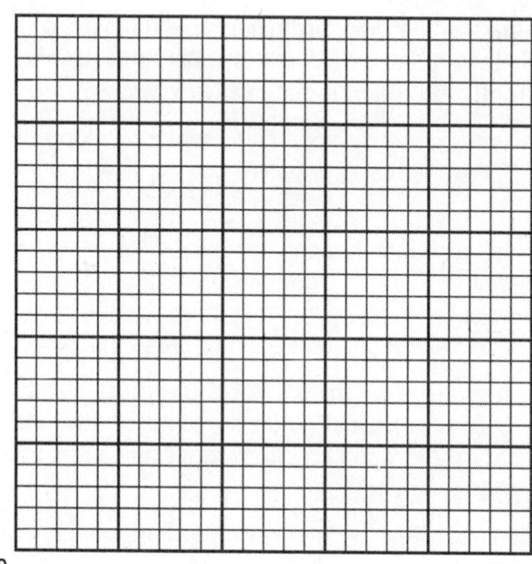

■ SHORT ANSWER AND ESSAY QUESTIONS

1. What are the four market models (or situations) which economists employ, and what are the major characteristics of each type of market?

2. Describe in detail four characteristics of pure competition.

3. If pure competition is so rare in practice, why are students of economics asked to study it?

4. Explain how the firm in a purely competitive industry sees the demand for the product it produces in terms of the

(a) price elasticity of demand,

(b) relationship of average to marginal revenue, and

(c) behavior of total, average, and marginal revenues as the output of the firm increases.

5. Describe the total-revenue–total-cost approach to profit maximization.

6. Compare and contrast the total-revenue–total-cost approach with the marginal-revenue–marginal-cost approach to profit maximization. Are the two approaches consistent?

7. Explain the MR = MC rule and its three characteristics.

8. Why does the purely competitive firm want to maximize total profit but not its per unit profit?

9. Why is a firm willing to produce at a loss in the short run if the loss is no greater than the fixed costs of the firm?

10. Explain how the short-run supply of an individual firm and of the purely competitive industry are determined.

11. What determines the equilibrium price and output of a purely competitive industry in the short run? Will economic profits in the industry be positive or negative?

12. Why do the MC = MR rule and MC = ***P*** rule mean the same thing under conditions of pure competition?

13. What are the important distinctions between the short run and the long run and between equilibrium in the short run and in the long run in a competitive industry?

14. When is the purely competitive industry in long-run equilibrium? What forces the purely competitive firm into this position?

15. What is a constant-cost industry? What is an increasing-cost industry? Under what economic conditions is each likely to be found? What will be the nature of the long-run supply curve in each of these industries?

16. When has an economy achieved the most efficient use of its scarce resources? What two kinds of efficiency are necessary if the economy is to make the most efficient use of its resources?

17. Why is it said that a purely competitive economy is an efficient economy?

18. What did Adam Smith mean when he said that self-interest and competition bring about results which are in the best interest of the economy as a whole without government regulation or interference?

19. Even if an economy is purely competitive, the allocation of resources may not be ideal. Why?

20. Does pure competition *always* promote both the use of the most efficient technological methods of production and the development of better methods?

ANSWERS

Chapter 23 Pure Competition

FILL-IN QUESTIONS

1. *a.* pure competition; *b.* pure monopoly; *c.* monopolistic competition; *d.* oligopoly (any order a–d)
2. number, standardized, differentiated, enter
3. *a.* a large number of sellers; *b.* a standardized product; *c.* firms are price takers, not price makers; *d.* free entry and exit of firms
4. taker, elastic
5. revenue, average, total, marginal
6. is constant, equal to
7. minus, equal to, break-even
8. maximum, minimum, equal to
9. variable
10. marginal, above
11. sum, short-run
12. quantity supplied, quantity supplied
13. fixed, variable
14. average, average, minimum
15. normal, economic, losses
16. increasing-, upsloping
17. decreasing-, downsloping
18. average, minimum
19. marginal
20. *a.* The system does not accurately measure spillover costs and benefits or provide public goods; *b.* It does not entail the use of the most efficient productive techniques; *c.* It may limit large-scale production to achieve economies of scale; *d.* It may not provide a range of product choice for consumers

TRUE-FALSE QUESTIONS

1. F, p. 467
2. T, pp. 467-468
3. T, p. 468
4. T, p. 468
5. F, p. 469
6. T, pp. 470-471
7. F, p. 469
8. F, p. 471
9. T, p. 471
10. F, p. 471
11. T, p. 472
12. T, pp. 473-474
13. F, p. 474
14. T, pp. 474-476
15. F, p. 478
16. T, p. 479
17. T, p. 480
18. T, pp. 484-485
19. T, p. 482
20. F, p. 482
21. T, pp. 485-488
22. T, p. 487
23. T, p. 487
24. T, p. 487
25. F, p. 489

MULTIPLE-CHOICE QUESTIONS

1. d, p. 468
2. a, p. 469
3. a, p. 469
4. b, pp. 468-469
5. c, pp. 469-470
6. c, pp. 470-471
7. b, p. 471
8. b, p. 478
9. b, p. 480
10. b, p. 475
11. a, pp. 476-477
12. d, pp. 475-476
13. a, pp. 475-476
14. c, p. 476
15. c, pp. 471, 476-477
16. b, pp. 472-475
17. c, pp. 472-475
18. d, pp. 472-475
19. c, pp. 472, 474
20. c, pp. 474, 480
21. c, p. 483
22. c, pp. 484-485
23. a, p. 484
24. d, p. 485
25. c, pp. 484-485
26. a, p. 482
27. a, pp. 485-486
28. b, p. 487
29. d, p. 489
30. a, pp. 489-490

PROBLEMS

1. Number of firms: d, a, c, b; Type of product: e, n, f, e, or f; Control over price: m, h, g, g; Conditions of entry: i, j, k, l; Nonprice competition: m, g, h, g, or h
2. *a.* Average revenue: all are \$10.00; Total revenue: \$0, 10.00, 20.00, 30.00, 40.00, 50.00, 60.00; Marginal revenue: all are \$10; *b.* yes, because price (average revenue) is constant and equal to marginal revenue; *c.* infinity; *d.* they are equal; *e.* see Figure 23-1 of the text for an example; *f.* horizontal, \$10; *g.* constant, constant
3. *a.* (see following table); *b.* 7, 380; *c.* see Figure 23-2 of the text for an example

	Market price = \$200	
Output	**Revenue**	**Profit**
0	0	\$−300
1	200	−200
2	400	−50
3	600	90
4	800	210
5	1,000	300
6	1,200	360
7	1,400	380
8	1,600	350
9	1,800	260
10	2,000	100

4. *a.* 0, 5, 7 (last answer is the same as 3b); *b.* average total cost, output; (1) \$146 (\$200 − \$146 = \$54), (\$54 × 7 = \$378); (2) \$140 (\$120 − \$140 = −\$20), (−\$20 × 5 = −\$100); *c.* see Figure 23-3 of the text for an example
5. *a.* see following table

Price	Quantity supplied	Profit
$360	10	$1,700
290	9	1,071
230	8	592
180	7	238
140	6	0
110	5	−150
80	4	−272
60	0	−300

b. (1) Quantity supplied: 1,000, 900, 800, 700, 600, 500, 400; (2) (*a*) 180, (*b*) 7, (*c*) 238, (*d*) enter, profits in the industry will attract them into the industry

6. *a.* 140; *b.* 6; *c.* 133 = 800 [the total quantity demanded at $140 divided by 6 (the output of each firm)]; *d.* 150 = 900 divided by 6

7. *a.* The curve is a horizontal line (see Figure 23-10 in the text); *b.* the curve slopes upward (see Figure 23-11 in the text)

SHORT ANSWER AND ESSAY QUESTIONS

1. pp. 467-468
2. pp. 467-468
3. p. 469
4. pp. 469-471
5. pp. 471-472
6. pp. 471-474
7. pp. 473-474
8. p. 474
9. pp. 476-477
10. pp. 478, 480-481
11. p. 480
12. p. 474
13. pp. 481-484
14. pp. 482-484
15. p. 484-485
16. pp. 485-486
17. pp. 487-488
18. p. 488
19. pp. 489-490
20. p. 490

CHAPTER 24

Pure Monopoly

Chapter 23 discussed pure competition, a market structure in which there are a very large number of sellers. This chapter looks at the other end of the spectrum and examines ***pure monopoly,*** a market structure in which there is a *single seller.* Like pure competition, pure monopoly is rarely found in the U.S. economy. Nevertheless, important industries such as those providing utilities (electricity, cable television, or local telephone service) are close to being pure monopolies, and they play a key role in the allocation of resources and the production of goods and services in the economy.

It is possible for a single seller or pure monopolist to dominate an industry if firms are prevented in some way from entering the industry. Factors that restrict firms from entering an industry are referred to as ***barriers to entry.*** The second part of this chapter is devoted to a description of the more important types of these barriers, such as economies of scale, patents and licenses, control of essential resources, and strategies for product pricing. Remember that barriers to entry not only make it possible for monopoly to exist in the economy, but they also explain why so many markets are oligopolies (the market structure you will study in the next chapter).

Like Chapter 23, this chapter answers certain questions about the firm: What output will the firm produce? What price will it charge? and What will be the profit received by the firm? In answering these questions for the monopoly firm and in comparing pure competition and pure monopoly, note the following:

1. Both the competitive and monopoly firm try to maximize profits by producing the output at which *marginal cost and marginal revenue are equal.*

2. The individual firm in a perfectly competitive industry sees a perfectly price elastic demand for its product at the going market price because it is but one of many firms in the industry, but the monopolist sees a market demand schedule which is less than perfectly price elastic because *the monopolist is the industry.* The former, therefore, has *only* an output policy and is a price taker, but the latter is able to determine the price at which it will sell its product and is a price maker.

3. When demand is perfectly price elastic, price is equal to marginal revenue and is constant, but when demand is less than perfectly price elastic, marginal revenue is less than price and both decrease as the output of the firm increases.

4. Because entry is blocked in the long run, firms cannot enter a monopolistic industry to compete away profits as they can under conditions of pure competition.

This chapter has three other goals that deserve your study time and careful attention. One goal is to evaluate ***economic efficiency*** under pure monopoly. Here the purely competitive industry that you read about in Chapter 23 serves as the standard for comparison. You will learn that unlike the purely competitive industry, pure monopoly does not result in allocative efficiency. Although the inefficiencies of monopoly are offset or reduced by economies of scale and technological progress, they are reinforced by the presence of X-inefficiency and rent-seeking expenditures.

The second goal is to discuss the possible *pricing strategies* of the pure monopolist. The monopolist may be able to set multiple prices for the same product even when the price differences are not justified by cost differences, a situation called ***price discrimination.*** This type of pricing power works only under certain conditions, and when it is effective it results in higher profits for the monopolist and also greater output.

The pricing power and ineffiency of the pure monpolist have made it a target for *government regulation.* Therefore, the last section of this chapter discusses the third goal, which is to explain the economic choices a regulatory agency faces when they must determine the maximum price that a public utility will be allowed to charge for its product. Here you will learn about the ***socially optimum price*** and the ***fair-return price*** and their effects on both allocative efficiency and profits. You will also discover the difficult economic dilemma regulatory officials face as they decide what prices they should permit a monopolist to charge.

■ CHECKLIST

When you have studied this chapter you should be able to

☐ Define pure monopoly based on five characteristics.
☐ Give several examples of monopoly and explain its importance.
☐ List and explain four potential barriers that would prevent or deter the entry of new firms into an industry.
☐ Define a natural monopoly using an average total-cost curve.
☐ Compare the demand curve for the pure monopolist with that of the purely competitive firm.

□ Compute marginal revenue when you are given the demand for the monopolist's product.
□ Explain the relationship between the price the monopolist charges and the marginal revenue from the sale of an additional unit of the product.
□ Explain why the monopolist is a price maker.
□ Use elasticity to identify the region of the demand curve where the monopolist produces, and give reasons for setting price and output in this region.
□ State the rule which explains what output the monopolist will produce and the price that will be charged.
□ Determine the profit-maximizing output and price for the pure monopolist when you are given the demand and cost data.
□ Explain why there is no supply curve for the pure monopolist.
□ Counter two popular misconceptions about the price charged and the profit target in pure monpoly.
□ Explain why monopolists can experience losses.
□ Compare the economic effects of pure monopoly in terms of price, output, productive efficiency, allocative efficiency, and the distribution of income with a purely competitive industry producing the same product.
□ Discuss the cost complications caused by economies of scale, X-inefficiency, rent-seeking behavior, and technological advance for pure monopoly and a purely competitive industry.
□ List three general policy options for dealing with the economic inefficiency of monopoly.
□ Define and give examples of price discrimination.
□ List three conditions that are necessary for price discrimination to exist.
□ Explain the economic consequences of price discrimination.
□ Use graphical analysis to identify the socially optimal price and the fair-return price for the regulated monopoly (public utility).
□ Explain the dilemma of regulation based on your graphical analysis of a regulated monopoly.

■ CHAPTER OUTLINE

1. Pure monopoly is a market structure in which a single firm sells a product for which there are no close substitutes. These characteristics make the monpoly firm a ***price maker*** rather than a price taker, as was the case for the purely competitive firm. Entry into the industry is blocked, and there can be nonprice competition through advertising to influence the demand for the product.
   a. Examples of monopolies typically include regulated public utilities such as firms providing electricity, natural gas, local telephone service, and cable television, but they can also be unregulated, such as the De Beers diamond syndicate.
   b. While monopoly is relatively *rare,* it is still important because monopoly firms account for about 5–6 percent of domestic output, and it is useful for understanding the economic effects of other market structures—oligopoly and monopolistic competition—where there is some degree of monopoly power.

2. Pure monopoly (and oligopoly) can exist in the long run only if potential competitors find there are *barriers* which prevent their entry into the industry.
   a. Four barriers that can prevent or restrict entry into an industry are
   (1) economies of scale, which makes one large firm the lowest cost producer instead of having many small competitive firms;
   (2) legal restrictions through patents and licenses that give a firm exclusive right over the sale of a product;
   (3) the ownership or control of essential resources; and
   (4) pricing and other strategic practices, such as price cuts, advertising campaigns, and producing excess capacity, all of which can deter entry.
   b. Entry barriers are seldom perfect in preventing the entry of new firms, and efficient production may, in some cases, require that firms be prevented from entering an industry.

3. The ***demand curve*** of the pure monopolist is *downsloping* because the monopolist is the industry. By contrast, the purely competitive firm has a horizontal (perfectly price elastic) demand curve because it is only one of many small firms in an industry. There are several implications of the downsloping shape of the monopolist's demand curve.
   a. The monopolist can increase sales only by lowering product price; thus *price will exceed marginal revenue* for every unit of output but the first.
   b. The monopolist will have a pricing policy, or is a *price maker*, the purely competitive firm has no price policy and is a price taker.
   c. The monopolist will avoid setting price in the inelastic segment of its demand curve because total revenue will be decreasing and marginal revenue will be negative; price will be set in the *elastic* portion of the demand curve.

4. The output and price determination of the profit-maximizing pure monopolist entails several considerations.
   a. Monopoly power in the sale of a product does not necessarily affect the prices that the monopolist pays for resources or the costs of production; an assumption is made in this chapter that the monopolist hires resources in a competitive market and uses the same technology as competitive firms.
   b. The monopolist produces that output at which *marginal cost and marginal revenue are equal* and charges a price at which this profit-maximizing output can be sold.
   c. The monopolist has *no supply curve* because there is no unique relationship between price and quantity supplied; price and quantity supplied will change when demand and marginal revenue change. By contrast, a purely competitive firm has a supply curve that is the portion of the marginal cost curve above average variable cost, and there is a unique relationship between price and quantity supplied.
   d. Two popular misconceptions about monopolists are that they charge as high a price as is possible and that they seek maximum profit per unit of output.

e. The monopolist is *not guaranteed a profit* and can experience losses because of weak demand for a product or high costs of production.

5. Pure monopoly has significant economic effects on the economy when compared to outcomes that would be produced in a purely competitive market.

a. The pure monopolist charges a *higher price* and *produces less output* than would be produced by a purely competitive industry. Pure monopoly is *neither productively efficient* because price is greater than the minimum of average cost, *nor* is it *allocatively efficient* because price is greater than marginal cost.

b. Monopoly contributes to income inequality in the economy.

c. A monopolist may have lower or higher average costs than a pure competitor producing the same product would have.

(1) If there are ***economies of scale*** in the production of the product, the monopolist is able to produce the good or service at a lower long-run average cost than a large number of small pure competitors could produce it.

(2) If a monopolist is more susceptible to ***X-inefficiency*** than a purely competitive firm, its long-run average costs at every level of output are higher than what those of a purely competitive firm would be.

(3) ***Rent-seeking expenditures*** in the form of legal fees, lobbying, and public-relations expenses to obtain or maintain a monopoly position add nothing to output, but increase costs.

(4) The monopoly market structure is *not* likely to be technologically progressive because there is little incentive for the monopolist to produce a new and more advanced product. The threat of potential competition, however, may stimulate more research and technological advances than would typically be the case, but it is often designed to restrict entry and maintain the monopoly position.

d. The policy options for dealing with the economic inefficiency of monopoly include the use of antitrust laws and the breakup of firms, the regulation of price, output, and profits of the monopolist, and ignoring the monopoly because its position is short lived.

6. To increase profits a pure monopolist may engage in ***price discrimination*** by charging different prices to different buyers of the same product (when the price differences do not represent differences in the costs of producing the product).

a. To discriminate, the seller must have some monopoly power, be capable of separating buyers into groups which have different price elasticities of demand, and be able to prevent the resale of the product from one group to another group.

b. The seller charges each group the highest price that group would be willing to pay for the product rather than go without it. Discrimination increases not only the profits but also the output of the monopolist.

c. Price discrimination is common in the U.S. economy.

7. The prices charged by monopolists are often *regulated* by governments to reduce the misallocation of resources.

a. A ceiling price determined by the intersection of the marginal-cost and demand schedules is the socially optimum price and improves the allocation of resources.

b. This ceiling may force the firm to produce at a loss, and therefore government may set the ceiling at a level determined by the intersection of the average cost and demand schedules to allow the monopolist a fair return.

c. The dilemma of regulation is that the socially optimum price may cause losses for the monopolist, and a fair-return price results in a less efficient allocation of resources.

■ HINTS AND TIPS

1. Make sure you understand how pure monopoly differs from pure competition. Here are key distinctions: (a) The monopolist's demand curve is downsloping, not horizontal as in pure competition; (b) the monopolist's marginal revenue is less than price (or average revenue) for each level of output except the first, whereas in pure competition marginal revenue equals price; (c) the monopoly firm is a price maker, not a price taker as in pure competition; (d) *the firm is the industry* in monopoly, but not in pure competition; (e) there is the potential for long-run economic profits in pure monopoly, but purely competitive firms will only break even in the long run; and (f) there is no supply curve for a pure monopoly, but there is one for the purely competitive firm.

2. A key similarity between a profit-maximizing pure monopolist and a purely competitive firm is that both types of firms will produce up to that output level at which marginal revenue equals marginal cost (MR = MC).

3. Figure 24-3 helps explain why the profit-maximizing monopolist will always want to select some price and quantity combination in the *elastic* and not in the *inelastic* portion of the demand. In the inelastic portion, total revenue declines and marginal revenue is negative.

4. Drawing the marginal revenue curve for a monopolist with a linear demand curve is easy if you remember that the marginal revenue curve will always be a straight line that intersects the quantity axis at half of the level of output as the demand curve. (See Figure 24-3.)

5. Spend extra time studying Figure 24-8 and reading the related discussion. It will help you see how price discrimination results in more profits, a greater output, and a higher price for some consumers and lower prices for other consumers.

■ IMPORTANT TERMS

pure monopoly
barrier to entry
natural monopoly
rent-seeking behavior
price discrimination
socially optimal price
fair-return price
dilemma of regulation

SELF-TEST

■ **FILL-IN QUESTIONS**

1. Pure monopoly is an industry in which a single firm is the sole producer of a product for which there are no close (substitutes, complements) ____________ and into which entry in the long run is (easy, difficult, blocked) ____________.

2. What are the four most important types of barriers to entry?

a. ____________

b. ____________

c. ____________

d. ____________

3. If there are substantial economies of scale in the production of a product, a small-scale firm will find it difficult to enter into and survive in an industry because its average costs will be (greater, less) ____________ than those of established firms, and a firm will find it (easy, difficult) ____________ to start out on a large scale because it will be nearly impossible to acquire the needed financing.

4. Public utility companies tend to be (nonprofit organizations, natural monopolies) ____________, and they receive their franchises from and tend to be (owned, regulated) ____________ by governments.

5. Legal barriers to entry by government include granting an inventor the exclusive right to produce a product for 20 years, or a (license, patent) ____________ and limiting entry into an industry or occupation through its issuing of a ____________. Other barriers to entry include the ownership of essential (markets, resources) ____________ and strategic changes in product (price, regulation) ____________.

6. The incidence of pure monopoly is relatively (rare, common) ____________ because eventually new developments in technology (strengthen, weaken) ____________ monopoly power or (substitute, complementary) ____________ products are developed.

7. The demand schedule confronting the pure monopolist is (perfectly elastic, downward sloping) ____________. This means that marginal revenue is (greater, less) ____________ than average revenue (or price) and that both marginal revenue and average revenue (increase, decrease) ____________ as output increases.

8. When demand is price elastic, a decrease in price will (increase, decrease) ____________ total revenue, but when demand is price inelastic, a decrease in price will ____________ total revenue. The demand curve for the purely competitive firm is (horizontal, downsloping) ____________, but it is ____________ for the monopolist. The profit-maximizing monopolist will want to set price in the price (elastic, inelastic) ____________ portion of its demand curve.

9. The supply curve for a purely competitive firm is the portion of the (average variable cost, marginal cost) ____________ curve that lies above the ____________ curve. The supply curve for the monopolist (is the same, does not exist) ____________.

10. When the economic profit of a monopolist is a maximum, (marginal, average) ____________ revenue equals ____________ cost and price is (greater, less) ____________ than marginal cost.

11. Two common misconceptions about pure monopoly are that it charges the (lowest, highest) ____________ price possible and seeks the maximum (normal, per unit) ____________ profit.

12. The pure monopolist (is, is not) ____________ guaranteed an economic profit; in fact, the pure monopolist can experience economic losses in the (short run, long run) ____________ because of (strong, weak) ____________ demand for the monopoly product.

13. The monopolist will typically charge a (lower, higher) ____________ price and produce (less, more) ____________ output and is (less, more) ____________ efficient than if the product was produced in a purely competitive industry.

a. The monopolist is inefficient *productively* because the average (variable, total) ____________ cost of producing it is not a (maximum, minimum) ____________.

b. It is inefficient *allocatively* because (marginal revenue, price) ____________ is not equal to (marginal, total) ____________ cost.

c. Monopolies seem to result in a greater inequality in the distribution of income because the owners of monopolies are largely in the (upper, middle, lower) ____________ income groups.

14. Resources can be said to be more efficiently allocated by pure competition than by pure monopoly only if the purely competitive firm and the monopoly have the same (costs, revenues) ______________, and they will not be the same if the monopolist

a. by virtue of being a large firm enjoys (economies, diseconomies) ______________ of scale not available to a pure competitor;

b. is more susceptible to X-(efficiency, inefficiency) ______________ than pure competitors;

c. may need to make (liability, rent-seeking) ______________ expenditures to obtain or maintain monopoly privileges granted by government; and,

d. reduces costs through adopting (higher prices, new technology) ______________.

15. Three general policy options to reduce the economic (efficiency, inefficiency) ______________ of monopolies are to file charges against it through (liability, antitrust) ______________ laws, have government regulate it if it is a (conglomerate, natural monopoly) ______________, or ignore it if it is short lived.

16. Price discrimination occurs whenever a product is sold at different (markets, prices) ______________, and these differences are not equal to the differences in the (revenue from, cost of) ______________ producing the product.

17. Price discrimination is possible only when the following three conditions exist:

a. ______________________________

b. ______________________________

c. ______________________________

18. The two economic consequences of a monopolist's use of price discrimination are a(n) (increase, decrease) ______________ in profits and a(n) ______________ in the output.

19. If the monopolist were regulated and a socially optimal price for the product were sought, the price would be set equal to (marginal, average total) ______________ cost. Such a legal price would achieve (productive, allocative) ______________ efficiency but might result in losses for the monopolist.

20. If a regulated monopolist is allowed to earn a fair return, the ceiling price for the product would be set equal to (marginal, average total) ______________ cost. Such a legal price falls short of (allocative, productive) ______________ efficiency.

■ TRUE-FALSE QUESTIONS

Circle the T if the statement is true, the F if it is false.

1. The pure monopolist produces a product for which there are no close substitutes. **T F**

2. The weaker the barriers to entry into an industry, the more competition there will be in the industry, other things equal. **T F**

3. Barriers to entry are rarely complete for the monopolist. **T F**

4. A monopolist may create an entry barrier by price cutting or substantially increasing the advertising of its product. **T F**

5. The monopolist can increase the sale of its product if it charges a lower price. **T F**

6. As a monopolist increases its output, it finds that its total revenue at first decreases, and that after some output level is reached, its total revenue begins to increase. **T F**

7. A purely competitive firm is a price taker but a monopolist is a price maker. **T F**

8. A monopolist will not voluntarily sell at a price at which the demand for its product is inelastic. **T F**

9. The monopolist determines the profit-maximizing output by producing that output at which marginal cost and marginal revenue are equal and sets the product price equal to marginal cost and marginal revenue at that output. **T F**

10. The supply curve for a monopolist is the upsloping portion of the marginal cost curve which lies above the average variable cost. **T F**

11. A monopolist will charge the highest price it can get. **T F**

12. A monopolist seeks maximum total profits, not maximum unit profits. **T F**

13. Pure monopoly guarantees economic profits. **T F**

14. Resources are misallocated by monopoly because price is not equal to marginal cost. **T F**

15. One of the economic effects of monopoly is less income inequality. **T F**

16. When there are substantial economies of scale in the production of a product, the monopolist may charge a price that is lower than the price that would prevail if the product were produced by a purely competitive industry. **T F**

17. The purely competitive firm is more likely to be affected by X-inefficiency than a monopolist. **T F**

18. Rent-seeking expenditures that monopolists make to obtain or maintain monopoly privilege have no effect on the firm's costs. **T F**

19. The general view of economists is that a pure monopoly is efficient because it has strong incentive to be technologically progressive. **T F**

20. One general policy option for a monopoly that creates substantial economic inefficiency and is long lasting is to directly regulate its prices and operation. **T F**

21. Price discrimination occurs when a given product is sold at more than one price and these price differences are not justified by cost differences. **T F**

22. A discriminating monopolist will produce a larger output than a nondiscriminating monopolist. **T F**

23. The regulated utility is likely to make an economic profit when price is set to achieve the most efficient allocation of resources (*P* = MC). **T F**

24. A fair-return price for a regulated utility would have price set to equal average cost. **T F**

25. The dilemma of monopoly regulation is that the production by a monopolist of an output which causes no misallocation of resources may force the monopolist to suffer an economic loss. **T F**

MULTIPLE-CHOICE QUESTIONS

Circle the letter that corresponds to the best answer.

1. Which would be defining characteristics of pure monpoly?
(a) The firm does no advertising and it sells a standardized product.
(b) No close substitutes for the product exist and there is one seller.
(c) The firm can easily enter into or exit from the industry and profits are guaranteed.
(d) The firm holds a patent and is technologically progressive.

2. A barrier to entry that signficantly contributes to the establishment of a monopoly would be
(a) economies of scale
(b) price-taking behavior
(c) technological progress
(d) X-inefficiency

3. The demand curve for the pure monopolist is
(a) perfectly price elastic
(b) perfectly price inelastic
(c) downsloping
(d) upsloping

4. Which of the following is true with respect to the demand data confronting a monopolist?
(a) Marginal revenue is greater than average revenue.
(b) Marginal revenue decreases as average revenue decreases.
(c) Demand is perfectly price elastic.
(d) Average revenue (or price) increases as the output of the firm increases.

5. When the monopolist is maximizing total profits *or* minimizing losses,
(a) total revenue is greater than total cost
(b) average revenue is greater than average total cost
(c) average revenue is greater than marginal cost
(d) average total cost is less than marginal cost

6. At which of the following combinations of price and marginal revenue is the price elasticity of demand less than 1?
(a) Price equals \$102, marginal revenue equals \$42.
(b) Price equals \$92, marginal revenue equals \$22.
(c) Price equals \$82, marginal revenue equals \$2.
(d) Price equals \$72, marginal revenue equals −\$18.

7. Monopolists' profits may be positive, negative, or zero
(a) in the short run
(b) in the long run
(c) in both the short run and long run
(d) where marginal cost equals marginal revenue and where average total cost is less than demand

8. At present output a monopolist determines that its marginal cost is \$18 and its marginal revenue is \$21. The monopolist will maximize profits or minimize losses by
(a) increasing price while keeping output constant
(b) decreasing price and increasing output
(c) decreasing both price and output
(d) increasing both price and output

Answer Questions 9, 10, 11, and 12 based on the demand and cost data for a pure monopolist given in the following table.

Output	Price	Total cost
0	\$1,000	\$ 500
1	600	520
2	500	580
3	400	700
4	300	1,000
5	200	1,500

9. How many units of output will the profit-maximizing monopolist produce?
(a) 1
(b) 2
(c) 3
(d) 4

10. The profit-maximizing monopolist would set its price at
(a) \$120
(b) \$200
(c) \$233
(d) \$400

11. If the monopolist could sell each unit of the product at the maximum price, the buyer of that unit would be willing to pay for it, and if the monopolist sold 4 units, total revenue would be
(a) \$1,200
(b) \$1,800
(c) \$2,000
(d) \$2,800

12. If the monopolist were forced to produce the socially optimal output by the imposition of a ceiling price, the ceiling price would have to be
(a) \$200
(b) \$300
(c) \$400
(d) \$500

13. The supply curve for a pure monopolist
(a) is the portion of the marginal cost curve that lies above the average variable cost curve
(b) is perfectly price elastic at the market price
(c) is upsloping
(d) does not exist

14. The analysis of monopoly indicates that the monopolist
(a) will charge the highest price it can get
(b) will seek to maximize total profits
(c) is guaranteed an economic profit
(d) is only interested in normal profit

15. When compared with the purely competitive industry with identical costs of production, a monopolist will charge a
(a) higher price and produce more output
(b) lower price and produce more output
(c) lower price and produce less output
(d) higher price and produce less output

16. At the equilibrium level of output, a monopolist does *not produce* the product as efficiently as is possible because
(a) the average total cost of producing it is not a minimum
(b) the marginal cost of producing the last unit is less than its price
(c) it is earning a profit
(d) average revenue is greater than the cost of producing an extra unit of output

17. Which will tend to increase the inefficiencies of the monopoly producer?
(a) price-taking behavior
(b) rent-seeking behavior
(c) economies of scale
(d) technological progress

18. Which is one of the conditions that must be realized before a seller finds that price discrimination is workable?
(a) The demand for the product is perfectly elastic.
(b) The seller must be able to segment the market.
(c) The buyer must be able to resell the product.
(d) The product must be a service.

19. If a monopolist engages in price discrimination rather than charging all buyers the same price, its
(a) profits and its output are greater
(b) profits and its output are smaller
(c) profits are greater and its output is smaller
(d) profits are smaller and its output is greater

Answer Questions 20, 21, 22, and 23 based on the demand and cost data for a pure monopolist given in the following table.

20. The profit-maximizing output and price for this monopolist would be
(a) 5 units and a $450 price
(b) 6 units and a $400 price
(c) 7 units and a $350 price
(d) 8 units and a $300 price

Quantity demanded	Price	Total cost
0	$700	$ 300
1	650	400
2	600	450
3	550	510
4	500	590
5	450	700
6	400	840
7	350	1,020
8	300	1,250
9	250	1,540
10	200	1,900

In answering Questions 21 and 22, assume this monopolist is able to engage in price discrimination and sell each unit of the product at a price equal to the maximum price the buyer of that unit would be willing to pay.

21. The marginal revenue that the price discriminating monopolist obtains from the sale of an additional unit is equal to
(a) total revenue
(b) average cost
(c) unit cost
(d) price

22. The profit-maximizing output for the price discriminating monopolist would be
(a) 6 units
(b) 7 units
(c) 8 units
(d) 9 units

23. How much greater would the total economic profits be for the discriminating monopolist than the nondiscriminating monopolist?
(a) $720
(b) $830
(c) $990
(d) $1,070

Question 24 is based on the following graph.

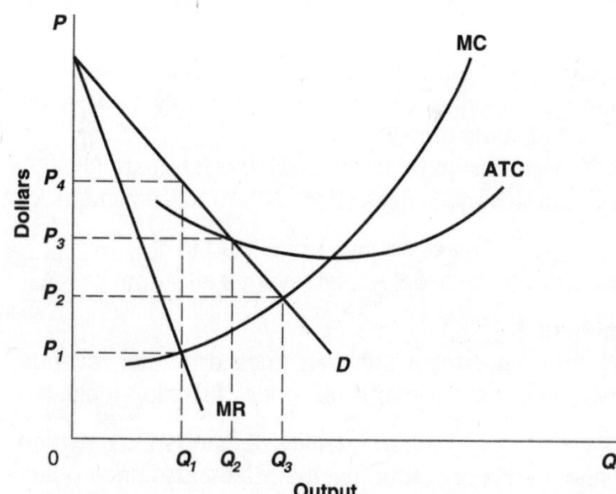

24. The price and output combination for the unregulated profit-maximizing monopoly compared with the socially optimal price and output combination for the regulated monopoly would be, respectively,

(a) P_4 and Q_1 versus P_3 and Q_2
(b) P_4 and Q_1 versus P_2 and Q_3
(c) P_3 and Q_2 versus P_4 and Q_1
(d) P_2 and Q_3 versus P_3 and Q_2

25. A monopolist who is limited by the imposition of a ceiling price to a fair return sells the product at a price equal to
(a) average total cost
(b) average variable cost
(c) marginal cost
(d) average fixed cost

■ PROBLEMS

1. The demand schedule for the product produced by a monopolist is given in the following table.

Quantity demanded	Price	Total revenue	Marginal revenue	Price elasticity
0	$700	$____		
1	650	____	$____	____
2	600	____	____	____
3	550	____	____	____
4	500	____	____	____
5	450	____	____	____
6	400	____	____	____
7	350	____	____	____
8	300	____	____	____
9	250	____	____	____
10	200	____	____	____
11	150	____	____	____
12	100	____	____	____
13	50	____	____	____
14	0	____	____	____

a. Complete the table by computing total revenue, marginal revenue, and the price elasticity of demand (use midpoints formula).
b. The relationships in the table indicate that
(1) total revenue rises from $0 to a maximum of $________ as price falls from $700 to $________, and as price falls to $0, total revenue falls from its maximum to $________;
(2) the relationship between price and total revenue suggests that demand is price (elastic, inelastic) ____________ when quantity demanded is between 0 and 7 units of output, but that demand is price (elastic, inelastic) ____________ when quantity demanded is between 8 units and 14 units;
(3) when demand is price elastic and total revenue rises from $0 to a maximum, marginal revenue is (negative, positive) ____________, but when demand is price inelastic and total revenue falls from its maximum, marginal revenue is ____________.
c. Use the data in the previous table and the graph on page 277 to plot and graph the demand curve and the marginal revenue curve for the monopolist. Indicate the portion of the demand curve that is price elastic and the portion that is price inelastic.

2. The following table shows demand and cost data for a pure monopolist.

Quantity	Price	Total revenue	Marginal revenue	Total cost	Marginal cost
0	$17	$____		$10	
1	16	____	$____	18	$____
2	15	____	____	23	____
3	14	____	____	25	____
4	13	____	____	27	____
5	12	____	____	28	____
6	11	____	____	32	____
7	10	____	____	40	____
8	9	____	____	50	____
9	8	____	____	64	____
10	7	____	____	80	____

a. Complete the table by filling in the column for total revenue, marginal revenue, and marginal cost.
b. Answer the next three questions using the data you calculated in the table.
(1) What output will the monopolist produce? ____________
(2) What price will the monopolist charge? ____________
(3) What total profit will the monopolist receive at the profit-maximizing level of output? ____________

3. Now assume that the pure monopolist in problem 2 is able to engage in price discrimination and sell each unit of the product at a price equal to the maximum price the buyer of that unit of the product would be willing to pay.
a. Complete the table on page 277 by computing total revenue and marginal revenue.
b. From the table it can be seen that
(1) the marginal revenue which the discriminating monopolist obtains from the sale of an additional unit is equal to the ____________;
(2) using the same table of costs, the discriminating monopolist would produce ____________ units of the product, charge the buyer of the last unit of product produced a price of $____________, and obtain a total economic profit of $____________;
(3) If the pure monopolist is able to engage in price discrimination its profits will be (larger, smaller, the same) ____________ and it will produce an output that is (larger, smaller, the same) ____________.

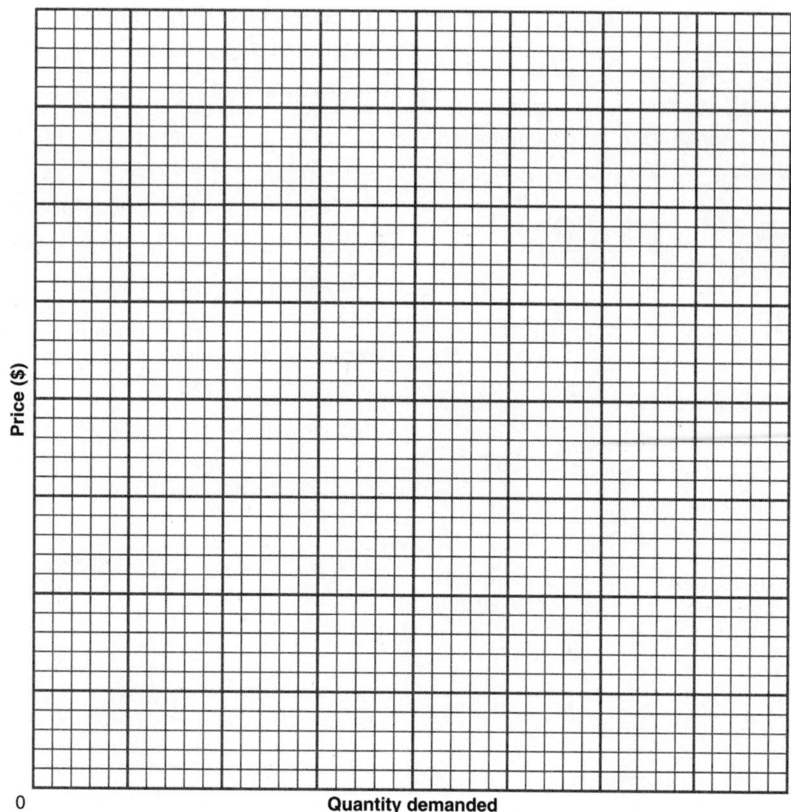

Quantity	Price	Total revenue	Marginal revenue	Total cost	Marginal cost
0	$17	$____		$10	
1	16	____	$____	18	$____
2	15	____	____	23	____
3	14	____	____	25	____
4	13	____	____	27	____
5	12	____	____	28	____
6	11	____	____	32	____
7	10	____	____	40	____
8	9	____	____	50	____
9	8	____	____	64	____
10	7	____	____	80	____

4. In the following table are cost and demand data for a pure monopolist.

Quantity demanded	Price	Marginal revenue	Average cost	Marginal cost
0	$17.50			
1	16.00	$16.00	$24.00	$24.00
2	14.50	13.00	15.00	6.00
3	13.00	10.00	11.67	5.00
4	11.50	7.00	10.50	7.00
5	10.00	4.00	10.00	8.00
6	8.50	1.00	9.75	8.50
7	7.00	−2.00	9.64	9.00
8	5.50	−5.00	9.34	9.25
9	4.00	−8.00	9.36	9.50

a. An unregulated monopolist would produce ________ units of this product, sell it at a price of $__________, and receive a total profit of $______________.

b. If this monopolist were regulated and the maximum price it could charge were set equal to marginal cost, it would produce ______________ units of a product, sell it at a price of $____________, and receive a total profit of $________________. Such regulation would either ______________ the firm or require that the regulating government ______________ the firm.

c. If the monopolist were not regulated and were allowed to engage in price discrimination by charging the maximum price it could obtain for each unit sold, it would produce 6 units (because the marginal revenue from the 6th unit and the marginal cost of the 6th unit would both be $8.50). Its total revenue would be $__________, its total costs would be $__________, and its total profit would be $______________.

d. If the monopolist were regulated and allowed to charge a fair-return price, it would produce __________ units of product, charge a price of $______________, and receive a profit of $______________.

e. From which situation—**a, b,** or **d**—does the most efficient allocation of resources result? ____________
From which situation does the least efficient allocation

result? ________________ In practice, government would probably select situation ________________

5. Identify whether the following long-run conditions apply to a firm under pure monopoly (**M**), pure competition (**C**), or both. Put the appropriate letter(s) (**M** or **C**) next to the condition.

a. There is the potential for long-run profits because price is greater than or equal to average total cost. _____

b. The firm's demand curve is perfectly elastic. _____

c. The firm maximizes profits at the output level where MC = MR. _____

d. The firm exhibits productive efficiency because price is equal to the minimum average total cost. _____

e. Price is greater than marginal revenue for each output level except the first. _____

f. There is an optimal allocation of resources because price is equal to marginal cost. _____

■ SHORT ANSWER AND ESSAY QUESTIONS

1. What is pure monopoly? Why is it studied if it is so rare in practice?

2. What is meant by a barrier to entry? What kinds of such barriers are there? How important are they in pure competition, pure monopoly, monopolistic competition, and oligopoly?

3. Why are the economies of scale a barrier to entry?

4. Why are most natural monopolies also public utilities? What does government hope to achieve by granting exclusive franchises to and regulating such natural monopolies?

5. How do patents and licenses create barriers to entry? Cite examples.

6. How can the monopolist use changes in price and other strategic actions to maintain a monopoly position?

7. Compare the pure monopolist and the individual pure competitor with respect to
(a) the demand schedule,
(b) the marginal-revenue schedule,
(c) the relationship between marginal revenue and average revenue,
(d) price policy, and
(e) the ability to administer (or set) price.

8. Explain why marginal revenue is always less than average revenue when demand is less than perfectly elastic.

9. Suppose a pure monopolist discovered it was producing and selling an output at which the demand for its product was inelastic. Explain why a decrease in its output would increase its economic profits.

10. How does the profit-maximizing monopolist determine what output to produce? What price will it charge?

11. Why is there no supply curve for a monopoly?

12. Why does the monopolist not charge the highest possible price for the product?

13. Why does the monopolist not set the price for the product in such a way that average profit is a maximum?

14. Why are some monopolies unprofitable?

15. In what sense is resource allocation and production more efficient under conditions of pure competition than under monopoly conditions?

16. How does monopoly allegedly affect the distribution of income in the economy and why does monopoly seemingly have this effect on income distribution in the U.S. economy?

17. Why are some monopolies unprofitable in the short run? What will be the long-run profit condition for most monopolies?

18. Explain how economies of scale offset some of the economic inefficiency of a monopoly. Evaluate the importance of this factor in reducing a monopolist's cost.

19. What is X-inefficiency? How does it affect the cost of production for the monopolist?

20. A monopolist will often engage in rent-seeking behavior. Explain what this means and how it changes a monopolist's cost.

21. Evaluate this statement from an economic perspective: "A pure monopoly has great incentive to discover and use new technology."

22. What is meant by price discrimination? Define it. What conditions must be realized before it is workable?

23. Explain how a monopolist who discriminates would determine what price to charge for each unit of the product sold (or to charge each group of buyers).

24. How does price discrimination affect the profits and the output of the monopolist? How does it affect consumers?

25. How do public utility regulatory agencies attempt to eliminate the misallocation of resources that results from monopoly? Explain the dilemma that almost invariably confronts the agency in this endeavor, and explain why a fair-return policy only reduces but does not eliminate misallocation.

ANSWERS

Chapter 24 Pure Monopoly

FILL-IN QUESTIONS

1. substitutes, blocked

2. *a.* the economies of scale; *b.* patents and licenses; *c.* ownership of essential resources; *d.* pricing and other strategic barriers (any order *a–d*)

3. greater, difficult
4. natural monopolies, regulated
5. patent, license, resources, price
6. rare, weaken, substitute
7. downsloping, less, decrease
8. increase, decrease, horizontal, downsloping, elastic
9. marginal cost, average variable cost, does not exist
10. marginal, marginal, greater
11. highest, per unit
12. is not, short run, weak
13. higher, less, less; *a.* total, minimum; *b.* price, marginal; *c.* upper
14. costs; *a.* economies; *b.* inefficiency; *c.* rent-seeking; *d.* new technology
15. inefficiency, antitrust, natural monopoly
16. prices, cost of
17. *a.* the seller has some monopoly power; *b.* the seller is able to separate buyers into groups which have different elasticities of demand for the product; *c.* the original buyers cannot resell the product
18. increase, increase
19. marginal, allocative
20. average total, allocative

TRUE-FALSE QUESTIONS

1. T, p. 493
2. T, p. 495
3. T, P. 497
4. T, p. 497
5. T, p. 499
6. F, pp. 499-500
7. T, p. 499
8. T, p. 500
9. F, p. 501
10. F, pp. 501-503
11. F, p. 503
12. T, p. 503
13. F, p. 503
14. T, pp. 504-505
15. F, p. 505
16. T, pp. 505-506
17. F, p. 506
18. F, p. 506
19. F, p. 506
20. T, p. 507
21. T, p. 507
22. T, pp. 508-510
23. F, pp. 510-512
24. T, p. 512
25. T, p. 512

MULTIPLE-CHOICE QUESTIONS

1. b, p. 493
2. a, pp. 495-496
3. c, p. 498
4. b, p. 499
5. c, pp. 500-501
6. d, p. 500
7. a, pp. 503-504
8. b, p. 501
9. c, p. 501
10. d, p. 501
11. b, p. 508
12. b, p. 505
13. d, pp. 501-503
14. b, p. 501
15. d, pp. 504-505
16. a, pp. 504-505
17. b, p. 506
18. b, pp. 507-508
19. a, pp. 508-509
20. b, p. 501
21. d, p. 509
22. c, pp. 508-509
23. c, p. 508
24. b, pp. 504-505
25. a, pp. 510-512

PROBLEMS

1. *a.* Total revenue: $0, 650, 1,200, 1,650, 2,000, 2,250, 2,400, 2,450, 2,400, 2,250, 2,000, 1,650, 1,200, 650, 0; Marginal revenue: $650, 550, 450, 350, 250, 150, 50, −50, −150, −250, −350, −450, −550, −650; Price elasticity: 27, 8.33, 4.60, 3.00, 2.11, 1.55, 1.15, .87, .65, .47, .33, .22, .12, .04 *b.* (1) $2,450, $350, 0, (2) elastic, inelastic, (3) positive, negative *c.* see Figure 24-3a in the text as an example
2. *a.* Total revenue: $0, 16, 30, 42, 52, 60, 66, 70, 72, 72, 70; Marginal revenue: $16, 14, 12, 10, 8, 6, 4, 2, 0, −2; Marginal cost: $8, 5, 2, 2, 1, 4, 8, 10, 14, 16 *b.* (1) 6, (2) $11, (3) $34 (TR of $66 minus TC of $32)
3. *a.* Total revenue: $0, 16, 31, 45, 58, 70, 81, 91, 100, 108, 115; Marginal revenue: $16, 15, 14, 13, 12, 11, 10, 9, 8, 7; Marginal cost: $8, 5, 2, 2, 1, 4, 8, 10, 14, 16; *b.* (1) price, (2) 7, $10; $51 (TR of $91 minus TC of $40), (3) larger, larger
4. *a.* 4, 11.50, 4.00; *b.* 6, 8.50, −7.50, bankrupt, subsidize; *c.* 73.50, 58.50, 15.00; *d.* 5, 10.00, zero; *e.* b or c, a, d
5. *a.* M; *b.* C; *c.* C, M; *d.* C; *e.* M; *f.* C

SHORT ANSWER AND ESSAY QUESTIONS

1. pp. 493-494
2. p. 495
3. pp. 495-496
4. pp. 495-496
5. p. 496
6. p. 497
7. pp. 498-499
8. p. 500
9. p. 500
10. p. 501
11. pp. 501-503
12. p. 503
13. p. 503
14. pp. 503-504
15. pp. 504-505
16. p. 505
17. pp. 503-504
18. pp. 505-506
19. p. 506
20. p. 506
21. pp. 506-507
22. pp. 507-508
23. pp. 508-510
24. pp. 508-510
25. pp. 510-512

CHAPTER 25

Monopolistic Competition and Oligopoly

This chapter is the last of the three chapters on price and output determination under different market structures. Here two market structures—monopolistic competition and oligopoly—that fall in between the extremes of pure competition and pure monopoly are examined. Both structures are important because each offers a description of most firms and industries more typically found in the U.S. economy than was the case with pure competition or pure monopoly.

Monopolistically competitive firms are quite prevalent because most retail establishments, such as grocery stores or restaurants, fall into the monopolistically competitive category. In such industries, there are a relatively large number of competitors, so no one firm has a large market share, firms sell differentiated products, and each firm has only limited pricing power.

A key section in the monopolistic competition part of the chapter focuses on the demand curve for the monopolistically competitive firm. You should now know how and why this demand curve differs from that found in pure competition and pure monopoly. In this connection it is also important to understand that as the individual firm changes the character of the product, it produces or changes the extent to which it promotes the sale of its product, both the costs of the firm and the demand for its product will change. A firm confronts a different demand curve every time it alters its product or its promotion of the product.

With the product and promotional campaign of the firm given, the price-output analysis of the monopolistic competitor is relatively simple. In the short run, this analysis is identical with the analysis of the price-output decision of the pure monopolist in the short run. It is only in the long run that the competitive element makes itself apparent: The entry (or exit) of firms forces the price the firm charges down (up) toward the level of average cost. This price is not equal either to minimum average cost or to marginal cost; consequently, monopolistic competition, on these two scores, can be said to be less efficient than pure competition.

This chapter also discusses ***nonprice competition*** under monopolistic competition. This topic is covered for several reasons. In monopolistically competitive industries, a part of the competitive effort of individual firms is devoted to product differentiation, product development, and advertising. Each firm has three things to manipulate—price, product, and advertising—in trying to maximize profits. Although monopolistic competition has been characterized as inefficient, some of the positive features and results of nonprice competition may offset some of the inefficiencies of this market structure.

The concept of ***oligopoly*** is fairly easy to grasp: a few firms that are mutually interdependent and that dominate the market for a product. The underlying causes of oligopoly are economies of scales, barriers to entry, and mergers, subjects you read about before. Economists use concentration ratios and the Herfindahl index to measure the degree of firm dominance of an industry, but as with most economic measures you studied in previous chapters, they are subject to several shortcomings.

What is more difficult to grasp is oligopoly behavior. The game theory overview should help you understand *what is meant* by mutual interdependence and *why it exists* in an oligopoly. If you can do this, you will be well on the road to understanding why specific conclusions cannot be reached about the price and output determination of individual firms. You will also see why oligopolists are loath to engage in price competition and why they frequently resort to ***collusion*** to set prices and sometimes use nonprice competition to determine market share. Collusion does not give firms complete protection from the rigors of competition because there are incentives to cheat on collusive agreements.

There is no standard model of oligopoly because of the diversity of markets and the uncertainty caused by mutual interdependence among firms. Chapter 25, however, does present three variants of *oligopoly models* that cover the range of market situations. The ***kinked demand curve*** model is the first variant. It explains why, in the absence of collusion, oligopolists will not raise or lower their prices even when their costs change. But the kinked demand curve does not explain what price oligopolists will set; it only explains why price, once set, will be relatively inflexible.

The second model examines how oligopolists resort to collusion to set price. The collusion can be overt, as in a cartel agreement, or the collusion can be covert, as in a secret agreement. The history of the OPEC international cartel is a classic example of how covert collusion can work in practice and how obstacles to collusion can eventually weaken the power of a cartel.

A third model of oligopoly is also noteworthy. In some industries a dominant firm serves as the *price leader* for other firms. In this price leadership model there is no overt collusion, only tacit understandings among firms involved in this industry. Also, in this model there are infrequent price changes, price and output announcements made by the lead firm for other firms to follow, and limits placed on pricing to prevent entry. Such covert collusion, however, can be undermined at times by price wars among firms.

The next to last section of the chapter looks at the role of ***advertising*** in oligopoly. Advertising, product differentiation, and product development are often the means the oligopolist uses, instead of price, to compete. Drawing firm conclusions about the effect of advertising in oligopoly (and also monopolistic competition) is difficult. Reasonable arguments can be made that advertising is both beneficial and costly for consumers and for efficiency in the U.S. economy.

Compared with pure competition, oligopoly does not result in allocative or productive efficiency. Nevertheless, the qualifications noted at the end of the chapter may offset some of oligopoly's shortcomings.

■ CHECKLIST

When you have studied this chapter you should be able to

☐ List the three features of monopolistic competition.
☐ Cite three characteristics that follow from having relatively large numbers of sellers in monopolistic competition.
☐ Describe four aspects and one major implication of product differentiation.
☐ Describe the entry and exit conditions in monopolistic competition.
☐ State the role of nonprice competition and advertising in monopolistic competition.
☐ Compare the firm's demand curve under monopolistic competition with a firm's demand curve in pure competition and pure monopoly.
☐ Determine the output of and the price charged by a monopolistic competitor in the short run when given cost and demand data.
☐ Explain why the price charged by a monopolistic competitor will in the long run tend to equal average cost and result in only a normal profit.
☐ Cite two real-world complications that may affect the outcome for monopolistically competitive firms in the long run.
☐ Show graphically how the typical firm in monopolistic competition achieves neither productive nor allocative efficiency and how excess capacity occurs.
☐ Describe the two principal types of nonprice competition.
☐ Explain why monopolistic competition is more complex in practice than is expressed in a simple economic model.
☐ Supply a basic definition of oligopoly.
☐ Describe the characteristics of oligopolies in terms of the number of producers, type of product, control over price, and interdependence.
☐ Explain how entry barriers and mergers contribute to the existence of oligopolies.
☐ Define concentration ratio and cite its shortcomings.
☐ Use the Herfindahl index to assess the distribution of market power among dominant firms in an oligopoly.
☐ Use game theory to analyze the pricing behavior of oligopolists.
☐ Explain the three features of oligopoly from a game theory perspective.
☐ List three distinct pricing models for oligopoly, and cite two reasons why there is no standard model of oligopoly.
☐ Use the kinked demand theory to explain the tendency for prices to be inflexible in a noncollusive model oligopoly.
☐ Describe the price and output conditions for a collusive pricing model of oligopoly.
☐ Give an example of overt collusion using the OPEC cartel.
☐ Describe covert collusion using the electrical equipment conspiracy, and cite other recent examples of covert collusion.
☐ List five obstacles to collusion.
☐ Use the history of OPEC to illustrate how obstacles to collusion eventually weakened OPEC.
☐ Describe the price leadership model of oligopoly, the types of leadership tactics, and the effect of price wars.
☐ Explain why oligopolists use advertising.
☐ Cite the potential positive and negative effects of advertising.
☐ Compare oligopoly to other market structures in terms of allocative and productive efficiency.

■ CHAPTER OUTLINE

1. ***Monopolistic competition*** has several defining characteristics; this market structure is found in many industries.

a. The relatively large number of sellers means that each has a small market share, there is no collusion, and firms take actions that are independent of each other.
b. Monopolistic competition exhibits product differentiation. This differentiation may take the form of differences in product attributes, services to customers, location and accessibility, brand names, and packaging. One implication of product differentiation is that monopolistically competitive firms have some control over price.
c. Entry into the industry or exit from it is relatively easy.
d. In addition to price competition, monopolistically competitive firms also use nonprice competition in the form of product differentiation and advertising.
e. Monopolistically competitive firms are found throughout the economy, and examples include grocery stores, gasoline stations, and restaurants.

2. Assume that the products the firms in the industry produce and the amounts of promotional activity in which they engage are given.

a. The *demand curve* confronting each firm will be highly but not perfectly price elastic because each firm has many competitors who produce close but not perfect substitutes for the product it produces.
(1) Comparing the demand curve for the monopolistic competitor to other market structures suggests that it is not perfectly elastic, as is the case with the pure competitor, but it is also more elastic than the demand curve of the pure monopolist.

(2) The degree of elasticity, however, for each monopolistic competitor will depend on the number of rivals and the extent of product differentiation.
b. In the *short run* the individual firm will produce the output at which marginal cost and marginal revenue are equal and charge the price at which the output can be sold; either profits or losses may result in the short run.
c. In the *long run* the entry and exodus of firms will *tend* to change the demand for the product of the individual firm in such a way that profits are eliminated. (Price and average costs are made equal to each other.)

3. Monopolistic competition among firms producing a given product and engaged in a given amount of promotional activity results in *less economic efficiency* and more excess capacity than does pure competition.
a. The typical monopolistically competitive firm achieves neither allocative nor productive efficiency.
(1) The average cost of each firm is equal in the long run to its price, but the industry does not realize allocative efficiency because output is smaller than the output at which marginal cost and price are equal.
(2) The industry does not realize productive efficiency because the output is smaller than the output at which average cost is a minimum.
b. There will be excess capacity because firms are producing less output than would be produced at the minimum of average total cost. Monopolistically competitive industries have many firms operating below optimal capacity.

4. In addition to setting its price and output so that its profit is maximized, each monopolistically competitive firm also attempts to differentiate its product and to promote or advertise it to increase the firm's profit; these additional activities give rise to nonprice competition among firms.
a. ***Product differentiation*** means that the monopolistically competitive firms will offer consumers a wide range of types, style, brands, and quality variants of a product; this expansion of consumer choice may offset the wastes of monopolistic competition.
b. *Product development* is an attempt by firms to improve a product, and it serves as a form of nonprice competition; to the extent that improved products contribute to consumer welfare, this type of nonprice competition among monopolistic firms may also offset some of the wastes of competition.
c. Monopolistic competition is more complex than the simple model presented in the chapter because the firm must constantly juggle three factors—price, product characteristics, and advertising—in seeking to maximize profits.

5. ***Oligopoly*** is frequently encountered in the U.S. economy.
a. It is composed of a few firms that dominate an industry and sell a standardized or differentiated product.
b. Oligopolistic industries may produce standardized (homogeneous) or differentiated products.
c. Oligopolistic firms control price. There is also mutual interdependence because firms must consider the reaction of rivals to any change in price, output, product characteristic, or advertising.
d. Barriers to entry such as economies of scale or ownership and control over raw materials can explain the existence of oligopoly.
e. Some industries have become oligopolistic not from internal growth but from external factors such as mergers.
f. Concentration of the industry among a few large producers can be measured in several ways.
(1) A ***concentration ratio*** gives the percentage of an industry's total sales provided by the largest firms. If the four largest firms account for 40 percent or more of the industry output, the industry is considered oligopolistic. Shortcomings of this measure include the imprecise definition of the market area and failure to take into account interindustry competition or import competition.
(2) The ***Herfindahl index*** more accurately measures concentration because it takes into account the market shares held by each firm. It is the sum of the squared percentage market shares of all firms in the industry.

6. Insight into the pricing behavior of oligopolists can be gained by thinking of the oligopoly situation as a game of strategy. This ***game theory*** overview leads to three conclusions.
a. Firms in an oligopolistic industry are mutually interdependent and must consider the actions of rivals when they make price decisions.
b. Oligopoly often leads to overt or covert collusion among the firms to fix prices or to coordinate pricing because competition among oligopolists results in low prices and profits; collusion helps maintain higher prices and profits.
c. Collusion creates incentive to cheat among oligopolists.

7. The economic analysis of oligopoly is difficult because oligopoly actually covers many different market situations and mutual interdependence makes it difficult for an oligopolist to estimate a demand curve. Nevertheless, two important characteristics of oligopoly are inflexible prices and simultaneous price changes by oligopolistic firms. An analysis of three oligopoly models helps explain the various pricing practice of oligopolists.
a. In the kinked demand model there is no collusion.
(1) Each firm believes that when it lowers its price its rivals will lower their prices, and when it increases its price its rivals will not increase their prices.
(2) The firm is therefore reluctant to change its price for fear of decreasing its profits.
(3) The model has two shortcomings: It does not explain how the going price gets set, and prices are not as rigid as the model implies.
b. The game theory perspective suggests that mutual interdependence of oligopolists encourages firms to collude to maintain or to increase prices and profits.

(1) Firms that collude tend to set their prices and joint output at the same level a pure monopolist would set them.
(2) Collusion may be overt, as in a cartel agreement. The OPEC cartel is an example of effective overt collusion during the 1970s.
(3) The electrical equipment conspiracy of 1960 is an example of covert collusion whereby tacit understandings between firms set price or market share.
(4) Examples of overt collusion are common and have included bid rigging on milk prices for schools or fixing worldwide prices for a livestock feed additive.
(5) At least six obstacles make it difficult for firms to collude or maintain collusive arrangements: difference in demand and cost among firms, the number of firms in the arrangement, incentives to cheat, changing economic conditions, potential for entry by other firms, and legal restrictions and penalties.
(6) Obstacles to collusion explain the decline in the OPEC cartel during the 1980s, including such factors as new suppliers and declining demand.

c. ***Price leadership*** is a form of covert collusion in which one firm initiates price changes and the other firms in the industry follow the lead. Three price leadership tactics have been observed.
(1) Price adjustments tend to be made infrequently as cost and demand conditions change to a significant degree.
(2) The price leader announces the price change in various ways, through speeches, announcement, or other such activities.
(3) The price set may not maximize short-run profits for the industry, especially if the industry wants to prevent entry by other firms.

8. Oligopolistic firms often avoid price competition but engage in ***nonprice competition*** through product development and advertising to determine each firm's market share for two reasons: Price cuts are easily duplicated, but nonprice competition is more unique; and oligopolists have greater financial resources to devote to advertising and product development.

a. The potential positive effects of advertising include providing low-cost information to consumers that reduces search time and monopoly power, thus enhancing economic efficiency.

b. The potential negative effects of advertising include manipulating consumers to pay higher prices, serving as a barrier to entry into an industry, and offsetting campaigns that raise product costs and prices.

c. A graphical analysis using average total cost curves shows no general conclusion about the effect of advertising on price, competition, and efficiency.

9. To compare the efficiency of an oligopoly with other market structures is difficult.

a. Many economists think that oligopoly price and output characteristics are similar to monopoly; oligopoly firms may set output where price exceeds marginal cost and average total cost. It is thus neither allocatively efficient (***P*** = MC) nor productively efficient (***P*** = minimum ATC).

b. This view must be qualified because of increased foreign competition to oligopolistic firms, the use of limit pricing that sets prices at less than the profit-maximizing price, and the technological advances arising from this market structure.

■ HINTS AND TIPS

1. Review the four basic market models in Table 23-1 so you see how monopolistic competition and oligopoly compare with the other market models on five characteristics.

2. The same MC = MR rule for maximizing profits or minimizing losses for the firm that you learned about in previous chapters is now used to determine output and price in monopolistic competition in certain oligopoly models. If you understood how the rule applied under pure competition and pure monopoly, you should have no trouble applying it to monopolistic competition and oligopoly.

3. Make sure you know how to interpret Figure 25-2 because it is the most important graph in the first half of the chapter. It illustrates why a representative firm in monopolistic competition just breaks even in the long run, and earns just normal rather than economic profits. It also shows how economic inefficiency in monopolistic competition produces excess capacity.

4. Where is the kink in the kinked demand model? To find out, practice drawing the model. Then use Figure 25-4 to check your answer. Explain to yourself what each line means in the graph.

5. Price and output determination under collusive oligopoly or a cartel is essentially the same as that for pure monopoly.

■ IMPORTANT TERMS

advertising	**Herfindahl index**
monopolistic competition	**interindustry competition**
product differentiation	**import competition**
nonprice competition	**game theory model**
excess capacity	**collusion**
oligopoly	**kinked demand curve**
homogeneous oligopoly	**price war**
differentiated oligopoly	**cartel**
mutual interdependence	**tacit understandings**
concentration ratio	**price leadership**

SELF-TEST

■ FILL-IN QUESTIONS

1. In a monopolistically competitive market, there are a relatively (large, small) ____________ number of producers who sell (standardized, differentiated) ____________ products. Entry into such a market is relatively (difficult, easy) ______________. The number of firms means that each one has a (large, small) ______________ market share, the firms (do, do not) ______________ collude, and they operate in a(n) (independent, dependent) ______________ manner.

2. Monopolistic competition features product differentiation in the following forms:

a. ______________

b. ______________

c. ______________

d. ______________

One implication of this product differentiation is that each firm has (no, limited, complete) ______________ control over the price.

3. In the *short run* for a monopolistically competitive firm,

a. the demand curve will be (more, less) __________ elastic than that facing a monopolist and __________ elastic than that facing a pure competitor;

b. the elasticity of this demand curve will depend on

(1) ______________ and

(2) ______________; and

c. it will produce the output level where marginal cost is (less than, equal to, greater than) ______________ marginal revenue.

4. In the long run for a monopolistically competitive industry,

a. the *entry* of new firms will (increase, decrease) ______________ the demand for the product produced by each firm in the industry and ______________ the elasticity of that demand.

b. the price charged by the individual firm will tend to equal (average, marginal) ______________ cost, its economic profits will tend to be (positive, zero) ______________, and its average cost will be (greater, less) ______________ than the minimum average cost of producing and promoting the product.

5. Although representative firms in monopolistic competition tend to earn (economic, normal) ______________ profits in the long run, there can be complications that may result in firms earning ______________ profits in the long run. Some firms may achieve a degree of product differentiation that (can, cannot) ______________ be duplicated by other firms. There may be (collusion, barriers to entry) ______________ that prevent penetration of the market by other firms.

6. In monopolistic competition, price is (less than, equal to, greater than) ______________ marginal cost, and so the market structure (does, does not) ______________ yield allocative efficiency. Also, average total cost is (less than, equal to, greater than) ______________ the minimum of average total cost, and so the market structure (does, does not) ______________ result in (allocative, productive) ______________ efficiency.

7. In the long run, the monopolistic competitor tries to earn economic profits by using (price, nonprice) ______________ competition in the form of product differentiation and advertising. Product differentiation and product development tend to result in the consumer being offered a (wider, narrower) ______________ variety of goods at any given time and (less, more) ______________ useful goods over a period of time.

8. The more complex model of monopolistic competition suggests that in seeking to maximize profits, each firm juggles the factors of (losses, price) ______________, changes in (collusion, product) ______________, and decisions about (controls, advertising) ______________ until the firm feels no further change in the variables will result in greater profit.

9. In an oligopoly (many, a few) ______________ large firms produce either a differentiated or a (heterogeneous, homogeneous) ______________ product, and entry into such an industry is (easy, difficult) ______________. The oligopolistic firm is a price (maker, taker) ______________ and there is mutual (independence, interdependence) ______________ among firms in an industry. The existence of oligopoly can be explained by (exit, entry) ______________ barriers and by (markets, mergers) ______________.

10. The percentage of the total industry sales accounted for by the top four firms in an industry is known as a four-firm (Herfindahl index, concentration ratio) ______________, whereas summing the squared percentage market shares of each firm in the industry is the way to calculate the ______________.

11. The basics of the pricing behavior of oligopolists can be understood from a (game, advertising) ______________ theory perspective. Oligopoly consists of a few firms that are mutually (funded, interdependent) ______________. This means that when setting the price of its product, each producer (does, does not) ______________ consider the reaction of its rivals. The monopolist (does, does not) ______________ face this problem because it has no rivals, and the pure competitor, or monopolistic competitor, ______________ faces the problem because it has many rivals.

12. It is difficult to use formal economic analysis to explain the prices and outputs of oligopolists because oligopoly encompasses (diverse, similar) ______________ market situation(s), and when firms are mutually interdependent, each firm is (certain, uncertain) ______________ about how its rivals will react when it changes the price of its product. Despite the analytical problems, oligopoly prices tend to be (flexible, inflexible) ______________ and oligopolists tend to change their prices (independently, together) ______________.

13. The noncolluding oligopolist has a kinked demand curve that

a. is highly (elastic, inelastic) ______________ at prices above the current or going price and tends to be only slightly ______________ or (elastic, inelastic) ______________ below that price.

b. is drawn on the assumption that if the oligopolist raises its price its rivals (will, will not) ______________ raise their prices or if it lowers its price its rivals ______________ lower their prices.

c. has an associated marginal-(cost, revenue) ______________ curve with a gap, such that small changes in the marginal-______________ curve do not change the price the oligopolist will charge.

14. A situation in which firms in an industry reach an agreement to fix prices, divide up the market, or otherwise restrict competition among them is called (monopolistic competition, collusion) ______________. In this case, the prices they set and their combined output tend to be the same as that found with pure (competition, monopoly) ______________.

15. A formal written agreement among sellers in which the price and the total output of the product and each seller's share of the market are specified is a (cartel, duopoly) ______________. It is a form of (covert, overt) ______________ collusion, and an example would be (ADM, OPEC) ______________. The electrical equipment conspiracy of 1960 is an example of (overt, covert) ______________ collusion, as are tacit understandings.

16. Six obstacles to collusion among oligopolists are

a. ______________

b. ______________

c. ______________

d. ______________

e. ______________

f. ______________

17. The power of OPEC has declined in recent decades because of problems with (duopoly, collusion) ______________. The increase in oil prices during the 1970s (attracted, discouraged) ______________ new entrants into oil production. A recession and increased use of alternative energy sources led to a(n) (increase, decrease) ______________ in the demand for oil during the early 1980s. Also, there was (fair play, cheating) ______________ among the cartel members due to their different economic conditions.

18. When one firm in an oligopoly is almost always the first to change its price and the other firms change their prices after the firm has changed its price, the oligopoly model is called the (price war, price leadership) ______________ model. The tactics of this model include (infrequent, frequent) ______________ price changes, announcements of such price changes, and (limit, no limit) ______________ pricing. One event that can undermine this model is (price leadership, price wars) ______________.

19. There tends to be very little (price, nonprice) ______________ competition among oligopolists and a great deal of ______________ competition such as product development and advertising used to determine each firm's share of the market.

a. The positive view of advertising contends that it is (efficient, inefficient) ______________ because it provides important information that (increases, reduces) ______________ search costs, and information about competing goods ______________ monopoly power.

b. The negative view of advertising suggests that it is (inefficient, efficient) ______________ because the advertising campaigns are (offsetting, reinforcing) ______________, the creation of brand loyalty serves as a barrier to (entry, exit) ______________, and consumers are persuaded to pay (lower, higher) ______________ prices than they would have paid otherwise.

20. Although it is difficult to evaluate the economic efficiency of oligopoly, when comparisons are made to pure competition, the conclusion drawn is that oligopoly (is, is not) ______________ allocatively efficient and (is, is not) ______________ productively efficient. The price and output behavior of the oligopolist is more likely to be similar to that found under (competition, monopoly) ______________.

■ TRUE-FALSE QUESTIONS

Circle the T if the statement is true, the F if it is false.

1. Monopolistic competitors have no control over the price of their products. T F

2. The firm's reputation for servicing or exchanging its product is a form of product differentiation under monopolistic competition. T F

3. Entry is relatively easy in pure competition, but there are significant barriers to entry in monopolistic competition. T F

4. The smaller the number of firms in an industry and the greater the extent of product differentiation, the greater will be the elasticity of the individual seller's demand curve. T F

5. The demand curve of the monopolistic competitor is most likely to be less elastic than the demand curve of the pure monopolist. T F

6. In the short run, firms that are monopolistically competitive may earn economic profits or incur losses. T F

7. The long-run equilibrium position in monopolistic competition would be where price is equal to marginal cost. T F

8. Representative firms in a monopolistically competitive market earn economic profits in the long run. T F

9. One reason why monopolistic competition is economically inefficient is that the average cost of producing the product is greater than the minimum average cost at which the product could be produced. T F

10. The wider the range of differentiated products offered to consumers by a monopolistically competitive industry, the less excess capacity there will be in that industry. T F

11. Successful product improvement by one firm has little or no effect on other firms under monopolistic competition. T F

12. The products produced by the firms in an oligopolistic industry may be either homogeneous (standardized) or differentiated. T F

13. Oligopolistic industries contain a few large firms that act independently of one another. T F

14. Concentration ratios include adjustments for interindustry competition in measuring concentration in an industry. T F

15. The Herfindahl index is the sum of the market shares of all firms in the industry. T F

16. Game theory analysis of oligopolist behavior suggests that oligopolists will not find any benefit in collusion. T F

17. One shortcoming of kinked demand analysis is that it does not explain how the going oligopoly price was established in the first place. T F

18. Collusion occurs when firms in an industry reach an overt or covert agreement to fix prices, divide or share the market, and in some way restrict competition among the firms. T F

19. Secret price concessions and other forms of cheating will strengthen collusion. T F

20. A cartel is usually a written agreement among firms which sets the price of the product and determines each firm's share of the market. T F

21. The practice of price leadership is almost always based on a formal written or oral agreement. T F

22. Limit pricing is the leadership tactic of limiting price increases to a certain percentage of the basic price of a product. T F

23. Those who contend that advertising contributes to the growth of monopoly power in the economy argue that the advertising by established firms creates barriers to the entry of new firms into an industry. T F

24. There tends to be rather general agreement among both critics and defenders of advertising that advertising increases the average cost of producing and promoting the product. T F

25. Oligopolies are allocatively and productively efficient. T F

■ MULTIPLE-CHOICE QUESTIONS

Circle the letter that corresponds to the best answer.

1. Which would be most characteristic of monopolistic competition?
- **(a)** collusion among firms
- **(b)** firms selling a homogeneous product
- **(c)** a relatively large number of firms
- **(d)** difficult entry into and exit from the industry

2. The concern that monopolistically competitive firms express about product attributes, services to customers, or brand names are aspects of
- **(a)** allocative efficiency in the industry
- **(b)** collusion in the industry
- **(c)** product differentiation
- **(d)** concentration ratios

3. The demand curve a monopolistically competitive firm faces is
- **(a)** perfectly elastic
- **(b)** perfectly inelastic
- **(c)** highly, but not perfectly inelastic
- **(d)** highly, but not perfectly elastic

4. In the short run, a typical monopolistically competitive firm will earn
- **(a)** only a normal profit
- **(b)** only an economic profit

(c) only an economic or normal profit
(d) an economic or normal profit or suffer an economic loss

5. A monopolistically competitive firm is producing at an output level in the short run where average total cost is $3.50, price is $3.00, marginal revenue is $1.50, and marginal cost is $1.50. This firm is operating
(a) with an economic loss in the short run
(b) with an economic profit in the short run
(c) at the break-even level of output in the short run
(d) at an inefficient level of output in the short run

6. If firms enter a monopolistically competitive industry, then we would expect the typical firm's demand curve to
(a) increase and the firm's price to increase
(b) decrease and the firm's price to decrease
(c) remain the same but the firm's price to increase
(d) remain the same and the firm's price to remain the same

Answer Questions 7, 8, 9, and 10 on the basis of the following diagram for a monopolistically competitive firm in short-run equilibrium.

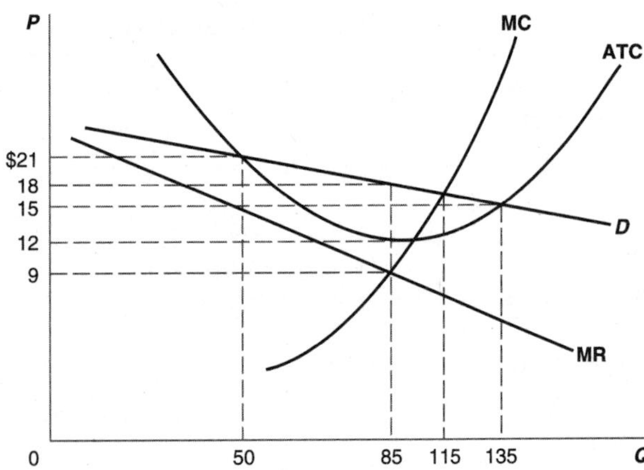

7. The firm's profit-maximizing price will be
(a) $9
(b) $12
(c) $15
(d) $18

8. The equilibrium output for this firm will be
(a) 50
(b) 85
(c) 115
(d) 135

9. This firm will realize an economic profit of
(a) $510
(b) $765
(c) $1,021
(d) $1,170

10. If firms enter this industry in the long run,
(a) demand will decrease
(b) demand will increase
(c) the marginal revenue curve will shift upward
(d) economic profits will increase

11. Given a representative firm in a typical monopolistically competitive industry, in the long run
(a) the firm will produce that output at which marginal cost and price are equal
(b) the elasticity of demand for the firm's product will be less than it was in the short run
(c) the number of competitors the firm faces will be greater than it was in the short run
(d) the economic profits being earned by the firm will tend to equal zero

12. *Productive* efficiency is not realized in monopolistic competition because production occurs where
(a) MR is greater than MC
(b) MR is less than MC
(c) ATC is greater than minimum ATC
(d) ATC is less than MR and greater than MC

13. The *underallocation* of resources in monopolistic competition means that at the profit-maximizing level of output, price is
(a) greater than MC
(b) less than MC
(c) less than MR
(d) greater than minimum ATC

14. Excess capacity occurs in a monopolistically competitive industry because firms
(a) advertise and promote their product
(b) charge a price that is less than marginal cost
(c) produce at an output level short of the least-cost output
(d) have a perfectly elastic demand for the products that they produce

15. Were a monopolistically competitive industry in long-run equilibrium, a firm in that industry might be able to increase its economic profits by
(a) increasing the price of its product
(b) increasing the amounts it spends to advertise its product
(c) decreasing the price of its product
(d) decreasing the output of its product

16. Which would be most characteristic of oligopoly?
(a) easy entry into the industry
(b) a few large producers
(c) product standardization
(d) no control over price

17. Mutual interdependence means that
(a) each firm produces a product similar but not identical to the products produced by its rivals
(b) each firm produces a product identical to the products produced by its rivals
(c) each firm must consider the reactions of its rivals when it determines its price policy
(d) each firm faces a perfectly elastic demand for its product

18. Which of the following contributes to the existence of oligopoly in an industry?
(a) low barriers to entry
(b) standardized products

(c) economies of scale
(d) elastic demand

19. One major problem with concentration ratios is that they fail to take into account
(a) the national market for products
(b) competition from imported products
(c) excess capacity in production
(d) mutual interdependence

20. Industry A is composed of four large firms that hold market shares of 40, 30, 20, and 10. The Herfindahl index for this industry is
(a) 100
(b) 1,000
(c) 3,000
(d) 4,500

Questions 21, 22, and 23 are based on the following payoff matrix for a duopoly in which the numbers indicate the profit in thousands of dollars for a high-price or a low-price strategy.

		Firm A	
		High-price	**Low-price**
Firm B	**High-price**	A = \$425 B = \$425	A = \$525 B = \$275
	Low-price	A = \$275 B = \$525	A = \$300 B = \$300

21. If both firms collude to maximize joint profits, the total profits for the two firms will be
(a) \$400,000
(b) \$800,000
(c) \$850,000
(d) \$950,000

22. Assume that Firm B adopts a low-price strategy while Firm A maintains a high-price strategy. Compared to the results from a high-price strategy for both firms, Firm B will now
(a) lose \$150,000 in profit and Firm A will gain \$150,000 in profit
(b) gain \$100,000 in profit and Firm A will lose \$150,000 in profit
(c) gain \$150,000 in profit and Firm A will lose \$100,000 in profit
(d) gain \$525,000 in profit and Firm A will lose \$275,000 in profit

23. If both firms operate independently and do not collude, the most likely profit is
(a) \$300,000 for Firm A and \$300,000 for Firm B
(b) \$525,000 for Firm A and \$275,000 for Firm B
(c) \$275,000 for Firm A and \$525,000 for Firm B
(d) \$425,000 for Firm A and \$425,000 for Firm B

24. The prices of products produced by oligopolies tend to be
(a) relatively flexible, and when firms change prices they are apt to change them at the same time
(b) relatively inflexible, and when firms change prices they are not apt to change them at the same time
(c) relatively inflexible, and when firms change prices they are apt to change them at the same time
(d) relatively flexible, and when firms change prices they are not apt to change them at the same time

25. If an individual oligopolist's demand curve is kinked, it is necessarily
(a) perfectly elastic at the going price
(b) less elastic above the going price than below it
(c) more elastic above the going price than below it
(d) of unitary elasticity at the going price

Use the following diagram to answer Question 26.

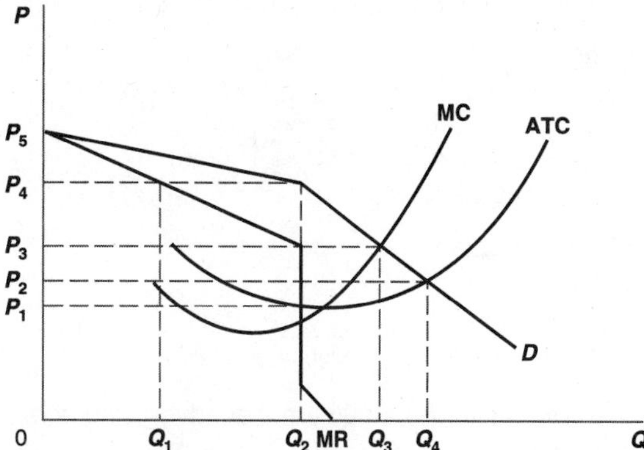

26. The profit-maximizing price and output for this oligopolistic firm is
(a) P_5 and Q_2
(b) P_4 and Q_2
(c) P_3 and Q_3
(d) P_2 and Q_4

27. What is the situation called whenever firms in an industry reach an agreement to fix prices, divide up the market, or otherwise restrict competition?
(a) interindustry competition
(b) incentive to cheat
(c) price leadership
(d) collusion

28. When oligopolists collude the results are generally
(a) greater output and higher price
(b) greater output and lower price
(c) smaller output and lower price
(d) smaller output and higher price

29. Which of the following constitutes an obstacle to collusion among oligopolists?
(a) a general business recession
(b) a small number of firms in the industry
(c) a homogeneous product
(d) the patent laws

30. To be successful, collusion requires that oligopolists be able to
(a) keep prices and profits as low as possible
(b) block or restrict the entry of new producers
(c) reduce legal obstacles that protect market power
(d) keep the domestic economy from experiencing high inflation

31. Which is a typical tactic that has been used by the price leader in the price leadership model of oligopoly?

(a) limit pricing
(b) frequent price changes
(c) starting a price war with competitors
(d) giving no announcement of a price change

32. Market shares in oligopolistic industries are typically determined on the basis of
(a) product development and advertising
(b) covert collusion and cartels
(c) tacit understandings
(d) joint profit maximization

Answer Questions 33 and 34 based on the following graph.

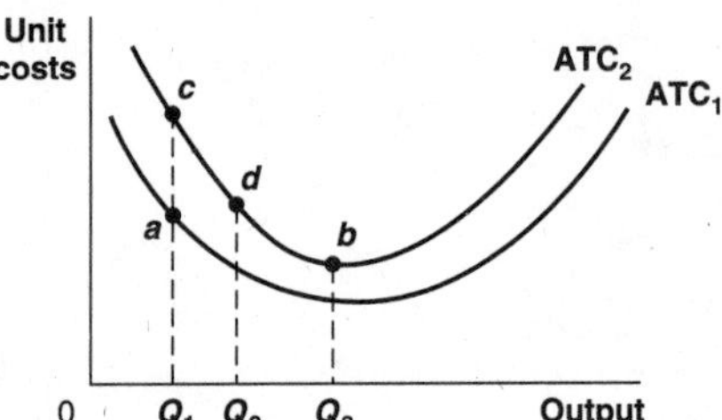

33. Those who make the argument that advertising is *efficient* think that it
(a) lowers unit costs and increases the level of output (i.e., moves from point ***a*** to ***b***)
(b) increases cost curves from **ATC_1** to **ATC_2** and decreases output levels (i.e., moves from point ***b*** to point ***c***)
(c) lowers costs from **ATC_2** to **ATC_1**, but leaves output unchanged (i.e., at point ***a***)
(d) lowers costs and increases output by moving downward along an existing cost curve (i.e., from point ***c*** to ***b***)

34. Those who make the argument that advertising is *inefficient* think that it
(a) has no effect on costs or output levels
(b) decreases output and costs (i.e., moves from point ***d*** to ***a***)
(c) raises costs without affecting output because of the offsetting effect of competitor's ads (i.e., moves from point ***a*** to ***c***)
(d) raises costs and lowers output because it offends many potential customers (i.e., from point ***b*** to ***a***)

35. Many economists would conclude that in a highly oligopolistic market there is
(a) allocative efficiency, but not productive efficiency
(b) productive efficiency, but not allocative efficiency
(c) both allocative and productive efficiency
(d) neither allocative nor productive efficiency

■ PROBLEMS

1. Assume that the short-run cost and demand data given in the following table confront a monopolistic competitor selling a given product and engaged in a given amount of product promotion.

Output	Total cost	Marginal cost	Quantity demanded	Price	Marginal revenue
0	$ 50		0	$120	
1	80	$____	1	110	$____
2	90	____	2	100	____
3	110	____	3	90	____
4	140	____	4	80	____
5	180	____	5	70	____
6	230	____	6	60	____
7	290	____	7	50	____
8	360	____	8	40	____
9	440	____	9	30	____
10	530	____	10	20	____

a. Compute the marginal cost and marginal revenue of each unit of output and enter these figures in the table.

b. In the short run the firm will (1) produce ________ units of output, (2) sell its output at a price of $________________, and (3) have a total economic profit of $________________.

c. In the long run, (1) the demand for the firm's product will ________________, (2) until the price of the product equals ________________, and (3) the total economic profits of the firm are ____________.

2. Match the following descriptions to one of the six graphs on page 291. Indicate on each graph the area of economic profit or loss or state if the firm is just making normal profits.

a. a purely competitive firm in earning economic profits in the short run Graph _____

b. a purely competitive firm in long-run equilibrium Graph _____

c. a natural monopoly Graph _____

d. a monopolistically competitive firm earning economic profits in the short run Graph _____

e. a monopolistically competitive firm experiencing economic losses in the short run Graph _____

f. a monopolistically competitive firm in long-run equilibrium Graph _____

3. Consider the following payoff matrix in which the numbers indicate the profit in millions of dollars for a duopoly based on either a high-price or a low-price strategy.

		Firm X High-price	Firm X Low-price
Firm Y	High-price	X = $200 Y = $200	X = $250 Y = $ 50
	Low-price	X = $ 50 Y = $250	X = $ 50 Y = $ 50

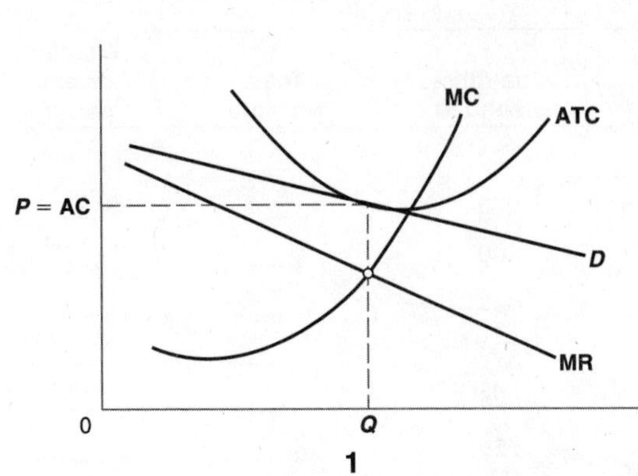

1

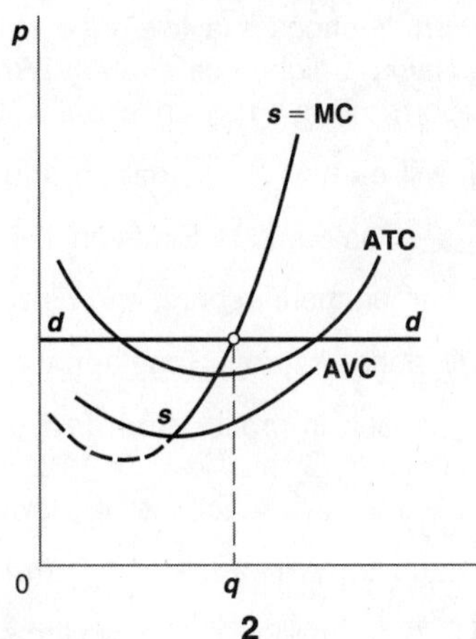

2

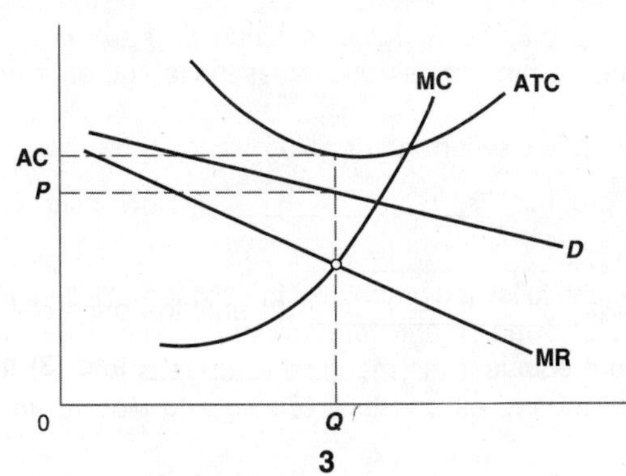

3

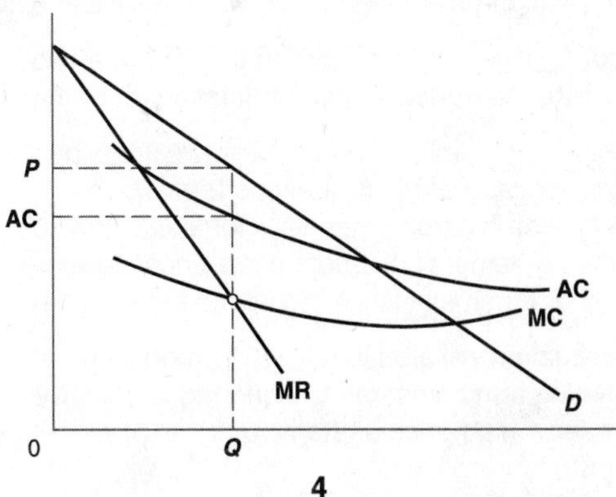

4

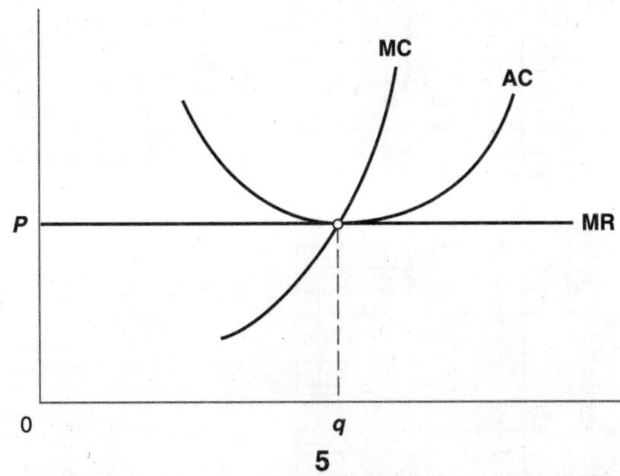

5

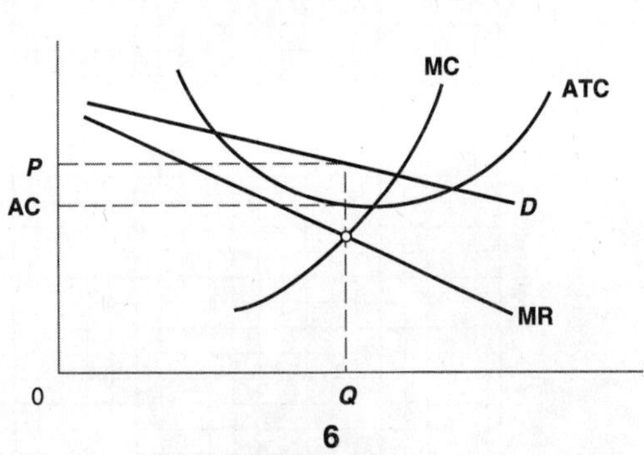

6

a. ***Situation 1:*** Each firm chooses a high-price strategy. ***Result:*** Each firm will earn $______ million in profit for a total of $______ million for the two firms.

b. ***Situation 2:*** Firm X chooses a low-price strategy while Firm Y maintains a high-price strategy. ***Result:*** Firm X will earn $_______ million and Firm Y will earn $_____ million. Compared to Situation 1, Firm X has an incentive to cut prices because it will earn $_____ million more in profit and Firm Y will earn $_____ million less in profit. Together, the firms will earn $_____ million in profit, which is $_____ million less than in Situation 1.

c. *Situation 3:* Firm Y chooses a low-price strategy while Firm X maintains a high-price strategy. ***Result:*** Compare to Situation 1. Firm Y has an incentive to cut prices because it will earn $______ million and Firm X will earn $______. Compared to Situation 1, Firm Y will earn $______ million more in profit and Firm X will earn $______ million less in profit. Together, the firms will earn $______ million in profit, which is $______ less than in Situation 1.

d. *Situation 4:* Each firm chooses a low-price strategy. ***Result:*** Each firm will earn $______ million in profit for a total of $______ million for the two firms. This total is $______ less than in Situation 1.

e. *Conclusions:*

(1) The two firms have a strong incentive to collude and adopt the high-price strategy because there is the potential for $______ million more in profit for the two firms than with a low-price strategy (Situation 4), or the potential for $______ million more for the two firms than with a mixed-price strategy (Situations 2 or 3).

(2) There is also a strong incentive for each firm to cheat on the agreement and adopt a low-price strategy when the other firm maintains a high-price strategy because this situation will produce $______ more in profit for the cheating firm compared to honoring a collusive agreement for a high-price strategy.

4. The kinked demand schedule which an oligopolist believes confronts the firm is presented in the following table.

Price	Quantity demanded	Total revenue	Marginal revenue per unit
$2.90	100	$______	
2.80	200	______	$______
2.70	300	______	______
2.60	400	______	______
2.50	500	______	______
2.40	525	______	______
2.30	550	______	______
2.20	575	______	______
2.10	600	______	______

a. Compute the oligopolist's total revenue at each of the nine prices and enter these figures in the table.

b. Also compute marginal revenue *for each unit* between the nine prices and enter these figures in the table.

c. What is the current, or going, price for the oligopolist's product? $______________ How much is it selling? ______________

d. On the following graph, plot the oligopolist's demand curve and marginal-revenue curve. Connect the demand points and the marginal-revenue points with as straight a line as possible. (Be sure to plot the mar-

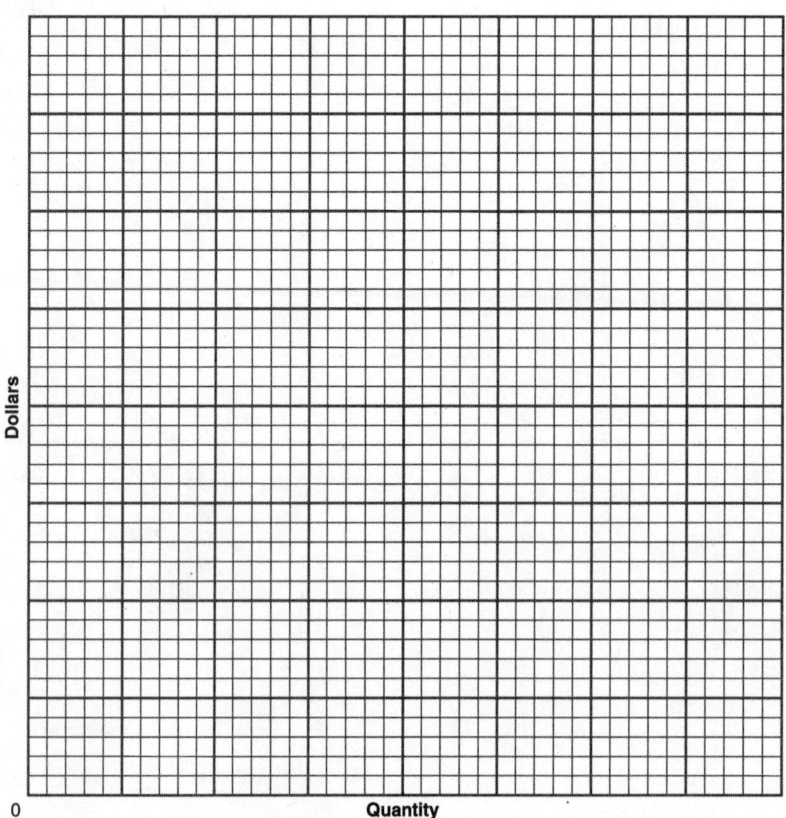

ginal-revenue figures at the average of the two quantities involved, that is, at 150, 250, 350, 450, 512.5, 537.5, 562.5, and 587.5.)

e. Assume that the marginal-cost schedule of the oligopolist is given in columns 1 and 2 of the following table. Plot the marginal-cost curve on the graph on which demand and marginal revenue were plotted.

(1) Output	(2) MC	(3) MC′	(4) MC″
150	$1.40	$1.90	$.40
250	1.30	1.80	.30
350	1.40	1.90	.40
450	1.50	2.00	.50
512½	1.60	2.10	.60
537½	1.70	2.20	.70
562½	1.80	2.30	.80
587½	1.90	2.40	.90

(1) Given demand and marginal cost, what price should the oligopolist charge to maximize profits? $__________ How many units of product will it sell at this price? __________

(2) If the marginal-cost schedule changed from that shown in columns 1 and 2 to that shown in columns 1 and 3, what price should it charge? $__________

What level of output will it produce? __________

How have profits changed as a result of the change in costs? __________

Plot the new marginal-cost curve on the graph.

(3) If the marginal-cost curve schedule changed from that shown in columns 1 and 2 to that shown in columns 1 and 4, what price should it charge? $__________

What level of output will it produce? __________

How have profits changed as a result of the change in costs? __________

Plot the new marginal-cost curve on the graph.

5. An oligopoly producing a homogeneous product is composed of three firms. Assume that these three firms have identical cost schedules. Assume also that if any one of these firms sets a price for the product, the other two firms charge the same price. As long as the firms all charge the same price they will share the market equally, and the quantity demanded of each will be the same.

At the bottom of the page is the total-cost schedule of one of these firms and the demand schedule that confronts it when the other firms charge the same price as this firm.

a. Complete the marginal-cost and marginal-revenue schedules facing the firm.

b. What price would this firm set if it wished to maximize its profits? __________

c. How much would

(1) it sell at this price? __________

(2) its profits be at this price? $__________

d. What would be the industry's

(1) total output at this price? __________

(2) joint profits at this price? $__________

e. Is there any other price this firm can set, assuming that the other two firms charge the same price, which would result in a greater joint profit for them? __________

If so, what is that price? $__________

f. If these three firms colluded in order to maximize their joint profit, what price would they charge? $__________

■ SHORT ANSWER AND ESSAY QUESTIONS

1. What are the three characteristics of monopolistic competition?

2. What is meant by product differentiation? By what methods can products be differentiated?

3. How does product differentiation affect the kind of competition and the degree of monopoly in monopolistic competition?

4. Describe the elasticity of the demand curve faced by a monopolistically competitive firm in the short run.

Output	Total cost	Marginal cost	Price	Quantity demanded	Marginal revenue
0	$ 0		$140	0	
1	30	$____	130	1	$____
2	50	____	120	2	____
3	80	____	110	3	____
4	120	____	100	4	____
5	170	____	90	5	____
6	230	____	80	6	____
7	300	____	70	7	____
8	380	____	60	8	____

5. Assume that the firm is producing a given product and is engaged in a given amount of promotional activity. What two factors determine how elastic the demand curve will be for a monopolistic competitor?

6. At what level of output will the monopolistic competitor produce in the short run? What price will it charge for its product? Draw a graph to help explain your answer.

7. What determines whether a monopolistically competitive firm will earn economic profits or suffer economic losses in the short run?

8. What will be the level of economic profit that the monopolistic competitor will *tend* to receive in the long run? What forces economic profits toward this level? Why is this just a *tendency*?

9. What are two complications that would explain why the representative firm may not earn only a normal profit in the long run and may earn economic profits?

10. Use the concepts of allocative and productive efficiency to explain excess capacity and the level of prices under monopolistic competition.

11. Describe the methods, other than price cutting, that a monopolistic competitor can use to protect and increase its economic profits in the long run.

12. Identify the ways in which product differentiation and product development may offset the economic inefficiency associated with monopolistic competition.

13. What are the essential characteristics of an oligopoly? How does oligopoly differ from pure competition, pure monopoly, and monopolistic competition?

14. Explain how the concentration ratio in a particular industry is computed. What is the relationship between this ratio and fewness? What are the shortcomings of the concentration ratio as a measure of the extent of competition in an industry?

15. What is the Herfindahl index? How can it be used to correct problems with concentration ratios?

16. How can game theory be used to explain price behavior under oligopoly? What do mutual interdependence and collusion mean with respect to oligopoly?

17. Why is it difficult to use one standard model to explain the prices charged by and the outputs of oligopolists?

18. How can the kinked demand curve be used to explain why oligopoly prices are relatively inflexible?

19. Suppose a few firms produce a homogeneous product, have identical cost curves, and charge the same price. How will the price they set, their combined output of the product, and their joint profit compare with what would be found in the same industry if it were a pure monopoly with several plants?

20. Why do oligopolists find it advantageous to collude? What are the obstacles to collusion?

21. What is the price leadership model, and what leadership tactics do oligopolistic firms use?

22. Why do oligopolists engage in little price competition and in extensive product development and advertising?

23. How is it possible for consumers to get a lower price on a product with advertising than they would in its absence?

24. Explain how the advertising efforts of firms may be offsetting and lead to higher prices for consumers.

25. Evaluate the economic efficiency of the oligopoly market structure. What qualifications should be noted for the evaluation?

ANSWERS

Chapter 25 Monopolistic Competition and Oligopoly

FILL-IN QUESTIONS

1. large, differentiated, easy, small, do not, independent
2. *a.* product attributes; *b.* services; *c.* location; *d.* brand names and packaging; limited
3. *a.* more, less; *b.* (1) number of rivals the firm has, (2) the degree of product differentiation; *c.* equal to
4. *a.* decrease, increase; *b.* average, zero, greater
5. normal, economic, cannot, barriers to entry
6. greater than, does not, greater than, productive
7. nonprice, wider, more
8. price, product, advertising
9. a few, homogeneous, difficult, maker, interdependence, entry, mergers
10. concentration ratio, Herfindahl index
11. game, interdependent, does, does not, does not
12. diverse, uncertain, inflexible, together
13. *a.* elastic, elastic, inelastic; *b.* will not, will; *c.* revenue, cost
14. collusion, monopoly
15. cartel, overt, OPEC, covert
16. *a.* demand and cost differences; *b.* a large number of firms; *c.* cheating (secret price cutting); *d.* a recession; *e.* potential entry; *f.* legal obstacles (antitrust laws)
17. collusion, attracted, decrease, cheating
18. price leadership, infrequent, limit, price wars
19. price, nonprice; *a.* efficient, reduces, reduces; *b.* inefficient, offsetting, entry, higher
20. is not, is not, monopoly

TRUE-FALSE QUESTIONS

1. F, p. 517	**10.** F, p. 521	**19.** F, p. 532
2. T, p. 516	**11.** F, p. 522	**20.** T, p. 531
3. F, p. 517	**12.** T, p. 522	**21.** F, p. 533
4. F, pp. 517-518	**13.** F, p. 523	**22.** F, pp. 533-534
5. F, p. 517	**14.** F, pp. 524-525	**23.** T, p. 535
6. T, p. 518	**15.** F, p. 525	**24.** T, p. 536
7. F, p. 518	**16.** F, p. 526	**25.** F, p. 537
8. F, pp. 518-520	**17.** T, p. 529	
9. T, p. 520	**18.** T, pp. 530-531	

MULTIPLE-CHOICE QUESTIONS

1. c, p. 516	**6.** b, p. 518	**11.** d, pp. 518-520
2. c, pp. 516-517	**7.** d, pp. 518-519	**12.** c, p. 520
3. d, p. 517	**8.** b, pp. 518-519	**13.** a, p. 520
4. d, p. 518	**9.** a, pp. 518-519	**14.** c, p. 520
5. a, pp. 518-519	**10.** a, pp. 518-519	**15.** b, p. 521

16. b, p. 523
17. c, p. 523
18. c, p. 523
19. b, p. 525
20. c, p. 525
21. c, p. 526
22. b, p. 526
23. a, p. 526
24. c, p. 527
25. c, p. 529
26. b, pp. 527-529
27. d, p. 530
28. d, p. 530
29. a, p. 532
30. b, p. 532
31. a, pp. 533-534
32. a, p. 534
33. a, p. 538
34. c, p. 538
35. d, p. 537

PROBLEMS

1. *a.* Marginal cost: $30, 10, 20, 30, 40, 50, 60, 70, 80, 90, Marginal revenue: $110, 90, 70, 50, 30, 10, −10, −30, −50, −70; *b.* (1) 4, (2) $80, (3) $180; *c.* (1) decrease, (2) average cost, (3) equal to zero
2. *a.* 2; *b.* 5; *c.* 4; *d.* 6; *e.* 3; *f.* 1
3. *a.* 200, 400; *b.* 250, 50, 50, 150, 300, 100; *c.* 250, 50, 50, 150, 300, 100; *d.* 50, 100, 300; *e.* (1) 300, 100, (2) 50
4. *a.* Total revenue: 290, 560, 810, 1,040, 1,250, 1,260, 1,265, 1,265, 1,260; *b.* Marginal revenue: 2.70, 2.50, 2.30, 2.10, 0.40, 0.20, 0, −0.20; *c.* 2.50, 500; *e.* (1) 2.50, 500, (2) 2.50, 500, they have decreased; (3) 2.50, 500, they have increased.
5. *a.* Marginal cost: $30, 20, 30, 40, 50, 60, 70, 80; Marginal revenue: $130, 110, 90, 70, 50, 30, 10, −10; *b.* $90; *c.* (1) 5, (2) $280; *d.* (1) 15, (2) $840; *e.* no; *f.* $90

SHORT ANSWER AND ESSAY QUESTIONS

1. p. 516
2. pp. 516-517
3. p. 517
4. p. 517
5. pp. 517-518
6. pp. 518-519
7. pp. 518-519
8. pp. 518-519
9. pp. 520-521
10. p. 520
11. p. 521
12. p. 522
13. pp. 522-523
14. pp. 524-525
15. p. 525
16. pp. 526-527
17. p. 527
18. pp. 527-529
19. p. 530
20. pp. 530, 532-533
21. pp. 533-534
22. p. 534
23. pp. 536, 538
24. pp. 536, 538
25. pp. 537-538

CHAPTER **26**

Technology, R&D, and Efficiency

A market economy is not static but subject to change over time. One of the dynamic forces affecting an economy and the particular industries in it is *technological advance.* This advance occurs over a very long time and allows firms to introduce new products and adopt new methods of production.

The chapter begins by discussing the three-step process that constitutes technological advance: *invention, innovation,* and *diffusion.* Here the text describes many real-world examples of how technological change has affected firms and industries. You will also find out that research and development (R&D) expenditures by firms and government play an integral role in directly supporting this technological advance. The traditional view of economists was that technological advance was something external to the economy, but most contemporary economists think that technological advance is integral to capitalism and arises from the intense rivalry among firms.

Entrepreneurs and other innovators play a major role in encouraging innovation and technological change. Entrepreneurs typically form small companies—***startups***—to create and introduce new products and production techniques. In this activity entrepreneurs assume personal financial risk, but if they are successful, they can be highly rewarded in the marketplace. There are also innovators within existing firms who can use R&D work to develop new products. University and government research can also contribute output that can be useful for fostering technological advance.

A major section of this chapter analyzes how the firm determines the optimal amount of R&D spending. The decision is made by equating marginal benefit with marginal cost. The marginal cost is measured by the interest-rate cost-of-funds that the firm borrows or obtains from other sources to finance its R&D expenditures. The expected rate of return from the last dollar spent on R&D is the measure of marginal benefit. You should remember that the outcomes from R&D spending are only expected, not guaranteed for the firm.

Technological changes can increase a firm's profit in two ways. Recall that profit is simply the difference between total revenue and total cost. ***Product innovation*** can increase revenues because people buy more products from the innovative firm. These increased revenues will increase profits, assuming that costs stay the same. ***Process innovation*** can also increase profits by reducing costs. This type of innovation leads to better methods for producing a product and decreases the average total cost for the firm.

One problem with technological advance is that it encourages *imitation.* Successful innovative firms are often emulated by others. This imitation problem can be especially threatening to innovative, smaller firms because they can be challenged by the dominant firms in the industry. However, a firm has some advantages in taking the lead in innovation. Several advantages protect and reward the firm. Legal protections include patents, copyrights, and trademarks; other advantages are early brand-name recognition or the potential for a profitable buyout.

You spent the past three chapters learning about differences in the four market structures. Now you may be wondering whether one market structure is better suited than another for encouraging technological progress. The answer is clearly mixed because each structure has its strengths and shortcomings. The *inverted-U theory* gives you an even better framework for figuring out the optimal industry structure for R&D.

The chapter ends by returning to the issue of economic efficiency, a topic discussed throughout the text. Technological advance has a double benefit because it enhances both ***productive efficiency*** and ***allocative efficiency.*** Productive efficiency increases from process innovation that reduces production costs. Allocative efficiency increases because product innovation gives consumers more choice and gives society a more desired mix of products. The efficiency results are not automatic, and the outcome may depend on whether innovation strengthens or weakens monopoly power.

■ CHECKLIST

When you have studied this chapter you should be able to

☐ Define technological advance.
☐ Describe each of the three steps in technological advance.
☐ Explain the role of research and development (R&D) in technological advance.
☐ Contrast the traditional with the modern view of technological advance.
☐ Distinguish between entrepreneurs and other innovators and between startups and innovation with existing firms.

☐ Explain how innovators are rewarded for anticipating the future.
☐ Describe the role that universities and government play in fostering technological advance.
☐ Identify five means for financing R&D that are available to firms.
☐ Describe and show graphically with an example how the optimal level of R&D expenditures is determined.
☐ Explain how product innovation can increase profits by increasing revenues.
☐ Describe how process innovation can increase profits by reducing costs.
☐ Explain the imitation problem for firms.
☐ Identify six protections or advantages of being the first to develop a new product or process.
☐ Evaluate which of the four market structures are best suited to technological advance.
☐ Explain the inverted-U theory and its implications for technological progress.
☐ Describe how technological advance enhances both productive and allocative efficiency.
☐ Explain how innovation may lead to creative destruction and describe the criticisms of this view.

■ CHAPTER OUTLINE

1. ***Technological advance*** involves the development of new and improved products and new and improved ways of producing and distributing the products. It is a three-step process of invention, innovation, and diffusion.

a. ***Invention*** is the most basic part of technological advance and involves the discovery of a product or process. Governments encourage invention by granting the inventor a patent, which is an exclusive right to sell a product.

b. ***Innovation*** is the first successful commercial use of a new product or method or the creation of a new form of business. There are two major types: product innovation, which involves new and improved products or services, and process innovation, which involves new and improved production or distribution methods. Innovation is an important factor in competition because it can enable a firm to leapfrog competitors by making their products or methods obsolete.

c. ***Diffusion*** is the spread of an innovation through imitation or copying. New and existing firms copy or imitate successful innovation of other firms to profit from new opportunities or to protect their profits.

d. In business, research and development (R&D) includes work and expenditures directed toward invention, innovation, and diffusion. Government also supports R&D through defense expenditures and the funding of other activities.

e. The traditional view of technological advance was that it was external to the economy. It was a random force to which the economy adjusted and depended on the advance of science. The modern view is that technological advance is internal to capitalism. Intense rivalry among individuals and firms motivates them to seek and exploit new or expand existing opportunities for profit. Entrepreneurs and other innovators are the drivers of technological advance.

2. The ***entrepreneur*** is an initiator, innovator, and risk bearer. Other innovators are key people involved in the pursuit of innovation but who do not bear personal financial risk.

a. Entrepreneurs often form small new companies called ***startups,*** which are firms that create and introduce a new product or production technique.

b. Innovators are found within existing corporations. R&D work in major corporations has resulted in technological improvements, often by splitting off units to form innovative firms.

c. Innovators attempt to anticipate future needs. Product innovation and development are creative activities with both nonmonetary and monetary rewards. More resources for further innovation by entrepreneurs often comes from past successes. Those businesses that have succeeded in meeting consumer wants are given the opportunity to produce goods and services for the market.

d. New scientific knowledge is important to technological advance. Entrepreneurs study the scientific results from university and government laboratories to find those with commercial applicability.

3. The optimal amount of R&D for the firm depends on the marginal benefit and marginal cost of R&D activity. To earn the greatest profit, the firm will expand an activity until its marginal benefit equals its marginal cost.

a. Several sources are available for financing firms' R&D activities: bank loans, bonds, retained earnings, venture capital, or personal savings. A firm's marginal cost of these funds is an interest rate *i.*

b. A firm's marginal benefit of R&D is its expected profit (or return) from the last dollar spent on R&D.

c. The optimal amount of R&D in marginal-cost and marginal-benefit analysis is the point where the interest-rate cost-of-funds (marginal-cost) curve and the expected-rate-of-return (marginal-benefit) curve intersect. R&D expenditures can be justified only if the expected return equals or exceeds the cost of financing it. The firm expects positive outcomes from R&D, but the results are not guaranteed.

4. Technological change can increase a firm's profit in two ways.

a. The firm can increase revenues through *product innovation.* From a utility perspective, consumers will purchase a new product only if it increases total utility from their limited income. The purchases of the product increase the firm's revenues. Note three other points.

(1) Consumer acceptance of a new product depends on both its marginal utility and price.

(2) Many new products are not successful, so the firm fails to realize the expected return.

(3) Most product innovations are small or incremental improvements to existing products, not major changes.

b. *Process innovation,* the introduction of better ways to make products, is another way to increase profit and obtain a positive return on R&D expenditures. It results in a shift upward in the firm's total product curve and a shift downward in the firm's average total cost curve, which increase the firm's profit.

5. The *imitation problem* is that the rivals of a firm may copy or emulate the firm's product or process and thus decrease the profit from the innovator's R&D effort. When a dominant firm quickly imitates the successful new product of smaller competitors with the goal of becoming the second firm to adopt the innovation, it is using a fast-second strategy.

a. Taking the lead in innovation offers the firm several protections and potential advantages.

(1) Patents limit imitation and protect profits over time.

(2) Copyrights and trademarks reduce direct copying and increase the incentive for product innovation.

(3) Brand names may provide a major marketing asset.

(4) Trade secrets and learning by doing give firms an advantage.

(5) The time lags between innovation and diffusion give innovators time to make substantial economic profits.

(6) There is the potential purchase of the innovating firm by a larger firm at a high price.

6. Certain market structures may be best suited to foster technological progress.

a. Each structure has strengths and limitations.

(1) ***Pure competition:*** Strong competition gives firms the reason to innovate, but the expected rate of return on R&D may be low or negative for a pure competitor.

(2) ***Monopolistic competition:*** These firms have a strong profit incentive to develop and differentiate products, but they have limited ability to obtain inexpensive R&D financing. It is also difficult for these firms to extract large profits because the barriers to entry are relatively easy.

(3) ***Oligopoly:*** Although the size of firms makes them capable of promoting technological progress, there is little reason for them to introduce costly new technology and new products when they earn large economic profit without doing it.

(4) ***Pure monopoly:*** This firm has little incentive to engage in R&D because its high profit is protected by high barriers to entry.

b. ***Inverted-U theory*** suggests that R&D effort is weak in industries with very low concentration (pure competition) and very high concentration (pure monopoly). The optimal industry structure for R&D is one in which expected returns on R&D spending are high and funds are readily available and inexpensive to finance it. This generally occurs in industries with a few firms that are absolutely and relatively large, but the concentration ratio is not so high as to limit strong competition by smaller firms.

c. General support for the inverted-U theory comes from industry studies. The optimal market structure for technological advance appears to be an industry with a mix of large oligopolistic firms (a 40–60 percent concentration ratio) and several highly innovative smaller firms. The technical characteristics of an industry, however, may be a more important factor influencing R&D and its structure.

7. Technological advance enhances ***economic efficiency.***

a. *Process innovation* improves productive efficiency by increasing the productivity of inputs and reducing average total costs.

b. *Product* (or service) *innovation* enhances allocative efficiency by giving society a more-preferred mixture of goods and services.

(1) The efficiency gain from innovation, however, can be reduced if patents and the advantages of being first lead to monopoly power.

(2) Monopoly power, however, can be reduced or destroyed by innovation because it provides competition where there was none.

c. Innovation may foster ***creative destruction,*** whereby the creation of new products and production methods simultaneously destroys the monopoly positions of firms protecting existing products and methods. This view is expressed by Joseph Schumpeter, and there are many examples of it in business history. Another view suggests that creative destruction is not inevitable or automatic. In general, innovation improves economic efficiency, but in some cases it can increase monopoly power.

■ HINTS AND TIPS

1. The section of the chapter on a firm's optimal amount of R&D uses marginal-cost and marginal-benefit analysis similar to what you saw in previous chapters. In this case, the interest rate or expected return is graphed on the vertical axis and the amount of R&D spending on the horizontal axis. The only difference from previous MB-MC graphs is that the marginal cost in this example is assumed to be constant at the given interest rate. **It is graphed as a horizontal line.** The expected-rate-of-return curve is downward sloping because there are fewer opportunities for R&D expenditures with higher expected rates of return than at lower expected rates of return.

2. The explanation for how new products gain acceptance by consumers is based on the marginal utility theory that you learned about in Chapter 21. Be sure to review the text discussion of Table 21-1 before reading about the example in Table 26-1.

3. When new processes are developed, they can increase a firm's total product curve and decrease a firm's average total cost curve. Review the section in Chapter 22 in "Shifting the Cost Curves" to understand these points.

■ IMPORTANT TERMS

technological advance
very long run
invention
patents
innovation (product and process)
diffusion
startups
venture capital
interest-rate cost-of-funds curve

expected-rate-of-return curve
optimal amount of R&D
imitation problem
fast-second strategy
inverted-U theory of R&D
creative destruction

SELF-TEST

■ FILL-IN QUESTIONS

1. Technological advance is a three-step process of

a. ______________________

b. ______________________

c. ______________________

2. The first discovery of a product or process is (innovation, invention) ______________, whereas the first commercial introduction of a new product or process is ______________; patent protection is available for (invention, innovation) ______________ but not ______________. The spread of an innovation through imitation or copying is (trademarking, diffusion) ______________.

3. The development of new or improved products is (process, product) ______________ innovation; the development of new or improved production or distribution methods is ______________ innovation.

4. The traditional view of technological advance was that it was (internal, external) ______________ to the economy, but the modern view is that technological advance is ______________. In the modern view, technological advance arises from (scientific progress, rivalry among firms) ______________, but the traditional view holds that it arises from ______________ that is largely (internal, external) ______________ to the market system.

5. The individual who is an initiator, innovator, and risk bearer who combines resources in unique ways to produce new goods and services is called an (entrepreneur, intrapreneur) ______________, but an individual who promotes entrepreneurship within existing corporations is called an ______________. Entrepreneurs tend to form (large, small) ______________ companies called startups, and if they are successful they will receive ______________ monetary rewards.

6. Past successes often give entrepreneurs access to (more, less) ______________ resources for further innovation because the market economy (punishes, rewards) ______________ those businesses that meet consumer wants.

7. To earn the greatest profit from R&D spending, the firm should expand the activity until its marginal benefit is (greater than, less than, equal to) ______________ its marginal cost, but a firm should cut back its R&D if its marginal benefit is ______________ its marginal cost.

8. The five ways a firm can obtain funding to finance R&D spending are

a. ______________________

b. ______________________

c. ______________________

d. ______________________

e. ______________________

9. Product innovation will tend to increase a firm's profit by increasing the (costs, revenues) ______________ of the firm; process innovation will tend to increase a firm's profit by reducing the (costs, revenues) ______________ of the firm.

10. Consumer acceptance of a new product depends on its marginal utility (and, or) ______________ its price. The expected return that motivates product innovation (is, is not) ______________ always realized. Most product innovations are (major, minor) ______________ improvements to existing products.

11. Process innovation results in a shift (downward, upward) ______________ in the firm's total product curve and a shift ______________ in the firm's average-total-cost curve, which in turn (increases, decreases) ______________ the firm's profit.

12. The imitation problem is that the rivals of a firm may copy or emulate the firm's product or process and thus (increase, decrease) ______________ the profit from the innovator's R&D effort. When a dominant firm quickly imitates the successful new product of smaller competitors with the goal of becoming the second firm to adopt the innovation, it is using a (second-best, fast-second) ______________ strategy.

13. An example of legal protection for taking the lead in innovation would be (copyrights, trade secrets) ______________, but a nonlegal advantage might come from (patents, learning by doing) ______________.

14. In regard to R&D, purely competitive firms tend to be (less, more) ______________ complacent than monopolists, but the expected rate of return for a pure competitor may be (high, low) ______________, and they (may, may not) ______________ be able to finance R&D.

15. Monopolistically competitive firms have a (weak, strong) ________________ profit incentive to develop and differentiate products, but they have (extensive, limited) ________________ ability to obtain inexpensive R&D financing, and it is (difficult, easy) ________________ for these firms to extract large profits because the barriers to entry are relatively (high, low) ________________.

16. The size of oligopolistic firms makes them (capable, incapable) ________________ of promoting technological progress, but there is (much, little) ________________ reason for them to introduce costly new technology and new products when they earn (small, large) ________________ economic profit without doing it.

17. Pure monopoly has a (strong, weak) ________________ incentive to engage in R&D because its high profit is protected by (low, high) ________________ barriers to entry. This type of firm views R&D spending as a(n) (offensive, defensive) ________________ move to protect the monopoly from new products that would undercut its monopoly position.

18. Inverted-U theory suggests that R&D effort is at best (strong, weak) ________________ in industries with very low and very high concentrations. The optimal industry structure for R&D is one in which expected returns on R&D spending are (low, high) ________________ and funds are readily available and inexpensive to finance it. This generally occurs in industries with (many, a few) ________________ firms that are absolutely and relatively large, but the concentration ratio is not so high as to limit strong competition by smaller firms.

19. Technological advance increases the productivity of inputs, and by reducing average total costs it enhances (allocative, productive) ________________ efficiency; when it gives society a more-preferred mixture of goods and services it enhances ________________ efficiency. The efficiency gain from innovation can be (increased, decreased) ________________ if patents and the advantages of being first lead to monopoly power, but it can be ________________ if innovation provides competition where there was none.

20. Innovation may foster creative destruction, where the (destruction, creation) ________________ of new products and production methods simultaneously leads to the ________________ of the monopoly positions of firms protecting existing products and methods. Another view, however, suggests that creative destruction (is, is not) ________________ automatic. In general, innovation improves economic efficiency, but in some cases it can increase monopoly power.

■ TRUE-FALSE QUESTIONS

Circle the T if the statement is true, the F if it is false.

1. Technological advance consists of new and improved goods and services and new and improved production or distribution processes. **T F**

2. In economists' models, technological advance occurs in the short run, not the long run. **T F**

3. Invention is the first successful commercial introduction of a new product. **T F**

4. Firms channel a majority of their R&D expenditures to innovation and imitation rather than to basic scientific research. **T F**

5. Historically, most economists viewed technological advance as a predictable and internal force to which the economy adjusted. **T F**

6. The modern view of economists is that capitalism is the driving force of technological advance and such advance occurs in response to profit incentives within the economy. **T F**

7. The entrepreneur is an innovator but not a risk bearer. **T F**

8. Startups are small companies focused on creating and introducing a new product or using a new production or distribution technique. **T F**

9. The only innovators are entrepreneurs. **T F**

10. The market entrusts the production of goods and services to businesses which have consistently succeeded in fulfilling consumer wants. **T F**

11. Research and development rarely occur outside the labs of major corporations. **T F**

12. When entrepreneurs use personal savings to finance the R&D for a new venture, the marginal cost of financing is zero. **T F**

13. The optimal amount of R&D spending for the firm occurs where its expected return is greater than its interest-rate cost of funds to finance it. **T F**

14. Most firms are guaranteed a profitable outcome when making an R&D expenditure because the decisions are carefully evaluated. **T F**

15. A new product succeeds when it provides consumers with higher marginal utility per dollar spent than do existing products. **T F**

16. Most product innovations consist of major changes to existing products and are not incremental improvements. **T F**

17. Process innovation increases the firm's total product, lowers its average total cost, and increases its profit. **T F**

18. Imitation poses no problems for innovators because there are patent and trademark protections for their innovations. **T F**

19. A fast-second strategy involves letting the dominant firm set the price of the product and then letting smaller firms quickly undercut that price. **T F**

20. Pure competition is the best market structure for encouraging R&D and innovation. **T F**

21. One major shortcoming of monopolistic competition in promoting technological progress is its limited ability to secure inexpensive financing for R&D. **T F**

22. The inverted-U theory suggests that R&D effort is strongest in very low-concentration industries and weakest in very high-concentration industries. **T F**

23. The technical and scientific characteristics of an industry may be more important than its structure in determining R&D spending and innovation. **T F**

24. Technological advance enhances productive efficiency but not allocative efficiency. **T F**

25. Creative destruction is the process the inventor goes through in developing new products and innovations. **T F**

■ MULTIPLE-CHOICE QUESTIONS

Circle the letter that corresponds to the best answer.

1. The period in which technology can change and in which firms can introduce entirely new products is the
(a) short run
(b) very short run
(c) long run
(d) very long run

2. Technological progress is a three-step process of
(a) creation, pricing, and marketing
(b) invention, innovation, and diffusion
(c) manufacturing, venturing, and promotion
(d) startups, imitation, and creative destruction

3. The first discovery of a product or process through the use of imagination, ingenious thinking, and experimentation and the first proof that it will work is
(a) process innovation
(b) product innovation
(c) creative destruction
(d) invention

4. From the time of application, patents have a uniform duration of
(a) 10 years
(b) 15 years
(c) 20 years
(d) 25 years

5. Innovation is a major factor in competition because it can
(a) be patented to protect the investment of the developers
(b) enable firms to make competitors' products obsolete
(c) guarantee the monopoly position of innovative firms
(d) reduce research and development costs for firms

6. What idea is best illustrated by the example of McDonald's successfully introducing the fast-food hamburger and then that idea being adopted by other firms such as Burger King and Wendy's?
(a) startups
(b) diffusion
(c) invention
(d) fast-second strategy

7. About what percentage of GDP in the United States is spent on research and development?
(a) 2.5 percent
(b) 5 percent
(c) 7.5 percent
(d) 10 percent

8. The modern view of technological advance is that it is
(a) rooted in the independent advancement of science
(b) best stimulated through government R&D spending
(c) a result of intense rivalry among individuals and firms
(d) a random outside force to which the economy adjusts

9. The major difference between entrepreneurs and other innovators is that
(a) innovators work in teams, but entrepreneurs do not
(b) innovators manage startups, but entrepreneurs do not
(c) entrepreneurs bear personal financial risk, but innovators do not
(d) entrepreneurs invent new products and processes, but innovators do not

10. Past successes in developing products often means that entrepreneurs and innovative firms
(a) have access to more private resources for further innovation
(b) have access to less private resources for further innovation
(c) have access to more public support for further innovation
(d) experience no change in the availability of private or public resources for further innovation

Questions 11, 12, and 13 are based on the following table showing the expected rate of return, R&D spending, and interest-rate cost of funds for a hypothetical firm.

Expected rate of return (%)	R&D (millions of $)	Interest-rate cost of funds (%)
15	20	9
13	40	9
11	60	9
9	80	9
7	100	9

11. In a supply and demand graph, the interest-rate-cost-of-funds curve would be a(n)
(a) vertical line at 9%
(b) horizontal line at 9%
(c) upward sloping line over the 15 to 7% range
(d) downward sloping line over the 15 to 7% range

12. The optimal amount of R&D would be
(a) $40 million
(b) $60 million
(c) $80 million
(d) $100 million

13. If interest-rate cost of funds rose to 13%, the optimal amount of R&D spending would be
(a) $40 million
(b) $60 million
(c) $80 million
(d) $100 million

14. Product innovation tends to increase the profits of firms primarily by
(a) decreasing the firm's average costs
(b) increasing the firm's total revenue
(c) decreasing marginal utility per dollar spent
(d) increasing the success of R&D spending

15. Consumers will buy a new product only if
(a) it has a lower marginal utility per dollar spent than another product
(b) there is a substantial budget for promotion and marketing
(c) it can be sold at a lower price than that for a competing product
(d) it increases the total utility they obtain from their limited income

16. Process innovation produces a(n)
(a) downward shift in the total-product curve and an upshift in the average-cost curve
(b) upward shift in the total-product curve and a downshift in the average-cost curve
(c) upward shift in both the total-product and average-cost curves
(d) downward shift in both the total-product and average-cost curves

17. Some dominant firms in an industry use a fast-second strategy that involves
(a) developing two products to compete with rivals
(b) cutting the development time for the introduction of a new product
(c) moving quickly to buy the second largest firm in the industry to gain larger market share
(d) letting smaller firms initiate new products and then quickly imitating the success

18. One legal protection for taking the lead in innovation is
(a) venture capital
(b) trademarks
(c) trade secrets
(d) mergers

19. One major advantage of being the first to develop a product is the
(a) use of the fast-second strategy
(b) increase in retained earnings
(c) lower interest-rate costs of funds
(d) potential for profitable buyouts

20. Which firm has a strong incentive for product development and differentiation?
(a) a monopolistically competitive firm
(b) a purely competitive firm
(c) an oligopolistic firm
(d) a pure monopoly

21. In which market structure is there the least incentive to engage in R&D?
(a) a monopolistically competitive firm
(b) a purely competitive firm
(c) an oligopolistic firm
(d) a pure monopoly

22. The inverted-U theory suggests that R&D effort is at best weak in
(a) low-concentration industries only
(b) high-concentration industries only
(c) low- and high-concentration industries
(d) low- to middle-concentration industries

23. The optimal market structure for technological advance seems to be an industry in which there
(a) are many purely competitive firms
(b) are monopolists closely regulated by government
(c) is a mix of large oligopolistic firms with several small and highly innovative firms
(d) is a mix of monopolistically competitive firms and a few large monopolists in industries with high capital costs

24. Technological advance as embodied in process innovation typically
(a) decreases allocative efficiency
(b) increases allocative efficiency
(c) decreases productive efficiency
(d) increases productive efficiency

25. Why did Joseph Schumpeter view capitalism as a process of "creative destruction"?
(a) Innovation would lead to monopoly power and thus destroy the economy.
(b) The creation of new products and production methods would destroy the market for existing products.
(c) Invention would create new products, but diffusion would destroy many potentially good ideas.
(d) Firms are being creative with the learning by doing, but this spirit is destroyed by the inability of firms to finance R&D expenditures.

■ PROBLEMS

1. Match the terms with the phrase using the appropriate number

1. invention 2. innovation 3. diffusion

a. Imitation of the Chrysler Corporation's Jeep Grand Cherokee with sport utilities developed by other auto companies ________
b. The first working model of the microchip ________
c. Computers and word processing software that eliminate the need for typewriters ________

d. Adoption of the Boston Market's concept of oven-roasted chicken as an item on the menu at KFC ________

e. The creation of the first electric lightbulb ________

f. Development of a new brand of carpet by DuPont ________

2. Use the following table, which shows the rate of return and R&D spending for a hypothetical firm.

Expected rate of return (%)	R&D (millions of $)
24	3
20	6
16	9
12	12
9	15
6	18
3	21

a. Assume the interest-rate cost of funds is 12%. The optimal amount of R&D expenditures will be $________ million. At this amount, the marginal cost of R&D spending is ________% and the marginal benefit (the expected rate of return) is ________%.

b. Graph the marginal cost and marginal benefit curves of R&D spending in the graph below. Be sure to label the axes.

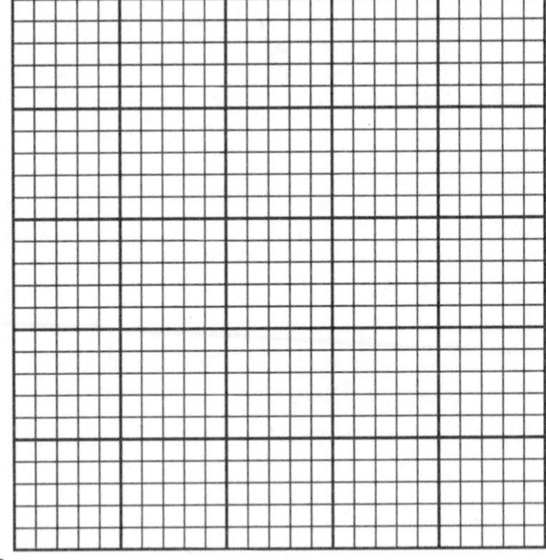

c. Now assume that the interest-rate cost of funds falls to 6%. The optimal amount of spending will be $________ million. For this amount of R&D spending, the marginal cost of R&D spending is ________% and the marginal benefit (expected rate of return) is ________%.

d. Show on the graph above how the interest-rate cost-of-funds curve changed in the answer that you gave for **b.**

3. Following are two average-total-cost schedules for a firm. The first schedule (ATC_1) shows the cost of producing the product at five levels of output before a new innovation. The second schedule (ATC_2) shows the average total cost at the five output levels after the innovation.

Output	Before ATC_1	After ATC_2
10	$30	$27
20	25	18
30	18	14
40	22	19
50	28	26

a. Plot the average-cost curves for the schedules on the following graph.

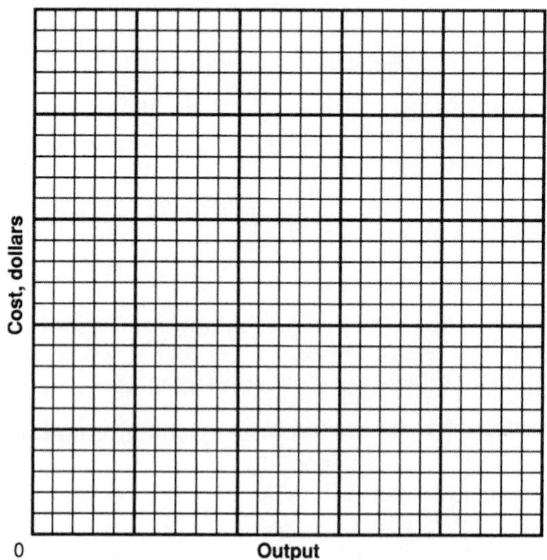

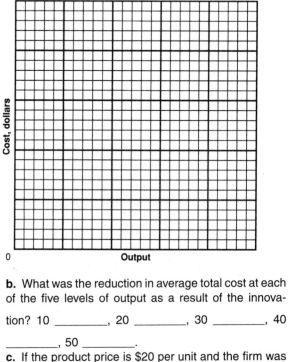

b. What was the reduction in average total cost at each of the five levels of output as a result of the innovation? 10 ________, 20 ________, 30 ________, 40 ________, 50 ________.

c. If the product price is $20 per unit and the firm was producing at 30 units of output, the profit for the firm before the innovation was $________. At this level of output, the profit after the innovation was $________.

■ SHORT ANSWER AND ESSAY QUESTIONS

1. Give a definition of technological advance. According to economists, what role does time play in the definition?

2. Explain and give examples of invention. What does government do to protect it?

3. How does innovation differ from invention and diffusion? How does innovation affect competition among firms?

4. Compare and contrast the modern view of technological advance with the traditional view.

5. In what ways to entrepreneurs differ from other innovators? In what types of business does each tend to work? How have the characteristics of entrepreneurs changed over time?

6. What does it mean that "innovators try to anticipate the future?" What are the economic consequences of this effort?

7. Why do entrepreneurs and other innovators actively study the scientific output of universities and government laboratories?

8. Explain how the firm decides on the optimal amount of research and development. Use a marginal-cost and marginal-benefit graph in your explanation.

9. What are the many different sources of funding to finance firms' R&D expenditures? If an entrepreneur uses personal funds, is there a cost for financing?

10. Why might many R&D expenditures be affordable but not worthwhile? Are outcomes from R&D guaranteed?

11. Describe how a firm's revenues and profits are increased through product innovation. Why does consumer acceptance of a new product depend on both its marginal utility and price?

12. Explain how process innovation reduces cost and increases profits. Illustrate the point graphically using a total-product and average-cost curve graph.

13. Describe the fast-second strategy and give an example of it.

14. What is the imitation problem resulting from technological advance?

15. Describe the legal protections and potential advantages of taking the lead in innovation.

16. Compare and contrast the suitability of different market structures for fostering technological advance.

17. Explain the basic conclusions from inverted-U theory. What will be the optimal market structure for technological progress?

18. How does technological advance enhance economic efficiency? Distinguish between its effects on productive efficiency and allocative efficiency.

19. How might innovation create or reduce monopoly power? Why might both effects be possible?

20. Explain the idea of creative destruction as championed by Joseph Schumpeter. What are the objections to that idea?

ANSWERS

Chapter 26 Technology, R&D, and Efficiency

FILL-IN QUESTIONS

1. *a.* invention, *b.* innovation, *c.* diffusion
2. invention, innovation, invention, innovation, diffusion
3. product, process
4. external, internal, rivalry among firms, scientific progress, external
5. entrepreneur, intrapreneurs, small, large
6. more, rewards
7. equal to, less than
8. *a.* bank loans; *b.* bonds; *c.* retained earnings; *d.* venture capital; *e.* personal savings (any order for *a–e*)
9. revenues, costs
10. and, is not, minor
11. upward, downward, increases
12. decrease, fast-second
13. copyrights, learning by doing
14. less, low, may not
15. strong, limited, difficult, low
16. capable, little, large
17. weak, high, defensive
18. weak, high, a few
19. productive, allocative, decreased, increased
20. creation, destruction, is not

TRUE-FALSE QUESTIONS

1. T, p. 541
2. F, p. 541
3. F, p. 542
4. T, p. 543
5. F, p. 543
6. T, pp. 543-544
7. F, p. 544
8. T, p. 544
9. F, p. 544
10. T, p. 545
11. F, p. 545
12. F, p. 546
13. F, p. 548
14. F, p. 548
15. T, pp. 549-550
16. F, p. 550-551
17. T, pp. 550-551
18. F, pp. 551-553
19. F, p. 551
20. F, pp. 553-554
21. T, p. 554
22. F, p. 555
23. T, p. 556
24. F, pp. 556-558
25. F, pp. 558-559

MULTIPLE-CHOICE QUESTIONS

1. d, p. 541
2. b, p. 542
3. d, p. 542
4. c, p. 542
5. b, p. 542
6. b, p. 542
7. a, p. 542
8. c, p. 543
9. c, p. 544
10. a, p. 545
11. b, pp. 546-547
12. c, p. 548
13. a, p. 548
14. b, pp. 549-550
15. d, p. 549
16. b, pp. 550-551
17. d, p. 551
18. b, pp. 551-552
19. d, p. 552
20. a, p. 554
21. d, p. 554
22. c, p. 555
23. c, pp. 555-556
24. d, p. 557
25. b, pp. 558-559

PROBLEMS

1. *a.* 3; *b.* 1; *c.* 2; *d.* 3; *e.* 1; *f.* 2
2. *a.* 12, 12, 12; *b.* similar to Figure 26-5 in the text; *c.* 18, 6, 6; *d.* horizontal interest-rate cost-of-funds curve will drop from 12 to 6%
3. *a.* Put output on the horizontal axis, and put average cost on the vertical axis. Plot the set of points. Connect the set with lines; *b.* 3, 7, 4, 3, 2; *c.* Before: TR is \$600 (30 × \$20), TC is \$540 (30 × \$18), profit is \$60; After: TR is \$600, TC is \$420 (30 × \$14), profit is \$180.

SHORT ANSWER AND ESSAY QUESTIONS

1. p. 541
2. p. 542
3. p. 542
4. pp. 543-544
5. p. 544
6. pp. 544-545
7. p. 545
8. pp. 546-548
9. p. 546
10. p. 548
11. pp. 549-550
12. pp. 550-551
13. p. 551
14. p. 551
15. pp. 551-552
16. pp. 553-554
17. pp. 555-556
18. pp. 556-558
19. p. 558
20. pp. 558-559

CHAPTER **27**

The Demand for Resources

This chapter is the first of three which examine the market for resources. Resource markets are those in which employers of the resources are the demanders and the owners of the resources are the suppliers. As you already know, the demand for and the supply of a resource will determine the resource price and the quantities employed in a competitive market.

Chapter 27 focuses on the demand or employer side of the resource market, offering a general explanation of what determines demand for *any resource but not for any particular resource.* Chapters 28 and 29 discuss the characteristic of the market for particular resources—labor, capital, land, or entrepreneurial ability—and present the supply side of the resource market.

The resource market is important for several reasons, as you will learn in the first section of the chapter. Resource prices determine what resource suppliers (or households) receive in exchange for their resources and thus the income of households. Prices allocate resources to their most efficient uses and encourage the least costly methods of production in our economy. Many public policy issues also involve resource pricing, such as setting a minimum wage.

The next section of the chapter focuses on the marginal productivity theory of resource demand. You know from previous chapters that when a firm wishes to maximize its profits, it produces that output at which marginal revenue and marginal cost are equal. But how much of each resource does the firm hire if it wishes to maximize its profits? You will learn that the firm hires that amount of each resource at which the marginal revenue product and the marginal resource cost of that resource are equal.

There is another similarity between the output and the resource markets for the firm. Recall that the competitive firm's supply curve is a portion of its marginal-cost curve. The purely competitive firm's demand curve for a resource is a portion of its marginal-revenue-product curve. Just as cost is the important determinant of supply, the revenue derived from the use of a resource is the important factor determining the demand for that resource in a competitive market for resources.

The next major section of the chapter presents the ***determinants of resource demand.*** Three major ones are discussed—changes in product demand, productivity, and the prices of other resources. The last determinant is the most complicated one to understand in terms of its effect on resource demand because you must consider whether the other resources are substitutes or complements and the underlying factors affecting them.

This chapter also has a section on the *elasticity of resource demand,* which is no different from the elasticity concept you learned about in Chapter 2. In this case, it is the percentage change in quantity demanded of the resource to a percentage change in the price of the resource. As you will discover, the four factors that affect elasticity are the rate at which the marginal product of the resource declines, the availability of other substitute resources, the elasticity of product demand, and the ratio of resource cost to total cost.

Most of the chapter examines the situation in which there is only one variable resource. The next-to-last section of the chapter, however, offers a general perspective on the combination of resources the firm will choose to use when multiple inputs are used and all inputs are variable. Two rules are presented. The *least-cost rule* states that the firm will minimize costs when the last dollar spent on each resource results in the same marginal product. The *profit-maximizing rule* means that in a competitive market the firm will maximize its profits when each resource is used so that its marginal product is equal to its price. The second rule is equally important because a firm that employs the quantity of resources that maximizes its profits also produces the output that maximizes its profits and is thus producing at least cost.

The marginal productivity theory of resource demand is not without criticism, as you will learn in the last section of the chapter. If resource prices reflect marginal productivity, then this relationship can produce income inequality in society. In addition, market imperfection may skew the distribution of income.

■ CHECKLIST

When you have studied this chapter you should be able to

☐ Present four reasons for studying resource pricing.
☐ Explain why the demand for an economic resource is a derived demand.
☐ Define marginal revenue product.
☐ Determine the marginal-revenue-product schedule of a resource used to produce a product which is sold in a purely competitive market when you are given the relevant data.

□ Define marginal resource cost.
□ State the rule used by a profit-maximizing firm to determine how much of a resource it will employ.
□ Apply the MRP = MRC rule to determine the quantity of a resource a firm will hire when you are given the necessary data.
□ Explain why the marginal-revenue-product schedule of a resource is the firm's demand for the resource.
□ Find the marginal-revenue-product schedule of a resource used to produce a product which is sold in an imperfectly competitive market when you are given the necessary data.
□ Derive the market demand for a resource.
□ List the three factors which would change a firm's demand for a resource.
□ Predict the effect of an increase or decrease in each of the three factors affecting resource demand on the demand of a firm for a resource.
□ Give examples of the practical significance of the determinants of labor demand.
□ Enumerate the four determinants of the price elasticity of demand for a resource.
□ Describe how a change in each of the four determinants of the resource price elasticity would change the price elasticity of demand for a resource.
□ State the rule used by a firm to determine the least-cost combination of resources.
□ Use the least-cost rule to find the least-cost combination of resources for production when you are given the necessary data.
□ State the rule used by a profit-maximizing firm to determine how much of each of several resources to employ.
□ Apply the profit-maximizing rule to determine the quantity of each resource a firm will hire when you are given the necessary data.
□ Explain the marginal productivity theory of income distribution.
□ Give two criticisms of the marginal productivity theory of income distribution.

■ CHAPTER OUTLINE

1. The study of what determines the prices of resources is *important* because resource prices influence the size of individual incomes and the resulting distribution of income. They allocate scarce resources and affect the way in which firms combine resources to produce their products. They also raise ethical questions about the distribution of income.

2. Economists generally agree on the basic principles of resource pricing, but the complexities of different resource markets make these principles difficult to apply.

3. The ***demand*** for a single resource depends on (or is derived from) the demand for the goods and services it can produce.

a. Because resource demand is a ***derived demand,*** the demand for a single resource depends on the marginal productivity of the resource and the market price of the good or service it is used to produce.

b. Marginal revenue product combines these two factors—the marginal product of a resource and the market price of the product it produces—into a single useful tool.

c. A firm will hire a resource up to the quantity at which the marginal revenue product of the resource is equal to its marginal resource cost: MRP = MRC.

d. The firm's marginal-revenue-product schedule for a resource is that firm's demand schedule for the resource.

e. If a firm sells its output in an *imperfectly competitive market,* the more the firm sells the lower becomes the price of the product. This causes the firm's marginal-revenue-product (resource demand) schedule to be less elastic than it would be if the firm sold its output in a purely competitive market.

f. The market (or total) demand for a resource is the horizontal summation of the demand schedules of all firms employing the resource.

4. *Changes in the demand* for the product being produced, changes in the productivity of the resource, and changes in the prices of other resources will tend to *change the demand for a resource.*

a. A change in the demand for a product produced by a resource such as labor will change the demand of a firm for labor in the same direction.

b. A change in the productivity of a resource such as labor (caused by an increase in the quantity of other resources such as capital, technological improvements, and improvement in resource quality) will change the demand of a firm for the resource in the same direction.

c. A change in the price of a

(1) *substitute* resource will change the demand for a resource such as labor in the same direction if the substitution effect outweighs the output effect and in the opposite direction if the output effect outweighs the substitution effect;

(2) *complementary* resource will change the demand for a resource such as labor in the opposite direction.

d. There are many real-world applications of the determinants of labor demand. The chapter discusses the reasons for changes in the demand for auto, fast-food, computer, office, defense, and contingent workers in recent years.

5. The ***price elasticity of resource demand*** measures the sensitivity of producers to changes in resource prices.

a. Four possible factors affect the price elasticity of resource demand:

(1) the rate at which the marginal product of the resource declines—the slower the rate, the more elastic the resource demand;

(2) the ease of substitution of other resources—the more good substitute resources that are available, the more elastic the demand for the resource;

(3) the elasticity of the demand for the product that the resource produces—the more elastic the product demand, the more elastic the resource demand;

(4) the ratio of labor cost to total cost—the greater the ratio of labor cost to total cost, the greater the price elasticity of demand for labor.

6. Firms typically employ more than one resource in producing a product.
   a. The firm employing resources in purely competitive markets is hiring resources in the *least-cost* combination when the ratio of the marginal product of a resource to its price is the same for all the resources the firm hires.
   b. The firm is hiring resources in the *most profitable* combination if it hires resources in a purely competitive market when the *marginal revenue product of each resource is equal to the price of that resource.*
   c. A numerical example illustrates the least-cost and profit-maximizing rules for a firm that employs resources in purely competitive markets.

7. The marginal productivity theory of *income distribution* seems to result in an equitable distribution of income because each unit of a resource receives a payment equal to its marginal contribution to the firm's revenue. The theory has at least two serious faults.
   a. The distribution of income will be unequal because resources are unequally distributed among individuals in the economy.
   b. The income of those who supply resources will not be based on their marginal productivities if there is monopsony or monopoly in the resource markets of the economy.

■ HINTS AND TIPS

1. The list of important terms for Chapter 27 is relatively short, but included in the list are two very important concepts—***marginal revenue product*** and ***marginal resource cost***—which you must grasp if you are to understand how much of a resource a firm will hire. These two concepts are similar to, but not identical with, the marginal-revenue and marginal-cost concepts used in the study of product markets and in the explanation of the quantity of output a firm will produce.

Marginal revenue and marginal cost are, respectively, the change in the firm's total revenue and the change in the firm's total cost when it produces and sells an additional unit of **output.** Marginal revenue product and marginal resource cost are, respectively, the change in the firm's total revenue and the change in the firm's total cost when it hires an additional unit of **input.** Note that the two new concepts deal with changes in revenue and costs as a consequence of hiring more of a **resource.**

2. The marginal revenue product (MRP) of a resource is simply the marginal product of the resource (MP) times price of the product that resource produces (***P***), or MRP = MP × ***P***. Under pure competition, MP changes, but ***P*** is constant as more resources are added to production. Under imperfect competition, both MP and ***P*** change as more resources are added, and thus each variable (MP and ***P***) affects MRP. Compare the data in Tables 27-1 and 27-2 in the textbook to see this difference.

3. Make sure you understand the rule MRP = MRC. A firm will hire one more unit of a resource only so long as the resource adds more to the firm's revenues than it does to its costs. If MRP > MRC, the firm will hire more resources. If MRP < MRC, the firm will cut back on resource use.

4. It can be perplexing to figure out what outcome will result from a change in the price of a substitute resource (capital) on the demand for another resource (labor). It is easy to understand why the demand for labor might decrease if the price of capital decreases because cheaper capital would be substituted for labor. It is harder to explain why the opposite may be true. That insight requires an understanding of both the ***substitution effect*** and the ***output effect.*** Find out how one effect may offset the other.

5. The profit-maximizing rule for a combination of resources may seem difficult, but it is relatively simple. Just remember that the price of any resource must be equal to its marginal revenue product, and thus **the ratio must always equal 1.**

■ IMPORTANT TERMS

derived demand
marginal product
marginal revenue product
marginal resource cost
MRP = MRC rule
substitution effect
output effect
least-cost combination of resources
profit-maximizing combination of resources
marginal productivity theory of income distribution

SELF-TEST

■ FILL-IN QUESTIONS

1. Resource prices allocate (revenues, resources) ______ and are one factor that determine household (incomes, costs) ______ and business ______.

2. The demand for a resource is a (constant, derived) ______ demand that depends on the (productivity, cost) ______ of the resource and the (cost, price) ______ of the product made from the resource.

3. A firm will find it profitable to hire units of a resource up to the quantity at which the marginal revenue (cost, product) ______ equals the marginal resource ______.

4. If the firm hires the resource in a purely competitive market, the marginal resource (cost, product) ______ will be (greater than, less than, equal to) ______ the price of the resource.

5. A firm's demand schedule for a resource is the firm's marginal revenue (cost, product) ______________ schedule for that resource because both indicate the quantities of the resource the firm will employ at various resource (costs, prices) ______________.

6. A producer in an imperfectly competitive market finds that the more of a resource it employs, the (higher, lower) ______________ becomes the price at which it can sell its product. As a consequence, the (supply, demand) ______________ schedule for the resource is (more, less) ______________ elastic than it would be if the output were sold in a purely competitive market.

7. Adding the quantity demanded for the resource at each and every price for each firm using the resource gives the market (supply, demand) ______________ curve for the resource.

8. The demand for a resource will change if the (demand, supply) ______________ of the product the resource produces changes, if the (productivity, price) ______________ of the resource changes, or if the (price, elasticity) ______________ of other resources change.

9. If the demand for a product increases, then the demand for the resource that produces that product will (increase, decrease) ______________. Conversely, if the demand for a product decreases, then the demand for the resource that produces that product will ______________.

10. When the productivity of a resource falls, the demand for the resource (rises, falls) ______________, but when the productivity of a resource rises, the demand for the resource ______________.

11. The output of the firm being constant, a decrease in the price of resource A will induce the firm to hire (more, less) ______________ of resource A and ______________ of other resources; this is called the (substitution, output) ______________ effect. But if the decrease in the price of A results in lower total costs and an increase in output, the firm may hire (more, less) ______________ of both resources; this is called the (substitution, output) ______________ effect.

12. A decrease in the price of a complementary resource will cause the demand for labor to (increase, decrease) ______________, but an increase in the price of a complementary resource will cause the demand for labor to ______________.

13. The four determinants of the price elasticity of demand for a resource are the rate at which the marginal (cost, product) ______________ of the resource decreases, the ease with which other resources can be (substitutes, complements) ______________ for it, the price elasticity of (supply, demand) ______________ for the product the resource produces, and the ratio of resource (demand, cost) ______________ to total (demand, cost) ______________.

14. If the marginal product of labor declines slowly when added to a fixed stock of capital, the demand curve for labor (MRP) will decline (rapidly, slowly) ______________ and will tend to be highly (elastic, inelastic) ______________.

15. The larger the number of good substitutes available for a resource, the (greater, less) ______________ will be the elasticity of demand for a resource.

16. Suppose a firm employs resources in purely competitive markets. If the firm wishes to produce any given amount of its output in the least costly way, the ratio of the marginal (cost, product) ______________ of each resource to its (demand, price) ______________ must be the same for all resources.

17. A firm that hires resources in purely competitive markets is employing the combination of resources which will result in maximum profits for the firm when the marginal (revenue product, resource cost) ______________ of every resource is equal to its (demand, price) ______________.

18. If the marginal revenue product of a resource is equal to the price of that resource, the marginal revenue product divided by its price is equal to (1, infinity) ______________.

19. In the marginal productivity theory, the distribution of income is an equitable one because each unit of each resource is paid an amount equal to its (total, marginal) ______________ contribution to the firm's (revenues, costs) ______________.

20. The marginal productivity theory rests on the assumption of (competitive, imperfect) ______________ markets. In the real world, there are market imperfections because of employer pricing or monopoly power, so wage rates and other resource prices (do, do not) ______________ measure contributions to domestic output.

■ TRUE-FALSE QUESTIONS

Circle the T if the statement is true, the F if it is false.

1. In the resource markets of the economy resources are demanded by business firms and supplied by households. **T F**

2. The prices of resources are an important factor in the determination of resource allocation. **T F**

3. The demand for a resource is a derived demand based on the demand for the product it produces. **T F**

4. A resource which is highly productive will always be in great demand. **T F**

5. A firm's demand schedule for a resource is the firm's marginal-revenue-product schedule for the resource. **T F**

6. It will be profitable for a firm to hire additional units of labor resources up to the point where the marginal revenue product of labor is equal to its marginal resource cost. **T F**

7. A firm with one worker can produce 30 units of a product that sells for $4 a unit, but the same firm with two workers can produce 70 units of that product. The marginal revenue product of the second worker is $400. **T F**

8. The marginal revenue product of a purely competitive seller will fall because marginal product diminishes and product price falls as output increases. **T F**

9. A producer's demand schedule for a resource will be more elastic if the firm sells its product in a purely competitive market than it would be if it sold the product in an imperfectly competitive market. **T F**

10. The market demand for a particular resource is the sum of the individual demands of all firms that employ that resource. **T F**

11. An increase in the price of a resource will cause the demand for the resource to decrease. **T F**

12. The demand curve for labor will increase when the demand for (and price of) the product produced by that labor increases. **T F**

13. There is an inverse relationship between the productivity of labor and the demand for labor. **T F**

14. The demand for a resource will be increased with improvements in its quality. **T F**

15. When two resources are substitutes for each other, both the substitution effect and the output effect of a decrease in the price of one of these resources operate to increase the quantity of the other resource employed by the firm. **T F**

16. The output effect of an increase in the price of a resource increases the quantity demanded of that resource. **T F**

17. If two resources are complementary, an increase in the price of one will reduce the demand for the other. **T F**

18. The faster the rate at which the marginal product of a variable resource declines, the greater will be the price elasticity of demand for that resource. **T F**

19. The larger the number of good substitute resources available, the less will be the elasticity of demand for a particular resource. **T F**

20. The greater the elasticity of product demand, the greater the elasticity of resource demand. **T F**

21. The demand for labor will be less elastic when labor is a smaller proportion of the total cost of producing a product. **T F**

Use the following information as the basis for answering Questions 22 and 23. The marginal revenue product and price of resource A are $12 and a constant $2, respectively, and the marginal revenue product and price of resource B are $25 and a constant $5, respectively. The firm sells its product at a constant price of $1.

22. The firm should decrease the amount of A and increase the amount of B it employs if it wishes to decrease its total cost without affecting its total output. **T F**

23. If the firm wishes to maximize its profits, it should increase its employment of both A and B until their marginal revenue products fall to $2 and $5, respectively. **T F**

24. The marginal productivity theory of income distribution results in an equitable distribution if resource markets are competitive. **T F**

25. The marginal productivity theory rests on the assumption of imperfectly competitive markets. **T F**

■ MULTIPLE-CHOICE QUESTIONS

Circle the letter that corresponds to the best answer.

1. The prices paid for resources affect
(a) the money incomes of households in the economy
(b) the allocation of resources among different firms and industries in the economy
(c) the quantities of different resources employed to produce a particular product
(d) all of the above

2. The study of the pricing of resources tends to be complex because
(a) supply and demand do not determine resource prices
(b) economists do not agree on the basic principles of resource pricing
(c) the basic principles of resource pricing must be varied and adjusted when applied to particular resource markets
(d) resource pricing is essentially an ethical question

3. The demand for a resource is *derived* from the
(a) marginal productivity of the resource and price of the good or service produced from it
(b) marginal productivity of the resource and the price of the resource
(c) price of the resource and the price of the good or service produced from it
(d) price of the resource and the quantity of the resource demanded

4. The law of diminishing returns explains why
(a) the MRP of an input in a purely competitive market decreases as a firm increases the quantity of an employed resource

(b) the MRC of an input in a purely competitive market decreases as a firm increases the quantity of an employed resource
(c) resource demand is a derived demand
(d) there are substitution and output effects for resources

Answer Questions 5, 6, and 7 on the basis of the information in the following table for a purely competitive market.

Number of workers	Total product	Product price ($)
0	0	4
1	16	4
2	26	4
3	34	4
4	40	4
5	44	4

5. At a wage rate of $15, the firm will choose to employ
(a) 2 workers
(b) 3 workers
(c) 4 workers
(d) 5 workers

6. At a wage rate of $30, the firm will choose to employ
(a) 2 workers
(b) 3 workers
(c) 4 workers
(d) 5 workers

7. If the product price increases to a constant $8, then at a wage rate of $30 the firm will choose to employ
(a) 2 workers
(b) 3 workers
(c) 4 workers
(d) 5 workers

Use the following total-product and marginal-product schedules for a resource to answer Questions 8, 9, 10, and 11. Assume that the quantities of other resources the firm employs remain constant.

Units of resource	Total product	Marginal product
0	0	—
1	8	8
2	14	6
3	18	4
4	21	3
5	23	2

8. If the product the firm produces sells for a constant $3 per unit, the marginal revenue product of the 4th unit of the resource is
(a) $3
(b) $6
(c) $9
(d) $12

9. If the firm's product sells for a constant $3 per unit and the price of the resource is a constant $15, the firm will employ how many units of the resource?
(a) 2
(b) 3
(c) 4
(d) 5

10. If the firm can sell 14 units of output at a price of $1 per unit and 18 units of output at a price of $0.90 per unit, the marginal revenue product of the 3rd unit of the resource is
(a) $4
(b) $3.60
(c) $2.20
(d) $0.40

11. If the firm can sell 8 units at a price of $1.50, 14 units at a price of $1.00, 18 units at a price of $0.90, 21 units at a price of $0.70, and 23 units at a price of $0.50, then the firm is
(a) maximizing profits at a product price of $0.50
(b) minimizing its costs at a product price of $1.00
(c) selling in an imperfectly competitive market
(d) selling in a purely competitive market

12. As a firm that sells its product in an imperfectly competitive market increases the quantity of a resource it employs, the marginal revenue product of that resource falls because
(a) the price paid by the firm for the resource falls
(b) the marginal product of the resource falls
(c) the price at which the firm sells its product falls
(d) both the marginal product and the price at which the firm sells its product fall

13. Which of the following would increase a firm's demand for a particular resource?
(a) an increase in the prices of complementary resources used by the firm
(b) a decrease in the demand for the firm's product
(c) an increase in the productivity of the resource
(d) an increase in the price of the particular resource

14. The substitution effect indicates that a firm will use
(a) more of an input whose relative price has decreased
(b) more of an input whose relative price has increased
(c) less of an input whose relative price has decreased
(d) less of an input whose relative price has remained constant

15. Suppose resource A and resource B are substitutes and the price of A increases. If the output effect is greater than the substitution effect,
(a) the quantity of A employed by the firm will increase and the quantity of B employed will decrease
(b) the quantity of both A and B employed by the firm will decrease
(c) the quantity of both A and B employed by the firm will increase
(d) the quantity of A employed will decrease and the quantity of B employed will increase

16. Two resource inputs, capital and labor, are complementary and used in fixed proportions. A decrease in the price of capital will
(a) increase the demand for labor
(b) decrease the demand for labor
(c) decrease the quantity demanded for labor
(d) have no effect because the relationship is fixed

17. Which of the following would result in an increase in the elasticity of demand for a particular resource?
(a) an increase in the rate at which the marginal product of that resource declines
(b) a decrease in the elasticity of demand for the product which the resource helps to produce
(c) an increase in the percentage of the firm's total costs accounted for by the resource
(d) a decrease in the number of other resources which are good substitutes for the particular resource

18. The demand for labor would most likely become more inelastic as a result of an increase in the
(a) elasticity of the demand for the product that the labor produces
(b) time for employers to make technological changes or purchase new equipment
(c) proportion of labor costs to total costs
(d) rate at which marginal revenue product declines

19. A firm is allocating its expenditure for resources in a way that will result in the least total cost of producing any given output when the
(a) amount the firm spends on each resource is the same
(b) marginal revenue product of each resource is the same
(c) marginal product of each resource is the same
(d) marginal product per dollar spent on the last unit of each resource is the same

20. A business is employing inputs such that the marginal product of labor is 20 and the marginal product of capital is 45. The price of labor is $10 and the price of capital is $15. If the business wants to minimize costs, then it should
(a) use more labor and less capital
(b) use less labor and less capital
(c) use less labor and more capital
(d) make no change in resource use

21. Assume that a profit-maximizing computer disk manufacturer is employing resources so that the MRP of the last unit hired for resource X is $240 and the MRP of the last unit hired for resource Y is $150. The price of resource X is $80 and the price of resource Y is $50. The firm should
(a) hire more of resource X and less of resource Y
(b) hire less of resource X and more of resource Y
(c) hire less of both resource X and resource Y
(d) hire more of both resource X and resource Y

22. A firm that hires resources in a purely competitive market is *not* maximizing its profits when
(a) the marginal revenue product of every resource is equal to 1
(b) the marginal revenue product of every resource is equal to its price
(c) the ratio of the marginal revenue product of every resource to its price is equal to 1
(d) the ratio of the price of every resource to its marginal revenue product is equal to 1

23. Assume that a purely competitive firm uses two resources—labor (*L*) and capital (*C*)—to produce a product. In which situation would the firm be maximizing profit?

	MRP_L	MRP_C	P_L	P_C
(a)	10	20	30	40
(b)	10	20	10	20
(c)	15	15	10	10
(d)	30	40	10	5

24. In the marginal productivity theory of income distribution, when all markets are purely competitive, each unit of each resource receives a money payment equal to
(a) its marginal product
(b) its marginal revenue product
(c) the needs of the resource owner
(d) the payments received by each of the units of the other resources in the economy

25. A major criticism of the marginal productivity theory of income distribution is that
(a) labor markets are often subject to imperfect competition
(b) the theory suggests that there eventually will be equality in incomes
(c) purely competitive firms are only interested in profit maximization
(d) the demand for labor resources are price elastic

■ PROBLEMS

1. The table below shows the total production a firm will be able to obtain if it employs varying amounts of resource

Quantity of resource A employed	Total product	Marginal product of A	Total revenue	Marginal revenue product of A
0	0		$____	
1	12	____	____	$____
2	22	____	____	____
3	30	____	____	____
4	36	____	____	____
5	40	____	____	____
6	42	____	____	____
7	43	____	____	____

A while the amounts of the other resources the firm employs remain constant.

a. Compute the marginal product of each of the seven units of resource A and enter these figures in the table.

b. Assume the product the firm produces sells in the market for $1.50 per unit. Compute the total revenue of the firm at each of the eight levels of output and the marginal revenue product of each of the seven units of resource A. Enter these figures in the table.

c. On the basis of your computations, complete the firm's demand schedule for resource A by indicating in the following table how many units of resource A the firm would employ at the given prices.

Price of A	Quantity of A demanded
$21.00	____
18.00	____
15.00	____
12.00	____
9.00	____
6.00	____
3.00	____
1.50	____

2. In the table below are the marginal product data for resource B. Assume that the quantities of other resources employed by the firm remain constant.

a. Compute the total product (output) of the firm for each of the seven quantities of resource B employed and enter these figures in the table.

b. Assume that the firm sells its output in an imperfectly competitive market and that the prices at which it can sell its product are those given in the table. Compute and enter in the table

(1) the total revenue for each of the seven quantities of B employed.

(2) the marginal revenue product of each of the seven units of resource B.

c. How many units of B would the firm employ if the market price of B were

(1) $25? ____

(2) $20? ____

(3) $15? ____

(4) $9? ____

(5) $5? ____

(6) $1? ____

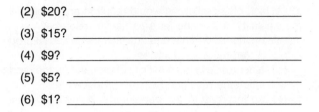

3. Use the following total-product schedule as a resource to answer questions **a, b,** and **c.** Assume that the quantities of other resources the firm employs remain constant.

Units of resource	Total product
0	0
1	15
2	28
3	38
4	43
5	46

a. If the firm's product sells for a constant $2 per unit, what is the marginal revenue product of the second unit of the resource? ____

b. If the firm's product sells for a constant $2 and the price of the resource is $10, how many units of the resource will the firm employ? ____

c. If the firm can sell 15 units of output at a price of $2.00 and 28 units of output at a price of $1.50, what is the marginal revenue product of the second unit of the resource? ____

4. In the space to the right of each of the following, indicate whether the change would tend to increase (+) or decrease (−) a firm's demand for a particular resource.

a. An increase in the demand for the firm's product ____

b. A decrease in the price of the firm's output ____

c. An increase in the productivity of the resource ____

d. An increase in the price of a substitute resource when the output effect is greater than the substitution effect ____

Quantity of resource B employed	Marginal product of B	Total product	Product price	Total revenue	Marginal revenue product of B
0	—	0		$0.00	—
1	22	____	$1.00	____	$____
2	21	____	.90	____	____
3	19	____	.80	____	____
4	16	____	.70	____	____
5	12	____	.60	____	____
6	7	____	.50	____	____
7	1	____	.40	____	____

Quantity of resource C employed	Marginal product of C	Marginal revenue product of C	Quantity of resource D employed	Marginal product of D	Marginal revenue product of D
1	10	$5.00	1	21	$10.50
2	8	4.00	2	18	9.00
3	6	3.00	3	15	7.50
4	5	2.50	4	12	6.00
5	4	2.00	5	9	4.50
6	3	1.50	6	6	3.00
7	2	1.00	7	3	1.50

e. A decrease in the price of a complementary resource _____

f. A decrease in the price of a substitute resource when the substitution effect is greater than the output effect _____

5. The table above shows the marginal-product and marginal-revenue-product schedules for resource C and resource D. Both resources are variable and are employed in purely competitive markets. The price of C is $2 and the price of D is $3. (Assume that the productivity of each resource is independent of the quantity of the other.)

a. The least-cost combination of C and D that would enable the firm to produce

(1) 64 units of its product is _____ C and _____ D.

(2) 99 units of its product is _____ C and _____ D.

b. The profit-maximizing combination of C and D is _____ C and _____ D.

c. When the firm employs the profit-maximizing combination of C and D, it is also employing C and D in the least-cost combination because _____ equals _____.

d. Examination of the figures in the table reveals that the firm sells its product in a _____ competitive market at a price of $_____.

e. Employing the profit-maximizing combination of C and D, the firm's

(1) total output is _____.

(2) total revenue is $_____.

(3) total cost is $_____.

(4) total profit is $_____.

■ SHORT ANSWER AND ESSAY QUESTIONS

1. Give four reasons why it is important to study resource pricing.

2. How does the demand for a product differ from the demand for a resource? Explain why the demand for a resource is a derived demand.

3. What two factors determine the strength of the demand for a resource?

4. Explain why firms that wish to maximize their profits follow the MRP = MRC rule.

5. What effect do marginal product and marginal price have on a firm's resource demand curve under pure competition and under imperfect competition?

6. Why is the demand schedule for a resource less elastic when the firm sells its product in an imperfectly competitive market than when it sells it in a purely competitive market?

7. How do you derive the market demand for a resource?

8. Identify and describe three factors that will cause the demand for a resource to increase or decrease. Give examples of how each factor influences changes in demand.

9. What is the difference between the substitution effect and the output effect?

10. If the price of capital falls, what will happen to the demand for labor if capital and labor are substitutes in production? Describe what happens when the substitution effect outweighs the output effect and when the output effect outweighs the substitution effect. What can you conclude?

11. Why does a change in the price of a complementary resource cause the demand for labor to change in the opposite direction?

12. Describe four real-world applications of how changes in the determinants of labor demand affected the demand for labor.

13. What are the four factors that determine the elasticity of demand for a resource?

14. Use an example to explain what happens to elasticity when there are many substitute resources compared to when there are few.

15. How can the ratio of labor cost to the total cost influence how producers react to changes in the price of labor?

16. Assume that a firm employs resources in purely competitive markets. How does the firm know that it is spending money on resources in such a way that it can produce a given output for the least total cost?

17. Why is minimizing cost not sufficient for maximizing profit for a firm?

18. When is a firm that employs resources in purely competitive markets using these resources in amounts that will maximize the profits of the firm?

19. What is the marginal productivity theory of income distribution? What ethical proposition must be accepted if this distribution is to be fair and equitable?

20. What are the two major shortcomings of the marginal productivity theory of income distribution?

ANSWERS

Chapter 27 The Demand for Resources

FILL-IN QUESTIONS

1. resources, incomes, costs
2. derived, productivity, price
3. product, cost
4. cost, equal to
5. product, prices
6. lower, demand, less
7. demand
8. demand, productivity, price
9. increase, decrease
10. falls, rises
11. more, less, substitution, more, output
12. increase, decrease
13. product, substitutes, demand, cost, cost
14. slowly, elastic
15. greater
16. product, price
17. revenue product, price
18. 1
19. marginal, revenues
20. competitive, do not

TRUE-FALSE QUESTIONS

1. T, p. 564
2. T, p. 564
3. T, p. 565
4. F, p. 565
5. T, p. 567
6. T, pp. 566-567
7. F, p. 566
8. F, p. 568
9. T, pp. 568-569
10. T, p. 569
11. F, pp. 571-572
12. T, pp. 569-570
13. F, p. 570
14. T, p. 570
15. F, pp. 570-571
16. F, p. 570
17. T, p. 571
18. F, p. 573
19. F, p. 573
20. T, pp. 573-574
21. T, p. 574
22. F, pp. 574-575
23. T, p. 575
24. F, p. 578
25. F, p. 578

MULTIPLE-CHOICE QUESTIONS

1. d, pp. 564-565
2. c, p. 565
3. a, p. 565
4. a, pp. 565-566
5. d, pp. 566-567
6. b, pp. 566-567
7. d, pp. 566-567
8. c, pp. 565-566
9. a, pp. 565-567
10. c, p. 568
11. c, p. 568
12. d, p. 568
13. c, p. 570
14. a, p. 570
15. b, pp. 570-571
16. a, p. 571
17. c, p. 574
18. d, p. 573
19. d, p. 574
20. c, pp. 574-575
21. d, p. 575
22. a, p. 575
23. b, p. 575
24. b, p. 578
25. a, p. 578

PROBLEMS

1. *a.* Marginal product of A: 12, 10, 8, 6, 4, 2, 1; *b.* Total revenue: 0, 18.00, 33.00, 45.00, 54.00, 60.00, 63.00, 64.50; Marginal revenue product of A: 18.00, 15.00, 12.00, 9.00, 6.00, 3.00, 1.50; *c.* 0, 1, 2, 3, 4, 5, 6, 7
2. *a.* Total product: 22, 43, 62, 78, 90, 97, 98; *b.* (1) Total revenue: 22.00, 38.70, 49.60, 54.60, 54.00, 48.50, 39.20; (2) Marginal revenue product of B: 22.00, 16.70, 10.90, 5.00, −0.60, −5.50, −9.30; *c.* (1) 0, (2) 1, (3) 2, (4) 3, (5) 4, (6) 4
3. *a.* \$26. The second worker increases TP by 13 units. 13 × \$2 = \$26; *b.* 4 units. The marginal product of the fourth resource is 5 units of output (5 × \$2 = \$10). Thus MRP = \$10 and MRC = \$10 when the fourth resource is employed; *c.* \$12. The total revenue from 1 unit is \$30.00 (15 × \$2.00). The total revenue with 2 units is \$42 (28 × \$1.50). The difference is the MRP of the second unit.
4. *a.* +; *b.* −; *c.* +; *d.* − *e.* +; *f.* −
5. *a.* (1) 1, 3; (2) 3, 5; *b.* 5, 6; *c.* The marginal product of C divided by its price, the marginal product of D divided by its price; *d.* purely, \$.50; *e.* (1) 114, (2) \$57, (3) \$28, (4) \$29

SHORT ANSWER AND ESSAY QUESTIONS

1. pp. 564-565
2. pp. 564-565
3. pp. 565-566
4. pp. 566-567
5. pp. 567-569
6. pp. 568-569
7. p. 569
8. pp. 569-572
9. p. 570
10. pp. 570-571
11. p. 571
12. p. 572
13. pp. 573-574
14. p. 573
15. p. 574
16. pp. 574-575
17. p. 575
18. p. 575
19. p. 578
20. p. 578

CHAPTER **28**

Wage Determination

The preceding chapter explained the demand for *any* resource in a competitive resource market. Chapter 28 builds on this explanation and uses demand and supply analysis to describe what determines the quantity of a *particular* resource—***labor***—and the price paid for it—***wages***—in different types of markets.

The chapter begins by defining terms and briefly discussing the general level of wages in the United States and other advanced economies. Here you will learn about the role that productivity plays in explaining the long-run growth of real wages and the increased demand for labor over time. You will also discover two reasons, one related to productivity and the other to wage pressure, why real wage growth has stagnated in the United States in recent years.

Recall from Chapters 23–25 that in the product market, the degree of competition has a significant influence on how prices are determined and what output is produced. Similarly, in a labor resource market, the degree of competition directly affects the determination of wage rates and the level of employment. The main purpose of Chapter 28, therefore, is to explain how wage rates and the quantity of labor employed are determined in labor markets that vary in competitiveness.

Six types of labor markets are discussed in the chapter: (1) the competitive market, in which the number of employers is large and labor is nonunionized; (2) the monopsony market, in which a single employer hires labor under competitive (nonunion) conditions; (3) a market in which a union controls the supply of labor, the number of employers is large, and the union attempts to increase the total demand for labor; (4) a similar market in which the union attempts to reduce the total supply of labor; (5) another similar market in which the union attempts to obtain a wage rate that is above the competitive-equilibrium level by threatening to strike; and (6) the bilateral monopoly market, in which a single employer faces a labor supply controlled by a single union.

What is important for you to learn is how the characteristics of each labor market affect wage rates and employment. In the competitive or monopsony labor market, there is no union, and the determination of the wage rate and employment will be quite definite although different for each market. In the next four types of labor markets, **unions** control the supply of labor, and thus the outcomes for wage rates and employment will be less definite. If the demand for labor is competitive, the wage rate and the amount of employment will depend on how successful the union is in increasing the demand for labor, restricting the supply of labor, or setting a wage rate that employers will accept. If there is both a union and one employer (a bilateral monopoly), wages and employment will fall within certain limits, but exactly where will depend on the bargaining power of the union or the employer.

Three other issues related to labor markets are discussed in the last three sections of the chapter. First, for many years the Federal government has set a legal *minimum wage* for labor. The chapter uses supply and demand analysis to make the case for and against the minimum wage and then discusses its real-world effects. Second, wage rates are not homogeneous and differ across workers and occupations. The chapter presents three important reasons why these ***wage differentials*** exist. Third, there is a *principal-agent problem* in most types of employment that may lead to shirking on the job. Different pay schemes have been devised to tie worker pay to performance in an effort to overcome this problem. Each of these issues should be of direct interest to you and deepen your understanding about how labor markets work.

■ CHECKLIST

When you have studied this chapter you should be able to

- ☐ Define wages (or the wage rate).
- ☐ Distinguish between nominal and real wages.
- ☐ List five reasons for high productivity in the United States and other advanced economies.
- ☐ Describe the long-run relationship between real wages and productivity in the United States.
- ☐ Cite the two factors contributing to the secular growth in real wages in the United States and evaluate the importance of each one.
- ☐ Discuss several reasons for the apparent stagnation of real wage growth in the United States in recent years.
- ☐ Define the three characteristics of a competitive labor market.
- ☐ Use demand and supply graphs to explain wage rates and the equilibrium level of employment in competitive labor markets.
- ☐ Define the three characteristics of a labor market monopsony and compare it with the competitive labor market.

☐ Use demand and supply graphs to explain wage rates and the equilibrium level of employment in the monopsony model.
☐ Explain why the marginal resource cost exceeds the wage rate in monopsony.
☐ Cite three types of union models.
☐ Identify three strategies that labor unions use to increase the demand for labor and the effects of the strategies on wage rates and employment.
☐ Explain and illustrate graphically the effects of actions taken by craft unions to decrease the supply of labor on wages and the employment of workers.
☐ Explain and illustrate graphically how the organization of workers by an industrial union in a previously competitive labor market would affect the wage rate and the employment level.
☐ Describe evidence of the effect of unions on wage increases and two reasons that might mitigate unemployment effects from wage increases.
☐ Use a graph to explain why the equilibrium wage rate and employment level is indeterminate when a labor market is a bilateral monopoly and to predict the range within which the wage rate will be found.
☐ Present the case for and the case against a legally established minimum wage.
☐ List the three major factors which explain why wage differentials exist.
☐ Describe two reasons why groups of workers in the labor force with similar characteristics may earn different wages.
☐ Explain the nonmonetary aspect of job differences.
☐ Cite four reasons for labor market imperfections.
☐ Describe the principal-agent problem.
☐ Identify four pay schemes employers use to prevent shirking or to tie worker pay to performance.
☐ Explain how "solutions" to principal-agent problems sometimes yield undesirable results.

■ CHAPTER OUTLINE

1. A wage (or the wage rate) is the price paid per unit of time for any type of labor and can be measured either in money or in real terms. Earnings are equal to the wage multiplied by the amount of time worked.

2. The general (or average) level of real wages in the United States and other advanced economies is high because the demand for labor has been great relative to the supply of labor.

a. The demand for labor in the United States and advanced economies has been strong because labor has been highly productive, and it has been highly productive for several major reasons—substantial quantities of capital goods and natural resources, technological advancement, improvements in labor quality, and other intangible factors (management techniques, business environment, and size of the domestic market).

b. The real hourly wage rate and output per hour of labor are closely and directly related to each other, and real income per worker can increase only at the same rate as output per worker.

c. The increases in the demand for labor that have resulted from the increased productivity of labor over time have been greater than the increase in the supply of labor in the United States, and as a result the real wage rate in the United States has increased in the long run.

d. But there has been stagnation in the growth of real wages since 1979. Among the possible factors are falling rates of capital accumulation, shifts in labor to the low-productivity service sector, changes in the skill level and composition of the labor force, and the globalization of production.

3. The wage rate received by a specific type of labor depends on the demand for and the supply of that labor and the competitiveness of the market in which that type of labor is hired. In a *purely competitive* and nonunionized labor market, the total demand for and the total supply of labor determine the wage rate. From the point of view of the individual firm, the supply of labor is perfectly elastic at this wage rate (that is, the marginal labor cost is equal to the wage rate) and the firm will hire the amount of labor at which the marginal revenue product of labor is equal to its marginal labor cost.

4. In a *monopsonistic* and nonunionized labor market, the firm's marginal labor costs are greater than the wage rates it must pay to obtain various amounts of labor. It hires the amount of labor at which marginal labor cost and the marginal revenue product of labor are equal. Both the wage rate and the level of employment are less than they would be under purely competitive conditions.

a. Note that if the firm employs resources in imperfectly competitive markets, it is hiring resources in the least-cost combination when the ratio of the marginal product of a resource to its marginal resource cost is the same for all resources, and

b. it is hiring resources in the most profitable combination when the marginal revenue product of each resource is equal to its marginal resource cost.

5. In labor markets in which ***labor unions*** represent workers, the unions attempt to raise wages in three ways.

a. The union can increase the demand for labor by increasing the demand for the products that the union workers produce, by increasing productivity, and by increasing the prices of resources which are substitutes for the labor provided by the members of the union.

b. An exclusive or craft union will seek to increase wages by reducing the supply of labor. Occupational licensing is another means of restricting the supply of a particular type of labor.

c. An inclusive or industrial union will try to increase wages by forcing employers to pay wages in excess of the equilibrium rate which would prevail in a purely competitive labor market.

d. Labor unions are aware that their actions to increase wage rates may also increase the unemployment of their members and may, therefore, limit their demands for higher wages, but the unemployment effect of higher wages is lessened by increases in and a relatively inelastic demand for labor.

6. In a labor market characterized by ***bilateral monopoly,*** the wage rate depends, within certain limits, on the relative bargaining power of the union and of the employer.

7. Whether ***minimum wage*** laws reduce poverty is a debatable question, but the evidence suggests that while they increase the incomes of employed workers they also reduce the number of workers employed.

8. Differences in wages exist among workers for three major reasons.

a. Workers are not homogeneous, and they can be thought of as falling into many *noncompeting* occupational groups. The wages for each group differ because of
(1) differences in the abilities or skills possessed by workers, the number of workers in each group, and the demand for those abilities or skills in the labor market, and
(2) investment in human capital by workers through education and training.

b. Jobs also vary in difficulty and attractiveness, and thus higher wages may be necessary to compensate for less desirable aspects of some jobs.

c. Workers are not perfectly mobile because of market imperfections arising from lack of job information, geographic immobilities, union or government restraints, and discrimination.

9. Wage payments in labor markets are often more complex in practice and are often designed to make a connection between worker pay and performance.

a. A ***principal-agent problem*** arises when the interest of agents (workers) diverge from the interest of the principal (firms). For example, ***shirking*** on the job can occur if workers give less than the desired level of performance for pay received.

b. Firms can try to reduce shirking by monitoring worker activity, but this monitoring is costly; therefore, ***incentive pay plans*** are adopted by firms to tie worker compensation more closely to performance. Among the various incentive schemes are
(1) piece rate payments, commissions, royalties, bonuses, and profit sharing plans, and
(2) efficiency wages that pay workers above-market wages to get greater effort.

c. Sometimes the "solutions" to principal-agent problems lead to negative results. Commissions may cause employees to pad bills; changes in work rules may demoralize workers.

■ HINTS AND TIPS

1. The reason why the market supply curve for labor rises in competitive markets is based on an economic concept from Chapter 2 that you may want to review. To obtain more workers, firms must increase wages to cover the ***opportunity cost*** of time spent on other alternatives (other employment, household work, or leisure).

2. In monopsony, the marginal resource cost exceeds the wage rate (and the marginal-resource-cost curve lies above the supply curve of labor). The relationship is difficult to understand, so you should pay careful attention to the discussion of Table 28-2 and Figure 28-4.

3. To illustrate the differences in the three union models presented in this chapter, draw supply and demand graphs of each model.

4. The chapter presents the positive economic explanations for the differences in wages between occupations. Remember that whether these wage differentials are "fair" is a normative question. (See Chapter 1 for the positive and normative distinction.)

■ IMPORTANT TERMS

wage (rate)	**bilateral monopoly**
earnings	**minimum wage**
nominal wages	**wage differentials**
real wages	**noncompeting groups**
competitive labor market	**human capital investment**
monopsony	**compensating differences**
exclusive unionism	**principal-agent problem**
occupational licensure	**shirking**
inclusive unionism	**incentive pay plan**

SELF-TEST

■ FILL-IN QUESTIONS

1. The price paid for labor per unit of time is the (piece, wage) ______ rate. The earnings of labor are equal to the ______ rate (divided, multiplied) ______ by the amount of time worked.

2. The amount of money received per hour or day by a worker is the (nominal, real) ______ wage, while the purchasing power of that money is the ______ wage.

3. The general level of wages is high in the United States and other advanced economies because the demand for labor in these economies is (weak, strong) ______ relative to the supply of labor.

4. United States labor tends to be highly productive, among other reasons, because it has access to relatively large amounts of (consumer, capital) ______ goods, abundant (financial, natural) ______ resources, a high-quality (service sector, labor force) ______, and superior (military, technology) ______.

5. There is a close (short-run, long-run) ______ relationship between output per labor hour and real hourly wages in the United States. This reflects the fact that real income (earnings) per worker can only increase at about (a slower, a faster, the same) _______________ rate as output per worker over time.

6. Some reasons that have been given to explain the stagnation in real wages since 1979 in the United States are the (faster, slower) _______________ rate of growth in productivity due in part to _______________ rates of capital accumulation and the (upward, downward) _______________ pressure on wages due to globalization of production.

7. In a competitive labor market,

a. the supply curve slopes upward from left to right because it is necessary for employers to pay (higher, lower) _______________ wages to attract workers from alternative employment. The market supply curve rises because it is a(n) (average cost, opportunity cost) _______________ curve.

b. the demand is the sum of the marginal (revenue product, resource cost) _______________ schedules of all firms hiring this type of labor.

c. the wage rate will equal the rate at which the total quantity of labor demanded is (less than, equal to, greater than) _______________ the total quantity of labor supplied.

8. Insofar as an individual firm hiring labor in a competitive market is concerned, the supply of labor is perfectly (elastic, inelastic) _______________ because the individual firm is unable to affect the wage rate it must pay. The firm will hire that quantity of labor at which the wage rate, or marginal labor cost, is (less than, equal to, greater than) _______________ the marginal revenue product.

9. A monopsonist employing labor in a market which is competitive on the supply side will hire that amount of labor at which marginal revenue product is (less than, equal to, greater than) _______________ marginal labor cost. In such a market, the marginal labor cost is (less, greater) _______________ than the wage rate, so the employer will pay a wage rate which is _______________ than both the marginal revenue product of labor and the marginal labor cost.

10. A monopsonist facing a competitive supply of labor

a. is employing the combination of resources that enables it to produce any given output in the least costly way when the marginal product of every resource (divided, multiplied) _______________ by its marginal resource cost is the same for all resources.

b. is employing the combination of resources that maximizes its profits when the marginal revenue product of every resource is (equal to, greater than) _______________ its marginal resource cost or when the marginal revenue product of each resource (divided, multiplied) _______________ by its marginal resource cost is equal to (infinity, 1) _______________.

11. When compared with a competitive labor market, a market dominated by a monopsonist results in (higher, lower) _______________ wage rates and in (more, less) _______________ employment.

12. The basic objective of labor unions is to increase wages, and they attempt to accomplish this goal either by increasing the (demand for, supply of) _______________ labor, restricting the _______________ labor, or imposing a(n) (below, above) _______________-equilibrium wage rate on employers.

13. Labor unions can increase the demand for the services of their members by increasing the (demand for, supply of) _______________ the products they produce, by increasing the (number, productivity) _______________ of their members, and by (increasing, decreasing) _______________ the prices of resources which are substitutes for the services supplied by their members.

14. Restricting the supply of labor to increase wages is the general policy of (exclusive, inclusive) _______________ unionism, and imposing above-equilibrium wage rates is the strategy used in _______________ unionism. An example of exclusive unionism is (an industrial, a craft) _______________ union, while an example of inclusive unionism would be _______________ union.

15. If craft unions are successful in increasing wages, employment in the craft or industry will (increase, decrease) _______________, but this effect on members may lead unions to _______________ their wage demands. Unions, however, will not worry too much about the effect on employment from the higher wage rates if the economy is growing or if the demand for labor is relatively (elastic, inelastic) _______________.

16. In a labor market which is a bilateral monopoly, the monopsonist will try to pay a wage (less, greater) _______________ than marginal revenue product of labor; the union will ask for some wage _______________ than the competitive and monopsonist equilibrium wage. Within these limits, the (wage rate, elasticity) _______________ of labor will depend on the relative bargaining strength of the union and the monopsonist.

17. In competitive labor markets, the effect of imposing an effective minimum wage rate, ignoring any shock effects, is to (increase, decrease) _______________ the wage rate and to _______________ employment; in monopolistic labor markets, the effect is to (increase, decrease) ________________ the wage rate and to ________________ employment.

18. After a minimum wage rise, employed workers at the new minimum wage generally experience a(n) (increase, decrease) ________________ in their income, but the employment of less productive workers will ________________ and the incomes of these workers will (increase, decrease) ________________. Thus, the research evidence suggests that the overall antipoverty effect from increasing the minimum wage is a(n) (positive, uncertain) ________________ one.

19. Actual wage rates received by different workers tend to differ because workers (are, are not) ________________ homogeneous, jobs (vary, do not vary) ________________ in attractiveness, and labor markets may be (perfect, imperfect) ________________.

20. Another explanation for wage differentials is that the total labor force is composed of a number of (competing, noncompeting) ________________ groups of workers. Wages differ among these groups as a consequence of differences in (ability, wealth) ________________ and because of different investments in (the stock market, human capital) ________________.

21. Within each of these noncompeting groups, some workers receive higher wages than others to compensate these workers for the less desirable (monetary, nonmonetary) ________________ aspects of a job. These wage differentials are called (monopsony, compensating) ________________ differences.

22. Another reason that workers performing identical jobs often receive different wages is due to market imperfections such as lack of information about (investments, jobs) ________________, geographic (mobility, immobility) ________________, union or government (subsidies, restraints) ________________, and (taxes, discrimination) ________________.

23. Firms, or parties, who hire others to achieve their objectives may be regarded as (agents, principals) ________________, while workers, or parties, who are hired to advance firms' interests can be regarded as the firms' ________________. The objective of a firm is to maximize (wages, profits) ________________ and workers to help a firm achieve that objective in return for ________________, but when the interests of a firm and the workers diverge, a principal-agent problem is created.

24. An example of this type of problem is a situation in which workers provide less than the agreed amount of work effort on the job, which is called (licensure, shirking) ________________. To prevent this situation, firms can closely monitor job (pay, performance) ________________, but this is costly; therefore, firms offer different incentive ________________ plans.

25. Examples of such pay-for-performance schemes include (efficiency, piece) ________________ rate payments, commissions and royalties, bonuses and profit sharing, and ________________ wages, which means that workers are paid above equilibrium wages to encourage greater work effort. Such plans must be designed with care because of possible (positive, negative) ________________ side effects.

■ TRUE-FALSE QUESTIONS

Circle the T if the statement is true, the F if it is false.

1. If you received a 5% increase in your nominal wage and the price level increased by 3%, then your real wage has increased by 8%. **T F**

2. The general level of wages is high in the United States and other advanced economies because the supply of labor is large relative to the demand for it. **T F**

3. One reason for the high productivity of labor in the United States and other advanced economies is access to large amounts of capital equipment. **T F**

4. Real income per worker can increase only at about the same rate as output per worker. **T F**

5. Real wages in the United States have significantly increased since 1979 because of higher productivity growth. **T F**

6. If an individual firm employs labor in a competitive market, it finds that its marginal labor cost is equal to the wage rate in that market. **T F**

7. Given a purely competitive employer's demand for labor, a lower wage will result in more workers being hired. **T F**

8. Both monopsonists and firms hiring labor in purely competitive markets hire labor up to the quantity at which the marginal revenue product of labor and marginal labor cost are equal. **T F**

9. Increasing the productivity of labor will tend to increase the demand for labor. **T F**

10. One strategy unions use to bolster the demand for union workers is to lobby against a higher minimum wage for nonunion workers. **T F**

11. Restricting the supply of labor is a means of increasing wage rates more commonly used by craft unions than by industrial unions. **T F**

12. Occupational licensing is a means of increasing the supply of specific kinds of labor. **T F**

13. Unions that seek to organize all available or potential workers in an industry are called craft unions. **T F**

14. The imposition of an above-equilibrium wage rate will cause employment to fall off more when the demand for labor is inelastic than it will when the demand is elastic. **T F**

15. Union members are paid wage rates which on the average are greater by 10% or more than the wage rates paid to nonunion members. **T F**

16. The actions of both exclusive and inclusive unions that raise the wage rates paid to them by competitive employers of labor also cause, other things remaining constant, an increase in the employment of their members. **T F**

17. In a bilateral monopoly, the negotiated wage will be below the competitive equilibrium wage in that labor market. **T F**

18. If a labor market is purely competitive, the imposition of an effective minimum wage will increase the wage rate paid and decrease employment in that market. **T F**

19. When an effective minimum wage is imposed on a monopsonist, the wage rate paid by the firm will increase and the number of workers employed by it may also increase. **T F**

20. An increase in the minimum wage rate in the U.S. economy tends to increase the unemployment of teenagers and others in low-wage occupations. **T F**

21. Actual wage rates received in different labor markets tend to differ because the demands for particular types of labor relative to their supplies differ. **T F**

22. Wage differentials that are used to compensate workers for unpleasant aspects of a job are called efficiency wages. **T F**

23. Market imperfections which impede workers from moving from lower- to higher-paying jobs help explain wage differentials. **T F**

24. Shirking is an example of a principal-agent problem. **T F**

25. There are examples of solutions that have been implemented to solve principal-agent problems that produce negative results. **T F**

■ MULTIPLE-CHOICE QUESTIONS

Circle the letter that corresponds to the best answer.

1. Real wages would decline if the
(a) prices of goods and services rose more rapidly than nominal-wage rates
(b) prices of goods and services rose less rapidly than nominal-wage rates
(c) prices of goods and services and wage rates both rose
(d) prices of goods and services and wage rates both fell

2. The basic explanation for high real wages in the United States and other industrially advanced economies is that the
(a) price levels in these nations have increased at a faster rate than nominal wages
(b) governments in these nations have imposed effective minimum wage laws to improve the conditions of labor
(c) demand for labor in these nations is quite large relative to the supply of labor
(d) supply of labor in these nations is quite large relative to the demand for labor

3. A characteristic of a purely competitive labor market would be
(a) firms hiring different types of labor
(b) workers supplying labor under a union contract
(c) wage taker behavior by the firms
(d) price maker behavior by the firms

4. The supply curve for labor in a purely competitive market is upward sloping because
(a) opportunity costs are rising
(b) the marginal resource cost is constant
(c) the wage rate paid to workers falls
(d) the marginal revenue product rises

5. The individual firm which hires labor under purely competitive conditions faces a supply curve for labor which
(a) is perfectly inelastic
(b) is of unitary elasticity
(c) is perfectly elastic
(d) slopes upward from left to right

6. All of the following are characteristics of a monopsonist *except:*
(a) there is only a single buyer of a particular kind of labor
(b) the type of labor is relatively immobile
(c) the wage rate it must pay workers varies directly with the number of workers it employs
(d) the supply curve is the marginal resource cost curve

7. A monopsonist pays a wage rate which is
(a) greater than the marginal revenue product of labor
(b) equal to the marginal revenue product of labor
(c) equal to the firm's marginal labor cost
(d) less than the marginal revenue product of labor

8. If a firm employs resources in imperfectly competitive markets, to maximize its profits the marginal revenue product of each resource must equal
(a) its marginal product
(b) its marginal resource cost
(c) its price
(d) 1

9. Compared with a purely competitive labor market, a monopsonistic market will result in
(a) higher wage rates and a higher level of employment
(b) higher wage rates and a lower level of employment
(c) lower wage rates and a higher level of employment
(d) lower wage rates and a lower level of employment

10. The labor market for nurses in a small community that has two hospitals would be best described as
(a) monopolistically competitive
(b) a bilateral monopoly
(c) an oligopsony
(d) an oligopoly

11. Higher wage rates and a higher level of employment are the usual consequences of
(a) inclusive unionism
(b) exclusive unionism
(c) an above-equilibrium wage rate
(d) an increase in the productivity of labor

12. Which would increase the demand for a particular type of labor?
(a) a decrease in the wages of that type of labor
(b) an increase in the prices of those resources which are substitutes for that type of labor
(c) an increase in the prices of the resources which are complements to that type of labor
(d) a decrease in the demand for the products produced by that type of labor

13. Occupational licensing laws have the economic effect of
(a) increasing the demand for labor
(b) decreasing the supply of labor
(c) strengthening the bargaining position of an industrial union
(d) weakening the bargaining position of a craft union

14. Industrial unions typically attempt to increase wage rates by
(a) imposing an above-equilibrium wage rate on employers
(b) increasing the demand for labor
(c) decreasing the supply of labor
(d) forming a bilateral monopoly

Answer Questions 15, 16, and 17 using the data in the following table.

Wage rate	Quantity of labor supplied	Marginal labor cost	Marginal revenue product of labor
$10	0	—	$18
11	100	$11	17
12	200	13	16
13	300	15	15
14	400	17	14
15	500	19	13
16	600	21	12

15. If the firm employing labor were a monopsonist, the wage rate and the quantity of labor employed would be, respectively,
(a) $14 and 300
(b) $13 and 400
(c) $14 and 400
(d) $13 and 300

16. But if the market for this labor were purely competitive, the wage rate and the quantity of labor employed would be, respectively,
(a) $14 and 300
(b) $13 and 400
(c) $14 and 400
(d) $13 and 300

17. If the firm employing labor were a monopsonist and the workers were represented by an industrial union, the wage rate would be
(a) between $13 and $14
(b) between $13 and $15
(c) between $14 and $15
(d) below $13 or above $15

*Answer Questions 18, 19, 20, and 21 on the basis of the following labor market diagram, where **D** is the demand curve for labor, **S** is the supply curve for labor, and **MRC** is the marginal resource (labor) cost.*

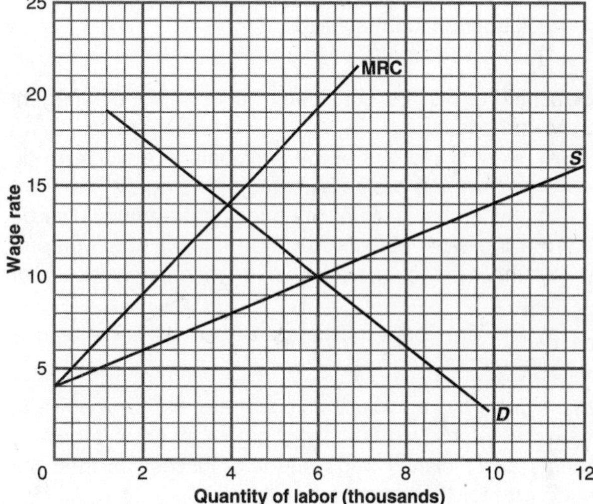

18. If this were a purely competitive labor market, the number of workers hired and the wage rate in equilibrium would be
(a) 4,000 and $14
(b) 4,000 and $8
(c) 6,000 and $10
(d) 8,000 and $12

19. If this were a monopsonistic labor market, the number of workers hired and the wage rate in equilibrium would be
(a) 4,000 and $14
(b) 4,000 and $8
(c) 6,000 and $10
(d) 8,000 and $12

20. Suppose an inclusive union seeks to maximize the employment of workers with the monopsonist. If successful, the number of workers employed and the wage rate would be
(a) 4,000 and $14
(b) 6,000 and $12
(c) 6,000 and $10
(d) 8,000 and $12

21. If the market were characterized as a bilateral monopoly, the number of workers hired and the wage rate in equilibrium would be

(a) 6,000 and $10
(b) 4,000 and $14
(c) 4,000 and $8
(d) indeterminate

22. The major reason that major league baseball players receive an average salary of over $1 million a year and teachers receive an average salary of about $40,000 a year can best be explained in terms of
(a) noncompeting labor groups
(b) compensating differences
(c) lack of job information
(d) discrimination

23. The fact that unskilled construction workers typically receive higher wages than bank clerks is best explained in terms of
(a) noncompeting labor groups
(b) compensating differences
(c) geographic immobilities
(d) union restraints

24. Shirking can be considered to be a principal-agent problem because
(a) work objectives of the principals (the workers) diverge from the profit objectives of the agent (the firm)
(b) profit objectives of the principal (the firm) diverge from the work objectives of the agents (the workers)
(c) the firm is operating in an oligopsonistic labor market
(d) the firm pays efficiency wages to workers in a labor market

25. A firm pays an equilibrium wage of $10 an hour and the workers produce 10 units of output an hour. If the firm adopts an efficiency wage and it is successful, then the wage rate for these workers will
(a) rise and output will fall
(b) fall and output will rise
(c) rise and output will rise
(d) fall and output will fall

■ PROBLEMS

1. Suppose a single firm has for a particular type of labor the marginal-revenue-product schedule given in the following table.

Number of units of labor	MRP of labor
1	$15
2	14
3	13
4	12
5	11
6	10
7	9
8	8

a. Assume there are 100 firms with the same marginal-revenue-product schedules for this particular type of labor. Compute the total or market demand for this labor by completing column 1 in the following table.

(1) Quantity of labor demanded	(2) Wage rate	(3) Quantity of labor supplied
_____	$15	850
_____	14	800
_____	13	750
_____	12	700
_____	11	650
_____	10	600
_____	9	550
_____	8	500

b. Using the supply schedule for labor given in columns 2 and 3,
(1) what will be the equilibrium wage rate? $_______
(2) what will be the total amount of labor hired in the market? _______________

c. The individual firm will
(1) have a marginal labor cost of $_______________.
(2) employ _______________ units of labor.
(3) pay a wage of $_______________.

d. On the following graph, plot the market demand and supply curves for labor and indicate the equilibrium wage rate and the total quantity of labor employed.

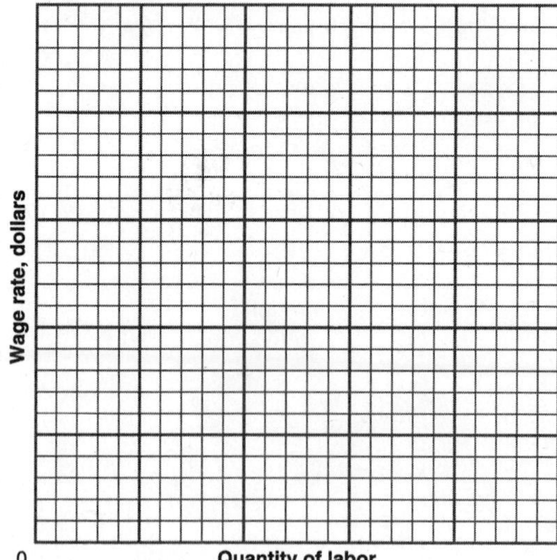

e. On the graph in column 1 on page 325, plot the individual firm's demand curve for labor, the supply curve for labor, and the marginal-labor-cost curve which confronts the individual firm, and indicate the quantity of labor the firm will hire and the wage it will pay.

f. The imposition of a $12 minimum wage rate would change the total amount of labor hired in this market to _______________.

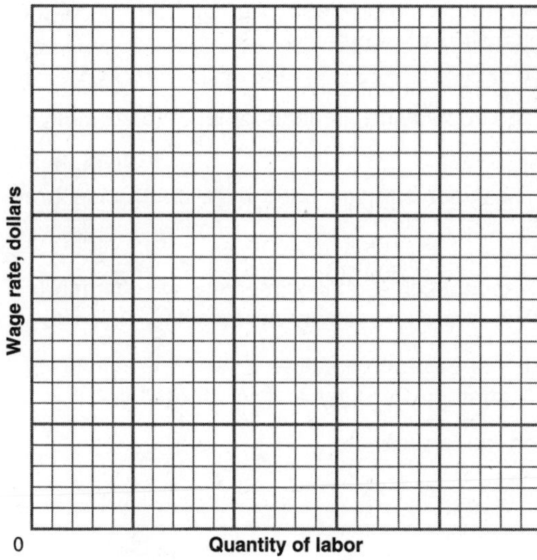

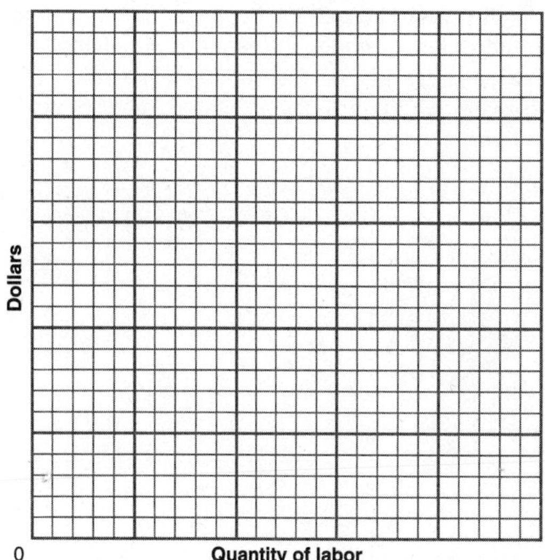

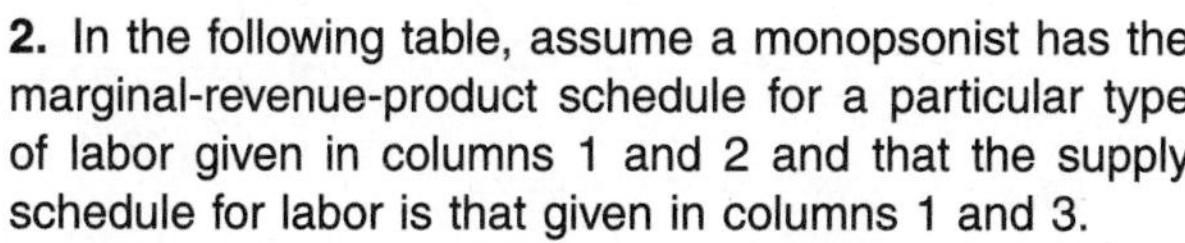

2. In the following table, assume a monopsonist has the marginal-revenue-product schedule for a particular type of labor given in columns 1 and 2 and that the supply schedule for labor is that given in columns 1 and 3.

(1) Number of labor units	(2) MRP of labor	(3) Wage rate	(4) Total labor cost	(5) Marginal labor cost
0		$ 2	$____	
1	$36	4	____	$____
2	32	6	____	____
3	28	8	____	____
4	24	10	____	____
5	20	12	____	____
6	16	14	____	____
7	12	16	____	____
8	8	18	____	____

a. Compute the firm's total labor costs at each level of employment and the marginal labor cost of each unit of labor, and enter these figures in columns 4 and 5.
b. The firm will

(1) hire ____________________ units of labor.

(2) pay a wage of $____________________.
(3) have a marginal revenue product for labor of

$____________ for the last unit of labor employed.
c. Plot the marginal revenue product of labor, the supply curve for labor, and the marginal-labor-cost curve on the following graph and indicate the quantity of labor the firm will employ and the wage it will pay.
d. If this firm's labor market were competitive, there

would be at least____________________ units hired at

a wage of at least $____________________.

3. Assume that the employees of the monopsonist in problem 2 organize a strong industrial union. The union demands a wage rate of $16 for its members, and the monopsonist decides to pay this wage because a strike would be too costly.
a. In the following table, compute the supply schedule for labor which now confronts the monopsonist by completing column 2.

(1) Number of labor units	(2) Wage rate	(3) Total labor cost	(4) Marginal labor cost
1	$____	$____	
2	____	____	$____
3	____	____	____
4	____	____	____
5	____	____	____
6	____	____	____
7	____	____	____
8	____	____	____

b. Compute the total labor cost and the marginal labor cost at each level of employment and enter these figures in columns 3 and 4.

c. The firm will hire ____________ units of labor, pay

a wage of $____________, and pay total wages of

$____________.
d. As a result of unionization, the wage rate has

____________________, the level of

employment has ____________________, and the earnings of labor have ____________________.

e. On the graph below plot the firm's marginal revenue product of labor schedule, the labor supply schedule, and the marginal-labor-cost schedule. Indicate also the wage rate the firm will pay and the number of workers it will hire.

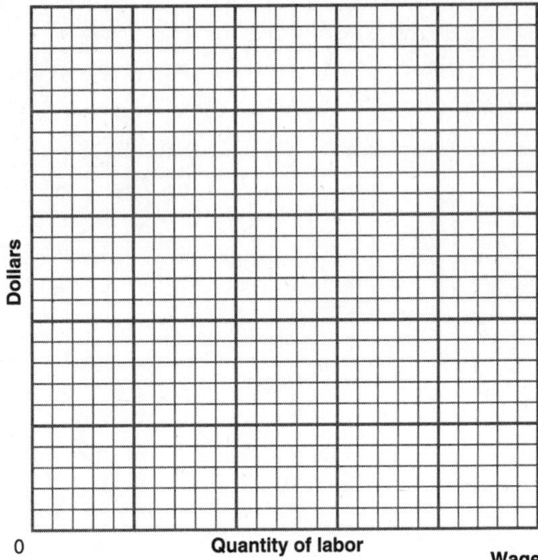

4. Match the following descriptions to the one of the six accompanying graphs below.

a. A bilateral monopoly Graph _____

b. The supply and demand for labor for a purely competitive firm Graph _____

c. The labor strategy used by a craft union to raise wages Graph _____

d. A monopsonistic labor market Graph _____

e. The strategy used by an industrial union to raise wages above a competitive level Graph _____

f. A strategy used by a union to get people to buy union-made products Graph _____

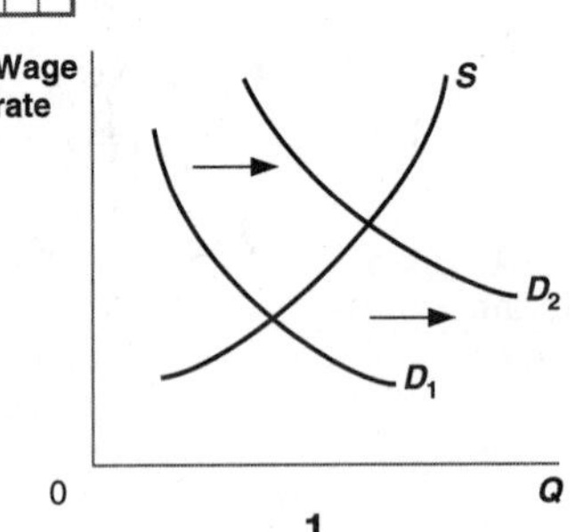

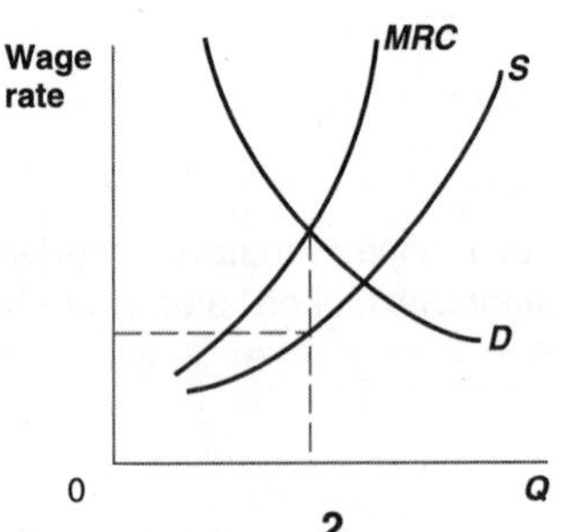

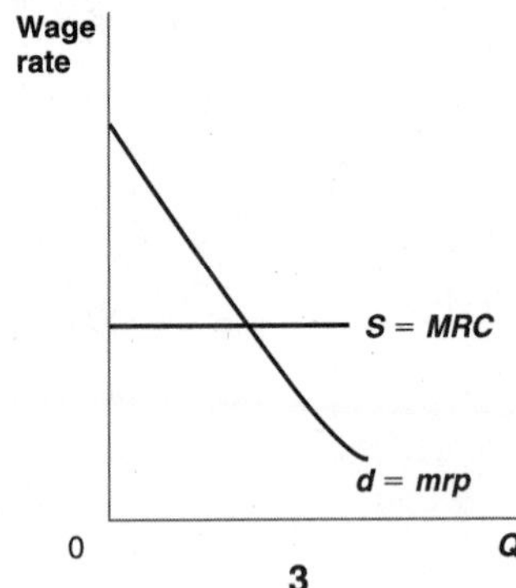

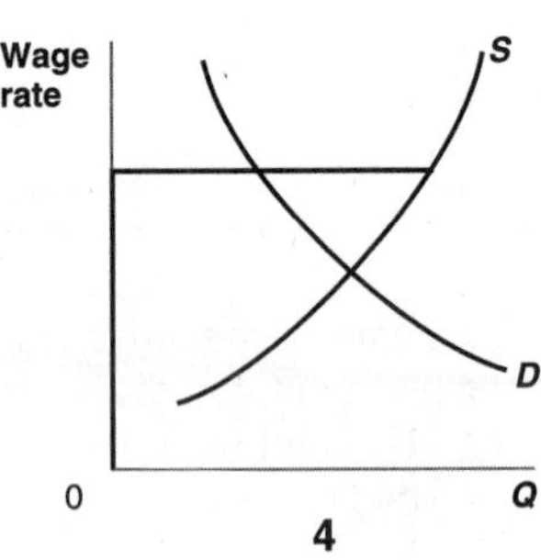

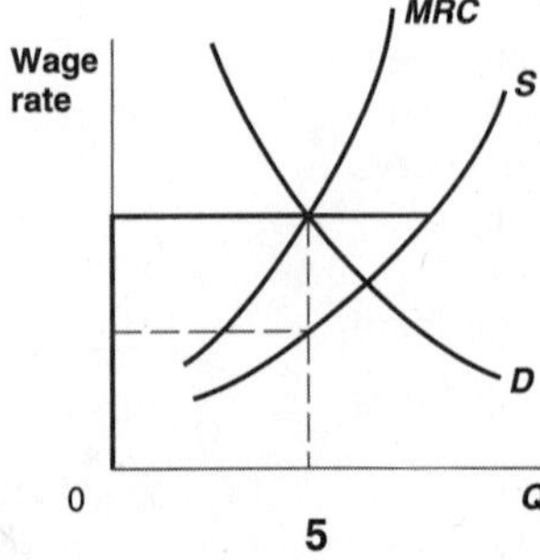

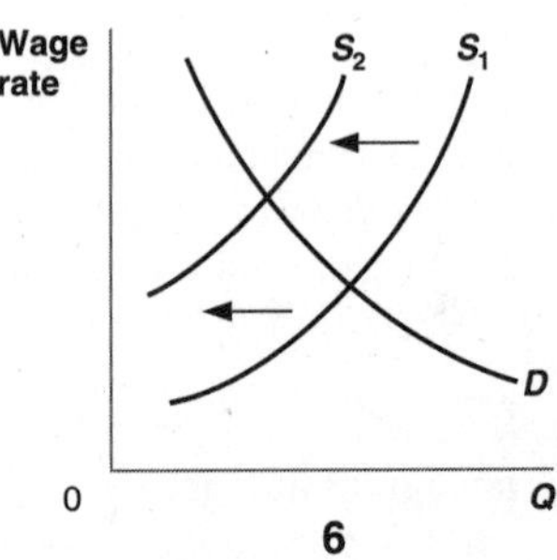

SHORT ANSWER AND ESSAY QUESTIONS

1. What is meant by the term wages? What is the difference between real wages and nominal wages?

2. How does the level of wages in the United States compare with other foreign nations?

3. Explain why the productivity of the U.S. labor force increased in the past to its present high level.

4. Why has the level of real wages continued to increase even though the supply of labor has continually increased?

5. What economic reasons have been given for the stagnation in real wages in the United States since 1979?

6. In the competitive model, what determines the market demand for labor and the wage rate? What kind of supply situation do all firms as a group confront? What kind of supply situation does the individual firm confront? Why?

7. In the monopsony model, what determines employment and the wage rate? What kind of supply situation does the monopsonist face? Why? How does the wage rate paid and the level of employment compare with what would result if the market were competitive?

8. In what sense is a worker who is hired by a monopsonist "exploited" and one who is employed in a competitive labor market "justly" rewarded? Why do monopsonists wish to restrict employment?

9. When supply is less than perfectly elastic, marginal labor cost is greater than the wage rate. Why?

10. What basic methods do labor unions use to try to increase the wages their members receive? If these methods are successful in raising wages, 'what effect do they have on employment?

11. What three methods might labor use to increase the demand for labor? If these methods are successful, what effects do they have on wage rates and employment?

12. When labor unions attempt to restrict the supply of labor to increase wage rates, what devices do they use to do this for the economy as a whole, and what means do they use to restrict the supply of a given type of worker?

13. How do industrial unions attempt to increase wage rates, and what effect does this method of increasing wages have on employment in the industry affected?

14. Both exclusive and inclusive unions are able to raise the wage rates their members receive. Why might unions limit or temper their demands for higher wages? What two factors determine the extent to which they will or will not reduce their demands for higher wages?

15. What is bilateral monopoly? What determines wage rates in a labor market of this type?

16. What is the effect of minimum wage laws on wage rates and employment in
(a) competitive labor markets,
(b) monopsony labor markets, and
(c) the economy as a whole?

17. What is meant by the term "noncompeting" groups in a labor market? What two factors tend to explain wage differentials in noncompeting groups?

18. How are wages used to equalize differences in the characteristics of jobs? Give examples.

19. Describe four types of imperfections in labor markets. Discuss how these imperfections contribute to wage differentials.

20. Explain what is meant by the principal-agent problem, and relate it to shirking. What are the different pay incentive plans that are correct for shirking on the job? How does profit sharing reduce shirking? What is the reason for efficiency wages?

ANSWERS

Chapter 28 Wage Determination

FILL-IN QUESTIONS

1. wage, wage, multiplied
2. nominal, real
3. strong
4. capital, natural, labor force, technology
5. long-run, the same
6. slower, slower, downward
7. *a.* higher, opportunity cost; *b.* revenue product; *c.* equal to
8. elastic, equal to
9. equal to, greater, less
10. *a.* divided; *b.* equal to, divided, 1
11. lower, less
12. demand for, supply of, above
13. demand for, productivity, increasing
14. exclusive, inclusive, a craft, an industrial
15. decrease, decrease, inelastic
16. less, greater, wage rate
17. increase, decrease, increase, increase
18. increase, decrease, decrease, uncertain
19. are not, vary, imperfect
20. noncompeting, ability, human capital
21. nonmonetary, compensating
22. jobs, immobility, restraints, discrimination
23. principals, agents, profits, wages
24. shirking, performance, pay
25. piece, efficiency, negative

TRUE-FALSE QUESTIONS

1. F, p. 582
2. F, pp. 582-583
3. T, p. 583
4. T, pp. 583-584
5. F, p. 584
6. T, p. 587
7. T, pp. 585-587
8. T, pp. 585-588
9. T, p. 590
10. F, pp. 590-591
11. T, p. 591
12. F, p. 591
13. F, p. 591
14. F, p. 593
15. T, p. 592
16. F, p. 592
17. F, pp. 593-594
18. T, p. 594
19. T, p. 594
20. T, pp. 594-595
21. T, p. 595
22. F, p. 596
23. T, pp. 596-597
24. T, pp. 597-598
25. T, p. 600

MULTIPLE-CHOICE QUESTIONS

1. a, p. 582
2. c, pp. 582-583
3. c, p. 585
4. a, p. 585
5. c, p. 586
6. d, p. 587
7. d, pp. 588-589
8. b, p. 588
9. d, p. 589
10. c, p. 589
11. d, p. 590
12. b, pp. 590-591
13. b, p. 591
14. a, p. 592
15. d, pp. 588-589
16. c, pp. 588-589
17. b, p. 593
18. c, pp. 588-589
19. b, pp. 588-589
20. c, p. 586
21. d, p. 593
22. a, p. 595
23. b, p. 596
24. b, pp. 597-598
25. c, pp. 599-600

PROBLEMS

1. *a.* Quantity of labor demanded: 100, 200, 300, 400, 500, 600, 700, 800; *b.* (1) 10.00, (2) 600; *c.* (1) 10.00, (2) 6, (3) 10.00; *f.* 400

2. *a.* Total labor cost: 0, 4.00, 12.00, 24.00, 40.00, 60.00, 84.00, 112.00, 144.00, Marginal labor cost: 4.00, 8.00, 12.00, 16.00, 20.00, 24.00, 28.00, 32.00; *b.* (1) 5, (2) 12.00, (3) 20.00, *d.* 6, 14.00

3. *a.* Wage rate: 16.00, 16.00, 16.00, 16.00, 16.00, 16.00, 16.00, 16.00; *b.* Total labor cost: 16.00, 32.00, 48.00, 64.00, 80.00, 96.00, 112.00, 128.00; Marginal labor cost: 16.00, 16.00, 16.00, 16.00, 16.00, 16.00, 16.00; *c.* (1) 6, (2) 16.00, (3) 96.00; *d.* increased, increased, increased

4. *a.* 5; *b.* 3; *c.* 6; *d.* 2; *e.* 4; *f.* 1

SHORT ANSWER AND ESSAY QUESTIONS

1. p. 582
2. pp. 582-583
3. p. 583
4. p. 584
5. p. 584
6. pp. 585-587
7. pp. 587-589
8. pp. 587-589
9. pp. 587-588
10. p. 590
11. pp. 590-591
12. p. 591
13. pp. 591-592
14. pp. 592-593
15. pp. 593-594
16. pp. 594-595
17. pp. 595-596
18. p. 596
19. pp. 596-597
20. pp. 597-600

CHAPTER 29

Rent, Interest, and Profit

Chapter 29 concludes the study of the prices of resources by examining rent, interest, and profits. There is nothing especially difficult about Chapter 29. By now you should understand that the marginal revenue product of a resource determines the demand for that resource and that this understanding can be applied to the demand for land and capital. It will be on the supply side of the land market that you will encounter whatever difficulties there are. The supply of **land** is unique because it is perfectly *inelastic:* Changes in rent do not change the quantity of land which will be supplied. Demand, given the quantity of land available, is thus the sole determinant of rent. Of course land varies in productivity and can be used for different purposes, but these are merely the factors which explain why the rent on all lands is not the same.

Capital, as the economist defines it, means capital goods. Is the rate of interest, then, the price paid for the use of capital goods? No, not quite. Capital is not one kind of good; it is many different kinds. In order to be able to talk about the price paid for the use of capital goods, there must be a simple way of adding up different kinds of capital goods. The simple way is to measure the quantity of capital goods in terms of money. The interest rate is, then, the price paid for the use of money (or of financial capital).

The *interest rate* is determined by the *demand for and supply of loanable funds* in the economy. In a simplified model, businesses are the primary demanders of loanable funds because they want to use this financial capital to buy capital goods (e.g., equipment, machinery, factories, etc.). As with the demand for any good or service, the greater the price of using loanable funds (the interest rate), the smaller the amount of loanable funds that firms will be able and willing to borrow. A business will most likely borrow funds and make an investment in capital goods if the expected rate of return on the investment is greater than the interest rate. Therefore, the lower the interest rate, the greater the opportunities for profitable investments and the greater the amount of loanable funds demanded.

On the *supply* side, households are the typical suppliers of loanable funds. At a higher rate of interest, households are willing to supply more loanable funds than at lower interest rates because of the weighing of present consumption to future consumption. Most consumers prefer present consumption, but they would be willing to forgo this current use of funds and make them available for loan if there is compensation in the form of interest payments. Thus, the greater the interest rate, the more saving by households, which in turn creates a greater supply of loanable funds.

The intersection of the demand curve and the supply curve for loanable funds determines the *equilibrium* rate of interest, or the price of loanable funds, and the equilibrium quantity. This relationship is illustrated in Figure 29-2. The demand and supply curves of loanable funds can also shift due to a variety of factors. For example, there could be an increase in the rates of return on investments, which would increase the demand for loanable funds at each and every interest rate; changes in the tax laws could make savings more attractive and this change would increase the supply of loanable funds. Note too that while in the simplified model businesses are the demanders and households the suppliers of loanable funds, in reality these sectors can operate on both sides of the market.

When it comes to *profits,* supply and demand analysis fails the economist. Profits are not merely a wage for a particular type of labor, rather, they are rewards for taking risks and the gains of the monopolist. Such things as "the quantity of risk taken" or "the quantity of effort required to establish a monopoly" simply cannot be measured; consequently, it is impossible to talk about the demand for or the supply of them. Nevertheless, profits are important in the economy. They are largely rewards for doing things that have to be done if the economy is to allocate resources efficiently and to progress and develop; they are the lure or the bait which makes people willing to take the risks that result in efficiency and progress.

The final section of Chapter 29 answers two questions about the U.S. economy. What part of the national income goes to workers and what part goes to capitalists—those who provide the economy with land, capital goods, and entrepreneurial ability? And have the shares going to workers and to capitalists changed since 1900? You may be surprised to learn that the lion's share—about 80%—of the national income goes to workers today and went to workers at the beginning of the century and that only about 20% of national income goes to the capitalists today or went to them in 1900.

■ CHECKLIST

When you have studied this chapter you should be able to

- ☐ Define economic rent.
- ☐ Explain why supply of land does not affect economic rent.
- ☐ Illustrate how changes in demand determine economic rent.

☐ Explain why land rent is a surplus payment.
☐ Give the rationale for a single tax on land proposed by Henry George.
☐ State four criticisms of the single tax on land.
☐ Illustrate graphically how productivity differences affect land rent.
☐ Contrast society's and a firm's perspective on economic rent.
☐ Define interest and state two aspects about it.
☐ Describe the loanable funds theory of interest using supply and demand.
☐ Show how the equilibrium rate of interest is established in the loanable funds market using supply and demand analysis.
☐ Explain why the supply of loanable funds curve has a positive slope.
☐ Explain why the demand for loanable funds curve has a negative slope.
☐ List factors that change the supply or demand for loanable funds.
☐ Distinguish between a change in demand or supply and a change in quantity demanded or supplied as applied to the loanable funds market.
☐ Identify the different sides that participants (households, businesses, or government) take in the demand or supply of loanable funds.
☐ List five reasons why interest rates differ.
☐ Define the pure rate of interest and state how it is measured.
☐ Explain how the interest rate affects investment spending, total output, the allocation of capital, and research and development (R&D) spending.
☐ Distinguish between real and nominal interest rates.
☐ Distinguish between nominal and real wages.
☐ Use graphical analysis to explain the three effects of usury laws.
☐ Distinguish between economic and normal profit.
☐ Describe the return to the entrepreneurial ability in terms of economic and normal profit.
☐ List three sources of economic profit.
☐ Explain the relationship between insurable and uninsurable risk and economic profit.
☐ Describe how innovation affects economic profit.
☐ Discuss the influence of monopoly on economic profit.
☐ Identify two functions of profits for the economy.
☐ List in percentage terms the sources of national income.
☐ Describe the change in labor's and capital's income share since 1900.

■ CHAPTER OUTLINE

1. ***Economic rent*** is the price paid for the use of land or natural resources whose supply is perfectly inelastic.

a. The supply of land is perfectly inelastic because it is virtually fixed in the quantity available. Supply has no influence in determining economic rent.

b. Demand is the active determinant of economic rent. As demand increases or decreases, economic rent will increase or decrease given the perfectly inelastic supply of land.

c. Economic rent serves no incentive function given the fixed supply of land. It is not necessary to increase economic rent to bring forth more quantity, as is the case with other natural resources. Economists, therefore, consider economic rent a ***surplus payment.***

d. Socialists have argued that land rent is unearned income and that either land should be nationalized or land rents should be taxed away.

(1) Henry George, in his 1879 book *Progress and Poverty,* called for a single tax on land as the sole source of government tax revenue.

(2) Critics of the single tax cite its inadequacy for meeting government needs, the difficulty of identifying the portion of rent in incomes, the conflicting interpretations of unearned income, and adverse equity effects arising from changes in land ownership.

e. Economic rents on different types of land vary because different plots of land vary in productivity.

f. From society's perspective, economic rent is a surplus payment, but from a firm's perspective, economic rent is a cost. Firms must pay economic rent to bid the land it wants to use for its production away from alternative uses.

2. The ***interest rate*** is the price paid for the use of money. The ***loanable funds theory of interest*** describes how the interest rate is determined by the demand for and supply of loanable funds. The intersection of the demand for and supply of loanable funds determines the equilibrium interest rate and the quantity of funds loaned.

a. The ***supply*** of loanable funds is generally provided by households through savings. There is a positive relationship between the interest rate and the quantity of loanable funds supplied. The supply curve, however, may be relatively inelastic and thus not very responsive to changes in the interest rate.

b. The ***demand*** for loanable funds typically comes from businesses for investment in capital goods. There is an inverse relationship between the interest rate and the quantity of loanable funds demanded. Lower interest rates provide more profitable investment opportunities; higher interest rates reduce investment.

c. There are some extensions to the simplified model of the loanable funds market.

(1) Financial institutions serve as intermediaries in the supply and demand market for loanable funds.

(2) The supply of funds can change because of changes in factors that affect the thriftiness of households.

(3) The demand for funds can change because of changes in the rate of return on potential investments.

(4) Households and businesses can operate on both sides of the market—as both demanders and suppliers of loanable funds. Government also participates on both sides of the loanable fund market.

d. It is convenient to speak as if there were one interest rate, but actually there are a range of rates. These rates differ because of difference in five factors: risk, maturity, loan size, taxability, and market imperfections.

e. When economists talk about "the interest rate," they are referring to the pure rate of interest which is best measured by the interest paid on long-term and riskless securities, such as 30-year bonds of the U.S. government.

f. The interest rate plays several roles in the economy.
(1) It affects the total output because of the inverse relationship between interest rate and investment spending; government often tries to influence the interest rate to achieve its policy goals.
(2) It rations (allocates) financial and real capital among competing firms and determines the composition of the total output of capital goods.
(3) It changes the level and composition of spending on research and development.
These effects are based on changes in the real interest rate, which is the rate expressed in inflation-adjusted dollars, not the nominal interest rate, which is the rate expressed in current dollars.

g. Usury laws specify a maximum interest rate for loans. They were passed to limit borrowing costs, but they can have other effects. First, they may cause a shortage of credit, which is then given only the most worthy borrower. Second, borrowers gain from paying less for credit and borrowers lose from receiving less interest income. Third,it creates inefficiency in the economy because funds get directed to less-productive investments.

3. ***Economic profit*** is what remains of the firm's revenue after all its explicit and implicit opportunity costs have been deducted.

a. Profit is a payment for entrepreneurial ability. Normal profit is the payment necessary to keep the entrepreneur in current work and is thus a cost. Economic profit is the residual payment to the entrepreneur from total revenues after all other costs have been subtracted.

b. Profits come from three basic sources that reflect the dynamic nature of real-world capitalism:
(1) rewards for assuming uninsurable risk that arises from changes in economic conditions, the structure of the economy, and government policy.
(2) a return for assuming the uncertainties inherent in innovation; and
(3) surpluses which firms obtain from the exploitation of monopoly power.

c. The expectation of profit serves several functions in the economy. Profits encourage businesses to innovate, and this innovation contributes to economic growth. Profits (and losses) guide businesses to produce products and to use resources in the way desired by society.

4. National income is distributed among wages, rent, interest, and profit. Using a broad definition, the share of national income going to labor is about 80%. The share going to capitalists is about 20%. These percentages have remained relatively stable since 1900.

■ HINTS AND TIPS

1. Although this chapter focuses on three resource payments (rent, interest, and profit), the discussion is much simpler and easier to understand than it was for the one resource payment (wages) in the previous chapter. It will help if you think of this chapter as three minichapters.

2. Use a supply and demand graph for land to explain to yourself why land rent is ***surplus payment.*** Draw a vertical (perfectly inelastic) supply curve and a downsloping demand curve. Identify the price and quantity combination where the two curves intersect. Then draw a new demand curve showing an increase in demand. What happens to price? (It increases.) What happens to quantity? (No change.) Changes in land rent perform no incentive function for the economy because they bring forth no more supply of land. Land rents are unnecessary (surplus) payments for the economy.

3. The loanable funds theory of interest will be easy to understand if you think of it as an application of supply and demand analysis. You need to remember, however, who are the suppliers and who are the demanders of loanable funds. In this simplified model, the *suppliers* of loanable funds are *households* who have a different quantity of savings to make available for loans at different interest rates; the higher the interest rate, the greater the quantity of loanable funds supplied. The *demanders* of loanable funds are *businesses* that want to borrow a quantity of money at each interest rate; the higher the interest rate, the smaller the quantity of loanable funds demanded for investment purposes.

4. Remember that it is the expectation, not the certainty, of profit that drives the entrepreneur. The generation of profit involves risk taking by the entrepreneur. You should distinguish, however, between risks that are insurable and those which are not. A major source of profit for the entrepreneur comes from the uninsurable risks that the entrepreneur is willing to assume in an uncertain world.

■ IMPORTANT TERMS

economic rent
incentive function
single-tax movement
the loanable funds theory of interest
pure rate of interest
nominal interest rate
real interest rate
usury laws
explicit costs
implicit costs
normal profit
economic (pure) profit
static economy
insurable risks
uninsurable risks

SELF-TEST

■ FILL-IN QUESTIONS

1. Economic rent is the price paid for the use of (labor, land) ______________ and (capital, natural) ______________ resources which are completely (fixed, variable) ______________ in supply.

2. The active determinant of economic rent is (demand, supply) ______________ and the passive determinant is ______________.

3. Economic rent does not bring forth more supply and serves no (profit, incentive) ______________ function. Economists consider economic rent a (tax, surplus) ______________ payment which is not necessary to ensure that land is available to the economy.

4. Socialists argue that land rents are (earned, unearned) ______________ incomes. Henry George called for a single (price, tax) ______________ on land to transfer economic rent to government because it would not affect the amount of land. One criticism of George's proposal is that it would not generate enough (revenue, profit) ______________.

5. Rents on different pieces of land are not the same because land differs in (price, productivity) ______________.

6. From society's perspective, land rent is a (surplus payment, cost) ______________, but from a firm's perspective, land rent is a ______________ because land (is a free good, has alternative uses) ______________.

7. The price paid for the use of money is (profit, interest) ______________. It is typically stated as a (price, percentage) ______________ of the amount borrowed. Money (is, is not) ______________ an economic resource because money ______________ productive.

8. Money or financial capital is obtained in the (mutual, loanable) ______________ funds market. At the equilibrium rate of interest, the quantity demanded for loanable funds is (greater than, equal to, less than) ______________ the quantity supplied of loanable funds.

9. The quantity supplied of loanable funds is (inversely, directly) ______________ related to the interest rate while the quantity demanded for loanable funds is ______________ related to the interest rate.

10. With a higher interest rate, there are (greater, fewer) ______________ opportunities for profitable investment and hence a (larger, smaller) ______________ quantity demanded for loanable funds.

11. An increase in the thriftiness of households will result in a(n) (increase, decrease) ______________ in the (supply, demand) ______________ of loanable funds. Anything that increases the rate of return on potential investments will (increase, decrease) ______________ the (supply, demand) ______________ of loanable funds.

12. State five reasons why there is a range of interest rates:

a. ______________________________

b. ______________________________

c. ______________________________

d. ______________________________

e. ______________________________

13. Economists often talk of the (loan, pure) ______________ rate of interest. It is approximated by the interest paid on (short-term, long-term) ______________ U.S. government bonds.

14. A higher equilibrium interest rate often (increases, decreases) ______________ business borrowing for investment and thus ______________ total spending in the economy, whereas a lower equilibrium interest rate (increases, decreases) ______________ business borrowing and thus ______________ total spending in the economy.

15. The rate of interest expressed in purchasing power, or inflation-adjusted dollars, is the (real, nominal) ______________ interest rate, while the rate of interest expressed in dollars of current value is the ______________ interest rate.

16. Laws which state the maximum interest rate at which loans can be made are called (antitrust, usury) ______________ laws. These laws cause (market, nonmarket) ______________ rationing of credit that favors (lenders, borrowers) ______________ and leads to (less, more) ______________ economic efficiency in the allocation of credit.

17. The difference between total revenue and total cost is (economic, normal) ______________ profit. The minimum payment for the entrepreneur to keep him or her in the current line of business is (economic, normal) ______________ profit. The excess of total revenue above total cost is (economic, normal) ______________ profit.

18. Economic profit is a reward for either assuming (insurable, uninsurable) ______________ risk or for dealing with the uncertainty of (taxation, innovation) ______________.

19. Economic profit over time can also arise from (pure competition, monopoly) ______________, and this source of profit is typically based on (increased, decreased)

______________ output, ______________ prices above competitive levels, and (increased, decreased) ______________ economic efficiency.

20. Defining labor income broadly to include both wages and salaries and proprietors' income, the labor share of national income total is about (20%, 50%, 80%) __________, while capitalist share of income is about __________. The share of income going to capitalists has (increased, decreased, remained stable) ______________ since 1900.

■ TRUE-FALSE QUESTIONS

Circle the T if the statement is true, the F if it is false.

1. Rent is the price paid for use of capital resources. **T F**

2. The determination of economic rent for land and other natural resources is based on a demand curve that is perfectly inelastic. **T F**

3. Rent is a surplus payment because it does not perform an incentive function. **T F**

4. Rent is unique because it is not determined by demand and supply. **T F**

5. Henry George argued in *Progress and Poverty* that the increasing land rents would produce more unearned income for landowners which could then be taxed by government. **T F**

6. Critics of the single tax on land argue that it would bring in too much revenue for the government. **T F**

7. For individual producers, rental payments are a surplus payment, but for society they are a cost. **T F**

8. Money is an economic resource and the interest rate is the price paid for this resource. **T F**

9. The quantity of loanable funds demanded is inversely related to the interest rate. **T F**

10. The quantity of loanable funds supplied is directly related to the interest rate. **T F**

11. An increase in the demand for loanable funds would tend to increase the interest rate. **T F**

12. An increase in the rate of return on investments would most likely increase the supply of loanable funds. **T F**

13. Other things equal, long-term loans usually command lower rates of interest than do short-term loans. **T F**

14. The pure rate of interest is best approximated by the interest paid on long-term bonds with very low risk, such as the 30-year U.S. Treasury bond. **T F**

15. A higher equilibrium interest rate discourages business borrowing for investment, reducing investment and total spending. **T F**

16. The interest rate rations the supply of loanable funds to investment projects whose rate of return will be less than the interest rate. **T F**

17. If the nominal rate of interest is 6% and the inflation rate is 3%, the real rate of interest is 9%. **T F**

18. Usury laws result in a shortage of loanable funds and nonmarket rationing in credit markets. **T F**

19. Lenders or banks are the main beneficiaries of usury laws. **T F**

20. If the economists' definition of profit were used, total profit in the economy would be greater than would be the case if the accountants' definition were used. **T F**

21. A normal profit is the minimum payment the entrepreneur must receive to induce him or her to provide the firm with entrepreneurial ability. **T F**

22. It is the static competitive economy that gives rise to economic profit. **T F**

23. Insurable risk is one of the sources of economic profit. **T F**

24. Profits arising from monopoly are more socially desirable than profits arising from uncertainty. **T F**

25. Profits influence both the level of economic output and the allocation of resources among alternative uses. **T F**

■ MULTIPLE-CHOICE QUESTIONS

Circle the letter that corresponds to the best answer.

1. Which of the following do economists consider a productive economic resource?
   (a) money capital
   (b) capital goods
   (c) interest
   (d) profit

2. The price paid for a natural resource that is completely fixed in supply is
   (a) profit
   (b) interest
   (c) rent
   (d) a risk payment

3. In total, the supply of land is
   (a) perfectly inelastic
   (b) of unitary elasticity
   (c) perfectly elastic
   (d) elastic but not perfectly elastic

4. Which of the following is a characteristic of the tax proposed by Henry George?
   (a) It would be equal to 20% of all land rent.
   (b) It would be the only tax levied by government.
   (c) It would reduce the supply of land.
   (d) It would reduce rents paid by the amount of the tax.

5. A major criticism of the single tax on land is that it would
(a) bring in more tax revenues than is necessary to finance all current government spending
(b) not distinguish between payments for the use of land and those for improvements to land
(c) take into account the history of ownership of the land in determining the tax
(d) not tax "unearned" income

6. Which of the following is true?
(a) The greater the demand for land, the greater the supply of land.
(b) A windfall profits tax on the increases in the profits of petroleum producers was proposed by Henry George.
(c) Individual users of land have to pay a rent to its owners because that land has alternative uses.
(d) The less productive a particular piece of land is, the greater will be the rent its owner is able to earn from it.

7. The economic rent from land will increase, *ceteris paribus,* whenever the
(a) price of land decreases
(b) demand for land increases
(c) demand for land decreases
(d) supply curve for land increases

8. When the supply curve for land lies entirely to the right of the demand curve,
(a) landowners will receive an economic rent
(b) landowners will not receive an economic rent
(c) the interest rate on land will increase
(d) the interest rate on land will decrease

9. The upsloping supply of loanable funds is best explained by the idea that most people prefer
(a) current consumption to future consumption
(b) future consumption to present consumption
(c) saving over consumption
(d) investment over saving

10. Why is the demand for loanable funds downsloping?
(a) At lower interest rates, fewer investment projects will be profitable to businesses, and hence a small quantity of loanable funds will be demanded.
(b) At lower interest rates, more investment projects will be profitable to businesses, and hence a small quantity of loanable funds will be demanded.
(c) At higher interest rates, more investment projects will be profitable to businesses, and hence a large quantity of loanable funds will be demanded.
(d) At higher interest rates, fewer investment projects will be profitable to businesses, and hence a small quantity of loanable funds will be demanded.

11. In the competitive market for loanable funds, when the quantity of funds demanded exceeds the quantity supplied, then the
(a) interest rate will decrease
(b) interest rate will increase
(c) demand curve will increase
(d) supply curve will decrease

12. A decrease in the productivity of capital goods will, *ceteris paribus,*
(a) increase the supply of loanable funds
(b) decrease the supply of loanable funds
(c) increase the demand for loanable funds
(d) decrease the demand for loanable funds

13. Which of the following would tend to result in a lower interest rate?
(a) the greater the risk involved
(b) the shorter the length of the loan
(c) the smaller the amount of the loan
(d) the greater the monopoly power of the lender

14. What is the most likely reason why a lender would prefer a high-quality municipal bond that pays a 6% rate of interest as compared to a high-quality corporate bond paying 8%?
(a) The municipal bond is tax-exempt.
(b) The municipal bond is a long-term investment.
(c) The corporate bond is safer than the municipal bond.
(d) The municipal bond is easier to purchase than a corporate bond.

15. The pure rate of interest is best approximated by the interest paid on
(a) consumer credit cards
(b) tax-exempt municipal bonds
(c) 90-day Treasury bills
(d) 30-year Treasury bonds

16. If the annual rate of interest were 18% and the rate of return a firm expects to earn annually by building a new plant were 20%, the firm would
(a) not build the new plant
(b) build the new plant
(c) have to toss a coin to decide whether to build the new plant
(d) not be able to determine from these figures whether to build the plant

Questions 17 and 18 refer to the following data.

Expected rate of return	Amount of capital goods investment (in billions)
19%	$220
17	250
15	300
13	360
11	430
9	500

17. If the interest rate is 13%,
(a) $300 billion of investment will be undertaken
(b) $360 billion of investment will be undertaken
(c) $430 billion of investment will be undertaken
(d) $500 billion of investment will be undertaken

18. An increase in the interest rate from 15% to 17% would
(a) increase investment by $40 billion
(b) increase investment by $50 billion
(c) decrease investment by $50 billion
(d) decrease investment by $40 billion

19. Which of the following is the definition of a usury law? It is a law that specifies the
(a) alternative uses of surplus government land
(b) tax rate on interest paid for state and municipal bonds
(c) maximum interest rate at which loans can be made
(d) interest paid on long-term, virtually riskless bonds of the U.S. government

20. Which would be a likely economic effect of a usury law?
(a) There would be an increase in economic efficiency.
(b) There would be a decrease in the rationing of credit.
(c) Creditworthy borrowers would lose and lenders would gain.
(d) Creditworthy borrowers would gain and lenders would lose.

21. Which is the minimum return or payment necessary to retain the entrepreneur in some specific line of production?
(a) normal profit
(b) explicit cost
(c) real interest rate
(d) pure rate of interest

22. Which of the following is an economic cost?
(a) uninsurable risk
(b) normal profit
(c) economic profit
(d) monopoly profit

23. One basic reason why there is economic profit is that
(a) risks are insurable
(b) economies are static
(c) there is innovation
(d) there are purely competitive markets

24. Monopoly profit is typically based on
(a) uncertainty and innovation
(b) insurable and uninsurable risk
(c) productivity and economic efficiency
(d) reduced output and above-competitive prices

25. Since 1900, the share of national income
(a) has increased for capitalists, but decreased for labor
(b) has decreased for capitalists, but increased for labor
(c) has increased for capitalists and for labor
(d) has remained relatively constant for capitalists and labor

■ PROBLEMS

1. Assume that the quantity of a certain type of land available is 300,000 acres and the demand for this land is that given in the following table.

Pure land rent, per acre	Land demanded, acres
$350	100,000
300	200,000
250	300,000
200	400,000
150	500,000
100	600,000
50	700,000

a. The pure rent on this land will be $____________.

b. The total quantity of land rented will be ____________ ____________ acres.

c. On the graph below, plot the supply and demand curves for this land and indicate the pure rent for land and the quantity of land rented.

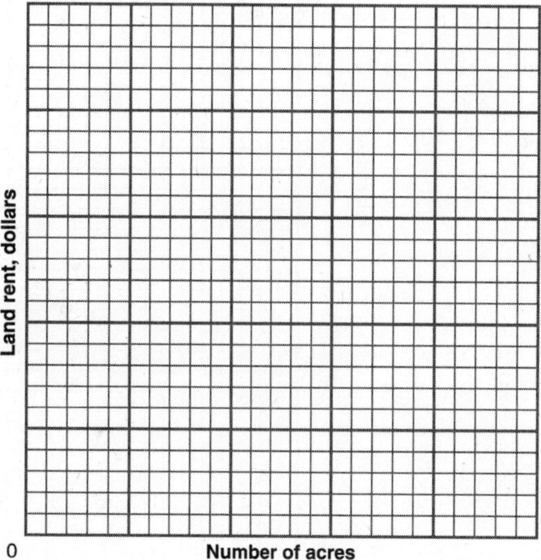

d. If landowners were taxed at a rate of $250 per acre for their land, the pure rent on this land after taxes would be $____________ but the number of acres rented would be ____________.

2. The following schedule shows interest rates (column 1), the associated quantity demand of loanable funds (column 2), and the quantity supplied of loanable funds (column 4) in billions of dollars at those interest rates.

Interest rate (1)	Quantity demanded (2)	(3)	Quantity supplied (4)	(5)
12	50	______	260	______
10	100	______	240	______
8	150	______	220	______
6	200	______	200	______
4	250	______	180	______
2	300	______	160	______

a. Plot the demand and supply schedule on the graph on the next page. (The interest rate is measured along the vertical axis and the quantity demanded or supplied is measured on the horizontal axis.)

(1) The equilibrium interest rate is ________%. The quantity demanded is $____________ billion and the quantity supplied is $____________ billion.

(2) At an interest rate of 10%, the quantity demanded of loanable funds is $____________ billion and the quantity supplied of loanable funds is $____________

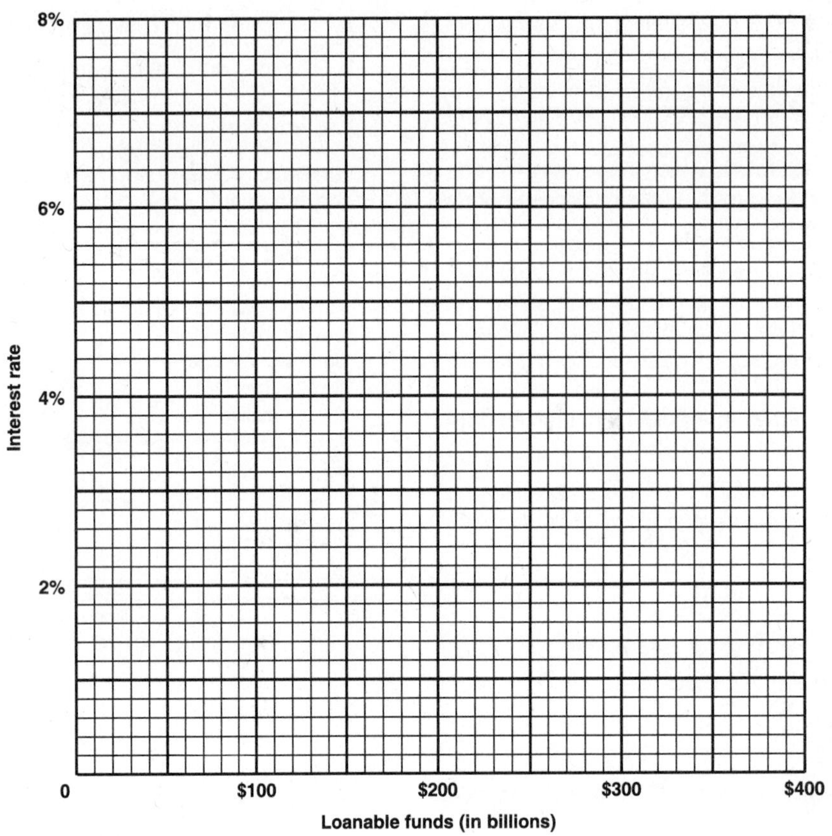

billion. There is an excess of loanable funds of $__________ billion.

(3) At an interest rate of 4%, the quantity demanded of loanable funds is $__________ billion and the quantity supplied of loanable funds is $__________ billion. There is a shortage of loanable funds of $__________ billion.

b. If technology improves and the demand for loanable funds increases by $70 billion at each interest rate, then the new equilibrium interest rate will be _____% and the equilibrium quantity of loanable funds will be $__________ billion. Fill in the new demand schedule in column 3 of the table on page 335, and plot this new demand curve on the graph.

c. Then, because of changes in the tax laws, households become more thrifty by $140 at each interest rate. The new equilibrium interest rate will be _____% and the new equilibrium quantity of loanable funds will be $__________ billion. Fill in the new supply schedule in column 5 of the table, and plot this new supply curve on the graph.

3. Firms make investment decisions based on the rate of return and the interest rate.

a. In each of the following simple cases, calculate the rate of return on an investment.

(1) You invest in a new machine that costs $2,000 but which is expected to increase total revenues by $2,075 in 1 year. __________

(2) You invest in a new piece of equipment that costs $150,000 but which is expected to increase total revenues in 1 year by $160,000. __________

(3) You invest in a new plant that costs $3 million and which is expected to increase total revenues in 1 year by $3.5 million. __________

b. Given each of the following interest rates, would you make an investment in situations 1, 2, and 3?

(1) An interest rate of 5% __________

(2) An interest rate of 8% __________

(3) An interest rate of 15% __________

4. The following table shows estimated wages and salaries, proprietors' income, corporate profits, interest, rent, and the national income of the United States in 1997.

Wages and salaries	$4,703 billion
Proprietors' income	545 billion
Corporate profits	804 billion
Interest	450 billion
Rent	148 billion
National income	6,650 billion

a. Wages and salaries were _____% of the national income.

b. Labor's share of the national income was _____% and capital's share was _____%.

■ SHORT ANSWER AND ESSAY QUESTIONS

1. Explain what determines the economic rent paid for the use of land. What is unique about the supply of land?

2. Why is land rent a surplus payment?

3. What economic difficulties would be encountered if the government adopted Henry George's single tax proposal as a means of confiscating this surplus? What do the critics think of the concept of a single tax on land?

4. Even though land rent is an economic surplus payment, it is also an economic cost for the individual use of land. Why and how can it be both an economic surplus payment and an economic cost?

5. Explain what determines (a) the amount of loanable funds that households are willing to supply, (b) the amount that businesses wish to demand, and (c) how these desires are resolved in the market for loanable funds.

6. How might a change in productivity affect the interest rate? How might a change in the tax laws affect household savings and the interest rate? What are the implications if the supply curve for loanable funds is highly inelastic?

7. What is the connection between the rate of return on a capital goods investment and the interest rate? Give examples of possible investment situations.

8. Why are there actually many different rates in the economy at any given time?

9. What is the pure rate of interest? How is it approximated?

10. What important functions does the rate of interest perform in the economy?

11. What is the difference between the nominal and the real interest rate? How does each one affect investment spending or decisions about research and development?

12. What are economic profits? In what way are profits a return to entrepreneurial ability?

13. Why would there be no economic profits in a purely competitive and static economy?

14. Why is the distinction between insurable and uninsurable risk important from a profit perspective? What are three sources that contribute to uninsurable risk?

15. How does economic profit arise from innovation?

16. "The risks which an entrepreneur assumes arise because of uncertainties which are external to the firm and because of uncertainties which are developed by the initiative of the firm itself." Explain.

17. Explain why profit arising from monopoly is not socially desirable, while profit arising from uncertainty is socially desirable.

18. What part of the U.S. national income is wages and salaries, and what part is labor income? Why do your answers to these questions differ?

19. What part of the national income is the income of capitalists? What kinds of income are capitalist income?

20. What have been the historical trends in the shares of national income that are wages and salaries, labor income, and capitalist income?

ANSWERS

Chapter 29 Rent, Interest, and Profit

FILL-IN QUESTIONS

1. land, natural, fixed
2. demand, supply
3. incentive, surplus
4. unearned, tax, revenue
5. productivity
6. surplus payment, cost, has alternative uses
7. interest, percentage, is not, is not
8. loanable, equal to
9. directly, inversely
10. fewer, smaller
11. increase, supply, increase, demand
12. *a.* risk; *b.* length of loan; *c.* amount of loan; *d.* tax status of loan (or investment); *e.* market imperfections (any order for a–e)
13. pure, long-term
14. decreases, decreases, increases, increases
15. real, nominal
16. usury, nomarket, borrowers, less
17. economic, normal, economic
18. uninsurable, innovation
19. monopoly, decreased, increased, decreased
20. 80%, 20%, remained stable

TRUE-FALSE QUESTIONS

1. F, p. 604
2. F, p. 604
3. T, p. 605
4. F, p. 604
5. T, p. 605
6. F, p. 605
7. F, p. 606
8. F, p. 607
9. T, pp. 607-608
10. T, p. 607
11. T, p. 608
12. F, p. 608
13. F, p. 609
14. T, p. 609
15. T, p. 610
16. F, p. 610
17. F, p. 610
18. T, p. 611
19. F, p. 611
20. F, p. 612
21. T, p. 612
22. F, p. 612
23. F, pp. 612-613
24. F, p. 613
25. T, pp. 613-614

MULTIPLE-CHOICE QUESTIONS

1. b, p. 607
2. c, p. 604
3. a, p. 604
4. b, p. 605
5. b, p. 605
6. c, p. 606
7. b, p. 604
8. b, p. 604
9. a, p. 607
10. d, p. 608
11. b, pp. 607-608
12. d, p. 608
13. b, p. 609
14. a, p. 609
15. d, p. 609
16. b, p. 610
17. b, p. 610
18. c, p. 610
19. c, p. 611
20. d, p. 611
21. a, p. 612
22. b, p. 612
23. c, p. 613
24. d, p. 613
25. d, p. 615

PROBLEMS

1. *a.* 250; *b.* 300,000; *d.* 0, 300,000
2. *a.* (1) 6, 200, 200; (2) 100, 240, 140; (3) 250, 180, 70; *b.* 8, 220; 120, 170, 220, 270, 320, 370; *c.* 4, 320; 400, 380, 360, 340, 320, 300
3. *a.* (1) 3.75; (2) 6.67; (3) 16.67; *b.* (1) 2, 3; (2) 3; (3) 3
4. *a.* 71; *b.* 79, 21

SHORT ANSWER AND ESSAY QUESTIONS

1. p. 604
2. p. 605
3. pp. 605-606
4. p. 606
5. pp. 607-608
6. p. 608
7. p. 610
8. p. 609
9. p. 609
10. pp. 609-610
11. p. 610
12. p. 612
13. p. 612
14. pp. 612-613
15. p. 613
16. pp. 612-613
17. p. 613
18. pp. 614-615
19. pp. 614-615
20. pp. 614-615

CHAPTER **30**

Government and Market Failure: Public Goods, Externalities, and Information Problems

This chapter is the first of two to take a more extensive look at the economic role of government that was introduced in Chapter 5. The primary focus of this chapter is ***market failures*** that occur in our economy. These failures often result in government intervention in the economy to provide public goods and services, to address externality problems such as pollution, and to improve the quality and amount of information for buyers and sellers in the private markets.

The chapter begins by reviewing the characteristics of public goods. Recall from Chapter 5 that a private good is divisible and subject to the exclusion principle, whereas a ***public good*** is indivisible and not subject to exclusion. What is new in Chapter 30 is that you are shown how the demand curve and schedule for a public good are constructed and how the optimal allocation of a public good is determined. You should also note how the demand and supply curves for a public good are related to collective marginal benefit and the marginal cost of providing the good.

Governments use ***benefit-cost analysis*** to determine whether they should or should not undertake some specific action—a particular project or program. This type of analysis forces government to estimate both the marginal costs and the marginal benefits of the project or program, to expand its activities only where the additional benefits exceed the added costs, and to reduce or eliminate programs and projects when the marginal costs exceed the marginal benefits. This analysis, however, depends on the ability to measure benefits and costs with some degree of accuracy.

The second topic of the chapter is ***externalities,*** a situation in which a cost is incurred or a benefit is obtained by a party that was not involved in the market transactions. You learned in Chapter 5 that one role of government is to reduce the spillover costs to society from negative externalities and to increase the spillover benefits to society from positive externalities. This general point is now modified by the ***Coase theorem,*** which suggests that there are situations in which government intervention is not required. Individual bargaining can settle most externality problems when there is clear ownership of property rights, the number of people involved is small, and the costs of bargaining are minimal. When these conditions do not hold, government action with direct controls or specific taxes may be necessary to solve the problem. You discover that it may even be possible for the government to create a ***market*** for externality rights and that there is a rule for the optimal reduction of an externality.

Pollution is a prime example of a negative externality and is the focus of the third topic in the chapter. There are many types of pollution, but their causes stem from the *law of conservation of matter and energy.* The production of goods and services uses resources that ultimately become waste (matter or energy) that our environment is not able to reabsorb. Over the years, the government has developed a number of antipollution policies. In this chapter you will learn about two national ones: the *Superfund law of 1980* and the *Clean Air Act of 1990.* You will also discover how the market forces of supply and demand in the recycling market help reduce some of the demands for the dumping of solid waste in landfills.

Another type of market failure you will encounter in the last major section of this chapter is asymmetric information. You probably never thought about the role of information in the functioning of markets, but you will discover how important information is to both buyers and sellers. For example, buyers need some assurance about the measurement standards or quality of products that they purchase, be it gasoline or medical care. The government may intervene in some markets to ensure that this information is made available to buyers.

Inadequate information in markets creates problems for sellers, too. In certain markets, such as insurance, sellers experience a *moral hazard problem* because buyers change their behavior and become less careful, and the change in behavior makes the insurance more costly to sellers. There is also an *adverse selection problem* in the insurance market because those buyers most likely to benefit (higher-risk buyers) are more likely to purchase the insurance; therefore this group imposes higher costs on sellers than if the riskers were more widely spread among the population. Actions of sellers to screen buyers means that fewer people will be covered by insurance, and it creates a situation that may lead to the provision of social insurance by government. Government may also provide better information about workplace safety or enforce safety standards to address information problems in resource markets.

You should not finish this chapter with the sole thought that all market failures require government intervention and direct control. Some problems do require a specific government action, but other problems may be handled more efficiently or in a more optimal way through individual negotiations, lawsuits, or the use of market incentives. What is important for you to understand is the range of solutions to different market and information failures and the rationale for government intervention to correct them.

■ CHECKLIST

When you have studied this chapter you should be able to

☐ Compare the characteristics of a public good with a private good.
☐ Calculate the demand for a public good when given tabular data.
☐ Explain how marginal benefit is reflected in the demand for a public good.
☐ Describe the relationship between marginal cost and the supply of a public good.
☐ Identify on a graph where there is an overallocation, an underallocation, and an optimal allocation of a public good.
☐ Use benefit-cost analysis to determine the extent to which government should apply resources to a project or program when you are given the cost and benefit data.
☐ Define and give examples of positive and negative externalities (spillovers).
☐ Use supply and demand graphs to illustrate how spillover costs and spillover benefits affect the allocation of resources.
☐ State the conditions that are necessary for the Coase theorem, and give an example of its use.
☐ Explain how liability rules and lawsuits are used to resolve externality problems.
☐ Identify two means government uses to achieve allocative efficiency when there are spillover costs.
☐ Describe three options government uses to correct for the underallocation of resources when there are spillover benefits that are large and diffuse.
☐ Determine the price a government agency should charge in a market for pollution rights when you are given the necessary data.
☐ Compare the advantages of a market for pollution rights to direct controls.
☐ Explain and illustrate with a graph a rule for determining the optimal reduction of a negative externality.
☐ Describe the dimensions of the pollution problem.
☐ Cite four major causes of the pollution problem.
☐ Discuss the purpose and results of the Superfund law of 1980.
☐ Identify four major provisions of the Clean Air Act of 1990.
☐ Explain how pollution rights are traded under the Clean Air Act.
☐ Describe the solid waste disposal problem and the reason for interest in recycling.
☐ Explain how a market for recyclable input works using a supply and demand graph.
☐ Define the terms "information failure" and "asymmetric information."
☐ Explain how inadequate information about sellers can cause market failures, and give two examples of ways that the government resolves these problems.
☐ Define the terms "moral hazard" and "adverse selection."
☐ Describe and give examples of how inadequate information about buyers can cause moral hazard, adverse selection, and workplace safety problems.
☐ Cite an example of a way that information difficulties are overcome without government intervention.

■ CHAPTER OUTLINE

1. The characteristics of a private good are that it is divisible and subject to the exclusion principle, whereby those who are unable to pay for the good or service are excluded from enjoying the benefits of the provision of the good or service; in contrast, a public (collective) good such as national defense is indivisible and not subject to exclusion—once it is provided for one person it is available for all.

a. The *demand* for a public good is determined by summing the prices that people are willing to pay collectively for the last unit of the public good at each possible quantity demanded, whereas the demand for a private good is determined by summing the quantities demanded at each possible price. The *demand curve* for a public good is downsloping because of the law of diminishing marginal utility.

b. The *supply curve* for a public good is upsloping because of the law of diminishing returns; additional units supplied reflect increasing marginal costs.

c. The *optimal allocation* of a public good is determined by the intersection of the supply and demand curves.

(1) If the marginal benefit exceeds the marginal cost, there is an underallocation of a public good,

(2) but if the marginal cost exceeds the marginal benefit there will be an overallocation.

(3) Only when the marginal benefits equal the marginal costs is there an optimal allocation of public goods.

d. *Benefit-cost analysis* may be used by government to determine whether it should employ resources for a project and to decide the total quantity of resources it should devote to a project. Additional resources should be devoted to a project only so long as the marginal benefit to society from using the additional resources for the project exceeds the marginal costs to society of the additional resources or where the total benefits minus the total costs are at a maximum.

2. *Market failure* can arise from externalities or spillovers, whereby a third party bears a portion of the cost associated with the production or consumption of a good or service.

a. ***Spillover costs,*** or negative externalities, result in an overallocation of resources to the production of a product. All the costs associated with the product are not reflected in the supply curve. The producer's supply curve lies to the right of the full-cost supply curve.

b. ***Spillover benefits,*** or positive externalities, result in an underallocation of resources to the production of a product. All the benefits associated with the product are not reflected in the demand curve. The demand curve lies to the left of the full-benefits demand curve.

c. Individual bargaining can be used to correct negative externalities or to encourage positive externalities. The *Coase theorem* suggests that private negotiations rather than government intervention should be the course of action if there is clear ownership of the property, the number of people involved is small, and the costs of bargaining is minimal. When these conditions do not hold, however, it may be necessary for government intervention.

d. It is possible to resolve disputes that arise from externalities through the *legal system.* This system defines property rights and specifies liability rules that can be used for lawsuits to cover externality disputes. This method also has limitations because of the expense, the length of time to resolve the dispute, and the uncertainty of the outcomes.

e. When there is the potential for severe harm to common resources, such as air or water, and when the situation involves a large number of people, two types of government intervention may be necessary.

(1) *Direct controls* use legislation to ban or to limit the activities that produce a negative externality. These actions reduce the supply of the products that create the negative externalities to levels that are allocatively efficient.

(2) *Specific taxes* are also applied to productive activity that create negative externalities. These taxes increase the cost of production, and thus decrease the supply to levels that are allocatively efficient.

f. When there are *spillover benefits,* other government actions may be necessary to correct for the underallocation of resources.

(1) The government can provide subsidies to buyers to encourage purchase or consumption of a good or service.

(2) The government might also offer subsidies to producers to reduce the cost of production and increase output of a good or service.

(3) When spillover benefits are extremely large, government may provide the good or service.

g. Another solution has been to create a ***market for externality rights*** or to internalize the spillover cost or benefit in a private market. For example, with a pollution problem in a region,

(1) the government (a pollution-control agency) might set the limit for the amount of pollution permitted, which means that the supply curve is perfectly inelastic (vertical) at some level of pollution;

(2) the demand curve would reflect the willingness of polluters to pay for the right to pollute at different prices for pollution rights;

(3) and the price for pollution rights would be determined by the intersection of the demand and supply curves.

(4) Given a fixed supply curve, an increase in demand because of economic growth in the region would increase the price of pollution rights.

h. In most cases, it is not allocatively efficient to eliminate completely the production of goods that create negative externalities. From society's perspective, the optimal reduction of a negative externality occurs where the marginal cost to society and the marginal benefit of reducing the externality are equal (MB = MC). Over time, there may be shifts in the marginal-cost and marginal-benefit curves that change the optimal level.

3. *Pollution* is a prime example of a major negative externality in our industrial society.

a. The dimensions of the problem are extensive and include air pollution, water pollution, toxic waste, solid-waste disposal, oil spills, and potential changes to the climate.

b. The causes of the pollution problem relate to the *law of conservation of matter and energy.* Matter used for production of goods and services ultimately gets transformed into waste (in the form of matter or energy) after it is consumed. The waste creates a problem if there is an imbalance between it and the capacity of the environment to reabsorb the waste. Population density, rising per capita consumption, changing technology, the abuse of common resources, and economic incentives are all factors contributing to the pollution problem.

c. Antipollution policy in the United States is complex.

(1) The ***Superfund law of 1980*** uses direct controls, specific taxes, and liability rules to correct the toxic waste problem.

(2) The ***Clean Air Act of 1990*** uses direct controls through uniform emission standards to limit the amount of air pollution. The act covers toxic chemicals, urban smog, motor vehicle emissions, ozone depletion, and acid rain. The act also permits some trading of pollution rights to reduce acid rain.

d. Solid waste is usually deposited in garbage dumps or incinerated. Dumps and incinerators, however, create negative externalities, and they are becoming increasingly expensive. The situation has created a market for recycled items to help reduce this pollution problem. Government can use either demand or supply incentives to encourage recycling as an alternative to dumping or incineration of solid waste.

4. Economic inefficiency from information failures can occur in markets. These information failures arise from ***asymmetric information***—unequal knowledge that is held by parties to a market transaction.

a. When information involving sellers is incomplete, inaccurate, or very costly, there will be market failures. For example, in the market for gasoline, consumers need accurate information about the amount and quality of gasoline they purchase. In the market for medical service, it is important that consumers have some assurances about the credentials of physicians. These information failures are remedied by government through such actions as establishing measurement standards and by testing and licensing.

b. Inadequate information involving buyers creates market failures.

(1) A market may produce less than the optimal amount of goods and services from society's perspective because of a ***moral hazard problem,*** which

results when buyers alter their behavior and increase the costs of sellers. For example, the provision of insurance may cause the insured to be less cautious. (2) An ***adverse selection problem*** also occurs in many markets. In the case of insurance, the buyers most likely to need or benefit from insurance are the ones most likely to purchase it. These higher-risk buyers impose higher costs on sellers. Sellers then screen out the higher-risk buyers, but this action reduces the population covered by insurance in the private market. In some cases, government may establish a social insurance system that is designed to cover a much broader group of the population than would be covered by the private insurers, such as with social security. (3) Market failures occur in resource markets when there is inadequate information for workers about the health hazards or safety of a workplace. Government can act to correct these problems by publishing health and safety information or by forcing businesses to provide more information. The more typical approach to this problem has been the enforcement of standards for health and safety on the job.

c. Government does not always need to intervene in the private market to address information problems. Businesses can adopt policies to correct these problems, and some firms or other organizations can specialize in providing important market information for buyers or sellers.

■ HINTS AND TIPS

1. Review the discussion of public goods and externalities in Chapter 5.

2. Make sure you understand the difference between the demand for public goods (collective demand) and the market demand for a product. To determine market demand, add the quantities demanded at each possible price, and with the demand for public goods, add the prices people collectively are willing to pay for the last unit of the public good at each possible quantity demanded.

3. Table 30-3 is important because it summarizes the private actions and government policies that correct for the problems of spillover costs or benefits. The government can influence the allocation of resources in a private market by taking actions that increase or decrease demand or supply.

4. Problems occur because information in a market is sometimes asymmetric, which means that there is *unequal* information for sellers or buyers about product price, quality, or other product conditions. Use the examples in the text to help you distinguish between the different types of information problems created by sellers or buyers.

■ IMPORTANT TERMS

public good
benefit-cost analysis
marginal cost equals marginal benefit rule
positive or negative externality (spillover)
Coase theorem
market for externality rights
optimal reduction of an externality
law of conservation of matter and energy
Superfund law of 1980
Clean Air Act of 1990
asymmetric information
moral hazard problem
adverse selection problem

SELF-TEST

■ FILL-IN QUESTIONS

1. A public good is one which is (divisible, indivisible) _______________ and one for which the exclusion principle (does, does not) _______________ apply.

2. With a private good you add together the (prices, quantities demanded) _______________ people are willing to pay at each possible (price, quantity demanded) _______________, whereas with a public good you add together the (prices, quantities demanded) _______________ people are willing to pay for the last unit of the public good at each possible (price, quantity demanded) _______________.

3. The demand curve for a public good slopes downward because of the law of diminishing marginal (returns, utility) _______________; the supply curve for a public good is upsloping because of the law of diminishing _______________. The demand curve for a public good is, in essence, a marginal-(benefit, cost) _______________ curve; the supply curve for a public good reflects rising marginal _______________. The optimal quantity of a public good will be shown by the intersection of the collective demand and supply curve, which means that marginal (benefit, cost) _______________ of the last unit equals that unit's marginal _______________.

4. In applying benefit-cost analysis, government should use more resources in the production of public goods if the marginal (cost, benefit) _______________ from the additional public goods exceed the marginal _______________ that results from having fewer public goods. This rule will determine which plan from a benefit-cost analysis will result in the (maximum, minimum) _______________ net benefit to society.

5. One objective of government is to correct for market failures called spillovers or (internalities, externalities) _______________. If there is a cost to an individual or group that is a third party to the market transaction, it is a (positive, negative) ______________ externality or a spillover (benefit, cost) ______________. If there is a benefit to an individual or group that is a third party to a market transaction, it is a (positive, negative) ______________ externality or a spillover (benefit, cost) ______________.

6. When there are spillover costs in competitive markets, the result is an (over, under) ______________ allocation of resources to the production of the good or service. When there are spillover benefits, the result is an (over, under) ______________ allocation of resources to the production of the good or service.

7. The (liability, Coase) ______________ theorem suggests when there are negative or positive externalities in situations in which the ownership of property is (undefined, defined) ______________, the number of people involved is (large, small) ______________, and the costs of bargaining are (major, minor) ______________, then government intervention (is, is not) ______________ required.

8. The legal system is also important for settling externality disputes between individuals because settling it defines (political, property) ______________ rights and specifies (business, liability) ______________ rules that can be used for lawsuits. This method, however, has limitations because of its cost, the length of time, and the (certainty, uncertainty) ______________ of the result.

9. Government may use direct controls to reduce spillover (benefits, costs) ______________ by passing legislation that restricts business activity. In other cases, the government may (subsidize, tax) ______________ a producer.

10. The government may correct for the underallocation of resources where spillover (costs, benefits) ______________ are large and diffuse. This objective can be achieved by (taxing, subsidizing) ______________ buyers or producers and through government (provision, consumption) ______________ of a good or service.

11. One novel policy solution to a spillover cost problem such as pollution is to create a (market, government) ______________ for externality rights.

a. For example, a region may have a set amount of acceptable air pollution, so the supply curve for the air pollution rights would be perfectly (elastic, inelastic) ______________.

b. The demand curve for air pollution rights would be (up, down) ______________ sloping and intersect the supply curve to determine the (quantity, price) ______________ for the right to pollute the air in that area.

c. If the demand for air pollution rights increased over time, then the price would (rise, fall, stay the same) ______________, but the quantity supplied would ______________.

12. Reducing negative externalities comes at a "price" to society, and therefore society must decide how much of a decrease it wants to (buy, sell) "______________." Further abatement of a negative externality increases economic efficiency if the marginal cost is (greater than, equal to, less than) ______________ the marginal benefit, but it is economically inefficient if the marginal benefit is ______________ the marginal cost. The optimal reduction of a negative externality occurs where the society's marginal benefit is (greater than, equal to, less than) ______________ society's marginal cost.

13. The pollution problem stems from the law of (consumption, conservation) ______________ of matter and energy. Matter used for production of goods and services ultimately gets transformed into (consumption, waste) ______________, which is another form of matter or energy that the (consumer, environment) ______________ may not be able to reabsorb.

14. The United States and most other nations have experienced pollution problems because of (increases, decreases) ______________ in population density, ______________ in per capita consumption, changes in (laws, technology) ______________ that have negative externalities, and the Tragedy of the (Firm, Commons) ______________, which lead to an overuse of public resources.

15. To correct the toxic waste problem, Congress passed the (Clear Air Act of 1990, Superfund law of 1980) ______________. It established (indirect, direct) ______________ controls, specific (taxes, subsidies) ______________, and (transportation, liability) ______________ rules for toxic waste. The (Clean Air Act of 1990, Superfund law of 1980) ______________ ______________ imposes uniform (price, emission) ______________ standards to limit the amount of air pollution and (prohibits, permits) ______________ the trading of pollution rights.

16. One way the government can increase the recyling of solid waste is to (decrease, increase) ______________ the demand for recycled inputs in the production process or ______________ the incentives to supply recycled products.

17. Markets can produce failures because of (symmetric, asymmetric) ________________ information. When information involving sellers is (complete, incomplete) ________________ or obtaining such information is (costless, costly) ________________, the market will (under, over) ________________allocate resources to the production of that good or service. To correct such problems in the gasoline market, the government establishes quality (prices, standards) ________________. In the medical market, the government protects consumers by (taxing, licensing) ________________ physicians.

18. Inadequate information involving buyers can lead to two problems. First, if a market situation arises whereby buyers alter their behavior and increase the cost to sellers, a(n) (adverse selection, moral hazard) ________________ ________________ problem is created. Second, if buyers withhold information from sellers that would impose a large cost on sellers, a(n) ________________ problem is created. The moral hazard problem occurs (at the same time, after) ________________ a person makes a purchase, but the adverse selection problem occurs ________________ the buyer makes a purchase.

19. Another example of information failure occurs in labor markets in which there is incomplete or inadequate information about (productivity, safety) ________________. The government will intervene in these situations to enforce (quotas, standards) ________________ or provide (health care, information) ________________ related to workplace hazards.

20. Private businesses overcome some information problems about the reliability or quantity through (prices, warranties) ________________ for products or the (penalizing, franchising) ________________ of businesses that make them more uniform. Some businesses and organizations also collect and publish product information that is useful for (sellers, buyers) ________________. Despite these actions, there may still be need for government actions to correct (wage, information) ________________ problems and to promote an efficient allocation of society's scarce resources.

■ TRUE-FALSE QUESTIONS

Circle the T if the statement is true, the F if it is false.

1. The exclusion principle applies to public goods but not to private goods. **T F**

2. When determining the demand for a public good, you add the prices people are willing to pay collectively for the last unit of the public good at each possible quantity demanded. **T F**

3. When the marginal benefit of a public good exceeds the marginal cost, there will be an overallocation of resources to that public good use. **T F**

4. The optimal allocation of a public good is determined by the rule that marginal cost (MC) equals marginal revenue (MR). **T F**

5. "Reducing government spending" means the same as "economy in government." **T F**

6. A spillover is a cost or benefit accruing to an individual or group—a third party—which is external to the market transaction. **T F**

7. In a competitive product market and in the absence of spillover costs, the supply curve or schedule reflects the costs of producing the product. **T F**

8. If demand and supply reflected all the benefits and costs of a product, the equilibrium output of a competitive market would be identical with its optimal output. **T F**

9. There is an underallocation of resources to the production of a commodity when negative externalities are present. **T F**

10. The inclusion of the spillover benefits would increase the demand for a product. **T F**

11. When spillover costs are involved in the production of a product, more resources are allocated to the production of that product and more of the product is produced than is optimal or most efficient. **T F**

12. The Coase theorem suggests that government intervention is required whenever there are negative or positive externalities. **T F**

13. Lawsuits and liability rules create externality problems instead of helping resolve them. **T F**

14. Taxes that are imposed on businesses which create an externality will lower the marginal cost of production and increase supply. **T F**

15. Subsidizing the firms producing goods which provide spillover benefits will usually result in a better allocation of resources. **T F**

16. One solution to the negative externalities caused by pollution is to create a market for pollution rights in which the social costs of pollution are turned into private costs. **T F**

17. In the market for pollution rights, if a government agency sets a fixed level for pollution, the supply curve of pollution rights will be perfectly elastic. **T F**

18. If a society has marginal costs of $10 for pollution abatement and the marginal benefit of pollution abatement is $8, to achieve an optimal amount of the pollution it should increase the amount of pollution abatement. **T F**

19. Pollution is caused almost exclusively by profit-seeking business firms. **T F**

20. The Superfund law of 1980 uses direct controls and specific taxes to address the problem of toxic waste. **T F**

21. The Clean Air Act of 1990 permits the trading of emission credits between electric utilities and the trading of pollution rights between polluters. **T F**

22. If the government provides a subsidy to producers of recycled paper products, the demand for recycled paper *products* should increase. **T F**

23. The inspection of meat products by the Federal government for quality is justified on the grounds that it reduces the costs of obtaining information in the market for meat. **T F**

24. If the provision of government health insurance encourages people to take more health risks, it has created a moral hazard. **T F**

25. Adverse selection problems primarily result when the government begins enforcing standards for safety in the workplace. **T F**

■ MULTIPLE-CHOICE QUESTIONS

Circle the letter that corresponds to the best answer.

1. How do public goods differ from private goods? Public goods
- **(a)** are divisible
- **(b)** are subject to the exclusion principle
- **(c)** are divisible and subject to the exclusion principle
- **(d)** are *not* divisible and *not* subject to the exclusion principle

Answer Questions 2, 3, 4, and 5 on the basis of the following information for a public good. $\boldsymbol{P_1}$ *and* $\boldsymbol{P_2}$ *represent the prices individuals 1 and 2, the only two people in the society, are willing to pay for the last unit of a public good.* $\boldsymbol{P_c}$ *represents the price (or collective willingness to pay) for a public good, and* $\boldsymbol{Q_s}$ *represents the quantity supplied of the public good at those prices.*

Q_d	P_1	P_2	P_c	Q_s
1	$4	$5	$9	5
2	3	4	7	4
3	2	3	5	3
4	1	2	3	2
5	0	1	1	1

2. This society is willing to pay what amount for the first unit of the public good?
- **(a)** $10
- **(b)** $9
- **(c)** $8
- **(d)** $7

3. This society is willing to pay what amount for the third unit of the public good?
- **(a)** $5
- **(b)** $6
- **(c)** $7
- **(d)** $8

4. Given the supply curve $\boldsymbol{Q_s}$, the optimal price and quantity of the public good in this society will be
- **(a)** $9 and 5 units
- **(b)** $5 and 3 units
- **(c)** $5 and 4 units
- **(d)** $3 and 2 units

5. If this good were a private good instead of a public good, the total quantity demanded at the $4 price would be
- **(a)** 3 units
- **(b)** 4 units
- **(c)** 5 units
- **(d)** 6 units

Answer Questions 6, 7, and 8 for a public good on the basis of the following graph.

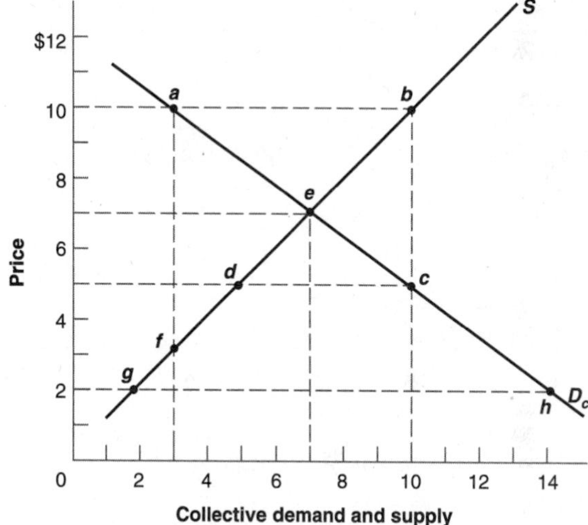

6. Where the marginal benefits equal the collective marginal costs is represented by point
- **(a)** *b*
- **(b)** *c*
- **(c)** *d*
- **(d)** *e*

7. Which line segment would indicate the amount by which the marginal benefit of this public good is less than the marginal cost?
- **(a)** *ab*
- **(b)** *bc*
- **(c)** *fa*
- **(d)** *gh*

8. If 3 units of this public good are produced, the marginal
- **(a)** cost of $10 is greater than the marginal benefit of $3
- **(b)** cost of $10 is greater than the marginal benefit of $5
- **(c)** benefit of $10 is greater than the marginal cost of $5
- **(d)** benefit of $10 is greater than the marginal cost of $3

9. Assume that a government is considering a new antipollution program and may choose to include in this program any number of four different projects. The marginal cost and the marginal benefits of each of the four projects are given below. What total amount should this government spend on the antipollution program?

(a) $2 million
(b) $7 million
(c) $17 million
(d) $37 million

Project	Marginal cost	Marginal benefit
#1	$ 2 million	$ 5 million
#2	5 million	7 million
#3	10 million	9 million
#4	20 million	15 million

10. When the production and consumption of a product entail spillover costs, a competitive product market results in a(n)

(a) underallocation of resources to the product
(b) overallocation of resources to the product
(c) optimal allocation of resources to the product
(d) higher price for the product

11. A spillover benefit in the production of some product will result in

(a) overproduction
(b) underproduction
(c) the optimal level of production if consumers are price takers
(d) the optimal level of production if consumers are utility maximizers

Use the following graph which shows the supply and demand for a product to answer Questions 12, 13, and 14.

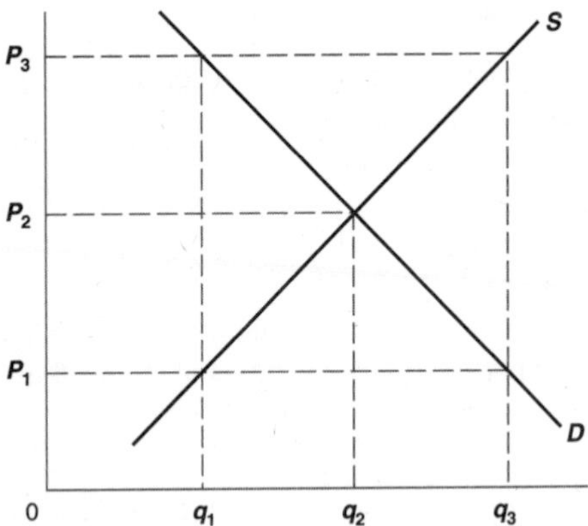

12. If there are neither spillover costs nor spillover benefits, the output which results in the optimal allocation of resources to the production of this product is

(a) q_1
(b) q_2
(c) q_3
(d) 0

13. If the market for a product was in equilibrium at output level q_2 but the optimal level of output for society was at q_1, the government could correct for this

(a) spillover cost with a subsidy to consumers
(b) spillover cost with a subsidy to producers
(c) spillover benefit with a subsidy to producers
(d) spillover cost with a tax on producers

14. If the market for a product was in equilibrium at output level q_2 but the optimal level of output for society was at q_3, the government could correct for this

(a) overallocation of resources by direct controls on consumers
(b) underallocation of resources through taxes on producers
(c) overallocation of resources through a market for externality rights
(d) underallocation of resources through subsidy to producers

15. One condition for the Coase theorem to hold is that there be

(a) clear ownership of the property rights
(b) a large number of people involved in the dispute
(c) active government intervention to solve the externality problem
(d) a sizeable cost for bargaining to settle the dispute between the private parties

16. Which of the following would be the most effective strategy for addressing a problem such as acid rain, which stems from the pollution of coal-burning electric utilities?

(a) private negotiations between property owners and the utilities
(b) lawsuits filed against the utilities by property owners
(c) asking consumers to reduce electricity consumption
(d) government taxes on utility emissions

17. If government were to sell pollution rights, an increase in the demand for pollution rights would

(a) increase both the quantity of pollutants discharged and the market price of pollution rights
(b) increase the quantity discharged and have no effect on the market price
(c) have no effect on the quantity discharged and increase the market price
(d) have no effect on either the quantity discharged or the market price

Use the following table to answer Questions 18, 19, and 20. The data in the table show the marginal costs and marginal benefits to a city for five different levels of pollution abatement.

Quantity of pollution abatement	Marginal cost	Marginal benefit
500 tons	$500,000	$100,000
400 tons	300,000	150,000
300 tons	200,000	200,000
200 tons	100,000	300,000
100 tons	50,000	400,000

18. If the city seeks an optimal reduction of the externality, it will select how many tons of pollution abatement?

(a) 100
(b) 300
(c) 400
(d) 500

19. If the marginal benefit of pollution abatement increased by $150,000 at each level because of the community's desire to attract more profitable and cleaner industry, the optimal level of pollution abatement in tons would be

(a) 200
(b) 300
(c) 400
(d) 500

20. What would cause the optimal level of pollution abatement to be 200 tons?

(a) technological improvement in production that decreases marginal costs by $150,000 at each level
(b) an increase in the health risk from this pollution that increases marginal benefits by $200,000 at each level
(c) the need to replace old pollution monitoring equipment with new equipment that increases marginal costs by $200,000 at each level
(d) reduction in the public demand for pollution control that decreases marginal benefits by $100,000 at each level

21. Which has contributed to the pollution problem in the United States?

(a) declining population density
(b) rising prices for gasoline and oil
(c) a higher standard of living
(d) less use of plastic and aluminum containers

22. Results from the Superfund law of 1980 indicate that it

(a) reduced major sources of pollution by 95%, but the fund is now exhausted and reauthorization is uncertain
(b) raised billions from the chemical industry to treat toxic waste, but progress is slow and legal negotiations over dump sites drain funds
(c) made recycling the most economical method for handling waste in many communities, but citizen compliance is limited and depends on economic incentives
(d) established uniform emission standards that are being paid for out of the fund, but legal action is sometimes necessary to get cooperation from companies

23. The Clean Air Act of 1990

(a) permits the exchange of pollution rights within firms and between firms in an area
(b) sets stricter limits on the dumping of garbage in landfills
(c) funds research on applications of the law of conservation of matter and energy
(d) forces companies to clean up toxic waste dumps

24. Which would tend to increase the demand for recycled paper?

(a) an increase in the price of regular paper
(b) an increase in taxes on all paper production
(c) a decrease in interest in protecting the environment
(d) a decrease in subsidies for all paper production

25. If Congress adopted an increase in government insurance on bank deposits, this action would create a moral hazard problem because it may

(a) lead to careful screening of depositors and the source of their funds
(b) restrict the amount of deposits made by bank customers
(c) encourage bank officers to make riskier loans
(d) reduce bank investments in real estate

■ PROBLEMS

1. Data on two individuals' preferences for a public good are reflected in the following table. P_1 and P_2 represent the prices individuals 1 and 2, the only two people in the society, are willing to pay for the last unit of the public good.

Quantity	P_1	P_2
1	$6	$6
2	5	5
3	4	4
4	3	3
5	2	2
6	1	1

a. Complete the table below showing the collective demand for the public good in this society.

Q_d	Price	Q_s
1	$____	7
2	____	6
3	____	5
4	____	4
5	____	3
6	____	2

b. Given the supply schedule for this public good as shown by the Q_s column, the optimal quantity of this public good is __________ units and the optimal price is $__________.

c. When 3 units of this public good are produced, the perceived marginal benefit is $________ and the marginal cost is $__________; there will be an (overallocation, underallocation) __________ of resources to this public good.

d. When 6 units of this public good are produced, the perceived marginal benefit is $__________ and the marginal cost is $__________; there is an (underallocation, overallocation) ________ of resources to this public good.

2. Imagine that a state government is considering constructing a new highway to link its two largest cities. Its estimate of the total costs and the total benefits of building 2-, 4-, 6-, and 8-lane highways between the two cities are shown in the table at the top of page 338. (All figures are in millions of dollars.)

Project	Total cost	Marginal cost	Total benefit	Marginal benefit
No highway	$ 0		$ 0	
2-lane highway	500	$ _____	650	$ _____
4-lane highway	680	_____	750	_____
6-lane highway	760	_____	800	_____
8-lane highway	860	_____	825	_____

a. Compute the marginal cost and the marginal benefit of the 2-, 4-, 6-, and 8-lane highways.

b. Will it benefit the state to allocate resources to construct a highway? _____________

c. If the state builds a highway,

(1) it should be a _____________-lane highway.

(2) the total cost will be $_____________ million.

(3) the total benefit will be $_____________ million.

(4) the *net* benefit will be $_____________ million.

3. The following graph shows the demand and supply curves for a product bought and sold in a competitive market. Assume that there are no spillover benefits or costs.

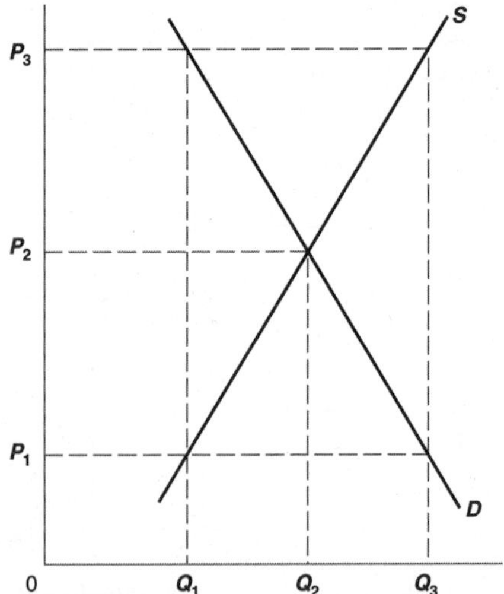

a. Were this market to produce an output of Q_1, there would be an (optimal, under, over) _____________ allocation of resources to the production of this product.

b. Were this market to produce Q_3, there would be an _____________ allocation of resources to this product.

c. The equilibrium output is _________________, and at this output there is an _________________ allocation of resources.

4. The two graphs in column 2 show product demand and supply curves that do *not* reflect either the spillover costs of producing the product or the spillover benefits obtained from its consumption.

a. On the first graph, draw in another curve that reflects the inclusion of spillover *costs.*

(1) Government might force the (demand for, supply of) _____________________ the product to reflect the spillover costs of producing it by (taxing, subsidizing) _________________ the producers.

(2) The inclusion of spillover costs in the total cost of producing the product (increases, decreases) _________________ the output of the product and _________________ its price.

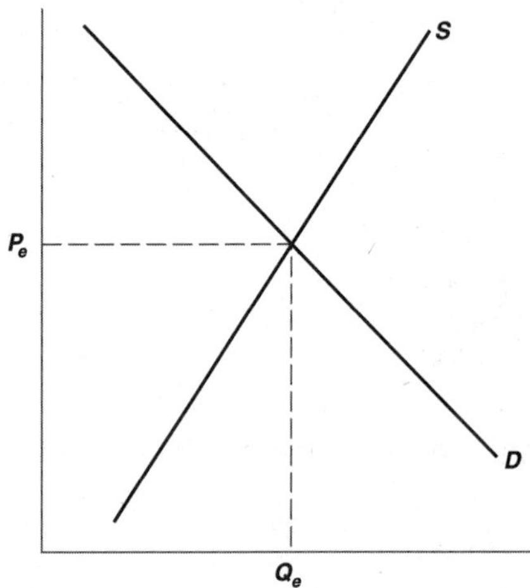

b. On the second graph, draw in a demand curve that reflects the inclusion of spillover *benefits.*

(1) Indicate on the graph the output that is optimal when spillover benefits are included.

(2) To bring about the production of this optimal output, government might (tax, subsidize) _____________ the consumers of this product, which would (increase, decrease) _____________ the demand of the product.

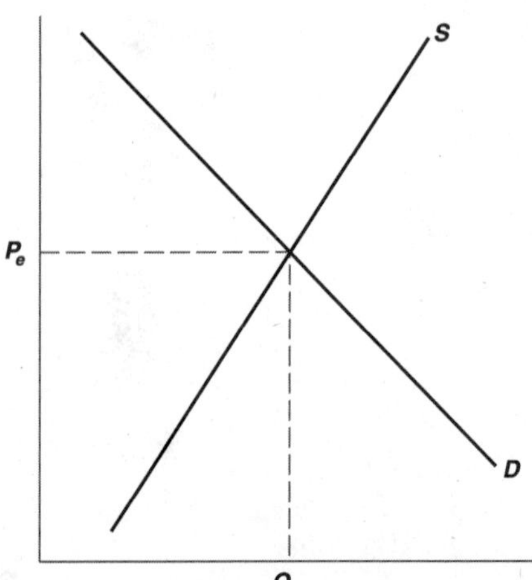

(3) This optimal output is (greater than, less than, equal to) ________________ Q_e; and the price of the product is (above, below, equal to) ______________ P_e.

5. Assume the atmosphere of Cuyahoga County, Ohio (the Cleveland metropolitan area), is able to reabsorb 1,500 tons of pollutants per year. The following schedule shows the price polluters would be willing to pay for the right to dispose of 1 ton of pollutants per year and the total quantity of pollutants they would wish to dispose of at each price.

a. If there were no emission fee, polluters would put ______________ tons of pollutants in the air each year, and this quantity of pollutants would exceed the ability of nature to reabsorb them by ______________ tons.

Price (per ton of pollutant rights)	Total quantity of pollutant rights demanded (tons)
$ 0	4,000
1,000	3,500
2,000	3,000
3,000	2,500
4,000	2,000
5,000	1,500
6,000	1,000
7,000	500

b. To reduce pollution to the capacity of the atmosphere to recycle pollutants, an emission fee of $____________ per ton should be set.

c. Were this emission fee set, the total emission fees set would be $______________.

d. Were the quantity of pollution rights demanded at each price to increase by 500 tons, the emission fee could be increased by $______________ and total emission fees collected would increase by $________.

■ SHORT ANSWER AND ESSAY QUESTIONS

1. What are the basic characteristics of public goods?

2. How do public goods differ from private goods?

3. Contrast how you construct the demand curve for a public good with the procedure for constructing the demand curve for a private good using individual demand schedules.

4. Explain the relationship between the marginal cost and benefit of a public good when there is an underallocation, an overallocation, and an optimal allocation of resources for the provision of the public good.

5. Describe benefit-cost analysis, and state the rules used to make decisions from a marginal and a total perspective.

6. Is "economy in government" the same as "reduced government spending"? Explain the distinction.

7. What are externalities and spillovers? Give examples of positive externalities and negative externalities.

8. Under what conditions might it be worthwhile for the government to intervene or not to intervene to settle a spillover problem?

9. Should the government intervene in an externality dispute between two property owners over the use of one party's land? Should government intervene in the case of acid rain?

10. How do lawsuits and liability rules resolve externality problems? How would these actions be justified?

11. What actions can government take to correct for spillover costs in a market?

12. How do you create a market for externality rights in the case of pollution? What are some advantages and limitations of this approach to the pollution problem?

13. What rule can society use to determine the optimal level of pollution abatement? What is the problem with this approach?

14. Outline the dimensions of the pollution problem in the United States. Why has this problem developed? What is the specific cause of the pollution problem?

15. Discuss the major features of the Superfund law of 1980 and the Clean Air Act of 1990. What features of a market for externalities are built into the Clean Air Act?

16. Why is solid-waste disposal of national concern? How is recycling a partial alternative to it? How does a market for recyclable items work?

17. Describe how inadequate information about sellers creates market problems for buyers. Give examples.

18. Explain what is meant by a "moral hazard problem" and describe how it affects sellers. Give some examples of the application of this problem.

19. How can the market for insurance result in an adverse selection problem? What actions might government take to correct this information problem?

20. In what way does workplace safety become an information problem? How might this problem be resolved by government or businesses?

ANSWERS

Chapter 30 Government and Market Failure: Public Goods, Externalities, and Information Problems

FILL-IN QUESTIONS

1. indivisible, does not
2. quantities demanded, price, prices, quantity demanded
3. utility, returns, benefit, cost, benefit, cost
4. benefit, cost, maximum
5. externalities, negative, cost, positive, benefit
6. over, under
7. Coase, defined, small, minor, is not
8. property, liability, uncertainty

9. costs, tax
10. benefits, subsidizing, provision
11. market, *a.* inelastic; *b.* down, price; *c.* rise, stay the same
12. buy, less than, less than, equal to
13. conservation, waste, environment
14. increases, increases, technology, Commons
15. Superfund law, direct, taxes, liability, Clean Air Act of 1990, emission, permits
16. increase, increase
17. asymmetric, incomplete, costly, under, standards, licensing
18. moral hazard, adverse selection, after, at the same time
19. safety, standards, information
20. warranties, franchising, buyers, information

TRUE-FALSE QUESTIONS

1. F, pp. 620-621	**10.** T, p. 625	**19.** F, pp. 631-632
2. T, p. 622	**11.** T, pp. 624-625	**20.** T, p. 632
3. F, P. 624	**12.** F, p. 625	**21.** T, p. 633
4. F, p. 624	**13.** F, p. 626	**22.** F, pp. 634-635
5. F, p. 624	**14.** F, p. 627	**23.** T, p. 636
6. T, p. 624	**15.** T, p. 627	**24.** T, p. 637
7. T, p. 624	**16.** T, pp. 628-629	**25.** F, pp. 637-639
8. T, pp. 624-625	**17.** F, p. 628	
9. F, p. 624	**18.** F, pp. 629-630	

MULTIPLE-CHOICE QUESTIONS

1. d, pp. 620-621	**10.** b, p. 624	**19.** c, pp. 630-631
2. b, pp. 621-622	**11.** b, p. 624	**20.** c, pp. 630-631
3. a, pp. 621-622	**12.** b, p. 625	**21.** c, pp. 631-632
4. b, pp. 621-623	**13.** d, p. 627	**22.** b, pp. 632-633
5. a, pp. 621-623	**14.** d, p. 627	**23.** a, p. 633
6. d, pp. 621-623	**15.** a, p. 625	**24.** a, p. 634
7. b, pp. 621-623	**16.** d, p. 627	**25.** c, p. 637
8. d, pp. 621-623	**17.** c, pp. 628-629	
9. b, pp. 623-624	**18.** b, p. 630	

PROBLEMS

1. *a.* $12, 10, 8, 6, 4, 2; *b.* 4, 6; *c.* 8, 4, underallocation; *d.* 2, 10, overallocation
2. *a.* Marginal cost: $500, $180, $80, $100; Marginal benefit: $650, $100, $50, $25; *b.* yes; *c.* (1) 2, (2) $500, (3) $650, (4) $150
3. *a.* under; *b.* over; *c.* Q_2, optimal
4. *a.* (1) supply of, taxing, (2) decreases, increases; *b.* (2) subsidize, increase, (3) greater than, above
5. *a.* 4,000, 2,500; *b.* 5,000; *c.* 7,500,000; *d.* 1,000, 1,500,000

SHORT ANSWER AND ESSAY QUESTIONS

1. pp. 620-621	**8.** pp. 625-626	**15.** pp. 632-633
2. pp. 620-621	**9.** pp. 625-626	**16.** pp. 633-635
3. pp. 621-622	**10.** pp. 626-627	**17.** pp. 636-637
4. pp. 623-624	**11.** pp. 626-627	**18.** p. 637
5. pp. 623-624	**12.** pp. 628-629	**19.** pp. 637-639
6. p. 624	**13.** pp. 629-630	**20.** p. 639
7. p. 624	**14.** pp. 631-632	

CHAPTER **31**

Public Choice Theory and Taxation

Although both Chapters 30 and 31 analyze the role of government in the economy, they look at government from an opposite perspective. Chapter 30 discussed market failure issues and what actions government takes to correct these market problems. Chapter 31 now examines government failure, or why government makes inefficient use of the scarce resources. For this explanation, you will first be introduced to ***public choice theory,*** or the economic analysis of public decision making. Later in the chapter you will learn more about ***public finance,*** which covers such topics as the principles of taxation and the economic effects of specific taxes.

Many public decisions are made by *majority voting,* but this decision-making procedure may distort the true preferences of society. In the first section of the chapter you will find out how majority voting may lead to inefficient outcomes in the provision of public goods. In some choices, the benefits of a public good are greater than the costs, but the majority votes against it. In other choices, the benefits outweigh the costs, but the provision of the public good is supported by the majority vote. Although actions by interest groups and the use of logrolling may tend to reduce inefficiencies created by majority rule, the final result depends on the circumstances of the decision.

Also note that there is a *paradox of voting* from majority voting. Depending on how a vote or election is arranged, it is possible for majority rule to produce choices that are inconsistent with the ranking of preferences among voters. You should spend time working through the example in the textbook so you understand how opposing outcomes can result from majority rule. You should also learn why the median voters strongly influence the result of a vote or an election when there is majority rule. In fact, the *median-voter model* is very useful for explaining why the middle position on issues is often adopted in public decisions.

The second section of Chapter 31 discusses other reasons for *inefficiencies* by government. Here you will learn that (1) special-interest effects and rent-seeking behavior impair public decisions; (2) politicians often have a strong incentive to adopt an economic policy that has clear benefits to voters, but hidden or uncertain costs; (3) public choice is more limited and less flexible than private choice because it entails voting for or accepting a "bundle" of programs, some good and some bad; and (4) bureaucratic inefficiencies in the public sector arise from the lack of the economic incentives and competitive pressures found in the private sector.

Chapter 31 then switches from public choice theory to public finance for further insights about government and, in particular, about *taxation.* In the third section of the chapter you learn the economic principles used in levying taxes. You also learn about the *regressive, progressive,* and *proportional* classifications for taxes and how most U.S. taxes fit into this classification scheme.

The *tax incidence* and *efficiency loss of a tax* are described in the fourth section of the chapter. Incidence means "who ends up paying the tax." As you will discover, the elasticities of demand and of supply determine how much of the tax will be paid by buyers and how much of it will be paid by sellers. No matter who pays the tax, however, there is an efficiency loss to society from the tax, the size of which is also affected by the elasticities of demand and of supply. With this knowledge, you are now ready to study the probable incidence of five taxes—personal income, corporate income, sales, excise, and property—that are used to raise most of the tax revenue for government in the United States.

The final two sections of the chapter discuss *tax issues.* The fifth section looks at tax reform in two areas: proposals for a national *value-added tax (VAT)* and a *flat tax* on Federal income. The sixth section explores the question of whether an increase in the role of government reduces or expands the freedoms of individuals. The authors present both the conservative case of those who argue that expanded government reduces personal freedom and the liberal case of those who contend that it may create individual freedom.

■ CHECKLIST

When you have studied this chapter you should be able to

☐ Explain the purpose of public choice theory and the topics it covers.
☐ Illustrate how majority voting procedures can produce inefficient outcomes when the vote is "yes" or the vote is "no."
☐ Describe how interest groups and political logrolling affect the efficiency of outcomes from voting.
☐ Give an example of the paradox of voting.
☐ Describe the median-voter model, its applicability to the real world, and two implications of the model.
☐ Explain the meaning of the phrase "public sector failure" and cite examples.

☐ Give an example of a special-interest effect and an example of rent-seeking behavior.
☐ Describe the economic problem that arises when a political decision involves clear benefits and hidden costs.
☐ Compare the type of choices consumers make in the private market with the type of choices citizens make.
☐ Contrast the incentives for economic efficiency in private business with those found in the public agencies and bureaucracies.
☐ Discuss how government and markets are imperfect in allocating resources.
☐ Distinguish between the ability-to-pay principle of taxation and the benefits-received principle of taxation.
☐ Determine whether a tax is regressive, progressive, or proportional when you are given the necessary data.
☐ Describe the progressivity, regressivity, and proportionality of the five major kinds of taxes used in the United States.
☐ Illustrate with a supply and demand graph how the price elasticity of demand and supply affects tax incidence.
☐ Describe the efficiency loss of a tax using a supply and demand graph.
☐ Explain the effects of price elasticity of demand or supply on the efficiency loss of a tax.
☐ Evaluate the probable incidence of the personal income, corporate income, sales and excise, and property taxes.
☐ Describe the progressivity of the U.S. tax structure overall and at the Federal, state, and local levels.
☐ Explain the advantages and disadvantages of a value-added tax.
☐ Discuss the pros and cons of a flat-tax rate on Federal income.
☐ Present the case for and present the case against the proposition that an expanded public sector reduces personal freedom.

CHAPTER OUTLINE

1. Critics of the government argue that it has failed to find solutions for many problems of society and that it is very inefficient in its use of society's scarce resources. This chapter first analyzes economic decisions made by government from *public choice* perspective, turns to the issue of *public finance,* and then examines the economics of taxation.

2. Most decisions about government activity are made collectively through *majority voting,* but the procedure is not without problems.

a. Voting outcomes may be economically inefficient in cases where voters reject a public good whose total benefits exceed total costs or fail to reject a public good whose total costs are greater than the total benefits. These inefficiencies can be resolved sometimes by
(1) the formation of special interest groups that work to overcome inefficient outcomes, or
(2) the use of logrolling, in which votes are traded to secure a favorable and efficient decision,
(3) but logrolling can also lead to inefficient decisions.

b. The ***paradox of voting*** suggests that the public may not be able to make consistent choices that reflect its preferences.

c. Based on the ***median-voter model,*** it is suggested that the person or groups holding the middle position on an issue will likely determine the outcome from a majority rule election. Public decisions tend to reflect the median view.

3. Public choice theory suggests that the *public sector has failed* because the process it uses to make decisions is inherently weak and results in an economically inefficient allocation of resources.

a. The weakness of the decision-making process in the public sector and the resulting inefficient allocation of resources is often the result of pressures exerted on Congress and the bureaucracy by special interests and other groups.
(1) There can be a ***special-interest effect*** in which a small number of people obtain a government program or policy giving them large gains at the expense of a large number of people who individually suffer small losses. This special-interest effect is also present in pork-barrel politics because a government program will mostly benefit one constituency.
(2) ***Rent-seeking behavior*** is reflected in appeals to government for special benefits or treatment at the taxpayers' or someone else's expense. Government can dispense such rents through laws, rules, hiring, and purchases.

b. Those seeking election to public office frequently favor programs whose benefits are clear and immediate and whose costs are uncertain and deferred, even when the benefits are less than the costs. Conversely, they frequently oppose programs whose costs are clear and immediate and whose benefits are uncertain and deferred, even when the benefits are greater than the costs.

c. There are limited and bundle choices in political decisions. When citizens must vote for candidates who represent different but complete programs, the voters are unable to select those parts of a program which they favor and to reject the other parts of the program.

d. It is argued that the public sector (unlike the private sector) is inefficient because those employed there are offered no incentive to be efficient, there is no way to measure efficiency in the public sector, and government bureaucrats can join with the special-interest groups to block budget cuts or lobby for increased funding.

e. Just as the private or market sector of the economy does not allocate resources perfectly, the public sector does not perform its functions perfectly; the imperfections of both sectors make it difficult to determine which sector will provide a particular good or service more efficiently.

4. The financing of public goods and services through *taxation* also raises an important question about how the tax burden is allocated among people.

a. The ***benefits-received principle*** and the ***ability-to-pay principle*** are widely used to determine how the tax bill should be apportioned among the economy's citizens.

(1) The benefits-received principle suggests that those people who benefit most from public goods should pay for them.

(2) The ability-to-pay principle states that taxes for the support of public goods should be tied to the income and wealth of people or their ability to pay.

b. Taxes can be classified as *progressive, regressive,* or *proportional* according to the way in which the average tax *rate* changes as incomes change.

(1) The average tax rate increases as income increases with a ***progressive tax,*** it decreases as income increases with a ***regressive tax,*** and it remains the same as income increases with a ***proportional tax.***

(2) In the United States, the personal income tax tends to be mildly progressive, the corporate income tax is proportional, and the payroll, sales, and property taxes are regressive.

5. ***Tax incidence*** and the ***efficiency loss of a tax*** are also important in discussion of public finance.

a. The ***price elasticities of demand and supply*** determine the incidence of a sales or excise tax.

(1) The imposition of such a tax on a product decreases the supply of the product and increases its price. The amount of the price increase is the portion of the tax paid by the buyer; the seller pays the rest.

(2) The price elasticities of demand and supply for a product affect the portions paid by buyers and sellers: **(a)** the more elastic the demand, the greater the portion paid by the seller; **(b)** the more inelastic the demand, the smaller the portion paid by the seller; **(c)** the more elastic the supply, the greater the portion paid by the buyer; and **(d)** the more inelastic the supply, the smaller the portion paid by the buyer.

b. There is an efficiency loss from taxation. This loss occurs because there is a reduction in output, despite the fact that the marginal benefits of that output are greater than the marginal cost. Thus, the consumption and production of the taxed product have been reduced below the optimal level by the tax.

(1) The degree of the efficiency loss of a sales or an excise tax depends on the elasticities of supply and demand. Other things equal, the greater the elasticity of supply and demand, the greater the efficiency loss of a sales or an excise tax; consequently, the total tax burden to society may not be equal even though two taxes produce equal tax revenue.

(2) Other tax goals, however, may be more important than minimizing efficiency losses from taxes. These goals may include redistributing income or reducing negative externalities.

c. A tax levied on one person or group of persons may be shifted partially or completely to another person or group; and to the extent that a tax can be shifted or passed on through lower prices paid or higher prices received, its incidence is passed on to others. Table 31-2 in the text summarizes the probable shifting and incidence of the personal income tax, corporate income tax, general sales tax, specific excise taxes, and property taxes.

d. The overall U.S. tax structure is only slightly progressive and has little effect on the distribution of income because progressive taxes are generally offset by regressive taxes; however, estimates of the progressivity of the tax system depend on the assumed incidence of various taxes and transfer payments made by governments to reduce income inequality in the United States.

6. In recent years, two *tax issues* have been discussed in the United States.

a. Pressure to improve the performance of the U.S. economy and industry has resulted in debates over tax changes to reduce consumption, increase savings, and stimulate investment in capital goods. The adoption of a ***value-added tax (VAT)*** on consumer goods and the reduction or elimination of the personal income or corporate income tax have been considered to achieve these objectives. The VAT penalizes consumption and should encourage saving. Increased saving should stimulate investment and economic growth.

b. The complexity of the Federal tax code also contributes to economic inefficiency because it requires time to keep records and calculate taxes owed. Proponents of the ***flat tax*** would simplify the code by having a single tax rate applied to individuals and businesses; the tax would encourage saving and investment because it would not tax capital gains or income on saving.

c. Critics of the VAT and flat tax contend that either one is regressive and would reduce the overall progressivity of the Federal tax system. Critics also cite transition costs to the economy from tax changes: a general price increase resulting from the adoption of the VAT, and the losses of tax deductions from the flat tax may alter spending and housing valuations.

7. The nature and amount of government activity and the extent of individual freedom may be related.

a. Conservatives argue that the cost of government entails not only the economic cost from a growing public sector but also a cost in terms of reduced economic freedom for the individual because government now makes more of the decisions over economic activity.

b. Liberals counter that the conservative position is subject to the fallacy of limited decisions. If government activity expands, this does not necessarily mean that there is less private decision making because the range of choices can be expanded by increased governmental activity.

■ HINTS AND TIPS

1. The first part of the chapter presents public choice theory, but this theory has many practical applications to politics. As you read about the reasons for inefficient voting outcomes, the influence of special-interest groups, political logrolling, the median-voter model, rent-seeking behavior, limited and bundled choices, and public sector failures, see if you can apply the ideas to current public issues at the local, state, or Federal level. Also ask your instructor for current examples of the ideas from public choice theory.

2. Remember that what happens to the ***average tax rate*** as income increases determines whether a tax is progressive, regressive, or proportional. The average tax rate increases for progressive taxes, decreases for regressive taxes, and remains the same for proportional taxes as income increases.

3. This chapter applies supply, demand, and elasticity concepts to taxation issues. Chapter 20 is worth checking to review your understanding of elasticity. Figure 31-5 and the related discussion in the text are crucially important for understanding the efficiency loss from a tax.

■ IMPORTANT TERMS

public choice theory	**ability-to-pay principle**
public finance	**progressive tax**
logrolling	**regressive tax**
paradox of voting	**proportional tax**
median-voter model	**tax incidence**
public sector failure	**efficiency loss of a tax**
special-interest effect	**value-added tax (VAT)**
rent-seeking behavior	**flat tax**
benefits-received principle	**fallacy of limited decisions**

SELF TEST

■ FILL-IN QUESTIONS

1. The economic analysis of government decisions and the economic problems created by the public sector are topics studied under the theory of public (finance, choice) _______________.

2. Many collective decisions are made on the basis of (minority, majority) _______________ voting. One problem with this voting system is that it results in (efficient, inefficient) _______________ voting outcomes because it fails to incorporate the strength of (individual, majority) _______________ preferences. Voters may defeat a proposal even though the total costs are (less than, greater than) _______________ the total benefits, or they accept a proposal even though the total costs are _______________ the total benefits.

3. The voting problem might be resolved or reversed through the influence of (interest, social) _______________ groups or through political (primaries, logrolling) _______________.

4. Another problem with this voting system is a situation in which the public may not be able to rank its preferences with consistency; this is called the (fallacy, paradox) _______________ of voting.

5. There are also insights into majority voting based on the (motor-voter, median-voter) _______________ model, whereby the person holding the (lower, middle, upper) _______________ position is likely to determine the outcome from an election.

6. When governments use resources to attempt to solve problems and the employment of these resources (does, does not) _______________ result in solutions to these problems, there has been (private, public) _______________ sector failure. This means that there are shortcomings in government which promote economic (efficiency, inefficiency) _______________.

7. One reason for this type of failure is that there can be a special-interest effect whereby a (large, small) _______________ number of people benefit from a government program at the expense of a _______________ number of persons who individually suffer (large, small) _______________ losses.

8. Inefficiencies can also be caused by an appeal to government for special benefits at taxpayers' or someone else's expense that is called (revealed preferences, rent-seeking behavior) _______________.

9. Another reason for the failure is that the benefits from a government program or project are often (clear, hidden) _______________ to citizens or groups, but the costs are frequently _______________ when legislation is passed or programs are funded.

10. There can also be inefficencies in government because voters or elected representatives have to accept political choices that are (limited, unlimited) _______________ and (bundled, unbundled) _______________, which means government legislation forces voters or elected representatives to take the bad programs with the good programs.

11. The incentives for economic efficiency tend to be stronger in the (private, public) _______________ sector because there is a profit incentive in the _______________ sector but not a similar incentive in the (private, public) _______________ sector. As a result, there tends to be (more, less) _______________ government bureaucracy and _______________ efficient use of scarce resources.

12. Although the public sector can experience (market, government) _______________ failure, the private sector can also experience _______________ failure, and thus both government and markets can be considered (perfect, imperfect) ______________ economic institutions.

13. The tax philosophy which asserts that households and businesses should purchase public goods and services in about the same way as private goods and services are bought is the (ability-to-pay, benefits-received) ______________ principle of taxation, but the tax philosophy that the tax burden should be based on a person's wealth or income is the ______________ principle of taxation.

14. If the average tax rate remains constant as income increases, the tax is (regressive, progressive, proportional) ______________. If the average tax rate decreases as income increases, the tax is ______________. If the average tax rate increases as income increases, the tax is (regressive, progressive, proportional) ______________.

15. In the United States, the Federal personal income tax is (regressive, progressive, proportional) ______________, but sales taxes, property taxes, and payroll taxes are ______________. If all shareholders bear the burden of the corporate income tax, then it is (regressive, progressive, proportional) ______________, but if part of the tax is passed on to consumers in higher prices, then the tax is ______________.

16. The income that people lose as a result of paying a tax is called tax (avoidance, incidence) ______________. When an excise tax is placed on a product, the supply curve will (increase, decrease) ______________, or shift to the (right, left) ______________. The amount the product price rises as a result of the tax is the portion of the tax burden borne by (buyers, sellers) ______________, and the difference between the original price and the after-tax price is the portion of the tax burden borne by ______________.

17. The incidence of an excise tax primarily depends on the (price, income) ______________ elasticity of demand and of supply. The buyer's portion of the tax is larger the (more, less) ______________ elastic the demand and the ______________ elastic the supply. The seller's portion of the tax is larger the (more, less) ______________ elastic the demand and the ______________ elastic the supply.

18. When an excise tax reduces the consumption and production of the taxed product below the level of economic efficiency, there is an efficiency (gain, loss) ______________ of the tax. Other things equal, the greater the elasticity of supply and demand, the (greater, less) ______________ the efficiency (gain, loss) ______________ of the tax.

19. There can be goals to tax policy besides minimizing efficiency losses. One goal is to (cut, redistribute) ______________ income. Another goal is to reduce (negative, positive) ______________ externalities.

20. What is the probable incidence of each of the following taxes?

a. Personal income tax: ______________

____

b. Sales and excise tax: ______________

____

c. Corporate income tax: ______________

____

d. Property tax: ______________

____

21. The Federal tax system is generally (progressive, regressive, proportional) ______________, state and local tax systems are generally ______________, and overall the U.S. tax system is slightly ______________, but these conditions depend on the incidence of the taxes. The tax system has a relatively (large, small) ______________ effect on the distribution of income in the United States, but income inequality is (increased, decreased) ______________ by transfer payments made by governments.

22. A tax on the difference between the value of a firm's sales and the value of its purchases from other firms is a(n) (excise, value-added) ______________ tax. The advantage of this tax is that it would penalize (saving, consumption, investment) ______________ and encourage ______________ and ______________, thus increasing economic growth.

23. The complexity of the tax code has resulted in calls for a tax that would be a fixed percentage of taxable income, or a(n) (elastic, flat) ______________ tax. Under this tax, income or capital gains from saving (would, would not) ______________ be taxed. Society would presumably save (more, less) ______________, invest ______________ and consume (more, less) ______________, thus increasing economic growth.

24. Critics of the VAT and flat tax contend that these tax reforms would (increase, decrease) ______________ the progressivity of Federal taxation and thus ______________ after-tax income inequality. Some individuals might be hurt by this tax because of the (increase, decrease) ______________ in allowable tax deductions, tax preparation firms might experience a ______________ in business, and the general price level might (increase, decrease) ______________.

25. Many conservatives argue that a larger public sector also diminishes (social, economic) ______________ freedom. Liberals counter that to believe that more governmental activity necessarily decreases private decision making and economic activity is an example of the fallacy of (composition, limited decisions) ______________.

■ TRUE-FALSE QUESTIONS

Circle the T if the statement is true, the F if it is false.

1. Majority voting may produce outcomes that are economically inefficient because it fails to take into account the strength of preferences of the individual voter. **T F**

2. Logrolling will always diminish economic efficiency in government. **T F**

3. The paradox of voting is that majority voting will result in consistent choices which reflect the preferences of the public. **T F**

4. The proposition that the person holding the middle position on an issue will likely determine the outcome of an election is suggested by the median-voter model. **T F**

5. There is a failure in the public sector whenever a governmental program or activity has been expanded to the level at which the marginal social cost exceeds the marginal social benefit. **T F**

6. Those concerned with public choice theory argue that the special-interest effect tends to reduce public sector failures because the pressures exerted on government by one special-interest group are offset by the pressures brought to bear by other special-interest groups. **T F**

7. The appeal to government for special benefits at taxpayers' or someone else's expense is called rent seeking. **T F**

8. When the costs of programs are hidden and the benefits are clear, vote-seeking politicians tend to reject economically justifiable programs. **T F**

9. The limited choice of citizens refers to the inability of individual voters to select the precise bundle of social goods and services that best satisfies the citizen's wants when he or she must vote for a candidate and the candidate's entire program. **T F**

10. Critics of government contend that there is a tendency for government bureaucracy to justify continued employment by finding new problems to solve. **T F**

11. When comparing government with markets, government is imperfect, whereas markets are perfect in efficiently allocating resources. **T F**

12. The chief difficulty in applying the benefits-received principle of taxation is determining who receives the benefit of many of the goods and services which government supplies. **T F**

13. The state and Federal taxes on gasoline are good examples of taxes levied on the benefits-received principle. **T F**

14. A tax is progressive when the average tax rate decreases as income increases. **T F**

15. A general sales tax is considered a proportional tax with respect to income. **T F**

16. When an excise tax is placed on a product bought and sold in a competitive market, the portion of the tax borne by the seller equals the amount of the tax less the rise in the price of product due to the tax. **T F**

17. The more elastic the demand for a good, the greater the portion of an excise tax on the good borne by the seller. **T F**

18. The efficiency loss of an excise tax is the gain in net benefits for the producers from the increase in the price of the product. **T F**

19. The degrees of efficiency loss from an excise tax vary from market to market and depend on the elasticities of supply and demand. **T F**

20. The probable incidence of the tax on rented apartment properties is on the landlord, not on the tenant. **T F**

21. The overall U.S. tax system is largely regressive. **T F**

22. A value-added tax is a tax on the difference between the value of goods sold by a firm and the value of the goods it purchases from other firms. **T F**

23. A flat tax is designed to simplify the tax code by setting an equal dollar amount of tax that all citizens would pay. **T F**

24. Major critics of the VAT and flat tax contend that they would encourage consumption at the expense of investment. **T F**

25. Both liberals and conservatives agree that the expansion of government's role in the economy has reduced personal freedom in the United States. **T F**

■ MULTIPLE-CHOICE QUESTIONS

Circle the letter that corresponds to the best answer.

1. Deficiencies in the processes used to make collective decisions in the public sector and economic inefficiencies caused by government are the primary focus of

(a) public finance
(b) public choice theory
(c) the study of tax incidence
(d) the study of tax shifting

2. The trading of votes to secure favorable outcomes on decisions which otherwise would be adverse is referred to as
(a) logrolling, and it increases economic efficiency
(b) logrolling, and it may increase or decrease economic efficiency
(c) rent-seeking behavior, and it decreases economic efficiency
(d) rent-seeking behavior, and it may increase or decrease economic efficiency

Answer Questions 3, 4, 5, and 6 on the basis of the following table, which shows the rankings of the public goods by three voters: A, B, and C.

Public good	Voter *A*	Voter *B*	Voter *C*
Dam	1	2	3
School	3	1	2
Road	2	3	1

3. In a choice between a dam and the school,
(a) a majority of voters favor the dam
(b) a majority of voters favor the school
(c) a majority of voters favor both the dam and the school
(d) there is no majority of votes for either the dam or the school

4. In a choice between a road and a dam,
(a) a majority of voters favor the dam
(b) a majority of voters favor the road
(c) a majority of voters favor both the dam and the road
(d) there is no majority of votes for either the road or the dam

5. In a choice between a school and a road,
(a) a majority of voters favor the road
(b) a majority of voters favor the school
(c) a majority of voters favor both the road and the school
(d) there is no majority of votes for either the road or the school

6. What do the rankings in the table indicate about choices made under majority rule? Majority voting
(a) reflects irrational preferences
(b) produces inconsistent choices
(c) produces consistent choices in spite of irrational preferences
(d) results in economically efficient outcomes because they have been influenced by special interests

7. The idea that the person holding the middle position will in a sense determine the outcome of an election is suggested by the
(a) rent-seeking behavior
(b) paradox of voting
(c) median-voter model
(d) fallacy of limited decisions

8. Actions that groups take to seek government legislation which puts tariffs on foreign products to limit foreign competition or which gives tax breaks to specific corporations would best be an example of
(a) how the median-voter model works
(b) how political choices are bundled
(c) rent-seeking behavior
(d) the paradox of voting

9. It is difficult to determine whether provision for a particular good or service should be assigned to the private or public sector of the economy because the
(a) institutions in both sectors function efficiently
(b) markets function efficiently and the agencies of government perform imperfectly
(c) markets are faulty and government agencies function with much greater efficiency
(d) institutions in both sectors are imperfect

10. Which is true of the ability-to-pay principle as applied in the United States?
(a) It is less widely applied than the benefits-received principle.
(b) Tax incidence is generally taken as the measure of the ability to pay.
(c) Gasoline taxes are based on this principle.
(d) As an individual's income increases, taxes paid increase both absolutely and relatively.

11. Taxing people according to the principle of ability to pay would be most characteristic of
(a) a payroll tax
(b) a value-added tax
(c) a general sales tax
(d) a progressive income tax

12. With a regressive tax, as income
(a) increases, the tax rate remains the same
(b) decreases, the tax rate decreases
(c) increases, the tax rate increases
(d) increases, the tax rate decreases

13. Which tends to be a progressive tax in the United States?
(a) income tax
(b) property tax
(c) sales tax
(d) payroll tax

14. In a competitive market, the portion of an excise tax borne by a buyer is equal to the
(a) amount the price of the product rises as a result of the tax
(b) amount of the tax
(c) amount of the tax less the amount the price of the product rises as a result of the tax
(d) amount of the tax plus the amount the price of the product rises as a result of the tax

15. Which statement is correct?
(a) The more elastic the supply, the greater the portion of an excise tax borne by the seller.

(b) The more elastic the demand, the greater the portion of an excise tax borne by the seller.
(c) The more inelastic the supply, the greater the portion of an excise tax borne by the buyer.
(d) The more inelastic the demand, the greater the portion of an excise tax borne by the seller.

Answer Questions 16, 17, 18 and 19 based on the following graph of an excise tax imposed by government.

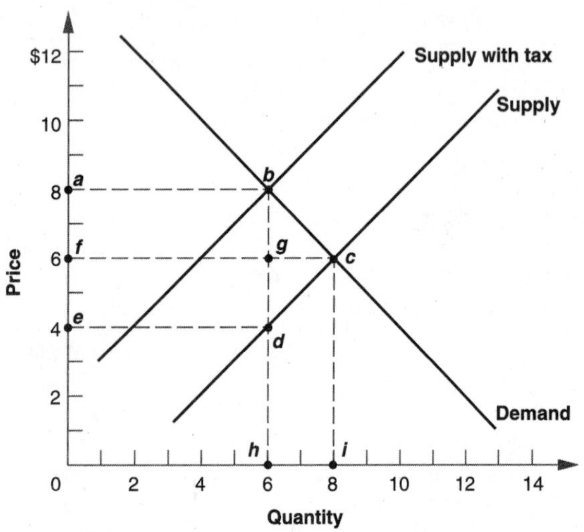

16. What is the amount of the excise tax paid by the seller in terms of price per unit sold?
(a) $1
(b) $2
(c) $3
(d) $4

17. The amount of the excise tax paid by consumers is
(a) $2
(b) $6
(c) $12
(d) $16

18. The tax revenue for government is represented by area
(a) ***abde***
(b) ***abgf***
(c) ***fgde***
(d) ***abcde***

19. The efficiency loss of the tax is represented by area
(a) ***bgc***
(b) ***bdc***
(c) ***abcf***
(d) ***hbci***

20. The efficiency loss of an excise tax is
(a) greater, the greater the elasticity of supply and demand
(b) greater, the less the elasticity of supply and demand
(c) less, the greater the elasticity of supply and demand
(d) not affected by the elasticity of supply and demand

21. Which tax is the most difficult to shift to others?
(a) personal income tax
(b) corporate income tax
(c) specific excise taxes
(d) business property taxes

22. The Federal tax system is
(a) proportional, while state and local tax structures are largely progressive
(b) progressive, while state and local tax structures are largely regressive
(c) regressive, while state and local tax structures are largely proportional
(d) proportional, while state and local tax structures are largely progressive

23. A value-added tax as used by many countries would basically tax a firm's
(a) revenue from the sale of a product
(b) revenue from the sale of a product less the resource cost
(c) purchase of resources that the firm makes to produce a product
(d) value of the capital goods and property resources held by the firm

24. Supporters of the VAT and flat-tax proposals contend that they would
(a) decrease consumption, but critics of these reforms contend that they would increase the progressivity of Federal taxation
(b) decrease saving and investment, but critics of these reforms contend that they would decrease the progressivity of Federal taxation
(c) increase saving and investment, but critics of these reforms contend that they would decrease the progressivity of Federal taxation
(d) increase consumption, but critics of these reforms contend that they would decrease the progressivity of Federal taxation

25. The statement that "government extends the range of free choice for members of a society when it provides public goods and services" serves to illustrate
(a) rent-seeking behavior
(b) the median-voter model
(c) the benefits-received principle
(d) the fallacy of limited decisions

■ PROBLEMS

1. The table at the top of page 359 shows the demand and supply schedules for copra in the New Hebrides Islands.
a. Before a tax is imposed on copra, its equilibrium price is $______________.
b. The government of New Hebrides now imposes an excise tax of $.60 per pound on copra. Complete the after-tax supply schedule in the right-hand column of the table.
c. After the imposition of the tax, the equilibrium price of copra is $____________.
d. Of the $.60 tax, the amount borne by
(1) the buyer is $___________ or ___________%.
(2) the seller is $___________ or ___________%.

Quantity demanded (pounds)	Price (per pound)	Before-tax quantity supplied (pounds)	After-tax quantity supplied (pounds)
150	$4.60	900	_____
200	4.40	800	_____
250	4.20	700	_____
300	4.00	600	_____
350	3.80	500	_____
400	3.60	400	_____
450	3.40	300	0
500	3.20	200	0
550	3.00	100	0

2. On the following graph, draw a perfectly elastic demand curve and a normal upsloping supply curve for a product. Now impose an excise tax on the product, and draw the new supply curve that would result.

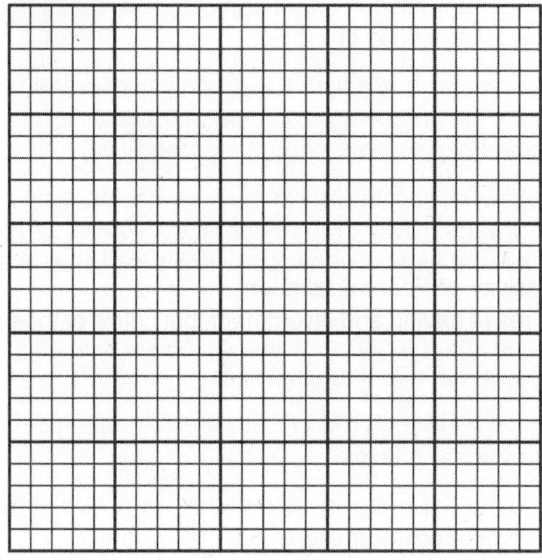

0

a. As a consequence of the tax, the price of the product has _____________.

b. It can be concluded that when demand is perfectly elastic, the buyer bears _________________ of the tax and the seller bears _________________ of the tax.

c. Thus the *more* elastic the demand, the ___________ is the portion of the tax borne by the buyer and the ____________________ is the portion borne by the seller.

d. But the *less* elastic the demand, the ____________ is the portion borne by the buyer and the ______________ is the portion borne by the seller.

3. In the following graph, draw a perfectly elastic supply curve and a normal downsloping demand curve. Impose an excise tax on the product, and draw the new supply curve.

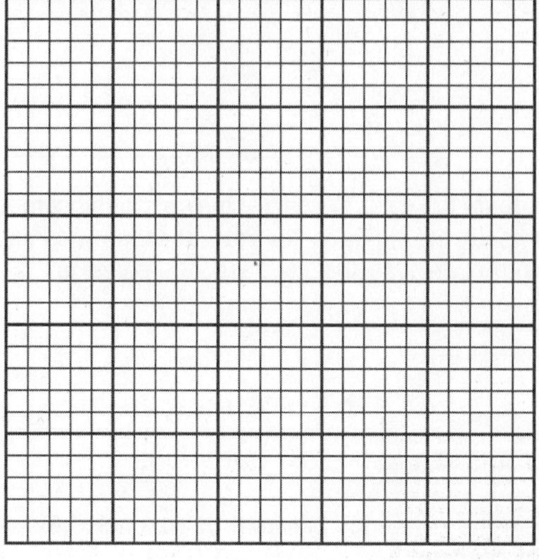

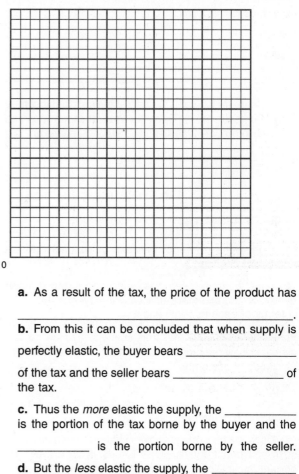

0

a. As a result of the tax, the price of the product has ____.

b. From this it can be concluded that when supply is perfectly elastic, the buyer bears _______________ of the tax and the seller bears __________________ of the tax.

c. Thus the *more* elastic the supply, the ___________ is the portion of the tax borne by the buyer and the ____________ is the portion borne by the seller.

d. But the *less* elastic the supply, the ____________ is the portion borne by the buyer and the _________________ is the portion borne by the seller.

4. The table below shows five levels of taxable income and the amount that would be paid at each of the five levels under three tax laws: ***A***, ***B***, and ***C***. Compute for each of the three tax laws the *average* rate of taxation at each of the four remaining income levels. Indicate whether the tax is regressive, proportional, progressive, or some combination thereof.

	Tax A		*Tax B*		*Tax C*	
Income	**Tax paid**	**Av. tax rate %**	**Tax paid**	**Av. tax rate %**	**Tax paid**	**Av. tax rate %**
$ 1,500	45.00	3 %	30.00	2 %	135.00	9 %
3,000	90.00	_____	90.00	_____	240.00	_____
5,000	150.00	_____	150.00	_____	350.00	_____
7,500	225.00	_____	187.50	_____	450.00	_____
10,000	300.00	_____	200.00	_____	500.00	_____
Type of tax:	_____________		_____________		_____________	

5. Assume a state government levies a 4% sales tax on all consumption expenditures. Consumption expenditures at six income levels are shown in the following table.

Income	Consumption expenditures	Sales tax paid	Average tax rate, %
$ 5,000	$5,000	$200	4.0
6,000	5,800	232	3.9
7,000	6,600	____	____
8,000	7,400	____	____
9,000	8,200	____	____
10,000	9,000	____	____

a. Compute the sales tax paid at the next four incomes.
b. Compute the average tax rate at these incomes.
c. Using income as the tax base, the sales tax is a ________________ tax.

SHORT ANSWER AND ESSAY QUESTIONS

1. Explain the difference between public choice theory and public finance.

2. Why has there been dissatisfaction with government decisions and economic efficiency in government?

3. What is the relationship between majority voting and the efficiency of outcomes from an election? How do special-interest groups or the use of logrolling influence the efficiency of outcomes?

4. Why is there a paradox with majority voting? Do the outcomes from majority voting suggest that voters are irrational in their preferences?

5. Describe how median voters influence the election results and debates over public issues. What are two important implications of the median voter model?

6. Explain what is meant by "public sector failure." Is it related to market failure and externalities?

7. Public choice theory suggests that there are a number of reasons for public sector failures. What are the reasons? Explain how each would tend to result in the inefficient allocation of the economy's resources.

8. It is generally agreed that "national defense must lie in the public sector while wheat production can best be accomplished in the private sector." Why is there no agreement on where many other goods or services should be produced?

9. What are the two basic philosophies for apportioning the tax burden in the United States? Explain each one.

10. What are the difficulties encountered in putting the two basic tax philosophies into practice?

11. Explain the difference among progressive, regressive, and proportional taxes. Which types of taxes fall into each of these categories?

12. Explain the effect the imposition of an excise tax has on the supply of a product that is bought and sold in a competitive market.

13. Illustrate with a supply and demand graph what part of an excise tax is passed on to the buyer and what part is borne by the seller. What determines the division of the tax between the buyer and the seller?

14. What is the relationship between the price elasticity of demand for a commodity and the portion of an excise tax on a commodity borne by the buyer and the seller?

15. What is the relationship between the price elasticity of supply and the incidence of an excise tax?

16. How does an excise tax produce an efficiency loss for society? Explain and illustrate with a supply and demand graph.

17. How is the efficiency loss from an excise tax affected by the elasticity of supply or demand? All else equal, shouldn't the total tax burden be equal for two taxes that produce equal revenues?

18. For whom is the tax shifted, and on whom is the tax incidence for the personal income tax, corporate income tax, sales and excise taxes, and the property tax?

19. What general conclusion can be drawn about the progressivity or regressivity of the Federal tax system, taxation by state and local governments, and the overall U.S. tax system?

20. Describe the probable incidence of the five major types of taxes in the United States.

21. What is a value-added tax? Compare the value-added tax to other types of taxes.

22. What is the flat tax, and how would it work? What arguments do supporters make for this tax reform?

23. Explain the major criticisms of proposals for a value-added or a flat tax.

24. Do you think government limits or expands personal freedom? Do you think the government's role in the economy should be increased or decreased?

25. What is meant by the term the "fallacy" of limited decisions?

ANSWERS

Chapter 31 Public Choice Theory and Taxation

FILL-IN QUESTIONS

1. choice
2. majority, inefficient, individual, less than, greater than
3. interest, logrolling
4. paradox
5. median-voter, middle
6. does not, public, inefficiency
7. small, large, small
8. rent-seeking behavior
9. clear, hidden

10. limited, bundled
11. private, private, public, more, less
12. government, market, imperfect
13. benefits-received, ability-to-pay
14. proportional, regressive, progressive
15. progressive, regressive, proportional, regressive
16. incidence, decrease, left, buyers, sellers
17. price, less, more, more, less
18. loss, greater, loss
19. redistribute, negative
20. *a.* the persons on whom it is levied; *b.* sales tax: consumer; excise tax: the firm and/or its customers; *c.* either the firm or its customers; *d.* owners when they occupy their own residences, tenants who rent residences from the owners, and consumers who buy the products produced on business property
21. progressive, regressive, progressive, small, decreased
22. value-added, consumption, saving, investment (either order for last two)
23. flat, would not, more, more, less
24. decrease, increase, decrease, decrease, increase
25. economic, limited decisions

TRUE-FALSE QUESTIONS

1. T, pp. 644-645
2. F, p. 645
3. F, pp. 645-646
4. T, p. 646
5. T, pp. 647-648
6. F, p. 648
7. T, p. 648
8. F, p. 648
9. T, p. 649
10. T, p. 649
11. F, p. 650
12. T, pp. 650-651
13. T, p. 650
14. F, p. 651
15. F, p. 652
16. T, pp. 652-653
17. T, pp. 653-654
18. F, p. 654
19. T, pp. 654-655
20. F, p. 656
21. F, p. 657
22. T, p. 657
23. F, p. 658
24. F, pp. 658-659
25. F, pp. 659-660

MULTIPLE-CHOICE QUESTIONS

1. b, p. 643
2. b, p. 645
3. b, pp. 645-646
4. a, pp. 645-646
5. a, pp. 645-646
6. b, p. 646
7. c, p. 646
8. c, p. 648
9. d, p. 650
10. d, p. 651
11. d, pp. 651-652
12. d, p. 651
13. a, pp. 651-652
14. a, pp. 652-653
15. b, pp. 653-654
16. b, pp. 652-653
17. c, pp. 652-653
18. a, p. 654
19. b, p. 654
20. a, pp. 654-655
21. a, p. 655
22. b, pp. 656-657
23. b, pp. 657-658
24. c, pp. 658-659
25. c, p. 659

PROBLEMS

1. *a.* \$3.60; *b.* (reading down) 600, 500, 400, 300, 200, 100; *c.* \$4.00; *d.* (1) \$.40, 67, (2) \$.20, 33
2. *a.* not changed; *b.* none, all; *c.* smaller, larger; *d.* larger, smaller
3. *a.* increased by the amount of the tax; *b.* all, none; *c.* larger, smaller; *d.* smaller, larger
4. Tax A: 3, 3, 3, 3, proportional; Tax B: 3, 3, 2.5, 2, combination; Tax C: 8, 7, 6, 5, regressive
5. *a.* \$264, 296, 328, 360; *b.* 3.8, 3.7, 3.64, 3.6; *c.* regressive

SHORT ANSWER AND ESSAY QUESTIONS

1. p. 643
2. p. 643
3. pp. 643-645
4. pp. 645-646
5. pp. 646-647
6. p. 647
7. pp. 647-649
8. p. 650
9. pp. 650-651
10. pp. 650-651
11. pp. 651-652
12. pp. 652-653
13. pp. 652-654
14. pp. 653-654
15. p. 654
16. p. 654
17. pp. 654-655
18. pp. 655-656
19. pp. 656-657
20. pp. 655-656
21. pp. 657-658
22. p. 658
23. pp. 658-659
24. pp. 659-660
25. p. 659

CHAPTER **32**

Antitrust Policy and Regulation

Chapter 32 examines issues related to monopoly and government regulation in output markets. These issues are important for you to study because they affect product prices, economic efficiency, and social welfare. Note from the first section that the term "monopoly" as used in this chapter does *not* mean pure or absolute monopoly; it means control of a large percentage of the total supply by one of the suppliers—*industrial concentration.* Actually, in the U.S. economy there is no such thing as pure monopoly, just degrees of industrial concentration.

Over the years the Federal government has taken action to curb or limit industrial concentration in U.S. business. The *Sherman Act* of 1890 was the first major ***antitrust law*** passed in the United States. As you will learn, it was followed in later years by other important antitrust legislation and the establishment of regulatory agencies.

The chapter also discusses major antitrust issues and evaluates the effectiveness of antitrust laws. Several issues of interpretation address whether business should be judged for antitrust violations on the basis of behavior or structure and what the relevant definition of a market is. You will also learn about how antitrust policy conflicts with the achievement of other economic goals. The effectiveness of antitrust policy is also evaluated in the chapter from the perspective of market structure, ***mergers,*** and ***price fixing.***

The Federal government has also undertaken to regulate industries that appeared to be *natural monopolies,* beginning with the railroads in 1887. This regulation by agencies and commissions has, however, at least three serious problems of which you should be aware. One problem is that some of the regulated industries may not be natural monopolies at all and would be competitive industries if they were left unregulated. From this problem comes the legal cartel theory of regulation: Many industries want to be regulated so that competition among the firms in the industry will be reduced and the profits of these firms increased.

A consequence of the problems encountered in regulating industries has been the trend in recent years to *deregulate* a few of the industries previously regulated by agencies or commissions. Many regulated industries—airlines, trucking, banking, railroad, natural gas, television, and telecommunications—were deregulated in the 1970s or 1980s. The controversies surrounding the deregulation of several U.S. industries are presented, as well as the economic outcomes. Here you will learn that despite the predictions of the critics, deregulation has been beneficial generally for consumers and the economy.

Beginning in the early 1960s, a host of new agencies and commissions began to engage in regulation different from the regulation of the prices charged by and the services offered by specific industries. Critics of social regulation contend that it is costly and that the marginal costs exceed the benefits. Although *social regulation* does increase product prices and indirectly reduces worker productivity, supporters of this type of regulation argue that the social benefits over time will exceed the costs. You should spend time understanding both sides of this issue.

The final section of the chapter examines *industrial policy*—actions the government takes to promote the economic health of industries or firms. As you will learn, both past and recent economic history contain many examples of such policies that government has used to help specific industries or businesses. Whether this policy is justified or beneficial to the economy is a matter of current debate. Critics of industrial policy contend that the policy is not needed, foreign examples show many failures, and it encourages special interests and political favoritism. Supporters contend that it encourages technological development and enhances efficiency.

When you finish this chapter, you should conclude that antitrust, regulation, and industrial policy are controversial areas for the U.S. economy. Antitrust and regulation raise issues and questions about the role of government in maintaining competition and restricting certain business practices in a market economy. Industrial policy raises the issue of whether the government should take actions to promote the economic vitality of specific businesses or industries. How we deal with the issues and answer the questions will affect the quality of our lives and the economic efficiency of businesses and the economy.

■ CHECKLIST

When you have studied this chapter you should be able to

☐ Define the term industrial concentration and explain how it is used in this chapter.
☐ Cite four arguments in the case against industrial concentration.
☐ State four arguments in defense of industrial concentration.
☐ Outline the major provisions of each of the following
- Sherman Act
- Clayton Act

- Federal Trade Commission Act
- Wheeler-Lea Act
- Celler-Kefauver Act

☐ Contrast the behavior and structural approaches to the enforcement of antitrust laws for judging the competitiveness of an industry.
☐ Explain the importance of market definition in the interpretation of antitrust laws.
☐ Give three examples of how strict enforcement of antitrust law may conflict with another economic goal.
☐ Generalize about the application of antitrust laws to existing market structure, mergers, and price fixing.
☐ Distinguish among a horizontal, vertical, and conglomerate merger.
☐ Explain the use of the Herfindahl index for merger guidelines.
☐ Cite recent examples of price fixing.
☐ Define a natural monopoly, and explain how it is related to the public interest theory of regulation.
☐ State the three problems that have been encountered in the economic regulation of industries by agencies and commissions.
☐ Distinguish between the public interest and legal cartel theories of regulation.
☐ Explain the controversies and outcomes from deregulation of selected U.S. industries in the 1970s and 1980s.
☐ Contrast industrial (or economic) regulation with social regulation.
☐ State three distinguishing features of social regulation.
☐ Present the critics' case against social regulation.
☐ Describe three economic implications of social regulation.
☐ Make the case for social regulation by discussing the benefits and citing data.
☐ Give historical and recent examples of industrial policy in the United States.
☐ Explain arguments for and against industrial policy.

■ CHAPTER OUTLINE

1. The term ***industrial concentration,*** as used in this chapter, means a situation in which a small number of firms control all or a substantial percentage of the total output of a major industry. Business firms may be large in either an absolute or a relative sense, and in many cases they are larger in both senses. Chapter 32 is concerned with firms large in both senses.

2. Whether industrial concentration is beneficial or detrimental to the U.S. economy is debatable. A case can be made against industrial concentration, but industrial concentration can also be defended.

a. Many argue that industrial concentration results in a misallocation of resources; it is not needed for firms to achieve the economies of scale, and it does not lead to technological progress. It contributes to income inequality in the economy, and it is politically dangerous.
b. But others argue that industrial concentration is often faced by interindustry and foreign competition, offers superior products, large firms are necessary if they are to achieve the economies of scale in producing goods and services, and concentrated industries promote a high rate of technological progress.

3. Government policies toward industrial concentration have not been clear and consistent; *legislation* and *policy,* however, for the most part have been aimed at restricting concentration and promoting competition.

a. Following the Civil War, the expansion of the U.S. economy brought with it the creation of trusts (or industrial concentration) in many industries; the fear of the trusts resulted in the enactment of antitrust legislation.
b. The ***Sherman Act*** of 1890 was the first antitrust legislation and made monopolization and restraint of trade criminal offenses.
c. In 1914 the ***Clayton Act*** outlawed a number of specific techniques by which monopolies or oligopolies had been created.
d. During the same year Congress passed the ***Federal Trade Commission Act,*** which established the ***Federal Trade Commission (FTC)*** to investigate unfair practices that might lead to the development of monopoly power. In 1938 it amended this act by passing the ***Wheeler-Lea Act*** to prohibit deceptive practices (including false and misleading advertising and misrepresentation of products).
e. In 1950 passage of the ***Celler-Kefauver Act*** plugged a loophole in the Clayton Act and prohibited mergers that might lead to a substantial reduction in competition.

4. The effectiveness of antitrust laws in preventing monopoly and maintaining competition has depended on judicial interpretation of the laws and enforcement of these laws by Federal agencies.

a. Two issues have arisen in the *judicial interpretation* of the antitrust laws.
(1) The first issue is whether an industry should be judged on the basis of its highly concentrated structure or on the basis of its market behavior. Today, most economists and antitrust enforcers adopt a rule of reason approach that bases antitrust action on market behavior, not structure.
(2) The second issue is whether to use a broad or narrow definition of the market in which firms sell their products.
b. An enforcement issue is the potential *conflict* of antitrust policy with other desirable economic goals, such as maintaining a balance of trade, supporting the defense industry, or encouraging new technologies.
c. Whether the antitrust laws have been *effective* is a difficult question to answer. The application of the laws to existing market structures, to the three types of mergers, and to price fixing has ranged from lenient to strict:
(1) for existing market structures, it has been lenient;
(2) for horizontal, vertical, or conglomerate mergers, it usually varies by the type of merger and the particulars of a case, but merger guidelines are based on the Herfindahl index (the sum of the squared values of market shares within an industry);
(3) for price fixing, it has been strict, and as a consequence price fixing is now often done in secret or

through the use of informal collusion in the form of price leadership or cost-plus pricing.

5. In addition to the enactment of the antitrust laws, government has undertaken to *regulate natural monopolies.*

a. If a single producer can provide a good or service at a lower average cost (because of economies of scale) than several producers, competition is not economical and a ***natural monopoly*** exists. Government may either produce the good or service or (following the public interest theory) regulate private producers of the product for the benefit of the public.

b. The effectiveness of the regulation of business firms by regulatory agencies has been criticized for three principal reasons.

(1) It is argued that regulation increases costs and leads to an inefficient allocation of resources and higher prices.

(2) It is also contended that the regulatory agencies have been "captured" by the regulated industries and protect them rather than the public.

(3) It can be argued that some of the regulated industries are not natural monopolies and would be competitive if they were not regulated.

c. The legal cartel theory of regulation is that potentially competitive industries want and support the regulation of their industries in order to increase the profits of the firms in the industries by limiting competition among them.

6. The three criticisms of the regulation of industries and the *legal cartel theory of regulation* led, beginning in the 1970s, to the *deregulation* of a number of industries in the United States: airlines, trucking, banking, railroad, natural gas, television, and telecommunications.

a. Critics of deregulation contended that it would result in higher prices, less output, and poorer service. Concerns were also raised about increasing industrial concentration and instability in business.

b. The overall evidence, however, shows deregulation to be generally positive for U.S. consumers and the economy. Prices and production costs have fallen and output has increased.

7. Beginning in the early 1960s, ***social regulation*** developed and resulted in the creation of additional regulatory agencies.

a. This regulation differed in several ways from the older regulation of specific industries and aimed to improve quality of life in the United States.

b. While the objectives of the new regulation are desirable, the overall costs for both program administration and compliance costs can be high; most of the costs, however, are compliance costs, which are about 20 times administrative costs.

c. Critics argue that this social regulation is inefficient because

(1) regulatory standards and objectives are poorly drawn and targeted;

(2) the rules and regulations are made based on limited and inadequate information;

(3) there are unintended secondary effects from the regulation that boost product costs;

(4) regulatory agencies tend to attract "overzealous" workers who believe in regulation.

d. The economic consequences of social regulation are that it increases product prices, it may slow the rate of product innovation, and it may lessen competition.

e. The defenders of social regulation contend that it is needed to fight serious and neglected problems, such as job and auto safety or environment pollution, and that the social benefits, if they can be measured, will over time exceed the costs.

8. ***Industrial policy***—actions taken by government to promote the economic health or interests of firms or industries—has been considered in recent years.

a. There are many historical examples of industrial policy such as granting free land to railroads to promote rail building and westward expansion, and the subsidies given to U.S. agriculture.

b. Recent examples of industrial policy include loans and trade restrictions to help the auto industry, the synfuels program of the 1970s to encourage development of alternative fuels, loans to foreign buyers of U.S. products through the ***Export-Import Bank,*** the formation of Sematech for production of semiconductors, and government aid to businesses producing flat-glass panels for microcomputers.

c. Industrial policy is controversial. Critics contend that industrial policy is not needed: Foreign experience shows it to be ineffective, and government is not capable of picking winners and losers in industry and will wind up subsidizing certain businesses or industries at taxpayer expense. Supporters of industrial policy believe that it reduces the risks of developing new technology and ultimately enhances dynamic efficiency.

■ HINTS AND TIPS

1. Whether industrial concentration is a real threat to efficient resource allocation and technological progress in the United States is certainly a debatable question. Chapter 32 does not attempt to answer the question; however, it is important for you to see that there are good and plausible arguments on both sides of the question.

2. A section of the chapter discusses several Federal antitrust laws. After looking at this section, many students ask, "Am I expected to know these laws?" The answer is yes, you should have an understanding of these laws. A related question asked is, "Why should I know them?" To examine current economic issues, you need to know how the problem arose, what actions have been taken over time to solve it, and what the outcomes are. Also, many of these major antitrust laws are enforced to some degree today and may affect a business for which you may work.

3. The Herfindahl index was first introduced in Chapter 25. Reread that material if you cannot remember what the index is. In Chapter 32 you learn how the index is used for merger guidelines.

4. This chapter discusses controversies about many topics—industrial concentration, antitrust policy, industrial regulation, deregulation, social regulation, and industrial policy. To help understand these controversies and get an overview, make a table showing the pro and con positions for each issue. See problems **1, 5,** and **6** for examples.

■ IMPORTANT TERMS

antitrust law
industrial regulation
social regulation
industrial policy
industrial concentration
interindustry competition
foreign competition
potential competition
Sherman Act
Clayton Act
tying agreement
interlocking directorate
Federal Trade Commission (FTC)
cease-and-desist order
Wheeler-Lea Act
Celler-Kefauver Act
U.S. Steel case
rule of reason
Alcoa case
DuPont cellophane case
horizontal merger
vertical merger
conglomerate merger
per se violations
natural monopoly
public interest theory of regulation
legal cartel theory of regulation

SELF-TEST

■ FILL-IN QUESTIONS

1. As used in this chapter, "industrial concentration" means that (many, a few) ________________ firms control all or a substantial portion of the output of a major industry. This chapter is concerned with firms which in absolute size are (large, small) ______________, and relative to the market they are ______________.

2. Those who argue the case against industrial concentration assert that it results in an (efficient, inefficient) ________________ allocation of resources, (slows, speeds) __________ the rate of technological progress, contributes to the (equal, unequal) ______________ distribution of income, and creates political (consensus, dangers) ______________ in the United States.

3. Those who defend industrial concentration contend that it produces (inferior, superior) ______________ products, the critics (under, over) ______________ estimate the extent of competition, large firms are necessary to achieve (economies, diseconomies) ______________ of scale, and the large firms are conducive to a (rapid, slow) ______________ rate of technological progress.

4. The two techniques of Federal control that have been adopted as substitutes for or to maintain competition in markets are

a. ________________________________

b. ________________________________

5. Antitrust legislation in 1890 that made it illegal to monopolize or restrain trade between the states or between nations was the (Clayton, Sherman) ______________ Act. Legislation passed in 1914 that prohibited such practices as price discrimination, acquisition of the stock of competing corporations, tying contracts, and interlocking directorates was the (Clayton, Sherman) ______________ Act.

6. The 1914 act that had set up an agency to investigate unfair competitive practices, hold public hearings on such complaints, and issue cease-and-desist orders was the (Clayton, Federal Trade Commission) ______________ Act.

7. The 1938 antitrust act that had the effect of prohibiting false and misleading advertising was the (Celler-Kefauver, Wheeler-Lea) ______________ Act, while the act that plugged a loophole in the Clayton Act by banning the acquisition of assets of one firm by another when it would lessen competition was the ______________ Act.

8. When the judicial courts used the rule of reason to evaluate industrial concentration by U.S. Steel in 1920, they were judging the firm on the basis of its market (behavior, structure) ______________, but when the courts made a decision to break up Alcoa in 1945, they were judging the firm on the basis of its market ______________. Since 1945, the courts have returned to evaluating a firm on the basis of its market (behavior, structure) ______________.

9. One major issue of interpretation in antitrust law is the definition of a market. The firm's market share will appear small if the courts define a market (narrowly, broadly) ______________, but the firm's market share will appear large if the courts define a market share ______________. In 1956, the courts ruled that although DuPont sold nearly all the cellophane produced in the United States, it (did, did not) ______________ dominate the market for flexible packaging materials.

10. Other desirable economic goals (complement, conflict with) ______________ antitrust policy. Strict enforcement of antitrust laws may (help, hurt) ______________ efforts to achieve a favorable balance of trade, may ______________ the defense industry adjustment to reduced government spending, and may ______________ the development of new technologies.

11. A merger between two competitors selling similar products in the same market is a (vertical, horizontal, conglomerate) ______________ merger; a ______________ merger occurs among firms at different stages in the production process of the same industry; a _______________ merger results when a firm in one industry is purchased by a firm in an unrelated industry. The (Sherman, Herfindahl) _______________ index is used as a guideline for mergers.

12. A natural monopoly exists when a single firm is able to supply the entire market at a (higher, lower) _____________ average cost than a number of competing firms. In the United States, many of these natural monopolies are controlled by (business cartels, regulatory commissions) _______________.

13. The three major criticisms of regulation of industries by a government agency or commission are

a. The regulated firms have no incentive to lower their costs because the commission will then require them to (raise, lower) _______________ their prices, and because the prices they are allowed to charge are based on the value of their capital equipment, firms tend to make uneconomical substitutions of (labor, capital) _______________ for _______________.

b. The regulatory commissions have been (independent of, controlled by) _______________ the industries they were supposed to regulate.

c. Regulation has been applied to industries that (are, are not) _______________ natural monopolies, which in the absence of regulation would be more competitive.

14. The public interest theory of regulation assumes that the objective of regulating an industry is to (encourage, discourage) _______________ the abuses of monopoly power. An alternative theory assumes firms wish to be regulated because it enables them to form, and the regulatory commission helps them to create, a profitable and legal (conglomerate, cartel) _______________.

15. The available evidence indicates that deregulation of many industries which began in the 1970s generally resulted in (decreased, increased) _______________ prices because _______________ competition among firms led to _______________ costs and _______________ output.

16. The concern with the conditions under which goods and services are produced, the impact of production on society, and the physical quality of products is the focus of (industrial, social) _______________ regulation. It applies to (more, fewer) _______________ firms, affects day-to-day production to a (greater, lesser) _______________ extent, and has expanded more (rapidly, slowly) _______________ than (social, industrial) _______________ regulation.

17. The costs of social regulation which include salaries paid to employees of regulatory agencies are (compliance, administrative) _______________ costs, and the expenses incurred by businesses and state and local governments in meeting the requirements of the regulatory laws are _______________ costs. The latter costs have been estimated to be about (5, 20) _________ times those of the former. Critics of social legislation contend that its marginal costs are (greater, less) _______________ than its marginal benefits.

18. Two of many economic effects of social regulation are that it tends to (increase, decrease) _______________ product prices and tends to _______________ worker productivity, and it also may (increase, decrease) _______________ the rate of innovation and may _______________ competition in the economy.

19. Supporters of social regulation hold that there are (minor, major) _______________ problems government must deal with. In this view, the relevant economic test for judging whether social regulation is worthwhile is whether the benefits are (greater, less) _______________ than the costs and not just the high level of (costs, benefits) _______________.

20. A government policy that is designed to promote the economic health of specific firms or industries is called (antitrust, industrial) _______________ policy.

a. Critics contend such policy is not needed because foreign experience with such policy has produced many (successes, failures) _______________, and winners and losers are better decided by the (government, market) _______________.

b. Proponents believe that this policy (increases, decreases) _______________ risks of applying new technology and _______________ the international competitiveness of the economy.

■ TRUE-FALSE QUESTIONS

Circle the T if the statement is true, the F it is false.

1. The term “industrial concentration” in this chapter is taken to mean a situation in which a single firm or a small number of firms control the major portion of the output of an industry. **T F**

2. It is clear that on balance, industrial concentration is detrimental to the functioning of the U.S. economy. **T F**

3. Those who defend industrial concentration contend that it is technologically more progressive than smaller firms. **T F**

4. Potential competition acts as a restraint on the price and output decisions of firms possessing market power. **T F**

5. Achieving minimum average total cost may require such a high level of output that competition among a large number of firms is inefficient. **T F**

6. Industrial concentration and "trusts" developed in the U.S. economy during the two decades preceding the American Civil War. **T F**

7. In 1920 the courts applied the rule of reason to the U.S. Steel Corporation and decided that the corporation possessed monopoly power and had unreasonably restrained trade. **T F**

8. Those who believe an industry should be judged on the basis of its structure contend that any industry with a monopolistic structure must behave like a monopolist. **T F**

9. The market for DuPont's product was broadly defined by the courts in the DuPont cellophane case of 1956. **T F**

10. Strict enforcement of antitrust laws will generally complement the economic objective of achieving a favorable balance of trade. **T F**

11. A horizontal merger is a merger between firms at different stages of the production process. **T F**

12. The Herfindahl index is the sum of the squared values of the market shares within an industry. **T F**

13. To gain a conviction under *per se violations,* the party making the charge must show that the conspiracy to fix prices actually succeeded or caused damage. **T F**

14. There is substantial evidence that antitrust policy has *not* been effective in identifying and prosecuting price fixing by businesses. **T F**

15. Public ownership rather than public regulation has been the primary means used in the United States to ensure that the behavior of natural monopolists is socially acceptable. **T F**

16. The rationale underlying the public interest theory of regulation of natural monopolies is to allow the consumers of their goods or services to benefit from the economies of scale. **T F**

17. Regulated firms, because the prices they are allowed to charge are set to enable them to earn a "fair" return over their costs, have a strong incentive to reduce their costs. **T F**

18. From the perspective of the legal cartel theory of regulation, some firms want to be regulated by government. **T F**

19. Deregulation of industries over the past two decades has resulted in large gains in economic efficiency for the U.S. economy. **T F**

20. Those who favor social regulation believe that it is needed in order to improve the quality of life in the United States. **T F**

21. Critics of social regulation argue that its marginal costs exceed its marginal benefits. **T F**

22. Social regulation tends to lower product prices and raise worker productivity. **T F**

23. Actions taken by government to promote the economic health of an industry or a specific firm is called industrial regulation. **T F**

24. The Export-Import Bank is a prime example of social regulation. **T F**

25. A critic of industrial policy would question whether government bureaucracy has the ability to pick the winners and losers while deciding which industries the government should help. **T F**

■ MULTIPLE-CHOICE QUESTIONS

Circle the letter that corresponds to the best answer.

1. "Industrial concentration" in this chapter refers to which one of the following?
- **(a)** firms that are absolutely large
- **(b)** firms that are relatively large
- **(c)** firms that are either absolutely or relatively large
- **(d)** firms that are both absolutely and relatively large

2. Which is part of the case *against* industrial concentration? Industrial concentration
- **(a)** leads to income equality
- **(b)** results in lower per unit costs
- **(c)** is greater than it needs to be to achieve economies of scale
- **(d)** produces economic profits that are used for research and technological development

3. An essential part of the defense of industrial concentration is that the power of large businesses is decreased by
- **(a)** the misallocation of resources
- **(b)** inferior product development
- **(c)** a rising standard of living
- **(d)** interindustry competition

4. Which law stated that contracts and conspiracies in restraint of trade, monopolies, attempts to monopolize, and conspiracies to monopolize are illegal?
- **(a)** Sherman Act
- **(b)** Clayton Act
- **(c)** Federal Trade Commission Act
- **(d)** Wheeler-Lea Act

5. Which act specifically outlawed tying contracts and interlocking directorates?
- **(a)** Sherman Act
- **(b)** Clayton Act
- **(c)** Federal Trade Commission Act
- **(d)** Wheeler-Lea Act

6. Which act has given the Federal Trade Commission the task of preventing false and misleading advertising and the misrepresentation of products?
- **(a)** Sherman Act
- **(b)** Clayton Act
- **(c)** Federal Trade Commission Act
- **(d)** Wheeler-Lea Act

7. Which act banned the acquisition of a firm's assets by a competing firm when the acquisition would tend to reduce competition?

(a) Celler-Kefauver Act
(b) Wheeler-Lea Act
(c) Clayton Act
(d) Federal Trade Commission Act

8. The argument that an industry which is highly concentrated will behave like a monopolist and the Alcoa court case of 1945 suggest that the application of antitrust laws should be based on industry

(a) behavior
(b) structure
(c) efficiency
(d) rule of reason

9. The merger of a firm in one industry with a firm in an unrelated industry is called a

(a) horizontal merger
(b) vertical merger
(c) secondary merger
(d) conglomerate merger

10. Toward which of the following has the application of the antitrust laws been the strictest in recent years?

(a) existing market structures
(b) conglomerate mergers
(c) mergers in which one of the firms is on the verge of bankruptcy
(d) price fixing

11. An industry has four firms, each with a market share of 25%. There is no foreign competition, entry into the industry is difficult, and no firm is on the verge of bankruptcy. If two of the firms in the industry sought to merge, this action would most likely be opposed by the government because the Herfindahl index for the industry is

(a) 2,000 and the merger would increase the index by 1,000
(b) 2,500 and the merger would increase the index by 1,000
(c) 2,500 and the merger would increase the index by 1,250
(d) 3,000 and the merger would increase the index by 1,250

12. When the government or other party making the charge can show that there was a conspiracy to fix prices, even if the conspiracy did not succeed, this would be an example of

(a) a tying contract
(b) a per se violation
(c) the rule of reason
(d) the legal cartel theory

13. Antitrust laws have been most effective in

(a) breaking up monopolies
(b) prosecuting price fixing in business
(c) expanding industrial concentration
(d) blocking entry of foreign competition in domestic markets

14. An example of industrial or public regulation would be the

(a) Federal Communications Commission
(b) Food and Drug Administration
(c) Occupational Safety and Health Administration
(d) Environmental Protection Agency

15. Legislation designed to regulate natural monopolies would be based on which theory of regulation?

(a) cartel
(b) public interest
(c) X-inefficiency
(d) public ownership

16. Those who oppose the regulation of industry by regulatory agencies contend that

(a) many of the regulated industries are natural monopolies
(b) the regulatory agencies may favor industry because they are often staffed by former industry executives
(c) regulation contributes to an increase in the number of mergers in industries
(d) regulation helps moderate costs and improves efficiency in the production of a good or service produced by the regulated industry

17. The legal cartel theory of regulation

(a) would allow the forces of demand and supply to determine the rate (prices) of the good or service
(b) would attempt to protect the public from abuses of monopoly power
(c) assumes that the regulated industry wishes to be regulated
(d) assumes that both the demand for and supply of the good or service produced by the regulated industry are perfectly inelastic

18. Critics of the deregulation of industry argued that (among other things) deregulation would lead to

(a) lower prices for the products produced by the industry
(b) more competition in the industry
(c) a decline in the quantity of the product produced by the industry
(d) an increase in bureaucratic inefficiencies in that industry

19. The overall effect of deregulation in U.S. industry over the past decades has resulted in

(a) higher prices, higher costs, and decreased output
(b) higher prices and costs, but increased output
(c) lower prices and costs, but decreased output
(d) lower prices, lower costs, and increased output

20. Which is a concern of social regulation?

(a) the prices charged for goods
(b) the service provided to the public
(c) the conditions under which goods are manufactured
(d) the impact on business profits from the production of goods

21. Those costs businesses and state and local government incur in meeting the requirement of regulatory commissions are referred to as

(a) administrative costs
(b) compliance costs

(c) containment costs
(d) per unit costs

22. Which is engaged in social regulation?
(a) the Federal Trade Commission
(b) the Interstate Commerce Commission
(c) the Environmental Protection Agency
(d) the Federal Energy Regulatory Commission

23. Which is a major criticism leveled against social regulation by its opponents?
(a) It is procompetitive.
(b) It will decrease the rate of innovation in the economy.
(c) It will increase the amount of price fixing among businesses.
(d) It will require too long a time for it to achieve its objectives.

24. Supporters of social regulation contend that
(a) there is a pressing need to reduce the number of mergers in U.S. business
(b) the presence of natural monopoly requires strong regulatory action by government
(c) the social benefits will over time exceed the social costs
(d) administrative and compliance costs are often exaggerated

25. Opponents of industrial policy contend that it
(a) reduces the private risk of exploring and applying new technology
(b) enhances economic efficiency in the economy
(c) encourages government support of declining industries
(d) fosters the development of complementary products and industries

■ PROBLEMS

1. A case can be made *for* and *against* industrial concentration. In the blank spaces below, indicate the for and against views on whether industrial concentration would increase or decrease each characteristic. Mark an **I** for increase and **D** for decrease in the blank space. If the text states nothing about the likely effect, mark an **N**.

	For	Against
a. prices	_____	_____
b. output	_____	_____
c. product innovation	_____	_____
d. competition	_____	_____
e. income inequality	_____	_____
f. technological progress	_____	_____
g. political danger	_____	_____

2. Following is a list of Federal laws. Next is a series of provisions found in Federal laws. Match each law with the appropriate provision by placing the appropriate capital letter after each provision.

A. Sherman Act
B. Clayton Act
C. Federal Trade Commission Act
D. Wheeler-Lea Act
E. Celler-Kefauver Act

a. Established a commission to investigate and prevent unfair methods of competition _____
b. Made monopoly and restraint of trade illegal and criminal _____
c. Prohibited the acquisition of the assets of a firm by another firm when such an acquisition will lessen competition _____
d. Had the effect of prohibiting false and misleading advertising and the misrepresentation of products _____
e. Clarified the Sherman Act and outlawed specific techniques or devices used to create monopolies and restrain trade _____

3. Indicate with the letter **L** for leniently and the letter **S** for strictly how the antitrust laws tend to be applied to each of the following.
a. Vertical mergers in which each of the merging firms sells a small portion of the total output of its industry _____
b. Price fixing by a firm in an industry _____
c. Conglomerate mergers _____
d. Existing market structures in which no firm sells 60% or more of the total output of its industry _____
e. Horizontal mergers in which the merged firms would sell a large portion of the total output of their industry and no one of the firms is on the verge of bankruptcy _____
f. Action by firms in an industry to divide up sales _____
g. Horizontal mergers where one of the firms is on the verge of bankruptcy _____

4. The following table contains data on five different industries and the market shares for each firm in the industry. Assume that there is no foreign competition, entry into the industry is difficult, and that no firm in each industry is on the verge of bankruptcy.

	Market share of firms in industry						**Herfindahl**
Industry	**1**	**2**	**3**	**4**	**5**	**6**	**index**
A	35	25	15	11	10	4	_____
B	30	25	25	20	—	—	_____
C	20	20	20	15	15	10	_____
D	60	25	15	—	—	—	_____
E	22	21	20	18	12	7	_____

a. In the last column, calculate the Herfindahl index.

b. The industry with the most concentration is Industry ______________, and the industry with the least monopoly power is Industry ____________.

c. If the *sixth* firm in Industry A sought to merge with the *fifth* firm in that industry, then the government (would, would not) ______________ be likely to challenge the merger. The Herfindahl index for this industry is ______________, which is higher than the merger guideline of ______________ points used by the government, but the merger increases the index by only ____________ points.

d. If the *fourth* firm in Industry B sought to merge with the *third* firm in that industry, then the government (would, would not) ____________ be likely to challenge the merger. The Herfindahl index for this industry is ______________, which is higher than the merger guideline of the government, and the merger increases the index by ______________ points.

e. A *conglomerate* merger between the *fourth* firm in Industry C and the *fourth* firm in Industry E (would, would not) ______________ likely be challenged by the government. The Herfindahl index would (increase, remain the same) ____________________ with this merger.

f. If a *vertical* merger between the *first* firm in Industry B with the *first* firm in Industry D lessened competition in each industry, then the merger (would, would not) ____________ likely be challenged by the government, but the merger ________________ likely be challenged if it did not lessen competition in each industry.

5. The deregulation in U.S. business that began in the 1970s was controversial and had its supporters and opponents. In the blank spaces below, indicate the effect that deregulation was to have had on each characteristic from a pro and a con perspective. Mark an **I** for increase and **D** for decrease. If the text states nothing about this effect, mark an **N**.

	Pro	Con
a. prices	_____	_____
b. output	_____	_____
c. competition	_____	_____
d. service	_____	_____
e. safety	_____	_____

6. Social regulation has had its critics and defenders. In the blank spaces in the following table, indicate the effect that critics and defenders thought social regulation would have on each characteristic. Mark an **I** for increase and **D** for decrease. If the text states nothing about this effect, mark an **N**.

	Critics	Defenders
a. prices	_____	_____
b. output	_____	_____
c. competition	_____	_____
d. product innovation	_____	_____
e. net benefits to society	_____	_____

■ SHORT ANSWER AND ESSAY QUESTIONS

1. Compare and contrast the terms "pure monopoly" and "industrial concentration." How is the latter term used in this chapter?

2. What are the chief arguments in the case against industrial concentration?

3. What are the chief arguments in defense of industrial concentration?

4. What are the historical background to and the main provisions of the Sherman Act?

5. The Clayton Act and the Federal Trade Commission Act amended or elaborated the provisions of the Sherman Act, and both aimed at preventing rather than punishing monopoly. What were the chief provisions of each act, and how did they attempt to prevent monopoly? In what two ways is the FTC Act important?

6. What loophole in the Clayton Act did the Celler-Kefauver Act plug in 1950, and how did it alter the coverage of the antitrust laws with respect to mergers?

7. Contrast the two different approaches to the application of the antitrust laws that are illustrated by the decisions of the courts in the U.S. Steel and Alcoa cases.

8. Why is defining the market an important issue in the application of the antitrust laws? How did the courts define the market in the case brought against DuPont for monopolizing the market for cellophane?

9. Cite and discuss three examples of how strict enforcement of antitrust laws can conflict with other economic objectives.

10. How are the antitrust laws applied today to (*a*) existing market structures, (*b*) horizontal mergers, (*c*) vertical mergers, (*d*) conglomerate mergers, and (*e*) price fixing? What are the guidelines used for mergers?

11. What are per se violations? Give five examples of recent price-fixing investigations and court cases.

12. What is a natural monopoly? What two alternative ways can it be used to ensure that it behaves in a socially acceptable fashion?

13. Explain the three major criticisms leveled against public interest regulation as it is practiced by commissions and agencies in the United States.

14. What is the legal cartel theory of regulation? Contrast it with the public interest theory of regulation.

15. Why were a number of industries in the U.S. economy deregulated beginning in the 1970s? What have been the economic effects of deregulation?

16. How does social regulation differ from industrial (or public) regulation? What is the objective of this type of regulation, its three principal concerns, and its three distinguishing features?

17. What are the two types of costs of social regulation? How do these costs compare?

18. Why do critics of social regulation argue that the marginal costs exceed the marginal benefits?

19. What are three economic implications of social regulation?

20. What is industrial policy? What arguments do supporters and critics make about industrial policy?

ANSWERS

Chapter 32 Antitrust Policy and Regulation

FILL-IN QUESTIONS

1. a few, large, large
2. inefficient, slows, unequal, dangers
3. superior, under, economies, rapid
4. *a.* establishing regulatory agencies; *b.* passing antitrust laws (either order for a and b)
5. Sherman, Clayton
6. Federal Trade Commission
7. Wheeler-Lea, Celler-Kefauver
8. behavior, structure, behavior
9. broadly, narrowly, did not
10. conflict, hurt, hurt, hurt
11. horizontal, vertical, conglomerate, Herfindahl
12. lower, regulatory commissions
13. *a.* lower, capital, labor; *b.* controlled by; *c.* are not
14. discourage, cartel
15. decreased, increased, decreased, increased
16. social, more, greater, rapidly, industrial
17. administrative, compliance, 20, greater
18. increase, decrease, decrease, decrease
19. major, greater, costs
20. industrial; *a.* failures, market; *b.* decreases, increases

TRUE-FALSE QUESTIONS

1. T, pp. 664-665
2. F, p. 666
3. T, p. 666
4. T, p. 666
5. T, p. 666
6. F, p. 667
7. F, p. 668
8. T, p. 669
9. T, p. 669
10. F, p. 669
11. F, p. 671
12. T, p. 671
13. F, pp. 671-672
14. F, p. 672
15. F, p. 673
16. T, p. 673
17. F, p. 673
18. T, p. 674
19. T, pp. 674-675
20. T, p. 676
21. T, p. 676
22. F, p. 677
23. F, p. 678
24. F, p. 679
25. T, pp. 680-681

MULTIPLE-CHOICE QUESTIONS

1. d, p. 665
2. c, p. 665
3. d, p. 666
4. a, p. 667
5. b, pp. 667-668
6. d, p. 668
7. a, p. 668
8. b, pp. 668-669
9. d, p. 671
10. d, pp. 671-672
11. c, p. 671
12. b, pp. 671-672
13. b, p. 672
14. a, p. 673
15. b, p. 673
16. b, p. 673
17. c, p. 674
18. c, p. 674
19. d, pp. 674-675
20. c, p. 675
21. b, p. 676
22. c, p. 675
23. b, p. 677
24. c, p. 677
25. c, p. 681

PROBLEMS

1. *a.* D, I; *b.* I, D; *c.* I, D; *d.* I, D; *e.* N, D; *f.* I, D; *g.* N, I
2. *a.* C; *b.* A; *c.* E; *d.* D; *e.* B
3. *a.* L; *b.* S; *c.* L; *d.* L; *e.* S; *f.* S; *g.* L
4. *a.* 2,312, 2,550, 1,750, 4,450, 1,842; *b.* D, C; *c.* would not, 2,312, 1,800, 80; *d.* would, 2,550, 1,000; *e.* would not, remain the same; *f.* would, would not
5. *a.* D, I; *b.* I, D; *c.* I, D or I; *d.* N, D; *e.* N, D
6. *a.* I, N; *b.* D, N; *c.* D, N; *d.* D, N; *e.* D, I

SHORT ANSWER AND ESSAY QUESTIONS

1. pp. 664-665
2. pp. 665-666
3. p. 666
4. p. 667
5. pp. 667-668
6. p. 668
7. pp. 668-669
8. p. 669
9. pp. 669-670
10. pp. 670-672
11. pp. 671-672
12. pp. 672-673
13. pp. 673-674
14. pp. 673-674
15. pp. 674-675
16. pp. 675-676
17. p. 676
18. p. 676
19. p. 677
20. pp. 678, 680-681

CHAPTER 33

Agriculture: Economics and Policy

Agriculture is a large and vital part of the U.S. and world economy, and so it merits the special attention it receives in Chapter 33. As you will learn, the economics of agriculture and farm policies of the Federal government are of concern not only to those directly engaged in farming, but also to U.S. consumers and businesses who purchase farm products and to U.S. taxpayers who subsidize farm incomes. Agriculture is also important in the world economy because each nation must find a way to feed its population, and domestic farm policies designed to enhance farm incomes often lead to distortions in world trade and economic inefficiency in world agricultural production.

The chapter begins by examining both the ***short-run farm problem*** and the ***long-run farm problem*** in U.S. agriculture. The short-run problem is that farm prices and incomes have fluctuated sharply from year to year. The long-run problem is that agriculture is a declining industry, and as a consequence, farm incomes have fallen over time. To understand the causes of each problem, you will have to use the concept of inelastic demand and use your knowledge of how demand and supply determine price in a competitive market. The effort you put into the study of these tools in previous chapters will now pay a dividend: an understanding of the causes of a real-world problem and the policies designed to solve the problem.

The agricultural policies of the Federal government have been directed at enhancing and stabilizing farm incomes by supporting farm prices. In connection with the support of farm prices, you are introduced to the ***parity concept.*** Once you understand parity and recognize that the parity price in the past has been above what the competitive price would have been, you will come to some important conclusions. Consumers paid higher prices for and consumed smaller quantities of the various farm products, and at the prices supported by the Federal government, there were surpluses of these products. The Federal government bought these surpluses to keep the price above the competitive market price. The purchases of the surpluses were financed by U.S. taxpayers. To eliminate these surpluses, government looked for ways to increase the demand for or to decrease the supply of these commodities. Programs to increase demand and decrease supply were put into effect, but they failed to eliminate the annual surpluses.

Over the past 60 years, farm policies have not worked well and have been criticized for several reasons. First, the policies confuse the *symptoms* of the problem (low farm prices and incomes) with the *causes* of the problem (resource allocation). Second, the costly farm subsidies are also misguided because they tend to benefit the high-income instead of the low-income farmer. Third, some policies of the Federal government contradict or offset other policies designed to help farmers.

The *politics of farm policy* can also be studied from the public choice perspective first presented in Chapter 31. In this chapter you will learn why costly farm programs have been supported by political leaders and subsidized by the Federal government for so many years. Nevertheless, the political backing for farm price supports is declining because of a reduction in the farm population and related political representation, pressures to balance the Federal budget, and negative publicity about problems with excessive subsidies. There is also international pressure to reduce farm price supports in all nations to eliminate distortions in world trade and improve worldwide economic efficiency.

The chapter concludes with a discussion of the recent reform of agricultural policy in the United States. The ***Freedom to Farm Act*** of 1996 was a historic change that eliminated price supports and acreage allotments for many major agricultural products. In return, U.S. farmers will receive income payments until the year 2002 to help them make the transition to working in a more competitive market. The outcomes from this reform are expected to be positive for both the economy and farmers, and it will be interesting for you to follow the developments.

■ CHECKLIST

When you have studied this chapter you should be able to

☐ Give five reasons why it is important to study the economics of U.S. agriculture.
☐ List four causes of the short-run problem in agriculture.
☐ Explain why the demand for agricultural products is price inelastic.
☐ Cite a reason for the fluctuation in agricultural output.
☐ Discuss what accounts for the fluctuations in domestic demand for agricultural products.
☐ Describe the stability of foreign demand for agricultural products.
☐ Identify the two major factors contributing to the long-run problem in U.S. agriculture.
☐ Describe how technological change affects the long-run supply of agricultural products.

☐ Give two reasons why increases in demand lag increases in supply over time in U.S. agriculture.
☐ Use a supply and demand graph to illustrate the long-run problem in U.S. agriculture.
☐ Give cost estimates of the size of U.S. farm subsidies in recent years.
☐ Present several arguments in support of Federal assistance to agriculture.
☐ Define the parity ratio and explain its significance to agricultural policy.
☐ Use a supply and demand graph to identify the economic effects of price supports for agricultural products on output, farm income, consumer and taxpayer expenditures, economic efficiency, the environment, and international trade.
☐ Give examples of how the Federal government restricts supply and bolsters demand for farm products.
☐ Present three criticisms of U.S. agricultural policy.
☐ Use insights from public choice theory to discuss the politics of agricultural legislation and expenditures by the Federal government for farm programs.
☐ Give four reasons to support a prediction that farm subsidies will decline in the future.
☐ Explain the effects of agricultural policy in the European Union (EU) and in the United States on world trade in agricultural products.
☐ Describe the major features of the Freedom to Farm Act of 1996.

■ CHAPTER OUTLINE

1. The economic analysis of U.S. agriculture is important for at least *five reasons:* It is the nation's largest industry, it is a real-world example of the purely competitive model, it illustrates the economic effects of government intervention in markets, it reflects changes in global markets, and it highlights aspects of public choice theory.

2. The farm problem is both a *short-run* and a *long-run farm problem:* The short-run problem is the frequent sharp changes in the incomes of farmers from one year to the next; the long-run problem is the tendency for farm prices and incomes to lag behind the upward trend of prices and incomes in the rest of the economy.

a. The causes of the *short-run* (income-instability) problem are the inelastic demand for farm products, fluctuations in the output of agricultural products, fluctuations in the domestic demand, and the unstable foreign demand which result in relatively large changes in agricultural prices and farm incomes.

b. The causes of the *long-run* problem (low farm income and farm prices) stem from two basic factors:
(1) the *supply* of agricultural products increased significantly over most of this century because of technological advances in agriculture, and
(2) the *demand* for agricultural products failed to match the large increase in supply even though there were large increases in income (and population) because the demand for agricultural products is *income* inelastic (that is, increases in income lead to less than proportionate increases in expenditures on farm products).

3. Since the 1930s, farmers have been able to obtain various forms of public aid, but the primary purposes of the Federal government subsidies have been to enhance and stabilize farm prices and incomes.

a. Several arguments are used to justify these expenditures, such as the poor incomes of farmers, the importance of the family farm, the hazards of farming, and market power problems.

b. The cornerstone of Federal policy to raise farm prices is the concept of *parity* (or the parity price), which would give the farmer year after year the same real income per unit of output.

c. Historically, farm policy supported farm prices at some percentage of the parity price. But because the supported price was almost always above the market price, government had to support the price by purchasing and accumulating surpluses of agricultural products; while farmers gained from this policy, there were losses for consumers and society, and problems were created in the environment and the international sector.

d. To reduce the annual and accumulated surpluses, government attempted to
(1) reduce the output (or supply) of farm products by ***acreage allotment*** and soil bank ***programs*** and
(2) expand the demand for farm products by finding new uses for farm products, expanding domestic demand, and increasing the foreign demand for agricultural commodities.

4. Agricultural policies designed to stabilize farm incomes and prices have not worked well over the past 60 years. The subsidies have been subject to criticisms, political debate, and recent reform.

a. There are three basic *criticisms of agricultural subsidies.*
(1) Farm programs have confused the *symptoms* of the problem (low farm product and low farm incomes) with the *causes* of the problem (resource allocation) and have encouraged people to stay in agriculture.
(2) The major benefits from farm programs are *misguided* because low-income farmers often receive small government subsidies while high-income farmers often receive large government subsidies; price supports also affect land values and become a subsidy for owners of farm land who rent their land and do not farm.
(3) The various farm programs of the Federal government have often *offset* or contradicted each other.

b. The *politics of agricultural policy* explain why costly and extensive subsidies have persisted in the United States.
(1) Four insights from public choice theory serve to explain this development: ***rent-seeking behavior*** by farm groups, the ***special-interest effect*** that impairs public decision making, political ***logrolling*** to turn negative outcomes into positive outcomes, and the *clear benefits and hidden costs* of farm programs.
(2) Changing politics also explains why there has been a reduction in the political support for agricultural subsidies—the decline in farm population and political

power, the pressure to balance the Federal budget, and the negative publicity from the excesses of farm programs.

(3) The United States also is committed to reducing agricultural subsidies worldwide because they *distort world trade.* For example, price supports for agriculture in the ***European Union (EU)*** lead to higher trade barriers to restrict agricultural imports, give incentives for domestic overproduction, lead to demand for export subsidies, and make these markets less attractive for farmers in the United States and developing nations. A 1994 international agreement was designed to reduce farm price supports by 20% and agricultural trade barriers by 15% by the year 2000.

c. The Freedom to Farm Act of 1996 changed 60 years of U.S. farm policy. The law ended price supports and acreage allotments for eight agricultural commodities. Income payments will be made to farmers through the year 2002 to help them make the transition to a more competitive market. The change is expected to increase agricultural output, crop diversity, and risk management by farmers.

■ HINTS AND TIPS

1. This chapter applies several economic ideas—supply and demand, elasticity, price controls, and public choice theory—that you learned about in previous chapters. If your understanding of these ideas is weak, review supply and demand in Chapter 3, elasticity and price controls in Chapter 20, and public choice theory in Chapter 31.

2. There is a short-run and a long-run problem in agriculture. Make sure you understand the distinction. The short-run problem involves the year-to-year change in the prices of farm products and farm incomes. The long-run problem is that changes in supply and demand over time have made agriculture a declining industry in the U.S. economy.

3. Figure 33-6 and the related discussion are very important to study. The figure illustrates the economic effects that agricultural price supports have on different groups and the overall economy.

■ IMPORTANT TERMS

short-run farm problem	**price supports**
long-run farm problem	**acreage allotment programs**
parity concept	**Freedom to Farm Act**
parity ratio	

SELF-TEST

■ FILL-IN QUESTIONS

1. It is important to study the economics of U.S. agriculture for at least five reasons; it is one of the (largest, smallest) ______________ industries in the nation; it provides a real-world example of pure (monopoly, competition) ______________; it demonstrates the intended and unintended effects of (consumer, government) ______________ policies that interfere with forces of supply and demand; it reflects the (decreased, increased) ______________ globalization of agricultural markets; and it illustrates aspects of (public, private) ______________ choice theory.

2. The basic cause of the short-run problems in agriculture is the (elastic, inelastic) ______________ demand for farm products. This demand occurs because farm products have few good (complements, substitutes) ______________ and because of rapidly diminishing marginal (product, utility) ______________.

3. The inelastic demand for farm products contributes to unstable farm prices and incomes because relatively (large, small) ______________ changes in the output of farm products result in relatively ______________ changes in prices and incomes and because relatively ______________ changes in domestic or foreign demand result in relatively ______________ changes in prices and incomes.

4. From a long-run perspective, the (demand for, supply of) ______________ agricultural products increased greatly over the past 60 years because of technological progress, but the ______________ agricultural products did not increase by as much, in large part because food demand is income (elastic, inelastic) ______________ and because the rate of population increase has not matched the increase in production.

5. Four arguments used to justify expenditures for farm subsidies are: the (inelastic, low) ______________ income of farmers, the (cost, value) ______________ of the family farm as a U.S. institution; the (rent-seeking, hazards) ______________ of farming from many natural disasters, and the fact that the farmers sell their output in (purely, imperfectly) ______________ competitive markets and purchase their inputs in ______________ competitive markets.

6. If farmers were to receive a parity price for a product, year after year a given output would enable them to acquire a (fixed, increased) ______________ amount of goods and services.

7. If the government supports farm prices at an above-equilibrium level, the results will be (shortages, surpluses) ______________ which the government must (buy, sell) ______________ to maintain prices at their support level.

8. With price support programs, farmers (benefit, are hurt) ______________ and consumers ______________. The incomes of farmers (increase, decrease) ______________, while the price consumers pay for products ______________ and the quantities of the agricultural product that they purchase ______________.

9. Society also is hurt by farm price support programs because they encourage economic (efficiency, inefficiency) ______________, an (over, under) ______________ allocation of resources to agriculture, and a (small, large) ______________ government bureaucracy for agriculture.

10. Agricultural price supports have (increased, decreased) ______________ domestic agricultural production and ______________ the use of inputs such as pesticides and fertilizers, resulting in (positive, negative) ______________ effects on the environment.

11. The above-equilibrium price supports make U.S. agricultural markets (more, less) ______________ attractive to foreign producers who try to sell ______________ of their agricultural products in the United States. This activity is likely to (increase, decrease) ______________ trade barriers, and ______________ the efficiency of U.S. agriculture. The trade barriers will have a (negative, positive) ______________ effect on developing nations, which are often dependent on worldwide agricultural markets.

12. To bring the equilibrium level of prices in the market up to their support level, government has attempted to (increase, decrease) ______________ the demand for and to ______________ the supply of farm products.

13. To decrease supply, the Federal government has used (acreage allotment, rent-seeking) ______________ programs. To increase demand, the Federal government has encouraged (new, old) ______________ uses for agricultural products and sought to increase domestic and foreign (supply, demand) ______________ for agricultural products through the domestic food stamps program or the foreign Food for Peace program.

14. The policies of government to support agricultural prices and income (have, have not) ______________ worked well over the past 60 years because they have confused the symptoms of the farm problem, which are (high, low) ______________ prices and incomes, with the root cause of the problem, which is (efficient, inefficient) ______________ allocation of resources.

15. There are two other criticisms. Much of the benefits from farm subsidies go to (high, low) ______________-income farmers instead of ______________-income farmers. The effects of price support programs of the Federal government are (reinforced, offset) ______________ by other government programs.

16. Despite these criticisms, farm policies have received strong support in Congress over the years, the result of which can be explained by insights from (monopoly, public choice) ______________ theory. When farm groups lobby for Federal programs that transfer income to them, they are exhibiting (parity, rent-seeking) ______________ behavior. There is also a special-interest effect because the costs to individual taxpayers are (large, small) ______________ but the benefits to farmers are ______________ from farm programs.

17. In addition, when agricultural groups or farm-state politicians trade votes to turn negative into positive outcomes, they are using political (allotments, logrolling) ______________. Another public choice problem with farm subsidies is that the benefits of farm programs are (clear, hidden) ______________, while much of the costs are ______________ in the form of higher consumer prices for agricultural products.

18. Factors that explain the change in support for farm subsidies are the (increase, decrease) ______________ in the farm population and rural representation in Congress and the ______________ in pressure to balance the Federal budget. There has also been (positive, negative) ______________ publicity from the excesses of farm subsidies and the ______________ effects of farm subsidies on world agricultural trade.

19. The effects of supports for the prices of agricultural products by the European Community have (increased, decreased) ______________ incentives for domestic production in the member nations, ______________ export subsidies for farm products in member nations, ______________ sales of U.S. agricultural products to the European Community, ______________ world prices for agricultural products.

20. The Freedom to Farm Act aimed to (expand, eliminate) ______________ price supports for eight farm crops and ______________ acreage allotments for these crops. In return, farmers will receive transition (price supports, income payments) ______________ through the year 2002. The act is expected to (decrease, increase) ______________ farm output and ______________ the variability in farm product prices and farm incomes.

■ TRUE-FALSE QUESTIONS

Circle the T if the statement is true, the F if it is false.

1. The short-run farm problem is the sharp year-to-year fluctuations in farm prices and farm incomes that frequently occur. **T F**

2. The demand for farm products is price elastic. **T F**

3. The quantities of agricultural commodities produced tend to be fairly *insensitive* to changes in agricultural prices because a large percentage of farmers' total costs are variable. **T F**

4. The foreign demand for farm products is relatively stable. **T F**

5. Appreciation of the dollar will tend to increase the demand for farm products. **T F**

6. The supply of agricultural products has tended to increase more rapidly than the demand for these products in the United States. **T F**

7. Most of the recent technological advances in agriculture have been initiated by farmers. **T F**

8. The demand for farm products is income elastic. **T F**

9. The long-run farm problem is that the incomes of farmers have been low relative to incomes in the economy as a whole. **T F**

10. The size of the farm population in the United States has declined in both relative and absolute terms since about 1930. **T F**

11. The major aim of agricultural policy in the United States for the past 60 years was to support agricultural prices and incomes. **T F**

12. Between 1990–1996, Federal expenditures for farm price and income support programs were relatively small and cost only $1 billion a year. **T F**

13. If the prices paid by farmers were 500% higher than in the base year and the price received by farmers were 400% higher than in the base year, the parity ratio would be 125%. **T F**

14. Application of the parity concept to farm prices causes farm prices to decline and results in agricultural surpluses. **T F**

15. When government supports farm prices at above-equilibrium levels, it can reduce the annual surpluses of agricultural commodities either by increasing the supply or by decreasing the demand for them. **T F**

16. The acreage allotment program was designed to decrease the supply of farm products. **T F**

17. Restricting the number of acres which farmers use to grow agricultural products has not been a very successful method of reducing surpluses because farmers tend to cultivate their land more intensively when the acreage is reduced. **T F**

18. Public policy has been effective in alleviating the resource allocation problem in U.S. agriculture, not just the symptoms. **T F**

19. The price-income support programs for agriculture have given the most benefit to those farmers with the least need for the government assistance. **T F**

20. A political action committee organized by a group of sugar beet farmers to lobby Congress for subsidies for sugar beets is an example of political logrolling. **T F**

21. The reason that farmers, who are a small proportion of the population, can impose a large cost to taxpayers in the form of agricultural subsidies is because the cost imposed on each individual taxpayer is small and not given much attention by each taxpayer. **T F**

22. One hidden cost of agricultural price support programs is the higher prices that consumers pay for the product. **T F**

23. The decline in farm population and related political representation in rural areas is one reason why political support for farm subsidies has increased. **T F**

24. Domestic farm subsidies distort world trade and contribute to the inefficiencies in the international allocation of agricultural resources. **T F**

25. The Freedom to Farm Act gave farmers a substantial increase in agricultural price supports in return for a reduction in acreage allotments for agricultural products. **T F**

■ MULTIPLE-CHOICE QUESTIONS

Circle the letter that corresponds to the best answer.

1. The inelasticity of demand for agricultural products can be explained by
- **(a)** parity ratio
- **(b)** economies of scale
- **(c)** rent-seeking behavior
- **(d)** diminishing marginal utility

2. The inelastic demand for agricultural products means that relatively small increases in output will result in a relatively
- **(a)** small increase in farm prices and incomes
- **(b)** large decrease in farm prices and incomes
- **(c)** small decrease in farm prices and a relatively large increase in farm incomes
- **(d)** large increase in farm prices and a relatively small decrease in farm incomes

3. One reason for the year-to-year instability of agricultural product prices is
- **(a)** stable production of domestic agricultural products
- **(b)** stable production of foreign agricultural products
- **(c)** fluctuations in incomes received for agricultural products
- **(d)** fluctuations in the domestic demand for agricultural products

4. The reason that large declines in farm prices do not significantly reduce farm production in the short run is that farmers'

(a) fixed costs are high relative to their variable costs
(b) variable costs are high relative to their fixed costs
(c) prices received are greater than prices paid for agricultural products
(d) prices paid are greater than prices received for agricultural products

5. If, over time, the increases in the supply of an agricultural product are much greater than the increases in demand for it, the supply and demand model would suggest that the product price

(a) and quantity will both increase
(b) and quantity will both decrease
(c) will increase, but the quantity will decrease
(d) will decrease, but the quantity will increase

6. Which is a significant reason why increases in demand for agricultural products have been relatively small?

(a) Increases in the population of the United States have been greater than increases in the productivity of agriculture.
(b) Increases in the population of the United States have been greater than decreases in the productivity of agriculture.
(c) Increases in the incomes of U.S. consumers result in less than proportionate increases in their spending on agricultural products.
(d) Increases in the incomes of U.S. consumers result in more than proportionate increases in their spending on agricultural products.

7. Given an inelastic demand for farm products, a greater increase in the

(a) demand for such products relative to the supply creates a persistent downward pressure on farm incomes
(b) supply for such products relative to the demand creates a persistent upward pressure on farm incomes
(c) supply for such products relative to the demand creates a persistent downward pressure on farm incomes
(d) demand for such products relative to the supply creates a persistent downward pressure on agricultural product prices

8. As a consequence of the migration out of farming over the years, agricultural income per farm household

(a) has decreased relative to nonfarm incomes
(b) has increased relative to nonfarm incomes
(c) is now significantly greater than nonfarm income
(d) is now significantly less than nonfarm income

9. Between 1990 and 1996, U.S. farmers received an average annual subsidy from the Federal government of

(a) $1.5 billion
(b) $5.5 billion
(c) $10.5 billion
(d) $15.5 billion

10. Which is a major rationale for public aid for agriculture in the United States?

(a) Farmers are more affected by competition from foreign producers than other parts of the economy.
(b) Farmers sell their products in highly competitive markets and buy resources in highly imperfect markets.
(c) Technological progress in farming has greatly increased the demand for farm products.
(d) The demand for farm products is income elastic.

11. Farm parity means that over time,

(a) the real income of the farmer remains constant
(b) a given output will furnish the farmer with a constant amount of real income
(c) the purchasing power of the farmer's nominal income remains constant
(d) the nominal income of the farmer will buy a constant amount of goods and services

12. If the index of prices paid by farmers were 1,000 and the prices received by farmers were 600, then the parity ratio would be

(a) 2.1
(b) 1.7
(c) 0.6
(d) 0.4

13. The necessary consequence of the government's support of agricultural prices at an above-equilibrium level is

(a) a surplus of agricultural products
(b) increased consumption of agricultural products
(c) reduced production of agricultural products
(d) the destruction of agricultural products

14. Another consequence of having government support farm prices at an above-equilibrium level is that consumers pay higher prices for farm products and

(a) consume more of these products and pay higher taxes
(b) consume less of these products and pay higher taxes
(c) consume more of these products and pay lower taxes
(d) consume less of these products and pay lower taxes

Use the graph below to answer Questions 15, 16, and 17. ***D*** *is the demand for and* ***S*** *is the supply of a certain product.*

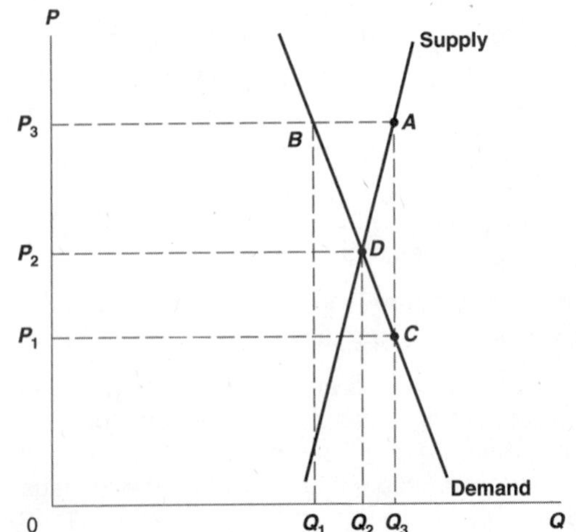

15. If the Federal government supported the price of this product at P_3, the total amount it would have to spend to purchase the surplus of the product would be
(a) $0Q_3AP_3$
(b) Q_1Q_3AB
(c) P_1CAP_3
(d) $0Q_1BP_3$

16. With a support price of P_3, the total income of producers of the product will be
(a) $0Q_3AP_3$
(b) $0Q_1BP_3$
(c) $0Q_3CP_1$
(d) $0Q_2DP_2$

17. With a support price of P_3, the amount spent by consumers will be
(a) $0Q_3AP_3$
(b) $0Q_1BP_3$
(c) $0Q_2DP_2$
(d) Q_1Q_3AB

*Answer Questions 18, 19, and 20 on the basis of the demand and supply schedules for agricultural product **Z** as shown below.*

Pounds of Z demanded	Price	Pounds of Z supplied
850	$1.30	1,150
900	1.20	1,100
950	1.10	1,050
1,000	1.00	1,000
1,050	.90	950
1,100	.80	900
1,150	.70	850

18. If the Federal government supports the price of **Z** at $1.30 a pound, then at this price, there is
(a) a surplus of 200 pounds of **Z**
(b) a surplus of 300 pounds of **Z**
(c) a surplus of 400 pounds of **Z**
(d) a shortage of 400 pounds of **Z**

19. With a Federal price support of $1.30 a pound, consumers spend
(a) $1,040, the Federal government spends $410, and farmers receive income from product **Z** of $1,450
(b) $1,105, the Federal government spends $390, and farmers receive income from product **Z** of $1,495
(c) $1,296, the Federal government spends $240, and farmers receive income from product **Z** of $1,320
(d) $1,045, the Federal government spends $110, and farmers receive income from product **Z** of $1,155

20. If instead of supporting the price the Federal government took actions to increase demand by 150 units at each price and to decrease supply by 150 units at each price, then the equilibrium price would be
(a) $1.00 and the income of farmers would be $1,000
(b) $1.10 and the income of farmers would be $1,320
(c) $1.20 and the income of farmers would be $1,260
(d) $1.30 and the income of farmers would be $1,300

21. To help eliminate the agricultural surpluses created by farm subsidies, the Federal government has tried to
(a) increase supply and demand
(b) decrease supply and demand
(c) increase supply and decrease demand
(d) decrease supply and increase demand

22. Which is a major criticism of agricultural subsidies?
(a) Restricting agricultural output increases farm prices but reduces farm incomes when demand is inelastic.
(b) The principal beneficiaries of these subsidies have been farmers with low incomes who would be better off in another type of work.
(c) They fail to treat the underlying problem of the misallocation of resources between agriculture and the rest of the economy.
(d) They duplicate other economic policies that are designed to increase the prices for agricultural products.

23. When farmers and farm organizations lobby Congress for a larger appropriation for agricultural price and income programs, according to public choice theory this action would be an example of
(a) confusing symptoms with causes
(b) misguided subsidies
(c) rent-seeking behavior
(d) political logrolling

24. Which has been a consequence of protective trade barriers for agricultural products established by the European Union (EU)?
(a) higher prices for U.S. agricultural products
(b) restriction of exports of EU agricultural products
(c) lower worldwide prices for agricultural products
(d) more sales of U.S. agricultural products to the EU

25. A major feature of the Freedom to Farm Act was the
(a) expansion of acreage allotments for farmers
(b) elimination of agricultural price supports for many crops
(c) bolstering of the domestic and foreign demand for U.S. agricultural products
(d) improving of the parity ratio so that the prices farmers paid for their inputs were similar to the prices farmers received for their output

■ PROBLEMS

1. The following table is a demand schedule for agricultural product **X**.

(1) Price	(2) Bushels of X demanded	(3) Bushels of X demanded
$2.00	600	580
1.80	620	600
1.60	640	620
1.40	660	640
1.20	680	660
1.00	700	680
.80	720	700
.60	740	720

a. Is demand elastic or inelastic in the price range given? ______________________

b. If the amount of **X** produced should increase from 600 to 700 bushels, the income of producers of **X** would ______ from $______ to $______; an increase of ______% in the amount of **X** produced would cause income to ______ by ______%.

c. If the amount of **X** produced were 700 bushels and the demand for **X** decreased from that shown in columns 1 and 2 to that shown in columns 1 and 3, the price of **X** would ______ from $______ to $______; the income of farmers would ______ from $______ to $______.

d. Assume that the government supports a price of $1.80, that the demand for **X** is that shown in columns 1 and 2, and that farmers grow 720 bushels of **X**.

(1) At the supported price there will be a surplus of ______ bushels of **X**.

(2) If the government buys this surplus at the support price the cost to the taxpayers of purchasing the surplus is $ ______.

(3) The total income of the farmers producing product **X** when they receive the support price of $1.80 per bushel for their entire crop of 720 bushels is $______.

(4) Had farmers sold the crop of 720 bushels at the free-market price, the price of **X** would be only $______ per bushel, and the total income of these farmers would be $ ______.

(5) The gain to farmers producing **X** from the price-support program is therefore $______.

(6) In addition to the cost to taxpayers of purchasing the surplus, consumers pay a price that is $______ greater than the free-market price and receive a quantity of **X** that is ______ bushels less than they would have received in a free market.

2. The following table gives the index of prices farmers paid in three different years. The price farmers received in year 1, the base year, for a certain agricultural product was $3.50 per bushel.

Year	Index of prices paid	Parity price	Price received	Parity ratio
1	100	$3.50	$3.50	100%
2	120	______	3.78	______%
3	200	______	5.25	______%

a. Compute the parity price of the product in years 2 and 3 and enter them in the table.

b. The prices received for the product in each year are also shown in the table. Complete the table by computing the parity *ratio* in years 2 and 3. (*Hint:* It is *not* necessary to construct an index of prices received in order to compute the parity ratio. This ratio can be computed by dividing the price received by the parity price.)

3. The demand schedule for agricultural product **Y** is given in columns 1 and 2 of the following table.

(1) Price	(2) Bales of Y demanded	(3) Bales of Y demanded
$5.00	40,000	41,000
4.75	40,200	41,200
4.50	40,400	41,400
4.25	40,600	41,600
4.00	40,800	41,800
3.75	41,000	42,000
3.50	41,200	42,200

a. If farmers were persuaded by the government to reduce the size of their crop from 41,000 to 40,000 bales, the income of farmers would ______ from $______ to $______.

b. If the crop remained constant at 41,000 bales and the demand for **Y** increased to that shown in columns 1 and 3, the income of farmers would ______ from $______ to $______.

4. Suppose the demand for sow jowls during a certain period of time was that shown in the table below and the Federal government wished to support the price of sow jowls at $.70 a pound.

Price (per pound)	Quantity demanded (pounds)
$1.00	1,000
.90	1,020
.80	1,040
.70	1,060
.60	1,080
.50	1,100
.40	1,120

a. If the output of sow jowls were 1,100 pounds during that period of time, the market price of sow jowls would be $______ and the Federal government would (buy, sell) ______ (how many) ______ pounds of sow jowls.

b. But if the output were 1,000 pounds during that period of time, the market price of sow jowls would be $______ and the Federal government would not have to intervene.

■ SHORT ANSWER AND ESSAY QUESTIONS

1. Why are the economics of agriculture and agricultural policy important topics for study?

2. What is the short-run farm problem and what are its causes?

3. Why does the demand for agricultural products tend to be inelastic? What are the implications for agriculture?

4. What have been the specific causes of the large increases in the supply of agricultural products since World War I?

5. Why has the demand for agricultural products failed to increase at the same rate as the supply of these products?

6. Explain why the farm population tends to be relatively immobile.

7. What is meant by "the farm program"? What particular aspect of the farm program has traditionally received the major attention of farmers and their representatives in Congress?

8. Why do agricultural interests claim that farmers have a special right to aid from the Federal government?

9. Explain the concept of parity and the parity ratio.

10. Why is the result of government-supported prices invariably a surplus of farm commodities?

11. What are the effects of farm price support programs on farmers, consumers, and resource allocation in the economy?

12. Identify and describe three ways that society at large loses from farm price support programs.

13. Explain how U.S. farm policy may cause environmental problems.

14. Discuss the effects of farm price support programs on international trade and developing nations.

15. What programs has the government used to try to restrict farm production? Why have these programs been relatively unsuccessful in limiting agricultural production?

16. How has the Federal government tried to increase the demand for farm products?

17. Explain the three major criticisms of agricultural subsidies.

18. How can public choice theory explain the persistence of Federal government support for farm subsidies for so many decades? Discuss the application of rent-seeking behavior, the special-interest effect, political logrolling, and hidden costs to subsidies for agriculture.

19. What domestic and international factors are contributing to the reduction in political support for agricultural subsidies?

20. What are the key features of the Freedom to Farm Act passed by Congress in 1996? How does it handle agricultural price support and income payments? What are the expected outcomes from this reform?

ANSWERS

Chapter 33 Agriculture: Economics and Policy

FILL-IN QUESTIONS

1. largest, competition, government, increased, public
2. inelastic, substitutes, utility
3. small, large, small, large
4. supply of, demand for, inelastic
5. low, value, hazards, purely , imperfectly
6. fixed
7. surpluses, buy
8. benefit, are hurt, increase, increase, decrease
9. inefficiency, over, large
10. increased, increased, negative
11. more, more, increase, decrease, negative
12. increase, decrease
13. acreage-allotment, new, demand
14. have not, low, inefficient
15. high, low, offset
16. public choice, rent-seeking, small, large
17. logrolling, clear, hidden
18. decrease, increase, negative, negative
19. increased, increased, decreased, decreased
20. eliminate, eliminate, income payments, increase, increase

TRUE-FALSE QUESTIONS

1. T, p. 684
2. F, p. 685
3. F, p. 686
4. F, pp. 686-687
5. F, p. 686
6. T, p. 687
7. F, p. 687
8. F, pp. 687-688
9. T, pp. 687-688
10. T, p. 688
11. T, pp. 689-690
12. F, p. 689
13. F, p. 690
14. F, pp. 690-691
15. F, p. 693
16. T, p. 693
17. T, p. 693
18. F, p. 694
19. T, p. 694
20. F, pp. 694-695
21. T, pp. 694-695
22. T, p. 695
23. F, p. 695
24. T, p. 696
25. F, pp. 696-697

MULTIPLE-CHOICE QUESTIONS

1. d, p. 685
2. b, pp. 685-686
3. d, p. 686
4. a, p. 686
5. d, pp. 687-688
6. c, pp. 687-688
7. c, p. 688
8. b, p. 689
9. b, p. 689
10. b, pp. 689-690
11. b, p. 690
12. c, p. 690
13. a, pp. 690-691
14. b, pp. 691-692
15. b, pp. 690-692
16. a, pp. 690-692
17. b, pp. 690-692
18. b, pp. 690-691
19. b, pp. 690-692
20. d, p. 693
21. d, p. 693
22. c, p. 694
23. c, pp. 694-695
24. c, p. 696
25. b, p. 696

PROBLEMS

1. *a.* increase; *b.* decrease, 1,200.00, 700.00, 16.67, decrease, 41.67; *c.* fall, 1.00, 0.80, fall, 700.00, 560.00; *d.* (1) 100, (2) 180, (3) 1,296, (4) 0.80, 576, (5) 720, (6) 1.00, 100
2. *a.* 4.20, 7.00; *b.* 90, 75
3. *a.* increase, 153,750.00, 200,000.00; *b.* increase, 153,750.00, 205,000.00
4. *a.* .50, buy, 40; *b.* 1.00

SHORT ANSWER AND ESSAY QUESTIONS

1. p. 684
2. pp. 684-685
3. p. 685
4. p. 687
5. pp. 687-688
6. p. 689
7. p. 689
8. pp. 689-690
9. p. 690
10. pp. 690-691
11. pp. 691-692
12. p. 692
13. p. 692
14. pp. 692-693
15. p. 693
16. p. 693
17. p. 694
18. pp. 694-695
19. pp. 695-696
20. p. 696

CHAPTER **34**

Income Inequality and Poverty

Chapter 34 examines another current problem in the economy of the United States: the unequal distribution of total income and poverty in the nation. Recall from Chapter 5 that the market system does not produce an equal distribution of income, so an economic function of government is income redistribution. Now you will learn about the extent of the income distribution problem and the actions government has taken to address it.

The chapter begins with a look at the facts of ***income inequality.*** You will discover that there is substantial income inequality in the United States, and it has increased in recent decades. You will also find out about the probable reasons for this growing income inequality and how it is measured with the ***Lorenz curve.*** You should also note that the degree of income inequality will vary according to the time period considered and the redistributive effect of taxes and public transfer payments on personal income.

The chapter also discusses the multiple *factors that contribute to income inequality.* The seven causes that are described should indicate to you that there is no simple explanation for why some people have more income than others. It is certainly not the result of some grand conspiracy; it can be attributed to ability differences, education and training, discrimination, preferences for jobs and risk, wealth, market power, and luck.

A case can be made for both income equality and income inequality. Few people, however, would advocate that there should be an absolutely equal distribution of income. The question to be decided is not one of inequality or equality but of how much or how little inequality there should be. A major insight from the chapter is that there is a fundamental tradeoff between equality and efficiency in the economy. If the society wants more equality, it will have to give up some economic efficiency in the form of less output and employment.

Much of the concern with income distribution focuses on the issue of ***poverty.*** In the later sections of the chapter you will learn about the extent of the poverty problem, who poverty affects, and the actions government has taken to alleviate it. Poverty and other income problems are addressed through the Federal government's *income-maintenance system.* This system consists of *social insurance programs,* such as social security, and *public assistance* or *welfare programs,* such as *Aid to Families with Dependent Children.* Each program was designed to meet the needs of different groups, either those who are poor or those who need to stabilize their incomes.

It is the welfare programs which have drawn the most extensive criticisms over the years, so the final sections of the chapter examine *public assistance programs.* There are many criticisms of these programs that have to do with their high cost, poor work incentives, and other concerns. Although you will find that it is not possible to design the perfect public assistance program because of conflicting goals, attempts have been made in recent years to reform the current system. This discontent with the public assistance system spawned several reforms that you will read about, such as workfare plans and the *Personal Responsibility Act* passed by Congress in 1996.

■ CHECKLIST

When you have studied this chapter you should be able to

☐ Present data from the textbook to support the conclusion that there is considerable income inequality in the United States.
☐ Report what has happened to the distribution of income in the United States in time periods since 1929.
☐ Identify three probable causes of growing income inequality in the past three decades.
☐ State what is measured on each axis when a Lorenz curve is used to describe the degree of income inequality and what area measures the extent of income inequality.
☐ Discuss the effects of time on income mobility and the distribution of income.
☐ Describe the effects of government redistribution on income equality in the United States.
☐ List and discuss the seven causes of an unequal distribution of income.
☐ Use the utility concept to argue the case for income inequality.
☐ Make the case for income inequality based on incentives and efficiency.
☐ Explain the tradeoff between equality and efficiency that is at the heart of the debate over how much income inequality is desirable.
☐ Define poverty using current government standards.
☐ Identify the groups in which poverty is concentrated.
☐ Describe the trends in the poverty rate since 1960.
☐ Give three reasons why poverty tends to be invisible.
☐ Contrast social insurance with public assistance.
☐ List three social insurance and four public assistance programs.

☐ Identify other public assistance programs that basically are in-kind transfers.
☐ Compare and contrast the characteristics of three hypothetical public assistance plans.
☐ State six major criticisms of the public assistance system.
☐ Describe the major features of state workfare plans for public assistance.
☐ Explain the key provisions of the Personal Responsibility Act of 1996.

■ CHAPTER OUTLINE

1. There is considerable ***income inequality*** in the U.S. economy.

a. The extent of the inequality can be seen by examining a personal-distribution-of-income table.

b. Since 1929 the real incomes received by all income classes have increased, and between 1929 and 1947 the relative distribution of personal income changed to reduce income inequality. From 1947–1969 there was a slight increase in the equality of income distribution, but from 1969–1996, the distribution of income moved to less equality.

c. Several factors have been cited as probable reasons for growing income inequality in the United States over the past three decades:

(1) increased demand for highly skilled workers compared with less-skilled workers;

(2) changed demographics from the influx of less-skilled baby boomers in the labor force, the increase in dual incomes among high-wage households, and more single-parent households earning less income; and

(3) a fall in wages and job security because of more import competition, the influx of less-skilled immigrants into the labor force, and a decline in unionism.

d. The degree of income inequality can be shown with a ***Lorenz curve.*** The percentage of families is plotted on the horizontal axis and the percentage of income is plotted on the vertical axis. The diagonal line between the two axes represents a perfectly equal distribution of income. A Lorenz curve that is bowed to the right from the diagonal shows income inequality.

2. Looking at income data over a longer time period than a single year shows that there is considerably less income inequality. In fact, there is significant individual and family *mobility* in income over time. The longer the time period, the more equal the distribution of income.

3. *Government redistribution* also has an effect on income distribution. The distribution of income can be examined after taxes and transfer payments are taken into account. When this adjustment is made, the distribution of income is more equal. Transfer payments account for most of the reduction in income inequality.

4. The impersonal market system does not necessarily result in a just or fair distribution of income; at least *seven factors explain why income inequality exists:*

(1) the distribution of abilities and skills of people;

(2) differences in education and training;

(3) discrimination in labor markets;

(4) preferences of certain types of jobs and willingness to accept risk on the job;

(5) inequalities in the distribution of wealth;

(6) market power in either resource or product markets; and

(7) other factors, such as luck, personal connections, and misfortunes.

5. The important question which society must answer is not whether there will or will not be income inequality but what is the best amount of inequality.

a. Those who argue for *equality* contend that it leads to the maximum satisfaction of consumer wants (utility) in the economy.

b. But those who argue for *inequality* contend that equality would reduce the incentives to work, save, invest, and take risks, and that these incentives are needed if the economy is to be efficient to produce as large an output (and income) as it is possible for it to produce from its available resources.

c. In the United States there is a tradeoff between economic equality and economic efficiency. A more nearly equal distribution of income results in less economic efficiency (a smaller domestic output) and greater economic efficiency leads to a more unequal distribution of income. The debate over the right amount of inequality depends, therefore, on how much output society is willing to sacrifice to reduce income inequality.

6. Aside from inequality in the distribution of income, there is a great concern today with the problem of ***poverty*** in the United States.

a. Using the generally accepted definition of poverty, 13.7% of the people in the U.S. economy lived in poverty in 1996.

b. The poor tend to be concentrated among certain groups, such as blacks, Hispanics, female-headed families, and children.

c. The poverty rate has varied over time, as shown in the text in Figure 34-4. It fell significantly from 1959–1969 and has ranged from about 11 to 15% since 1969.

d. Poverty in the United States tends to be invisible because the pool of poor people changes, the poor are isolated in large cities, and the poor do not have a political voice.

7. The ***income-maintenance system*** of the United States is intended to reduce poverty and includes both social insurance and ***public assistance (welfare) programs.***

a. OASDHI ***(Old Age, Survivors and Disability Health Insurance,*** also known as social security) and ***Medicare*** are the principal ***social insurance programs*** and are financed by taxes levied on employers and employees. The ***unemployment insurance*** programs maintained by the states and financed by taxes on employers are also a part of the social insurance program of the United States.

b. The public assistance programs include SSI (***Supplemental Security Income***), AFDC (***Aid to families***

with dependent children), food stamps, and ***Medicaid.*** Other public assistance programs provide ***in-kind transfer,*** such as education, job training, and housing assistance for the poor.

8. The ideal public assistance program has three basic goals: getting people out of poverty, providing incentives to work, having a reasonable cost. These goals can conflict, however, as three hypothetical public assistance plans illustrate.

a. In any plan, a family would be guaranteed a minimum income and the subsidy to a family would decrease as its earned income increases. But a comparison of three alternative plans reveals that the guaranteed income, the ***(benefit-reduction) rate*** at which the subsidy declines as earned income increases, and the ***(break-even) income*** at which the subsidy is no longer paid may differ.

b. The comparison of the plans also indicates there is a conflict among the goals of taking families out of poverty, maintaining incentives to work, and keeping the costs of the plan at a reasonable level, and that a tradeoff among the three goals is necessary because no one plan can achieve all three goals.

9. The public assistance system has been subject to criticisms over the years and has undergone recent reforms.

a. The many criticisms include administrative inefficiency, serious inequities in state welfare benefits, a lack of incentives to work, creating a culture of government dependency, breaking up families, fostering social divisiveness, and requiring a high cost.

b. Two approaches have been taken to reform welfare. (1) Workfare plans adopted by many states focus primarily on the AFDC program. Under these plans, public assistance recipients would be provided with education, training, health benefits, and work activities to help move them from public assistance to employment. (2) The ***Personal Responsibility Act*** of 1996 eliminated the Federal government's guarantee of cash assistance for poor families. In its place, states were given payments from the Federal government to operate their own public assistance systems. Limits were placed on the number of years that a person could receive AFDC benefits. Work requirements and restrictive provisions were also added for those receiving public assistance. The act has both supporters and critics.

■ HINTS AND TIPS

1. The distribution of income often raises issues of ***normative economics.*** For example, you may hear some people say that "no person should be allowed to make that much money" when a high salary is reported in the media for a sports star or business executive. This chapter, however, focuses on ***positive economics*** and offers some explanations for why there are wide differences in the distribution of income and why there is poverty. Look for those explanations based on positive economics.

2. The Lorenz curve looks more complicated than it really is. The curve shows how the percentage of income is distributed across the percentage of families. The easiest way to learn about the curve is to use income and family data to construct one. Problem 1 in this chapter will help you with that objective.

3. Public assistance plans differ in two ways because there are two variables that affect the outcomes: the size of the *minimum annual income* and the difference in the *benefit-reduction rate.* Problem 2 in this chapter illustrates how those two variables affect the outcomes from a plan.

■ IMPORTANT TERMS

income inequality
Lorenz curve
income mobility
noncash transfers
equality vs. efficiency tradeoff
poverty rate
entitlement programs
social insurance programs
Old Age, Survivors, and Disability Health Insurance (OASDHI)
Medicare
poverty
unemployment insurance (compensation)
public assistance (welfare) programs
Supplemental Security Income (SSI)
Aid to families with dependent children (AFDC)
food stamp program
Medicaid
Earned Income Tax Credit
Personal Responsibility Act

SELF-TEST

■ FILL-IN QUESTIONS

1. The data on the distribution of personal income by families suggest that there is considerable income (equality, inequality) ______________ in the United States. The data show that (7.6, 10.3) __________% of families have annual incomes of $100,000 or more, while __________% of families have an annual income of less than $10,000.

2. From 1929 to 1947, the percentage of total before-tax income received by the top quintile of families (increased, decreased) ________________, and the percentages received by the other four quintiles ________________. Since 1969, the distribution of income by quintiles has become (more, less) ______________ unequal.

3. The causes of the growing inequality of incomes are due to (more, less) ____________ demand for highly skilled workers, entrance into the labor force of ______________-experienced baby boomers, and ______________ families headed by single-wage earners. Other factors include (more, less) ______________ international competition that reduced the average wage of low-skilled workers,

_______________ immigration that increased the number of low-income families, and _______________ unionism.

4. Income inequality can be portrayed graphically by drawing a (Phillips, Lorenz) _______________ curve.

a. When such a curve is plotted, the cumulative percentage of (income, families) _______________ is measured along the horizontal axis, and the cumulative percentage of _______________ is measured along the vertical axis.

b. The curve which would show a completely (perfectly) equal distribution of income is a diagonal line which would run from the (lower, upper) _______________ left to the _______________ right corner of the graph.

c. The extent or degree of income inequality is measured by the area which lies between the line of complete equality and the (horizontal axis, Lorenz curve) _______________.

5. One major limitation with census data on the distribution of income in the United States is that the income-accounting period is too (short, long) _______________. There appears to be significant income (mobility, loss) _______________ over time. Also, the longer the time period considered, the (more, less) _______________ equal is the distribution of income.

6. The tax system and the transfer programs in the U.S. economy significantly (reduce, expand) _______________ the degree of inequality in the distribution of income. The distribution of household income is substantially less equal (before, after) _______________ taxes and transfers are taken into account and substantially more equal _______________ taxes and transfers are taken into account.

7. The important factors which explain (or cause) income inequality are differences in _______________, education and _______________, labor market _______________, differences in job tastes and _______________, the unequal distribution of _______________, market _______________, and _______________, connections, and misfortune.

8. Those who argue for the equal distribution of income contend that it results in the maximization of total (income, utility) _______________ in the economy, while those who argue for the unequal distribution of income believe it results in a greater total _______________.

9. The fundamental tradeoff is between equality and (welfare, efficiency) _______________. This means that less income equality leads to a (greater, smaller) _______________ total output, and a larger total output requires (more, less) _______________ income inequality.

10. The economic problem for a society that wants more equality is how to (minimize, maximize) _______________ the adverse effects on economic efficiency. Recent studies suggest that the (gain, loss) _______________ from the redistribution of income may be higher than originally thought.

11. Using the more or less official definition of poverty for 1996, the poor included any family of four with an income of less than ($16,036; $21,389) _______________ and any individual with an income of less than ($7,995; $10,354) _______________ a year. In 1996, about (7, 14) _______________% of the population or about (36, 54) _______________ million people were poor.

12. Poverty tends to be concentrated among the (young, elderly) _______________, among (whites, blacks and Hispanics) _______________ and in families headed by (men, women) _______________.

13. In the affluent economy of the United States, much of the poverty in the country is (visible, invisible) _______________ because the poverty pool (stays the same, changes) _______________ from year to year, the poor are often isolated in (small, large) _______________ cities, and the poor do not have a political voice.

14. One part of the income-maintenance system in the United States consists of social insurance programs such as (OASDHI, AFDC) _______________, (Medicare, Medicaid) _______________, and (employment, unemployment) _______________ compensation.

15. The other part of the income-maintenance system consists of public assistance or welfare programs such as (OASDHI, SSI) _______________, (AFDC, SEC) _______________, (Medicare, Medicaid) _______________, and the food stamp program. Other public assistance programs also provide help in the form of (cash, noncash) _______________ transfers, such as housing and education assistance.

16. An ideal public assistance program would try to achieve three goals at the same time: The plan should get individuals and families off or out of (Medicare, poverty) _______________, provide work (insurance, incentives) _______________, and ensure that the program (benefits, costs) _______________ are reasonable. In reality, these goals are (complementary, conflicting) _______________.

17. The two common elements of a public assistance plan are a (maximum, minimum) ______________ annual income provided by the government if the family earned no income and a (cost-benefit, benefit-reduction) ________________ rate which specifies the rate at which the transfer payment would be cut if earned income increases.

18. The criticisms of welfare are that there are administrative (efficiencies, inefficiencies) ______________, differences in welfare payments across states are (equitable, inequitable) ______________, and there is a lack of work (insurance, incentives) ______________. Other criticisms include a culture of welfare (equality, dependency) ______________, the incentives for families to (form, break up) ______________, the social (divisiveness, cohesion) ______________ between those working and those on welfare, and the (low, high) ______________ program costs.

19. Recent welfare reforms have included a variety of state-sponsored (food stamp, workfare) ______________ plans. These states use (OASDHI, AFDC) ___________ payments to provide work, training, and education to help people move from public assistance to work.

20. In 1996, the Congress passed a major welfare reform, the (Family Support, Personal Responsibility) ___________________ Act. It set a lifetime limit of (5, 10) __________ years for receiving AFDC payments and required able-bodied adults to work after (2, 4) _______ years of receiving assistance. Supporters of the law contend that it will end the culture of (compensation, welfare) ______________, whereas critics think that it places the (responsibility, blame) ______________ for poverty on its victims.

■ TRUE-FALSE QUESTIONS

Circle the T if the statement is true, the F if it is false.

1. If you knew the average income in the United States, you would know a great deal about income inequality in the United States. **T F**

2. The data on the distribution of personal income by families in the United States indicates that there is considerable income inequality. **T F**

3. There was a significant increase in income inequality in the 1929–1969 period. **T F**

4. The distribution of income was essentially the same in 1996 as it was in 1969. **T F**

5. The greater demand for highly skilled and highly educated workers is probably the significant contributor to the growing income inequality of the past three decades. **T F**

6. Growing income inequality means that the "rich are getting richer" in terms of absolute income. **T F**

7. In a Lorenz curve, the percentage of families in each income class is measured along the horizontal axis and the percentage of total income received by those families is measured on the vertical axis. **T F**

8. Income mobility is the movement of individuals or families from one income quintile to another over time. **T F**

9. Income is less than equally distributed over a longer time period than a shorter time period. **T F**

10. The distribution of income in the United States *after* taxes and transfers are taken into account is more equal than it is *before* taxes and transfers are taken into account. **T F**

11. Differences in tastes for market work relative to nonmarket activities is one reason for income differences in the United States. **T F**

12. The ownership of wealth is fairly equally distributed across households in the United States. **T F**

13. The basic argument for an equal distribution of income is that income equality is necessary if consumer satisfaction (utility) is to be maximized. **T F**

14. Those who favor equality in the distribution of income contend that it will lead to stronger incentives to work, save, and invest and thus to a greater national income and output. **T F**

15. In the tradeoff between equality and economic efficiency, an increase in equality will lead to an increase in efficiency. **T F**

16. Using the government definition of poverty, approximately 14% of the population was poor in 1996. **T F**

17. The incidence of poverty is very high among female-headed families. **T F**

18. OASDHI, Medicare, and unemployment compensation are public assistance or welfare programs. **T F**

19. Social insurance programs provide benefits for those who are unable to earn income because of permanent handicaps or who have no or very low income and also have dependent children. **T F**

20. The benefit-reduction rate is the rate at which government benefits decrease as the earned income of a family increases. **T F**

21. The lower the benefit-reduction rate, the smaller the incentives to earn additional income. **T F**

22. In comparing welfare plans, it is possible to achieve simultaneously the three goals of eliminating poverty, maintaining work incentives, and holding down program costs. **T F**

23. Those who have been critical of welfare contend that it creates dependency on government and reduces the motivation to work. **T F**

24. Workfare plans are basically designed to provide public funds for transportation so that people on welfare can get to work. **T F**

25. The Personal Responsibility Act was designed to reduce the dependence of the elderly on social security. **T F**

■ MULTIPLE-CHOICE QUESTIONS

Circle the letter that corresponds to the best answer.

1. Recent data on the personal distribution of income in the United States indicate that
(a) average incomes are falling
(b) average incomes are constant
(c) there is considerable income equality
(d) there is considerable income inequality

2. In 1996, the top 5% of families received about what percentage of total income before taxes?
(a) 10%
(b) 20%
(c) 30%
(d) 40%

3. Which of the following would be evidence of a decrease in income inequality in the United States?
(a) a decrease in the percentage of total personal income received by the lowest quintile
(b) an increase in the percentage of total personal income received by the highest quintile
(c) an increase in the percentage of total personal income received by the four lowest quintiles
(d) a decrease in the percentage of total personal income received by the four lowest quintiles

4. Since 1969, there has been
(a) a decrease in the percentage of total personal income received by the highest quintile
(b) an increase in the percentage of total personal income received by the lowest quintile
(c) an increase in the percentage of total personal income received by the highest quintile
(d) no significant change in the percentage of total personal income received by any of the five quintiles

5. When a Lorenz curve has been drawn, the degree of income inequality in an economy is measured by the
(a) slope of the diagonal that runs from the southwest to the northeast corner of the diagram
(b) slope of the Lorenz curve
(c) area between the Lorenz curve and the axes of the graph
(d) area between the Lorenz curve and the southwest-northeast diagonal

Use the following graph to answer Questions 6, 7, 8, and 9. The graph shows four different Lorenz curves (1, 2, 3, and 4).

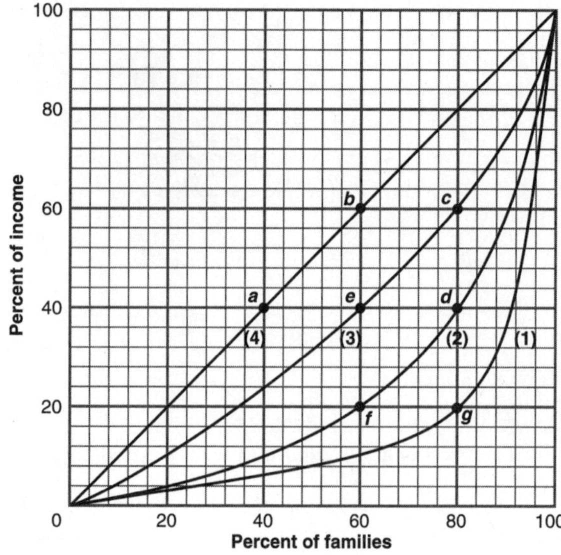

6. The greatest increase in income *equality* would occur with a shift in a Lorenz curve from
(a) 1 to 2
(b) 1 to 4
(c) 4 to 1
(d) 3 to 1

7. What point indicates that 80% of the families receive only 40% of the income?
(a) *c*
(b) *d*
(c) *e*
(d) *g*

8. The movement from point ***b*** to point ***f*** in the graph would indicate that
(a) 60% of families now receive 40% of income instead of 60% of income
(b) 60% of income goes to 20% of families instead of 60% of families
(c) 20% of income goes to 20% of families instead of 60% of families
(d) 60% of families now receive 20% of income instead of 60% of income

9. Which change would indicate that there has been an increase in income *inequality*? A movement from point
(a) ***b*** to ***a***
(b) ***g*** to ***d***
(c) ***g*** to ***f***
(d) ***e*** to ***d***

10. Suppose that Laura earns $5,000 in year 1 and $50,000 in year 2, while Kristin earns $50,000 in year 1 and only $5,000 in year 2. Is there income inequality for the two individuals?
(a) Both the annual and the 2-year data indicate equality.
(b) Both the annual and the 2-year data indicate inequality.
(c) The annual data indicate inequality, but 2-year data indicate equality.
(d) The annual data indicate equality, but 2-year data indicate inequality.

11. The empirical data indicate that the tax system and the transfer programs of the government

(a) significantly reduce the degree of inequality in the distribution of income
(b) produce only a slight reduction in the degree of inequality in the distribution of income
(c) significantly increase the degree of inequality in the distribution of income
(d) produce only a slight increase in the degree of inequality in the distribution of income

12. Most of the contribution to government redistribution of income comes from

(a) taxes
(b) transfers
(c) income mobility
(d) unemployment insurance

13. Which is one cause of unequal income distribution in the United States?

(a) an equitable distribution of wealth and property
(b) differences in education and training
(c) the high levels of noncash transfers
(d) the low benefit-reduction rate

14. The fact that some individuals are willing to take riskier jobs or assume more risk in their business is one major reason why there are differences in

(a) social insurance programs
(b) entitlement programs
(c) welfare
(d) income

15. Suppose Ms. Anne obtains 5 units of utility from the last dollar of income received by her, and Mr. Charles obtains 8 units of utility from the last dollar of his income. Those who favor an equal distribution of income would

(a) advocate redistributing income from Charles to Anne
(b) advocate redistributing income from Anne to Charles
(c) be content with this distribution of income between Anne and Charles
(d) argue that any redistribution of income between them would increase total utility

16. The case for income inequality is primarily made on the basis that income inequality

(a) is reduced by the transfer payment programs for the poor
(b) is necessary to maintain incentives to work and produce output
(c) depends on luck and chance, which cannot be corrected by government action
(d) is created by education and training programs that distort the distribution of income

17. The debate over income redistribution focuses on the tradeoff between equality and

(a) efficiency
(b) unemployment
(c) economic growth
(d) economic freedom

18. The leaky bucket analogy is used to describe the

(a) welfare reform mess
(b) trends in the poverty rate
(c) economic loss from income redistribution programs
(d) piecemeal approach toward income maintenance programs

19. The officially accepted poverty line for a family of four in 1996 was about

(a) $ 7,363
(b) $ 8,590
(c) $10,121
(d) $16,036

20. In 1996, which group had the smallest percentage in poverty?

(a) Hispanics
(b) families headed by women
(c) children under 18 years of age
(d) the elderly (65 years and older)

21. An example of a social insurance program would be

(a) Medicare
(b) Medicaid
(c) food stamps
(d) Aid to families with dependent children

22. Which of the following is designed to provide a nationwide minimum income for the aged, the blind, and the disabled?

(a) SSI
(b) FFS
(c) AFDC
(d) OASDHI

23. The goals of welfare plans often conflict because it is difficult to construct a plan that

(a) provides reasonable income levels and incentives to work for the poor, but is not too costly
(b) is not subject to substantial administrative costs and bureaucratic red tape
(c) does not discriminate against those individuals with similar circumstances, but who have similar needs
(d) promotes family unity and does not create a "culture of poverty" among the participants in the program

24. Which is a major criticism of the welfare system that led to recent reforms? Welfare payments

(a) give incentives for people to work but not to save for periods of unemployment
(b) create dependency on government and reduce personal responsibility
(c) encourage the formation of families and enables them to get more welfare benefits
(d) fail to provide a minimum income for the aged, blind, and disabled

25. Workfare plans of several states

(a) provide a high level of guaranteed income for low-income working families
(b) provide education and job training opportunities for welfare recipients to help and require them to become employed
(c) decrease the level of support for social security programs and transfer the funds to improve the Aid to families with dependent children program
(d) substitute the payment of cash for the use of food stamps for those willing to go to work

■ PROBLEMS

1. The distribution of personal income among families in a hypothetical economy is shown in the table at the bottom of the page.

a. Complete the table by computing the

(1) percentage of all families in each income class and all lower classes; enter these figures in column 4.

(2) percentage of total income received by each income class and all lower classes; enter these figures in column 5.

b. From the distribution of income data in columns 4 and 5, it can be seen that

(1) families with less than $15,000 a year income constitute the lowest ______% of all families and receive ______% of the total income.

(2) families with incomes of $50,000 a year or more constitute the highest ______% of all families and receive ______% of the total income.

c. Use the figures you entered in columns 4 and 5 to draw a Lorenz curve on the graph on page 391. (Plot the seven points and the zero-zero point and connect them with a smooth curve.) Be sure to label the axes.

(1) Draw a diagonal line which would indicate complete equality in the distribution of income.

(2) Shade the area of the graph that shows the degree of income inequality.

2. The following table contains different possible earned incomes for a family of a certain size.

Earned income	Transfer payment	Total income
$ 0	$5,000	$5,000
5,000	____	____
10,000	____	____
15,000	____	____
20,000	____	____
25,000	____	____

a. Assume that $5,000 is the minimum annual income provided by government for a family of this size and that the benefit-reduction rate is 20%. Enter the transfer payment and the total income at each of the five remaining earned-income levels. (*Hint*: 20% of $5,000 is $1,000.)

(1) This program retains strong incentives to work because whenever the family earns an additional $5,000 its total income increases by $______.

(2) But this program is costly because the family receives a subsidy until its earned income, the break-even income, is ______.

b. To reduce the break-even income, the benefit-reduction rate is raised to 50%. Complete the following table.

Earned income	Transfer payment	Total income
$ 0	$5,000	$5,000
2,500	____	____
5,000	____	____
7,500	____	____
10,000	____	____

(1) This program is less costly than the previous one because the family only receives a subsidy until it earns the break-even income of $______,

(2) but the incentives to work are less because whenever the family earns an additional $5,000 its total income increases by only $______.

c. Both the previous two welfare programs had a minimum annual income of only $5,000. Assume that the minimum annual income is raised to $7,500 and the benefit-reduction rate is kept at 50%. Complete the following table.

Earned income	Transfer payment	Total income
$ 0	$7,500	$7,500
3,000	____	____
6,000	____	____
9,000	____	____
12,000	____	____
15,000	____	____

(1) Personal income class	(2) Percentage of all families in this class	(3) Percentage of total income received by this class	(4) Percentage of all families in this and all lower classes	(5) Percentage of total income received by this and all lower classes
Under $10,000	18	4	____	____
$10,000–$14,999	12	6	____	____
$15,000–$24,999	14	12	____	____
$25,000–$34,999	17	14	____	____
$35,000–$49,999	19	15	____	____
$50,000–$74,999	11	20	____	____
$75,000 and over	9	29	____	____

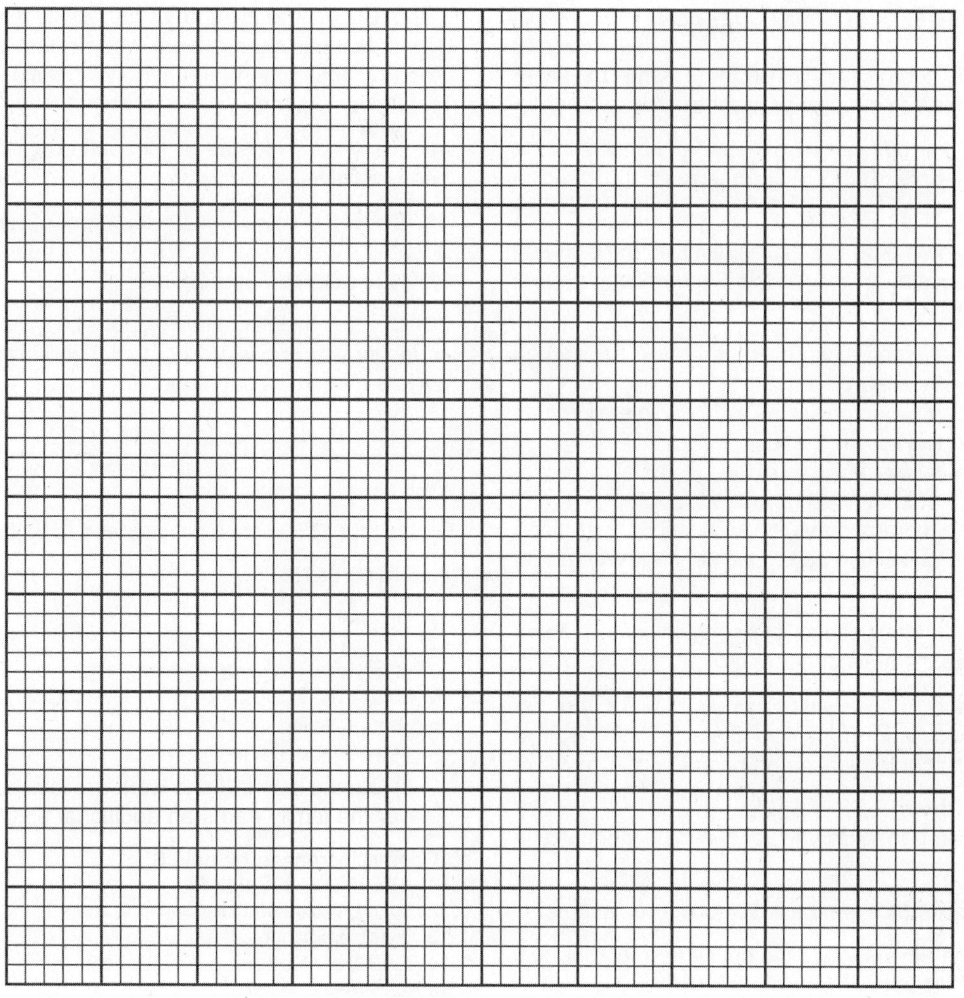

(1) This program is more costly than the previous one because the break-even income has risen to $____________.

(2) The incentives to earn additional income are no better in this program than in the previous one. But to improve these incentives by reducing the benefit-reduction rate to 40% would raise the break-even income to (divide the minimum annual income by the benefit-reduction rate) $_______________.

d. To summarize:

(1) Given the minimum annual income provided by government, the lower the benefit-reduction rate the (greater, less) ________________ are the incentives to earn additional income and the (greater, less) ______________ is the break-even income and the cost of the welfare program,

(2) and given the benefit-reduction rate, the greater the minimum annual income, the (greater, less) ______________ is the break-even income and the cost of the program,

(3) but to reduce the break-even income and the cost of the program requires either a(n) (increase, decrease) ______________ in the benefit-reduction rate or a(n) ______________ in the minimum annual income.

3. Match the terms with the phrase using the appropriate number.

1. entitlement programs
2. noncash transfers
3. public assistance programs
4. social insurance programs

a. Government programs such as social insurance, food stamps, Medicare, and Medicaid that guarantee particular levels of transfer payments to all who fit the programs' criteria. ______

b. Government programs that pay benefits to those who are unable to earn income (because of permanent handicaps or because they have very low incomes). ______

c. Government transfer payments in the form of goods and services rather than money. ______

d. Government programs that replace earnings lost when people retire or are temporarily unemployed. ______

SHORT ANSWER AND ESSAY QUESTIONS

1. How much income inequality is there in the U.S. economy? Cite figures to support your conclusion.

2. How has the distribution of income changed in the United States since 1929? What has been the trend in income distribution since 1969?

3. What are three probable explanations for the increase in income inequality in the United States over the past three decades?

4. What is measured along each of the two axes when a Lorenz curve is drawn?
(a) If the distribution of income were completely equal, what would the Lorenz curve look like?
(b) If one family received all of the income of the economy, what would the Lorenz curve look like?
(c) After the Lorenz curve for an economy has been drawn, how is the degree of income inequality in that economy measured?

5. Explain how time affects the distribution of income and interpretations of income trends.

6. What effect do taxes and transfers have on the distribution of income in the United States? How much of this change in the distribution of income is the result of the transfer payments made by government?

7. What seven factors contribute to income inequality in the United States?

8. State the case for an equal distribution of income.

9. Explain the advantage to the nation from an unequal distribution of income.

10. What is the fundamental tradeoff involving income inequality? Explain the leaky bucket analogy.

11. What is poverty? What is the minimum income level below which the Federal government defines a person or family as "in poverty"? How many people and what percentage of the U.S. population are "in poverty" using this definition?

12. What characteristics—other than the small amounts of money they have to spend—do the greatest concentrations of the poor families of the nation *tend* to have?

13. What have been the trends in the poverty rate since 1960? In the 1980s and 1990s?

14. Why does poverty in the United States tend to be invisible or hidden?

15. Explain the difference between social insurance and public assistance (or welfare). List and briefly describe three social insurance and the public assistance programs that constitute the income-maintenance system of the United States.

16. What are the three goals of an ideal welfare program? Explain why there is a conflict among these goals—why all three goals cannot be achieved simultaneously.

17. Explain how poverty and the unequal distribution of income would be reduced by three hypothetical welfare plans. Be sure to include in your explanation the definition of the minimum annual income that would be provided by government, the benefit-reduction rate, and the break-even income.

18. State six criticisms of the welfare system that have been made in recent years.

19. Describe some major features of workfare plans adopted by some states. What have been some results from the adoption of these plans?

20. Discuss the Personal Responsibility Act of 1996. Describe the key provisions of the act and explain what supporters and critics say about it.

ANSWERS

Chapter 34 Income Inequality and Poverty

FILL-IN QUESTIONS

1. inequality, 10.3, 7.6
2. decreased, increased, more
3. more, less, more, more, more, less
4. Lorenz; *a.* families, income; *b.* lower, upper; *c.* Lorenz curve
5. short, mobility, more
6. reduce, before, after
7. ability, training, discrimination, risks, wealth, power, luck
8. utility, income
9. efficiency, greater, more
10. minimize, loss
11. $16,036, $7,995, 14, 36
12. young, blacks and Hispanics, women
13. invisible, changes, large
14. OASDHI, Medicare, unemployment
15. SSI, AFDC, Medicaid, noncash
16. poverty, incentives, costs, conflicting
17. minimum, benefit-reduction
18. inefficiencies, inequitable, incentives, dependency, break up, divisiveness, high
19. workfare, AFDC
20. Personal Responsibility, 5, 2, welfare, blame

TRUE-FALSE QUESTIONS

1. F, pp. 701-702
2. T, pp. 701-702
3. F, p. 702
4. F, pp. 702-703
5. T, p. 703
6. T, p. 704
7. T, p. 704
8. T, pp. 704-705
9. F, p. 705
10. T, p. 705
11. T, p. 707
12. F, p. 707
13. T, pp. 708-709
14. F, pp. 708-709
15. F, pp. 709-710
16. T, p. 710
17. T, pp. 710-711
18. F, pp. 712-713
19. F, p. 713
20. T, p. 714
21. F, p. 714
22. F, pp. 714-715
23. T, pp. 716-717
24. F, p. 717
25. F, p. 717

MULTIPLE-CHOICE QUESTIONS

1. d, pp. 701-702
2. b, p. 702
3. c, pp. 702-703
4. c, pp. 702-703
5. d, p. 704
6. b, p. 704
7. b, p. 704
8. d, p. 704
9. d, p. 704
10. c, pp. 704-705
11. a, p. 705
12. b, p. 705
13. b, pp. 705-707
14. d, pp. 705-707
15. b, p. 708-709
16. b, p. 709
17. a, pp. 709-710
18. c, p. 709
19. d, p. 710
20. d, p. 711
21. a, pp. 712-713
22. a, p. 713
23. a, p. 714
24. b, pp. 716-717
25. b, p. 717

PROBLEMS

1. *a.* (1) column 4: 18, 30, 44, 61, 80, 91, 100, (2) column 5: 4, 10, 22, 36, 51, 71, 100; *b.* (1) 30, 10, (2) 20, 49
2. *a.* Transfer payment: 4,000, 3,000, 2,000, 1,000, 0; Total income: 9,000, 13,000, 17,000, 21,000, 25,000, (1) 4,000, (2) 25,000; *b.* Transfer payment: 3,750, 2,500, 1,250, 0; Total income: 6,250, 7,500, 8,750, 10,000, (1) 10,000, (2) 2,500; *c.* Transfer payment: 6,000, 4,500, 3,000, 1,500, 0; Total income: 9,000, 10,500, 12,000, 13,500, 15,000, (1) 15,000, (2) 18,750; *d.* (1) greater, greater, (2) greater, (3) increase, decrease
3. *a.* 1; *b.* 3; *c.* 2; *d.* 4

SHORT ANSWER AND ESSAY QUESTIONS

1. pp. 701-702, 705-707
2. pp. 702-703
3. pp. 703-704
4. p. 704
5. pp. 704-705
6. p. 705
7. pp. 705-707
8. pp. 708-709
9. p. 709
10. pp. 709-710
11. p. 710
12. pp. 710-711
13. pp. 710-711
14. p. 711
15. pp. 712-714
16. pp. 714-715
17. pp. 714-715
18. pp. 716-717
19. p. 717
20. pp. 717-718

CHAPTER **35**

The Economics of Health Care

Health care has been a topic of major national debate in recent years. One reason is that health care costs have risen. Another reason is that fewer people in the United States are being covered by the health care system or they have only limited access to health care. The first four sections of the chapter discuss the rising costs and limited access problems of the U.S. health care system. The economics you learned in previous chapters will now be put to good use in analyzing these twin problems of health care.

The explanations for the first problem—the rapid rise in costs—relies on your prior knowledge of supply and demand. Before you can appreciate the demand and supply factors that influence health care costs, however, you need to recognize the *peculiar features* of the market for health care that make it different from the other markets with which you are familiar. Society is reluctant to ration health care based solely on price or income, as is the case with most products. The market is also subject to asymmetric information between the buyer (patient) and seller (health care provider), with the seller making most of the decisions about the amount of services to be consumed and the prices to be paid. Medical care generates spillover benefits that may lead to underproduction in the private market and require some government intervention to achieve efficient allocation of resources. The system of third-party payments reduces the price to buyers and distorts the traditional price signals of the marketplace.

With this background in mind, you are ready to read about the ***demand*** for health care. The demand factors have significantly increased the cost of health care. Health care is relatively price insensitive, so increases in price result in little reduction in the quantity consumed. The demand for health care has increased as per capita incomes increased because health care is a normal good. Adding to the demand pressures are an aging population, unhealthy lifestyles, and the practices of physicians that are influenced by medical ethics and a fee-for-payment system. The medical insurance system also contributes to increased demand by reducing the costs to the consumer, as does the Federal government with its tax subsidy of employer-financed health insurance.

Supply has not increased at the same rate as demand in health care. Although the supply of physicians has increased, it has had little effect on reducing health care costs. Health care is also an area of slow productivity growth because of the personal attention required for services. Also, the development and use of new medical technology have increased cost pressures in health care rather than reduced them.

The proposed *reforms* for the health care system that you will read about in the last section of the chapter focus on achieving universal coverage and cost containment. A number of schemes have been proposed to increase coverage. These include play-or-pay insurance programs for businesses, tax credits and vouchers, and a national health insurance system. Suggestions for cost containment call for increased uses of incentives, such as increased deductibles and copayments for medical services, the adoption of more managed care such as is found in health maintenance organizations, and tighter controls over Medicare payments based on specific classifications of treatments. The reform section concludes with a brief discussion of recent health care legislation considered by Congress.

■ CHECKLIST

When you have studied this chapter you should be able to

☐ Describe the major characteristics of the health care industry.
☐ State two problems with the health care system.
☐ Cite data on the dimensions of cost increases in health in absolute and relative terms.
☐ Discuss the quality of medical care in the United States.
☐ Give three economic implications of rising health care expenditures.
☐ Explain the basic problem with rising health care expenditures.
☐ Identify the reasons why people are medically uninsured and the consequences of such a condition.
☐ List four peculiarities of the market for health care.
☐ Discuss the demand factors which have increased health care costs over time.
☐ Explain how health insurance affects health care costs.
☐ Use supply and demand analysis to explain the rapid rise in health care expenditures.
☐ Identify the supply factors affecting the costs of health care.
☐ Evaluate the relative importance of demand and supply factors affecting health care.

□ Discuss proposals to reform the health care system so that there can be universal access.
□ Cite arguments for and against national health insurance.
□ Explain how incentives can be used to help contain health care costs.
□ Describe the major features of the Health Security Act proposal of the Clinton administration.
□ Discuss how Congress has addressed the issues of universal health coverage and medical savings accounts.

■ CHAPTER OUTLINE

1. The *health care industry* in the United States covers a broad range of services provided by doctors, hospitals, dentists, nursing homes, and medical laboratories. It employs about 9 million people, over 600,000 of whom are physicians. There are about 6,000 hospitals. Some 680 million visits are made to physicians each year.

2. Two major problems face the health care system. The *costs* of health care are high and growing rapidly. Some U.S. citizens do not have *access* to health care or adequate coverage by the system.

3. *Health care costs* are rising for many reasons.

a. Costs have risen in absolute and relative terms.
(1) Total health care spending pays for many items and is obtained from many sources, as shown in text Figure 35-1.
(2) Expenditures were 14% of domestic output in 1995 and may rise to 16% by the year 2000.
(3) The highest per capita health care expenditures in the world are in the United States.

b. There is general agreement that medical care in the United States is probably the best in the world, which is a consequence of its high expenditures for health care. That does not mean, however, that the United States is the healthiest nation. In fact, it ranks low internationally on many health indicators.

c. Rising health care expenditures and costs have negative economic effects that include
(1) reduced access and coverage for workers and others;
(2) labor market problems in the form of slower wage growth, less labor mobility, and more use of part-time or temporary workers; and
(3) adding to budget demands at all levels of government.

d. The basic problem is that there is an *overallocation* of resources to health care and less economic efficiency in the use of the nation's resources.

4. A large percentage of the population (about 16% in 1996) have *no medical coverage.* Those medically uninsured are generally the poor, although some young adults with good health choose not to buy insurance. Low-income workers and those employed in smaller businesses are less likely to be covered, or have limited coverage, because of the higher costs of health care for smaller firms.

5. There are many reasons for the rapid rise in health care costs.

a. The market for health care is different from other markets because of ethical-equity considerations, asymmetric information, spillover benefits, and third-party insurance.

b. Several ***demand factors*** have increased health care costs over time.
(1) Health care is a normal good with an income elasticity of about +1.0, so that spending on it will rise in proportion to per capita income. Health care is also price inelastic, which means that total health care spending will increase even as the price of health care rises.
(2) The aging population of the United States increases the demand for health care.
(3) Unhealthy lifestyles because of alcohol, tobacco, or drug abuse increases the demand for and spending on health care.
(4) Doctors can add to costs because there is ***asymmetric information***—the provider knows more than the buyer—and thus there is supplier-induced demand. Doctors have no strong incentive to reduce costs for the buyer and perhaps an economic interest in increasing them because they are paid on a *fee-for-service* basis. Two other doctor practices may contribute to increased costs: "defensive medicine" may be used to prevent possible lawsuits, and medical ethics require the best (and often the most expensive) procedures.

c. Although health insurance plays a positive role in giving people protection against health risks, it contributes to increased costs and demand for health care.
(1) It creates a ***moral hazard problem*** by encouraging some people to be less careful about their health and gives some people incentives to overconsume health care than would be the case without insurance.
(2) Health insurance financed by employers is exempt from both Federal income and payroll taxation. This ***tax subsidy*** increases the demand for health care.
(3) From a supply and demand perspective, health insurance reduces the price to the buyer below the no-insurance equilibrium price. This lower price induces more health care consumption and creates an efficiency or welfare loss for society.

d. ***Supply factors*** affect health care costs.
(1) Physicians have high incomes that add to medical costs, although it is difficult to identify what specific factors determine the high income levels.
(2) The productivity growth in health care has been slow.
(3) Most new medical technology has increased costs, despite the fact that some technological advances in medicine have decreased costs.

e. Only a relatively minor portion of the increase in health care costs can be attributed to increasing incomes, the aging of the population, or defensive medicine. The most likely explanations for the rise in health care costs are the use of new medical technology and a third-party system of insurance payments with little incentive to control costs.

6. *Reforms* for the health care system call for increased access to health care and cost containment.

a. There are three basic proposals for increasing access.
(1) ***"Play-or-pay"*** schemes would require all employers either to fund a basic health insurance program (play) or finance health care through a special payroll tax (pay).
(2) *Tax credits and vouchers* are another option designed to make health insurance more affordable for the poor.
(3) A ***national health insurance (NHI)*** program would provide universal coverage at no cost or at a low cost and would be financed out of tax revenues. The basic arguments for NHI are its simplicity, the choice of physician, the reduction in administrative costs, the improvement in labor market mobility, and increased government bargaining power to contain costs. Arguments against NHI are the ineffectiveness of price controls, increased waiting for doctors and tests, the inefficiency of the Federal government, and income redistribution problems.
b. To contain health care costs, alternatives that use incentives have been adopted.
(1) Insurance companies have increased deductibles and copayments to provide more incentives for consumers to reduce health expenditures.
(2) Managed care organizations are being more widely used to control health care costs and are of two types. ***Preferred provider organizations (PPOs)*** offer discounts to insurance companies and consumers who use them. ***Health maintenance organizations (HMOs)*** are prepaid health plans that closely monitor health care costs because they operate with a fixed budget.
(3) The *diagnosis-related-group (DRG)* system has been used to classify treatments and fix fees in an effort to reduce the costs of Medicare payments, although the DRG systems may also reduce the quality of care.
c. The status report on health care reform shows several recent developments. In 1993, the Clinton administration submitted the Health Security Act (HSA) to Congress. It would have provided universal insurance coverage for a standard package of benefits that would have been financed by employer mandates. The complexity of HSA and fears about the creation of a health bureaucracy contributed to its defeat. Since then, Congress has passed more modest health legislation that allows workers to maintain health insurance when changing jobs or becoming self-employed. Congress also authorized the trial use of medical savings accounts as a tax-deductible way for selected groups to pay for medical expenses.

■ HINTS AND TIPS

1. This chapter contains many health care terms (e.g., preferred provider organization) with which you may not be familiar. Make sure you review the meaning of each important term before reading the chapter and taking the self-test in this chapter.

2. The two economic ideas that are the most difficult to comprehend are asymmetric information and moral hazard. The buyer and seller information problems were discussed extensively in Chapter 30. To remember the meaning of these ideas, associate them with examples from the text or ones that you construct.

3. This chapter uses the concepts of income elasticity and price elasticity of demand to explain the demand for health care. Reread the text discussion of these concepts in Chapter 20 if you cannot recall how these elasticities are defined.

4. The graphical presentation of a market with and without health insurance (Figure 35-3) is a relatively straightforward application of supply and demand. The one difficult concept is efficiency loss. This concept was originally discussed in Chapter 31 as it related to taxation; you will now see it applied to health care.

■ IMPORTANT TERMS

deductibles
copayments
fee-for-service
tax subsidy
"play or pay"
national health insurance
preferred provider organization (PPO)
health maintenance organization (HMO)
diagnosis-related-group (DRG)

SELF-TEST

■ FILL-IN QUESTIONS

1. The health care industry in the United States employs about (2, 9) __________ million people, about (300; 600) ______________ thousand of whom are physicians. There are more than (3,000; 6,000) ____________ hospitals.

2. The twin problems facing the health care system are high and rapidly growing (benefits, costs) ____________ and the fact that many U.S. citizens (do, do not) _______ have access to health care or adequate coverage by the system.

3. Health care spending was about (6, 12) ________% of domestic output in 1965 and was ________% of domestic output in 1995, a sizeable change. Compared to other nations, the United States has the (lowest, highest) ______________ level of per capita health care expenditures, and it is also the nation with the (slowest, fastest) ______________ growth in these expenditures.

4. The economic effects of rising health care costs are (more, less) ______________ access to health care and

______________ coverage for workers. There are labor market problems, such as (more, less) ______________ wage growth, ______________ labor mobility, and (more, less) ______________ use of temporary or part-time workers. Health care costs also create ______________ demands on the budgets of governments at the Federal, state, and local levels.

5. The basic problem with growing health care expenditures is that there is an (underallocation, overallocation) ______________ of resources to health care. The large expenditures for health care mean that at the margin, health care is worth (more, less) ______________ than alternative products that could have been produced with the resources.

6. The uninsured represent about (16, 32) _______% of the population. They are concentrated among the poor, many of whom work at (low-wage, high-wage) ______________ jobs, (do, do not) __________ qualify for Medicaid, and may work for (small, large) ______________ businesses. Others who are uninsured include (older, younger) ______________ adults in excellent health and people with (minor, major) ___________ health problems.

7. The market for health care is different from other markets because of (technology, ethical-equity) ________________ considerations, (symmetric, asymmetric) ______________ information, spillover (costs, benefits) ______________, and (first-party, third-party) ______________ insurance.

8. Health care is a(n) (inferior, normal, superior) ______________ good with an income elasticity of about (0, 1) ________. In this case, a 10% increase in incomes will result in a (1, 10) _______% increase in health care expenditures.

9. Health care is price (inelastic, elastic) ______________, with a coefficient estimated to be (0.2, 1.5) __________. The price elasticity of demand for health care means that a 10% increase in price would decrease health care spending by (2, 15) __________%.

10. Other factors increasing the demand for health care include an (older, younger) ______________ population and lifestyles that are often (entertaining, unhealthy) ______________.

11. The demand for health care is affected by the problem of asymmetric information in the practice of medicine, which means that the (demander, supplier) ______________ will decide the types and amount of health care to be consumed. Physicians (have, do not have) ______________ an incentive to reduce costs for the buyer and perhaps an economic interest in increasing them because they are paid on a (play-or-pay, fee-for-service) ______________ basis.

12. Increased demand and costs can arise from the practice of (offensive, defensive) ______________ medicine to limit the possibility of a lawsuit or from medical (insurance, ethics) ______________ that require the use of the best medical techniques by doctors.

13. Health insurance increases demand because it creates a moral (dilemma, hazard) ______________ problem. It makes people be (more, less) ______________ careful about their health and gives people incentives to (underconsume, overconsume) ______________ health care than they otherwise would without health insurance.

14. Health insurance financed by employers is (taxed, tax-exempt) ______________ at the Federal level. This (tax, tax subsidy) ______________ (increases, decreases) ______________ the demand for health care.

15. In a supply and demand analysis, health insurance (raises, lowers) ______________ the price to the buyer below the no-insurance equilibrium price. This (higher, lower) ______________ price induces (less, more) ______________ health care consumption and creates an efficiency (benefit, loss) ______________ for society.

16. The supply factors that affect health care costs include the (high, low) ______________ cost of physician services, (fast, slow) ______________ growth in productivity in health care, and the use of (new, old) ______________ medical technology.

17. Increasing access to health care could be achieved by a (fee-for-service, play-or-pay) ______________ requirement for all employers either to fund a basic health insurance program or pay a special payroll tax to finance health care for workers. Another option would be the use of tax (levies, credits) ______________ and vouchers to make health insurance more affordable for the poor.

18. A program that would provide universal coverage at no cost or at a low cost and would be financed out of tax revenues is (managed care, national health insurance) ______________.

a. Some of its advantages are that it is a simple and (direct, indirect) ______________ way to provide universal coverage, it allows patients to choose their own (insurance, physician) ______________, it (increases, decreases) ______________ administrative costs, it ______________ labor market mobility, and (increases, decreases) _______________ government bargaining power with medical care providers.

b. One argument against it is the ineffectiveness of price (ceilings, floors) _______________ on physician services. It may also (increase, decrease) _______________ waiting for doctors and tests, _______________ the inefficiency of the Federal government, and (increase, decrease) _______________ redistribution of income.

19. Actions have been taken to contain health care costs. Insurance companies have (increased, decreased) _______________ deductibles and copayments to provide incentives for consumers to reduce expenditures, and there has been _______________ use of preferred provider organizations (PPOs) to get consumers to use lower-cost health care providers. Businesses and other organizations have formed health maintenance organizations (HMOs) that have prepaid health plans and use a (fee-for-service, managed care) _______________ approach to control health costs. Medical treatments have been classified according to a diagnosis-related-group (DRG) system and the government has (fixed, variable) _______________ fee payments for each treatment.

20. Congress has considered several types of health legislation in recent years.

a. A 1993 proposal of the Clinton administration for health reform was the Health Security Act (HSA), which sought to provide (limited, universal) _______________ insurance coverage. Criticisms of the HSA were that it was too (simple, complex) _______________ and that it would (decrease, increase) _______________ costly government bureaucracy, so Congress (did, did not) _______________ pass it.

b. In 1996, Congress passed the Health Insurance Portability and Accountability Act that (requires, allows) _______________ workers to buy health insurance when they change jobs. Congress also introduced (dental, medical) _______________ savings accounts on a trial basis.

■ TRUE-FALSE QUESTIONS

Circle the T if the statement is true, the F if it is false.

1. The twin problems of health care are the rapidly rising cost of health care and the general decline in the quality of health care. **T F**

2. Medicaid is the nationwide Federal health care program available to social security beneficiaries and the disabled. **T F**

3. Per capita expenditures on health care are high in the United States but even higher in Japan and Britain. **T F**

4. Rising health care costs reduce workers' access to health care. **T F**

5. Increasing health care expenditures cause problems for the budget of Federal, state, and local governments. **T F**

6. Aggregate consumption of health care is so great that at the margin it is worth more than the alternative goods and services these resources could otherwise have produced. **T F**

7. About 40% of the population of the United States had no health insurance for the entire year in 1992. **T F**

8. Minimum-wage workers have health insurance because their insurance premiums are covered by the Federal government. **T F**

9. There is asymmetric information in the market for health care because the supplier (doctor) acts as the agent for the buyer (patient) and tells the buyer what health care service should be consumed. **T F**

10. The market for health care is characterized by spillover costs. **T F**

11. Third-party payments are a factor in the health care market because about three-fourths of all health care expenses are paid through public or private insurance. **T F**

12. The demand for health care is price elastic. **T F**

13. There is a strong incentive to underconsume health care because consumers have little information about the costs of medical treatments and doctors are paid on a fee-for-service basis. **T F**

14. "Defensive medicine" refers to the medical practice of physicians using preventive medicine to reduce illness and disease in patients. **T F**

15. Health care insurance is a means by which one pays a relatively small known cost for protection against an uncertain and much larger cost in the future. **T F**

16. A moral hazard problem arises from health insurance because those covered tend to take fewer health risks and consume less health care than would be the case without insurance. **T F**

17. The demand for health care is increased by a Federal tax policy that exempts employer-financed health insurance from taxation. **T F**

18. There is overwhelming evidence that the American Medical Association has purposely kept admissions to medical school artificially low to restrict the supply of doctors. **T F**

19. Productivity growth has been slow in the health care industry. **T F**

20. The development and use of new technology in health care has been a major factor in increasing the costs of health care. **T F**

21. The basic intent of reform proposals calling for tax credits and vouchers to pay for health insurance is to reduce or contain costs. **T F**

22. Proposals for national health insurance would provide a basic package of health care for each citizen at no direct charge or at a low-cost rate and would be financed out of tax revenues rather than health insurance premiums. **T F**

23. A problem with a government-imposed ceiling on the prices for physician services is that physicians can protect their incomes from fixed prices by altering the quantity and quality of care they give a patient. **T F**

24. The diagnostic-related-group (DRG) system is a health maintenance organization that specializes in the diagnosis of illnesses to reduce costs. **T F**

25. The growth of managed care organizations has transformed the medical industry into one dominated by large insurance and health care firms. **T F**

■ MULTIPLE-CHOICE QUESTIONS

Circle the letter that corresponds to the best answer.

1. The two major problems facing the health care system of the United States are
(a) the formation of health alliances and preferred provider organizations
(b) a decline in innovation and the rate of technological changes
(c) increasing supply and decreasing demand for health care
(d) access to health care and rapidly increasing costs

2. The health care industry employs about how many physicians?
(a) 50,000
(b) 100,000
(c) 600,000
(d) 1 million

3. What was total spending as a percentage of GDP in 1965 and in 1995?

	1965	1995
(a)	1	4
(b)	2	6
(c)	6	12
(d)	9	18

4. The contradiction about health care in the United States is that its
(a) medical care is the best in the world, but the nation ranks low on many health indicators
(b) expenditures for health care are modest, but medical care is the best in the world
(c) expenditures for health care are the highest in the world, but the quality of medical care is the worst of all industrial nations
(d) advances in medicine have fallen at a time when its need for better medicine has risen

5. Which is a labor market effect from rapidly rising health care costs?
(a) a decrease in the number of health care workers
(b) an increase in the rate of growth of real wages
(c) an increase in the use of part-time workers
(d) a decrease in the mobility of the labor force

6. Which person is most likely to be uninsured or ineligible for health insurance?
(a) a college professor working at a state university
(b) a part-time worker at a manufacturing plant
(c) an accountant employed by a large corporation
(d) a person who qualifies for Aid to Families with Dependent Children (AFDC)

7. Which would be considered a peculiarity of the market for health care?
(a) third-party payments
(b) employer mandates
(c) tax credits and vouchers
(d) fee-for-service payments

8. The demand for health care is
(a) price elastic
(b) price inelastic
(c) income elastic
(d) income inelastic

9. From an income perspective, health care is considered
(a) an inferior good
(b) a normal good
(c) a superior good
(d) a supply-induced good

10. Which is a demand factor in the market for health care?
(a) asymmetric information
(b) advance in new medical technology
(c) slow productivity growth in the health care industry
(d) the number of physicians graduating from medical school

11. Asymmetric information causes problems in the health care market because
(a) the buyer, not the supplier of health care services, makes most of the decisions about the amount and type of health care to be provided
(b) the supplier, not the buyer of the health care services, makes most of the decisions about the amount and type of health care to be provided
(c) government has less information than the health care providers and can inflate fees
(d) insurance companies, not the health care consumer, control deductibles and copayment policies

12. Which is a supply factor in the health care market?
(a) medical technology
(b) an aging population
(c) defensive medicine
(d) growing incomes

13. Unhealthy lifestyles may be encouraged by medical insurance because people figure that health insurance will cover illnesses or accidents. This attitude is characteristic of
(a) asymmetric information
(b) the play-or-pay problem

(c) a moral hazard problem
(d) a reduced access problem

Answer Questions 14, 15, 16, and 17 based on the following demand and supply graph of the market for health care.

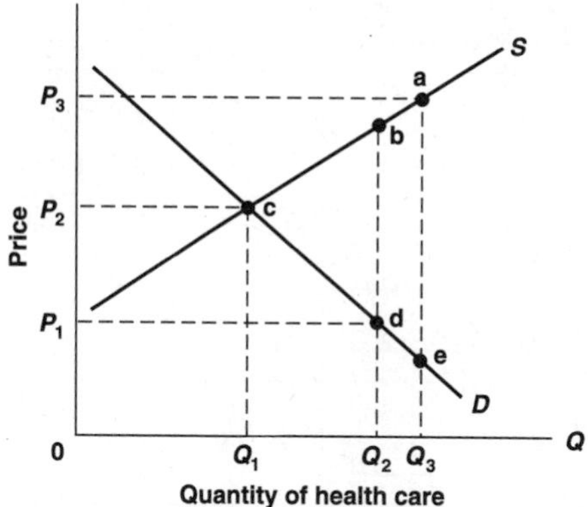

14. If there was no health insurance, the equilibrium price and quantity of health care would be
(a) P_1 and Q_2
(b) P_2 and Q_1
(c) P_2 and Q_2
(d) P_3 and Q_3

15. Assume that health insurance pays half the cost of health care. For the consumer, the price and quantity of health care consumed would be
(a) P_1 and Q_2
(b) P_2 and Q_2
(c) P_2 and Q_1
(d) P_3 and Q_3

16. With health insurance paying half the cost of health care, there is allocative
(a) efficiency because at Q_1 the marginal cost to society equals the marginal benefit
(b) efficiency because at Q_2 the marginal cost to society is less than the marginal benefit by the difference between points ***b*** and ***d***
(c) inefficiency because at Q_2 the marginal cost to society exceeds the marginal benefit by the difference between points ***b*** and ***d***
(d) inefficiency because at Q_3 the marginal cost to society exceeds the marginal benefit by the difference between points ***a*** and ***e***

17. The efficiency loss caused by the availability of health insurance is shown by area
(a) Q_1caQ_3
(b) Q_1cbQ_2
(c) ***cae***
(d) ***cbd***

18. Most experts attribute a major portion of the relative rise in health care spending to
(a) rising incomes
(b) an aging population
(c) advances in medical technology
(d) an increase in the number of physicians

19. The play-or-pay proposal for health care reform is intended to
(a) increase access to health care through the use of tax credits and vouchers as part of a national health insurance system
(b) expand health care coverage by requiring all employers to offer a health insurance program for workers or pay a special payroll tax for health care
(c) make states become a bigger player in health care reform by having the Federal government match state expenditures for health care and Medicaid
(d) reduce consumption of health care by increasing deductibles and copayments for health insurance

20. Which is primarily designed to increase access to health care rather than contain costs?
(a) national health insurance
(b) diagnosis-related-group system
(c) health maintenance organizations
(d) preferred provider organizations

21. A substantive criticism of national health insurance is that
(a) the Federal government provision of tax credits and vouchers for health care would be inefficient
(b) it establishes a diagnosis-related-group system for the payments of health provider services that is unnecessary and inefficient
(c) it increases deductibles and copayments that are borne by individuals, making health care more costly
(d) the Federal government does not have a good record of containing the costs of health care programs

22. Insurance companies often have policies that require the insured to pay the fixed portion (e.g., $500) of each year's health cost and a fixed percentage (e.g., 20%) of all additional costs. The expenditures by the insured are
(a) credits and vouchers
(b) deductibles and copayments
(c) fee-for-service payments
(d) diagnosis-related-group expenditures

23. An organization that requires hospitals and physicians to provide discounted prices for their services as a condition for inclusion in the insurance plan is a
(a) health maintenance organization
(b) preferred provider organization
(c) fee-for-service organization
(d) health alliance

24. The Health Security Act of the Clinton administration that was proposed in 1993 would have
(a) expanded the use of the fee-for-payment system
(b) made the participation of the employer voluntary
(c) used health alliances to provide universal coverage
(d) limited the number of preferred provider organizations

25. With medical savings accounts for small business owners, the self-employed, and the uninsured, consumers
(a) make tax-deductible contributions to the accounts and then use the funds to pay for health care expenditures

(b) contract with health maintenance organizations and use the accounts to get medical services at the lowest possible rate
(c) obtain discounted prices for health care services that are provided by the diagnosis-related-group system
(d) deposit money in a bank and receive a certificate of deposit that is indexed to the inflation rate for health care

■ PROBLEMS

1. Following is a table showing a supply and demand schedule for health care. In the left column is the price of health care. The middle column shows the quantity demanded (Q_d) for health care. The right column shows the quantity supplied (Q_s) of health care.

Price ($)	Q_d	Q_s
3,000	100	500
2,500	200	400
2,000	300	300
1,500	400	200
1,000	500	100

a. Assume that there is no health insurance in this market. At a price of $2,000, the quantity demanded will be ______________ units of health care and the quantity supplied will be ______________ units. There will be (a surplus, a shortage, equilibrium) ______________ in this market for health care at ______________ units.
b. Now assume that health insurance cuts the price of health care in half for the consumer. The new price to the consumer will be $__________ and the quantity consumed will be ______________ units. At this level of quantity, the marginal cost to society of a unit of health care is $ ______________ while the marginal benefit is ______________.
c. Draw a supply and demand graph in the following graph based on the data in the preceding table. Make sure to label the axes and identify prices and quantities.
(1) Show the equilibrium point in a market without health insurance and label it as point *a*.
(2) Show the price to the consumer and quantity consumed when health insurance covers half the cost of health care. At this quantity, indicate the marginal cost to society of this unit of health care and label it at point *b*. Also, indicate the marginal benefit to society of this unit of health care and label it as point *c*.
(3) Indicate the area of efficiency loss when health insurance covers half the cost of health care.

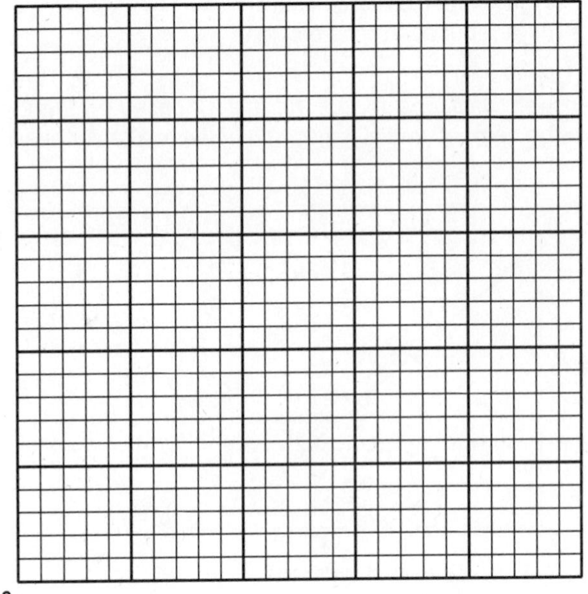
0

2. In the situations that follow indicate whether the events primarily affect the demand (*D*) for health care or the supply (*S*) of health care. Also, indicate whether it would increase (+) or decrease (−) the demand for or supply of health care.

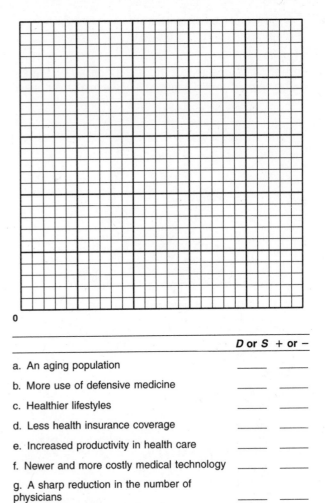

	D or *S*	+ or −
a. An aging population	____	____
b. More use of defensive medicine	____	____
c. Healthier lifestyles	____	____
d. Less health insurance coverage	____	____
e. Increased productivity in health care	____	____
f. Newer and more costly medical technology	____	____
g. A sharp reduction in the number of physicians	____	____
h. A tax subsidy to consumers to cover health care	____	____
i. Rising per capita incomes	____	____
j. More use of a fee-for-service payment system	____	____

3. Match the terms with the phrase using the appropriate number.

1. copayments
2. play-or-pay
3. diagnosis-related-group system
4. preferred provider organization
5. health maintenance organization
6. deductibles

a. A unit set up by insurance companies that requires hospitals and physicians to provide discounted prices for their services as a condition for being included in the insurance plan ____
b. The percentage of cost that an insured individual pays while the insurer pays the remainder ____
c. A health care organization that contracts with employers, insurance companies, and other groups to provide health care for their workers or others who are insured ____

d. The dollar sum of costs that an insured individual must pay before the insurer begins to pay _____

e. An arrangement that gives the hospital a fixed payment for treating each patient with the payments based on hundreds of detailed health categories for patient conditions and needs _____

f. A way to expand health coverage by requiring employers to either provide insurance for their workers or be assessed a special payroll tax to finance insurance for uncovered workers _____

■ SHORT ANSWER AND ESSAY QUESTIONS

1. Define and describe the major features of the health care industry.

2. Explain the relationship between the cost of and access to health care.

3. What are the dimensions of the cost increases in health care in absolute and relative terms?

4. How do health care expenditures in the United States compare with other industrialized nations?

5. What are the economic implications of rising health care costs?

6. Why is the aggregate consumption of health care in the United States a basic problem?

7. Who are the uninsured in the United States? What are the characteristics of the uninsured?

8. What are four peculiarities of the market for health care?

9. How does income and price elasticity affect the demand for health care?

10. In what ways do an aging population and unhealthy lifestyles influence and shape the demand for health care?

11. Why is there asymmetric information in health care? How does it affect consumption and the cost of health care?

12. What role does health insurance play in affecting health care costs? Explain the advantages and disadvantages of health insurance.

13. Why might physicians' high incomes have nothing to do with supply restrictions?

14. How have changes in medical technology affected health care costs?

15. What is the relative importance of demand and supply factors in affecting the rise in health care costs?

16. How would play-or-pay or tax credit and voucher reforms be used to achieve universal access to health care?

17. Discuss the arguments for and against national health insurance.

18. What actions have insurance companies and the Federal government taken to reduce or contain health care costs?

19. What were the major features of the Health Security Act (HSA) of 1993 proposed by the Clinton administration? What were the criticisms of the Health Security Act?

20. Describe and assess the two reforms for health care passed by Congress in 1996. What are the prospects for new reforms?

ANSWERS

Chapter 35 The Economics of Health Care

FILL-IN QUESTIONS

1. 9, 600, 6,000
2. costs, do not
3. 6, 14, highest, fastest
4. less, less, less, less, more, more
5. overallocation, less
6. 16, low-wage, do not, small, younger, major
7. ethical-equity, asymmetric, benefits, third-party
8. normal, 1, 10
9. inelastic, 0.2, 2
10. older, unhealthy
11. supplier, do not have, fee-for-service
12. defensive, ethics
13. hazard, less, overconsume
14. tax-exempt, tax subsidy, increases
15. lowers, lower, more, loss
16. high, slow, new
17. play-or-pay, credits
18. national health insurance; *a.* direct, physician, decreases, increases, increases; *b.* ceilings, increase, increase, increase
19. increased, increased, managed care, fixed
20. *a.* universal, complex, increase, did not; *b.* allows, medical

TRUE-FALSE QUESTIONS

1. F, pp. 721-722
2. F, p. 723
3. F, p. 723
4. T, p. 724
5. T, pp. 724-725
6. F, p. 725
7. F, p. 725
8. F, p. 725
9. T, p. 726
10. F, p. 726
11. T, p. 726
12. F, p. 727
13. F, pp. 726-727
14. F, p. 728
15. T, p. 728
16. F, p. 728
17. T, p. 729
18. F, p. 730
19. T, pp. 730-731
20. T, p. 731
21. F, p. 732
22. T, p. 732
23. T, p. 733
24. F, p. 734
25. T, p. 736

MULTIPLE-CHOICE QUESTIONS

1. d, p. 722
2. c, p. 721
3. c, p. 723
4. a, pp. 723-724
5. d, p. 724
6. b, p. 725
7. a, p. 726
8. b, p. 727
9. b, p. 726
10. a, p. 727
11. b, p. 727
12. a, p. 731
13. c, p. 728
14. b, p. 729
15. a, pp. 729-730
16. c, pp. 729-730
17. d, pp. 729-730
18. c, p. 731
19. b, p. 732
20. a, p. 732
21. d, p. 733
22. b, p. 733
23. b, p. 734
24. c, p. 734
25. a, p. 735

PROBLEMS

1. *a.* 300, 300, equilibrium, 300; *b.* 1,000, 500, 3,000, 1,000; *c.* (1) the intersection of price of $2,000 and quantity of 300, (2) point **b** is the intersection of $3,000 and quantity of 500 units, and point **c** is the intersection of $1,000 and quantity of 500 units, (3) the area of efficiency loss is the area in the triangle outlined point **a, b,** and **c.**

2. *a.* D, +; *b.* D, +; *c.* D, −; *d.* D, −; *e.* S, +; *f.* S, −; *g.* S, −; *h.* D, +; *i.* D, +; *j.* D, +

3. *a.* 4; *b.* 1; *c.* 5; *d.* 6; *e.* 3; *f.* 2

SHORT ANSWER AND ESSAY QUESTIONS

1. p. 721
2. pp. 721-722
3. pp. 722-723
4. p. 723
5. pp. 724-725
6. p. 725
7. pp. 725-726
8. p. 726
9. pp. 726-727
10. p. 727
11. p. 727
12. pp. 728-729
13. p. 730
14. p. 731
15. p. 731
16. p. 732
17. pp. 732-733
18. pp. 733-736
19. pp. 734-736
20. pp. 735-736

CHAPTER **36**

Labor Market Issues: Unionism, Discrimination, Immigration

Chapter 36 completes the examination of government and current economic problems by looking at three major issues in labor markets: unionism, discrimination, and immigration. Unions and labor-management relations are frequently in the news for one reason or another, such as strikes, new labor legislation, wage increases, employee wage concessions, union demands, and collective bargaining. In Chapter 34 discrimination was cited as a factor contributing to poverty, but Chapter 36 now extends the discussion by analyzing discrimination in labor markets. Immigration allows labor resources to move between nations and has economic effects on both the sending and receiving nation.

The ***labor union*** is an important economic institution in the U.S. economy. Some 17 million workers covering about 16% of the labor force belong to unions. Unions typically focus on specific economic objectives such as improving pay, hours, and working conditions. Union members are more likely to work in government or to be employed in transportation, construction, manufacturing, and mining industries. In spite of its importance, unionism has been on the decline since the mid-1950s, and Chapter 36 offers several explanations for this trend.

In Chapter 28 you learned how unions directly and indirectly seek to influence wage rates. The impact of the union on its own membership, on employers, and on the economy is more than just a matter of wages, it involves a *contract* between a union and an employer. This chapter discusses collective bargaining to give you some insights about the union goals and other issues over which employers and employees bargain. Another important idea discussed is that labor-management relations involve more than the periodic signing of a contract, they also involve the day-to-day relations between the union and the employer and the new issues not settled in the contract but which must be resolved under the general provisions of the contract.

The chapter elaborates on the economic effects of unions on the economy. Unions affect their members' wage rates relative to nonunionized workers' wage rates. Unions may also improve the productivity of labor and therefore economic efficiency in the economy. Just how unions affect these economic variables is largely uncertain and debatable. The authors of the text present both sides of the issues and draw conclusions from the empirical evidence.

Discrimination has always been present in labor markets in the form of wage, employment, occupational, or human capital discrimination. This discrimination causes significant costs for individuals who earn lower wages or have fewer work opportunities than would otherwise be the case. There are also costs to society because valuable labor resources are being inefficiently used.

The economic analysis of labor-market discrimination gives you several insights into this significant problem. The ***taste-for-discrimination model*** explains the hiring practices of prejudiced employers and the effects on the wages and employment of discriminated groups. You will also learn how ***statistical discrimination,*** which bases decisions on average characteristics, may disadvantage individuals. The ***crowding model of occupational discrimination*** described in the chapter also explains how occupational segregation affects pay and output in an economy.

The government has taken actions and adopted policies to counter discrimination in labor markets. Perhaps the most controversial form of government intervention has been ***affirmative action.*** You will examine the current debate over affirmative action and learn what supporters and critics have to say about it. You will also learn about recent legal and political developments related to this controversy.

The final major part of the chapter discusses the economics of *immigration,* which moves labor resources from one nation to another. The migration of workers from a poorer nation (such as Mexico) to a richer nation (such as the United States) economically affects wage rates, unemployment, output, and business incomes in the two nations. The method used to analyze the effects of this immigration is similar to the analysis of unions and discrimination you studied earlier in the chapter. The conclusions drawn about immigration using the supply and demand analysis are definite, but as you discover at the end of the chapter, the real world is more complicated, so any conclusions will be modified.

■ CHECKLIST

When you have studied this chapter you should be able to

□ Identify the number and percentage of union members and the major union organizations.
□ Explain the meaning of business unionism.
□ Describe the characteristics of workers belonging to unions.

☐ State how unions have declined since the mid-1950s.
☐ Present two hypotheses to explain unionism's decline.
☐ Explain the four basic areas covered by a work agreement in collective bargaining.
☐ Describe the bargaining process and major labor relations law.
☐ Draw conclusions about the effects of unions on the wages of workers.
☐ Identify three negative effects unions might have on productivity and efficiency.
☐ Use a supply and demand model to show how a union might lead to a misallocation of labor resources and reduced output.
☐ List three positive effects unions might have on productivity and efficiency.
☐ Identify how unions increase, the two ways in which they decrease, and the inequality with which the earnings of labor are distributed.
☐ Describe four types of labor market discrimination.
☐ Illustrate the cost of discrimination with a production possibilities curve.
☐ Use a wage equation to explain the taste-for-discrimination model in labor markets.
☐ Use a supply and demand graph to illustrate the taste-for-discrimination model in labor markets.
☐ Explain and give an example of statistical discrimination.
☐ Use the crowding model of occupational discrimination to explain why certain groups receive lower wages and why the labor is more efficiently allocated when occupational segregation is eliminated.
☐ Identify three types of antidiscrimination policies.
☐ Discuss the arguments for and against affirmative action.
☐ Describe recent legal and political developments in affirmative action.
☐ Give estimates of the number of legal and illegal immigrants entering the United States in recent years.
☐ Use a supply and demand model to explain the effects of worker migration from a poor to a rich nation on wage rates, output, and incomes.
☐ Explain how four complicating factors modify the effects of migration on the two economies.
☐ Describe two contrasting views of the effects of immigration on the United States.

■ CHAPTER OUTLINE

1. About 17 million workers in the United States belong to *unions,* and they account for only about 16% of wage and salary workers. Most union workers are members of the American Federation of Labor and Congress of Industrial Organizations (AFL-CIO).

a. Most unions have adopted a philosophy of business unionism that focuses on the economic objectives of higher pay, shorter work hours, and improved working conditions.

b. Occupation and industry are important factors that explain who belongs to unions. The rate of unionization is high in government, transportation, construction, manufacturing, and mining. Men, blacks, and those living in urban areas are more likely to be union members.

c. Union membership has declined since the mid-1950s, when about 25% of the workforce was unionized. Two complementary hypotheses explain the decline.

(1) The ***structural-change hypothesis*** is that changes in the structure of the economy and the labor force have limited the expansion of union membership.

(2) The ***managerial-opposition hypothesis*** is that the opposition of management to unions increased because union firms were thought to be less profitable than nonunion firms. The policies management used against unions decreased union membership.

2. ***Collective bargaining*** between labor and management results in collective bargaining (or work) agreements between them.

a. The work agreements reached take many different forms, but usually cover four basic areas: union status (open, closed, or agency shops) and managerial prerogatives; wages and hours; seniority and job protection; and grievance procedures.

b. This bargaining process on a new contract typically occurs in the 60-day period before the end of the existing contract. After the deadline, a union can strike, or there can be a lockout by the firm. Most contract agreements are compromises; strikes, lockouts, and violence are rare. The National Labor Relations Act specifies legal and illegal practices in collective bargaining, and the National Labor Relations Board is authorized to investigate unfair labor practices.

3. Labor unions have *economic effects.*

a. While unions have increased the wages of their members relative to the wages of nonunion members, they have had little or no effect on the average level of real wages in the economy.

b. Whether unions result in more or less *efficiency* and an increase or a decrease in the productivity of labor is a two-sided question.

(1) The *negative* view is that unions decrease efficiency by featherbedding and work rules, engaging in strikes, and fostering a misallocation of labor resources.

(2) The *positive* view is that unions increase efficiency by having a shock effect on management performance, reducing worker turnover, and by informally transferring skills from the more- to the less-skilled workers fostered by the seniority system.

(3) The empirical evidence is mixed, showing that unions have increased labor productivity in some industries but decreased it in others. There is no generally accepted conclusion as to the effect of unions on the productivity of labor in the economy.

4. *Discrimination* in labor markets occurs when equivalent labor resources that make equal productive contributions are given different pay or treatment. Discrimination affects the earnings of women and minorities in the labor market.

a. Labor market discrimination against a group can occur in four ways: lower wages; inferior employment treatment in hiring, promotions, assignments, and working conditions; restrictions or prohibitions that limit entry or mobility in occupations; and less access to opportunities for investments in education and training or other forms of human capital.

b. Discrimination has private and social costs. It transfers income and benefits from one group to another. It also reduces the output and income of the economy by operating as an artificial barrier to competition.

5. The economic analysis of discrimination provides some insights even though the issue is complex and multifaceted.

a. The *taste-for-discrimination model* explains prejudice using demand theory. The model assumes that a prejudiced employer is willing to pay a "price" to avoid interactions with a nonpreferred group.

(1) The discrimination coefficient measures in monetary units the cost of the employer's prejudice. An employer will hire nonpreferred workers only if their wage rates are below those of the preferred workers by an amount at least equal to the discrimination coefficient.

(2) In the supply and demand model for nonpreferred workers, an increase in the prejudice of employers will decrease the demand for this labor, the number of workers, and their wage rate. A decrease in the prejudice of employers will increase the demand for this labor, the number employed, and the wage rate.

(3) The taste-for-discrimination model suggests that in the very long run, competition will reduce discrimination, but critics question this conclusion, given the insufficient progress in reducing discrimination over time in the United States.

b. ***Statistical discrimination*** involves judging people based on the average characteristics of the group to which they belong instead of productivity or personal characteristics. In labor markets, employers may stereotype workers by applying the average characteristics of the group in work assessments of individual members of that group. The practice may be profitable and on average it may produce correct decisions, but fails to take into account the individual skills and capabilities and limits opportunities for workers.

c. The practice of ***occupational segregation*** suggests that women and minorities are crowded into a small number of occupations. In this crowding model, the supply of these workers is large relative to the demand for them, and thus their wage rates and incomes are lower in these crowded occupations. Eliminating the occupation segregation would raise wage rates and incomes for these workers and also increase the economy's output.

6. The government can try to *correct the discrimination problem* by promoting a growing economy, improving the education and training of women and minorities, and creating policies that restrict or eliminate discriminatory practices.

a. *Affirmative action* involves special efforts by employers to increase employment and promotion opportunities for groups which have and continue to experience discrimination.

(1) Arguments for affirmative action include the need to close the pay and socioeconomic gap for women and minorities and the need to counter long-lasting prejudice and discriminatory employment practices. Eliminating discrimination will also improve economic efficiency and economic growth.

(2) The opposing view is that economic efficiency is reduced because employers are forced to hire less qualified workers. Hiring quotas and preferential treatment are considered a form of reverse discrimination. Some opponents suggest that affirmative action increases hostility and resentment in the workplace and mistakenly leads people to attribute work success not to their personal contributions but to protected status.

b. Affirmative action has been subject to legal and political attacks in recent years. The Supreme Court declared some affirmative action programs illegal because they promote reverse discrimination. The courts have also limited the application of race-based preferences in Federal programs. Congress has debated the issue, and the Clinton administration halted some minority programs that gave contracting preferences to minorities.

7. The *immigration* of workers into the United States is a controversial issue because this international movement of labor has economic effects on the U.S. economy.

a. During the 1990s, about 850,000 legal immigrants and 100,000 illegal immigrants entered the United States each year. About one-third of the recent population growth is from immigration.

b. The economic effects of immigration can be shown in a two-nation model, one poorer and one richer.

(1) The movement of workers from a poorer economy raises the average wages of workers in the poorer nation and lowers the average wage rates in the richer nation. Domestic output in the poorer nation will decline and domestic output in the richer nation will expand, but the net effect from a world perspective is an increase in output and economic efficiency.

(2) The incomes of businesses in the richer nation will increase but decrease in the poorer nation; the richer nation gains "cheap" labor and the poorer nation loses "cheap" labor.

c. These conclusions must be modified to take into account other factors.

(1) There is a cost to migration for workers that will reduce the world gain in output.

(2) Remittances reduce the gains for the richer nation. If immigrant workers remit some of their increased wages to relatives in the poorer nation, then some gain for the domestic economy is lost. The return of immigrants to the poorer nation (backflows) alters gains and losses.

(3) The model assumes full employment in both nations. If there is unemployment or underemployment in the poorer nation, it can increase domestic output when the surplus workers emigrate.

(4) Immigration can affect tax revenues and government spending. If immigrants take advantage of welfare benefits in the richer nation, it imposes an additional cost on the richer nation.

d. The positive view of immigration considers it a source of economic progress for a nation, but the negative view is that it causes socioeconomic problems that hinder a nation.

■ HINTS AND TIPS

1. This chapter deals with three issues—unions, discrimination, and immigration—that can provoke emotional reactions. Make sure you remember the distinction between *positive* and *normative* economics made in Chapter 1. The purpose of Chapter 36 is to analyze and explain the economics of unions, discrimination, and immigration (*what is*), and not the ideal world (*what ought to be*).

2. The effects of discrimination are illustrated by the production possibilities curve you first learned about in Chapter 2. In this model discrimination is similar to unemployment in the economy.

3. Although three different issues are discussed in this chapter, the supply and demand graphs comparing the gains and losses of different groups are quite similar (Figures 36-2, 36-5, and 36-6). In each graph, the wage rate is plotted on the vertical axis and the quantity of labor is on the horizontal axis. Each graph shows how segmentation of a labor market affects the wage rate, employment, and domestic output. Problems 3, 4, and 5 in this chapter will help you master this material.

■ IMPORTANT TERMS

American Federation of Labor-Congress of Industrial Organizations (AFL-CIO)
independent unions
business unionism
structural-change hypothesis
managerial-opposition hypothesis
collective bargaining
closed shop
union shop
agency shop
right-to-work laws
open shop
strike
lockout
National Labor Relations Act
National Labor Relations Board
collective voice
exit mechanism
voice mechanism
labor market discrimination
wage discrimination
employment discrimination
occupational discrimination
human-capital discrimination
taste-for-discrimination model
discrimination coefficient
statistical discrimination
occupational segregation
affirmative action
reverse discrimination
legal immigrants
illegal immigrants

SELF TEST

■ FILL-IN QUESTIONS

1. About (17, 34) __________ million workers belong to labor unions in the United States. This number represents about (16, 32) __________% of wage and salary workers.

2. The rate of unionization is (low, high) __________ among workers in government, transportation, construction, manufacturing, and mining, and it is __________ among protective service workers, machine operators, and craft workers. Men are (more, less) __________ likely to be union members than women; blacks are __________ likely to be union members than whites; and those in urban areas are __________ likely to be union members than in other locations.

3. Since the mid-1950s, union membership as a percentage of the labor force has (increased, decreased) __________ and the number of unionized workers has __________.

4. Two complementary hypotheses can be used to explain the changes in the size of union membership. The (structural-change, managerial-opposition) __________ hypothesis suggests that conditions unfavorable to the expansion of unions have occurred in the economy and labor; the __________ hypothesis suggests that union growth has been deterred by the policies of firms to limit or dissuade workers from joining unions.

5. A typical work agreement between a union and an employer covers the following four basic areas:

a. __________

b. __________

c. __________

d. __________

6. Unionization of workers in the U.S. economy has tended to (increase, decrease, have no effect on) __________ the wage rates of union members, to __________ the wage rates of nonunion workers, and to __________ the average level of real wage rates received by all workers.

7. Unions have a negative effect on productivity and efficiency in the economy to the extent that they engage in (collective bargaining, featherbedding) __________ and impose (a shock effect, work rules) __________ on their employers, participate in (training with, strikes against) __________ their employers, or impose (above, below) __________-equilibrium wage rates on employers that lead to misallocation of labor resources.

8. Unions have a positive effect of productivity and efficiency in the economy. The increased wage rate can have a(n) (income, shock) __________ effect that induces employers to substitute capital for labor and hasten their search for technologies that (increase, decrease) __________ the costs of production. Unions can

also (increase, decrease) ______________ labor turnover, and the seniority system can ______________ informal training of younger workers by older workers.

9. Discrimination relating to the labor market occurs when women or minorities having (the same, inferior) ______________ abilities, education, training, and experience as men or white workers are given ______________ treatment with respect to hiring, occupational choice, education and training, promotion, and wage rates. Studies of the differences in earnings between men and women and blacks and whites find that about (half, three-fourths) ______________ can be explained by factors such as age, education, and training, but about (one-fourth, half) ______________ are unexplained and due largely to discrimination.

10. The four principal kinds of economic discrimination are

a. ______________________________

b. ______________________________

c. ______________________________

d. ______________________________

11. Discrimination will (increase, decrease) ______________ the wages of workers in the discriminated group and ______________ the wage of workers in the nondiscriminated group; it ______________ economic efficiency and ______________ total output in the economy.

12. In the taste-for-discrimination model, the discrimination coefficient *d* measures the (utility, disutility) ______________ that prejudiced employers experience when they must interact with those they are biased against. This coefficient is measured in monetary units and becomes part of the (benefit, cost) ______________ of hiring nonpreferred workers. The prejudiced employer will hire nonpreferred workers only if their wage rate is at least (above, below) ______________ the amount of the preferred workers by the amount of the discrimination coefficient.

13. An increase in the prejudice of employers against nonpreferred workers will (increase, decrease) ______________ their wage rate and the number employed; a decrease in the prejudice of employers against nonpreferred workers will (increase, decrease) ______________ their wage rate and the number employed.

14. When employers base employment decisions about individuals on the average characteristics of groups of workers, this is (reverse, statistical) ______________ discrimination. The decisions that firms make based on this type of discrimination may be (irrational, rational) ______________ and profitable, on average, but hurt individuals for whom the averages (do, do not) ______________ apply.

15. The occupational discrimination that pushes women and blacks into a small number of occupations in which the supply of labor is large relative to the demand for it is explained by the (managerial-opposition, crowding) ______________ model. Because supply is large relative to demand, wages and incomes in these occupations are (high, low) ______________. The reduction or elimination of this occupational discrimination would result in a (more, less) ______________ efficient allocation of the labor resources of the economy and a(n) (expansion, contraction) ______________ in the domestic output.

16. Those who support affirmative action say that (equal, preferential) ______________ treatment is needed to help women and minorities compensate for decades of discrimination. They also argue that affirmative action (increases, decreases) ______________ economic efficiency, but opponents argue that it ______________ economic efficiency and causes (statistical, reverse) ______________ discrimination.

17. The annual number of legal immigrants to the United States in the 1990s was about (450; 850) ______________ thousand. About one- (tenth, third) ______________ of the population growth can be attributed to immigration.

18. In the rich nation, the movement of workers from a poor nation to a rich nation tends to (increase, decrease) ______________ domestic output, to ______________ wage rates, and to (increase, decrease) ______________ business incomes; in the poor nation it tends to ______________ domestic output, to (increase, decrease) ______________ wage rates, and to ______________ business incomes; in the world it tends to (increase, decrease) ______________ the real output of goods and services.

19. List the four complications that may modify the conclusions reached in question 18.

a. ______________________________

b. ______________________________

c. ______________________________

d. ______________________________

20. Supporters of immigration argue that immigrant workers (increase, decrease) ______________ the supply of products with their labor and ______________ the demand for products with their incomes, but opponents of immigration contend that immigrants (increase, decrease) ______________ the burden of welfare and ______________ the wages of domestic workers. These views, however, are too (complex, simplistic) ______________ because assessing the net benefits of immigration depends on the number of immigrants, their education, skills, work ethic, and other factors.

■ TRUE-FALSE QUESTIONS

Circle the T if the statement is true, the F if it is false.

1. Most union members in the United States belong to independent unions. **T F**

2. The rate of unionization is high in transportation, construction, and manufacturing industries. **T F**

3. Union membership has been slowly and steadily rising since the 1950s. **T F**

4. The managerial-opposition hypothesis argues that structural changes in the economy have limited management opposition to unions. **T F**

5. Collective bargaining between labor and management means no more than deciding on the wage rates employees will receive during the life of the contract. **T F**

6 The wages of union members exceed the wages of nonunion members on the average by more than 40%. **T F**

7. Strikes in the U.S. economy result in little lost work time and reductions in total output. **T F**

8. The loss of output in the U.S. economy resulting from increases in wage rates imposed by unions on employers is relatively large. **T F**

9. The seniority system, its advocates argue, expands the informal training of less-skilled, younger workers and improves the productivity of a firm's workforce. **T F**

10. It is generally agreed that unions decrease the productivity of labor in the U.S. economy. **T F**

11. Labor market discrimination occurs when equivalent labor resources are paid or treated differently even though their productive contributions are equal. **T F**

12. Almost all the differences in the earnings between men and women and blacks and whites can be explained by discrimination. **T F**

13. Sexual and racial harassment would be considered part of human-capital discrimination. **T F**

14. Discrimination redistributes income and reduces the economy's output. **T F**

15. In the taste-for-discrimination model, employer preference for discrimination is measured in dollars by discrimination coefficient *d*. These employers will hire nonpreferred workers only if their wages are at least *d* dollars below the wages of preferred workers. **T F**

16. In the taste-for-discrimination model, a decline in the prejudice of employers will decrease the demand for black workers and lower the black wage rate and the ratio of black to white wages. **T F**

17. Statistical discrimination occurs when employers base employment decisions about individuals on the average characteristics of groups of workers. **T F**

18. Tight labor markets tend to increase discrimination and stereotyping rather than reduce them. **T F**

19. The crowding model of occupational segregation shows how white males earn higher earnings at the expense of women and minorities, who are restricted to a limited number of occupations. **T F**

20. More than 10 million immigrants enter the United States each year, about half of whom are legal and the other half illegal. **T F**

21. Supply and demand analysis suggests that the movement of workers from a poor to a rich country decreases domestic output in the rich country and increases domestic output in the poor country. **T F**

22. An increase in the mobility of labor from one nation to other nations tends to increase the world's output of goods and services. **T F**

23. Mexican workers who have migrated to the United States and send remittances to their families in Mexico increase the gain to domestic output in the United States and reduce it in Mexico. **T F**

24. When unemployed or underemployed labor from a poor nation migrate to a rich nation, the poor nation suffers a loss in domestic output because it loses workers. **T F**

25. Immigration will always harm a nation because it reduces the wages of workers in the domestic economy and thus reduces national income. **T F**

■ MULTIPLE-CHOICE QUESTIONS

Circle the letter that corresponds to the best answer.

1. About what percent of employed wage and salary workers in the United States belong to unions?
- **(a)** 8%
- **(b)** 16%
- **(c)** 24%
- **(d)** 32%

2. The rate of unionization is highest in
- **(a)** services
- **(b)** retail trade
- **(c)** government
- **(d)** manufacturing

3. The decline in union membership in the United States in recent years can be explained by the
- **(a)** managerial-growth hypothesis
- **(b)** structural-change hypothesis
- **(c)** relative-income hypothesis
- **(d)** complementary-expansion hypothesis

4. If workers at the time they are hired have a choice of joining the union and paying dues or of not joining the union and paying no dues, there exists
- **(a)** a union shop

(b) an open shop
(c) a nonunion shop
(d) a closed shop

5. A major responsibility of the National Labor Relations Board is to
(a) enforce right-to-work laws
(b) keep unions from becoming politically active
(c) investigate unfair labor practices under labor law
(d) maintain labor peace between the AFL and CIO

6. Unionization has tended to
(a) increase the wages of union workers and decrease the wages of nonunion workers
(b) increase the wages of nonunion workers and decrease the wages of union workers
(c) increase the wages of both union and nonunion workers
(d) increase the average level of real wages in the economy

7. Which tends to decrease (to have a negative effect on) productivity and efficiency in the economy?
(a) the seniority system
(b) reduced labor turnover
(c) featherbedding and union-imposed work rules
(d) the shock effect of higher union-imposed wage rates

8. The higher wages imposed on employers in a unionized labor market tend to result in
(a) lower wage rates in nonunionized labor markets and a decline in domestic output
(b) lower wage rates in nonunionized labor markets and an expansion in domestic output
(c) higher wage rates in nonunionized labor markets and a decline in domestic output
(d) higher wage rates in nonunionized labor markets and an expansion in domestic output

9. The reallocation of labor from employment where its MRP is $50,000 to employment where its MRP is $40,000 will
(a) increase the output of the economy by $10,000
(b) increase the output of the economy by $90,000
(c) decrease the output of the economy by $10,000
(d) decrease the output of the economy by $90,000

10. Which tends to increase (have a positive effect on) productivity and efficiency in the economy?
(a) strikes
(b) reduced labor turnover
(c) featherbedding and union-imposed work rules
(d) the unionization of a particular labor market

11. A wage increase imposed by unions on employers has a shock effect if it induces employers to
(a) decrease the substitution of capital for labor
(b) slow their search for productivity-increasing technologies
(c) speed their employment of productive techniques that reduce their costs
(d) lockout workers to encourage bargaining

12. Unions tend to reduce labor turnover by providing workers with all but one of the following. Which one?
(a) an exit mechanism
(b) a voice mechanism
(c) a collective voice
(d) a wage advantage

13. What form of discrimination is indicated by a report from the U.S. Department of Labor that states the unemployment rate for blacks is double that for whites?
(a) occupational discrimination
(b) employment discrimination
(c) human-capital discrimination
(d) wage discrimination

14. A study by a labor economist finds that 12% of blacks and 22% of whites completed 4 or more years of college. These data are evidence of
(a) occupational discrimination
(b) employment discrimination
(c) human-capital discrimination
(d) wage discrimination

15. In the production possibilities model, the effect of discrimination can be illustrated by a
(a) point outside the frontier
(b) point inside the frontier
(c) point on the frontier
(d) shift out from the frontier

16. In a supply and demand model of the labor market for nonpreferred workers, an increase in employer prejudice will
(a) increase supply, raise the wage rate, and decrease the employment of these workers
(b) decrease supply, lower the wage rate, and decrease employment of these workers
(c) decrease demand, lower the wage rate, and decrease the employment of these workers
(d) increase demand, raise the wage rate, and increase the employment of these workers

17. Suppose the market wage rate for a preferred worker is $12 and the monetary value of disutility the employer attached to hiring a nonpreferred worker is $3. The employer will be indifferent between either type of worker when the wage rate for nonpreferred workers is
(a) $15
(b) $12
(c) $9
(d) $3

18. When people are judged on the basis of the average characteristics of the group to which they belong rather than on their own personal characteristics or productivity, this is
(a) human-capital discrimination
(b) occupational discrimination
(c) employment discrimination
(d) statistical discrimination

19. The crowding of women and minorities into certain occupations results in
(a) higher wages and more efficient allocation of labor resources
(b) lower wages and less efficient allocation of labor resources

(c) lower wages, but more efficient allocation of labor resources
(d) lower wages, but no effect on the efficient allocation of labor resources

20. Supporters of affirmative action believe that
(a) improved social equity is worth the price society must pay in the form of a lowered domestic output
(b) preferential treatment is necessary to eliminate bias and is a good strategy for increasing economic efficiency
(c) it decreases human-capital discrimination but increases statistical discrimination
(d) it decreases occupational discrimination but increases wage discrimination

21. About what percentage of recent population growth in the United States can be attributed to immigration?
(a) 10%
(b) 33%
(c) 67%
(d) 90%

22. The elimination of barriers to the international flow of labor tends to
(a) lower the wage rates for all labor
(b) raise the wage rates for all labor
(c) increase worldwide efficiency
(d) decrease worldwide efficiency

23. If there is full employment in both nations, the effect of the migration of workers from a poor to a rich nation is to increase the
(a) average wage rate in the rich nation
(b) domestic output in the rich nation
(c) business incomes in the poor nation
(d) domestic output in the poor nation

24. Which of the following would increase the gains realized in the world from the migration of workers?
(a) the explicit and implicit costs of migration
(b) the remittances of workers to their native countries
(c) the migration of unemployed workers to nations in which they find employment
(d) the migration of employed workers to nations in which the taxes they pay are less than the welfare benefits they receive

25. From a strictly economic perspective, nations seeking to maximize net benefits from immigration should
(a) expand immigration because it benefits society with a greater supply of products and increased demand for them
(b) contract immigration because the benefits are minor and it reduces the wage rates of domestic workers
(c) expand immigration until its marginal benefits equal its marginal costs
(d) contract immigration until the extra welfare cost for taxpayers is zero

■ PROBLEMS

1. Match the union term with the phrase using the appropriate number.

1. lockout
2. union shop
3. closed shop
4. right-to-work laws
5. open shop
6. agency shop
7. National Labor Relations Act
8. collective bargaining

a. Employer can hire union or nonunion workers. _____
b. Acts by states to make compulsory union membership, or the union shop, illegal. _____
c. A worker must be a member of the union before he or she is eligible for employment in the firm. _____
d. First passed as the Wagner Act of 1935 and sets forth the dos and don'ts of union and management-labor practices. _____
e. Requires a worker to pay union dues or donate an equivalent amount to charity. _____
f. A firm forbids the workers from returning to work until a new contract is signed. _____
g. Permits the employer to hire nonunion workers, but provides that these workers must join the union within a specified period or relinquish their jobs. _____
h. The negotiations of labor contracts. _____

2. Suppose there are two identical labor markets in the economy. The supply of workers and the demand for workers in each of these markets are shown in the following table.

Quantity of labor demanded	Wage rate (MRP of labor)	Quantity of labor supplied
1	$100	7
2	90	6
3	80	5
4	70	4
5	60	3
6	50	2
7	40	1

a. In each of the two labor markets the equilibrium wage rate in a competitive labor market would be $_____________ and employment would be _____________ workers.
b. Now suppose that in the first of these labor markets workers form a union and the union imposes an above-equilibrium wage rate of $90 on employers.
(1) Employment in the unionized labor market will (rise, fall) _____________ to _____________ workers; and
(2) the output produced by workers employed by the firms in the unionized labor market will (expand, contract) _____________ by $_____________.
c. If the workers displaced by the unionization of the first labor market all enter and find employment in the second labor market which remains nonunionized and competitive,

(1) the wage rate in the second labor market will (rise, fall) ______________ to $______________.
(2) the output produced by the workers employed by firms in the second labor market will (expand, contract) ______________ by $ ______________.
d. While the total employment of labor in the two labor markets has remained constant, the total output produced by the employers in the two labor markets has (expanded, contracted) ______________ by $______________.

3. Match the discrimination terms with the phrase using the appropriate number.

1. statistical discrimination
2. human-capital discrimination
3. employment discrimination
4. affirmative action
5. reverse discrimination
6. wage discrimination
7. occupational discrimination
8. occupational segregation

a. The crowding of women, blacks, and certain ethnic groups into less desirable, lower-paying occupations. _____
b. The payment of a lower wage to members of particular groups than to white males for the same work. _____
c. Inferior treatment in hiring, promotions, and work assignments for a particular group of workers. _____
d. Judging an individual on the basis of the average characteristics of the group to which the individual belongs rather than the individual's characteristics. _____
e. The view that preferential treatment associated with affirmative action efforts constitutes discrimination against other groups. _____
f. The denial of equal access to productivity-enhancing education and training to members of particular groups. _____
g. Policies and programs that establish targets of increased employment and promotion for women and minorities. _____
h. The arbitrary restriction of particular groups from entering more desirable higher-paying occupations. _____

4. Suppose there are only three labor markets in the economy and each market is perfectly competitive. The following table contains the demand (or marginal-revenue-product) schedule for labor in each of these three markets.
a. Assume there are 24 million homogeneous workers in the economy and that 12 million of these workers are male and 12 million are female.
(1) If the 12 million female workers can be employed only in the labor market Z, for them all to find employment the hourly wage rate must be $______________.

Wage rate (marginal revenue product of labor per hour)	Quantity of labor (millions per hour)
$11	4
10	5
9	6
8	7
7	8
6	9
5	10
4	11
3	12

(2) If of the 12 million male workers 6 million are employed in labor market X and 6 million are employed in labor market Y, the hourly wage rate in labor markets X and Y will be $ ______________.
b. Imagine now that the impediment to the employment of females in labor markets X and Y is removed and that as a result (and because the demand and marginal revenue product of labor is the same in all three markets) 8 million workers find employment in each labor market.
(1) In labor market Z (in which only females had previously been employed)
(a) the hourly wage rate will rise to $______________.
(b) the *decrease* in national output that results from the decrease in employment from 12 million to 8 million workers is equal to the loss of the marginal revenue products of the workers no longer employed, and it totals $ ______________.
(2) In labor market X and in labor market Y (in each of which only males had previously been employed)
(a) the hourly wage rate will fall to $ ______________.
(b) the *increase* in national output that results from the increase in employment from 6 million to 8 million workers is equal to the marginal revenue products of the additional workers employed; the gain in *each* of these markets is $______________ million, and the total gain in the two markets is $ ______________.
(c) the *net* gain to society from the reallocation of female workers is $ ______________ million.

5. The following two tables show the demands for labor and the levels of domestic output that can be produced at each level of employment in two countries, ***A*** and ***B***.

Country A		
Wage rate	**Quantity of labor demanded**	**Real output**
$20	95	$1,900
18	100	1,990
16	105	2,070
14	110	2,140
12	115	2,200
10	120	2,250
8	125	2,290

	Country B	
Wage rate	**Quantity of labor demanded**	**Real output**
$20	10	$200
18	15	290
16	20	370
14	25	440
12	30	500
10	35	550
8	40	590

a. If there were full employment in both countries and if

(1) the labor force in Country ***A*** were 110, the wage rate in Country ***A*** would be $ ______________.

(2) the labor force in Country ***B*** were 40, the wage rate in Country ***B*** would be $ ______________.

b. With these labor forces and wage rates

(1) total wages paid in ***A*** would be $______________ and the incomes of businesses (capitalists) in ***A*** would be $______________. (*Hint:* Subtract total wages paid from the real output.)

(2) total wages paid in ***B*** would be $______________ and business incomes in ***B*** would be $______________.

c. Assume the difference between the wage rates in the two countries induces 5 workers to migrate from ***B*** to ***A***. So long as both countries maintain full employment,

(1) the wage rate in ***A*** would (rise, fall) ______________ to $______________,

(2) and the wage rate in ***B*** would ______________ to $ ______________.

d. The movement of workers from ***B*** to ***A*** would

(1) (increase, decrease) ______________ the output of ***A*** by $______________,

(2) (increase, decrease) ______________ the output of ***B*** by $______________, and

(3) (increase, decrease) ______________ their combined (and the world's) output by $______________.

e. This movement of workers from ***B*** to ***A*** also (increased, decreased) ______________ business incomes in ***A*** by $______________ and (increased, decreased) ______________ business incomes in ***B*** by $______________.

■ SHORT ANSWER AND ESSAY QUESTIONS

1. Describe the current status of unions in the United States and the major union organization.

2. What is business unionism in the United States? How does it differ from the European approach to unions?

3. Who belongs to unions? Answer in terms of the types of industries and occupations and the personal characteristics of workers.

4. What evidence is there that the labor movement in the United States has declined? What are two possible causes of this decline?

5. What are the four basic areas usually covered in the collective-bargaining agreement between management and labor?

6. What four arguments does labor (management) use in demanding (resisting) higher wages? Why are these arguments two-edged?

7. How large is the union wage advantage in the United States? How has the unionization of many labor markets affected the average level of real wages in the U.S. economy?

8. By what basic means do unions have a positive and a negative effect on economic efficiency in the economy? What appears to have been the overall effect of unions on economic efficiency in the U.S. economy?

9. What effect does the unionization of a particular labor market have on the wage rate in that market, wage rates in other labor markets, and the total output of the economy?

10. Explain how unions reduce labor turnover and improve the skills of younger workers.

11. Define labor market discrimination. How much of the differences in the earning of workers is explained by discrimination?

12. Describe the four types of labor market discrimination, and give an example of each type.

13. Describe the cost of discrimination to society. Illustrate the cost using a production possibilities curve.

14. How can discrimination be viewed as resulting from a preference or taste for which the prejudiced employer is willing to pay? What will determine whether the prejudiced employer hires nonpreferred workers in this model?

15. How do changes in employer prejudice affect wage rates for nonpreferred workers and the ratio of wages between preferred and nonpreferred workers?

16. Explain the concept of statistical discrimination and give an example of it. How can it lead to discrimination even in the absence of prejudice?

17. Describe the economic effects of occupational segregation on the wages of women and minorities. How does this type of segregation affect the domestic output of the economy?

18. What three types of antidiscrimination policies have been used in the United States? Distinguish between direct and indirect policies.

19. Explain the arguments for and against affirmative action. Does affirmative action increase or decrease economic efficiency?

20. How has the Supreme Court viewed affirmative action in recent years? What views have been expressed by Congress and the president?

21. Describe the number of legal and illegal immigrants who entered the United States annually during the 1990s. What has been the effect of this immigration on population growth?

22. Construct a supply and demand model to explain the effects of the migration of labor from a poorer nation to a richer nation. Give your answer in terms of the effects on wage rate, domestic output, and business incomes in the two nations.

23. What four complications make it necessary to modify the conclusions that you reached in question 22? Explain how each of these complications alters your conclusion.

24. Why would the elimination of international barriers to the mobility of labor increase worldwide efficiency?

25. Contrast the positive view with the negative view of immigration. Why are these two views too simplistic?

ANSWERS

Chapter 36 Labor-Market Issues: Unionism, Discrimination, Immigration

FILL-IN QUESTIONS

1. 17, 16
2. high, high, more, more, more
3. decreased, decreased
4. structural-change, managerial-opposition
5. *a.* the degree of recognition and status accorded the union and the prerogatives of management; *b.* wages and hours; *c.* seniority and job opportunities; *d.* a procedure for settling grievances (any order for a–d)
6. increase, decrease, have no effect on
7. featherbedding, work rules, strikes against, above
8. shock, decrease, decrease, increase
9. the same, inferior, half, half
10. *a.* wage discrimination; *b.* employment discrimination; *c.* human-capital discrimination; *d.* occupational discrimination (any order for a–d)
11. decrease, increase, decreases, decreases
12. disutility, cost, below
13. decrease, increase
14. statistical, rational, do not
15. crowding, low, more, expansion
16. preferential, increases, decreases, reverse
17. 850, third
18. increase, decrease, increase, decrease, increase, decrease, increase
19. *a.* including the costs of migration; *b.* remittances and backflows; *c.* the amounts of unemployment in the two nations; *d.* the fiscal aspects in the country receiving the immigrants (any order for a–d)
20. increase, increase, increase, decrease, simplistic

TRUE-FALSE QUESTIONS

1. F, p. 739
2. T, p. 740
3. F, p. 741
4. F, p. 741
5. F, pp. 741-742
6. F, p. 743
7. T, p. 744
8. F, p. 745
9. T, p. 746
10. F, p. 746
11. T, p. 747
12. F, p. 747
13. F, p. 748
14. T, p. 748
15. T, p. 749
16. F, pp. 749-750
17. T, p. 750
18. F, p. 753
19. T, p. 751-752
20. F, p. 755
21. F, p. 755-756
22. T, p. 756
23. F, p. 756
24. F, p. 758
25. F, p. 758

MULTIPLE-CHOICE QUESTIONS

1. b, p. 739
2. c, p. 740
3. b, p. 741
4. b, p. 742
5. c, p. 743
6. a, p. 743
7. c, p. 744
8. a, pp. 744-745
9. c, pp. 744-745
10. b, p. 746
11. c, p. 745-746
12. a, p. 746
13. b, p. 748
14. c, p. 748
15. b, p. 748
16. c, p. 749-750
17. c, p. 749
18. d, p. 750
19. b, p. 751-752
20. b, p. 753-754
21. b, p. 755
22. c, p. 756
23. b, p. 756
24. c, p. 758
25. c, p. 758

PROBLEMS

1. *a.* 5; *b.* 4; *c.* 3; *d.* 7; *e.* 6; *f.* 1; *g.* 2; *h.* 8
2. *a.* 70, 4; *b.* (1) fall, 2, (2) contract, 150; *c.* (1) fall, 50 (2) expand, 110; *d.* contracted, 40
3. *a.* 8; *b.* 6; *c.* 3; *d.* 1; *e.* 5; *f.* 2; *g.* 4; *h.* 7
4. *a.* (1) 3, (2) 9; *b.* (1) (*a*) 7, (*b*) 18, (2) (*a*) 7, (*b*) 15, 30, (*c*) 12
5. *a.* (1) 14, (2) 8; *b.* (1) 1,540, 600, (2) 320, 270; *c.* (1) fall, 12, (2) rise, 10; *d.* (1) increase, 60, (2) decrease, 40, (3) increase, 20; *e.* increased, 220, decreased, 70

SHORT ANSWER AND ESSAY QUESTIONS

1. p. 739
2. pp. 739-740
3. pp. 740-741
4. p. 741
5. pp. 741-742
6. p. 742
7. p. 743
8. pp. 744-746
9. pp. 744-745
10. p. 746
11. p. 747
12. p. 748
13. p. 748
14. p. 749
15. pp. 749-750
16. pp. 750-751
17. pp. 751-752
18. pp. 752-753
19. pp. 753-754
20. p. 754
21. p. 755
22. pp. 755-756
23. pp. 756-758
24. p. 756
25. p. 758

CHAPTER **37**

International Trade

In Chapter 6 you learned about the role of the United States in the global economy and the basic principles of international trade. Chapter 37 extends that analysis in several ways. It gives you a more advanced understanding of comparative advantage. It uses the tools of supply and demand to explain the equilibrium prices and quantities of imports and exports and the economic effects of tariffs and quotas. It examines the fallacious arguments for trade protectionism and the cost of this protection on U.S. society.

After a brief review of the facts of international trade presented in Chapter 6, the text uses graphical analysis to explain why nations trade: to take advantage of the benefits of specialization. Nations specialize in and export those goods and services in the production of which they have a ***comparative advantage.*** A comparative advantage means that the opportunity cost of producing a particular good or service is lower in that nation than in another nation. These nations will avoid producing and importing the goods and services that other nations have a comparative advantage in producing. In this way all nations are able to obtain products which are produced as inexpensively as possible. Put another way, when nations specialize in those products in which they have a comparative advantage, the world as a whole can obtain more goods and services from its resources; each nation of the world can enjoy a standard of living higher than it would have if it did not specialize and export and import.

The principle of comparative advantage tells us why nations trade, but what determines the ***equilibrium prices*** and ***quantities*** of the imports and exports resulting from trade? To answer this question, the text uses the supply and demand analysis, originally presented in Chapter 3, to explain equilibrium in the world market for a product. A simplified two-nation and one-product model of trade is used to construct export supply curves and import demand curves for each nation. Equilibrium occurs where one nation's export supply curve intersects another nation's import demand curve.

Regardless of the advantages of specialization and trade among nations, people in the United States and throughout the world for well over 200 years have debated whether ***free trade*** or ***protection*** was the better policy for their nation. Economists took part in this debate and, with few exceptions, argued for free trade and against protection. Those who favor free trade contend that free trade benefits both the nation and the world as a whole. "Free traders" argue that tariffs, import quotas, and other barriers to international trade prevent or reduce specialization and decrease both a nation's and the world's production and standard of living.

But nations have and continue to erect *barriers to trade* with other nations. The latter part of this chapter focuses attention on (1) what motivates nations to impose tariffs and to limit the quantities of goods imported from abroad; (2) the economic effects of protection on a nation's own prosperity and on the prosperity of the world economy; (3) the kinds of arguments those who favor protection use to support their position (on what grounds do they base their contention that their nation will benefit from the erection of barriers which reduce imports from foreign nations); and (4) the costs of protectionism for the United States.

The chapter's final section is a brief review of the *international trade policy* of the United States. Three general approaches to trade policy are identified in the discussion. First, the United States has participated in a generalized liberalization of trade as a result of ***General Agreements on Tariffs and Trade (GATT)*** negotiations and regional accords such as the ***North American Free Trade Agreement (NAFTA).*** Second, the United States has pursued an aggressive policy of promoting exports. The U.S. government has subsidized exports, supported export-oriented industries, and lobbied other nations to purchase U.S. exports, all in an effort to increase U.S. exports. Third, bilateral negotiations have been conducted between the United States and other nations. In recent years, the United States has held bilateral negotiations with China and Japan to resolve major trade disputes.

Whether the direction of the international trade policy in the United States will be toward freer trade or more protectionism is a question that gets debated as each new trade issue is presented to the U.S. public. The decision on each issue may well depend on your understanding of the advantages of free trade and the costs of trade protection for the nation and the world economy.

■ CHECKLIST

When you have studied this chapter you should be able to

☐ Cite some key facts about international trade.
☐ State the two economic circumstances which make it desirable for nations to specialize and trade.
☐ Compute the costs of producing two commodities when you are given the necessary data in a two-nation example.

□ Determine which nation has the comparative advantage in the production of each commodity using the cost data you computed for the two-nation example.
□ Calculate the range in which the terms of trade will occur in the two-nation example.
□ Explain how nations benefit from trade and specialization based on the two-nation example.
□ Discuss how increasing costs affect specialization in the two-nation example.
□ Restate the case for free trade.
□ Construct domestic supply and demand curves for two nations that trade a product.
□ Construct export supply and import demand curves for two nations that trade a product.
□ Use supply and demand analysis to explain how the equilibrium prices and quantities of exports and imports are determined for two nations that trade a product.
□ Identify the four principal types of artificial barriers to international trade and the motive for erecting these barriers.
□ Explain the economic effects of a protective tariff on resource allocation, the price of the commodity, the total production of the commodity, and the outputs of foreign and domestic producers of the commodity.
□ Analyze the economic effects of an import quota and compare them with the economic effects of a tariff.
□ Enumerate six arguments used to support the case for protection and find the weakness in each argument.
□ Offer a summation of the arguments for and against trade protection.
□ Discuss the costs of trade protectionism for society.
□ Explain how trade protectionism affects income distribution.
□ Describe actions taken to promote trade liberalization.
□ Cite examples of export promotion undertaken by the United States.
□ Discuss the issues involved in the bilateral trade negotiations of the United States.

■ CHAPTER OUTLINE

1. Some facts about international trade presented in Chapter 6 are worth reviewing.

a. About 12% of the total output of the United States is accounted for by exports of goods and services, a percentage which has more than doubled since 1965. The percentage of exports is much higher in other industrially advanced nations (e.g., 56% in the Netherlands, 38% in Canada), but the size of the U.S. economy means that it has the largest volume of imports and exports in the world.

b. The United States has a trade deficit in goods, a trade surplus in services, and a trade deficit in goods and services.

c. The principal exports of the United States are chemicals, computers, consumer durables, and aircraft, while its major imports are petroleum, automobiles, and clothing. Most of the trade occurs with other industrially advanced nations. Canada is the largest trading partner for the United States.

d. Factors that have facilitated trade since World War II include improvements in transportation and communications technology along with a general decline in tariffs and worldwide conflict.

e. The major participants in international trade are the United States, Japan, and the nations of western Europe. Newer participants include the "Asian tigers" (Hong Kong, Singapore, South Korea, and Taiwan) and China. The collapse of the former Soviet Union has changed trade patterns for Russia and the nations of eastern Europe.

f. International trade policy has been a subject of recent concern as evidenced by the North American Free Trade Agreement (NAFTA), the conclusion of negotiations on the General Agreements on Tariffs and Trade (GATT), and bilateral negotiations between the United States and Japan.

2. Specialization and trade among nations is advantageous because the world's resources are not evenly distributed and the efficient production of different commodities necessitates different methods and combinations of resources.

3. The principle of *comparative advantage*, first presented in Chapter 6 to explain the gains from trade, can now be reexamined with the aid of graphical analysis.

a. Suppose the world is composed of only two nations, each of which is capable of producing two different commodities and in which the production possibilities curves are different straight lines (whose opportunity cost ratios are constant but different).

(1) With different opportunity cost ratios, each nation will have a comparative (cost) advantage in the production of one of the two commodities, and if the world is to use its resources economically, each nation must specialize in the commodity in the production of which it has a comparative advantage.

(2) The ratio at which one product is traded for another—the terms of trade—lies between the opportunity cost ratios of the two nations.

b. Each nation gains from this trade because specialization permits a greater total output from the same resources and a better allocation of the world's resources.

c. If opportunity cost ratios in the two nations are not constant (if there is increasing cost), specialization may not be complete.

d. The basic argument for free trade among nations is that it leads to a better allocation of resources and a higher standard of living in the world, but it also increases competition and deters monopoly in these nations.

4. *Supply and demand analysis* can be used to explain how the equilibrium price and quantity of exports and imports for a product (e.g., aluminum) are determined when there is trade between two nations (e.g., the United States and Canada).

a. For the United States, there will be domestic supply and demand as well as export supply and import demand for aluminum.

(1) The price and quantity of aluminum are determined by the intersection of the *domestic* demand and supply curves in a world without trade.

(2) In a world with trade, the ***export supply curve*** for the United States shows the amount of aluminum that U.S. producers will export at each world price above the domestic equilibrium price. U.S. exports will increase when the world price rises relative to the domestic price.
(3) The ***import demand curve*** for the United States shows the amount of aluminum that U.S. citizens will import at each world price below the domestic equilibrium price. U.S. imports will increase when world prices fall relative to the domestic price.
b. For Canada, there will be domestic supply and demand as well as export supply and import demand for aluminum. The description of these supply and demand curves is similar for those of the United States described in point **a**.
c. The *equilibrium* world price and equilibrium world levels of exports and imports can be determined with further supply and demand analysis. The export supply curves of the two nations can be plotted on one graph. The import demand curves of both nations can be plotted on the same graph. In this two-nation model, equilibrium will be achieved when one nation's import demand curve intersects another nation's export supply curve.

5. Nations, however, limit international trade by erecting *artificial barriers.* Tariffs, import quotas, a variety of nontariff barriers, and voluntary export restrictions are the principal barriers to trade.
a. Special-interest groups benefit from protection and persuade their nations to erect trade barriers, but the costs to consumers of this protection exceed the benefits to the economy.
b. The imposition of a ***tariff*** on a good imported from abroad has both direct and indirect effects on an economy.
(1) The tariff increases the domestic price of the good, reduces its domestic consumption, expands its domestic production, decreases foreign production, and transfers income from domestic consumers to government.
(2) It also reduces the income of foreign producers and the ability of foreign nations to purchase goods and services in the nation imposing the tariff, causes the contraction of relatively efficient industries in that nation, decreases world trade, and lowers the real output of goods and services.
c. The imposition of a *quota* on an imported product has the same direct and indirect effects as that of a tariff on that product, with the exception that a tariff generates revenue for government use whereas an import quota transfers that revenue to foreign producers.

6. The arguments for *protectionism* are many, but often they are of questionable validity.
a. The military self-sufficiency argument can be challenged because it is difficult to determine which industry is "vital" to national defense and must be protected; it would be more efficient economically to provide a direct subsidy to military producers rather than impose a tariff.
b. Trade barriers do not necessarily increase domestic employment because
(1) imports may eliminate some jobs, but create others, so imports may change only the composition of employment, not the overall level of employment;
(2) the exports of one nation become the imports of another, so tariff barriers can be viewed as "beggar thy neighbor" policies;
(3) other nations are likely to retaliate against the imposition of trade barriers that will reduce domestic output and employment; and
(4) they create a less efficient allocation of resources by shielding protected domestic industries from the rigors of competition.
c. Using tariff barriers to permit diversification for stability in the economy is not necessary for advanced economies such as the United States, and there may be economic costs to diversification in developing nations.
d. It is alleged that infant industries need protection until they are sufficiently large to compete, but the argument may not apply to developed economies: It is difficult to select which industries will prosper; protectionism tends to persist long after it is needed; and direct subsidies may be more economically efficient. For advanced nations, a variant of this argument is strategic trade policy. It justifies barriers that protect the investment in high risk, growth industries for a nation, but these policies often lead to retaliation and similar policies from other trading nations.
e. Sometimes protection is sought against the "dumping" of excess foreign goods on U.S. markets. Dumping is a legitimate concern and is restricted under U.S. trade law, but to use dumping as an excuse for widespread tariff protection is unjustified and the number of documented cases is few. If foreign companies are more efficient (low cost) producers, what may appear to be dumping may actually be comparative advantage at work.
f. Protection is sometimes sought because of the cheap foreign labor argument; it should be realized that nations gain from trade based on comparative advantage, and without trade, living standards will be lower.
g. In summary, most protectionist arguments are fallacious or based on half-truths. The only points that have some validity, under certain conditions, are the infant industry and military-sufficiency arguments, but both are subject to abuse. The historical evidence suggests that free trade promotes and protectionism deters prosperity and economic growth in the world.

7. There are *costs to trade protectionism* for the United States.
a. There is a significant cost to society:
(1) It raises product prices by raising the imported price of the product, causes some consumers to switch to higher-priced domestic products, and increases the price of domestic products.
(2) The benefits for businesses and workers from trade protection are outweighed by the costs to U.S. society. The net cost to U.S. citizens was more than $15 billion annually in the mid-1990s.

b. There is an effect on income distribution because import restrictions are more costly for low-income families than for high-income families.

8. The *trade policies* of the United States in recent years can be categorized in three ways.

a. The United States has participated in regional and global agreements to liberalize trade. Two examples are the North American Free Trade Agreement (NAFTA) and the completion of the Uruguay round of the General Agreements on Tariffs and Trade (GATT).

b. Export promotion policies have included governmental lobbying for contracts, relaxation of export controls, advantageous loans through the U.S. Export-Import Bank, increased support for an industrial policy, and retaliatory tariffs.

c. Bilateral trade negotiations have been used to resolve trade differences with trading partners. These negotiations were used with China over most-favored-nation status and with Japan over persistent trade deficits.

■ HINTS AND TIPS

1. In the discussion of comparative advantage, the assumption of a constant-cost ratio means the production possibilities "curves" for each nation can be drawn as straight lines. The slope of the line in each nation is the opportunity cost of one product (wheat) in terms of the other product (coffee). The reciprocal of the slope of each line is the opportunity cost of the other product (coffee) in terms of the first product (wheat).

2. The export supply and import demand curves in Figures 37-3 and 37-4 in the text look different from the typical supply and demand curves that you have seen so far, so you should understand how they are constructed. The export supply and import demand curves for a nation do not intersect. Each curve meets at the price point on the *Y* axis showing the equilibrium price for domestic supply and demand. At this point there are no exports or imports.

a. The *export supply curve* is upsloping from that point because as world prices rise above the domestic equilibrium price, there will be increasing domestic surpluses produced by a nation that can be exported. The export supply curve reflects the positive relationship between rising world prices (above the domestic equilibrium price) and the increasing quantity of exports.

b. The *import demand curve* is downsloping from the domestic equilibrium price because as world prices fall below the domestic equilibrium price, there will be increasing domestic shortages that need to be covered by increasing imports. The import demand curve reflects the inverse relationship between falling world prices (below the domestic price) and the increasing quantity of imports.

3. One of the most interesting sections of the chapter discusses the arguments for and against trade protection. You have probably heard people give one or more of the arguments for trade protection, but now you have a chance to use your economic reasoning to expose the weaknesses in these arguments. Most are half-truths and special pleadings.

■ IMPORTANT TERMS

labor-intensive goods
land-intensive goods
capital-intensive goods
cost ratio
principle of comparative advantage
terms of trade
trading possibilities line
gains from trade
world price
domestic price
export supply curve
import demand curve
tariff
revenue tariff
protective tariff
import quota
nontariff barrier
voluntary export restriction
strategic trade policy
dumping
World Trade Organization
export controls
export subsidy
most-favored-nation (MFN) status

SELF-TEST

■ FILL-IN QUESTIONS

1. Exports of goods and services account for about (12, 24) ____________% of total output in the United States and have more than (doubled, quadrupled) ______________ since 1965.

2. Other industrially advanced nations such as the Netherlands and Canada have a (larger, smaller) ______________ percentage of imports and exports than the United States, but the United States' volume makes it the world's (largest, smallest) ______________ importing and exporting nation.

3. Nations tend to trade among themselves because the distribution of economic resources among them is (even, uneven) ______________ and the efficient production of various goods and services necessitates (the same, different) ______________ technologies or combinations of resources.

4. Comparative advantage means total world output will be greatest when each good is produced by that nation having the (highest, lowest) ______________ opportunity cost. The nations of the world tend to specialize in the production of those goods in which they (have, do not have) ______________ a comparative advantage and then export them, and they import those goods in which they ______________ a comparative advantage in production.

5. If the cost ratio in country X is 4 Panama hats equal 1 pound of bananas, while in country Y 3 Panama hats equal 1 pound of bananas, then

a. country X hats are relatively (expensive, inexpensive) ________________ and bananas relatively ________________,

b. country Y hats are relatively (expensive, inexpensive) ________________ and bananas relatively ________________,

c. X has a comparative advantage and should specialize in the production of (bananas, hats) ________________, and Y has a comparative advantage and should specialize in the production of ________________.

d. when X and Y specialize and trade, the terms of trade will be somewhere between (1, 2, 3, 4) __________ and __________ hats for each pound of bananas and will depend on world demand and supply for hats and bananas.

e. When the actual terms of trade turn out to be 3 1/2 hats for 1 pound of bananas, the cost of obtaining

(1) 1 Panama hat has been decreased from (2/7, 1/3) __________ to __________ pounds of bananas in Y.

(2) 1 pound of bananas has been decreased from (3 1/2, 4) ________ to ________ Panama hats in X.

f. International specialization will not be complete if the opportunity cost of producing either good (rises, falls) ______________ as a nation produces more of it.

6. The basic argument for free trade based on the principle of (bilateral negotiations, comparative advantage) ________________ is that it results in a (more, less) ________________ efficient allocation of resources and a (lower, higher) ________________ standard of living.

7. The world equilibrium price is determined by the interaction of (domestic, world) ________________ supply and demand, while the domestic equilibrium price is determined by ________________ supply and demand.

8. When world prices fall relative to domestic prices in a nation, the nation will (increase, decrease) ________________ its imports, and when world prices rise relative to domestic prices, the nation will ________________ its exports.

9. In a two-nation model for a product, the equilibrium price and quantity of imports and exports occurs where one nation's import demand intersects another nation's export (supply, demand) ________________ curve. In a highly competitive world market, there can be (multiple, only one) ________________ price(s) for a standardized product.

10. Excise taxes on imported products are (quotas, tariffs) ________________, whereas limits on the maximum amount of a product that can be imported are import ________________. Tariffs applied to a product not produced domestically are (protective, revenue) ________________ tariffs, but tariffs designed to shield domestic producers from foreign competition are ________________ tariffs.

11. There are other types of trade barriers. Imports that are restricted through the use of a licensing requirement or bureaucratic red tape are (tariff, nontariff) ________________ barriers. When foreign firms voluntarily limit their exports to another country, this would represent a voluntary (import, export) ______________ restraint.

12. Nations erect barriers to international trade to benefit the economic positions of (consumers, domestic producers) ________________ even though these barriers (increase, decrease) ________________ economic efficiency and trade among nations and the benefits to that nation are (greater, less) ________________ than the costs to it.

13. When the United States imposes a tariff on a good which is imported from abroad, the price of that good in the United States will (increase, decrease) ________________, the total purchases of the good in the United States will ________________, the output of U.S. producers of the good will (increase, decrease) ________________, and the output of foreign producers will ________________. The ability of foreigners to buy goods and services in the United States will (increase, decrease) ________________ and, as a result, output and employment in U.S. industries that sell goods and services abroad will ________________.

14. When comparing the effects of a tariff with the effects of a quota to restrict the U.S. imports of a product, the basic difference is that with a (tariff, quota) ________________ the U.S. government will receive revenue, but with a ________________ foreign producers will receive the revenue.

15. List the six arguments which protectionists use to justify trade barriers.

a. ____

b. ____

c. ____

d. ____

e. ____

f. ____

16. Most arguments for protectionism are (strong, weak) _______________ and are designed to benefit (consumers, domestic producers) _______________. If these arguments were followed, it would create (losses, gains) _______________ for protected industries and their workers at the expense of _______________ for the economy.

17. Protectionism will raise the price of a product by (increasing, decreasing) _______________ the imported price of the product, _______________ consumer purchases of the domestically produced product, and thus _______________ the demand and the price of the domestically produced product.

18. Studies indicate that the cost to consumers of protected products are substantially (less, greater) _______________ than the benefits to producers and government. Import restrictions also hurt low-income consumers (more, less) _______________ than high-income consumers.

19. Participation of the United States in the General Agreements on Tariffs and Trade (GATT) is an example of (export promotion, trade liberalization) _______________, whereas increased government funding for the U.S. Import-Export Bank is an example of _______________; both activities are part of the U.S. international trade policies.

20. Another U.S. trade policy is to hold discussions on trade issues directly with particular nations using (regional agreements, bilateral negotiations) _______________ _______________. Examples of this policy would be the annual review of most-favored-nation status for (Japan, China) _______________ and the discussion about the large trade deficit with _______________.

■ TRUE-FALSE QUESTIONS

Circle the T if the statement is true, the F if it is false.

1. The bulk of U.S. export and import trade is with other industrially advanced nations. **T F**

2. Two factors serve as the economic basis for world trade: the even distribution of resources and the fact that efficient production of various goods requires similar techniques or combinations of resources. **T F**

3. Mutually advantageous specialization and trade are possible between any two nations if they have the same domestic opportunity-cost ratios for any two products. **T F**

4. The principle of comparative advantage is that total output will be greatest when each good is produced by that nation which has the higher domestic opportunity cost. **T F**

5. By specializing based on comparative advantage, nations can obtain larger real incomes with fixed amounts of resources. **T F**

6. The terms of trade determine how the increase in world output resulting from comparative advantage is shared by trading nations. **T F**

7. Increasing production costs tend to prevent specialization among trading nations from being complete. **T F**

8. Trade among nations tends to bring about a more efficient use of the world's resources and a higher level of material well-being. **T F**

9. Free trade among nations tends to increase monopoly and lessen competition in these nations. **T F**

10. A nation will export a particular product if the world price is less than the domestic price. **T F**

11. In a two-country model, equilibrium in world prices and quantities of exports and imports will occur where one nation's export supply curve intersects the other nation's import demand curve. **T F**

12. A tariff on coffee in the United States is an example of a protective tariff. **T F**

13. The imposition of a tariff on a good imported from abroad will raise the price of the good and lower the quantity of how much of that good is bought and sold. **T F**

14. The major difference between a tariff and a quota on an imported product is that a quota produces revenue for the government. **T F**

15. To advocate tariffs which would protect domestic producers of goods and materials essential to national defense is to substitute a political-military objective for the economic objectives of efficiently allocating resources. **T F**

16. Tariffs and import quotas meant to achieve domestic full employment achieve short-run domestic goals by making trading partners poorer. **T F**

17. One-crop economies may be able to make themselves more stable and diversified by imposing tariffs on goods imported from abroad, but these tariffs are also apt to lower the standard of living in these economies. **T F**

18. Protection against the "dumping" of foreign goods at low prices on the U.S. market is one good reason for widespread, permanent tariffs. **T F**

19. The only argument for tariffs that has, in the appropriate circumstances, any economic justification is the increase-domestic-employment argument. **T F**

20. The cost of protecting U.S. firms and employees from foreign competition is the rise in the prices of products produced in the United States, and this cost almost always exceeds its benefits. **T F**

21. Trade protectionism has no effect on income distribution. **T F**

22. An example of trade liberalization is General Agreements on Tariffs and Trade (GATT). **T F**

23. The World Trade Organization was established by the United Nations to encourage purchases of products from developing nations. **T F**

24. It is a myth that the global marketplace is a battleground for supremacy where one nation wins and the other loses. Every nation is both a seller and buyer in the world market. Gains from trade come from the increased consumable output shared by the trading countries. **T F**

25. The United States uses bilateral trade negotiations to resolve trade disputes with the U.S. Export-Import Bank. **T F**

■ MULTIPLE-CHOICE QUESTIONS

Circle the letter that corresponds to the best answer.

1. Which nation leads the world in the volume of exports and imports?
(a) Japan
(b) Germany
(c) United States
(d) United Kingdom

2. Which group of nations dominates world trade?
(a) Saudi Arabia and other OPEC nations
(b) Hong Kong, Singapore, South Korea, and Taiwan
(c) United States, Japan, and the nations of western Europe
(d) China, Russia, and the nations of eastern Europe

3. Nations need to engage in trade because
(a) world resources are evenly distributed among nations
(b) world resources are unevenly distributed among nations
(c) all products are produced from the same technology
(d) all products are produced from the same combinations of resources

Use the following tables to answer Questions 4, 5, 6, and 7.

NEPAL PRODUCTION POSSIBILITIES TABLE

	Production alternatives					
Product	**A**	**B**	**C**	**D**	**E**	**F**
Yak fat	0	4	8	12	16	20
Camel hides	40	32	24	16	8	0

KASHMIR PRODUCTION POSSIBILITIES TABLE

	Production alternatives					
Product	**A**	**B**	**C**	**D**	**E**	**F**
Yak fat	0	3	6	9	12	15
Camel hides	60	48	36	24	12	0

4. The data in the table show that production in
(a) both Nepal and Kashmir are subject to increasing opportunity costs
(b) both Nepal and Kashmir are subject to constant opportunity costs
(c) Nepal is subject to increasing opportunity costs and Kashmir to constant opportunity costs
(d) Kashmir is subject to increasing opportunity costs and Nepal to constant opportunity costs

5. If Nepal and Kashmir engage in trade, the terms of trade will be
(a) between 2 and 4 camel hides for 1 unit of yak fat
(b) between 1/3 and 1/2 units of yak fat for 1 camel hide
(c) between 3 and 4 units of yak fat for 1 camel hide
(d) between 2 and 4 units of yak fat for 1 camel hide

6. Assume that prior to specialization and trade Nepal and Kashmir both choose production possibility C. Now if each specializes according to its comparative advantage, the resulting gains from specialization and trade will be
(a) 6 units of yak fat
(b) 8 units of yak fat
(c) 6 units of yak fat and 8 camel hides
(d) 8 units of yak fat and 6 camel hides

7. Each nation produced only one product in accordance with its comparative advantage, and the terms of trade were set at 3 camel hides for 1 unit of yak fat. In this case, Nepal could obtain a maximum combination of 8 units of yak fat and
(a) 12 camel hides
(b) 24 camel hides
(c) 36 camel hides
(d) 48 camel hides

8. What happens to a nation's imports or exports of a product when world prices rise relative to domestic prices?
(a) Imports of the product increase.
(b) Imports of the product stay the same.
(c) Exports of the product increase.
(d) Exports of the product decrease.

9. What happens to a nation's imports or exports of a product when world prices fall relative to domestic prices?
(a) Imports of the product increase.
(b) Imports of the product decrease.
(c) Exports of the product increase.
(d) Exports of the product stay the same.

10. Which one of the following is characteristic of tariffs?
(a) They prevent the importation of goods from abroad.
(b) They specify the maximum amounts of specific commodities which may be imported during a given period of time.
(c) They often protect domestic producers from foreign competition.
(d) They enable nations to reduce their exports and increase their imports during periods of depression.

11. The motive for barriers to the importation of goods and services from abroad is to
(a) improve economic efficiency in that nation
(b) protect and benefit domestic producers of those goods and services
(c) reduce the prices of the goods and services produced in that nation
(d) expand the export of goods and services to foreign nations

12. When a tariff is imposed on a good imported from abroad,

(a) the demand for the good increases
(b) the demand for the good decreases
(c) the supply of the good increases
(d) the supply of the good decreases

Answer Questions 13, 14, 15, 16, and 17 on the basis of the following diagram, where S_d *and* D_d *are the domestic supply and demand for a product and* P_w *is the world price of that product.*

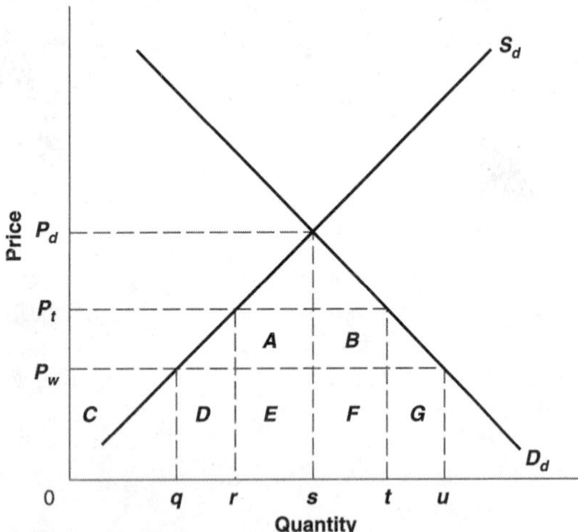

13. In a closed economy (without international trade), the equilibrium price would be

(a) P_d, but in an open economy, the equilibrium price will be P_t
(b) P_d, but in an open economy, the equilibrium price will be P_w
(c) P_w, but in an open economy, the equilibrium price will be P_d
(d) P_w, but in an open economy, the equilibrium price will be P_t

14. If there is free trade in this economy and no tariffs, the total revenue going to the foreign producers is represented by

(a) area ***C***
(b) areas ***A*** and ***B*** combined
(c) areas ***A, B, E,*** and ***F*** combined
(d) areas ***D, E, F,*** and ***G*** combined

15. If a per unit tariff was imposed in the amount of P_wP_t then domestic producers would supply

(a) ***q*** units and foreign producers would supply ***qu*** units
(b) ***s*** units and foreign producers would supply ***su*** units
(c) ***r*** units and foreign producers would supply ***rt*** units
(d) ***t*** units and foreign producers would supply ***tu*** units

16. Given a per unit tariff in the amount of P_wP_t, the amount of the tariff revenue paid by consumers of this product is represented by

(a) area ***A***
(b) area ***B***
(c) areas ***A*** and ***B*** combined
(d) areas ***D, E, F,*** and ***G*** combined

17. Assume an import quota of ***rt*** units is imposed on the foreign nation producing this product. The amount of *total* revenue going to foreign producers is represented by areas

(a) $A + B$
(b) $E + F$
(c) $A + B + E + F$
(d) $D + E + F + G$

18. Tariffs lead to

(a) the contraction of relatively efficient industries
(b) an overallocation of resources to relatively efficient industries
(c) an increase in the foreign demand for domestically produced goods
(d) an underallocation of resources to relatively inefficient industries

19. "The nation needs to protect itself from foreign countries that sell their products in our domestic markets at less than the cost of production." This quotation would be most closely associated with which protectionist argument?

(a) diversification for stability
(b) increase domestic employment
(c) protection against dumping
(d) cheap foreign labor

20. Which argument for protection is the least fallacious and most pertinent in the United States today?

(a) the military self-sufficiency argument
(b) the increase-domestic-employment argument
(c) the cheap foreign labor argument
(d) the infant industry argument

21. Which of the following is the likely result of the United States using tariffs to protect its high wages and standard of living from cheap foreign labor?

(a) an increase in U.S. exports
(b) a rise in the U.S. real GDP
(c) a decrease in the average productivity of U.S. workers
(d) a decrease in the quantity of labor employed by industries producing the goods on which tariffs have been levied

22. Which is a likely result of imposing tariffs to increase domestic employment?

(a) a short-run increase in domestic employment in import industries
(b) a decrease in the tariff rates of foreign nations
(c) a long-run reallocation of workers from export industries to protected domestic industries
(d) a decrease in consumer prices

23. The infant industry argument for tariffs

(a) is especially pertinent for the European Economic Community
(b) generally results in tariffs that are removed after the infant industry has matured
(c) makes it rather easy to determine which infant industries will become mature industries with comparative advantages in producing their goods
(d) might better be replaced by an argument for outright subsidies for infant industries

24. Trade protectionism is costly to consumers because
(a) the price of the imported good rises
(b) the supply of the imported good increases
(c) import competition increases for domestically produced goods
(d) consumers shift purchases away from domestically produced goods

25. What international trade policy has the United States pursued in recent years?
(a) increasing the level of tariffs
(b) increasing import quotas
(c) export promotion
(d) import subsidies

■ PROBLEMS

1. Shown below are the production possibilities curves for two nations: the United States and Chile. Suppose these two nations do not currently engage in international trade or specialization, and suppose that points ***A*** and ***a*** show the combinations of wheat and copper they now produce and consume.

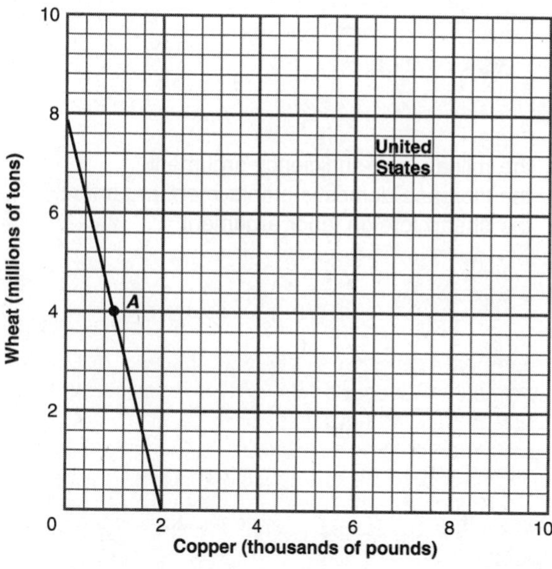

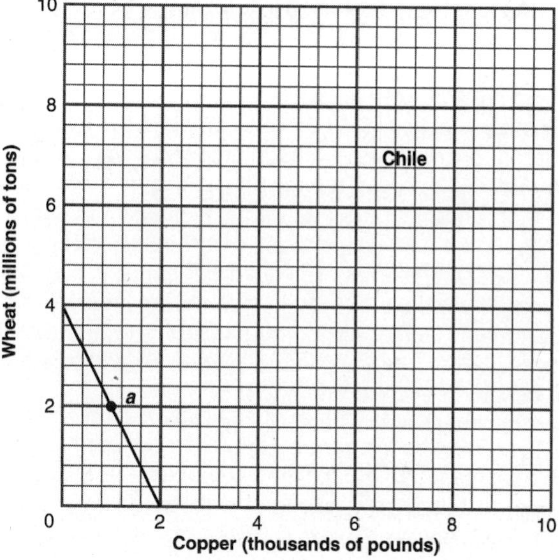

a. The straightness of the two curves indicates that the cost ratios in the two nations are (changing, constant) ______________.

b. Examination of the two curves reveals that the cost ratio in

(1) the United States is ______________ million tons of wheat for ______________ thousand pounds of copper.

(2) Chile is ______________ million tons of wheat for ______________ thousand pounds of copper.

c. If these two nations were to specialize and trade wheat for copper,

(1) The United States would specialize in the production of wheat because ______________

______________.

(2) Chile would specialize in the production of copper because ______________.

d. The terms of trade, if specialization and trade occur, will be greater than 2 and less than 4 million tons of wheat for 1,000 pounds of copper because ______

______________.

e. Assume the terms of trade turn out to be 3 million tons of wheat for 1,000 pounds of copper. Draw in the trading possibilities curve for the United States and Chile.

f. With these trading possibilities curves, suppose the United States decides to consume 5 million tons of wheat and 1,000 pounds of copper while Chile decides to consume 3 million tons of wheat and 1,000 pounds of copper. The gains from trade to

(1) the United States are ______________ million tons of wheat and __________ thousand pounds of copper.

(2) Chile are ______________ million tons of wheat and

______________ thousand pounds of copper.

2. Following are tables showing the domestic supply and demand schedule and the export supply and import demand schedule for two nations (**A** and **B**).

NATION A

Price	Q_{dd}	Q_{sd}	Q_{di}	Q_{se}
$3.00	100	300	0	200
2.50	150	250	0	100
2.00	200	200	0	0
1.50	250	150	100	0
1.00	300	100	200	0

a. For nation **A,** the first column of the table is the price of a product. The second column is the quantity demanded domestically (***Q_{dd}***). The third column is the quantity supplied domestically (***Q_{sd}***). The fourth column is the quantity demanded for imports (***Q_{di}***). The fifth column is the quantity of exports supplied (***Q_{se}***).

(1) At a price of \$2.00, there (will, will not) ______ be a surplus or shortage and there ______ be exports or imports.
(2) At a price of \$3.00, there will be a domestic (shortage, surplus) ______ of ______ units. This domestic ______ will be eliminated by (exports, imports) ______ of ______ units.
(3) At a price of \$1.00, there will be a domestic (shortage, surplus) ______ of ______ units. This domestic ______ will be eliminated by (exports, imports) ______ of ______ units.

b. For nation **B,** the first column is the price of a product. The second column is the quantity demanded domestically (***Q_{dd}***). The third column is the quantity supplied domestically (***Q_{sd}***). The fourth column is the quantity demanded for imports (***Q_{di}***). The fifth column is the quantity of exports supplied (***Q_{se}***).

NATION B

Price	Q_{dd}	Q_{sd}	Q_{di}	Q_{se}
\$2.50	100	300	0	200
2.00	150	250	0	100
1.50	200	200	0	0
1.00	250	150	100	0

(1) At a price of \$1.50, there (will, will not) ______ be a surplus or shortage and there ______ be exports or imports.
(2) At a price of \$2.50, there will be a domestic (shortage, surplus) ______ of ______ units. This domestic ______ will be eliminated by (exports, imports) ______ of ______ units.
(3) At a price of \$1.00, there will be a domestic (shortage, surplus) ______ of ______ units. This domestic ______ will be eliminated by (exports, imports) ______ of ______ units.

c. The following table shows a schedule of the import demand in Nation **A** and the export supply in Nation **B** at various prices. The first column is the price of the product. The second column is the quantity demanded for imports (***Q_{diA}***) in Nation **A**. The third column is the quantity of exports supplied (***Q_{seB}***) in Nation **B.**

Price	Q_{diA}	Q_{seB}
\$2.00	0	100
1.75	50	50
1.50	100	0

(1) If the world price is \$2.00, then Nation **(A, B)** ______ will want to import ______ units and Nation ______ will want to export ______ units of the product.
(2) If the world price is \$1.75, then Nation **(A, B)** ______ will want to import ______ units and Nation ______ will want to export ______ units of the product.
(3) If the world price is \$1.50, then Nation **(A, B)** ______ will want to import ______ units and Nation ______ will want to export ______ units of the product.

3. The following table shows the quantities of woolen gloves demanded (***D***) in the United States at several different prices (***P***). Also shown in the table are the quantities of woolen gloves that would be supplied by U.S. producers (***S_a***) and the quantities that would be supplied by foreign producers (***S_f***) at the nine different prices.

P	*D*	S_a	S_f	S_t	S'_f	S'_t
\$2.60	450	275	475	____	____	____
2.40	500	250	450	____	____	____
2.20	550	225	425	____	____	____
2.00	600	200	400	____	____	____
1.80	650	175	375	____	____	____
1.60	700	150	350	____	____	____
1.40	750	125	325	____	____	____
1.20	800	0	300	____	____	____
1.00	850	0	0	____	____	____

a. Compute and enter in the table the total quantities that would be supplied (***S_t***) by U.S. and foreign producers at each of the prices.
b. If the market for woolen gloves in the United States is a competitive one the equilibrium price for woolen gloves is \$______ and the equilibrium quantity is ______.
c. Suppose now that the United States government imposes an 80 cent (\$.80) tariff per pair of gloves on all gloves imported into the United States from abroad. Compute and enter into the table the quantities that would be supplied (***S'_t***) by foreign producers at the nine different prices. (*Hint:* If foreign producers were willing to supply 300 pairs at a price of \$1.20 when there was no tariff and they are now willing to supply 300 pairs at \$2.00 (the \$.80 per pair tariff plus the \$1.20 they will receive for themselves). The quantities supplied at each of the other prices may be found in a similar fashion.)
d. Compute and enter into the table the total quantities that would be supplied (***S'_t***) by U.S. and foreign producers at each of the nine prices.
e. As a result of the imposition of the tariff the equilibrium price has risen to \$______ and the equilibrium quantity has fallen to ______.
f. The number of pairs sold by

(1) U.S. producers has (increased, decreased) ______________ by ______________.
(2) foreign producers has (increased, decreased) ______________ by ______________.

g. The total revenues (after the payment of the tariff) of
(1) U.S. producers—who *do not* pay the tariff—have (increased, decreased) ______________ by $________.
(2) foreign producers—who *do* pay the tariff—have (increased, decreased) ______________ by $________.

h. The total amount spent by U.S. buyers of woolen gloves has ______________ by $__________.

i. The total number of dollars earned by foreigners has ______________ by $____________, and, as a result, the total foreign demand for goods and services produced in the United States will ______________ by $____________.

j. The tariff revenue of the United States government has ______________ by $______________.

k. If an import quota were imposed that had the same effect as the tariff on price and output, the amount of the tariff revenue, $______________, would now be received as revenue by ______________ producers.

■ SHORT ANSWER AND ESSAY QUESTIONS

1. Describe the quantity of imports and exports for the United States in absolute and relative terms. How has the quantity of imports and exports changed over time?

2. What are the major imports and exports of the United States? With which nations does the United States trade?

3. What role does the United States play in international trade? Who are the other major players in international trade?

4. What two facts—one dealing with the distribution of the world's resources and the other related to the technology of producing different products—are the basis for the trade among nations?

5. Explain
(a) the theory or principle of comparative advantage;
(b) what is meant by and what determines the terms of trade; and
(c) the gains from trade.

6. What is the case for free trade?

7. Explain how the equilibrium prices and quantities of exports and imports are determined.

8. Why will exports in a nation increase when world prices rise relative to domestic prices?

9. What motivates nations to erect barriers to the importation of goods from abroad, and what types of barriers do they erect?

10. Suppose the United States increases the tariff on automobiles imported from Germany (and other foreign countries). What is the effect of this tariff-rate increase on
(a) the price of automobiles in the United States;
(b) the total number of cars sold in the United States during a year;
(c) the number of cars produced by and employment in the German automobile industry;
(d) production by and employment in the U.S. automobile industry;
(e) German income obtained by selling cars in the United States;
(f) the German demand for goods produced in the U.S.;
(g) the production of and employment in those U.S. industries which now export goods to Germany;
(h) the standards of living in the U.S. and in Germany;
(i) the allocation of resources in the U.S. economy; and
(j) the allocation of the world's resources?

11. Compare and contrast the economic effects of a tariff with the economic effects of an import quota on a product.

12. Critically evaluate the military self-sufficiency and infant industry arguments (including strategic trade policy) as a basis for protectionism.

13. Can a strong case for protectionism be made on the basis of one of the following reasons: increasing domestic employment, diversifying for stability, defending against the "dumping" of products, or shielding domestic workers from competition from "cheap" foreign labor? Summarize the case for and the case against protectionism.

14. How costly have trade barriers been for the United States? What are the costs to society? What are the benefits from trade barriers?

15. What is the effect of trade protectionism on income distribution in society? Explain, and give an example.

16. Describe the three types of international trade policies the United States conducts.

17. What are the major provisions of the General Agreements on Tariffs and Trade (GATT)?

18. Describe at least three examples of how the United States has pursued a trade policy of aggressive export promotion in recent years.

19. What are the issues involved in the renewal of most-favored-nation status for China?

20. Why did the United States participate in bilateral negotiations with Japan in recent years? What were the arguments and the results?

ANSWERS

Chapter 37 International Trade

FILL-IN QUESTIONS

1. 12, doubled
2. larger, largest

3. uneven, different
4. lowest, have, do not have
5. *a.* inexpensive, expensive; *b.* expensive, inexpensive; *c.* hats, bananas; *d.* 3, 4; *e.* (1) 1/3, 2/7, (2) 4, 3 1/2; *f.* rises
6. comparative advantage, more, higher
7. world, domestic
8. increase, increase
9. supply, only one
10. tariffs, quotas, revenue, protective
11. nontariff, export
12. domestic producers, decrease, less
13. increase, decrease, increase, decrease, decrease, decrease
14. tariff, quota
15. *a.* military self-sufficiency; *b.* infant industry; *c.* increase domestic employment; *d.* diversification for stability; *e.* protection against dumping; *f.* cheap foreign labor (any order for a–f)
16. weak, domestic producers, gains, losses
17. increasing, increasing, increasing
18. greater, more
19. trade liberalization, export promotion
20. bilateral negotiations, China, Japan

TRUE-FALSE QUESTIONS

1. T, p. 765
2. F, pp. 765-766
3. F, pp. 766-768
4. F, p. 767
5. T, p. 771
6. T, p. 768
7. T, pp. 770-771
8. T, p. 771
9. F, p. 771
10. F, pp. 771-774
11. T, pp. 774-775
12. F, p. 775
13. T, pp. 775-776
14. F, p. 777
15. T, p. 777
16. T, pp. 777-778
17. T, p. 778
18. F, p. 779
19. F, p. 780
20. T, pp. 781-782
21. F, p. 782
22. T, p. 782
23. F, p. 783
24. T, p. 783
25. F, pp. 783-785

MULTIPLE-CHOICE QUESTIONS

1. c, p. 764
2. c, p. 765
3. b, p. 765
4. b, p. 767
5. a, pp. 767-768
6. a, pp. 768-770
7. c, pp. 768-770
8. c, pp. 771-774
9. a, pp. 771-774
10. c, p. 775
11. b, pp. 775-777
12. d, pp. 775-776
13. b, pp. 775-776
14. d, p. 776
15. c, p. 776
16. c, p. 776
17. c, p. 777
18. a, pp. 776-777
19. c, p. 779
20. a, p. 780
21. c, p. 780
22. c, pp. 777-778
23. d, pp. 778-779
24. a, p. 781
25. c, pp. 783-785

PROBLEMS

1. *a.* constant; *b.* (1) 8, 2, (2) 4, 2; *c.* (1) it has a comparative advantage in producing wheat (its cost of producing wheat is less than Chile's), (2) it has a comparative advantage in producing copper (its cost of producing copper is less than the United States'); *d.* one of the two nations would be unwilling to trade if the terms of trade are outside this range; *f.* (1) 1, 0, (2) 1, 0
2. *a.* (1) will not, will not, (2) surplus, 200, surplus, exports, 200, (3) shortage, 200, shortage, imports, 200; *b.* (1) will not, will not, (2) surplus, 200, surplus, exports, 200, (3) shortage, 100, shortage, imports, 100; *c.* (1) A, 0, B, 100, (2) A, 50, B, 50, (3) A, 100, B, 0
3. *a.* 750, 700, 650, 600, 550, 500, 450, 300, 0; *b.* $2.00, 600; *c.* 375, 350, 325, 300, 0, 0, 0, 0, 0; *d.* 650, 600, 550, 500, 175, 150, 125, 0, 0; *e.* $2.20, 550; *f.* (1) increased, 25, (2) decreased, 75; *g.* (1) increased, $95, (2) decreased, $345; *h.* increased, $10; *i.* decreased, $345, decreased, $345; *j.* increased, $260; *k.* $260, foreign

SHORT ANSWER AND ESSAY QUESTIONS

1. pp. 764-765
2. p. 765
3. p. 765
4. pp. 765-766
5. pp. 767-770
6. p. 771
7. pp. 774-775
8. pp. 772-773
9. pp. 775-777
10. pp. 775-777
11. p. 777
12. pp. 777-779
13. pp. 777-780
14. pp. 781-782
15. p. 782
16. pp. 782-783
17. pp. 782-783
18. p. 783
19. pp. 783-785
20. p. 785

CHAPTER 38

Exchange Rates, the Balance of Payments, and Trade Deficits

In the last chapter you learned *why* nations engage in international trade and *why* they erect barriers to trade with other nations. In Chapter 38 you will learn *how* nations using different currencies are able to trade with each other.

The means nations use to overcome the difficulties that result from the use of different currencies is fairly simple. When the residents of a nation (its consumers, business firms, or governments) wish to buy goods or services or real or financial assets from, make loans or gifts to, or pay interest and dividends to the residents of other nations, they *buy* some of the currency used in that nation. They pay for the foreign money with some of their own currency. In other words, they *exchange* their own currency for foreign currency.

When the residents of a nation sell goods or services or real or financial assets to, receive loans or gifts from, or are paid dividends or interest by the residents of foreign nations and obtain foreign currencies, they **sell** this foreign currency—often called foreign exchange—in return for some of their own currency. That is, they **exchange** foreign currency for their own currency.

The markets in which one currency is sold and is paid for with another currency are called ***foreign exchange markets.*** The price that is paid (in one currency) for a unit of another currency is called the ***foreign exchange rate*** (or the ***rate of exchange***). And like most prices, the foreign exchange rate for any foreign currency is determined by the demand for and the supply of that foreign currency.

As you know from Chapter 37, nations buy and sell large quantities of goods and services across national boundaries. But the residents of these nations also buy and sell such financial assets as stocks and bonds and such real assets as land and capital goods in other nations, and the governments and individuals in one nation make gifts (remittances) in other nations. At the end of a year, nations summarize their foreign transactions with the rest of the world. This summary is called the nation's *international balance of payments:* a record of how it obtained foreign currency during the year and what it did with this foreign currency.

Of course, all foreign currency obtained was used for some purpose—it did not evaporate—consequently the balance of payments *always* balances. The international balance of payments is an extremely important and useful device for understanding the amounts and kinds of international transactions in which the residents of a nation engage. But it also enables us to understand the meaning of a balance of payments imbalance (a deficit or a surplus), the causes of these imbalances, and how to deal with them.

Probably the most difficult section of this chapter is concerned with ***balance of payments deficits*** and ***surpluses.*** A balance of payments deficit (surplus) is found when the receipts of foreign currency are less (greater) than the payments of foreign currency and the nation must reduce (expand) its official reserves to make the balance of payments balance. Pay particular attention to the way in which a system of *flexible* exchange rates and a system of *fixed* exchange rates will correct balance of payments deficits and surpluses and the advantages and disadvantages of these two alternative methods of eliminating imbalances.

As examples of these two types of exchange-rate systems, the third section of the chapter examines the gold standard, the Bretton Woods system, and the managed floating exchange-rate system. In the first two systems exchange rates are fixed, and in the third system exchange rates are fixed in the short run (to obtain the advantages of fixed exchange rates) and flexible in the long run (to enable nations to correct balance of payments deficits and surpluses).

The final section of the chapter examines the ***trade deficits*** of the United States during the 1990s. As you will learn, these deficits were the result of several factors—differences in national growth rates, large Federal budget deficits, and a declining saving rate—that contributed to imports rising faster than exports. They also have several implications, such as increased current consumption at the possible expense of future consumption and increased U.S. indebtedness to foreigners.

■ CHECKLIST

When you have studied this chapter you should be able to

☐ Explain how U.S. exports create a foreign demand for dollars that in turn generates a supply of foreign currencies.
☐ Describe how U.S. imports create a domestic demand for foreign currencies that in turn generates a supply of dollars.
☐ Give a definition of a nation's international balance of payments.
☐ Use the items in the current account to calculate the balance of trade, balance on goods and services, and balance on the current account when given the necessary data.

□ Describe how balance is achieved in the capital account.
□ Explain the relationship between the current account, capital account, and official reserves account.
□ Indicate how the official reserve account is used to determine whether there is a balance of payment deficit or surplus.
□ Use a supply and demand graph to illustrate how a flexible exchange-rate system works to establish the price and quantity of a currency.
□ Describe the depreciation and appreciation of a nation's currency under a flexible exchange-rate system.
□ Identify the five principal determinants of the demand for and supply of a particular foreign currency and explain how they alter exchange rates.
□ List three disadvantages of flexible exchange rates.
□ Use a supply and demand graph to illustrate how a fixed exchange-rate system functions.
□ Discuss the objectives and limitations of using official reserves, trade policies, exchange controls, and domestic stabilization policies to maintain a fixed exchange rate.
□ Identify three different exchange-rate systems used by the world's nations in recent years.
□ List three conditions a nation had to fulfill if it were to be on the gold standard.
□ Explain how the gold standard worked to maintain fixed exchange rates.
□ Give reasons for the demise of the gold standard.
□ Explain how the Bretton Woods system attempted to stabilize exchange rates and establish orderly changes in exchange rates for correcting balance of payment deficits.
□ State reasons for the demise of the Bretton Woods system.
□ Describe the current system of managed floating exchange rates.
□ Discuss the pros and cons of the system of managed floating exchange rates.
□ Describe the causes of recent trade deficits in the United States.
□ Explain the economic implications of recent trade deficits in the United States.

■ CHAPTER OUTLINE

1. Trade between two nations differs from domestic trade because the nations use different currencies. This problem is resolved by the existence of *foreign exchange markets,* in which the currency used by one nation can be purchased and paid for with the currency of the other nation.

a. United States exports create a foreign demand for dollars, and the satisfaction of this demand increases the supply of foreign currencies in the foreign exchange market.

b. United States imports create a domestic demand for foreign currencies, and meeting this demand decreases the supplies of foreign currencies in the foreign exchange market.

2. The ***international balance of payments*** for a nation is an annual record of all its transactions with the other nations in the world; it records all the payments received from and made to the rest of the world.

a. The ***current account*** section of a nation's international balance of payments records its trade in currently produced goods and services. Within this section

(1) the trade balance of the nation is equal to its exports of goods (merchandise) less its imports of goods (merchandise);

(2) the balance on goods and services is equal to its exports of goods and services less its imports of goods and services; and

(3) the balance on the current account is equal to its balance on goods and services plus its net investment income (dividends and interest) from other nations and its net private and public transfers to other nations, and minus this balance may be either a surplus or a deficit.

b. The ***capital account*** section of a nation's international balance of payments records its sales of real and financial assets (which earn it foreign currencies) and its purchases of real and financial assets (which use up foreign currencies). The nation has a ***capital account surplus (deficit)*** if its sales are greater (less) than its purchases of real and financial assets.

c. The ***official reserves*** account consists of the foreign currencies owned by the central bank. These reserves decrease when they are used to finance a net deficit on the combined current and capital accounts. The reserves increase when a nation has a net surplus on its current and capital account. The three components of the balance of payments—the current account, the capital account, and the official reserves account—must equal zero.

d. A nation has a balance of payments *deficit* when imbalances in the combined current and capital accounts lead to a decrease in official reserves. A balance of payments *surplus* arises when imbalances in the combined current and capital accounts result in an increase in official reserves.

3. There are flexible (floating) and fixed *exchange-rate systems* that nations use to correct imbalances in the balance of payments. If the foreign exchange rate *floats freely,* the demand for and the supply of foreign exchange determine foreign exchange rates. The exchange rate for any foreign currency is the rate at which the quantity of that currency demanded is equal to the quantity of it supplied.

a. A change in the demand for or the supply of a foreign currency will cause a change in the exchange rate for that currency. When there is an increase in the price paid in dollars for a foreign currency, the dollar has depreciated and the foreign currency has appreciated in value. Conversely, when there is an decrease in the price paid in dollars for a foreign currency, the dollar has appreciated and the foreign currency has depreciated in value.

b. Changes in the demand for or supply of a foreign currency are largely the result of changes in tastes, relative incomes, relative price levels, relative interest rates, and speculation.

c. Flexible exchange rates can be used to eliminate a balance of payments deficit or surplus.

(1) When a nation has a payment deficit, foreign exchange rates will increase, thus making foreign goods and services more expensive and decreasing imports.

These events will make a nation's goods and services less expensive for foreigners to buy, thus increasing exports.

(2) With a payment surplus, the exchange rates will increase, thus making foreign goods and services less expensive and increasing imports. This situation makes a nation's goods and services more expensive for foreigners to buy, thus decreasing exports.

d. But a flexible exchange-rate system increases the uncertainties exporters, importers, and investors face, thus reducing international trade. This system also changes the terms of trade and creates instability in domestic economies.

4. When nations *fix* (or peg) foreign exchange rates, the governments of these nations must intervene in the foreign exchange markets to prevent shortages and surpluses caused by shifts in demand and supply.

a. One way a nation can stabilize foreign exchange is for its government to sell its reserves of a foreign currency in exchange for its own currency (or gold) when there is a shortage of the foreign currency. Conversely, a government would buy a foreign currency in exchange for its own currency (or gold) when there is a surplus of the foreign currency; however, currency reserves may be limited and inadequate for handling large and persistent deficits or surpluses, so it may use other means to maintain fixed exchange rates.

(1) A nation might adopt trade policies that discourage imports and encourage exports.

(2) A nation might impose exchange rate controls and rationing, but these policies tend to distort trade, lead to government favoritism, restrict consumer choice, and create black markets.

b. Another way a nation can stabilize foreign exchange rates is to use monetary and fiscal policy to reduce its national income and price level and raise interest rates relative to those in other nations. These events would lead to a decrease in demand for and increase in the supply of different foreign currencies.

5. In their recent history, the nations of the world have used three different exchange-rate systems.

a. Under the ***gold standard,*** each nation must define its currency in terms of a quantity of gold, maintain a fixed relationship between its gold and its money supply, and allow gold to be imported or exported without restrictions.

(1) The potential gold flows between nations would ensure that exchange rates remained fixed.

(2) Payment deficits and surpluses would be eliminated through macroeconomic adjustments. For example, if a nation has a balance of payments deficit and gold flowing out of the country, its money supply would decrease. This event would increase interest rates and decrease total spending, output, employment, and the price level. The opposite would happen in the other country because it has a payments surplus. The changes in both nations would eliminate any payments deficit or surplus.

(3) During the worldwide depression of the 1930s nations felt that remaining on the gold standard threatened their recoveries, and the policy of devaluating their currencies to boost exports led to the breakdown and abandonment of the gold standard.

b. From the end of World War II until 1971 the ***Bretton Woods system,*** committed to the adjustable-peg system of exchange rates and managed by the ***International Monetary Fund (IMF),*** kept foreign exchange rates relatively stable.

(1) The adjustable-peg system required the United States to sell gold to other member nations at a fixed price and the other members of the IMF to define their monetary units in terms of either gold or dollars (which established fixed exchange rates among the currencies of all member nations) and required the other member nations to keep the exchange rates for their currencies from rising by selling foreign currencies, selling gold, or borrowing on a short-term basis from the IMF.

(2) The system also provided for orderly changes in exchange rates to correct a fundamental imbalance (persistent and sizable balance of payments deficits) by allowing a nation to devalue its currency (increase its defined gold or dollar equivalent).

(3) The other nations of the world used gold and dollars as their international monetary reserves in the Bretton Woods system. For these reserves to grow, the United States had to continue to have balance of payments deficits, but to continue the convertibility of dollars into gold it had to reduce the deficits, and, faced with this dilemma, in 1971 the United States suspended the convertibility of the dollar, brought an end to the Bretton Woods system of fixed exchange rates, and allowed the exchange rates for the dollar and the other currencies to float.

c. Exchange rates today are managed by individual nations to avoid short-term fluctuations and allowed to float in the long term to correct balance of payments deficits and surpluses. This new system of ***managed floating exchange rates*** is favored by some and criticized by others.

(1) Its proponents contend that this system has not led to any decrease in world trade and has enabled the world to adjust to severe economic shocks.

(2) Its critics argue that it has resulted in volatile exchange rates, has not reduced balance of payments deficits and surpluses, and is a "nonsystem" that a nation may use to achieve its own domestic economic goals.

6. During the 1990s, the United States has had large and persistent trade deficits.

a. These trade deficits were the result of several factors:

(1) more rapid growth in the domestic economy than in the economies of several major trading partners, which caused imports to rise more than exports;

(2) recent large deficits in the Federal budget which drove up real interest rates, increased the international value of the dollar, and increased imports and decreased exports; and

(3) a decline in the rate of saving and a capital account surplus, which allowed U.S. citizens to consume more imported goods.

b. The trade deficits of the United States have had two principal effects: They increased current domestic consumption and allowed the nation to operate outside its production possibilities frontier, and they increased the indebtedness of U.S. citizens to foreigners. A possible implication of these persistent trade deficits is that they will lead to permanent debt and foreign ownership of domestic assets, or large sacrifices of future domestic consumption.

■ HINTS AND TIPS

1. The chapter is filled with many new terms, some of which are just special words used in international economics to mean things with which you are already familiar. Other terms are new to you, so you must spend time learning them if you are to understand the chapter.

2. The terms *depreciation* and *appreciation* can be confusing when applied to foreign exchange markets.

a. First, know the related terms. "Depreciate" means decrease or fall, whereas "appreciate" means increase or rise.

b. Second, think of depreciation or appreciation in terms of quantities:

(1) what *decreases* when the currency of Country A *depreciates* is the *quantity* of Country B's currency that can be purchased for *1 unit* of Country A's currency;

(2) what increases when the currency of Country A *appreciates* is the *quantity* of Country B's currency that can be purchased for *1 unit* of Country A's currency.

c. Third, consider the effect of changes in exchange rates:

(1) when the exchange rate for Country B's currency *rises,* this means that Country A's currency has *depreciated* in value because 1 unit of Country A's currency will now purchase a smaller quantity of Country B's currency;

(2) when the exchange rate for Country B's currency *falls,* this means that Country A's currency has *appreciated* in value because 1 unit of Country A's currency will now purchase a larger quantity of Country B's currency.

3. The meaning of the balance of payments can be confusing also because of the number of accounts in the balance sheet. Remember that the balance of payments must always balance and sum to zero because one account in the balance of payments can be in surplus, but it will be offset by a deficit in another account. However, when people talk about a *balance of payments surplus* or *deficit,* they are referring to the sum of the current and capital account balances. If the total is positive, there is a balance of payments surplus, but if it is negative, there is a balance of payments deficit.

■ IMPORTANT TERMS

international balance of payments
current account
trade balance
balance on goods and services
balance on current account
capital account
balance on the capital account
official reserves
balance of payments deficit
balance of payments surplus
flexible (floating) exchange-rate system
fixed exchange-rate system
purchasing power parity theory
gold standard
devaluation
Bretton Woods system
International Monetary Fund (IMF)
managed floating exchange rate

SELF-TEST

■ FILL-IN QUESTIONS

1. The rate of exchange for the French franc is the amount in (francs, dollars) ______ which a U.S. citizen must pay to obtain 1 (franc, dollar) ______. If the rate of exchange for the French franc is (5 francs, $.20) ______, the rate of exchange for the U.S. dollar is ______.

2. U.S. exports create a foreign (demand for, supply of) ______ dollars and generate a ______ foreign currencies owned by U.S. banks and available to domestic buyers; U.S. imports create a domestic (demand for, supply of) ______ foreign currencies and reduces the ______ foreign currencies held by U.S. banks and available for domestic consumers.

3. The balance of payments of a nation records all payments (domestic, foreign) ______ residents make to and receive from ______ residents. Any transaction that *earns* foreign exchange for that nation is a (debit, credit) ______, and any transaction that *uses up* foreign exchange is a ______. A debit is shown with a (+, −) ______ sign, and a credit is shown with a ______ sign.

4. If a nation has a deficit in its balance of trade, its exports are (greater, less) ______ than its imports of goods, and if it has a deficit in its balance on goods and services, its exports of these items are ______ than its imports of them. The current account is equal to the balance on goods and services (plus, minus) ______ net investment income and ______ net transfers.

5. The capital account records the capital inflows and capital outflows of a nation. The capital inflows are the expenditures made (in that nation, abroad) ______ by residents of (that nation, other nations) __________ __________, and the capital outflows are the expenditures made (in that nation, abroad) __________ by residents of (that nation, other nations) __________ __________ for real and financial assets. A nation has a capital account surplus when its capital account inflows are (greater, less) __________ than its outflows.

6. A nation may finance a current account deficit by (buying, selling) __________ assets or by (borrowing, lending) __________ abroad and may use a current account surplus to (buy, sell) __________ assets or to (borrow, lend) __________ abroad.

7. The official reserves of a nation are the quantities of (foreign currencies, its own money) __________ owned by its central bank. If that nation has a deficit on the current and capital accounts, its official reserves (increase, decrease) __________, but with a surplus on the current and capital accounts, its official reserves __________. The sum of the current, capital, and official reserve accounts must equal (0, 1) __________.

8. A country has a balance of payments deficit if the sum of its current and capital accounts balance is (positive, negative) __________ and its official reserves (increase, decrease) __________. A country has a payments surplus when the sum of its current and capital accounts balance is (positive, negative) __________ and its official reserves (increase, decrease) __________.

9. If foreign exchange rates float freely and a nation has a balance of payments *deficit*, that nation's currency in the foreign exchange markets will (appreciate, depreciate) __________ and foreign currencies will __________. As a result of these changes in foreign exchange rates, the nation's imports will (increase, decrease) __________, its exports will __________, and the size of its deficit will (increase, decrease) __________.

10. What effect would each of the following have on the appreciation (**A**) or depreciation (**D**) of the French franc in the foreign exchange market (*ceteris paribus*)?

a. The increased preference in the United States for domestic wines over wines produced in France: _____

b. A rise in the U.S. national income: _____

c. An increase in the price level in France: _____

d. A rise in real interest rates in the United States: _____

e. The belief of speculators in France that the dollar will appreciate in the foreign exchange market: _____

11. There are three disadvantages of freely floating foreign exchange rates: the risks and uncertainties associated with flexible rates tend to (expand, diminish) __________ trade between nations; when a nation's currency depreciates, its terms of trade with other nations are (worsened, improved) __________; and fluctuating exports and imports can (stabilize, destabilize) __________ an economy.

12. To fix or peg the rate of exchange for the German mark when the exchange rate for the mark is rising, the United States would (buy, sell) __________ marks in exchange for dollars, and when the exchange rate for the mark is falling, the United States would __________ marks in exchange for dollars.

13. Under a fixed exchange-rate system, a nation with a balance of payments deficit might attempt to eliminate the deficit by (taxing, subsidizing) __________ imports or by __________ exports. The nation might use exchange controls and ration foreign exchange among those who wish to (export, import) __________ goods and services and require all those who __________ goods and services to sell the foreign exchange they earn to the (businesses, government) __________.

14. If the United States has a payments deficit with Japan and the exchange rate for the Japanese yen is rising, under a fixed exchange-rate system the United States might adopt (expansionary, contractionary) __________ fiscal and monetary policies to reduce the demand for the yen, but this would bring about (inflation, recession) __________ in the United States.

15. When the nations of the world were on the gold standard exchange, rates were relatively (stable, unstable) __________. When a nation had a payments deficit, gold flowed (into, out of) __________ the nation, its money supply (increased, decreased) __________, its interest rates __________, and output, employment, income, and perhaps prices (increased, decreased) __________; thus its payments deficit __________.

16. The Bretton Woods system was established to bring about (flexible, fixed) __________ exchange rates. Under the Bretton Woods system, a member nation defined its monetary unit in terms of (oil, gold) __________ or dollars. Each member nation stabilized the exchange rate for its currency and prevented it from rising by (buying, selling) __________ foreign currency which it obtained from its official reserves, by (buying, selling) _______________ gold or by (borrowing from, lending to) _______________ the International Monetary Fund. A nation with a deeply rooted payments deficit could (devalue, revalue) _______________ its currency. The system was designed so that in the short run exchange rates would be (stable, flexible) _______________ enough to promote international trade and in the long run they would be _______________ enough to correct balance of payments imbalances.

17. The role of the dollar as a component of international monetary reserves under Bretton Woods produced a dilemma. For the dollar to remain an acceptable international monetary reserve, the U.S. payments deficits had to be (eliminated, continued) _______________, but for international monetary reserves to grow to accommodate world trade, the U.S payments deficits had to be _______________. These deficits caused an acceptability problem because they resulted in a(n) (decrease, increase) _______________ in the foreign holding of U.S. dollars and a(n) _______________ in the U.S. reserves of gold, which contributed to a(n) (decrease, increase) _______________ in the ability of the United States to convert dollars into gold and the willingness of foreigners to hold dollars as if they were as good as gold. In 1971, the United States essentially ended this system when it (adopted, suspended) _______________ the convertibility of dollars into gold and allowed the value of the dollar to be determined by markets.

18. Since then the international monetary system has moved to a system of managed (fixed, floating) _______________ exchange rates. This means that exchange rates of nations are (restricted from, free to) _______________ find their equilibrium market levels, but nations may occasionally (leave, intervene in) _______________ the foreign exchange markets to stabilize or alter market exchange rates.

19. The advantages of the current system are that the growth of trade (was, was not) _______________ accommodated as well as under the Bretton Woods system and that it has survived much economic (stability, turbulence) _______________. Its disadvantages are its (equilibrium, volatility) _______________ and the lack of guidelines for nations that make it a (bureaucracy, nonsystem) _______________.

20. The major problem with foreign trade in the United States concerns U.S. merchandise and current account (surpluses, deficits) _______________ which were brought about by the sharp increases in its (exports, imports) _______________ and the small increases in its _______________. One cause has been (stronger, weaker) _______________ economic growth in the United States relative to _______________ economic growth in Europe and Japan which would (increase, decrease) _______________ U.S. imports more than exports. Other contributing factors are (small, large) _______________ deficits in the annual Federal budget and a (rising, falling) _______________ saving rate. One effect of the trade deficits of the United States has been (decreased, increased) _______________ current domestic consumption that allows the nation to operate outside its production possibility frontier, and another effect was a (rise, fall) _______________ in the indebtedness of U.S. citizens to foreigners.

■ TRUE-FALSE QUESTIONS

Circle the T if the statement is true, the F if it is false.

1. The importation of goods and services by U.S. citizens from abroad creates a supply of dollars in the foreign exchange market. **T F**

2. The international balance of payments of the United States records all the payments its residents receive from and make to the residents of foreign nations. **T F**

3. Exports are a debit item and are shown with a plus sign (+), and imports are a credit item and are shown with a minus sign (−) in the international balance of payments of a nation. **T F**

4. The United States would have a balance of payments surplus if the balances on its current and capital accounts were positive. **T F**

5. Any nation with a balance of payments deficit must reduce its official reserves. **T F**

6. The sum of a nation's current account balance, its capital account balance, and the change in its official reserves in any year is always equal to zero. **T F**

7. The purchasing power parity theory basically explains why there is an inverse relationship between the price of dollars and the quantity demanded. **T F**

8. The expectations of speculators in the United States that the exchange rate for the Japanese yen will fall in the future will increase the supply of yen in the foreign exchange market and decrease the exchange rate for the yen. **T F**

9. If a nation has a balance of payments deficit and exchange rates are flexible, the price of that nation's currency in the foreign exchange markets will fall; this will reduce its imports and increase its exports. **T F**

10. Were the United States' terms of trade with Nigeria to worsen, Nigeria would obtain a greater quantity of U.S.

goods and services for every barrel of oil it exported to the United States. **T F**

11. If a nation wishes to fix (or peg) the foreign exchange rate for the Swiss franc, it must buy Swiss francs with its own currency when the rate of exchange for the Swiss franc rises. **T F**

12. If exchange rates are stable or fixed and a nation has a payments surplus, prices and currency incomes in that nation will tend to rise. **T F**

13. A nation using exchange controls to eliminate a balance of payments surplus might depreciate its currency. **T F**

14. If country A defined its currency as worth 100 grains of gold and country B defined its currency as worth 20 grains of gold, then, ignoring packing, insuring, and shipping charges, 5 units of country A's currency would be worth 1 unit of country B's currency. **T F**

15. Under the gold standard, the potential free flow of gold between nations would result in exchange rates which are fixed. **T F**

16. In the Bretton Woods system, a nation could not devalue its currency by more than 10% without the permission of the International Monetary Fund. **T F**

17. In the Bretton Woods system, a nation with persistent balance of payments surpluses had an undervalued currency and should have increased the pegged value of its currency. **T F**

18. To accommodate expanding world trade in the Bretton Woods system, the U.S. dollar served as a reserve medium of exchange and the United States ran persistent balance of payments deficits. **T F**

19. A basic shortcoming of the Bretton Woods system was its inability to bring about the changes in exchange rates needed to correct persistent payments deficits and surpluses. **T F**

20. Using the managed floating system of exchange rates, a nation with a persistent balance of payments surplus should allow the value of its currency in foreign exchange markets to decrease. **T F**

21. Two criticisms of the current managed floating exchange-rate system are its potential for volatility and its lack of clear policy rules or guidelines for nations to manage exchange rates. **T F**

22. The foreign trade deficits experienced by the U.S. economy in the 1990s were caused by sharp increases in U.S. exports and slight increases in U.S. imports. **T F**

23. Improved economic growth in the major economies of the major trading partners of the United States would tend to worsen the trade deficit. **T F**

24. High real interest rates in the United States would tend to increase the attractiveness of financial investment in the United States to foreigners and the foreign demand for U.S. dollars. **T F**

25. The negative net exports of the United States have increased the indebtedness of U.S. citizens to foreigners. **T F**

■ MULTIPLE-CHOICE QUESTIONS

Circle the letter that corresponds to the best answer.

1. If a U.S. citizen could buy £25,000 for $100,000, the rate of exchange for the pound would be
(a) $40
(b) $25
(c) $4
(d) $.25

2. U.S. residents demand foreign currencies to
(a) produce goods and services exported to foreign countries
(b) pay for goods and services imported from foreign countries
(c) receive interest payments on investments in the United States
(d) have foreigners make real and financial investments in the United States

3. A nation's balance of trade is equal to its exports less its imports of
(a) goods
(b) goods and services
(c) financial assets
(d) official reserves

4. A nation's balance on the current account is equal to its exports less its imports of
(a) goods and services
(b) goods and services, plus U.S. purchases of assets abroad
(c) goods and services, plus net investment income and net transfers
(d) goods and services, minus foreign purchases of assets in the United States

5. The net investment income of the United States in its international balance of payment is the
(a) interest income it receives from foreign residents
(b) dividends it receives from foreign residents
(c) excess of interest and dividends it receives from foreign residents over what it paid to them
(d) excess of public and private transfer payments it receives from foreign residents over what it paid to them

6. A nation may be able to correct or eliminate a persistent (long-term) balance of payments deficit by
(a) lowering the barriers on imported goods
(b) reducing the international value of its currency
(c) expanding its national income
(d) reducing its official reserves

7. If exchange rates float freely, the exchange rate for any currency is determined by the
(a) demand for it
(b) supply of it
(c) demand for and the supply of it
(d) official reserves that back it

8. If a nation had a balance of payments surplus and exchange rates floated freely, the foreign exchange rate for its currency would

(a) rise, its exports would increase, and its imports would decrease
(b) rise, its exports would decrease, and its imports would increase
(c) fall, its exports would increase, and its imports would decrease
(d) fall, its exports would decrease, and its imports would increase

9. Assuming exchange rates are flexible, which of the following should increase the dollar price of the Swedish krona?

(a) a rate of inflation greater in Sweden than in the United States
(b) real interest rate increases greater in Sweden than in the United States
(c) national income increases greater in Sweden than in the United States
(d) the increased preference of Swedish citizens for U.S. automobiles over Swedish automobiles

10. Which of the following would be one of the results associated with the use of freely floating foreign exchange rates to correct a nation's balance of payments surplus?

(a) The nation's terms of trade with other nations would be worsened.
(b) Importers in the nation who had made contracts for the future delivery of goods would find that they had to pay a higher price than expected for the goods.
(c) If the nation were at full employment, the decrease in exports and the increase in imports would be inflationary.
(d) Exporters in the nation would find their sales abroad had decreased.

11. When exchange rates are fixed and a nation at full employment has a balance of payments surplus, the result in that nation will be

(a) a declining price level
(b) falling currency income
(c) inflation
(d) rising real income

12. The use of exchange controls to eliminate a nation's balance of payments deficit results in decreasing the nation's

(a) imports
(b) exports
(c) price level
(d) income

13. Which condition did a nation have to fulfill if it were to be under the gold standard?

(a) use only gold as a medium of exchange
(b) maintain a flexible relationship between its gold stock and its currency supply
(c) allow gold to be freely exported from and imported into the nation
(d) define its monetary unit in terms of a fixed quantity of dollars

14. If the nations of the world were on the gold standard and one nation has a balance of payments surplus,

(a) foreign exchange rates in that nation would rise
(b) gold would tend to be imported into that country
(c) the level of prices in that country would fall
(d) employment and output in that country would fall

15. Which was the principal disadvantage of the gold standard?

(a) unstable foreign exchange rates
(b) persistent payments imbalances
(c) the uncertainties and decreased trade that resulted from the depreciation of gold
(d) the domestic macroeconomic adjustments experienced by a nation with a payments deficit or surplus

16. The objective of the adjustable-peg system was exchange rates which were

(a) adjustable in the short run and fixed in the long run
(b) adjustable in both the short and long run
(c) fixed in both the short and long run
(d) fixed in the short run and adjustable in the long run

17. Which is the best definition of international monetary reserves in the Bretton Woods system?

(a) gold
(b) dollars
(c) gold and dollars
(d) gold, dollars, and British pounds

18. The major dilemma created by the persistent U.S. payments deficits under the Bretton Woods system was that to maintain the status of the dollar as an acceptable international monetary reserve, the deficits had to

(a) decrease, but to expand reserves to accommodate world trade, the deficits had to continue
(b) continue, but to expand reserves to accommodate world trade, the deficits had to be eliminated
(c) increase, but to expand reserves to accommodate world trade, the deficits had to be reduced
(d) decrease, but to expand reserves to accommodate world trade, the deficits had to be eliminated

19. "Floating" the dollar means

(a) the value of the dollar is determined by the demand for and the supply of the dollar
(b) the dollar price of gold has been increased
(c) the price of the dollar has been allowed to crawl upward at the rate of one-fourth of 1% a month
(d) the IMF decreased the value of the dollar by 10%

20. A system of managed floating exchange rates

(a) allows nations to stabilize exchange rates in the short term
(b) requires nations to stabilize exchange rates in the long term
(c) entails stable exchange rates in both the short and long term
(d) fixes exchange rates at market levels

21. Floating exchange rates

(a) tend to correct balance of payments imbalances
(b) reduce the uncertainties and risks associated with international trade

(c) increase the world's need for international monetary reserves
(d) tend to expand the volume of world trade

22. The foreign trade problem facing the United States is
(a) its balance of trade and current account surpluses
(b) its balance of trade deficit and current account surpluses
(c) its balance of trade and current account deficits
(d) its balance of trade surplus and current account deficit

23. Which is one of the causes of the growth of U.S. trade deficits during the 1990s?
(a) protective tariffs imposed by the United States
(b) slower economic growth in the United States
(c) direct foreign investment in the United States
(d) a declining saving rate in the United States

24. What would be the effect on U.S. imports and exports when the United States experiences strong economic growth but its major trading partners experience sluggish economic growth?
(a) U.S. imports will increase more than U.S. exports
(b) U.S. exports will increase more than U.S. imports
(c) U.S. imports will decrease but U.S. exports will increase
(d) there will be no effect on U.S. imports and exports

25. Two major outcomes from the trade deficits of the 1990s were
(a) decreased domestic consumption and U.S. indebtedness
(b) increased domestic consumption and U.S. indebtedness
(c) increased domestic consumption but decreased U.S. indebtedness
(d) decreased domestic consumption but increased U.S. indebtedness

■ PROBLEMS

1. Assume a U.S. exporter sells $3 million worth of wheat to an importer in Colombia. If the rate of exchange for the Colombian peso is $.02 (2 cents), the wheat has a total value of 150 million pesos.

a. There are two ways the importer in Colombia may pay for the wheat. It might write a check for 150 million pesos drawn on its bank in Botogá and send it to the U.S. exporter.

(1) The American exporter would then sell the check to its bank in New Orleans and its demand deposit there would increase by $________ million.

(2) This New Orleans bank now sells the check for 150 million pesos to a correspondent bank (a U.S. commercial bank that keeps an account in the Botogá bank).

(a) The New Orleans bank's account in the correspondent bank increases by ________ million (dollars, pesos) ________; and

(b) the correspondent bank's account in the Botogá bank increases by ________ million (pesos, dollars) ________.

b. The second way for the importer to pay for the wheat is to buy from its bank in Botogá a draft on a U.S. bank for $3 million, pay for this draft by writing a check for 150 million pesos drawn on the Botogá bank, and send the draft to the U.S. exporter.

(1) The U.S. exporter would then deposit the draft in its account in the New Orleans bank and its demand deposit account there would increase by $________ million.

(2) The New Orleans bank collects the amount of the draft from the U.S. bank on which it is drawn through the Federal Reserve Banks.

(a) Its account at the Fed increases by $________ million; and

(b) the account of the bank on which the draft was drawn decreases by $________ million.

c. Regardless of the way used by the Colombian importer to pay for the wheat,

(1) the export of the wheat created a (demand for, supply of) ________ dollars and a ________ pesos.

(2) The number of dollars owned by the U.S. exporter has (increased, decreased) ________ and the number of pesos owned by the Colombian importer has ________.

2. The following table contains hypothetical international balance of payments data for the United States. All figures are in billions.

Current account		
(1) U.S. merchandise exports	$+150	
(2) U.S. merchandise imports	−200	
(3) Balance of trade		____
(4) U.S. exports of services	+75	
(5) U.S. imports of services	−60	
(6) Balance on goods and services		____
(7) Net investment income	+12	
(8) Net transfers	−7	
(9) Balance on current account		____
Capital account		
(10) Capital inflows to the U.S.	+80	
(11) Capital outflows from the U.S.	−55	
(12) Balance on capital account		____
(13) Current and capital account balance		____
(14) Official reserves		____
		$ 0

a. Compute with the appropriate sign (+ or −) and enter in the table the six missing items.

b. The United States had a payments (deficit, surplus) ________ of $________.

3. The following table shows the supply and demand schedules for the British pound.

Quantity of pounds supplied	Price	Quantity of pounds demanded
400	$5.00	100
360	4.50	200
300	4.00	300
286	3.50	400
267	3.00	500
240	2.50	620
200	2.00	788

a. If the exchange rates are flexible
(1) what will be the rate of exchange for the pound? $__________
(2) what will be the rate of exchange for the dollar? £__________
(3) how many pounds will be purchased in the market? __________
(4) how many dollars will be purchased in the market? __________

b. If the U.S. government wished to fix or peg the price of the pound at $5.00, it would have to (buy, sell) __________ (how many) __________ pounds for $__________.

c. And if the British government wishes to fix the price of the dollar at £2/5, it would have to (buy, sell) __________ (how many) __________ pounds for $__________.

SHORT ANSWER AND ESSAY QUESTIONS

1. What is foreign exchange and the foreign exchange rate? Who are the demanders and suppliers of a particular foreign exchange, say, the French franc? Why is a buyer (demander) in the foreign exchange markets always a seller (supplier) also?

2. What is meant when it is said that "A nation's exports pay for its imports"? Do nations pay for all their imports with exports?

3. What is an international balance of payments? What are the principal sections in a nation's international balance of payments, and what are the principal "balances" to be found in it?

4. How can a nation finance a current account deficit, and what can it do with a current account surplus?

5. How does a nation finance a balance of payments deficit, and what does it do with a balance of payments surplus?

6. What types of events cause the exchange rate for a foreign currency to appreciate or to depreciate? How will each event affect the exchange rate for a foreign currency and for a nation's own currency?

7. How can freely floating foreign exchange rates eliminate balance of payments deficits and surpluses? What are the problems associated with this method of correcting payments imbalances?

8. How may a nation use its international monetary reserves to fix or peg foreign exchange rates? Be precise. How does a nation obtain or acquire these monetary reserves?

9. What kinds of trade controls may nations with payments deficits use to eliminate their deficits?

10. How can foreign exchange controls be used to restore international equilibrium? Why do such exchange controls necessarily involve the rationing of foreign exchange? What effect do these controls have on prices, output, and employment in nations that use them?

11. If foreign exchange rates are fixed, what kind of domestic macroeconomic adjustments are required to eliminate a payments deficit? To eliminate a payments surplus?

12. When were the major nations on the gold standard? How did the international gold standard correct payments imbalances?

13. What were the disadvantages of the gold standard for eliminating payments deficits and surpluses?

14. What did nations use as international monetary reserves under the Bretton Woods system? Why was the dollar used by nations as an international money, and how could they acquire additional dollars?

15. Explain the dilemma created by the need for expanding international monetary reserves and for maintaining the status of the dollar.

16. Why and how did the United States shatter the Bretton Woods system in 1971?

17. Explain what is meant by a managed floating system of foreign exchange rates. When are exchange rates managed and when are they allowed to float?

18. Explain the arguments of the proponents and the critics of the managed floating system.

19. What were the causes of the trade deficits of the United States during the 1990s?

20. What were the effects of the trade deficits of the 1990s on the U.S. economy?

ANSWERS

Chapter 38 Exchange Rates, the Balance of Payments, and Trade Deficits

FILL-IN QUESTIONS

1. dollars, franc, $.20, 5 francs
2. demand for, supply of, demand for, supply of
3. domestic, foreign, credit, debit, −, +
4. less, less, plus, minus
5. in that nation, other nations, abroad, that nation, greater

6. selling, borrowing, buy, lend
7. foreign currencies, decrease, increase, zero
8. negative, decrease, positive, increase
9. depreciate, appreciate, decrease, increase, decrease
10. *a.* D; *b.* A; *c.* D; *d.* D; *e.* D
11. diminish, worsened, destabilize
12. sell, buy
13. taxing, subsidizing, import, export, government
14. contractionary, recession
15. stable, out of, decreased, increased, decreased, decreased
16. fixed, gold, buying, selling, borrowing from, devalue, stable, flexible
17. eliminated, continued, increase, decrease, decrease, suspended
18. floating, free to, intervene in
19. was, turbulence, volatility, nonsystem
20. deficits, imports, exports, stronger, weaker, increase, large, falling, increased, rise

TRUE-FALSE QUESTIONS

1. T, pp. 789-791	**10.** T, p. 799	**19.** T, p. 803
2. T, p. 791	**11.** F, pp. 799-800	**20.** F, pp. 804-805
3. F, pp. 791-792	**12.** T, p. 800	**21.** T, p. 805
4. T, pp. 792-794	**13.** F, p. 800	**22.** F, pp. 806-807
5. T, p. 794	**14.** F, p. 801	**23.** F, p. 806
6. T, p. 794	**15.** T, p. 801	**24.** T, p. 806
7. F, p. 796	**16.** T, p. 803	**25.** T, p. 807
8. T, pp. 796-797	**17.** T, p. 803	
9. T, pp. 797-798	**18.** T, p. 803	

MULTIPLE-CHOICE QUESTIONS

1. c, pp. 789-790	**10.** d, pp. 798-799	**19.** a, p. 804
2. b, pp. 790-791	**11.** c, pp. 799-801	**20.** a, pp. 804-805
3. a, p. 792	**12.** a, p. 800	**21.** a, pp. 804-805
4. c, pp. 792-793	**13.** c, p. 801	**22.** c, pp. 806-807
5. c, p. 792	**14.** b, pp. 801-802	**23.** d, pp. 806-807
6. b, pp. 797-798	**15.** d, pp. 801-802	**24.** a, pp. 806-807
7. c, p. 794	**16.** d, pp. 802-803	**25.** b, p. 807
8. b, pp. 797-798	**17.** c, p. 803	
9. b, pp. 796-797	**18.** a, p. 803	

PROBLEMS

1. *a.* (1) 3, (2) (a) 3, dollars, (b) 150, pesos; *b.* (1) 3, (2) (a) 3, (b) 3; *c.* (1) demand for, supply of, (2) increased, decreased
2. *a.* −50, −35, −30, +25, −5, +5; *b.* deficit, 5
3. *a.* (1) 4.00, (2) 1/4, (3) 300, (4) 1,200; *b.* buy, 300, 1,500; *c.* sell, 380, 950

SHORT ANSWER AND ESSAY QUESTIONS

1. pp. 789-791	**8.** pp. 799-800	**15.** p. 803
2. p. 791	**9.** p. 800	**16.** pp. 803-805
3. pp. 791-794	**10.** p. 800	**17.** pp. 804-805
4. p. 794	**11.** p. 800	**18.** p. 805
5. p. 794	**12.** pp. 801-802	**19.** pp. 806-807
6. pp. 795-797	**13.** p. 802	**20.** p. 807
7. pp. 797-799	**14.** pp. 802-803	

CHAPTER 39

The Economics of the Developing Countries

This chapter looks at the critical problem of raising the *standard of living* in ***developing countries*** (DVCs) of the world. About three-fourths of the world's population live in these 107 nations. The development problems in these nations are extensive: low literacy rates, low levels of industrialization, high dependence on agriculture, rapid rates of population growth, and widespread poverty. In addition, the income gap between these developing nations and the 26 industrially advanced nations of the world is growing.

Economic growth in both developing and ***industrially advanced countries*** (IACs) requires that the economic resources base be expanded and these resources be used efficiently. As you will discover in one of the major sections of the chapter, developing nations trying to apply these principles face *obstacles* quite different from those that limit growth in the United States and other industrially advanced nations. Developing nations have many problems with natural, human, and capital resources and with technology, all of which combine to hinder economic growth. In addition, certain social, cultural, and institutional factors create a poor environment for economic development.

These obstacles do not mean that it is impossible to increase the living standards of these DVCs. What they do indicate is that to encourage growth, the DVCs must do things that do not need to be done in the United States or other industrially advanced nations. Population pressures need to be managed, and labor resources have to be better used. Steps must be taken to encourage capital investment. Governments must take an active role in promoting economic growth and limiting the public sector problems for economic development. Dramatic changes in social practices and institutions are required. If these and other actions are not taken, it may not be possible to reduce the major obstacles to growth and break the vicious circle of poverty in the DVCs.

No matter how successful the DVCs are in overcoming these obstacles, they still will not be able to grow very rapidly without the help of industrially advanced countries. These countries can lower trade barriers that limit sales of products from developing countries, and they can provide foreign aid in the form of government grants and loans. This foreign aid is subject to criticism, and it is declining, as you will learn from the chapter. The banks, corporations, and other businesses in industrially advanced nations can provide private capital in the form of loans or direct foreign investment. These private capital flows are also subject to problems, as the debt crisis of the 1980s illustrates. This crisis is now over, and changes have been made, but the conditions for another crisis also exist.

The final section of the chapter is a fitting ending to the discussion of economic problems in developing nations. It focuses on specific policies to promote economic growth in the DVCs and examines the issue from two sides. One side offers a set of policies from the perspective of developing countries, and the other side lists things industrially advanced countries can do to foster economic growth in developing nations.

■ CHECKLIST

When you have studied this chapter you should be able to

☐ Describe income disparity among nations.
☐ Compare industrially advanced countries (IACs) and developing countries (DVCs) in terms of economic growth and population.
☐ Discuss the human implications of poverty in DVCs.
☐ Identify two basic avenues for economic growth in IACs and DVCs.
☐ Describe natural resource problems in DVCs.
☐ Identify the three specific problems related to human resources that plague the DVCs.
☐ Explain the difficulties for economic growth that are created by population growth in DVCs.
☐ Compare the traditional and demographic transition view of population and economic growth in DVCs.
☐ Describe the conditions of unemployment and underemployment in DVCs.
☐ State reasons for low labor productivity in DVCs.
☐ Present three reasons for the emphasis on capital formation in the DVCs.
☐ Identify obstacles to domestic capital formation through saving.
☐ List obstacles to domestic capital formation through investment.
☐ Explain why transferring the technologies used in the industrially advanced countries to the DVCs may not be a realistic method of improving the technology of the latter nations.
☐ Identify three potential sociocultural factors that can inhibit economic growth.
☐ Describe the institutional obstacles to growth.
☐ Explain why poverty in the poor nations is a vicious circle.

□ List five reasons why governments in the DVCs will have to play a crucial role if the vicious circle of poverty is to be broken.
□ Describe the problems with the public sector in fostering economic development.
□ Identify the three ways the industrially advanced countries may help the DVCs grow economically.
□ Explain the importance of a reduction in international trade barriers to economic growth in DVCs.
□ Describe the two sources of foreign aid for DVCs.
□ Give three criticisms of foreign aid to DVCs.
□ Explain why foreign aid to DVCs has declined.
□ Describe what groups in IACs provide private capital to DVCs.
□ Give four reasons for the debt crisis of the 1980s.
□ Explain how the debt crisis was resolved in the 1990s.
□ Evaluate the prospects for future debt problems in DVCs.
□ Discuss nine DVC policies for promoting economic growth.
□ Explain five actions that IACs can take to encourage growth in DVCs.

■ CHAPTER OUTLINE

1. There is considerable income inequality among countries. The richest 20% of the world's population receive about 83% of the world's income.

Countries can also be classified into two main groups. *Industrially advanced countries* (IACs) are characterized by well-developed market economies based on large stocks of capital goods, advanced technology for production, and well-educated workers. Among these 26 high-income nations are the United States, Canada, Japan, Australia, New Zealand, and most of the nations of western Europe. These countries averaged $24,930 per capita income in 1995.

Developing countries (DVCs) are poor, not highly industrialized, heavily dependent on agriculture, have high population growth, and have low rates of literacy. These countries comprise about three-fourths of the world's population. Of the 107 DVCs, 68 are middle-income countries with an average income per capita of $2,390; 49 low-income countries have an average income per capita of $430. This latter group is dominated by India, China, and most of the sub-Saharan nations of Africa.

a. There are disparities in the growth rates of nations, resulting in sizable income gaps. Some DVC nations have been able to improve their economic conditions over time and become IACs. Other DVCs are now showing high rates of economic growth, but still other DVCs have experienced a decline in economic growth and standard of living. If growth rates were the same for high- and low-income nations, the gap in per capita income would widen because the income base is higher in high-income nations.

b. The human implications of extreme poverty are important. Compared with IACs, DVCs have not only lower per capita incomes but also lower life expectancies, higher infant mortality, lower literacy rates, more of the labor force in agriculture, and fewer nonhuman sources of energy.

2. Economic growth requires that DVCs use their existing resources more efficiently and that they expand their available supplies of resources. The physical, human, and socioeconomic conditions in these nations are the reasons why DVCs experience different rates of economic growth.

a. Many DVCs possess inadequate *natural resources.* This limited resource base is an obstacle to growth. Also, the agricultural products which DVCs typically export are subject to significant price variation on the world market, creating variations in national income.

b. The circumstances for *human resources* in DVCs is difficult for three reasons.

(1) DVCs tend to be overpopulated and have high rates of population growth. These growing populations reduce the DVCs' capacity to save, invest, and increase productivity. They also overuse land and natural resources, and the migration of rural workers to cities creates urban problems.

(2) DVCs often experience both unemployment and underemployment, which wastes labor resources.

(3) DVCs have low levels of labor productivity because of insufficient physical capital and lack of investment in human capital.

c. DVCs have an inadequate amount of ***capital goods,*** and so find it difficult to accumulate capital. Domestic capital formation occurs through saving and investing. The potential for saving is low in many DVCs because the nations are too poor to save. There is also capital flight of saving from DVCs to more stable IACs. The investment obstacles include a lack of investors and entrepreneurs and a lack of incentives to invest in DVC economies. The infrastructure is poor in many DVCs.

d. ***Technological advance*** is slow in DVCs. Although these nations might adopt the technologies of industrial nations, these technologies are not always appropriate for the resource endowments of the DVCs, so they must learn to develop and use their own technologies.

e. It is difficult for DVCs to alter the *social, cultural,* and *institutional* factors to create a good environment for achieving economic growth.

3. In summary, DVCs save little and therefore invest little in real and human capital because they are poor, and because they do not invest, their outputs per capita remain low and they remain poor. Even if the vicious circle were to be broken, a rapid increase in population would leave the standard of living unchanged.

4. There are differing views about the role that government plays in fostering economic growth in DVCs.

a. The positive view holds that in the initial stages of economic development, government action is needed to help overcome such obstacles as the lack of law and order, entrepreneurship, and infrastructure. Government policies may also assist capital formation and help resolve social and institutional problems.

b. Problems and disadvantages with government involvement in promoting growth include bureaucratic impediments, corruption, maladministration, and the importance of political objectives over economic goals. Central planning does not work because it restricts competition and individual incentives, which are important ingredients in the growth process.

5. Industrially advanced nations of the world can help the DVCs develop in a number of ways.

a. They can lower the trade barriers which prevent the DVCs from selling their products in the developed countries.

b. Loans and grants from governments and international organizations such as the World Bank also enable the DVCs to accumulate capital. This foreign aid has been criticized because it increases dependency, bureaucracy, and corruption. For these reasons, and because of the end of the cold war, foreign aid to DVCs is declining.

c. DVCs can also receive flows of private capital from IACs. These flows come from banks, corporations, and financial investment companies.

(1) In the 1980s, DVCs experienced a debt crisis in which they found they could not repay their loans. The factors contributing to this crisis were high prices for imported oil, a tight monetary policy in the United States, an appreciating dollar, and unproductive investments by DVCs. The flow of private lending and investments in DVCs virtually ceased during this period.

(2) In the 1990s, the flow of private lending and investing increased as DVC debts were restructured and some DVC economies were reformed to control budget deficits and inflation. More of the flows are now in the form of direct foreign investment in DVCs rather than loans to their governments; however, the flow of most private capital goes to selective nations, and it is still not certain that the debt crisis is over in some DVCs.

6. There are several policies that DVCs and IACs might undertake to foster economic development in DVCs. Two perspectives are offered.

a. DVC policies for promoting growth include establishing the rule of law, opening economies to international trade, controlling population growth, encouraging direct foreign investment, building human capital, making peace with neighbors, establishing independent central banks, making realistic exchange-rate policies, and privatizing state industries.

b. IAC policies for encouraging economic growth in DVCs are directing foreign aid to the poorest of the DVCs, reducing tariffs and import quotas, providing debt relief to DVCs, allowing more low-skilled immigration and discouraging brain drains, and limiting arm sales to DVCs.

■ HINTS AND TIPS

1. This chapter offers a comprehensive look at the various factors affecting growth and economic development. No one factor explains why some nations prosper and others remain poor. The chapter should give you insights into how natural, human, and capital resources together with government policies may influence a nation's economic development.

2. Several economic and demographic statistics for comparing rich and poor nations appear in the chapter's tables. You need not memorize the numbers, but you should try to get a sense of the magnitude of the differences between IACs and DVCs on several key indicators. To do this, ask yourself questions calling for relative comparisons. For example, how many times larger is per capita income in IACs than in low-income DVCs? Answer: 58 times greater ($24,930/$430 = 58).

3. The chapter ends with policy suggestions for increasing economic growth in DVCs. Be sure to look at these policies from the perspective of both DVCs and IACs. Identify those that you think are most important, and explain your reasoning.

■ IMPORTANT TERMS

industrially advanced countries (IACs)
developing countries (DVCs)
demographic transition view
underemployment
brain drain
capital flight
infrastructure
capital-saving technology
capital-using technology
the will to develop
capricious universe view
land reform
vicious circle of poverty
World Bank
direct foreign investment

SELF-TEST

■ FILL-IN QUESTIONS

1. There is considerable income inequality among nations. The richest 20% of the world's population receive about (43, 83) ____________% of world income, while the poorest 20% of the world's population receive about (1, 10) ____________% of world income.

2. High-income nations can be classified as (industrially advanced, developing) ______________ countries, or (IACs, DVCs) ______________, and the middle- or low-income nations as ______________ countries, or (DVCs, IACs) __________. In 1995, the average income per capita in high-income nations was ($24,930, $55,460) ______________, in middle-income nations it was ($2,390, $9,650) ______________, and in low-income nations it was ($430, $5,170) ______________.

3. IACs have a (higher, lower) ______________ starting base for per capita income than DVCs, so the same percentage growth rate for both IACs and DVCs means a(n) (increase, decrease) _______________ in the absolute income gap.

4. Low per capita income in DVCs means that there is (lower, higher) _______________ life expectancies, _______________ adult literacy, (lower, higher) _______________ daily calorie supply, _______________ energy consumption, and (lower, higher) _______________ infant mortality.

5. The process for economic growth is the same for IACs and DVCs. It involves (less, more) _______________ efficient use of existing resources and obtaining _______________ productive resources.

6. The distribution of natural resources among DVCs is (even, uneven) _______________; many DVCs lack vital natural resources. Although oil resources have been used for economic growth in (OPEC, DVCs) _______________, IACS own or control much of the natural resources in _______________. Also, exports of products from DVCs are subject to (small, large) _______________ price fluctuations in the world market, and that tends to make DVC incomes (more, less) _______________ stable.

7. In terms of human resources,

a. many DVCs are (under, over) _______________ populated and have (higher, lower) _______________ population growth rates than IACs. Rapid population growth can cause per capita income to (increase, decrease) _______________.

b. In DVCs, many people are unable to find jobs, so there is (underemployment, unemployment) _______________, and many people are employed for fewer hours than they desire or work at odd jobs, so there is _______________.

c. In DVCs, labor productivity is very (high, low) _______________, partly because these countries have not been able to invest in (stocks and bonds, human capital) _______________; when the best-trained workers leave DVCs to work in IACs, there is a (demographic transition, brain drain) _______________ that contributes to the decline in skill level and productivity.

8. Capital accumulation is critical to the development of DVCs. If there were more capital goods, this would improve (natural resources, labor productivity) _______________ and help boost per capita output. An increase in capital goods is necessary because the (demand for, supply of) _______________ arable land is limited. The process of capital formation is cumulative, investment increases the (output, natural resources) _______________ of the economy, and this in turn makes it possible for the economy to save more and invest more in capital goods.

9. The formation of domestic capital requires that a nation save and invest.

a. Saving is difficult in DVCs because of a (high, low) _______________ potential for saving, and investment is difficult because of (many, few) _______________ investors or entrepreneurs, and (strong, weak) _______________ incentives to invest. The is also the problem of private savings being transferred to IACs; this transfer is called (brain drain, capital flight) _______________.

b. Many DVCs do not have the infrastructure or (private, public) _______________ capital goods that are necessary for productive _______________ investment by businesses.

c. Nonfinancial (or in-kind) investment involves the transfer of surplus labor from (agriculture, industry) _______________ to the improvement of agricultural facilities or the infrastructure.

10. The technologies used in the advanced industrial countries might be borrowed by and used in the DVCs, but

a. the technologies used in the advanced countries are based on a labor force that is (skilled, unskilled) _______________, labor that is relatively (abundant, scarce) _______________, and capital that is relatively _______________, and their technologies tend to be (labor, capital) _______________-using, while

b. the technologies required in developing countries must be based on a labor force that is (skilled, unskilled) _______________, labor that is relatively (abundant, scarce) _______________, and capital that is relatively _______________, and their technologies tend to be (labor, capital) _______________-using.

c. If technological advances make it possible to replace a worn-out plow, costing $10 when new, with a new $5 plow, the technological advance is capital (saving, using) _______________.

11. Other obstacles to economic growth in DVCs include those dealing with problems of national unity, religion, and customs, or (institutional, sociocultural) _______________ problems, and those dealing with such issues as political corruption, poor school systems, and land reform, or _______________ problems.

12. In most DVCs, there is a vicious circle of poverty. Saving is low because the income per capita is (high, low) _______________, and because saving is low, investment in real and human capital is ______________. For this reason the productivity of labor and output (income) per capita remain (high, low) ______________.

13. List five ways that government can serve a positive role in fostering economic growth in DVCs, especially during the early phases of growth:

a. ______________________________________

b. ______________________________________

c. ______________________________________

d. ______________________________________

e. ______________________________________

14. Government involvement in the economy of DVCs creates public sector problems because government bureaucracy can (foster, impede) ______________ social and economic change, government planners can give too much emphasis to (political, economic) ______________ objectives, and there can be (good, poor) ______________ administration and corruption.

15. Three major ways that IACs can assist in the economic development in DVCs is by (increasing, decreasing) ______________ international trade barriers, ______________ foreign aid, and ______________ the flow of private capital investment.

16. Direct foreign aid for DVCs generally comes from individual nations in the form of (private, public) ______________ loans, grants, and programs. It can also come from the (Bank of America, World Bank), ______________ which is supported by (12, 180) ________ member nations. This organization is a (first, last) ______________ resort lending agency for DVCs and provides (military, technical) ______________ assistance for DVCs.

17. Foreign aid has been criticized in recent years because it may (increase, decrease) ______________ dependency in a nation instead of creating self-sustained growth, may ______________ government bureaucracy and control over a nation's economy, and may ______________ the misuse of funds or corruption. These criticisms and the end of the cold war have led to a(n) ______________ in the amount of foreign aid to DVCs.

18. The causes of the DVC debt problem were due to world events during the 1970s and early 1980s. Oil prices (rose, fell) ______________ during the 1970s, and thus the borrowing needs of DVCs ______________ to pay for imported oil. In the early 1980s, the United States had a(n) (tight, easy) ______________ monetary policy that increased interest rates and the cost to DVCs of servicing debts. The international value of the dollar (appreciated, depreciated) ______________, which meant that DVCs had to pay (more, less) ______________ for imports and receive ______________ in return for exports. Some DVCs borrowed funds and used them for (consumption, investment) ______________ that was not productive.

19. Actions taken to resolve the debt crisis have (raised, lowered) ______________ foreign private investment in DVCs in the 1990s. The reason for this change is that many DVCs have reformed their economies and adopted policies that (limit, encourage) ______________ economic growth and ______________ direct foreign investment. Nevertheless, the flow of private capital to DVCs is (selective, widespread) ______________, and it is (correct, premature) ______________ to say that the crisis is resolved.

20. DVCs can adopt policies to encourage economic growth. They can (open, close) ______________ economies to international trade, (encourage, discourage) ______________ direct foreign investment and the development of human capital, and (expand, control) ______________ population growth. IACs can also adopt policies to help DVCs. They can (raise, lower) ______________ trade barriers, (encourage, discourage) ______________ immigration of the brightest and best-educated, and direct foreign aid to the (middle-income, low-income) ______________ DVCs.

■ TRUE-FALSE QUESTIONS

Circle the T if the statement is true, the F if it is false.

1. The richest 20% of the world's population receive about 50% of the world's income while the poorest 20% receive only about 20% of the world's income. **T F**

2. Developing countries generally have high unemployment, low literacy rates, rapid population growth, and a labor force committed to agricultural production. **T F**

3. The United States has about 5% of the world's population and produces about one-fourth of the world's output. **T F**

4. The absolute income gap between DVCs and industrially advanced countries has decreased over the past 30 years. **T F**

5. Economic growth in both IACs and DVCs requires using economic resources more efficiently and increasing the supplies of some of these resources. **T F**

6. It is impossible to achieve a high standard of living with a small supply of natural resources. **T F**

7. DVCs have low population densities and low population growth relative to IACs. **T F**

8. The demographic transition view of population growth is that rising incomes must first be achieved and only then will slower population growth follow. **T F**

9. A major factor contributing to the high unemployment rates in urban areas of DVCs is the fact that the migration from rural areas to cities has greatly exceeded the growth of urban job opportunities. **T F**

10. Saving in DVCs is a smaller percentage of domestic output than in IACs, and this is the chief reason total saving in DVCs is small. **T F**

11. Before private investment can be increased in DVCs, it is necessary to reduce the amount of investment in infrastructure. **T F**

12. Technological advances in DVCs will be made rapidly because the advances do not require pushing forward the frontiers of technological knowledge, and the technologies used in IACs can be easily transferred to all DVCs. **T F**

13. When technological advances are capital saving, it is possible for an economy to increase its productivity without any *net* investment in capital goods. **T F**

14. A critical, but intangible, ingredient in economic development is the "will to develop." **T F**

15. The capricious universe view is that there is a strong correlation between individual effort and results. **T F**

16. Land reform is one of the institutional obstacles to economic growth in many developing countries. **T F**

17. The situation in which poor nations stay poor because they are poor is a description of the vicious circle of poverty. **T F**

18. The creation of an adequate infrastructure in a nation is primarily the responsibility of the private sector. **T F**

19. Governments always play a positive role in fostering the economic growth of DVCs. **T F**

20. One effective way that IACs can help DVCs is to raise trade barriers so that DVCs become more self-sufficient. **T F**

21. The World Bank is the organization to which DVCs turn for the majority of foreign aid, loans, and grants. **T F**

22. Two reasons why foreign aid is viewed as harmful are that it tends to promote dependency and reduce market activity. **T F**

23. One reason for the debt crisis of the 1980s is that loans to DVCs frequently went to projects that were not productive investments. **T F**

24. In recent years, a smaller proportion of private capital flows to DVCs has been direct foreign investment rather than loans to DVC governments. **T F**

25. One policy suggested for promoting economic growth in DVCs is the establishment of independent central banks (where they do not already exist) to keep inflation in check and control the money supply. **T F**

■ MULTIPLE-CHOICE QUESTIONS

Circle the letter that corresponds to the best answer.

1. Data on per capita income from the nations of the world indicate that there is considerable
- **(a)** income equality
- **(b)** income inequality
- **(c)** stability in the income growth
- **(d)** deterioration in incomes for most developing nations

2. Which nation would be considered a developing nation?
- **(a)** India
- **(b)** Italy
- **(c)** Singapore
- **(d)** New Zealand

3. If the per capita income is $600 a year in a DVC and $12,000 in an IAC, then a 2% growth rate in each nation will increase the absolute income gap by
- **(a)** $120
- **(b)** $228
- **(c)** $240
- **(d)** $252

4. A DVC would probably exhibit a high level of
- **(a)** literacy
- **(b)** life expectancy
- **(c)** infant mortality
- **(d)** per capita energy consumption

5. The essential paths for economic growth in any nation are expanding the
- **(a)** size of the population and improving agriculture
- **(b)** role of government and providing jobs for the unemployed
- **(c)** supplies of resources and using existing resources more efficiently
- **(d)** amount of tax subsidies to business and tax credits for business investment

6. Based on the rule of 70, if the United States has an annual rate of population increase of 1% and a DVC has one of 2%, how many years will it take for the population to double in each nation?
- **(a)** 140 years for the United States and 70 years for the DVC
- **(b)** 35 years for the United States and 70 years for the DVC
- **(c)** 70 years for the United States and 35 years for the DVC
- **(d)** 70 years for the United States and 140 years for the DVC

7. Assume the total real output of a developing country increases from $100 billion to $115.5 billion while its population expands from 200 to 210 million people. Real per capital income has increased by
- **(a)** $50

(b) $100
(c) $150
(d) $200

8. An increase in the total output of consumer goods in a DVC may not increase the average standard of living because it may increase
(a) capital flight
(b) population growth
(c) disguised unemployment
(d) the quality of the labor force

9. Which best describes unemployment found in DVCs?
(a) the cyclical fluctuations in the nation's economy
(b) the migration of agricultural workers from rural areas to seek jobs in urban areas
(c) workers being laid off by large domestic or multinational corporations during periods of economic instability
(d) the education and training of workers in the wrong types of jobs and for which there is little demand

10. Which is an obstacle to economic growth in DVCs?
(a) the low demand for natural resources
(b) the low supply of capital goods
(c) the decline in demographic transition
(d) a fall in population growth

11. Which is a reason for placing special emphasis on capital accumulation in DVCs?
(a) the flexible supply of arable land in DVCs
(b) the high productivity of workers in DVCs
(c) the high marginal benefits of capital goods
(d) the greater opportunities for capital flight

12. Which is a factor limiting saving in DVCs?
(a) The output of the economy is too low to permit a large volume of saving.
(b) Those who do save make their savings available only to their families.
(c) Governments control the banking system and set low interest rates.
(d) There is an equal distribution of income in most nations.

13. When citizens of developing countries transfer savings to or invest savings in industrially advanced countries, this is referred to as
(a) brain drain
(b) capital flight
(c) savings potential
(d) in-kind investment

14. Which is a major obstacle to capital formation in DVCs?
(a) lack of oil resources
(b) lack of entrepreneurs
(c) lack of government price supports for products
(d) an excess of opportunities for financial investments

15. If it is cheaper to use a new fertilizer that is better adapted to a nation's topography, this is an example of
(a) a capital-using technology
(b) a capital-saving technology
(c) capital consumption
(d) private capital flows

16. Which is an example of infrastructure?
(a) a farm
(b) a steel plant
(c) an electric power plant
(d) a deposit in a financial institution

17. Which seems to be the most acute *institutional* problem that needs to be resolved by many DVCs?
(a) development of strong labor unions
(b) an increase in natural resources
(c) the adoption of birth control
(d) land reform

18. Which is a major positive role for government in the early stage of economic development?
(a) providing an adequate infrastructure
(b) conducting central economic planning
(c) improving the efficiency of tax collection
(d) creating marketing boards for export products

19. In recent years, many DVCs have come to realize that
(a) there are few disadvantages from government involvement in economic development
(b) competition and economic incentives for individuals are necessary for economic growth
(c) the World Bank is an institutional barrier to economic growth
(d) private capital is not essential for economic growth

20. Industrially advanced countries can best help DVCs by
(a) letting them raise tariffs and quotas to protect domestic markets
(b) reducing foreign grant aid but increasing loan aid
(c) increasing the flows of private capital
(d) increasing control over their capital markets

21. The major objective of the World Bank is to
(a) maximize its profits for its worldwide shareholders
(b) assist developing countries in achieving economic growth
(c) provide financial backing for the operation of the United Nations
(d) maintain stable exchange rates in the currencies of developing countries

22. A major criticism of foreign aid to developing nations is that it
(a) provides incentives for capital flight
(b) is capital using rather than capital saving
(c) encourages growth in government bureaucracy
(d) gives too much power and control to the World Bank

23. An event that occurred in the early 1980s that contributed to the debt crisis in DVCs was a
(a) sharp decline in the price of oil charged by OPEC
(b) depreciation in the international value of the dollar
(c) tight monetary policy in the United States
(d) fall in interest rates in Japan

24. A suggested policy for DVCs to implement that promotes economic growth is
(a) reducing the control of monetary policy by central banks

(b) obtaining more low-interest loans from the World Bank
(c) encouraging more direct foreign investment
(d) expanding state industries

25. Which is a suggested policy for industrially advanced countries to adopt to foster economic growth in DVCs?
(a) increased appreciation of currencies in DVCs
(b) increased debt relief in DVCs
(c) elimination of the International Monetary Fund
(d) elimination of the OPEC oil cartel

PROBLEMS

1. Suppose that the real per capita income in the average industrially advanced country is $8,000 per year and in the average DVC $500 per year.

a. The gap between their standards of living is $__________ per year.

b. If GDP per capita were to grow at a rate of 5% during a year in both the industrially advanced and the DVC,
(1) the standard of living in the IACs would rise to $__________ in a year;
(2) the standard of living in the DVCs would rise to $__________ in a year; and
(3) the gap between their standards of living would (narrow, widen) __________ to $________ in a year.

2. While economic conditions are not identical in all DVCs, certain conditions are common to or typical of most of them. In the space after each of the following characteristics, indicate briefly the nature of this characteristic in most DVCs.

a. Standard of living (per capita income): __________
b. Average life expectancy: __________
c. Extent of unemployment: __________
d. Literacy: __________
e. Technology: __________
f. Percentage of the population engaged in agriculture: __________
g. Size of the population relative to the land and capital available: __________
h. The birthrates and death rates: __________
i. Quality of the labor force: __________
j. Amount of capital equipment relative to the labor force: __________
k. Level of saving: __________
l. Incentive to invest: __________
m. Amount of infrastructure: __________
n. Extent of industrialization: __________
o. Size and quality of the entrepreneurial class and the supervisory class: __________
p. Per capita public expenditures for education and per capita energy consumption: __________
q. Per capita consumption of food: __________
r. Disease and malnutrition: __________

3. Suppose it takes a minimum of 5 units of food to keep a person alive for a year, the population can double itself every 10 years, and the food supply can increase every 10 years by an amount equal to what it was in the beginning (year 0).

a. Assume that both the population and the food supply grow at these rates. Complete the following table by computing the size of the population and the food supply in years 10 through 60.

Year	Food supply	Population
0	200	20
10	____	____
20	____	____
30	____	____
40	____	____
50	____	____
60	____	____

b. What happens to the relationship between the food supply and the population in the 30th year? __________

c. What would actually prevent the population from growing at this rate following the 30th year? __________

d. Assuming that the actual population growth in the years following the 30th does not outrun the food supply, what would be the size of the population in
(1) Year 40: __________
(2) Year 50: __________
(3) Year 60: __________

e. Explain why the standard of living failed to increase in the years following the 30th even though the food supply increased by 75% between years 30 and 60.

____

SHORT ANSWER AND ESSAY QUESTIONS

1. What is the degree of income inequality among nations of the world?

2. How do the overall level of economic growth per capita and the rates of economic growth compare among rich

nations and poor countries? Why does the income gap widen?

3. What are the human implications of poverty found in DVCs? (Use the socioeconomic indicators in Table 39-3 of the text to contrast the quality of life in IACs and DVCs).

4. Describe the basic paths of economic growth. Do these avenues differ for IACs and DVCs?

5. How would you describe the natural resource situation for DVCs? In what ways do price fluctuations affect DVC exports? Is a weak natural resource base an obstacle to economic growth?

6. Describe the implications of the high rate of growth in population and its effects on the standard of living. Can the standard of living be raised merely by increasing the output of consumer goods in DVCs? What is the meaning of the cliché "the rich get richer and the poor get children," and how does it apply to DVCs?

7. Compare and contrast the traditional view of population and economic growth with the demographic transition view.

8. What is the distinction between unemployment and underemployment? How do these concepts apply to DVCs?

9. What are the reasons for the low level of labor productivity in DVCs?

10. How does the brain drain affect DVCs?

11. What are the reasons for placing special emphasis on capital accumulation as a means of promoting economic growth in DVCs?

12. Why is domestic capital accumulation difficult in DVCs? Answer in terms of both the saving side and the investment side of capital accumulation. Is there capital flight from DVCs?

13. In addition to the obstacles which limit domestic investment, what other obstacles tend to limit the flow of foreign capital into DVCs? What role does infrastructure play in capital formation?

14. How might the DVCs improve their technology without engaging in slow and expensive research? Why might this be an inappropriate method of improving the technology used in the DVCs?

15. What is meant by the "will to develop"? How is it related to social and institutional change in DVCs?

16. Explain the vicious circle of poverty in the DVCs. How does population growth make an escape from this vicious circle difficult?

17. Why is the role of government expected to be a positive one in the early phases of development in DVCs? What have been the problems with the involvement of government in economic development?

18. What are three ways that IACs help DVCs?

19. How is it possible for the United States to assist DVCs without spending a penny on foreign aid? Is this type of aid sufficient to ensure rapid and substantial development in DVCs?

20. Discuss the World Bank in terms of its purposes, characteristics, sources of funds, promotion of private capital flows, and success. What are its affiliates and their purposes?

21. Discuss three criticisms of foreign aid to DVCs.

22. Describe the dimension and basic causes of the DVC debt crisis.

23. In the 1990s, what were the results and reforms from the debt crisis for DVCs?

24. Describe the variety of suggested policies that DVCs can adopt to promote economic growth.

25. Explain what IACs can do to assist DVCs in fostering economic growth.

ANSWERS

Chapter 39 The Economics of Developing Countries

FILL-IN QUESTIONS

1. 83, 1
2. industrially advanced, IACs, developing, DVCs, $24,930; $2,390; $430
3. higher, increase
4. lower, lower, lower, lower, higher
5. more, more
6. uneven, OPEC, DVCs, large, less
7. *a.* over, higher, decrease; *b.* unemployment, underemployment; *c.* low, human capital, brain drain
8. *a.* labor productivity, supply of, output
9. *a.* low, few, weak, capital flight; *b.* public, private; *c.* agriculture
10. *a.* skilled, scarce, abundant, capital; *b.* unskilled, abundant, scarce, labor; *c.* saving
11. sociocultural, institutional
12. low, low, low
13. *a.* establishing effective law and order; *b.*encouraging entrepreneurship; *c.* improving the infrastructure; *d.* promoting saving and investment; *e.* dealing with the social-institutional obstacles (any order for *a–e*)
14. impede, political, poor
15. decreasing, increasing, increasing
16. public, World Bank, 180, last, technical
17. increase, increase, increase, decrease
18. rose, rose, tight, appreciated, more less, investment
19. raised, encourage, encourage, selective, premature
20. open, encourage, control, lower, discourage, low-income

TRUE-FALSE QUESTIONS

1. F, pp. 812-813
2. T, pp. 812-813
3. T, p. 813
4. F, p. 813
5. T, p. 815
6. F, pp. 815-816
7. F, p. 818
8. T, p. 818
9. T, p. 818
10. F, pp. 819-820
11. F, p. 820
12. F, p. 821
13. T, p. 821
14. T, p. 821
15. F, p. 822
16. T, p. 822
17. T, pp. 822-823
18. F, p. 824
19. F, p. 824
20. F, p. 825
21. F, pp. 825-826
22. T, p. 826
23. T, p. 827
24. F, p. 828
25. T, pp. 828-829

MULTIPLE-CHOICE QUESTIONS

1. b, pp. 812-813
2. a, pp. 812-814
3. b, p. 813
4. c, pp. 814-815
5. c, p. 815
6. c, pp. 816-818
7. a, p. 816
8. b, p. 816
9. b, p. 818
10. b, p. 819
11. c, p. 819
12. a, pp. 819-820
13. b, p. 820
14. b, p. 820
15. b, p. 821
16. c, p. 820
17. d, p. 822
18. a, pp. 820, 824
19. b, p. 825
20. c, p. 825
21. b, p. 826
22. c, p. 826
23. c, p. 827
24. c, p. 829
25. b, pp. 829-830

PROBLEMS

1. *a.* 7,500; *b.* (1) 8,400, (2) 525, (3) widen, 7,875

2. *a.* low; *b.* short; *c.* widespread; *d.* low; *e.* primitive; *f.* large; *g.* large; *h.* high; *i.* poor; *j.* small; *k.* low; *l.* absent; *m.* small; *n.* small, *o.* small and poor; *p.* small; *q.* low; *r.* common

3. *a.* Food supply: 400, 600, 800, 1,000, 1,200, 1,400; Population: 40, 80, 160, 320, 640, 1,280; *b.* the food supply is just able to support the population; *c.* the inability of the food supply to support a population growing at this rate; *d.* (1) 200, (2) 240, (3) 280; *e.* the population increased as rapidly as the food supply

SHORT ANSWER AND ESSAY QUESTIONS

1. pp. 812-813
2. p. 813
3. pp. 813-815
4. p. 815
5. pp. 815-816
6. pp. 816-817
7. p. 818
8. p. 818
9. pp. 818-819
10. p. 819
11. p. 819
12. pp. 819-820
13. pp. 820-821
14. p. 821
15. p. 821
16. pp. 822-823
17. pp. 823-825
18. p. 825
19. p. 825
20. p. 826
21. pp. 826-827
22. p. 827
23. pp. 827-828
24. pp. 828-829
25. pp. 829-830

CHAPTER 40

Transition Economies: Russia and China

In the years following the Russian Revolution of 1917, many people in the United States were convinced that the economic system of the Soviet Union was unworkable and that it would break down sooner or later—proof that Marx and Lenin were unrealistic dreamers—and that the reconversion of the Soviet economy to a market system would follow. Now, over 80 years after the revolution, the Russian economy is being transformed into a market economy and a democracy.

China is also undergoing a rapid transition from a centrally planned economy to a market-based economy, but its experience differs from that of Russia. The transition in China has been longer and more gradual. The economic outcomes have also been very positive, with strong economic growth, rising productivity, and a significantly increased standard of living; however, problems remain because the Communist party retains dictatorial political control and economic development is uneven throughout the country.

Chapter 40 provides insights into the profound turn of events in both Russia and China. The first two sections of the chapter explain the basic ideas behind *Marxian ideology,* which gave rise to these command economies. They also discuss two basic institutional features of the former Soviet Union and pre-reform China: These economies operated under a system of state ownership of property resources; central planning was used to set prices, restrict consumption, and direct investment to heavy industry and the military.

Although central planning served as a powerful form of economic decision making in the former Soviet Union and pre-reform China, it had two serious problems, as you will discover in the third section. The first problem was one of *coordination*, which resulted in production bottlenecks and managers and bureaucrats missing production targets. Central planning also created an *incentive problem* because it sent out incorrect and inadequate signals for directing the efficient allocation of an economy's resources and gave workers little reason to work hard. The lack of incentives killed entrepreneurship and stifled innovation and technological advance.

The slowing of economic growth in the Soviet economy in the 1970s and 1980s set the stage for the failure of communism and the *collapse* of its command economy. Certainly other factors contributed to the economy's deterioration, as you will discover in the fourth section of the chapter. Production was of poor quality, and there were inadequate or limited consumer goods to meet consumer demand. The economy was overly burdened by government leaders' desire to support a large military. Agricultural inefficiencies were a drain on resources and restricted investment for other sectors of the economy.

The fifth section of the chapter explains the five elements of market reform in the Russian economy and its problems and prospects. The transition has led to the privatization of property resources, the promotion of competition, the decontrol of prices, and better connections to the international economy. The hyperinflation problem was solved by the establishment of a Russian central bank and the adoption of an anti-inflation monetary policy. Other problems continue to plague the economy. Real output, as well as living standards, fell significantly during the transition. Income inequality has grown, and government instability and social unrest give organized crime the opportunity to flourish. In spite of these problems, Russia is likely to succeed in becoming an advanced market economy, but much work remains to be done.

The market reform in China is the focus of the sixth section of the chapter. As already noted, China's reform efforts differed significantly from those of Russia because they started earlier and have been more gradual and experimental. Partial decontrol of land and prices in agriculture unleashed the rural economy and made it more market oriented. State-owned enterprises are being consolidated and forced to become more competitive and operate like corporations. The formation of private businesses has been encouraged. New foreign investment is encouraged to help capital formation and to gain access to advanced technology.

The results from Chinese economic reforms have been impressive, as described in the final section of the chapter. The economy has grown at a 9% annual rate since 1978. The standard of living has risen fourfold and at a much faster rate than population growth. Nevertheless, China's transition to a market economy continues to face significant problems. Property rights are ill-defined. The economy has experienced periods of high inflation and is not well-integrated into the world economy. Economic development across the nation is uneven, and the average income remains low by DVC standards.

The transformations of Russian and Chinese economies into market economies are among the most important economic events of recent decades. The sweeping changes in these economies from centrally planned economies to market economies should deepen your understanding of the principles of economics and how the market system works. These dramatic developments are a fitting topic to conclude your study of economics.

■ CHECKLIST

When you have studied this chapter you should be able to

☐ Outline the key elements of Marxian ideology.
☐ Identify two institutional characteristics of the former Soviet Union (prior to collapse) and China (prior to market reforms).
☐ Make seven generalizations about the central planning goals and techniques in the former Soviet Union and China.
☐ Compare how a market economy coordinates economic activity with how it works in a centrally planned economy.
☐ Explain how a market economy provides incentives and the problems with incentives in a centrally planned economy.
☐ Identify five factors that contributed to the collapse of the Soviet economy.
☐ List five factors that are important for the transition of Russia's economy to a market economy.
☐ Explain the effects of privatization in Russia.
☐ Use a supply and demand graph to discuss the difficulties that price reforms pose in the Russian transition.
☐ Describe the promotion of competition in Russia.
☐ Explain the importance of Russia joining the world economy.
☐ Describe the need for price-level stabilization in Russia.
☐ Explain two major problems the Russian economy has experienced during the transition.
☐ Evaluate the future prospects for Russia's transition to a market economy.
☐ Contrast China's path to market reforms with that of Russia.
☐ Describe agricultural and price reform in China.
☐ Discuss the reform of urban industries and the use of special economic zones in China.
☐ Describe how the Chinese government has developed supporting institutions and transformed state-owned enterprises.
☐ State the positive outcomes from the reform of the Chinese economy.
☐ Identify four significant problems in the Chinese transition to a market economy.

■ CHAPTER OUTLINE

1. The centrally planned economies of the former Soviet Union and pre-reform China were based on Marxian ideology. The government was viewed as a dictatorship of the proletariat (or working class) and the peasantry. Especially important was the Marxian concept of a ***labor theory of value,*** which held that only labor creates value in production and that profits are a surplus value expropriated from workers by capitalists who, because of the institution of private property, were able to control the means of production (capital goods). The purpose of communism was to overthrow capitalism and end this exploitation of workers (and peasants) by eliminating private property and creating a classless society.

2. The two major institutional features of the pre-collapse Soviet and pre-reform Chinese economies were ***state-owned enterprises*** of all property resources and ***central economic planning.*** The command economy based most economic decisions on bureaucrats' choices rather than relying on market forces to direct economic activity.

a. The central planning functioned differently in the former Soviet Union and pre-reform China.

(1) The former Soviet Union attached great importance to rapid industrialization and military strength, whereas China emphasized rural development.

(2) Each economy overcommitted its available resources, and they often missed planning targets.

(3) Each economy mobilized resources by increasing the quantity of resources rather than using given resources more productively.

(4) Directives were used rather than markets and prices to allocate inputs for production in each economy.

(5) Government fixed and controlled prices.

(6) Each economy emphasized self-sufficiency of the nation, viewed capitalist nations as hostile, and restricted trade.

(7) Each economy passively used monetary and fiscal policies; unemployment was limited or disguised; the price level was controlled through government price fixing.

3. There are two basic problems with a centrally planned economy.

a. The *coordination problem* involves the difficulty of coordinating the economy's many interdependent segments and avoiding the chain reaction that would result from a bottleneck in any one of the segments. This coordination problem became even more difficult as the economy grew larger and more complex, and more economic decisions had to be made in the production process. There were also inadequate measures of economic performance to determine the degree of success or failure of enterprises or to give clear signals to the economy.

b. The second problem was *economic incentives.* In a command economy, incentives are ineffective for encouraging economic initiative and work and for directing the most efficient use of productive resources. In a market economy, profits and losses signal what firms should produce, how they should produce, and how productive resources should be allocated to best meet the wants of a nation. Central planning in the two economies also lacked entrepreneurship and stifled innovation, both of which are important forces for achieving long-term economic growth. Individual workers lacked much motivation to work hard because pay was limited and there were either few consumer goods to buy or they were of low quality.

4. The *collapse of the Soviet economy* stemmed largely from the failure of central economic planning.

a. Economic growth declined in the 1970s and 1980s. Real output also fell sharply in the few years before the country's breakup.

b. Technology in manufacturing lagged by western standards, and consumer goods were of poor quality.

c. Consumers received few material benefits from years of sacrifice for rapid industrialization and the military, and consumer goods were in short supply.
d. The large financial burden for military expenditures diverted valuable resources from the production of consumer and capital goods to military production.
e. Agriculture acted as a drag on economic growth and hurt productivity in other sectors of the economy.

5. The *transition* of the former Soviet Union, particularly Russia, from a centrally planned to a market economy is occurring in several ways.
a. A market economy relies on private property rights and limited government control of business. Private property rights have been established to encourage entrepreneurship, and much government property has been transferred to private ownership. This privatization was initially achieved through government distribution of vouchers that could be used to purchase businesses; it is now done through the direct sale of state enterprises. This change has stimulated foreign investment and the flow of foreign capital to Russia; however, market reforms in agriculture have been limited.
b. Soviet government controls on prices led to a serious misallocation of resources and poor economic incentives. Most price controls were eliminated (about 90%) in 1992, so prices for goods and services were free to change and reflect relative scarcities. The value of the ruble is now established by supply and demand on foreign exchange markets.
c. For a market economy to work properly, competition must be promoted by splitting up or restructuring large state-owned enterprises to reduce the potential for monopoly power from having one privatized business in an industry. Progress in this area has been slow, but joint ventures and foreign investment may stimulate more business competition in the Russian economy.
d. The Soviet economy was restricted from actively participating in international trade. Action has been taken to open the economy to international trade and finance by making the ruble a convertible currency.
e. The transition to a market economy brought hyperinflation. Contributing factors included price decontrols, the ruble overhang (excess currency saved when there were few consumer goods to purchase), large government budget deficits, and the printing of money to finance the deficits. A Russian central bank has been created, and an anti-inflation money policy was adopted to eliminate hyperinflation and keep prices relatively stable.
f. Several major problems continue to affect the transition.
(1) Real output and living standards fell during the reforms, although the decline bottomed out in 1992. Inflation, reduced international trade, bankruptcy and the closing of state enterprises, and the massive reallocation of resources and reductions in government and military spending precipitated the decline in output.
(2) Economic inequality and social costs increased during the transition. Market reforms enriched some groups and hurt others. Economic insecurity and instability resulting from the transition raised tensions among workers and other groups, reduced the quality of life and life expectancy, and stimulated the rise of organized crime and "crony" capitalism.
g. The *prospects* for Russia's transition to a market economy are still a matter of concern. The pessimistic view is that the government remains weak in enforcing laws, public debt is mounting, and there is an inability to provide basic public services. Excessive government spending and borrowing combined with a banking crisis might lead to a collapse of the economy. The more optimistic view is that the fall in real output has ended and that the rate of inflation is now under control. Market reforms are now taking hold, and the economy will eventually prosper. Although the transitional problems are present, prospects are good for Russia to become an advanced market economy.

6. The path of *economic reform in China* differed significantly from that in Russia. China's market reforms began earlier and were more gradual and experimental. The Communist Party in China retained dictatorial control, while in Russia the party was replaced with democratic leadership. Russia has privatized much of the economy and sold off state enterprises, whereas China has protected its state enterprises while encouraging competing private enterprises. Russia experienced a significant decline in real output; China's output has continued to grow at high rates.
a. Agricultural reform in China began in 1978 with the leasing of land to individual farmers and permission to sell the output at competitive rather than government-controlled prices. This decollectivization and price reform provided a market basis for Chinese agriculture and the economy and released labor resources to private rural manufacturing firms (township and village enterprises).
b. Market reforms were also established in urban industries to give state-owned enterprises (SOEs) more control over production and employment. Enterprises could retain profits and sell more of their output at market prices rather than government-set prices. Urban collectives were formed that operated as private firms jointly owned by managers and workers. The collectives competed strongly with state enterprises and stimulated productivity in the economy.
c. Special enterprise zones were established that were open to foreign investment, private ownership, and international trade. They attracted foreign capital and increased Chinese exports. These areas undercut the support for central planning.
d. Supporting institutions have been developed to facilitate the transition to a market economy. The Chinese central bank was established to regulate the banking system and control the money supply. The enterprise tax system replaced the profit transfer from state enterprises. Foreign exchange can be swapped as needed between enterprises. A stock market has been established.
e. State-owned enterprises have been transformed; they operate more like corporations and respond to

market needs rather than to social directives. The major SOEs have been consolidated into 1,000 enterprises. Government plans call for stock to be issued and for the SOEs to become shareholder owned and operate like corporations, with the government retaining control. Other SOEs will be sold or permitted to go bankrupt.

7. There are positive outcomes from China's market-based reforms, but the transition to a market economy is still incomplete.

a. China has an impressive record of growth. It has averaged 9% annually since 1978, among the highest on record for such a period. Real output and incomes have quadrupled in less than two decades. Capital formation has increased productivity, and labor resources have been shifted from lower areas of productivity (agriculture) to higher areas of productivity (manufacturing). International trade has expanded exports and the imports of critical consumer and capital goods. Foreign investment has resulted in access to new technology that can be used to further increase productivity.

b. There are economic problems in China's development.

(1) Property rights are incomplete because the privatization of farmland is opposed by the Communist Party, and such a policy leads to less investment in agriculture.

(2) China has experienced periods of high inflation because the financial and monetary control system is weak. The banking system is owed substantial sums by state-owned enterprises.

(3) China is not fully integrated into the world economy. It is not a member of the World Trade Organization, and it has high tariffs on many products. There is weak enforcement of intellectual property rights.

(4) Economic growth is geographically uneven throughout China. Hong Kong is now part of China and has high per capita income. Although people living in enterprise zones and the coastal areas near Hong Kong have experienced substantial growth in incomes and living standards, people in poorer regions still receive low incomes. Overall, China is still considered a low-income developing country.

■ HINTS AND TIPS

1. This chapter applies your knowledge of economics to explain the transformation of Russia and China from centrally planned to market-oriented economies. Throughout this chapter you will be comparing a market economy with a command economy. Review Chapter 4 before you read this chapter to make sure you have a good understanding of how capitalism works and its major characteristics.

2. View the chapter as a culminating exercise in your study of economics that gives you a chance to *review, apply,* and *integrate* many of the economic concepts and ideas you learned from the text. Only a few terms and concepts will be new to you in this chapter (they apply to Marxian ideology or the reforms in China or Russia).

3. Supply and demand analysis is used to explain price controls in Figure 40-1 in the text. The figure differs from those you saw in a previous chapter (Chapter 3) because there are two supply curves. One is vertical (perfectly inelastic) because it assumes fixed government control of production and no effect on quantity supplied as price controls are lifted. The upsloping supply curve shows an increase in quantity supplied as price controls are lifted.

■ IMPORTANT TERMS

labor theory of value
surplus value
state ownership
central economic planning
coordination problem
incentive problem
township and village enterprises
state-owned enterprises
urban collectives
special economic zones

SELF-TEST

■ FILL-IN QUESTIONS

1. The ideology behind the central planning in the former Soviet Union and pre-reform China was that the value of any commodity is determined by the amount of (capital, labor) ________________ required to produce it. In capitalist economies, capital was (privately, publicly) ________________ owned, and capitalists exploited workers by paying them a wage that was (greater than, less than) ________________ the value of their production and obtained (shortage, surplus) ________________ value at the expense of workers.

2. In a communist economy, capital and other property resources would be (publicly, privately) ________________ owned and society would be (segregated, classless) ________________. The Communist Party would serve as the representative of the (capitalists, proletariat) ________________ and peasantry and would redistribute the surplus value of workers in the form of (tax cuts, subsidies) ________________ for public and quasipublic goods. In reality, the Communist Party was (democratic, a dictatorship) ________________.

3. One major institution of the former Soviet Union and pre-reform China was the ownership of property resources by (the state, property owners) ________________. Another institutional feature was (central, decentralized) ________________ economic planning.

4. Economic planning in the former Soviet Union and pre-reform China functioned in several ways. In the former

Soviet Union, plans sought to achieve rapid (population growth, industrialization) ______________ and provision of (civilian, military) ______________ goods. In China, emphasis was on (urban, rural) ______________ development. In both nations, the planning policies created an (over, under)______________commitment of the economy's resources and resulted in an ______________ production of goods for consumers.

5. Economic growth was achieved by (importing, mobilizing) ______________ resources and by reallocating surplus labor from (industry, agriculture) ______________ to ______________. The government allocated inputs among industries by (prices, directives) ______________, and the government set fixed ______________ for goods and services and inputs.

6. Each nation also viewed itself as a (capitalist, socialist) ______________ nation surrounded by hostile ______________ nations, and central plans were designed to achieve economic (freedom, self-sufficiency) ______________. Macroeconomic policies were (active, passive) ______________.

7. Coordination and decision making in a market economy are (centralized, decentralized) ______________, but in the Soviet and pre-reform Chinese economies it was ______________. The market system tends to produce a reasonably (efficient, inefficient) ______________ allocation of resources, but in centrally planned economies it was ______________ and resulted in production bottlenecks and failures to meet many production targets. Central planning became (more, less) ______________ complex and difficult as each economy grew and changed over time. Indicators of economic performance were (adequate, inadequate) ______________ for determining the success or failure of economic activities.

8. Another problem with central planning was that economic incentives were (effective, ineffective) ______________ for encouraging work or for giving signals to planners for efficient allocation of resources in the economy. The centrally planned system also lacked the (production targets, entrepreneurship) ______________ which is so important to technological advance. Innovation (fostered, lagged) ______________ because there was no competition.

9. A number of factors contributed to the collapse of the Soviet economy. The economy experienced (rise, decline) ______________ in economic growth in the 1970s and 1980s. Consumer goods were of (good, poor) ______________ quality, and there were widespread (shortages, surpluses) ______________. There was a large (consumer, military) ______________ burden on the economy that diverted resources from the production of (consumer, investment) ______________ goods. Agriculture was (efficient, inefficient) ______________ and (helped, hurt) ______________ economic growth and productivity in other sectors of the economy.

10. The Russian transition to a market economy has resulted in major reforms. Property rights have been (revoked, established) ______________, and government property has been transferred to (foreign, private) ______________ ownership. In Soviet Russia, the prices of goods and services were kept at low levels through price (competition, controls) ______________, so the marginal cost of a product (was, was not) ______________ equal to its marginal benefit. This pricing policy led to (efficient, inefficient) ______________ use of resources to make products and to (surpluses, shortages) ______________ of many consumer goods. Today, most prices in Russia are (still fixed, free to vary) ______________ ______________.

11. Russia is also promoting competition by (forming, dismantling) ______________ state-owned enterprises to reduce the potential for (rivalry, monopoly) ______________. Russia has (opened, closed) ______________ the economy to international trade and finance. One example of this policy is making the ruble a (fixed, convertible) ______________ currency on international markets.

12. The Russian transition to a market economy was accompanied by (inflation, deflation) ______________. It was high because of price (controls, decontrols) ______________, a ruble (under, over) ______________hang, and government budget (surpluses, deficits) ______________. In response to this problem, the nation created an independent central (account, bank) ______________ to provide control over (fiscal, monetary) ______________ policy.

13. Major problems remain for Russia's transition. There has been a (falling, rising) ______________ level of real output and a ______________ standard of living. Economic inequality has (increased, decreased) ______________ and led to ______________ economic security and (increased, decreased) ______________ and ______________ crime.

14. Compared with Russia, China's market reforms began (later, earlier) ______________ and were more (rapid, gradual) ______________. China asserts that communist dictatorship and markets are (incompatible, compatible) ______________, while Russia views them as ______________. China instituted its market reforms and experienced (growth, depression) ______________, while Russia experienced ______________ in its transition to a market economy. Russia (sold, protected) ______________ state enterprises, while China ______________ them but encouraged competing private enterprises.

15. Agricultural reform in China began in 1978 with the (selling, leasing) ______________ of land to individual farmers and permission for ______________ the agriculture products at (market, government) ______________ prices. The reform released (capital, labor) ______________ resources to private rural manufacturing firms called township and village enterprises.

16. Market reforms were also established in Chinese urban industries to give state-owned enterprises (less, more) ______________ decision making about production and employment. Urban (cartels, collectives) ______________ were formed that operated as private firms jointly owned by managers and workers. The competition of state and nonstate enterprises (increased, decreased) ______________ productivity and innovation in the economy.

17. China created special economic zones that were (open, closed) ______________ to foreign investment, private ownership, and international trade. A Chinese central bank was established to regulate the (trading, banking) ______________ system and control the (import, money) ______________ supply. Profit transfers from state enterprises to the central government were replaced with an enterprise (spending, tax) ______________ system. Foreign exchange can be (hoarded, swapped) ______________ as needed between enterprises.

18. There has been a transformation of Chinese state-owned enterprises (SOEs). They operate more like (bureaucracies, corporations) ______________ and respond to (social directive, the market) ______________. Plans call for the major 100 SOEs to issue (money, stock) ______________ and operate more like corporations under government control. Other smaller SOEs will be (bought, sold) ______________ by the government or permitted to go bankrupt.

19. The transition to a market economy in China shows positive outcomes. Economic growth in China averaged (2, 9) __________% annually since 1978. Real output and income have (doubled, quadrupled) ______________ in less than two decades. China's real GDP and real income have grown much (more, less) ______________ rapidly than its population.

20. Problems remain with China's transition. Privatization of farmland is (supported, opposed) ______________ by the Communist Party, and this policy leads to (more, less) ______________ investment in agriculture. Limited financial and monetary control has resulted in periods of severe (inflation, deflation) ______________. Substantial sums are (paid, owed) ______________ by state-owned enterprises to the banking system. China (is, is not) ______________ fully integrated into the world economy, ______________ a member of the World Trade Organization, and has (low, high) ______________ tariffs on many products. Economic growth is (even, uneven) ______________, and China is still considered a (low, middle) ______________-income developing country.

■ TRUE-FALSE QUESTIONS

Circle the T if the statement is true, the F if it is false.

1. The labor theory of value is the Marxian idea that the value of any good is determined solely by the amount of labor required for its production. **T F**

2. Surplus value in Marxian ideology is the value or price of a commodity at equilibrium in a competitive market. **T F**

3. The economies of the former Soviet Union and pre-reform China were characterized by state ownership of resources and authoritarian central planning. **T F**

4. The former Soviet Union was dedicated to the task of rapid industrialization and building economic self-sufficiency. **T F**

5. Pre-reform China emphasized rural economic development. **T F**

6. Economic resources tended to be undercommitted in both the former Soviet Union and pre-reform China. **T F**

7. Both the former Soviet Union and pre-reform China actively used monetary and fiscal policies to manipulate levels of employment, output, and prices. **T F**

8. A centrally planned economy is significantly affected by missed production targets and bottlenecks. **T F**

9. The problems of central planning become easier and less complex as an economy grows over time. **T F**

10. Profit is the key indicator of success and failure in a centrally planned economy. **T F**

11. Central planning provided weak or inaccurate incentives for allocating resources to achieve economic efficiency and encourage hard work. **T F**

12. Centrally planned economies encourage entrepreneurship and technological advance under the directive of the Communist Party. **T F**

13. In the former Soviet Union, greater productivity and technological progress in the civilian sector were often sacrificed or limited by the demands to support a large military. **T F**

14. As part of the transition to a market economy, Russia has taken major steps to privatize its economy and establish property rights. **T F**

15. Price decontrol was a minor problem in the conversion of the Russian economy to capitalism because the prices the Soviet government established over the years were very similar to the economic value established in a competitive market. **T F**

16. The transition to a market economy in Russia has required the breakup of large industries and coordinated actions to promote competition. **T F**

17. A major accomplishment during the Russian transition to a market economy was limited inflation because of balanced budgets and a tight control of the money supply. **T F**

18. Two major problems Russia experienced during its transition to capitalism were a decline in the standard of living and increased economic inequality. **T F**

19. The Chinese economy used a "shock" approach to economic reform to make its transition to a market economy. **T F**

20. Collectivization and price controls were instrumental in strengthening production incentives and moving the Chinese economy toward a market-based agriculture. **T F**

21. The Chinese government has encouraged the formation of nonstate enterprises, called urban collectives, which are jointly owned by workers and managers. **T F**

22. China has created special economic zones that are open to foreign investment, private ownership, and international trade. **T F**

23. A major limitation of Chinese economic reform is the failure to create a stock market for the exchange of shares of newly created corporations. **T F**

24. China's economic growth has declined over the past two decades because of the instability caused by its economic reforms. **T F**

25. One continuing economic problem in China is the uneven regional economic development. **T F**

■ MULTIPLE-CHOICE QUESTIONS

Circle the letter that corresponds to the best answer.

1. Which was an element in Marxian ideology?
(a) the creation of surplus value by government
(b) dictatorship over the business class
(c) the private ownership of property
(d) the labor theory of value

2. Marxian ideology was highly critical of capitalist societies because in those societies capitalists
(a) reduced the productivity of workers by not investing their profits in new capital goods
(b) paid workers a wage that was less than the value of their production
(c) shared surplus value with the government
(d) were not taxed as much as the workers

3. The institution that was most characteristic of the former Soviet Union and pre-reform China was
(a) private ownership of property
(b) authoritarian central planning
(c) a system of markets and prices
(d) consumer sovereignty

4. Industrialization, rapid economic growth, and military strength in the former Soviet Union and pre-reform China were primarily achieved by
(a) mobilizing larger quantities of resources
(b) joining the international economy
(c) making currencies convertible
(d) using an easy-money policy

5. Both the former Soviet Union and pre-reform China viewed themselves as socialist nations surrounded by hostile capitalist nations, and as a consequence central planning stressed the need for
(a) hoarding gold
(b) flexible prices
(c) consumer sovereignty
(d) economic self-sufficiency

6. In the former Soviet Union and pre-reform China, monetary policy
(a) was active and fiscal policy was passive
(b) was passive and fiscal policy was active
(c) and fiscal policy were both passive
(d) and fiscal policy were both active

7. In the system of central planning, the outputs of some industries became the inputs for other industries, but a failure of one industry to meet its production target would cause
(a) widespread unemployment
(b) inflation in wholesale and retail prices
(c) profit declines and potential bankruptcy of firms
(d) a chain reaction of production problems and bottlenecks

8. What was the major success indicator for Soviet and Chinese state enterprises?
- **(a)** profits
- **(b)** the level of prices
- **(c)** production targets
- **(d)** the enterprise tax

9. The centrally planned system in the former Soviet Union and pre-reform China lacked
- **(a)** price controls
- **(b)** entrepreneurship
- **(c)** economic growth
- **(d)** allocation by directives

10. In the last year or two before the Soviet economic system collapsed, real output
- **(a)** increased slightly
- **(b)** decreased significantly
- **(c)** remained relatively constant
- **(d)** increased faster than the rate of population growth

11. Which was evidence of the Soviet economy's economic failure?
- **(a)** a tight monetary policy
- **(b)** an oversupply of most products
- **(c)** the poor quality of consumer goods
- **(d)** higher productivity in agriculture than industry

12. What was the size of expenditures for the military as a percentage of domestic output in the former Soviet Union (**SU**) and the United States (**U.S.**)?

	SU %	U.S., %
(a)	26–30	18
(b)	21–25	12
(c)	15–20	6
(d)	10–14	3

13. Which was a cause of low productivity in agriculture in the former Soviet Union?
- **(a)** inability to make productive use of the abundance of good farmland in the country
- **(b)** failure to construct an effective incentive system for agriculture
- **(c)** increase in the length of the growing season
- **(d)** overuse of certain chemical fertilizers on crops

14. Which helped Russia make a transition to a market economy?
- **(a)** ruble overhang
- **(b)** price controls
- **(c)** privatization
- **(d)** hyperinflation

15. The effect of price controls on most consumer goods in the former Soviet Union was that
- **(a)** surpluses developed because the quantity consumers demanded was greater than the quantity supplied at the price set by government
- **(b)** prices fell because the quantity consumers demanded was greater than the quantity supplied
- **(c)** prices rose because the quantity consumers demanded was less than the quantity supplied
- **(d)** shortages developed because the quantity consumers demanded was greater than the quantity supplied at the price set by government

16. Which set of factors most likely contributed to hyperinflation as Russia made its transition to a market economy?
- **(a)** the breakup of state monopolies, land reform, and the poor quality of consumer goods
- **(b)** increased military spending, investment in new technology, and the convertibility of the ruble
- **(c)** central planning, production targets, and production bottlenecks
- **(d)** government deficits, the ruble overhang, and price decontrols

17. Which two significant problems did Russia encounter in its transition to a market system?
- **(a)** rising taxes and increasing life expectancies
- **(b)** a loose monetary policy and a strict fiscal policy
- **(c)** falling real output and declining living standards
- **(d)** greater military spending and more environmental pollution

18. Compared with Russia, market reforms in China
- **(a)** occurred over a longer time and were more gradual
- **(b)** focused primarily on industry rather than agriculture
- **(c)** relied more on monetary policy than fiscal policy
- **(d)** were less successful and more disruptive

19. The key elements of the 1978–1984 rural economic reforms in China
- **(a)** were passive macroeconomic policies
- **(b)** was formation of special economic zones
- **(c)** were foreign investment and loans to state-owned enterprises
- **(d)** were decollectivization and creation of a two-track price system

20. Privately owned rural manufacturing firms in China are called
- **(a)** town and village enterprises
- **(b)** special economic zones
- **(c)** incentive collectives
- **(d)** farm cooperatives

21. Chinese enterprises in urban areas that are jointly owned by their managers and workers are
- **(a)** industrial unions
- **(b)** urban collectives
- **(c)** business operating units
- **(d)** manufacturing cooperatives

22. Which would be a supporting institution for market reform in China?
- **(a)** a price control authority
- **(b)** a profit transfer system
- **(c)** a farm collective
- **(d)** a central bank

23. Since market reforms began, real output and real income in China have
- **(a)** doubled
- **(b)** tripled
- **(c)** quadrupled
- **(d)** quintupled

24. The shift of employment from agriculture toward rural and urban manufacturing in China has increased
 (a) inflation
 (b) productivity
 (c) bankruptcies
 (d) unemployment

25. One significant problem China faces in its transition to a market economy is
 (a) establishing a stock market
 (b) establishing a central bank
 (c) incomplete privatization of land
 (d) creation of special economic zones

■ PROBLEMS

1. In the following table are several major institutions and characteristics of a capitalistic economy, such as that in the United States, and a centrally planned economy, such as that in the former Soviet Union or pre-reform China. In the appropriate space, name the corresponding institution or characteristic of the other economy.

Capitalist institution or characteristic	Socialist institution or characteristic
a. ______________	labor theory of value
b. ______________	surplus value
c. private ownership of economic resources	______________
d. a market economy	______________
e. ______________	state-owned enterprises
f. privately owned farms	______________
g. ______________	government price controls
h. ______________	passive macroeconomic policies
i. representative democracy	______________

2. Answer the following set of questions based on the table below. The columns show the price, quantity demanded (Q_d) by consumers, and a fixed quantity supplied by government (Q_{s1}) for a product in the former Soviet Union. The column for Q_{s2} shows the supply curve for the product *after* privatization in the industry producing the product.

Price (in rubles)	Q_d	Q_{s1}	Q_{s2}
90	25	25	55
80	30	25	50
70	35	25	45
60	40	25	40
50	45	25	35
40	50	25	30
30	55	25	25

a. When only the government supplies the product as shown in the Q_{s1} schedule, the equilibrium price will be ______________ rubles and the equilibrium quantity will be ______________ units.

b. If the government tries to make the product more accessible to lower-income consumers by setting the price at 30 rubles, then the quantity demanded will be ______________ units and the quantity supplied will be ______________ units, producing a shortage of ______________ units.

c. If the government decontrolled prices but did not privatize industry, then prices would rise to ______________ rubles and the government would still produce ______________ units.

d. With privatization, there will be a new quantity supplied schedule (Q_{s2}). The equilibrium price will be ______________ rubles and the equilibrium quantity will be ______________ units. The equilibrium price has risen by ______________ rubles and the equilibrium quantity by ______________ units.

3. Match the terms from China's economic reform with the phrase using the appropriate number.

1. special economic zone
2. urban collective
3. two-track price system
4. town and village enterprises
5. enterprise tax system
6. state-owned enterprise

a. Privately owned rural manufacturing firms ________

b. Replaced the system of profit transfers from state enterprises to the central government ________

c. Areas in coastal regions that are open to foreign investment, private ownership, and international trade ________

d. Nonstate enterprises jointly owned by managers and their work forces in urban areas ________

e. Gives farmers ability to sell output at market-determined prices ________

f. Enterprises that are controlled by the government ________

■ SHORT ANSWER AND ESSAY QUESTIONS

1. What are the essential features of Marxian ideology on which the Soviet Union's command economy was based?

2. What were the two principal economic institutions of the pre-reform and pre-collapse economies of China and Russia? How do these institutions compare with those in the United States?

3. Describe how central planning functioned in the former Soviet Union and pre-reform China. What generalizations can you make about resource use, directives, prices, self-sufficiency, and macroeconomic policies?

4. Why does central planning result in a coordination problem? Compare the operation of central planning with the use of markets and prices for economic decision making.

5. How does central economic planning produce a significant incentive problem? What types of economic incentives for business, workers, and consumers exist in a market economy? How are those incentives different in a centrally planned economy?

6. Discuss the five factors that help explain or contributed to the collapse of the Soviet economy.

7. What action has Russia taken to privatize the economy?

8. Why was there a need for price reform in Russia in its transition to a market economy? What has been the *general* effect of this change? Use a supply and demand graph to explain the effect of the price decontrol on a specific product.

9. Discuss what is being done in Russia to promote competition. To what extent are public monopolies a problem?

10. What major problem is confronting Russia as it seeks to join the world economy?

11. How have high rates of inflation affected Russia's transition to a market economy? What has been the shift in macroeconomic policy?

12. What major problems has Russia encountered in its transition to a market economy?

13. Evaluate the prospects for the transformation of Russia into a market economy.

14. How did China's approach to market reforms differ from that in Russia?

15. Describe how China has tried to transform agriculture and rural production.

16. What market-based changes has the Chinese government made in urban industries?

17. What actions has the Chinese government taken to encourage foreign investment and establish institutions that support a market-based economy?

18. Describe the economic transformation of state-owned enterprises in China.

19. What are the positive outcomes of China's economic reform?

20. Discuss four significant economic problems that China continues to face in its transition to a market economy.

ANSWERS

Chapter 40 Transition Economies: Russia and China

FILL-IN QUESTIONS

1. labor, privately, less than, surplus
2. publicly, classless, proletariat, subsidies, a dictatorship
3. the state, central
4. industrialization, military, rural, over, under
5. mobilizing, agriculture, industry, directives, prices
6. socialist, capitalist, self-sufficiency, passive
7. decentralized, centralized, efficient, inefficient, more, inadequate
8. ineffective, entrepreneurship, lagged
9. decline, poor, shortages, military, consumer, inefficient, hurt
10. established, private, controls, was not, inefficient, shortages, free to vary
11. dismantling, monopoly, opened, convertible
12. inflation, decontrols, over, deficits, bank, monetary
13. falling, falling, increased, decreased, increased
14. earlier, gradual, compatible, incompatible, growth, depression, sold, protected
15. leasing, selling, market, labor
16. more, collectives, increased
17. open, banking, money, tax, swapped
18. corporations, the market, stock, sold
19. 9, quadrupled, more
20. opposed, less, inflation, owed, is not, is not, high, uneven, low

TRUE-FALSE QUESTIONS

1. T, p. 835
2. F, p. 835
3. T, pp. 835-836
4. T, p. 836
5. T, p. 836
6. F, p. 836
7. F, pp. 836-837
8. T, p. 837
9. F, p. 837
10. F, pp. 837-838
11. T, pp. 837-838
12. F, pp. 837-838
13. T, p. 839
14. T, pp. 839-840
15. F, pp. 840-841
16. T, p. 841
17. F, p. 841
18. T, pp. 841-842
19. F, p. 843
20. F, pp. 843-844
21. T, p. 844
22. T, p. 844
23. F, p. 844
24. F, p. 845
25. T, pp. 846-847

MULTIPLE-CHOICE QUESTIONS

1. d, p. 835
2. b, p. 835
3. b, pp. 835-836
4. a, p. 836
5. d, p. 836
6. c, pp. 836-837
7. d, p. 837
8. c, pp. 837-838
9. b, p. 838
10. b, p. 839
11. c, p. 839
12. c, p. 839
13. b, p. 839
14. c, pp. 839-840
15. d, p. 840
16. d, p. 841
17. c, pp. 841-842
18. a, p. 843
19. d, pp. 843-844
20. a, p. 844
21. b, p. 844
22. d, p. 844
23. c, p. 845
24. b, p. 845
25. c, p. 845

PROBLEMS

1. *a.* supply and demand; *b.* profit; *c.* state ownership of resources; *d.* command or centrally planned economy; *e.* corporations; *f.* collective farms or agricultural cooperatives; *g.* competitive markets and flexible prices; *h.* active or discretionary macroeconomic policies; *i.* dictatorship by the Communist Party
2. a. 90, 25; *b.* 55, 25, 30; *c.* 90, 25; *d.* 60, 40, 30, 15
3. a. 4; *b.* 5; *c.* 1; *d.* 2; *e.* 3; *f.* 6

SHORT ANSWER AND ESSAY QUESTIONS

1. pp. 834-835
2. pp. 835-836
3. pp. 836-837
4. p. 837
5. pp. 837-838
6. pp. 838-839
7. pp. 839-840
8. pp. 840-841
9. p. 841
10. p. 841
11. p. 841
12. pp. 841-842
13. pp. 842-843
14. p. 843
15. pp. 843-844
16. p. 844
17. p. 844
18. p. 844
19. p. 845
20. pp. 845-847

Glossary

Note: Terms in *italic* type are defined separately in this glossary.

A

Ability-to-pay principle The idea that those who have greater income (or wealth) should pay a greater proportion of it as taxes than those who have less income (or wealth).

Abstraction Elimination of irrelevant and noneconomic facts to obtain an *economic principle.*

Acreage allotment program A pre-1996 government program which determined the total number of acres to be used in producing (reduced amounts of) various agricultural products and allocated the acres among individual farmers; these farmers had to limit their plantings to the allotted number of acres to obtain *price supports* for their crops.

Actual budget A listing of amounts spent by the *Federal government* (to purchase goods and services and for *transfer payments*) and the amounts of tax revenue collected by it in any (fiscal) year.

Actual deficit The size of the Federal government's *budget deficit* actually recorded in any particular year.

Actual investment The amount which *firms* do invest; equal to *planned investment* plus *unplanned investment.*

Actual reserves The funds which a bank has on deposit at the *Federal Reserve Bank* of its district (plus its *vault cash*).

Adaptive expectations theory The idea that people determine their expectations about future events (for example, inflation) on the basis of past and present events (rates of inflation) and only change their expectations as events unfold.

Adjustable pegs The device used in the *Bretton Woods system* to alter *exchange rates* in an orderly way to eliminate persistent payments deficits and surpluses. Each nation defined its monetary unit in terms of (pegged it to) gold or the dollar, kept the *rate of exchange* for its money stable in the short run, and adjusted its rate in the long run when faced with international payments disequilibrium.

Adverse selection problem A problem arising when information known to one party to a contract is not known to the other party, causing the latter to incur major costs. Example: Individuals who have the poorest health are more likely to buy health insurance.

Advertising A seller's activities in communicating its message about its product to potential buyers.

AFDC (See *Aid to families with dependent children program.*)

Affirmative action Policies and programs which establish targets of increased employment and promotion for women and minorities.

AFL-CIO An acronym for the American Federation of Labor-Congress of Industrial Organizations; the largest federation of *labor unions* in the United States.

Aggregate demand A schedule or curve which shows the total quantity of goods and services demanded (purchased) at different *price levels.*

Aggregate demand–aggregate supply model The macroeconomic model which uses *aggregate demand* and *aggregate supply* to determine and explain the *price level* and the real *domestic output.*

Aggregate expenditures The total amount spent for final goods and services in the economy.

Aggregate expenditures–domestic output approach Determination of the *equilibrium gross domestic product* by finding the real GDP at which aggregate expenditures equal *domestic output.*

Aggregate expenditures schedule A schedule or curve showing the total amount spent for final goods and services at different levels of GDP.

Aggregate supply A schedule or curve showing the total quantity of goods and services supplied (produced) at different *price levels.*

Aggregation Combining individual units or data into one unit or number. For example, all prices of individual goods and services are combined into a *price level,* or all units of output are aggregated into *real gross domestic product.*

Aid to families with dependent children (AFDC) program A state-administered and partly federally funded program in the United States which provides aid to families in which dependent children do not have the support of a parent because of the parent's death, disability, or desertion.

Alcoa case A 1945 case in which the courts ruled that the possession of monopoly power, no matter how reasonably that power had been used, was a violation of the antitrust laws; temporarily overturned the *rule of reason* applied in the *U.S. Steel case.*

Allocative efficiency The apportionment of resources among firms and industries to obtain the production of the products most wanted by society (consumers); the output of each product at which its *marginal cost* and *price* or *marginal benefit* are equal.

Annually balanced budget A budget in which government expenditures and tax collections are equal each year.
Anticipated inflation Increases in the price level (*inflation*) which occur at the expected rate.
Antitrust laws Legislation (including the *Sherman Act* and *Clayton Act*) which prohibit anticompetitive business activities such as *price fixing,* bid rigging, monopolization, and *tying contracts.*
Antitrust policy The use of the *antitrust laws* to promote *competition* and *economic efficiency.*
Applied economics (See *Policy economics.*)
Appreciation (of the dollar) An increase in the value of the dollar relative to the currency of another nation so that a dollar buys a larger amount of the foreign currency and thus of foreign goods.
"Asian tigers" The newly industrialized and rapidly growing economies of Hong Kong, Singapore, South Korea, and Taiwan.
Asset Anything of monetary value owned by a firm or individual.
Asset demand for money The amount of *money* people want to hold as a *store of value;* this amount varies inversely with the *rate of interest.*
Asymmetric information A situation in which one party to a market transaction has much more information about a product or service than the other; the result may be an under- or overallocation of resources.
Authoritarian capitalism An economic system in which property resources are privately owned and government extensively directs and controls the economy.
Average fixed cost A firm's total *fixed cost* divided by output (the quantity of product produced).
Average product The total output produced per unit of a *resource* employed (*total product* divided by the quantity of that employed resource).
Average propensity to consume Fraction (or percentage) of *disposable income* which households plan to spend for consumer goods and services; *consumption* divided by *disposable income.*
Average propensity to save Fraction (or percentage) of *disposable income* which households save; *saving* divided by *disposable income.*
Average revenue Total revenue from the sale of a product divided by the quantity of the product sold (demanded); equal to the price at which the product is sold when all units of the product are sold at the same price.
Average tax rate Total tax paid divided by total (taxable) income, as a percentage.
Average total cost A firm's *total cost* divided by output (the quantity of product produced); equal to *average fixed cost* plus *average variable cost.*
Average variable cost A firm's total *variable cost* divided by output (the quantity of product produced).

B

Backflows The return of workers to the countries from which they originally migrated.
Balanced-budget amendment Proposed constitutional amendment that would require Congress to balance the Federal budget annually.
Balanced-budget multiplier The extent to which an equal change in government spending and taxes changes *equilibrium gross domestic product;* always has a value of 1 since it is equal to the amount of the equal changes in *G* and *T.*
Balance of payments (See *International balance of payments.*)
Balance of payments deficit The amount by which the sum of the *balance on current account* and the *balance on the capital account* is negative in a year.
Balance of payments surplus The amount by which the sum of the *balance on current account* and the *balance on the capital account* is positive in a year.
Balance on current account The exports of goods and services of a nation less its imports of goods and services plus its *net investment income* and *net transfers* in a year.
Balance on goods and services The exports of goods and services of a nation less its imports of goods and services in a year.
Balance on the capital account The *capital inflows* of a nation less its *capital outflows.*
Balance sheet A statement of the *assets, liabilities,* and *net worth* of a firm or individual at some given time.
Bank deposits The deposits which individuals or firms have at banks (or thrifts) or which banks have at the *Federal Reserve Banks.*
Bankers' bank A bank which accepts the deposits of and makes loans to *depository institutions;* in the United States, a *Federal Reserve Bank.*
Bank reserves The deposits of commercial banks and thrifts at *Federal Reserve Banks* plus bank and thrift *vault cash.*
Barrier to entry Anything which artificially prevents the entry of firms into an industry.
Barter The exchange of one good or service for another good or service.
Base year The year with which other years are compared when an index is constructed, for example, the base year for a *price index.*
Benefit-cost analysis Comparing the *marginal benefits* of a government project or program with the *marginal costs* to decide whether or not to employ resources in that project or program and to what extent.
Benefit-reduction rate The percentage by which subsidy benefits in a *public assistance program* are reduced as earned income rises.
Benefits-received principle The idea that those who receive the benefits of goods and services provided by government should pay the taxes required to finance them.
Bilateral monopoly A market in which there is a single seller (*monopoly*) and a single buyer (*monopsony*).
Board of Governors The 7-member group which supervises and controls the money and banking system of the United States; the Board of Governors of the Federal Reserve System; the Federal Reserve Board.
Bond A financial device through which a borrower (a firm or government) is obligated to pay the principle and interest on a loan at a specific date in the future.
Brain drain The emigration of highly educated, highly skilled workers from a country.

Break-even income The level of *disposable income* at which *households* plan to consume (spend) all their income and to save none of it; also denotes that level of earned income at which subsidy payments become zero in an income transfer program.

Break-even output Any output at which a (competitive) firm's *total cost* and *total revenue* are equal; an output at which it has neither an *economic profit* nor a loss; at which it has only a *normal profit.*

Bretton Woods system The international monetary system developed after World War II in which *adjustable pegs* were employed, the *International Monetary Fund* helped to stabilize foreign exchange rates, and gold and the dollar were used as *international monetary reserves.*

Budget deficit The amount by which the expenditures of the Federal government exceed its revenues in any year.

Budget line A line which shows the different combinations of two products a consumer can purchase with a specific money income, given the products' prices.

Budget restraint The limit which the size of a consumer's income (and the prices which must be paid for goods and services) imposes on the ability of that consumer to obtain goods and services.

Budget surplus The amount by which the revenues of the Federal government exceed its expenditures in any year.

Built-in stabilizer A mechanism which increases government's budget deficit (or reduces its surplus) during a recession and increases government's budget surplus (or reduces its deficit) during inflation without any action by policymakers; the tax system is one such mechanism.

Business cycle Recurring increases and decreases in the level of economic activity over periods of years. Consists of peak, *recession,* trough, and recovery phases.

Business firm (See *Firm.*)

Business unionism Labor unionism which concerns itself with such practical and short-run objectives as higher wages, shorter hours, and improved working conditions.

C

Capital Human-made resources (buildings, machinery, and equipment) used to produce goods and services; goods which do not directly satisfy human wants; also called capital goods.

Capital account The section of a nation's *international balance of payments* statement in which the foreign purchases of assets in the United States (producing money *capital inflows*) and U.S. purchases of assets abroad (producing money *capital outflows* of that nation) are recorded.

Capital account deficit A negative *balance on the capital account.*

Capital account surplus A positive *balance on the capital account.*

Capital flight The transfer of savings from developing countries to industrially advanced countries to avoid government expropriation, taxation, and high rates of inflation or to realize better investment opportunities.

Capital gain The gain realized when securities or properties are sold for a price greater than the price paid for them.

Capital goods (See *Capital.*)

Capital inflow The expenditures made by the residents of foreign nations to purchase real and financial capital from the residents of a nation.

Capital-intensive commodity A product which requires a relatively large amount of *capital* to produce.

Capitalism (See *Pure capitalism.*)

Capital outflow The expenditures made by the residents of a nation to purchase real and financial capital from the residents of foreign nations.

Capital-saving technological advance An improvement in *technology* which permits a greater quantity of a product to be produced with a specific amount of *capital* (or permits the same amount of the product to be produced with a smaller amount of capital).

Capital stock The total available *capital* in a nation.

Capital-using technological advance An improvement in *technology* which requires the use of a greater amount of *capital* to produce a specific quantity of a product.

Cartel A formal agreement among firms in an industry to set the price of a product and the outputs of the individual firms or to divide the market for the product geographically.

Causation A relationship in which the occurrence of one or more events brings about another event.

CEA (See *Council of Economic Advisers.*)

Cease-and-desist order An order from a court or government agency to a corporation or individual to stop engaging in a specified practice.

Ceiling price (See *Price ceiling.*)

Celler-Kefauver Act The Federal act of 1950 that amended the *Clayton Act* by prohibiting the acquisition of the assets of one firm by another firm when the effect would be to lessen competition.

Central bank A bank whose chief function is the control of the nation's *money supply;* in the United States, the *Federal Reserve System.*

Central economic planning Government determination of the objectives of the economy and how resources will be directed to attain those objectives.

***Ceteris paribus* assumption** (See *"Other things equal" assumption.*)

Change in demand A change in the *quantity demanded* of a good or service at every price; a shift of the *demand curve* to the left or right.

Change in supply A change in the *quantity supplied* of a good or service at every price; a shift of the *supply curve* to the left or right.

Checkable deposit Any deposit in a *commercial bank* or *thrift institution* against which a check may be written; includes *demand deposits.*

Checking account A *checkable deposit* in a *commercial bank* or *thrift institution.*

Check clearing The process by which funds are transferred from the checking accounts of the writers of checks to the checking accounts of the recipients of the checks.

Circular flow model The flow of resources from *households* to *firms* and of products from firms to households. These flows are accompanied by reverse flows of money from firms to households and from households to firms.
Civil Rights Act of 1964 Title VII of this law outlaws discrimination based on race, color, religion, gender, or national origin in hiring, promoting, and compensating workers.
Classical economics The macroeconomic generalizations accepted by most economists before the 1930s which led to the conclusion that a capitalistic economy was self-regulating and therefore would usually employ its resources fully.
Clayton Act The Federal antitrust act of 1914 which strengthened the *Sherman Act* by making it illegal for firms to engage in certain specified practices.
Closed economy An economy which neither exports nor imports goods and services.
Closed shop A place of employment where only workers who are already members of a labor union may be hired.
Coase theorem The idea first stated by economist Ronald Coase that *spillover* problems may be resolved through private negotiations of the affected parties.
Coincidence of wants A situation in which the good or service which one trader desires to obtain is the same as that which another trader desires to give up, and an item which the second trader wishes to acquire is the same as that which the first trader desires to surrender.
COLA (See *Cost-of-living adjustment.*)
Collective bargaining The negotiation of labor contracts between *labor unions* and *firms* or government entities.
Collective voice The function a *labor union* performs for its members as a group when it communicates their problems and grievances to management and presses management for a satisfactory resolution.
Collusion A situation in which firms act together and in agreement (collude) to fix prices, divide a market, or otherwise restrict competition.
Command economy An economic system (method of organization) in which property resources are publicly owned and government uses *central economic planning* to direct and coordinate economic activities.
Commercial bank A firm which engages in the business of banking (accepts deposits, offers checking accounts, and makes loans).
Commercial banking system All *commercial banks* and *thrift institutions* as a group.
Communism (See *Command economy.*)
Comparative advantage A lower relative or comparative cost than another producer.
Compensating differences Differences in the *wages* received by workers in different jobs to compensate for nonmonetary differences in the jobs.
Compensation to employees *Wages* and salaries plus *wage and salary supplements* paid by employers to workers.
Competing goods (See *Substitute goods.*)
Competition The presence in a market of a large number of independent buyers and sellers competing with one another and the freedom of buyers and sellers to enter and leave the market.
Competitive industry's short-run supply curve The horizontal summation of the short-run supply curves of the *firms* in a purely competitive industry (see *Pure competition*); a curve which shows the total quantities offered for sale at various prices by the firms in an industry in the short run.
Competitive labor market A resource market in which a large number of (noncolluding) firms demand a particular type of labor supplied by a large number of nonunion workers.
Complementary goods Products and services which are used together; when the price of one falls the demand for the other increases (and conversely).
Complex multiplier The *multiplier* which exists when changes in the *gross domestic product* change *net taxes* and *imports,* as well as *saving.*
Concentration ratio The percentage of the total sales of an *industry* made by the four (or some other number) largest sellers in the industry.
Conglomerate combination A group of *plants* owned by a single *firm* and engaged at one or more stages in the production of different products (of products that do not compete with each other).
Conglomerate merger The merger of a *firm* in one *industry* with a firm in another industry or region (with a firm which is not a supplier, customer, or competitor).
Constant-cost industry An industry in which expansion by the entry of new firms has no effect on the prices firms in the industry must pay for resources and thus no effect on production costs.
Consumer goods Products and services which satisfy human wants directly.
Consumer price index (CPI) An index which measures the prices of a fixed "market basket" of some 300 goods and services bought by a "typical" consumer.
Consumer sovereignty Determination by consumers of the types and quantities of goods and services which will be produced with the scarce resources of the economy; consumer direction of production through dollar votes.
Consumer surplus The difference between what a consumer (or consumers) is willing to pay for an additional unit of a product or service and its market price; the triangular area below the demand curve and above the market price.
Consumption of fixed capital Estimate of the amount of *capital* worn out or used up (consumed) in producing the *gross domestic product;* also called *depreciation.*
Consumption schedule A schedule showing the amounts *households* plan to spend for *consumer goods* at different levels of *disposable income.*
Contractionary fiscal policy A decrease in *government expenditures* for goods and services, an increase in *net taxes,* or some combination of the two, for the purpose of decreasing *aggregate demand* and thus controlling inflation.
Coordination failure A situation in which people do not reach a mutually beneficial outcome because they lack

some way to jointly coordinate their actions; a possible cause of macroeconomic instability.

Copayment The percentage of (say, health care) costs which an insured individual pays while the insurer pays the remainder.

Copyright A legal protection provided to developers and publishers of books, computer software, videos, and musical compositions against copying of their works by others.

Corporate income tax A tax levied on the net income (profit) of corporations.

Corporation A legal entity ("person") chartered by a state or the Federal government which is distinct and separate from the individuals who own it.

Correlation A systematic and dependable association between two sets of data (two kinds of events); does not itself indicate causation.

Cost-of-living adjustment (COLA) An automatic increase in the incomes (wages) of workers when inflation occurs; guaranteed by a collective bargaining contract between firms and workers.

Cost-push inflation Increases in the price level (inflation) resulting from an increase in resource costs (for example, higher wage rates and raw material prices) and hence in *per-unit production costs;* inflation caused by reductions in *aggregate supply.*

Cost ratio An equality showing the number of units of two products which can be produced with the same resources; the cost ratio 1 corn ≡ 3 olives shows that the resources required to produce 3 units of olives must be shifted to corn production to produce 1 unit of corn.

Council of Economic Advisers A group of three persons that advises and assists the President of the United States on economic matters (including the preparation of the annual *Economic Report of the President*).

Craft union A labor union which limits its membership to workers with a particular skill (craft).

Creative destruction The hypothesis that the creation of new products and production methods simultaneously destroys the market power of existing monopolies.

Credit An accounting item which increases the value of an asset (such as the foreign money owned by the residents of a nation).

Credit union An association of persons who have a common tie (such as being employees of the same firm or members of the same labor union) which sells shares to (accepts deposits from) its members and makes loans to them.

Cross elasticity of demand The ratio of the percentage change in *quantity demanded* of one good to the percentage change in the price of some other good. A positive coefficient indicates the two products are *substitute goods;* a negative coefficient indicates they are *complementary goods.*

Crowding model of occupational discrimination A model of labor markets suggesting that *occupational discrimination* has kept many women and minorities out of high-paying occupations and forced them into a limited number of low-paying occupations.

Crowding-out effect A rise in interest rates and a resulting decrease in *planned investment* caused by the Federal government's increased borrowing in the money market.

Currency Coins and paper money.

Currency appreciation (See *Exchange rate appreciation.*)

Currency depreciation (See *Exchange rate depreciation.*)

Current account The section in a nation's *international balance of payments* which records its exports and imports of goods and services, its *net investment income,* and its *net transfers.*

Customary economy (See *Traditional economy.*)

Cyclical deficit A Federal *budget deficit* which is caused by a recession and the consequent decline in tax revenues.

Cyclical unemployment A type of *unemployment* caused by insufficient total spending (or by insufficient *aggregate demand*).

Cyclically balanced budget The equality of *government expenditures* and *net tax collections* over the course of a *business cycle;* deficits incurred during periods of recession are offset by surpluses obtained during periods of prosperity (inflation).

D

Debit An accounting item which decreases the value of an asset (such as the foreign money owned by the residents of a nation).

Declining industry An industry in which *economic profits* are negative (losses are incurred) and which will, therefore, decrease its output as firms leave it.

Decreasing-cost industry An industry in which expansion through the entry of firms decreases the prices firms in the industry must pay for resources and therefore decreases their production costs.

Deductible The dollar sum of (for example, health care) costs which an insured individual must pay before the insurer begins to pay.

Deduction Reasoning from assumptions to conclusions; a method of reasoning which first develops a hypothesis (an assumption) and then tests the hypothesis with economic facts.

Deflating Finding the *real gross domestic product* by decreasing the dollar value of the GDP for a year in which prices were higher than in the *base year.*

Deflation A decline in the economy's *price level.*

Demand A schedule showing the amounts of a good or service buyers (or a buyer) wish to purchase at various prices during some time period.

Demand curve A curve illustrating *demand.*

Demand deposit A deposit in a *commercial bank* or *thrift* against which checks may be written; a *checkable deposit.*

Demand-deposit multiplier (See *Monetary multiplier.*)

Demand factor (in growth) The increase in the level of *aggregate demand* which brings about the *economic growth* made possible by an increase in the production potential of the economy.

Demand management The use of *fiscal policy* and *monetary policy* to increase or decrease *aggregate demand.*

Demand-pull inflation Increases in the price level (inflation) resulting from an excess of demand over output at the existing price level, caused by an increase in *aggregate demand.*

Dependent variable A variable which changes as a consequence of a change in some other (independent) variable; the "effect" or outcome.

Depository institutions Firms which accept the deposits of *money* of the public (businesses and persons); *commercial banks, savings and loan associations, mutual savings banks,* and *credit unions.*

Depreciation (See *Consumption of fixed capital.*)

Depreciation (of the dollar) A decrease in the value of the dollar relative to another currency so that a dollar buys a smaller amount of the foreign currency and therefore of foreign goods.

Derived demand The demand for a resource which depends on the demand for the products it can be used to produce.

Determinants of aggregate demand Factors such as consumption spending, *investment,* government spending, and *net exports* which, if they change, shift the *aggregate demand curve.*

Determinants of aggregate supply Factors such as input prices, *productivity,* and the legal-institutional environment which, if they change, shift the *aggregate supply curve.*

Determinants of demand Factors other than its price which determine the quantities demanded of a good or service.

Determinants of supply Factors other than its price which determine the quantities supplied of a good or service.

Devaluation A decrease in the governmentally defined value of a currency.

Developing countries Many countries of Africa, Asia, and Latin America which are characterized by a lack of capital goods, use of nonadvanced technologies, low literacy rates, high unemployment, rapid population growth, and labor forces heavily committed to agriculture.

Differentiated oligopoly An *oligopoly* in which the firms produce a *differentiated product.*

Differentiated product A product which differs physically or in some other way from the similar products produced by other firms; a product such that buyers are not indifferent to the seller when the price charged by all sellers is the same.

Diffusion The spread of an *innovation* through its widespread imitation.

Dilemma of regulation The tradeoff a *regulatory agency* faces in setting the maximum legal price a monopolist may charge: The *socially optimal price* is below *average total cost* (and either bankrupts the *firm* or requires that it be subsidized), while the higher *fair-return price* does not produce *allocative efficiency.*

Diminishing marginal returns (See *Law of diminishing returns.*)

Direct foreign investment The building of new factories (or the purchase of existing capital) in a particular nation by corporations of other nations.

Direct relationship The relationship between two variables which change in the same direction, for example, product price and quantity supplied.

Discount rate The interest rate which the *Federal Reserve Banks* charge on the loans they make to *commercial banks* and *thrift institutions.*

Discouraged workers Employees who have left the *labor force* because they have been unable to find employment.

Discrimination According individuals or groups inferior treatment in hiring, occupational access, education and training, promotion, wage rates, or working conditions, even though they have the same abilities, education and skills, and work experience as other workers.

Discrimination coefficient A measure of the cost or disutility of prejudice; the monetary amount an employer is willing to pay to hire a preferred worker rather than a nonpreferred worker.

Discretionary fiscal policy Deliberate changes in taxes (tax rates) and government spending by Congress to promote full-employment, price stability, and economic growth.

Diseconomies of scale Increase in the *average total cost* of producing a product as the *firm* expands the size of its *plant* (its output) in the *long run.*

Disinflation A reduction in the rate of *inflation.*

Disposable income *Personal income* less personal taxes; income available for *personal consumption expenditures* and *personal saving.*

Dissaving Spending for consumer goods and services in excess of *disposable income;* the amount by which *personal consumption expenditures* exceed disposable income.

Dividends Payments by a corporation of all or part of its profit to its stockholders (the corporate owners).

Division of labor Dividing the work required to produce a product into a number of different tasks which are performed by different workers; *specialization* of workers.

Dollar votes The "votes" which consumers and entrepreneurs cast for the production of consumer and capital goods, respectively, when they purchase them in product and resource markets.

Domestic capital formation Addition to a nation's stock of *capital* by saving and investing part of its own domestic output.

Domestic output *Gross* (or net) *domestic product;* the total output of *final goods and services* produced in the economy.

Domestic price The price of a good or service within a country, determined by domestic demand and supply.

Double taxation The taxation of both corporate net income (profits) and the *dividends* paid from this net income when they become the personal income of households.

Dumping The sale of products below cost in a foreign country or below the prices charged at home.

DuPont cellophane case The antitrust case brought against DuPont in which the U.S. Supreme Court ruled (in 1956) that while DuPont had a monopoly in the narrowly defined market for cellophane, it did not monopolize the more broadly defined market for flexible packaging materials. It was thus not guilty of violating the *Sherman Act.*

Durable good A consumer good with an expected life (use) of 3 or more years.

Dynamic efficiency The development over time of less costly production techniques, improved products, and new products; technological progress.

E

E-cash Electronic money; an entry (usable as money) stored in a computer or a stored-value card ("smart card").

Earned Income Tax Credit A Federal tax credit for low-income working families designed to encourage labor force participation.

Earnings The money income received by a worker; equal to the *wage* (rate) multiplied by the amount of time worked.

Easy money policy Federal Reserve System actions to increase the *money supply* to lower interest rates and expand *real GDP.*

Economic analysis Deriving *economic principles* from relevant economic facts.

Economic concentration A description or measure of the degree to which an industry is monopolistic or competitive. (See *Concentration ratio.*)

Economic cost A payment which must be made to obtain and retain the services of a *resource;* the income a firm must provide to a resource supplier to attract the resource away from an alternative use; equal to the quantity of other products which cannot be produced when resources are instead used to make a particular product.

Economic efficiency Obtaining the socially optimal amounts of goods and services using minimum necessary resources; entails both *productive efficiency* and *allocative efficiency.*

Economic growth (1) An outward shift in the *production possibilities curve* which results from an increase in resource quantity or quality or an improvement in *technology;* (2) an increase either in real output (*gross domestic product*) or in real output per capita.

Economic integration Cooperation among and the complete or partial unification of the economies of different nations; the elimination of barriers to trade among these nations; the bringing together of the markets in each of the separate economies to form one large (a common) market.

Economic law (See *Economic principle.*)

Economic model A simplified picture of economic reality; an abstract generalization.

Economic perspective A viewpoint which envisions individuals and institutions making rational decisions by comparing the marginal benefits and marginal costs associated with their actions.

Economic policy A course of action intended to correct or avoid a problem.

Economic principle A widely accepted generalization about the economic behavior of individuals and institutions.

Economic profit The *total revenue* of a firm less all its *economic costs;* also called "pure profit" and "above normal profit."

Economic regulation (See *Industrial regulation.*)

Economic rent The price paid for the use of land and other natural resources, the supply of which is fixed (*perfectly inelastic*).

Economic resources The *land, labor, capital,* and *entrepreneurial ability* which are used in the production of goods and services; productive agents; factors of production.

Economics The social science dealing with the use of scarce resources to obtain the maximum satisfaction of society's virtually unlimited material wants.

Economic theory Deriving *economic principles* from relevant economic facts; an *economic principle.*

Economic system A particular set of institutional arrangements and a coordinating mechanism for solving the economizing problem; a method of organizing an economy; of which the *market economy, command economy,* and *traditional economy* are three general types.

Economies of scale Reductions in the *average total cost* of producing a product as the firm expands the size of plant (its output) in the *long run;* the economies of mass production.

Economizing problem The choices necessitated because society's material wants for goods and services are unlimited but the *resources* available to satisfy these wants are limited (scarce).

Efficiency factors (in growth) The capacity of an economy to combine resources effectively to achieve growth of real output which the *supply factors* (of growth) make possible.

Efficiency loss of a tax The loss of net benefits to society because a tax reduces the production and consumption of a taxed good below the level of allocative efficiency.

Efficient allocation of resources That allocation of the resources of an economy among the production of different products which leads to the maximum satisfaction of the wants of consumers; producing the socially optimal mix of output with society's scarce resources.

Efficiency wage A wage which minimizes wage costs per unit of output.

Elastic demand Product or resource demand whose *price elasticity* is greater than 1; means the resulting change in *quantity demanded* is greater than the percentage change in *price.*

Elasticity coefficient The number obtained when the percentage change in *quantity demanded* (or supplied) is divided by the percentage change in the *price* of the commodity.

Elasticity formula (See *Price elasticity of demand.*)

Elastic supply Product or resource supply whose price elasticity is greater than 1; means the resulting change in quantity supplied is greater than the percentage change in price.

Employment Act of 1946 Federal legislation that committed the Federal government to the maintenance of economic stability (a high level of employment, a stable price level, and economic growth); established the *Council of Economic Advisers* and the *Joint Economic Committee;* and required an annual economic report of the President to Congress.

Employment rate The percentage of the *labor force* employed at any time.

Employment discrimination Inferior treatment in hiring, promotions, work assignments, and such for a particular group of employees.

Entitlement programs Government programs such as *social insurance, food stamps, Medicare,* and *Medicaid* which guarantee particular levels of *transfer payments* to all who fit the programs' criteria.

Entrepreneurial ability The human resources which combine the other resources to produce a product, make nonroutine decisions, innovate, and bear risks.

Equality versus efficiency tradeoff The decrease in *economic efficiency* which may accompany a decrease in *income inequality;* the presumption that some income inequality is required to achieve economic efficiency.

Equal Pay Act of 1963 Federal government legislation making it illegal to pay men and women different wage rates if they do equal work on jobs, the performance of which requires equal skill, effort, and responsibility, and which are performed under similar working conditions.

Equation of exchange $MV = PQ$, in which M is the supply of money, V is the *velocity of money,* P is the *price level,* and Q is the physical volume of *final goods and services* produced.

Equilibrium real domestic output The *gross domestic product* at which the total quantity of final goods and ser-vices purchased (*aggregate expenditures*) is equal to the total quantity of final goods and services produced (the real domestic output); the real domestic output at which the *aggregate demand curve* intersects the *aggregate supply curve.*

Equilibrium price The *price* in a competitive market at which the *quantity demanded* and the *quantity supplied* are equal; where there is neither a *shortage* nor a *surplus;* and where there is no tendency for price to rise or fall.

Equilibrium price level The price level at which the *aggregate demand curve* intersects the *aggregate supply curve.*

Equilibrium quantity (1) The quantity demanded and supplied at the equilibrium price in a competitive market; (2) the profit-maximizing output of a firm.

European Union (EU) An association of European nations initiated in 1958 which has eliminated tariffs and import quotas that existed among them, established common tariffs for goods imported from outside the member nations, allowed the free movement of labor and capital among them, and created other common economic policies.

Excess capacity Plant resources which are underused when imperfectly competitive firms produce less output than that associated with achieving minimum average total cost.

Excess reserves The amount by which a bank or thrift's *actual reserves* exceed its *required reserves;* actual reserves minus required reserves.

Exchange control (See *Foreign exchange control.*)

Exchange rate The *rate of exchange* of one nation's currency for another nation's currency.

Exchange-rate appreciation An increase in the value of a nation's currency in foreign exchange markets; an increase in the *rate of exchange* for foreign currencies.

Exchange-rate depreciation A decrease in the value of a nation's currency in foreign exchange markets; a decrease in the *rate of exchange* for foreign currencies.

Exchange-rate determinant Any factor other than the *rate of exchange* which determines a currency's demand and supply in the *foreign exchange market.*

Excise tax A tax levied on the production of a specific product or on the quantity of the product purchased.

Exclusion principle The ability to exclude those who do not pay for a product from receiving its benefits.

Exclusive unionism The practice of a *labor union* of restricting the supply of skilled union labor to increase the wages received by union members; the policies typically employed by a *craft union.*

Exhaustive expenditure An expenditure by government resulting directly in the employment of *economic resources* and in the absorption by government of the goods and services those resources produce; a *government purchase.*

Exit mechanism The process of leaving a job and searching for another one as a means of improving one's working conditions.

Expanding industry An industry whose firms earn *economic profits* and which experience an increase in output as new firms enter the industry.

Expansionary fiscal policy An increase in *government expenditures* for goods and services, a decrease in *net taxes,* or some combination of the two for the purpose of increasing *aggregate demand* and expanding real output.

Expectations The anticipations of consumers, firms, and others about future economic conditions.

Expected rate of return The increase in profit a firm anticipates it will obtain by purchasing capital (or engaging in research and development), expressed as a percentage of the total cost of the investment (or R&D) activity.

Expenditures approach The method which adds all expenditures made for *final goods and services* to measure the *gross domestic product.*

Expenditures-output approach (See *Aggregate expenditures-domestic output approach.*)

Explicit cost The monetary payment a *firm* must make to an outsider to obtain a *resource.*

Export controls The limitation or prohibition of the export of certain products on the basis of foreign policy or national security objectives.

Export-Import Bank A Federal institution which provides interest-rate subsidies to foreign borrowers who buy U.S. exports on credit.

Exports Goods and services produced in a nation and sold to customers in other nations.

Export subsidies Government payments to domestic producers to enable them to reduce the *price* of a good or service to foreign buyers.

Export supply curve An upsloping curve showing the amount of a product domestic firms will export at each *world price* above the *domestic price.*
Export transactions A sale of a good or service which increases the amount of foreign currency flowing to the citizens, firms, and governments of a nation.
External benefit (See *Spillover benefit.*)
External cost (See *Spillover cost.*)
External debt Private or public debt owed to foreign citizens, firms, and institutions.
Externality (See *Spillover.*)

F

Face value The dollar or cents value stamped on a U.S. coin.
Factors of production *Economic resources: land, capital, labor,* and *entrepreneurial ability.*
Fair-return price The price of a product which enables its producer to obtain a *normal profit* and which is equal to the *average total cost* of producing it.
Fallacy of composition Incorrectly reasoning that what is true for the individual (or part) is necessarily true for the group (or whole).
Fallacy of limited decisions The false notion that there are a limited number of economic decisions to be made so that, if government makes more decisions, there will be fewer private decisions to render.
Farm problem Technological advance, coupled with a price-inelastic and relatively constant demand, have made agriculture a *declining industry;* also, the tendency for farm income to fluctuate sharply from year to year.
FDIC (See *Federal Deposit Insurance Corporation.*)
Federal Advisory Committee The group of 12 commercial bankers that advises the Board of Governors on banking policy.
Federal Deposit Insurance Corporation (FDIC) The Federally chartered corporation which insures the deposit liabilities of *commercial banks* and *thrift institutions.*
Federal funds rate The interest rate banks and other depository institutions charge one another on overnight loans made out of their *excess reserves.*
Federal government The government of the United States, as distinct from the state and local governments.
Federal Open Market Committee (FOMC) The 12-member group that determines the purchase-and-sale policies of the *Federal Reserve Banks* in the market for U.S. government securities.
Federal Reserve Banks The 12 banks chartered by the U.S. government to control the *money supply* and perform other functions. (See *Central bank, Quasipublic bank,* and *Banker's bank.*)
Federal Reserve Notes Paper money issued by the *Federal Reserve Banks.*
Federal Trade Commission (FTC) The commission of 5 members established by the *Federal Trade Commission Act* of 1914 to investigate unfair competitive practices of firms, to hold hearings on the complaints of such practices, and to issue *cease-and-desist orders* when firms were found to engage in such practices.
Federal Trade Commission Act The Federal act of 1914 which established the *Federal Trade Commission.*
Feedback effects (of monetary policy) The effects that a change in the money supply will have (because it affects the interest rate, planned investment, and the equilibrium GDP) on the demand for money, which is itself directly related to the GDP.
Fiat money Anything which is *money* because government has decreed it to be money.
Final goods and services Goods and services which have been purchased for final use and not for resale or further processing or manufacturing.
Financial capital (See *Money capital.*)
Firm An organization which employs resources to produce a good or service for profit and owns and operates one or more *plants.*
Fiscal federalism The system of transfers (grants) by which the Federal government shares its revenues with state and local governments.
Fiscal policy Changes in government spending and tax collections designed to achieve a full-employment and noninflationary domestic output; also called *discretionary fiscal policy.*
Five fundamental economic questions The 5 questions which every economy must answer: how much to produce, what to produce, how to produce it, how to divide the total output, and how to ensure economic flexibility.
Fixed cost Any cost which in total does not change when the *firm* changes its output; the cost of *fixed resources.*
Fixed exchange rate A *rate of exchange* which is set in some way and hence prevented from rising or falling with changes in currency supply and demand.
Fixed resource Any resource whose quantity cannot be changed by a firm in the *short run.*
Flexible exchange rate A *rate of exchange* determined by the international demand for and supply of a nation's money; a rate free to rise or fall (to float).
Floating exchange rate (See *Flexible exchange rate.*)
Food stamp program A program permitting low-income persons to purchase for less than their retail value, or to obtain without cost, coupons that can be exchanged for food items at retail stores.
Foreign competition (See *Import competition.*)
Foreign exchange control The control a government may exercise over the quantity of foreign currency demanded by its citizens and firms and over the *rates of exchange* in order to limit its *outpayments* to its *inpayments* (to eliminate a *payments deficit*).
Foreign exchange market A market in which the money (currency) of one nation can be used to purchase (can be exchanged for) the money of another nation.
Foreign exchange rate (See *Rate of exchange.*)
Foreign purchase effect The inverse relationship between the *net exports* of an economy and its price level relative to foreign price levels.
45-degree line A line along which the value of *GDP* (measured horizontally) is equal to the value of *aggregate expenditures* (measured vertically).
Fractional reserve A *reserve ratio* that is less than 100 percent of the deposit liabilities of a *commercial bank* or *thrift institution.*

Freedom of choice The freedom of owners of property resources to employ or dispose of them as they see fit, of workers to enter any line of work for which they are qualified, and of consumers to spend their incomes in a manner which they think is appropriate.

Freedom of enterprise The freedom of *firms* to obtain economic resources, to use these resources to produce products of the firm's own choosing, and to sell their products in markets of their choice.

"Freedom to Farm" Act A law passed in 1996 which revamped 60 years of U.S. farm policy by ending *price supports* and *acreage allotments* for wheat, corn, barley, oats, sorghum, rye, cotton, and rice.

Free-rider problem The inability of potential providers of an economically desirable but indivisible good or service to obtain payment from those who benefit because the *exclusion principle* is not applicable.

Free trade The absence of artificial (government-imposed) barriers to trade among individuals and firms in different nations.

Frictional unemployment A type of unemployment caused by workers voluntarily changing jobs and by temporary layoffs; unemployed workers between jobs.

Fringe benefits The rewards other than *wages* which employees receive from their employers; include pensions, medical and dental insurance, paid vacations, and sick leaves.

Full employment (1) Use of all available resources to produce want-satisfying goods and services. (2) The situation when the *unemployment rate* is equal to the *full-employment unemployment rate* and there is *frictional* and *structural* but no *cyclical unemployment* (and the *real output* of the economy equals its *potential real output*).

Full-employment budget A comparison of the government expenditures and tax collections which would occur if the economy operated at *full employment* throughout the year.

Full-employment unemployment rate The *unemployment rate* at which there is no *cyclical unemployment* of the *labor force;* equal to about 5.5 percent in the United States because some *frictional* and *structural unemployment* are unavoidable.

Full production Employment of available resources so that the maximum amount of (or total value of) goods and services is produced; occurs when both *productive efficiency* and *allocative efficiency* are realized.

Functional distribution of income The manner in which *national income* is divided among the functions performed to earn it (or the kinds of resources provided to earn it); the division of national income into wages and salaries, proprietors' income, corporate profits, interest, and rent.

Functional finance The use of *fiscal policy* to achieve a noninflationary full employment *gross domestic product* without regard to the effect on the *public debt.*

G

G-7 Nations A group of seven major industrial nations (the United States, Japan, Germany, United Kingdom, France, Italy, and Canada) whose leaders meet regularly to discuss common economic problems and try to coordinate economic policies. (Recently has also included Russia, making it unofficially the G-8.)

Gains from trade The extra output which trading partners obtain through specialization of production and exchange of goods and services.

Game theory A means of analyzing the pricing behavior of oligopolists using the theory of strategy associated with games such as chess and bridge.

GDP (See *Gross domestic product.*)

GDP deflator The *price index* found by dividing *nominal GDP* by *real GDP;* a price index used to adjust money (or nominal) GDP to real GDP.

GDP gap The amount by which actual *gross domestic product* falls below *potential gross domestic product.*

General Agreement on Tariffs and Trade (GATT) The international agreement reached in 1947 in which 23 nations agreed to give equal and nondiscriminatory treatment to the other nations, to reduce tariff rates by multinational negotiations, and to eliminate *import quotas.* Now includes most nations and has become the *World Trade Organization.*

Generalization Statement of the nature of the relation between two or more sets of facts.

Gold standard A historical system of fixed exchange rates in which nations defined their currency in terms of gold, maintained a fixed relationship between their stock of gold and their money supplies, and allowed gold to be freely exported and imported.

Government purchases Disbursements of money by government for which government receives a currently produced good or service in return; the expenditures of all governments in the economy for *final goods and services.*

Government transfer payment The disbursement of money (or goods and services) by government for which government receives no currently produced good or service in return.

Grievance procedure The methods used by a *labor union* and a *firm* to settle disputes which arise during the life of the collective bargaining agreement between them.

Gross domestic product (GDP) The total market value of all *final goods and services* produced annually within the boundaries of the United States, whether by U.S. or foreign-supplied resources.

Gross private domestic investment Expenditures for newly produced *capital goods* (such as machinery, equipment, tools, and buildings) and for additions to inventories.

Guiding function of prices The ability of price changes to bring about changes in the quantities of products and resources demanded and supplied.

H

Health maintenance organization (HMO) Health care providers which contract with employers, insurance companies, labor unions, or governmental units to provide health care for their workers or others who are insured.

Herfindahl index A measure of the concentration and competitiveness of an industry; calculated as the sum of the squared percentage market shares of the individual firms.

Homogeneous oligopoly An *oligopoly* in which the firms produce a *standardized product.*

Horizontal axis The "left-right" or "west-east" axis on a graph or grid.

Horizontal combination A group of *plants* in the same stage of production which are owned by a single *firm.*

Horizontal merger The merger into a single *firm* of two firms producing the same product and selling it in the same geographical market.

Horizontal range The horizontal segment of the *aggregate-supply curve* along which the price level is constant as real domestic output changes.

Household An economic unit (of one or more persons) which provides the economy with resources and uses the income received to purchase goods and services that satisfy material wants.

Human capital The accumulation of prior investments in education, training, health, and other factors which increase productivity.

Human-capital discrimination The denial to members of particular groups of equal access to productivity-enhancing education and training.

Human-capital investment Any expenditure undertaken to improve the education, skills, health, or mobility of workers, with an expectation of greater productivity and thus a positive return on the investment.

Hyperinflation A very rapid rise in the price level.

Hypothesis A tentative, untested economic principle.

I

Illegal immigrant A person who enters a country without the country's permission for purpose of residing there.

IMF (See *International Monetary Fund.*)

Immobility The inability or unwillingness of a worker to move from one geographic area or occupation to another or from a lower-paying job to a higher-paying job.

Imperfect competition All market structures except *pure competition;* includes *monopoly, monopolistic competition,* and *oligopoly.*

Implicit cost The monetary income a *firm* sacrifices when it uses a resource it owns rather than supplying the resource in the market; equal to what the resource could have earned in the best-paying alternative employment.

Import competition The competition which domestic firms encounter from the products and services of foreign producers.

Import demand curve A downsloping curve showing the amount of a product which an economy will import at each *world price* below the *domestic price.*

Import quota A limit imposed by a nation on the quantity (or total value) of a good which may be imported during some period of time.

Imports Spending by individuals, *firms,* and governments for goods and services produced in foreign nations.

Import transaction The purchase of a good or service which decreases the amount of foreign money held by citizens, firms, and governments of a nation.

Incentive function of price The inducement which an increase in the price of a commodity gives to sellers to make more of it available (and conversely for a decrease in price); and the inducement which an increase in price offers to buyers to purchase smaller quantities (and conversely for a decrease in price).

Incentive pay plan A compensation structure which ties worker pay directly to performance. Such plans include piece rates, bonuses, commissions, and profit sharing.

Inclusive unionism The practice of a labor union of including as members all workers employed in an industry.

Income approach The method that adds all the income generated by the production of *final goods and services* to measure the *gross domestic product.*

Income effect A change in the price of a product changes a consumer's *real income* (*purchasing power*) and thus the quantity of the product purchased.

Income elasticity of demand The ratio of the percentage change in the *quantity demanded* of a good to a percentage change in consumer income; measures the responsiveness of consumer purchases to income changes.

Income inequality The unequal distribution of an economy's total income among persons or families.

Income-maintenance system Government programs designed to eliminate poverty and reduce inequality in the distribution of income.

Increase in demand An increase in the *quantity demanded* of a good or service at every price; a shift of the *demand curve* to the right.

Increase in supply An increase in the *quantity supplied* of a good or service at every price; a shift of the *supply curve* to the right.

Increasing-cost industry An *industry* in which expansion through the entry of new firms increases the prices *firms* in the industry must pay for resources and therefore increases their production costs.

Increasing marginal returns An increase in the *marginal product* of a resource as successive units of the resource are employed.

Independent goods Products or services for which there is no relationship between the price of one and the demand for the other; when the price of one rises or falls, the demand for the other remains constant.

Independent variable The variable causing a change in some other (dependent) variable.

Independent unions U.S. unions which are not affiliated with the AFL-CIO.

Indifference curve A curve showing the different combinations of two products which give a consumer the same satisfaction or *utility.*

Indifference map A set of *indifference curves,* each representing a different level of *utility,* and which together show the preferences of the consumer.

Indirect business taxes Such taxes as *sales, excise,* and business *property taxes,* license fees, and *tariffs* which firms treat as costs of producing a product and pass on (in whole or in part) to buyers by charging higher prices.

Individual demand The demand schedule or *demand curve* of a single buyer.

Individual supply The supply schedule or *supply curve* of a single seller.

Induction A method of reasoning which proceeds from facts to *generalization.*
Industrial concentration A situation in which a single firm or a small number of firms produces the major portion of an industry's output; fewness of producers within industries.
Industrially advanced countries High-income countries such as the United States, Canada, Japan, and the nations of western Europe which have highly developed *market economies* based on large stocks of technologically advanced capital goods and skilled labor forces.
Industrial policy Any policy by which government takes a direct and active role in promoting specific firms or industries for purposes of expanding their output and achieving economic growth; called "technology policy" when its goal is to promote *technological advance.*
Industrial regulation The older and more traditional type of regulation in which government is concerned with the prices charged and the services provided the public in specific industries: in contrast to *social regulation.*
Industrial union A *labor union* which accepts as members all workers employed in a particular industry (or by a particular firm).
Industry A group of (one or more) *firms* which produces identical or similar products.
Inelastic demand Product or resource demand for which the *price elasticity coefficient* is less than 1; means the resulting percentage change in *quantity demanded* is less than the percentage change in *price.*
Inelastic supply Product or resource supply for which the price elasticity coefficient is less than 1; the percentage change in *quantity supplied* is less than the percentage change in *price.*
Inferior good A good or service whose consumption declines as income rises (and conversely), price remaining constant.
Inflating Determining *real gross domestic product* by increasing the dollar value of the *nominal gross domestic product* produced in a year in which prices are lower than in a *base year.*
Inflation A rise in the general level of prices in an economy.
Inflation premium The component of the *nominal interest rate* which reflects anticipated inflation.
Inflationary expectations The belief of workers, firms, and consumers that substantial inflation will occur in the future.
Inflationary gap The amount by which the *aggregate expenditures schedule* must shift downward to decrease the *nominal GDP* to its full-employment noninflationary level.
Infrastructure The capital goods usually provided by the *public sector* for the use of its citizens and firms (for example, highways, bridges, transit systems, wastewater treatment facilities, municipal water systems, and airports).
Injection An addition of spending to the income-expenditure stream: *investment, government purchases,* and *net exports.*
Injunction A court order directing a person or organization not to perform a certain act because the act would do irreparable damage to some other person or persons; a restraining order.
In-kind investment (See *Nonfinancial investment.*)
In-kind transfer The distribution by government of goods and services to individuals and for which the government receives no currently produced good or service in return; a *government transfer payment* made in goods or ser-vices rather than in money; also called a noncash transfer.
Innovation The first commercially successful introduction of a new product, the use of a new method of production, or the creation of a new form of business organization.
Inpayments The receipts of its own or foreign money which individuals, firms, and governments of one nation obtain from the sale of goods and services abroad, or as investment income, *remittances,* and *capitals inflows* from abroad.
Insider-outsider theory The hypothesis that nominal wages are inflexible downward because firms are aware that workers ("insiders") who retain employment during recession may refuse to work cooperatively with previously unemployed workers ("outsiders") who offer to work for less than the current wage.
Insurable risk An event which would result in a loss but whose frequency of occurrence can be estimated with considerable accuracy; insurance companies are willing to sell insurance against such losses.
Interest The payment made for the use of money (of borrowed funds).
Interest income Payments of income to those who supply the economy with *capital.*
Interest rate The annual rate at which interest is paid; a percentage of the borrowed amount.
Interest-rate effect The tendency for increases in the *price level* to increase the demand for money, raise interest rates, and, as a result, reduce total spending in the economy (and the reverse for price level decreases).
Interindustry competition The competition for sales between the products of one industry and the products of another industry.
Interlocking directorate A situation in which one or more members of the board of directors of a *corporation* are also on the board of directors of a competing corporation; illegal under the *Clayton Act.*
Intermediate goods Products which are purchased for resale or further processing or manufacturing.
Intermediate range The upsloping segment of the *aggregate supply curve* lying between the *horizontal range* and the *vertical range.*
Internally held public debt *Public debt* owed to citizens, firms, and institutions of the same nation issuing the debt.
International balance of payments A summary of all the transactions which took place between the individuals, firms, and government unit of one nation and those in all other nations during a year.
International balance of payments deficit (See *Balance of payments deficit.*)
International balance of payments surplus (See *Balance of payments surplus.*)

International Bank for Reconstruction and Development (See *World Bank.*)
International gold standard (See *Gold standard.*)
International Monetary Fund (IMF) The international association of nations which was formed after World War II to make loans of foreign monies to nations with temporary *payments deficits* and, until the early 1970s, to administer the *adjustable pegs;* it now mainly makes loans to nations facing possible defaults on private and government loans.
International monetary reserves The foreign currencies and such assets as gold a nation may use to settle a *payments deficit.*
International value of the dollar The price which must be paid in foreign currency (money) to obtain one U.S. dollar.
Intrinsic value The market value of the metal within a coin.
Invention The first discovery of a product or process through the use of imagination, ingenious thinking, and experimentation and the first proof that it will work.
Inventories Goods which have been produced but are still unsold.
Inverse relationship The relationship between two variables which change in opposite directions, for example, product price and quantity demanded.
Inverted-U theory A theory saying that, other things equal, *R&D* expenditures as a percentage of sales rise with industry concentration, reach a peak at a *concentration ratio* of about 50 percent, and then fall as concentration further increases.
Investment Spending for the production and accumulation of *capital* and additions to inventories.
Investment goods Same as *capital.*
Investment schedule A curve or schedule which shows the amounts firms plan to invest at various possible values of *real gross domestic product.*
Investment-demand curve A curve which shows the amount of *investment* demanded by an economy at a series of *real interest rates.*
Investment in human capital (See *Human-capital investment.*)
Invisible hand The tendency of firms and resource suppliers seeking to further their own self-interests in competitive markets to also promote the interest of society as a whole.

J

Joint Economic Committee (JEC) Committee of Senators and Representatives which investigates economic problems of national interest.

K

Keynesian economics The macroeconomic generalizations which lead to the conclusion that a capitalistic economy is characterized by macroeconomic instability and that *fiscal policy* and *monetary policy* can be used to promote *full employment, price-level stability,* and *economic growth.*
Keynesianism The philosophical, ideological, and analytical views pertaining to *Keynesian economics.*
Kinked demand curve The demand curve for a noncollusive oligopolist, which is based on the assumption that rivals will follow a price decrease and will ignore a price increase.

L

Labor The physical and mental talents and efforts of people which are used to produce goods and services.
Labor force Persons 16 years of age and older who are not in institutions and who are employed or are unemployed (and seeking work).
Labor force participation rate The percentage of the working-age population which is actually in the *labor force.*
Labor-intensive commodity A product requiring a relatively large amount of *labor* to produce.
Labor productivity Total output divided by the quantity of labor employed to produce it; the *average product* of labor or output per worker per hour.
Labor theory of value The Marxian idea that the economic value of any commodity is determined solely by the amount of labor required to produce it.
Labor union A group of workers organized to advance the interests of the group (to increase wages, shorten the hours worked, improve working conditions, and so on).
Laffer curve A curve showing the relationship between tax rates and the tax revenues of government and on which there is a tax rate (between 0 and 100 percent) where tax revenues are a maximum.
Laissez faire capitalism (See *Pure capitalism.*)
Land Natural resources ("free gifts of nature") used to produce goods and services.
Land-intensive commodity A product requiring a relatively large amount of land to produce.
Law of demand The principle that, other things equal, an increase in a product's price will reduce the quantity of it demanded; and conversely for a decrease in price.
Law of diminishing marginal utility As a consumer increases the consumption of a good or service, the *marginal utility* obtained from each additional unit of the good or service decreases.
Law of diminishing returns As successive increments of a *variable resource* are added to a *fixed resource,* the *marginal product* of the *variable resource* will eventually decrease.
Law of increasing opportunity costs As the production of a good increases, the *opportunity cost* of producing an additional unit rises.
Law of supply The principle that, other things equal, an increase in the price of a product will increase the quantity of it supplied; and conversely for a price decrease.
Leakage (1) A withdrawal of potential spending from the income-expenditures stream via *saving,* tax payments, or *imports.* (2) A withdrawal which reduces the lending potential of the banking system.
Leakages-injections approach Determination of the equilibrium *gross domestic product* by finding the real GDP at which *leakages* are equal to *injections.*

Least-cost combination of resources The quantity of each resource a firm must employ in order to produce a particular output at the lowest total cost; the combination at which the ratio of the *marginal product* of a resource to its *marginal resource cost* (to its *price* if the resource is employed in a competitive market) is the same for the last dollar spent on each resource employed.

Legal cartel theory of regulation The hypothesis that some industries seek regulation or want to maintain regulation so they may form or maintain a legal *cartel.*

Legal immigrant A person who lawfully enters a country for the purpose of residing there.

Legal reserves The minimum amount a *depository institution* must keep on deposit with the *Federal Reserve Bank* in its district, or in *vault cash.*

Legal tender Anything which government says must be accepted in payment of a debt.

Lending potential of an individual commercial bank The amount by which a single bank can safely increase the *money supply* by making new loans to (or buying securities from) the public; equal to the bank's excess reserves.

Lending potential of the banking system The amount by which the banking system can increase the money supply by making new loans to (or buying securities from) the public; equal to the *excess reserves* of the banking system multiplied by the *monetary multiplier.*

Liability A debt with a monetary value; an amount owed by a firm or an individual.

Limited liability Restriction of the maximum loss to a predetermined amount for the owners (stockholders) of a *corporation;* the maximum loss is the amount they paid for their shares of stock.

Limited-liability company An unincorporated business whose owners are protected by *limited liability.*

Line-item veto The presidential power to delete specific expenditure items from spending legislation passed by Congress.

Liquidity *Money* or things which can be quickly and easily converted into money with little or no loss of purchasing power.

Loanable funds *Money* available for lending and borrowing.

Loanable funds theory of interest The concept that the supply of and demand for *loanable funds* determine the equilibrium rate of interest.

Lockout An action by a firm which forbids workers to return to work until a new collective bargaining contract is signed; a means of imposing costs (lost wages) on union workers in a collective bargaining dispute.

Logrolling The trading of votes by legislators to secure favorable outcomes on decisions concerning the provision of *public goods* and *quasipublic goods.*

Long run (1) In *microeconomics,* a period of time long enough to enable producers of a product to change the quantities of all the resources they employ; period in which all resources and costs are variable and no resources or costs are fixed. (2) In *macroeconomics,* a period sufficiently long for *nominal wages* and other input prices to change in response to a change in the nation's *price level.*

Long-run aggregate supply curve The *aggregate supply curve* associated with a time period in which input prices (especially *nominal wages*) are fully responsive to changes in the *price level.*

Long-run competitive equilibrium The price at which firms in *pure competition* neither obtain *economic profit* nor suffer losses in the *long run* and the total quantity demanded and supplied at that price are equal; a price equal to the minimum long-run *average total cost* of producing the product.

Long-run farm problem The tendency for agriculture to be a declining industry as technological progress increases supply relative to an inelastic and slowly increasing demand.

Long-run supply A schedule or curve showing the prices at which a *purely competitive industry* will make various quantities of the product available in the *long run.*

Lorenz curve A curve showing the distribution of income in an economy; the cumulated percentage of families (income receivers) is measured along the horizontal axis and cumulated percentage of income is measured along the vertical axis.

Lump-sum tax A tax which is a constant amount (the tax revenue of government is the same) at all levels of GDP.

M

M1 The most narrowly defined *money supply;* the *currency* and *checkable deposits* not owned by the *Federal government, Federal Reserve Banks,* or *depository institutions.*

M2 A more broadly defined money supply; equal to *M*1 plus *noncheckable savings deposits, money market deposit accounts,* small *time deposits* (deposits of less than $100,000), and individual *money market mutual fund balances.*

M3 Very broadly defined *money supply;* equal to *M*2 plus large *time deposits* (deposits of $100,000 or more).

Macroeconomics The part of economics concerned with the economy as a whole; with such major aggregates as the household, business, and governmental sectors; and with measures of the total economy.

Managed floating exchange rate An *exchange rate* which is allowed to change (float) as a result of changes in currency supply and demand but at times is altered (managed) by governments via their buying and selling of particular currencies.

Managerial-opposition hypothesis An explanation which attributes the relative decline of unionism in the United States to the increased and more aggressive opposition of management to unions.

Managerial prerogatives The decisions which management of the firm has the sole right to make; often enumerated in the labor contract (work agreement) between a *labor union* and a *firm.*

Marginal analysis The comparison of marginal ("extra" or "additional") benefits and marginal costs, usually for decision making.

Marginal benefit The extra (additional) benefit of consuming one more unit of some good or service; the change in total benefit when one more unit is consumed.

Marginal cost The extra (additional) cost of producing one more unit of output; equal to the change in *total cost* divided by the change in output (and in the short run to the change in total *variable cost* divided by the change in output).

Marginal labor cost The amount total labor cost increases when a *firm* employs one additional unit of labor (the quantity of other resources employed remaining constant); equal to the change in the total cost of labor divided by the change in the quantity of labor employed.

Marginal product The additional output produced when one additional unit of a resource is employed (the quantity of all other resources employed remaining constant); equal to the change in total product divided by the change in the quantity of a resource employed.

Marginal productivity theory of income distribution The contention that the distribution of income is equitable when each unit of each resource receives a money payment equal to its marginal contribution to the firm's revenue (its *marginal revenue product*).

Marginal propensity to consume The fraction of any change in *disposable income* spent for *consumer goods;* equal to the change in consumption divided by the change in disposable income.

Marginal propensity to save The fraction of any change in *disposable income* which households save; equal to the change in *saving* divided by the change in disposable income.

Marginal rate of substitution The rate at which a consumer is prepared to substitute one good for another (from a given combination of goods) and remain equally satisfied (have the same *total utility*); equal to the slope of a consumer's *indifference curve* at each point on the curve.

Marginal resource cost The amount the total cost of employing a *resource* increases when a firm employs one additional unit of the resource (the quantity of all other resource employed remaining constant); equal to the change in the *total cost* of the resource divided by the change in the quantity of the resource employed.

Marginal revenue The change in *total revenue* which results from the sale of one additional unit of a firm's product; equal to the change in total revenue divided by the change in the quantity of the product sold.

Marginal-revenue—marginal-cost approach A method of determining the total output at which *economic profit* is a maximum (or losses a minimum) by comparing the *marginal revenue* and the *marginal cost* of each additional unit of output.

Marginal revenue product The change in a firm's *total revenue* when it employs one additional unit of a resource (the quantity of all other resources employed remaining constant); equal to the change in total revenue divided by the change in the quantity of the resource employed.

Marginal tax rate The tax rate paid on each additional dollar of income.

Marginal utility The extra *utility* a consumer obtains from the consumption of one additional unit of a good or service; equal to the change in total utility divided by the change in the quantity consumed.

Market Any institution or mechanism which brings together buyers (demanders) and sellers (suppliers) of a particular good or service.

Market demand (See *Total demand.*)

Market economy An economy in which only the private decisions of consumers, resource suppliers, and firms determine how resources are allocated; the market system.

Market failure The failure of a market to bring about the allocation of resources which best satisfies the wants of society. In particular, the over- or underallocation of resources to the production of a particular good or service because of *spillovers* or informational problems and because markets fail to provide desired *public goods.*

Market for externality rights A market in which firms can buy rights to pollute the environment; the price of such rights is determined by the demand for the right to pollute and a *perfectly inelastic supply* of such rights (the latter determined by the quantity of pollution which the environment can assimilate).

Market period A period in which producers of a product are unable to change the quantity produced in response to a change in its price; in which there is a *perfectly inelastic supply.*

Market socialism An *economic system* (method of organization) in which property resources are publicly owned *and* markets and prices are used to direct and coordinate economic activities.

Market system All the product and resource markets of a *market economy* and the relationships among them; a method which allows the prices determined in these markets to allocate the economy's scarce resources and to communicate and coordinate the decisions made by consumers, firms, and resource suppliers.

Median-voter model The view that under majority rule the median (middle) voter will be in the dominant position to determine the outcome of an election.

Medicaid A Federal program that helps finance the medical expenses of individuals covered by the *Supplemental Security Income* and *Aid to Families with Dependent Children* programs.

Medicare A Federal program which is financed by *payroll taxes* and provides for (1) compulsory hospital insurance for senior citizens and (2) low-cost voluntary insurance to help older Americans pay physicians' fees.

Medium of exchange Items sellers generally accept and buyers generally use to pay for a good or service; *money;* a convenient means of exchanging goods and services without engaging in *barter.*

Merger The combination of two (or more) firms into a single firm.

Microeconomics The part of economics concerned with such individual units as *industries, firms,* and *households;* and with individual markets, particular prices, and specific goods and services.

Minimum wage The lowest *wage* employers may legally pay for an hour of work.

Mixed capitalism An economy in which both government and private decisions determine how resources are allocated.

Monetarism The macroeconomic view that the main cause of changes in aggregate output and the price level are fluctuations in the *money supply;* advocates of a *monetary rule.*

Monetary multiplier The multiple of its *excess reserves* by which the banking system can expand *demand deposits* and thus the *money supply* by making new loans (or buying securities); and equal to 1 divided by the *required reserve ratio.*

Monetary policy A central bank's changing of the *money supply* to influence interest rates and assist the economy in achieving a full-employment, noninflationary level of total output.

Monetary rule The rule suggested by *monetarism;* the *money supply* should be expanded each year at the same annual rate as the potential rate of growth of the *real gross domestic product;* the supply of money should be increased steadily from 3 to 5 percent per year.

Money Any item which generally is acceptable to sellers in exchange for goods and services.

Money capital Money available to purchase *capital.*

Money income (See *Nominal income.*)

Money interest rate The *nominal interest rate;* the interest rate which includes an *inflationary premium* (if any).

Money market The market in which the demand for and the supply of money determine the *interest rate* (or the level of interest rates) in the economy.

Money market deposit account (MMDA) Interest-earning accounts at *banks* and *thrift institutions,* which pool the funds of depositors to buy various short-term securities.

Money market mutual funds (MMMF) Interest-bearing accounts offered by investment companies, which pool depositors' funds for the purchase of short-term securities; depositors may write checks in minimum amounts or more against their accounts.

Money supply Narrowly defined *M*1; more broadly defined, *M*2 and *M*3.

Money wage (See *Nominal wage.*)

Money wage rate (See *Nominal wage.*)

Monopolistic competition A market structure in which many firms sell a *differentiated product,* into which entry is relatively easy, in which the firm has some control over its product price, and in which there is considerable *nonprice competition.*

Monopoly A market structure in which the number of sellers is so small that each seller is able to influence the total supply and the price of the good or service. (Also see *Pure monopoly.*)

Monopsony A market structure in which there is only a single buyer of a good, service, or resource.

Moral hazard problem The possibility that individuals or institutions will change their behavior as the result of a contract or agreement; for example, a bank whose deposits are insured against loss may make riskier loans and investments.

Most-favored-nation (MFN) status An agreement by the United States to allow some other nation's *exports* into the United States at the lowest tariff level levied by the United States, then or at any later time.

MR = MC rule A firm will maximize its profit (or minimize its losses) by producing that output at which *marginal revenue* and *marginal cost* are equal, provided product price is equal to or greater than *average variable cost.*

MRP = MRC rule To maximize profit (or minimize losses) a firm should employ that quantity of a resource at which its *marginal revenue product* (MRP) is equal to its *marginal resource cost* (MRC), the latter being the wage rate in pure competition.

Multinational corporation A firm which owns production facilities in other countries and produces and sells its product abroad.

Multiple counting Wrongly including the value of *intermediate goods* in the *gross domestic product;* counting the same good or service more than once.

Multiplier The ratio of a change in the *equilibrium GDP* to the change in *investment* or in any other component of *aggregate expenditures* or *aggregate demand;* the number by which a change in any component of aggregate expenditures or aggregate demand must be multiplied to find the resulting change in the equilibrium GDP.

Multiplier effect The effect on equilibrium GDP of a change in *aggregate expenditures* or *aggregate demand* (caused by a change in the *consumption schedule, investment, government expenditures,* or *net exports*).

Mutual interdependence A situation in which a change in price strategy (or in some other strategy) by one firm will affect the sales and profits of another firm (or other firms); any firm which makes such a change can expect the other rivals to react to the change.

Mutual savings bank A firm without stockholders which accepts deposits primarily from small individual savers and lends primarily to individuals to finance the purchases of autos and residences.

Mutually exclusive goals Two or more goals which conflict and cannot be achieved simultaneously.

N

National bank A *commercial bank* authorized to operate by the U.S. government.

National health insurance (NHI) A proposed program in which the Federal government would provide a basic package of health care to all citizens at no direct charge or at a low cost-sharing level. Financing would be out of general tax revenues.

National income Total income earned by resource suppliers for their contributions to *gross national product;* equal to the gross domestic product minus *nonincome charges,* minus *net foreign factor income.*

National income accounting The techniques used to measure the overall production of the economy and other related variables for the nation as a whole.

National Labor Relations Act (Wagner Act of 1935) As amended, the basic labor-relations law in the United States; defines the legal rights of unions and management and identifies unfair union and management labor practices; established the *National Labor Relations Board.*

National Labor Relations Board (NLRB) The board established by the *National Labor Relations Act* of 1935 to investigate unfair labor practices, to issue *cease-and-desist orders,* and to conduct elections among employees to determine if they wish to be represented by a *labor union.*

Natural monopoly An industry in which *economies of scale* are so great the product can be produced by one firm at a lower average total cost than if the product were produced by more than one firm.

Natural rate hypothesis The idea that the economy is stable in the long run at the *natural rate of unemployment;* views the long-run *Phillips Curve* as vertical at the *natural rate of unemployment.*

Natural rate of unemployment The *full-employment unemployment rate;* the unemployment rate occurring when there is no *cyclical unemployment* and the economy is achieving its *potential output;* the unemployment rate at which actual inflation equals expected inflation.

Near-money Financial assets, the most important of which are *noncheckable savings accounts, time deposits,* and U.S. short-term securities and savings bonds, which are not a medium of exchange but can be readily converted into money.

Negative relationship (See *Inverse relationship.*)

Net domestic product *Gross domestic product* less the part of the year's output which is needed to replace the *capital goods* worn out in producing the output; the nation's total output available for consumption or additions to the *capital stock.*

Net export effect The idea that the impact of a change in *monetary policy* or *fiscal policy* will be strengthened or weakened by the consequent change in *net exports;* the change in net exports occurs because of changes in real interest rates, which affect exchange rates.

Net exports *Exports* minus *imports.*

Net foreign factor income Payments by a nation of resource income to the rest of the world minus receipts of resource income from the rest of the world.

Net investment income The interest and dividend income received by the residents of a nation from residents of other nations less the interest and dividend payments made by the residents of that nation to the residents of other nations.

Net private domestic investment *Gross private domestic investment* less *consumption of fixed capital;* the addition to the nation's stock of *capital* during a year.

Net taxes The taxes collected by government less *government transfer payments.*

Net transfers The personal and government transfer payments made by one nation to residents of foreign nations, less the personal and government transfer payments received from residents of foreign nations.

Net worth The total *assets* less the total *liabilities* of a firm or an individual; the claims of the owners of a firm against its total assets.

New classical economics The theory that, although unanticipated price level changes may create macroeconomic instability in the short run, the economy is stable at the full-employment level of domestic output in the long run because prices and wages adjust automatically to correct movements away from the full employment, noninflationary output.

NLRB (See *National Labor Relations Board.*)

Nominal gross domestic product (GDP) The *GDP* measured in terms of the price level at the time of measurement (unadjusted for *inflation*).

Nominal income The number of dollars received by an individual or group for its resources during some period of time.

Nominal interest rate The interest rate expressed in terms of annual amounts currently charged for interest and not adjusted for inflation.

Nominal wage The amount of money received by a worker per unit of time (hour, day, etc.); money wage.

Noncash transfer A *government transfer payment* in the form of goods and services rather than money, for example, housing assistance and job training; also called in-kind transfers.

Noncheckable savings account A *savings account* against which a check can *not* be written.

Noncollusive oligopoly An *oligopoly* in which the firms do not agree to act together in determining the price of the product and the output each firm will produce.

Noncompeting groups Groups of workers in the economy who do not compete with each other for employment because the skill and training of the workers in one group are substantially different from those in other groups.

Nondiscretionary fiscal policy (See *Built-in stabilizer*).

Nondurable good A *consumer good* with an expected life (use) of less than 3 years.

Nonexhaustive expenditure An expenditure by government which does not result directly in the employment of economic resources or the production of goods and services; see *Government transfer payment.*

Nonfinancial investment An investment which does not require *households* to save a part of their money incomes; but which uses surplus (unproductive) labor to build *capital goods.*

Nonincome charges *Consumption of fixed capital* and *indirect business taxes;* amounts subtracted from *GDP* (along with *net foreign factor income*) in determining *national income.*

Nonincome determinants of consumption and saving All influences on *consumption* and *saving* other than the level of *GDP.*

Noninterest determinants of investment All influences on the level of investment spending other than the *interest rate.*

Noninvestment transaction An expenditure for stocks, bonds, or second-hand *capital goods.*

Nonmarket transactions The production of goods and services excluded in the measurement of the *gross domestic product* because they are not bought and sold.

Nonprice competition Distinguishing one's product by means of *product differentiation* and then *advertising* the distinguished product to consumers.

Nonproduction transaction The purchase and sale of any item which is not a currently produced good or service.

Nontariff barriers All barriers other than *protective tariffs* which nations erect to impede international trade: include *import quotas,* licensing requirements, unreasonable product-quality standards, and unnecessary red tape in customs procedures.

Normal good A good or service whose consumption increases when income increases and falls when income decreases, price remaining constant.

Normal profit The payment made by a firm to obtain and retain *entrepreneurial ability;* the minimum income which entrepreneurial ability must receive to induce it to perform entrepreneurial functions for a firm.

Normative economics That part of economics involving value judgments about what the economy should be like; concerned with identifying economic goals and promoting them via public policies.

North American Free Trade Agreement (NAFTA) A 1993 agreement establishing, over a 15-year period, a free trade zone composed of Canada, Mexico, and the United States.

O

OASDHI (See *Old Age, Survivors, and Disability Health Insurance.*)

Occupational discrimination Arbitrary restriction of particular groups from entering the more desirable higher-paying occupations.

Occupational licensure The laws of state or local governments which require a worker to satisfy certain specified requirements and obtain a license from a licensing board before engaging in a particular occupation.

Occupational segregation Crowding women or minorities into less desirable, lower-paying occupations.

Official reserves Foreign currencies owned by the central bank of a nation.

Okun's Law The generalization that any one percentage point rise in the *unemployment rate* above the *full-employment unemployment rate* will increase the GDP gap by 2 percent of the *potential output* (GDP) of the economy.

Old Age, Survivors, and Disability Health Insurance The social program in the United States financed by Federal *payroll taxes* on employers and employees and designed to replace some of the *earnings* lost when workers retire, die, or become unable to work.

Oligopoly A market structure in which a few firms sell either a *standardized* or *differentiated product,* into which entry is difficult, in which the firm has limited control over product price because of *mutual interdependence* (except when there is collusion among firms), and in which there is typically *nonprice competition.*

Oligopsony A market in which there are only a few buyers.

OPEC An acronym for the *Organization of Petroleum Exporting Countries.*

Open economy An economy which exports and imports goods and services.

Open-market operations The buying and selling of U.S. government securities by the *Federal Reserve Banks* for purposes of carrying out *monetary policy.*

Open shop A place of employment in which the employer may hire nonunion workers and in which the workers need not become members of a *labor union.*

Opportunity cost The amount of other products which must be forgone or sacrificed to produce a unit of a product.

Organization of Petroleum Exporting Nations (OPEC) The cartel formed in 1970 by 13 oil-producing countries to control the price and quantity of crude oil exported by its members, and which accounts for a large proportion of the world's export of oil.

Other things equal assumption The assumption that factors other than those being considered are held constant.

Outpayments The expenditures of its own or foreign currency which the individuals, firms, and governments of one nation make to purchase goods and services, for *remittances,* as investment income, and *capital outflows* abroad.

Output effect An increase in the price of one input will increase a firm's production costs and reduce its level of output, thus reducing the demand for other inputs; conversely for a decrease in the price of the input.

P

Paper money Pieces of paper used as a *medium of exchange;* in the United States, *Federal Reserve Notes.*

Paradox of voting A situation whereby paired-choice voting by majority rule fails to provide a consistent ranking of society's preferences for *public goods* or services.

Parity concept The idea that year after year a specific output of a farm product should enable a farmer to acquire a constant amount of nonagricultural goods and services.

Parity ratio The ratio of the price received by farmers from the sale of an agricultural commodity to the prices of other goods paid by them; usually expressed as a percentage; used as a rationale for *price supports.*

Partnership An unincorporated firm owned and operated by two or more persons.

Patent An exclusive right to inventors to produce and sell a new product or machine for a set period of time.

Payments deficit (See *Balance of payments deficit.*)

Payments surplus (See *Balance of payments surplus.*)

Payroll tax A tax levied on employers of labor equal to a percentage of all or part of the wages and salaries paid by them; and on employees equal to a percentage of all or part of the wages and salaries received by them.

Per capita GDP *Gross domestic product* (GDP) per person; the average GDP of a population.

Per capita income A nation's total income per person; the average income of a population.

Perfectly elastic demand Product or resource demand in which *quantity demanded* can be of any amount at a particular *price;* graphs as a horizontal *demand curve.*

Perfectly elastic supply Product or resource supply in which *quantity supplied* can be of any amount at a particular *price;* graphs as a horizontal *supply curve.*

Perfectly inelastic demand Product or resource demand in which *price* can be of any amount at a particular quantity of the product or resource demanded; *quantity demanded* does not respond to a change in price; graphs as a vertical *demand curve.*

Perfectly inelastic supply Product or resource supply in which *price* can be of any amount at a particular quantity of the product or resource demanded; *quantity supplied* does not respond to a change in price; graphs as a vertical *supply curve.*

Per se violations Collusive actions, such as attempts by firms to fix prices or divide a market, which are violations of the *antitrust laws* even if the actions are unsuccessful.

Personal consumption expenditures The expenditures of *households* for *durable* and *nondurable consumer goods* and services.

Personal distribution of income The manner in which the economy's *personal* or *disposable income* is divided among different income classes or different households.

Personal income The earned and unearned income available to resource suppliers and others before the payment of *personal taxes.*

Personal income tax A tax levied on the *taxable income* of individuals, households, and unincorporated firms.

Personal Responsibility Act A 1996 law that eliminated the Federal government's 6-decade-long guarantee of cash assistance for poor families, whether adults in the family work or not; sets a limit of 5 years on receiving AFDC benefits and requires able-bodied adults to work after 2 years to continue to receive public assistance.

Personal saving The *personal income* of households less *personal taxes* and *personal consumption expenditures; disposable income* not spent for *consumer goods.*

Per-unit production cost The average production cost of a particular level of output; total input cost divided by units of output.

Phillips Curve A curve showing the relationship between the *unemployment rate* (on the horizontal axis) and the annual rate of increase in the *price level* (on the vertical axis).

Planned economy An economy in which government determines how resources are allocated.

Planned investment The amount which *firms* plan or intend to invest.

Plant A physical establishment which performs one or more functions in the production, fabrication, and distribution of goods and services.

"Play or pay" A means of expanding health insurance coverage by requiring employers to either provide insurance for their workers or pay a special *payroll tax* to finance insurance for uncovered workers.

***P* = MC rule** A purely competitive firm will maximize its profit or minimize its loss by producing that output at which the *price* of the product is equal to *marginal cost,* provided that price is equal to or greater than *average variable cost* in the short run and equal to or greater than *average total cost* in the long run.

Policy economics The formulation of courses of action to bring about desired economic outcomes or to prevent undesired occurrences.

Political business cycle The alleged tendency of Congress to destabilize the economy by reducing taxes and increasing government expenditures before elections and to raise taxes and lower expenditures after elections.

Positive economics The analysis of facts or data to establish scientific generalizations about economic behavior.

Positive relationship Direct relationship between two variables.

***Post hoc, ergo propter hoc* fallacy** Incorrectly reasoning that when one event precedes another the first event must have caused the second event.

Potential competition New competitors which may be induced to enter an industry if firms now in that industry are receiving large *economic profits.*

Potential output The real output (*GDP*) an economy can produce when it fully employs its available resources.

Poverty A situation in which the basic needs of an individual or family exceed the means to satisfy them.

Poverty rate The percentage of the population with incomes below the official poverty income levels established by the Federal government.

Preferred provider organization (PPO) The doctors and hospitals that agree to provide health care to insured individuals at rates negotiated with an insurer.

Premature inflation A type of inflation which sometimes occurs before the economy has reached *full employment.*

Price The amount of money needed to buy a particular good, service, or resource.

Price ceiling A legally established maximum price for a good or service.

Price discrimination The selling of a product to different buyers at different prices when the price differences are not justified by differences in cost.

Price elasticity of demand The ratio of the percentage change in *quantity demanded* of a product or resource to the percentage change in its *price;* a measure of the responsiveness of buyers to a change in the price of a product or resource.

Price elasticity of supply The ratio of the percentage change in *quantity supplied* of a product or resource to the percentage change in its *price;* the responsiveness of producers to a change in the price of a product or resource.

Price fixing The conspiring by two or more firms to set the price of their products; an illegal practice under the *Sherman Act.*

Price floor A legally determined price above the *equilibrium price.*

Price index An index number which shows how the weighted average price of a "market basket" of goods changes through time.

Price leadership An informal method which firms in an *oligopoly* may employ to set the price of their product: one firm (the leader) is the first to announce a change in price, and the other firms (the followers) soon announce identical or similar changes.

Price level The weighted average of the prices of all the final goods and services produced in an economy.

Price-level surprises Unanticipated changes in the price level.

Price maker A seller (or buyer) of a product or resource which is able to affect the product or resource price by changing the amount it sells (or buys).

Price-level stability A steadiness of the price level from one period to the next; zero or low annual inflation; also called "price stability."

Price support A minimum price which government allows sellers to receive for a good or service; a legally established or maintained minimum price.

Price taker A seller (or buyer) of a product or resource who is unable to affect the price at which a product or resource sells by changing the amount it sells (or buys).

Price-wage flexibility Changes in the *prices* of products and in the *wages* paid to workers; the ability of prices and wages to rise or fall.

Price war Successive and continued decreases in the prices charged by the firms in an oligopolistic industry; each firm lowers its price below rivals' prices, hoping to increase its sales and revenues at its rivals expense.

Prime interest rate The *interest rate* banks charge their most creditworthy borrowers, for example, large corporations with excellent financing credentials.

Principal-agent problem A conflict of interest which occurs when agents (workers or managers) pursue their own objectives to the detriment of the principals' (stockholders) goals.

Private good A good or service which is subject to the *exclusion principle* and which is provided by privately owned firms to consumers who are willing to pay for it.

Private property The right of private persons and firms to obtain, own, control, employ, dispose of, and bequeath *land, capital,* and other property.

Private sector The *households* and business *firms* of the economy.

Process innovation The development and use of a new or improved production or distribution method.

Product differentiation A strategy in which one firm's product is distinguished from competing products by means of its design, related services, quality, location, or other attributes (except price).

Product innovation The development and sale of a new or improved product (or service).

Production possibilities curve A curve showing the different combinations of two goods or services that can be produced in a *full-employment, full-production* economy in which the available supplies of resources and technology are fixed.

Productive efficiency The production of a good in the least costly way; occurs when production takes place at the output at which *average total cost* is a minimum and at which *marginal product* per dollar's worth of input is the same for all inputs.

Productivity A measure of average output or real output per unit of input. For example, the productivity of labor may be found by dividing real output by hours of work.

Productivity slowdown The decline in the rate at which *labor productivity* in the United States has increased in recent decades.

Product market A market in which products are sold by *firms* and bought by *households.*

Profit The return to the resource *entrepreneurial ability* (see *Normal profit*); *total revenue* minus *total cost* (see *Economic profit*).

Profit-maximizing combination of resources The quantity of each resource a firm must employ to maximize its profit or minimize its loss; the combination in which the *marginal revenue product* of each resource is equal to its *marginal resource cost* (to its *price* if the resource is employed in a competitive market).

Profit sharing plan A compensation device through which workers receive part of their pay in the form of a share of their employer's profit (if any).

Progressive tax A tax whose *average tax rate* increases as the taxpayer's income increases and decreases as the taxpayer's income decreases.

Property tax A tax on the value of property (*capital, land,* stocks and bonds, and other *assets*) owned by *firms* and *households.*

Proportional tax A tax whose *average tax rate* remains constant as the taxpayer's income increases or decreases.

Proprietor's income The net income of the owners of unincorporated firms (proprietorships and partnerships).

Protective tariff A *tariff* designed to shield domestic producers of a good or service from the competition of foreign producers.

Public assistance programs Government programs which pay benefits to those who are unable to earn income (because of permanent handicaps or because they have very low income and dependent children); financed by general tax revenues and viewed as public charity (rather than earned rights).

Public choice theory The economic analysis of collective and government decision making, politics, and the democratic process.

Public debt The total amount owed by the Federal government to the owners of government securities; equal to the sum of past government *budget deficits* less government *budget surpluses.*

Public finance The branch of economics which analyzes government revenues and expenditures.

Public good A good or service which is indivisible and to which the *exclusion principle* does not apply; a good or service with these characteristics provided by government.

Public interest theory of regulation The presumption that the purpose of the regulation of an *industry* is to protect the public (consumers) from abuse of the power possessed by *natural monopolies.*

Public sector The part of the economy which contains all government entities; government.

Public sector failure Inefficiencies in resource allocation caused by problems in the operation of the public sector (government); occurs because of rent-seeking pressure by special-interest groups, short-sighted political behavior, limited and bundled choices, and bureaucratic inefficiencies.

Public utility A firm which produces an essential good or service, has obtained from a government the right to be the sole supplier of the good or service in the area, and is regulated by that government to prevent the abuse of its monopoly power.

Purchasing power The amount of goods and services which a monetary unit of income can buy.

Purchasing power parity The idea that exchange rates between nations equate the purchasing power of various currencies; exchange rates between any two nations adjust to reflect the price-level differences between the countries.

Pure capitalism An economic system in which property resources are privately owned and markets and prices are used to direct and coordinate economic activities.

Pure competition A market structure in which a very large number of firms sell a *standardized product,* into which entry is very easy, in which the individual seller has no control over the product price, and in which there is no nonprice competition; a market characterized by a very large number of buyers and sellers.

Pure monopoly A market structure in which one firm sells a unique product, into which entry is blocked, in which the single firm has considerable control over product price, and in which *nonprice competition* may or may not be found.

Pure profit (See *Economic profit.*)

Pure rate of interest An essentially risk-free, long-term interest rate which is free of the influence of market imperfections.

Q

Quantity demanded The amount of a good or service buyers (or a buyer) desire to purchase at a particular price during some period.

Quantity supplied The amount of a good or service producers (or a producer) offer to sell at a particular price during some period.

Quasipublic bank A bank which is privately owned but governmently (publicly) controlled; each of the U.S. *Federal Reserve Banks.*

Quasipublic good A good or service to which the *exclusion principle* could apply but which has such a large *spillover benefit* that government sponsors its production to prevent an underallocation of resources.

R

R&D Research and development activities undertaken to bring about *technological progress.*

Ratchet effect The tendency for the *price level* to rise when *aggregate demand* increases but not fall when aggregate demand declines.

Rate of exchange The price paid in one's own money to acquire one unit of a foreign currency; the rate at which the money of one nation is exchanged for the money of another nation.

Rate of return The gain in net revenue divided by the cost of an investment or a *R&D* expenditure; expressed as a percentage.

Rational expectations theory The hypothesis that firms and households expect monetary and fiscal policies to have certain effects on the economy and (in pursuit of their own self-interests) take actions which make those policies ineffective.

Rationing function of prices The ability of market forces in a competitive market to equalize *quantity demanded* and *quantity supplied* and to eliminate shortages and surpluses via changes in prices.

Real-balances effect The tendency for increases in the price level to lower the real value (or purchasing power) of financial assets with fixed money value and, as a result, to reduce total spending; and conversely for decreases in the price level; also called the *wealth effect.*

Real business cycle theory A theory that *business cycles* result from changes in technology and resource availability, which affect *productivity* and thus increase or decrease *long-run aggregate supply.*

Real capital (See *Capital.*)

Real gross domestic product (GDP) *Gross domestic product* adjusted for inflation; gross domestic product in a year divided by the *GDP deflator* for that year, expressed as a decimal.

Real GDP (See *Real gross domestic product.*)

Real income The amount of goods and services which can be purchased with *nominal income* during some period of time; nominal income adjusted for inflation.

Real interest rate The interest rate expressed in dollars of constant value (adjusted for *inflation*); and equal to the *nominal interest rate* less the expected rate of inflation.

Real wage The amount of goods and services a worker can purchase with his or her *nominal wage;* the purchasing power of the nominal wage.

Recession A period of declining real GDP, accompanied by lower real income and higher unemployment.

Recessionary gap The amount by which the *aggregate expenditures schedule* must shift upward to increase the *real GDP* to its full-employment, noninflationary level.

Reciprocal Trade Agreements Act A 1934 Federal law which gave the President the authority to negotiate up to 50 percent lower tariffs with foreign nations that agreed to reduce their tariffs on U.S. goods (and which incorporated the *most-favored-nation clause*).

Refinancing the public debt Paying owners of maturing government securities with money obtained by selling new securities or with new securities.

Regressive tax A tax whose *average tax rate* decreases as the taxpayer's income increases, and increases as the taxpayer's income decreases.

Regulatory agency An agency, commission, or board established by the Federal government or a state government to control the prices charged and the services offered by a natural monopoly.

Rental income The payments (income) received by those who supply *land* to the economy.

Rent-seeking behavior The actions by persons, firms, or unions to gain special benefits from government at the taxpayers' or someone else's expense.

Required reserves The funds which banks and thrifts must deposit with the *Federal Reserve Bank* (or hold as *vault cash*) to meet the legal *reserve requirement;* a fixed percentage of the bank or thrift's checkable deposits.

Reserve requirement The specified minimum percentage of its checkable deposits which a bank or thrift must keep on deposit at the Federal Reserve Bank in its district, or in *vault cash.*

Resource market A market in which *households* sell and *firms* buy resources or the services of resources.

Retiring the public debt Reducing the size of the *public debt* by paying money to owners of maturing U.S. government securities.

Revaluation An increase in the governmentally defined value of its currency relative to other nations' currencies.

Revenue tariff A *tariff* designed to produce income for the Federal government.

Reverse discrimination The view that the preferential treatment associated with *affirmative action* efforts constitutes discrimination against other groups.

Right-to-work law A state law (in about 20 states) which makes it illegal to require a worker to join a *labor union* in order to retain his or her job; laws which make *union shops* illegal.

Roundabout production The construction and use of *capital* to aid in the production of *consumer goods.*

Rule of reason The rule stated and applied in the *U.S. Steel case* that only combinations and contracts unreasonably restraining trade are subject to actions under the antitrust laws and that size and possession of monopoly power are not themselves illegal.

Rule of 70 A method for determining the number of years it will take for some measure to double, given its annual percentage increase. Example: To determine the number of years it will take for the *price level* to double; divide 70 by the annual rate of *inflation.*

S

Sales tax A tax levied on the cost (at retail) of a broad group of products.

Saving Disposable income not spent for consumer goods; equal to *disposable income* minus *personal consumption expenditures.*

Savings deposit An interest-bearing deposit which normally can be withdrawn by the depositor at any time.

Savings and Loan association (S&L) A firm which accepts deposits primarily from small individual savers and lends primarily to individuals to finance purchases such as autos and homes; now nearly indistinguishable from a *commercial bank.*

Saving schedule A schedule which shows the amounts *households* plan to save (plan not to spend for *consumer goods*), at different levels of *disposable income.*

Savings institution A *thrift institution.*

Say's law The largely discredited macroeconomic generalization that the production of goods and service (supply) creates an equal *demand* for these goods and service.

Scarce resources The limited quantities of *land, capital, labor,* and *entrepreneurial ability* which are never sufficient to satisfy the virtually unlimited material wants of humans.

Seasonal variations Increases and decreases in the level of economic activity within a single year, caused by a change in the season.

Secular trend Long-term tendency; change in some variable over a very long period of years.

Self-interest That which each firm, property owner, worker, and consumer believes is best for itself and seeks to obtain.

Seniority The length of time a worker has been employed absolutely or relative to other workers; may be used to determine which workers will be laid off when there is insufficient work for them all, and who will be rehired when more work becomes available.

Separation of ownership and control The fact that different groups of people own a *corporation* (the stockholders) and manage it (the directors and officers).

Service An (intangible) act or use for which a consumer, firm, or government is willing to pay.

Sherman Act The Federal antitrust act of 1890 which made monopoly and conspiracies to restrain trade criminal offenses.

Shirking Actions by workers to increase their *utility* or well-being by neglecting or evading work.

Shut-down case The circumstance in which a firm would experience a loss greater than its total *fixed cost* if it were to produce any output greater than zero; alternatively, a situation in which a firm would cease to operate when the *price* at which it can sell its product is less than its *average variable cost.*

Shortage The amount by which the *quantity demanded* of a product exceeds the *quantity supplied* at a particular (below-equilibrium) price.

Short run (1) In *microeconomics,* a period of time in which producers are able to change the quantity of some but not all of the resources they employ; a period in which some resources (usually plant) are fixed and some are variable. (2) In *macroeconomics,* a period in which nominal wages and other input prices do not change in response to a change in the price level.

Short-run aggregate supply curve An aggregate supply curve relevant to a time period in which input prices (particularly *nominal wages*) do not change in response to changes in the *price level.*

Short-run supply curve A supply curve which shows the quantity of a product a firm in a purely competitive industry will offer to sell at various prices in the *short run;* the portion of the firm's short-run marginal cost curve which lies above its *average variable cost* curve.

Short-run competitive equilibrium The price at which the total quantity of a product supplied in the *short run* in a purely competitive industry equals the total quantity of the product demanded and which is equal to or greater than *average variable cost.*

Short-run farm problem The sharp year-to-year changes in the prices of agricultural products and in the incomes of farmers.

Simple multiplier The *multiplier* in an economy in which government collects no *net taxes,* there are no *imports,* and *investment* is independent of the level of income; equal to 1 divided by the *marginal propensity to save.*

Slope of a line The ratio of the vertical change (the rise or fall) to the horizontal change (the run) between any two points on a line. The slope of an upward sloping line is positive, reflecting a direct relationship between two variables; the slope of a downward sloping line is negative, reflecting an inverse relationship between two variables.

Smoot-Hawley Tariff Act Legislation passed in 1930 which established very high tariffs. Its objective was to reduce imports and stimulate the domestic economy, but it only resulted in retaliatory tariffs by other nations.

Social accounting (*See National income accounting.*)

Social insurance programs The programs which replace some of the earnings lost when people retire or are temporarily unemployed, which are financed by *payroll taxes,* and which are viewed as earned rights (rather than charity).

Socially optimal price The price of a product which results in the most efficient allocation of an economy's resources and is equal to the *marginal cost* of the product.
Social regulation The regulation by which government is concerned with the conditions under which goods and services are produced, their physical characteristics, and the impact of their production on society; in contrast to *industrial regulation.*
Social security program (See *Old Age, Survivorship, and Disability Health Insurance* program.)
Sole proprietorship An unincorporated *firm* owned and operated by one person.
Special economic zones Regions of China open to foreign investment, private ownership, and relatively free international trade.
Special-interest effect Any result of government promotion of the interests (goals) of a small groups at the expense of a much larger group.
Specialization The use of the resources of an individual, a firm, a region, or a nation to produce one or a few goods and services.
Speculation The activity of buying or selling with the motive of later reselling or rebuying for profit.
Spillover A benefit or cost from production or consumption, accruing without compensation to nonbuyers and nonsellers of the product (see *Spillover benefit; Spillover costs*).
Spillover benefit A benefit obtained without compensation by third parties from the production or consumption of sellers or buyers. Example: A beekeeper benefits when a neighboring farmer plants clover.
Spillover cost A cost imposed without compensation on third parties by the production or consumption of sellers or buyers. Example: A manufacturer dumps toxic chemicals into a river, killing the fish sport fishers seek.
SSI (See *Supplemental Security Income.*)
Stagflation Inflation accompanied by stagnation in the rate of growth of output and an increase in unemployment in the economy; simultaneous increases in the *price level* and the *unemployment rate.*
Standardized product A product for which buyers are indifferent to the seller from whom they purchase it so long as the price charged by all sellers is the same; a product for which all units of the product are identical and thus perfect substitutes for each other.
Startup (firm) A new firm focused on creating and introducing a particular new product or employing a specific new production or distribution method.
State bank A *commercial bank* authorized by a state government to engage in the business of banking.
State-owned enterprises Businesses which are owned by government; the major types of enterprises in Russia and China before their transitions to the market system.
Statistical discrimination Judging an individual on the basis of the average characteristic of the group to which the person belongs rather than on personal characteristics.
Stock (corporate) An ownership share in a corporation.
Store of value An *asset* set aside for future use; one of the three functions of *money.*
Strategic trade policy The use of trade barriers to reduce the risk inherent in product development by domestic firms, particularly that involving advanced technology.
Strike The withholding of labor services by an organized group of workers (a *labor union*).
Structural-change hypothesis The explanation which attributes the decline of unionism in the United States to changes in the structure of the economy and of the labor force.
Structural deficit The extent to which the Federal government's expenditures exceed its tax revenues when the economy is at full employment (or the extent to which its current expenditures exceed the projected tax revenues which would accrue if the economy were at full employment); also known as a full-employment budget deficit.
Structural unemployment Unemployment of workers whose skills are not demanded by employers, they lack sufficient skill to obtain employment, or they cannot easily move to locations where jobs are available.
Subsidy A payment of funds (or goods and services) by a government, firm, or household for which it receives no good or service in return; when made by a government, it is a *government transfer payment.*
Substitute goods Products or services which can be used in place of each other. When the price of one falls the demand for the other falls, and conversely with an increase of price.
Substitution effect (1) A change in the price of a *consumer good* changes the relative expensiveness of that good and hence changes the consumer's willingness to buy it rather than other goods. (2) The effect of a change in the price of a *resource* on the quantity of the resource employed by a firm, assuming no change in its output.
Sunk cost A cost which has been incurred and cannot be recovered.
Superfund Law Federal legislation of 1980 which taxes manufacturers of toxic products and uses the revenues to finance the cleanup of toxic-waste sites; assigns liability for improperly dumped waste to the firms producing, transporting, and dumping that waste.
Superior good (See *Normal good.*)
Supplementary Security Income program A federally financed and administered program which provides a uniform nationwide minimum income for the aged, blind, and disabled who do not qualify for benefits under *the Old Age, Survivors, and Disability Health Insurance* or *unemployment insurance* program in the United States.
Supply A schedule showing the amounts of a good or service sellers (or a seller) will offer at various prices during some period.
Supply curve A curve illustrating *supply.*
Supply factor (in growth) An increase in the availability of a resource, an improvement in its quality, or an expansion of technological knowledge which makes it possible for an economy to produce a greater output of goods and services.
Supply shock An event which increases production costs, decreases *aggregate supply,* reduces *real GDP,* and increases *unemployment.*

Supply-side economics A view of macroeconomics which emphasizes the role of costs and *aggregate supply* in explaining *inflation, unemployment,* and *economic growth.*

Surplus The amount by which the *quantity supplied* of a product exceeds the *quantity demanded* at a specific (above-equilibrium) price.

Surplus payment A payment to a resource which is not required to ensure the availability of the resource, for example, land rent.

Surplus value A Marxian term; the amount by which the value of a worker's daily output exceeds the worker's daily wage; workers' output appropriated by capitalists as profit.

T

Tacit collusion Any method by an oligopolist to set prices and outputs which does not involve outright (or overt) *collusion; price leadership* is an example.

Tariff A tax imposed by a nation on an imported good.

Taste-for-discrimination model A theory of discrimination which views discrimination as a preference for which an employer is willing to pay.

Tax An involuntary payment of money (or goods and services) to a government by a *household* or *firm* for which the household or firm receives no good or service directly in return.

Tax incidence The person or group who ends up paying a tax.

Tax subsidy A grant in the form of reduced taxes through favorable tax treatment; for example, employer-paid health insurance is exempt from Federal income and payroll taxes.

Tax-transfer disincentives Decreases in the incentives to work, save, invest, innovate, and take risks which allegedly result from high *marginal tax rates* and *transfer-payments.*

Technology The body of knowledge and techniques which can be used to produce goods and services from *economic resources.*

Technological advance New and better goods and services and new and better ways of producing or distributing them.

Terms of trade The rate at which units of one product can be exchanged for units of another product; the price of a good or service; the amount of one good or service which must be given up to obtain one unit of another good or service.

Theory of human capital Generalization that *wage differentials* are the result of differences in the amount of *human-capital investment,* and that the incomes of lower paid workers are increased by increasing the amount of such investment.

Thrift institution A *savings and loan association, mutual savings bank,* or *credit union.*

Tight money policy *Federal Reserve System* actions which contract, or restrict, the growth of the nation's *money supply* for the purpose of reducing or eliminating inflation.

Till money (See *Vault cash.*)

Time deposit An interest-earning deposit in a *commercial bank* or *thrift institution* which the depositor can withdraw without penalty after the end of a specified period.

Token money Coins having a *face value* greater than their *intrinsic value.*

Total cost The sum of *fixed cost* and *variable cost.*

Total demand The demand schedule or the *demand curve* of all buyers of a good or service; also called market demand.

Total demand for money The sum of the *transactions demand for money* and the *asset demand for money.*

Total product The total output of a particular good or service produced by a firm (or a group of firms or the entire economy).

Total revenue The total number of dollars received by a firm (or firms) from the sale of a product; equal to the total expenditures for the product produced by the firm (or firms); equal to the quantity sold (demanded) multiplied by the price at which it is sold.

Total-revenue test A test to determine elasticity of *demand* between any two prices: Demand is elastic if *total revenue* moves in the opposite direction as price; it is inelastic when it moves in the same direction as price; and it is of unitary elasticity when it does not change when price changes.

Total spending The total amount buyers of goods and services spend or plan to spend; also called *aggregate expenditures.*

Total supply The supply schedule or the supply curve of all sellers of a good or service; also called market supply.

Total utility The total amount of satisfaction derived from the consumption of a single product or a combination of products.

Township and village enterprises Privately owned rural manufacturing firms in China.

Trade balance The export of goods (or goods and services) of a nation less its imports of goods (or goods and services).

Trade bloc A group of nations which lowers or abolishes trade barriers among members. Examples include the *European Union* and the nations of the *North American Free Trade Agreement.*

Trade controls *Tariffs, export subsidies, import quotas,* and other means a nation may use to reduce *imports* and expand *exports.*

Trade deficit The amount by which a nation's *imports* of goods (or goods and services) exceed its *exports* of goods (or goods and services).

Trademark A legal protection which gives the originators of a product an exclusive right to use the brand name.

Tradeoffs The sacrifice of some or all of one economic goal, good, or service to achieve some other goal, good, or service.

Trade surplus The amount by which a nation's exports of goods (or goods and services) exceed its imports of goods (or goods and services).

Trading possibilities line A line which shows the different combinations of two products an economy is able to obtain (consume) when it specializes in the production of one product and trades (exports) it to obtain the other product.

Traditional economy An economic system in which traditions and customs determine how the economy will use its scarce resources.

Transactions demand for money The amount of money people want to hold for use as a *medium of exchange* (to make payments), and which varies directly with the *nominal GDP.*

Transfer payment A payment of *money* (or goods and services) by a government to a *household* or *firm* for which the payer receives no good or service directly in return.

Tying contract A promise made by a buyer when allowed to purchase a product from a seller that it will purchase certain other products from the same seller; a practice forbidden by the *Clayton Act.*

U

Unanticipated inflation Increases in the price level (*inflation*) at a rate greater than expected.

Underemployment (1) Failure to produce the maximum amount of goods and services which can be produced from the resources employed; failure to achieve *full production.* (2) A situation in which workers are employed in positions requiring less than the amount of education and skill than they have.

Undistributed corporate profits After-tax corporate profits not distributed as dividends to stockholders; corporate or business saving; also called retained earnings.

Unemployment Failure to use all available *economic resources* to produce goods and services; failure of the economy to fully employ its *labor force.*

Unemployment compensation (See *Unemployment insurance.*)

Unemployment insurance The social insurance program which in the United States is financed by state *payroll taxes* on employers and makes income available to workers who become unemployed and are unable to find jobs.

Unemployment rate The percentage of the *labor force* unemployed at any time.

Uninsurable risk An event which would result in a loss and whose occurrence is uncontrollable and unpredictable; insurance companies are not willing to sell insurance against such a loss.

Union shop A place of employment where the employer may hire either *labor union* members or nonmembers but where nonmembers must become members within a specified period of time or lose their jobs.

Unit elasticity Demand or supply for which the *elasticity coefficient* is equal to 1; means the percentage change in the quantity demanded or supplied is equal to the percentage change in price.

Unit labor cost Labor costs per unit of output; total labor cost divided by total output; also equal to the *nominal wage rate* divided by the *average product* of labor.

Unit of account A standard unit in which prices can be stated and the value of goods and services can be compared; one of the three functions of *money.*

Unlimited liability Absence of any limits on the maximum amount which an individual (usually a business owner) may become legally required to pay.

Unlimited wants The insatiable desire of consumers for goods and services which will give them satisfaction or *utility.*

Unplanned investment Actual investment less *planned investment;* increases or decreases in the *inventories* of firms resulting from production greater than sales.

Urban collectives Chinese enterprises jointly owned by their managers and their workforces, located in urban areas.

Uruguay Round The eighth and most recent round of trade negotiations under *GATT* (now the *World Trade Organization*).

U.S. Steel case The antitrust action brought by the Federal government against the U.S. Steel Corporation, in which the courts ruled (in 1920) that only unreasonable restraints of trade were illegal and that size and the possession of monopoly power were not violations of the antitrust laws.

Usury laws State laws which specify the maximum legal interest rate at which loans can be made.

Utility The want-satisfying power of a good or service; the satisfaction or pleasure a consumer obtains from the consumption of a good or service (or from the consumption of a collection of goods and services).

Utility-maximizing rule To obtain the greatest *utility* the consumer should allocate *money income* so that the last dollar spent on each good or service yields the same marginal utility.

V

Value added The value of the product sold by a *firm* less the value of the products (materials) purchased and used by the firm to produce the product.

Value-added tax A tax imposed on the difference between the value of the products sold by a firm and the value of the goods purchased from other firms to produce the product.

Value judgment Opinion of what is desirable or undesirable; belief regarding what ought or ought not to be (regarding what is right or just and wrong or unjust).

Value of money The quantity of goods and services for which a unit of money (a dollar) can be exchanged; the purchasing power of a unit of money; the reciprocal of the *price level.*

Variable cost A cost which in total increases when the firm increases its output and decreases when it reduces its output.

VAT (See *Value-added tax.*)

Vault cash The *currency* a bank has in its vault and cash drawers.

Velocity The number of times per year the average dollar in the *money supply* is spent for *final goods and services;* nominal GDP divided by the money supply.

Venture capital That part of household saving used to finance high-risk business ventures in exchange for shares of the profit if the business endeavors succeed.

Vertical axis The "up-down" or "north-south" axis on a graph or grid.

Vertical combination A group of *plants* engaged in different stages of the production of a final product and owned by a single *firm.*
Vertical intercept The point at which a line meets the vertical axis of a graph.
Vertical merger The merger of one or more *firms* engaged in different stages of the production of a final product.
Vertical range The vertical segment of the aggregate supply curve along which the economy is at full capacity.
Very long run A period in which *technology* can change and in which *firms* can introduce new products.
Vicious circle of poverty A problem common in some developing countries in which their low per capita incomes are an obstacle to realizing the levels of saving and investment requisite to acceptable rates of economic growth.
Voice mechanism Communication by workers through their union to resolve grievances with an employer.
Voluntary export restrictions Voluntary limitations by countries or firms of their exports to a particular foreign nation to avoid enactment of formal trade barriers by that nation.

W

Wage The price paid for the use or services of *labor* per unit of time (per hour, per day, and so on).
Wage differential The difference between the *wage* received by one worker or group of workers and that received by another worker or group of workers.
Wage discrimination The payment of a lower wage to members of particular groups than to preferred workers for the same work.
Wage rate (See *Wage.*)
Wages The income of those who supply the economy with *labor.*
Wealth effect (See *Real balances effect.*)
Welfare programs (See *Public assistance programs.*)
Wheeler-Lea Act The Federal act of 1938 which amended the *Federal Trade Commission Act* by prohibiting and giving the commission power to investigate unfair and deceptive acts or practices of commerce (such as false and misleading advertising and the misrepresentation of products).
"Will to develop" Wanting economic growth strongly enough to change from old to new ways of doing things.
World Bank A bank which lends (and guarantees loans) to developing nations to help them increase their *capital stock* and thus achieve *economic growth;* formally, the International Bank for Reconstruction and Development.
World price The international market price of a good or service, determined by world demand and supply.
World Trade Organization An organization established in 1994 to replace *GATT* to oversee the provisions of the *Uruguay round* and resolve any disputes stemming therefrom.

X

X-inefficiency Failure to produce any specific output at the lowest average (and total) cost possible.

Answers to Key Questions*

Chapter 1

1-1 This behavior can be explained in terms of marginal costs and marginal benefits. At a standard restaurant, items are priced individually—they have a positive marginal cost. If you order more, it will cost you more. You order until the marginal benefit from the extra food no longer exceeds the marginal cost. At a buffet you pay a flat fee no matter how much you eat. Once the fee is paid, additional food items have a zero marginal cost. You therefore continue to eat until your marginal benefit becomes zero.

1-5 Economic theory consists of factually supported generalizations about economic behavior. Economists use two methods to obtain sound theory: induction and deduction. In *deduction* the economist starts with a hypothesis and tests it for accuracy by gathering and examining facts. In *induction,* the economist starts by gathering facts and then examines their relationships, so as to extract a cause and effect pattern: a theory. Regardless of how derived, economic theory enables policymakers to formulate economic policy relevant to real-world goals and problems.

As for the quotation, the opposite is true; any theory not supported by facts is not a good theory. Good economic theory is empirically grounded; it is based on facts and so is highly practical.

1-7 (a), (d), and (f) are macro; (b), (c), and (e) are micro.

1-8 (a) and (c) are positive; (b) and (d) are normative.

1-9 (a) The fallacy of composition is the mistake of believing that something true for an individual part is necessarily true for the whole. Example: A single auto producer can increase its profits by lowering its price and taking business away from its competitors. But matched price cuts by all auto manufacturers will not necessarily yield higher industry profits. (b) The "after this, therefore because of this" fallacy is incorrectly reasoning that when one event precedes another, the first event *necessarily* caused the second. Example: Interest rates rise, followed by an increase in the rate of inflation, leading to the erroneous conclusion that the rise in interest rates caused the inflation. Actually, higher interest rates slow inflation.

Cause-and-effect relationships are difficult to isolate because "other things" are continually changing.

Appendix 1-2 (a) More tickets are bought at each price; the line shifts to the right. (b) and (c) Fewer tickets are bought at each price; the line shifts to the left.

Appendix 1-3 Income column: \$0; \$5,000; \$10,000, \$15,000; \$20,000. Saving column: −\$500; 0; \$500; \$1,000; \$1,500. Slope = 0.1 (= \$1,000 − \$500)/(\$15,000 − \$10,000). Vertical intercept = −500. The slope shows the amount saving will increase for every \$1 increase in income; the intercept shows the amount of saving (dissaving) occurring when income is zero. Equation: $S = -\$500 + 0.1Y$ (where S is saving and Y is income). Saving will be \$750 at the \$12,500 income level.

Appendix 1-6 Slopes: at $A = +4$; at $B = 0$; at $C = -40$.

Chapter 2

2-5 Economics deals with the "limited resources–unlimited wants" problem. Unemployment represents valuable resources which could have been used to produce more goods and services—to meet more wants and ease the economizing problem.

Allocative efficiency means that resources are being used to produce the goods and services most wanted by society. The economy is then located at the optimal point on its production possibilities curve where marginal benefit equals marginal cost for each good. *Productive efficiency* means the least costly production techniques are being used to produce wanted goods and services. Example: manual typewriters produced using the least-cost techniques but for which there is no demand.

2-6 (a) See curve *EDCBA* below. The assumptions are full employment and productive efficiency, fixed supplies of resources, and fixed technology.

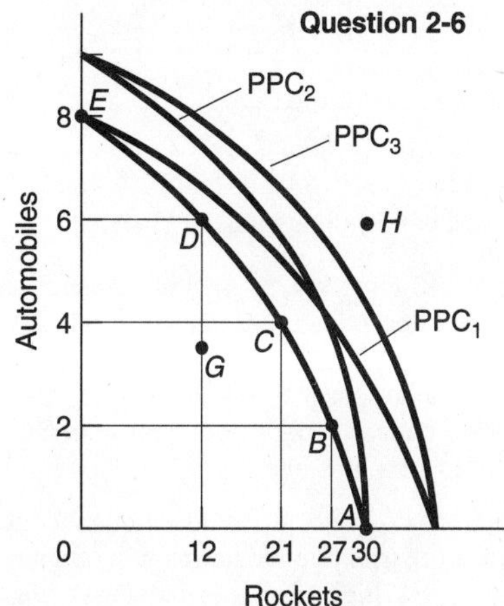

(b) 4.5 rockets; .33 automobiles, as determined from the table. Increasing opportunity costs are reflected in the concave-from-the-origin shape of the curve. This means the economy must give up larger and larger amounts of rockets to get constant added amounts of automobiles—and vice versa.

(c) It must obtain full employment and productive efficiency.

2-9 The marginal benefit curve is downsloping; MB falls as more of a product is consumed because additional units of a good yield less satisfaction than previous units. The marginal cost curve is upsloping; MC increases as more of a product is produced because additional units require the use of increasingly unsuitable

*Prepared by Campbell McConnell and Stanley Brue.

resources. The optimal amount of a particular product occurs where MB equals MC. If MC exceeds MB, fewer resources should be allocated to this use. The resources are more valuable in some alternative use (as reflected in the higher MC) than in this use (as reflected in the lower MB).

2-10 See the answer for Question 2-6. *G* indicates unemployment, productive inefficiency, or both. *H* is at present unattainable. Economic growth—through more inputs, better inputs, improved technology—must be achieved to attain *H.*

2-11 See the answer for Question 2-6. PPC_1 shows improved rocket technology. PPC_2 shows improved auto technology. PPC_3 shows improved technology in producing both products.

Chapter 3

3-2 Demand increases in (a), (c), (e), and (f); decreases in (b) and (d).

3-5 Supply increases in (a), (d), (e), and (g); decreases in (b), (c), and (f).

3-7 Data, from top to bottom: −13; −7; 0; +7; +14; and +21. (a) P_e = $4.00; Q_e = 75,000. Equilibrium occurs where there is neither a shortage nor surplus of wheat. At the immediately lower price of $3.70, there is a shortage of 7,000 bushels. At the immediately higher price of $4.30, there is a surplus of 7,000 bushels.

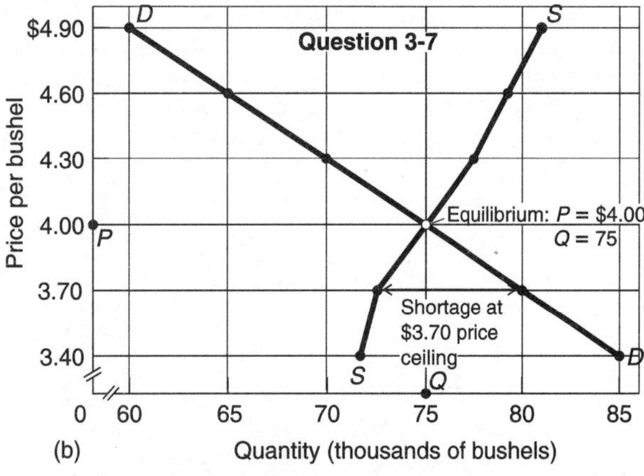

(b)

(c) Because at $3.40 there will be a 13,000 bushel shortage which will drive the price up. Because at $4.90 there will be a 21,000 bushel surplus which will drive the price down. Quotation is incorrect; just the opposite is true.
(d) A $3.70 ceiling causes a persistent shortage. Government might want to suppress inflation.

3-8 (a) Price up; quantity down; (b) Price down; quantity down; (c) Price down; quantity up; (d) Price indeterminate; quantity up; (e) Price up; quantity up; (f) Price down; quantity indeterminate; (g) Price up; quantity indeterminate; (h) Price indeterminate and quantity down.

Chapter 4

4-2 "Roundabout" production means using capital goods in the production process, enabling producers to obtain more output than through direct production. The direct way to produce a corn crop is to scatter seed about in an unplowed field. The roundabout way is to plow, fertilize, harrow, and till the field using machinery and then use a seed drill to sow the seeds in rows at the correct depth. The higher yield per acre will more than compensate the farmer for the cost of using the capital goods.

To increase the capital stock at full employment, the current production of consumer goods must decrease. Moving along the production possibilities curve toward more capital goods comes at the expense of current consumption.

No, it can use its previously unemployed resources to produce more capital goods, without sacrificing consumption goods. It can move from a point inside the curve to a point on it, thus obtaining more capital goods.

4-8 (a) Technique 2. Because it produces the output with least cost ($34 compared to $35 each for the other two). Economic profit will be $6 = ($40 −$34), which will cause the industry to expand. Expansion will continue until prices decline to where total revenue is $34 (equal to total cost).
(b) Adopt technique 4 because its cost is now lowest at $32.
(c) Technique 1 because its cost is now lowest at $27.50.
(d) The statement is logical. Increasing scarcity causes prices to rise. Firms ignoring higher resource prices will become high-cost producers and be competed out of business by firms switching to the less expensive inputs. The market system forces producers to conserve on the use of highly scarce resources. Question 8c confirms this: Technique 1 was adopted because labor had become less expensive.

4-10 The quest for profit led firms to produce these goods. Producers looked for and found the least-cost combination of resources in producing their output. Resource suppliers, seeking income, made these resources available. Consumers, through their dollar votes, ultimately decide on what will continue to be produced.

Chapter 5

5-2 The distribution of income is quite unequal. The highest 20 percent of the residents receive 10 times more income than the lowest 20 percent.

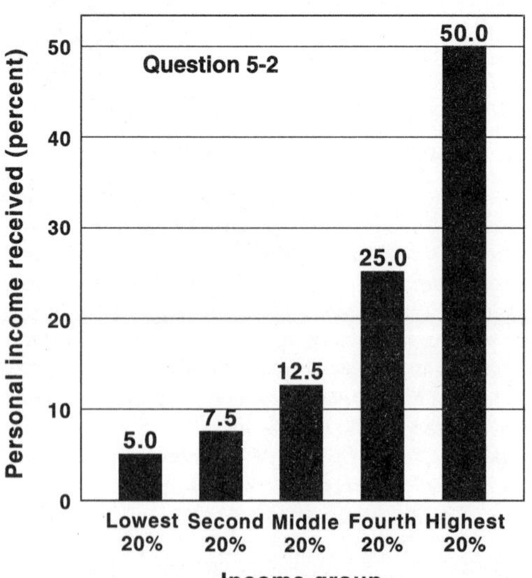

5-4 Sole proprietorship, partnership, and corporation.

Proprietorship advantages: easy to start and provides maximum freedom for the proprietor to do what she or he thinks best. Proprietorship disadvantages: limited financial resources; the owner must be a Jack-or-Jill-of-all-trades; and unlimited liability.

Partnership advantages: easy to organize; greater specialization of management; and greater financial resources. Disadvantages: financial resources are still limited; unlimited liability; possibility of disagreement among the partners; and precarious continuity.

Corporation advantages: can raise large amounts of money by issuing stocks and bonds; limited liability; continuity.

Corporation disadvantages: red tape and expense in incorporating; potential for abuse of stockholder and bondholder funds; double taxation of profits; separation of ownership and control.

The dominant role of corporations stems from the advantages cited, particularly unlimited liability and ability to raise money.

5-9 Public goods are indivisible (they are produced in such large units that they cannot be sold to individuals) and the exclusion principle does not apply to them (once the goods are produced nobody—including free riders—can be excluded from the goods' benefits). The free-rider problem explains the significance of the exclusion principle. The exclusion principle separates goods and services which private firms will supply (because those who do not pay for them can be excluded from their benefits) and goods and services which government must supply (because people can obtain the benefits without paying). Government must levy taxes to get revenues to pay for public goods.

5-10 On the curve, the only way to obtain more public goods is to reduce the production of private goods (from *C* to *B*).

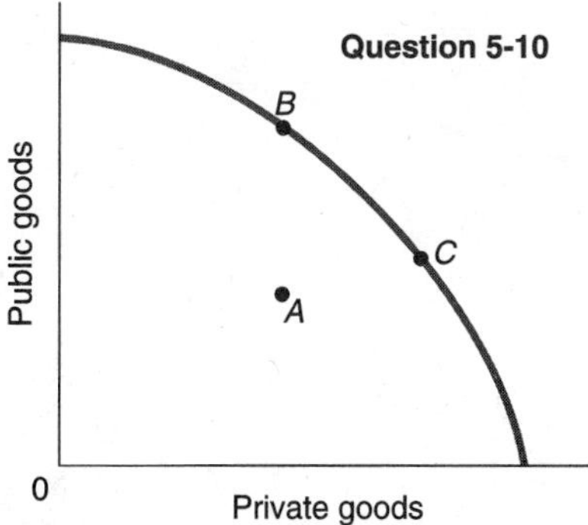

An economy operating inside the curve can expand the production of public goods without sacrificing private goods (say, from *A* to *B*) by making use of unemployed resources.

5-15 Total tax = $13,000; marginal tax rate = 40%; average tax rate = 26%. This is a progressive tax; the average tax rate rises as income goes up.

Chapter 6

6-3 Greater exporting increases domestic output and thus increases revenues to domestic exporting firms. Because these firms would employ more resources, household income would rise. Households would then use part of their greater income to buy more imported goods (imports would rise).

United States exports in 1996 were $612 billion (flow 13) and imports were $803 billion (flow 16).

Flow 14 must equal flow 13. Flow 15 must equal flow 16.

6-4 (a) Yes, because the opportunity cost of radios is less (1R ≡ 1C) in South Korea than in the United States (1R ≡ 2C). South Korea should produce radios and the United States should produce chemicals.

(b) If they specialize, the United States can produce 20 tons of chemicals and South Korea can produce 30,000 radios. Before specialization South Korea produced alternative B and the United States alternative U for a total of 28,000 radios (24,000 + 4,000) and 18 tons of chemicals (6 tons + 12 tons). The gain is 2,000 radios and 2 tons of chemicals.

(c) The limits of the terms of trade are determined by the comparative cost conditions in each country before trade: 1R ≡ 1C in South Korea and 1R ≡ 2C in the United States. The terms of trade must be somewhere between these two ratios for trade to occur.

If the terms of trade are 1R ≡ $1\frac{1}{2}$C, South Korea would end up with 26,000 radios (= 30,000 − 4,000) and 6 tons of chemicals. The United States would have 4,000 radios and 14 tons of chemicals (= 20 − 6). South Korea has gained 2,000 radios. The United States has gained 2 tons of chemicals.

(d) Yes, the world is obtaining more output from its fixed resources.

6-6 The first part of this statement is incorrect. U.S. exports create a domestic *supply* of foreign currencies, not a domestic demand for them. The second part of the statement is accurate. The foreign demand for dollars (from U.S. exports) generates a supply of foreign currencies to the United States.

A decline in U.S. incomes or a weakening of U.S. preferences for foreign goods would reduce U.S. imports, reducing U.S. demand for foreign currencies. These currencies would depreciate (the dollar would appreciate). Dollar appreciation means U.S. exports would decline and U.S. imports would increase.

6-10 GATT is the General Agreement on Tariffs and Trade. It affects nearly everyone around the globe because its trade liberalization applies to 120 nations. Major outcomes: reduced tariffs and quotas, liberalized trade in services, lower agricultural subsidies, enhanced protection of intellectual property rights, creation of the World Trade Organization. The EU and NAFTA are free-trade blocs. GATT reduces tariffs and liberalizes trade for nearly *all* nations. The ascendancy of the EU and the passage of NAFTA undoubtedly encourage nations to reach the latest GATT agreement. The tariff reductions within the EU and NAFTA apply only to sellers from other nations in the blocs. The GATT provisions reduce trade barriers facing *all* exporting nations, including those outside the trade blocs.

Chapter 7

7-3 They are excluded because the dollar value of final goods includes the dollar value of intermediate goods. If intermediate goods were counted, then multiple counting would occur. The value of steel (intermediate good) used in autos is included in the price of the auto (the final product).

This value is not included in GDP because such sales and purchases simply transfer the ownership of existing assets; such sales and purchases are not themselves (economic) investment and thus should not be counted as production of final goods and services.

Used furniture was produced in some previous year; it was counted as GDP then. Its resale does not measure new production.

NDP is GDP less depreciation—the physical capital used up in producing this year's output.

7-6 When gross investment exceeds depreciation, net investment is positive and production capacity expands; the economy ends the year with more physical capital than it started with. When gross investment equals depreciation, net investment is zero and production capacity is said to be static; the economy ends the year with the same amount of physical capital. When depreciation exceeds gross investment, net investment is negative and production capacity declines; the economy ends the year with less physical capital.

The first statement is wrong. Just because *net* investment was a minus $6 billion in 1933 does not mean the economy produced no new capital goods in that year. It simply means depreciation exceeded gross investment by $6 billion. So the economy ended the year with $6 billion less capital.

The second statement is correct. If only one $20 spade is bought by a construction firm in the entire economy in a year and no other physical capital is bought, then gross investment is $20—a positive amount. This is true even if *net* investment is highly negative, because depreciation is well above $20. If not even this $20 spade had been bought, then gross investment would have been zero. But gross investment can never be *less* than zero.

7-8 (a) GDP = $388; NDP = $361; (b) NI = $339; (c) PI = $291; (d) DI = $265.

7-11 Price index for 1984 = 62.5; 60 percent; real GDP for 1984 = $112,000 and real GDP for 1992 = $352,000.

7-12 Values for real GDP, top to bottom of the column: $2,206.5 (inflating); $2,695.1 (inflating); $3,133.8 (inflating); $3,905.6 (inflating); $5,864.8 (inflating); $6,739.7 (deflating).

Chapter 8

8-1 The four phases of a typical business cycle, starting at the bottom, are trough, recovery, peak, and recession. As seen in Figure 8-1, the length of a complete cycle varies from about 2 to 3 years to as long as 15 years.

Normally there is a pre-Christmas spurt in production and sales and a January slackening. This normal seasonal variation does not signal boom or recession. From decade to decade, the long-term trend (the secular trend) of the U.S. economy has been upward. A period of no GDP growth thus does not mean that all is normal but that the economy is operating below its trend growth of output.

Because durable goods last, consumers can postpone buying replacements. This happens when people are worried about a recession and whether there will be a paycheck next month. And firms will soon stop producing what people are not buying. Durable goods industries therefore suffer large output declines during recessions. In contrast, consumers cannot long postpone the buying of nondurables such as food; therefore recessions only slightly reduce nondurable output.

8-3 Labor force = 230 [= 500 − (120 + 150)]; official unemployment rate = 10% [= (23/230) × 100].

8-5 GDP gap = 8% [= (9 − 5) × 2]; forgone output = $40 billion (= 8% of $500 billion).

8-7 This year's rate of inflation is 10% or [(121 −110)/110] × 100.

Dividing 70 by the annual percentage rate of increase of any variable (for instance, the rate of inflation or population growth) will give the approximate number of years for doubling of the variable.

(a) 35 years (= 70/2); (b) 14 years (= 70/5); (c) 7 years (= 70/10).

Chapter 9

9-6 Data for completing the table (top to bottom). Consumption: $244; $260; $276; $292; $308; $324; $340; $356; $372. APC: 1.02; 1.00; .99; .97; .96; .95; .94; .94; .93. APS: −.02; .00; .01; .03; .04; .05; .06; .06; .07. MPC: .80 throughout. MPS: .20 throughout.

(a) See the graphs at the top of the next column.

(b) Break-even income = $260. Households dissave by borrowing or using past savings.

(c) Technically, the APC diminishes and the APS increases because the consumption and saving schedules have positive and negative vertical intercepts respectively (Appendix to Chapter 1). MPC and MPS measure *changes* in consumption and saving as income changes; they are the

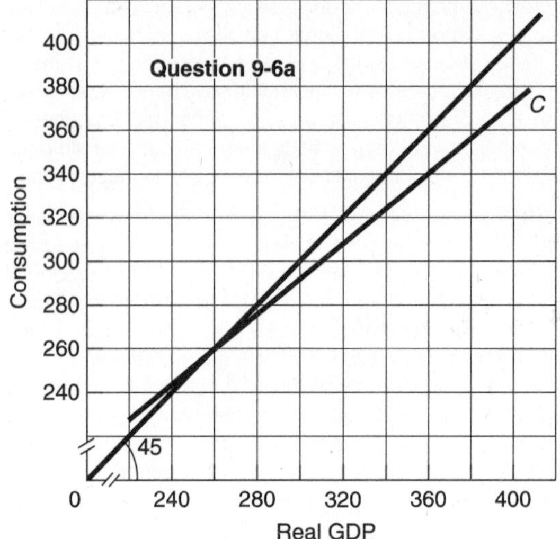

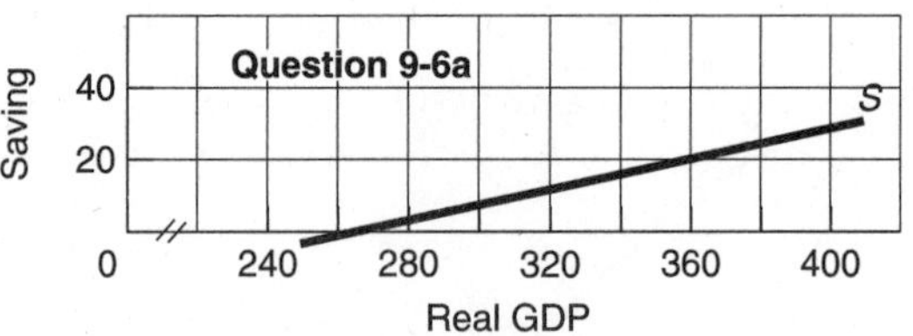

slopes of the consumption and saving schedules. For straight-line consumption and saving schedules, these slopes do not change as the level of income changes; the slopes and thus the MPC and MPS remain constant.

9-8 See the graph. Aggregate investment: (a) $20 billion; (b) $30 billion; (c) $40 billion. This is the investment-demand curve because we have applied the rule of undertaking all investment up to the point where the expected rate of return, *r*, equals the interest rate, *i*.

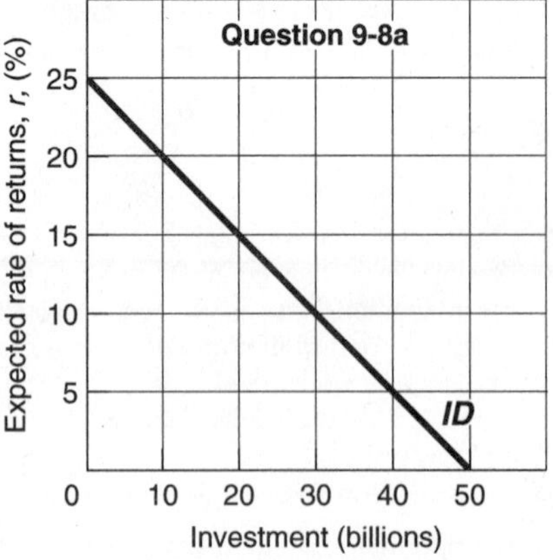

9-10 Saving data for completing the table (top to bottom): $−4; $0; $4; $8; $12; $16; $20; $24; $28.

Equilibrium GDP = $340 billion, determined where (1) aggregate expenditures equal GDP (*C* of $324 billion + *I* of $16 billion = GDP of $340 billion); or (2) where planned *I* = S (*I* of $16 billion = *S* of $16 billion). Equilibrium level of employment = 65 million; MPC = .8; MPS = .2.

9-11 At the $380 billion level of GDP, planned saving = $24 billion; planned investment = $16 billion (from the question). This deficiency of $8 billion of planned investment causes an unplanned $8 billion *increase* in inventories. Actual investment is

$24 billion (= $16 billion of planned investment *plus* $8 billion of unplanned inventory investment), matching the $24 billion of actual saving.

At the $300 billion level of GDP, saving = $8 billion; planned investment = $16 billion (from the question). This excess of $8 billion of planned investment causes an unplanned $8 billion *decline* in inventories. Actual investment is $8 billion (= $16 billion of planned investment *minus* $8 billion of unplanned inventory disinvestment) matching the actual saving of $8 billion.

When unplanned investments in inventories occur, as at the $380 billion level of GDP, businesses revise their production plans downward and GDP falls. When unintended disinvestments in inventories occur, as at the $300 billion level of GDP, businesses revise their production plans upward and GDP rises. Equilibrium GDP—in this case, $340 billion—occurs where planned investment equals saving.

Chapter 10

10-2 The multiplier effect is the magnified increase in equilibrium GDP that occurs when any component of aggregate expenditures changes. The greater the MPC (the smaller the MPS), the greater the multiplier.

MPS = 0, multiplier = infinity; MPS = .4, multiplier = 2.5; MPS = .6, multiplier = 1.67; MPS = 1; multiplier = 1.

MPC = 1; multiplier = infinity; MPC = .9, multiplier = 10; MPC = .67; multiplier = 3; MPC = .5, multiplier = 2; MPC = 0, multiplier = 1.

MPC = .8: Change in GDP = $40 billion (= $8 billion × multiplier of 5); MPC = .67: change in GDP = $24 billion ($8 billion × multiplier of 3). The simple multiplier takes account of only the leakage of saving. The complex multiplier also takes account of leakages of taxes and imports, making the complex multiplier less than the simple multiplier.

10-5 (a) Equilibrium GDP for closed economy = $400 billion. (b) Net export data for column 5 (top to bottom): $−10 billion in each space. Aggregate expenditure data for column 6 (top to bottom): $230; $270; $310; $350; $390; $430; $470; $510. Equilibrium GDP for the open economy is $350 billion, $50 billion below the $400 billion equilibrium GDP for the closed economy. The $−10 billion of net exports is a leakage which reduces equilibrium GDP by $50 billion. Imports = $40 billion: Aggregate expenditures in the private open economy would fall by $10 billion at each GDP level and the new equilibrium GDP would be $300 billion. Imports = $20 billion: Aggregate expenditures would increase by $10 billion; new equilibrium GDP would be $400 billion. Exports constant, increases in imports reduce GDP; decreases in imports increase GDP.
(d) Since every rise of $50 billion in GDP increases aggregate expenditures by $40 billion, the MPC is .8 and so the multiplier is 5.

10-8 The addition of $20 billion of government expenditures and $20 billion of personal taxes increases equilibrium GDP from $350 to $370 billion. The $20 billion increase in *G raises* equilibrium GDP by $100 billion (= $20 billion × the multiplier of 5); the $20 billion increase in *T reduces* consumption by $16 billion (= $20 billion × the MPC of .8). This $16 billion decline in turn reduces equilibrium GDP by $80 billion (= $16 billion × multiplier of 5). The net change from adding government is $20 billion (= $100 billion −$80 billion.).

10-10 (a) A recessionary gap. Equilibrium GDP is $600 billion, while full employment GDP is $700 billion. Employment will be 20 million less than at full employment. Aggregate expenditures would have to increase by $20 billion (= $700 billion − $680 billion) at each level of GDP to eliminate the recessionary gap.
(b) An inflationary gap. Aggregate expenditures will be excessive, causing demand-pull inflation. Aggregate expenditures would have to *fall* by $20 billion (= $520 billion − $500 billion) at each level of GDP to eliminate the inflationary gap.
(c) MPC = .8 (= $40 billion/$50 billion); MPS = .2 (= 1 −.8); multiplier = 5 (= 1/.2).

Chapter 11

11-4 (a) See the graph. Equilibrium price level = 200. Equilibrium real output = $300 billion. No, the full-capacity level of GDP is $400 billion, where the AS curve becomes vertical.

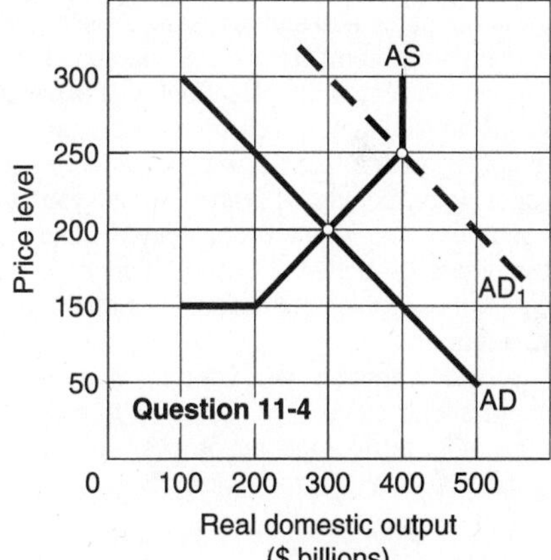

(b) At a price level of 150, real GDP supplied is a maximum of $200 billion, less than the real GDP demanded of $400 billion. The shortage of real output will drive the price level up. At a price level of 250, real GDP supplied is $400 billion, which is more than the real GDP demanded of $200 billion. The surplus of real output will drive down the price level. Equilibrium occurs at the price level at which AS and AD intersect.
(c) See the graph. Increases in consumer, investment, government, or net export spending might shift the AD curve rightward. New equilibrium price level = 250. New equilibrium GDP = $400 billion. The intermediate range.

11-5 (a) Productivity = 2.67 (= 300/112.5). (b) Per-unit cost of production = $.75 (= $2 × 112.5/300). (c) New per-unit production cost = $1.13. The AS curve would shift leftward. The price level would rise and real output would decrease; (d) New per-unit cost of production = $0.375 ($2 × 112.5/600). AS curve shifts to the right; price level declines and real output increases.

11-7 (a) AD curve left; (b) AD curve right; (c) AS curve left; (d) AD curve right; (e) AD curve left; (f) AD curve right; (g) AS curve right; (h) AD curve right; (i) AS curve right; (j) AS curve left; (k) AD curve right; AS curve left; (l) AD curve left; (m) AS curve right.

11-9 (a) Price level rises and no change in real output; (b) price level drops and real output increases; (c) price level does not change, but real output rises; (d) price level does not change, but real output declines; (e) price level increases, but the change in real output is indeterminate; (f) price level does not change, but real output declines.

Chapter 12

12-2 Increase in government spending = $5 billion. Initial spending of $5 billion is still required, but only .8 (= MPC) of a tax cut will be spent. So tax cut = $5/.8 = $6.25 billion. Because part of the tax reduction ($1.25 billion) is saved, not spent. Combination: a $1 billion increase in government spending and a $5 billion tax cut.

12-3 Reduce government spending, increase taxes, or some combination of both. See Figure 12-2. If the price level is flexible downward, it will fall. In the real world, the goal is to reduce *inflation*—to keep prices from rising so rapidly—not to reduce the *price level.* A "conservative" economist might favor cuts in government spending since this would reduce the size of government. A "liberal" economist might favor a tax hike; it would preserve government spending programs.

12-7 The *full-employment budget* is a budget which indicates the amount the Federal deficit or surplus would be *if* the economy operated at full employment throughout the year (whether or not it did). This budget is a useful measure of fiscal policy. An increase in a full-employment deficit (or a decrease in a full-employment surplus) indicates that fiscal policy is expansionary. A decrease in full-employment deficit (or an increase in a full-employment surplus) means that fiscal policy is contractionary. The actual budget simply compares *G* and *T* for the year. A *structural deficit* is another name for a full-employment deficit. A cyclical deficit is the difference between *G* and *T* caused by tax revenues being below those which are collected when the economy is at full employment.

At GDP_f, the structural deficit is *ab* and the cyclical deficit is zero. Government should raise *T* or reduce *G* to eliminate this deficit, but it may want to take this action over several years to avoid pushing the economy into recession.

12-9 It takes time to ascertain the direction in which the economy is moving (recognition lag), to get a fiscal policy enacted into law (administrative lag), and for the policy to have its full effect on the economy (operational lag). Meanwhile, other factors may change, rendering inappropriate a particular fiscal policy. Nevertheless, discretionary fiscal policy is a valuable tool in preventing severe recession or severe demand-pull inflation.

A political business cycle is the concept that politicians are more interested in reelection than in stabilizing the economy. Before the election, they enact tax cuts and spending increases to please voters even though this may fuel inflation. After the election, they apply the brakes to restrain inflation; the economy will slow and unemployment will rise. In this view the political process creates economic instability.

The crowding-out effect is the reduction in investment spending caused by the increase in interest rates arising from an increase in government spending, financed by borrowing. The increase in *G* was designed to increase AD but the resulting increase in interest rates may decrease *I*. Thus the impact of the expansionary fiscal policy may be reduced.

The net export effect also arises from the higher interest rates accompanying expansionary fiscal policy. The higher interest rates make U.S. bonds more attractive to foreign buyers. The inflow of foreign currency to buy dollars to purchase the bonds drives up the international value of the dollar, making imports less expensive for the United States, and U.S. exports more expensive for people abroad. Net exports in the United States decline, and like the crowding-out effect, diminish the expansionary fiscal policy.

Chapter 13

13-4 *M*1 = currency (in circulation) + checkable deposits. The largest component of *M*1 is checkable deposits. If the face value of a coin were not greater than its intrinsic (metallic) value, people would remove coins from circulation and sell them for their metallic content. *M*2 = *M*1 + noncheckable savings deposits + money market deposit accounts + small time deposits + money market mutual fund balances. *M*3 = *M*2 + large time deposits (those of $100,000 or more). Near-monies include the components of *M*2 and *M*3 not included in *M*1 and, secondly, other less liquid assets such as Savings bonds and Treasury bills.

Near-monies represent wealth; the more wealth people have, the more they are likely to spend out of current income. Also, the fact that near-monies are liquid adds to potential economic instability. People may cash in their near-monies and spend the proceeds while the monetary authorities are trying to stem inflation by reducing the money supply. Finally, near-monies can complicate monetary policy because *M*1, *M*2, and *M*3 do not always change in the same direction.

The argument for including noncheckable savings deposits in a definition of money is that saving deposits can quickly be transferred to a checking account or withdrawn as cash and spent.

13-6 In the first case, the value of the dollar in year 2, relative to year 1 is $.80 (= 1/1.25); in the second case the value is $2 (= 1/.50). Generalization: The price level and the value of the dollar are inversely related.

13-7 (a) The level of nominal GDP. The higher this level, the greater the amount of money demanded for transactions. (b) The interest rate. The higher the interest rate, the smaller the amount of money demanded as an asset.

On a graph measuring the interest rate vertically and the amount of money demanded horizontally, the two demand for money curves can be summed horizontally to get the total demand for money. This total demand shows the total amount of money demanded at each interest rate. The equilibrium interest rate is determined at the intersection of the total demand for money curve and the supply of money curve.

(a) Expanded use of credit cards: transaction demand for money declines; total demand for money declines; interest rate falls. (b) Shortening of worker pay periods: transaction demand for money declines; total demand for money declines; interest rate falls. (c) Increase in nominal GDP: transaction demand for money increases; total demand for money increases; interest rate rises.

Chapter 14

14-2 Reserves provide the Fed a means of controlling the money supply. It is through increasing and decreasing excess reserves that the Fed is able to achieve a money supply of the size it thinks best for the economy.

Reserves are assets of commercial banks because these funds are cash belonging to them; they are a claim the commercial banks have against the Federal Reserve Bank. Reserves deposited at the Fed are a liability to the Fed because they are funds it owes; they are claims which commercial banks have against it.

Excess reserves are the amount by which actual reserves exceed required reserves: Excess reserves = actual reserves − required reserves. Commercial banks can safely lend excess reserves, thereby increasing the money supply.

14-4 Banks add to checking account balances when they make loans; these checkable deposits are part of the money supply. People pay off loans by writing checks: checkable deposits fall, meaning the money supply drops. Money is "destroyed."

14-8 (a) $2,000. Column 1 of Assets (top to bottom): $22,000; $38,000; $42,000. Column 1 of Liabilities: $102,000.
(b) $2,000. The bank has lent out its excess reserves, creating $2,000 of new demand-deposit money.
(c) Column 2) of assets (top to bottom): $20,000; $38,000; $42,000. Column 2 of Liabilities: $100,000.
(d) $7,000.

14-13 (a) Required reserves = $50 billion (= 25% of $200 billion); so excess reserves = $2 billion (= $52 billion − $50 billion). Maximum amount banking system can lend = $8 billion (= 1/.25 × 2 billion). Column (1) of Assets data (top to bottom): $52 billion; $48 billion; $108 billion. Column (1) of Liabilities data: $208 billion. Monetary multiplier = 4 (= 1/.25).
(b) Required reserves = $40 billion (= 20% of $200 billion); so excess reserves = $12 billion (= $52 billion − $40 billion). Maximum amount banking system can lend = $60 billion (= 1/.20 × $12 billion). Column (1) data for Assets after loans (top to bottom): $52 billion; $48 billion; $160 billion. Column (1) data for Liabilities after loans: $260 billion. Monetary multiplier = 5 (= 1/.20). The decrease in the reserve ratio increases the banking system's excess reserves from $2 billion to $12 billion and increases the size of the monetary multiplier from 4 to 5. Lending capacity become 5 × $12 = $60 billion.

Chapter 15

15-2 (a) Column (1) data, top to bottom: (Commercial banks) $34; $60; $60; $150; $4; (Fed banks) $60; $4; $34; $3; $27.
(b) Column (2) data: (Commercial banks) $30; $60; $60; $147; $3; (Fed banks) $57; $3; $30; $3; $27.
(c) Column (3) data (top to bottom): $35; $58; $60; $150; $3; (Fed banks) $62; $3; $35; $3; $27.
(d1) Money supply (demand deposits) directly changes only in (b), where it decreases by $3 billion; (d2) See balance sheets; (d3) Money-creating potential of the banking system increases by $5 billion in (a); decreases by $12 billion in (b) (not by $15 billion—the writing of $3 billion of checks by the public to buy bonds reduces demand deposits by $3 billion, thus freeing $0.6 billion of reserves. Three billion dollars minus $0.6 billion equals $2.4 billion of reduced reserves, and this multiplied by the monetary multiplier of 5 equals $12 billion); and increases by $10 billion in (c).

15-3 (a) Increase the reserve ratio. This would increase the size of required reserves. If the commercial banks were fully loaned up, they would have to call in loans. The money supply would decrease, interest rates would rise, and aggregate demand would decline.
(b) Increase the discount rate. This would decrease commercial bank borrowing from the Fed. Actual reserves of the commercial banks would fall, as would excess reserves and lending. The money supply would drop, interest rates would rise, and aggregate demand would decline.
(c) Sell government securities in the open market. Buyers of the bonds would write checks to the Fed on their demand deposits. When these checks cleared, reserves would flow from the banking system to the Fed. The decline in reserves would reduce the money supply, which would increase interest rates and reduce aggregate demand.

15-4 The basic objective of monetary policy is to assist the economy in achieving a full-employment, noninflationary level of total output. Changes in the money supply affect interest rates, which affect investment spending and therefore aggregate demand.

(a) A steep demand curve for money makes monetary policy more effective since the steepness of the curve means that only a relatively small change in the money supply is needed to produce large changes in interest rates. A relatively flat investment demand curve aids monetary policy since it means that only a small change in the interest rate is sufficient to change investment sharply. (b) A high MPC (low MPS) yields a large income multiplier, meaning that a relatively small initial change in spending will multiply into a larger change in GDP.

An easy money policy increases the money supply. The increase in GDP resulting from an easy money policy will also increase the transactions demand for money, partially offsetting the reduction in the interest rate associated with the initial increase in the money supply. Overall, investment spending, aggregate demand, and GDP will not rise by as much. The reverse is true for a tight money policy.

15-5 The Federal funds interest rate is the interest rate banks charge one another on overnight loans needed to meet the reserve requirement. The prime interest rate is the interest rate banks charge on loans to their most creditworthy customers. The tighter the monetary policy, the less the supply of excess reserves in the banking system and the higher the Federal funds rate.

The Fed wanted to reduce excess reserves, slowing the growth of the money supply. This would slow the expansion of aggregate demand and keep inflation from occurring. The prime interest rate went up.

15-6 The intent of a tight money policy would be shown as a leftward shift of the aggregate demand curve and a decline in the price level (or, in the real world, a reduction in the rate of inflation). In an open economy, the interest rate hike resulting from the tight money policy would entice people abroad to buy U.S. securities. Because they would need U.S. dollars to buy these securities, the international demand for dollars would rise, causing the dollar to appreciate. Net exports would fall, pushing the aggregate demand curve farther leftward than in the closed economy.

Chapter 16

16-3 (a) $280; $220. When the price level rises from 100 to 125 [in aggregate supply schedule AS(P_{100})], producers experience higher prices for their products. Because nominal wages are constant, profits rise and producers increase output to Q = $280. When the price level decreases from 100 to 75, profits decline and producers adjust their output to Q = $75. These are short-run responses to changes in the price level.
(b) $250; $250. In the long run, a rise in the price level to 125 leads to nominal wage increases. The AS(P_{100}) changes to AS(P_{125}) and Q returns to $250, now at a price level of 125. In the long run, a decrease in the price level to 75 leads to lower nominal wages, yielding aggregate supply schedule AS(P_{75}). Equilibrium Q returns to $250, now at a price level of 75.
(c) Graphically, the explanation is identical to Figure 16-1b. Short run AS: P_1 = 100; P_2 = 125; P_3 = 75; and Q_1 = $250; Q_2 = 280; Q_3 = $220. Long-run aggregate supply = Q_1 = $250 at each of the three price levels.

16-4 (a) See Figure 16-4 in the chapter. Short run: The aggregate supply curve shifts to the left, the price level rises, and real output declines. Long run: The aggregate supply curve shifts back rightward (due to declining nominal wages), the price level falls, and real output increases.
(b) See Figure 16-3. Short run: The aggregate demand curve shifts to the right, and both the price level and real output increase. Long run: The aggregate supply curve shifts to the left (due to higher nominal wages), the price level rises, and real output declines.
(c) See Figure 16-5. Short run: The aggregate demand curve shifts to the left, both the price level and real output decline. Long run: The aggregate supply curve shifts to the right, the price level falls further, and real output increases.

16-6 Adaptive expectations: People form their expectations of future inflation on the basis of previous and present rates of inflation and only gradually change their expectations as experience unfolds. Rational expectations: People form their expectations by predicting what inflation will be in the future.

With adaptive expectations, an increase in inflation reduces the unemployment rate since prices rise but nominal wages for a time stay constant; thus higher inflation is associated with lower unemployment rates. This is not possible with rational expectations since workers anticipate the higher inflation and immediately take action to increase their nominal wages to avoid suffering a decline in real wages.

Both types of expectations result in a vertical long-run Phillips Curve because workers either *eventually* (adaptive expectations) or *immediately* (rational expectations) adjust their expectations of inflation to the actual rate of inflation. Therefore, no tradeoff between inflation and the unemployment rate exist in the long run.

16-8 Taxes and transfers reduce incentives to work; the economy is overregulated. The Laffer Curve relates tax revenues to tax rates and suggests that tax revenues first rise as tax rates increase, reach a maximum at some particular tax rate, and then decline as tax rates further increase. This curve reflects the supply-side tenet that high taxes create disincentives to work and thus to earn income; reduced income reduces income tax revenue.

Chapter 17

17-1 (a) Classical economists envisioned the AS curve as being perfectly vertical. When prices fall, real profits do not decrease because wage rates fall in the same proportion. With constant real profits, firms have no reason to change the quantities of output they supply. Keynesians viewed the AS curve as being horizontal at outputs less than the full-employment output. Declines in aggregate demand in this range do not change the price level because wages and prices are assumed to be inflexible downward.

(b) Classical economists viewed AD as stable so long as the monetary authorities hold the money supply constant. Therefore inflation and deflation are unlikely. Keynesians viewed the AD curve as unstable—even if the money supply is constant—since investment spending is volatile. Decreases in AD can cause a recession; rapid increases in AD can cause demand-pull inflation. The Keynesian view seems more consistent with the facts of the Great Depression; in that period, real output declined by nearly 40 percent in the United States and remained low for a decade.

17-4 Velocity = 3.5. They will cut back on their spending to try to restore their desired ratio of money to other items of wealth. Nominal GDP will have to fall to $266 billion (= $76 billion of money supply × 3.5) to restore equilibrium.

17-7 See the graph and the decline in aggregate demand from AD_1 to AD_2. RET view: The economy anticipates the decline in the price level and immediately moves from *a* to *d*. Mainstream view: The economy first moves from *a* to *b* and then to *c*. In view of historical evidence, the mainstream view seems more plausible to us than the RET view; only when aggregate demand shifts from AD_2 to AD_1 will full-employment output Q_1 be restored.

17-13 (a) RET; (b) MAIN; (c) MON; (d) MAIN; (e) MON.

Chapter 18

18-2 There are four supply factors, a demand factor, and an efficiency factor in explaining economic growth. (1) Supply factors: the quantity and quality of natural resources, the quantity and quality of human resources, the stock of capital goods, and technology. (2) Demand factor: maintaining full employment. (3) Efficiency factor: productive and allocative efficiency.

In the long run, a nation must expand its production capacity in order to grow (supply side). But aggregate demand must also expand (demand side) or the extra capacity will stand idle. Economic growth depends on an enhanced ability to produce *and* a greater willingness to buy.

The supply side of economic growth is illustrated by the outward expansion of the production possibilities curve, as from *AB* to *CD* in Figure 18-1. The demand side of economic growth is shown by the movement from a point on *AB* to an optimal point on *CD*, as from *a* to, say, *b* in the figure.

18-3 Growth rate of real GDP = 4 percent (= $31,200 − $30,000)/$30,000). GDP per capita in year 1 = $300 (= $30,000/100). GDP per capita in year 2 = $305.88 (= $31,200/102). Growth rate of GDP per capita is 1.96 percent = ($305.88 − $300)/300).

Question 17-7

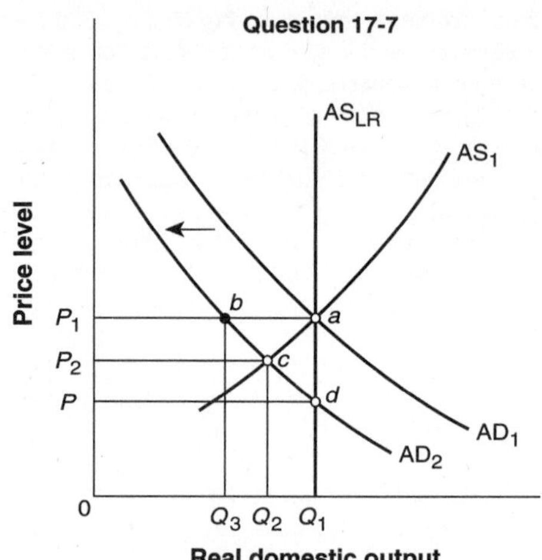

Question 18-3

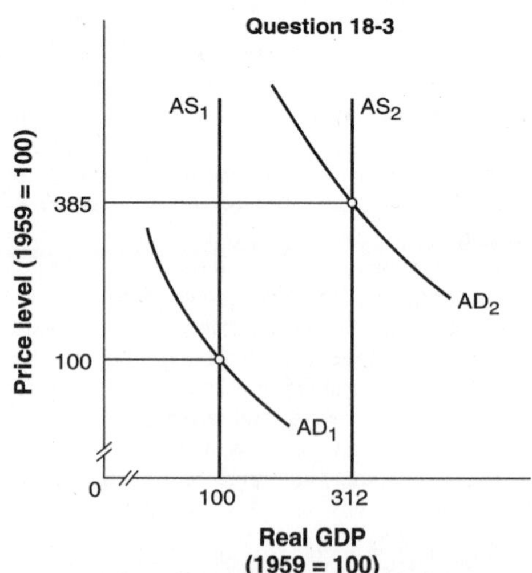

"One Possible Graphical Solution"

In the graph, AD_1 and AS_1 intersect for 1959 at a price level of 100 and GDP of 100. The 1997 AD_2 and AS_2 intersect at a price level of 385 (an increase of 285 percent) and at a real GDP of $312 (an increase of 212 percent).

18-5 Increase in labor inputs: 33 percent; increase in labor productivity: 67 percent.

Refer to Table 18-2. Productivity increasing factors in descending order: (1) Technological advance—the discovery of new knowledge which results in the combining of resources in more productive ways. (2) The quantity of capital. (3) Education and training. Since 1940 the proportion of those in the labor force with a high school education has doubled from 40 to 80 percent. And those with a college education have more than doubled from under 10 percent to 20 percent. (4) Economies of scale and (5) improved resource allocation. Workers have been moving out of lower productivity jobs to higher productivity jobs. Part of this is associated with the increased efficiency often derived from production in larger plants in which specialization of labor and productivity-increasing methods are possible.

18-8 Declines in labor quality; a slowing of technological process; declining investment spending as a percentage of GDP; high energy prices during the 1970s and 1980s; and lagging growth of service productivity. The main consequence of the slowdown is a slower rise in the U.S. standard of living (slower increases in real GDP per capita). Other outcomes are greater inflation and loss of competitiveness in world markets.

We are generally optimistic about a resurgence of productivity growth. The most recent productivity growth rates are higher than the averages of the slowdown years. Energy prices are stable and inflation is under control; the baby-boomers are becoming more experienced workers; a surge of innovation is occurring in computers and telecommunications; real interest rates remain low, prompting purchases of capital goods; and international trade barriers are declining. All these factors may result in faster productivity growth than in the slowdown years.

Chapter 19

19-1 (a) There is practically no potential for using fiscal policy as a stabilization tool under an annually balanced budget. In an economic downturn, tax revenues fall. To keep the budget in balance, fiscal policy would require the government to reduce its spending or increase its tax rates, adding to the deficiency in spending and accelerating the downturn. If the economy were booming and tax revenues were mounting, to keep the budget balanced fiscal policy would have to increase government spending or reduce taxes, thus adding to the already excessive demand and accelerating the inflationary pressures. An annually balanced budget would intensify cyclical ups and downs.

(b) A cyclically balanced budget would be countercyclical, as it should be, since it would bolster demand by lowering taxes and increasing government spending during a recession and restrain demand by raising taxes and reducing government spending during an inflationary boom. However, because boom and bust are not always of equal intensity and duration, budget surpluses during the upswing need not automatically match budget deficits during the downswing. Requiring the budget to be balanced over the cycle may necessitate inappropriate changes in tax rates or levels of government expenditures.

(c) Functional finance pays no attention to the balance of deficits and surpluses annually or over the cycle. What counts is the maintenance of a noninflationary full-employment level of spending. Balancing the economy is what counts, not the budget.

19-3 Two ways of measuring the public debt: (1) measure its absolute size; (2) measure its size as a percentage of GDP.

An internally held debt is one in which the bondholders live in the nation having the debt; an externally held debt is one in which the bondholders are citizens of other nations. Paying off an internally held debt would involve boosting taxes or reducing other government spending and using the proceeds to buy the government bonds. This would present a problem of income distribution because holders of the government bonds generally have higher incomes than the average taxpayer. But paying off an internally held debt would not burden the economy as a whole—the money used to pay off the debt would stay within the domestic economy.

In paying off an externally held debt people abroad would use the proceeds of the bonds sales to buy goods from the country paying off its external debt. That nation would have to send some of its output abroad to be consumed by others (with no imported goods in exchange).

Refinancing the public debt simply means rolling over outstanding debt—selling "new" bonds to retire maturing bonds.

19-7 Economists do not, in general, view the large public debt as a burden for future generations. Future generations not only inherit the public debt, they inherit the bonds which constitute the public debt. They also inherit public capital goods, some of which were financed by the debt.

There is one way the debt can be a burden to future generations. Unlike tax financing, debt financing may drive up interest rates since government must compete with private firms for funds in the bond market. Higher interest rates will crowd out some private investment, resulting in a smaller stock of future capital goods and thus a less productive economy for future generations to inherit.

19-8 Cause and effect chain: Government borrowing to finance the debt competes with private borrowing and drives up the interest rate; the higher interest rate induces an inflow of foreign money to buy the now higher-return U.S. bonds; to buy the bonds, the foreign financiers must first buy dollars; the demand for dollars rises and the dollar appreciates; U.S. exports fall and U.S. imports rise; a U.S. trade deficit results.

The U.S. public often blames the large trade deficits on the trade policies of other countries—particularly Japan. But, as noted in the scenario just described, a substantial portion of the large U.S. *trade* deficits may have resulted from the U.S. policy of running large *budget* deficits for the past decade or more.

Chapter 20

20-2 See the graph accompanying the answer to 20-4. Elasticities, top to bottom: 3; 1.4; .714; .333. Slope does not measure elasticity. This demand curve has a constant slope of −1 (= −1/1), but elasticity declines as we move down the curve. When the initial price is high and initial quantity is low, a unit change in price is a *low* percentage change while a unit change in quantity is a *high* percentage change. The percentage change in quantity exceeds the percentage change in price, making demand elastic. When the initial price is low and initial quantity is high, a unit change in price is a *high* percentage change while a unit change in quantity is a *low* percentage change. The percentage change in quantity is less than the percentage change in price, making demand inelastic.

20-4 See the graph at the top of the next page. Total revenue data, top to bottom: $5; $8; $9; $8; $5. When demand is elastic, price and total revenue move in the opposite direction. When demand is inelastic, price and total revenue move in the same direction.

20-5 Total revenue would increase in (c), (d), (e), and (f); decrease in (a) and (b); and remain the same in (g).

20-6 Substitutability, proportion of income, luxury versus necessity, and time. Elastic: (a), (c), (e), (g), (h), and (i). Inelastic: (b), (d), (f), and (j).

20-10 Supply was perfectly inelastic—vertical—at a quantity of 1 unit. The $82.5 million price was determined where the demand curve intersected this supply curve.

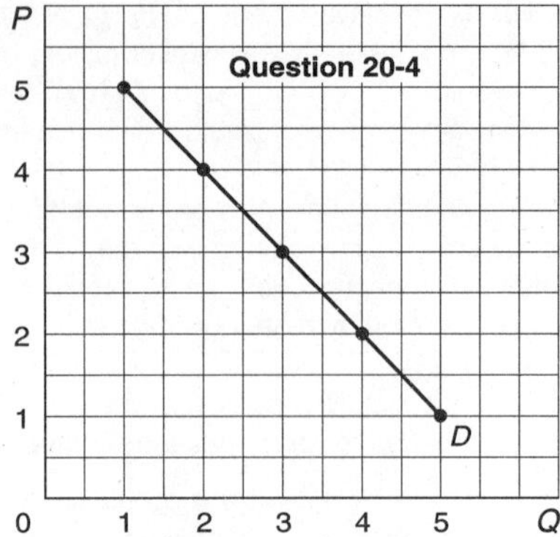

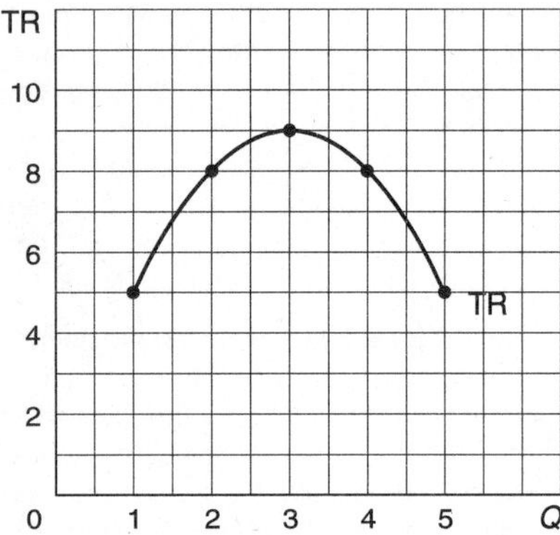

20-12 A and B are substitutes; C and D are complements.

20-13 All are normal goods—income and quantity demanded move in the same direction. These coefficients reveal that a 1 percent increase in income will increase the quantity of movies demanded by 3.4 percent, of dental services by 1.0 percent, and of clothing by 0.5 percent. A negative coefficient indicates an inferior good—income and quantity demanded move in the opposite direction.

Chapter 21

21-2 Missing total utility data, top to bottom: 18; 33. Missing marginal utility data, top to bottom: 7; 5; 1.

(a) A decreasing rate; because marginal utility is declining. (b) Disagree. The marginal utility of a unit beyond the first may be sufficiently great (relative to product price) to make it a worthwhile purchase. (c) Agree. This product's price could be so high relative to the first unit's marginal utility that the consumer would buy none of it.

21-4 (a) 4 units of A; 3 units of B; 3 units of C, and 0 units of D. (b) Save \$4. (c) 36/\$18 = 12/\$6 = 8/\$4 = 2/\$1. The marginal utility per dollar of the last unit of each product purchased is 2.

21-5 Buy 2 units of X and 5 units of Y. Marginal utility of last dollar spent will be equal at 4 (= 8/\$2 for X and 4/\$1 for Y) and the \$9 income will be spent. Total utility = 48 (= 10 + 8 for X plus 8 + 7 + 6 + 5 + 4 for Y). When the price of X falls to \$1, the quantity of X demanded increases from 2 to 4. Total utility is now 58 (= 10 + 8 + 6 + 4 for X plus 8 + 7 + 6 + 5 + 4 for Y).

Demand schedule: $P = \$2$; Q = 2. $P = \$1$; Q = 4.

Appendix 21-3 The tangency point places the consumer on the highest attainable indifference curve; it identifies the combination of goods yielding the highest total utility. All intersection points place the consumer on a lower indifference curve. MRS is the slope of the indifference curve; P_B/P_A is the slope of the budget line. Only at the tangency point are these two slopes equal. If MRS $> P_B/P_A$ or $MRS < P_B/P_A$, adjustments in the combination of products can be made to increase total utility (get to a higher indifference curve).

Chapter 22

22-2 Explicit costs: \$37,000 (= \$12,000 for the helper + \$5,000 of rent + \$20,000 of materials). Implicit costs: \$22,000 (= \$4,000 of forgone interest + \$15,000 of forgone salary + \$3,000 of entrepreneurship).

Accounting profit = \$35,000 (= \$72,000 of revenue − \$37,000 of explicit costs); Economic profit = \$13,000 (= \$72,000 − \$37,000 of explicit cost −\$22,000 of implicit costs).

22-4 Marginal product data, top to bottom: 15; 19; 17; 14; 9; 6; 3; −1. Average product data, top to bottom: 15; 17; 17; 16.25; 14.8; 13.33; 11.86; 10.25. Your diagram should have the same general characteristics as text Figure 22-2.

MP is the slope—the rate of change—of the TP curve. When TP is rising at an increasing rate, MP is positive and rising. When TP is rising at a diminishing rate, MP is positive but falling. When TP is falling, MP is negative and falling. AP rises when MP is above it; AP falls when MP is below it.

MP first rises because the fixed capital gets used more productively as added workers are employed. Each added worker contributes more to output than the previous worker because the firm is better able to use its fixed plant and equipment. As still more labor is added, the law of diminishing returns takes hold. Labor becomes so abundant relative to the fixed capital that congestion occurs and marginal product falls. At the extreme, the addition of labor so overcrowds the plant that the marginal product of still more labor is negative—total output falls.

Illustrated by Figure 22-6. Because labor is the only variable input and its price (its wage rate) is constant, MC is found by dividing the wage rate by MP. When MP is rising, MC is falling; when MP reaches its maximum, MC is at its minimum; when MP is falling, MC is rising.

22-7 The total fixed costs are all \$60. The total costs are all \$60 more than the total variable cost. The other columns are shown in Question 4 in Chapter 23.

(a) See the graph. Over the 0 to 4 range of output, the TVC and TC curves slope upward at a decreasing rate because of increasing marginal returns. The slopes of the curves then increase at an increasing rate as diminishing marginal returns occur.

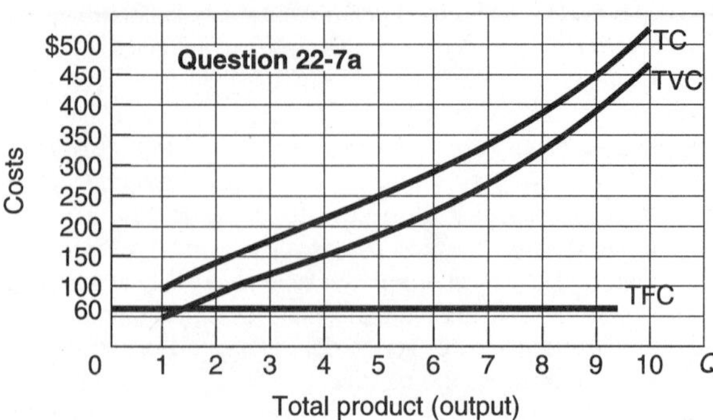

(b) See the graph. AFC (= TFC/Q) falls continuously since a fixed amount of capital cost is spread over more units of output. The MC (= change in TC/change in Q), AVC (= TVC/Q), and ATC (= TC/Q) curves are U-shaped, reflecting the influence of first increasing and then diminishing returns. The ATC curve sums AFC and AVC vertically. The ATC curve falls when the MC curve is below it;

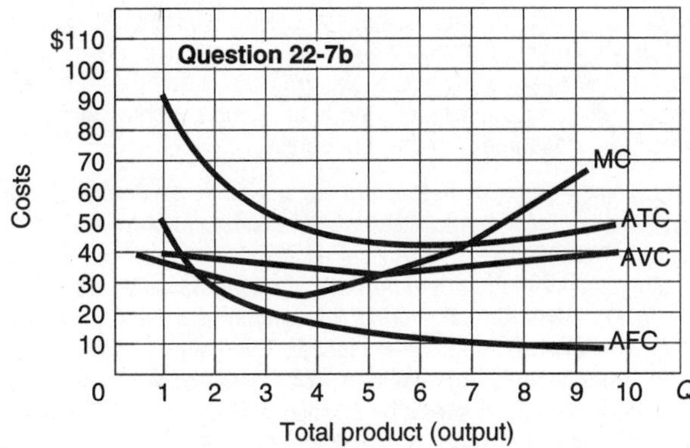

the ATC curve rises when the MC curve is above it. This means the MC curve must intersect the ATC curve at its lowest point. The same logic holds for the minimum point of the AVC curve.

(c1) If TFC had been $100 instead of $60, the AFC and ATC curves would be higher—by an amount equal to $40 divided by the specific output. Example: at 4 units, AVC = $25.00 [= ($60 + $40)/4]; and ATC = $62.50 [= ($210 + $40)/4]. The AVC and MC curves are not affected by changes in fixed costs.

(c2) If TVC had been $10 less at each output, MC would be $10 lower for the first unit of output but remain the same for the remaining output. The AVC and ATC curves would also be lower—by an amount equal to $10 divided by the specific output. Example: at 4 units of output, AVC = $35.00 [= ($150 − $10)/4], ATC = $50 [= ($210 − $10)/4]. The AFC curve would not be affected by the change in variable cost.

22-10 The long-run ATC curve is U-shaped. At first, long-run ATC falls as the firm expands and realizes economies of scale from labor and managerial specialization and the use of more efficient capital. The long-run ATC curve later turns upward when the enlarged firm experiences diseconomies of scale, usually resulting from managerial inefficiencies.

The MES (minimum efficient scale) is the smallest level of output needed to attain all economies of scale and minimum long-run ATC.

If long-run ATC drops quickly to its minimum cost which then extends over a long range of output, the industry will likely be composed of both large and small firms. If long-run ATC descends slowly to its minimum cost over a long range of output, the industry will likely be composed of a few large firms. If long-run ATC curve drops quickly to its minimum point and then rises abruptly, the industry will likely be composed of many small firms.

Chapter 23

23-3 Total revenue, top to bottom: 0; $2; $4; $6; $8; $10. Marginal revenue, top to bottom: $2, throughout.

(a) The industry is purely competitive—this firm is a “price taker.” The firm is so small relative to the size of the market that it can change its level of output without affecting the market price.

(b) See the graph.

(c) The firm’s demand curve is perfectly elastic; MR is constant and equal to *P*.

(d) Yes. Table: When output (quantity demanded) increases by 1 unit, total revenue increases by $2. This $2 increase is the marginal revenue. Figure: The change in TR is measured by the slope of the TR line, 2 (= $2/1 unit).

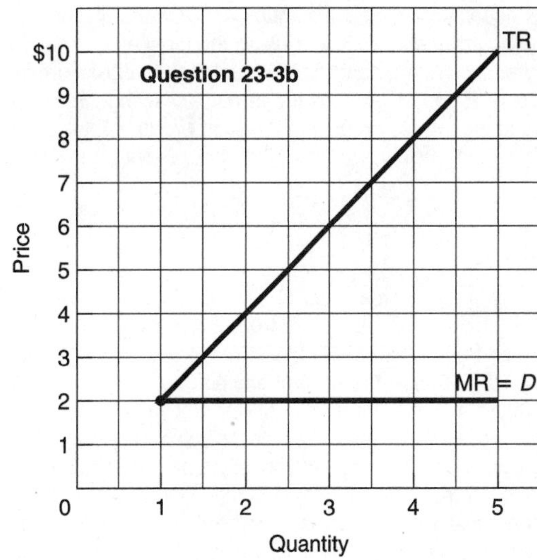

23-4 (a) No, because $32 is always less than AVC. If it did produce, its output would be 4—found by expanding output until MR no longer exceeds MC. By producing 4 units, it would lose $82 [= 4($32 − $52.50)]. By not producing, it would lose only its total fixed cost of $60.

(b) Yes, $41 exceeds AVC at the loss-minimizing output. Using the MR = MC rule it will produce 6 units. Loss per unit of output is $6.50 (= $41 − $47.50). Total loss = $39 (= 6 × $6.50), which is less than its total fixed cost of $60.

(c) Yes, $56 exceeds AVC (and ATC) at the loss-minimizing output. Using the MR = MC rule it will produce 8 units. Profit per unit = $7.87 (= $56 − $48.13); total profit = $62.96.

(d) Column (2) data, top to bottom: 0; 0; 5; 6; 7; 8; 9. Column (3) data, top to bottom, in dollars: −60; −60; −55; −39; −8; +63; +144.

(e) The firm will not produce if *P* < *AVC. When* P > AVC, the firm will produce in the short run at the quantity where *P* (= MR) is equal to its increasing MC. Therefore, the MC curve above the AVC curve is the firm’s short-run supply curve, it shows the quantity of output the firm will supply at each price level. See Figure 23-6 for a graphical illustration.

(f) Column (4) data, top to bottom: 0; 0; 7,500; 9,000; 10,500; 12,000, 13,500.

(g) Equilibrium price = $46; equilibrium output = 10,500. Each firm will produce 7 units. Loss per unit = $ 1.14, or $8 per firm. The industry will contract in the long run.

23-6 See Figures 23-8 and 23-9 and their legends. See Figure 23-11 for the supply curve for an increasing cost industry. The supply curve for a decreasing cost industry is below.

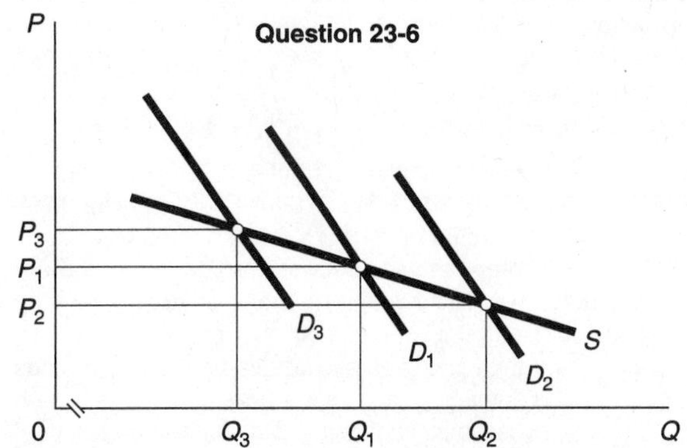

23-7 The equality of P and minimum ATC means the firm is achieving *productive efficiency;* it is using the most efficient technology and employing the least costly combination of resources. The equality of P and MC means the firm is achieving *allocative efficiency;* the industry is producing the right product in the right amount based on society's valuation of that product and other products.

Chapter 24

24-4 Total revenue, in order from $Q = 0$: $6.50, $12.00; $16.50; $20.00; $22.50; $24.00; $24.50; $24.00; $22.50. Marginal revenue in order from $Q = 1$: $6.50; $5.50; $4.50; $3.50; $2.50; $1.50; $.50; −$1.50. See the accompanying graph. Because TR is increasing at a diminishing rate, MR is declining. When TR turns downward, MR becomes negative. Marginal revenue is below D because demand is not perfectly elastic. Four units sell for $5.00 each, but three of these four could have been sold for $5.50 had the monopolist been satisfied to sell only three. Having decided to sell four, the monopolist had to lower the price of the first three from $5.50 to $5.00, sacrificing $.50 on each for a total of $1.50. This "loss" of $1.50 explains the difference between the $5.00 price obtained on the fourth unit of output and its marginal revenue of $3.50. Demand is elastic from $P =$ $6.50 to $P =$ $3.50, a range where TR is rising. The curve is of unitary elasticity at $P =$ $3.50, where TR is at its maximum. The curve is inelastic from then on as the price continues to decrease and TR is falling. When MR is positive, demand is elastic. When MR is zero, demand is of unitary elasticity. When MR is negative, demand is inelastic. If MC is zero, the monopolist should produce 7 units where MR is also zero. It would never produce where demand is inelastic because MR is negative there while MC is positive.

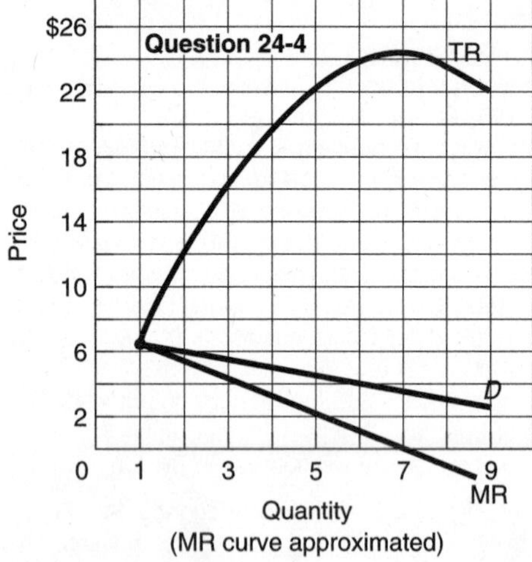

24-5 Total revenue data, top to bottom, in dollars: 0; 100; 166; 213; 252; 275; 288; 294; 296; 297; 290. Marginal revenue data, top to bottom, in dollars: 100; 66; 47; 39; 23; 13; 6; 2; 1; −7.

Price = $63; output = 4; profit = $42 [= 4($63 − 52.50)]. Your graph should have the same general appearance as Figure 24-4. At $Q = 4$, TR = $252 and TC = $210 [= 4($52.50)].

24-6 Perfect price discrimination: Output = 6. TR would be $420 (= $100 + $83 + $71 + $63 + $55 + $48). TC would be $285 [= 6($47.50)]. Profit would be $135 (= $420 − $285).

Your single diagram should combine Figures 24-8a and 24-8b in the chapter. The discriminating monopolist faces a demand curve which is also its MR curve. It will sell the first unit at f in Figure 24-8b and then sell each successive unit at lower prices (as shown on the demand curve) as it moves to Q_2 units, where D (= MR) = MC. Discriminating monopolist: Greater output; total revenue, and profits. Some consumers will pay a higher price under discriminating monopoly than with nondiscriminating monopoly; others, a lower price. Good features: greater output and improved allocative efficiency. Bad feature: more income is transferred from consumers to the monopolist.

24-11 No, the proposal does not consider that the output of the natural monopolist would still be at the suboptimal level where $P >$ MC. Too little would be produced and there would be an underallocation of resources. Theoretically, it would be more desirable to force the natural monopolist to charge a price equal to marginal cost and subsidize any losses. Even setting price equal to ATC would be an improvement over this proposal. This fair-return pricing would allow for a normal profit and ensure a greater production than the proposal would.

Chapter 25

25-2 Less elastic than a pure competitor and more elastic than a pure monopolist. Your graphs should look like Figures 23-12 and 25-1 in the chapters. Price is higher and output lower for the monopolistic competitor. Pure competition: $P =$ MC (allocative efficiency); $P =$ minimum ATC (productive efficiency). Monopolistic competition: $P >$ MC (allocative inefficiency) and $P >$ minimum ATC (productive inefficiency). Monopolistic competitors have excess capacity, meaning that fewer firms operating at capacity (where $P =$ minimum ATC) could supply the industry output.

25-7 A four-firm concentration ratio of 60 percent means the largest four firms in the industry account for 60 percent of sales; a four-firm concentration ratio of 90 percent means the largest four firms account for 90 percent of sales. Shortcomings: (1) they pertain to the nation as a whole, although relevant markets may be localized; (2) they do not account for interindustry competition; (3) the data are for U.S. products—imports are excluded; and (4) they don't reveal the dispersion of size among the top four firms.

Herfindahl index for A: 2400 (= 900 + 900 + 400 + 100 + 100). For B: 4300 (= 3600 + 625 + 25 + 25 + 25). We would expect Industry A to be more competitive than Industry B, where one firm dominates and two firms control 85 percent of the market.

25-8 The matrix shows the four possible profit outcomes for each of two firms, depending on which of two price strategies each follows. Example: If C sets price at $35 and D at $40, C's profits will be $59,000, and D's $55,000.

(a) C and D are interdependent because their profits depend not just on their own price, but also on the other firm's price.

(b) Likely outcome: Both firms will set price at $35. If either charged $40, it would be concerned the other would undercut the price and its profit by charging $35. At $35 for both, C's profit is $55,000; D's, $58,000.

(c) Through price collusion—agreeing to charge $40—each firm would achieve higher profit (C = $57,000; D = $60,000). But once both firms agree on $40, each sees it can increase its profit even more by secretly charging $35 while its rival charges $40.

25-9 Assumptions: (1) Rivals will match price cuts; (2) Rivals will ignore price increases. The gap in the MR curve results from the abrupt change in the slope of the demand curve at the going price. Firms will not change their price because they fear that if they do their total revenue and profits will fall. Shortcomings of the model: (1) It does not explain how the going price evolved in the first place; (2) it does not allow for price leadership and other forms of collusion.

25-11 Effect (1): Advertising may increase demand, allowing the firm to expand output and achieve economies of scale, meaning a lower ATC. Effect (2): Advertising is a business expense, implying a higher ATC. If (1) > (2), ATC will fall and consumers may benefit through lower prices. If (1) < (2), per unit cost will rise and consumers will likely face higher prices.

Chapter 26

26-4 (a) 5 percent; (b) no, because the 5 percent rate of return is less than the 6 percent interest rate; (c) yes, because the 5 percent the rate of return is now greater than the 4 percent interest rate.

26-5 (a) 50 million, where the interest-rate cost of funds *i* equals the expected rate of return *r*; (b) At \$20 million of R&D, *r* of 14 percent exceeds *i* of 8 percent; (c) at \$60 million, *r* of 6 percent is less than *i* of 8 percent.

26-6 (a) The person would now buy 5 units of product C and 0 units of A and B; (b) the MU/price ratio is what counts; a new product can be successful by having a high MU, a low price, or both relative to existing products.

26-8 (a) Total cost = \$40,000; average total cost = \$.80 (= \$4,000/5,000 units). (b) Total cost = \$4,000, average total cost = \$.667 (= \$4,000/6,000 units); (c) Process innovation can lower the average total cost of producing a particular output, meaning that society uses fewer resources in producing that output. Resources are freed from this production to produce more of other desirable goods. Society realizes extra output through a gain in efficiency.

Chapter 27

27-2 Marginal product data, top to bottom: 17; 14; 12; 10; 7; 5. Total revenue data, top to bottom: \$0; \$34; \$62; \$86; \$106; \$120; \$130. Marginal revenue product data, top to bottom: \$34; \$28; \$24; \$20; \$14; \$10.

(a) Two workers at \$27.95 because the MRP of the first worker is \$34 and the MRP of the second worker is \$28, both exceeding the \$27.95 wage. Four workers at \$19.95 because workers 1 through 4 have MRPs exceeding the \$19.95 wage. The fifth worker's MRP is only \$14, so he or she will not be hired.

(b) The demand schedule consists of the first and last columns of the table:

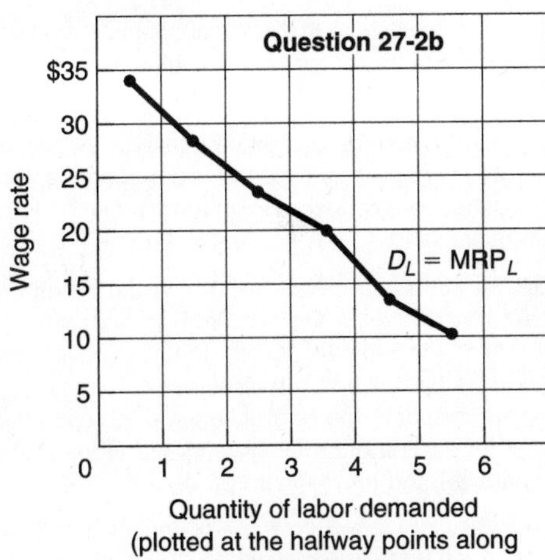

(c) Reconstruct the table. New product price data, top to bottom: \$2.20; \$2.15; \$2.10; \$2.05; \$2.00; \$1.95. New total revenue data, top to bottom: \$0; \$37.40; \$66.65; \$90.30; \$108.65; \$120.00; \$126.75. New marginal revenue product data, top to bottom: \$37.40; \$29.25; \$23.65; \$18.35; \$11.35; \$6.75. The new labor demand is less elastic. Here, MRP falls because of diminishing returns *and* because product price declines as output increases. A decrease in the wage rate will produce less of an increase in the quantity of labor demanded, because the output from the added labor will reduce product price and thus MRP.

27-3 Four factors: the rate at which the resource's MP declines; the ease of substituting other resources; elasticity of product demand; and the ratio of the resource cost to the total cost of production.

(a) Increases the demand for C. (b) The price increase for D will increase the demand for C through the *substitution effect,* but decrease the demand for all resources—including C—through the *output effect.* The net effect is uncertain; it depends on which effect outweighs the other. (c) Increases the elasticity of demand for C. (d) Increases the demand for C. (e) Increases the demand for C through the output effect. There is no substitution effect. (f) Reduces the elasticity of demand for C.

27-4 (a) 2 capital; 4 labor. $MP_L/P_L = 7/1$; $MP_C/P_C = 21/3 = 7/1$. (b) 7 capital and 7 labor. $MRP_L/_L = 1$ (= 1/1) = $MRP_C/P_C = 1$ (= 3/3). Output is 142 (= 96 from capital + 46 from labor). Economic profit is \$114 (= \$142 − \$28). Yes, least-cost production is part of maximizing profits—the profit-maximizing rule includes the least-cost rule.

27-5 (a) Use more of both; (b) use less labor and more capital; (c) use maximum profits obtained; (d) use less of both.

Chapter 28

28-3 See Figure 28-3 and its legend.

28-4 Total labor cost data, top to bottom: \$0; \$14; \$28; \$42; \$56; \$70; \$84. Marginal resource cost data: \$14, throughout.

(a) The labor supply curve and MRC curve coincide as a single horizontal line at the market wage rate of \$14. The firm can employ as much labor as it wants, each unit costing \$14; wage rate = MRC because the wage rate is constant to the firm.

(b) Graph: equilibrium is at the intersection of the MRP and MRC curves. Equilibrium wage rate = \$14; equilibrium level of employment = 4 units of labor. Explanation: From the tables: MRP exceeds MRC for each of the first four units of labor, but MRP is less than MRC for the fifth unit.

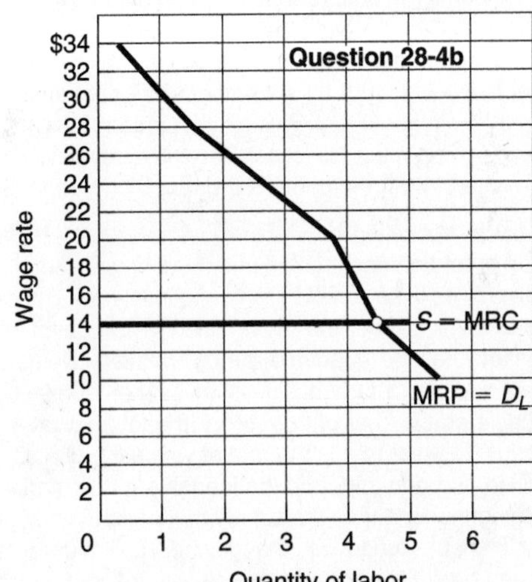

28-6 The monopsonist faces the market labor supply curve *S*—it is the only firm hiring this labor. MRC lies above *S* and rises more rapidly than *S* because all workers get the higher wage rate that is needed to attract each added worker. Equilibrium wage rate = $12; equilibrium employment = 3 (where MRP = MRC). The monopsonist can pay a below-competitive wage rate by restricting its employment.

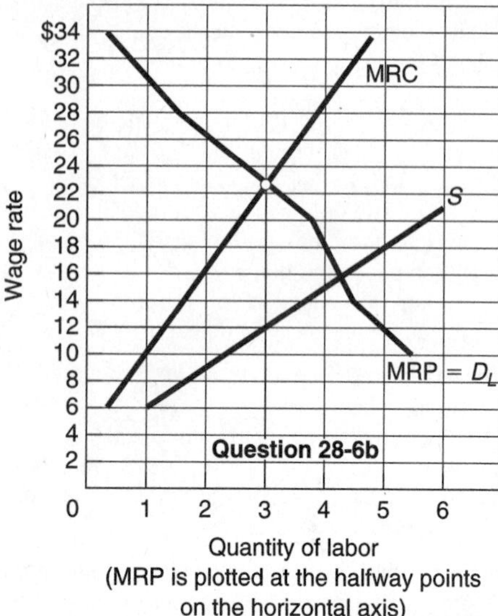

28-7 The union wage rate *Wc* becomes the firm's MRC, which we would show as a horizontal line to the left of *S*. Each unit of labor now adds only its own wage rate to the firm's costs. The firm will employ Q_c workers, the quantity of labor where MRP = MRC (= W_c); Q_c is greater than the Q_m workers it would employ if there were no union.

Chapter 29

29-2 Land is completely fixed in total supply. As population expands and the demand for land increases, rent first appears and then grows. From society's perspective this rent is a surplus payment unnecessary for ensuring that the land is available to the economy as a whole. If rent declined or disappeared, the same amount of land would be available. If it increased, no more land would be forthcoming. Thus, rent does not function as an incentive for adding land to the economy.

But land does have alternative uses. To get it to its most productive use, individuals and firms compete and the winners are those who pay the highest rent. To the high bidders, rent is a cost of production which must be covered by the revenue gained through the sale of the commodities produced on that land.

29-4 Supply is upsloping because households prefer present consumption to future consumption and must be enticed through higher interest rates to save more (consume less) now. The higher the interest rate, the greater the saving and the amount of money made available to the loanable funds market. Demand is downsloping because more business investment projects become profitable as the cost of borrowing (the interest rate) falls. The equilibrium interest rate is the rate at which the quantities of funds supplied and demanded in the loanable funds market are equal. Anything that changes the supply of loanable funds or the demand for loanable funds will change the equilibrium interest rate. Two examples: Higher taxes on interest income would reduce the supply of loanable funds and increase the equilibrium interest rate; a decrease in business optimism would reduce the expected return on investment, decrease the demand for loanable funds, and reduce the equilibrium interest rate.

29-6 The nominal interest rate is the interest rate stated in dollars of current value (unadjusted for inflation). The real interest rate is the nominal interest rate adjusted for inflation (or deflation). The real interest rate is more relevant for making investment decisions—it reflects the true cost of borrowing money. It is compared to the expected return on the investment in the decision process. Real interest rate = 4 percent (= 12 percent − 8 percent).

29-8 Accounting profit is what remains of a firm's total revenues after it has paid for all the factors of production employed by the firm (its explicit costs) but not for the use of the resources owned by the business itself. Economists also take into consideration implicit costs—the payment the owners could have received by using the resources they own in some other way. The economist adds these implicit costs to the accountant's explicit costs to arrive at total cost. Subtracting the total cost from total revenue results in a smaller profit (the economic profit) than the accountant's profit.

Sources of economic profit: (1) uninsurable risks; (2) innovations; and (3) monopoly.

(a) Profit from assuming uncertainties of innovation, as well as monopoly profit from the patent. (b) Monopoly profit arising from its locational advantage. (c) Profit from bearing the uninsurable risk of a change in demand (the change could have been unfavorable).

Chapter 30

30-1 (a) Private good, top to bottom: $P = \$8$, $Q = 1$; $P = \$7$, $Q = 2$; $P = \$6$, $Q = 4$; $P = \$5$, $Q = 7$; $P = \$4$, $Q = 10$; $P = \$3$, $Q = 13$; $P = \$2$, $Q = 16$; $P = \$1$, $Q = 19$. (b) Public good, top to bottom: $P = \$19$, $Q = 1$; $P = \$16$, $Q = 2$; $P = \$13$, $Q = 3$; $P = \$10$, $Q = 4$; $P = \$7$, $Q = 5$; $P = \$4$, $Q = 6$; $P = \$2$, $Q = 7$; $P = \$1$, $Q = 8$. The first schedule represents a horizontal summation of the individual demand curves; the second schedule represents a vertical summation of these curves. The market demand curve for the private good will determine—in combination with market supply—an actual price-quantity outcome in the marketplace. Because potential buyers of public goods do not reveal their individual preferences in the market, the collective demand curve for the public good is hypothetical or needs to be determined through "willingness to pay" studies.

30-2 Optimal quantity = 4. It is optimal because at 4 units the collective willingness to pay for the final unit of the good (= $10) matches the marginal cost of production (= $10).

30-3 Program B since the marginal benefit no longer exceeds marginal cost for programs which are larger in scope. Plan B is where net benefits—the excess of total benefits over total costs—are maximized.

30-4 Spillover costs are called negative externalities because they are *external* to the participants in the transaction and *reduce* the utility of affected third parties (thus "negative"). Spillover benefits are called positive externalities because they are *external* to the participants in the transaction and *increase* the utility of affected third parties (thus "positive"). See Figures 30-3 and 30-4. Compare (b) and (c) in Figure 30-4.

30-7 Reducing water flow from storm drains has a low marginal benefit, meaning the MB curve would be located far to the left of where it is in the text diagram. It will intersect the MC curve at a low amount of pollution abatement, indicating the optimal amount of pollution abatement (where MB = MC) is low. Any cyanide in public water sources could be deadly. Therefore, the marginal benefit of reducing cyanide is extremely high and the MB curve in the figure would be located to the extreme right where it would intersect the MC curve at or near 100 percent.

30-13 Moral hazard problem: (b) and (d). Adverse selection problem: (a), (c), and (e).

Chapter 31

31-2 The paradox is that majority voting does not always provide a clear and consistent picture of the public's preferences. Here the courthouse is preferred to the school and the park is preferred to the courthouse, so we would surmise that the park is preferred to the school. But paired-choice voting would show that the school is preferred to the park.

31-3 Project B (small reservoir wins) using a paired-choice vote. There is no "paradox of voting" problem here and B is the preference of the median voter. The two voters favoring No reservoir and Levees, respectively, will prefer Small reservoir—project B—to Medium or Large reservoir. The two voters preferring Large reservoir or Medium reservoir will prefer Small reservoir to Levees or No reservoir. The median voter's preference for B will prevail. However, the optimal size of the project from an economic perspective is C—it would provide a greater net benefit to society than B.

31-4 The electorate is faced with a small number of candidates, each of whom offers a broad range or "bundle" of proposed policies. Voters are then forced to choose the individual candidate whose bundle of policies most resembles their own. The chances of a perfect identity between a particular candidate's preferences and those of any voter are quite slim. As a result, the voter must purchase some unwanted public goods and services. This represents an inefficient allocation of resources.

Government bureaucracies do not function on the basis of profit, so the incentive for holding down costs is less than in the private sector. Also, because there is no profit-and-loss test of efficiency, it is difficult to determine whether public agencies are operating efficiently. Nor is there entry of competing entities to stimulate efficiency and develop improved public goods and services. Furthermore, wasteful expenditures can be maintained through the self-seeking lobbying of bureaucrats themselves, and the public budgetary process can reward rather than penalize inefficiency.

31-7 Average tax rates: 20; 15; and 13.3 percent. Regressive.

31-9 The incidence of an excise tax is likely to be primarily on consumers when demand is highly inelastic and primarily on producers when demand is elastic. The more elastic the supply, the greater the incidence of an excise tax on consumers and the less on producers.

The efficiency loss of a sales or excise tax is the net benefit society sacrifices because consumption and production of the taxed product are reduced below the level of allocative efficiency which would occur without the tax. Other things equal, the greater the elasticities of demand and supply, the greater the efficiency loss of a particular tax.

Chapter 32

32-2 Sherman Act: Section 1 prohibits conspiracies to restrain trade; Section 2 outlaws monopolization. Clayton Act (as amended by the Celler-Kefauver Act of 1950): Section 2 outlaws price discrimination; Section 3 forbids tying contracts; Section 7 prohibits mergers which substantially lessen competition; Section 8 prohibits interlocking directorates. The acts are enforced by the Department of Justice and Federal Trade Commission. Also, private firms can bring suit against other firms under these laws.

32-5 (a) They would block this horizontal merger (violation of Section 7 of the Clayton Act). (b) They would charge these firms with price fixing (violation of Section 1 of the Sherman Act). (c) They would allow this vertical merger, unless both firms had very large market shares. (d) They would allow this conglomerate merger.

32-10 Industries composed of natural monopolies subject to significant economies of scale. Regulation based on "fair-return" prices creates disincentives for firms to minimize costs since cost reductions lead regulators to force firms to charge a lower price. Regulated firms may also use "creative" accounting to boost costs and hide profits. Because regulatory commissions depend on information provided by the firms themselves and commission members are often recruited from the industry, the agencies may in effect be controlled by the firms they are supposed to oversee. Also, industrial regulation sometimes is applied to industries which are not natural monopolies. Because the calculation of a fair return is based on the value of the firm's capital, there is an incentive for regulated natural monopolies to increase allowable profits by uneconomically substituting capital for labor.

32-12 Industrial regulation is concerned with prices and service in specific industries whereas social regulation deals with the broader impact of business on consumers, workers, and third parties. Benefits: increased worker and product safety, less environmental damage, reduced economic discrimination. Two types of costs: administrative costs, because regulations must be administered by costly government agencies; compliance costs, because firms must increase spending to comply with regulations.

32-14 Industrial policy consists of direct government actions to aid specific firms or industries. Antitrust policy and industrial and social regulation restrict the conduct of firms, often increasing their costs or reducing their revenues. In contrast, industrial policy enhances profits, which is why targeted firms view it favorably. Example: A $1 billion Federal government plan to help U.S. firms compete with Japan in developing flat computer screens. Proponents contend industrial policy strengthens critical industries, speeds development of new technologies, increases labor productivity, and strengthens international competitiveness. Opponents charge that industrial policy can substitute the whims of politicians and bureaucrats for the hard scrutiny of entrepreneurs and business executives. They also point to failures of past industrial policies.

Chapter 33

33-1 First sentence: Shifts in the supply curve of agricultural goods (*changes in supply*) relative to fixed inelastic demand curves produce large changes in equilibrium prices. Second sentence: But these drastic changes in prices produce only small changes in equilibrium outputs (where *quantities demanded* equals *quantities supplied*) because demands are inelastic.

Because exports are volatile from one year to the next, they increase the instability of demand for farm products.

33-3 (a) Because the demand for most farm products is inelastic, the frequent fluctuations in supply brought about by weather and other factors have relatively small effects on quantity demanded, but large effects on equilibrium prices of farm products. Farmers' sales revenues and incomes therefore are unstable. (b) Technological innovations have decreased production costs, increased long-run supply for most agricultural goods, and reduced the prices of farm output. These declines in prices have put a downward pressure on farm income. (c) The modest long-run growth in the demand for farm products has not been sufficient to offset the expansion of supply, resulting in stagnant farm income. (d) Because the number of producers in most agricultural markets is high, it is difficult if not impossible for producers to collude as a way to limit supply and lessen fluctuations in prices and incomes or halt their long-run declines.

33-8 Price supports benefit farmers, harm consumers, impose costs on society, and contribute to problems in world agriculture. Farmers benefit because the prices they receive and the output they produce both increase, expanding their gross incomes. Consumers lose because the prices they pay for farm products rise and quantities purchased decline. Society as a whole bears several costs. Surpluses of farm products have to be bought and stored, leading to a greater burden on taxpayers. Domestic economic efficiency is lessened as the artificially high prices of farm products lead to an overallocation of resources to agriculture. The environment suffers: the greater use of pesticides and fertilizers contributes to water pollution; farm policies discourage crop rotation; and price supports encourage farming of environmentally sensitive land. The efficient use of world resources is also distorted because of the import tariffs or quotas which such programs often require. Finally, domestic overproduction leads to supply increases in international markets, decreasing prices and causing a decline in the gross incomes of foreign producers.

Chapter 34

34-2 See the figure. In this simple economy each person represents a complete income quintile—20 percent of the total population. The richest quintile (Al) receives 50 percent of total income; the poorest quintile (Ed) receives 5 percent.

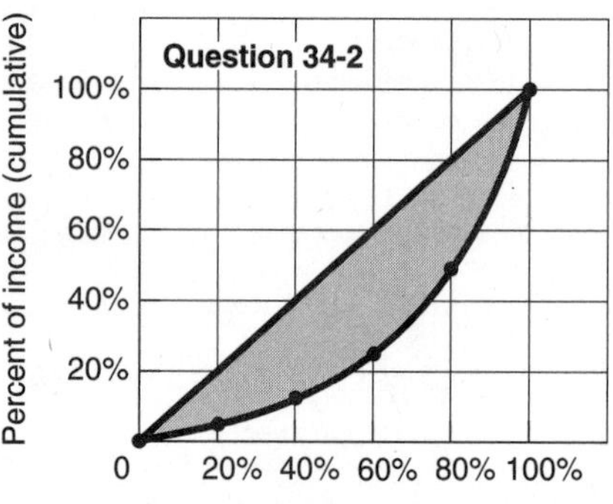

34-5 The reasons for income inequality may be grouped into 3 broad categories: unequal personal endowments, differences in individual character, and external social factors. The first is largely a matter of luck—some people possess high intelligence, particular talents, or physical dexterity which allow them to earn high incomes. Also, they may inherit property or be aided by the social status and financial resources of their parents. The second reason involves personal initiative—individuals may be willing to undergo costly training, accept risk, or tolerate unpleasant working conditions in the expectation of higher pay. They may also show high personal initiative on the job. The third factor relates to society as a whole. Market power and discrimination are two important social determinants of income inequality.

A high IQ normally does not lead to high income unless it is combined with personal initiative and favorable social circumstances. Inherited property—as long as it is competently managed—provides income irrespective of one's character and personal attributes. Both factors are largely a matter of luck to the recipient.

34-11 (a) Plan 1: Minimum income = \$4,000; benefit-reduction rate = 50 percent; break-even income = \$8,000 (= \$4,000/.5). Plan 2: Minimum income = \$4,000; benefit-reduction rate = 25 percent; break-even income = \$16,000 (= \$4,000/.25). Plan 3: Minimum income = \$8,000; benefit-reduction rate = 50 percent; break-even income = \$16,000 (= \$8,000/.5).
(b) Plan 3 is the most costly. Plan 1 is the least costly. Plan 3 is most effective in reducing poverty (although it has a higher benefit-reduction rate than Plan 2, its minimum income is higher). Plan 1 is least effective in reducing poverty. Plan 3 has the strongest disincentive to work (although it has the same benefit-reduction rate as Plan 1, its higher minimum income discourages work more). Plan 2 has the weakest disincentives to work (its minimum income and benefit-reduction rates are low).
(c) The only way to eliminate poverty is to provide a minimum income high enough to lift everyone from poverty, including people who cannot work or choose not to work. But this large minimum income reduces the incentive to work, expands the number of people receiving transfer payments, and substantially boosts overall program costs.

Chapter 35

35-2 The "twin problems" are rising prices for all and limited access (lack of insurance) for about 16 percent of the population. The problems are related since rising costs make insurance unaffordable for many individuals and families and make it difficult for some businesses to insure their workers.

35-7 Income elasticity is 1.0, suggesting that health care spending will rise proportionately with income. Price elasticity is only 0.2, meaning higher prices for health care services will increase total health care spending.

35-10 Health care insurance removes or greatly lessens a person's budget restraint at the time health care is purchased, raising health care utility per dollar spent and causing an overconsumption of health care. In Figure 35-3b, insurance reduces the price of health care at the time of purchase from P_u to P_i, increasing the quantity consumed from Q_u to Q_i. At Q_i the marginal cost of health care is represented by point *b* and exceeds the marginal benefit represented by *c*, indicating an overallocation of resources. The efficiency loss is area *cab.*

Chapter 36

36-4 Fifteen percent. The higher wages which unions achieve reduce employment, displace workers, and increase the marginal revenue product in the union sector. Labor supply increases in the nonunionized sector, reducing wages and decreasing marginal revenue product there. Because of the lower nonunion marginal revenue product, the workers added in the nonunion sector contribute less to GDP than they would have in the unionized sector. The gain of GDP in the nonunionized sector does not offset the loss of GDP in the unionized sector, so there is an overall efficiency loss.

36-7 (a) See the graph.
(b) The equilibrium Hispanic wage rate is \$12; the equilibrium quantity of Hispanic employment is 36,000 workers.
(c) The Hispanic-to-white wage ratio is .75 (= \$12/\$16).
(d) The employer will hire only white workers because the \$5 discrimination coefficient exceeds the \$4 difference between the wage rates of whites and Hispanics.
(e) The new equilibrium Hispanic wage rate is \$14 and the new equilibrium quantity of Hispanic employment is 44,000 workers. The Hispanic-white wage ratio rises to .875 (= \$16/\$14) because of the increased demand for

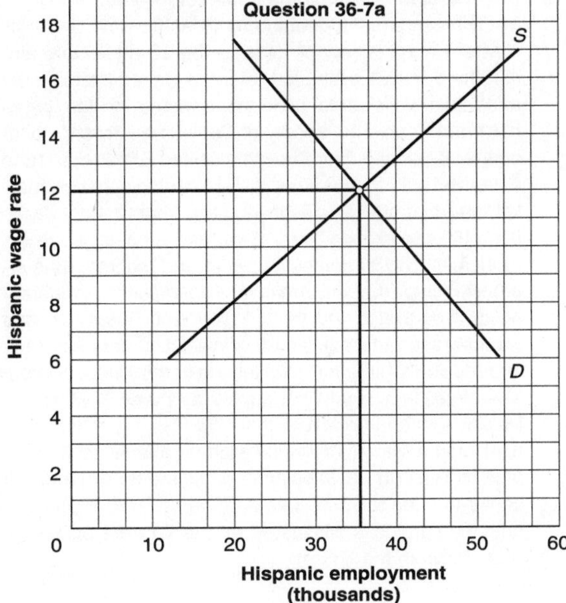

Hispanic labor in relation to the unchanging supply of Hispanic labor.

(f) The new equilibrium Hispanic wage rate is \$10 and the new equilibrium quantity of Hispanic employment is 20,000. This Hispanic-white wage ratio falls to .625 (= \$10/\$16).

36-9 See Figure 36-5. Discrimination against women in two of the three occupations will crowd women into the third occupation. Labor supply in the "men's occupations" (*X* and *Y*) decreases, making them high-wage occupations. Labor supply in the "women's occupation" (*Z*) increases, creating a low-wage occupation.

Eliminating occupational segregation would entice women into the high-wage occupations, increasing labor supply there and reducing it in the low-wage occupation. The wage rates in the three occupations would converge to *B*. Women would gain, men would lose. Society would gain because the increase in output in the expanding occupations would exceed the loss of output in the contracting occupation.

36-12 See Figure 36-6. Migration of labor from the low- to the high-income country increases labor supply in the high-income country and decreases it in the low-income country. Wages are equalized at W_e. Output and business income increase in the receiving country; decline in the sending country. World output increases: the output gain in the receiving country exceeds the output loss in the sending country.

(a) The gains to the receiving country will not materialize if the migrants are unemployed. (b) Remittances to the home country will decrease the income gain in the receiving country and reduce the income loss in the sending country. (c) If migrants who return to their home country have enhanced their skills, their temporary departure might be to the long-run advantage of the home country. (d) Young skilled migrants will increase output and likely be net taxpayers in the receiving country. Older or less skilled workers who are not so easily assimilated could be net recipients of government services.

In view of the sometimes large investments which sending countries have made in providing education and skills, there is a justification for levying a departure tax on such migrants. But if this tax were too high, it would infringe on a basic human right: the right to emigrate.

Chapter 37

37-4 (a) New Zealand's cost ratio is 1 plum ≡ 4 apples (or 1 apple ≡ $\frac{1}{4}$plum). Spain's cost ratio is 1 plum ≡ 1 apple (or 1 apple ≡ 1 plum).

(b) New Zealand should specialize in apples, Spain in plums.

(c) See the graphs.

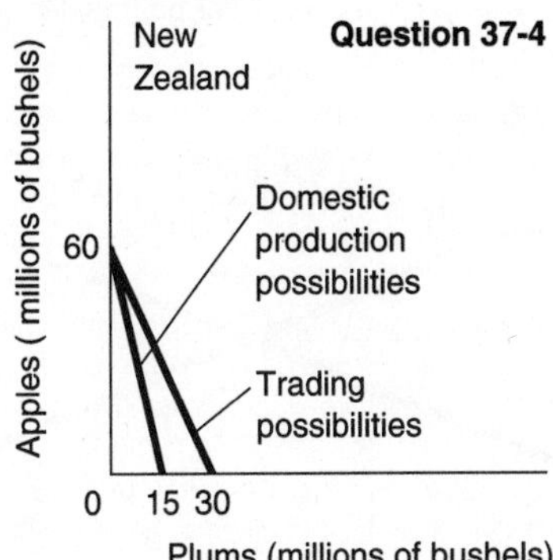

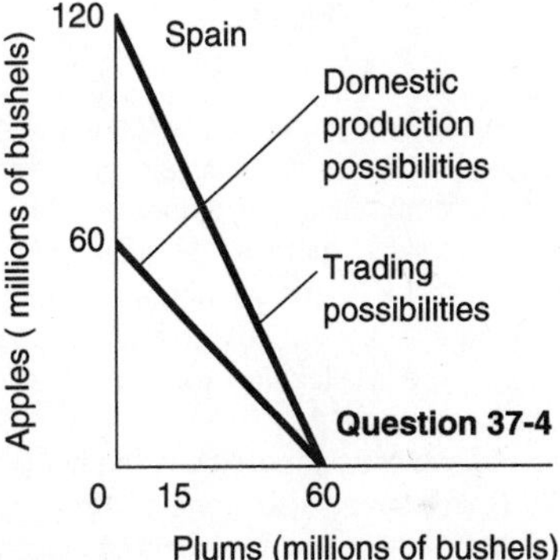

(d) Total production before specialization and trade: 40 apples (20 + 20) and 50 plums (10 + 40). After specialization and trade: 60 apples and 60 plums. Gain = 20 apples and 10 plums.

37-6 At \$1: import 15,000. At \$2: import 7,000. At \$3: no imports or exports. At \$4: export 6,000. At \$5: export 10,000.

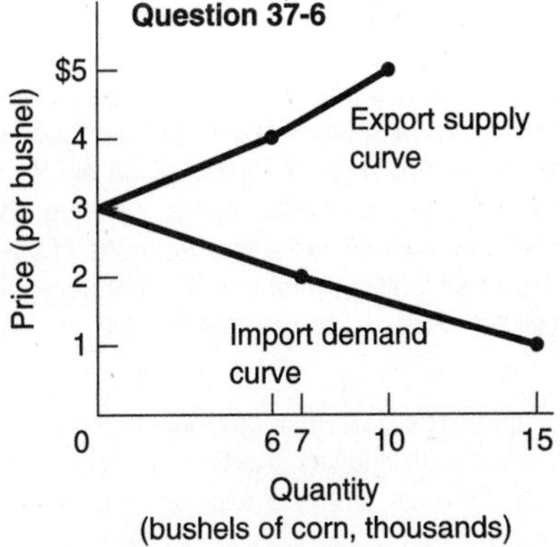

The United States will export corn; France will import it.

37-7 See the graph. The United States does not have a comparative advantage in this product because the world price P_w is below the U.S. domestic price P_d. Imports will reduce the price to P_w, increasing consumption from Q_c to Q_e and decreasing domestic production from Q_c to Q_a. See the graph. A tariff of P_wP_t (a) harms domestic consumers by increasing price from P_w to P_t and decreasing consumption from Q_e to Q_d; (b) aids domestic producers through the increase in price from P_w to P_t and the expansion of domestic production from Q_a to Q_b; (c) harms foreign exporters by decreasing exports from Q_aQ_e to Q_bQ_d.

An import quota of Q_bQ_d would have the same effects as the tariff, but there would be no tariff revenues to government from these imports; this revenue would in effect be transferred to foreign producers.

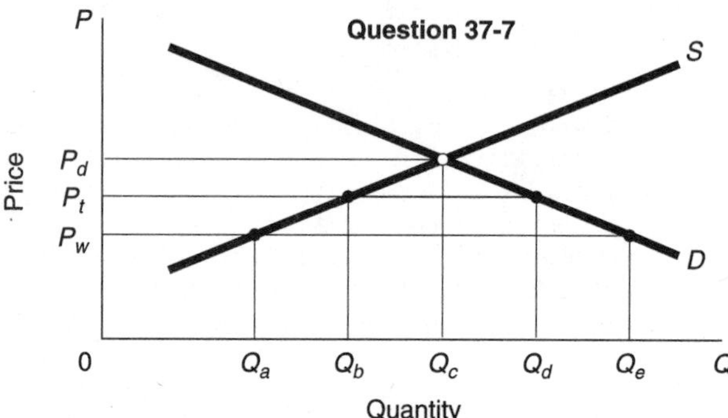

37-11 The major cost of trade protection is reduced efficiency borne by price increases by consumers. Prices of imported goods rise, decreasing levels of competition for domestic firms producing similar goods and allowing them to increase their prices. Prices of products using these goods as inputs also rise. Prices of all other goods increase as consumer spending patterns change. Also, resources are reallocated from more-efficient to less-efficient domestic industries.

The main benefit of protectionist policies is greater profits for the protected firms. Government also benefits from tariff revenues. But empirical studies find that the costs of protectionism greatly exceed the benefits, resulting in a large net cost—or efficiency loss—to society.

Chapter 38

38-2 A demand for francs is created in (a), (c), and (f). A supply of francs is created in (b), (d), (e), and (g).

38-3 Balance of trade = $10 billion surplus (= exports of goods of $40 billion minus imports of goods of $30 billion). Balance on goods and services = $15 billion surplus (= $55 billion of exports of goods and services minus $40 billion of imports of goods and services). Balance on current account = $20 billion surplus (= credits of $65 billion minus debits of $45 billion). Balance on capital account = $30 billion deficit (= Foreign purchases of assets in the United States of $10 billion minus U.S. purchases of assets abroad of $40 billion). Balance of payments = $10 billion deficit.

38-6 The U.S. demand for pesos is downsloping: When the peso depreciates in value (relative to the dollar), the United States find that Mexican goods and services are less expensive in dollar terms and purchase more of them, demanding a greater quantity of pesos in the process. The supply of pesos to the United States is upsloping: As the peso appreciates in value (relative to the dollar), U.S. goods and services become cheaper to Mexicans in peso terms. Mexicans buy more dollars to obtain more U.S. goods, supplying a larger quantity of pesos.

The peso appreciates in (a), (f), (g), and (h) and depreciates in (b), (c), (d), and (e).

38-10 See the graph illustrating the market for Zees.
(a) The decrease in demand for Zees from D_1 to D_2 will create a surplus (*bc*) of Zees at the $5 price. To maintain the $5 to Z1 exchange rate, the United States must undertake policies to shift the demand-for-Zee curve rightward or shift the supply-of-Zee curve leftward. To increase the demand for Zees, the United States could use dollars or gold to buy Zees in the foreign exchange market, employ trade policies to increase imports from Zeeonia, or enact expansionary fiscal and monetary policies to increased U.S. domestic output and income, thus increasing imports from Zeeonia. Expansionary monetary policy would also reduce the *supply* of Zees: Zeeons would respond to the resulting lower U.S. interest rates by reducing their financial investing in the United States. Therefore, they would not supply as many Zees to the foreign exchange market.
(b) Under a system of flexible exchange rates, the *bc* surplus of Zees (the U.S. balance of payments surplus) will cause the Zee to appreciate and the dollar to appreciate until the surplus is eliminated (at the $4 = Z1 exchange rate shown in the figure).

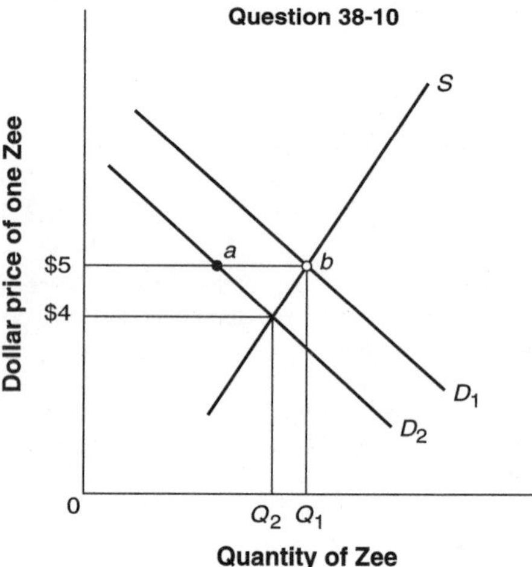

Chapter 39

39-3 Rise in per capita output gap = $135 (= 3% × $5,000 − 3% × $500).

39-6 Demographic transition view: Expanded output and income in developing countries will result in lower birthrates and slower growth of population. As incomes of primary family members expand, they begin to see the marginal cost of a larger family exceeding the marginal benefit. The policy emphasis should therefore be on economic growth; population growth will stabilize. Traditional view: Developing nations should reduce population growth as a first priority. Slow population growth enables the growth of per capita income.

39-7 Capital earns a higher return where it is scarce, *other things equal.* But, when comparing investment opportunities between IACs and DVCs, other things are not equal. Advanced factories filled with specialized equipment require a productive work force. IACs have an abundance of educated, experienced workers; these workers are scarce in DVCs. Also, IACs have extensive public infrastructures which increase the returns on private capital. Example: a network of highways makes it more profitable to produce goods which need to be widely transported. Finally, investment returns must be adjusted for risk. IACs have stable governments and "law and order," reducing the risk of capital being "nationalized" or pilfered by organized crime.

39-13 To describe countries such as Japan and South Korea, we would need to change labels on three boxes, leading to a change in the "results" boxes. "Rapid" population growth would change to "low" rate of population growth; "low" level of saving would change to "high" level of saving; "low" levels of investment in physical and human capital would change to "high" levels of investment in physical and human capital. These three changes would result in higher productivity and higher per capita income, which would produce a rising level of demand. Other factors: stable national government; homogeneous population; extensive investment in infrastructure; "will to develop"; strong private incentives.

Chapter 40

40-5 See Figure 40-1. Because Russia and China set prices and did not allow them to change as supply or demand shifted, prices were below the equilibrium price for most goods and services. When the fixed price, P_f, is below the equilibrium price, P_e, there will be a shortage since the quantity demanded will exceed the quantity supplied.

Black markets are common where prices are fixed below equilibrium levels. People can buy goods at the fixed government prices (or pay off clerks to save such goods to sell to them), and because of the shortages at the low fixed price, resell these goods at a much higher price to those unable to find the goods in government stores at the controlled prices. This reselling is said to occur on the black market.

40-6 Privatization of state-owned businesses; market-determined prices; promotion of competition; integration with the world economy; and price-level stabilization. These reforms are referred to as shock therapy because they were dramatic and quick rather than phased in over many years or decades. Russia's reform has been successful in privatizing the economy, establishing market-determined prices, and setting the stage for future prosperity. But the transition has resulted in declining living standards for many and increasing income inequality.

40-8 (a) leasing of land resulted in individually operated rather than collectivized farms; this greatly increased production incentives and boosted farm output. (b) Price reform established market-based prices. These higher-than-government prices provided incentives for enterprises to expand output; they also enabled market-determined allocation of resources to replace inefficient central planning. (c) Private rural and urban enterprises absorbed workers released by greater productivity in China's agricultural sector and established competition for China's state-owned enterprises. (d) The special economic zones—with their private corporations, free trade, and foreign investment—established the workability and benefits of "near-capitalism." (e) Corporatization focused the goals of state-owned enterprises on providing high-quality, minimum per-unit cost goods desired by consumers.